EXTREME SPEECH AND DEMOCRACY

Extreme Speech and Democracy

Editors

IVAN HARE

Barrister, Blackstone Chambers,
Former Fellow of Trinity College Cambridge

JAMES WEINSTEIN

Amelia D. Lewis Professor of Constitutional Law,
Sandra Day O'Connor College of Law
Arizona State University

OXFORD

UNIVERSITY PRESS

OXFORD
UNIVERSITY PRESS

Great Clarendon Street, Oxford OX2 6DP

Oxford University Press is a department of the University of Oxford.
It furthers the University's objective of excellence in research, scholarship,
and education by publishing worldwide in

Oxford New York

Auckland Cape Town Dar es Salaam Hong Kong Karachi
Kuala Lumpur Madrid Melbourne Mexico City Nairobi
New Delhi Shanghai Taipei Toronto

With offices in

Argentina Austria Brazil Chile Czech Republic France Greece
Guatemala Hungary Italy Japan Poland Portugal Singapore
South Korea Switzerland Thailand Turkey Ukraine Vietnam

Oxford is a registered trade mark of Oxford University Press
in the UK and in certain other countries

Published in the United States
by Oxford University Press Inc., New York

British Library Cataloguing in Publication Data

Data available

Library of Congress Cataloging in Publication Data

Extreme speech and democracy / editors Ivan Hare, James Weinstein.
  p. cm.
Includes index.
ISBN 978–0–19–954878–1
1. Freedom of speech. 2. Hate speech. I. Hare, Ivan. II. Weinstein, James, 1953–
K3254.E99 2008
342.08'53—dc22   2008048519

Typeset by Newgen Imaging Systems (P) Ltd., Chennai, India
Printed in Great Britain
on acid-free paper by
CPI Antony Rowe, Chippenham, Wiltshire

ISBN 978–0–19–954878–1
ISBN 978–0–19–960179–0 (pbk)

1 3 5 7 9 10 8 6 4 2

Foreword

*Ronald Dworkin**

What is the relationship between free speech and democracy? Is freedom of expression valued for democratic reasons primarily because it promotes an informed electorate? Or is there some deeper and more vital connection between free speech and democracy beyond this important instrumental concern? And what call does freedom of speech have on non-democratic states? Is it a universal human right that must be respected even in non-democratic societies? Or is it a norm that other cultures, drawing on different traditions, might properly reject as unsuitable for them? In this volume, a distinguished group of scholars, drawn both from different disciplines and from different democracies, shed light on the nature of the relationship between free speech and democracy by considering what limits, if any, may properly be imposed on freedom of expression in a free and democratic society. In addition, by focusing on the various justifications both for protecting and suppressing speech, including those not directly connected to democracy, the volume casts fresh light on why freedom of expression might be valued as a universal human right. In this Foreword I argue that freedom of speech is not just instrumental to democracy but constitutive of that practice and why, even apart from this intimate relationship with democracy, it is a universal human right.

The strong conviction that freedom of speech is a universal value is challenged today not only by freedom's oldest opponents (the despots and ruling thieves who fear it), but also by new enemies who claim to speak for justice not tyranny. These new enemies point to other values we respect, including self-determination, equality, and freedom from racial hatred and prejudice, as reasons why the right of free speech should now be demoted to a much lower grade of urgency and importance. In part, this new hostility reflects a reluctance to impose Western values on alien cultures. Can we reasonably expect peoples whose entire social structure and sense of national identity are based on the supreme authority of a particular religion to permit what they believe to be ridicule of that religion within their own borders?

Other critics insist that free speech is overvalued even within Western democracies, and particularly within the United States. When the Supreme Court

---

* This foreword is a development of a previously published article entitled: 'A New Map of Censorship' which was published in *Index on Censorship*, Issue 1/2/94; it also draws upon an article by the author published under the title 'The Right to Ridicule' in the New York Review of Books, vol. 53, no. 5, March 23, 2006.

ruled, in the *Skokie* case, that the Constitution's First Amendment protected neo-Nazis who wanted to carry swastikas through a town of Holocaust survivors in Illinois, many people of goodwill wondered how justice could require people to accept such a grotesque insult.[1] In the decades since the *Skokie* decision, moreover, Americans have become even more aware of the malign, chilling force of hate speech and hate gesture. That kind of speech seems particularly odious in universities, where it has been directed against women and minority students and has been fuelled by a backlash against the affirmative action and other special recruiting programmes such universities adopted to increase the number of such students.

Officials at some of these universities have adopted 'speech codes' to prohibit remarks that are sexist or derogatory of a particular race or religion or sexual orientation. A further attack on freedom of speech within democracies has been organized by those feminists, like Catherine MacKinnon, who are anxious to outlaw pornography or to make its publishers liable for punitive damages if a rapist or other criminal convinces a jury that pornography made him act as he did.[2] They say that pornography contributes to a general cultural environment in which women are treated only as sexual devices, and subordinated to men in every way. In this way, limits on free speech are said to be justified by the promotion of equality. The most recent strand in this debate has been the attempts of some Western democracies to punish speech which vilifies or offends religious minorities, in particular those minorities which have been implicated in terrorist activity. For example, in 2006 the United Kingdom enacted a law prohibiting incitement to religious hatred, and in 2005 several people called for the punishment of those who published cartoons in a Danish newspaper associating the Prophet Mohammed with terrorism and demanded censorship of these images in other countries.

These calls for censorship will strike many people as reasonable and signal, just for that reason, a new and particularly dangerous threat to free speech, for we are more likely to relax our defence of that freedom when its betrayers are foreign, or when the speech in question seems worthless or even vile. But if we do, then the principle is inevitably weakened, not just in such cases, but generally. So we must try to abstract from the particular challenges to free speech that now dominate the argument, and to return to the wider question I began by asking. Is free speech a universal human right, a right so important that we must work to secure it even in nations where it is unfamiliar and alien? Is it so important that we must tolerate, in its name, despicable and harmful speech in our own society?

I do not mean, by posing that last question, to agree that bad speech has had the malign consequences that have recently been claimed for it. Many of those claims are inflated and some are absurd. But if free speech really is as fundamental

---

[1] *Collin* v. *Smith* 447 F Supp 676, affirmed 578 F 2d 1197 (7th Cir, 1978).
[2] *Only Words* (London: HarperCollins, 1995).

as many of its defenders have supposed in the past, we must protect it even if it does have bad consequences, and we must be prepared to explain why. We must explain this, moreover, bearing in mind everything that, if we are right, must be tolerated. It may seem easy to defend the rights to investigative reporters exposing corruption or serious novelists exploring literary and intellectual boundaries. But free speech, if it is a universal right, also protects pornographers hawking pictures of naked women with their legs spread, and bigots sporting swastikas or white hoods and selling hatred.

We must start by recognizing that the most famous and honoured defence of free speech, John Stuart Mill's argument in *On Liberty*,[3] cannot support a right with that scope. Mill said that we should tolerate even the speech we hate because truth is most likely to emerge in a free intellectual combat from which no idea has been excluded. People with passionate religious convictions think they already know the truth, however, and they can hardly be expected to have more confidence in Mill's doubtful epistemology than in their own bibles. Nor could Mill's optimism justify, even to us, tolerating everything that those who believe free speech is a basic human right insist should be tolerated. Pornographic images hardly supply 'ideas' to any marketplace of thought; and history gives us little reason for expecting racist speech to contribute to its own refutation.

If freedom of speech is a basic right, this must be so not in virtue of instrumental arguments, like Mill's, which suppose that liberty is important because of its consequences. It must be so for reasons of basic principle. We can find that basic principle, moreover. We can find it in a condition of human dignity: it is illegitimate for governments to impose a collective or official decision on dissenting individuals, using the coercive powers of the state, unless that decision has been taken in a manner that respects each individual's status as a free and equal member of the community. People who believe in democracy think that it is fair to use the police power to enforce the law if the law has been adopted through democratic political procedures that express the majority's will. But though majoritarian procedures may be a necessary condition of political legitimacy, they are not a sufficient condition. Fair democracy requires what we might call a democratic background: it requires, for example, that every competent adult have a vote in deciding what the majority's will is. And it requires, further, that each citizen have not just a vote but a voice: a majority decision is not fair unless everyone has had a fair opportunity to express his or her attitudes or opinions or fears or tastes or presuppositions or prejudices or ideals, not just in the hope of influencing others (though that hope is crucially important), but also just to confirm his or her standing as a responsible agent in, rather than a passive victim of, collective action. The majority has no right to impose its will on someone who is forbidden to raise a voice in protest or argument or objection before the decision is taken.

---

[3] *On Liberty* (London: John W Parker & Son, 1859).

That is not the only reason for insisting on freedom of speech as a condition of political legitimacy; but it is a central one. It may be objected that in most democracies that right now has little value for many citizens: ordinary people, with no access to great newspapers or television broadcasts, have little chance to be heard. That is a genuine problem; it may be that genuine free speech requires more than just freedom from legal censorship. But that is hardly an excuse for denying at least that freedom and the dignity it confirms: we must try to find other ways of providing those without money or influence a real chance to make their voices heard.

This argument entails a great deal more than just that governments may not censor formal political speeches or writing. A community's legislation and policy are determined more by its moral and cultural environment, the mix of its people's opinions, prejudices, tastes, and attitudes than by editorial columns or party political broadcasts or stump political speeches. It is as unfair to impose a collective decision on someone who has not been allowed to contribute to that moral environment, by expressing his political or social convictions or tastes or prejudices informally, as on someone whose pamphlets against the decision were destroyed by the police. This is true no matter how offensive the majority takes these convictions or tastes or prejudices to be, nor how reasonable its objection is.

The temptation may be near overwhelming to make exceptions to that principle to declare that people have no right to pour the filth of pornography or race-hatred into the culture in which we all must live. But we cannot do that without forfeiting our moral title to force such people to bow to the collective judgments that do make their way into the statute books. We may and must protect women and homosexuals and members of minority groups from specific and damaging consequences of sexism, intolerance, and racism. We must protect them against unfairness and inequality in employment or education or housing or the criminal process, for example, and we may adopt laws to achieve that protection. But we must not try to intervene further upstream, by forbidding any expression of the attitudes or prejudices that we think nourish such unfairness or inequality, because if we intervene too soon in the process through which collective opinion is formed, we spoil the only democratic justification we have for insisting that everyone obey these laws, even those who hate and resent them.

So in a democracy no one, however powerful or impotent, can have a right not to be insulted or offended. Echoing arguments in favour of laws prohibiting racist and homophobic speech, it is often said that religion is special, because people's religious convictions are so central to their personalities that they should not be asked to tolerate ridicule of their beliefs, and might feel a religious duty to strike back at what they take to be a sacrilege. But just as we should not make an exception for insults based on race or sexual orientation if we expect bigots to accept the verdict of the majority once the majority has spoken in enacting legislation prohibiting racial and sexual orientation discrimination in employment, for instance, we cannot make an exception for religious insult if we want use law to protect the free exercise of religion in other ways. If we want to forbid the police from profiling people who look or dress like Muslims for special searches, for example, we cannot also forbid people from opposing that policy by claiming in cartoons or otherwise, that Islam is committed to terrorism, however misguided we think that opinion is. Certainly we should criticize the judgment and taste of such people. But religion must observe the principle of democracy, not the other way around.

Someone might now object that my argument shows, at most, only that free speech is essential to a democracy, and therefore does not show that it is a universal human right that may properly be claimed even in non-democratic societies. We may want to reply that democracy is itself a universal human right and that non-democratic societies are tyrannies. But we need not rely on that claim, because we can distinguish democracy, as a form of political organization, from the more basic obligation of government to treat all those subject to its dominion with equal concern, as all people whose lives matter. That plainly is a basic human right; and many of the more detailed human rights we all recognize flow from it. And so does a right of free speech. Even in a country ruled by prophets or generals in which ordinary citizens have no real vote, these citizens must nevertheless have the right to speak out, to cry for the attention or to buy the ear of those who will decide their fates, or simply to bear witness, out of self-respect if nothing else, to what they believe to be wicked or unfair. A government that deems them too corrupt or debased or ignoble even to be heard, except on penalty of death or jail, can hardly pretend that it counts their interests as part of its own.

It is tempting, as I said, to think that even if some liberty of speech must be counted a universal right, this right cannot be absolute; that those whose opinions are too threatening or base or contrary to the moral or religious consensus have forfeited any right to the concern on which the right rests. But such a reservation would destroy the principle: it would leave room only for the pointless grant of protection for ideas or tastes or prejudices that those in power approve, or in any case do not fear. We might have the power to silence those we despise, but it would be at the cost of political legitimacy, which is more important than they are.

Any such reservation would also be dangerous. Principle is indivisible, and we try to divide it at our peril. When we compromise on freedom because we think our immediate goals more important, we are likely to find that the power to exploit the compromise is not in our own hands after all, but in those of fanatical priests armed with fatwas and fanatical moralists with their own brand of hate.

Preface

This book has its origin in a conference which took place under the same title over a weekend in April 2007 at the University of Cambridge. We are very grateful to the Centre for Public Law in the Law Faculty and its Director, Christopher Forsyth, for hosting the conference and for placing the invaluable human resource of Felicity Eves at our disposal. We are also indebted to Clifford Chance LLP for their financial support for the conference and for the personal support provided by Michael Smyth. The British Academy funded the attendance of some of our overseas speakers. The conference sessions themselves were managed with great efficiency by the distinguished chairs: Baroness Perry, Sir Stephen Sedley, Sir Patrick Elias, Sir Jack Beatson, Professor David Feldman, and Michael Smyth. The conference also benefited from papers by Lord Goldsmith QC, David Feldman, Gavin Phillipson, and Joshua Rozenberg which do not appear in this volume.

We have used the time since the conference to expand the coverage of this collection and are delighted to have secured contributions from C. Edwin Baker, Ronald Dworkin, John Finnis, Steven Heyman, Pascal Mbongo, Peter Molnar, Amnon Reichman, L.W. Sumner, and Patrick Weil. These additional chapters have enabled us to cover more ground and to add the perspectives of other disciplines. However, extreme speech is a capacious subject making some selection as to subject matter inevitable. We would have liked to include a section on pornography (which some consider to be a form of hate speech against women), but for reasons of space were unable to do so.

We have been much aided by our research assistant, Kelly Frailing, who has checked references across an unusually broad range of sources with great skill and speed. We are also grateful to the staff at OUP for their enthusiastic welcome of the project and their encouragement and assistance since then: John Louth, Chris Champion, Alex Flach, Lucy Page, and Rebecca Smith.

This book is dedicated to our families.

Ivan Hare   James Weinstein
Blackstone Chambers   Sandra Day O'Connor College of Law
London   Arizona

Outline Contents

Table of Cases   xxvii
Table of Legislation   xxxix
Table of Conventions and International Instruments   xlix
List of Contributors   liii

General Introduction: Free Speech, Democracy, and the
Suppression of Extreme Speech Past and Present   1
James Weinstein and Ivan Hare

PART I: INTRODUCTION AND BACKGROUND

1. Freedom of Speech in a Globalized World   11
   Dieter Grimm

2. Extreme Speech, Public Order, and Democracy:
   Lessons from *The Masses*   23
   James Weinstein

3. Extreme Speech Under International and
   Regional Human Rights Standards   62
   Ivan Hare

4. An Overview of American Free Speech Doctrine and its
   Application to Extreme Speech   81
   James Weinstein

5. Hate Speech in the United Kingdom: An Historical Overview   92
   Sir David Williams QC

6. Extreme Speech and Liberalism   96
   Maleiha Malik

PART II: HATE SPEECH

7. Hate Speech   123
   Robert Post

8. Autonomy and Hate Speech   139
   C. Edwin Baker

9. Hate Speech, Public Discourse, and the First Amendment   158
   Steven J. Heyman

10. Wild-West Cowboys versus Cheese-Eating Surrender Monkeys:
    Some Problems in Comparative Approaches to Hate Speech   182
    Eric Heinze

11. Incitement and the Regulation of Hate Speech in Canada:
    A Philosophical Analysis   204
    L.W. Sumner

12. Hate Speech, Extreme Speech, and Collective Defamation in
    French Law   221
    Pascal Mbongo

13. Towards Improved Law and Policy on 'Hate Speech'—The
    'Clear and Present Danger' Test in Hungary   237
    Peter Molnar

14. Cumulative Jurisprudence and Hate Speech: Sexual Orientation
    and Analogies to Disability, Age, and Obesity   265
    Eric Heinze

        PART III: INCITEMENT TO RELIGIOUS HATRED
                  AND RELATED TOPICS

15. Blasphemy and Incitement to Religious Hatred:
    Free Speech Dogma and Doctrine   289
    Ivan Hare

16. The Danish Cartoons, Offensive Expression, and
    Democratic Legitimacy   311
    Ian Cram

17. Criminalizing Religiously Offensive Satire: Free Speech,
    Human Dignity, and Comparative Law   331
    Amnon Reichman

       PART IV: RELIGIOUS SPEECH AND EXPRESSIVE
       CONDUCT THAT OFFEND SECULAR VALUES

18. Religious Speech that Undermines Gender Equality   357
    Carolyn Evans

19. Homophobic Speech, Equality Denial, and Religious Expression   375
    Ian Leigh

20. Extreme Religious Dress: Perspectives on Veiling Controversies 400
    Dominic McGoldrick

21. Endorsing Discrimination Between Faiths: A Case of
    Extreme Speech?   430
    John Finnis

PART V INCITEMENT TO, AND GLORIFICATION OF, TERRORISM

22. Incitement to, and Glorification of, Terrorism 445
    Eric Barendt

23. The Terrorism Act 2006: Discouraging Terrorism 463
    Tufyal Choudhury

24. Radical Religious Speech: The Ingredients of a Binary World View 488
    Sara Savage and Jose Liht

PART VI HOLOCAUST DENIAL

25. 'On the Internet, Nobody Knows You're a Nazi': Some
    Comparative Legal Aspects of Holocaust Denial on the *WWW* 511
    David Fraser

26. Expanding Holocaust Denial and Legislation Against It 538
    Michael Whine

27. The Holocaust Denial Decision of the Federal Constitutional
    Court of Germany 557
    Dieter Grimm

28. The Politics of Memory: Bans and Commemorations 562
    Patrick Weil

PART VII GOVERNMENTAL AND SELF-REGULATION OF THE MEDIA

29. Shouting Fire
    From the Nanny State to the Heckler's Veto: The New
    Censorship and How to Counter It 583
    David Edgar

30. Extreme Speech and American Press Freedoms 598
    David J. Bodney

31. Extreme Speech and the Democratic Functions of the Mass Media 608
    Jacob Rowbottom

Index 631

Detailed Contents

Table of Cases   xxvii
Table of Legislation   xxxix
Table of Conventions and International Instruments   xlix
List of Contributors   liii

General Introduction: Free Speech, Democracy, and the
Suppression of Extreme Speech Past and Present   1
James Weinstein and Ivan Hare

   1. The Enduring yet Troubled Marriage of Free
      Speech and Democracy   1
   2. Is there a Lesson in this History?   5

PART I: INTRODUCTION AND BACKGROUND

1. **Freedom of Speech in a Globalized World**   11
   Dieter Grimm

   1. The Meaning of Freedom of Speech   11
      (i) Freedom of Expression   11
      (ii) Freedom of the Media   14
   2. Freedom of Speech Under Globalized Conditions   17
      (i) Protecting Religion from Speech?   17
      (ii) More Uniformity of Speech-Related Law?   19

2. **Extreme Speech, Public Order, and Democracy:**
   Lessons from *The Masses*   23
   James Weinstein

   1. Introduction   23
   2. The Core Free Speech Right of Democratic Participation 25
      (i) Popular Sovereignty   26
      (ii) The Individual Right of Political Participation   27
      (iii) Public Discourse   29
   3. Breaching the Core: *Hammond* v. *DPP*   30
      (i) Facts and Divisional Court Decision   30
      (ii) Identifying the Core Breach   32
      (iii) A Countervailing Right Not to be Insulted?   33
      (iv) Distinguishing Public Discourse from Personal Abuse   35

(v) What Went Wrong? 37

4. Object Lessons from the US   40

5. Another Core Breach?: *Norwood* v. *DPP*   44
     (i) Facts and Divisional Court Decision   44
     (ii) Excluding Anti-Democratic Speech from Public Discourse   47
     (iii) The Perils of Interpreting Ambiguous Political Rhetoric   50

6. Speech at the Periphery of the Core and
     the Strategy of Overprotection   52
     (i) 'Fighting Words'   53
     (ii) Advocacy of Law Violation   53
     (iii) Expression Offending Civility Norms   55
     (iv) Group Defamation   58

7. Conclusion   60

3. **Extreme Speech Under International and Regional
Human Rights Standards**   62
Ivan Hare

1. The History and Structure of International and Regional
     Human Rights Instruments   62
     (i) International Human Rights Instruments   63
     (ii) Regional Human Rights Instruments   65

2. Freedom of Expression   69
     (i) Freedom of Expression Under the ICCPR   69
     (ii) Freedom of Expression Under Regional Human Rights Instruments   72

3. The Effectiveness of International and Regional Human Rights
     Instruments in Protecting Extreme Speech   74

4. Conclusion   79

4. **An Overview of American Free Speech Doctrine and its
Application to Extreme Speech**   81
James Weinstein

1. The Rule against Content Discrimination   81

2. The Rule against Content Discrimination and its Application
     to Extreme Speech   84
     (i) Hate Speech   84
     (ii) Incitement to terrorism, Holocaust denial, and other forms of
         extreme speech   88

3. Methodological Differences   90

4. Conclusion   91

5. **Hate Speech in the United Kingdom: An Historical Overview**   92
Sir David Williams QC

6. **Extreme Speech and Liberalism** 96
   Maleiha Malik

   1. Introduction 96
   2. 'Who are the Extremists?' 97
   3. Legal and Non-Legal Responses to Extreme Speech 99
       (i) Criminalizing Extreme Speech: The Limits of Legal Regulation 99
       (ii) Non-Legal Responses to Hate Speech: Cultural Policy and Media
            Regulation 105
   4. Engaging with Extremists 107
       (i) Liberal Democracy as a 'Rational Liberal Consensus': Containing
           Doctrines that Are 'Irrational, Unreasonable, and Mad' 107
       (ii) Agonistic Respect: Creating Political Space for the Extremists 109
       (iii) 'Discourse Ethics': What Are the Rules of the Game
             When 'Engaging with Extremists'? 111
       (iv) Engaging with the 'Extremists' 113
       (v) Applying the 'Rules of the Game' to Extremists:
           Classification, Protection, and Critique 115
       (vi) Internal and External Critique of Extremists 117
       (vii) The Limits of Democratic Discourse 118
   5. Conclusion 120

PART II: HATE SPEECH

7. **Hate Speech** 123
   Robert Post

8. **Autonomy and Hate Speech** 139
   C. Edwin Baker

   1. Introduction 139
   2. Speaker Autonomy and State Legitimacy 142
   3. Objections and a Pragmatic Reply 146
   4. The Evils Restrictions May Cause 150
   5. Conclusion: Democracy's Necessary Faith in People 155

9. **Hate Speech, Public Discourse, and the First Amendment** 158
   Steven J. Heyman

   1. The Foundations and Limits of the First Amendment Freedom
      of Expression 159
   2. Should Public Hate Speech be Protected
      by the First Amendment? 165
       (i) The Impact of Public Hate Speech on Other Rights 165

(ii) Should Public Hate Speech be Protected Because
        of Its Political Character?   169
   (iii) Refining the Rights-Based Analysis of Public Hate Speech   177
   3. Conclusion   181

10. **Wild-West Cowboys versus Cheese-Eating Surrender Monkeys:
     Some Problems in Comparative Approaches to Hate Speech**   182
     Eric Heinze

     1. Introduction   182
     2. The Locus of Comparison   184
     3. Informal Power   187
     4. Formal Law   189
     5. Realism and Essentialism   190
     6. Formal and Substantive Freedoms: An Age-Old Dilemma   196
     7. Ahistoricism   200
     8. Conclusion   203

11. **Incitement and the Regulation of Hate Speech in
     Canada: A Philosophical Analysis**   204
     L. W. Sumner

     1. Mill's Tests   204
     2. The Harms of Hate Speech   207
     3. Promoting and Inciting   212
     4. Conclusion   219

12. **Hate Speech, Extreme Speech, and Collective
     Defamation in French Law**   221
     Pascal Mbongo

     1. Systematic Control of Hate Speech and Extreme Speech   222
        (i) Administrative Law   223
        (ii) Criminal Law   227
        (iii) General Observations   228
     2. A Particular Rigour for Certain Types of Speech   229
        (i) Overview of Collective Defamations   229
        (ii) Religious Abuse and Defamation   231
        (iii) Racial Abuse and Defamation   234

13. **Towards Improved Law and Policy on 'Hate Speech'—The
     'Clear and Present Danger' Test in Hungary**   237
     Peter Molnar

     1. Introduction   237

2. The Social Context of 'Hate Speech' in Hungary   239

3. The Application of the 'Clear and Present Danger Test' in Hungary   247

    (i) The 'Hate Speech' Decisions of the Hungarian Constitutional Court   247

    (ii) The *Hegedus Jr.* Case and Its Aftermath: The Failure Properly to Apply the Test   257

    (iii) The Prohibition of the Public Display of Certain Totalitarian Symbols   261

4. Conclusion   263

14. **Cumulative Jurisprudence and Hate Speech: Sexual Orientation and Analogies to Disability, Age, and Obesity**   265

Eric Heinze

1. Introduction   265

2. Sexual Minorities and Cumulative Jurisprudence   266

3. Cumulative or Contradictory?   272

4. Some Objections and Replies   280

5. Conclusion   284

PART III: INCITEMENT TO RELIGIOUS HATRED AND RELATED TOPICS

15. **Blasphemy and Incitement to Religious Hatred: Free Speech Dogma and Doctrine**   289

Ivan Hare

1. The Historical Relationship between Speech and the Protection of Religion: Blasphemy   289

2. Legislating Against Hate and the Repeal of the Law of Blasphemy   293

    (i) Incitement to Religious Hatred   294

    (ii) Repeal of the Law of Blasphemy   296

3. Free Speech Principle and the Protection of Religious Sensibilities 300

    (i) Blasphemy   301

    (ii) Incitement to Religious Hatred   305

4. Conclusion   310

16. **The Danish Cartoons, Offensive Expression, and Democratic Legitimacy**   311

Ian Cram

1. Introduction   311

2. Offensive Expression in European Convention
Jurisprudence—*Handyside* Rhetoric and Reality   314
3. The Margin of Appreciation and the Absence of Consensus   317
4. A 'Right' to be Protected from Offensive Expression?   319
5. Offence as a Contents-Based Ground for Restricting Expression   321
6. Expression about Islam as 'Political Speech'   323
7. The Problem of Gratuitously Insulting or Gratuitously
Offensive Speech   325
8. Putting the Breaks on Offensive Expression: Tipping Points
and the Concept of Democratic Legitimacy   327

17. **Criminalizing Religiously Offensive Satire:
Free Speech, Human Dignity, and Comparative Law**   331
Amnon Reichman

   1. Introduction   331
   2. The *Suszkin* Case   332
   3. Offensive Speech: Diverging Normative Justifications   333
   4. Offensive Speech: Is Religion Normatively Special?   337
   5. Citizens, State, and Speech   340
   6. The Cultural Significance of Speech   342
   7. Legal Cultures—Balancing Words   345
   8. Beyond Differences: The Doctrine of Fighting Words   348
   9. Some Heretical Reflections on Speech Theory
and the Role of Passion   350
   10. Conclusion   352

PART IV: RELIGIOUS SPEECH AND EXPRESSIVE CONDUCT THAT OFFEND SECULAR VALUES

18. **Religious Speech that Undermines Gender Equality**   357
Carolyn Evans

   1. Introduction   357
   2. Religious Speech that Offends against Gender Equality   358
     (i) Construction of Gendered Hierarchies   359
     (ii) Incitement or Condoning of Violence against Women   360
   3. Two Models of Speech   362
     (i) The Liberal Model   363
     (ii) A Religious Model   364
   4. Empowering Religious Women's Speech   368
     (i) The Importance of Religious Women's Speech   368
     (ii) Practical Strategies for Empowering Religious Women's Speech   370

5. Conclusion 373

19. **Homophobic Speech, Equality Denial, and Religious Expression** 375
    Ian Leigh

    1. Introduction 375
    2. Laws Prohibiting Homophobic Expression 379
    3. International Responses 380
    4. The UK Position 381
    5. The Status of Religiously-Motivated Speech 388
       (i) The *Hammond* Case 388
       (ii) The *Åke Green* Case 391
    6. Adjudicating Rights Conflicts 393
    7. Conclusion 398

20. **Extreme Religious Dress: Perspectives on Veiling Controversies** 400
    Dominic McGoldrick

    1. Introduction 400
    2. Speech and Religious Dress 401
    3. Human Rights Perspectives 402
       (i) Individual Applications to National Courts 402
       (ii) Individual Applications to International Human Rights Bodies 403
       (iii) Individual and Group Identities and Rights 405
       (iv) Minority Rights and Cultural Rights 406
       (v) The Right to Freedom of Religion 407
       (vi) Negative and Positive Aspects of a Human Right 408
       (vii) The Human Rights Context of Church–State Relations under the ECHR 409
       (viii) Limitations on Religious Freedoms on the Basis of the 'protection of public order' and the 'protection of the rights and freedoms of others' 410
    4. Educational Contexts 411
       (i) Children's Rights 411
       (ii) Teachers' Rights and Children's Rights 414
       (iii) Universities 416
    5. Discrimination 416
       (i) Religious Discrimination and Islamophobia 416
       (ii) Religious Discrimination and the European Union 418
       (iii) Racial Discrimination 419
       (iv) Gender Discrimination and Feminist Perspectives 420
       (v) Intersecting Discrimination 424
    6. Autonomy and Consent 424

7. Explaining Differential Human Rights Outcomes:
The Margin of Appreciation — 427
8. Locating the Debates on Religious Dress — 427

21. **Endorsing Discrimination Between Faiths: A Case of
Extreme Speech?** — 430
John Finnis

1. Legitimate, if not Necessary, School Ban on a Garment — 430
2. Necessary State Ban on a Party and Government — 433
3. A Certain Religion's Unacceptable Political Purposes — 437
4. Applying the Findings: Extreme Speech or Belated Warning? — 439

PART V: INCITEMENT TO, AND GLORIFICATION OF, TERRORISM

22. **Incitement to, and Glorification of, Terrorism** — 445
Eric Barendt

1. Introduction — 445
2. The Terrorism Act 2006 — 446
3. The Encouragement of Terrorism and Freedom of Speech — 447
4. Scanlon's Argument — 449
5. A Speaker's Right to Encourage Terrorism? — 451
6. Other Arguments — 452
7. *Brandenburg* v. *Ohio* — 454
   (i) The Words Used by the Speaker or Writer   455
   (ii) Advocacy Directed to Inciting or Producing Unlawful Action   456
   (iii) The Requirement of Imminent Unlawful Action   457
   (iv) Likely to Incite or Produce Unlawful Action   458
8. The *Brandenburg* Principle Inapplicable to
   Threats and Conspiracy — 459
9. The Relevance of *Terrorism* — 461

23. **The Terrorism Act 2006: Discouraging Terrorism** — 463
Tufyal Choudhury

1. Introduction — 463
2. The CONTEST Strategy — 465
3. The Terrorism Act 2006 — 466
4. The Radicalization Process — 473
5. The Counterproductive Potential of Counterterrorism Laws — 481
6. Conclusion — 486

24. **Radical Religious Speech: The Ingredients of a Binary World View** 488
    Sara Savage and Jose Liht

    1. Introduction: The Shaping Power of Language 488
    2. Structural Features of Islamist Radical Religious Discourse 489
        (i) Narrative 489
        (ii) Rhetorical Strategies 492
        (iii) Propositional, Word-Based Processing 495
        (iv) Intratextuality 496
        (v) Integrative Complexity 497
        (vi) Thinking as Arguing 498
        (vii) The Myth of Pure Evil 499
    3. The Appeal of Islamist Extreme Speech 500
    4. Implications 504
    5. Conclusion 507

PART VI: HOLOCAUST DENIAL

25. **'On the Internet, Nobody Knows You're a Nazi':**
    Some Comparative Legal Aspects of Holocaust Denial
    on the *WWW* 511
    David Fraser

    1. Introduction 511
    2. The Context of Holocaust Denial 514
    3. YAHOO!, the *WWW*, and French Legal Regulation
       of Holocaust Denial 521
    4. Canada: Zundel, the Web, and the Success (?) of Law 529
    5. Australia, the Law, and Holocaust Denial 534
    6. Conclusion 536

26. **Expanding Holocaust Denial and Legislation Against It** 538
    Michael Whine

    1. Holocaust Denial and the Internet 539
    2. International Agreements 541
    3. National Legislation 543
    4. Successful Prosecution 545
    5. The European Common Framework 547
    6. Recent Convictions 548
    7. The Iranian Government's Initiative 551
    8. David Irving 552
    9. Future Outcomes 553
    10. The Necessity of Holocaust Education 555

27. **The Holocaust Denial Decision of the Federal Constitutional Court of Germany** 557
Dieter Grimm

28. **The Politics of Memory: Bans and Commemorations** 562
Patrick Weil

    1. Introduction 562
    2. Permanent Elimination of Slavery in 1848 566
    3. Consecration of the Republic 568
    4. Commemorations and Bans with Respect to the Genocide of the Jews in Europe 571
    5. And Slavery...? 575

PART VII: GOVERNMENTAL AND SELF-REGULATION OF THE MEDIA

29. **Shouting Fire**
From the Nanny State to the Heckler's Veto: The New Censorship and How to Counter It 583
David Edgar

30. **Extreme Speech and American Press Freedoms** 598
David J. Bodney

    1. Introduction 598
    2. The Sedition Act 600
    3. *Near, Sullivan*, and *Brandenburg* 600
    4. Rhetorical Hyperbole, Vigorous Epithets, and Parody 603
    5. Incitement, True Threats, and Fighting Words 604
    6. The Marketplace and Evolving Norms of Civility 605

31. **Extreme Speech and the Democratic Functions of the Mass Media** 608
Jacob Rowbottom

    1. Media Freedom and Democracy 609
        (i) Public Watchdog 610
        (ii) Diverse Information and Ideas 613
    2. Extreme Speech and Media Regulation 618
        (i) The Broadcast Media 619
        (ii) The Press 626
    3. Conclusion 629

Index 631

Table of Cases

INTERNATIONAL CASES AND DECISIONS

Committee on the Elimination of Racial Discrimination (CERD)

Ahmad v Denmark CERD 16/99 72

Hagan v Australia CERD 26/02 72

LK v Netherlands CERD 4/91 72

Committee on the Elimination of Discrimination Against Women (CEDAW)

Rahime Kayhan v Turkey, Comm No 8/2005 .... 405, 420

European Court of Human Rights (ECtHR)

Abdulaziz, Cabales and Balkandali v United Kingdom (1985) 7 EHRR 471 422

Ahmed and Others v UK (2000) 29 EHRR 1 414

BH, MW, HP and GK v Austria Appl No 12774/87, 12 Oct 1989 76

Choudhury v UK (1991) 12 Hum Rts L J 172 309

Connors v UK (2005) 40 EHRR 9 403

Cyprus v Turkey (2002) 35 EHRR 731 76

Dahlab v Switzerland Appl No 42393/98, 15 Feb 2001 .... 404, 414, 415, 421, 422

Darby v Sweden (1990) 13 EHRR 774 272

De Becker v Belgium Appl No 214/56 (1958) 2 YB 79

Dudgeon v UK Appl No 7525/76, 22 Oct 1981 .... 189, 272, 318

Erdogdu and Ince v Turkey [1999] Appl No 25067/94, 8 July 1999 611

Fairfield v UK Appl No 24790/04, 8 Mar 2005 .... 44, 381, 389

Freedom and Democracy Party v Turkey, Appl No 23885/94,
   8 Dec 1999 226

Garaudy v France Appl No 65831/01, 24 Jun 2003 .... 73, 89, 381, 547, 561

Gay News and Lemon v United Kingdom (1982) 5 EHRR 123 304

Giniewski v France (2007) 45 EHRR 23 .... 74, 231–232, 305, 381

Glimmerveen & Hagenbeek v Netherlands Appl
   Nos 8348 & 8406/78 (1980) 18 D & R 187 .... 73, 84, 313, 381

Goodwin v UK (1996) 22 EHRR 123 316

Goodwin v UK (2002) 35 EHRR 18 406

Gündüz v Turkey (2005) 41 EHRR 5 .... 74, 305, 372, 380, 381, 426

H, W, P & K v Austria (1989)
   62 D & R 216 .... 73, 89

Handyside v UK (1976) 1 EHRR 737 .... 68, 228, 314–317, 318, 388, 389, 440

I A v Turkey (2007) 45 EHRR 30 .... 305, 313, 319, 325, 326, 327, 330

Inze v Austria, 28 Oct 1987, Ser A, No. 26 272

Jersild v Denmark (1995) 19 EHRR 1 .... 72, 73, 177, 191, 273, 317, 381,
                                                       440, 610–613, 616, 624

Kalac v Turkey (1999) 27 EHRR 552 414–415

Karaduman v Turkey (1993) 74 DR 93 .... 404, 436

Klein v Slovakia Appl No 72208/01, 31 Oct 2006 381

Kokkinakis v Greece (1994) 17 EHRR 397 .... 303, 320, 388

Konrad v Germany Appl No 35504/03, 18 Sep 2006 411

Lawless *v* Ireland (No 3) (1961) 1 EHRR 15 . . . . 67, 317
Lehideux and Isorni *v* France (1998) 30 EHRR 665 . . . . 73, 381
Lindon *v* France Appl No 21279/02, 22 Oct 2007 611
Lingens *v* Austria (1986) 8 EHRR 103 . . . . 78, 79
Marckx *v* Belgium Appl No 6833/74, 13 Jun 1979, Ser A, No. 13 272
Moscow Branch of the Salvation Army *v* Russia Appl No 72881/01, 5 Oct 2006 401
Muller *v* Switzerland (1991) 13 EHRR 212 318
Murphy *v* Ireland (2004) 38 EHRR 13 . . . . 316, 326, 327, 330, 388, 411
Nachova *v* Bulgaria Appl Nos 43577/98 & 43579/98, 6 Jul 2005 403
Norwood *v* UK Appl No 23131/03, (2004) 40 EHRR SE 111 . . . . 78, 84, 101
Oberschlick *v* Austria (1995) 19 EHRR 389 314
Observer and Guardian *v* UK (1992) 14 EHRR 153 609
Otto Preminger Institut *v* Austria (1994) 19 EHRR 34 . . . . 73–74, 89, 190, 191, 267,
273, 277, 279, 304, 305, 313, 314,
315, 319, 326, 327, 330, 397, 410
Plattform Artze fur das Leben *v* Austria (1998) 13 EHRR 204 320
Prager and Oberschlic *v* Austria (1996) 21 EHRR 1 611
Pretty *v* UK (2002) 35 EHRR 1 . . . . 406, 424
Refah Partisi (The Welfare Party) *v* Turkey (2002)
  (Chambers Opinion) 35 EHRR 3, (2003) 37
  EHRR 1 . . . . 47, 67, 324, 411, 435–436, 437, 438, 439, 441
Refah Partisi (No 2) *v* Turkey (2003) 37 EHRR 1 . . . . . . 434–436, 437, 438, 439, 440, 441
Şahin (Leyla) *v* Turkey (2007) 44 EHRR 5 . . . . 404, 405, 406, 410, 411, 416, 417,
422, 423, 432, 433, 434, 435, 437
Socialist Party *v* Turkey (1998) 27 EHRR 51 226
Sorenson *v* Denmark (2008) 46 EHRR 29 408
Stedman *v* UK (1997) 23 EHRR CD 168 414
Stoll *v* Switzerland Appl No 69698/01, 10 Dec 2007 611–612
Sunday Times *v* UK (1979) 2 EHRR 245 73
Sunday Times *v* UK (No 2) [1992] 14 EHRR 123 33
Sürek *v* Turkey Appl No 26682/95, 8 Jul 1999 . . . . 372, 611, 625
United Communist Party of Turkey *v* Turkey (1998) 26 EHRR 121 . . . . 67, 226
VgT Verein Gegen Tierfabriken *v* Swtzerland (2002) 34 EHRR 159 411
Von Hannover *v* Germany (2004) 16 BHRC 545 20
Wingrove *v* UK (1996) 24 EHRR 1 . . . . 74, 89, 128, 190, 191, 267, 273, 277,
300, 304, 305, 313, 314, 315,
316, 319, 326, 327, 330, 368, 410
Witzsch *v* Germany Appl No 7485/03, 13 Dec 2005 381
X *v* FRG (1982) 29 D & R 194 73
X and Y *v* Netherlands (1986) 8 EHRR 235 320
Yasar et al *v* Turkey Appl 42713/98, 23 Sep 2004 393

International Criminal Tribunal for Rwanda (ICTR)

Ferdinand Nahimana, Jean-Bosco Barayagwiza and Hassan Ngeze *v*
  The Prosecutor, Case No ICTR-99-52-A 264

United Nations Human Rights Committee (HRC)

Ballantyne, Davidson and McIntyre *v* Canada UN Doc
  CCPR/C/47/359/1989, 5 May 1993 407
Cha'are Shalom Ve Tsedek *v* France (2000) 9 BHRC 27 406
Faurisson *v* France (1996) 2 BHRC 1 . . . . 70, 71, 190, 380

Folgero *v* Norway (2007) 23 BHRC 227; [2007] ELR 557 414
Fressoz and Roire *v* France (1999) 5 BHRC 654 610
Hertzberg *v* Finland 61/79 77
Hudoyberganova *v* Uzbekistan UN Doc CCPR/C/82/D/931/2000,
    18 Jan 2004 405
Joslin *v* New Zealand, Communication No 902/1999,
    UN Doc A/57/40 (2002) 272
JRT and WG Party *v* Canada UN Doc A/38/40 71
Lehideux and Isornia *v* France (1998) 5 BHRC 540 610
Leirvag *v* Norway (2004) 19 BHRC 635 414
Ross *v* Canada (2001) 10 BHRC 219 71
Toonen *v* Australia, Communication No 488/1992,
    UN Doc CCPR/C/50/D/488/1992 (1994) 272
Young *v* Australia, Communication No 941/2000,
    UN Doc CCPR/C/78/D/941/2000 (2003) 272

NATIONAL CASES

Australia

Australian Capital Television Pty Ltd *v* Commonwealth (1992) 177 CLR 106 . . . . 11, 27
Coleman *v* Power (2004) 220 CLR 1 459
Jones *v* Töben [2002] FCA 1150 534
R *v* Sharkey (1949) 79 CLR 121 3
Theophanous *v* The Herald and Weekly Times Ltd (1994) 182 CLR 104 324

Austria

Gudenus case (Holocaust denial) 549
Honsik case, 2007 (Holocaust denial) 550

Belgium

Raes case, 2007 (Holocaust denial) 550

Canada

Chamberlain *v* Surrey School District No 36 [2002] 4 SCR 710 397
Hugh Owens *v* Saskatchewan Human Rights Commission
    [2006] SKCA 41 392
Mugesera *v* Canada (Minister of Citizenship and Immigration)
    2005 SCC 40 511
R *v* Ahenakew [2005] SJ No 459; [2006] SKQB 272; [2006]
    Sk. C. LEXIS 345 518
R *v* Keegstra [1990] 3 SCR 697 . . . . 72, 79, 125, 178, 205, 213, 217, 380, 394
R *v* Oakes (1986) 1 SCR 103 . . . . 13, 205, 206, 207, 394
R *v* Zundel [1992] 2 SCR 731 380
Reference re Same Sex Marriage [2004] 3 SCR 698 378
Ross *v* New Brunswick School District No 15 [1996] 1 SCR 825 380
Trinity Western University *v* British Columbia College of
    Teachers [2001] 1 SCR 772 . . . . 395, 396
Canadian Human Rights Tribunal
Sabina Citron and Canadian Human Rights Commission and
    Ernst Zündel and League for Human Rights of B'nai Brith
    Canada, Reasons for Decision, CHRT, T.D. 1/02 2002/01/18 . . . 529–533, 534, 535, 549

Warman *v* Kyburz 2003 CHRT 18 533

Denmark

Prophet Mohammed cartoons 2005 .... 17, 180, Ch 16, 312, 331, 349,
                                                 453, 551, 583, 592, 594, 608

France

Association J'Accuse, Acton Internationale pour le Justice
    (AIPJ) & UEJF *v* Nos Racines, TGI Paris, No. RG :02/57758,
    8 Aug 2002 529
CJL, Cour de Cassation, Ch Cr, No. Y 01-80, 134 FS-P+F Z 01-80 527
Dieudonné case 235–236
Edgar Morin case, Ct of Cassation, 1st Civ, Bull No. 395, 12 Jul 2006, 340 234–235
Faurisson case 1978 572
Faurisson/Badinter, TGI Paris, No. 9727603115, 13 Nov 1998 .... 517, 522, 527, 528
Gollnisch case (Holocaust denial) 549
La Ligue Contre Le Racisme et l'Antisémitisme-LICRA et l'Union
    des Étudiants Juifs de France-UEJF c La Société YAHOO! France,
    TGI Paris, RG :00/05308 521–529
Mohammed Cartoons (Charlie Hebdo), Cr Ct, Paris, 22 Mar 2007 232–233
Reynouard case (Holocaust denial), 2007 550
T, TGI Paris No. 0028602422, 26 Mar 2002 529
UEJF *v* SA Multimania Production devenue LYCOS France, CA Versailles,
    RG No. 00/05502, 16 May 2002 528

Germany

Federal Constitutional Court (BVerfGE)

54, 208, 219 (1980) 559
57, 295 (1981) 16
61, 1, 8 (1982) 559
85, 1, 15 (1991) 559
90, 241 (1994) Holocaust Denial case ....178, 190, Ch 27
93, 266, 299–303 (1995) 126, 560
101, 361 (1999) 20
2 BvR 1436/02, 24 Sep 2003 Ludin case 402, 410, 416
1 BvR 1626/07, 26 Feb 2008 Caroline case 21
Federal Supreme Court
BGHZ 75, 160, 162–3 (1980) 89, 558
Auschwitz trial, Frankfurt 1964/65 559
Germar Rudolf case (Holocaust denial), 2007 538

Greece

Plevris case (Holocaust denial) 550

Hungary

Hegedus Jr, Budapest Municipal Ct, Case No 13.B.423/2002/7, Municipal
    High Ct of Appeal Case Reg No 3.Bf.111/2003/10,
    Sup Ct BH 1997/165, 1998/521 ....255, 257–261
Constitutional Court
Dec 30/1992 .... 245, 247–257, 260
Dec 12/1999 251
Dec 14/2000 261

Dec 18/2004 . . . . 140, 250, 251–252
Dec 95/2008 260
Dec 98/2008 253

Ireland

Corway *v* Independent Newspapers (Ireland) Ltd [1999] 4 IR 484 302

Israel

Adalah *v* Ministry of the Interior (2006) H.C. 7052/03 13
Association for Civil Rights in Israel *v* Chairman of Central Elections
    Committee for Sixteenth Knesset HCJ 651/03 [2003] IsrSC 57(2) 62 354
Bachri *v* Movies' Review Council CA 316/03 [2003] IsrSC 58(1) 249 . . . . 349, 354
Central Elections Committee for Sixteenth Knesset *v* MK
    Tibby EA 11280/02 [2003] IsrSC 57(4) 1, 52–53 . . . . 332, 349
Conterm Ltd *v* Ministry of Finance, Department of Customs and
    VAT [1998] IscSC 52(1) 289 341
Daher *v* Minister of Interior HCJ 448/85 [1986] IsrSC 40(2) 701 346
Dayan *v* Wilk, Jerusalem District Commander HCJ 2481/93 [1994]
    IsrSC 48(2) 456 . . . . 346, 347
Disenchik *v* Attorney General CrimA 126/62 [1963] IsrSC 17(1) 179 346
Golan *v* Prison Services PPA 4463/94 [1996] IsrSC 50(4) 136 337
Gur-Aryeh *v* Second Television and Radio Authority HCJ 1514/01 [2001]
    IsrSC 55(4) 285 346
Israel *v* Suszkin CrimC (Jer) 436/97 [1997] IsrDC 97(5) 730 . . . . 332, 337, 348
Kidum Enterprise and Publishing (1981) Ltd *v* Broadcasting Authority
    HCJ 606/93 [1994] IsrSC 48(2) 1 349
Laor *v* Film & Play Review BD HCJ 14/96 [1987] IsrSC 41(1) 421 349
Levi *v* Southern Dis Commissioner HCJ 153/83 [1988] IsrSC 38(2) 393 . . . . 345, 347
Lishkat Menahaley Hashka'ot *v* Minister of Finance HCJ 1715/97
    [1997] ISCR 51(4) 367 345
Miller *v* Minister of Defense (1995) IsrSC 49(4) 94 337
Qa'adan *v* Israel Land Administration HCJ 6698/95 [2000] IsrSC 54(1) 258 354
Sa'ar *v* Interior Minister [1980] IsrSC 34(2) 169 347
Senesh *v* Broadcasting Authority Management Board HCJ 6126/94
    [1999] IsrSC 53(3) 817 353
Suszkin *v* Israel CrimA 697/98 [1998]
    IsrSC 52(3) 289 . . . . 332, 346, 347, 349, 350, 352, 353, 354
United Mizrahi Bank *v* Migdal Cooperative Village (1995)
    49 (4) P.D.221 13
Universal City Studios Inc *v* Film & Play Review BD HCJ
    806/88 [1989] IsrSC 43(2) 22 347

Netherlands

Janssen case, Dist Ct Hertogenbosch 21 Dec 2004 545
Verbeke case, Appeal 25 Nov 1997 545

New Zealand

Living Word Distributors Ltd *v* Human Rights Action Group Inc
    (Wellington) (1997) 4 HRNZ 9 394
Moonen *v* Film and Literature Board of Review [2000] 2 NZLR 9 394

Poland

Michalkiewicz case (Holocaust denial) 549–550

South Africa

Minister of Home Affairs and another *v* Fourie Case CCT 60/04, 1 Dec 2005 397
Islamic Unity Convention *v* Independent Broadcasting Authority
    2002 (4) SA 294 308

Spain

Constitutional Court, Pedro Varela (Holocaust denial case) 546

Sweden

Prosecutor General *v* Åke Ingemar Teodor Green, Sup Ct,
    Case B 1050-05, 29 Nov 2005 . . . . 377, 386, 391–393, 397, 398, 399

United Kingdom

Ali *v* Lord Grey School Governors [2006] UKHL 14; [2006] 2 AC 363 431
Animal Defenders International *v* Secretary of State for Culture,
    Media and Sport [2008] UKHL 15 . . . . 43, 61, 79
Apelogun Gabriels *v* London Borough of Lambeth (2006) ET 2301976/05 383
Application for Judicial Review by the Christian Institute and
    Others, Re [2007] NIQB 66 . . . . 308, 384
Attorney-General *v* Guardian Newspapers (No 2) [1990] 1 AC 109 609
Attorney-General *v* ITN [1995] 2 All ER 370 457
Attorney-General *v* News Group Newspapers Ltd [1987] 1 QB 1 457
Azmi *v* Kirklees MBC [2007] ICR 1154; [2007] ELR 339 415
Bowman, in re [1915] 2 Ch 447 292
Bowman *v* Secular Society Ltd [1917] AC 406 . . . . 292, 304, 312
Brutus *v* Cozens [1973] AC 854 . . . . 39, 309
Connolly *v* Director of Public Prosecutions [2007] EWHC 237
    (Admin); [2008] 1 WLR 276 309
De Costa *v* De Paz (1754) 2 Swanst 487 292
de Freitas *v* Permanent Secretary of Ministry of Agriculture, Fisheries
    Lands and Housing [1999] 1 AC 69 394
Dimmock *v* Secretary of State for Education and Skills [2007]
    EWHC 2288 (Admin), [2008] ELR 98 413
Director of Public Prosecutions *v* Collins [2006] UKHL 40;
    [2006] 1 WLR 2223 309
Eweida *v* British Airways Plc (2008) UKEAT/0123/08, unreported 419
Ghaidan *v* Godin-Mendoza [2004] UKHL 30; [2004] 2 AC 557 76
Gleaves *v* Deakin [1980] AC 477 301
Hammond *v* DPP [2004] EWHC 69 (Admin) 24, 30–40, 44, 46, 47, 60, 61,
                                                                       80, 381, 385, 388–391, 399
Henry *v* Robinson 1843 1 Brown 643 293
Houston *v* BBC [1995] SC 433 620
Hussain *v* Midland Cosmetic Sales Ltd [2002] EmpLR 713 424
Irving *v* Penguin Books Ltd & Deborah Lipstadt [2001] EWCA Civ 1197 . . . . . 517, 552–553
Jordan *v* Burgoyne [1963] 2 QB 744 93
Khanum *v* IBC Vehicles Ltd (1999) UKEAT/0685/98, unreported 424
Knuppfer *v* London Express News Ltd [1944] AC 116 58
Lynch *v* BBC [1983] NI 193 619

Mandla *v* Dowell Lee [1983] 2 AC 548 . . . . 100, 420
Matadeen *v* Pointu [1999] 1 AC 98 76
Norwood *v* DPP [2003] EWHC 1564
   (Admin) 24, 44–52, 60, 61, 78, 84, 85, 87, 101, 307
Pearce *v* Mayfield Secondary School Governing Body [2002] ICR 198 383
Percy *v* DPP [2001] EWHC Admin 1125 . . . . 39, 45
PF *v* Wilson 24 Oct 2002, unpublished 307
R *v* Aldred (1909) 22 Cox CC 1 93
R *v* Barrie [2005] EWCA Crim 1318; [2006] 1 Cr App R (S) 40 307
R *v* BBC, *ex p* Owen [1985] QB 1153 619
R *v* BBC, *ex p* ProLife Alliance [2004] 1 AC 185 80
R *v* BBC, *ex p* Referendum Party [1997] EMLR 605 619
R *v* Bow Street Magistrates' Court, *ex p* Choudhury [1991]
   1 QB 429 . . . . 293, 296, 301, 312
R *v* Bradlaugh (1883) 15 Cox CC 217 . . . . 127, 128, 296
R *v* Burns (1886) 16 Cox CC 355 . . . . 294, 301
R *v* Carlile (Mary) (1821) 1 St Tr NS 1033 303
R *v* Caunt (1947) unreported 294, 301
R *v* Chief Metropolitan Stipendiary Magistrate, *ex p* Choudhury
   see R *v* Bow Street Magistrates' Court, *ex p* Choudhury
R *v* El-Faisal [2004] EWCA Crim 456 446
R *v* F (Terrorism) [2007] 2 All ER 193, CA 462
R *v* Gathercole (1838) 2 Lew 237; 168 ER 1140 293
R *v* Gott (1922) 16 Cr App R 87 . . . . 303, 304
R *v* Hetherington (1841) 4 St Tr NS 563 292
R *v* Holbrook (1878) 4 QBD 42 301
R *v* Horseferry Road Metropolitan Stipendiary Magistrate,
   ex p Siadatin [1991] 1 QB 260 457
R *v* Keach (1665) 6 St Tr 701 301
R *v* Lemon [1979] AC 617, [1979] QB 10 (see also
   Whitehouse *v* Lemon) 127, 292, 299, 302, 612
R *v* Manley [1933] 1 KB 529 294
R *v* Moxon (1841) 4 St Tr NS 693 303
R *v* Osborne (1732) 2 Swanst 503n 294
R *v* Ramsay & Foote (1883) 15 Cox CC 231 . . . . 127, 292, 296
R *v* Secretary of State for Education and Employment, *ex p*
   Williamson [2005] UKHL 15; [2005] 2 AC 246 398
R *v* Shayler [2002] UKHL 11; [2003] 1 AC 247 . . . . 26, 43
R *v* Special Adjudicator, *ex p* Ullah [2004] UKHL 26; [2004] 2 AC 323 79
R *v* Taylor (1676) 3 Keb 607; 84 ER 906 290
R *v* Williams (1797) 26 St Tr 653 303
R *v* Woolston (1728) Fitzg 64; 94 ER 655 303
R (Begum) *v* Denbigh High School Governors [2006] UKHL 17;
   [2007] 1 AC 100 . . . . 412, 418, 427, 430, 432, 433,
                                       434, 435, 436, 437, 439
R (Daly) *v* Secretary of State for the Home Department [2001]
   UKHL 26, [2001] 2 AC 532 394
R (Farrakhan) *v* Secretary of State for the Home Department [2002]
   EWCA Civ 606; [2002] QB 1391 80
R (Playfoot (A Child)) *v* Millais School Governing Body [2007]
   EWHC 1698 (Admin) [2007] HRLR 34 412

R (Pro-Life Alliance) *v* British Broadcasting Corporation [2003]
UKHL 23, [2004] AC 185 . . . . 321–322, 622, 624
R (Ullah) *v* Special Adjudicator [2004] UKHL 26; [2004] 2 AC 323 43
R (Watkins Singh) *v* Governing Body of Aberdale Girls'
High School and Rhondda Cynon Taf Unitary Authority [2008] EWHC 1865 420
R (on the application of Boyd Hunt) *v* ITC [2002] EWHC 2296 619
R (on the application of Laporte) *v* Chief Constable of
Gloucestershire [2006] UKHL 55; [2007] 2 All ER 529 457
R (on the application of Stephen Green) *v* City of
Westminster Magistrates' Court & Ors [2007] EWHC 2785
(Admin) (Jerry Springer case) 289, 293, 297, 298,
299, 301, 302, 313, 612
R (on the application of X) *v* Headteacher of Y School
(2007) EWHC 298 (Admin); [2008] 1 All ER 249 412
Redmond-Bate *v* DPP (1999) 7 BHRC 375; [1999] Crim LR 998 . . . . 33, 95, 390
Taylor's case 1 Vent 293; 86 ER 189 291
Walker *v* Hussain [1996] IRLR 11 420
Whitehouse *v* Lemon [1979] AC 617, (1978) 68 Cr App R 38
(see also R *v* Lemon) 293–294, 299, 302, 312
Wilson *v* Independent Broadcasting Authority [1979] SC 351 619
Wilson *v* PF [2005] HCJAC97, 2005 SCCR 686 307

United States of America
Abrams *v* US 250 US 616 (1919) 41, 50, 51, 157, 169, 248, 253, 606
Adderley *v* Florida 385 US 39 (1966) 141
Am Booksellers Ass'n Inc *v* Hudnut 771 F 2d 323 (7th Cir, 1985) 88
Austin *v* Michigan Chamber of Commerce 494 US 652 (1990) 345
Beauharnais *v* Illinois 343 US 250 (1952) 59, 88, 141, 189, 333
Bethel School District *v* Fraser 478 US 675 (1986) 83
Bodett *v* Coxcom Inc 366 F 3d 736 (9th Cir, 2004) 383
Bond *v* Floyd 385 US 116 (1966) 52
Bonnell *v* Lorenzo 241 F 3d 800 (6th Cir, 2001) 83
Boos *v* Barry 485 US 312 (1988) 42, 83, 321, 345
Bose Corp *v* Consumers Union 466 US 485 (1984) 40, 336
Bowers *v* Hardwick 478 US 186 (1986) 271
Brandenburg *v* Ohio 395 US 444 (1969) 5, 25, 42, 43, 52, 53, 54, 82,
88, 89, 134, 155, 162, 165, 179, 251,
446, 454–461, 600–602, 605
Brown *v* Board of Education 347 US 483 (1954) 201, 270
Brown *v* Oklahoma 408 US 914 (1972) 53
Burson *v* Freeman 504 US 191 (1992) 345, 346
Cantwell *v* Connecticut 310 US 296 (1940) 35, 89, 133, 200, 201, 202, 308, 348
Cary *v* Brown 447 US 455 (1980) 345
Central Hudson Gas and Electric *v* Public Service Comm'n 47 US 557 (1980) 83
Chaplinsky *v* New Hampshire 315
US 568 (1942) 36, 82, 135, 162, 282, 328, 348, 349, 605
Citizen Publishing Co *v* Miller 205 513, 115 P 3d 107
Az App Ct (2005) 604, 605
City of Houston *v* Hill 482 US 451 (1987) 53
City of Ladue *v* Gilleo 512 US 43 (1994) 46, 85, 91

Cohen *v* California 403 US 15 (1971) 29, 56, 57, 82, 83, 132,
133, 135, 165, 166, 326, 327, 336
Collin *v* Smith 447 F Supp 676 (ND Ill, 1978),
aff'd 578 F 2d 1197 (7th Cir 1978), cert denied,
439 US 916 (1978) 87, 158, 166, 244, 347
Commonwealth *v* Davis 162 Mass 510 (1895), aff'd 167 US 43 (1897) 141
Commonwealth of Massachusetts *v* Fred A. Leuchter, Jr, Cambridge
Dist Ct, Cambridge, MA, 11 June 1991 539
Connick *v* Myers 461 US 138 (1983) 83
Cox *v* Louisiana 379 US 559 (1965) 141
Craig *v* Boren 429 US 190 (1976) 271
Curtis Publishing Co *v* Butts 388 US 130 (1967) 601, 603
De Shaney *v* Winnebago Social Services Dept 489 US 189 (1989) 194
Debs *v* US 249 US 211 (1919) 3, 24, 41, 50, 91, 134
Dennis *v* United States 341 US 494 (1951) 3, 24, 51, 91, 144, 150, 454
Dred Scott *v* Sandford 60 US (19 How) 393 (1857) 166
Dun & Bradstreet *v* Greenmoss Builders 472 US 749 (1985) 336
FCC *v* Pacifica Foundation 438 US 726 (1978) 317, 606
FEC *v* Wisconsin Right to Life, Inc 127 SCt 2652 (2007) 51
Fiske *v* Kansas 274 US 380 (1927) 52
Florida Star *v* B.J.F. 491 US 524 (1989) 160, 161
Forsyth County Georgia *v* Nationalist Movement 505 US 123 (1992) 347
Frohwerk *v* US 249 US 204 (1919) 50
Frontiero *v* Richardson 411 US 677 (1973) 271
Gentile *v* State Bar of Nevada 501 US 1030 (1991) 83
Gertz *v* Robert Welch, Inc 418 US 323 (1974) 59, 88, 165, 603
Giboney *v* Empire Storage & Ice Co 336 US 490 (1949) .141
Gitlow *v* New York 268 US 652 (1925) 3, 134, 170, 453
Gooding *v* Wilson 405 US 528 (1972) 53
Greenbelt Cooperative Publishing Association Inc *v* Bressler 398 US 6 (1970) 603
Greater New Orleans Broadcasting Ass'n *v* United States 527 US 173 (1999) 83
Heart of Atlanta Motel, Inc *v* United States 379 US 241 (1964) 193, 201
Hess *v* Indiana 414 US 105 (1973) 455, 457
Hughes *v* Superior Court 339 US 460 (1950) 141
Hustler Magazine *v* Falwell 485 US 46
(1988) 19, 29, 83, 132, 173, 251, 321,
327, 336, 351, 603, 604, 605
International Brotherhood of Teamsters, AFL *v*
Vogt, Inc 354 US 284 (1957) 141
Katzenbach *v* McClung 379 US 294 (1964) 193
Korematsu *v* US 323 US 214 (1944) 270, 283, 346
Lawrence *v* Texas 539 US 558 (2003) 271, 319
Letter Carriers *v* Austin 418 US 264 (1974) 57, 603
Lewis *v* City of New Orleans 408 US 913 (1972) 53
Loving *v* Virginia 388 US 1 (1967) 270
Marsh *v* Chambers 463 US 783 (1983) 199
Masses Publishing Co *v* Patten 244 F 535 (SDNY, 1917),
rev'd 246 F 24 (2nd Cir 1917) 24, 25, 38, 41, 43, 52, 53, 144
Miller *v* California 413 US 15 (1973) 82, 163, 192
NAACP *v* Claiborne Hardware Co 458 US 886 (1982) 455, 460
Nationalist Socialist Party *v* Skokie 432 US 43 (1977) 87

Near *v* Minnesota 283 US 697 (1931) 600–602
New York *v* Ferber 458 US 747 (1982) 82
New York Times *v* Sullivan 376 US 254 (1964) 2, 59, 88, 89, 132,
151, 165, 321, 333, 600–602, 603, 604, 607
New York Times Co *v* United States 403 US 713 (1971) 345, 602
Noto *v* US 367 US 290 (1961) 454
Nuxoll *v* Indian Prairie School Dist 523 F 3d 668 (7th Cir, 2008) 34, 59, 88
Paris Adult Theater I *v* Slaton 413 US 49 (1973) 163, 192
Patterson *v* Colorado 205 US 454 (1907) 141
Pennekamp *v* Florida 328 US 331 (1946) 134
Peterson *v* Hewlett-Packard Co 358 F 3d 599 (9th Cir, 2004) 383
Planned Parenthood of the Columbia/Williamette
   Inc *v* American Coalition of Life Activists 290 F 3d 1058
   (9th Cir, 2002) 456, 459
Plessy *v* Ferguson 163 US 537 (1896) 193, 201
Police Dep't of Chicago *v* Mosley 408 US 92 (1972) 42, 81, 86, 163, 189, 321, 333
R.A.V. *v* City of St Paul, Minnesota 505 US 377 (1992) 85, 86, 87, 89,
90, 163, 164, 165, 349, 380
Red Lion Broadcasting Co *v* FCC 395 US 367 (1969) 16
Reed *v* Reed 404 US 71 (1971) 271
Regan *v* Time, Inc 468 US 641 (1984) 81
Romer *v* Evans 517 US 620 (1996) 271
Rosenberger *v* Rector and Visitors of the University of
   Virginia 515 US 819 (1995) 82
Rosenfeld *v* New Jersey 408 US 901 (1972) 53
Roth *v* US 354 US 476 (1957) 26, 141
Schenck *v* US 249 US 47 (1919) 2, 41, 50, 248, 454
Simon & Schuster Inc *v* Members of the New York State Crime Victims
   Board 502 US 105 (1991) 321
Skokie *v* Nationalist Socialist Party 373 NE 2d 21 (Ill Sup Ct, 1978) 57, 87, 158, 165
Smith *v* Collin 439 US 916 (1978) (cert denied) 333
Speiser *v* Randall 357 US 513 (1958) 53
Terminiello *v* City of Chicago 337 US 1 (1949) 53, 75, 134, 607
Texas *v* Johnson 491 US 397 (1989) 57, 82, 86, 132
Time, Inc *v* Hill 385 US 374 (1967) 132
US *v* Abrams 250 US 616 (1919) 253
US *v* Dennis 813 F 2d (2nd Cir 1950), aff'd 341 US 494 (1951) 461
US *v* Eichman 496 US 310 (1990) 86
US *v* Kelner 534 F 2d 1020 (2nd Cir, 1976) 459
US *v* Rahman 189 F 3d 88 (2nd Cir, 1999) 460
US *v* Spock 416 F 2d 165 (1st Cir, 1969) 460
US *v* Virginia 518 US 515 (1996) 271
Virginia *v* Black 538 US 343 (2003) 57, 86, 158, 162,
165, 176, 179, 380
Walker *v* Colorado Springs Sun, Inc 538 P 2d 450 (Colo, 1975) 603
Watts *v* US 394 US 705 (1969) 82, 455, 458, 605
West Virginia State Board of Education *v* Barnette 319
   US 624 (1943) 155, 161
Whitney *v* California 274 US 357 (1927) 61, 252, 284, 336, 354, 453, 480
Widmar *v* Vincent 454 US 263 (1981) 366
Wisconsin *v* Mitchell 508 US 476 (1993) 283

Wisconsin *v* Yoder 406 US 203 (1972) 371
YAHOO! Inc *v* La Ligue Contre Le Racisme et l'Antisémitisme 145 F Supp
    2d 1168 (ND Cal 2001); 433 F 3d 1199, cert denied, 547 US 1163 (2006) 524, 525
Yates *v* US 354 US 298 (1957) 454
Zal *v* Steppe 968 F 2d 924 (9th Cir, 1992) 83

Table of Legislation

European Union

Treaty of Rome

Art 141 (ex Art 119) 77

Directives

Equal Pay 75/117 77

Equal Treatment 76/207 (now 2006/54) 77

Equal Treatment 2006/54 77

Equal Treatment in Employment and Occupation, Dir 2000/78/EC 77, 418

Art 2 418

Art 4(1) 378

Art 4(2) 378

Race or Ethnic Origin 2000/43 . . . . 77, 419–420

Television without Frontiers

Art 22 622

Framework Decision on Racism and Xenophobia, Apr 2007 . . . . . . 515, 547–548, 555, 561

Art 1 547

Art 1(c) 548

NATIONAL LEGISLATION

Australia

Constitution 534

Racial Discrimination Act

s 18C 534

s 18C(1)(a) 534

Austria

Prohibition Act

Art 3h 544

Belgium

Law of 23 Mar 1995

Art 1 544

Canada

Constitution 12

Charter of Rights and Freedoms 1982 (Sch B, Constitution Act 1982) 13, 79, 204, 205,
                                                                          263, 340

Art 1 . . . . 13, 204, 205, 392, 396

Art 2(a) 378, 396

Art 2(b) 79, 204, 205

Art 15 396

Criminal Code, R.S., 1985, ch. C-46

s 318(1) 217

s 319 309

s 319(1) 217, 379

s 319(2) 85, 125, 205, 213, 214, 216, 217, 379
s 319(3)(b) 379, 386
s 319(7) 205
Human Rights Act
s 2 530
s 13 533
s 13(1) 529
s 13(2) 529
National Registration Act 3
School Act RSBC 1996, c 412, s 76 397
Saskatchewan Human Rights Code, SS 1979, c S-24.1 392

Czech Republic
Constitution, as amended, 1992
Art 261a 544

China
Constitution 12
Art 35 11

Denmark
Penal Code
s 140 132
s 266(b) 58, 132

Estonia
Constitution 240

France
Constitution, 1958 . . . . 229, 420, 575
Art 89 570
Decree of 27 Apr 1848 (Elimination of slavery) 566, 577, 578, 579
Art 8 566
Law of 11 Feb 1851 566
Law of 28 May 1858 566
Law of 25 Feb 1875
Art 8 570
Law of 6 July 1880 (Selection of 14 July as a national holiday) 568
Law of 30 Jun 1881 (Freedom of Assembly) 570
Law of 29 July 1881 (Freedom of the Press) 227, 526, 570
Art 23 . . . . 526, 527
Art 23A 544
Art 24 . . . . 229, 526, 527
Art 24*bis* 526, 527, 544, 564
Art 29 227
Art 32 231
Art 33 229
Law of 14 Aug 1884 (Partial reform of constitutional law) 570

Law of 1889 (Nationality) 567
Law of 1905 (Law of Separation) 418
Law of 10 Jan 1936 (Fighter groups and private militia), as amended 1972, 1986 . . . 226, 227
Law of 19 Oct 1945 (Nationality Act) 567
Law of 16 July 1949 (Publications intended for young people)
    Art 14 223
Law of 1 July 1972 (Racist speech) 222
Law of 2 Oct 1981 (Establishing 8 May as a national holiday) 573, 577
Law of 1986 (Audiovisual communication) 224
Law of 31 Dec 1987 (Crimes against humanity) 574
Law of 29 Jan 1990 564
Law of 13 July 1990 (Loi Gayssot) 512, 513, 543, 564, 565, 574, 575, 577, 578, 579
    Art 9 564
Law of 17 June 1998 (Sexual offences) 223–224
Law of 10 July 2000 (Commemoration of victims of racist and antisemitic crimes) 577
Law of 29 Jan 2001 . . . . 563, 564, 566, 578
Law of 21 May 2001 (Taubira Law) 563, 564, 577, 578, 579
    Art 2 . . . . 562, 564
    Art 4 564
Law of 12 Jun 2001 (Religious sects) 236
Law of 30 Dec 2004 (Discrimination) 229, 413, 414, 418, 423, 424, 426
Law of 23 Feb 2005 (Contribution of repatriated French citizens) 563
    Art 4 . . . . 562, 565, 578
Penal Code 523
    Art 113-2 527
    Art 433-5-1 221
    Art 624-4 228
Cinematic Industry Code
    Art 19 (implemented by Decree of 23 Feb 1990) 224
Declaration of the Rights of Man and of the Citizen, 1789
    Art 10 . . . . 222, 574
    Art 11 222
Declaration on Art 27 ICCPR 403

Germany
Basic Law 21
    Art 1 560
    Art 2 560
    Art 5 . . . . 15, 558–560
    Art 8 . . . . 558, 560
    Art 18 14
    Art 21 14
Penal Code
    s 130 . . . . 58, 87, 544, 557, 558, 561
    s 130(1) 125, 134
    s 130(3) 557
    s 185 . . . . 557, 560, 561
    s 189 . . . . 557, 561
    ss 220a(1) 557

Statute on Assemblies
  s 5(4) 558
  s 6(1) 557
Weimar Constitution 12

Greece
Criminal Code, Law 927/1979 550

Hungary
Constitution 1948–1989 243
Civil Code, amendment of 2007 253
Criminal Code 243, 247
  Art 268 259
  Art 269 249
  Art 269(b) 259, 260, 261
Protection of Personal Data and Disclosure of Information of Public Interest,
  Act LXIII, 1992 245
Act IV, 1939 (Limitation of social and economic expansion of the Jews) 259
Act VIII, 1942 (Legal status of Israelite denomination) 259
Act XLV, 1993 on the amendment of Act IV, 1978 on the Criminal Code 262

Iceland
Criminal Code
  s 223a 379

India
Code of Criminal Procedure 1898 104
Penal Code
  s 295 104
  s 298 296

Ireland
Constitution
  Art 40(3)(1) 316

Israel
Basic Law: Human Dignity and Liberty, 1992 amended 1994 .... 333, 336, 337, 341
Penal Code, 1977
  §144D1(a) 332
  §173 (formerly s 149 Criminal Code Ordinance (Palestine) 332
  §386c 338
Prevention of Terror Ordinance, 1948
  §4(g) 332

Liechtenstein
Penal Code
  Art 283 545

Lithuania
Constitution 240

Criminal Code
  s 170 379

Luxembourg
Criminal Code (revised)
  Art 457-3 545

Netherlands
Criminal Code
  art 90 379
  art 137 . . . . 390, 545
  art 137(c) 58, 87, 379
  art 137d 379
  art 137(e) 379

New Zealand
Bill of Rights Act 1990 394
  s 3 395
  s 5 . . . . 392, 395
  s 6 395
  s 14 . . . . 392, 395
  s 19 392
Films, Videos and Publications Classification Act 1993
  s 3 394
Human Rights Act 1993
  s 21(1) 394

Norway
Criminal Code
  s 135a 379

Poland
Law on the Institute of National Remembrance, 1998
  Art 55 545

Portugal
Criminal Code
  Art 240(2) 546

Romania
Constitution 240
Penal Code
  Emergency Ordinance 31/2002 546

Russia
Constitution 240
Statute on Countering Extremist Activity, 2002 (amended 2006) 240

Slovak Republic
Criminal Code
  s 261 546

South Africa
Constitution 1996 12
    Art 16(2) 177
    Art 36 13

Sweden
Constitution 392
Criminal Code
    ch 16, s 8 391–393

Switzerland
Penal Code
    Art 261*bis* 514, 546

Turkey
Constitution 428, 429
    Art 2 429

United Kingdom
Act of Settlement 1700
    s 2 290
    s 3 290
Anti-Terrorism, Crime and Security Act 2001 306
    s 37 100
Bill of Rights 1689 2
Broadcasting Act 1990 297
    Sch 15 . . . . 298, 612
Canada Act 1982
    Sch B (Charter of Rights and Freedoms) 204
Civil Partnerships Act 2004
    s 6 378
Communications Act 2003 382
    Pt 3, ch 4 619
    s 319(2)(c) 619
    s 320 619
Contempt of Court Act 1981
    s 2(2) 457
Crime and Disorder Act 1998 . . . . 101, 539
    s 28 45
    s 31 . . . . 45, 306
Criminal Justice Act 2003
    s 146 382
Criminal Justice and Immigration Act 2008 . . . . 127, 309
    s 74 . . . . 376, 384
    s 79 . . . . 289, 612
    Sch 16 . . . . 309, 387
Criminal Justice and Public Order Act 1994 539
De Haeretico Comburendo, abolished 29 Car 2, c 9 .292

Defamation Act 1961
  s 8 302
Disaffection Act 1934 93
Ecclesiastical Courts Act 1813 292
Equality Act 2006 . . . . 383, 466
  s 52(4)(g) 437
Human Rights Act 1998 . . . . 2, 11, 43, 101, 313, 399, 431, 472
  s 3(1) 32
  s 4(4) 32
  s 4(6) 32
  s 5 32
  s 6 389
Incitement to Mutiny Act 1797 93
Local Government Act 1986
  s 2A ("section 28") 377, 591
Local Government Act 2000 377
Obscene Publications Act 1959 298
  s 1(1) 301
  s 2(4) 298, 301
Offences Against the Person Act 1861 446
Police Act 1996
  s 91 93
Public Order Act 1936 . . . . .3, 93
  s 5 . . . . 39, 103
Public Order Act 1986 (POA) 34, 37, 40, 43, 44, 54, 55, 60, 93,
                                                                289, 295, 306, 307, 309, 612
  Part 3 . . . . 85, 215
  Part 3A 102
  s 4 457
  s 4A 306
  s 5 . . . . 31, 39, 44, 78, 84, 101, 306, 389, 390, 399
  s 5(1) 31, 46, 389
  s 5(3) 45, 46
  s 5(3)(c) 31, 389
  s 6(3) 31
  ss 17–23 100
  s 17 . . . . 100, 612
  s 17A 295
  ss 18–23 295
  s 18 . . . . 85, 294
  s 19 . . . . 85, 612
  s 22 612
  s 27 613
  s 28 307
  ss 29B-F 613
  s 29B(1) 296
  s 29J 296, 386, 613
  s 29JA 387, 399

Race Relations Act 1965 . . . . 95, 215, 264, 294, 295
    s 6 99
Racial and Religious Hatred Act 2006 . . . . 94, 102, 289, 295, 296, 306,
                                                                      307, 384, 386, 597
    s 29B 372
    s 29J 47
Religious Disabilities Act 1846 292
Roman Catholic Emancipation Act 1829 292
School Standards and Framework Act 1998 431
Terrorism Act 2000 . . . . 484, 591, 597
    s 1 462
    s 1(1) 471
    s 1(2) 470
    s 1(4)(a) 471
    s 44 483
Terrorism Act 2006 . . . . 445, 446–447, 455, 456, 459, 461, Ch 23, 597
    s 1 . . . . 89, 96, 446, 464, 467, 468, 470, 477, 478, 481, 613
    s 1(2) 96, 446
    ss 1(2)(b), (c) 472
    s 1(2)(b)(ii) 457
    s 1(3) 96, 446
    ss 1(3)(a), (b) 468
    s 1(4) 446
    s 1(5) 447, 472
    s 1(5)(a) 471
    s 1(6) 447, 613
    s 2 . . . . 97, 446, 467, 468, 470
    s 2(2) 467
    s 2(3)(a) 467
    ss 2(4)(a), (b) 468
    s 2(7) 471
    s 2(9) 613
    s 3 . . . . 97, 446, 467, 613
    s 4 97
    s 17 472
    s 20 462
    s 20(2) 446, 468
    s 20(3) 470
    s 20(4)(b) 467
    s 20(6) 467
    s 21(5A)(b) 467
Theatres Act 1968 297
    s 2 298
    s 2(4) 298
Toleration Act 1689 292
Statutory Instruments
Employment Equality (Religion or Belief) Regulations 2003 . . . . 418, 420

reg 3(b)(iii) 418
Equality Act (Sexual Orientation) Regulations 2003, SI 2003/1661
    reg 5(1) 383
Equality Act (Sexual Orientation) Regulations (Northern Ireland) 2006 . . . . 308, 383
Public Order (Northern Ireland) Order 1987 . . . . 100, 295

United States of America

Constitution 1, 18, 52, 132, 159, 185, 194, 319, 334, 335, 338, 598
    Bill of Rights/ First Amendment, 1791 . . . . 1, 12, 16, 17, 35, 81, 82, 86, 87, 88,
                                    89, 91, 92, 132, 133, 137, 140, 141, 144, 155, 159–181,
                                    191, 192, 194, 195, 252, 256, 317, 321, 326, 333, 348,
                                    366, 368, 370, 394, 455, 456, 458, 460, 511, 525,
                                    529, 540, 554, 600, 602, 603, 604, 605
Fourteenth Amendment 159, 161
Declaration of Independence 598
Espionage Act 1917 . . . . 40, 41, 51
Sedition Act 1798 . . . . 1, 2, 600, 607
Smith Act 1940 . . . . 51, 91

Table of Conventions and International Instruments

African Charter on Human and Peoples' Rights (AfCHPR), 1981 . . . . 68–69, 74
    Arts 15–24 69
    Art 28 74
American Convention on Human Rights (AmCHR), 1978, OASTS No 36, 1144
    UNTS 243 . . . . 68, 74
    Art 13(5) 74, 125, 134
American Declaration on the Rights and Duties of Man, 1948 68
Arab Charter of Human Rights, 1994 . . . . 69, 74
    Art 1 74
    Art 4 69
    Art 26 74
    Arts 40–41 69
    Art 42(b) 69
Convention on the Elimination of all Forms of Discrimination Against
Women (CEDAW), 1979 . . . . 76, 418
Convention on the Elimination of Racial Discrimination, UN 417
Convention on the Prevention and Punishment of the Crime of Genocide, 1951 65
    Art 2 65
    Art 3 65
    Art 4 65
Convention on the Rights of the Child (CRC)
    Art 30 405
Council of Europe Convention on Cybercrime
    Additional Protocol, Art 6 540–541
Council of Europe Convention on the Prevention of Terrorism
(CECPT), 2005 . . . . 444, 468
    Art 1 464
    Art 5 470
    Art 5(1) 464
    Art 5(2) 464
Declaration on the Elimination of All Forms of Intolerance and of
Discrimination Based on Religion or Belief, UN, 1981 76
    Art 6 386
European Convention on Human Rights and Fundamental Freedoms
(ECHR), 1953 . . . . 20, 21, 62, 65–68, 69, 72–74, 75,
                               76, 92, 178, 222, 223, 402, 425, 430–431, 434, 436
    Art 1 . . . . 66, 282, 315, 318
    Art 5 67
    Art 6 67
    Art 8 . . . . 318, 404, 422

Art 9 . . . . 191, 276, 288, 301, 317, 318, 381, 382, 384,
                        386, 387, 390, 391, 392, 397, 401, 404, 411, 415, 422, 429
Art 9(1) 391
Art 9(2) 391, 405, 406, 429, 430, 433, 435
Art 10 . . . . 32, 39, 43, 45, 52, 67, 72–74, 77, 78, 79, 101,
                        191, 228, 302, 303, 311, 312, 313, 314, 323, 370, 378, 379, 381,
                        386, 387, 390, 391, 392, 404, 424, 438, 545, 559, 608, 609, 610, 622
Art 10(1) 314, 318, 370
Art 10(2) 67, 68, 77, 163, 311, 314, 317, 318, 370
Art 11 . . . . 67, 318, 406
Art 13 66
Art 14 . . . . 67, 270, 271, 311, 401, 404, 411, 415, 419, 435
Art 15 . . . . 67, 202, 282
Art 16 67
Art 17 . . . . 67, 73, 77, 78, 311, 545, 559
Art 18 67
Art 33 66
Art 34 66
Art 53 21
Art 57 67
First Protocol 66, 404, 415
Third Protocol 270
Fourth Protocol 66
Fifth Protocol 270
Sixth Protocol 66
Seventh Protocol 66
Eighth Protocol 270
Eleventh Protocol 66, 270
Twelfth Protocol 66, 401, 419
Thirteenth Protocol 66
International Covenant on Civil and Political Rights 1966 (ICCPR) 6 ILM 368, 999
    UNTS 171 . . . . 11, 62, 63–64, 69, 69–72, 75, 76, 393, 406, 425
    Part IV 64, 185
    Art 2 . . . . 63, 419
    Art 2(2) 282
    Art 3 419
    Art 4 . . . . 64, 202, 282
    Arts 6–25 64
    Art 18 . . . . 386, 401, 403, 404
    Art 18(2) 414
    Art 18(3) 405
    Art 19 . . . . 69–72, 386
    Art 19(3) 163, 267
    Art 19(3)(a) 70
    Art 20 . . . . 64, 69–72, 184, 185, 307, 382
    Art 20(2) 71, 125, 177, 184, 267, 271, 272
    Arts 26–27 64

Art 26 . . . . 401, 419
Art 27 . . . . 401, 404, 405
First Protocol 64
First Optional Protocol (OP1) 401, 405, 406
International Convention on the Elimination of all Forms of Racial
  Discrimination (ICERD), 1969, 5 ILM 352, 660 UNTS 195 . . . . 64–65, 71–72, 76
  Arts 2–5 64
  Art 4 . . . . 71–72, 125, 177, 185, 186, 267–268, 271, 272
  Art 4(b) 72
  Art 5 71
  Art 5(d)(viii) 72
  Art 8 65
  Arts 11–12 65
  Art 14 65
  Art 22 65
International Convention on the Suppression and Punishment of the
  Crime of Apartheid, 1973 76
International Covenant on Economic, Social and Cultural Rights (ICESCR) 69
  Art 2 419
  Art 3 419
International Criminal Court, Statute 513, 524
  Art 6 . . . . 546, 559
  Art 7 . . . . 546, 559
  Art 8 . . . . 546, 559
Nuremberg Tribunal 1945, Charter
  Art 6 227
Nuremberg Tribunal, Statute 542
  Art 9 521
Organization for Security and Cooperation in Europe (OSCE), Declarations 539
Stockholm International Forum on the Holocaust, Declaration, 2000 . . . . 539, 553
Universal Declaration on Human Rights (UDHR), 1948 . . . . 62, 69, 71, 279
  Art 1 280
  Art 2 280
  Art 7 280
  Art 19 62
  Art 28 280

List of Contributors

C. Edwin Baker, Nicholas F. Gallicchio Professor of Law, University of Pennsylvania and graduate of Stanford University and Yale Law School, is author of *Human Liberty and Freedom of Speech* (Oxford, 1987), *Advertising and a Democratic Press* (Princeton, 1994), *Media, Markets, and Democracy* (Cambridge, 2002) (winner of the 2002 McGannon Communications Policy Research Award), *Media Concentration and Democracy: Why Ownership Matters* (Cambridge, 2007), and many articles on free speech, equality, economics, property, and jurisprudence.

Eric Barendt is Goodman Professor of Media Law, UCL. He has written extensively on freedom of speech and on media law, notably *Freedom of Speech* (2nd edition, OUP, 2007), *Broadcasting Law* (OUP, 1995) and *Libel and the Media* (OUP, 1997). He is now working on a comparative study of the law relating to academic freedom.

David J. Bodney is a partner in the international law firm of Steptoe & Johnson LLP, where he practises media, constitutional and intellectual property law. Resident in the firm's Phoenix, Arizona office, Mr. Bodney also serves as adjunct faculty at Arizona State University's Sandra Day O'Connor College of Law and the Walter Cronkite School of Journalism and Telecommunication. He is a graduate of Yale College (B.A., cum laude) and the University of Virginia School of Law (J.D./M.A., Foreign Affairs).

Tufyal Choudhury is a lecturer in law at Durham University and a Research Associate at the Oxford Centre on Migration Policy and Society. He is also senior policy advisor to the Open Society Institute's 'Muslim in EU Cities' project and a member of the EU Network of Experts on Violent Radicalisation. He is author of *Muslim Identity Politics and Radicalisation* (2007) and co-author of *The Rules of the Game: Terrorism, Community and Human Rights* (2007).

Ian Cram is Professor of Comparative Constitutional Law and Director of the LLM Programme in International and European Human Rights Law at the School of Law, Leeds University. His teaching and research interests lie in public law with especial reference to comparative constitutional law and human rights.

Ronald Dworkin is Professor of Philosophy and Frank Henry Sommer Professor of Law at New York University, and formerly Professor of Jurisprudence at Oxford University College and University College, London. He is a Fellow of the British Academy, a member of the American Academy of Arts and Sciences, and Holberg Laureate 2007. Professor Dworkin is the author of many books and articles on philosophy and law, and is a frequent contributor to the New York Review of Books.

David Edgar is a playwright, whose recent plays include *Testing the Echo* (Out of Joint, 2008), *Playing with Fire* (National Theatre, 2005), *The Prisoner's Dilemma* (Royal Shakespeare Company, 2001), and an adaptation of Gitta Sereny's *Albert Speer* (National Theatre, 2000). He founded Britain's first post-graduate playwriting course, at the

University of Birmingham, in 1989, and was appointed Professor of Playwriting Studies in 1995. David Edgar is President of the Writers' Guild.

Carolyn Evans is Deputy Director of the Centre for Comparative Constitutional Studies and Associate Dean (Research) at the Melbourne Law School, Australia. She has published widely in the area of religious freedom including a leading work on *Religious Freedom under the European Court of Human Rights* (OUP, 2001) and also researches the domestic application of international human rights law, where her works include *Australian Bills of Rights* (LexisNexis, 2008).

John Finnis is Professor of Law & Legal Philosophy in the University of Oxford, Vice-Master and Professorial Fellow in University College Oxford, Biolchini Family Professor of Law at the University of Notre Dame du Lac, and a Fellow of the British Academy. His books include *Natural Law & Natural Rights* (1980), *Fundamentals of Ethics* (1983), and *Aquinas: Moral, Political & Legal Theory* (1998). He is a barrister of Gray's Inn and since 1970 has contributed and revised the title *Commonwealth and Dependencies* in *Halsbury's Laws of England*.

David Fraser is Professor of Law and Social Theory, University of Nottingham. His research focuses on legal aspects of National Socialism and the Shoah, legal regimes under Nazi occupation and anti-Jewish persecution, and the legal regulation of memory. He is the author most recently of *Law After Auschwitz: Towards A Jurisprudence of the Holocaust* (2005) and *The Fragility of Law: Constitutional Patriotism and the Jews of Belgium, 1940–1945* (2008).

Dieter Grimm teaches constitutional law at Humboldt University Berlin and at the Yale Law School. From 1987 to 1999 he was a Justice of the Federal Constitutional Court of Germany. From 2001 to 2007 he served as Director of the Wissenschaftskolleg zu Berlin, Institute for Advanced Study. He holds a law degree and a doctoral degree from the University of Frankfurt, an LL.M. degree from Harvard Law School and an LL.D. h.c. from the University of Toronto.

Ivan Hare is a practising barrister at Blackstone Chambers in London specializing in public law and human rights cases. He was previously a Fellow of Trinity College, Cambridge, and remains an Associate Fellow of the Centre for Public Law at the University. He has written widely on public law in general and on comparative free speech doctrine in particular. This is the second collection of essays he has edited for OUP.

Professor Eric Heinze teaches at Queen Mary, University of London. His books include *The Logic of Constitutional Rights* (2005), *The Logic of Liberal Rights* (2003), *The Logic of Equality* (2003), *Sexual Orientation: A Human Right* (1995) (Russian translation 2004), and *Of Innocence and Autonomy: Children, Sex and Human Rights* (2000). Recent articles appear in Oxford Journal of Legal Studies, Modern Law Review, Harvard Human Rights Law Journal, International Journal of Human Rights, Ratio Juris, Journal of Social & Legal Studies, Law & Critique, Legal Studies.

Steven J. Heyman is a professor at Chicago-Kent College of Law, Illinois Institute of Technology. In addition to many articles on legal and constitutional theory, he is the author of *Free Speech and Human Dignity* (Yale University Press, 2008) and the editor of *Hate Speech and the Constitution* (Garland/Rutledge, 1996).

Ian Leigh is Professor of Law and Co-Director of the Human Rights Centre at Durham University. His publications include *Religious Freedom in the Liberal State* (OUP, 2005) (with Rex Ahdar), *Making Rights Real: the Human Rights Act in it First Decade* (Hart, 2008) (with Roger Masterman) and the *Handbook on Human Rights and Fundamental Freedoms of Armed Forces Personnel,* (OSCE, 2008) (with Hans Born), as well as many academic journal articles and chapters in edited collections.

Dr. Jose Liht is Research Associate with the Psychology and Religion Research Group, Centre for Advanced Religious and Theological Studies, University of Cambridge. His teaching and research interests are in the changes that the mental representation of self, ingroups and outgroups undergo under threat conditions that require the help of others. His publications include 'Social psychological research and the prevention of religiously motivated violence' (2008), 'Identifying young Muslims vulnerable to recruitment for terrorism: Psychological theory and recommendations' (2008) and 'Integrative complexity in face-to-face negotiations between the Chiapas guerrillas and the Mexican Government' (2005).

Maleiha Malik is a Reader in Law at King's College, University of London. Her research focuses on the theory and practice of discrimination law, minority protection, and feminist theory. She is the co-author of *Discrimination Law: Theory and Practice* (Sweet and Maxwell, 2008). Her recent publications on free speech issues include 'Complex Equality: Muslim Women and the Headscarf' in Droit et Société (2008) and 'Engaging With Extremists' in International Relations (2008).

Pascal Mbongo is Professor of Law at the University of Poitiers Law School and Attorney at Law (Paris Bar). He teaches Constitutional Law, European Human Rights Law, Minorities Law and French Media Law. He writes widely on free speech law with an interdisciplinary approach (law, legal theory, linguistics, social sciences) of censorship and he's preparing an essay about legal issues relating to bad artistic and literary works.

Dominic McGoldrick is Professor of Public International Law, University of Liverpool. In 1999–2000 he was a Fulbright Distinguished Scholar at the Harvard Law School. He has authored four books: *The Human Rights Committee, International Relations Law of the European Union, From 9–11 to the Iraq War 2003* and *Human Rights and Religion—The Islamic Headscarf Debate in Europe.* He was a major contributor to and co-editor of *The Permanent International Criminal Court—Legal and Policy Issues.* Recent publications have concerned 'Multiculturalism and its Discontents', 'Culture, Cultures and Cultural Rights', 'Human Rights and Humanitarian Law in the UK Courts,' 'The Bosnian Genocide Case' and 'Terrorism and Human Rights Paradigms'.

Peter Molnar is Senior Research Fellow at Central European University's Center for Media and Communication Studies. From 1990 to 1998 he was a member of Hungarian Parliament. Since 2001 he has been a member of the Hungarian Radio-Television Board's Complaint Commission, as well as a legislative advisor since 2002. He has taught and lectured around the world for over 10 years, and has been a German Marshall, Fulbright, and Shorenstein Fellow. In 2007, the staged version of his novel 'Searchers' won awards for best alternative and independent play in Hungary.

Robert Post is the David Boies Professor of Law at the Yale Law School. He writes frequently in the area of freedom of speech. Books on this subject include (Editor), *Censorship and Silencing: Practices of Cultural Regulation* (Getty Research Institute for the History of Art and the Humanities: Issues & Debates 1998), and *Constitutional Domains: Democracy, Community, Management* (Harvard University Press 1995). Recent articles relevant to the subject of this book include 'Democracy and Equality', 603 The Annals of the American Academy of Political and Social Science 24 (2006), and 'Redenfreiheit, Menschenwürde und Demokratie', in Güntr Frankenberg and Peter Niesen, eds, Bilderverbot: Recht, Ethik, und Ästhetik der öffentlichen Darstellung (2004).

Amnon Reichman, a tenured Senior-Lecturer at the Faculty of Law, University of Haifa, holds an LL.B. (Hebrew University), LL.M. (Berkeley Law) and S.J.D (University of Toronto). His areas of expertise include constitutional and administrative law (Israeli and comparative), theories of human rights and judicial review, and law and culture (primarily law and cinema). His recent publications include analysing the role scholars play in constitutional adjudication (published in California Law Review), and the contours of judicial non-dependence (forthcoming in an edited volume published by The University of Toronto Press).

Jacob Rowbottom is a Lecturer in Law at the University of Cambridge, Fellow of King's College Cambridge, Assistant Director of the Centre for Public Law and barrister. He specialises in constitutional law, in particular looking at the regulation of the democratic process and the role of the media.

Dr. Sara Savage is Senior Research Associate with the Psychology and Religion Research Group, University of Cambridge. A social psychologist, her work focuses on the cognitive and group dynamics affecting young people vulnerable to violent radicalization, the worldview of young people (published in *Making Sense of Generation Y*, 2006), the social psychology of religious organizations (*Human Face of Church*, 2007), and conflict transformation among senior church leaders of differing religious orientations (*Transforming Conflict*, 2008).

L.W. Sumner is University Professor Emeritus in the Department of Philosophy at the University of Toronto. His teaching and research interests are in ethical theory, bioethics (especially end-of-life issues), political philosophy, and philosophy of law. He is the author of *Abortion and Moral Theory* (1981), *The Moral Foundation of Rights* (1987), *Welfare, Ethics, and Happiness* (1996), and *The Hateful and the Obscene: Studies in the Limits of Free Expression* (2004).

Patrick Weil is a senior research fellow at the French National Research Center in Paris (University of Paris1, Pantheon-Sorbonne). His most recent books are *Qu'est ce qu'un français? Histoire de la nationalité française depuis la Révolution,* Paris, Grasset, 2002 (in English *How to be French? A Nationality in the Making since 1789*, Duke University Press, 2008); *L'esclavage, la colonisation et après... France, Etats-Unis, Royaume-Uni* (co-editor with Stephane Dufoix), Paris, Presses Universitaires de France, 2005; and *Liberté, égalité, discriminations, l'identité nationale au regard de l'histoire*, Paris, Grasset, 2008.

James Weinstein is the Amelia D. Lewis Professor of Constitutional Law at the Sandra Day O'Connor College of Law at Arizona State University, and an Associate Fellow of the Centre for Public Law at the University of Cambridge. He is the author of *Hate Speech, Pornography and the Radical Attack on Free Speech Doctrine*, as well as numerous articles on free speech. Professor Weinstein has also litigated several significant free speech cases.

Michael Whine is Director, Government and International Affairs at the Community Security Trust, the defence agency of the Jewish community in the UK, and Director of the Defence and Group Relations Division of the Board of Deputies of British Jews, the representative body of the community. He acts as consultant on defence and security matters to the European Jewish Congress, and represents it at the Organisation for Security and Cooperation in Europe.

Sir David Williams QC was Vice-Chancellor of the University of Cambridge for seven years, President of Wolfson College in Cambridge for twelve years, and Rouse Ball Professor of English Law at Cambridge for nine years. He has written extensively in various areas of public law.

General Introduction: Free Speech, Democracy, and the Suppression of Extreme Speech Past and Present

James Weinstein and Ivan Hare

1. The Enduring yet Troubled Marriage of Free Speech and Democracy

Free speech and democracy have had a long and ambivalent relationship. From the dawn of modern democracy, it was recognized that the right of the people to criticize government, laws, and social conditions was inherent in the very concept of rule by the people. As James Madison, the architect of the United States Constitution, explained: in a democracy '[t]he people, not the government, possess the absolute sovereignty';[1] it therefore follows that the 'censorial power is in the people over the government and not in the government over the people'.[2] But also from the outset, democratic governments have claimed that there must be limits to such criticism: that speech can appropriately be suppressed when it becomes so extreme as to pass beyond the limits of legitimate protest. On this view, despite the First Amendment, ratified as part of the Bill of Rights in 1791, Congress passed the Sedition Act of 1798 which made it a crime to publish any 'false, scandalous, and malicious writing' with the intent to 'defame' the government or bring it 'into contempt or disrepute' or to excite against the government 'the hatred of the good people of the United States...'[3] Fourteen men, mostly prominent newspaper publishers critical of the Adams administration, were prosecuted under the Act during its two and a half years of existence.[4] In addition to publishers, Congressman Matthew Lyon, a member of the opposition

---

[1] Virginia Resolutions, in 4 J. Elliot (ed.), *Debates in the Several State Conventions on the Adoption of the Federal Constitution,* Vol. 4 (1836), 569–70.

[2] 4 Annals of Congress 934 (1794).

[3] Act of 14 July 1798, 1 Stat. 596.

[4] See A. Lewis, *Freedom for the Thought That We Hate: A Biography of the First Amendment* (New York: Basic Books, 2008), 12–3. By its own terms, the Act expired in March, 1801, coinciding with the end of Adams' first (and only) term in office.

Republican party, was convicted for accusing President Adams of having 'an unbounded thirst for ridiculous pomp, foolish adulation, and selfish avarice'.[5]

Although the Supreme Court never ruled on the validity of the Sedition Act, history has condemned the law as a violation of the basic right of free speech inherent in democracy.[6] But perhaps this verdict is unfair. As Jeremy Waldron reminds us in a recent article:

To many people, federal authority seemed weak and precarious in 1798. Public agitation by Colonel Lyon's supporters led to a brief uprising in Vermont, and there was a threat of considerable political violence elsewhere. George Washington was denounced as a thief and a traitor; John Jay was burned in effigy; Alexander Hamilton was stoned in the streets of New York; our hero, Matthew Lyon, attacked a Connecticut Federalist with fire tongs in the House of Representatives; and Republican militias armed and drilled openly, ready to stand against Federalist armies. Over everything, like a specter, hung fears of the Jacobin terror in France.

It was by no means obvious in those years—thought it seems obvious to us—that the authorities could afford to ignore venomous attacks on the structures and officers of government...That government could survive the published vituperations of the governed seemed more like a reckless act of faith than basic common sense.[7]

And so it has gone ever since. Though generally committed to free speech (both in theory and usually in practice as well), democratic societies have repeatedly repressed extreme speech that seems to present a 'clear and present danger' to some other basic societal value or goal.[8] In Britain, without the bulwark of the First Amendment and the practice of judicial review of primary legislation, free speech was more fragile than in the US.[9] The coercive power of the state was applied against Chartists and suffragettes campaigning for the extension of the franchise and against the nascent trade union movement.[10] During World War I

---

[5] R. N. Rosenfeld, *American Aurora: A Democratic-Republican Returns* (New York: St. Martin's Press, 1997), 526–7. See also *Lyon's case* 15 F. Cas. 1183 (C.C. Vt. 1798).

[6] 'Although the Sedition Act was never tested in this Court, the attack upon its validity has carried the day in the court of history.' *New York Times* v. *Sullivan* 376 US 254, 276 (1964).

[7] 'Free Speech & the Menace of Hysteria', 55 *New York Review of Books*, 28 May 2008 (reviewing Lewis n. 4 above).

[8] See *Schenck* v. *US* 249 US 47, 52 (1919).

[9] The only constitutional protection for free speech in Britain until the enactment of the Human Rights Act 1998 was the provision of the Bill of Rights 1689 that 'the Freedome of speech and debates or proceedings in Parlyament ought not to be impeached or questioned in any court or place out of Parlyament'. Before the democratic era, the full barbarity of the medieval criminal law was deployed against religious dissenters on the ground that their challenges undermined the sacred authority of the King and State. See I. Hare, ch. 15 in this volume.

[10] See B. Hilton, *A Mad, Bad, and Dangerous People? England 1783–1846* (Oxford: Clarendon Press, 2006), 612–21; K. W. Wedderburn, *The Worker and the Law*, 3rd edn. (London: Sweet & Maxwell, 1986) 512–8.

protestors in Australia,[11] New Zealand,[12] and Canada,[13] as well as in the United States[14] and in Britain,[15] were imprisoned for too vehemently—or perhaps too effectively—protesting against their country's involvement in the War to Make the World Safe for Democracy.[16] The following decades witnessed the suppression of the advocacy of extreme political ideas such as anarchism, fascism, and communism in various democracies throughout the world.[17] Though the content

[11] For instance, in 1916 in Perth members of the Industrial Workers of the World, including 83 year-old labour leader Montague Miller, were convicted of sedition for opposing conscription and the war. See J. Toscano, 'Australian anarchist history: Monty Miller', *Anarchist Age Weekly Review*, No. 215, 2 September 1996.

[12] For instance, in 1916 future Prime Minister of New Zealand, Peter Fraser, was imprisoned for sedition for opposing conscription during World War I. See 'Peter Fraser', *Encyclopaedia Britannica* online, <http://www.britannica.com/EBchecked/topic/217506/Peter-Fraser> (last accessed 21 August 2008).

[13] For instance, Michael Chartinoff, editor of the Ukrainian Social Democratic Party's newspaper *Robotchyi Narod*, was given a three-year jail sentence and fined $1000 under the War Measures Act for opposing militarism, accusing France of murdering pacifist Jean Jaures and quoting German socialist Karl Liebknecht. See J. Keshen, *Propaganda and Censorship during Canada's Great War* (Edmonton: U Alberta P, 1996), 88, 91. Canada also banned books portraying England in a poor light with respect to the amount of alcohol consumed there for fear that such descriptions would cause Canadians to question if the home country was worth saving. Temperance leader Rev. Benjamin Spence was arrested for possession of several copies of *The Fiddlers*, one of the banned works, though this prosecution was eventually dropped. Other banned books included those portraying Germany in a positive light and those portraying warfare realistically. Ibid., 97–8.

[14] See eg, *Debs* v. *US* 249 US 211 (1919), upholding the conviction of Socialist presidential candidate Eugene Debs for obstructing the draft by giving a speech in which he praised draft resisters.

[15] For instance, in 1916 William Gallacher, president of the Clyde Workers' Committee in Scotland, was convicted under the Defence of the Realm Act and sentenced to six months in prison for writing an article condemning British involvement in World War I. John Muir, the publisher of *The Worker*, the Clyde Worker's Committee journal in which the article was published, received a one-year sentence. See W. Gallacher, *In Revolt on the Clyde*, 4th edn. (London: Lawrence and Wishart, 1936). For speaking out against Britain's involvement in the war, philosopher Bertrand Russell was convicted under the Defence of the Realm Act on the charge of interfering with British foreign policy and spent six months in Brixton Prison. Russell had criticized the American Army for strikebreaking and suggested that his fellow citizens be wary of these soldiers. See J. Vellacott, *Bertrand Russell and the Pacifists in the First World War* (Brighton: Harvester Press, 1980).

[16] See Woodrow Wilson, War Messages, 65th Cong., 1st Sess. Senate Doc. No. 5, Serial No. 7264, Washington, D.C., 1917, declaring that 'The world must be made safe for democracy'.

[17] In Australia, a communist leader was convicted of sedition and sentenced to prison for telling a Sydney journalist that 'if Soviet Forces in pursuit of aggressors entered Australia, Australian workers would welcome them'. *R* v. *Sharkey* (1949) 79 CLR 121. In Canada during World War II, Camillien Houde, a former mayor of Montreal, was fined and imprisoned for sedition for publicly urging the men of Quebec to ignore the National Registration Act. See 'Innocents abroad', Time Magazine, 5 August 1946. In November 1940, the Swiss government dissolved the Swiss Nazi Party, noting that the party's activities endangered public order and created conflict. See P. N. Stearns, *The Encyclopedia of World History*, 6th edn. (New York: Houghton Mifflin, 2001). The Public Order Act 1936 was enacted in England during the rise of the British Union of Fascists in an effort to curb its activities as a political group. See K. D. Ewing and C. Gerty, *The Struggle for Civil Liberties: Political Freedom and the Rule of Law in Britain, 1914–1945* (Oxford: OUP, 2000), ch. 6. In the United States, a member of Left Wing Section of the Socialist Party was convicted under a law proscribing advocacy of criminal anarchy. See *Gitlow* v. *New York* 268 US 652 (1925). Later, leaders of the American Communist party were convicted under the Smith Act's prohibition against conspiracy to advocate the violent overthrow of the United States government for teaching Marxist doctrine. See *Dennis* v. *United States* 341 US 494 (1951).

of the banned speech may have differed, the basic problem remained the same: at what point, if any, does political and social criticism become so extreme and offensive to basic societal norms or so disruptive of critical social goals that it can legitimately be suppressed in a democratic society?

In this volume, a host of distinguished scholars drawn from a range of disciplines and different countries examine current attempts to suppress various types of extreme speech that many believe pose an unacceptable threat to essential values in modern multicultural democracies, or in some cases, to democracy itself. Extreme speech regulation breaks down into a number of categories and operates in different contexts. A particularly controversial category of extreme speech and one that has often been subject to legislation in contemporary democracies is hate speech. In its purest form, hate speech is simply expression which articulates hatred for another individual or group, usually based on a characteristic (such as race) which is perceived to be shared by members of the target group. Legal systems do not attempt to prohibit the expression of hate *simpliciter*. Rather hate speech regulation prohibits the speaker from using hate speech to achieve some further purpose: usually inciting others to hatred of the target group or seeking to encourage the audience to discriminate against them. Most of the recent developments in this field involve the extension of racial hate speech laws to speech based on other characteristics of the target group such as their religion or sexual orientation. The regulation of hate speech and the limits of such regulation in a democratic society are explored in Parts II and III of this collection, with the first of these sections focusing on hate speech in general and the second on incitement to religious hatred.

Religion is central to the topic of extreme speech regulation in another way: not only can speech (whether secular or itself religious) offend religious sensibilities, but religious expression has the capacity to offend secular, liberal values. For example, religious disapproval of homosexual relationships or religiously mandated dress codes (such as veiling for women) may easily come into conflict with the liberal commitment to equality. This topic is addressed in Part IV. At some point, extreme speech may cross the line into general criminal prohibitions on the inchoate offences of incitement to violence. A recent development has been to expand the traditional categories of incitement to lawless action by creating specific offences to deal with incitement to, or glorification of, terrorism. These issues are explored in Part V of this volume.

Prohibitions on the denial of crimes against humanity such as the Holocaust overlap with incitement to hatred against ethnic or religious groups, but raise distinct questions as well. These questions are explored in Part VI. Different considerations may apply to extreme speech across distinct media: the growth in far-right propaganda on the Internet is a prime example. Part VII considers the appropriate limits of governmental and self-imposed regulation of the media.

These controversies are not unique to the United States and the United Kingdom, but arise at various times and to a greater or lesser extent in every liberal democracy. Therefore, we have included contributions which address extreme speech in a number of other jurisdictions, including Germany, France, Hungary, Israel, Australia, and Canada. We have also attempted to widen the scope of the discussions beyond the academic legal community in order to reflect the inter-disciplinary nature of debates about extreme speech. In addition to law's usual companion, philosophy, we have incorporated contributions from the fields of history, psychology, and literature.

2. Is there a Lesson in this History?

The long history of suppression of extreme criticism of political or social con-ditions suggests that democracies tend to overreact to what at the time seemed to be imminent threats to core societal values or to projects such as the successful prosecution of a war upon which the fate of the nation is thought to depend.[18] Looking back from the perspective of the late 1960s at 50 years of judicially approved suppression of extreme speech, United States Supreme Court Justice William O. Douglas observed that though 'the threats were often loud' they were 'always puny and made serious only by judges so wedded to the status quo that critical analysis made them nervous'.[19] Is the same true of the 'extreme speech' that democratic governments attempt to suppress today and on which this book focuses? Will the threats that now seem clear and present also in retrospect be seen as greatly exaggerated? An argument can certainly be made that such is the case. There are, however, respectable arguments that the situation is different at least with respect to some types of extreme speech that plague contemporary multicultural societies. Almost all of the speech suppression of which we now repent involved extreme speech directed against government, laws, or public policy. Most of the controversial regulations with which this book deals involve, in contrast, bans on extreme speech directed towards other individuals, such as attacks on people's race, ethnicity, religion, or sexual orientation.[20]

There are several reasons why this difference might be significant. The first goes to the perceived necessity of the law. Thus, Waldron argues in the article quoted

---

[18] Shortly after World War I, Judge Learned Hand wrote of the need to develop free speech doctrine adequate to 'serve just a little to withstand the torrents of passion to which I suspect democracies will be found more subject than for example the whig autocracy of the 18th century'. Letter from Hand to Zechariah Chafee, 2 January 1921, as quoted in G. Gunther, 'Learned Hand and the Origins of Modern First Amendment Doctrine: Some Fragments of History' (1975) 27 *Stan. L. Rev.* 719, 770.

[19] *Brandenburg* v. *Ohio* 395 US 444, 454 (1969).

[20] Some regulations considered in this volume, eg, laws against glorification of terrorism, do target speech not usually aimed at groups of individuals, but like the extreme speech traditionally sup-pressed by government, usually involve attacks upon the state. Conversely, the expression targeted by bans on speech that insult or demean individuals on the basis of race, ethnicity, religion, or sexual orientation is rarely a mere rant against members of these groups but is almost always bound up with criticism of some government policy, eg, immigration laws or race-based minority preferences.

from above that prosecution of speech that threatened the public order, arguably needed to protect the fledging American republic, was no longer justified when government soon thereafter became strong. 'But', he asks 'is that true of the system of mutual respect among the members of racial groups' which in many multi-cultural democracies, including the United States, is 'a recent and fragile achievement? Can we complacently assume that it too is immune from serious disturbance, so that we need not worry about the cumulative effect of racist attacks'?[21]

Waldron's point has merit, so far as it goes. But such an analysis is deficient in its assumption that the test of the legitimacy of a speech restriction is exclusively, or even primarily, the need for such laws. While gratuitous restrictions on speech, particularly political speech, are obviously illegitimate, the converse is not true. Thus a speech restriction is not legitimate just because it is actually needed to promote some important societal interest. For instance, few would argue that suppression of anti-war protests is legitimate in a democratic society just because government can show, as it likely could in many cases, that these protests imperil the war effort by encouraging the enemy and dispiriting the country's troops. What Waldron's analysis omits is the crucial question of whether the restriction on speech is justified despite speakers' interests in expressing their views as well as the audience's interest in hearing these perspectives. Such fuller analysis, in turn, raises the question of precisely why free speech, particularly 'speech concerning the organisation and culture of society', is valued in a democracy.[22] If, as Waldron seems to assume, speech is valued primarily for reasons instrumental to demo-cracy, such as to 'help reveal, and remedy, abuses of power',[23] then it may well be appropriate to suppress speech in order to advance other social goals such as assuring 'the system of mutual respect among the members of racial groups'. But if free speech is valued not for such instrumental reasons, but rather as a right of each individual to participate in the discussion by which public opinion is formed, then excluding anyone from this discussion would compromise 'the sense of participation, identification, and legitimacy' on which democracy depends.[24] On this view of free speech, even a goal as important as promoting racial harmony would not seem to justify the suppression of racist ideas.

A related argument for distinguishing many of the contemporary restrictions on extreme speech from the discredited speech restrictions of the past is this: historically, laws suppressed the individual right of free speech in the name of some state interest such as maintenance of public order or the successful pros-ecution of a war; in contrast, contemporary regulations, with which this book is primarily concerned, narrowly limit the rights of the speaker in order to protect

---

[21] Waldron, n. 7 above.

[22] E. Barendt, *Freedom of Speech*, 2nd edn. (Oxford: OUP, 2005), 189.

[23] Waldron, n. 7 above.

[24] R.C. Post, *Constitutional Domains: Democracy, Community and Management* (Cambridge, MA: Harvard UP, 1995), 286.

the rights of other individuals not to suffer an affront to their dignity on the basis of a characteristic central to their personality such as their race, ethnicity, religion, or sexual orientation. This rationale in turn raises several crucial questions, including whether in a democratic society one truly has a right (as opposed to an inchoate interest) not to be demeaned by public discourse on bases such as these;[25] and if so, why vindication of this right justifies the infringement of the right of the speaker to participate in the political process.[26]

It is not, however, the purpose of this general introduction to reach a conclusion about these matters, nor is it the purpose of this book to persuade others to adopt any particular view on the legitimacy of the various restrictions discussed in these pages. Rather, this introduction is meant to sketch some of the key questions raised by the new generation of laws suppressing extreme speech in a prelude to what we believe is a stimulating collection of essays that consider these questions in detail and from many different perspectives.

---

[25] Most commentators do not regard human dignity as a free-standing human right: 'The notion that dignity can itself be a fundamental right is superficially appealing but ultimately unconvincing' (D. Feldman, 'Human Dignity as a Legal Value, Part I' [1999] *Pub. L.* 682 and 'Part II' [2000] *Pub. L.* 61). See further, E. Grant, 'Dignity and Equality' [2007] *Hum. Rts. L. Rev* 299; and J. Jones, ' "Common Constitutional Traditions": Can the Meaning of Human Dignity under German Law Guide the European Court of Justice?' [2004] *Pub. L.* 167. But see the South African Bill of Rights which provides in s. 10 that 'Everyone has inherent dignity and the right to have their dignity respected and protected'.

[26] Hate speech restrictions are typically under-theorized and rely on a shifting collection of justifications relating to public peace and order, non-discrimination, offensiveness, and human dignity often without any principled attempt to separate them out or address the free speech concerns they raise.

PART I

INTRODUCTION AND BACKGROUND

1

Freedom of Speech in a Globalized World

Dieter Grimm

1. The Meaning of Freedom of Speech

(i) Freedom of Expression

There is no democracy without public discourse and no public discourse without freedom of speech, freedom of the media, and freedom of information. And only if it contains both the active and the passive side—freedom to express one's own opinions and freedom to learn about the opinions of others—does the right constitute a comprehensive freedom of communication. In order to find out whether this liberty is recognized in a particular jurisdiction, it is not sufficient to consult a country's constitution or the international human rights documents it has ratified. Freedom of opinion can exist without being constitutionally guaranteed, and it can be constitutionally guaranteed without existing for the members of a society.

Most socialist constitutions contained a right to free speech. The Chinese Constitution contains it today in its Article 35. Many Islamic countries are among the signers of the International Covenant on Civil and Political Rights of 1966. On the other hand, the United Kingdom enjoyed freedom of speech long before the Human Rights Act of 1998. Australia, in turn, deliberately refused to adopt a bill of rights. But when the Australian Parliament passed a law prohibiting televised political advertising and instead allotted free time to parties and candidates, the Australian High Court measured this law against a constitutional right to free speech although no such right was to be found in the text of the constitution.[1]

The High Court reasoned that the constitution declares Australia to be a democracy, and that there is no way to be a democracy without recognition of freedom of speech. The right was therefore in the Court's view implied in the notion of democracy, at least in so far as political speech was concerned. The reverse conclusion—that freedom of speech implies democracy—however, would

---

[1] *Australian Capital Television Pty. Ltd.* v. *Commonwealth* (1992) 177 CLR 106.

not be true. We know of countries that recognize and respect a fundamental right to free speech without being democracies. Historically, constitutionalism is not necessarily linked with democracy. Germany before the Weimar Constitution is an example.

This is of some importance because it shows that freedom of speech does not derive its raison d'être from democracy. Before being a necessary element of self-government of a nation, free speech is a necessary element of individual self-determination and personal dignity, which is at the centre of the idea of fundamental rights. The twofold basis of freedom of speech—individual self-development and collective self-determination—plays a role when the question is raised which restrictions of speech are compatible with the constitutional guarantee. There can be no doubt that, despite its importance, freedom of speech is not an absolute right since speech can harm other liberties or protected interests.

Even a country whose constitution reads 'Congress shall make no law... abridging the freedom of speech', as does the First Amendment to the United States Constitution, recognizes that not all speech is protected. Yet, it is of great significance for what purpose or in whose interest the right can be limited. It makes a difference whether a constitution allows for limitations 'in the interest of the state, of society or of the collective' as the Chinese Constitution does, or whether a constitution declares that fundamental rights are 'subject only to such reasonable limits...as can be demonstrably justified in a free and democratic society', as the Canadian and the South African Constitutions proclaim.

But here again the constitutional text does not tell the whole story. The interpretation of the text and its application in concrete cases matters as well. There are countries with rather broad limitation clauses that are narrowly interpreted as in Germany. But there are also countries with a narrow limitation clause that do not prevent severe restrictions. Ultimately it is decisive whether the state claims the power to enforce an objective truth, be it religious or secular, and legitimates its rule by this pre-determined truth, or whether the state sees its ultimate end in serving the freedom of its citizens so that different beliefs co-exist and rule is legitimated by consensus.

Of crucial importance in a democracy is the answer to the question whether freedom of speech ought to be privileged over other fundamental rights because it is indispensable to democracy. Can it be called a preferred freedom whose function it is—as Robert Post describes the American position[2]—to maintain public discourse free from control of community norms such as mutual respect and civility? Or are such norms legitimate grounds for restrictions of freedom of speech as most European constitutions assume? If one accepts that freedom of speech has a double basis in democracy as well as in dignity it seems difficult to

---

[2] See chapter 7 in this volume.

privilege the democratic aspect and submit the individual dignity aspects to exigencies of democracy.

Moreover, not only freedom of speech but also personality rights are closely linked to democracy. Equality and dignity of human beings regardless of their gender, race, religion, and similar classifications are themselves democratic values. Protecting people's personality rights against offensive speech seems therefore to be a democratically legitimate cause for limitations. In the final analysis, everything depends on a fair balance between the rights and interests at stake. It is not sufficient to consider only the detrimental effects speech may have on other equally important rights. The detrimental effects limitations of speech might have on democratic discourse must also be considered. 'Chilling effects' that speech regulation is likely to have on speech ought to be avoided.

In order to strike a fair balance between freedom of speech, on the one hand, and other protected values, rights and interests, on the other, most countries have turned to the principle of proportionality, originally developed in German administrative law in the late nineteenth century and transformed into a constitutional principle by the German Constitutional Court in the 1950s.[3] From there it spread out to many jurisdictions all over the world. The Israeli Supreme Court uses it constantly.[4] The Canadian Supreme Court declared shortly after the adoption of the Charter of Rights and Freedoms in 1982 that the limitation clause in Article 1 means proportionality.[5] The South African Constitution of 1996 explicitly prescribes it in Article 36.

Only in the United States is free speech doctrine still more or less immune to proportionality. Instead of employing an explicit proportionality approach, courts in the United States apply various degrees of 'scrutiny' depending on the type of speech and the nature of the regulation at issue. In a recent assessment of the Supreme Court's free speech jurisprudence no less than eight such tests were enumerated.[6] The choice between them tends to become the decisive stage in decision making. Whether this approach is superior to proportionality in terms of predictability of outcome is not uncontested even in the United States.[7]

Special treatment of freedom of speech in the interest of democracy can, however, not only come in form of a privilege. It can also consist in discrimination against certain types of speech. This would be the case where freedom of speech is functionalized in the interest of democracy so that only speech favouring democracy is protected while speech criticizing or rejecting democracy can be

---

[3] See D. Grimm, 'Proportionality in Canadian and German Constitutional Jurisprudence' (2007) 57 *U. Toronto L.J.* 383.

[4] *United Mizrahi Bank* v. *Migdal Cooperative Village* (1995) 49 (4) P.D. 221; *Adalah* v. *Ministry of the Interior* (2006) H.C. 7052/03; see also A. Barak, 'Proportional Effect: the Israeli Experience' (2007) 57 *U. Toronto L.J.* 369.

[5] *R.* v. *Oakes* (1986) 1 S.C.R. 103.

[6] See P. Gewirtz, 'Privacy and Speech' (2001) *Sup. Ct. Rev.* 139.

[7] Ibid., and more generally, T. A. Aleinikoff, 'Constitutional Law in the Age of Balancing' (1987) 96 *Yale L.J.* 934.

prohibited. The twofold basis of freedom of speech in individual self-development and collective self-determination forbids such functionalization. Given democracy's many shortcomings the possibility of criticism is indispensable to democracy. Moreover, free speech is a value independent of democracy. Even rejection of democracy must be permitted.

But how can this be harmonized with the concept of militant democracy? The German Basic Law explicitly allows for a ban on certain political parties in Article 21 and even for a forfeiture of the freedom of speech in Article 18. Yet, these provisions do not forbid anti-democratic speech. The only ground for applying the measures is a party's or a person's attempt to overthrow the democratic system. Speech alone does not suffice. The explanation for this solution is the self-destruction of Germany's democracy in 1933 when the democratic system was abolished, not by a revolution, but through democratic means. Meanwhile, the concept of militant democracy has been adopted by other countries as well and begins to gain support even in the United States.[8]

(ii) Freedom of the Media

Basically, what is true for speech is also true for the media. However, freedom of the media is not just freedom of speech with a wider range through technical means of dissemination. Natural speech and media-based speech differ in a more fundamental respect. While everybody can express his opinion, not everybody can amplify his speech via the mass media. Media-based speech is therefore speech by a few for the many. Only the Internet has begun to change this situation. But apart from the Internet, control over the media creates opportunities to channel or suppress information and to advance one's own opinion while fighting the ideas of others. Media control is a basis of power.

This is why all dictatorships exercise total control over the media. But this is by no means a problem of totalitarian systems alone. Democratic regimes in which the success of parties and politicians depends largely on public opinion are no less interested in gaining control over the media. While the print media in democracies usually are in private hands and operate under private law, this is not necessarily so for the electronic media. In a number of democracies—and not only recently established ones—the electronic media are either state run or state controlled and more or less serve the interests of the ruling party instead of serving the interest of a democratic society destined for self-government.

If democracy is understood as a form of political rule in which the people are the principal and the rulers are the agents who come to power after a fair competition and are accountable for the way they exercise their mandate, state control over the media creates a problem. Democracy is not only about free elections. Free elections mean little when they are not embedded in a free communication process that

---

[8] See S. Issacharoff, 'Fragile Democracies' (2007) 120 *Harv. L. Rev.* 1405.

provides the electorate with the information necessary to make an informed choice or when access to the media can be denied to opposition candidates or parties. Media under the control of those who seek re-election are less likely to serve the electorate well.

There is, moreover, an even deeper reason for a separation between the media and government. Political participation culminates in the election. However, it is not limited to elections. Popular self-government not only requires a full range of information and viewpoints related to candidates and parties but also a forum where people can venture and exchange ideas independently of government interests; where the general public can get an unvarnished picture of its political, social, cultural, economic situation; where the development society takes can be observed and criticized unbiased by an 'official' point of view; and where society's various shortcomings and scandals can be exposed.

Mass media are not the only means to produce such a forum. Art, literature, academic writing, and teaching fulfil this essential democratic function in different ways. But because of the media's range, suggestive force, and accessibility, they are a particularly important part of the cultural system where knowledge is produced, disseminated and tested, opinions are shaped, standards of behaviour are set, world views influenced, and meaning is constructed. A society's awareness of its state of affairs and the quality of a democracy depend to no small degree on the way the mass media fulfil their function. This is all too easily forgotten by those who perceive of the media, particularly television, only as part of the entertainment business.

Freedom from state control is a precondition for a media system that is able to fulfil this essential democratic and cultural function. But it would be an error to assume that a private media system is sufficient to guarantee fulfilment of this function. Although private ownership is arguably sufficient to assure the proper functioning of the print media, this is apparently not the case for the electronic media. Just as state control opens the door for political influence, private ownership opens the door for commercial influence. Private television operates for profit and therefore tends to neglect the interests of a free and democratic society over the profit that cheap distraction promises.

This is why a purely negative understanding of the right to free media, focusing only on the menaces emanating from the state, is not sufficient to secure the service the media owe to a free and democratic society. Freedom of the media is a comprehensive freedom that protects them against any instrumentalization for external purposes, be they political or commercial. Unlike freedom of speech, freedom of the media is more than an individual right. It refers to a social function of vital interest for individual self-determination and collective self-government. But this function can only be fulfilled adequately if it is rendered freely.

The German Constitutional Court made this distinction explicit when it called the freedom of broadcasting, guaranteed in Article 5 of the Basic Law, a functional freedom that serves a particular purpose, as opposed to personal freedoms that are ends in themselves. It even spoke of a 'serving' freedom.[9] This may sound unfamiliar in the context of fundamental rights language. But it is a concept that remains within the realm of freedom since the purpose is itself a freedom purpose. Only the point of reference changes: freedom is not primarily the freedom of the owners of the media, but the freedom of the viewers and listeners to form their opinion, which in turn presupposes free media.

Since this freedom can be endangered not only by the state but also by the owners and journalists, its protection may justify limitations of the individual aspect of the right in the interest of the overall freedom of communication or the establishment of public television that is neither state controlled nor profit driven. As a functional freedom, media freedom does not include the right not to exercise this freedom, as is the case with most individual freedoms. Rather, the state has to secure the fulfilment of the function. As far as the danger for media freedom stems from the political side, the state is obliged to respect this freedom. As far as the danger stems from private actors, the state is obliged to protect it.

Understanding fundamental rights not only as obligations of the state to refrain from certain actions that would violate liberty but also as duties to actively protect liberty against menaces emanating from third parties is a genuine contribution of the German constitutional jurisprudence.[10] It does not only apply to freedom of the media, but to every liberty guaranteed in the Bill of Rights. It helps to make these guarantees real in times when freedom is as much endangered by private action and societal developments as by government interests. It finds more and more support in other countries, but is still rejected in the United States.

There is, however, at least one decision of the US Supreme Court that comes quite close to this understanding with respect to media rights, the *Red Lion* case.[11] It concerned the so-called fairness doctrine, which guaranteed persons who were personally attacked in the context of controversial public issues free time to defend themselves and, more generally, required broadcasters to present balanced discussion of public issues. In upholding the fairness doctrine, the Supreme Court rejected the claim by a broadcaster that the First Amendment allowed him to use the station in whatever way or for whatever purpose he liked.

In language very similar to the one used by the German Constitutional Court, the Supreme Court held that in the context of freedom of broadcasting, it is the First Amendment rights of the viewers and listeners, not the rights of the broadcasters, that are paramount. This was because freedom of broadcasting had a goal, namely producing an informed public capable of conducting its own affairs.

---

[9] BVerfGE 57, 295 (1981). This marked an important step in a long line of decisions, many of which can be found in English translation in *Decisions of the Bundesverfassungsgericht*, Vol. 2 (Baden-Baden: Nomos, 1998) 31, 199, 313, 386, 474, 587.

[10] See D. Grimm, 'The Protective Function of the State', in G. Nolte (ed.), *European and US Constitutionalism* (Cambridge: CUP, 2005), 137.

[11] *Red Lion Broadcasting Co. v. FCC* 395 US 367 (1969).

Justice White called it a 'collective right to have the medium function consistently with the ends and purposes of the First Amendment'.[12] Despite this sweeping language, the Supreme Court held only that Congress *may* regulate broadcasting. The German Constitutional Court, in contrast, concluded that parliament *must* regulate broadcasting.

2. Freedom of Speech Under Globalized Conditions

(i) Protecting Religion from Speech?

In a globalized world speech can be universally heard, as the Mohammed cartoons that appeared 2005 in a local Danish newspaper illustrate. Without the growing multiculturalism of European societies, these cartoons would not have garnered much attention. Without modern information technology, they would not have been universally noticed within days. In a globalized world speech can provoke universal reactions. Again the Danish cartoons are an example: 139 persons lost their life during the violent reactions following the publication and others were threatened with death; embassies were set on fire, Danish goods boycotted, and journalists were convicted and fined or fired.

It was not by chance that the immediate cause of these events was a religious issue. Religion re-appears on the scene after the end of the Cold War and the collapse of many atheist regimes that suppressed religious movements. One can observe a new politicization of religion, particularly of such religions that have not undergone the process of historicization and contextualization of divine revelation and sacred texts, have not learned to distinguish between the error and the erring person or to bridge doctrinal differences by a spirit of tolerance, and are neither accustomed to a secular state nor to a pluralistic society.

One of the consequences of the violent reactions to the Danish cartoons was a call for better protection of religious sensibilities. The demand came not only from Muslim groups but also from the Christian Churches and found some resonance with politicians as well. Some saw the solution in press self-censorship. Others asked for new laws. Since it will usually be through speech that religious feelings are hurt, increased legal protection against offending religious feelings will entail more restrictions on freedom of speech. This raises the question of whether liberal democracies can fulfil this demand without violating their constitutions.

Legal protection of God, of religious beliefs, doctrine, symbols, rituals, and services has a long tradition in the West. Blasphemy laws could at one time be found in every penal code. They did not protect any religion, but the Christian faith and the Christian God. Only recently were many of them repealed. What remained in place were provisions against disturbance of the public peace caused

---

[12] Ibid., 390.

by offensive speech against religion. Should the wheel be turned back and, in reaction to growing multiculturalism in Western societies, more protection of religion be furnished, but now in conformity with the anti-discrimination clauses in modern constitutions rather than limited to a certain faith?

The answer requires some reflection on the place of religion in the secular state. The secular state was the historical reaction to the devastating religious wars that followed the Reformation of the sixteenth century. After a long process with results differing from country to country, the state finally succeeded in pacifying religiously divided society by untying its bonds with one religion and making itself independent from a transcendent truth. Religious truth became a matter both of individual belief and individual choice. As little as dominant religious institutions may have liked this new arrangement in the beginning, they came to realize that freedom of religion depends greatly on state neutrality in questions of religious beliefs.

Some secular states understood themselves not only as religiously neutral, but as actually opposed to religion. For them privatization of religion meant more than the state's abstinence from interfering with religious affairs. It meant rather a confinement of religion to the private sphere and the denial of a public role. The French 'laïcité' shows traits of this attitude. Yet, this is not a necessary feature of the secular state. The United States Constitution has been interpreted as requiring strict separation of church and state, but does not deny religion a public role. In many European countries the state explicitly concedes churches a role in the public arena.

Today separation between state and religion does not necessarily mean antagonism. The secular state recognizes religious beliefs as an elementary human urge that seeks collective expression. Freedom of religion enjoys constitutional protection in both its individual and collective dimension. This includes self-determination of a religious group about the content and commands of its faith. The secular state does not oblige any religion to renounce its claim to be the only true one. But it does prevent every religion from imposing its truth on society as a whole. Each religion can retain its truth just because the state does not take a stand in questions of ultimate truth.

However, peaceful coexistence of mutually exclusive beliefs is not possible without limitation on religious freedom. But since freedom of religion is a fundamental right, the limitations must be determined by law in a democratic process, which in turn presupposes an unimpeded public discourse. This means that, in the secular state, religion cannot be exempted from criticism. Freedom of speech and freedom of the media is not less important than freedom of religion. The more a religious group claims public recognition and respect for its religious norms, the more it must be exposed to public discourse.

Consequently, there are some limits to protection of religious beliefs against speech. Every general prohibition requires a basis in the secular law. Negation or criticism of what a religion regards as sacred, and therefore immunized internally against any form of questioning, cannot be prohibited by the secular state. The secular state may not enforce religious taboos. It is not permissible to shield sacred figures, symbols, or practices against ridicule or mockery. This applies also to speech in the form of cartoons. Cartoons can make a genuine contribution to the public discourse essential to a free and democratic society.[13]

But what about religious feelings? A general prohibition against hurting religious feelings would put the public discourse at the mercy of the sensitivity of religious groups, and particularly of the most militant among them. The state has to protect every religion against violence. But religiously motivated violence caused by offensive speech is something different and cannot justify a prohibition of that speech. Moreover, since the number of religious groups is immense, and since any disturbance of their religious feelings can get global attention, what speech might have this effect would be completely unforeseeable. Such a norm could not be formulated in conformity with rule of law requirements.

Yet, the secular state is not the enemy of religion. It recognizes religion as a value that deserves protection. This is more than mere tolerance. There can be no doubt that instigation to hate ought to be prohibited when it is directed against religious groups, just as it is prohibited when racial or ethnic groups are the target. Likewise speech that degrades, denigrates, or humiliates persons because of their religion can be prohibited without a violation of the right to free speech. These limitations rest on secular rather than religious grounds and thus permit legislation that protects religion.

The problem is identifying the exact boundary between legitimate public discourse and objectionable speech. In this respect, Europe and America may differ from one another. In the United States there seems to be a tendency to assume that a multicultural and multireligious society needs more speech than a homogeneous society.[14] Every religious group must be free to persuade or attack others, but prepared to tolerate the same behaviour when they are the target. In Europe there is a tendency to assume that multicultural and multireligious societies are in need of more consideration among the various groups. Consequently, greater restriction of speech in the interest of peaceful coexistence seems justifiable.

(ii) More Uniformity of Speech-Related Law?

This difference raises the question whether the global challenges we face today require global answers in the law. The global recognition of human rights could

---

[13] See *Hustler Magazine* v. *Falwell* 485 US 46, 54 (1988), 'Despite their sometimes caustic nature, from the early cartoon portraying George Washington as an ass down to the present day, graphic depictions and satirical cartoons have played a prominent role in public and political debate.'

[14] See R. C. Post, 'Cultural Heterogeneity and Law: Pornography, Blasphemy, and the First Amendment' (1988) 76 *Cal. L. Rev.* 297. See generally, E. J. Eberle, *Dignity and Liberty: Constitutional Visions in Germany and the United States* (Westport, CT: Praeger, 2002).

create the impression that this question has already been answered in the affirmative. A closer look shows, however, that a consensus can be found only on a very high level of abstraction. Below this level the differences in understanding, interpreting, and enforcing human rights are great. Even within the Western legal tradition one can find a variety of approaches. Particularly when conflicts between different human rights occur, the solutions vary considerably from country to country.

A recent decision of the European Court of Human Rights about freedom of press illustrates this lack of consensus.[15] Some popular magazines had published photographs showing Princess Caroline of Monaco at public places, but in private activities such as shopping in a local outdoor-market, riding a bicycle on a public way, and sitting in a crowded restaurant with a companion. Caroline argued that only photographs showing her in her official capacity as Princess of Monaco could be published without her permission, whereas everything else, regardless of the location, belonged to her private sphere and was precluded from publication.

The case originated in the German courts where Caroline had sued for an injunction against further publication of the photographs and worked its way up to the Federal Constitutional Court.[16] This Court ruled that, on the one hand, privacy does not end at the walls of one's house or the fence of one's garden, but can extend to other places, provided that the person has a reasonable expectation not to be in the public eye. The Court denied, on the other hand, that such a reasonable expectation exists when a person visits busy places. There is a legitimate interest in public figures not only when they act in an official capacity but also in everyday situations. Here freedom of press prevails over privacy. So the Court denied relief to Caroline.

The European Court, to the contrary, adopted Caroline's position. It ruled that the spatial criterion for privacy was unsuitable and had to be replaced by the purely functional criterion of whether the depicted person appeared in an official capacity or not, and at the same time limited freedom of press to matters that contribute to a serious public discussion. Only when dealing with such matters does the press exercise a 'watchdog' function that justifies the protection of the Convention. All the rest was called mere sensation seeking. The European Court thus did not recognize a legitimate public interest in information about public figures in form of pictures of activities outside their official conduct. So Caroline won her case.

The two decisions contradict each other, not only in the result but also in reasoning. The understanding of the two fundamental rights at stake, privacy and freedom of press, differs fundamentally, and behind this difference a

---

[15] *Von Hannover* v. *Germany* (2004) 16 BHRC 545.

[16] BVerfGE 101, 361 (1999). For an English translation see B. S. Markesinis, *The German Law of Torts: A Comparative Introduction*, 4th edn. (Oxford: Hart Publishing, 2002); also at <http://www.utexas.edu/law/academics/centers/transnational/work_new/german/case.php?id=728> (last accessed 29 May 2008).

fundamentally different notion of the meaning and function of the two rights can be discerned. What the European Court regards as a violation of the European Convention is in the eyes of the Federal Constitutional Court a requirement of the German Constitution. A reconciliation seems difficult since the Convention ranks below the Basic Law and is therefore not applied by the Constitutional Court.[17]

There is, of course, a lot to say about the merits of the two decisions: their different view on the demarcation of the right to privacy; their different comprehension of the function of public discourse and the role of the media in society; the more democratic or more paternalistic attitude in determining what is a legitimate public interest; and the viewpoints they consider when it comes to balancing the competing interests. But all this is besides the point here. Rather the question is whether in conflicts involving freedom of speech and other important values, national solutions should be superseded by some uniform international solution.

This would not be a problem on the domestic level. Here a contradiction between the judgments of two courts on the same case finds its solution in the hierarchy within the judiciary. Regardless of the quality of argumentation, the decision of the higher court prevails. But there is no such hierarchy beyond the national level. The European Court of Human Rights is not an appellate court. It may not reverse the judgment of the national court. It can only declare it in violation of the Convention. The domestic judgment remains in place and the state is under a duty by public international law to create a situation compatible with the Convention.

The desirability of uniformity is particularly doubtful when the issue is not protecting the individual against government but when the case requires a balancing of two constitutionally protected liberties in a conflict between private parties. Regarding the conflict between freedom of press and privacy, one can find a great variety of solutions in Europe.[18] There are two extreme positions. In France, privacy usually prevails even in cases of scandals in which public figures are involved. In the UK, freedom of press usually prevails and thus a public figure has little chance to be protected in his or her privacy. Germany lies in the middle between these two extremes.

The European Court of Human Rights, moreover, has no mandate to harmonize the law in Europe. Its task is to assure that the member states of the European Council observe a basic standard of fundamental rights protection. Article 53 of the Convention underscores this when it says that the Convention ought not to be interpreted in a way which would limit or impair the fundamental rights guaranteed by the laws of member states. But what did the European Court

---

[17] For an attempt to find a solution to this conundrum, see the most recent Caroline decision of the Federal Constitutional Court of 26 February 2008, case number 1 BvR 1626/07.

[18] See E. Barendt, *Freedom of Speech*, 2nd edn. (Oxford: OUP, 2005), 230–46.

do in deciding the Caroline case? It set out to make one extreme position, namely the French, obligatory throughout Europe and thereby impaired freedom of press as understood in other countries.

Notwithstanding the process of globalization, most of the law is still part of the national culture. It is also the product of a democratic process in the country. Both elements contribute to its legitimacy and acceptance within the community where it is in force. National culture does not mean that the law is free from any foreign influence. The contrary is true. But it is a genuine amalgamation of national roots and foreign influences. The democratic process does not guarantee that fundamental rights are always respected by the national legislature. But the member states have created means of their own to correct mistakes.

National courts do not decide cases solely on the basis of domestic positive law. Rather, they do it within a doctrinal and methodological framework rooted in national traditions. And they operate within a cultural context and are embedded in an ongoing legal and general discourse. Together these conditions are less visible but often more effective than the formal boundaries. They help keep national judges in contact with their society. They function as a corrective against judicial imperialism and contribute to the acceptance of court decisions. Finally, domestic courts can be reprogrammed by the lawmaker or the constitution-maker.

All these constraints are either lacking or poorly developed in international adjudication. The international judge is, therefore, much freer than the national judge. The consequence should be more self-restraint by international courts. Freedom of speech is no exception. It is a value of highest importance. At the same time it remains an endangered right. Therefore, an additional guarantee by international law is important. But when it comes to concretizing the right and balancing it against other rights or interests, a variety of national solutions are compatible with the basic guarantee. Universal recognition of freedom of speech does not require uniform legal solutions or interpretation.

2

Extreme Speech, Public Order, and Democracy: Lessons from *The Masses*

*James Weinstein**

1. Introduction

The unique history and culture of each nation threatens to confound any attempt at cross-cultural constitutional normative critique. Even with respect to nations with similar legal cultures, a regulation anathema to a core constitutional principle of one country might be constitutional in another. For instance, a law requiring a license to operate a television set would in the US be a patently unconstitutional restriction on free speech and freedom of the press; yet in the UK, the very different traditions concerning ownership and financing of the broadcast media make such a requirement perfectly compatible with free speech norms.

Do the markedly different approaches in the US and the UK towards the regulation of hate speech and similar forms of extreme speech present a similar phenomenon? Might it be that while in the United States bans on the virulent public expression of racist ideas violate basic conceptions of free speech, historical and cultural differences make such restrictions in the UK, as well as in most of the rest of Europe, perfectly compatible with freedom of expression?[1] If so, it would be singularly inappropriate for anyone not intimately familiar with the history and culture of a particular jurisdiction to criticize judicial decisions on this subject. But while there can be no doubt that some of the disparity between America and other democracies with regard to hate speech regulation stems from historical and cultural differences, there remains a core free speech principle that

* I am grateful to Eric Barendt, Ivan Hare, David Kaye, and Jeffrie Murphy for their helpful comments and suggestions and to David Ferrucci and Kelly Frailing for their valuable research assistance.

[1] For an excellent discussion of American free speech exceptionalism both with respect to hate speech and more generally, see F. Schauer, 'The Exceptional First Amendment' in M. Ignatieff (ed.), *American Exceptionalism and Human Rights* (Princeton: Princeton UP, 2005). See also J. Weinstein, 'An Overview of American Free Speech Doctrine and its Application to Extreme Speech', in this volume.

must be respected in any democracy worthy of that name and against which the propriety of free speech decisions of any democracy can be measured.

After first describing this core free speech principle and its derivation from a basic precept of democratic self-governance, I will discuss two recent English cases: *Hammond* v. *DPP*[2] and *Norwood* v. *DPP*.[3] As I will demonstrate, *Hammond* upholds a breach of this core free speech principle, while *Norwood* arguably does so. Finally, I will discuss speech at the periphery of this core—expression that government can in principle punish consistently with basic precepts of democracy, but which may nonetheless require protection lest in practice the core right of democratic participation be impaired.

In the course of this discussion I will point out the systemic failures of English case law that have left the core free speech right vulnerable and will suggest ways to remedy this problem. In particular, I will draw upon hard learned lessons from the United States where for decades after it first began to grapple with free speech problems, the Supreme Court also failed to provide adequate protection for the dissent that must be permitted in any democratic society. Here we will meet the redoubtable Justice Oliver Wendell Holmes and his famous 'clear and present danger' test which permitted the government to imprison protestors, including Eugene Debs, the Socialist candidate for President of the United States, for vehemently condemning American involvement in World War I[4] and later to jail the leaders of the Communist Party for teaching Marxist-Leninist doctrine.[5]

Shortly before Justice Holmes developed the 'clear and present danger' test, Learned Hand, an aptly named federal District Court judge, took a quite different approach in deciding whether a postmaster could legally refuse to mail a radical monthly magazine called *The Masses* because of its vehemently anti-war cartoons and text. Hand found legally irrelevant what he admitted were persuasive arguments that the expression would impair the war effort by stimulating draft resistance. Instead, he held that the sole question before him was whether the expression was

within the scope of that right to criticize either by temperate reasoning, or by immoderate and indecent invective, which is normally the privilege of the individual in countries dependent upon the free expression of opinion as the ultimate source of authority.[6]

Finding the material to be within this core democratic individual right of freedom of expression, Hand rejected the government's attempt to suppress the magazine.

As in art and science, an idea in law can also be too far ahead of the times to be accepted: Hand's decision was soon reversed, with the Court of Appeals noting

[2] [2004] EWHC 69 (Admin).
[3] [2003] EWHC 1564 (Admin).
[4] *Debs* v. *US* 249 US 211 (1919).
[5] *Dennis* v. *US* 341 US 494 (1951).
[6] *Masses Publishing Co.* v. *Patten* 244 F 535, 539 (SDNY, 1917).

that if the 'natural and reasonable effect of what was said is to encourage resistance to a law', the publication could be suppressed.[7] It would be more than half a century before Hand's approach was largely vindicated in the Supreme Court's seminal *Brandenburg* opinion.[8]

These early American cases reached wrong results because they asked the wrong question and are thus instructive for judges in England and other democracies in the early stages of developing free speech doctrine. We will see that to build doctrine adequate to protect dissent that must be allowed in a democracy, the key question cannot be whether the speech at issue is likely to impair some important government interest. Rather, as Judge Hand emphasized, the crucial question is whether the speaker has a right to engage in this expression in a society premised on democratic self-governance.

2. The Core Free Speech Right of Democratic Participation

'Democracy' literally means 'rule by the people'.[9] But precisely what practices are necessary to constitute such a state of affairs is an extremely contentious question. Not only are there different theories about what democracy should entail, but like the free speech principle, the practice of democracy in various countries will vary according to each society's particular culture and history. Nonetheless, I think it is safe to say that whatever else rule by the people may require, virtually all modern democratic theorists agree that it has at least two essential components: 1) popular sovereignty—a state of affairs in which the people exercise ultimate control over their government[10] and 2) the right of each citizen to participate in the process by which society's collective decisions are made.[11]

---

[7] *Masses Publishing Co.* v. *Patten* 246 F 24, 38 (2nd Cir, 1917).

[8] *Brandenburg* v. *Ohio* 395 US 444 (1969).

[9] The term was first used in the fifth century BCE by the Greek historian Herodotus and combines the Greek words *demos* ('the people') and *kratein* ('to rule'). B. Holden, *Understanding Liberal Democracy*, 2nd edn. (New York: Harvester Wheatsheaf, 1993), 7.

[10] Barry Holden observes that '[d]emocracy, indeed, is often characterized as a political system in which the people are sovereign, or in which there is popular sovereignty' and that 'certainly the notion of popular sovereignty is very deeply embedded in democratic thought.' Ibid., 9. Holden thus defines democracy as 'a political system in which the whole people, positively or negatively, make, and are entitled to make, the basic determining decisions on important matters of public policy'. Ibid., 8.

[11] 'In liberal democratic theory conceptions of "the people" are to a crucial extent "individualist".... [Thus] such conceptions imply that "the people" is simply a collection of individuals.' Ibid., 14. 'Equality before the law leads to the demand that all men should also have the same share in making the law. This is the point where traditional liberalism and the democratic movement meet.' F. Hayek, *The Constitution of Liberty* (Chicago: Univ Chicago Press, 1960), 103. See also R. Dahl, *Preface to Democratic Theory* (Chicago: Univ Chicago Press, 1963), 37: 'An organization is democratic if and only if the process of arriving at governmental policy is compatible with the condition of popular sovereignty and the condition of political equality.'

(i) Popular Sovereignty

The commitment to popular sovereignty alone arguably creates a narrow but very powerful right of free speech. If the people are the ultimate source of political authority, they must be able to speak to each other about all matters within the scope of this authority, that is, on all matters of public concern. If, to the contrary, the government were able to prohibit speech on the ground that it will persuade the populace to formulate erroneous public policy, then the government, not the people, would be the ultimate sovereign. As James Madison argued over two centuries ago, a logical consequence of a commitment to popular sovereignty is that 'the censorial power is in the people over the Government, and not in the Government over the people'.[12] Or as the United States Supreme Court has more recently declared, an essential purpose of free speech is to 'assure unfettered interchange of ideas for the bringing about of political and social changes desired by the people'.[13]

It is also arguable, however, that the commitment to popular sovereignty alone may *not* be sufficient to produce a right of free speech. For what if the people in the exercise of their sovereignty decide to restrict advocacy of political change? And indeed, restrictions on extreme speech in democratic societies are often imposed not by some executive decree or police action, but by legislation truly expressing the will of the people. So the question becomes, can the people themselves consistently with a commitment to popular sovereignty restrict future exercises of their own sovereignty? This is an old[14] and difficult riddle not unlike the old Sunday school query about whether an omnipotent God can make a rock so heavy He can't lift it, or less celestially, Mill's famous discussion about whether liberty entails the right to sell oneself into slavery.[15] Fortunately, we need not attempt to resolve this difficult issue here, because the other necessary component of democracy—the individual right to participate in the political process—assures each person the right to participate in the speech by which we

---

[12] 4 Annals of Cong. 934 (1794).

[13] *Roth* v. *US* 354 US 476, 484 (1957). See also *R* v. *Shayler* [2002] UKHL 11, para. 21 (Lord Bingham): 'Modern democratic government means government of the people by the people for the people. But there can be no government by the people if they are ignorant of the issues to be resolved, the arguments for and against different solutions and the facts underlying those arguments'; A. Meiklejohn, *Free Speech and its Relation to Self-Government* (New York: Harper and Brothers, 1948), 26–7: 'The principle of freedom of speech springs from the necessities of the program of self-government.... It is a deduction from the basic American agreement that public issues shall be decided by universal suffrage'.

[14] Karl Popper notes that Plato implicitly raised it in his criticism of democracy and his story of the rise of the tyrant. See K. R. Popper, 1 *The Open Society and Its Enemies, Part I: The Spell of Plato* (Princeton, NJ: Princeton UP, 1950), 122. See also C. A. Auerbach, 'The Communist Control Act of 1954: A Proposed Legal-Political Theory of Free Speech' (1956) 23 *U. Chi. L. Rev.* 173, 191–3.

[15] 'On Liberty' in J. Gray, (ed.), *On Liberty and Other Essays* (Oxford: OUP, 1998), 113–14.

govern ourselves, even if a majority of the people wish to exclude some speakers or certain views from the conversation.

(ii) The Individual Right of Political Participation

A basic precept of Enlightenment philosophy posits that though individuals may differ in their natural talents and abilities, each of us is of equal moral worth.[16] Ever since the idea of moral equality was loosed upon the world, there has been perpetual debate about what precisely it entails. There is now general agreement, however, that this precept includes at least a formal or procedural right of each person to participate in the process by which public issues are decided.[17] This right of equal participation in the political process includes not just equal voting rights but embraces also the right of each citizen to participate in the discussion by which public opinion is formed:

The will of the community, in a democracy, is always created through a running discussion between majority and minority, through free consideration of arguments for and against a certain regulation of a subject matter. That discussion takes place not only in parliament, but also, and foremost, at political meetings, in newspapers, books, and other vehicles of public opinion. A democracy without public opinion is a contradiction in terms.[18]

---

[16] See, eg I. Kant, *The Metaphysics of Morals* Trans. M. Gregor (Cambridge: CUP, 1991 [1797]), 434–35; J. Locke, *Second Treatise of Government*, C. B. Macpherson (ed.), (Indianapolis, IN: Hackett Publishing Co. Inc., 1980), ch.2 §§ 4, 6, 8, 9, 52. See also the statement of Thomas Rainboro during the 1647 Putney debates: 'Really I think that the poorest he that is in England has a life to live as the richest he; and therefore truly, Sir, I think it's clear, that every man that is to live under a Government ought first by his own consent to put himself under that Government.' R. A. Licht, (ed.), *Old Rights and New* (Washington, D.C.: American Enterprise Institute, 1993), 54.

[17] As one of the most prominent contemporary democratic theorists has explained: 'The democratic process is generally believed to be justified on the ground that people are entitled to participate as political equals in making binding decisions, enforced by the state, on matters that have important consequences for their individual and collective interest.' R. Dahl, *Controlling Nuclear Weapons: Democracy versus Guardianship* (Syracuse, NY: Syracuse UP, 1985), 5.

[18] H. Kelsen, *A General Theory of Law and State* Trans. A. Wedberg (Cambridge, MA: Harvard UP, 1945), 287–88. See also Hayek (n. 11 above), 101:

Democracy is, above all, a process of forming opinion.... The conception that government should be guided by majority opinion makes sense only if that opinion is independent of government. The ideal of democracy rests on the belief that the view which will direct government emerges from an independent and spontaneous process. It requires, therefore, the existence of a large sphere independent of majority control in which the opinions of individuals are formed. There is a widespread consensus that for this reason the case for democracy and the case for freedom of speech are inseparable.

In accord with these views, the High Court of Australia found a right to engage in political speech implicit in the democratic structure of the Australian Constitution. See *Australian Capital Television Pty. Ltd.* v. *Commonwealth* (1992) 177 CLR 106, 139–40: '[T]he great underlying principle of the Constitution was that rights of individuals were sufficiently secured by ensuring an equal share in political power. Absent freedom of communication, there would be scant prospect of the exercise of that power.' (Mason, CJ, internal quotation marks omitted).

Such an opportunity for free and equal participation is vital to the legitimacy of the entire legal system.[19] If an individual is excluded from participating in public discourse because the government disagrees with the speaker's views or because it finds the ideas too disturbing or too dangerous, any decision taken as a result of that discussion would, as to such an excluded citizen, lack legitimacy. So if someone is barred from expressing a view on a proposed tax increase or on whether the nation goes to war, or on the country's immigration policy, to that extent and with respect to that citizen, the government is no democracy but rather an illegitimate autocracy.[20]

This commitment to equal participation protects audience interests as well. The analogue to this core speaker's right is the precept that, in dealing with people in their capacity as the ultimate governors of society, government must treat each member of the polity as an equal, rational, and autonomous agent. Thus it is a core democratic precept that government may not restrict speech on the ground that it might cause the audience to adopt some unwise or even disastrous social policy.[21] To do so would be contrary to the precept that the people, collectively, have a right to govern and, individually, have a right to participate freely and equally in this collective decision making. Like the speaker right just described, this is a true individual right, not just a collective one, intimately tied to political legitimacy. And for this reason, it does not matter how many people support the speech repressive measure, so long as there is one person who has not agreed to surrender the right to be treated as a rational agent with respect to the

---

[19] See R. M. Dworkin, Foreword, this volume. See also R. C. Post, 'Democracy, Popular Sovereignty, and Judicial Review' (1998) 86 *Cal. L. Rev.* 429, 434: 'Finding it implausible to postulate [as did Rousseau] that the particular wills of individuals can be determinably identified with the specific enactments of the state, [modern] critics have suggested that democratic self-government requires that the particular will of individuals be connected instead to the *system* by which these enactments are created. They have thus proposed that law making be rendered dependent upon popular opinion, and they postulated that a necessary condition for citizens to identify with public opinion is the guarantee that all can freely participate in the public deliberations by which public opinion is formed.'

[20] N. Bobbio, *Democracy and Dictatorship: The Nature and Limits of State Power* Trans. P. Kennealy (Minneapolis, MN: Minnesota UP, 1989), 137: 'Democratic forms of government are those in which the laws are made by the same people to whom they apply (and for that reason they are autonomous norms), while in autocratic forms of government the law-makers are different from those to whom the laws are addressed (and are therefore heteronomous norms).'

[21] This is not to say, of course, that every person in society is in fact either autonomous or capable of making rational decisions about public policy. Rather, this is an ascription growing out of the fact that the people in the democracy have a right to govern and that it would be oxymoronic to view the ultimate sovereigns in society as lacking the capacity to make rational decisions on matters within the sphere of their democratic authority. In other capacities, however, such as consumer or as medical patient or as any other type of decision maker outside of the political realm, government may, without violating the core precept of democracy I am describing, treat us in accord with the reality that we are not full rational beings and in many contexts not fully autonomous. For a fuller discussion of this point, see J. Weinstein, 'Fools, Knaves, and the Protection of Commercial Speech: A Response to Professor Redish' (2007) 41 *Loy. L.A. L. Rev.* 133, 162–67.

public discussion of social policy matters.[22] Thus the right to participate in discussion of public affairs both as a speaker and as a potential recipient of ideas is not, as Gordon Brown has suggested, forfeited or even diminished just because the speech in question 'offends mainstream opinion'.[23]

(iii) Public Discourse

These two essential components of democracy—popular sovereignty and the individual right of political participation—generate a right of every citizen to participate in the discussion by which the people govern themselves through the formation of public opinion. As Eric Barendt has noted, this speech includes more than 'political speech in the narrow sense' but more generally embraces 'speech concerning the organization and culture of society'.[24] Courts and commentators often refer to this core democratic speech as 'public discourse',[25] which is the term I will adopt in this chapter as shorthand for that democratic conversation in which every member of society has a right to participate.

It is not, however, just the content of the speech that determines whether expression forms part of public discourse. Equally important is whether the speech occurs in settings dedicated to democratic self-governance, such as in a public forum like Hyde Park Corner or a town square, or as in many democracies including the United States, the corners of public thoroughfares. In addition to places dedicated to public discourse, there are also media essential to this conversation, including newspapers, books, films, and magazines, and more recently the Internet. As Robert Post has observed, 'prerequisites for democracy are commonly met in modern industrial societies by... media [that] combine to

---

[22] Although formal equality is obviously a crucial value underlying the modern concept of democracy, it arguably does not securely anchor the right to participate in the political process as an individual right. If, as discussed above, text accompanying n. 15, the people can in an exercise of their sovereignty limit this sovereignty, then universal restrictions on political participation such as denying everyone the right to vote (either generally or for certain offices) or the right to participate in public discourse (either altogether or on certain topics) would not violate this equality norm. In contrast, even if consistent with both popular sovereignty and equality, such restrictions would obviously implicate the legitimacy of the entire system of government. Thus, so far as individual as opposed to collective interests are concerned, the 'normative essence' of democracy is the legitimation served by the opportunity of each individual to participate in the political process. See R. C. Post, *Constitutional Domains: Democracy, Community and Management* (Cambridge, MA: Harvard UP, 1995), 273.

[23] In reacting to the acquittal of two leaders of the British National Party for inciting racial hatred, Brown declared: 'Any preaching of religious or racial hatred will offend mainstream opinion in this country. We have got to do whatever we can to root it out from whatever quarter it comes.' See 'Tougher race hate laws considered', *BBC News*, 11 November, 2006, <http://news.bbc.co.uk/1/hi/uk_politics/6137722.stm> (last accessed 23 July 2008). This case is discussed below.

[24] *Freedom of Speech*, 2nd edn. (Oxford: OUP, 2005), 189.

[25] Eg *Hustler Magazine, Inc.* v. *Falwell* 485 US 46, 55 (1988); *Cohen* v. *California* 403 US 15, 22 (1971); Barendt (n. 24 above), 183, 186; A. Geddis, 'Free Speech Martyrs or Unreasonable Threats to Social Peace—"Insulting" Expression and Section 5 of the Public Order Act 1986' [2004] *Pub. L.* 853, 855, 870; Post (n. 22 above), 119–78.

form a structural skeleton that is necessary ... for public discourse to serve the constitutional value of democracy'.[26]

As important as democratic self-governance may be, not all settings can be dedicated to public discourse. Of necessity there will be some places, such as the courtroom, classroom, or the government workplace, dedicated to other purposes and here government has far more leeway to legitimately restrict speech. But in settings that do form part of the 'structural skeleton' necessary for democratic self-governance, speech will tend to be considered part of the public discourse regardless of its content.[27] And where the speech is both overtly political or otherwise concerns 'the organization and culture of society' *and* occurs in a setting dedicated or essential to democratic self-governance, such expression might be fairly characterized as core public discourse and as such has the strongest claim to be immune from government regulation because of its viewpoint.

Finally, I want to emphasize that participatory democracy is not the only reason for protecting speech. There are, in addition, such well known justifications as the search for truth and the promotion of individual autonomy. But unlike the right to participate in the speech by which we govern ourselves, there is no consensus that either of these justifications underlies the core of a free speech principle necessary to any free and democratic society, and for that reason I do not focus upon them in the following analysis. Nevertheless, it should be borne in mind that even though a speech regulation might not offend the core democratic precept that I have identified, it could violate some other important free speech value.

3. Breaching the Core: *Hammond* v. *DPP*

(i) Facts and Divisional Court Decision

In October 2001, Harry John Hammond, an Evangelical Christian preacher, travelled to the town square in Bournemouth, England where he began preaching while holding a large placard bearing the following statement: 'Stop Immorality', 'Stop Homosexuality', 'Stop Lesbianism'. The sign also contained the statement 'Jesus is Lord' on each of its four corners. A group of about 30 to 40 people gathered around Hammond, arguing and shouting. Some threw soil at him and at one point someone tried to pull the placard away from Hammond, causing him to fall backwards. When Hammond stood up again with the sign and resumed preaching, someone poured water on him. A police officer who witnessed these events spoke to Hammond and asked him to put down the sign and leave the area, but he refused. A few minutes later, after being approached by

---

[26] 'Recuperating First Amendment Doctrine' (1995) 47 *Stan. L. Rev.* 1249, 1276.
[27] See ibid 1253; J. Weinstein, *Hate Speech, Pornography, and the Radical Attack on Free Speech Doctrine* (Boulder, CO: Westview Press, 1999), 45–6.

several members of the public who were outraged that Hammond was not arrested, the officer arrested Hammond for 'provoking violence' in breach of the peace.[28]

Hammond was charged with violating Section 5 of the Public Order Act 1986, which makes it an offence to use 'any threatening, abusive or insulting words or behaviour, or disorderly behaviour or [to display] any writing, sign, or other visible representation which is threatening, abusive, or insulting within the hearing or sight of a person likely to be caused harassment, alarm or distress thereby'.[29] To obtain a conviction, the prosecution must show that the defendant intended his conduct to be 'threatening, abusive or insulting' or that he was aware that it may be so.[30] The Act allows the accused to defend against a charge by proving that his conduct was 'reasonable'.[31]

The Magistrates' Court found Hammond guilty of violating the Act. The justices ruled that that the statements on his sign were 'insulting' and 'caused distress to persons who were present'. In their view 'there was a pressing social need' for the restriction on Hammond's expression because Hammond's message implied that the gay and lesbian communities were immoral and because 'there is a need to show tolerance towards all sections of society'. Because in the justices' view Hammond's protest 'went beyond legitimate protest', 'was provoking violence and disorder' and 'interfered with the rights of others', the justices held that 'the restriction on his right to freedom of expression' imposed by application of the Act to his speech 'was a proportionate response' and that Hammond's display of his sign under these circumstances was 'not reasonable'. They fined him £300 pounds and ordered forfeiture of his sign.[32]

The Divisional Court dismissed Hammond's appeal. In an opinion by May LJ, the court held, though 'not without hesitation', that it was 'open to the justices' to reach the conclusion that the words on the placard were 'insulting' within the meaning of the Public Order Act. Noting that the message on the sign was 'not expressed in intemperate language', the court 'considered very carefully' whether it should conclude that the words on the sign were incapable of being held to be insulting. However, the court 'came to the clear conclusion' that the Magistrates' Court could find the words insulting 'not least because the words on the sign appear to relate homosexuality and lesbianism to immorality'.[33] In addition, the

---

[28] *Hammond* (n. 2 above), para. 5.

[29] Public Order Act 1986, s. 5(1).

[30] Ibid., s. 6(3).

[31] Ibid., s. 5(3)(c). For a helpful discussion of the background of the Public Order Act and free speech cases arising under it, see Geddis, n. 25 above.

[32] *Hammond* (n. 2 above), para. 19. The justices also made the following findings: One member of the public was 'disgusted' by the sign and found it 'annoying' and, though not personally insulted, felt that it was 'insulting to homosexuals and lesbians'; another bystander was 'upset, shocked and insulted by the sign'; a third found the sign 'insulting'; a homosexual who lived nearby was 'personally insulted' and his partner found the sign 'insulting and distressing'. Ibid., para. 5.

[33] Ibid., para. 32.

court found that that the justices 'considered the questions they were obliged to consider' both in relation to the Act and with respect to the right of freedom of expression under Article 10 of the European Convention on Human Rights (ECHR).[34] The court therefore also concluded that it was 'open to them [the magistrates]' to reach the conclusion that Hammond's conduct was 'not reasonable' and that therefore Hammond was not entitled to the defence provided by the act for making insulting statements.[35]

(ii) Identifying the Core Breach

Despite paying lip service to the 'cardinal importance of freedom of expression in a democratic society'[36] the decision dismissing the appeal was but the sad denouement of a saga in which Hammond's right to participate in public discourse was continually violated. His core free speech right was first violated by the failure of the police to protect him from physical assault, then compounded by his arrest, trial, and conviction for doing no more than expressing, in fairly innocuous terms, a dissenting view about the 'the organization and culture of society'. There can be no denying that Hammond's speech was on a matter of public concern. The morality of homosexual activity is a topic that has obvious relevance to current social policy matters such as the desirability of same sex marriage or the propriety of the ordination of homosexual clergy within the Anglican community, not to mention the culture and morality of British society in general. Nor can there be any doubt that Hammond was expressing his views in a setting dedicated to public discourse—the pedestrian area of a town square where speakers evidently are free to express their views on issues of the day. It would appear, then, that Hammond's speech lies at the heart of the expression that must be allowed in any free and democratic society.

The Divisional Court's rationale for holding that Hammond's expression 'went beyond legitimate protest' was that it was open to the justices to find his expression 'insulting'.[37] But such a rationale for excluding Hammond's expression from public discourse is grossly inadequate. To appreciate why this is so, it is crucial first to distinguish two ways in which expression may be insulting. Expression may be insulting because it conveys an idea in an insulting *manner*,

---

[34] The Human Rights Act 1998 requires courts to interpret legislation so far as possible to be compatible with Convention rights: s. 3(1). If it is unable to interpret a provision to be compatible with such a right, a court may issue a declaration of incompatibility: s. 4(4). Such a declaration, however, does not affect the validity, operation, or enforcement of the provision and is not binding on the parties in the proceeding in which it was made: s. 4(6). Though not using this precise language, the Magistrates' Court in substance found the application of s. 5 of the Public Order Act compatible with the right of freedom of expression under Article 10 of the Convention. See *Hammond* (n. 2 above), paras. 20, 27–28.

[35] Ibid., para. 33.   [36] Ibid.

[37] The court seems to acknowledge that if Hammond's speech was 'reasonable' then the police should have protected him against the angry crowd. Ibid., para. 7.

such as by the use of epithets, profanity, mockery, or demeaning caricature. Alternatively, expression may be insulting because the *idea* itself is insulting. Significantly, it was not the manner of Hammond's expression that was insulting: the sign contained no epithets or other insulting terms for homosexuals, nor did Hammond use profanity, mockery, or offensive caricature to express his ideas. Indeed, it is difficult to imagine how Hammond could have expressed the idea he wanted to convey in a more civil manner without obscuring its meaning.[38]

The message on Hammond's sign was thus insulting to certain members of the audience purely because of the idea it expressed—that homosexuality is immoral. Whether the government can, consistently with the core right of democratic participation, impose civility norms on public discourse by banning insulting or offensive forms of communication such as the use of epithets or inflammatory symbols is a difficult question which I shall consider below. But the proposition that speakers may be excluded from participating in public discourse because others may find their ideas insulting and therefore threaten or assault the speaker or otherwise breach the peace is patently inconsistent with the fundamental right to participate in the discussion by which people in a democratic society debate matters of public concern.

The Divisional Court quotes the European Court of Human Rights' (ECtHR) statement that because freedom of expression is 'one of the essential foundations of a democratic society', it must include the right not only to express 'ideas that are favourably received', but also those that 'offend, shock or disturb'.[39] And indeed, in modern, pluralistic democracies there are few matters worth debating that will not elicit a viewpoint that someone will find offensive, shocking, or disturbing. Therefore, as Sedley LJ, aptly observed, 'Freedom only to speak inoffensively is not worth having'.[40] But if one has the right to express as part of public discourse ideas that 'offend, shock or disturb', why does this right not extend to ideas that 'insult'?

(iii) A Countervailing Right Not to be Insulted?

There are hints in the *Hammond* decision that, unlike offensive, shocking, and disturbing ideas, insulting ideas can legitimately be excluded from public discourse because they violate the rights of others. Thus, without expressly relying on this ground, the Divisional Court refers to the justices' finding that 'Mr Hammonds's behaviour went beyond legitimate protest [because] it interfered with the rights of others.'[41] Although this position may have superficial appeal, it cannot withstand analysis.

---

[38] Accord, Geddis (n. 25 above), 865: 'The practical effect of the outcome to this case is that the speaker was left with no effective way of expressing his beliefs on the issue of same-sex relationships.'
[39] *Hammond* (n. 2 above), para. 15, quoting *Sunday Times* v. *UK* (No 2) [1992] 14 EHRR 123.
[40] *Redmond-Bate* v. *DPP* (1999) 7 BHRC 375, [1999] Crim LR 998.
[41] *Hammond* (n. 2 above), para. 19.

To begin with, as a technical matter, there is no general right in the UK to recover damages for insulting ideas expressed in public discourse. The absence of a private cause of action does not of itself prove that a right does not exist (personal rights can be protected solely by the criminal law). However, it does suggest that people have no actual right to be protected against the expression of insulting ideas in public discourse, but at most have some inchoate *interest* in not being insulted by such expression.[42] In addition, it is far from obvious that insulting ideas are categorically more injurious than offensive, shocking, or disturbing ideas in terms of the emotional injury they inflict. For instance, do homosexuals seeing a sign proclaiming that homosexuality is immoral suffer greater emotional injury than do people with loved ones fighting in Iraq who encounter anti-war protestors carrying signs supporting the insurgency? The court agrees that the interest people may have in not being offended, shocked, or disturbed by ideas expressed in public discourse does not outweigh the right of other individuals to express these views on matters of public concern or the audience's interest in hearing these ideas. The court, however, does not explain the basis for categorically deeming the injury caused by insulting ideas as more grievous than that caused by offensive, shocking, or disturbing ones, and it is difficult to imagine a principled rationale for this distinction.

Finally, the sheer number of ideas routinely expressed on hotly contested public issues likely to be considered insulting to someone suggests that the court did not really mean to imply that there is a general right not to be insulted by ideas which trumps the right to participate in public discourse. To list just a few examples of ideas regularly expressed in public discourse that will likely insult some member of the audience: the government officials who led us into the war in Iraq are incompetent; people who support free trade are greedy; women who have abortions commit infanticide; those who oppose same sex marriage are bigots; people who eat genetically modified food are foolish; those who wear fur are cruel; or foxhunters are, to use Mr Hammond's term, immoral. It is implausible, however, that in contemporary Britain a speaker would be arrested, tried, and convicted under the Public Order Act for holding up a sign in a public square with the message 'Foxhunting is Immoral', even if those insulted by the sign assaulted the speaker. But if this is true, then there is no general right not to be insulted by ideas expressed in public discourse that outweighs 'one of the essential foundations of a democratic society'.

Of course, it could be forcefully argued that sexual orientation is for most people more central to their personality than pursuits such as foxhunting. Accordingly, it may well be that condemning homosexuality as immoral insults homosexuals more profoundly than calling foxhunting immoral insults fox-hunters. But even if this is true, it is far from clear that the expression of the idea

---

[42] '[P]eople do not have a legal right to prevent criticism of their beliefs or for that matter their way of life'. *Nuxoll* v. *Indian Prairie School Dist.* 523 F. 3d 668, 672 (7th Cir, 2008) (Posner, J).

that homosexuality is immoral is sufficiently more insulting than most other insulting ideas to justify giving homosexuals a right not to encounter this perspective in public conversation. And by what criteria are law enforcement officials and judges to make such judgments? Whatever formal criteria they are instructed to use, it is naïve to believe that these decision makers will be able to measure the degree of insult free from their own views about the allegedly insulting idea. Or equally disastrous from a free speech point of view, even if police officers, jurors, and judges are able to keep their personal views at bay, their judgments will still likely be influenced by the dominant societal view about the idea at issue. For instance, it is highly doubtful that Hammond's conviction turned on some principled, objective assessment that the degree of insult in associating homosexuality with immorality transcended the garden-variety insults common in public discourse. It is much more likely that Hammond's expression was considered so insulting as to be 'beyond legitimate protest' because it profoundly offended the contemporary orthodoxy that homosexuality is not immoral.

There is nothing wrong with new dominant narratives replacing old ones. Social progress depends on such a process. But the core right of participatory democracy that we are considering requires that people remain free to challenge the new dominant narratives as well as remnants of old ones.

(iv) Distinguishing Public Discourse from Personal Abuse

But here I want to draw another important distinction. While the reality of life in a pluralistic modern democracy forecloses any general legal right not to be insulted by ideas expressed in public discourse such as in books, newspapers, or signs carried by protesters in a public square, the robust public conversation necessary to any democracy does not require that speakers be free to hurl insults at other individuals in face-to-face confrontations. The United States Supreme Court recognized this distinction nearly 70 years ago in *Cantwell* v. *Connecticut*,[43] a case with facts similar to *Hammond* but which reaches the opposite result.

Jesse Cantwell, a Jehovah's Witness proselytizing in a heavily Catholic neighbourhood, asked for and received permission from two men he passed on the street to play them a phonographic recording. The recording attacked all organized religion, but particularly the Roman Catholic Church, as 'the instruments of Satan'. The listeners, who were Catholic, were incensed. One later testified that he felt like striking Cantwell. Any further confrontation was avoided, however, when Cantwell packed up his record player and walked up the street. Cantwell was charged with, and convicted of, inciting breach of the peace.[44] The Supreme Court unanimously reversed the conviction on the ground that Cantwell's activity was protected by the First Amendment right to free speech. In

---

[43] 310 US 296 (1940).　　[44] Ibid., 301–03, 308–09.

doing so, it provided the following eloquent explanation why expression such as Cantwell's must be protected in a democracy:

> In the realm of religious faith, and in that of political belief, sharp differences arise. In both fields the tenets of one man may seem the rankest error to his neighbour. To persuade others to his own point of view, the pleader, as we know, at times, resorts to exaggeration, [and] to vilification .... But the people of this nation have ordained in the light of history, that, in spite of the probability of excesses and abuses, these liberties are, in the long view, essential to enlightened opinion and right conduct on the part of the citizens of a democracy.
>
> The essential characteristic of these liberties is, that under their shield many types of life, character, opinion, and belief can develop unmolested and unobstructed. Nowhere is this shield more necessary than in our own country for a people composed of many races and of many creeds.[45]

The Court emphasized, however, that the constitutional guarantee of free speech does not embrace 'profane, indecent, or abusive remarks *directed to the person of the hearer*' that are likely to provoke violence or disturb the peace. 'Resort to epithets or personal abuse', the Court emphasized, 'is not in any proper sense communication of information or opinion safeguarded by the Constitution ... '.[46] A year later, the Court confirmed that such 'fighting words' fell outside the protection of the First Amendment, upholding a breach of the peace conviction of a Jehovah's Witness who in a face-to-face confrontation called a law enforcement official 'a God damned racketeer', and 'a damned Fascist'.[47] The Court observed that such 'fighting words' are 'no essential part of any exposition of ideas' and thus 'any benefit that may be derived from them is clearly outweighed by the social interest in order and morality'.[48]

If Hammond had directed anti-gay epithets at a particular individual or even towards a group of individuals immediately in front of him, he could have been punished for his speech consistent with the core democratic precept underlying freedom of expression. In any system of freedom of expression there must be a line separating the highly protected realm of public discourse from the rest of the speech in human society, particularly those words that often accompany or even instigate disputes having little or nothing to do with public affairs. Defining the boundaries between highly protected public discourse, on the one hand, and speech that may be readily regulated or even suppressed consistent with core precepts of democracy, on the other, presents a problem of no little difficulty.[49] But branding expression as going 'beyond legitimate protest' just because it expresses an idea that some will likely find insulting is a formula for excluding perspectives that challenge society's 'sacred cows' and thus is inconsistent with the

---

[45] Ibid., 310.
[46] Ibid., 309–10 (emphasis added).
[47] *Chaplinsky* v. *New Hampshire* 315 US 568, 569 (1942).
[48] Ibid., 572.
[49] See Post (n. 22 above), 163–78.

fundamental individual right to participate in the formation of the public opinion by which social and political issues are ultimately decided in a democracy.

(v) What Went Wrong?

What accounts for a state of affairs in which a citizen in one of the world's oldest and proudest democracies has his core right violated at every level of the legal system? My diagnosis is that the core free speech right recognized in English free speech jurisprudence is both too weak and too indeterminate to adequately protect the public expression of ideas that 'offend, shock or disturb' dominant opinion. This is particularly true when the speaker is not an author of a book or newspaper columnist, but an ordinary citizen trying to express a dissenting view in the public square.

The primary defect of the *Hammond* decision is its failure to give the core free speech right to participate in public discourse the weight befitting a fundamental individual right. In the Divisional Court's view, the crucial question was whether Hammond's expression was in fact insulting, and thus in the final analysis the court dismisses the appeal because it found it 'open' to the magistrates to find 'as a matter of fact that the words displayed on the sign were insulting'. This approach assumes that the right to express one's view on a matter of public concern in a forum dedicated to such expression can be outweighed by various legitimate societal interests such as protecting people against insult, or even more prob-lematically as the magistrates held, by 'the need to show tolerance towards all sections of society'.[50]

This approach is both theoretically and pragmatically deficient. It is theoret-ically deficient because it fails to recognize that Hammond's activity involved the exercise of a fundamental right that cannot properly be outweighed even by important interests such as these. If public discourse were valued primarily because it is instrumental to some social goal such as truth discovery or, social stability, or even reasons instrumental to democracy such as assuring a well-informed electorate, then suppressing speech to promote important social objectives might, depending on the circumstances, be appropriate. Whether protecting people from the emotional upset caused by hearing insulting ideas crucial to one's identity, or guarding society from the ill effects of expression of intolerant ideas, outweighs the various benefits that free speech produces for society as a whole is a difficult question, and in light of the clash of largely incommensurate values it presents, one most likely not susceptible to a definite answer. But while many other forms of expression may be valued for their con-tribution to social welfare, public discourse is primarily valued not for such

---

[50] *Hammond* (n. 2 above), para. 19. Geddis suggests that in *Hammond* and other cases involving protestors charged under the Public Order Act, 'the courts have undertaken a pragmatic balancing exercise with respect to the costs and benefits of "insulting" expression . . . ' (n. 25 above), 869.

instrumental reasons, but because each individual has a right to participate in the discussion by which collective decisions are made. Moreover, because the right of political participation is intimately bound up with the legitimacy of the entire legal system, it is an individual right of fundamental importance that can properly be outweighed only in the most extraordinary circumstances.

To appreciate the proper weight of the individual interest in political participation, including the right to participate in public discourse, imagine that the US government tried to exclude anyone who has expressed opposition to the war in Iraq from voting in the next national election on the grounds that the participation of these voters might result in the precipitous withdrawal of troops with disastrous consequences for national security. We would not decide the propriety of this exclusion by 'balancing' the right to vote against even something as important as the nation's security interests. Nor would it matter if it were demonstrably true that abruptly withdrawing the troops would have terrible consequences for national security. Rather, we would say that the right to vote is so fundamental that it cannot be infringed even for such important reasons. Similarly, we would not think the right of individuals to protest against the United States' continued military involvement in Iraq could be properly outweighed because of the tendency of such speech both to dispirit our troops and encourage the insurgents to continue to fight, even if it could be shown that such expression will likely lead to greater casualties among US soldiers.[51]

What these examples show is that even weighty reasons are ordinarily not sufficient justification for infringing a fundamental individual right such as the right to participate in the democratic process. In contrast, as the foregoing discussion of 'fighting words' shows, outside of public discourse, protecting people from insult is a strong enough interest to justify banning insulting speech. But like the interest in preventing people from being offended, shocked, or disturbed, this interest is not nearly important enough to justify excluding someone from expressing an idea in public discourse. Building a tolerant society, particularly about matters as essential to one's identity as sexual orientation, is a laudable societal goal. But just as protecting the war effort is insufficient grounds for suppressing anti-war protest, promoting tolerance is insufficient grounds for suppressing public discourse critical of homosexuality.

---

[51] In his *Masses* opinion, Judge Hand wrote that it was 'unhappily true' that 'a virulent attack upon the war and those laws which have been enacted to assist its prosecution, may interfere with the success of the military forces of the United States' because such expressions 'enervate public feeling at home...and encourage the success of the enemies of the United States abroad'. He therefore concluded that there 'cannot be the slightest question of the mischievous effects of such agitation' on the war effort. He even agreed with the government's claim that harsh criticism of the war tended to 'promote a mutinous and insubordinate temper among the troops'. He held, however, that in the absence of the 'clearest' statement by Congress 'in the throes of a struggle for the very existence of the state' that it wanted to suppress such criticism, even these grave harms were insufficient to justify the infringement of the 'right to criticize' which is 'normally the privilege of the individual in countries dependent upon free expression of opinion as the ultimate source of authority'. *Masses Publishing Co.* (n. 6 above), 539–40.

Equally as problematic as the theoretical shortcomings of the *Hammond* decision is the uncertainty that this decision creates.[52] I argued above that there are no obvious principled criteria for distinguishing ideas expressed in public discourse that 'insult' from those that 'offend, shock or disturb'. But even if some theoretical basis for this dichotomy could be found, the distinction would be far too nice for practical administration and is thus likely to invite viewpoint discrimination by law enforcement officials. Nor does this distinction give sufficient guidance to speakers as to which controversial ideas can be safely expressed in public without risking arrest or prosecution. And as I have already discussed, these same problems would render impractical any attempt to distinguish profoundly insulting ideas from ordinarily insulting ones.

A related pragmatic problem is created by the severe limitations on reviewing courts which prevent them from overturning a finding by the trial court that the expression was 'insulting' or that the speaker's conduct was not 'reasonable'. The Divisional Court in *Hammond* treated the magistrates' conclusion that the message on Hammond's sign was 'insulting' within the meaning of section 5 of the Public Order Act as a finding of fact which could be set aside only if a reviewing court concludes the finding was 'perverse'.[53] The court also took a very deferential stance towards the magistrates' finding that Hammond's conduct was not 'reasonable'. Significantly, the court did not itself decide whether Hammond had a right under Article 10 of the ECHR to display his sign. Rather, it found only that the justices 'considered the questions which they were obliged to consider' with respect to this issue and reached a conclusion that was 'open to them' in finding that Hammond's conduct was not 'reasonable'.[54]

---

[52] Uncertainty is a problem seemingly endemic to English free speech jurisprudence generally, but particularly acute with respect to cases under s. 5 of the Public Order Act. For examples of uncertainty and lack of objectivity in English free speech jurisprudence and the viewpoint discrimination to which this leads, see I. Hare, 'Method and Objectivity in Free Speech Adjudication: Lessons from America' (2005) 54 *Int'l and Comp. L. Q.* 49, 86–7. With respect to s. 5 cases, see Geddis (n. 25 above), 861. Geddis notes that in allowing the appeal of a protestor convicted under that Act for engaging in 'insulting' conduct by burning an American flag near a US army base, the Divisional Court in *Percy* v. *DPP* [2001] EWHC Admin 1125, failed 'to lay down any clear guidelines as to when, or even whether, conduct such as the appellant's ought to be permitted'.

[53] *Hammond* (n. 2 above), para. 32. The culprit here is the decision of the House of Lords in *Cozens* v. *Brutus* [1973] AC 854 which held that the Divisional Court erred by treating the question of whether conduct was 'insulting' under s. 5 of the 1936 Public Order Act as a question of law rather than a question of fact. In his speech, Lord Reid held that the term 'insulting' (as well as the terms 'threatening' and 'abusive') should be given its 'ordinary meaning' and not construed 'as having a specially wide or a specially narrow meaning'. Ibid., 861, 862. Such an approach might be appropriate in s. 5 prosecutions involving conduct that is plainly not within the scope of public discourse such as the activity in *Cozens*. In that case a protestor interrupted a tennis match at Wimbledon by stepping out on to the court and then blowing a whistle and throwing leaflets before pushing a policeman out of the way and sitting down on the court. (The magistrates had held that this conduct was not 'insulting' within the meaning of the Act.) But where the Act is applied to public discourse such as a protest in a town square dedicated to such public discussion, Lord Reid's confidence that 'free speech [will not] be impaired' (ibid., 862) by treating the finding that the expression is insulting as a virtually unreviewable question of fact is misplaced.

[54] *Hammond* (n. 2 above), para. 33.

But as Andrew Geddis has observed, '[s]uch continued deference to the magistrates' ruling at trial is inappropriate in a post-HRA [Human Rights Act] era'.[55] As a practical matter, then, despite the court's acknowledgment that suppression of offensive, disturbing and shocking ideas is inconsistent with freedom of expression necessary to a democratic society, the *Hammond* decision and the precedent on which it builds puts the expression of all controversial ideas at risk of punishment under the Public Order Act.

The problem of the uncertainty of the term 'insult' and the unbridled discretion it gives law enforcement officials to suppress speech was recently underscored by the citation of a 15-year-old boy for carrying a sign reading 'Scientology is not a religion, it is a dangerous cult' in peaceful protest on the public sidewalk near the headquarters of the Church of Scientology in London. The boy was told by the police to put down the sign or face arrest or summons. When he refused to do so, the police confiscated his sign and issued a summons charging him with making insulting and abusive statements in violation of the Public Order Act. City of London Chief Superintendent Rob Bastable defended this action, explaining that the 'City of London Police upholds the right to demonstrate lawfully, but we have to balance that with the rights of all sections of the community not to be alarmed, distressed, or harassed as a result of others' actions'. Upon reviewing the case the Crown Prosecution Service dismissed the charge.[56]

4. Object Lessons from the US

The dangers of an uncertain legal standard for deciding whether participants in public discourse may be punished for controversial speech is demonstrated by the 'clear and present danger' test formulated by Justice Oliver Wendell Holmes to deal with convictions under the Espionage Act of protestors against American involvement in World War I for interfering with the war effort.[57] The problem

---

[55] Geddis (n. 25 above), 867. In Geddis' view, 'following the coming into force of the HRA, the Divisional Court should now conduct its own analysis of the Convention-compatibility of convicting the accused for his or her insulting conduct; rather than, in effect subcontracting this analysis to the trial court and intervening only when that body has failed to consider all the factors, or has strayed so far as to have acted unreasonably'. Ibid. American appellate courts, including the Supreme Court, have an obligation to review independently factual findings in free speech cases. See *Bose Corp.* v. *Consumers Union* 466 US 485 (1984).

[56] Protest teenager may face charges', *BBC News*, 21 May 2008, <http://news.bbc.co.uk/2/hi/uk_news/england/london/7412002.stm> (last accessed 9 July 2008); 'No charges over Scientology demo', *BBC News*, 23 May 2008, <http://news.bbc.co.uk/2/hi/uk_news/england/london/7416425.stm> (last accessed 9 July 2008). There was a suggestion that the police were particularly vigilant in suppressing insults against Scientology because of the large donations they receive from that organization. See B. Taylor, 'Police officers accepted gifts from Church of Scientology', the *Daily Mail*, 21 November 2006, <http://www.dailymail.co.uk/news/article-417782/Police-officers-accepted-gifts-Church-Scientology.html> (last accessed 9 July 2008).

[57] 'The question in every case is whether the words used are used in such circumstances and are of such a nature as to create a clear and present danger that they will bring about the substantive evils that Congress has a right to prevent.' *Schenck* v. *US* 249 US 47, 52 (1919). *Schenck* is the first

with this test was that it required the finder of fact, which in a criminal case would typically be a jury, to make guesses about the likely consequences of speech.[58] In contrast, two years earlier in his *Masses* opinion Judge Learned Hand had engaged in a more 'objective' and 'manageable'[59] analysis focusing 'upon the nature of the utterance itself'[60] to determine whether the speech was immune from punishment because 'part of that public opinion which is the final source of government in a democratic state'.[61] As Hand explained in a letter to Harvard law professor Zechariah Chafee:

I am not in love with Holmsesy's test and the reason is this. Once you admit that the matter is one of degree...you give Tomdickandharry, D.J. [district judge], so much latitude that the jig is up at once. [Even] the Nine Elder Statesmen [the Supreme Court] have not shown themselves wholly immune from the "herd instinct".... I own I should prefer a qualitative formula, hard, conventional, difficult to evade.[62]

In hindsight, it is apparent that the focus on the possible harmful consequences of the speech, rather than on whether the speech at issue was a part of the expression by which the people govern, led to the suppression of speech that must be allowed in a free and democratic society. There were over 2,000 prosecutions under the Espionage Act, with over 1,000 defendants convicted, most of them for harshly criticizing American involvement in World War I, including Eugene Debs,[63] who in

significant free speech decision rendered by the Supreme Court. Among other restrictions, the Espionage Act made it a crime to cause refusal of duty in the armed forces or willfully to obstruct the recruitment or enlistment service of the United States.

[58] In criticizing the clear and present danger test, Ernst Freund wrote: '[T]o be permitted to agitate at your own peril, subject to a jury's guessing at motive, tendency and possible effect makes the right of free speech a precarious gift'. E. Freund, *The New Republic*, 3 May 1919, reprinted in H. Kalven, 'Ernst Freund and the First Amendment Tradition: Professor Ernst Freund and *Debs v. United States*' (1973) 40 *U. Chi. L. Rev.* 235, 240.

[59] 'I do not altogether like the way Justice Holmes put the limitation. I think it is a little more manageable and quite adequate a distinction to say that there is an absolute and objective test to language.... I still prefer that which I attempted to state in my first "Masses" opinion, rather than to say that the connection between the words used and the evil aimed at should be "immediate and direct"'. Letter from Learned Hand to Zechariah Chafee, Jr., 3 December 1919, reprinted in G. Gunther, 'Learned Hand and the Origins of Modern First Amendment Doctrine: Some Fragments of History' (1975) 27 *Stan. L. Rev.* 719, 763.

[60] Letter from Learned Hand to Zechariah Chafee, Jr., 8 January 1920, reprinted in Gunther (n. 59 above), 765.

[61] *Masses.Publishing Co.* (n. 6 above), 540.

[62] Letter from Learned Hand to Zechariah Chafee, Jr., 2 January 1921, (in n. 59 above), 770.

[63] *Debs* (n. 4 above), per Holmes, J. Holmes later applied the clear and present danger test in a more speech protective way by stressing that impugned expression must present a danger of an 'immediate' evil. See *Abrams* v. *US* 250 US 616 (1919) (Holmes, J. dissenting). Though Holmes insisted that *Schenck* and *Debs* were 'rightly decided' (ibid., 627), it is difficult to see how the expression in *Abrams* presented more of a 'clear and present danger' than did the speech in *Schecnk* or *Debs*. See Weinstein (n. 27 above), 19. As Gerald Gunther has demonstrated, Holmes' greater sensitivity to free speech reflected in his *Abrams* dissent was in part due to criticism from Hand, especially Hand's admonition about the need to pay attention to the values of free speech. See n. 59 above, 741–42. Even after Holmes' *Abrams* dissent, Hand still thought the clear and present danger test inadequate as a matter of practical administration. Letter to Chafee in n. 59 above.

1912 had garnered nearly a million votes as the Socialist candidate for President of the United States.[64]

Speech that vigorously challenges the status quo—whether it be protests against American involvement in World War I, Communist critique of the foundations of the democratic state, or attacks on contemporary orthodoxies such as the commitment to multiculturalism, gender and racial equality, and gay rights—is likely to be given short shrift under vague and indeterminate standards such as whether speech creates a 'clear and present danger' or whether an idea is 'insulting'. Recognition that such uncertain standards are inadequate to the task of protecting speech vigorously challenging dominant opinion led the Supreme Court in 1969 to strengthen and objectify the test for punishing advocacy of violence and other forms of law violation. Influenced by Hand's approach of a half century before,[65] the test announced in *Brandenburg* v. *Ohio* focuses on the objective meaning of the speaker's language. Thus, the key question is now not whether the speech is likely to cause harm but whether the expression in question amounts to mere advocacy of law violation, in which case it retains First Amendment protection, or whether it crosses the line to actual incitement of lawlessness, in which case it is eligible for suppression. The 'clear and present danger' test is relegated to supplying prophylactic protection to the harmless inciter by requiring the government to show that even speech that is directed towards inciting imminent lawless conduct, and thus theoretically eligible for suppression, is in fact is likely to produce such conduct.[66] In the following years, the Court more generally 'bright lined' free speech doctrine by subjecting all content-based restriction of public discourse to 'strict scrutiny',[67] a test that almost always leads to the invalidation of the regulation.[68]

While other democracies may also have long traditions of free speech, none, not even the UK, has anywhere near the wealth of experience with judicial protection of this fundamental right as does the US. This experience offers valuable lessons for courts in other democracies on how adequately to protect the

---

[64] See K. Sullivan and G. Gunther, *Constitutional Law*, 16th edn. (New York: Foundation Press, 2007), 754, 756. See also the Espionage Act cases discussed below, text accompanying n. 92.

[65] For a discussion of earlier cases that adopted Hand's approach as a matter of statutory construction, thus laying the foundation for its adoption in *Brandenburg* as a matter of constitutional law, see Gunther (n. 59 above), 752–5.

[66] 395 US 444, 447–48 (1969). I discuss the import of the *Brandenburg* decision in more detail below.

[67] See *Police Dep't of Chicago* v. *Mosley* 408 US 92, 95 (1972): '[A]bove all else, the First Amendment means that government has no power to restrict expression because of its message, its ideas, its subject matter, or its content'; *Boos* v. *Barry* 485 US 312, 321 (1988): '[Our] cases indicate that...a content-based restriction on political speech in a public forum...must be subjected to the most exacting scrutiny. Thus, we have required the State to show that the "regulation is necessary to serve a compelling state interest and that it is narrowly drawn to achieve that end"'. For a discussion of the meaning of 'content-based' regulation as that term is used in American free speech doctrine, see Hare (n. 52 above), 50–4; Weinstein (n. 27 above), 35–8.

[68] See Weinstein, ibid, 39.

expression of controversial opinions against the reliable tendency of society to suppress ideas that offend dominant opinion. By failing to define a core area of speech essential to democratic government and then rigorously protecting this expression, English courts are repeating a mistake the United States Supreme Court made in the first half of the twentieth century that I have just described. To avoid this pitfall, English courts should focus on the nature of the speech in question to determine whether by virtue of its subject matter and setting, it is expression which by 'any latitude of interpretation' is 'part of that public opinion which is the final source of government in a democratic state'.[69] If it is, then this expression should be deemed immune from punishment unless some truly extraordinary circumstance requires its suppression. And in assessing whether such extraordinary circumstances are present, courts in other democracies should heed another lesson from the American experience: what at the time seemed like compelling reasons for suppressing speech were in retrospect recognized as inadequate. In looking back at the cases decided under the old clear-and-present danger test, Justice William O. Douglas observed that the danger presented by the speech in those cases was 'made serious only by judges so wedded to the status quo that critical analysis made them nervous'.[70]

Unlike their American colleagues, English judges do not have the power to invalidate legislation as unconstitutional. But they do have the authority to construe an Act of Parliament narrowly to prevent it from infringing the common law right of free speech.[71] Moreover, under the Human Rights Act 1998, English courts have a duty to interpret legislation as far as possible to be compatible with rights guaranteed under the ECHR.[72] To prevent the Public Order Act from

[69] *Masses Publishing Co.* (n. 6 above), 540.

[70] *Brandenburg* (n. 8 above), 454 (concurring opinion). Or as Learned Hand observed: '[W]hat seems [an] "immediate and direct" [threat of danger] today may seem very remote the next year even though the circumstances surrounding the utterance be unchanged'. Letter to Chafee (n. 62 above), 770.

[71] 'The fundamental right of free expression has been recognized at common law for many years'. *R. v. Shayler* (n. 13 above), para. 21 (Lord Bingham). See also Barendt (n. 24 above), 40–1. In this regard, it is interesting to note that in his *Masses* decision Judge Hand did not rely on the First Amendment but rather narrowly construed the Espionage Act in light of the core democratic principles implicated in that case. See *Masses Publishing Co.*, (n. 6 above), 538, 540.

[72] It is, however, far from certain that Hammond's expression would find protection under the ECtHR Article 10 jurisprudence. As Ivan Hare observes, the Strasbourg court's legal doctrines 'have effectively prevented the Convention from safeguarding extreme speech and, as a consequence, from providing meaningful protection to a robust concept of free speech in general terms', especially when speech challenges anti-discrimination norms. 'Extreme Speech under International and Regional Legal Standards', this volume. Although there is still some doubt on the issue, it would apparently be improper for English courts to interpret Article 10 independently as providing greater protection for the speech in question than is provided by ECtHR jurisprudence. While English courts are not obliged to follow ECtHR decisions as strictly binding precedent, 'in the absence of special circumstances our courts should follow any clear and constant jurisprudence from the Strasbourg court....' *Animal Defenders International* v. *Secretary of State for Culture, Media and Sport* [2008] UKHL 15, para. 37 (Lord Bingham). Accordingly, while it is 'of course open to member states to provide for rights more generous than those guaranteed by the Convention...such provision should not be the product of interpretation of the Convention by national courts, since the meaning of the Convention should be uniform throughout the states party to it. The duty of national courts is to keep pace with the

violating the core free speech right of democratic participation, when dealing with expression that is part of public discourse, courts should, at minimum, construe the term 'insulting' (as well as the term 'abusive') as applying only to expression that employs epithets or profanity to refer to an individual or group of individuals. An even better course might be to borrow a page from the US Supreme Court's 'fighting words' jurisprudence and construe these terms as having no application whatsoever to public discourse but only to face-to-face insults or abuse directed at a particular person or persons.[73] Not only would such an approach protect the right of dissenters to express controversial ideas, it would bring the operation of the Public Order Act back in line with the purpose for which it was primarily intended: 'to deal with hooligans who, say, pester and alarm people late at night'.[74] But whatever the precise solution, the Public Order Act's prohibition of 'abusive' or 'insulting' speech should be carefully confined in its application to public discourse.

5. Another Core Breach?: *Norwood* v. *DPP*

A second case suggesting that UK free speech doctrine is not adequate to the task of protecting the dissent necessary to any democracy is *Norwood* v. *DPP*. Decided by the Divisional Court just six months before *Hammond*, it too involved a prosecution for insulting speech under the Public Order Act.

(i) Facts and Divisional Court Decision

In November 2001, Mark Anthony Norwood placed a poster in the window of his flat located in a small rural town in Shropshire bearing the words: 'Islam out of Britain' and 'Protect the British people'. These slogans were superimposed on a reproduction of a photograph of the World Trade Center in flames and a crescent and star surrounded by a prohibition sign. Norwood was a regional organizer of the British National Party (BNP) which had distributed the poster to its members. In January 2002, a member of the public saw the poster in Norwood's window and complained to the police, who visited his flat and removed the poster.[75]

Strasbourg jurisprudence as it evolves over time: no more, but certainly no less.' *R (Ullah)* v. *Special Adjudicator* [2004] UKHL 26, para. 20 (Lord Bingham). But see Lord Scott's speech in *Animal Defenders*, above, paras. 44–45 arguing that English courts have greater authority to interpret the Convention independently from Strasbourg jurisprudence than stated by Lord Bingham.

[73] Such protection of public discourse could, alternatively, be accomplished by holding that unlike other forms of insulting or abusive speech such expression is 'reasonable'. Because Hammond had died before he could appeal to the ECtHR, the Court declared the application by his heirs inadmissible for lack of standing. *Fairfield* v. *UK*, App. No. 24790/04, 8 March 2005.

[74] Barendt (n. 24 above), 300. See also Geddis (n. 25 above), 872: '[T]he problem caused by individual dissenters is not the primary mischief targeted by s. 5. Their expression is only covered because it falls within the ambit of broad statutory language intended to deal with more blatant forms of anti-social conduct . . .'.

[75] *Norwood* (n. 3 above), paras. 5–8.

Norwood was charged under section 5 of the Public Order Act 1986 for making 'abusive' and 'insulting' statements likely to cause 'harassment, alarm, or distress' to another person. The prosecution further charged that the display of the poster was subject to an increased penalty because the violation was 'racially or religiously aggravated' under the sections 28 and 31 of the Crime and Disorder Act 1998 in that the offense was 'motivated (wholly or partly) by hostility towards members of a racial or religious group based on their membership in that group'.[76]

At trial in the Magistrates Court, the complaining witness testified that he had felt 'quite sick' when he saw the poster and thought the poster would cause offence. One police officer testified that he considered the poster to be 'in bad taste and inflammatory', while another stated that having worked in London, he knew that this kind of material could stir up distress and 'racial feeling'. There was no evidence that any Muslim had seen the sign. The prosecution argued that the message of the poster was threatening, abusive or insulting because it suggested that Muslims were not welcome in the UK. Norwood and the Chairman of the BNP testified that the poster referred to Muslim extremism in light of the 9/11 attacks and that it was a 'slogan against creeping Islamification'. The District Judge convicted Norwood and fined him £300, finding that the poster was abusive and insulting to Islam and to the followers of that religion; was likely to cause harassment, alarm, and distress; and was religiously motivated.[77]

The Divisional Court dismissed Norwood's appeal, finding all of the statutory elements of the offence and its aggravation had been adequately proved. Addressing the free speech issues presented by the case, Auld LJ explained that the defence under section 5(3) that the conduct was objectively reasonable necessarily includes consideration of the right to freedom of expression under Article 10 of the ECHR.[78] Drawing on the analysis of Hallet J in *Percy* v. *DPP*,[79] the Court explained that whether Norwood's conduct was objectively reasonable depended upon 'whether the accused's conduct went beyond legitimate protest and whether the behaviour had not formed part of an open expression of opinion on a matter of public interest, but had become disproportionate and unreasonable'.[80] So stated, portions of this test offer a basis for constructing doctrine that would adequately protect the core democratic right of free speech we are considering here. Particularly promising is the focus on whether or not 'the expression formed part of an open expression of opinion on a matter of public interest'.[81]

---

[76] Ibid., paras. 1–4.   [77] Ibid., paras. 9–13.
[78] Ibid., para. 35.   [79] N. 52 above.
[80] *Norwood* (n. 3 above), para. 37.
[81] More problematic is the inquiry whether the expression had become 'disproportionate and unreasonable'. Theoretical difficulties aside, 'beyond legitimate protest' and the 'disproportionate and unreasonable' standards are as a practical matter far too vague to supply would-be speakers, law enforcement officials or lower courts with the certainty needed to know what speech people have a right to engage in.

But any promise this formulation might have had for protecting core free speech rights from suppression under the Public Order Act was quickly dashed by the following qualification: 'If the prosecution has proved, as it must to obtain a conviction, that an accused's conduct was insulting and that he intended it to be, or was aware that it might be so, it would in most cases follow that his conduct was objectively unreasonable.' While the Court allows that it might be possible that the findings necessary to make out violation of section 5(1) would not preclude a defence of objective reasonableness under section 5(3), it emphasizes that '[s]uch circumstances are difficult to envision'. The half a loaf of free speech protection that the court momentarily holds out is thus quickly withdrawn, thereby effectively nullifying the potential of section 5(3) to provide any real protection to insulting speech that is part of public discourse.

As with *Hammond*, it is difficult to believe that the court meant to embrace the principle that the expression of an insulting idea in public discourse goes beyond 'legitimate protest' just because the speaker is aware that someone who hears the speech is likely to be insulted. Surely, an anti-war protestor would be aware that President George Bush might be insulted by a sign that 'Bush Lied and Our Soldiers Died' and indeed, may well intend that this expression should insult Bush. But, just as surely, that fact does not render this expression 'beyond legitimate protest'. Or suppose in the incident described above, the CPS had decided to prosecute the 15-year-old boy cited for displaying a sign in the street in front of the headquarters of the Church of Scientology declaring that 'Scientology is not a religion, it is a dangerous cult'. Would the court have really upheld his conviction against a free speech defence if the lower court found that the sign was in fact insulting to scientologists and the protestor was aware that it was likely to be insulting to some scientologists who saw the sign? Surely not. But given the broad statement in *Hammond* and *Norwood* that insulting speech even in public discourse is not legitimate protest, what principled basis would the court have to disallow these convictions?

By placing the sign in his window, Norwood was expressing his view about what should be done about the then recent attack on the World Trade Center by Islamic militants, and was utilizing a medium of expression apparently open to individuals in the UK to express their views.[82] This expression would thus seem to qualify as core public discourse or as the court put it, 'part of an open expression of opinion on a matter of public interest'. As just demonstrated, it is implausible that the court meant to cast this expression 'beyond legitimate protest' just because it was insulting. Nor will it do to argue that speech is no legitimate part of public discourse merely because it insults people because of their religion.

---

[82] Compare *City of Ladue v. Gilleo* 512 US 43, 47 (1994) where the US Supreme Court, in invalidating a city's nearly total ban on all residential signs, refers to the practice of placing political signs in the windows of one's home as a 'venerable means of communication that is both unique and important'.

Like expression that insults on the basis of sexual orientation, there is no obvious basis to conclude that religiously-based insults are categorically worse than other insulting ideas that pervade public discourse in multicultural democracies. More significantly, even if such insults could on some principled and relevant basis be considered more egregious than other types of insulting ideas in public discourse, the interest in not being insulted on the basis of one's religion would still not be great enough to justify preventing people from expressing these ideas, as Parliament recognized recently by passing the Religious Hatred Act. In outlawing threatening speech intended to stir up religious hatred, Parliament recognized that speech that merely insults people on the basis of their religion will often be part of legitimate public debate in a free and democratic society, and thus expressly exempted such expression from the scope of the law.[83] Still, unlike the poster in *Hammond*, there is at least an argument, though a very problematic one, that Norwood's expression did indeed transcend the bounds of legitimate protest in a democracy.

(ii) Excluding Anti-Democratic Speech from Public Discourse

It can be argued that advocacy of outcomes inconsistent with core democratic precepts should not be considered part of the highly protected speech by which people in a democracy govern themselves.[84] This argument is premised on the view that the basic precepts of democracy permit—or even require—a democratic state to prevent the institution of any substantive arrangement radically inconsistent with precepts of democracy. Such radically undemocratic outcomes may be resisted consistent with democracy even if brought about by democratic means such as a fair election or a constitutional amendment.[85] Thus, whatever other objections might be raised, it would hardly seem to betray democracy for an incumbent democratic government to refuse to recognize a newly elected

---

[83] 'Nothing in this Part shall be read or given effect in a way which prohibits or restricts discussion, criticism, or expression of antipathy, dislike, ridicule, insult, or abuse of particular religions or the beliefs of its adherents....' Racial and Religious Hatred Act 2006, s. 29J.

[84] I have previously considered this argument in 'Hate Speech, Viewpoint Neutrality, and the American Concept of Democracy' in T. Hensley (ed.) *The Boundaries of Freedom of Expression & Order in American Democracy* (Kent, OH: Kent UP, 2001), 161–66.

[85] The ECtHR adopted precisely this view in upholding Turkey's banning of a party because it sought to use the political process to institute an anti-democratic theocracy. See *Refah Partisi (The Welfare Party) v. Turkey*, (2003) 37 EHRR 1, para. 98: 'A political party may promote a change in the law or the legal and constitutional structures of the State on two conditions: first, the means used to that end must be legal and democratic; second the change proposed must itself be compatible with fundamental democratic principles.' See also *Refah Partisi (Welfare Party) v. Turkey*, (2002) (Chambers Opinion) 35 EHRR 3, para. 43: 'There can be no democracy where the people of a State, even by majority decision, waive their legislation and judicial powers in favour of an entity which is not responsible to the people it governs, whether it is secular or religious'; Barendt (n. 24 above), 169–70: 'the argument from democracy, which ... provides the best explanation for the protection of speech and also explains the preferred status for political speech, hardly warrants the application of these guarantees to discourse posing a serious threat to democracy itself.'

government with a mandate to abolish the democratic state and replace it with a theocracy, absolute monarchy, or the dictatorship of the proletariat.[86] Similarly, it would seem consistent with or even required by the basic precepts of democracy for a democratic state to refuse to implement a democratically enacted provision which, though not abolishing democracy *in toto*, is nonetheless radically inconsistent with some basic premise of democracy such as the right of each individual to participate in the political process. Thus it would not be undemocratic for a democracy to refuse to give effect to a constitutional amendment or referendum stripping certain citizens of the right to vote because of their race or religion or on any other basis that does not legitimately justify depriving individuals of their right to participate in the political process.

If certain substantive outcomes can be taken off the table because they are not within the power of the people in a democracy to implement consistent with core democratic precepts, it can be argued that express advocacy of these outcomes is not within the public discourse by which people in a democracy decide issues within the scope of their democratic authority. Of course, other possible free speech values, such as the search for truth or individual autonomy and self-realization, would likely be impaired by the exclusion of even radically anti-democratic speech from public discourse. And there are strong practical reasons for permitting the advocacy of even radically anti-democratic speech: the line between anti-democratic speech and speech that otherwise radically challenges the status quo is far too slippery for practical administration. Still, as a theoretical matter, it is at least arguable that express advocacy of policies antithetical to democracy is not a legitimate part of the public discourse by which people govern themselves and thus may be suppressed without violating the core democratic free speech principle under consideration in this chapter.[87]

---

[86] The issue of whether a democracy may, consistently with basic democratic precepts, refuse to implement radically anti-democratic provisions that have the support of a majority of the people raises a different question than whether such a refusal would offend popular sovereignty, a question briefly considered above in the text accompanying n. 15. For unlike naked popular sovereignty, even the thin concept of democracy we are considering here has an individual as well as a collective rights basis that prevents the majority from depriving any individual of the right to participate in the political process.

[87] A strong argument that such expression *is* in principle entitled to protection under a democracy rationale is that excluding people from expressing even a radical anti-democratic view in public discourse undermines the legitimating function of free speech. On this view, even someone advocating an outcome impossible in a democratic society benefits from the legitimation that participating in the process of democratic self-governance instils. Thus, excluding someone from arguing that an undemocratic, religious form of government such as sharia should be adopted makes the imposition of a secular, nondemocratic state on that speaker illegitimate. But even if this view is correct, it does not necessarily follow that exclusion of someone advocating a position impossible in a democratic society undermines legitimacy to the same extent as does excluding someone from advocating an outcome that is within the people's democratic authority. So even if suppression of radically anti-democratic speech does implicate political legitimacy, it still might not violate the core democratic precept we are investigating in this chapter. This is a difficult question that would require a more extensive investigation of political legitimacy and its relationship to free speech than is possible in this essay. But even if express advocacy of radically antidemocratic discourse is not entitled to the same level of protection as advocacy of substantive outcomes that are within the peoples' democratic

So does the message on Norwood's sign constitute radically anti-democratic advocacy that can arguably be excluded from public discourse consistent with this core democratic precept? Like many political slogans that appeal more to the emotions than to the intellect, it is not clear what 'Islam out of Britain—Protect the British People' means. As noted above, Norwood and the chairman of the BNP testified that it was a warning of the danger that 'Muslim extremism' and 'increasing Islamification' posed to Britain. Given the unmodified reference to Islam, this interpretation could reasonably be rejected. Rather, the poster would seem to express a condemnation of Islam in general and a warning that Islamic ideas and practices are a threat to the British way of life. Such a message may be offensive and even insulting to moderate Muslims and (to use the Court's term) to other 'right-thinking member[s] of society'. Nonetheless, the poster still expresses ideas relevant to matters within the people's collective decision-making authority, including immigration policy, whether there is a role for sharia in Britain, and the attitude state schools and other public institutions should adopt towards various Muslim customs, including the veiling of women and girls.[88] It is thus a perspective that, despite the offense or insult it may cause, must be allowed to be expressed in a democratic society. So if by placing this poster in his window Norwood meant to argue that Islam was a religion dangerous to the British way of life, punishing him for this expression would seem to violate the core democratic right to free speech.

The Divisional Court, however, interpreted the poster as conveying a more sinister message. In the court's view, the message did not merely condemn Islam as a religion but was rather an 'attack on all Muslims in this country, urging all who read it that followers of the Islamic religion here should be removed from it and warning that their presence here was a threat or a danger to the British people'.[89] Expelling an entire class of citizens from their country because of their beliefs, religious or otherwise, is inconsistent with the core democratic precept of free and equal participation in the political process that generates the core democratic free speech principle. Because such a substantive outcome is deeply inconsistent with this core democratic precept, it is, as we have seen, at least arguable that express advocacy of such an outcome can be deemed no legitimate part of the speech by which people in a democracy govern themselves.

authority, the legitimacy concerns arguably implicated by suppression of such speech suggest that it is in principle entitled to some substantial degree of protection. See Barendt (n. 24 above), 169–70, who writes that anti-democratic advocacy speech is properly suppressed only if it 'really threatens the stability of the state and its democratic order'. See also J. Rawls, *A Theory of Justice* (Cambridge, MA: Harvard UP, 1971), 219: 'while an intolerant sect does not itself have title to complain of intolerance, its freedom should be restricted only when the tolerant sincerely and with reason believe that their own security and that of the institutions of liberty are in danger. The tolerant should curb the intolerant only in this case.'

[88] See J. Finnis, 'Endorsing Discrimination Between Faiths: A Case of Extreme Speech?', this volume.
[89] *Norwood* (n. 3 above), para. 33.

So if Norwood's poster had expressly stated or unmistakably implied that all Muslims should be expelled from Britain because their religion poses a danger to society, punishing him for displaying the poster in public might not violate the core democratic free speech norm we are considering.[90] But the actual poster contains no such statement. Indeed, it does not say '*Muslims* out of Britain' but rather '*Islam* out of Britain'. The poster is thus readily susceptible to the interpretation that the influence of Islamic ideas and customs in Britain is dangerous, a view that no matter how offensive falls well short of advocating a radically anti-democratic outcome.[91] Thus, from the standpoint of protecting the right of dissent necessary to any democracy, the *Norwood* decision is troubling.

(iii) The Perils of Interpreting Ambiguous Political Rhetoric

The *Norwood* Court's uncharitable interpretation of ambiguous political rhetoric is reminiscent of the United States Supreme Court's response to radical anti-war speech when the Court first started to develop free speech doctrine at the beginning of the twentieth century. During World War I, the Court was faced with several cases involving provocative political rhetoric that could be fairly construed either as mere condemnation of America's involvement in that war or as urging men to refuse service in the armed forces in violation of the Espionage Act. In almost every case, the Court interpreted language harshly criticizing the war or admiring the courage of those who were willing to go to

---

[90] Even if the poster could be fairly interpreted as advocating a radically anti-democratic outcome and thus could arguably be legitimately excluded from public discourse and the rigorous protection that such expression must be provided in a democratic society, it does not follow that it is entitled to no protection. Rather, it might be entitled to a substantial degree of protection because its suppression would impair legitimacy (see n. 87 above) or some free speech value other than the core democratic right of political participation. And even if the suppression of Norwood's speech would not in principle violate any free speech value there are, as discussed in the text, serious pragmatic difficulties raised by suppressing even radically antidemocratic speech. So on the assumption that Norwood's poster actually advocated the removal of all Muslims from Britain, the question would then become whether the interest in protecting people from encountering insulting ideas, and the promotion of religious tolerance, together with combating what is at present the extremely remote danger that this expression might lead to the expulsion of Muslims, is sufficient grounds for suppressing this arguably non-core speech.

[91] Official BNP policy includes urging the prevention of any further immigration of Muslims to Britain and providing 'firm but voluntary incentives for [Muslim] immigrants and their descendants to return home'. See Rebuliding British Democracy: British National Party General Election 2005 Manifesto, 48 <http://news.bbc.co.uk/1/shared/bsp/hi/pdfs/BNP_uk_manifesto.pdf> (last accessed 11 July 2008). The descendants of Muslim immigrants obviously include British citizens. Adoption of a governmental programme offering even 'voluntary incentives' for the expatriation of citizens on account of their religion would seem radically inconsistent with basic democratic precepts and thus express advocacy of such a programme is arguably not a legitimate part of public discourse. The court, however, does not rely on this or any other official BNP policy in interpreting the poster as calling for the expulsion of Muslims from the UK. In any event, attributing agreement with (or even knowledge) of all party policies to rank and file members or even lower echelon leaders is extremely problematic. See *Whitney v. California* 274 US 357 (1927).

prison rather than be drafted as intending to urge draft resistance in violation of the Act.[92]

As discussed above, it is problematic enough as a theoretical matter to deem advocacy of radically anti-democratic policies as 'beyond legitimate protest' and thus undeserving of the strong protection afforded public discourse. But even if it is theoretically justifiable to exclude such speech from public discourse, pragmatic considerations dictate that only expression that both directly and unmistakably advocates radical anti-democratic social change should be cast beyond the pale of legitimate debate. As the Espionage cases suggest, allowing prosecutors, juries, and lower courts to construe ambiguous language as calling for some pernicious policy, a process that will ordinarily require the finder of fact to speculate about the speaker's motive in making the utterance, is a formula both for viewpoint discrimination and the suppression of legitimate dissent.[93] To obviate this problem with respect to utterances that the government claims go beyond legitimate criticism of the laws to advocacy of their violation, the US Supreme Court generally adopted Hand's approach of eschewing motive inquiry, focusing instead on an 'objective' analysis of the impugned language.[94] Such an objective approach is even more of a necessity in cases in which government tries to suppress speech because of its anti-democratic viewpoint.

Norwood, it is true, was a regional organizer of the BNP, an organization whose official policies are, at best, just this side of the line separating legit-imate and illegitimate political parties in a democratic society and whose unofficial policies and actual conduct may well cross that line.[95] But many of those convicted under the Espionage Act for condemning the American involvement in World War I or under the Smith Act during the McCarthy era were also members of political parties whose democratic *bona fides* could be doubted.[96] The immediate result of these American cases may have been the

[92] *Schenck*, n. 57 above; *Frohwerk* v. *US* 249 US 204 (1919); *Debs*, n. 4 above; *Abrams*, n. 63 above.

[93] In this regard it is instructive to note that in criticizing the 'clear and present danger' test, Learned Hand was concerned not only with the uncertainty inherent in the need to guess about the consequences of the speech, as discussed in text accompanying notes 59 to 62. In addition, he objected because the speaker's intent was a key element of the test and thus 'exposes all who discuss heated questions to an inquiry before a jury as to their purposes. That inquiry necessarily is of the widest scope and if their general attitude is singular and intransigent, my own belief is that a jury is an insufficient protection. I think it is precisely at those times when alone the freedom of speech becomes important as an institution, that the protection of a jury on such an issue is illusory.' Letter to Chafee, n. 60 above, 766. See also T. M. Scanlon, 'Freedom of Expression and Categories of Expression' (1979) 40 *U. Pitt. L. Rev.* 519, 546, who aptly observes that 'distinctions based on participant intent . . . are nearly always suspect'; *FEC* v. *Wisconsin Right to Life, Inc.* 127 SCt 2652, 2665 (2007) (plurality opinion per Robert, CJ), finding that the use of an 'intent-based test' to determine whether or not a political advertisement is legal would 'chill core political speech'.

[94] See discussion below, text accompanying notes 101 to 103.

[95] See S. Silver, 'Booted and suited: The BNP's nazism', <http://www.stopthebnp.org.uk/index.php?location=election&link=BNP36.htm>, (last accessed 14 July 2008), documenting, for example, incidents of BNP supporters violently attacking anti-racist demonstrators.

[96] See eg, *Abrams*, n. 63 above; *Dennis*, n. 5 above.

conviction of some unsavoury characters who in their hearts wanted to implement anti-democratic policies. But the legacy of these cases was free speech doctrine that provided inadequate protection to legitimate social protest in the decades that followed.[97]

Similarly, though it might not seem immediately objectionable that the Divisional Court gave Norwood's ambiguous expression a particularly malignant interpretation, there is nothing in the court's opinion to limit it to expression by members of extremist organizations. As a result, the *Norwood* decision puts in jeopardy any political statement that can be loosely construed as urging some deeply anti-democratic outcome.[98]

6. Speech at the Periphery of the Core and the Strategy of Overprotection

To round out this discussion of the core right of free speech that must be respected in any democracy, I want to identify several categories of speech that are beyond this democratic core (or like radically anti-democratic speech arguably not within it), but which may nevertheless require protection for pragmatic reasons.

---

[97] For instance, in 1923 an organizer for the Industrial Workers of the World (IWW) was convicted under a criminal syndicalism statute for advocating criminal activity for political ends. The evidence of such criminal syndicalism was the statement in the preamble to the organization's constitution that between the working class and the employing class 'a struggle must go on until the workers of the World organize as a class, take possession of the earth, and the machinery of production and abolish the wage system'. The Kansas Supreme Court affirmed the conviction but the US Supreme Court, edging slightly nearer to Hand's position in the *Masses* case, held this language insufficient to establish that the defendant advocated illegal conduct. *Fiske* v. *Kansas* 274 US 380 (1927). As late as 1966, a federal court upheld the Georgia State Legislature's refusal to seat Julian Bond, a black anti-war activist, for making statements such as he 'admired the courage of people who burned their draft cards' and for adhering to the statement 'We are in sympathy with, and support the men in this country who are unwilling to respond to a military draft.' In a significant step towards formally adopting Hand's 'objective' approach three years later in *Brandenburg*, the Supreme Court held that the legislature's exclusion of Bond for this reason violated his First Amendment rights. *Bond* v. *Floyd* 385 US 116 (1966). For a description of the unsatisfactory state of free speech jurisprudence in the early 1960s and the Warren Court's subsequent modification of doctrine to protect dissent that vehemently challenged segregation to the benefit of freedom of expression generally, see H. Kalven, *The Negro and the First Amendment* (Columbus, OH: The Ohio State UP, 1965). Kalven famously observed that blacks 'won back for us freedoms that the Communists seemed to have lost for us'. Ibid., 6.

[98] The ECtHR held Norwood's application inadmissible. Agreeing with the Divisional Court's assessment that the poster 'amounted to public of attack on all Muslims in the United Kingdom', the Court held that such a 'vehement attack against a religious group, linking the group as a whole with a grave act of terrorism, is incompatible with the values proclaimed and guaranteed by the Convention, notably tolerance, social peace and non-discrimination'. *Norwood* v. *UK*, Appl. No. 23131/03, 16 November 2004. For a trenchant critique of this unsatisfactory rationale for excluding speech from the protection of Article 10 of the Convention, see I. Hare, 'Crosses, Crescents and Sacred Cows: Criminalising Incitement to Religious Hatred' (2006) *Pub. L.* 521, 530–31.

(i) 'Fighting Words'

I have already mentioned that so called 'fighting words'—abusive epithets directed to others in a face-to-face confrontation—are not part of the core speech required in any democracy and how the United States Supreme Court formally excluded such expression from the American free speech principle. As Robert Post has perceptively observed, in excluding fighting words from First Amendment coverage, the Court was trying to distinguish a 'private fracas' from a 'public debate'.[99] But as with most legal dichotomies, this distinction becomes blurry at the margins. So while the use of personally abusive language between two people fighting over a parking space is plainly not part of the speech by which we govern ourselves, it is not so clear that face-to-face abuse can be punished when used in a heated political debate, or even in a personal confrontation with political overtones, without implicating the core right of political participation we are considering. During the turbulent civil rights and Vietnam war eras, the US Supreme Court employed on an ad hoc basis various techniques to provide protection to the use of personally directed insults in a political context but without overruling or even formally limiting its 'fighting words' doctrine.[100]

(ii) Advocacy of Law Violation

To provide prophylaxis to the core democratic free speech right we are considering, the United States Supreme Court has extended protection to advocacy of law violation when it occurs as part of a critique of social or political conditions. As Learned Hand explained in his *Masses* opinion, and as was implicit in the Court's Espionage Act cases just considered, direct and as explicit advocacy of law violation 'cannot by any latitude of interpretation be a part of that public opinion which is the final source of government in a democratic state'.[101] But those charged with advocating law violation in these cases did not do so in a vacuum, but rather as part of a vehement critique of social or political conditions, including condemnation of existing laws. And as the Court belatedly came to realize, 'where particular speech falls close to the line separating the lawful and the unlawful, the possibility of mistaken fact-finding... will create the danger that the legitimate utterance will be penalized'. This danger, in turn, will cause critics to 'steer far wider of the unlawful zone'[102] than is acceptable in a free and democratic society.

---

[99] Post (n. 22 above), 175.
[100] See, eg *Gooding* v. *Wilson* 405 US 518 (1972); *Rosenfeld* v. *New Jersey* 408 US 901 (1972); *Lewis* v. *City of New Orleans* 408 US 913 (1972); *Brown* v. *Oklahoma* 408 US 914 (1972). See also *Terminello* v. *Chicago* 337 US 1 (1949); *City of Houston* v. *Hill* 482 US 451 (1987).
[101] *Masses Publishing Co.* (n. 6 above), 540.
[102] *Speiser* v. *Randall* 357 US 513, 526 (1958).

Accordingly, in *Brandenburg* v. *Ohio*, the Court created breathing space for the exercise of core free speech rights. It held that mere advocacy of law violation forming part of social and political criticism was protected by the First Amendment. To be punishable advocacy of law violation must not just advocate violation of the law in the abstract or at some indefinite future time but must be 'directed to inciting or producing imminent lawless action' and, in addition, must be 'likely to produce such action'.[103]

Such strategic protection of speech advocating serious law violation does not, to my knowledge, exist in any other democracy, including the UK, as a young Muslim protestor recently discovered. In February, 2006, Mizanur Rahman took part in a demonstration in London protesting the publication of cartoons satirizing the prophet Mohammed in a Danish newspaper. He carried a placard saying 'Behead those who insult Islam' and 'Annihilate those who insult Islam' and shouted in a megaphone: 'We don't want to see [British troops] in Baghdad, in Iraq any more. We want to see them coming home in body bags, we want to see their blood running in the streets of Baghdad, we want to see their blood running in Fallujah. We want to see the Mujahideen shoot down their planes the way we shoot down birds, we want to see their tanks burn in the way we burn their flags.'[104] At trial Rahman apologized to the court, claimed had got 'carried away' in front of the crowd and said he was a 'nobody' whose words no one would take seriously.[105] He was convicted of stirring up racial hatred in violation of the Public Order Act and solicitation of murder and sentenced to 6 years in prison.[106]

The statements on Rahman's placard directly advocated murder and those shouted through the megaphone can reasonably be construed as doing so. As such, they can in principle be excluded from public discourse and subject to suppression or punishment without infringing the core democratic right to political participation. Still, as the US experience suggests, punishing mere advocacy of law violation that has no quality of incitement and which is unlikely to cause serious imminent harm may not leave enough 'breathing room' for vehement yet legitimate criticism of the status quo. And severe punishment, such as the six-year sentence in Rahman's case, will increase the potential for 'chilling' core political speech.

[103] *Brandenburg* (n. 8 above), 447–48. See above, text accompanying notes 65–66.
[104] 'Protestor "called for beheadings"', *BBC News*, 3 November 2006, <http://news.bbc.co.uk/1/hi/uk/6113874.stm> (last accessed 23 July 2008).
[105] R. Alleyne, 'Cartoon protestor guilty of race hate', *The Daily Telegraph*, 10 November 2006, <http://www.telegraph.co.uk/news/uknews/1533762/Cartoon-protester-guilty-of-race-hate.html> (last accessed 23 July 2008).
[106] P. Walker, 'Man guilty of inciting murder at cartoon protest', *The Guardian*, 5 July 2007. <http://www.guardian.co.uk/world/2007/jul/05/muhammadcartoons.uk> (last accessed 23 July 2008).

Because no one in principle has a fundamental right to advocate law violation,[107] it is appropriate in determining what degree of protection, if any, such expression should be given to weigh the benefits of such protection against its costs. This imprecise process will depend heavily on judicial intuition and will inevitably involve culturally dependent questions such as how much legitimate social criticism will likely be deterred in the absence of some degree of protection or, on the other side of the scale, the extent to which such protection will impair respect for the rule of law or might even contribute to the possibility that the crime being advocated will be committed. But in deciding whether or not to extend protection to advocacy of law violation, courts should be careful not to confuse deep offence with profound danger.

(iii) Expression Offending Civility Norms

I have already argued that any attempt to impose civility norms on public discourse by excluding offensive or insulting *ideas* is both theoretically and pragmatically inconsistent with the core democratic free speech right of each individual to participate in the formation of public opinion. The question I want to consider now is whether excluding expression from this discourse because the *manner* or *form* of the expression offends civility norms would similarly breach this core free speech right. To examine this question, let us once again consider the speech of BNP members which, if good for nothing else, at least provides us with textbook examples of expression that tests the limits of 'legitimate protest' in a democratic society.

In a speech to supporters at a Yorkshire pub, BNP chairman Nick Griffin referred to Islam as a 'wicked, vicious faith' that 'has expanded from a handful of cranky lunatics about 1,300 years ago'. He further claimed that white society was turning into a 'multi-racial hell hole'. Mark Collett, a party activist, compared asylum seekers to 'cockroaches', claiming that 'they're doing what cockroaches do because cockroaches can't help what they do, they just do it, like cats miaow and dogs bark'. He proclaimed: 'Let's show these ethnics the door in 2004'. For making these and other statements, Griffin and Collett were charged with stirring up racial hatred in violation of the Public Order Act of 1986, but after two jury trials were acquitted of all charges.[108]

The prosecution seems to have conceded that Griffin and Collett would have had a right to criticize Islam and to urge even ethnically-based immigration reform

---

[107] Or at least not one founded on participation in the democratic process. For an admirable attempt to find such a right in the individual autonomy interests of the audience, see T. M. Scanlon, 'A Theory of Freedom of Expression' (1972) 1 *Phil. & Pub. Affairs* 204. Scanlon repudiated this theory several years later in Scanlon, n. 93 above.

[108] 'BNP leader "said Islam is wicked"', *BBC News*, 3 November 2006, <http://news.bbc.co.uk/2/hi/uk_news/england/bradford/6113040.stm> (last accessed 9 July 2008); 'BNP leader cleared of race hate', *BBC News*, 10 November 2006, <http://news.bbc.co.uk/2/hi/uk_news/england/bradford/6135060.stm> (last accessed 9 July 2008).

in a calm, reasoned tone. It argued, however, that the speech in this case was beyond the pale of legitimate discourse because, rather than contributing to the debate on multiculturalism, the statements amounted to 'little more than crude racist rants'.[109] What apparently pushed this expression beyond the realm of legitimate public debate in the prosecution's view was not 'disapproval of another race' but doing so in 'such strong terms'.[110] On this view, it would have been perfectly legal if instead of saying that Islam was 'wicked, vicious faith', Griffin had taken a page from Robert Spencer's controversial book, *Islam Unveiled*, and charged that:

It would be too pessimistic to say that there are no peaceful strains of Islam, but it would be imprudent to ignore the fact that deeply imbedded in the central documents of the religion is an all-encompassing vision of a theocratic state that is fundamentally different from and opposed to the post-Enlightenment Christian values of the West.[111]

Any such attempt to distinguish legitimate public discourse and criminally punishable expression based upon its tone is highly problematic. If, as I have argued, the right to participate in public discourse is primarily valued because it is a necessary condition of political legitimacy, then restricting the tone of the expression might unduly interfere with this legitimization process. For many people the interest in expressing strong emotion about a public issue is every bit as important as conveying some precise idea. As the US Supreme Court has observed: 'Much linguistic expression serves a dual communicative function: it conveys not only ideas capable of relatively precise, detached expression but otherwise inexplicable emotions as well'.[112] Whether the imposition of civility norms on public discourse infringes the core right of democratic participation would thus seem to depend on whether the legitimating function of public discourse is properly measured primarily by the subjective perception of the speaker rather than by some more objective assessment of one's opportunity to participate freely and fairly in the public debate. This is a difficult issue about which I remain uncertain.

---

[109] <http://www.martinfrost.ws/htmlfiles/nov2006/bnp_trial.html> (last accessed 23 July 2008).

[110] The prosecutor, Rodney Jameson, QC, told the jury: 'We agree that freedom of expression is an important right but it cannot be unfettered. No society can permit disapproval of another race to be expressed in such strong terms that hatred be stirred up against people on the basis of race or ethnicity.' P. Stokes, 'White society is now a hell-hole, said BNP boss on race charges', *The Daily Telegraph*, 18 January 2006, <http://www.telegraph.co.uk/news/uknews/1508079/White-society-is-now-a-hell-hole,-said-BNP-boss-on-race-charges.html> (last accessed 23 July 2008). Whatever might be said about the propriety of imposition of such civility norm on public discourse, this was a particularly dubious case for doing so in that Griffin and Collett were not speaking to the public at large but to a small group of party supporters. Indeed, the general public became aware of these statements only because the meeting was secretly taped by an undercover BBC reporter making a documentary of the BNP. See 'Going Undercover in the BNP', *BBC News*, 15 July 2004, <http://news.bbc.co.uk/1/hi/magazine/3896213.stm> (last accessed 23 July 2008).

[111] *Islam Unveiled: Disturbing Questions about the World's Fastest-Growing Faith* (San Francisco: Encounter Books, 2003), 173.

[112] *Cohen* (n. 25 above), 26. See also J. Weinstein, 'Democracy, Sex and the First Amendment' (2007) 31 *N.Y.U. Rev. L. & Soc. Change* 865, 885–88.

I am certain, however, that it would both be impractical and perilous to the dissent that must be allowed in any democratic society to leave it to prosecutors, judges, and juries to separate legitimate public discourse from punishable expression based on their assessment of whether the idea is expressed in too 'strong terms' or constitutes a 'crude rant' rather than a rational exposition. Any attempt to exclude speech from public discourse because of its overly strong or crude manner of expression would likely end up primarily reflecting the decision-makers' views about the merits of the idea rather than some principled decision about its tone. So, for a combination of theoretical and pragmatic concerns, I think it might have been better for the trial court to have concluded that Griffin had as much a right to condemn Islam as a 'wicked, vicious faith' as Spencer had to characterize this religion as 'fundamentally ... opposed to the post-Enlight-enment Christian values of the West'.

This does not mean, however, that it is necessarily impractical for a democratic society to try to impose some minimal civility on public discourse. While the theoretical concerns would remain, it might at least be more manageable to try to exclude certain highly inflammatory words and symbols from public discourse, such as Collett's calling asylum seekers 'cockroaches' or, more problematically, Griffin's referring to the founders of Islam as 'lunatics'. The particular words and symbols that are deemed so offensive as to be excluded from public discourse would, of course, vary with the conventions and mores of each society as well as with the exact context in which these terms are used. But even this more limited attempt to impose civility norms on public discourse will implicate the core norm of democratic participation.

As the United States Supreme Court explained in upholding the right of an antiwar protestor to wear a jacket in public emblazoned with the message 'Fuck the Draft': 'we cannot indulge the facile assumption that one can forbid particular words without also running a substantial risk of suppressing ideas in the process'.[113] Aside from the emotive value to the speaker of using such certain words and symbols, there is an essential connection between the form and content of speech. Thus any restriction on words or symbols may impair a speaker's ability to express the precise idea he or she wants to convey. In addition, as the Court also noted, government 'might soon seize upon the censorship of certain words as a convenient guise for banning the expression of unpopular ideas'.[114] John Stuart Mill similarly recognized that uncivil language challenging the *status quo* will likely be considered more offensive than the same uncouth expression used to support those in power.[115]

For all these reasons, American free speech doctrine generally forbids the government from imposing even minimal civility norms on public discourse.[116] Protestors in America have a constitutional right to use profanity

---

[113] *Cohen* (n. 25 above), 26.   [114] Ibid.
[115] Mill (n. 15 above), 60–61.
[116] See Weinstein (n. 27 above), 47; Post (n. 22 above), 145–48.

or epithets,[117] to burn the American flag,[118] or crosses,[119] or to display Swastikas[120] as part of public discourse. While such complete suspension of civility norms may not in principle be required by the core free speech right essential to any democracy, every democracy should at least carefully consider whether the benefit gained by imposing such civility norms is worth the inevitable cost to free and open public debate.

(iv) Group Defamation

In addition to uttering the crude attack on Islam just considered, Griffin made scurrilous charges against Muslims. After talking about how Muslim gangs raped children in a Yorkshire town, he exclaimed:

The bastards that are in that gang, they are in prison so the public think it's all over. Well it's not. Because there's more of them. The police force and elected governors haven't done a damn thing about it. Their good book [the Koran] tells them that's acceptable. If you doubt it, go and buy a copy and you will find verse after verse and you can take any woman you want as long as it's not Muslim women .... These 18-, 19- and 25-year-old Asian Muslims are seducing and raping white girls in this town right now .... It's part of their plan for conquering countries. It's how they do it ... as the last whites try and find their way to the sea.[121]

Are such calumnies properly considered no legitimate part of the speech by which the people govern themselves in a democracy? A plausible argument for excluding speech like this from public discourse is that it is defamatory. Many democracies (though not the UK, which relies on a public order concept to suppress hate speech such as this)[122] have laws against group defamation, traditionally on the basis of race, ethnicity, religion, and more recently on the basis of sexual orientation.[123] The laws are usually defended as mere extensions of laws against defamation against individuals-laws which have long operated in every democracy. If defamatory statements about individuals can be prohibited without violating the

---

[117] *Cohen*, n. 25 above; *Letter Carriers* v. *Austin* 418 US 264 (1974).
[118] *Texas* v. *Johnson* 491 US 397 (1989).
[119] *Virginia* v. *Black* 538 US 343 (2003).
[120] *Skokie* v. *Nationalist Social Party* 373 NE 2d 21 (Ill Sup Ct, 1978).
[121] See Stokes (n. 110 above).
[122] Use of the group defamation concept as a basis of hate speech regulation is foreclosed in the UK by the exceedingly limited scope of group defamation under English law. See *Knuppfer* v. *London Express News Ltd* [1944] AC 116. (I am grateful to Ivan Hare for bringing this to my attention.) Such careful confinement of the reach of group defamation, then, is one instance in which the English judiciary was more protective of freedom of expression than was the US Supreme Court. See n. 124 below.
[123] See, eg, Article 266(b) of the Danish Penal Code, which outlaws statements 'threatening, insulting or degrading a group of persons on account of their race, colour, national or ethnic origin, faith or sexual orientation; s. 130 of the German Penal Code, prohibiting 'attacks on human dignity by insulting, maliciously maligning, or defaming part of the population'; and s. 137(c) of the Dutch Criminal Code, which forbids 'deliberately giv[ing] public expression to views insulting to a group of persons on account of their race, religion or conviction or sexual preference'.

core democratic right of political participation, then, the argument continues, so can defamatory statements about groups of individuals.[124]

The comparison to laws against individual defamation is, however, inapt. To begin with, unlike defamatory statements about individuals which will usually have no bearing on matters of public concern, defamatory statements about racial, ethnic, religious, or sexual orientation groups will almost always be inextricably linked with some larger social critique. True, if, as is now typically the case, only false statements of fact can be defamatory, then the prohibition against group defamation would in theory at least seem consistent with the core precept of democratic participation, for it would be difficult to argue that in principle one has a fundamental right to make false statements even in public discourse. Crucially, however, the bigoted statements that group defamation laws usually target are not statements of fact like those involved in individual defamation actions. Rather, they are typically non-falsifiable interpretations of data, statements which are more commonly called opinions.[125] For instance, when racists in the US impugn African-Americans by claiming that the reason there is a disproportionate number of blacks in American prisons is that blacks are genetically predisposed to criminal activity, they are not so much making a false statement of fact as they are interpreting data based on their world view. Though evaluative judgments such as these may not be the best inferences from the data, and in many cases may even be implausible, they are not susceptible to the same kind of definitive disproof as the typical statement in an individual defamation suit, for instance the statement that Jones is a thief.

The same is true of Griffin's statements about Muslims. The import of Griffin's claims is that sexual crimes committed by Muslims are propelled by edicts from the Koran and the desire of Muslims to take over Britain. It would seem, however, that in a democracy it is more appropriate for the court of public opinion rather than for a court of justice to render judgment on claims of this nature. It is thus arguable that suppression of views such as these violates the core right of each individual to express opinions on matters of public concern as well the right of the audience to hear and consider such perspectives. But even if it is in principle permissible in a democracy to punish group defamation of this sort,

---

[124] In 1952, a sharply divided US Supreme Court invoked precisely this rationale to uphold a group libel law prohibiting the publication of any material that 'portrays depravity, criminality, unchastity, or lack of virtue of a class of citizens, of any race, color, creed or religion which . . . exposes [such] citizens . . . to contempt, derision or obloquy'. *Beauharnais* v. *Illinois* 343 US 250. Although never formally overruled, in light of subsequent seismic changes in American free speech doctrine, especially the extension of First Amendment protection to libellous statements on matters of public concern in cases such as *New York Times* v. *Sullivan* 376 US 254 (1964) and *Gertz* v. *Robert Welch, Inc.* 418 US 323(1974), this decision is no longer good law. See *Nuxoll* (n. 42 above), 672 (Posner, J): '[T]hough *Beauharnais* . . . has never been overruled, no one thinks the First Amendment would today be interpreted to allow group defamation to be prohibited'. For a more detailed discussion of how subsequent decisions have sapped *Beauharnais* of all vitality, see Weinstein (n. 27 above), 56–9.

[125] See Weinstein (n. 84 above), 159–60.

experience in the US shows that it is most difficult to excise defamatory statements on matters of public concern from public discourse without significantly
impeding democratic self-governance.[126]

7. Conclusion

The core democratic right of citizens in England to express unpopular ideas in
public is insecure. To a considerable extent this insecurity is a product of the
uncertainty created by overly refined, abstract distinctions that are unworkable in
practice, such as the *Hammond* court's attempt to distinguish ideas that 'insult'
from those that 'offend, shock, or disturb'. Adding to this uncertainty is the
possibility, demonstrated by *Norwood*, that courts will ascribe the most pernicious
meaning to ambiguous language. As a result of this uncertainty, law enforcement
officials have enormous discretion to squelch protest, as shown by the recent
citation of a protestor for stating that Scientology is a cult, while citizens have
insufficient guidance about what ideas they can safely express in public without
fear of arrest or even conviction under the Public Order Act. Relatedly, the core
right of free speech is weakened by the lack of objective criteria for determining
whether one has a right to express unpopular ideas in public. The use of vague
standards and amorphous balancing tests that characterize English free speech
jurisprudence invite law enforcement officials, juries and even courts themselves
to decide cases on ideological grounds rather than on a principled basis.[127] Other
areas of the law may well be served by flexible standards or nuanced tests. But to
achieve the certainty and objectivity essential to protection of dissent in a
democratic society, free speech doctrine should employ rules that are 'hard,
conventional, difficult to evade'.[128]

   As much as these pragmatic considerations explain the insecure status of the
right to express unpopular views in public, a more profound cause is the insufficient weight that English courts have afforded this right. Rather than treating the
right to participate in public discourse as a fundamental individual right that can
be violated only in truly extraordinary circumstances, both *Hammond* and *Norwood* and the precedent they follow consider this right as properly outweighed by
various societal interests, such as preventing people from being insulted or by the
promotion of tolerance. This conception of the right of free speech seems to
reflect the dominant view among English jurists. In a recent House of Lord's

---

[126] See *Sullivan*, n. 124 above.

[127] '[W]here messages are proscribed because they are dangerous, balancing tests inevitably
become intertwined with the ideological predispositions of those doing the balancing—or if not
that, at least with the relative confidence or paranoia of the age in which they are doing it...'
J. H. Ely, 'Flag Desecration: A Case Study in the Roles of Categorization and Balancing in First
Amendment Analysis' (1975) 88 *Harv. L. Rev.* 1482, 1501.

[128] See text accompanying n. 62 above. See also Hare (n. 98 above), 526: '[Courts in the UK]
have not formulated a method which contains sufficient guarantees of judicial objectivity when the
court is confronted with the expression of what are frequently unappealing opinions'.

decision, one of the realm's most prominent and respected judges, Lord Bingham of Cornhill, writes that the 'fundamental rationale of the democratic process' is:

that if competing views, opinions, and policies are publicly debated and exposed to public scrutiny the good will over time drive out the bad and the true prevail over the false. It must be assumed that, given time, the public will make a sound choice when, in the course of the democratic process, it has the right to choose.[129]

On this view, free speech is valued not as a true individual right but as instrumental to the democratic process because it will help the electorate make a 'sound choice'.[130] Decisions like *Hammond* and *Norwood* are consistent with this conception of 'the fundamental rationale' of free speech in a democratic society. Although free speech may be an important policy goal, as such it is susceptible to being outweighed by other important policy considerations such as promoting tolerance or protecting people from insult. The balance, moreover, will tip sharply in favour of these other policy concerns if the goal of promoting 'sound choice' by the electorate will be only minimally impaired by suppression of the speech in question, as will be the case if the substance of the view some pesky protestor wants to express in the public square is readily available in media such as newspapers, books, or the Internet.

But with due respect to Lord Bingham, as important as these instrumental concerns may be, they do not constitute the 'fundamental rationale of the democratic process' underlying the right to free speech. What this perspective misses is the interest that each individual has in participating in the public discussion by which collective decisions are made, an interest that as I have emphasized throughout this chapter is vitally linked to legitimacy. Punishing Hammond for expressing the view that homosexuality is immoral may not significantly impair the search for truth nor interfere with the public making a 'sound choice'; but excluding him from participating in the public conversation about the morality of homosexuality undermines the legitimacy of any decision made by the people or their representatives relating to this issue.

In the early part of the twentieth century, Justice Louis Brandeis sagely observed that to formulate sound free speech doctrine, courts 'must bear in mind why a State is, ordinarily, denied the power to prohibit dissemination of social, economic, and political doctrine which a vast majority of citizens believes to be false and fraught with evil consequence'.[131] So long as English courts continue to conceive of the right to participate in public discourse as an important social goal enhancing the quality of the democratic process rather than as a fundamental individual right constitutive of democracy, there is little chance that they will devise doctrine adequate to protect the core right to free speech essential to any democratic society.

---

[129] *Animal Defenders* (n. 72 above), para. 28.

[130] This view is similar to Alexander Meiklejohn's position that the basic value of free speech is that it promotes 'the voting of wise decisions', (n. 13 above), 25. For a trenchant criticism of Meiklejohn's view, see Post (n. 22 above), 268–89.

[131] *Whitney* v. *California* (n. 91 above), 374, concurring opinion.

3

Extreme Speech Under International and Regional Human Rights Standards

Ivan Hare

Many of the contributions to this volume refer to international or regional human rights instruments, such as the International Covenant on Civil and Political Rights (ICCPR) or the European Convention on Human Rights (ECHR). Since some readers will be unfamiliar with the content and impact of these instruments, we include this chapter to provide an introduction to the origin and effectiveness of international and regional legal standards in the field of extreme speech. The chapter falls into the following parts. In Part 1, I provide a brief outline of the history and structure of international and regional human rights instruments. Part 2 contains an analysis of the provisions of these instruments dealing with freedom of expression in general and extreme speech in particular. Part 3 assesses the effectiveness of international legal standards in protecting free speech, focusing on the ECHR and the United Kingdom.

1. The History and Structure of International and Regional Human Rights Instruments

The international human rights movement really began in 1948 with the adoption of the Universal Declaration on Human Rights by the then recently formed General Assembly of the United Nations.[1] The Universal Declaration was, as its name indicated, not an enforceable international treaty, but an assertion of fundamental rights principles.[2] Nonetheless, the Declaration marked an important shift in the understanding of the nature of international law

[1] On the development of international human rights protection, see P. Sieghart, *The Lawful Rights of Mankind* (Oxford: OUP, 1985) and *International Law of Human Rights* (Oxford: Clarendon Press, 1983); and H. J. Steiner, P. Alston and R. Goodman, *International Human Rights in Context: Law, Politics, Morals*, 2nd edn. (Oxford: OUP, 2000), ch. 2.

[2] The Universal Declaration provides in Art 19 that everyone 'has the right to freedom of opinion and expression'.

(which had previously been described as the law of nations).[3] The growth of the concept of fundamental human rights meant that, for the first time, individuals (rather than states) could be the holders of international legal rights. Further, the plea of state sovereignty (that is, that matters taking place within the borders of a state were no concern of the international community) would no longer be sufficient defence to an action brought against a state party by an individual within its territory.[4]

(i) International Human Rights Instruments

(a) The International Covenant on Civil and Political Rights

The original intention of the United Nations was that binding international human rights instruments would follow the Declaration with reasonable speed. However, the great ideological divide which opened between the Soviet Union and its satellite states on the one hand and the United States and western European nations on the other and the substantial growth in the number of members of the United Nations led to immense delays in drafting and ratification. It also emerged that (in contrast to the Declaration which contained both) there would have to be separate human rights treaties for civil and political rights and for economic, social, and cultural rights.[5] The ICCPR was adopted by the UN in 1966 and entered into force in 1976.[6] As of January 2008, there were 160 state parties to the ICCPR.

Under Article 2 of the ICCPR, state parties undertake to respect and ensure the rights contained within it to those in its territory and subject to its jurisdiction and to provide recourse to a competent and independent authority to determine any alleged violation. As its name suggests, the ICCPR protects a fairly standard list of civil and political rights: the right to life; the right to be free from torture, cruel, inhuman, or degrading treatment or punishment; a ban on slavery and servitude, on imprisonment for failure to fulfil a contractual obligation, and on retrospective criminal liability; the right to liberty and security of the person; liberty of movement; equality before the law and due process rights; the right to privacy; the right to freedom of thought, conscience, and religion; the right to hold opinions and to freedom of expression; the right to freedom of association

---

[3] For a general history of international law, see S. C. Neff, 'A Short History of International Law', in M. D. Evans (ed.), *International Law* (Oxford: OUP, 2006).

[4] H. Lauterpacht, *International Law and Human Rights* (London: Stevens and Son, 1950), chs. 4 and 5.

[5] I. Hare, 'Social Rights as Fundamental Rights', in B. A. Hepple (ed.), *Social and Labour Rights in a Global Context: International and Comparative Perspectives* (Cambridge: CUP, 2002) and J. Wadham and R. Taylor, 'Bringing More Rights Home' (2002) *Eur. Hum. Rts. L. Rev.* 714.

[6] The best accounts of the ICCPR are S. Joseph, J. Schultz and M. Castan, *The International Covenant on Civil and Political Rights: Cases, Materials and Commentary*, 2nd edn. (Oxford: OUP, 2004) and M. Nowak, *The United Nations Covenant on Civil and Political Rights: CCPR Commentary*, 2nd edn. (Arlington, VA: N. P. Engel, 2005).

and of peaceful assembly; the right to participate in public affairs; the right to marry; and the right to protection as a minor.[7] All such rights are to be secured without any distinctions, such as to race, colour, sex, language, religion, political, or other opinion, national or social origin, property, birth, or other status and ethnic, religious, and linguistic minorities are to be protected.[8]

In common with other international legal instruments, state parties may enter reservations at the time of ratification.[9] In addition, the ICCPR makes provision for derogation in times of public emergency which threaten the life of the nation. No derogation is permitted in relation to certain Articles (such as the right to life, to be free from torture, or the right not to be held in slavery) and any permitted derogation must only be to the extent strictly required by the exigencies of the situation.[10]

The ICCPR also establishes a supervisory and enforcement body called the Human Rights Committee (HRC).[11] Under the ICCPR, the HRC has the power to consider inter-state complaints of violations of the Convention and the periodic reports of the state parties on their own compliance. Under the First Protocol to the ICCPR, 108 states have so far recognized a right of individual petition (in the form of 'communications') to the HRC. There is no provision for oral hearings before the HRC and its written procedures conclude with the Committee communicating its 'views' to the state party concerned and the individual complainant.[12]

(b) International Convention on the Elimination of All Forms of Racial Discrimination

The International Convention on the Elimination of All Forms of Racial Discrimination (ICERD) entered into force in 1969. ICERD has been ratified by 173 state parties. Under this Convention, the state parties condemn all forms of racial discrimination, undertake to pursue all reasonable measures to eliminate it, and to ensure that civil and political and social and economic rights are secured to all without such discrimination.[13] ICERD establishes a Committee on the

---

[7] Arts 6–25. [8] Arts 26–7.

[9] A reservation is a unilateral statement on signing or ratifying a treaty in which the state purports to exclude or modify the legal effect of provisions of the treaty with respect to that state (I. Brownlie, *Principles of Public International Law*, 6th edn. (Oxford: OUP, 2003), 583–7). As a result of the reservations, understandings, and declarations entered by the United States when it ratified the ICCPR in 1992, it is arguable that the ICCPR has no domestic impact (L. Henkin, 'US Ratification of Human Rights Conventions: The Ghost of Senator Bricker' (1995) 89 *Am. J. Int'l L.* 341, 346). The United Kingdom entered a reservation to Article 20 of the ICCPR which is discussed below at n. 41 and associated text.

[10] Art 4.

[11] Part IV of the ICCPR. See generally, D. McGoldrick, *The Human Rights Committee: Its Role in the Development of the International Covenant on Civil and Political Rights* (Oxford: Clarendon Press, 1994) and R. Burchill, S. Davidson and A. Conte, *Defining Civil and Political Rights: The Jurisprudence of the United Nations Human Rights Committee* (Aldershot: Ashgate, 2004).

[12] Art 5 of First Protocol to the ICCPR (1966). [13] Arts 2–5.

Elimination of Racial Discrimination which receives periodic reports from the state parties and makes recommendations and suggestions upon them to the UN General Assembly.[14] The ICERD Committee may receive inter-state complaints which are then referred to an *ad hoc* Conciliation Commission with a view to reaching an amicable solution.[15] If the state parties fail to reach an amicable solution, the matter may be referred to the International Court of Justice (ICJ).[16] ICERD also contains an optional right to permit individual petitions in response to which the Committee makes 'suggestions and recommendations' to the state party.[17]

(c) Convention on the Prevention and Punishment of the Crime of Genocide

The Convention on the Prevention and Punishment of the Crime of Genocide (the Genocide Convention) entered into force in 1951 and now has 133 state parties. Genocide is defined expansively to include causing a range of harms with the intent to destroy a 'national, ethnical, racial, or religious group'.[18] Under the Genocide Convention, state parties undertake to enact legislation to create the following offences: conspiracy to commit genocide and direct and public incitement to commit genocide.[19] Disputes between the state parties to the Convention are referred to the ICJ. Most of the states referred to in this collection are Parties to the Convention.[20]

(ii) Regional Human Rights Instruments

As indicated above, the most significant regional human rights instrument for the purposes of this collection is the ECHR. However, at the close of this section, brief reference is made to the other principal regional human rights instruments and where fuller discussions of their content may be found.

(a) The European Convention on Human Rights

The visible results of two world wars on its own soil in the first half of the twentieth century and, in particular, the slide into totalitarianism of Germany, Italy, and Spain in the 1930s led to the foundation in 1949 of the Council of Europe. The 10 founding members of the Council committed themselves to upholding the rule of law and the protection of fundamental freedoms.[21] The greatest monument to the Council is the ECHR or, to give it its full title, the

---

[14] Art 8. [15] Arts 11–12. [16] Art 22.

[17] Art 14. This procedure became active in 1982.

[18] Art 2. [19] Arts 3 and 4.

[20] The United States has reserved its right to withhold consent to disputes being referred to the ICJ.

[21] The founding members were Belgium, Denmark, France, Ireland, Italy, Luxembourg, the Netherlands, Norway, Sweden, and the United Kingdom.

European Convention on Human Rights and Fundamental Freedoms which came into force on 3 September 1953.[22] The ECHR was the first comprehensive human rights treaty in the world and provided the first mechanism for individual judicial redress. It remains the most comprehensive and developed system for supranational human rights protection.[23] The High Contracting Parties to the ECHR undertake to secure the rights and freedoms contained therein and to provide an effective remedy before a national authority for alleged violations.[24]

The ECHR protects the following rights: to life; to be free from inhuman and degrading treatment or punishment; to be free from slavery and forced labour; to liberty and security of the person; to a fair trial; to be free from retrospective criminal legislation; to respect for one's private and family life, home, and correspondence; to freedom of thought, conscience, and religion; to freedom of expression; to freedom of assembly and peaceful association; and to freedom to marry and found a family. The First Protocol to the ECHR contains the right to the enjoyment of possessions, the right to education, and the right to free elections. There are now a number of additional Protocols, including the Sixth and Thirteenth Protocols which abolish the death penalty, the Fourth and Seventh Protocols which provide a number of protections for aliens (including freedom of movement within a state and freedom to leave it, freedom from collective expulsion, and restrictions on individual expulsion), and the Twelfth Protocol which introduces a general prohibition on discrimination.

The institutional structure of the Council of Europe was established at Strasbourg and was originally threefold: the Committee of Ministers, the European Commission on Human Rights, and the European Court of Human Rights. However, the increasing popularity of petitioning Strasbourg and the expansion of the Council of Europe (to some 46 members in 2007) created an unacceptable back log of cases. The response was to streamline the procedure by eliminating the role of the Commission and replacing it with a single full-time Court.[25] Upon the introduction of these reforms in 1998, the right of individual petition and the acceptance of the jurisdiction of the Court were made compulsory.

There are two mechanisms provided by the Convention for its enforcement: complaints brought by other state parties and individual petition.[26] Inter-state

---

[22] The Convention was required to be ratified by 10 members before it entered into force. The UK was the first State Party to do so in March 1951.

[23] For a fuller summary of the operation of the ECHR, see H. Woolf, J. Jowell and A. Le Sueur, *De Smith's Judicial Review*, 6th edn. (London: Sweet & Maxwell, 2007), ch. 13. The history of the ECHR is described in A. W. B. Simpson, *Human Rights and the End of Empire* (Oxford: OUP, 2001). The substantive scope of the ECHR is set out in A. Lester, D. Pannick and S. Herberg (eds.), *Human Rights Law and Practice*, 3rd edn. (London: Butterworths, 2009); and P. Van Dijk, F. van Hoof, A. van Rijn and L. Zwaak, *Theory and Practice of the European Convention on Human Rights*, 4th edn. (Antwerp: Intersentia, 2006).

[24] Arts. 1 and 13.

[25] The new procedure is set out in Protocol 11 to the Convention which came into force on 1 November 1998.

[26] Arts. 33 and 34 respectively.

complaints have been very rare and it is individual petitions which have seen the greatest growth: from 138 in 1955 to over 41,000 in 2005.[27]

Like the ICCPR, parties may enter reservations at the time of ratification and may derogate from certain rights in times of national emergency.[28] In addition, there are several general limitations on the exercise of ECHR rights. Article 16 permits the state to impose restrictions on the political activities of aliens not-withstanding Articles 10, 11 and 14. Article 18 limits the restrictions permitted in the Convention to the purposes for which they have been prescribed. More importantly, Article 17 provides that:

Nothing in this Convention may be interpreted as implying for any state, group or person any right to engage in any activity or perform any act aimed at the destruction of any of the rights and freedoms set forth herein or at their limitation to any greater extent than is provided for in the Convention.

On occasion, the Court does not make express reference to Article 17, but nonetheless qualifies the protection of Convention rights by reference to the principle it enshrines.[29] The scope of this broad and troublesome provision (which is discussed further below) is tempered somewhat by the requirement that there be a link between the right abused and that which the state seeks to limit.[30]

One of the most important characteristics of the application of the Convention is the doctrine of the margin of appreciation. In essence, this doctrine permits the Court to accord some latitude to the state in how Convention rights are protected. This reflects the fact that the Court's role is subsidiary to that of the states in ensuring the protection of Convention rights. The doctrine is most often invoked in fields where there is no consensus across the Council of Europe about how a matter should be addressed.

The Court points out that the machinery of protection established by the Convention is subsidiary to the national systems safeguarding human rights ... The Convention leaves to each Contracting State, in the first place, the task of securing the rights and liberties it enshrines.

These observations apply, notably, to Art 10(2). In particular, it is not possible to find in the domestic law of the various Contracting States a uniform European conception of morals. The view taken by their respective laws of the requirements of morals varies from time to time and from place to place, especially in our era which is characterised by a rapid and far-reaching evolution of opinions on the subject. By reason of their direct and

---

[27] The Court produces an informative annual survey of its activities which is available at <http://www.echr.coe.int/ECHR/EN/Header/Reports+and+Statistics/Reports/Annual+surveys+of+activity/> (last accessed 29 July 2008).

[28] Arts. 57 and 15.

[29] For example, in relation to the dissolution of a political party and a challenge based on the Art 11 right to freedom of association, see *Refah Partisi (The Welfare Party)* v. *Turkey* (2003) 37 EHRR 1, para. 99 and *United Communist Party of Turkey* v. *Turkey* (1998) 26 EHRR 121.

[30] Thus, the Irish government could not rely on Article 17 to limit the Article 5 and 6 rights of members of the IRA where there was no suggestion that the IRA had abused Articles 5 and 6 in the course of its activities (*Lawless* v. *Ireland (No 3)* (1961) 1 EHRR 15, para. 7).

continuous contact with the vital forces of their countries, State authorities are in principle in a better position than the international judge to give an opinion on the exact content of these requirements as well as on the 'necessity' of a 'restriction' or 'penalty' intended to meet them.

Consequently, Art 10(2) leaves to the Contracting States a margin of appreciation. This margin is given both to the domestic legislator ('prescribed by law') and to the bodies, judicial amongst others, that are called upon to interpret and apply the laws in force . . . [31]

The doctrine of the margin of appreciation is discussed further below.

A distinct, but related, European development is the European Union Agency for Fundamental Rights which (since 2007) has taken over the role of the European Monitoring Centre on Racism and Xenophobia and has produced reports and studies on these issues within the Member States of the European Union (EU).[32]

(b) The American Convention on Human Rights

The American Convention on Human Rights (AmCHR) followed the American Declaration of the Rights and Duties of Man (1948) and both were produced under the auspices of the Organization of American States. The AmCHR entered into force in 1978. The AmCHR is in similar terms to the ECHR (although it contains a clause requiring progress towards the better protection of social and economic rights) and establishes an Inter-American Commission and a Court of Human Rights. There are currently 24 state parties. Given the political history of the region, the Inter-American Commission and Court have been occupied principally with widespread and gross human rights violations rather than individual complaints. This tendency is enhanced by the fact that there is no right of individual petition to the Court.[33]

(c) The African Charter on Human and Peoples' Rights

The African Charter on Human and Peoples' Rights (AfCHPR) was adopted by the members of the Organization of African Unity in 1981.[34] There are 53 state parties. The AfCHPR is unusual for its integrated treatment of economic, social,

---

[31] The doctrine was first set out by the Court in *Handyside* v. *United Kingdom* (1976) 1 EHRR 737, para. 48 which concerned an obscenity prosecution.

[32] Details of the Agency's work are available at <http://fra.europa.eu/fra/index.php> (last accessed 29 July 2008).

[33] For an account of the Inter-American system, see Steiner et al, *International Human Rights* (n. 1 above), 1020–62.

[34] See M. D. Evans and R. Murray (eds.), *The African Charter on Human and Peoples' Rights: The System in Practice, 1986–2000* (Cambridge: CUP, 2002); and F. Ouguergouz, *The African Charter of Human and Peoples' Rights: A Comprehensive Agenda for Human Dignity and Sustainable Democracy in Africa* (The Hague: Kluwer Law International, 2003).

and cultural rights as well as collective rights to development and to a satisfactory environment.[35] The Charter also contains a list of duties, some of which are described in greater detail below. The enforcement mechanism is still under-developed as the African Court of Human and Peoples' Rights has only recently been established. However, both states and individuals may bring complaints to the African Commission on Human and Peoples' Rights which may then make recommendations to the relevant state. State parties are also required to submit periodic reports on their compliance with the AfCHPR.[36]

(d) The Arab Charter of Human Rights

The League of Arab States was founded in 1944 and now comprises 22 member states. The Council of the League adopted the Arab Charter of Human Rights in 1994. The Charter is based on the UN Declaration, the ICCPR and the International Covenant on Economic, Social, and Cultural Rights (ICESCR). There is a general restriction clause in the usual terms.[37] The Charter provides for the establishment of a Committee of Experts on Human Rights to which the state parties shall submit periodic reports.[38] There have not yet been sufficient ratifications by state parties for the Charter to enter into force.[39]

2. Freedom of Expression

International and regional human rights instruments provide different levels of protection for different rights. For example, under both the ICCPR and the ECHR, the right to be free from torture or inhuman and degrading treatment or punishment is an absolute right. This means that there are no limitations or qualifications to the right set out on the face of the document and that states have no power to derogate from it even in times of emergency. By contrast, the right to freedom of expression is a qualified right: that is, the state may lawfully interfere with the right to freedom of expression in certain defined and limited circumstances. A state may also derogate from the right to freedom of expression in times of emergency.

(i) Freedom of Expression Under the ICCPR

The relevant provisions of the ICCPR for our purposes are Articles 19 and 20.

Article 19

---

[35] Arts 15–24.
[36] Steiner et al, *International Human Rights* (n. 1 above), 1062–83 provide more detail on the operation of the AfCHPR.
[37] Art. 4.   [38] Arts. 40–1
[39] Art. 42(b) requires ratification by seven state parties before it enters into effect.

...

2. Everyone shall have the right to freedom of expression...
3. The exercise of the rights provided for in paragraph 2 of this article carries with it special duties and responsibilities. It may therefore be subject to certain restrictions, but these shall only be such as are provided by law and are necessary:
   (a) For respect of the rights or reputations of others;
   (b) For the protection of national security or of public order (*ordre public*), or of public health or morals.

Article 20

1. Any propaganda for war shall be prohibited by law.
2. Any advocacy of national, racial, or religious hatred that constitutes incitement to discrimination, hostility or violence shall be prohibited by law.

The HRC takes the view that there is no inconsistency between these provisions and that the requirements of Article 20 are fully compatible with the right to freedom of expression contained in Article 19.[40] However, Article 20 is singular in that it is the only provision of the ICCPR which requires (rather then prohibits) action by the state parties. It is also striking that the HRC issued no General Comment on Article 20 until 1983. The United Kingdom has taken a different view from the HRC and entered a reservation to Article 20 which, in the interests of freedom of speech, provides that it regards its existing legislation as adequate to address concerns of public order and reserves the right not to introduce further legislation.[41]

The HRC has held that political speech is at the core of the forms of expression protected by Article 19. However, the HRC has provided very limited protection for extreme speech and has relied on a number of techniques to deny such protection in the leading cases. In some cases, the HRC relies on the express limitations in Article 19 itself (without reference to Article 20). Thus, in *Faurisson* v. *France*, the HRC upheld the conviction of Faurisson and his publisher for the offence under French law of denying the crimes against humanity established by the Nuremberg Tribunal.[42] In an interview, Faurisson (a former professor of literature at the Sorbonne) doubted the use of gas for the purposes of extermination in Nazi concentration camps. The HRC held that France could legitimately restrict freedom of expression on the ground expressly provided by Article 19(3)(a), that is, 'for respect of the rights or reputations of others' and that this reputational interest could extend to the collective reputation of a group. The

---

[40] HRC, General Comment 11, para. 2.
[41] CCPR/C/2/Rev. 3, 33. See D. Feldman, 'Freedom of Expression', in D. Harris and S. Joseph (eds.), *The International Covenant on Civil and Political Rights and United Kingdom Law* (Oxford: Clarendon Press, 1995). The UK is not alone in this and Australia, Belgium, Denmark, Finland, Iceland, Ireland, the Netherlands, New Zealand, Sweden, and the USA, among others, have also entered reservations to Article 20.
[42] (1996) 2 BHRC 1.

restriction was found to be necessary to ensure that members of the Jewish community could live without fear of anti-Semitism since the comments were of a nature to raise or strengthen antisemitic feelings (even if Faurisson had no intention of doing so).[43] The HRC did rely on Article 20 in *JRT and WG Party* v. *Canada* in which it upheld the decision to curtail the telephone facilities available to T and his party as a result of the antisemitic messages which he made available through the telephone system.[44] The HRC declared T's application inadmissible:

The opinions which Mr T seeks to disseminate through the telephone system clearly constitute the advocacy of racial or religious hatred which Canada has an obligation under article 20(2) of the Covenant to prohibit.

(a) CERD

CERD contains a more detailed requirement to enact and implement laws on racial vilification. Article 4 provides:

States Parties condemn all propaganda and all organizations which are based on ideas or theories of superiority of one race or group of persons of one colour or ethnic origin, or which attempt to justify or promote racial hatred and discrimination in any form, and undertake to adopt immediate and positive measures designed to eradicate all incitement to, or acts of, such discrimination and, to this end, with due regard to the principles embodied in the Universal Declaration of Human Rights and the rights expressly set forth in article 5 of this Convention, inter alia:

(a) Shall declare an offence punishable by law all dissemination of ideas based on racial superiority or hatred, incitement to racial discrimination, as well as all acts of violence or incitement to such acts against any race or group of persons of another colour or ethnic origin, and also the provision of any assistance to racist activities, including the financing thereof;
(b) Shall declare illegal and prohibit organizations, and also organized and all other propaganda activities, which promote and incite racial discrimination, and shall recognize participation in such organizations or activities as an offence punishable by law;
(c) Shall not permit public authorities or public institutions, national or local, to promote or incite racial discrimination.

In one sense, Article 4 is narrower than Article 20 of the ICCPR since, by definition, it only applies to racial hate speech. However, in other respects Article 4 goes substantially beyond the obligations imposed by the ICCPR. In particular, Article 4 requires criminal sanctions (rather than mere legal prohibition), extends to the dissemination of ideas based on racial superiority (as well as incitement to

---

[43] The HRC applied *Faurisson* in *Ross* v. *Canada* (2001) 10 BHRC 219 in which it upheld the transfer to a non-teaching post of a school teacher for publishing criticism of the Jewish faith (even though the criticism was lawful under Canadian law and he did not articulate it through his teaching).
[44] Doc A/38/40, p. 231.

discrimination or hatred), and requires the prohibition of organizations which promote or incite racial discrimination. The CERD Committee has stated its view that Article 4 is consistent with the protection of freedom of speech (which is itself a protected right referred to in Article 5(d)(viii) of ICERD).[45] The CERD Committee has repeatedly urged state parties to adopt legislation to comply with the full obligations contained in Article 4 and has criticized the governments of the UK and the USA for their reservations to the Convention.[46]

The CERD Committee's doctrine on the interpretation of Article 4 is very limited. Unsurprisingly, the Committee found a violation of Article 4 in a case where an individual was greeted by a group of residents with shouts of 'No more foreigners' and threats to burn down the housing he was being shown.[47] In other cases, the Committee has not addressed Article 4 directly.[48]

(ii) Freedom of Expression Under Regional Human Rights Instruments

As with the discussion above, this section will focus on the ECHR.

(a) The ECHR

Article 10 provides:

1. Everyone has the right to freedom of expression. This right shall include freedom to hold opinions and to receive and impart information and ideas without interference by public authority and regardless of frontiers. This article shall not prevent States from requiring the licensing of broadcasting, television or cinema enterprises.
2. The exercise of these freedoms, since it carries with it duties and responsibilities, may be subject to such formalities, conditions, restrictions or penalties as are prescribed by law and are necessary in a democratic society, in the interests of national security, territorial integrity or public safety, for the prevention of disorder or crime, for the protection of health or morals, for the protection of the reputation or rights of others,

---

[45] General Recommendation 15, para. 4. See K. Boyle and A. Baldaccini, 'A Critical Evaluation of International Human Rights Approaches to Racism', in S. Fredman (ed.), *Discrimination and Human Rights: The Case of Racism* (Oxford: OUP, 2001).

[46] General Recommendations 1 and 7. The ICERD Committee has expressed the view that the UK's reservation is not compatible with Article 4(b) (see CERD/C/SR.1430, 21 August 2000). A very significant number of states have entered reservations or declarations in relation to Article 4, including Australia, Austria, Belgium, France, Ireland, Italy, Japan, Switzerland, Thailand, and the USA.

[47] *LK* v. *Netherlands* (CERD 4/91). Both domestic and supra-national courts have made reference to CERD: for example, the Canadian Supreme Court in *R* v. *Keegstra* [1990] 3 SCR 697 and the ECtHR in *Jersild* v. *Denmark* (1995) 19 EHRR 1.

[48] *Ahmad* v. *Denmark* (CERD 16/99) and *Hagan* v. *Australia* (CERD 26/02) (a complaint by an aboriginal Australian about the naming of a stand at a Queensland sports ground which included the term 'Nigger' which was the nickname of the (white) sporting personality after whom the stand was named).

for preventing the disclosure of information received in confidence, or for maintaining the authority and impartiality of the judiciary.

The European Court of Human Rights (ECtHR) has accepted that certain forms of extreme speech are protected by Article 10, which covers not only information or ideas which are favourably received, but also those which would shock, offend, or disturb any sector of the population.[49] There are examples of the ECtHR providing protection for racist or antisemitic expression if the speech can be shown to be an aspect of a broader discussion of matters in the public interest. Thus in *Jersild* v. *Denmark*, the ECtHR held that the criminal conviction of a journalist for disseminating racist insults was disproportionate and in breach of Article 10.[50] Although the journalist had solicited the opinions in question and gave the most extreme of them prominence in the finished programme, they took place in a factual programme about racist ideology and the journalist dissociated himself from them. Similarly, in *Lehideux and Isorni* v. *France*, the ECtHR found a breach of Article 10 in relation to the applicants' convictions for implicitly defending the collaboration of the Vichy regime with the Nazis in an advertisement which presented a positive view of Marshal Petain.[51] The Court held that the advertisements were part of a debate about a controversial period of French history and the convictions were not necessary to protect the rights of others or to prevent disorder or crime.

However, the degree of protection for such speech is extremely limited. In the vast majority of cases, the ECtHR holds that extreme speech either falls outside the ECHR altogether or that restrictions on it are justifiable on the most limited evidence of potential harm. Thus although the journalist was protected in *Jersild*, the ECtHR was clear that the individual members of the extremist group interviewed by him were properly convicted of the dissemination of racist insults on the basis that their speech was taken outside the protection of Article 10 by the provisions of Article 17.[52] Further, the Court has held that speech which denies or seeks to revise certain clearly established historical facts (such as the Nazi Holocaust itself) is also carried outside the realm of protected speech by Article 17.[53] Article 17 is discussed further below.

The ECtHR has also been very reluctant to provide meaningful protection for speech which offends religious sensibilities.[54] Thus in *Otto Preminger Institut* v. *Austria*, the Court upheld the seizure and forfeiture of a film which portrayed the

---

[49] *Sunday Times* v. *United Kingdom* (1979) 2 EHRR 245, para. 65, and affirmed repeatedly since.
[50] N. 47 above, para. 35.
[51] (1998) 30 EHRR 665, para. 47.
[52] See further, *Glimmerveen & Hagenbeek* v. *Netherlands* (1980) 18 D & R 187; and *H, W, P & K* v. *Austria* Appl. No. 12774/87 (1989) 62 D & R 216.
[53] See further, *Garaudy* v. *France* Appl. No. 65831/01, 24 June 2003. In other cases (such as *X* v. *FRG* Appl. No. 9235/81 (1982) 29 D & R 194), restrictions on Holocaust denial have been justified as protecting the rights of others.
[54] These issues are discussed in greater detail in Hare, ch.15 in this volume.

founding figures of Christianity (and some other religions) in a deeply offensive manner.[55] Similarly, in *Wingrove* v. *UK*, the ECtHR upheld a refusal by the relevant broadcasting authority to classify a video depicting St Theresa in a state of sexual ecstasy as consistent with Article 10.[56] There is some evidence that the ECtHR may be prepared to reconsider some aspects of this doctrine and is moving towards a greater willingness to protect speech from restrictions in relations to sensitive matters of religion.[57]

(b) Other Regional Human Rights Instruments

The AmCHR qualifies the right to freedom of thought and expression with a prohibition on 'any advocacy of national, racial, or religious hatred that constitutes incitements to lawless violence or to any other similar action' on grounds of race, colour, religion, language, national origin, or similar status.[58] Among the duties contained in the AfCHPR is that 'to respect and consider his fellow beings without discrimination, and to maintain relations aimed at promoting, safeguarding, and reinforcing mutual respect and tolerance'.[59] For the reasons given above, there is no significant doctrine on the scope of these limitations or on free speech in general under the AmCHR, the AfCHPR or the Arab Charter. Indeed, the Arab Charter contains no right to freedom of expression, but does include a right to freedom of belief, thought, and opinion (Article 26). Article 1 of the Arab Charter also refers to the need to condemn and endeavour to eliminate all practices based on racism and Zionism.

3. The Effectiveness of International and Regional Human Rights Instruments in Protecting Extreme Speech

Parts of the explanation for the limited effectiveness of international and regional legal norms in protecting extreme speech are the same as the reasons why most such norms provide a very low level of protection for human rights generally.[60] These include, first, the fact that the system remains essentially voluntary and certain states (which are responsible for widespread human rights violations, but which are not recipients of western aid) have little incentive to subscribe to international norms. Even if they do adhere, a state may still not permit individual

---

[55] (1994) 19 EHRR 34.

[56] (1996) 24 EHRR 1.

[57] See *Gunduz* v. *Turkey* (2005) 41 EHRR 5, paras. 43–48 and *Giniewski* v. *France* (2007) 45 EHRR 23, paras. 50–2, discussed in Hare, ch. 15 in this volume.

[58] Art. 13(5) of the AmCHR.

[59] Art. 28 of the AfCHPR. For an account of free speech doctrine under the Charter, see Evans and Murray, *The African Charter* (n. 34 above), 219–25.

[60] D. Kennedy, 'The International Human Rights Movement: Part of the Problem?' (2002) 15 *Harv. Hum. Rts. J.* 101.

petition which is often the most effective way of challenging state action. Secondly, states may enter reservations to many of the substantive rights which may rob them of almost all content.[61] Thirdly, enforcement mechanisms remain weak and are generally in an advisory form with no requirement that the state should demonstrate compliance in order to remain a party to the system. Finally, many allegations of human rights violations are highly politically sensitive or compromising for the state in question.[62]

Other reasons arise from the historical background of the major human rights instruments. As stated above, the international system for human rights protection and the ECHR are very much a response to the legacy of the rise of fascism in Europe. The language of hatred and the mobilization of different media were deployed to singular effect by the authorities of Nazi Germany and this had a tangible impact on those who participated at the Nuremberg trials.

It is noteworthy that the 24 principal Nuremberg defendants (among whom were Hermann Goring and Martin Bormann (the latter in absentia)) included Julius Streicher, founding editor of *Der Stürmer*. Streicher did not hold office in the Nazi Party after 1940, but had used *Der Stürmer* as a tool for antisemitic propaganda throughout the 1930s. He was sentenced to death by hanging and the Judgment of the International Military Tribunal recorded:

For his 25 years of speaking, writing, and preaching hatred of the Jews, Streicher was widely known as "Jew-Baiter Number One". In his speeches and articles, week after week, month after month, he infected the German mind with the virus of anti-Semitism, and incited the German people to active persecution . . . Streicher's incitement to murder and extermination at the time when Jews in the East were being killed under the most horrible conditions clearly constitutes persecution on political and racial grounds in connection with war crimes, as defined by the Charter, and constitutes a crime against humanity.[63]

A further illustration is the experience of Robert H. Jackson who became a distinctive voice on the US Supreme Court after returning from his duties as Chief US Prosecutor at Nuremberg. The legacy of that experience is clear in his judgment in *Terminiello* v. *City of Chicago* in which he dissented from the majority's decision to quash Terminiello's conviction for causing offence by his speech at a mass demonstration, citing both *Mein Kampf* and Goebbels, Jackson J stated:[64]

We need not resort to speculation as to the purposes for which these tactics are calculated nor as to their consequence. Recent European history demonstrates both.

---

[61] See n. 41 above on the US reservation to the ICCPR.

[62] See Brownlie, *Principles* (n. 9 above), 556–7 and A. Cassese, *International Law*, 2nd edn. (Oxford: OUP, 2003), 386–91.

[63] See The Avalon Project at Yale Law School, Judgement: Streicher, available online at <http://www.yale.edu/lawweb/avalon/imt/proc/judstrei.htm> (last accessed 29 July 2008).

[64] 337 US 1 (1949), 23–4, 35.

Given this background, it is perhaps not surprising that those who enforce international human rights instruments and the ECHR are alive to the risk that free speech may be exercised in the interests of oppression as well as liberty.

A related, but in many ways distinct development, has been the growth of anti-discrimination norms at international and regional (and, of course, national) levels over the twentieth century.[65] It is striking that among the limited number of specific UN-sponsored Conventions and Declarations following the ICCPR are examples relating to race discrimination (CERD), the suppression of apartheid (International Convention on the Suppression and Punishment of the Crime of Apartheid (1973)), gender discrimination (Convention on the Elimination of All Forms of Discrimination Against Women (1979) (CEDAW)), and discrimination on the grounds of religion or belief (Declaration on the Elimination of All Forms of Intolerance and of Discrimination Based on Religion or Belief (1981)).[66] These documents tend to associate the suppression of speech which advocates discrimination with the realization of the goal of equality. On the basis of these and other developments, it is now strongly arguable that the protection against (at least) racial discrimination is an obligation *erga omnes*, that is, binding on all states and having the status of a peremptory norm.[67]

For all of these reasons, extreme speech (which so often emerges from those on the political far right) has been seen as alien, and to some extent antithetical, to the concerns of the international human rights movement. In light of this, it is perhaps unsurprising that in no case concerning restrictions imposed on speech has the HRC found in favour of a speaker associated with the extreme right.

These concerns are, of course, also reflected at the European level since all the largest of the early members of the Council of Europe (except the United Kingdom) had recent histories of totalitarianism and participation in genocide. The organs of the Council of Europe have often expressed their hostility towards the far right.[68] The growth of anti-discrimination norms is also paralleled at the European levels of the European Union and the Council of Europe. The principal component of the social policy of the European Union has been in the field of women's rights to equal pay and equal treatment in the

---

[65] See W. McKean, *Equality and Discrimination Under International Law* (Oxford: Clarendon Press, 1983). Lord Hoffmann, on behalf of the Privy Council, described equality before the law as 'one of the building blocks of democracy' which 'necessarily permeates any democratic constitution' and that treating like cases alike as 'a general axiom of rational behaviour' (*Matadeen* v. *Pointu* [1999] 1 AC 98, 109C-D). Lady Hale stated that the guarantee of equal treatment is 'essential to democracy' (*Ghaidan* v. *Godin-Mendoza* [2004] UKHL 30; [2004] 2 AC 557, para. 132). For an overview of the UK position, see K. Monaghan, *Equality Law* (Oxford: OUP, 2007) ch. 1.

[66] Sieghart, *International Law* (n. 1 above), 72–84.

[67] McKean, *Equality* (n. 65 above), 277–84. The ECtHR has held that discrimination on the grounds of race may constitute a breach of the prohibition on inhuman or degrading treatment (*Cyprus* v. *Turkey* (2002) 35 EHRR 731).

[68] For example, 'National Socialism is a totalitarian doctrine incompatible with democracy and human rights' (*BH, MW HP and GK* v. *Austria* Appl. No. 12774/87, 12 October 1989).

workplace.[69] The EU's concern to combat discrimination has now much expanded into the fields of race, age, disability, sexual orientation, and religion or belief.[70] The EU's initiatives of xenophobia are mentioned earlier in this chapter. Since 2001, the EU has been debating the terms of its Common Framework Decision on Racism and Xenophobia which will require EU States to take the necessary measures to ensure that inciting violence or hatred against a group on the grounds of race or religion and publicly condoning, denying, or grossly trivializing the crimes enforced by the Nuremberg Military Tribunal will be an offence.[71] As I also note above, the Council of Europe is seeking to add a more general right to be free from discrimination on a range of grounds to the list of rights contained in the ECHR.[72]

Of closer concern to free speech scholars are three distinct, but related, legal doctrines under the ECHR which have effectively prevented the Convention from safeguarding extreme speech and, as a consequence, from providing meaningful protection to a robust concept of free speech in general terms. These doctrines are addressed briefly below and are: the margin of appreciation, the interpretation adopted of the exception to Article 10 based on the 'rights of others', and Article 17 of the ECHR.

The first two of these matters are addressed extensively in the literature and can be dealt with briefly here. The margin of appreciation is described above and has attracted a great deal of justified criticism for its lack of precision as a legal concept.[73] These criticisms apply equally to free speech doctrine, but the application of the doctrine in Article 10 cases has been particularly generous where states are seeking to suppress extreme speech.[74] The flexibility of the concept of the 'rights of others' in Article 10(2) and the refusal of the ECtHR to exclude, for example, offence which may be caused to others permit the Court to limit speech in cases where the Court is unsympathetic to the motives of the speaker.[75]

---

[69] Originally Article 119 (and now Article 141) of the Treaty of Rome and Council Directives 75/117 (equal pay) and 76/207 (equal treatment) and now 2006/54 (C. Barnard, *EC Employment Law*, 3rd edn. (Oxford: OUP, 2006), 297–338). The European Court of Justice has expanded the scope of the equality principle and held that non-discrimination is a general principle of EU law (T. Tridimas, *The General Principles of EU Law*, 2nd edn. (Oxford: OUP, 2006), 59–135).

[70] Council Directives 2000/43 (race or ethnic origin) and 2000/78.

[71] Proposal for a Council Framework Decision on combating racism and Xenophobia, 8544/07, DROIPEN 34, Justice and Home Affairs Council of the European Union, Brussels, 17 April 2007. Further discussed in Whine, ch. 26 in this volume.

[72] See p. 66 above.

[73] See 'The Doctrine of the Margin of Appreciation Under the European Convention on Human Rights: Its Legitimacy in Theory and Application in Practice' (1998) 19 *Hum. Rts. L. J.* 1, and T. H. Jones, 'The Devaluation of Human Rights Under the European Convention' (1995) *Pub. L.* 430. The doctrine is defended by P. Mahoney, 'Universality versus Subsidiarity in the Strasbourg Case Law on Free Speech: Explaining Some Recent Judgments' (1997) 4 *Eur. Hum. Rts. L. Rev.* 364.

[74] Interestingly, after a brief flirtation (*Hertzberg* v. *Finland* (61/79)), the HRC has not relied on the margin of appreciation.

[75] Discussed further by Cram, ch. 16 in this volume.

Article 17 of the ECHR provides that nothing in the ECHR shall be interpreted as implying the right to engage in any activity or perform any act aimed at the destruction of any of the rights set out in the Convention.[76] This is not necessarily objectionable in itself, but it has been interpreted so widely that little room is left for extreme speech. A well-known example is *Norwood* v. *United Kingdom*.[77] Norwood was a member of the British National Party and had exhibited in the window of his house a sign depicting one of the towers of the World Trade Center in flames and a crescent and star surrounded by a prohibition sign. The poster carried the words 'Islam out of Britain' and 'Protect the British People'. He was convicted of an offence under the public order legislation and fined (a result confirmed on appeal to the Divisional Court).[78] The ECtHR declared Mr. Norwood's application under Article 10 to be inadmissible on the basis that the images he had displayed were a public attack on all Muslims in the United Kingdom and fell within Article 17:

Such a general, vehement attack against a religious group, linking the group as a whole with a grave act of terrorism, is incompatible with the values proclaimed and guaranteed by the Convention, notably tolerance, social peace and non-discrimination.[79]

For the reasons explored elsewhere in this collection,[80] this decision is contrary to free speech principle. The use made of Article 17 also demonstrates how little scope there is for reliance on Convention arguments when dealing with extreme speech. Several regrettable results flow from this. First, the ECtHR's reliance on Article 17 is incompatible with the Court's oft-repeated statements that Article 10 applies not only to speech which is favourably received, but also to that which offends, shocks, or disturbs the state or any sector of the population.[81] Secondly, the broad interpretation of Article 17 has the effect of excluding the speech in question from the protection of Article 10 altogether. This is particularly dangerous since it removes the need for the state to justify the interference with Convention rights and drastically reduces the Court's role in ensuring that any limitations are narrowly construed and convincingly established. Thirdly, the decision is contrary to earlier statements from the European Commission on Human Rights to the effect that Article 17 is strictly confined to those situations which threaten the democratic system of the state itself and even then is limited to the extent that the restriction is proportionate to the seriousness and duration of

---

[76] D. Keane, 'Attacking Hate Speech Under Article 17 of the European Convention on Human Rights' (2007) 25 *Neth. Q. Hum. Rts.* 641.

[77] Appl. No. 23131/03, 16 November 2004.

[78] *Norwood* v. *Director of Public Prosecutions* [2003] EWCH 1564 (Admin). Discussed in A. Geddis, 'Free Speech Martyrs or Unreasonable Threats to Social Peace?: 'Insulting' Expression and Section 5 of the Public Order Act 1986' [2004] *Pub. L.* 853, and I. Hare, 'Crosses, Crescents and Sacred Cows: Criminalizing Incitement to Religious Hatred' [2006] *Pub. L.* 520.

[79] N. 77 above.

[80] See Weinstein, ch. 2 in this volume.

[81] *Lingens* v. *Austria* (1986) 8 EHRR 103, para. 31 and repeated in numerous other cases.

the threat.[82] Fourthly, the decision creates a serious risk that the state will (especially in times of particular religious or cultural sensitivity) be able to restrict or prohibit with impunity the expression of unpopular views by those who do not espouse mainstream liberal positions. If this is permitted to occur, the essential contribution which pluralism, tolerance, and broadmindedness make to the definition of a democratic society under the Convention[83] is substantially negated. The Canadian Supreme Court has adopted a more mature approach in holding that extreme speech still falls within the protection of the Charter of Rights and Freedoms:

[I]t must be emphasized that the protection of extreme statements, even where they attack those principles underlying the freedom of expression, is not completely divorced from the aims of s. 2(b) of the Charter...[I]t is partly through clash with extreme and erroneous views that truth and the democratic vision remain vigorous and alive... [C]ondoning a democracy's collective decision to protect itself from certain types of expression may lead to a slippery slope on which encroachments on expression central to s. 2(b) values are permitted. To guard against such a result, the protection of communications virulently unsupportive of free expression values may be necessary in order to ensure that expression more compatible with these values is never justifiably limited.[84]

The above reasons go some way to explaining the mechanisms available to the ECtHR to prevent Article 10 being relied on by those who express extreme views. They also explain why those who wish to strengthen the protection of free speech in the United Kingdom will be disappointed if they seek to do so in reliance on international or European human rights instruments and doctrine.

4. Conclusion

There is no reason in principle why the UK courts should not develop the long-standing common law protections available to protect free speech beyond the limited baseline established by Strasbourg and international human rights bodies.[85]

---

[82] *De Becker* v. *Belgium* Appl. No. 214/56 (1958) 2 YB, para. 279. See J. Cooper and A. Marshall Williams: 'Hate Speech, Holocaust Denial and International Human Rights Law' [1999] *Eur. Hum. Rts. L. Rev.* 593, 605–7.

[83] *Lingens*, n. 81 above.

[84] *Keegstra* (n. 47 above), 765–6, *per* Dickson C.J.

[85] See the examples of common law systems in Canada, Australia, New Zealand, South Africa, and India developing the right to freedom of political expression discussed in I. Hare, 'Is the Privileged Position of Political Speech Justified?' in J. Beatson and Y. Cripps (eds.), *Freedom of Expression and Freedom of Information—Essays in Honour of Sir David Williams QC* (Oxford: Clarendon Press, 2000). There is continued controversy about the extent to which UK courts can depart from the decisions of the ECtHR interpreting the Convention (see *R* v. *Special Adjudicator, ex p Ullah* [2004] UKHL 26; [2004] 2 AC 323, para. 20 (Lord Bingham) and *Re P (AP)* [2008] UKHL 38; [2009] 1 AC 173 in which the House of Lords indicates that it may be appropriate for domestic courts to provide greater protection in some cases).

The obvious example is available in the sophisticated doctrine of the US Supreme Court under the First Amendment which has too often been rejected for historical or sociological reasons of limited relevance today.[86] This is not the place to explore the merits of US free speech doctrine, but there are two characteristics which require mention. The first is the vastly greater theoretical and principled sophistication of the Supreme Court's contribution which compares very favourably with its generally under-theorized UK equivalent.[87] However, the second and overwhelming merit of the Supreme Court's method is that it provides a structure for analysing free speech disputes which divorces judicial analysis from the merits of the speaker and their message. The Supreme Court's focus is on the nature of the restriction in question and, in particular, whether it is based on the content of the speech (which requires very powerful justification) or the viewpoint advanced by the speaker (which is almost always regarded as unconstitutional).[88] This has proved invaluable in extending protection to unpopular speakers which is itself fundamental to respecting the right to individual self-determination within the political system and to permitting free speech to play its essential invigorating role in any democracy.

[86] See I. Hare, 'Method and Objectivity in Free Speech Adjudication: Lessons from America' [2005] 54 *Int'l. & Comp. L. Q.* 49.

[87] See eg, *R (Farrakhan)* v. *Secretary of State for the Home Department* [2002] EWCA Civ 606; [2002] QB 1391, paras. 52–62 and 71–9; *Hammond* v. *DPP* [2004] EWHC 69 (Admin), and *R* v. *BBC, ex p ProLife Alliance* [2004] 1 AC 185 (on which, see I. Hare, 'Debating Abortion—The Right to Offend Gratuitously' (2003) 62 *Cambridge L. J.* 525 and E. Barendt, 'Free Speech and Abortion' [2003] *Pub. L.* 580).

[88] I. Hare, 'Method and Objectivity' (n. 86 above), 51–4 and 'Inflammatory Speech: Cross-Burning and the First Amendment' [2003] *Pub. L.* 408, 408–10; G. R. Stone, 'Content Regulation and the First Amendment' (1983) 25 *Wm. & Mary L. Rev.* 189; and P. B. Stephan, 'The First Amendment and Content Discrimination' (1982) 68 *Va. L. Rev.* 203.

4

An Overview of American Free Speech Doctrine and its Application to Extreme Speech

James Weinstein

As several papers in this volume note, the United States is an outlier in the strong protection it affords some of the most noxious forms of extreme speech imaginable.[1] Commentators are divided about whether the American approach should be adopted by other jurisdictions, a division that is reflected in this volume. In light of this controversy, a brief survey of American free speech doctrine is in order, especially as it relates to the regulation of the various forms of extreme speech considered in this book.

1. The Rule against Content Discrimination

The leitmotif of contemporary American free speech doctrine is its intense hostility to the content-based regulation of public discourse.[2] Content-based laws are ones in which the government seeks to regulate expression because of the message it conveys. Content-neutral regulations, in contrast, regulate speech for some reason unrelated to the message, such the time, place, or manner of the speech. A law forbidding anyone from speaking about abortion is content-based; one prohibiting the use of loudspeakers in residential neighbourhoods after 10.00 p.m.

---

[1] See eg, E. Heinze, 'Wild-West Cowboys versus Cheese-Eating Surrender Monkeys: Some Problems in Comparative Approaches to Hate Speech', in this volume. See also K. Boyle, 'Hate Speech: The United States Versus the Rest of the World?' (2001) 53 *Me. L. Rev.* 487; F. Schauer, 'The Exceptional First Amendment' in M. Ignatieff (ed.), *American Exceptionalism and Human Rights* (Princeton: Princeton UP, 2005).

[2] '[A]bove all else, the First Amendment means that government has no power to restrict expression because of its message, its ideas, its subject matter, or its content', *Police Dep't of Chicago* v. *Mosley* 408 US 92, 95 (1972); 'Regulations which permit the Government to discriminate on the basis of the content of the message cannot be tolerated under the First Amendment', *Regan* v. *Time, Inc.* 468 US 641, 648–49 (1984).

would be content neutral.[3] Content-based regulations come in different varieties, some worse than others from a First Amendment standpoint. The most 'egregious' type of content regulation is viewpoint discrimination.[4] Viewpoint discriminatory regulations, to quote the Supreme Court's cumbersome phrase, are ones based on 'the specific motivating ideology or the opinion or perspective of the speaker . . .'.[5] A law that prohibited anyone from proclaiming that abortion is murder, that the invasion of Iraq was unjustified, or that blacks are genetically inferior to whites would be considered viewpoint discriminatory.

A distinguishing feature of American free speech jurisprudence is that the rule against content discrimination extends not just to laws targeting particular ideas or subject matter, but also to regulations forbidding the use of highly offensive words or symbols. Thus in United States, an anti-war protestor has the right to wear a jacket in public bearing the message 'Fuck the Draft'[6] or to burn the American flag.[7] Such complete suspension of civility norms within the realm of public discourse is unique to American law.

It is crucial to note, however, that this rule against content regulation does not apply across the board to all human utterances in whatever context they may occur. To begin with, there are familiar content-based exceptions to First Amendment protection, including 'fighting words'[8] (ie, face-to-face insults), obscenity,[9] child pornography,[10] true threats,[11] and incitement to law violation that is likely to cause such conduct.[12] It is often mistakenly believed that if expression does not fall into one of these traditionally unprotected categories of speech, government is forbidden from regulating the content of the speech unless there is a compelling reason for doing so.[13] This is demonstrably not the

---

[3] For more on the distinction between content-based and content-neutral regulations, see J. Weinstein, *Hate Speech, Pornography, and the Radical Attack on Free Speech Doctrine* (Boulder, CO: Westview Press, 1999), 35–8. See also S. H. Williams, 'Content Discrimination and the First Amendment' (1991) 139 *U. Pa. L. Rev.* 615.

[4] See *Rosenberger* v. *Rector and Visitors of University of Virginia* 515 US 819, 829 (1995).

[5] Ibid.

[6] *Cohen* v. *California* 403 US 15, 26 (1971).

[7] *Texas* v. *Johnson* 491 US 397, 420 (1989).

[8] *Chaplinsky* v. *New Hampshire* 315 US 568, 572 (1942). For a discussion of the Supreme Court's 'fighting words' doctrine, see J. Weinstein, 'Extreme Speech, Public Order and Democracy: Lessons from *The Masses*', in this volume.

[9] *Miller* v. *California* 413 US 15, 36 (1973).

[10] *New York* v. *Ferber* 458 US 747, 774 (1982).

[11] *Watts* v. *United States* 394 US 705, 707 (1969).

[12] *Brandenburg* v. *Ohio* 395 US 444, 447 (1969).

[13] See eg, R. Smolla, *Smolla and Nimmer on Freedom of Speech: A Treatise on the First Amendment* § 3.03(1) (a) (Eagan, MN: Thompson/West, 1994): 'The "strict scrutiny test" is the "default standard" for measuring the content-based regulation of speech. This means that in cases in which speech is regulated on the basis of content, the strict scrutiny test will apply unless displaced by some other First Amendment standard.' The elements of the 'strict scrutiny' test are set forth in n. 20 below.

case.[14] Rather, the exceedingly rigorous protection against content discrimination applies primarily to expression on matters of public concern occurring in settings dedicated or essential to public discussion such as books, magazines, films, the Internet, or in public fora such as the speaker's corner of the park. The Supreme Court and commentators often refer to this highly protected expression as 'public discourse'.[15] In settings dedicated to some purpose other than public discourse, in contrast, such as those dedicated to effectuating government programmes in the government workplace, instruction in a state school classroom, or the administration of justice in the courtroom, the government has far greater leeway to regulate the content of speech. Thus government employees may be fired for speech disloyal to their superiors;[16] students and teachers in public schools can be commanded to stick to the subject matter of the class and to keep a civil tongue;[17] and lawyers can be fined or even imprisoned for using profanity in a judicial proceeding.[18] More controversially, the First Amendment allows the government considerable power to regulate the content of commercial advertising.[19]

The scope of the rule against content regulation is thus far narrower than many believe that it is or wish that it were. But within the relatively confined scope of its operation, the rule against content discrimination is powerful indeed. Content-based regulations of public discourse are subject to 'strict scrutiny',[20] a test that almost always leads to the invalidation of the regulation.[21] The strength and clarity of this rule yield a definite answer about whether most of the regulation of

---

[14] See F. Schauer, 'The Boundaries of the First Amendment: A Preliminary Exploration of Constitutional Salience' (2003) 117 *Harv. L. Rev.* 1765, 1768: '[E]ven the briefest glimpse at the vast universe of widely accepted content-based restrictions on communication reveals that the speech with which the First Amendment deals is the exception and the speech that may routinely be regulated is the rule.' See also Weinstein (n. 3 above), 47–9; R. C. Post, 'Recuperating First Amendment Doctrine' (1995) 47 *Stan. L. Rev.* 1249, 1276.

[15] See eg, *Hustler Magazine, Inc.* v. *Falwell* 485 US 46, 55 (1988); *Cohen* v. *California* 403 US 15, 22 (1971); R. C. Post, *Constitutional Domains: Democracy, Community and Management* (Cambridge, MA: Harvard UP, 1995) 119–78.

[16] See *Connick* v. *Myers* 461 US 138 (1983).

[17] See *Bethel Sch. Dist.* v. *Fraser* 478 US 675, 685 (1986); *Bonnell* v. *Lorenzo* 241 F 3d 800, 820–1 (6th Cir, 2001).

[18] See *Gentile* v. *State Bar of Nevada* 501 US 1030, 1071 (1991); *Zal* v. *Steppe* 968 F 2d 924, 928 (9th Cir, 1992).

[19] See *Central Hudson Gas and Electric* v. *Public Service Comm'n* 47 US 557 (1980). Though the lesser degree of protection that *Central Hudson* provides commercial speech has been vigorously criticized by commentators as well as several justices, it has not been overruled. See *Greater New Orleans Broadcasting Ass'n* v. *United States* 527 US 173, 184 (1999). See also J. Weinstein, 'Fools, Knaves and the Protection of Commercial Speech: A Response to Professor Redish' (2007) 41 *Loy. L. A. L. Rev.* 133, 133–4 n. 3.

[20] See eg, *Boos* v. *Barry* 485 US 312, 321 (1988): '[Our] cases indicate that . . . a content-based restriction on political speech in a public forum . . . must be subjected to the most exacting scrutiny. Thus, we have required the State to show that the regulation is necessary to serve a compelling state interest and that it is narrowly drawn to achieve that end.' (internal quotation marks omitted).

[21] See Weinstein (n. 3 above), 39.

'extreme speech' considered in this volume would pass muster under the First Amendment: as content-based regulation of public discourse, they would be held unconstitutional.

2. The Rule against Content Discrimination and its Application to Extreme Speech

(i) Hate Speech

Hate speech bans, generally considered acceptable in virtually every democracy other than the United States,[22] provide a good example of extreme speech regulation that would be summarily invalidated under contemporary American free speech jurisprudence. To appreciate this stark difference, let us consider how a recent British hate speech case, *Norwood* v. *DPP*,[23] would have been decided in the United States.

Shortly after the attacks on the World Trade Center on 11 September 2001, Mark Norwood, a regional coordinator of the British National Party, an extreme right wing political organization, placed a poster in the window of his flat in a small rural town bearing the words: 'Islam out of Britain' and 'Protect the British people' superimposed on a reproduction of a photograph of the World Trade Center in flames and a crescent and star surrounded by a prohibition sign.[24] Norwood was convicted of making 'abusive' and 'insulting' statements likely to cause 'harassment, alarm or distress' to another person in violation of s. 5 of the Public Order Act 1986. This violation was found to be 'racially or religiously aggravated' because 'motivated (wholly or partly) by hostility towards members of a racial or religious group based on their membership in that group'.[25] The Divisional Court upheld Norwood's conviction, finding that this expression 'went beyond legitimate protest',[26] and the European Court of Human Rights declared his application inadmissible.[27]

Suppose that shortly after the 9/11 attacks a member of a neo-Nazi organization was charged by the City of Los Angeles under an ordinance similar to the Public Order Act 1986 for placing in the window of his apartment a sign with the same background as Norwood's, but with the message 'Protect the American People—Islam out of the US'. Since the offence is based on the message conveyed by the sign—an 'insulting' statement likely to cause 'harassment, alarm, or

---

[22] See eg, *Glimmerveen & Hagenbeek* v. *Netherlands* Appl. Nos. 8348/78 and 8406/78 (1979) 18 D & R 187; *Norwood* v. *UK*, Appl. No. 23131/03, 16 November 2004. See also Heinze (n. 1 above); Schauer, (n. 1 above), 33: '[T]here appears to be a strong international consensus that the principles of freedom of expression are either overridden or irrelevant when what is being expressed is racial, ethnic, or religious hatred.'

[23] [2003] EWHC 1564 (Admin).   [24] Ibid., paras. 6–7.
[25] Ibid., paras. 1–4, 12–3.   [26] Ibid., para. 37.
[27] *Norwood* v. *UK*, n. 22 above.

distress' to others—rather than, say, on some aesthetic concern about the size of the poster—the application of the law would be considered content based.[28] Indeed, to the extent the sentence was enhanced because the expression was motivated by 'hostility towards members of a racial or religious group based on their membership in that group' the application of the ordinance would likely be regarded as viewpoint discriminatory.[29] Crucially, because the message is on a matter of public concern—what should be done to prevent further terrorist attacks—and is expressed in a setting essential to democratic self-government,[30] the poster would be considered public discourse. As such it would be immune from suppression due to its content unless the government could offer some extraordinary justification for its suppression and, in addition, could show that the regulation was both narrrowly drawn and necessary to achieve this goal.[31]

While protecting people from insult within public discourse, especially on the basis of their race, ethnicity, or religion, might be a legitimate government interest, it is certainly not a compelling one. In contrast, promoting tolerance and harmony among different groups in society and assuring vulnerable minorities that the majority does not share the extreme views about them expressed by bigots is a much more important interest that might arguably be considered 'compelling'. But as the Supreme Court has emphasized,[32] government has effective measures at its disposal other than speech suppression to accomplish these worthy goals, including engaging in its own speech to counter these odious ideas.

R.A.V. v. *City of St. Paul* documents contemporary free speech doctrine's intense hostility to viewpoint discriminatory speech regulation, including laws that attempt to suppress virulent racist expression.[33] In that case, a juvenile was convicted under a local hate speech ordinance for burning a cross on a black family's lawn.[34] (In the United States, a burning cross is a symbol of the Ku Klux

---

[28] In *Norwood* the Divisional Court interpreted the poster as advocating that all Muslims be expelled from Britain. *Norwood* (n. 23 above), para. 33.

[29] Thus laws like the UK's prohibition against threatening, abusive, or insulting words or written material intended and likely to 'stir up racial hatred' (Public Order Act 1986, part III, ss. 18, 19) or Canada's law against wilfully promoting 'hatred against any . . . section of the public distinguished by colour, race, or ethnic origin' (Canadian Criminal Code, s. 319(2)) would likely be facially invalidated as viewpoint discriminatory.

[30] See *City of Ladue* v. *Gilleo* 512 US 43, 47 (1994) in which the US Supreme Court, in invalidating a city's nearly total ban on all residential signs, refers to the practice of placing political signs in the windows of one's home as a 'venerable means of communication that is both unique and important'.

[31] See n. 20 above.

[32] See text accompanying n. 39 below.

[33] 505 US 377 (1992).

[34] The ordinance provided: 'Whoever places on public or private property a symbol, object, appellation, characterization or graffiti, including, but not limited to, a burning cross or Nazi swastika, which one knows or has reasonable grounds to know arouses anger, alarm or resentment in others on the basis of race, color, creed, religion, or gender commits disorderly conduct and shall be guilty of a misdemeanor.' St. Paul, Minn., Legis. Code § 292.02 (1990).

Klan, and when directed to a particular individual can constitute a threat that violence will ensue.[35]) Recognizing that, as drafted, the ordinance at issue was unconstitutionally overbroad because it reached protected as well as unprotected speech, the Minnesota Supreme Court construed the ordinance as applying only to 'fighting words', those face-to-face insults that the Supreme Court had long held to be beyond of the scope of First Amendment protection.[36]

Despite this limiting construction, Justice Antonin Scalia, writing for a bare majority of the Court, held that by singling out only certain fighting words for proscription, the city was engaging in unconstitutional viewpoint discrimination. As evidence of such viewpoint discrimination, the Court pointed to the Minnesota court's acknowledgement that the statute was aimed at 'messages based on virulent notions of racial supremacy' as well as the court's and the city's explanation that the statute was 'directed at expression of group hatred'.[37] Having found that the statute thus 'regulates expression based on hostility towards its protected ideological content', the Court subjected the regulation to strict scrutiny.[38] The Court acknowledged that 'ensur[ing] the basic human rights of members of groups that have been subject to discrimination, including the right of such groups to live in peace wherever they wish', was a compelling governmental interest. The Court emphasized, however, that the 'existence of adequate content-neutral alternatives' to achieve this end made this viewpoint-based restriction on speech not 'reasonably necessary' and thus unconstitutional.[39]

R.A.V. teaches two lessons. The first is that the prohibition against viewpoint discrimination is so central to the framework of American free speech doctrine that it applies not just to public discourse and other forms of protected speech, but also to speech beyond the scope of First Amendment protection. The second lesson—and the one particularly relevant to the question of the constitutionality of hate speech laws—is that the basic First Amendment precept that '[t]here is an "equality of status in the field of ideas" '[40] extends to the expression of racist ideas, including 'virulent notions of racial supremacy'.[41] Thus, under the First Amendment, the most offensive expression of racist ideology is on an equal footing with arguments for or against higher taxes, the legality of abortion, or the legitimacy of the war in Iraq.[42]

---

35 See n. 44 below.

36 *R.A.V.* (n. 33 above), 380–1.

37 Ibid., 392 (internal quotation marks omitted).

38 Ibid., 395–6.

39 Ibid.

40 *Mosley* (n. 2 above), 96 quoting A. Meiklejohn, *Political Freedom: The Constitutional Powers of The People* (New York: OUP, 1948), 27.

41 *R.A.V.* (n. 33 above), 392.

42 A few years earlier in upholding the right to burn an American flag as means of political protest, the Court stated: 'The First Amendment does not guarantee that other concepts virtually sacred to our Nation as a whole—such as the principle that discrimination on the basis of race is odious and destructive—will go unquestioned in the market-place of ideas.' *Texas* v. *Johnson* (n. 7 above), 418. See also *United States* v. *Eichman* 496 US 310, 318 (1990): 'We are aware that desecration of the flag

A subsequent cross burning case, *Virginia* v. *Black*,[43] though arguably weakening *R.A.V.'s* rule against viewpoint discriminatory regulation of *unprotected* speech, reaffirms the view that expression of racist ideas within public discourse is fully protected. Recognizing that cross burning directed at an individual, such as a cross burned on another's lawn,[44] can represent 'a particularly virulent form of intimidation', the Court allowed government to single out this subset of a category of unprotected speech ('true threats') for prohibition.[45] In doing so, however, that the Court emphasized that in other contexts, such as when displayed at a Klan rally, burning crosses are 'potent symbols of shared group identity and ideology'[46] and as such constitute 'core political speech' fully protected by the First Amendment despite the 'sense of anger or hatred' this symbol arouses.[47]

Norwood, *R.A.V.*, and *Black* all involve regulations proscribing hate speech under a public order rationale. A different ground for banning hate speech is the prevention of group defamation, traditionally on the basis of race, ethnicity, and religion (though sexual orientation has recently been added to the prohibition in several jurisdictions).[48] In 1952, the US Supreme Court upheld a group libel law

---

is deeply offensive to many. But the same might be said, for example, of virulent ethnic and religious epithets'. Thus in accordance with the suspension of civility norms described in text accompanying nn. 6–7, not only does the First Amendment protect the right to express racist ideas in public discourse, but it also protects the right to use 'virulent ethnic and religious epithets' in that context as well. A decade before the Supreme Court confirmed in *R.A.V.* that there is no hate speech exception to First Amendment protection, lower courts came to the same conclusion in upholding the right of neo-Nazi's to march in Skokie, despite the large number of Holocaust survivors who lived there. See *Collin* v. *Smith* 447 F Supp 676 (NDI11), *aff'd*, 578 F 2d 1197 (7th Cir, 1978); *Skokie* v. *Nationalist Socialist Party* 373 NE 2d 21 (Illinois S Ct, 1978). See also *Nationalist Socialist Party* v. *Skokie* 432 US 43 (1977), vacating for lack of procedural safeguards an injunction prohibiting the National Socialist Party from parading in party uniform, displaying the swastika, or distributing anti-Semitic literature.

[43] 538 US 343 (2003).

[44] 'The person who burns a cross directed at a particular person often is making a serious threat, meant to coerce the victim to comply with the Klan's wishes unless the victim is willing to risk the wrath of the Klan.' Ibid., 357.

[45] Ibid., 363. Souter, Kennedy, and Ginsburg, JJ., dissented on this point, finding the special proscription of unprotected cross burning to be inconsistent with *R.A.V.*: 'A content-based proscription of cross burning ... may be a subtle effort to ban not only the intensity of the intimidation cross burning causes when done to threaten, but also the particular message of white supremacy that is broadcast even by nonthreatening cross burning.' Ibid., 384.

[46] Ibid., 356.

[47] Ibid., 365–6 (opinion of O'Connor J., joined by Rehnquist, CJ, and Stevens and Breyer, JJ.). See also opinion of Souter, J., joined by Kennedy and Ginsburg, JJ., arguing that even when used as a threat the burning cross contains an 'ideological message of white Protestant supremacy' and thus singling the symbol out for special proscription violates the First Amendment. Ibid., 381. For further discussion of this case, see I. Hare, 'Inflammatory Speech: Cross Burning and the First Amendment' [2003] *Pub. L.* 408.

[48] See eg, s. 130 of the German Penal Code, prohibiting 'attacks on human dignity by insulting, maliciously maligning, or defaming segments of the population'; and s. 137(c) of the Dutch Criminal Code, which forbids 'deliberately giv[ing] public expression to views insulting to a group of persons on account of their race, religion or conviction or sexual preference'.

in *Beauharnais* v. *Illinois*.[49] This decision has never formally been overruled. However, the extension of First Amendment protection to libellous statements on matters of public concern to the extent necessary to ensure that defamation laws do not impede 'uninhibited, robust, and wide-open' debate on public issues[50] has sapped this decision of vitality.[51] As Judge Richard Posner has recently observed: '[T]hough *Beauharnais*...has never been overruled, no one thinks the First Amendment would today be interpreted to allow group defamation to be prohibited'.[52]

(ii) Incitement to terrorism, Holocaust denial, and other forms of extreme speech

In addition to hate speech, others types of extreme speech are likely to be afforded greater constitutional protection in the United States than in other democracies. A particularly topical example is speech that promotes terrorism. In the United States, speakers engaged in public discourse may not be punished for advocating criminal activity or violence, including terrorism, unless the government can show that this advocacy is both 'directed to inciting or producing imminent lawless action' and 'is likely to incite or produce such action'.[53] Under this standard, a

---

[49] 343 US 250 (1952). The law at issue prohibited the publication of any material that 'portrays depravity, criminality, unchastity, or lack of virtue of a class of citizens, of any race, color, creed or religion which...exposes [such] citizens...to contempt, derision or obloquy'. See ibid., 251.

[50] *New York Times* v. *Sullivan* 376 US 254, 270, 279–80 (1964), holding that a public official may not recover damages for a defamatory statement relating to his official conduct unless he proves that the statement was made with knowledge that it was false or with reckless disregard of whether it was false or not. See also *Gertz* v. *Robert Welch, Inc* 418 US 323, 349 (1974), forbidding imposition of liability in a defamation suit brought by a private person regarding false statements on a matter of public concern without a finding of fault and proof of actual damages.

[51] See eg, *Am. Booksellers Ass'n Inc.* v. *Hudnut* 771 F 2d 323, 331 n.3 (7th Cir, 1985), noting that a previous decision of this court had 'concluded that cases such as *New York Times v. Sullivan* had so washed away the foundations of *Beauharnais* that it could not be considered authoritative'.

[52] *Nuxoll* v. *Indian Prairie School Dist.* 523 F 3d 668, 672 (7th Cir, 2008). For a more detailed discussion of why *Beauharnais* is no longer good law, see Weinstein (n. 3 above), 56–9; Post (n. 15 above), 112–3.

[53] *Brandenburg* (n. 12 above), 447. The defendant in *Brandenburg* was a leader of the Ku Klux Klan who proclaimed that 'some revengeance' might have to be taken if the federal government kept oppressing the white race. He made this statement at a Klan rally at which a cross was burned and derogatory statements about blacks and Jews were made by other participants; in another speech the defendant himself said 'I believe the nigger should be returned to Africa, the Jew returned to Israel.' Ibid. 446–7 and and n. 1. Because of the cross burning and the racist remarks, it is commonly though mistakenly believed that *Brandenburg* held that hate speech is protected by the First Amendment. See eg, J. Waldron, 'Free Speech & the Menace of Hysteria', 55 *New York Review of Books*, 28 May 2008, claiming that *Brandenburg* 'held that hate speech, like seditious speech, is protected' unless it meets the test established in that case. The defendant in *Brandenburg*, however, was not charged under a hate speech statute but under the Ohio Criminal Syndicalism statute for 'advocat[ing]...the duty, necessity, or propriety of crime, sabotage, violence, or unlawful methods of terrorism as a means of accomplishing industrial or political reform'. See Brandenburg (n. 12 above), 444–5. Thus, the question of whether hate speech was protected by the First Amendment was not at issue in that case, and in holding the Ohio statute unconstitutional because it punished 'mere advocacy' of criminal activity, the Court said nothing about that issue.

provision such as Britain's recent law making it a crime intentionally or recklessly to publish a statement 'that is likely to be understood by some or all of the members of the public to whom it is published as a direct or indirect encouragement' to commit acts of terrorism[54] would be unconstitutional. Similarly, laws that restrict public discourse to protect religious sensibilities or laws against blasphemy, though constitutionally permissible in Europe,[55] would founder on the First Amendment's rule against content and viewpoint discrimination.[56]

It is also fairly certain that restrictions prohibiting Holocaust denial enacted in Germany, France, and Austria and upheld both domestically[57] and by the European Court of Human Rights,[58] would be found unconstitutional in the United States.[59] The Supreme Court has sent mixed signals about whether false statements of fact in public discourse are inherently valuable or are protected only for pragmatic reasons such as creating 'breathing space' for true factual statements.[60] But whatever the reason, modern First Amendment doctrine has

---

Though demonstrably not a hate speech case, *Brandenburg's* strong protection of advocacy of lawless conduct does severely limit a rationale often invoked for the suppression of hate speech: it would forbid government from banning hate speech because it fears that the expression of racist ideas might persuade people to illegally discriminate against minorities or even to commit violence against them, unless it could be proved that the speech in question 'is directed to inciting or producing imminent lawless action and is likely to incite or produce such action'. *Brandenburg* thus leaves room only for an extremely narrow hate speech statute aimed at the persuasive effect of the speech. And even this tiny bit of constitutional space is likely closed by *R.A.V's* proscription against viewpoint discriminatory regulation of unprotected speech.

[54] Terrorism Act 2006, s. 1.

[55] See eg, *Wingrove* v. *UK* (1997) 24 EHRR 1; *Otto Preminger Institut* v. *Austria* (1994) 19 EHRR 34.

[56] Indeed, decades before the rule against content discrimination was formalized, the Supreme Court protected the right of a Jehovah's witness to play a phonograph recording on the streets of a predominately Catholic neighbourhood attacking all organized religion, but particularly the Roman Catholic Church, as 'the instruments of Satan'. See *Cantwell v. Connecticut* 310 US 296, 309 (1940). A prohibition of blasphemy, especially a law protecting one particular religion as was the case with UK's recently repealed blasphemy law (discussed in I. Hare, 'Blasphemy and Incitement to Religous Hatred: Free Speech Dogma and Doctrine', in this volume,) would also likely violate the anti-establishment provision of the First Amendment.

[57] See eg, the decision of the *Bundesgerichtshof,* Germany's Constitutional Court, BGHZ 75, 160, 162–3 (1980), discussed in D. Grimm, 'The Holocaust Denial Decision of the Federal Constitutional Court of Germany', in this volume.

[58] See eg, *Garaudy* v. *France* Appl. No. 65831/01 (2003); *H, W, P & K* v. *Austria* Appl. No. 12774/87 (1989) 62 D & R 216.

[59] For an excellent discussion of the First Amendment obstacles to proscribing Holocaust denial, see J. D. Varat, 'Deception and the First Amendment: A Central, Complex, and Somewhat Curious Relationship' (2006) 53 *UCLA L. Rev.* 1107, 1116–9.

[60] Compare *Sullivan* (n. 50 above), 279 n. 19: 'Even a false statement may be deemed to make a valuable contribution to public debate, since it brings about "the clearer perception and livelier impression of truth, produced by its collision with error"', citing J. S. Mill, *On Liberty* (Oxford: Blackwell, 1947),15 and J. Milton, 'Areopagitica', in *Prose Works*, Vol. II (New Haven, CT: Yale, 1959), 561, with *Gertz* (n. 50 above), 340: 'there is no constitutional value in false statements of fact. Neither the intentional lie nor the careless error materially advances society's interest in uninhibited, robust, and wide-open debate on public issues' (citation and internal quotation marks omitted).

extended considerable protection to false factual statements in public discourse.[61] Thus for a mixture of theoretical and practical reasons, the Court would probably find that the most salient harm caused by Holocaust denial that government can legitimately address[62]—the infliction of psychic injury on Holocaust survivors and their families—is not weighty enough to justify the suppression of even false statements within public discourse.[63]

3. Methodological Differences

American free speech doctrine differs from that of other democracies not just in substance and result, but also in its form and texture. Whereas other jurisdictions tend to employ soft, flexible standards that balance the free speech interest at issue in a particular case against the government's interest in suppressing the speech,[64] American doctrine is characterized by hard-edged, determinative rules.[65] As a general jurisprudential matter, rigid rules and flexible standards each has its strengths and weaknesses: inflexible rules supply certainty and confine discretion, but their rigidity can sometimes lead to results contrary to their underlying purpose; flexible standards, in contrast, provide individualized justice and can avoid perverse outcomes, but tend to create uncertainty and allow law enforcement officials and judges to smuggle their own ideology into the analysis.

Whatever the merits of flexible standards in other areas of the law, with respect to free speech doctrine, the Supreme Court has decided in light of long experience[66] in favour of rules which are 'hard, conventional, difficult to evade'.[67] This

---

[61] See text accompanying nn. 50–1 above.

[62] Justifying suppression of false statements in public discourse on the grounds that the audience might be misled into believing the Holocaust did not occur would likely be deemed inconsistent with the basic precept that when addressed as the ultimate governors of society engaged in public discourse, the audience must be considered rational and autonomous agents able to discern truth from lies. See J. Weinstein, 'Speech Categorization and the Limits of First Amendment Formalism: Lessons from *Nike v. Kasky*' (2004) 54 *Case W. Res. L. Rev.* 1091, 1104–5, esp. n. 64.

[63] In addition, any law that specifically outlawed Holocaust denial on this rationale might well run into the *R.A.V.* problem of underinclusiveness discussed above.

[64] See eg, Schauer (n. 1 above), 31, contrasting the American emphasis on 'rule-based categorization' to the 'more flexible and open-ended balancing approach that generally rides under the banner of "proportionality"' that mark the approach of the Canadian, South African, and European courts; E. Barendt, 'Freedom of Expression in the United Kingdom Under the Human Rights Act 1998' [2008] NZLR 243, 261.

[65] See I. Hare, 'Method & Objectivity in Free Speech Adjudication: Lessons from America' (2005) 54 *Int'l & Comp. L. Q.* 49, 61–78; J. Weinstein, 'Free Speech, Abortion Access, and the Problem of Judicial Viewpoint Discrimination' (1996) 29 *U.C. Davis L. Rev.* 471, 481–5.

[66] Primarily decades of experience with the uncertain 'clear and present danger test' that failed adequately to protect dissent from the onslaught of popular sentiment. See Weinstein (n. 3 above), 16–26.

[67] Letter from Learned Hand to Zechariah Chafee, Jr., 2 January 1921, reprinted in G. Gunther, 'Learned Hand and the Origins of Modern First Amendment Doctrine: Some Fragments of History' (1975) 27 *Stan. L. Rev.* 719, 770.

preference is based on the importance of people knowing with adequate certainty what they can safely say and the need to confine the discretion of law enforcement officials. In defending the rigidity of the rule against content discrimination, Justice Sandra Day O'Connor wrote:

But though our rule has flaws, it has substantial merit as well. It is a rule, in an area where fairly precise rules are better than more discretionary and more subjective balancing tests. On a theoretical level, it reflects important insights into the meaning of the free speech principle—for instance, that content-based speech restrictions are especially likely to be improper attempts to value some forms of speech over others, or are particularly susceptible to being used by the government to distort public debate.[68]

4. Conclusion

It is interesting to contemplate why American First Amendment doctrine affords extreme speech greater protection than does the free speech jurisprudence of other democracies.[69] Perhaps it is because Americans have a greater distrust of government. Or perhaps the difference stems from American law's deep and abiding natural rights tradition, in contrast to the more utilitarian views that predominate in many other democracies. But whatever role such profound cultural differences might play, a key part of the explanation is more prosaic: the nearly a century of experience that courts in the United States have had in formulating free speech doctrine, a wealth of experience that the courts of no other nation can come close to matching. Profoundly influencing contemporary doctrine is the Supreme Court's dismal failure during the first half of the twentieth century to protect speech that must be allowed in any democratic society, such as the right to protest against the nation's involvement in a war[70] or to radically critique the country's economic and political foundations.[71] So what might look like senseless overprotection of speech to many Europeans (and many Americans as well), in fact reflects hard-learned lessons about what is needed to adequately protect the right of dissent in a democratic society.

---

[68] *City of Ladue* v. *Gilleo* (n. 30 above), 60.

[69] For an excellent discussion of the reasons that may underlie American free speech exceptionalism, see Schauer (n. 1 above), 43–53.

[70] See eg, *Debs* v. *US* 249 US 211 (1919), upholding the conviction of Socialist presidential candidate Eugene Debs for obstructing the draft for giving a speech in which he praised draft resisters.

[71] See *Dennis* v. *United States* 341 US 494 (1951), upholding the convictions of leaders of the American Communist party for teaching Marxist doctrine in violation of the Smith Act's prohibition against conspiracy to advocate the violent overthrow of the United States government. For a more detailed discussion of how the failure of First Amendment doctrine to protect dissent during the first half of the twentieth century led to the construction of more protective doctrine in the latter part of that century, see Weinstein (n. 8 above).

5

Hate Speech in the United Kingdom: An Historical Overview

Sir David Williams QC

'Hate speech' has been described by one writer as 'the generic term that has come to embrace the use of speech attacks based on race, ethnicity, religion, and sexual orientation or preference'.[1] In the United States the legal battles over hate speech have highlighted several First Amendment issues, with the effect of permitting regulation 'in only a small number of closely confined circumstances' including, for instance, 'restrictions on fighting words that present a clear and present danger of violence'.[2]

In the United Kingdom, where we have only recently seen the formal incorporation of the European Convention on Human Rights into domestic law, issues of 'hate speech' have arisen over the centuries in a variety of contexts. There is no accepted generic term to embrace the battles of the past, and the restrictions which have arisen emerged from many statutes as well as from the common law itself. A number of surviving laws impinging on free speech have been modified and changed or have fallen into disuse.[3] Eric Barendt pointed to one example when he stated that the survival of sedition as a common law crime 'has only been rendered tolerable in Britain and other Commonwealth jurisdictions by numerous refinements and qualifications'.[4]

There were few efforts in the last century to invoke sedition in the courts of the United Kingdom, and it was only in the early years of the century that a trial judge was confident enough to assert that it 'is a weapon that is not often taken down from the armoury in which it hangs, but it is a necessary accompaniment to

---

[1] R. A. Smolla, *Free Speech in an Open Society* (New York: Knopf, 1992), 152. Professor Smolla devoted ch. 6 of his book to 'Hate Speech: Tolerating Intolerance'.

[2] Ibid., 167.

[3] See I. Brownlie and D. G. T. Williams, 'Judicial Legislation in Criminal Law' 1964 (42) *Can. Bar Rev.* 561, 578–90.

[4] *Freedom of Speech*, 2nd edn. (Oxford: OUP, 2005), paperback edn. 2007, 163. See D. Feldman, *Civil Liberties and Human Rights in England and Wales*, 2nd edn., (Oxford: OUP, 2002), 897–98. Now abolished by s. 73 of the Coroners and Justice Act 2009.

every civilized government'.[5] Given the uncertain bounds of the offence of sedition, it is not surprising that it was rarely invoked, but the corollary of its decline was parliamentary readiness to intervene by statute to combat particular manifestations of what might have been covered by the common law offence.

Offences of incitement have arisen in different contexts. The Incitement to Mutiny Act 1797 was enacted in the wake of naval mutinies. It was rarely invoked, though it was revived in the context of industrial disputes early on in the last century, and it was finally repealed in 1998. Still on the books but rarely invoked are the Incitement to Disaffection Act 1934, which was also aimed at protecting members of the armed forces, and—now enshrined in section 91 of the Police Act 1996—the offence of inciting disaffection among the police. None of these specific offences necessarily raises questions of hate speech, but the potential is there as it is with the wider offences built around threatening, abusive, and insulting words or behaviour which were provided for in the Public Order Act 1936 and are now in the Public Order Act 1986. In an apparent prosecution for hate speech in *Jordan* v. *Burgoyne*,[6] the defendant was convicted because of claims at a public meeting that 'Hitler was right' and remarks about 'world Jewry'; but the parliamentary response was to seek a further crime of incitement to racial hatred.

The first statute to provide for incitement to racial hatred was in 1965, but the process of enactment was slow and there were many arguments against such a law based on difficulties of definition, on problems about discretion in prosecutions, and on misgivings from the standpoint of free speech.[7] *The Times* commented in a leading article that the new offence departed from the principle that the law 'does not concern itself immediately with the content of speeches or writings or with the opinions they parade; it does concern itself with their probable effects on public order'.[8] Gladstone, in his first term as Prime Minister, had adhered to the same principle when, in the face of an outburst of republican sentiments, he referred to 'a great and just unwillingness' in the United Kingdom 'to interfere with the expression of any opinion that is not attended with danger to the public peace'.[9] It is significant that from the outset the law on racial incitement has been expressly linked to public order legislation—which at first sight might seem incongruous but could nevertheless influence the decision whether or not to prosecute.

Where the offence of racial incitement could be interpreted as a further effort to give substance to the general concept of sedition as developed through the common law, the offence of incitement to religious hatred has emerged from the

---

[5] *R* v. *Aldred* (1909) 22 Cox CC I. The defendant wrote about the trial in *Rex* v. *Aldred* (Glasgow: Strickland Press, 1948), and the comment by the trial judge (Coleridge J.) is quoted at 10.

[6] [1963] 2 QB 744. See Barendt's comments in n. 4 above, 299.

[7] See D. G. T. Williams, 'Racial Incitement and Public Order' (1966) *Crim. L. Rev.* 320.

[8] 31 May 1963, 13.

[9] Parl. Deb., 3rd series, Vol. 205, cc. 574–5, 24 March 1871.

evolution and narrowing of the offence of blasphemy. In his preface to a comprehensive study of the law of blasphemy, Leonard W. Levy commented that the subject 'forms the basis, at least implicitly, for a study of the struggle for intellectual liberty in general and religious liberty in particular'.[10] In a careful analysis of blasphemous libel, David Feldman recognized the enormous difficulty of definition—it 'can be said, as a rough guide, that matter is blasphemous if it denies the truth of Christian doctrine, or of the Bible, or vilifies God or Jesus, in terms of wanton and unnecessary profanity which are likely to shock and outrage the feelings of ordinary Christians'[11]—and the enormous difficulty of selecting appropriate occasions when prosecutions might be undertaken.[12] The Law Commission reported on blasphemy in 1985 and, recognizing the almost insuperable difficulties, it proposed the abolition of the offence; and a majority of the Commissioners declined to recommend a statutory replacement such as an offence of inciting religious hatred.[13]

The events of 11 September 2001, however, stimulated strong pressure for legislation introducing an offence of religious incitement. There had been such an offence in Northern Ireland since 1970,[14] but it was now proposed that there should be such an offence elsewhere in the United Kingdom. A provision for this was inserted in the Anti-terrorism, Crime, and Security Bill 2001 but it was dropped during the parliamentary proceedings after objections based on problems of enforcement were raised. The idea was not dropped, however, and it was discussed at length by a Select Committee of the House of Lords which reported in 2003.[15] Thereafter there were new attempts to legislate, and these finally resulted in only modified success in the Racial and Religious Hatred Act 2006. The House of Lords, in its legislative capacity, persuaded the House of Commons to accept significant amendments of the original proposals.[16] Nevertheless there is now an offence of incitement to religious hatred on the books, adding to a line of crimes of incitement which have crept in after the decline of both sedition and blasphemy.

Even a brief survey, such as this, of the emergence of common law and statute law in the context of what might be loosely described as 'hate speech', does

---

[10] *Blasphemy, Verbal Offence against the Sacred, from Moses to Salman Rushdie* (New York: Knopf, 1993), x.

[11] See n. 4 above, 907.

[12] Ibid., 907–21.

[13] The Law Commission (Law Com. No. 145), Criminal Law: Offences against Religion and Public Worship, HC 442 (18 June 1985). A detailed history of the offence appears in the Law Commission's Working Paper No 79, Offences against Religion and Public Worship (April 1981), 2.2 to 2.25 and 3.1 to 3.9.

[14] See P. M. Leopold, 'Incitement to Hatred—The History of a Controversial Criminal Offence' (1977) *Pub. L.* 389, 399–402; B. Hadfield, 'The Prevention of Incitement to Religious Hatred—An Article of Faith?' (1984) 35 *N. Ir. Legal Q.* 231.

[15] Religious Offences in England and Wales, HL Paper 95–1, 10 April 2003.

[16] I. Hare, 'Crosses, Crescents and Sacred Cows: Criminalising Incitement to Religious Hatred' (2006) *Pub. L.* 521, 524. Blasphemy offences were abolished by statute in 2008.

remind one of the unavoidable issues of free speech and democracy. Reference has already been made to Gladstone's cautionary remarks about the undesirability of restrictions on free speech in the absence of danger to the public peace.[17] He added that we should trust 'the notorious good sense and loyalty of the mass of the people' and that we should avoid giving false importance to those responsible for foolish opinions. Moreover, when there are problems of scope and definition, as there are in racial incitement and more vividly in religious incitement, there can be a 'chilling effect' or 'self-censorship motivated by fear that robust expressions of opinion may be judged to have overstepped an undefined boundary and become the subject of prosecution'.[18] In the parliamentary debates which led to the Race Relations Act 1965, introducing a new offence of racial incitement, a former Home Secretary spoke of the 'age-old battle' to say 'distasteful, unacceptable, provocative, antagonistic things'.[19] This assertion was echoed judicially by Lord Justice Sedley when he said that free speech allowed for 'not only the inoffensive but the irritating, the contentious, the eccentric, the heretical, the unwelcome and the provocative provided it does not tend to provoke violence'.[20]

The arguments about free speech have been considered in the context of both racial and religious incitement.[21] There are those who claim that to have laws on such incitement is important symbolically, even if prosecutions are rare; but there is the risk of legislating in response to a particular emergency or challenge and then retaining or adapting the legislation in different circumstances altogether. In addition, it is unwise to legislate as almost a panic reaction to unexpected events or new perceptions. The law relating to public order and freedom of expression generally is sufficient to meet the unexpected, and additions to the law need full consultation and consideration before legislation is undertaken.

---

[17] See n. 9 above.

[18] Report of the Select Committee of the House of Lords (n. 15 above), para. 82, 26.

[19] Parl. Deb., House of Commons, Vol. 711, cc. 966–8, 3 May 1965 (Henry Brooke).

[20] *Redmond-Bate* v. *Director of Public Prosecutions* (1999) *Crim. L. Rev.* 998, 999. The case concerned police action to stop three women preaching on the steps of Wakefield Cathedral before a crowd of people, some of whom were hostile.

[21] See eg, Barendt (n. 4 above), ch. 5; n. 16 above, 526–38; Sir D. Williams, 'Toleration, Religion and the Law', in *Civilisations and Public Law, Vol. LXXIX* (Athens: European Public Law Center, 2005), 523, 533–5. The latter article covers similar ground to that covered in this chapter.

6

Extreme Speech and Liberalism

Maleiha Malik

1. Introduction

There have been a number of high profile attempts at criminalizing 'extreme speech' in the last five years, many of which were a response to the post-September 11 political context. First, there was the attempt to criminalize hate speech against Muslims (who were not fully protected by incitement to racial hatred legislation) by introducing incitement to religious hatred legislation.[1] There have also been more direct attempts to focus on 'extreme' political speech through the criminalization of speech that can be said to be a 'glorification of terrorism' (which have now been enacted in the Terrorism Act 2006). For example, section 1 of the Terrorism Act introduces an offence of encouragement of terrorism which is defined as applying to statements that are likely to be understood by members of the public as inducement to acts of terrorism, and inducement is further defined as glorification of terrorism.[2] There have been mixed motives in the move towards criminalizing 'hate speech' in recent times.

---

[1] K. Goodall, 'Incitement to Religious Hatred: All Talk and No Substance?' (2007) 70(1) *Modern L. Rev.* 89.

[2] Terrorism Act 2006, s. 1 states, *inter alia*: 'This section applies to a statement that is likely to be understood by some or all of the members of the public to whom it is published as a direct or indirect encouragement or other inducement to them to the commission, preparation, or instigation of acts of terrorism or Convention offences.'

S. 1(2): 'A person commits an offence if—(a) he publishes a statement to which this section applies or causes another to publish such a statement; and (b) at the time he publishes it or causes it to be published, he—(i) intends members of the public to be directly or indirectly encouraged or otherwise induced by the statement to commit, prepare, or instigate acts of terrorism or Convention offences; or (iii) is reckless as to whether members of the public will be directly or indirectly encouraged or otherwise induced by the statement to commit, prepare, or instigate such acts or offences.'

S. 1(3): 'For the purposes of this section, the statements that are likely to be understood by members of the public as indirectly encouraging the commission or preparation of acts of terrorism or Convention offences include every statement which—(a) glorifies the commission or preparation (whether in the past, in the future or generally) of such acts or offences; and (b) is a statement from which those members of the public could reasonably be expected to infer that what is being glorified is being glorified as conduct that should be emulated by them in existing circumstances.'

On the one hand, the introduction of a new offence of incitement to religious hatred was motivated by a desire to protect vulnerable Muslim minorities from hate speech. On the other hand, there was a simultaneous impetus to regulate the speech of some Muslims that was deemed to be 'extremist' because of its advocacy of illiberal ideas or because it offered public support for acts of political violence by non-state actors in Britain and abroad. Within this debate there was very little discussion about what constitutes 'extreme speech'. Nor was there any detailed discussion of whether the use of the criminal law could deliver the goals of (a) protecting minorities against 'extreme' hate speech; or (b) deterring minorities from 'extreme' speech that could be said to constitute 'glorification of terrorism'.

Contemporary discussions about 'extreme speech' have tended to focus on whether it is appropriate to use the criminal law to regulate speech or on the extension of incitement to racial hatred provisions to cover religious groups. This discussion has left two important gaps. First of all, it has failed to analyse how liberal democracies can identify 'extremist speech'. Secondly, this debate has neglected to consider whether there are non-legal responses to 'extreme speech' which are a more appropriate response than legal regulation. This article undertakes an exploratory discussion of these often neglected topics in discussions about extreme speech in liberal democracies. Section 2 makes more explicit the often implicit assumption that we can easily identify 'extremists' in liberal democracies. Section 3 goes on to examine the application of legal and non-legal regulation to the problem of extreme speech. Finally, section 4 sets out a policy of 'engaging with extremists' as an alternative to the legal regulation of extreme speech.

2. 'Who are the Extremists?'

On what basis can a liberal democracy deem certain viewpoints or ideas to be 'extremist'? What does it mean for an individual or group to be 'extremist'? Contemporary academic and media commentators use 'extremist' in their discussions with great confidence. However, the term 'extremist' remains surprisingly under-theorized. There is some discussion of extremist politics in liberal democracies in the context of the rise of fascism and communism in twentieth-century Europe.[3] Whether or not an individual or a group is extreme will depend on the comparator against which they are being evaluated, that is, extremism is a relational concept. It follows that the norm against which the ideas, values, or conduct of the group is being compared is a critical part of the analysis of whether or not they are 'extremist'. In Western democracies, the obvious comparator is

---

[3] G. Capoccia, *Defending Democracy: Reactions to Extremism in Interwar Europe* (Baltimore: John Hopkins UP, 2005).

provided by the common consensus that politics should be governed by the principles of liberal democracy.

In this chapter, I set out some reservations about the naïve appeal to liberal democracy as the panacea in the search for 'common values'. Despite these reservations, there are good reasons for looking to liberalism as the comparator against which to define extremism. There is a considerable consensus that common public life and political values in Western states must take the principles of liberal democracy as foundational political values. Moreover, the motivation to engage with illiberal doctrines is justified from within the paradigm of liberalism: that is, it is based on the liberal premise that political principles should command the consent of all citizens. Therefore, in this analysis the core values of liberal democracy are taken as the normative standard against which extremism is defined. These core values include the well-established individual civil and political rights as set out in human rights and constitutional documents, for example, freedom from torture, freedom of expression, freedom of association, and freedom from arbitrary discrimination. These are individual rights and norms. How easily can they be applied in the context of groups that reject liberal principles?

Liberal theory is more comfortable dealing with the individual action of a one-off extremist individual. This may be easier to tolerate because he or she can be seen to be solitary figure. Once we move from the solitary figure to an organized group, there is a subtle shift in the analysis. A social or political group that is perceived to be 'extremist' raises distinct and difficult issues because it is seen to be a viable challenge to social and political power.[4] Moreover, collective action is a more difficult conceptual category for liberal politics, although recent work by theorists has provided a more complex structure within which to analyse groups.[5] However, as stated earlier, this focus on individual rights needs to be translated into an analysis that can be applied to groups. One source for this transformation from the individual to the group is the work of writers such as Benhabib who have identified three core values taken to be foundational norms which should bind groups in a liberal democracy:[6]

(1) Egalitarian reciprocity: Women, and members of cultural, religious, linguistic, and other minorities must not, in virtue of their membership status, be entitled to lesser degrees of civil, political, economic, and cultural rights than the majority.

---

[4] M. Walzer, *On Toleration* (London: Yale UP, 1997), 8–9.

[5] See eg, the work of Joseph Raz, who includes community within his account of what constitutes an autonomous life, in *The Morality of Freedom* (Oxford: Clarendon Press, 1988). An alternative approach to the analysis of groups in political theory is the work of Iris Marion Young, who argues that the concept of justice needs to be re-cast to include the way in which special types of injustice such as, inter alia, oppression and cultural alienation have a more significant impact on some social groups. See *Justice and the Politics of Difference* (Princeton, NJ: Princeton UP, 1990).

[6] S. Benhabib, *The Claims of Culture: Equality and Diversity in the Global Era* (Princeton, NJ: Princeton UP, 2002), 19.

(2) Voluntary self-ascription: Group membership must permit maximal forms of self-identification and self-ascription possible. Such self-identification may be contested, but the state should not grant the right to define and control group membership to the group alone.

(3) Freedom of exit and association: There must be unrestricted freedom to exit from the group, although such exit may be accompanied by loss of certain group privileges.

These three principles serve a number of important functions in this analysis of how liberal democracy should engage with extremists. First, these principles act as a marker for determining whether or not a particular group is 'extreme'. Of course, the degree of deviation from these norms will vary depending on the precise nature of group. Many groups that draw their ideas from non-liberal political traditions or from traditional cultures and religions will often breach the first principle. Some may go even further and breach the second and third principle: they may seek to restrict the ability to join and identify with the group; and they may seek to prevent individuals from leaving the group. This spectrum usefully provides a way of distinguishing between different types of groups. It also provides a mechanism for tracking movement within a group from more 'extreme' to 'mainstream' political values. Second, these three principles are a pre-condition to any group entering into public discourse in a liberal democracy. They also, therefore, provide an agreed procedural framework within which there can be public engagement with extremist groups. Finally, these principles set the minimal standard of protection that the State must guarantee for vulnerable individuals within groups, for example, women and children. They apply even in those cases where an illiberal social group does not want to participate in main-stream society. For example, the mistreatment of women by individuals within a group is already unlawful. In addition, a group that mistreats women may also be in breach of the principle of egalitarian reciprocity which could in turn act as a trigger for State regulation of the group to protect the individual rights of its women citizens.

3. Legal and Non-Legal Responses to Extreme Speech

(i) Criminalizing Extreme Speech: The Limits of Legal Regulation

There has been a criminal offence of incitement to racial hatred since the early race relations legislation (Race Relations Act 1965, section 6). This was introduced against a background of increased post-war immigration from the Commonwealth, and the prospect of the rise of a far-right political movement and later Powellism.[7]

---

[7] For discussion, see A. Lester and G. Bindman, *Race and Law* (Harmondsworth: Penguin, 1972), 344–60 and 417–8.

Here, it is worth observing that the recurring theme of race as a 'public order' problem, rather than a concern with the rights of dignities of minorities, provided the background for the early regulation of racist speech. This concern with public order is reflected in the language and context of the early incitement offence which, as commentators have noted, shared a lineage with the earlier common law offences of sedition and mischief which also focused on (i) intention; (ii) raising discontent amongst those to whom the speech is addressed; and (iii) promoting hostility between different classes of such subjects.[8] The current offence of incitement to racial hatred draws on these roots and is now explicitly placed within the context of public order (Public Order Act 1986 (POA), sections 17–23). There have been very few prosecutions under these provisions. Under the original legislation, it was essential that the incitement to hatred was within Britain. This jurisdictional limiting condition was removed by the Anti-terrorism, Crime, and Security Act 2001.[9] The removal of this jurisdictional limit has meant that it has been possible to prosecute those who have called for the killing of members of a racial group outside Britain. Incitement to religious hatred is prohibited under the Public Order (Northern Ireland) Order 1987, although there have not been a significant number of prosecutions under this provision either.[10]

A central issue in understanding the protection afforded by the current incitement to racial hatred provisions has been the groups that are protected under these provisions. The POA provisions on incitement to racial hatred have replicated the definition of racial group that was developed in *Mandla* v. *Dowell Lee*,[11] with the consequence that they have also replicated the anomalies of that definition which cover ethnic religious minorities (for example, Jews and Sikhs) but not non-ethnic, religious minorities (for example, Rastafarians and Muslims). Since 11 September, in the light of clear evidence of increasing prejudice and hostility against Muslims,[12] as well as organized far-right activity that targeted Muslims for attack, this anomaly has become even more problematic. It is worth observing that politically organized racists had clearly responded to this loophole and the events of 11 September and 7 July to target Muslims for hatred and violence.[13] Despite the application of this anomaly, there is also case law that

---

[8] I. Hare, 'Crosses, Crescents and Sacred Cows: Criminalising Incitement to Religious Hatred' (2006) *Pub. L.* 521. Hare notes this overlap and cites Stephen's definition of sedition which includes 'an intention [. . .] to raise discontent or disaffection amongst Her Majesty's subjects, or to promote feelings of ill-will and hostility between different classes of such subjects', 522.

[9] S. 37 that 'In section 17 of the Public Order Act 1986 (c. 64) (racial hatred defined by reference to a group of persons)'.

[10] See T. Murphy, 'Incitement to Hatred: Lessons from Northern Ireland', in S. Coliver (ed.), *Sriking a Balance: Hate Speech, Freedom of Expression and Non-Discrimination* (Essex: Art. 19, 1992).

[11] [1983] 2 AC 548.

[12] D. Abrams and D. M. Houston, 'Equality, Diversity and Prejudice in Britain', Report for the Cabinet Office Equalities Review 2006, Centre for the Study of Group Processes (Kent: Univ Kent, 2006).

[13] See analysis of the anti-Muslim politics of the BNP in Goodall (n. 1 above) 94.

suggests that anti-Muslim incitement could still fall within the definition of 'racial hatred' under the current legislation.[14]

The European Court of Human Rights' (ECtHR) analysis of the overlap between racial and religious hatred confirms this approach. In *Norwood* v. *DPP*, a man displayed a sign in his shop window which stated 'Islam out of Britain—Protect the British People', and a symbol of the crescent and star with a prohibition sign. He was prosecuted under the POA, section 5 which criminalizes 'any writing, sign, or other visible representation which is threatening, abusive, or insulting, within the hearing or sight of a person likely to be caused harassment, alarm, distress thereby.' He was also charged with the religiously aggravated version of the POA, section 5 offence with is contained in the Crime and Disorder Act 1998. The man's appeal from conviction to the High Court was not allowed, as the Court found that the restriction on speech did not breach the Human Rights Act 1998 or the European Convention (ECHR) freedom of speech provisions.[15] He appealed to the ECtHR which found that there had been no breach of the Article 10 free speech provision. The Court held that there was a legitimate interest in protecting religious groups from this type of 'hate speech' and in promoting the ECHR values of tolerance, social peace, and non-discrimination.[16] The ECtHR's approach fits in with the general trend to use the criminal law to address the most serious forms of hate speech, as illustrated by the recommendation of a recent opinion of the Parliamentary Assembly of the Council of Europe which has endorsed this strategy.[17] Significantly, the recommendations also emphasized that blasphemy should not be criminalized.

In the UK, legislation to protect minorities from hate speech has been one of the most controversial issues in the debate about freedom of expression in the last few years. The issue became topical following government proposals in 2003/4 to close a gap in existing incitement to racial hatred legislation, which did not extend sufficient coverage to Muslims. At around the same time as Parliament was debating whether to extend hate speech protection to Muslims, and senior ministers of state were discussing the nikab, Dominic Abrams and Diane Houston published their research for the Cabinet Office's National Survey on Prejudice 2006, which found that Muslims are the social group at the highest risk of prejudice, discrimination, and hatred.[18]

The British Government's response to the challenge of prejudice and hatred against Muslims was to extend the incitement to racial hatred provisions to religion. To this end, they introduced the Racial and Religious Hatred Bill in June

[14] Ibid., 96–8.

[15] *Norwood* v. *DPP* (2003) WL 21491815.

[16] *Norwood* v. *UK* (2004) 40 EHRR SE 111.

[17] 'Blasphemy, religious insults and hate speech against persons on the grounds of their religion Opinion' Committee on Legal Affairs and Human Rights, Rapporteur: Mr. J. Bartumeau Cassany (Andorra, Socialist Group, Doc. 11319, 25 June 2007), paras. 7–8.

[18] See n. 12 above.

2005,[19] which sought to add hatred on the grounds of religion to the existing racial incitement provisions. In the debates that preceded the introduction of the Racial and Religious Hatred Act 2006, the advocates of the extension of incitement legislation to protect Muslims argued that principle and justice justified protection for vulnerable Muslim minorities. Seumas Milne wrote that 'targeting Muslims is a way round existing race hate legislation, as well as drawing on the most poisonous prejudices and conflict of our era'.[20] Three years later, he observed that the mainstream media was promoting anti-Muslim prejudice with language, and in ways, that would be unacceptable in relation to any other social group. Milne concluded, 'What has given the anti-Muslim onslaught particular force is that many secular liberals have convinced themselves that since Islam is an ideology rather than an ethnicity—and because they see themselves as defending liberal values—they are on the righteous side of racism.'[21]

There was, however, a significant media and political campaign against the bill which has been described by Fenwick and Phillipson as 'ill informed'.[22] Parliament approved the amended version and passed the Racial and Religious Hatred Act on 31 January 2006, which created a new Part 3A of the Public Order Act 1986 which is the offence of incitement to religious hatred.

The acceptance of the amendments to this Bill (the new part 3A) has meant that it is now in a different form to the provisions on incitement to racial hatred. The assessment of whether this is a welcome development has been mixed. Kay Goodall argues that: 'The legislative history in Britain and Northern Ireland suggests that the new Part 3A will be almost unenforceable. Without a confession, it will be very difficult to prove the purposive intention. [...] The Lords have pruned this statute so hard they have left it a stump'.[23] Ivan Hare, on the other hand, argues that there are important freedom of speech concerns that justify either no legislation or very narrow legislation in drafting incitement to religious hatred provisions. He cites the fact that race and religion are different; and also that once hate speech is extended to religion this will let in a claim by a number of different groups such as gays and women. Hare concludes that:

the United Kingdom already has ample general criminal law provisions to deal with incitement to hatred and any public order consequences which may follow from it and therefore has no need of further restrictions which are certain to make us less free and are likely to prove to be counter-productive [...]. Perhaps then, the only merit of the proposal is that it may provoke further reflection on the desirability of the existing prohibition on incitement to hatred on racial grounds.[24]

---

[19] Bill 11, 54/1 introduced to the House of Common on 9 June 2005.
[20] 'The struggle is no longer against religion, but within it', *The Guardian*, 16 December 2004.
[21] 'This onslaught risks turning into a racist witch-hunt', *The Guardian*, 20 September 2007.
[22] H. Fenwick and G. Phillipson, *Media Freedom under the Human Rights Act* (Oxford: OUP, 2006), 517.
[23] See n. 1 above, 113.   [24] See n. 8 above, 538.

This final point reinforces the views of those, like Eric Heinze, who argue that existing hate crimes legislation favours some powerful groups (and viewpoints) over others, and that the only consistent principled approach is to abolish all hate speech statutes.[25]

Some opponents of the incitement campaign argued that extending legislation to religion was a 'step too far'. They did not argue for the repeal of the incitement to racial hatred provisions, which would have been a principled and consistent position for free speech advocates. Instead, they relied on arguments which sought to distinguish between race and religion, while comedians were wheeled out to protest that they would not be allowed to make mad mullah jokes. Helen Fenwick and Gavin Phillipson, authors of *Media Freedom under the Human Rights Act* have commented that whilst the 'determination to protect freedom of expression in the increasingly contested and important area of religious belief is heartening, it must be said that much of the criticism is ill informed and equates the proposed new offense to blasphemy law'.[26]

The debate between advocates and opponents to incitement legislation failed to address the question about whether criminalizing incitement to hatred is an effective means of protecting vulnerable minorities against hate speech in the first place. The existing incitement to racial hatred provisions have not been a resounding success: there have been very few prosecutions; there have also been some high profile 'failures', which have provided a propaganda opportunity for organized racists. In this context it is worth asking whether the criminal law model of 'incitement to hatred' is an appropriate paradigm. An analysis of the historical origins of the law in this area suggests that there are deep-rooted structural reasons for the difficulties that arise when incitement to hatred legislation is used to protect minorities from hate speech.

The common law offences of blasphemy and seditious libel have provided some of the conceptual means of distinguishing between acceptable expression and expression that should be regulated as a potential risk to public order. These were, however, not sufficient to address the problem of organized political activity that specifically targeted a vulnerable religious or racial minority. Therefore, in the 1930s when there was a threat to Jews from organized fascist activity, legislation in the form of the Public Order Act 1936 was passed to prohibit words or behaviour that was likely to lead to a breach of the peace. When the Public Order Act was passed in 1936, as a direct response to the British Union of Fascists, the most important provision was section 5 which made it an offence for any person, in any public place or at any public meeting, to use 'threatening, abusive, or insulting words or behaviour, with intent to provoke a breach of the peace or whereby a breach of the peace is likely to be occasioned'. This replicated the formula which had become a standard way in which the common law of sedition

---

[25] E. Heinze, 'Viewpoint Absolutism and Hate Speech' (2006) 69(4) *Modern L. Rev.* 543.
[26] See n. 22 above, 517.

had proscribed words and conduct which were a threat to public order. This model of 'sedition' is also to be found in older colonial criminal codes which were used to control and censor colonial subjects. If we look back to Britain as an empire, it is clear that the use of the criminal law of incitement to hatred has an even earlier origin. During this period, incitement to hatred legislation was used extensively to ban a wide range of material that was deemed to be overly critical of Western civilization.[27] This particular use of incitement to hatred legislation ensured that the British were able to suppress dissent within the communities over which they exercised colonial rule. One interesting example of this concerned the publication of the book Angāre, an anthology of short stories by four young Indian writers published in 1932. Shabana Mahmud's article on the history surrounding the confiscation and destruction of Angāre, 'Angāre and the Founding of the Progressive Writers Association', provides some useful lessons for the present.[28] Angāre was written by a group of young Indian writers and provided the foundations for the subsequent 'Progressive Writers Movement' which was set up in India in the late 1930s. Some of the short stories in Angāre were an 'internal critique' of patriarchal practices within the Muslim community, whilst others were critical of colonial rule. The publication of Angāre was met by widespread protests and it also led to 'fatwas' from the religious clergy. The British government used the Code of Criminal Procedure 1898 to confiscate and destroy copies of Angāre, claiming that it was a threat to public order and seditious. On 15 March 1933, the British banned the book using section 295 of the Indian Penal Code which read:

Whoever with deliberate and malicious intention of outraging the religious feelings of any class of His Majesty's subjects by words, either spoken or written, or by visible representations insults or attempts to insult the religion or the religious beliefs of that class, shall be punished with imprisonment of either description for a term which may extend to two years, or with a fine, or both.

The banning of Angāre illustrates a number of themes that are relevant to current debates. First, this incident highlights the way in which incitement to hatred legislation was used as a form of colonial governance rather than a means to ensure equality, respect, and dignity of minorities. Second, it shows the way in which incitement legislation can be used by those in power to oppress the speech of powerless minorities. In the immediate context in which Angāre was censored, there was a convergence between the colonial authorities and the patriarchal male Muslim clergy. These two powerful groups formed an alliance to use incitement to religious hatred legislation to suppress criticism of British colonial rule as well as criticism of the male religious leaders.

---

[27] G. N. Barrier, *Banned—Controversial Literature and Political Control in British India, 1907–1947* (Columbia, MO: Univ of Missouri Press, 1974).
[28] (1996) 30 *Modern Asian Studies* 447.

Given these origins, it should not surprise us that incitement legislation often fails to protect powerless minorities. The debate about criminalizing incitement to religious hatred has been a costly distraction from a much-needed discussion about how to address the very real harm caused by hate speech. Within this debate, it is essential to identify the precise source of the risk of harm. The most powerful source of hate speech against vulnerable minorities such as Muslims is, as Seumas Milne argues, mainstream public discourse. This type of speech and representation cannot be addressed through incitement to hatred provisions. What is needed is the exercise of responsible speech by those who have power, especially politicians and the media. The recent proposals by the government to extend protection from hate speech to other protected groups, such as gays and lesbians, are a sign of the commitment to take a zero tolerance approach to homophobic hate speech.[29] However, this approach does not overcome the objections to criminalizing hate speech which have been set out earlier, and which have motivated criticism by writers such as Ivan Hare and Eric Heinz. Therefore, we need to think more imaginatively about a range of non-legal responses to hate speech rather than relying exclusively on the criminal law. These responses could, for example, include forms of cultural policy which would build capacity within minority communities to participate in public debates.

(ii) Non-Legal Responses to Hate Speech: Cultural Policy and Media Regulation

A sole focus on the use of the criminal law to protect minorities—especially given the controversial domestic debates on incitement to racial and religious hatred legislation—hinders a more detailed analysis of whether the criminal law is an appropriate or sufficient response to hate speech. As stated earlier, there are very few prosecutions under these criminal provisions. There is also increasing concern that provisions such as incitement to racial and religious hatred are used more frequently to criminalize the speech of minorities rather than protect them from hate speech. This asymmetry of power, and risk of disproportionately criminal-izing minorities, suggests that incitement provisions offer protection with one hand, whilst at the same time taking away the rights of these minorities to exercise freedom of speech.[30]

There are, also, arguments in support of the view that free speech rather than the restriction of speech is a key value for minorities. David Richards, for example, argues that the American scepticism of allowing group-based harms (such as hate speech) that justify restrictions on constitutionally protected free speech, cannot be

---

[29] See Criminal Justice and Immigration Bill 2008 introduced on 11 January 2008 (HL Bill 16 07–08). S. 126 introduces an amendment to the POA which would criminalize hate speech on the grounds of sexual orientation on the same terms as hate speech on the grounds of religion.

[30] See n. 22 above, ch. 9.

fully explained in terms of its concern for democracy. Richards argues that there is an additional factor that explains the US approach. On his analysis, free speech is a critical constitutional and legal tool for minorities who have suffered injustice: it allows them to criticize and challenge dehumanising stereotypes. This is because free speech 'empowers the legitimacy and integrity of the politics of identity in the reasonable understanding and remedy of structural injustice of group and national identity whose political power has rested on invisibility and unspeakability of such injustice'.[31] This alternative approach to the relationship between free speech and minority protection encourages a focus on the structural disadvantage of minorities who are the targets of hate speech. It also suggests that the appropriate response to hate speech directed at minorities is not criminalization, but rather enabling more speech by minorities. This shifts the argument from strategies of law towards non-legal strategies of cultural policies that create capacity in minorities to respond to hate speech through developing what Richards calls a 'personal moral voice': '[i]t is because such voice is personal (not based on the state's judgements of group-based harms) that it has the moral authority and integrity that it has in addressing the terms of structural injustice.'[32] It can, therefore, be argued that the goals of non-discrimination are reflected in the state interest in allowing minorities to develop a 'personal voice' and to give them more opportunities for speech. This is also compatible with the liberal free speech principle because although a liberal state cannot easily interfere with free speech, it can prioritize a concern with the autonomy and wellbeing of individuals who are victims of hate speech, and use investment and cultural policy to develop their capacity to respond to speech. In order to do this, there may be a need for some regulation although this need not be legal (and especially not criminal) regulation. It is significant that incitement to racial or religious hatred targets the most extreme forms of speech. Whilst these are serious forms of hate speech, it is also the case that there is prejudice and stereotyping in the mainstream media which, in many cases, will have a more widespread influence. Prejudice and stereotypes in the mainstream media may in fact be more pernicious because these views and representations are 'normalized' and 'presented as the ordinary truth about the world in which we live'. This is one of the issues in the debate about pornography (which can be analysed as a form of hate speech against women). The use of media regulation may, therefore, be a more successful way of addressing this 'normalized' source of hate speech. For example, Clause 12 of the Press Complaints Commission Code of Practice which deals with discriminatory speech states that:

(i) the press must avoid prejudicial or pejorative references to an individual's race, colour, religion, gender, sexual orientation or to physical or mental illness or disability; (ii) Details of an individual's race, colour, religion, sexual orientation, physical or mental illness or disability must be avoided unless genuinely relevant to the story.

---

[31] D. A. J. Richards, *Free Speech and the Politics of Identity* (Oxford: OUP, 1999), 237.
[32] Ibid., 242.

A greater use of this provision, and the use of third-party support to assist individuals through the recently established Equality and Human Rights Commission, may allow the creation of a public sphere that is more conducive to allowing the participation of minorities in public debate.[33] This, however, leads to a problem of identifying which groups are legitimate partners to participate in public debate, and how that debate should be framed. There will be a need to draw limits about who constitutes legitimate partners for debate and dialogue. The next section examines these issues in the context of contemporary discussions about 'extreme speech'.

4. Engaging with Extremists[34]

(i) Liberal Democracy as a 'Rational Liberal Consensus': Containing Doctrines that Are 'Irrational, Unreasonable, and Mad'

Section 2 set out some of the criteria that can be used to identify 'extremists' in a liberal democracy. Section 3 argued that in some cases a policy which focuses on non-legal responses—such as cultural policy or 'engagement'—may be a better solution to extreme speech than a sole focus on criminalization. This section focuses on how a liberal democracy can 'engage' with groups that are 'extremists'. How should liberal political theory respond to these groups? How should liberal democracies design 'dialogue' or 'engagement' with these groups? What are the limits to 'engaging with extremists'?

The approach of traditional liberal political theory to the problem of extremism is to invoke the public-private dichotomy. As a number of commentators (most notably John Rawls) have argued, there are certain recognisable constraints to public reason that do not apply in the context of the private sphere. Rawls' most significant move has been from a substantive theory of justice towards a 'political' theory of justice which is based on a 'political' rather than substantive concept of the person. Rawls' political liberalism is no longer concerned with making substantive claims about morality: its aim is to generate an overlapping consensus around which a number of substantive comprehensive concepts of the good can agree and which will generate the substantive 'political principles' for organizing political and legal institutions. Each comprehensive doctrine recognizes that it cannot insist on its own vision in the face of diversity and so this overlapping consensus is a compromise *modus vivendi*.[35]

---

[33] For a discussion of these issues in the context of media freedom see J. Rowbottom, 'Media Freedom and Political Debate in the Digital Era' (2006) 69(4) *Modern Law Rev.* 489.

[34] This discussion draws on work that is discussed in more detail in M. Malik, 'Engaging with Extremists' (2008) 22(1) *Int'l. Relations* 85.

[35] Rawls also applies his 'domestic theory' in an international context by exploring the appropriate of liberal nation states to illiberal nations in.*Political Liberalism* (New York: Columbia UP, 1993).

Obviously, Rawls' political liberalism gives us an immediate solution to our problem. It limits public debate to those comprehensive doctrines that recognize the limits imposed by: (a) deep diversity and pluralism; and (b) public reason. Rawls' political liberalism replicates the traditional public-private dichotomy. Rawls is forced into this conclusion because of the 'shallow' foundations on which he builds his theory of political liberalism: he has a political conception of the person and he asks individuals to endorse his principles of justice as part of their political rather than substantive (or ethical) personality. Yet, the hard cases are precisely those where a social group is not reasonable in the Rawlsian sense: that is, where it refuses to accept the private-public dichotomy or it wants to insist on the truth of its comprehensive doctrine in the public sphere. It is worth noting that Rawls concedes that some groups will be unreasonable: that is, they will insist that their comprehensive doctrine should be the basis for organizing the public sphere irrespective of the fact that other individuals have opposing and incompatible beliefs. Rawls concludes that these are 'irrational or mad' doctrines and therefore, a liberal democracy may have to abandon engagement with these doctrines using public reason and instead act to contain these 'irrational or mad' doctrines.[36]

In some cases, the appropriate response to 'extremists' who advocate or enact violence may be prohibition or criminalization. However, Rawls' analysis moves too quickly towards an abandonment of public reason and engagement with a wider range of groups who reject liberalism but also, at the same time, reject violence. Most significantly, Rawls' theory very quickly labels these doctrines as 'irrational and mad' and therefore incapable of entering into a debate in the public sphere. Such dismissive attitudes towards the claims of actual individuals and groups in liberal democracies makes this an inappropriate theory for our analysis. We need a way of thinking about democratic politics that is able to link our discussions of justice and political legitimacy to the reality of political claims and struggles: we need to do justice to both the impetus towards theorizing whilst at the same time taking seriously the reality of the most pressing democratic struggles in our times. In the present context, this political struggle is often by those 'extremists' who seek to enter public discourse, and yet whose claims seem, at first sight, to be irreconcilable with liberal democratic politics. Does liberal political theory have the resources to meet this particular challenge?

Traditional liberal political theory does not seem to be well-suited to respond to these emerging forms of politics for three important reasons. First, there is the problem created by the liberal insistence on the public-private dichotomy. The standard response of liberal democracies to extremism generally, and religious extremism in particular, is to invoke the public-private dichotomy: a commitment

---

[36] 'Political liberalism also supposes that a reasonable comprehensive doctrine does not reject the essentials of a democratic regime. Of course, a society may also contain unreasonable and irrational, and even mad, comprehensive doctrines. In their case the problem is to contain them so that they do not undermine the unity and justice of society.' Ibid., xvi–xvii.

to liberty in the private sphere whilst at the same time insisting that illiberal viewpoints have no role in public reason or the design of public institutions. There are of course different versions of this 'liberal compromise' but in its traditional Rawlsian form it would lead to the exclusion of many extremist groups from the political sphere. This answer seems especially ill-suited to respond to claims that there should be accommodation of their needs as a social group in the public sphere. There is a further problem. The claims of some social groups who want accommodation in the public sphere are often incompatible with liberalism. Moreover, these groups often draw on sets of ideas and values that challenge the very identity of the sovereign liberal state. There is sometimes an assumption in traditional liberal politics that political institutions and actors within liberal democracies assume that a collective political identity will be coterminous with a sovereign state. Recent political formation at the European Union level, and the politics of 'globalization', has challenged some of these assumptions. Some social groups also draw on ideas and allegiances that often transcend national boundaries which makes it problematic for them to fit within traditional liberal theory.[37]

For all these reasons, traditional Rawlsian-style liberalism is inappropriate to meet the contemporary challenge of extremism. Is there any way of formulating a political response to the problem of illiberal and unreasonable groups that does not move so quickly from optimistic engagement through public reason to prohibition through the defeatist exercise of coercion? Is there a way of slowing down the process of public discourse before we have to reach the conclusion of 'no dialogue with extremists'?

(ii) Agonistic Respect: Creating Political Space for the Extremists

The traditional approach of liberal political theory as represented by Rawls presents liberal democracy as 'rational consensus'. It protects the 'purity' and certainty of a homogenous political identity of its citizens through seeking their agreement on key values that will govern political life. However, as we have seen the real challenge is to find a way to respond to those individuals and groups that seem to have values that are at best radically different and at worst incompatible with common liberal values. We need a strategy that allows liberal principles to be extended to these intractable and incomprehensible differences. This second strategy, of using a more expansive definition of democracy to accommodate a wider range of permissible ideas within the public sphere, introduces the risk of

---

[37] Faisal Devji, for example, argues that the key to understanding movements such as al-Qaeda, lies in the global nature of its cause—as with environmentalists: 'The issues of concern to them are strictly global. They cannot be dealt with by solutions at a national level, or even by internationalist solutions—those take too long.' See J. Sutherland, 'The ideas interview: Faisal Devji', *The Guardian*, 17 October 2005. For a detailed discussion of these ideas, see F. Devji, *Landscapes of the Jihad: Militancy, Morality, Modernity* (London: Hurst & Co., 2005).

uncertainty. However, this destabilization of existing political identities can be an advantage in some contexts. It can yield more complex forms of democratic politics which are more appropriate where citizens have widely different sets of beliefs whilst at the same time retaining a core set of liberal commitments. There are two important routes into this more complex form of democratic politics. First, there is the work of William E. Connolly, who introduces the concept of 'agonistic respect' into a definition of liberal democracy.[38] Agonistic respect has three important implications for democratic politics. First, agonistic democracy emphasizes the importance of a complex notion of political identity, but it does not seek rational consensus as a goal. Secondly, agonistic respect welcomes the introduction of 'difference' into the public sphere rather than relegating it to the private sphere. In this sense, it is distinct from the 'political minimalism of democratic individualism' such as the theory of Rawls which constitutes an overlapping rational consensus in the public sphere based on the public-private dichotomy.[39] Third, agonistic respect moves beyond limiting democratic politics to a territorial state and recognizes that an individual's political identity may transcend national boundaries by drawing on transnational allegiances.[40]

The first two features open up political space to disagreement rather than enforcing consensus; and use politics as a way of enabling the expression of identity in the public sphere. In this way, they provide a more appropriate paradigm for analysing the place of radically 'different' groups in liberal politics. It prevents democratic politics becoming a sphere within which liberalism becomes a dogma. This analysis treats 'difference' in the realm of ideas as an advantage rather than a problem. In this way, established concepts can be problematized and debated in exactly the way that was envisaged by classical liberalism's invocation of a market place of ideas. Moreover, this strategy provides some place for new ideas to be debated in a common public dialogue. The third feature, non-territorial democratization, explicitly de-links liberal democracy from geographical limits thereby providing an ideal paradigm for considering the 'global context' of extremism. In these ways, a form of democratic politics based on agonistic respect

---

[38] W. E. Connolly, *Identity\Difference: Democratic Negotiations of Political Paradox* (Minneapolis: Univ Minnesota Press, 2002).

[39] 'In contrast to the conventional view that the sanctity of the individual in a constitutional regime is best protected by restricting politics to its bare essentials, democratic agonism contends that spaces in which differences may constitute themselves as contending identities are today most effectively established by political means. In a world of closely woven interdependencies, distance must be generated by political means if it is to be at all.' Ibid., xi.

[40] '[...] agonistic democracy challenges the confinement of democracy to the governmental institutions of the territorial state. The politics of identity\difference flows beneath, through, and over the boundaries of the state. It overflows state boundaries when the state constitutes a set of differences to protect the certainty of its collective identity and whenever the established identity of a sovereign state itself becomes an object of politicization. "Nonterritorial democratization" provides one way to ventilate and supplement the institutional politics of territorial democracy under contemporary conditions of global life. Nonterritorial democratization, I suspect, has become a precondition for the health of contemporary territorial democracy.' Ibid.

seems an attractive model for theorizing the place of contemporary extremist groups in a liberal democracy.

Connolly treats this constant tension and problematizing of core values as a means strengthening liberal values.[41] Yet, a failure to have a minimal consensus or agreement on core values also carries with it certain risks. Connolly acknowledges this risk when he states that there is a danger of agonistic democracy and respect collapsing into political chaos. To address this defect, he distinguishes between agonistic respect and agonistic democracy: agonistic respect cannot be institutionalized into liberal democratic politics in a linear and simple way.[42] There is a need for further mediating principles that can provide some guidance, or inspiration, towards a positive vision. These agreed principles need to establish a common framework for liberal politics, within which difference is accommodated, rather than prescribing the content of political debate. This requires an agreed framework for debate between different ideas rather than a substantive agreement on universal values. The focus on procedure rather than substantive agreement suggests that theories of deliberative democracy may be a useful supplement to 'agonistic respect'. Like the concept of agonistic democracy, these theories give priority to public debate between competing doctrines thereby providing a more expansive political space for accommodating difference. Yet, at the same time, deliberative democracy also provides a structured ethical framework for this discussion that must be endorsed by all those who seek to participate in public discourse in liberal democracies.[43]

(iii) 'Discourse Ethics': What Are the Rules of the Game When 'Engaging with Extremists'?

There are important similarities between traditional models of liberal democracy such as those of John Rawls and the work of writers such as Habermas who favour a process of deliberative democracy guided by 'discourse ethics'. Both these traditions (Rawls' public reason and Habermas' deliberative democracy) come together around a common and agreed agenda which is relevant for our discussion. This

---

[41] 'The temptation to covert difference into heresy often flows from the effort to conceal uncertainties in one's faith or identity, projecting them onto others as evils' and what is needed he argues is '[...] to treat one's own faith as contestable in one's own eyes, not just to affirm that it is so in the eyes of others.' Ibid., xxiii.

[42] 'I do not talk much about "agonistic democracy" in this book, even though some have placed it under that generic label. Rather, I explore the benefits of folding *agonistic respect* into identity difference relations in a democratic state. The difference is critical. "Agonistic democracy" could be interpreted as a model in which no positive vision is enunciated and contestation takes priority over every other aspect of politics. I doubt that anybody actually endorses such a view. "Agonistic respect" on the other hand, is a civic virtue that allows people to honor different final sources, to cultivate reciprocal respect across difference, and to negotiate larger assemblages to set general policies.' Ibid., xxv–xxvi.

[43] For a review and critical comments on Connolly see J. M. Schwartz, 'Book Review: The Ethos of Pluralization by William E. Connolly' (May 1997) 59(2) *J. Politics* 618.

view is summarized by Benhabib as 'the legitimation of political power and the examination of the justice of institutions to be a public process, open to all citizens. The idea that the justice of institutions be "in the public's eye," so to speak—to be open to scrutiny, examination, and reflection—is fundamental.'[44]

Nevertheless, there are important differences between democracy based on 'public reason' and 'deliberative process'. As stated both Rawls' model of public reason and his political liberalism make a sharp division between the public and the private sphere. His standard of public reasons does not apply to private debate or the deliberation of associations such as churches (and analogous institutions) which are treated as part of the background culture for deliberation.[45] This locates public reasons within political institutions rather than in public culture more widely. Models of deliberative democracy provide a more expansive way of defining the public sphere. This means that this model: (a) encourages discourse about the lines separating the public from the private sphere; (b) also locates the public sphere in civic society and is therefore more sensitive to the interaction between the two; and (c) focuses on fluid processes for forming opinions in the public sphere.[46] Most importantly, unlike the Rawlsian model, this way of thinking about democracy opens up some room for connecting national (or international) public discussion and politics with the more private (individual or group) claims of social groups. However, this space is not unregulated in a way that might be seen to be problematic for 'agonistic democracy'. For theories of deliberative democracy, significantly, this space for a more fluid process is subject to the important constraints imposed by discourse ethics. These ethical principles (or discourse ethics) treat the values of individual freedom and autonomy as universal principles that bind all individuals and societies. There are two aspects to these foundational principles. First, universal moral respect: that is, recognizing the right of all beings capable of speech and action to be participants in the moral conversation. Secondly, egalitarian reciprocity: each individual should have the right to speech acts, to initiate conversations and new topics and to ask for justifications for the model itself.[47] More specifically, these foundational principles of liberalism generate three important constraints on any process of deliberative democracy: (a) egalitarian reciprocity; (b) voluntary self-ascription; and (c) freedom of exit and association.[48] These are the three foundational principles that were used as the comparative benchmark (the liberal norm) against which to define extremism.

The advocacy of these limited universal principles of discourse ethics is a major compromise to the principle of agonistic respect which explicitly rejects claims to universality in favour of a 'pluralization of ethical sources in public life'.[49] This compromise represents an attempt at pluralization of public discourse whilst at

---

[44] See n. 6 above, 108.
[45] See n. 35 above, 215.
[46] See n. 6 above, 109.
[47] Ibid., 107.
[48] Ibid., 131–2.
[49] See n. 38 above, xxi.

the same time recognizing the need for constraints that prevent a total abrogation of liberal values. As stated earlier, this compromise allows the translations of the principle of agonistic respect into institutionalized liberal politics. It also allows us to examine more closely the relationship between liberal politics and extremism.

Important consequences follow from modelling the process of discourse in this way. This analysis generates a wider definition of the public sphere. Public discourses that are linked to the wider culture are significant and provide a more expansive definition of the 'civic point of view'. The public space for engaging with extremists is much wider than the predominant focus on national political and legal institutions in traditional liberal political theory and gives an important role to the media and the wider civic community.

Thus, the process of engagement with extremists can be 'slowed down' by moving away from understanding democracy as rational consensus towards more complex forms of democratic politics. Seyla Benhabib has summarized this slowing down in the following terms:

In discourse ethics, autonomy is seen as a moral as well as a political principle; this requires that we create public practices, dialogues, and spaces in civil society around controversial normative questions in which all those affected can participate. It is fundamental to autonomy that the collective practices in which we participate may be seen as the outcome of our legitimate processes of deliberation. As opposed to the privileging of legal regulation and adjudication in the political liberalism model, deliberative democracy would expand the moral/political dialogue into the civil public sphere. Deliberative democracy sees the free public sphere of civil society as the principal arena for the articulation, contestation, and resolution of normative discourses.[50]

(iv) Engaging with the 'Extremists'

A focus on process (normative syntax) in a way that distinguishes it from substantive moral content (normative justification) is critical. The process of articulating reasons in public will not just be a matter of legitimizing political norms that are an outcome of the process (important though this is). In addition, the mere fact of being part of the process is critical because it can enhance the virtues of democratic citizenship by enlarging the perspectives of the participants by acculturating/socializing those who are engaged in dialogue in the process of public reasoning and exchange. It seems clear that many of the groups that are characterized as radical or extreme have in fact sought to enter into public processes of deliberation. They give interviews to the media or they are involved in other forms of participation in the public sphere. It may be the case that for some radical groups this may be an instrumental strategy to advance anti-democratic and illiberal goals: they may be 'wolves in sheep's clothing'. This public dissembling may mask the reality of a set of ideas that remain 'illiberal, unreasonable, and mad'. The process of

---

[50] See n. 6 above, 114–5.

deliberative democracy starts from the fact that extremist groups want to enter the public space to debate with others and make political demands. 'Agonistic democracy' makes greater public space for these groups and draws them in whilst at the same time 'discourse ethics' present these groups with minimal but clear criteria about the conditions which bind all those who participate in public discourse.

Agreement, between different actors in the public sphere, can take a number of different forms:

(1) Procedural agreement: agreeing on the minimum requirements and normative basis for entering into political discourse based on principles such as universal humanity or egalitarian reciprocity;

(2) Principled substantive agreement: the outcome of argument which rests on identical reasons and that are able to convince parties in the same way; and

(3) Compromised agreement: a compromise and negotiated solution based on different reasons between the various parties to the discourse; (Rawls' overlapping consensus/*modus vivendi* would fall into this category).

One way of sifting through the claims of extremist groups is to ask whether they are willing to reach a procedural agreement on the three principles of discourse ethics. In dramatic cases, a group may be rejectionist and refuse to accept these conditions or it may consistently breach or deviate from the principles of discourse ethics. In these cases discourse ethics provides a basis for exclusion, justified criticism or withholding public funding. Where a group accepts discourse ethics as a pre-condition for entering into a liberal public discourse, there may be different motivations for their acquiescence. What is critical is that the agreement of the extremist group to the normative syntax of discourse, procedural agreement (1) is not merely a strategic posture. At this stage, the extremist group needs to accept that their participation in democratic discourse must be based on normative foundations: the meta-principles of universal humanity and egalitarian reciprocity; voluntary self-ascription; and freedom of association and exit. This is the minimal core idea of deliberative democracy that all individuals and groups have to accept as a precondition of participating in liberal public discourse.

Some groups that seem to be extremist could go further. Their ideologies may provide them with the internal resources to reach a more substantive agreement to liberal principles as part of principled substantive agreements (2).[51] There is, therefore, a possibility of substantive convergence between what seem to be illiberal groups and liberal principles.[52]

---

[51] J. Habermas, 'Three Normative Models of Democracy', in S. Benhabib (ed.), *Democracy and Difference: Contesting the Boundaries of the Political* (Princeton, NJ: Princeton UP, 1996).

[52] So, eg, it might be possible to argue that there is some analogy between the requirements of the principle of universal humanity that all individuals have a right to enter into dialogue and the principle of freedom of opinion (hurriyat al-ray) or the right to freedom of exit and the principle of freedom of religion (al-hurriya al-diniyaa). See M. H. Kamali, *Freedom of Expression in Islam* (Cambridge: Islamic Texts Society, 1997).

In some cases, extremist groups may accept the procedural limits of discourse ethics, but may be entering into democratic processes with strategic and opportunistic goals. These groups may enter into compromise agreements (3) on a range of substantive issues that are not based on a substantive commitment to liberalism. The compromises that are inherent in public dialogue between extremist groups and other citizens are often pejoratively labelled a modus vivendi. Critics of 'compromise agreements' often argue that this is an insufficient basis on which to build a stable community. This critique, however, underestimates the ways in which strategic compromises may sometimes have transformative potential. There is a more complex relationship between the public and private sphere than traditional liberal theory is willing to concede. The political and private identity of individuals, although not identical, are related in important ways.[53] The politics of recognition, and the fact that identity is formed dialogically, works both ways: just as a private identity is important to our understanding of the public sphere, so the public sphere will influence a private identity. The public (structural) context within which a private identity operates has important causal consequences: it will influence not only whether and how a private identity is formed, but also the way in which this identity can manifest itself in the lives of individuals. Over a period of time, through processes of public deliberation, a strategic compromise may become transformed into principled substantive agreement. Providing space for such transformation requires an understanding that democratic processes are intrinsically important (whilst also being limited by the normative principles of ethics), rather than merely an instrument for advancing policy goals. It also requires a reformulation of what constitutes public understanding and agreement when there is a public dialogue between radically different beliefs.[54] Strategic compromises sometimes contain within them the prospect of a more fundamental transformation of all participants, through moral learning of all those who participate in processes of public dialogue and deliberative democracy.[55]

(v) Applying the 'Rules of the Game' to Extremists: Classification, Protection, and Critique

Deliberative democracy encourages a process of 'engaging with extremists' within the constraints of discourse ethics. As stated earlier, deliberative democracy is based on two core values. First, universal moral respect: that is, recognising the right of all beings capable of speech and action to be participants in the moral

[53] M. Malik, 'Faith and the State of Jurisprudence', in P. Oliver, S. Douglas-Scott, and V. Tadros (eds.), *Faith in Law: Essays in Legal Theory* (Oxford: Hart Publishing, 2000).
[54] M. Malik 'Justice', in D. Ford, B. Quash, and J. Martin Soskice (eds.), *In Fields of Faith: Theology and Religious Studies for the Twenty-First Century* (Cambridge: CUP, 2005).
[55] '[...] the parties do not modify the framework to achieve unanimity, although they may when conflicts are not so deep. Rather, they modify their conflicting interpretations of the framework so that each can recognize the other's moral values and framework so that each can recognize the other's moral values and standards as part of it' J. Bohman, quoted in n. 6 above, 145.

conversation. Secondly, egalitarian reciprocity: that is, each individual should have the right to speech acts, to initiate conversations and new topics, and to ask for justifications for the model itself.[56] In the nature of groups, these principles generate a framework of discourse ethics that is a precondition for all participants in public discourse: egalitarian reciprocity (women and other minorities must not, in virtue of their membership status, be entitled to lesser rights); voluntary self-ascription (group membership must permit the maximal forms of self-identification and self-ascription possible); and freedom of exit and association (there must be unrestricted freedom to exit from the group, although such exit may be accompanied by loss of certain group privileges). One practical advantage of this framework is that it performs three key functions in the process of engaging with extremists.

First, this analysis enables the classification of extremists. The principles of deliberative democracy and discourse ethics act as markers for determining whether or not a particular group is 'extreme'. Of course, the degree of deviation from these norms will vary depending on the precise nature of group. Many groups that draw their ideas from traditional cultures and religions will often breach the first principle, especially the requirements on gender equality. Some may go even further and breach the second and third principle: they may seek to restrict the ability to join and identify with the group; and they may seek to prevent individuals from leaving the group. This spectrum usefully provides a way of distinguishing between different types of extremist groups. It also provides a mechanism for tracking movement within a group from more 'extreme' to 'mainstream' political values.

Secondly, this framework provides protection for vulnerable individuals who may be at risk from extremist ideas and practices. It provides the minimal standard of care that the State must guarantee for vulnerable individuals within groups, for example, women and children. This protection will apply even in those cases where an illiberal social group does not want to participate in main-stream society. For example, the mistreatment of women by a group in breach of the principle of egalitarian reciprocity will provide a trigger for state regulation of the group to safeguard the individual rights of its citizens. Therefore, these principles provide guidance on a recurring problem about the extent to which a liberal state should tolerate illiberal practices and groups. It also allows extremist groups to be legitimately held to account, and criticized, for any harm that they cause to vulnerable group members such as women.

Thirdly, and finally, this framework permits and facilitates liberal critique of extremist groups without excluding them from the public sphere. Agonistic respect and deliberative democracy make more public space for differences in values. They allow extremist groups to introduce their ideas into the public

---

[56] Ibid., 107.

sphere. Yet, at the same time, the specific conditions of discourse ethics provide the limiting conditions which perform the functions of classification and protection to compensate for harm caused by extremists.[57]

(vi) Internal and External Critique of Extremists

Agonistic respect and deliberative democracy make more public space for difference in ideology and values: they allow extremist groups to introduce their ideas into the public sphere. Does this strategy of engaging with extremists undermine the 'critical' edge of discourse in the public sphere? Does agonistic respect collapse into uncritical acceptance of difference? Does liberal politics have to accommodate all illiberal practices in the name of tolerance and 'respect'? It does not follow that this political process of engaging with extremists requires an uncritical acceptance for all their ideas. In fact, an automatic grant of approval can sometimes collapse into condescension rather than a genuine engagement with the ideas of extremist groups.[58] The challenge for anyone offering a liberal critique of extremism is to strike a balance between two goals: (a) inclusion and understanding of new ideas in the public sphere; and (b) maintaining an authentic critical perspective towards these new ideas. Most extremist groups will contain not just one but a plurality of ideas and arguments. Some of these ideas and voices have been, and are, backed by existing power structures whilst others are relatively silent, do not have access to public space and are struggling for recognition. Once this complexity is accepted, there is the possibility of a critique of extremist groups by insiders who want to launch an internal dissent from within the group; and by outsiders who want to criticize the foundational ideas of the group.

In addition, and perhaps more controversially, once we accept that there is a diversity of views within extremist groups this is exactly the space where 'outsiders' can play a pivotal role.[59] The fact that these principles of deliberative democracy apply within a group opens up the possibility of a role for criticism by

---

[57] C. Taylor, 'Multiculturalism and the Politics of Recognition', in A. Gutman (ed.), *Multiculturalism: Examining the Politics of Recognition*,(Princeton, NJ: Princeton UP, 1994), 64–71.

[58] As Charles Taylor has noticed, such an uncritical acceptance can be patronising and therefore a breach, rather than a requirement of, liberal principles of 'recognition' of minorities. Ibid.

[59] A particularly British example illustrates the willingness of secular commentators to undertake exactly this task. Seumas Milne writing in *The Guardian* on 16 December 2004 suggested that this balance is possible. He argues that existing political movements can form alliances with religious groups such as Muslims without compromising a critical stance on issues such as gender and sexuality. See n. 20 above. His colleague Polly Toynbee—often and unfairly portrayed as being hostile towards Islam—is more sceptical. She poses the dilemma faced by liberal democrats in its most vivid form: 'Atheists, feminists, and anti-racists are paralysed by Islam. Whichever way they turn, they find themselves at risk of alliances with undesirables of every nasty hue.' She quite rightly and perceptively insists that 'Muslims must also accept the right of others to criticise religions without smearing any critic as racist.' 'We must be free to criticize without being called racist', *The Guardian*, 18 August 2004.

'outsiders'. In fact, one of the most significant contributions that outsiders can make is to 'hold the line' by providing a detailed and constructive critique of extremist groups where there has been a breach of a key principle, for example, equality for women. These external critics often provide the most prescient and invaluable critique of extremists. Insiders who are 'internal dissenters' within an extremist group seeking to reaffirm a principle such as egalitarian reciprocity can turn to this critique as a precious source of information and ideas. In this way, there is the possibility of an overlap between an external and internal critique of extremist groups around the normative principles of deliberative democracy. Such alliances based on normative principles challenge the assumption that agonistic respect has to yield a fragmentary form of identity politics. Mainstream political movements and established political parties need to reach out to excluded and marginalized groups; they will have to relinquish some of their tighter disciplines in favour of greater plurality in the realm of ideas, objectives, and policies; and they should allow more autonomy for their individual members and political representatives.[60] These strategies may also usefully limit the damaging fragmentation of politics that is often a by-product of 'identity politics'.

(vii) The Limits of Democratic Discourse

The previous analysis has assumed that the universalist ideas of discourse ethics are a sound basis on which to frame our public discourse. This leaves open the question of what happens when liberal democracies themselves breach these principles or misuse democratic discourse as an instrumental means for achieving other strategic goals. The opportunistic use or misuse of the concepts of liberal democracy as a chimera for exercising hegemony over individuals and groups, whether in the domestic or international context, is a real risk. This is a longstanding critique of liberal universalism. It is argued that universalism in political theory is in reality the exercise of hegemony over the powerless.[61] Liberalism, it is

---

[60] In developing politics along this line, there is a need to consider the distinction between aspiration and reality that was summarized by Weber as a 'realistic passion' and 'sterile excitement'. Passion and reaching for the ideal is essential to the political vocation, he argues, but it needs to be based on a sense of individual responsibility, judgment, and a sense of reality M. Weber, 'Politics as a Vocation', in W. G. Runciman (ed.), *Max Weber: Selections in Translation* Trans. E. Matthews (Cambridge: CUP, 1978).

[61] 'In effect, between a relationship of power and a strategy of struggle there is a reciprocal appeal, a perpetual linking and a perpetual reversal. At every moment the relationship of power may become a confrontation between two adversaries. Equally, the relationship between adversaries in society may, at every moment, give place to the putting into operation of mechanisms of power. The consequence of this instability is the ability to decipher the same events and the same transformations either from inside the history of struggle or from the standpoint of the power relationships. The interpretations which result will not consist of the same elements of meaning or the same links or the same types of intelligibility although they refer to the same historical fabric, and each of the two analyses must have reference to the other. In fact, it is precisely the disparities between the two readings which make visible those fundamental phenomena of "domination" which are present in a

argued, is able to mask its own ideological foundations by presenting itself as the neutral truth about the world in which we live.[62] We therefore need to be vigilant about the way in which what seem to be objective universalist principles such as autonomy and equality can in reality operate, in both domestic and international politics, as a way of preserving the power and dominance of Western democracies. This warning about the misuse of liberal universalism is important in both the domestic and international context.

In the domestic context, there is a specific risk that the call for an agreement on common and shared liberal values will be used as a way of 'disciplining' new minorities. Where a group draws upon religion for its ideology, it can be especially problematic because the function of religious ideas and personal transformation is in fact to challenge established norms and social structures. This problem is exacerbated in the context of a religion such as Islam which is commonly represented as falling outside the 'Western' canon and incompatible with liberal democracy.[63] There is a risk that any analysis of religious extremism and liberal democracy may replicate some of these stubborn and recurring methods of racializing non-Christian minorities as a group who it is claimed cannot assimilate into the values of democracy and tolerance.

In the international context, too, there are increasing reasons to be vigilant about the misuse of the concept of liberal democracy. There is a disjuncture between the appeal to liberal principles as a justification for the exercise of humanitarian intervention or as a legitimation for the use of armed force and the reality of practice. Advocacy of liberal democracy is not always matched by the consistent application of these principles in international politics. The flagrant abuse of the core principles of freedom and autonomy in high profile abuses of human rights in Guantanamo Bay or Abu Ghraib will make it impossible to present discourse ethics as the viable framework for a domestic or international dialogue with social groups who are labelled as extremist.[64] Moreover, these dramatic and flagrant abuses of human rights raise a more challenging issue. Liberal democracies may confidently present themselves as the vanguards of the principles of universal humanity and egalitarian reciprocity, but in practice they

large number of human societies.' The Subject and Power', in M. Foucault, *Beyond Structuralism and Hermeneutics* (Chicago: Univ Chicago, 1982), 208.

[62] See C. Taylor, 'Interpretation and the Sciences of Man', in *Philosophy and the Human Sciences: Philosophical Papers 2* (Cambridge: CUP, 1985).

[63] It is worth observing that during moments of national crisis, other religious minorities, such as Jews, have also been 'racialized' as a group that cannot be assimilated into liberal democracies. For example, public discourse of the new Jewish immigrants from Eastern Europe to Britain between 1890 and 1920 often cited their adherence to the Old Testament and religious law as evidence of their inability to accept the core British values of democracy. See D. Herman, ' "An Unfortunate Coincidence": Jews and Jewishness in Twentieth Century English Judicial Discourse' (2006) 33(2) *J. of Law and Society* 277, 284. See also the discussion of antisemitism in C. Holmes, *Anti-Semitism and British Society 1876–1939* (London: Edward Arnold, 1979) and J. Garrard, *The English and Immigration 1880–1910* (London: OUP, 1971).

[64] D. Rose, *Guantanamo: America's War on Human Rights* (London: Faber and Faber, 2004).

do not consistently meet their own self-professed criteria. It may turn out that those who fail to meet the criteria of deliberative democracy (the extremists) are not only 'out there': they may be closer to home than we had at first imagined. A process of 'engaging with extremists' may, therefore, provide an invaluable and more wide-ranging opportunity to affirm and apply liberal values in domestic and international politics.

5. Conclusion

The debate about the appropriate response to 'extreme speech' has predominantly focused on the criminal law to prohibit incitement to hatred against vulnerable minorities or to address the problem of the 'glorification of terrorism'. This debate has failed to make clear what constitutes 'extreme speech' in a liberal democracy. The focus on the use of the criminal law has also neglected 'engagement' as an alternative to criminalization. Traditional models of liberalism that define democracy as the creation of a public liberal consensus are not, however, an appropriate basis for political engagement with contemporary extremist groups. An alternative way of defining the goals of liberal politics based on the concepts of 'agonistic respect', 'deliberative democracy', and 'discourse ethics' is necessary to develop policies of 'engagement' that are a viable alternative to the criminalization of extreme speech. Agonistic respect and deliberative democracy create political space for extremist groups. At the same time, the principles of discourse ethics contain the potential harm caused by extremist ideas and practices. This range of ideas provides a basis for developing a range of non-legal responses to contemporary challenges of extreme speech in liberal democracies.

PART II
HATE SPEECH

7

Hate Speech

Robert Post

The OED teaches us the connection between hate speech and the overall theme of this volume, *Extreme Speech*. 'Hate,' we learn, is 'an emotion of extreme dislike or aversion; detestation, abhorrence, hatred.'[1] A draft OED addition of December 2002 defines 'hate speech' as 'speech expressing hatred or intolerance of other social groups, especially on the basis of race or sexuality.'[2] To prohibit hate speech, then, is to forbid expression of 'extreme' intolerance or 'extreme' dislike. The qualification 'extreme' is prerequisite because intolerance and dislike are necessary human emotions which no legal order could pretend to abolish. We *should* be intolerant of injustice and we *should* dislike the needless suffering of the innocent.

When do these otherwise appropriate emotions become so 'extreme' as to deserve legal suppression? What, for example, are we to make of Walt Whitman's exhortation to 'hate tyrants,'[3] or Charles William Eliot's inaugural Address as President of Harvard College, in which he observed that 'Americans, as a rule, hate disabilities of all sorts, whether religious, political, or social'?[4] Is it *wrong* for Americans to hate tyrants or to hate rules that exclude persons on the basis of religion, political belief, or social class? Perhaps, as an American presidential candidate once remarked when accepting the nomination of the Republican Party, 'Extremism in the defense of liberty is no vice; moderation in the pursuit of justice is no virtue.'[5]

---

[1] OED, online entry for 'hate', <http://dictionary.oed.com/cgi/entry/50103052?query_type=word&queryword=hate&first=1&max_to_show=10&sort_type=alpha&result_place=1&search_id=qKFU-s00SSN-13607&hilite=50103052> (last accessed 19 June 2008).

[2] OED, online entry for 'hate speech', <http://dictionary.oed.com/cgi/entry/50103052/50103052se10?single=1&query_type=word&queryword=hath+speech&first=1&max_to_show=10&hilite=50103052se10> (last accessed 19 June 2008).

[3] W. Whitman, *Leaves of Grass: His Original Edition* (Carbondale, IL: Southern Illinois UP, 1959 [1855]), 10.

[4] C. W. Eliot, (ed.), *Addresses at the Inauguration of Charles William Eliot as President of Harvard College, Tuesday, October 19, 1869.* (Cambridge: Sever and Francis, 1869), 49.

[5] B. M. Goldwater, 'Acceptance Speech in San Francisco, Cal., July 17, 1964', in G. Bush (ed.), *Campaign Speeches of America Presidential Candidates 1948–1984* (New York: Ungar Publishing Company, 1985), 134, 141.

Hatred, in its proper place, would seem socially desirable. The great English philologist William Jones, for example, once wrote to a correspondent that 'I hate favouritism.'[6] Jones believed that while the '*tender* passions' like '*love, pity, desire*' 'produce in the arts what we call the *beautiful*,' 'the *terrible* passions,' like '*hate, anger, fear . . .* are productive of the *sublime*'.[7] Edmund Burke, who knew something about the sublime, observed that 'They will never love where they ought to love, who do not hate where they ought to hate.'[8] And Burke would not let the matter stop there. In speeches on the impeachment of Warren Hastings, Burke avowed that 'Some say, you ought to hate the crime and love the criminal. No, that is the language of false morality; you ought to hate the crime and criminal, if the crime is of magnitude.'[9]

The indispensability of hatred to law was a major theme of the great Sir James FitzJames Stephen, who believed that 'the infliction of punishment by law gives definite expression and a solemn ratification and justification to the hatred which is excited by the commission of the offense, and which constitutes the moral or popular as distinguished from the conscientious sanction of that part of morality which is also sanctioned by the criminal law.'[10] 'Love and hatred,' Stephen wrote, 'imply each other as much as convex and concave.'[11] He considered 'unqualified denunciations' of hatred to be 'as ill-judged as unqualified denunciations of sexual passion'.[12]

Christian pieties to the contrary notwithstanding, hatred is plainly an extreme and troublesome human emotion, 'deeply rooted in human nature,'[13] that can serve constructive social purposes. When the law seeks to suppress hate—and hence hate speech—it is not because hate *as such* ought to be proscribed. It is instead because the law is intolerant of hatred when it is expressed in particular circumstances. But what are these circumstances?

The oldest and most venerable legal prohibition of hate is that contained in the law of seditious libel, which prohibits 'all writings . . . which tend to bring into hatred or contempt the King, the Government, or the constitution as by law established.'[14] Seditious libel was to be suppressed because, as Machiavelli advised

---

[6] Sir William Jones to J. Shore, Esq. 1789, in *Lord Teignmouth, Memoirs of the Life, Writings, and Correspondence, of Sir William Jones* (London: J Hatchard, 1804), 322–23.

[7] '*An Essay on the Arts, Commonly Called Imitative*', in Lord Teignmouth (ed.), *The Works of Sir William Jones* (London: John Stockdale, 1807), 379–80.

[8] E. Burke, 'Fourth Letter on the Proposals for Peace with Regicide Directory of France: With Preliminary Correspondence', in E. Burke (ed.), *The Works of the Right Honorable Edmund Burke*, 3rd edn. (Boston: Little, Brown, 1869), 90.

[9] E. Burke, '*Speeches in the Impeachment of Warren Hastings, Esquire, Late Governor-General of Bengal*' in ibid., 277. 'We hate the crime, and we hate the criminal ten times more; and if I use indignant language, if I use the language of scorn and horror with respect to the criminal, I use the language that becomes me.'

[10] J. F. Stephen, *A History of the Criminal Law of England: Vol. II* (London: Macmillan, 1883), 81. 'I think it highly desirable that criminals should be hated, that the punishments inflicted upon them should be so contrived as to give expression to that hatred, and to justify it so far as the public provision of means for expressing and gratifying a healthy natural sentiment can justify and encourage it.'

[11] Ibid., 82.   [12] Ibid.   [13] Ibid.

[14] H. C. Folkard, *The Law of Slander and Libel*, 7th edn. (London: Butterworth & Co., 1908), 371.

in the first English translation of *The Prince*, rulers ought to 'take a care not to incur contempt or hatred'.[15] Law traditionally condemned hatred in analogous circumstances: it punished speech expressed 'with a view ... to bring into hatred and contempt the administration of justice,'[16] for example, and also defamatory speech 'tending to expose' a person 'to publick hatred, contempt, or ridicule'.[17]

After a century of attempted genocides, law today tends to condemn the expression of hatred in the context of religious, racial, or ethnic groups.[18] The International Covenant on Civil and Political Rights (ICCPR) prohibits 'any advocacy of national, racial, or religious hatred that constitutes incitement to discrimination, hostility, or violence.'[19] The International Convention on Elimination of All Forms of Racial Discrimination (ICERD) condemns speech attempting 'to justify or promote racial hatred and discrimination in any form.'[20] The American Convention on Human Rights prohibits 'any advocacy of national, racial, or religious hatred that constitutes incitements to lawless violence.'[21] Canadian legislation prohibits the 'promotion of hatred ... towards any section of the public distinguished by colour, race, religion, or ethnic origin.'[22] The German penal code forbids speech that 'incites hatred against parts of the population' in a manner 'liable to disturb public peace.'[23]

All legal attempts to suppress hatred, whether of racial groups or of the King, must face a profound conceptual difficulty. They must distinguish hatred from ordinary dislike or disagreement. Even those who believe that hatred should be punished because it is 'extreme' would readily concede that disagreement, even disagreement that stems from dislike, ought to be protected because it is the lifeblood of politics. What Habermas calls communicative action cannot proceed at all without contestation and disagreement. But when does normal dislike become punishable hatred? To appreciate the difficulty, consider the 1792 conviction of Thomas Paine for seditious libel on the ground that the *Rights of Man* brought 'into hatred and contempt' the 'present Sovereign Lord the King and the Parliament of this kingdom, and the constitution, laws, and government

---

[15] N. Machiavelli, *Machiavel's Discourses Upon the First Decade of T. Livius, To Which is Added His Prince* Trans. E. Dacres (London, 1674), 598.

[16] T. Starkie, *A Treatise on the Law of Slander, Libel Scandalum Magnatum and False Rumours* (London: W. Clarke and Sons, 1813), 535.

[17] B. Wilson (ed.), *The Works of James Wilson, Vol. III* (Philadelphia: Bronson and Chauncey, 1804), 73. See n. 14 above, 67. Libel is defined as 'a publication, without justification or lawful excuse, which is calculated to injure the reputation of another, by exposing him to hatred, contempt, or ridicule.'

[18] M. Rosenfeld, 'Hate Speech in Constitutional Jurisprudence: A Comparative Analysis' (2003) 24 *Cardozo L. Rev.* 1523.

[19] ICCPR, Art. 20(2), 6 I.L. M. 368, 999 U.N.T.S. 171. See S. Farrior, 'Molding the Matrix: The Historical and Theoretical Foundations of International Law Concerning Hate Speech' (1996) 14 *Berkley J. Int'l L.* 1.

[20] ICERD, Art. 4, 5 I.L.M. 352, 660 U.N.T.S. 195.

[21] Art. 13(5), O.A.S.T.S. No. 36, 1144 U.N.T.S. 243.

[22] Criminal Code, R.S.C. ch. C-46, § 319(2) (1980). See *R.* v. *Keegstra* [1990] 3 SCR 697.

[23] Penal Code, s. 130 (1). See W. Brugger, 'Ban or Protection of Hate Speech? Some Observations Based on German and American Law' (2002) 17 *Tulane Eur. & Civ. L. F.* 1, 5.

thereof.'[24] We now regard *The Rights of Man* as an example of normal disagreement, not hatred.

How can we distinguish critique that is too extreme, that ought to be condemned as hatred, from mere disagreement?[25] The problem arises just as much in the context of contemporary hate speech regulation as it does in the context of seditious libel. Is speech attacking Islamic fundamentalism for its homophobia and suppression of women hate speech or critique? Is it hate speech or critique to attack the Catholic Church for its pedophiliac priests or for its position on abortion? Are the criticisms of African Americans by William Julius Wilson[26] or Shelby Steele[27] or Louis Farrakhan[28] hate speech or critique? Is the pacifist argument that 'Soldiers are murderers'[29] hate speech or critique?

---

[24] J. Ridgway (ed.), *The Speeches of The Hon. Thomas Erskine, Vol. II* (London: S. Gosnell, 1810), 5. The jury convicted even before the closing arguments. Stephen summarizes Erskine's famous defence as:

> A man who publishes what he really believes to be true from a desire to benefit mankind, does not act from a bad motive, however erroneous his opinions may be, and however harshly they may be expressed. Therefore, no publication of any opinions really entertained is criminal unless the publisher wishes to injure mankind.

See n. 10 above, 364. Stephen comments: 'Practically the inference would be that there ought to be no prosecutions for seditious libel at all unless the matter published obviously tended to provoke people to commit some definite crime, or unless it contained definite attacks upon individual character. This is not unlike the conclusion at which we have in practice arrived in these days.'

[25] We should recall in this context the famous remarks of Lord Chesterfield to the House of Lords, supposedly written by Samuel Johnson:

> One of the greatest blessings, my Lords, we enjoy is liberty; but every good in this life has its alloy of evil: licentiousness is the alloy of liberty, it is an ebullition, an excrescence; it is a speck upon the eye of the political body, but which I can never touch but with a gentle, with a trembling hand, lest I destroy the body, lest I injure the eye upon which it is apt to appear.
>
> There is such a connection between licentiousness and liberty, that is not easy to correct the one, without dangerously wounding the other: it is extreme hard to distinguish the true limit between them: like a changeable silk, we can easily see there are two different colours, but we cannot easily discover where the one ends, or where the other begins.

Quoted in Ridgway (n. 24 above), 148–49.

[26] W. J. Wilson, 'Social Research and the Underclass Debate' (1989) 43 *Bull. Am. Acad. Arts & Sci.* 30, 32, noting the 'chronic, self-perpetuating pathology . . . of the ghetto', including 'problems of crime, sexual exploitation, teenage pregnancy, alcoholism, drug addiction, and other forms of self-destructive behaviour.'

[27] S. Steele, *The Content of Our Character: A New Vision of Race in America* (New York: St Martin's Press, 1990), 50. Blacks come 'to the mainstream in the first place with a lower stock of self-esteem' that makes for a kind of 'opportunity aversion' which 'minimalizes opportunity to the point where it can be ignored. In black communities the most obvious entrepreneurial opportunities are routinely ignored. It is often outsiders or the latest wave of immigrants who own the shops, restaurants, cleaners, gas stations, and even the homes and apartments. Education is a troubled area in black communities for numerous reasons, but certainly one of them is that many black children are not truly imbued with the idea that learning is virtually the same as opportunity.'

[28] See 'Black Power, Foul and Fragrant', *The Economist*, 12 October 1985, 25. Farrakhan's 'basic message . . . is to call on America's large black underclass to stop accepting a position at the bottom of the pile. Stop depending on drugs and drink, he says, and try to be self-reliant; look after your children; clean up the slum where you live; have love for yourself, your family, your community.'

[29] 93 BVerfGE 266 (1995).

Moderns are rightly embarrassed by the notion that simple disagreement can be taken as conclusive evidence of extremism or hatred. We tend to regard the capacity to deny each other's 'self-evident truths' as constitutive of dialogue, which alone can justify the validity of ideas. Laws that punish the bare assertion of some propositional truth, like those which punish Holocaust denial or the assertion of racial inferiority, are rare and always problematic. Almost all regulations of hate speech therefore define hate speech *both* in terms of expressions of dislike or abhorrence *and* in terms of some additional element that is thought to identify the unique presence of extreme hate and hence to justify legal intervention. Although hate speech regulations come in innumerable varieties, this additional element comes in roughly two distinct kinds: sometimes it emphasizes the manner of speech and sometimes it emphasizes the likelihood of causing contingent harm like violence or discrimination.

In the first variation, hate speech legislation conceives itself as punishing speech not merely because of its content, but because of its style of presentation. Hate speech is defined as speech that is formulated in a way that insults, offends, or degrades. The distinction between content and style is apparent in the history of English blasphemy law, which for centuries prohibited expression that offered 'some indignity unto God himself.'[30] As with seditious libel, British law originally defined blasphemous speech on the basis of its substantive content. It punished 'as an offence any general denial of the truth of Christianity, without reference to the language or temper in which such denial is conveyed.'[31] About the middle of the 19th century, however, British blasphemy law began to evolve.

In 1883, Lord Coleridge explained that whatever the 'old cases' may have said 'the mere denial of the truth of Christianity is not enough to constitute the offence of blasphemy.'[32] He defined the crime of blasphemous libel instead as the publication of communications 'calculated and intended to insult the feelings and the deepest religious convictions of the great majority of the persons amongst whom we live.'[33] The point of blasphemy regulation was thus altered so that the law would prevent 'outrages to the general feeling of propriety among the persons amongst whom we live.'[34] 'If the decencies of controversy are observed, even the fundamentals of religion may be attacked without the writer being guilty of blasphemy.'[35] This was essentially the status of the crime of blasphemous libel until its recent repeal.[36] The crime prohibited 'any contemptuous, reviling, scurrilous or ludicrous matter relating to God, Jesus Christ, or the Bible,' but

---

[30] S. Johnson, *A Dictionary of the English Language* (London: W. Strahan, 1756).
[31] Commissioners on Criminal Law, *Sixth Report* 83 (1841).
[32] *R* v. *Ramsay & Foote* (1883) 15 Cox CC 231, 236.
[33] *R* v. *Bradlaugh* (1883) 15 Cox CC 217, 230.
[34] Ibid., 231.
[35] *R* v. *Ramsay & Foote* (1883) 15 Cox CC 238.
[36] *R* v. *Lemon* [1979] AC 617. British laws prohibiting blasphemy were repealed by the Criminal Justice and Immigration Act, 2008, ch. 5, § 79. The repeal took effect on 8 July 2008.

provided that opinions hostile to Christianity may be expressed in a 'decent and moderate' manner.[37]

Much hate speech regulation follows an analogous logic. It permits statements about race, nationality, and religion, so long as such speech maintains a 'decent and moderate' manner. It penalizes speech that inflicts 'outrages to the general feeling of propriety among the persons amongst whom we live.'[38] The question, therefore, is how law can distinguish between, on the one hand, speech which respects 'the decencies of controversy,' and, on the other hand, speech which is outrageous and therefore hate inducing. If this distinction is not determined by the substantive content of the speech, how can it be drawn? I suggest that the distinction can be maintained only by reference to ambient social norms which allow us to distinguish speech that is outrageous from speech that is respectful.[39]

Sociologists teach us that social norms can be very important to the identities of persons. They are, so to speak, internalized into the very identity of persons who have been well-socialized into a culture. The best description of this process of socialization is by the American theoretician George Herbert Mead, who wrote:

What goes to make up the organized self is the organization of the attitudes which are common to the group. A person is a personality because he belongs to a community, because he takes over the institutions of that community into his own conduct. He takes its language as a medium by which he gets his personality, and then through a process of taking the different roles that all the others furnish he comes to get the attitude of the members of the community. Such, in a certain sense, is the structure of a man's personality...The structure, then, on which the self is built is this response which is common to all, for one has to be a member of a community to be a self.[40]

For the sake of terminological simplicity, I shall use the term 'norms' to refer to the group attitudes that we all carry around in us all the time and that form the foundation and possibility of our very 'selves,' and I shall use the term 'community' to refer to the form of social organization that is created and sustained by such norms.

It is by reference to norms that a well-socialized person in any culture can tell whether any given communication is 'extreme,' meaning that the communication violates essential standards of civility and hence is vulnerable to legal sanction. The law commonly enforces social norms of this kind, as for example when it prohibits defamation, invasions of privacy, intentional infliction of emotional distress, flag burning, and so on.

---

[37] *Wingrove* v. *UK* (1997) 24 EHRR 1, 7.

[38] *R* v. *Bradlaugh* (1883) 15 Cox CC 217, 231.

[39] See R. C. Post, 'Racist Speech, Democracy, and the First Amendment' (1991) 32 *Wm. & Mary L. Rev.* 267.

[40] G. H. Mead, *Mind, Self, and Society from the Standpoint of a Social Behaviorist* Ed. C. W. Morris (Chicago: UCP, 1962), 162.

We should note five aspects of these norms. First, norms are not merely subjective; they are instead 'intersubjective', because they refer to attitudes and standards that persons have a right to expect from others. So, for example, when Charles Taylor refers to 'dignity' as rooted in 'our sense of ourselves as commanding (attitudinal) respect,'[41] he means, first, that dignity depends upon communal norms that define respect as between persons in a given community, and, second, that the right to dignity is not merely subjective, but involves claims that members of a community place upon other members of the community by virtue of the shared norms of the community.

Second, norms are not merely instilled during processes of primary socialization in the family, but are also continuously reinforced through forms of social interaction that sociologists like Erving Goffman have demonstrated pervade every aspect of ordinary social life. When these forms of social interaction are disrupted, so are the identities of well-socialized members of a culture. If others act in ways that persistently violate the norms that define my dignity, I find myself threatened, demeaned, perhaps even deranged. The health of our personality, therefore, depends in no small degree upon the observance of community norms.

Third, the totality of a culture's norms defines 'its distinctive shape, its unique identity.'[42] There is thus a reciprocity between individual identity and the cultural identity of a community. Fourth, norms are shared and yet evolve over time. Norms are like a language that conveys meaning because of common expectations but that nevertheless changes over time. Fifth, precisely because norms evolve, they are intrinsically contestable. There are constant struggles over the developing meaning of shared standards and expectations. As a consequence, cultures tend to establish institutions that offer authoritative interpretations of norms: schools are one such institution; another is the law.

To quickly summarize this line of thought, I suggest that 'community' identifies a particular way in which social organization is created, which is by internalizing norms into the identities of persons. Because some such internalization must occur for a person to have a 'self,' community is a primary form of social organization. Healthy human beings always inhabit a community, which they value as they value themselves. But because norms are always in a historical process of evolution, the norms that define community are always threatened, always slipping away, which is why societies have institutions, like schools and the law, to enforce and stabilize norms. Hate speech regulation, like the regulation in preceding centuries of seditious libel, blasphemy, contempt of court, or defamation, exemplifies the aspiration of law to enforce norms that it regards as especially important for community and personal identity.

---

[41] C. Taylor, *Sources of the Self: The Making of the Modern Identity* (Cambridge: CUP, 1989), 15.
[42] K. T. Erikson, *Wayward Puritans: A Study in the Sociology of Deviance* (New York: John Wiley, 1966), 11.

Patrick Devlin offered the classic expression of the assumptions underlying this aspiration. Devlin famously argued that law should be used to enforce the organic norms that define a society's culture:

[S]ociety means a community of ideas; without shared ideas on politics, morals, and ethics no society can exist . . . If men and women try to create a society in which there is no fundamental agreement about good and evil they will fail; if, having based it on common agreement, the agreement goes, the society will disintegrate. For society is not something that is kept together physically; it is held by the invisible bonds of common thought . . . A common morality is part of the bondage. The bondage is part of the price of society; and mankind, which needs society, must pay its price.[43]

Once we understand, however, that norms enforced by law are not fixed and singular in the way that Devlin imagines, but instead are constantly evolving, we can also see that law must continuously choose what kind of community it will sustain. It must always decide whether to reinforce existing norms or to allow for the growth of new norms.[44]

Anthropologists of law express this point by noting that culture is 'never a closed, entirely coherent system but contains within it polyvalent, contestable messages, images, and actions.'[45] Culture is 'a site of social differences and struggles,'[46] so that it is impossible 'to conceive of cultural identity apart from the arenas of contest in which questions of identity arise and are perforce answered.'[47] Law that seeks to enforce the 'common morality' of society must thus intervene into controversies about norms. Law is not innocent in the manner imagined by Devlin. It is rarely a question of *whether* we shall inhabit a common community with a common morality; it is usually instead a question of *what kind of* community we shall inhabit and of *which kind of* morality we shall hold in common.

This suggests that whenever law chooses to enforce cultural norms, as for example by enforcing norms that distinguish hate speech from normal disagreement, law hegemonically imposes a particular vision of these norms. Hate speech regulation imagines itself as simply enforcing the given and natural norms of a decent society, á la Devlin; but from a sociological or anthropological point of view we know that law is always actually enforcing the mores of the dominant group that controls the content of law. For every Machiavelli who urges law to prohibit speech that induces hatred of the state, there is a Walt Whitman who urges us to 'hate tyrants.'

---

[43] P. Devlin, *The Enforcement of Morals* (London: OUP, 1965), 10.

[44] R. C. Post, 'Law and Cultural Conflict' (2003) 78 *Chi-Kent L. Rev.* 485.

[45] S. E. Merry, 'Law, Culture, and Cultural Appropriation' (1998) 10 *Yale J. L. & Human.* 575, 582.

[46] R. Johnson, 'What Is Cultural Studies Anyway?' (1987) 16 *Soc. Text* 38, 39.

[47] C. J. Greenhouse, 'Constructive Approaches to Law, Culture, and Identity' (1994) 28 *Law & Soc'y Rev.* 1231, 1240; see M. Sunder, 'Cultural Dissent' (2001) 54 *Stan. L. Rev.* 495, 514–16.

The point was well expressed in debates 78 years ago in the British Parliament during a previous attempt to abolish Great Britain's blasphemy law, which at that time allowed religious dissent only so long as 'the decencies of controversy' were observed. It was recognized that 'what it really comes to is that, where opinions are strongly held by an educated man, those opinions will be expressed in a way which the law cannot touch, while those expressed by an uneducated man, simply because he is uneducated, will come under the penalties of the law.'[48]

[48] 234 Parl. Deb. H.C. (5th Ser.) 535 (1930) (remarks of Mr. Kingsley Griffith); see also ibid., 499:

We have writers today who can commit the offence of blasphemy with impunity, if the offence of blasphemy is an attack on the Christian religion. There are men like Sir Arthur Keith, Mr. H. G. Wells, Mr. Bertrand Russell, Mr. Aldous Huxley, and others who are able to attack the Christian religion without any danger whatever of their being prosecuted, while poor men, expressing the same point of view more bluntly and crudely, expose themselves to fine and imprisonment. That is a thoroughly unsatisfactory state of the law. After all, if one concedes the right to attack religion . . . one has to concede to the people who care to do this thing the right to choose their style of doing it. Different styles are needed for different circumstances and different audiences. I do not suppose the kind of style that would go down in a select circle in the West End would be effective amongst the democracy of the East End.

(remarks of Mr. Thurtle); see also ibid., 558 (remarks of Mr. Lansbury). When the law purports to impose what it regards as a 'natural' distinction between liberty and license, between proper discussion and abuse, it tends to justify itself like this:

There are no questions of more intense and awful interest than those which concern the relations between the Creator and the beings of his creation; and although as a matter of discretion and prudence, it might be better to leave the discussion of such matters to those who, from their education and habits, are most likely to form correct conclusions, yet it cannot be doubted that any man has a right, not merely to judge for himself on such subjects, but also legally speaking to publish his opinions for the benefit of others. When learned and acute men enter upon these discussions with such laudable motives, their very controversies, even where one of the antagonists must necessarily be mistaken, so far from producing mischief, must in general tend to the advancement of truth, and the establishment of religion on the firmest and most stable foundations. The very absurdity and folly of an ignorant man, who professes to teach and enlighten the rest of mankind are usually so gross as to render his errors harmless; but be this as it may, the law interferes not with his blunders so long as they are honest ones, justly considering that society is more than compensated for the partial and limited mischiefs which may arise from the mistaken endeavours of honest ignorance, by the splendid advantages which result to religion and to truth, from the exertions of free and unfettered minds. It is the mischievous abuse of this state of intellectual liberty which calls for penal censure. The law visits not the honest errors, but the malice of mankind. A willful intention to pervert, insult, and mislead others, by means of licentious and contumelious abuse applied to sacred objects, or by willful misrepresentations or artful sophistry, calculated to mislead the ignorant and unwary, is the criterion and test of guilt. A malicious and mischievous intention, or what is equivalent to such an intention, in law, as well as morals, a state of apathy and indifference to the interests of society, is the broad boundary between right and wrong.

If it can be collected from the circumstances of the publication, from a display of offensive levity, from contumelious and abusive expressions applied to sacred persons or subjects, that the design of the author was to occasion that mischief to which the matter which he published immediately tends, to destroy or even to weaken men's sense of religious or moral obligations, to insult those who believe, by casting contumelious abuse and ridicule upon their doctrine, or to bring the established religion and form of worship into disgrace and contempt, the offense against society is complete.

In n. 14 above, 362–63.

Suppressing speech that is highly offensive to religious groups is the aim of the blasphemy statutes that characterize most European states. Even so tolerant a state as Denmark possesses a blasphemy statute that punishes 'any person who, in public, ridicules or insults the dogmas or worship of any lawfully existing religious community.'[49] These laws serve the same sociological function as Denmark's hate speech statutes, which punish 'any person who, publicly ... makes a statement ... insulting or degrading a group of persons on account of their race ...'.[50] Both statutes necessarily distinguish speech that merely expresses disagreement from speech that degrades. Neither statute punishes speech that expresses critique, but each sanctions speech that insults.

I suggest that Danish statutes must draw this distinction by reference to the social norms that in Denmark define respect. But once we understand that even in Denmark such norms are contested, we can also see that both blasphemy and hate speech regulation must necessarily enforce social norms that represent the well-socialized intuitions of the hegemonic class that controls the content of the law. This would be true even in a society that purported to adopt a 'multicultural' perspective enforcing norms of respect among disparate groups.[51] European legal systems tend to be quite comfortable using law to enforce such hegemonic community norms.

By contrast, the First Amendment to the United States Constitution prohibits the punishment of blasphemous speech as well as hate speech. This is because the American First Amendment tends to regard speech necessary for the maintenance of democratic legitimacy, which I shall call 'public discourse,' as a unique domain in which the state is constitutionally prohibited from enforcing community norms.[52] Most customary legal efforts to enforce such norms—the torts of defamation,[53] invasion of privacy,[54] intentional infliction of emotional distress,[55] outrageous or indecent speech,[56] or the crimes of seditious libel[57] or flag burning[58]—are subject to severe constitutional restrictions.

We may ask why the United States Constitution prohibits the enforcement of community norms within public discourse, especially since such enforcement is ordinarily regarded as a common and necessary task of the legal system. The

---

[49] Danish Criminal Code, s.140. See R. N. Winfield, 'An Editorial Controversy Metastasizing: Denmark's Hate Speech Laws' (Spring 2006) 24 *Communications Lawyer* 35.

[50] Danish Criminal Code, s. 266(b).

[51] R. C. Post, 'Democratic Constitutionalism and Cultural Heterogeneity' (2000) 25 *Australian J. Leg. Phil.* 185; R. C. Post, 'Cultural Heterogeneity and Law: Pornography, Blasphemy, and the First Amendment' (1988) 76 *Cal. L. Rev.* 297.

[52] See R. C. Post, 'The Constitutional Concept of Public Discourse: Outrageous Opinion, Democratic Deliberation, and *Hustler Magazine v. Falwell*' (1990) 103 *Harv. L. Rev.* 601.

[53] See *New York Times* v. *Sullivan* 376 US 254 (1964).

[54] See *Time, Inc.* v. *Hill* 385 US 374 (1967).

[55] See *Hustler Magazine* v. *Falwell* 485 US 46 (1988).

[56] See *Cohen* v. *California* 403 US 15 (1971).

[57] See *New York Times* v. *Sullivan* 376 US 254 (1964).

[58] See *Texas* v. *Johnson* 491 US 397 (1989).

explanation offered by our Supreme Court is that in the United States public discourse is an arena for the competition of many distinct communities, each trying to capture the law to impose its own particular norms. The Court has therefore interpreted the Free Speech Clause of the First Amendment in a manner analogous to the Amendment's Establishment Clause, which requires government to be neutral as between the many different religious sects that in America have sought to control the state. Since the 1940s, the Supreme Court has been reluctant to allow the state to enforce community norms in public discourse. In effect the First Amendment pressures the state to be neutral with respect to the many competing communities that seek to control the law by enforcing their own particular ways of distinguishing decency from indecency, critique from hatred:

In the realm of religious faith, and in that of political belief, sharp differences arise. In both fields the tenets of one man may seem the rankest error to his neighbor. To persuade others to his own point of view, the pleader, as we know, at times, resorts to exaggeration, to vilification of men who have been, or are, prominent in church or state, and even to false statement. But the people of this nation have ordained in the light of history, that, in spite of the probability of excesses and abuses, these liberties are, in the long view, essential to enlightened opinion and right conduct on the part of the citizens of a democracy.

The essential characteristic of these liberties is, that under their shield many types of life, character, opinion, and belief can develop unmolested and unobstructed. Nowhere is this shield more necessary than in our own country for a people composed of many races and of many creeds.[59]

In America, unlike Europe, constitutional protections for freedom of speech have been interpreted to create a 'marketplace of communities' as well as a marketplace of ideas.[60] Respect for the equality of diverse communities underlies the American constitutional conclusion that social norms of civility, which always reflect the view of some particular community, may not be used to regulate speech within public discourse.[61] American constitutional law is concerned to protect public discourse as a sphere that remains equally open to all communities, to all potential visions of the good and the decent. It is for this reason that the American First Amendment holds that in public discourse 'one man's vulgarity is another's lyric.'[62]

The second major justification for hate speech regulation does not purport to enforce community norms. There is a large class of hate speech legislation that seeks to distinguish speech expressing extreme abhorrence that is likely to cause harmful effects, like discrimination or violence, from speech with identical content that is not likely to produce such empirical effects. The former is suppressed as hate speech; the latter is not. This is the form of hate speech regulation that is embodied

---

[59] See eg, *Cantwell* v. *Connecticut* 310 US 296, 310 (1940).
[60] See n. 52 above, 634–35.
[61] See R. C. Post, 'Community and the First Amendment' (1997) 29 *Ariz. St. L. J.* 473.
[62] *Cohen* v. *California* 403 US 15, 25 (1971).

in the German statute I mentioned earlier[63] as well as in the American Convention on Human Rights.[64] Such regulation imagines itself as preventing actual, contingent, measurable harms.

Of course every legal system suppresses speech that causes evil consequences. But there is always an important preliminary question about how tightly the causal connection between speech and its possible effects must be drawn before speech can constitutionally be sanctioned. In the United States, content-based restrictions on speech in public discourse cannot be imposed merely on the ground that speech might tend to cause future harm. 'Speech is often provocative and challenging.... [But it] is nevertheless protected against censorship or punishment, unless shown likely to produce a clear and present danger of a serious substantive evil that rises far above public inconvenience, annoyance, or unrest.'[65]

The justification for this unusual legal rule is the fear that permitting a more lax causal connection would invite the government to fabricate pretexts for suppressing speech. A classic historical example of such abuse was the suppression of the advocacy of Communist doctrine on the grounds that such advocacy might cause a future revolution.[66] In the early years of the 20th century, suppression of dissident speech was justified on the basis of what later became known as the 'bad tendency' test, which permitted the censorship of speech that had the general tendency to cause social harms.[67] The stringent requirement that speech must have a very tight causal connection to contingent empirical harms before it can be suppressed emerged when this 'bad tendency' test was repudiated.[68]

There is no doubt that speech which conveys messages of extreme abhorrence may be causally related to harmful effects, like violence or discrimination. But in most cases such speech merely has the tendency to cause these harmful effects.[69] Hate speech regulation that suppresses speech because of this bad tendency would not be permitted in the United States, because the causal connection between the speech and its consequences would be too attenuated to pass constitutional muster. In most countries, by contrast, speech that causes harm can be regulated even if the casual connection between speech and harm is very loose. Most countries have not repudiated the bad tendency test.

That having been said, it is striking that in its actual operation hate speech regulation reaches only a very tiny subset of speech that actually has the tendency to cause the harmful effects of discrimination and violence. Take, for example, the claim that hate speech can be regulated because it causes discrimination against

---

[63] See n. 23 above.   [64] See n. 21 above.

[65] *Terminiello* v. *Chicago* 337 US 1, 4 (1949).

[66] *Gitlow* v. *New York* 268 US 652, 669 (1925).

[67] Ibid., *Debs* v. *United States*, 249 US 211 (1919).

[68] See eg, *Pennekamp* v. *Florida* 328 US 331, 335 (1946).

[69] Speech conveying messages of hate that is more directly and immediately connected to these harms can usually be punished as incitement to violence or discrimination. See *Brandenburg* v. *Ohio* 395 US 444, 447 (1969).

racial groups. Much expression has the tendency to cause this evil. Consider a reputable scientist who publishes an article in a respected scientific journal purporting to demonstrate a correlation between race and crime. Surely such an article would have the genuine tendency to contribute to discrimination, far more so than the crude expression that is ordinarily punished under the rubric of hate speech. Yet it is all but unimaginable that such an article would be suppressed as hate speech. This would be true even if the scientist were to republish his findings in a popular magazine, and even if the policy implications of the article were potentially far more harmful to norms of racial equality than the ranting of a street corner bigot.

The point can be generalized. Sober, rational communication, communication that conforms to the 'decencies of controversy', is extremely unlikely to be suppressed as hate speech, even if it manifestly has the tendency to cause discrimination. It does not take clairvoyance to know that professional or even popular sociological articles analysing Islamic terror cells will not be punished as hate speech. Nor will elite discussions of racial violence or the burdens of immigration. This strongly suggests that laws prohibiting hate speech that purport to regulate only such speech as will cause contingent effects like discrimination do not in fact punish all speech that has the tendency to cause these effects. They actually suppress only the subset of such speech that *also* violates social norms of respect. It appears, therefore, that such laws are not driven as much by the need to eliminate the objective harms of discrimination as by the more urgent need to suppress speech that violates social norms of respect.

The same could be said with regard to laws that seek to suppress hate speech because such speech 'causes' violence. Once again, we can better appreciate the sociological ecology of such laws if we examine a less recent and controversial example. In 19th-century Britain, it was said that blasphemy could be suppressed because its 'sufferance would be the endurance of brawls. When the law is moved against such writers, it is not persecution: it is a defence of the public tranquility and decency.'[70] We now have no difficulty distinguishing between blasphemy and brawls. But two hundred years ago, British law could not make this distinction because it experienced as disorderly and potentially disruptive the violation of the norms of propriety that blasphemy law sought to protect.

When the norms protected by hate speech regulation are violated, we also tend to conceptualize that violation as 'mainly conduct and little speech'.[71] We are easily moved to claim that 'the lewd and obscene, the profane, the libelous, and the insulting or 'fighting' words...tend to incite an immediate breach of the peace'.[72] The sociological point is that we experience the violation of social norms

[70] F. L. Holt, *The Law of Libel* (London: J Butterworth and Son, 1816), 71.
[71] *Cohen* v. *California* 403 US 15, 27(1971), Blackmun, J. dissenting.
[72] *Chaplinsky* v. *New Hampshire* 315 US 568, 572 (1942).

as disorderly and provocative. This is because the maintenance of social norms is essential to the maintenance of social order.

Just as 19th-century Britons experienced the denial of Christian truths as inherently likely to cause violence, so we experience hate speech as inherently likely to cause violence. It should be obvious, however, that this experience does not demonstrate the connection between hate speech and the empirical, contingent fact of violence. It instead underscores the subjective sense of disorder that arises whenever social norms of propriety or civility are violated. Of course we could regulate hate speech like any other incitement to commit a crime, like any speech that creates a clear and present danger of imminent illegality. But hate speech regulation is distinctive in that it seeks to repress speech merely because it has 'the tendency' to produce violence or disorder. Law that seeks to suppress speech with this 'tendency' is in reality law that seeks to suppress violations of essential social norms.

If we were truly serious about prohibiting speech that might cause actual racial or ethnic or national violence, we would proscribe much more than what is currently classified as hate speech. We would proscribe all manner of cinema, novels, and popular entertainment. That hate speech regulation does not reach anywhere near so far suggests that, sociologically speaking, hate speech regulation is most essentially about suppressing speech that violates civility norms. We may tell a story about the connection between hate speech and violence, but the actual shape of the law suggests that we are instead using law to enforce norms of propriety in sensitive areas like race, nationality, and ethnicity. Even the branch of hate speech regulation that purports to turn on objective and empirical facts, like the causation of discrimination or violence, turns out on closer inspection to participate in the venerable tradition of using law to enforce essential community norms.

When law uses community norms to restrict participation in public discourse, it limits the capacity of persons to contribute to the formation of 'that public opinion which is the final source of government in a democratic state'.[73] This may have significant negative social consequences if a society is heterogeneous and encompasses distinct communities with distinct norms,[74] such that the law's exclusions are perceived to be hegemonic and unjustified. To the extent that in any given society free participation in public discourse is necessary for the maintenance of democratic legitimacy,[75] these consequences may include the loss of democratic authority. Under such conditions the enforcement of community norms in public discourse, which the law undertakes in order to promote normative social solidarity of the kind theorized by Devlin, can have the counterintuitive effect of undermining democratic cohesion.

---

[73] L. Hand, J in *Masses Publishing Co.* v. *Patten* 244 F. 535, 540 (S.D.N.Y.) rev'd, 246 F. 24 (2d Cir., 1917).

[74] See Post n. 44 above.

[75] See R. C. Post, 'Democracy and Equality' (2006) 603 *Annals Am. Acad. Pol. & Soc. Sci.* 24.

Different societies will negotiate these possible untoward consequences differently in light of the imperatives and burdens of their own histories. They will differently balance the use of law to sustain essential norms of civility against the use of law to safeguard the capacity of members of diverse domestic cultures freely to express themselves in public discourse. It is in this light that I believe we should assess the rather stark differences between European and American jurisprudences of hate speech.

To explain these differences is the work of comparative sociology. I am no sociologist, but I would offer two hypotheses for further exploration. The first is that highly ingrained and idiosyncratic American values like individualism and mistrust of government combine to put intense pressure on public discourse to legitimate governmental authority in the United States. It is possible that the American First Amendment is so highly speech protective because public discourse in the United States has the extraordinarily difficult task of ensuring democratic legitimacy in a climate of comparatively severe suspicion and distrust. Nothing like this climate would seem to exist in Europe, where democracy is a comparative newcomer to millennia-old forms of highly deferential structures of political governance. European habits of deference to political authority are to American eyes conspicuously evident in the toleration accorded to a European Union that everyone agrees suffers from great democratic deficits. This toleration would be all but inconceivable in the United States. If this contrast is correct, it suggests that European states do not experience the same pressure to keep the communicative public sphere open to individual participation as does the United States, because democratic legitimation is a less pressing issue in Europe.

The contrast between European and American hate speech regulation should be understood not only in terms of the relative need to maintain democratic legitimation in Europe and America, but also in terms of the relative imperative on the two continents of sustaining community identity. Nations will negotiate the tension between democracy and community in light of a felt necessity to enforce shared community norms prerequisite for maintaining social solidarity. My second hypothesis is that this latter necessity is experienced quite differently in the United States than in Europe.

In the United States deeply engrained norms of individualism, which drive what I earlier referred to as the marketplace of communities, tend to undermine common norms of civility, most certainly in the area of speech regulation.[76] This is not true in Europe, as Jim Whitman demonstrates. Whitman argues that European law 'levels up' by extending 'historically high-status norms throughout the population',[77] whereas American law 'levels down' by enabling a 'free and

---

[76] See Post, 'Cultural Heterogeneity' n. 51 above.

[77] J. Q. Whitman, 'The Two Western Cultures of Privacy: Dignity Versus Liberty' (2004) 113 *Yale L. J.* 1151, 1166.

aggressive display of disrespect' that expresses a uniquely American understanding of 'the political constitution of our form of egalitarian society'.[78]

   There are several possible explanations for this difference. It could be that in Europe elite norms retain a hegemonic status that they have lost in America, perhaps because of our populism, or because of our ethnic diversity. Or it could be that American norms of discourse affirmatively valorize disrespect so that, in Whitman's words, '[i]t is important to us, as political actors in everyday life, to refuse to show respect'.[79] Whatever the explanation, I suggest that Americans feel far less pressure to use law to protect the norms at issue in hate speech regulation than do their European counterparts, because American community identity depends far less on the maintenance of these norms than does European community identity.

   The distinct approaches adopted by Europe and America toward the legal regulation of hate speech no doubt reflect both the different role that public discourse plays in underwriting democratic legitimation in the two continents, and also the distinctly different levels of commitment that citizens of the two continents experience with regard to the felt imperative of maintaining norms of respect constitutive of social solidarity.

---

   [78] J. Q. Whitman, 'Enforcing Civility and Respect: Three Societies' (2000) 109 *Yale L. J.* 1279, 1397.
   [79] Ibid.

8

Autonomy and Hate Speech

*C. Edwin Baker**

1. Introduction

Given the evils of hate, any argument for protecting it is, at best, an uphill effort and, at worst, simply misguided. Many people either accept or, at least, wonder whether they should accept, an argument that goes something like this:

Anyone sensitive to the horror of genocide knows that hate pervades the atmosphere at such times. Few goals can rank higher than preventing genocide and the murderous racial conflicts presented to the world during the twentieth century. Moreover, it is difficult to find any value in the freedom to engage in racist hate speech. Important but ultimately less significant values such as free speech cannot, for any sensitive person, lead to any pause in outlawing the speech that contributes to these horrors. Whether or not the ban will be effective in even a few cases at preventing genocide or racial violence, the mere possibility that it will more than justifies the ban.

As an advocate of almost absolute protection of free speech, I should explain the grounds for my valuation of free speech and rejection of the above claim. That explanation, it turns out, is too ambitious for this essay. Nevertheless, Part 2 describes but does not defend a theory of why racist or hate speech should be protected—a theory that I believe provides the best, though often unrecognized, explanation of existing American case law but one that is surely a controversial, probably minority, view even in the United States.

Most readers will realize, as do I, that these theoretical grounds do not really answer my imagined proponent of regulation. Thus, Part 3 describes the empirical evidence that would cause me to abandon the theory described in Part 2, at least in the context of some category of racist or hate speech, but then gives reasons to doubt that this evidence will be forthcoming. In the end, this essay is more a call for more knowledge—I stand ready to be shown that the relevant evidence overrides my doubts about the efficacy of suppression.

* Versions of this paper were presented at conferences on hate speech at Cardozo Law School in November, 2005 and the Central European University in April, 2006. I received helpful comments from many people but particularly Peter Molnar and Monroe Price.

But given the inevitable empirical uncertainties in evaluating such evidence, Part 3 does not answer the last sentence of the imagined argument for regulation set forth above about the mere *possibility* of making a contribution toward prevention. Thus, the final part of this essay offers a different answer: it considers reasons to expect, as a practical matter, that hate speech *regulation* is more likely to contribute to genocidal events and major events of racial violence than to reduce them. These historical horrors help justify, or so I suggest, greater protection for speech. My hypothesis is that the empirical investigation supports the gamble that strong speech protection leads to better results.

Before beginning, however, I offer the following preface. Constantly, references to 'American exceptionalism' are made in discussions of free speech. Usually the suggestion is that the United States is extremely protective of free speech, disregarding most contrary values, while Europeans, although generally protective of core speech freedoms, have a margin of appreciation that also recognizes other important values that it considers in determining the extent of protection of speech—basically an approach Americans call 'balancing'. This suggestion of difference is, at best, overblown. First, in many contexts many Europeans—including some Justices on the European Court of Justice—favour something close to what has been portrayed as the strongly speech-protective American position. For example, a 2004 decision of the Hungarian Constitutional Court followed its earlier 1992 decision in repeatedly invoking the American 'clear and present danger' test in finding unconstitutional a law that punished speech provoking racial hate.[1] In contrast, many if not most American First Amendment scholars and courts favour 'balancing' that is quite like what is portrayed as the European approach.[2]

Moreover, though some Americans—I am one—favour the strongly speech-protective approach identified with American exceptionalism, that approach has been in the United States a 'fighting faith' that often has not (yet) prevailed. Admittedly, the last half of the twentieth century saw generally increasing judicial protection of speech in America. Still, earlier in the twentieth century, American courts regularly approved limits, jailing or fining people for their speech activities. All sorts of expression have been prohibited and punished—speech favouring socialism, communism, anarchism,[3] and an even more mainstream political

---

[1] Hungarian Constitutional Court, Decision 18/2004 (v. 25). AB, available at: <http://www. mkab.hu/content/en/en3/09360304.htm> (last accessed 24 July 2008).

[2] Virtually all First Amendment opinions of Chief Justice Burger or Justice Powell adopt a form of balancing, which has received one of its best defences in S. H. Shiffrin, *The First Amendment, Democracy, and Romance* (Cambridge, MA: Harvard UP, 1990), an approach that would probably require reversal of many of the great modern First Amendment opinions in which no hint of balancing occurs. See C. E. Baker, 'Harm, Liberty, and Free Speech' (1997) 70(4) *S. Cal. L. Rev.* 979.

[3] See cases described in Z. Chafee, Jr., *Free Speech in the United States* (Cambridge, MA: Harvard UP, 1964), esp. ch. 2, 36–107.

editorial;[4] racist speech[5] or sexually explicit speech;[6] publication and sale of great novels;[7] feminist materials important for sex education;[8] labour picketing[9] and public assemblies.[10] And to this day, the First Amendment, which applies only to governmental not private activity, does not protect people from being fired by private employers for their speech or political associations.

Interestingly, putting aside official legal doctrine, some political scientists have concluded that in practice as opposed to rhetoric the United States is not exceptional in the way these comments suggest. The impression of one commentator is that, as 'compared to nine European democracies, the US has imposed the most severe legal and social "obstacles to political dissent" '.[11] Later this chapter will raise doubts about causal claims. Still, I cannot help wondering if the extraordinarily sad state not only of American foreign policy but also of domestic policies, which have left the US with greater income inequality than any other industrialized democratic country, reflects in part the historically *inadequate* protection of speech freedom in the United States. How would our politics have gone if we had not suppressed labour activists from early in our history, the liberal internationalists during or after World War I, or wiped progressive thinkers out of the universities and cultural industries during the McCarthy period, a cleansing that took decades to repair? Much of Zachariah Chafee's classic book on free speech can be read as supporting his speculative comment that greater respect for free speech at the time of World War I might have led to a better treaty after the war, to support in the United States for the League of Nations, and to 'save[ing]

---

[4] An editorial cartoon criticizing political corruption was the basis for a fine, with the Court refusing to hear the publisher's offer to prove its truth. *Patterson* v. *Colorado* 205 US 454 (1907).

[5] *Beauharnais* v. *Illinois* 343 US 250 (1952).

[6] *Roth* v. *United States* 354 US 476 (1957).

[7] Courts upheld eg, bans on Theodore Drieser's *American Tragedy* in 1930, Lillian Smith's *Strange Fruit* in 1945, Edmund Wilson's *Memories of Hecate County* in 1947 and Erskine Caldwell's *God's Little Acre* in 1950. See T. I. Emerson, *The System of Freedom of Expression* (New York: Random House, 1970), 468–70. Beyond the judicial approval of censorship of specific books was, of course, the effect of this potential on what was written and deleted. This censorship of great—as well as not so great—literature in the United States is well and exhaustively described in E. de Grazia, *Girls Lean Back Everywhere: The Law of Obscenity and the Assault on Genius* (New York: Random House, 1992).

[8] Most famous is Margaret Sanger's persecution under the Comstock laws for trying to circulate birth control information. M. A. Blanchard, 'The American Urge to Censor: Freedom of Expression Versus the Desire to Sanitize—from Anthony Comstock to 2 Live Crew' 33 (1992) *Wm. & Mary L. Rev.* 741, 766–78.

[9] *Giboney* v. *Empire Storage & Ice Co.* 336 US 490 (1949); *Hughes* v. *Superior Court* 339 US 460 (1950); *International Brotherhood of Teamsters, AFL* v. *Vogt, Inc.* 354 US 284 (1957).

[10] A conviction for public speaking in a public place was famously affirmed by Justice Holmes in the now discredited decision of *Commonwealth* v. *Davis* 162 Mass. 510 (1895), aff'd 167 US 43 (1897) and later echoed in decisions such as *Cox* v. *Louisiana* 379 US 559 (1965), upholding an ordinance that prohibited picketing near a courthouse, though reversing conviction because of selective application of the statute against defendants, and *Adderley* v. *Florida* 385 US 39 (1966), upholding the conviction for peacefully demonstrating outside a county jail.

[11] R. J. Goldstein, *Political Repression in Modern America: From 1870 to the Present* (Cambridge, MA: Schenkman, 1978), xiv, quoting R. A. Dahl (ed.), *Political Oppositions in Western Democracies* (New Haven, CT: Yale UP, 1966), xvi, 390–2.

English children from German bombs in 1941'.[12] In any event, though prominent advocates of rather absolutist speech freedom may come from American
scholars and jurists, identifying that position with an American and as contrasted
with a European reality is exaggerated. Still, relatively absolutist protection is the
view that my comments endorse.

2. Speaker Autonomy and State Legitimacy

My premises are: (i) that the legitimacy of the state depends on its respect for
people's equality and autonomy and (ii) that as a purely formal matter, the state
only respects people's autonomy if it allows people in their speech to express their
own values—no matter what these values are and irrespective of how this
expressive content harms other people or makes government processes or
achieving governmental aims difficult. Achievement of more substantive aims,
such as helping people experience fulfilment and dignity, must occur with a legal
structure that as a formal matter respects people's equality and autonomy.

The conception of autonomy that the state must respect is, as noted, in a sense
formal not *substantive*.[13] A legal order must ascribe autonomy to people generally,
usually withdrawing this attribution only to the extent of involvement in institutional structures or frameworks steered by mechanisms other than communication and a person's choices. The state cannot coherently *ask* a person to obey its
laws unless it treats the person as capable of making choices for herself, for
example, the choice to obey the law.[14] As so conceived, respect for a person's
autonomy is in general an on/off value. A government regulation either is or is
not consistent with the required respect. A person is not treated as formally
autonomous if the law denies her the right to use her own expression to embody
her views. As used here, formal autonomy has an activity or choice, not a result or
resource-oriented, focus. (I have gone further and argued that she also must have
a general right over the value-expressive uses of herself—her own body—but that
raises interpretive difficulties not necessary to examine here.) Moreover, meeting
the requirement of respecting her choice autonomy, granting this expressive right,
creates no actual or even potential conflict with respect for others' formal
autonomy, that is, no conflict with recognizing their equivalent choice or
expressive rights with respect to their body or speech. Law's respect for formal
autonomy of one person never denies respect for the formal autonomy (or, for
that matter, the formal equality) of another.

---

[12] See n. 3 above, xiii, 561–2.

[13] C. E. Baker, 'Autonomy and Informational Privacy, or Gossip: The Central Meaning of the
First Amendment' (2004) 21(2) *Soc. Phil. & Pol'y*, 215.

[14] Seeing the law this way represents the most important transformative element of H. L. A.
Hart's transformation of positivism. See H. L. A. Hart, *The Concept of Law*, 2nd edn. (Oxford:
Clarendon Press, 1994 [1961]); C. E. Baker, 'Hart's Transformation of Positivism' (ms, 2008).

In contrast to respect for a person's formal autonomy as an absolute requirement of legal legitimacy, a central aim of a democratic state should be to promote people's *substantive autonomy*. Substantive autonomy involves a person's actual capacity and opportunities to lead the best, most meaningful, self-directed life possible. Laws that advance one person's substantive autonomy—by allocating resources to her or providing her information, for example—often reduce the substantive autonomy of another person. In making policy choices, a state is properly influenced but not controlled by substantively egalitarian aims, welfare maximizing considerations, and various inevitably non-neutral collective self-definitional or majoritarian values. These policy or legal choices, as compared to others the state might make, inevitably favour some people's substantive autonomy over that of others.

Democratic legitimacy, I believe, and certainly the civil libertarian commitment, requires that, in advancing people's substantive autonomy as well as in advancing substantive egalitarian aims and other proper policy goals, the legal order neither have the purpose to nor use general means that disrespect people's formal autonomy (or their formal equality). On this view, respect for free speech is a proper constraint on the choice of collective or legal means to advance legitimate policy goals. Typically racist hate speech embodies the speaker's at least momentary view of the world and, to that extent, expresses her values. Of course, *her speech* does not respect others' equality or dignity. It is not, however, her but the state's legitimacy that is at stake in evaluating the content of the legal order. Law's purposeful restrictions on her racist or hate speech violate her formal autonomy, while her hate speech does not interfere with or contradict anyone else's formal autonomy even if her speech does cause injuries that sometimes include undermining others' substantive autonomy. For this reason, prohibitions on racist or hate speech should generally be impermissible—even if arguably permissible in special, usually institutionally bound, limited contexts where the speaker has no claimed right to act autonomously, such as when, as an employee, she has given up her autonomy in order to meet role demands that are inconsistent with expressions of racism.

Admittedly, other influential theories of free speech could lead to different conclusions—or different explanations for similar conclusions. Pragmatic balancers are likely to treat the notion of formal autonomy as incoherent or lacking moral appeal and instead seek to advance people's substantive autonomy, possibly in a roughly egalitarian manner, or to advance other substantive goals. Undoubtedly, the mere expression of racist hate speech can cause real injuries and has the potential to stimulate further harms. As will be noted below, however, those disparaged by hate speech might well be better off without legal restrictions on the speech. Without offering any sympathy for the racists, the pragmatic balancer could plausibly come out on either side in this debate about legal restrictions on hate speech.[15]

[15] S. H. Shiffrin, *Dissent, Injustice, and the Meanings of America* (Princeton, NJ: Princeton UP, 1999), 49–87.

Equally interesting is another foundational approach to free speech. Some view free speech guarantees as a necessary implication of democracy—with the scope of protection limited by its rationale.[16] To many thoughtful observers, this democratic basis for the protected legal status of speech suggests justifiable restrictions on at least some racist hate speech. The assertion is that the content of racist speech contradicts the democratic premise—an equality in being self-governing. For example, hate speech that portrays a particular group as unfit to participate in the governing process or that advocates crimes against members of a particular group rejects basic premises of democracy. The critique observes that the hate speech does not take a position *within* democratic discourse but rather aims at thwarting democracy and democracy's discourses by means of actual or expressive exclusion. For this reason, it is argued, hate speech can be prohibited.

In the past, a number of jurists have accepted roughly the above view—arguing that anti-democratic speech is permissibly prohibited. Judge Learned Hand treated counselling or advocacy of law violation as inconsistent with the democratic methods of change and, therefore, properly made illegal.[17] Justice Felix Frankfurter explained that communists' speech ranked low on any scale of values.[18] Presumably the low ranking occurred because the communists recommended change by non-democratic means; for that reason, their speech was not 'political' within Frankfurter's understanding of democratic practice. Robert Bork likewise denied that advocacy of law violation—for example, advocacy of revolution or even peaceful civil disobedience—could be 'political speech,' which is the only category that he would protect.[19] At mid-century, Carl Auerbach argued that the basic postulate behind the First Amendment allows Congress to 'exclude from the struggle', to restrict the speech of, 'those groups which, if victorious, would crush democracy and impose totalitarianism'.[20] Such arguments could apply equally to racist hate speech, at least to the extent the speech rejects the premise of democratic inclusion.

Others argue, however, that this conclusion does not follow, or at least does not follow for 'our' (meaning the American) particular version of democracy.[21] They claim that all speech, no matter how disrespectful of others, that is part of public

---

[16] A. Meiklejohn, *Political Freedom: The Constitutional Powers of the People* (New York: Harper, 1960).

[17] *Masses Publishing Co.* v. *Patten* 244 Fed. 535 (S.D.N.Y. 1917).

[18] *Dennis* v. *United States* 341 US 494 (1951), J. Frankfurter, concurring.

[19] R. Bork, 'Neutral Principles and Some First Amendment Problems' (1971) 47 *Ind. L.J.* 1, 20, 29–31. At about the time of publication, Bork in a lecture given at Yale Law School, argued, as I remember it, for an even more restrictive interpretation of the scope of political speech.

[20] 'The Communist Control Act of 1954: A Proposed Legal-Political Theory of Free Speech' (1956) 23 *U. Chi. L. Rev.* 173, 189.

[21] R. C. Post, 'Hate Speech' in this volume; R. C. Post, *Constitutional Domains: Democracy, Community, Management* (Cambridge, MA: Harvard UP, 1995), 119–78; J. Weinstein, 'Hate Speech, Viewpoint Neutrality, and the American Concept of Democracy', in T. R. Hensley (ed.), *The Boundaries of Freedom of Expression & Order in American Democracy* (Kent, OH: Kent State UP, 2001), 146–69; J. Weinstein, 'Extreme Speech, Public Order and Democracy: Lessons from *The Masses* in this volume'.

discourse, merits protection, possibly absolute protection. Even if emphatic about locating the basis of free speech in democracy, 'our' conception of democracy often seems premised on people's autonomously arriving at their own political views— that is, arriving at their views without legal restriction on the public discourse leading to those views. A person must be able to explore (advocate or hear) even views inconsistent with democracy in order to formulate her own commitments, although this strong protection of speech applies only to speech that is part of public discourse, which seemingly covers only speech evocative of possible public issues and which is part of a possible public sphere or public discourse.

This view has undeniable strengths both interpretatively and normatively and may very well reach the same conclusion about most regulation of hate speech as does my emphasis on formal autonomy. Still, unlike a theory grounded on respect for individual autonomy, this democratic approach does not give protection to speech not characterized as part of public discourse. (Interestingly, though for different reasons, both the autonomy and the democratic discourse approaches either completely or largely deny protection to 'commercial speech'.) My theoretical objection to this view relates to its initial premise—that we should protect speech fundamentally because the protection is essential to democracy or, more precisely, to the conception of democracy that we accept. My question is *why* are we so concerned with democracy? Why does democracy provide a foundational premise? (The strategy of my question is the expectation that any sound normative answer to this inquiry will both explain the proper contours of democracy and show that an explanation of the *nature and significance* of democracy's contribution to the legitimacy of the legal order requires and reflects acceptance of value premises that go beyond the structure of the political order to matters such as protection of even non-political self-expression.)

One response could attempt to avoid the normative question and merely say— perhaps for the United States but maybe not for those European countries that restrict hate speech—that we are not only in fact deeply committed to democracy but also that *our* conception of democracy requires virtually complete citizen autonomy within public discourse. This essentially sociological response, however, leaves two problems. First, it does not answer the sceptic, the person who wonders why we should be committed to democracy, particularly *our* conception of democracy, especially given 'the sheer stupidity of the policies of this nation'.[22] Second, and even more fundamentally, to the extent that we do in fact adopt laws punishing hate speech—even if invalidated by courts—it seems that *our* conception of democracy is at least contested. It even seems that, in the view of the majority, our conception of democracy is more like the one that Justice Frankfurter and Judge Hand describe than the one Professors Post and Weinstein propose. They may be right but they need a normative, not merely sociological, rationale for their position.

[22] A. Meiklejohn, 'The First Amendment Is an Absolute' (1961) *Sup. Ct. Rev.* 245, 263.

Instead of the contextual sociological claim, I have argued that the best answer to this normative question of what it is about democracy that justifies our allegiance is that democracy is the *only* political order that embodies a normative principle of equal respect for people's right to be engaged in self-determination when self-determination occurs at the group level, leads to legal allocation of resources, and involves coercion—that is, is the only form of government that respects people as free and equal in the process of choosing laws. But if legitimacy (or the justification of legal obligation) requires respect for people's right of self-determination, there is no reason why this required respect applies only when people act to decide about the collective but not when they act to decide about themselves. If this is right, the fundamental status of each person's equality and autonomy provides *both* the normative basis for democracy and a set of normative principles that democratic laws must not violate. These values both require democracy and require limits on democracy. The logic of this rationale for democracy does not so much place free speech at the centre of democracy but rather locates democracy as an off-shoot of respect for free speech or, more specifically, respect for individual autonomy (and equality). Respect for ascribed autonomy is both definitive of, and a restriction on, the scope of both free speech and democracy. Thus, I reject an emphasis on democratic foundations for free speech in favour of this more basic premise of respect for the individual's autonomy to which the law must conform even as it pursues practices that favour people's substantive autonomy. On this basis, the legal order must respect the autonomy even of the individual who would deny such respect to others in the community—the law must respect the freedom of the racist to express her views.

3. Objections and a Pragmatic Reply

Abstract theory is fine. But a convincing case that a different approach to free speech might prevent occurrences such as the Holocaust, more recent genocides like that in Rwanda, or other virulent, murderous practices would lead me—and I suppose any person of good will—to revise abstract commitments that counsel against legal prohibitions of racist speech. So the natural question is: what evidence or argument would such a convincing case require?

First, some historical evidence is available. So the question becomes: what specific historical evidence should be tellingly relevant to us today? Germany's experience with Nazism is often noted in explaining their current prohibitions on hate speech but it is less clear that this history shows that these prohibitions are *now* needed. Historical accounts might find that racist hate speech was prominent in periods leading up to the genocide. But that finding would clearly not be enough. It would not show whether this speech was causal or merely symptomatic, maybe even usefully symptomatic (in exposing a problem that needed to be dealt with), of deeper underlying forces. And it would not show whether, even if causal in that historical context, it would be so under different historical conditions—for example, the conditions that exist in modern democracies. Moreover, even if historically causal and potentially causal again, racist speech takes many forms and occurs in many contexts. Thus, the account would need to show, in addition, that *the specific hate speech* that proposed legal regulations would effectively prevent was at least a contributing cause of virulent racist or genocidal practices. Support for this last empirical issue—that the restriction would be effective in dealing with the particularly relevant racist speech—will be much harder than a showing of correlation or even cause. Or, alternatively, the account could be convincing in some other way, possibly by showing that the symbolism implicit in the speech prohibitions would be effective at combating racism, again a difficult claim to make with confidence. (Many countries that have experienced the worst racist violence have, in fact, had such prohibitions without successfully preventing racist or genocidal results.[23])

Still, even in the absence of good empirical evidence, a causal claim about racist hate speech—at least as a contributing cause within a longer chain of causation—seems plausible. Genocide or virulent racial discrimination presumably reflects attitudes. It is difficult to understand how such attitudes could first arise and then persist if not in some way embodied in people's communications, their expression. Of course, such expression is unlikely to arise out of nothing. Material conditions and social orientations that are not themselves equivalent to the expression of racism are also likely to be a central part of the causal chain. If so, the question becomes where in this causal chain, where in its fight against virulent racism, should a legal order target its intervention(s)?

The seriousness of the evil surely justifies multiple interventions if their multiplicity increases the likelihood of favourable outcomes. Still, pragmatically to justify hate speech regulation seems to require that the following be shown:

(i) hate speech occurs in cases of genocide or virulent racial discrimination—a demonstration that usually, maybe always, can be made;

(ii) as a causal matter, hate speech—or, more specifically, the hate speech that would be outlawed by hate speech regulation—contributes to these evils. The more general version of this claim is probably right, although the more specific claim about the specific hate speech that would be barred is considerably more speculative. Evidence on the point is seldom offered and, I suspect, seldom would any offering be fully convincing.

Even if these two points are right, the argument for legal prohibitions also requires persuasive support for the following additional claims:

(iii) legal prohibitions of hate speech would actually be an effective place (even if not the exclusive place) to intervene in the causal chain: I have seen little

---

[23] I was told at the conferences where this paper was presented that both Rwanda before the genocide and Nazi and pre-Nazi Germany are examples.

empirical evidence supporting this claim. Below I will suggest doubts that
this argumentative burden can be met;

(iv) these legal bars on hate speech would not reduce the efficaciousness or
likelihood of other (legal or social) interventions that would be more effective
in preventing virulent racist acts; or, at least, that any negative effects would
not be greater than any benefits the bars on hate speech provide; and

(v) enactment of the hate speech prohibitions will not have other 'costs'—
unrelated to race but possibly related to the extent or nature of democracy
and to human freedom—that are greater than the net benefits of these means
in comparison with or in addition to other means for combating daunting
racial evils.

An assessment of these five essentially empirical matters is crucial. I will put aside
the fifth, assume the first two *arguendo*, and focus on the third and fourth.

The third point requires two doubtful claims. It must assume that political
forces will be able to secure adoption and sufficient enforcement of the needed
prohibitions on hate speech *in those situations* where the prohibitions are needed
and could be causally effective as a means to prevent virulent racism or genocide.
Clearly, many places in the modern world have adopted such prohibitions. The
possibility is real, however, that the prohibitions will be adopted and enforced
only in places where and because they are not needed. Still, maybe the proper
purpose of international conventions requiring their adoption is precisely to add
to the political pressure to adopt such restrictions, thereby increasing the likelihood of their adoption where needed.

Even more problematic, to be an effective place to intervene, adopted prohibitions must be efficacious in reducing the likelihood of serious racist evils. Most
obviously, this result probably requires sufficient enforcement of the prohibitions
against the relevant targets. Maybe, however, their mere adoption could help create
a cultural climate where racist speech, and even more importantly, virulent racist
practices, are unacceptable. The question of whether to expect effective enforcement is made more difficult because it is not clear at what stage enforcement would
be meaningful in preventing the polity from devolving in an unacceptably racist
direction or whether enforcement could be effective at reversing cultural directions. Active enforcement (against appropriate targets) is likely only if racist groups
have not become too established. By the time Nazis were gaining power, or during
the year immediately preceding the genocide in Rwanda, effective enforcement
was unlikely. At the relevant time, enforcement would likely be blocked, create a
backlash against the enforcers and sympathy for the 'suppressed' racists, or as will
be discussed below, be enforced primarily against 'unpatriotic' or 'racist' speech of
those most needing protection—Jews or Tutsis, for example, or against African-
Americans in the United States or Algerians in France.

Thus, the hope of those favouring hate speech prohibitions must be that
enforcement will be meaningful and effective at a quite early stage. Pessimism

about this speculative hope seems justified. First are generic doubts about the likelihood of effective legal enforcement. More important, however, is the likelihood that at this most relevant stage the speech that meaningfully contributes to developing or sustaining racism will be subtle, quotidian and, to many people, seemingly inoffensive or at least not 'seriously' offensive speech. This speech is likely to fly under the legal radar screen and, in any event, meaningful enforcement of prohibitions against this speech is even less likely. Thus, even given a belief that racist speech contributes significantly to virulent racism and genocidal practice, my hypothesis is that at earlier stages legal prohibitions will not cover or be effectively enforced against the most relevant speech and at later stages enforcement will not occur, will be counter-productive in creating martyrs for a racist cause, or will focus on the wrong targets.

Even if there is reason to doubt the effectiveness of legal prohibitions in preventing the reign of racist practices, the horrific evil feared (as well as the noxious quality of speech properly covered by a prohibition) recommends that error should be on the side of caution. Here is where the fourth point about possible negative effects of restrictions on hate speech, preliminarily suggested by some comments above, is crucial. Caution is often given as a reason to prohibit hate speech. This reason, however, depends crucially on rejecting two further real empirical possibilities: (i) that the prohibitions themselves will contribute to the racist nature of society and (ii) that adoption of hate speech prohibitions will make other, more effective interventions against the development of a racist, genocidal culture or polity less likely or less effective. Of course, the opposite empirical results are possible. Advocacy of and then adoption of hate speech prohibitions and pressure for their enforcement could invigorate anti-racist politics that makes other, maybe even more significant interventions, more likely. This scenario is, however, at best questionable. And, if the first possibility turns out to be true, adoption of hate speech prohibitions could contribute to the evil outcomes that a country must try to prevent. That is, official legal suppression of 'evil' speech could generate the very evil that motivates suppression.

Given these alternative empirical possibilities, the debate is not between idealistic but uncaring 'liberal' defenders of free speech and fierce opponents of the worst forms of racism. Rather, the pragmatic debate is about different empirical predictions concerning the most effective strategy for opposing racism. Empirical evidence of which scenario is most likely should be welcome. Maybe the evidence exists, though I do not know of it at a level where confidence in a particular conclusion is warranted. Thus, Part 4 describes considerations supporting the empirical hypothesis that speech prohibition will actually exacerbate racist practice. Finally, if the issue remains in doubt, I will consider which direction merits our gamble.

Before engaging in that discussion, however, I will describe an example of when such an exacerbation hypothesis was invoked in a judicial decision. In the late 1940s and early 1950s, the United States prosecuted leaders of the Communist

Party for what could be benignly characterized as advocating (teaching), or conspiracy to teach, the necessity and propriety of violent means to achieve a proletarian dictatorship (though some justices, without any relevant evidence, gave the speech at issue a more malignant characterization). When their convictions were affirmed by the Supreme Court in *Dennis* v. *United States*, Justice Douglas in dissent powerfully asserted:

Communism in the world scene is no bogeyman; but Communism as a political faction or party in this country plainly is. Communism has been so thoroughly exposed in this country that it has been crippled as a political force. *Free speech* has destroyed it as an effective political party.[24] (emphasis added)

Essentially Douglas' account claims 'exceptionalism' for the American response to communism. The claim is implicitly two-fold: that the American response was to rely on free speech and that this response was more effective than other responses tried elsewhere in the world. Unfortunately, specifics of Douglas' historical account and causal claim are either doubtful or much too simplistic. Nevertheless, Douglas illustrates the logic of a view that favouring free speech provides a central aspect of the best response to a major evil to which objectionable speech is said to contribute. Crucially, nothing in Douglas's argument for allowing the expression of evil views counsels neutrality toward or even social toleration of those objectionable revolutionary views. The same lack of social toleration even more obviously applies to the expression of racial hatred. Nothing about legally allowing the speech—either in the *Dennis* case or in the hate speech context—suggests that the views expressed do not present a serious threat to the existence of an acceptable world. Rather, the *pragmatic* claim is that to allow people the option to express their dreadful views is less dangerous than to attempt to outlaw this expression.

4. The Evils Restrictions May Cause

Finally, consider reasons that hate speech prohibitions are likely to backfire. My hypothesis has two reciprocal prongs. First, as an empirical matter, my suspicion is that the prohibitions will not be effective at reducing the chances of horrendous results. That point has been discussed above. Second, also as an empirical matter, my suspicion is that prohibitions on hate speech will actually exacerbate problems, will increase the likelihood of horrendous results. I consider six interrelated points that suggest this suspicion.

First, prohibitions on hate speech may divert energy from and dampen the sense of necessity of the more vital activity of responding expressively to and critiquing racist views. Prohibitions, to the extent that they take overt expression of racism out of public discourse, create a danger about which John Stuart Mill

---

[24] *Dennis* v. *United States* 341 US 494, 588 (1951).

warned. Without people having the experience of responding to and opposing expressions of misguided views, truth is in danger of becoming sterile dogma, ineffective for good because people will have lost the ability to justify and explain the truth when challenged.[25] This point—the need for any noxious doctrine that exists within a community to be publicly expressed and then persuasively rejected—was probably the underlying lesson offered by Justice Douglas' account of the discursive defeat of communism in the United States.

Here is a place to repeat the point that, even if human rights, including the right of everyone to express her views no matter how horrifying, require rejecting legal prohibitions of hate speech, this legal toleration does not imply neutrality or complacency toward the evil views. Neutrality or *social* toleration is the opposite of what society needs. In any free discussion—or in wide-open debate where speech may be 'vehement, caustic, and sometimes unpleasantly sharp' in its attacks[26]—conversational partners (or political opponents) should be committed to each being able to express her view. But the response of the other can be: 'no, your view is entirely unacceptable, it is wrong for the following reasons, and I will do everything within my (legal) power to prevent it from being realized'. Despite conservative objections, people *should seek political correctness*, like all forms of correctness. Of course, ideal responses to the people whom a person believes are offering evil counsels is a subject too extensive to take up here, but I should note that I am hardly recommending retributivist responses or denial of rights. Still, to the extent they are able, people should reject, not tolerate, evil counsels and evil endeavours. Specifically, people should condemn the racist expression and react accordingly to the people who purvey it.

As an empirical hypothesis, I suggest that more active (and thus more effective) opposition to racist views is likely to come from social practices of not tolerating racist expression than from laws making it illegal. People in positions of power or authority do and should lose their influence, and often even their position of authority, for public or exposed private racist expression. Society should be and apparently is prepared to maintain strong social norms rejecting racist viewpoints. I fear, however, that such social practices would be weakened or even replaced by laws prohibiting racist expression. Legal prosecutions focus on the wrong issues— legal requirements, legal line drawing, propriety of prosecution of this rather than other cases. In any minimally decent society that legally permits hate speech, such expression of hate reflexively creates, for those who object to racism, a platform to explain and justify their objections. This expressive activity may provide the greatest safeguard against racist cultures and polities. In contrast, repression creates a platform for racists to claim victim-hood and to appeal to the many who value liberty to oppose the suppression of their freedom, shearing off the energy of a significant group from the chorus that condemns the racist views.

[25] *On Liberty* (London: J. W. Parker and Son, 1859), ch. 2.
[26] *New York Times Co.* v. *Sullivan* 376 US 254, 270 (1964).

Second is a closely related point. By causing racism to (largely) go underground, speech prohibitions are likely to obscure the extent of the problem and
the location or the human or social carriers of the problem, thereby reducing both
the perceived necessity and the likely effectiveness of opposition to racism. My
experience has been that among those people who are likely targets of hate speech
but who still favour free speech, the reason most often given for favouring speech
is the advantage of 'knowing the enemy'. Knowledge of the existence, views, and,
importantly, the identity of those with racist attitudes increases the capacity of
those potentially subject to racist harms to protect themselves and to make
meaningful rhetorical, strategic, political, and legal responses.

Third, speech prohibitions can increase (or create) racist individuals' or groups'
sense of oppression and, thereby, their rage and belief that they must act. There is
an empirical issue of whether prohibitions on racist speech do more to prevent
than to fan the development of racist attitudes. I only speculate here, but I suggest
that the causes are deeper and the prohibitions may do little. If this suggestion is
right, the primary immediate effect of the speech prohibition may be simply to
suppress (or to attempt to suppress) people's expression of their racist views. The
primary dynamic consequence of suppression is to outrage and alienate those
suppressed. They reasonably experience the majority (that is, those who back the
law) and the legal order as specifically denying their basic rights, their right to
express their truthfully held views in the public sphere (or in whatever contexts
the specific law applies) while everyone else has this freedom. For this reason, they
may conclude, they can no longer accord allegiance to (or view as legitimate) this
legal order. That is, the prohibition is likely to increase the virulence of their views
and their self-understanding of being treated unjustly by a legal order that they
see as coddling those whom they despise. Under these conditions, those whose
speech the prohibitions make illegal are likely to feel increasingly justified in using
any means—including violent or illegal means—to pursue their values. Essentially, this is the point of Thomas Emerson's fourth, often neglected reason to
protect free speech.[27] Speech freedom, he argues, helps create a balance between
stability and change, which reduces the likelihood that pent-up anger, when
almost inevitably it *eventually* expresses itself, will be expressed with irrational
violence. The prediction is that even if speech prohibitions decrease the short
term level of expression of the forbidden views, they will increase the likelihood
that those views will periodically be expressed by violent outbreaks.

Fourth, prohibiting verbal *expression* of any values—even the most offensive
views such as expression that denies democratic values or calls for violent or illegal
actions—in the context of discourses where verbal responses are possible, is likely
to reduce the democratic cultural self-understanding that conflicts are to be dealt
with as a political rather than violent struggle. This self-understanding, as

---

[27] *The System of Freedom of Expression*, (n. 7 above), 7; T. I Emerson. *Toward a General Theory of
the First Amendment* (New York: Random House, 1966), 11–5.

suggested earlier, helps decrease the likelihood (without eliminating the danger) that racism will be expressed in overt violence. This is basically Ralf Dahrendorf's vision that the idea of democracy is not to embody the naive goal to eliminate conflict but rather to move society's inevitable real conflicts from the plane of violence to the plane of politics.[28]

Fifth, a political programme of enacting and enforcing hate speech prohibitions runs the danger of diverting political energy from arguably more meaningful political responses to the underlying causes of racism. Often the purveyors of racism have themselves experienced forms of social or material discrimination (or deprivation)—and sometimes they even list their depressed material condition as evidence justifying their racist views. Changing these material conditions is crucial. Though full consideration of the causes of racism is far beyond the scope of this talk (and my understanding), social and material conditions, including those that generate feelings of economic and social marginalization, are likely contexts in which racial resentment flourishes. Changing these conditions, combined with creating contexts that can defuse racist attitudes, could make a significant difference to the likelihood of outbreaks of racial violence as well as to the commonality of attitudes of racial hate. Though the prospects of successful suppression of hate speech may not be good, may even exacerbate the problem, the possibility of reducing (though probably not eliminating) underlying causes may be real. Political energy should be devoted to this task.

Anti-censorship feminists made a similar point in debates about regulation of pornography. Although their substantive views about pornography varied greatly, the anti-censorship feminists were united in the view both that the existing social order operates to oppress women in many spheres and that a strategy of trying to suppress pornography was a misdirection of their political energy.[29] Similarly, the more meaningful political responses to racism include fighting racism within public discourse, referred to in the first point above, but also efforts to change social conditions that generate the alienation of groups among which racism flourishes. Equally important are policy endeavours aimed at integrating into the culture and economy those groups that are typical targets of racist oppression. Effective enforcement of laws prohibiting discrimination in employment and education, as well as affirmative recruitment of typical targets of racism, could help change the material conditions that create racial oppression. The goal should be to change the material conditions that reflect, breed, and sustain racial hatred.

As an example of wrongly directed energies, I have observed corporate leaders showing their liberality by favouring suppression of hate speech (which, in any event, is not conducive to a good business climate). They thereby seem to be

---

[28] *Class and Class Conflict in Industrial Society* (Stanford, CA: Stanford UP, 1959).

[29] C. Meyer, 'Sex, Sin, and Women's Liberation: Against Porn-Suppression' (1994) 72 *Tex. L. Rev.* 1097; N. Strossen, 'A Feminist Critique of "the" Feminist Critique of Pornography' (1993) 79 *Va. L. Rev.* 1099.

(I expect are) caring people who as individuals are opposed to racism. These same leaders, however, often oppose civil rights laws that would force their firms to take responsibility for lack of minorities in their workforce or discrimination against minorities on the job. It is hard to avoid the view that this politics favours the superficial, and for these businesses, the inexpensive remedy over real material responses to underlying social conditions that contribute to racism and racial subordination.[30]

Finally, a prohibition on even a narrowly formulated category of hate speech embodies a principle that will be hard to circumscribe. There are two problems here. First, these laws are likely to be abused by those in power, who will often be able to characterize the speech or politics of their opponents as amounting to hate speech or its equivalent. Consider possible characterizations: that labour agitators ferment class hatred and, potentially, class violence; lesbians ferment hatred of and violence against men; black nationalists make racist attacks on whites; Algerians insult the French; et cetera. Nadine Strossen has argued that the typical use of laws prohibiting hate speech or related offenses to honour, even if adopted to protect minority groups, is to defend dominant groups and punish minority group members or suppress their speech.[31] Minorities in Ethiopia were punished under hate speech laws for their criticisms of Ethiopia's dominant ethnic group.[32] That is, hate speech prohibitions have been continually used to punish activists among oppressed groups for the criticism of dominant groups.

The second problem involves the slippery slope both in application of these categories and use of the justification. Any principle that allows restrictions on speech that preaches hate will be hard to contain. Suppression of other 'harmful' speech to deal with other nasty problems will seem similar. Few laws aiming to restrict speech cannot receive as a justification that the law responds to real harms. But most laws restricting speech see application only or primarily against marginal individuals and groups—the outsiders or dissenters who should be the primary beneficiaries of speech protection.[33] A real danger to free speech is that prohibitions on hate speech, justified because of the serious harm the expression can cause, are likely to justify other restrictions on the basis of arguments about other purported harms with the net effect of further subordinating the disempowered.

Even without any certainty that the prohibitions will have meaningfully beneficial effects, caution might at first seem to justify prohibitions of hate speech. If, however, the six points listed here are right, that is precisely the wrong

---

[30] See a similar suggestion in J. Weinstein, *Hate Speech, Pornography, and the Radical Attack on Free Speech Doctrine* (Boulder, CO: Westview Press, 1999), 155–6.

[31] 'Hate Speech and Pornography: Do We Have to Choose Between Freedom of Speech and Equality?' (1996) 46 *Case Western Reserve L. Rev.* 449, 465–70.

[32] This observation was made at the conference in Budapest (see n. 1 above) by an activist focused on Africa.

[33] See Shiffrin, n. 15 above.

conclusion. Instead, if these points are right, caution would accept the necessity of some real harms out of a realistic fear that prohibitions would overall be counter-productive and lead to even worse results. Those six reasons were: (1) allowing and then combating hate speech discursively is the only real way to keep alive the understanding of the evil of racial hatred; (2) forcing hate speech underground obscures the extent and location of the problem to which society must respond; (3) suppression of hate speech is likely to increase racists' sense of oppression and their willingness to express their views violently; (4) suppression is likely to reduce the societal self-understanding that democracy means not eliminating conflict through suppression—what Justice Jackson described as the unanimity of the graveyard[34]—but rather moving conflict from the plane of violence to the plane of politics; (5) legal prohibition and enforcement of laws against hate speech are likely to divert political energies away from more effective and meaningful responses, especially those directed at changing material conditions in which racism festers; (6) the principle justifying prohibitions and the specific laws prohibiting hate speech are likely to be abused, creating a slippery slope to results contrary to the needs of victims of racial hatred (including jailing the subjects of racial hatred for their verbal responses) and to the needs of other marginalized groups.

5. Conclusion: Democracy's Necessary Faith in People

Thus, my fear is that the precedent of punishing racial hate speech, even punishing loosely defined genocidal speech, may itself contribute to tragedy. For example, as I understand the facts, the International Tribunal's conviction of Rwandan radio broadcasters for genocide based on their speech, speech which was integrated into the actual practice of murder much like that of the leader of a pack of gunmen who directs her subordinates as to whom to shoot, was proper and would have been proper under the relevant US free speech doctrine relating to intentional creation of a clear and present danger of crime.[35] The First Amendment does not protect a person in using speech in an attempt to commit a crime.[36] The speaker who gives orders to her associated gunmen is properly treated as having participated in any murder they commit. However, conviction for genocide of the Rwandan newspaper publisher, Hassan Ngeze, who periodically published racist diatribes against his group's traditional oppressors, who purported to speak in defence of a historically subordinated group, under circumstances where the traditionally subordinated group was apparently under

---

[34] *West Virginia State Board of Education* v. *Barnette* 319 US 624, 641 (1943).

[35] *Brandenburg* v. *Ohio* 395 US 444 (1969).

[36] H. A. Linde, '"Clear and Present Danger" Reexamined: Dissonance in the *Brandenburg* Concerto' (1970) 22 *Stan.L. Rev.* 1163.

armed attack by those oppressors, and who published his views substantially before the occurrence of the genocidal murders, sets a troubling precedent.[37]

As I see it, if cycles of oppression and societal violence are to be broken, a society desperately needs to create a culture of open expression where all views, especially the most extreme views, are openly expressed and debated. In contrast, legal prohibitions on racist speech—to the extent that they would (often did) exist where 'needed' but given how much and against whom these laws most likely would be (or were) enforced—would not have prevented the occurrence of the genocide in Rwanda or elsewhere. But the mere existence of International Tribunal's precedent of jailing this publisher is likely to be used—I have been told informally, has been used—by those in power in African countries at a similar stage in the development of civil society and of democracy, to suppress expression of opposition groups. The precedent might even be used (or more accurately, 'abused') to justify punishment of 'disrespectful' or 'inaccurate' speech about those in power. The impact of this precedent on a nation, through its impact on press freedom, can be hugely significant. Any consequent lack of free press will contribute greatly to the likelihood of corruption in existing governments and to making any replacements of ruling elites much more likely to come only through violence. If my fears are right, the International Tribunal could have hardly given Africa a worse present.

My main pragmatic point, I suppose, is to doubt the validity of the hypothesis that a legal prohibition of (necessarily only some) racist speech, speech which admittedly occurs in contexts that produce genocidal results, would contribute to preventing such events. More specifically, the empirical suppositions justifying this opposition to hate speech regulation are: (1) Speech prohibitions will be ineffective. Contexts in which genocide practices occur are ones in which enforcement of hate speech prohibitions will not occur and the development of such contexts will not be effectively prevented by earlier attempts to legally suppress hate speech. Too many bigoted practices and expressions will fly below the radar screen of any speech prohibitions. (2) Regulation of hate speech may affirmatively contribute to the rise of racist genocidal cultures or polities. (3) A key (though hardly the only) element in the most effective strategy of preventing the rise of such a culture or polity is to provide for more robust protection of speech.

As a concluding comment, I want to indicate awareness of the fact that hate speech causes many real harms, many real injuries. Though I reject the conclusion, these injuries could plausibly justify suppression of hate speech even if suppression were not a wise way to respond to the most dramatic evils of racism. For two reasons, this chapter does not address arguments for suppression of hate speech based on these other injuries. First, much of the commentary explaining

---

[37] See *Prosecutor* v. *Nahimana, Barayagwiza, and Ngeze*, No. ICTR-99-52-T (December 3, 2003); C. E. Baker, 'Genocide, Press Freedom, and the Case of Hassan Ngeze' (2004), available at <http://papers.ssrn.com/sol3/papers.cfm?abstract_id=480762> (last accessed 24 July 2008).

America's exceptionalism, its (purportedly) greater protection of speech, especially of hate speech, involves Europe's twentieth-century close-up experience with fascism and the Holocaust. I wanted therefore in this chapter to rebut the suggestion that some countries have reasons to restrict hate speech different from the reasons operable in the United States. Thus, I needed to argue that this historical experience does not justify, whether or not it explains, a purportedly different European evaluation of free speech. In this regard, I might note that the single most defining element of the American experience, continually reflected in countless aspects of American law, especially in our policy failures, is the legacy of African-American slavery and the American civil war. Europe hardly has a monopoly on hate, on hate speech, or on racism. But to the extent that America has made any progress on this front, free speech protections have likely played a large role.

Second, though the argument that racist speech causes real harms is surely right, that point is hardly unique to racist speech. Real harms are caused by most speech that judges or legislatures consider as possible bases for legal liability or punishment.[38] Here is not the place to discuss the point, but one or both of the reasons given here to protect speech—either normative views that protection is necessary to justify the legitimacy of the legal order or pragmatic arguments about bad consequences of accepting the propriety of regulation—justifies a speech protective stance despite the harms speech can and does cause. This is especially true given the inevitable errors of identifying what speech causes greater harms than benefits and given the inevitable chilling effect of speech regulation on valuable speech.

Justice Holmes argued that our theory of free speech 'is an experiment, as all life is an experiment'. It is a 'wager...based on imperfect knowledge'.[39] Given the lack of adequate evidence for any certainty about the guess whether suppression or freedom provides the best security, I think wisdom requires that choice favour liberty. Liberty is the choice if people are fundamentally good and worthy of respect; suppression is the choice if the opposite holds factually. We are worthy of intellectual attention and concern only if the former is true. For this reason, recognizing that the guess may turn out to be wrong, I would rather have hazarded the guess that justifies a concern with the circumstances and future of humanity. Only then would being right in the guess matter. Moreover, I suspect, given that the answer is not writ in stone, that guess can be a self-fulfilling prophesy. If so, it is clear which prophesy should be favoured.

[38] See Baker (n. 3 above), 979–82, 986–8.
[39] *Abrams* v. *United States* 250 US 616, 624 (1919), dissenting opinion.

9

Hate Speech, Public Discourse, and the First Amendment

*Steven J. Heyman**

In contrast to the law of many other liberal democratic nations, American law holds that constitutional protections for free expression extend to public speech that promotes hatred against racial, ethnic, and religious groups. The classic decision is *Collin* v. *Smith*. In that case a neo-Nazi group announced plans to hold a march in Skokie, Illinois, a Chicago suburb with a large Jewish population. The town responded by adopting several ordinances that outlawed demonstrations and other forms of expression that intentionally 'promote and incite hatred against persons by reason of their race, national origin, or religion'. In *Collin*, the US Court of Appeals for the Seventh Circuit acknowledged that speech of this sort was 'repugnant to the core values' of a civilized society, and that the march might well result in 'the infliction of psychic trauma' on the Jewish residents of Skokie—a group that included several thousand Holocaust survivors. Nevertheless, the court maintained that the Nazi demonstration was 'indistinguishable in principle' from other forms of political agitation that might anger or offend others. For this reason, the court concluded that the march fell within the constitutional guarantee of freedom of speech.[1] Similarly, the US Supreme Court has recently declared that individuals who publicly burn a cross to express racial hatred are engaged in a form of 'lawful political speech at the core of what the First Amendment is designed to protect'.[2] Many American constitutional scholars take the same position.[3]

* This essay is adapted from S. J. Heyman, *Free Speech and Human Dignity* (New Haven: Yale UP, 2008), esp. ch. 10. Thanks to Kate Baldwin, Anita Bernstein, Vincent Blasi, Michael Curtis, Paul Finkleman, Sarah Harding, Robert Post, James Weinstein, David Williams, and Susan Williams for their comments on earlier versions.
[1] *Collin* v. *Smith* 578 F.2d 1197, 1200, 1205–06, 1210 (7th Cir,), *cert. denied*, 439 US 916 (1978). For a related state decision, see *Village of Skokie* v. *National Socialist Party of America* 373 N.E.2d 21 (Ill. 1978).

[2] *Virginia* v. *Black* 538 US 343, 365 (2003).

[3] See eg, R. C. Post, *Constitutional Domains: Democracy, Community, Management* (Cambridge, MA: Harvard UP, 1995) 291–331, hereinafter Post, *Constitutional Domains*; C. R. Sunstein,

In this essay, I offer an alternative understanding of hate speech, public discourse, and the constitutional right to free expression. In Part 1, I outline a general theory of the First Amendment. On this view, freedom of speech is rooted in respect for the autonomy and dignity of human beings. But the same values that justify free speech also give rise to other fundamental rights which are entitled to protection under the law. In Part 2, I use this rights-based theory to argue that the Constitution should not protect public hate speech such as the Nazi march in Skokie, on the grounds that this speech invades the fundamental rights of its targets and that it falls outside of a proper understanding of the political discourse protected by the First Amendment.

1. The Foundations and Limits of the First Amendment Freedom of Expression

In developing a general theory of when speech should be protected, it is natural to begin with the constitutional text. The First Amendment provides that 'Congress shall make no law...abridging the freedom of speech, or of the press'. At first glance, this language appears to grant absolute protection to free expression. When we consider the background and development of this provision, however, a very different story emerges.[4] Eighteenth-century American thought was deeply influenced by the liberal theory of natural rights and the social contract—a theory that was set forth in the works of John Locke and that was popularized by later writers such as John Trenchard and Thomas Gordon, the radical Whig authors of *Cato's Letters*.[5] According to this theory, freedom of speech was an inherent right of human nature and republican citizenship. Like all rights, however, this freedom was limited by the fundamental rights of others, such as the right to reputation. This natural rights understanding of free expression was embodied in the first state declarations of rights, which in turn provided the model for the First Amendment. And the same conception appears to have been held by the framers of the Fourteenth Amendment, which became the vehicle for protecting the liberties in the Bill of Rights against infringement by the state governments.

The natural rights background of the First and Fourteenth Amendments suggests a normative standard for assessing the legitimacy of restrictions on expression: whether they are necessary to protect the basic rights of others. Although this principle was widely held at the time that the Bill of Rights and the Reconstruction

Democracy and the Problem of Free Speech (New York: Free Press, 1993), 184–7; R. C. Post, 'Hate Speech', ch. 7 in this volume, hereinafter Post, 'Hate Speech'.

[4] For a fuller exploration of the history recounted in the following four paragraphs, see S. J. Heyman, *Free Speech and Human Dignity* (Cambridge, MA: Harvard UP, 2008), chs. 1–2, hereinafter Heyman, *Free Speech*.

[5] See eg, J. Locke, *Two Treatises of Government* Ed. P. Laslett (Cambridge, CUP: 1988 [1698]), hereinafter Locke, *Government*; J. Trenchard and T. Gordon, *Cato's Letters, or Essays on Liberty, Civil and Religious, and Other Important Subjects* Ed. R. Hamowy (Indianapolis: Liberty Fund, 1995 [1724]), hereinafter *Cato's Letters*.

Amendments were adopted, it no longer plays a central role in American consti-
tutional jurisprudence. One can trace this change to developments after the Civil
War. During the late nineteenth and early twentieth centuries, the traditional
American belief in natural rights gave way to a fundamentally different conception
of law. According to this view—which was championed by legal positivists such as
Oliver Wendell Holmes, Jr., as well as by progressive scholars such as Roscoe
Pound—the purpose of law was not to protect inherent rights, but rather to
promote social welfare as defined by the community or the state.

Under the influence of this view, American law recharacterized First Amendment problems as conflicts between the 'social interest' in free speech and other
'social interests'. During the course of the twentieth century, it became clear that
an interest-balancing approach of this sort failed to provide adequate protection
for free speech, especially in times of national crisis. Over time, American law has
once more come to view freedom of speech as a fundamental right. But this
revival of rights in First Amendment jurisprudence has not extended to the values
that may be endangered by speech.

As a result of these developments, First Amendment problems are now
understood as conflicts between *the right to free expression* and various *social
interests*—a term within which the rights of others have been absorbed. When the
issue is understood in this way, we seem to face a tragic choice, in which we can
protect freedom of speech only at the expense of other rights, and can safeguard
those rights only by sacrificing freedom of speech.

The best way to escape from this dilemma, I believe, is to return to a rights-
based conception of the First Amendment. On this view, freedom of speech is a
fundamental right. At the same time, that freedom is limited by the rights of
others. Speech that infringes those rights may be regulated by narrowly drawn
laws, except in situations where the value of the speech is sufficient to justify the
injuries it causes.

The difference between this theory and the conventional understanding of the
First Amendment clearly emerges if one considers the case of *Florida Star* v. *B.J.F.*
A Florida jury awarded a rape victim $100,000 in damages for the invasion of her
privacy that resulted when the defendant newspaper published her name in
violation of state law. On appeal, the Supreme Court overturned this award under
the First Amendment. Writing for a six-to-three majority, Justice Thurgood
Marshall framed the issue as a conflict between the First Amendment right to
freedom of the press and the 'state interest[s]' in protecting the privacy and safety
of rape victims. Under the Court's decisions, a state can impose restrictions on the
content of expression only if it can show that a particular regulation is necessary to
promote a compelling state interest. Finding that the state had failed to meet this
highly demanding standard, Marshall held that the regulation was unconstitutional as applied to the facts of *Florida Star*.[6]

---

[6] 491 US 524, 529, 533–4, 537–41 (1989).

How would this case look from a rights-based perspective? On this view, it is clear that the purpose of the Florida statute was not to protect the interests of the state but rather to protect the rights of the victim. The case involved a clash between two sets of rights—the First Amendment rights of the newspaper and the public on one hand, and the victim's rights to privacy and personal security on the other. In resolving such a conflict, the Court should not apply a standard that is heavily weighted toward one side of the balance, but should assess the competing rights in an evenhanded manner. In a situation like this, disclosing the victim's name constitutes a serious invasion of her privacy and may also threaten her personal safety. Moreover, publishing her name does little to promote the public interest, at least in cases like *Florida Star*, in which no one had been arrested or charged with the crime. It follows that, in cases like this, the law should be allowed to shield the identities of sexual assault victims. In this way, the rights-based approach seeks to reconcile freedom of speech with other important values such as privacy.

To make an approach like this work, it is necessary to formulate a general account of the rights that people have, and to show where freedom of speech and other rights fit within this framework. Here I wish to briefly outline a view that I have developed in depth elsewhere.[7] This view draws on the natural rights theory that informed the adoption of the Bill of Rights and the Fourteenth Amendment, as well as on our contemporary understanding of rights. According to this view, rights are based on respect for human freedom and dignity. Rights represent what it means for people to be free in different areas of human life, including (1) the external world; (2) the internal realm of thought and feeling; (3) the social and political domain; and (4) 'the sphere of intellect and spirit'.[8] These four elements of liberty provide the leading justifications for freedom of expression. At the same time, they also support other fundamental rights that impose some limits on that freedom.

External rights. Our idea of liberty begins with what it means to be free in the external world. From this perspective, freedom of thought can be seen as an aspect of personal security, or the right to control one's own mind and body, free from unwarranted interference by others.[9] Likewise, freedom of speech can be understood as a form of outward liberty, or the ability to act as one likes.[10] But other individuals also have a right to personal security. In addition, the community has a collective right to freedom from violence.[11] Speech violates these rights when it

---

[7] See Heyman, *Free Speech* (n. 4 above), chs. 3–5.

[8] *West Virginia State Board of Education. v. Barnette* 319 US 624, 642 (1943).

[9] See eg, St. George Tucker, *Of the Right of Conscience; and of the Freedom of Speech, and of the Press,* in W. Blackstone, *Commentaries on the Laws of England, Vol. 1,* note G, 3 (Philadelphia: Young & Small, 1803).

[10] See eg, *Cato's Letters* (n. 5 above), No. 62, 429.

[11] For a defence of the claim that collective rights find some recognition within the liberal tradition, see Heyman, *Free Speech* (n. 4 above), 40–2. On the community's right to the peace, see 50–1.

constitutes an assault or a threat of violence; when it amounts to 'fighting words'; or when it is intended and likely to incite its audience to lawless action.[12]

Rights of personality. A second justification for free expression is that it is essential to individual self-realization.[13] It follows that unjustified restrictions on speech are wrongful not only because they impose limits on external freedom, but also because they interfere with the ability of individuals to develop and express their own personalities. But the value of individual personality also gives rise to other rights, including privacy, reputation, personal dignity, and emotional tranquillity (a right that is protected by the tort doctrine that affords a remedy for the intentional and unjustified infliction of severe emotional distress).[14]

Rights of citizenship. A third rationale holds that freedom of speech is vital to democratic self-government.[15] When free speech is understood in this way, it should be regarded as a *relational right*—that is, a right to interact with others in a particular way or to participate in a shared activity. The right to take part in democratic deliberation therefore carries with it a duty to respect the corresponding rights of other citizens and of the community itself.

Rights of intellectual and spiritual freedom. In these ways, the same values that underlie freedom of expression also point to certain limitations on that freedom. The same is true of the fourth argument for free speech—that it is necessary for the pursuit of truth.[16] This pursuit takes place on both an individual and a social level. To the extent that this activity involves interaction with others, or has an impact on them, it should also be exercised with due regard for their rights.

The right to equality. In addition to these four categories of substantive rights, individuals have a right to equality. Much of contemporary First Amendment jurisprudence is based on the notion that all individuals have an equal right to express their views and to engage in public debate.[17] At the same time, the idea of equality also lies at the heart of many other rights that are protected by the Constitution as well as by federal, state, and local civil rights laws.

---

[12] For decisions holding these forms of speech unprotected by the First Amendment, see *Virginia* v. *Black* 538 US 343, 359–60 (2003), threats; *Chaplinsky* v. *New Hampshire* 315 US 568, 572 (1942), 'insulting or "fighting" words'; *Brandenburg* v. *Ohio* 395 US 444, 447 (1969) (per curiam), incitement.

[13] For leading accounts of free speech as self-realization, see C. E. Baker, *Human Liberty and Freedom of Speech* (Oxford, OUP: 1989); M. H. Redish, *Freedom of Expression: A Critical Analysis* (Charlottesville, VA: Michie Co, 1984); D. A. J. Richards, *Toleration and the Constitution* (New York: OUP, 1986), 165–230; T. I. Emerson, 'Toward a General Theory of the First Amendment' (1963) 72 *Yale L.J.* 877, 879–81.

[14] For exploration of these rights, see Heyman, *Free Speech* (n. 4 above), 55–7, 149–63, privacy; 57–9, 73–7, reputation; 144–6, personal dignity; 54–5, emotional tranquility.

[15] See eg, A. Meiklejohn, *Political Freedom* (New York: Harper & Bros., 1960); R. C. Post, *Constitutional Domains*, n. 3 above; Sunstein, n. 3 above; R. Bork, 'Neutral Principles and Some First Amendment Problems' (1971) 47 *Ind. L. J.* 1, 20–35.

[16] See eg, J. S. Mill, *On Liberty* Ed. D. Spitz (New York: W. W. Norton, 1975 [1859]), ch 2.

[17] See eg, K. L. Karst, 'Equality as a Central Principle in the First Amendment' (1975) 43 *U. Chi. L. Rev.* 20, discussing the doctrine of content neutrality; S. H. Williams, 'Content Discrimination and the First Amendment' (1991) 139 *U. Pa. L. Rev.* 615, 666–76, same.

In short, freedom of speech should be understood within a broader framework of rights based on human dignity and autonomy. Although free speech is a fundamental right, it must be exercised with due respect for the fundamental rights of others. Speech that invades those rights may be regulated by law except in cases where the value of the speech outweighs the injuries that it causes.

Let me conclude this discussion with three observations. First, while I offer this view as a normative theory of the First Amendment, I believe that it can also illuminate existing American law. To a large extent, the Supreme Court's current jurisprudence is based on the doctrine of content neutrality. That doctrine holds that, 'above all else, the First Amendment means that government has no power to restrict expression because of its message, its ideas, its subject matter, or its content'.[18] If this principle were applied literally, however, the government would be unable to regulate speech even when it causes serious harm to individuals or to society. For this reason, the Court has carved out a number of exceptions to the content neutrality doctrine.[19] Yet the Justices have never succeeded in explaining the rationale for these exceptions or in squaring them with the general rule.[20] By contrast, I believe that the view I have presented—which holds that free speech is limited by the rights of others—is capable of offering a more coherent and principled explanation for why such categories of speech as incitement and defamation should be denied constitutional protection. At the same time, the theory provides a basis for criticizing existing doctrine. For example, the theory suggests that laws to protect personal privacy, such as the regulation in *Florida Star*, should often be sustained under the First Amendment. On the other hand, the theory can also be used to challenge the Supreme Court's obscenity doctrine, which allows states to ban sexually explicit material on the ground that it offends the community's moral standards, without any showing that the material violates the rights of others.[21]

Second, reforming First Amendment jurisprudence in the way that I propose would bring American law closer to the view that prevails in many other liberal democratic nations, where it is commonly accepted that the law must seek to reconcile freedom of expression with other rights.[22] This idea also finds recognition in international human rights law, where it appears in documents such as the European Convention on Human Rights and the International Covenant on Civil and Political Rights (ICCPR).[23]

---

[18] *Police Department of Chicago* v. *Mosley* 408 US 92, 95 (1972).

[19] See eg, *R.A.V.* v. *City of St. Paul* 505 US 377, 382–83 (1992), discussing exceptions such as defamation, fighting words, and obscenity.

[20] For a critique of the Court's doctrine, see Heyman, *Free Speech* (n. 4 above), ch. 6.

[21] See *Miller* v. *California* 413 US 15 (1973); *Paris Adult Theater I* v. *Slaton* 413 US 49 (1973).

[22] See eg, E. Barendt, *Freedom of Speech*, 2nd edn. (Oxford: OUP, 2005), 39–73, 205–26; R. J. Krotoszynski, Jr., *The First Amendment in Cross-Cultural Perspective: A Comparative Legal Analysis of the Freedom of Speech* (New York: NYU Press, 2006).

[23] See European Convention on Human Rights Art 10(2); International Covenant on Civil and Political Rights Art 19(3), hereinafter ICCPR.

Finally, the rights-based theory helps to explain why the law should be allowed to restrict *private hate speech*, by which I mean hate speech that is addressed to specific individuals or small groups of people. For example, hanging a noose over a tree as a warning to African Americans to stay away may amount to a threat of violence.[24] Private hate speech can also violate laws against fighting words, incitement, intentional infliction of emotional distress, invasion of privacy, and discrimination in education, housing, and employment. Speech of this sort generally lacks sufficient value to outweigh the injuries it causes to its targets.[25] Under the rights-based approach, it follows that the expression should not be protected by the First Amendment.[26] Current American constitutional law reaches the same result and allows the state to ban such expression, at least if it does so pursuant to general laws that restrict an entire category of unprotected speech.[27]

[24] See eg, R. G. Jones, 'In Louisiana, a tree, a fight and a question of justice', *The New York Times*, 19 September 2007, describing an incident at a high school in Jena, Louisiana, that led to severe racial tensions. The US House of Representatives has passed a 'sense of the House' resolution condemning the hanging of nooses to intimidate others, and urging that 'any criminal violations should be vigorously prosecuted'. H. Res. 826, 110th Congress, adopted 5 December 2007.

[25] First, a ban on private hate speech imposes only a slight restriction on external liberty in comparison with the severity of the injuries that flow from the speech. Second, while a speaker might feel that the expression promotes his self-realization, this value can be largely or wholly satisfied through thought or expression that is not communicated to the targets, unless the speaker defines his self-realization in terms of negating the rights of others. But this cannot count as a reason for protecting the speech. On the approach I have sketched, the balancing of rights is subject to a crucial constraint: an asserted right can derive no value from its negation of another right. If rights like personal security, personality, and equality have positive value, the negation of those rights cannot also have such value. See Heyman, *Free Speech* (n. 4 above), 70–1. Finally, as I explain in Part 2, hate speech should not be protected because of its contribution to political discourse or the search for truth.

[26] See Heyman *Free Speech* (n. 4 above), 165–6.

[27] See *R.A.V.* v. *City of St. Paul* 505 US 377, 379–80 and n. 1, 388, 395–6 (1992). In *R.A.V.*, however, the Supreme Court ruled five to four that a state may not draw distinctions *within* an unprotected category by subjecting speech based on group hatred to more stringent regulation than other speech in the same category. According to Justice Antonin Scalia, selective restrictions of this sort—such as laws that ban insulting or fighting words only when based on race, religion, or gender—amount to a form of content or viewpoint discrimination forbidden by the First Amendment. See 383–84, 391–96. At the same time, however, Scalia conceded that some instances of speech that fall within an unprotected category may cause greater injury than others. In such cases, the government may choose to regulate only the most harmful acts of speech without violating the rule against content discrimination. See 388–89. But this raises the obvious question of whether the laws that Scalia condemns can be justified on the same ground: that they seek to regulate only the most harmful instances of fighting words. There are several reasons for believing that insults based on race, gender, or religion cause greater harm than insults in general. First, unlike insults that express merely personal dislike, group-based insults often deny the very humanity of their targets. In this way, they inflict a deeper injury. Second, in an important sense, such insults are directed not only against specific individuals, but also against the group in general. For this reason, they may injure more people and may provoke violence on a broader scale. By exacerbating tensions between groups, such insults may also have a greater impact on the community as a whole. And all of these injuries are heightened when the insults are directed against members of groups that historically have been subjected to discrimination and oppression. Thus, the reasons for restricting fighting words and other unprotected categories are particularly powerful when applied to hate speech, and the state should be allowed to subject it to greater regulation. For a fuller critique of the *R.A.V.* opinion, see S. J. Heyman, 'Spheres of Autonomy: Reforming the Content Neutrality Doctrine in First Amendment Jurisprudence' (2002) 10 *Wm. & Mary Bill of Rts. J.* 647, 689–98, 710–4. For a recent

2. Should Public Hate Speech be Protected by the First Amendment?

Now let us return to the question with which we started: the problem of public hate speech. Suppose that, as in the *Skokie* case, a group of neo-Nazis or Klansmen decides to march in full regalia through a Jewish or African American neighbourhood, in order to express profound hatred of those groups, or to urge that they be subjected to segregation, deportation, genocide, or other extreme forms of discrimination or oppression.[28] Should expression of this sort be protected under the First Amendment? Of course, the freedom to engage in political discourse is a basic right in a democratic society. But this right is not absolute. For example, under the Supreme Court's decisions, political speech is not protected when it amounts to a true threat of violence, when it incites its audience to imminent lawbreaking, when it recklessly defames a public figure, or when it negligently defames a private person.[29] On the account I have given, these forms of speech may be restricted to protect the rights of others. The question is whether the same is true of public hate speech such as a Nazi or Ku Klux Klan demonstration. Under the rights-based approach, one should first ask whether the march would infringe the rights of other individuals or the community, and then consider whether it should nevertheless be protected because of its political character.

(i) The Impact of Public Hate Speech on Other Rights

Personal security. In view of the history of violence by Nazis and the Klan, the march is likely—and may very well be intended—to undermine the personal security of the groups against whom it is directed. However, unless the speech clearly amounts to a threat or incitement to violence, its impact on personal security should not be regarded as sufficient to justify regulation.

---

decision that partially retreats from *R.A.V.*, see *Virginia* v. *Black* 538 US 343 (2003). In that case, the Court held that a state could subject threats that were expressed through cross burning to greater regulation than other threats on the ground that cross burning constitutes 'a particularly virulent form of intimidation'. 363.

[28] The Skokie controversy generated a rich and extensive literature. See eg, L. C. Bollinger, *The Tolerant Society: Freedom of Speech and Extremist Speech in America* (New York: OUP, 1986); D. Downs, *Nazis in Skokie: Freedom, Community, and the First Amendment* (Notre Dame: Univ of Notre Dame Press, 1985); A. Neier, *Defending My Enemy: American Nazis in Skokie, Illinois, and the Risks of Freedom* (New York: Dutton, 1979); R. Cohen-Almagor, 'Harm Principle, Offense Principle, and the Skokie Affair' (1993) 41 *Pol. Stud.* 453; D. A. Farber, 'Civilizing Public Discourse: An Essay on Professor Bickel, Justice Harlan, and the Enduring Significance of *Cohen v. California*' 1980 *Duke L.J.* 283.

[29] See eg, *Virginia* v. *Black* 538 US 343, 359–60 (2003), threats; *Brandenburg* v. *Ohio* 395 US 444, 447 (1969) (per curiam), incitement; *New York Times Co.* v. *Sullivan* 376 US 254, 279–80 (1964), defamation of public officials; *Gertz* v. *Robert Welch, Inc.* 418 US 323, 347 (1974), defamation of private figures.

Rights of personality. The march does, however, constitute a serious infringement of the personality rights of its targets. By treating them not as persons but as inferior beings who may be oppressed or murdered, the march may inflict severe distress or even lasting trauma on many members of the group. Whether or not it does so, it constitutes a fundamental attack on their right to personal dignity.[30]

In response, it may be said that the targets can avoid this attack simply by staying away from the march.[31] This objection might be persuasive if the speech took place out of public view. By contrast, speech that is political and that occurs in a public place is intended and must be deemed to be communicated to the public at large, not merely to those who happen to be present at the time. As citizens, minority-group members have a responsibility to attend to the political speech of others, while as the targets of such expression they have a compelling reason to do so. Thus, even if they were to stay away from the march, they could hardly avoid its impact.

It is true, as Justice John Marshall Harlan observes in *Cohen* v. *California,* that in public we are 'often ... subject to objectionable speech' and that public discourse may not be restricted merely because it causes offence to others.[32] In my view, however, it would be a serious mistake to hold that personality is entitled to no protection in the public realm. Individuals do not cease to be persons when they participate in the public life of the community, and they should not be required to wholly sacrifice their personality rights to do so.[33] One can hardly imagine a form of public discourse that injures those rights more deeply than does hate speech.

The right to recognition. Above all, hate speech violates what I shall call the right to recognition. Rights are rooted in respect for personhood. It follows that an individual cannot enjoy rights in relation to others unless they recognize him as a person.[34] Recognition is the most fundamental right that individuals have, a right

---

[30] For an account of this right, see Heyman, *Free Speech* (n. 4 above), 144–6.

[31] See *Collin* v. *Smith* 578 F.2d 1197, 1207 (7th Cir,), *cert. denied* 439 US 916 (1978).

[32] 403 US 15, 21 (1971), internal quotation marks and citation omitted.

[33] Harlan acknowledges this point to some extent when he observes that restrictions on speech may be justified where 'substantial privacy interests are being invaded in an essentially intolerable manner'. Ibid. Although he speaks of 'privacy,' it seems reasonable to extend his statement to other personality rights as well, such as personal dignity and emotional well-being.

[34] This idea is clear not only in the natural rights tradition, but also in the rhetoric of racism itself. A classic statement appears in the *Dred Scott* case. In holding that the descendants of African slaves could never become citizens of the United States, Chief Justice Roger Taney asserted that, at the time the Constitution was adopted, blacks were universally 'regarded as beings of an inferior order, and altogether unfit to associate with the white race, either in social or political relations; and so far inferior, that they had no rights which the white man was bound to respect; and that the negro might justly and lawfully be reduced to slavery for his benefit'. *Dred Scott* v. *Sandford,* 60 US (19 How.) 393, 407 (1857). Of course, during the 1930s and 1940s, the Nazis regarded Jews and other groups as subhuman. For a more recent example, see N. D. Kristof, 'The Face of Genocide', *The New York Times,* 19 November 2006, reporting that Arab militiamen in Darfur (a region of Sudan) have justified the rape and extermination of black Africans by telling them, 'You blacks are not human .... We can do anything we want to you.'

that lies at the basis of all their other rights. At the same time, mutual recognition is the bond that constitutes the political community. For these reasons, individuals have a duty to recognize one another as human beings and citizens. Hate speech violates this duty in a way that profoundly affects both the targets themselves and the society as a whole.

The concept of recognition has deep roots in the natural rights tradition.[35] An early version may be found in the writings of Thomas Hobbes. According to Hobbes, the law of nature dictates that individuals should establish peaceful relations with one another in order to escape from the state of nature, which he represents as a condition of universal hostility, a war of all against all. From this basic principle, he derives a variety of more specific obligations, including a duty to recognize the equality of others. As he explains, 'If Nature . . . have made men equall; that equalitie is to be acknowledged: or if Nature have made men unequall; yet because men that think themselves equall, will not enter into conditions of Peace, but upon Equall termes, such equalitie must be admitted. And therefore [it is a law of Nature,] *That every man acknowledge other for his Equall by Nature*'.[36] From this proposition, Hobbes develops the further rule that individuals must not arrogantly claim for themselves greater rights than they are willing to allow others. Finally, in a passage that bears most directly on the problem of hate speech, he holds that it constitutes a violation of natural law for any person by word or deed to '*declare Hatred, or Contempt of another*', because 'all signs of hatred, or contempt, provoke to fight'. This evil, he notes, may be caused not only by insults against individuals themselves, but also by expressions of contempt for the various groups to which they belong.[37]

Locke also condemns speech that denies the equal rights of others. According to Locke, the freedom and dignity of human beings derive from their nature as 'rational creatures' who are capable of directing their own actions.[38] Reason is also the basis of the law of nature, which teaches that, because all are free and equal, no one should wrongfully harm another. In this way, reason forms a natural bond of community between people. Locke describes the social contract in similar terms, as a 'mutual agreement' among persons who regard one another as free and equal, without any 'Subordination or Subjection' between them. Through the social contract, individuals establish a community for the mutual preservation of their rights—a community that necessarily supposes that its members recognize one another as human beings and citizens.[39]

[35] As I explain below, this concept also plays an important role in contemporary political theory.

[36] T. Hobbes, *Leviathan*, Ed. R. Tuck (Cambridge: CUP, 1991 [1651]), ch. XIV, 91–2; ch. XV, 107. Although he argues in the alternative here, Hobbes himself holds that 'all men are equall' by nature. Ibid., ch. XV, 107; ch. XIII, 86–7.

[37] Ibid., ch. XV, 107–8; ch. XIII, 88.

[38] See J. Locke, 'Of the Conduct of the Understanding' in Eds. R. W. Grant and N. Tarcov, *Some Thoughts Concerning Education and Of the Conduct of the Understanding* (Indianpolis: Hackett, 1996 [1706]), § 6, 178; Locke, *Government* (n. 5 above), Bk. II, §§ 6, 63, 91, 163.

[39] See Locke, *Government* (n. 5 above), Bk. II, §§ 4, 6, 100, 102, 123, 172.

In contrast to Hobbes, Locke was a strong advocate of freedom of thought and belief. In *A Letter Concerning Toleration*, he explores the scope of this freedom in connection with one of the most controversial issues of his time, the problem of conflict and coexistence between religious groups. Locke maintains that individuals have an inalienable right to hold and express their beliefs. At the same time, he argues that this liberty does not extend to speech that refuses to acknowledge the duty to tolerate others, or that asserts a claim to superiority or dominion over them within civil society—a claim that the speakers presumably intend to make good whenever they have the power to do so. Locke argues that speech of this sort 'undermine[s] the Foundations of Society' and should not receive legal protection.[40]

The concept of recognition finds its fullest development in the philosophy of G. W. F. Hegel. Hegel depicts human beings in a state of nature as separate and independent individuals, each of whom regards himself in an egoistic way as the sole, absolute value. When one of these individuals comes face to face with another, he finds his selfhood threatened. This gives rise to a struggle for recognition, in which each party seeks to demonstrate his superiority by subjugating or destroying the other. According to Hegel, this conflict can be resolved only through mutual recognition, a condition of reciprocity in which each individual comes to know himself in the other. Mutual recognition is the basis of personhood, rights, and the state. Within the state, 'man is recognized and treated as a *free* and *rational* being, a *person*'. Conversely, 'the individual ... makes himself worthy of this recognition' by obeying the law and 'acknowledging each as the recognizedly free person he wishes to be himself'. In this way, reciprocal recognition lies at the foundation of a society based on 'rational freedom and genuine civic respect'. Although Hegel does not explicitly address the problem of speech that denies recognition to others, his account sheds a good deal of light on this phenomenon. In particular, we can understand hate speech as reflecting the stage of consciousness in which individuals find themselves deeply threatened by the selfhood of others and respond by trying to dominate or destroy them. Thus, hate speech clearly conflicts with what Hegel regards as the basic principle underlying the system of rights: the duty to '*respect others as persons*'.[41]

---

[40] See J. Locke, *A Letter Concerning Toleration* Ed. J. Tully, Trans. W. Popple (Indianpolis: Hackett, 1983 [1689]), 26–7, 33, 49–50. Similar language appears in Spinoza's classic defence of freedom of speech and thought. Spinoza maintains that the true end of government is 'to enable [individuals] to develope [sic] their minds and bodies in security, and to employ their reason unshackled,' and he formulates many of the basic civil libertarian objections to censorship. B. Spinoza, *A Theologico-Political Treatise* Trans. R. H. M. Elwes (New York: Dover Publications, 1951 [1670]). ch. XX, 259. At the same time, however, he argues that the law may restrict the expression of opinions that 'by their very nature nullify the [social] compact.' Ibid., 260.

[41] G. W. F. Hegel, *Philosophy of Subjective Spirit, Volume 3* Ed. and Trans. M. J. Petry (Dordrecht: D. Reidel, 1978 [1830, 1845]), §§ 430–9, § 432A); G. W. F. Hegel, *Lectures on Natural Right and Political Science* Trans. J. M. Stewart and P. C. Hodgson (Berkeley: Univ of California Press, 1995), § 124; G. W. F. Hegel, *Elements of the Philosophy of Right* Ed. A. W. Wood, Trans. H. B. Nisbet (Cambridge: CUP, 1991 [1820]), §§ 36, 57R. For a comprehensive discussion of Hegel's view, see

In these ways, the concept of recognition plays a central role in natural rights theory. On this view, the most basic function of speech is to assert one's status and to demand recognition from others as a person and a member of the community.[42] Conversely, one has a duty to accord such recognition to others. This duty is violated by public hate speech, such as a Nazi march through a Jewish neighbourhood. By denying recognition to others, the speech also attacks their rights to personal security, dignity, equality, and emotional tranquillity.

(ii) Should Public Hate Speech be Protected Because of Its Political Character?

For all of these reasons, public hate speech should be regarded as presumptively wrongful. Under the rights-based approach, the next question is whether the value of this speech outweighs its impact on the rights of others. In particular, should the speech be protected on the ground that it is intended as a contribution to public discourse?

The way one answers this question will be strongly influenced by one's conception of political speech. According to two of the leading theories in this area—Justice Holmes's vision of the marketplace of ideas and Robert C. Post's theory of public discourse—no principled distinction can be drawn between public hate speech and other forms of political expression. In this section, I criticize these two theories and propose an alternative view of public discourse as speech that takes place within a community that is based on mutual recognition. From this perspective, public hate speech is not entitled to constitutional protection because it violates the principles that should govern democratic debate.

Holmes's theory of the marketplace of ideas. In *Abrams* v. *United States*, Holmes declared that 'the best test of truth is the power of the thought to get itself accepted in the competition of the market'.[43] On this view, the ideas contained in

---

R. R. Williams, *Hegel's Ethics of Recognition* (Berkeley: Univ of California Press, 1997). For other recent works on the concept of recognition, see A. Honneth, *Disrespect: The Normative Foundations of Critical Theory* (Cambridge: Polity Press, 2007); A. Honneth, *The Struggle for Recognition: The Moral Grammar of Social Conflicts* Trans. J. Anderson (Cambridge, MA; MIT Press, 1996), hereinafter Honneth, *Struggle*; P. Ricœur, *The Course of Recognition* Trans. D. Pellauer (Cambridge, MA: Harvard UP, 2005); and the essays by Charles Taylor, Jürgen Habermas, and others in A. Guttman (ed.), *Multiculturalism: Examining the Politics of Recognition* (Princeton: Princeton UP, 1994).

[42] See I. Kant, *The Metaphysics of Morals* Trans. M. Gregor (Cambridge: CUP, 1991 [1797]), *236, explaining that the most basic right and duty one has is to 'assert one's worth as a man in relation to others,' by insisting that they treat oneself not as a mere means but also as an end. In recent decades, this form of speech has been exemplified by the civil rights movement, the women's movement, and the gay rights movement. On the fight for recognition as a social and political struggle, see D. Cornell, *The Imaginary Domain: Abortion, Pornography and Sexual Harassment* (London: Routledge, 1995), ch. 3; Honneth, *Struggle*, n. 41 above; *Multiculturalism*, n. 41 above.

[43] *Abrams* v. *United States* 250 US 616, 630 (1919), J. Holmes, dissenting.

hate speech are no less worthy of consideration than any other beliefs. Whether or not those ideas prevail should be determined by the marketplace itself.[44]

Holmes's view is subject to serious objections, however. Individuals regarded as market participants pursue their own private good. Thus, the consumers in a marketplace of ideas would tend to 'buy' those ideas that accorded with their own interests, and the ideas that prevailed in the marketplace would be those that reflected the interests of the greatest number of people. But the result would merely be the self-interested belief of the majority, rather than an objective truth or one that was capable of being shared by the society as a whole. Indeed, since interests tend to be opposed to one another, the ideas that triumph in the marketplace may well conflict with the most fundamental interests or rights of some members of the society. There is no justification for regarding this process as 'the best test of truth'.

These objections to Holmes's position are especially serious in the case of hate speech. To take an extreme case, consider the idea that genocide should be committed against a relatively small and powerless group within the society. Nothing in the marketplace model precludes the possibility that this idea could prevail if a majority of citizens found that it accorded with their interests and beliefs.[45] Plainly, however, this idea would merely represent the subjective views of the majority, not a truth that in principle could be accepted by all reasonable persons within the society, including members of the target group itself. For these reasons, Holmes's view is unconvincing. An adequate understanding of political speech must be found elsewhere.[46]

Post's theory of public discourse. In recent years, no one has developed a richer or more illuminating theory of the First Amendment than Robert Post. According to this theory, constitutional principles apply in different ways within different areas of social life. Post identifies three distinct 'domains' or 'forms of social order' that 'are especially relevant to understanding [American] constitutional law' in general and First Amendment jurisprudence in particular. The first domain, which he calls *community*, is a form of social life that is governed by 'shared mores and norms'. The second domain, *management*, 'organizes social life instrumentally to achieve specific objectives'. The third domain is *democracy*, which embodies the value of collective self-determination. As Post explains, '[C]ollective self-determination occurs when through participation or potential participation in public

---

[44] See *Gitlow* v. *New York* 268 US 652, 673 (1925), J. Holmes, dissenting, 'If in the long run the beliefs expressed in proletarian dictatorship are destined to be accepted by the dominant forces of the community, the only meaning of free speech is that they should be given their chance and have their way.'

[45] See A. M. Bickel, *The Morality of Consent* (New Haven: Yale UP, 1975), 70–2, 76–7.

[46] For a variety of perspectives on Holmes and the marketplace of ideas, see Baker, n. 13 above, ch. 1; F. Schauer, *Free Speech: A Philosophical Enquiry* (Cambridge: CUP, 1982), ch. 2; J. B. White, *Living Speech: Resisting the Empire of Force* (Princeton: Princeton UP, 2006), 29–38; V. Blasi, 'Holmes and the Marketplace of Ideas' 2004 *Sup. Ct. Rev.* 1; T. C. Grey, 'Holmes, Pragmatism, and Democracy' (1992) 71 *Or. L. Rev.* 521; R. A. Posner, 'The Speech Market and the Legacy of *Schenck*', in L. C. Bollinger and G. R. Stone (eds.), *Eternally Vigilant: Free Speech in the Modern Era* (Chicago: Univ. of Chicago Press, 2002).

discourse, the citizens of a state come to identify with the actions and decisions of their government.' More broadly, public discourse is the medium through which independent citizens come together to shape their common identity and to 'choose the forms of their communal life'. In these ways, public discourse functions 'to reconcile, to the extent possible, the will of individuals with the general will'. In a formulation that Post adopts from Jean Piaget, '"The essence of democracy resides in its attitude towards law as a product of the collective will, and not as something emanating from a transcendent will or from the authority established by divine right. It is therefore the essence of democracy to replace the unilateral respect of authority by the mutual respect of autonomous wills." '[47]

For Post, a central purpose of the First Amendment is to protect speech that is relevant to democratic self-governance. Although the state should often be allowed to regulate speech within other domains, the contemporary American understanding of free speech requires that public discourse 'be as free from legal constraint as is feasible to sustain' so that citizens can fully engage in collective self-determination.[48]

This theory of the First Amendment leads Post to adopt a complex and nuanced approach to the problem of hate speech. The state, he suggests, may forbid 'certain kinds of racist communications in *nonpublic* speech,' on the ground that they conflict with the community's standards of civility and respect or on the ground that they interfere with the accomplishment of legitimate objectives within managerial domains. For example, he would permit some restrictions on hate speech within the workplace as well as within organizations such as state universities.[49]

By contrast, Post contends that 'racist speech is and ought to be immune from regulation within public discourse'. '[T]he value of self-determination,' he writes, 'requires that public discourse be open to the opinions of all.' 'If the state were to forbid the expression of a particular idea, the government would become, with respect to individuals holding that idea, heteronomous and nondemocratic.' This would violate the fundamental principle that (in the words of John Rawls) citizens should be treated ' "in ways consistent with their being viewed as free and equal persons." '[50] It follows that, under the First

---

[47] Post, *Constitutional Domains* (n. 3 above), 1–2, 187–8, 299, 300, 302, 330; R. C. Post, 'Community and the First Amendment' (1997) 29 *Ariz. St. L.J.* 473, 481, hereinafter Post, 'Community'. The quotation is taken from J. Piaget, *The Moral Judgment of the Child* Trans. M. Gabain (Glencoe, IL: Free Press, 1948), 366.

[48] Post, *Constitutional Domains* (n. 3 above), 330.

[49] Ibid., 311–2, 323–9 (emphasis added).

[50] Ibid., 304, 327, quoting J. Rawls, 'Justice as Fairness: Political Not Metaphysical' (1985) 14 *Phil. & Pub. Aff.* 223, 230; see also R. C. Post, 'Equality and Autonomy in First Amendment Jurisprudence' (1997) 95 *Mich. L. Rev.* 1517, 1530–2, 1534, book review, asserting that 'the state's obligation to treat ideas as if they were equal derives from the equal respect that the state owes to speakers as participants in the process of democratic self-governance'.

Amendment, the state has no power to restrict public forms of hate speech like the Nazi march in Skokie.[51]

The problem with Post's argument is that it fails to come to terms with the distinctive nature of hate speech. Because hate speech denies recognition to other citizens, it is plainly incompatible with Piaget's description of democracy as founded on 'the mutual respect of autonomous wills,' as well as with Post's 'image of independent citizens deliberating together to form public opinion'.[52] Hate speech disrespects the autonomy of others and refuses to deliberate with them. In these ways, it tends to undermine rather than to promote the formation of a genuinely common will.

This discussion suggests that Post's account of the preconditions of public discourse is incomplete. Although individuals have a right to take part in public discourse, they also have a duty to respect other citizens as equal participants in that discourse. In other words, it is not enough that the *state* should view individuals as free and equal; citizens must also view *one another* in this light. Only in this way can public discourse serve the functions that Post attributes to it: to reconcile individual and collective autonomy by promoting the development of a shared identity and a common will.

According to Post, any effort to mandate respect for others within public discourse would subordinate democracy to the demands of a very different realm, that of community. In Post's terms, a community is 'a social formation that inculcates norms into the very identities of its members'. These norms or 'civility rules' prescribe the forms of respect that individuals are obligated to show one another. In ordinary social life, the law enforces these norms by regulating speech as well as conduct—for example, by means of 'such communicative torts as defamation, invasion of privacy, and infliction of emotional distress'. By means of these torts, 'the common law not only protects the integrity of the personality of individual community members, but also serves authoritatively to articulate a community's norms and hence to define a community's identity'. As Post explains, however, while the domain of community regards individual identity as the product of social norms, the domain of democracy conceives of individuals as autonomous actors who are capable of collectively defining their identity and shaping their common life. For this reason, he holds that the legal enforcement of civility rules must be suspended within public discourse, so that citizens can freely engage in collective self-determination. Public discourse must be as free from legal

---

[51] Post, *Constitutional Domains* (n. 3 above), 303. I should emphasize that Post makes this claim in an American context, and that the claim is not necessarily meant to apply to other nations. On Post's view, the problem of hate speech involves a tension between 'the maintenance of democracy legitimacy' and 'the felt necessity to enforce shared community norms' in order to sustain a community's identity; and different societies will resolve this tension in different ways. Post, 'Hate Speech', (n. 3 above), 136–8.

[52] Post, *Constitutional Domains* (n. 3 above), 330.

restriction as possible, so as not to constrain 'the boundless possibility of social self-constitution'.[53]

But this argument does not justify Post's view that the state should have no power to regulate racist speech in public discourse. First, as I argue below, a law regulating political hate speech need not be understood as imposing the norms of community on democratic deliberation. On the contrary, the duty to respect others can be understood as an integral feature of public discourse itself. Second, and more fundamentally, I believe that Post is mistaken when he asserts that standards of dignity and respect merely 'reflect the [norms] of some particular community'—norms whose enforcement must be suspended so that citizens can freely determine how they wish to live.[54] Instead, while specific forms of respect differ from one community to another, the requirement that individuals recognize one another as human beings and community members is not simply a contingent or conventional one, but is inherent in the very idea of a community. A collection of individuals who did not regard one another in this way would not be a community at all. It follows that restrictions on recognition-denying speech do not limit our freedom to collectively 'choose the forms of our communal life' by compelling us to adhere to the conventions of a particular society. To put the point another way, Post overstates the case when he describes our ability to shape our common life as 'boundless'. For example, no society can legitimately adopt extreme racist measures such as forced segregation, deportation, or genocide, for such measures would violate the most basic duties a society has to those subject to its jurisdiction. Thus, a ban on hate speech should not be regarded as restricting the legitimate scope of democratic self-governance merely because it precludes a society from considering or adopting policies of this sort.[55]

Although Post believes that democratic debate must be protected from the imposition of civility rules, he recognizes that in some ways democracy depends on the observance of those rules: '[B]ecause the identity of democratic citizens will have been formed by reference to community norms, speech in violation of civility rules will characteristically be perceived as both irrational and coercive.' This leads to what he calls the 'paradox of public discourse': 'the First Amendment, in the name of democracy, suspends legal enforcement of the very civility rules that make rational deliberation possible'. It follows that democracy 'depends in some measure on the spontaneous persistence of civility'. 'In the absence of such persistence, the use of legal regulation to enforce community standards of civility may be required as an unfortunate but necessary option of last resort.'[56]

[53] Ibid., 300–1. Post defends this view most fully in his essay on *Hustler Magazine* v. *Falwell* 485 US 46 (1988), which appears ibid.,119–78.

[54] Post, 'Hate Speech' (n. 3 above), 133.

[55] For similar arguments, see J. Weinstein, *Hate Speech, Pornography, and the Radical Attack on Free Speech Doctrine* (Boulder, CO: Westview Press, 1999), 172–6, hereinafter Weinstein, *Radical Attack*; L. Lessig, 'Post Constitutionalism,' (1996) 94 *Mich. L. Rev.* 1422, 1462–5, reviewing *Constitutional Domains*.

[56] Post, *Constitutional Domains* (n. 3 above), 301; see also 144–8.

In this way, Post qualifies his broad view that norms of dignity and respect may not be enforced within public discourse. For two reasons, however, this qualification fails to adequately reconcile the demands of free speech and human dignity. First, Post makes clear that limits of this sort are exceptional and that they can be applied only at the 'periphery' of the realm of public discourse, not at its 'core'. For example, while he would allow the state to ban fighting words in a face-to-face setting, he would reject legal restrictions on the use of racial epithets in public discourse.[57] Second, Post represents the duty to respect others as an external limitation on public discourse, one that is imported from the domain of community and that is at odds with the principles that govern democracy. I want to argue, on the contrary, that this duty is internal to the realm of public discourse itself.[58]

Public discourse and mutual recognition. In contrast to both Holmes and Post, I believe that political speech is best understood as discourse among individuals who recognize one another as free and equal persons and members of the community. In addition to classical natural rights theorists such as Locke (whose views I discussed above), this view can find support in the work of contemporary theorists such as Alexander Meiklejohn and Jürgen Habermas.

According to Meiklejohn, the First Amendment protects free speech because it is essential to democratic deliberation. He elaborates this view by reference to the traditional town meeting, in which citizens gather to debate and act on matters of public concern. In this meeting, every individual 'has a right and a duty to think his own thoughts, to express them, and to listen to the arguments of others'. Free speech must be protected so that the community can reach the wisest and most fully informed decisions on the issues that come before it. This means that no view 'shall be denied a hearing because it is on one side of the issue rather than another' or because others think it false or dangerous. At the same time, however, Meiklejohn stresses that speakers can be required to observe certain rules of order. These rules do not abridge freedom of speech, but rather make reasoned deliberation possible. In particular, Meiklejohn observes that '[i]f a speaker . . . is abusive or in other ways threatens to defeat the purpose of the meeting, he may be and should be declared "out of order" '.[59]

This position reflects Meiklejohn's conception of the nature of a democratic community. '[U]nder our form of government,' he asserts, 'every citizen has . . . a right to . . . dignity—the dignity of men who govern themselves.' Self-government is possible only on the basis of mutual respect among persons who regard one another as free and equal citizens engaged in 'a common enterprise.' These ideas lie at the heart of Meiklejohn's account of political freedom of speech.[60]

---

[57] Ibid., 177, 311–2, 322–3, 443 n. 112, 447 n. 149; Post, 'Community' (n. 47 above), 483.

[58] For a critique of Post's broader view that personality rights cannot be enforced within public discourse, see Heyman, *Free Speech* (n. 4 above), 276 n. 56.

[59] Meiklejohn (n. 15) above, 24–8.

[60] Ibid., 25, 68–70. In an illuminating intellectual biography, the historian Lance Banning attributes a similar view to Madison. As 'a *revolutionary* statesman,' Banning writes, Madison was

The relationship between speech and mutual recognition also plays an important role in the work of Habermas, perhaps the leading contemporary theorist of public discourse. '[T]he democratic constitutional state,' Habermas observes, 'understands itself as an association of free and equal persons.' 'Such an association is structured by relations of mutual recognition in which each person can expect to be respected by all as free and equal. Each and every person should receive a three-fold recognition: they should receive equal protection and equal respect in their integrity as irreplaceable individuals, as members of ethnic or cultural groups, and as citizens, that is, as members of the political community.'[61]

For Habermas, these relations of mutual recognition are the foundation of rights: '[A]ll rights ultimately stem from the system of rights that free and equal legal subjects would mutually accord to one another.' People are entitled to a wide range of basic rights, from individual rights such as life, liberty, bodily integrity, and personal dignity, to political rights such as freedom of expression, which allow everyone to 'participate in the processes of opinion- and will-formation in which citizens exercise their *political autonomy*.' Habermas characterizes these political rights as forms of 'communicative freedom'—a term he applies to activities that seek to achieve mutual understanding through reasoned discourse. These activities are essential in order to generate legitimate law in accord with what he calls the 'discourse principle', which holds that laws and other norms are valid insofar as 'all possibly affected persons could agree [to them] as participants in rational discourses'.[62]

Habermas maintains that political communication instantiates the discourse principle in two ways. From a *cognitive perspective*, public discourse operates to 'filter reasons and information, topics and contributions in such a way that the outcome of a discourse enjoys a presumption of rational acceptability.' At the same time, public discourse 'has the *practical sense* of establishing relations of mutual understanding that are "violence-free," ' in the sense that participants seek uncoerced agreement rather than dominating or manipulating others. Accordingly, Habermas describes the forms of communication that constitute political discourse as 'structures of mutual recognition'.[63]

'genuinely dedicated to a special concept of how decisions should be made in a republic. He believed that a republic ultimately rests on mutual respect among its citizens and on a recognition on the part of all that they are the constituents of a community of mutually regarding equals, participators in a polity that asks them to be conscious that they are, at once, the rulers and the ruled'. *The Sacred Fire of Liberty: James Madison and the Founding of the Federal Republic* (Ithaca, NY: Cornell UP, 1995), 287.

[61] J. Habermas, *Between Facts and Norms: Contributions to a Discourse Theory of Law and Democracy* Trans. W. Rehg (Cambridge, MA: MIT Press, 1996), 496–97. Michael Walzer also emphasizes the relationship between recognition and citizenship. 'The experience of citizenship,' he writes, 'requires the prior acknowledgment that everyone is a citizen—a public form of simple recognition...What is necessary is that the idea of citizenship be shared among some group of people who recognize one another's title and provide some social space within which the title can be acted out.' *Spheres of Justice: A Defense of Pluralism and Equality* (New York: Free Press, 1983), 277.

[62] Habermas (ibid.), 88, 107, 110, 119, 122–3, 125–7, 409.

[63] Ibid., 147–4, 151, 409. In discussing 'violence-free' relations, Habermas draws on the work of Hannah Arendt, ibid., 147–8. For a valuable effort to work out the implications of Habermas's views

In these ways, Meiklejohn and Habermas provide support for the view that political speech should be understood as discourse between individuals who recognize one another as free and equal persons and members of the community.[64] This view dovetails with the general theory of rights I have presented, which holds that rights are founded on the duty to respect the autonomy and dignity of human beings—a duty that applies not merely to the state but also to individuals.[65]

From this perspective, the Supreme Court was mistaken in *Virginia* v. *Black* when it declared that cross burning and other forms of public hate speech should be regarded as 'lawful political speech at the core of what the First Amendment is designed to protect'. Instead, hate speech transgresses the most basic ground rules of public discourse. To use Meiklejohn's language, hate speech may be regarded as a form of abuse that violates the rules of order that make democratic deliberation possible. In Habermasian terms, one can argue that hate speech is not an instance of 'communicative freedom' oriented toward mutual understanding. Rather, the aim of hate speech is to dominate and subordinate others. In this way it is inconsistent with those 'relations of mutual recognition in which each person can expect to be respected by all as free and equal'.[66]

---

for First Amendment theory, see L. B. Solum, 'Freedom of Communicative Action: A Theory of the First Amendment Freedom of Speech' (1989) 83 *Nw. U. L. Rev.* 54.

[64] The law-and-literature scholar James Boyd White expresses this view in eloquent terms: 'To imagine people as speaking is to imagine them in some deep sense as equals, for it is to recognize that each person has her own place in the world, her own mind and her own experience, her own right to express the meanings she finds in existence, from her own perspective. It is to create a polity based upon communication across difference, committing us to the acknowledgment of the reality of the experience of others.' N. 46 above, 42. White adds that racist speech is an 'especially destructive form' of discourse because it denies its targets 'their inherent right to grow and develop as unique and uniquely valuable human beings. In this way racism has kinship with the language and motives of war . . . which reduces whole nations, with all their people . . . to objects of fear and hate.' 209.

[65] This point, which is axiomatic in the natural rights tradition, is stressed by Habermas as well. See Habermas (n. 61 above), 174, 457.

[66] *Virginia* v. *Black* 538 US 343, 365 (2003); Habermas (n. 61 above), 496. Following Kant, Habermas holds that although the law can regulate external conduct, it cannot compel individuals to act from good motives or to hold particular attitudes. Ibid., 83–4, 130, 499; see Kant, *Metaphysics of Morals* (n. 42 above), *214, *218–9, *230, *239. It follows that the 'law cannot oblige its addressees to use individual rights [such as freedom of speech] in ways oriented to reaching understanding,' even though it is only by using their political rights in this way that they can achieve the ends of communicative freedom. Habermas (n. 61 above), 130, 461. In my view, a ban on public hate speech would not violate these strictures against coercion. Such a law would not compel individuals to hold any attitude or to act from any motive. Instead, it would simply prohibit a particular form of external conduct, namely, the act of speaking in a way that violates the rights of others. In this sense, laws against hate speech do not coerce belief any more than do laws against any other kind of wrongful speech. Insofar as hate speech laws are justified to protect the rights of others, they also should not be regarded as inconsistent with Habermas's view that democratic deliberation should involve 'noncoercive communication.' Ibid., 147. On the contrary, hate speech laws promote such communication by excluding the 'violence' that consists in invading the rights of others. Ibid., 148. In this way, such laws can help us to move toward the 'structures of undamaged intersubjectivity' that Habermas regards as essential for 'unleash[ing] the generative force of communicative freedom'. Ibid., 148, 151.

It follows that, in principle, public hate speech does not fall within the First Amendment right to political freedom of speech. Instead, as I have suggested, that right should be understood as a *relational* one, that is, as a right to participate in a certain kind of interaction with others. Political free speech is a right to interact with others as free and equal citizens who are engaged in discourse on matters of common concern. Because this is a right to take part in a cooperative activity, it carries with it a duty to respect the rights of other participants.[67] Thus, the duty to refrain from speech that denies recognition to others is not one that is imposed on public discourse from the outside, but one that is inherent in the concept of political freedom of speech.[68]

(iii) Refining the Rights-Based Analysis of Public Hate Speech

In this part of the essay, I have argued that, by denying recognition to others, public hate speech violates the fundamental rights of its targets as well as the principles of democratic deliberation. For these reasons, the speech does not deserve constitutional protection.

This conclusion is consistent with the view taken by the international community. For example, the ICCPR requires nations to prohibit '[a]ny advocacy of national, racial, or religious hatred that constitutes incitement to discrimination, hostility, or violence'. Other international agreements take the same position. Many liberal democratic nations have enacted laws restricting certain forms of public hate speech, and they regard those laws as consonant with national and international guarantees of freedom of expression.[69]

---

[67] This discussion also lends support to another argument that many scholars have made: that hate speech tends to silence its targets and undermine their right to free expression. Because political discourse involves interaction with others, an individual cannot fully engage in such discourse unless other citizens are willing to interact with her and take her views seriously. By refusing to engage in discourse with their targets and by dissuading other citizens from doing so, hate speakers curtail the ability of target-group members to take part in democratic deliberation. Hate speech can also silence its targets by diminishing their sense of personal security and by attacking their dignity in ways that discourage them from full participation in the life of the community. These considerations suggest that hate speech regulation is justified not only to secure other rights but also to protect freedom of expression itself.

[68] Similar considerations lead to the conclusion that public hate speech should not be protected because of its contribution to the pursuit of truth. Under the First Amendment, individuals must be free to determine their own thoughts and beliefs. In addition, they must be free to join with others in a shared search for truth. In order to do so, however, they must recognize others as reasonable beings who are capable of participating in a common enterprise. By denying recognition to others, hate speech tends to defeat rather than promote the social pursuit of truth. For a fuller discussion of the relationship between mutual recognition and the search for truth, see S. J. Heyman, 'Hate Speech and the Theory of Free Expression', S. J. Heyman (ed.), *Hate Speech and the Constitution* (New York: Garland Publishing, 1996), lxii–lxiii. For the reasons given earlier, public hate speech is also not entitled to protection as a form of external liberty or individual self-realization. See n. 25 above.

[69] ICCPR (n. 23 above), Art. 20(2); see also eg, International Convention on the Elimination of All Forms of Racial Discrimination Art. 4 (similar provision); S. Afr. Const., § 16(2), stating that freedom of expression does not extend to 'advocacy of hatred that is based on race, ethnicity, gender, or religion, and that constitutes incitement to cause harm'; *Jersild* v. *Denmark*, 19 Eur. Ct. H.R. 1

My position on public hate speech is subject to four important qualifications. First, to be meaningful and effective, rights must be realized within a concrete social order.[70] Thus, the right to recognition can provide a justification for hate speech laws only if it is accepted by a particular society. It follows that the controversy over hate speech cannot be resolved purely on the level of legal theory or doctrine but must also play out in the political arena. Those who support or oppose hate speech laws must persuade the community to adopt their views. The courts should allow this debate to proceed and not be too forward in imposing a solution. In particular, they should not reject hate speech laws out of hand on the ground that they are inconsistent with the American understanding of freedom of speech. As the ongoing debate over the issue makes clear, this understanding is not a monolithic one. Moreover, a society's conception of free speech and other rights evolves over time. If the community comes to believe that individuals have a fundamental right to respect as human beings and citizens, and if (as I have tried to show) this right is justified in principle, the courts should not simply hold that no such right exists. Instead, as in other cases, they should consider whether hate speech regulation is justified in view of the competing rights at stake.

Second, in determining whether regulation is appropriate, courts and legislatures must take into account not only the substantive value of the rights, but also practical and institutional considerations. For example, hate speech laws are acceptable only if they can be drafted in a way that clearly distinguishes between lawful and unlawful conduct. Moreover, such laws should not be adopted if they are unnecessary or if they are likely to be counterproductive, for example, by provoking a backlash against minority groups.[71]

This discussion leads to a third qualification. On the view I have presented, the law is justified in regulating public hate speech when it causes concrete and serious injury to other rights that are recognized by the community and when such regulation makes sense from a practical standpoint. But whether this is true will vary from one situation to another. It follows that context is crucial in assessing the constitutionality and desirability of hate speech regulation.

This point becomes clear when we consider several variations on the problem of public hate speech. First, suppose that the Ku Klux Klan burns a cross in the front yard of an African American family's house, in order to terrorize the family

---

(1994), indicating that some restrictions on racist speech are compatible with European Convention on Human Rights; *R.* v. *Keegstra*, [1990] 3 S.C.R. 697 (Can.), upholding a ban on willful promotion of hatred against racial, ethnic, and religious groups; Holocaust Denial Case, 90 BverfGE 241 (Germany 1994), in D. P. Kommers, *The Constitutional Jurisprudence of the Federal Republic of Germany*, 2nd edn. (Durham: Duke UP, 1997), 382. For an overview of the legal approaches taken by the United States and other Western democracies, see M. Rosenfeld, 'Hate Speech in Constitutional Jurisprudence: A Comparative Analysis' (2003) 24 *Cardozo L. Rev.* 1523.

[70] See Heyman, *Free Speech* (n. 4 above), 42.

[71] See eg, S. H. Shiffrin, *Dissent, Injustice, and the Meanings of America* (Princeton, NJ: Princeton UP, 1999) 80–6. For a thoughtful and balanced exploration of the costs and benefits of hate speech regulation, see Weinstein, *Radical Attack*, n. 55 above.

and force them to move. On the view I have presented, this conduct may be banned like other forms of private hate speech that invades its targets' rights to personal security, property, personality, or equality. Under the Supreme Court's decisions, the state clearly has the power to ban this act of expression.[72]

Now imagine that the cross burning was also intended to convey an ideological message to African Americans and to the public in general—say, a message that blacks are inferior and degraded beings who have no place in a white nation. In that case, the expression would also have a political dimension. It seems clear, however, that we would still have no difficulty in holding the expression unprotected by the First Amendment. Although the cross burning was meant to express a political position, this does nothing to ameliorate the injuries that the family members suffer. On the contrary, it aggravates those injuries, for in this case the speech also violates their rights of citizenship by attacking their status as members of the community.

Now suppose that, as in *Brandenburg* v. *Ohio*, the Klan burns a cross at a small rally on a private farm that is not visible to others.[73] Although this conduct may be intended to deny recognition to African Americans, it does so in a way that has far less impact on their rights. At the same time, the cross burning has some value as a means of self-expression and affirmation of group identity. Although those values are not strong enough to justify First Amendment protection for cross burning in front of a family's house, they are sufficient to justify protection in the context of a rally of this sort.

The case I have been focusing on—a march by Nazis or Klansmen through a Jewish or African American neighbourhood—falls between these two extremes. How this issue should be resolved depends on one's assessment of the value of the speech and its impact on other rights. As I have indicated, my own judgment is that this speech causes profound injury to its targets and that it fails to meet the minimum standards of respect that citizens are entitled to demand of one another in public discourse. For these reasons I would hold the speech unprotected by the First Amendment. This conclusion is far from inevitable, however. One could accept the rights-based approach and nevertheless reach the opposite result if one thought that the injuries inflicted by the speech were not concrete and serious enough to justify depriving it of constitutional protection. Ultimately, the issue will turn on whether one believes that allowing the speech or restricting it will best promote the values of human freedom and dignity.[74]

---

[72] See eg, *Virginia* v. *Black* 538 US 343 (2003).

[73] 395 US 444, 445–7 (1969) (per curiam).

[74] An even more difficult problem arises from the publication of hate propaganda in the form of written materials or by means of the broadcast media or the Internet. On one hand, these forms of expression are less confrontational than a Skokie-type march and have a less direct and immediate impact on the targets. On the other hand, because the speech is more widely distributed, it may have a more far reaching effect on them and their status in the society. On balance, I am inclined to deny constitutional protection to these forms of hate speech as well—a position that accords with the view that is commonly taken outside the United States, see n. 69 above and accompanying text.

It follows that controversial issues like hate speech need not be resolved in an all-or-nothing fashion. We can allow regulation of public hate speech in situations where we believe it causes the most serious injury to other rights, while protecting it in other situations. I believe that a view like this, which is sensitive to context, is preferable to one that holds that speech may never (or hardly ever) be regulated on the basis of its content.

Fourth, while people have a right to be free from hate speech, they have no right to be free from expression that challenges their ideas or beliefs. This distinction goes to the heart of the recent controversy over Danish newspaper cartoons that depicted the Prophet Muhammad in ways that many Muslims found blasphemous and disrespectful and that sparked protests and rioting in countries around the world.[75] Although some of the cartoons' critics described them as hate speech against Muslims, this charge was unfounded. Many of the drawings were innocuous and were regarded as offensive only because they violated a belief held by some Islamic sects that forbids any representation of the prophet. In a liberal democratic society, however, public discourse may not be restricted merely because it fails to conform to the religious principles of some members of the society.[76] Several of the other cartoons—such as a drawing of the prophet wearing a turban shaped like a bomb, and another showing him holding a dagger while standing in front of two women clad in burkas—were more provocative. Nevertheless, those drawings did not attack the humanity of Muslims or call for any form of violence or discrimination against them. Instead, these drawings were intended to criticize those aspects of Islamic culture or belief that the artists viewed as promoting terrorism or the subordination of women. This does not constitute hate speech. It is true that religious beliefs are central to many people's identity and that an attack on those beliefs may therefore be experienced as an attack on their personality. But insofar as one's identity is based on beliefs of this sort, it must be open to revision and transformation in light of criticism. For the liberal tradition, this is an essential part of what it means to be rational and autonomous. The right to criticize one's own tradition as well as the views of others is fundamental to the liberal conception of free speech.[77] It follows that such speech falls within the principle of free expression.[78]

In short, individuals must enjoy absolute freedom to advocate and debate ideas, so long as they refrain from attacking the rights of others or their status as human

[75] For a fascinating discussion of this controversy, see R. C. Post, 'Religion and Freedom of Speech: Portraits of Muhammad' (2007) 14 *Constellations* 72.

[76] Ibid., 81.

[77] Similar considerations apply to the controversy over Salman Rushdie's novel, *The Satanic Verses*—a controversy which was rekindled by the British Government's decision to grant him a knighthood. See eg, 'Iran assails Britain for honoring novelist', *The New York Times*, 18 June 2007.

[78] Courts in Denmark and France have rejected lawsuits claiming that it was unlawful to publish the Muhammad cartoons. See J. M. Olsen, 'Danish court rejects suit against paper that printed prophet cartoons', *The Washington Post*, 27 October 2006; 'Prophet cartoons ruled not offensive', *The Australian*, 24 March 2007.

beings and members of the community. To use Habermas's language, speech may never be restricted merely because of its cognitive content, but only when it is directed in a practical way toward violating the rights of others.[79]

This distinction also provides the key to a proper approach to the ongoing controversy over campus speech codes. As academic institutions, colleges and universities should promote the broadest freedom of intellectual inquiry. At the same time, they are communities whose members owe one another a minimum degree of respect. This point is by no means limited to hate speech, but extends to all forms of speech and conduct that wrongfully abuse or harass others. However, it is reasonable to believe that hate speech causes greater injury than many other forms of disrespectful speech and conduct.[80] Thus, it is appropriate for academic institutions to adopt policies that treat hate speech as an especially serious breach of the community's standards of conduct. At the same time, such policies must be carefully drawn to avoid interfering with the legitimate expression of ideas. Once more, context is important: as Post has suggested, it may be reasonable to apply different rules to the dormitories, classrooms, and open spaces of universities.[81]

3. Conclusion

American courts hold that public hate speech must be protected because there is no principled way to distinguish it from other forms of political discourse—a category of speech that lies at the heart of the First Amendment. In this essay, I have argued that this view is incorrect for two reasons. First, public hate speech invades the rights of its targets, especially the right to recognition as a human being and a member of the community. And second, this form of speech violates the basic rules that should govern democratic debate, which depends on mutual respect among free and equal citizens. It follows that, as a matter of principle, public hate speech is not entitled to constitutional protection. Interpreting the First Amendment in this way would not only allow American law to reconcile the competing demands of free speech and human dignity, it would also bring that law into harmony with the principles accepted by other liberal democratic nations and the international community.

---

[79] See Habermas (n. 61 above), 151. For this reason, scientific inquiry should also receive the broadest constitutional protection, even when it reaches conclusions that some consider derogatory. For a similar view, see M. J. Matsuda, 'Public Response to Racist Speech: Considering the Victim's Story', in M. J. Matsuda, C. Lawrence III, R. Delgado, and K. W. Crenshaw, *Words that Wound: Critical Race Theory, Assaultive Speech and the First Amendment* (Boulder, CO: Westview Press, 1993), 40–1.
[80] See n. 27 above.
[81] See Post, *Constitutional Domains* (n. 3 above), 329.

10

Wild-West Cowboys versus Cheese-Eating Surrender Monkeys: Some Problems in Comparative Approaches to Hate Speech

Eric Heinze

1. Introduction

European conferences on hate speech follow a similar pattern. A few Americans make impassioned speeches about the values of freedom and democracy. The Europeans dutifully listen and applaud. Then come tea and biscuits, where the pros and cons of various positions are exchanged with tepid enthusiasm. All delegates are then thanked for having attended an event that 'will surely provide food for thought'. The Europeans depart with the same views they held when they arrived; and the Americans leave crestfallen from a missionary venture that failed to convert a single soul.

European debates on hate speech are likely to remain a trans-Atlantic affair. Few issues divide so blatantly into one approach followed under US law, pitted against an opposite approach in Europe and, effectively, the rest of the world. But it is questionable whether the trans-Atlantic dialogue is going well. Many Europeans view American tolerance of hate speech as another quirk from across the pond: 'Americans prize liberty above everything, even above dignity. Perhaps that wild-west freedom is good for them, but it's not for the rest of us.' To many European eyes, the American approach reflects the callousness that one would expect from a country that maintains a racially discriminatory death penalty,[1] shuns essential social and economic protections for the needy,[2] or commits torture under the guise of 'extraordinary renditions'.[3] And impressions in the

---

[1] See eg, 'Conclusions and Recommendations of the Committee on the Elimination of Racial Discrimination: United States of America', UN Doc A/56/18 (2001), para. 396.

[2] See generally, e.g, Institute for Research on Poverty, <http://www.irp.wisc.edu/> (last accessed 12 June 2008).

[3] See eg, Amnesty International, 'State of the World's Human Rights: United States of America', in *Amnesty International Report 2008*, <http://thereport.amnesty.org/eng/Regions/Americas/United-States-of-America> (last accessed 12 June 2008).

other direction are no better. Any red-blooded Yank will see European hate speech bans as hypocritical posturing from a continent of cheese-eating surrender monkeys who cheerfully sacrifice liberty for any paltry measure of security, or even for sheer decorum.

Although Euro-American comparisons are frequent, and sometimes gentler, little attention has been paid to questions of comparative method. Given the limited enforcement of hate speech bans in Europe, and given that freedoms of speech are, practically speaking, very similar in the United States and Western Europe, one might wonder whether a trans-Atlantic comparison serves any purpose at all. Yet various contributions in this collection suggest that the sheer differences in principle are of intrinsic interest. Under the case law of the US Supreme Court, hate speech bans are effectively inconsistent with free speech. European legislatures and courts have found hate speech bans to be compatible with individual freedom, and even affirmatively required to promote it. It is tempting to believe that those surface differences in legal norms must somehow correlate to deeper cultural differences. While some real cultural differences are, no doubt, at work, we must avoid simplistic understandings of them.

In this chapter, I shall argue that seemingly black-and-white differences in US and European approaches to hate speech turn grey once they are situated within their societies' political and social contexts. As a *descriptive* matter, trans-Atlantic differences on the regulation of extreme speech point to genuine, but still very limited, cultural differences. Therefore, as a *prescriptive* matter, we should avoid hasty conclusions to the effect that the abolition of bans 'may be fine for Americans, but could never work for Europeans'.

Precisely because of my doubts about fundamental cultural differences on this issue, I might just as easily have drawn the opposite prescriptive conclusion: if the underlying cultural differences between European and American approaches to speech are really rather minor, then there are no reasons why hate speech bans could not be *adopted* as easily in the US as in Europe. I shall suggest, however, that there are reasons other than cultural difference for not drawing that conclusion. I shall argue that, in terms of broader cultural histories and attitudes, no particular stance is inevitable for either side of the Atlantic. Questions about whether to adopt hate speech bans should therefore be decided on grounds of democratic principle.

Using Robert Post's chapter in this collection as a point of departure, I shall examine some problems of trans-Atlantic comparison arising at the intersection of formal law and social life. Comparative analysis is indispensable, but we must avoid what I shall identify as the twin traps of cultural essentialism and ahistoricism. We must apply legal realism to some of the formalisms of free-speech doctrine. I begin by inquiring into the specific interest of a comparison between the US and Europe. In rejecting hate speech bans, the US contrasts with most of the world's legal systems. Why, then, focus on a comparison to Europe? Next, I consider Post's notion of institutional, anti-democratic elitism, and the role it plays on both sides of the Atlantic, either to promote or to combat restrictions on speech. I then turn to Post's concept of the 'public sphere', and its relevance to hate speech bans. I compare 'formalist' and 'realist' understandings of the public sphere, and the problems of cultural essentialism that can arise if we fail to distinguish them. Finally, I examine an assumption underlying hate speech bans, namely, that formal restrictions on freedom serve to enhance substantive freedoms. I argue that, just as black-letter norms must be read in a broader social context, they must also be situated within their historical context; just as a legal-realist analysis is required to overcome essentialism, it also serves to avoid ahistoricism in transnational comparisons.

2. The Locus of Comparison

Whom shall we compare with whom? The title of a 2001 article by the human rights advocate Kevin Boyle hits the nail on the head: 'Hate Speech: The United States Versus the Rest of the World?'[4] The 1960s witnessed worldwide acceptance of hate speech bans as set forth in international human rights treaties. Boyle and other scholars[5] deemed that initiative successful: virtually all states had adopted national, regional or international restrictions on hate speech.[6] The US is the one major power that has continued to oppose hate speech bans.[7]

For example, Article 20(2) of the International Covenant on Civil and Political Rights (ICCPR) provides that 'any advocacy of national, racial or religious hatred that constitutes incitement to discrimination, hostility, or violence shall be prohibited by law'.[8] The US was the one major power opposed to that provision. The US did not ratify the ICCPR until 1992[9]—'very late', in Boyle's view.[10] Upon submitting its instrument of ratification, the US included a reservation stating '[t]hat Article 20 does not authorize or require legislation or other action by the United States that would restrict the right of free speech and association

---

[4] (2001) 53 *Me. L. Rev.* 487.

[5] See eg, M. J. Matsuda, 'Public Response to Racist Speech: Considering the Victim's Story', in M. J. Matsuda, C. Lawrence III, R. Delgado, and K. W. Crenshaw (eds.), *Words that Wound: Critical Race Theory, Assaultive Speech and the First Amendment* (Boulder, CO: Westview Press, 1993), 17, praising an 'international consensus' on hate speech bans; J. Stefancic and R. Delgado, 'A Shifting Balance: Freedom of Expression and Hate-Speech Restriction' (1993) 78 *Iowa L. Rev.* 737, examining national jurisdictions in reviewing *Striking a Balance: Hate Speech, Freedom of Expression and Non-Discrimination* (Sandra Coliver, K. Boyle and F. D'Souza, eds., London: Art. 19, 1992).

[6] For a critical account of that global consensus, challenging in particular the views of Matsuda and Delgado, see E. Heinze, 'Truth and Myth in Critical Race Theory and LatCrit: Human Rights and the Ethnocentrism of Anti-Ethnocentrism' (2008) 20 *Nat'l Black L.J.* 107.

[7] See n. 4 above, 493–6.

[8] 993 U.N.T.S. 3, entered into force 3 January 1976. For information on states parties, see eg, Office of the United Nations High Commissioner for Human Rights (UNHCHR), <http://www2.ohchr.org/english/bodies/ratification/4.htm> (last accessed 13 June 2008).

[9] UNHCHR in ibid., 8.

[10] See n. 4 above, 493.

protected by the Constitution and laws of the United States'.[11] The US thereby collapsed the international norms binding upon its national free-speech laws into a tautology (or a vacuity). The reservation meant that the US would recognize any requirements arising under ICCPR Article 20 as binding upon the US only to the extent that the US Constitution would be interpreted by the Supreme Court to permit precisely the same requirements. The Supreme Court *may,* of course, uphold domestic legislation adopted pursuant to an ICCPR obligation. However, under the reservation, the Supreme Court remains free *not* to do so; or indeed to reverse an earlier decision to do so. Contrary to the treaty's aim to create internationally binding obligations, the US reservation consigns the ultimate question of the binding character of those obligations to its domestic judiciary.

The United Nations Human Rights Committee, which supervises states parties' adherence to the ICCPR,[12] has adopted no detailed view about whether that reservation violates the object and purpose of the Covenant.[13] Instead, in its first report on the United States in 1995, it stated, in general terms, that it 'regrets the extent' of the US 'reservations, declarations, and understandings. . . . [T]aken together, they intended to ensure that the United States has accepted only what is already the law of the United States.'[14]

Article 4 of the International Convention on the Elimination of All Forms of Racial Discrimination (CERD)[15], described by Boyle as 'more radical and far-reaching',[16] requires that states parties,

(a) Shall declare an offence punishable by law all dissemination of ideas based on racial superiority or hatred, incitement to racial discrimination, as well as all acts of violence or incitement to such acts against any race or group of persons of another colour of ethnic origin . . .

[11] See information on reservations, understandings and declarations of states parties to the ICCPR, provided by the Office of the United Nations High Commissioner for Human Rights (UNHCHR), <http://www2.ohchr.org/english/bodies/ratification/4_1.htm> (last accessed 13 June 2008). Interestingly, some other democracies, such as Australia, Belgium, New Zealand, and the United Kingdom submitted similar reservations. Their statements have received less attention, however, presumably because those states' domestic laws do in fact concede some ground to hate speech bans. See UNHCHR in this note.

[12] See ICCPR, pt. IV, providing for the establishment of the UN Human Rights Committee.

[13] But see UN Human Rights Committee, 'General Comment 24 (52)', UN Doc CCPR/C/21/Rev.1/Add.6 (1994), concerning inter alia issues relating to reservations made upon ratification or accession to the Covenant. In para. 1, the Committee criticizes reservations which, in their number, content or scope, would 'undermine the effective implementation of the covenant and tend to weaken respect for the obligations of states parties'. According to Boyle, General Comment 24 is 'widely regarded' as having been published in anticipation of the first US submission of 1994. See n. 4 above, 495.

[14] UN Human Rights Committee, 'Concluding Observations of the Human Rights Committee: United States of America,' UN Doc A/50/40 (1995), para. 279.

[15] 660 U.N.T.S. 195, entered into force 4 January 1969. For information on states parties, see eg, Office of the United Nations High Commissioner for Human Rights (UNHCHR) <http://www2.ohchr.org/english/bodies/ratification/2.htm> (last accessed 13 June 2008).

[16] See n. 4 above, 496.

(b) Shall declare illegal and prohibit organizations, and also organized and all other propaganda activities, which promote and incite racial discrimination, and shall recognize participation in such organizations or activities as an offence punishable by law.'

The US ratified CERD in 1994, almost three decades after it had been opened for signature.[17] The government again included a reservation precluding any effect on speech more restrictive than that of the US Constitution.[18]

States parties' performance under CERD is monitored by the UN Committee on the Elimination of Racial Discrimination. In its 2001 report on the US, the Committee stated that it was 'particularly concerned' about the US 'reservation on the implementation of Article 4'.[19] The report continued,

[T]he prohibition of dissemination of all ideas based upon racial superiority or hatred is compatible with the right to freedom of opinion and expression, given that a citizen's exercise of this right carries special duties and responsibilities, among which is the obligation not to disseminate racist ideas. The Committee recommends that the State party review its legislation in view of the new requirements of preventing and combating racial discrimination, and adopt regulations extending the protection against acts of racial discrimination, in accordance with article 4 of the Convention.[20]

The US position on hate speech looks increasingly like an anomaly. It may seem arbitrary, then, to a compare only *Europe* with the US. In their overall conception, European hate speech bans differ little from those of many non-European states. Australia, Canada, India, or South Africa also have Western-style democracies with hate speech bans, and can provide interesting contrasts to the American civil liberties position. Why, then, focus on Europe? The post-World War II emergence of European democracies, within integrated Council of Europe and EU systems, has made Europe a 'centre of gravity'—a crucial political and cultural counter-weight to the US. I shall therefore examine a Euro-American divide, while noting that the basic observations in this chapter would apply to other states.

The distinction between European and American centres of gravity arises in various contexts. On issues as diverse as the death penalty or the welfare state, recent decades have seen Europe and the US grow ever further apart. And yet, even on those issues, trans-Atlantic differences can turn out to be hazier than superficial comparisons would suggest. For example, not all American jurisdictions provide for the death penalty, nor are all identical in their levels of social

[17] See UNHCHR in n. 8 above.
[18] See UNHCHR in n. 11 above.
[19] UN Committee on the Elimination of Racial Discrimination, 'Conclusions and Recommendations of the Committee on the Elimination of Racial Discrimination: United States of America', UN Doc A/56/18 (2001), para. 391.
[20] Ibid.

services, so comparisons between Council of Europe jurisdictions and 'the American approach' become more complex from the outset.

On hate speech, by contrast, the Euro-American divide seems absolute. All European states maintain at least minimal hate speech regulation pursuant to national, European, or international law.[21] Meanwhile, over several decades, the US Supreme Court has moved strongly towards a civil-libertarian position, as described both by Robert Post and by James Weinstein and Ivan Hare in their contributions to this collection. When the dominant norms on free speech appear to divide Western democracies so starkly, it becomes tempting to assume that the difference reflects a deeper cultural divide—an unbridgeable chasm between European and American attitudes towards rights, freedom, pluralism, or democracy. I shall argue, however, that such conclusions may be exaggerated insofar as the deeper social and cultural realities are far subtler than the yes-or-no black-letter norms ('Europe requires bans, the US forbids them') might suggest.

3. Informal Power

Blasphemy laws provide a useful point of reference. Rooted in age-old religious doctrine, they have been salvaged by today's secular European democracies on grounds similar to the secular rationales invoked to justify hate speech bans.[22] Post cites the example of Denmark, a state often seen as progressive in the protection of human rights. He observes that, albeit arising from different histories and social contexts, blasphemy laws and hate speech bans are functionally equivalent. Both kinds of statutes require that government officials pass judgment on the intrinsic merits of ideas, distinguishing 'speech that merely expresses disagreement from speech that degrades'.[23] Neither type of ban 'punishes speech that expresses critique, but each sanctions speech that insults'.[24] That distinction, in turn, can be drawn 'only by reference to the social norms that in Denmark define respect'.[25] The same observation applies to bans in any state.

On Post's view, the state withdraws those decisions from open, public debate when it enforces blasphemy laws or hate speech bans:

Once we understand that even in Denmark such norms are contested, we can also see that both blasphemy and hate speech regulation must necessarily enforce social norms that represent the well-socialized intuitions of the hegemonic class that controls the content of

---

[21] See n. 4 above. In some cases, the law is still in flux. See eg, A. Sajó and M. Rosenfeld, 'Spreading Liberal Constitutionalism: An Inquiry into the Fate of Free Speech Rights in New Democracies', in S. Choudhry (ed.), *The Migration of Constitutional Ideas* (Cambridge: CUP, 2006), 156–77, examining Hungary.

[22] See eg, E. Heinze, 'Viewpoint Absolutism and Hate Speech' (2006) 69 *Modern L. Rev.* 543, 557–9.

[23] 'Hate Speech', ch. 7 in this volume.

[24] Ibid.   [25] Ibid.

the law. This would be true even in a society that purported to adopt a 'multicultural' perspective enforcing norms of respect among disparate groups.[26]

In the United States today, no blasphemy law could survive judicial review on the secular rationale of not causing offence.[27] Even purely secular hate speech bans fail First Amendment scrutiny, insofar as they regulate communication within public discourse solely on grounds that the speech is offensive.

A preliminary point arises from Post's suspicion towards 'the hegemonic class that controls the content' of European hate speech bans. To be sure, a hegemonic class controls speech as much in the US as in Europe. On both continents, an elite exercises disproportionate control over informal, social spheres as well as formal, legal ones. In 2003, Cable News Network's (CNN) reporter Christiane Aman-pour claimed that the network had been '"intimidated" by the Bush adminis-tration in its coverage of the war in Iraq'.[28] She maintained that CNN had 'muzzled' her through 'a combination of the White House and the high-profile success of the controversial pro-war news network, Rupert Murdoch-owned Fox News'. In her view, 'the administration and its foot soldiers at Fox News' had imposed 'a climate of fear and self-censorship in terms of the kind of broadcast work we did'.[29] Similarly, the BBC's director general, Greg Dyke, had been 'shocked' by 'how unquestioning the [US] broadcast news media was during this war.'[30]

If a 'hegemonic class' includes agents beyond the specific members of the government or the judiciary, then Amanpour and Dyke certainly point to an American hegemonic class that is able to censor speech of paramount public and political importance, whilst avoiding (as one would expect a hegemonic class to be able to do) any formal conflicts with the American Constitution's guarantee of free speech, which restrict only government, but not powerful non-govermental institutions such as CNN.

In today's world, even that distinction between 'governmental' and 'non-governmental' institutions is arbitrary. The news media count among our most vital links to government. Our opinions about what government is, does, and should be are shaped more by the media than any other force. When an elite exercises covert control over the content of broadcasts, that informal control is arguably more pernicious than control through formal laws limiting speech. The latter may be inappropriate for a democratic society, but at least the laws will be public, open to scrutiny and debate. The covert controls described by Amanpour and Dyke, if detected at all, may be inferred only obliquely and after the fact. The most dangerous controls are the ones we cannot see.

---

[26] Ibid., internal citations omitted.   [27] Ibid.
[28] J. Plunkett, 'CNN star reporter attacks war coverage', *The Guardian*, 16 September 2003, <http://www.guardian.co.uk/media/2003/sep/16/broadcasting.Iraqandthemedia> (last accessed 13 June 2008).
[29] Ibid.   [30] Ibid.

4. Formal Law

To be sure, Post makes no claim to be assessing the informal operation of hegemonic elites. His interest in hate speech bans follows their customary form, as formal law through which governments adopt an official, moral choice broadly condemning certain expressions of intolerance. In that context, 'hegemonic class' generally equates with 'governing elites in their official governing capacity'.

Then let us consider America's judicial elite. In the 1952 case of *Beauharnais* v. *Illinois*,[31] decided over a decade before the US Supreme Court had taken a more civil-libertarian approach, a majority of the Court adopted the concept of group defamation to uphold a law that banned any publication that 'portrays depravity, criminality, unchastity, or lack of virtue of a class of citizen of any race, colour, creed, or religion'. There is no evidence that the Court's ruling met with the overall disapproval of the American people, who presumably still resembled Europeans in thinking that government has a role to play in curbing at least some forms of provocative speech.

Nor, by the time the Court had changed course, was it obvious that the Justices were speaking for a majority of Americans. Quite the contrary. Central to the Court's position in recent years is the view that the Constitution protects minority views from majority pressures.[32] (The same can be said of other individual, higher-law rights, which, today, are expected not merely to rubber-stamp majority opinion, but to insulate individuals from majorities.[33]) Admittedly, a generation or two now having passed, the current position may well represent the majority US view today.[34] The fact remains that the requirement of government neutrality in the public sphere was introduced by the Court acting as an elite corps irrespective of, if not actively opposing, the majority will. In other words, both the US and European approaches are the products of elites—as is, of course, virtually all law today.

Still, Post's suspicions about European elitism are not without foundation. An attraction of the American civil liberties position (and this is perhaps how Post's views should be read) is that its elitism has a crucially anti-elitist strain: the only viewpoint it imposes is that government may not officially impose viewpoints

---

[31] *Beauharnais* v. *Illinois* 343 US 250 (1952).

[32] James Weinstein has rightly pointed out that it is in the early 1970s that the US Supreme Court begins to adopt concepts of 'content neutrality', 'viewpoint discrimination', and the requirement that government cite a 'compelling' interest if it is to regulate speech on grounds of its viewpoint. See eg, *Police Dept. Of City of Chicago* v. *Mosley* 408 US 92 (1972).

[33] See eg, *Dudgeon* v. *United Kingdom* (Appl. No. 7525/76), judgment of 22 October 1981, ECHR., Ser. A., No. 45, finding that majority disapproval of homosexuality in Northern Ireland did not justify criminal penalties. See generally eg, R. Dworkin, *Taking Rights Seriously* (London: Duckworth, 1977).

[34] See eg, L. B. Nielsen, *License to Harass: Law, Hierarchy and Offensive Public Speech* (Princeton: Princeton UP, 2004), suggesting ambivalence towards legal regulation of hate speech in the US, even among target groups.

within the overall sphere of public discourse. European legal systems use the law to punish one intellectual position (such as offence to religion,[35] or Holocaust denial,[36] or a belief in the superiority of heterosexuality[37]) in order to impose, coercively, a contrary opinion (such as, respectively, the need to protect religious feelings, or to honour the memory of Holocaust victims, or to combat homophobia). European elitism uses state coercion to penalize offensive viewpoints, and thus to enforce the viewpoint that certain viewpoints are, as a matter of law, superior or inferior.

But the problems raised by Amanpour and Dyke do not go away so easily. They were speaking about a particular issue arising at a sensitive time—important, for sure, but not necessarily typical of the more ordinary, everyday sphere of American public discourse. Post's interest is in the character of the public sphere as an arena for the robust exchange of views and ideas. A comparison of formal norms might certainly suggest that US law endows the American public sphere with a freedom qualitatively superior, from a civil-libertarian perspective, to a European sphere in which states coerce, through threat of legal penalties, the silencing of certain provocative or offensive views. The real question, then, is: how do those differences in formal norms reflect real freedoms of expression, as actually exercised, in Europe and the US?

5. Realism and Essentialism

Post describes an ideal of 'public discourse', in civil-libertarian terms, as 'a unique domain in which the state is constitutionally prohibited from enforcing community norms'.[38] He claims that, in the United States, 'public discourse is an arena for the competition of many distinct communities, each trying to capture the law to impose its own particular norms'.

Of course, 'public discourse' as 'an arena for the competition of many distinct communities' is no American invention. It has long stood as an aim of law in European states. The increasingly secular, post-Westphalian European order arose largely from devastating wars of religion.[39] John Locke came to argue that it was 'toleration' that must stand as 'the chief characteristic mark of the true

---

[35] See eg, *Otto-Preminger-Institut* v. *Austria* (Appl. No. 13470/87), ECHR, Ser. A, No. 295-A [1994]; *Wingrove* v. *United Kingdom* (Appl. No. 17419/90), ECHR 60 [1996].

[36] See eg, the German 'Auschwitzlüge' (Holocaust denial) case, BVerfG 90, 241 (1994); *Faurisson* v. *France*, Communication No. 550/1993, UN Doc CCPR/C/58/D/550/1993 (1996).

[37] See eg, J. P. Loof, 'Freedom of Expression and Religiously-Based Ideas on Homosexuality: European and Dutch Standards', in T. Loenen and J. Goldschmidt (eds.), *Religious Pluralism and Human Rights* (Antwerp: Intersentia, 2007), 267–78. But see, critically, E. Heinze, 'Towards the Abolition of Hate Speech Bans', in Loenen & Goldschmidt, ibid, 295–309.

[38] See n. 23 above, p. 132.

[39] For a classic account, recall F. Schiller, *Geschichte des dreissigjährigen Krieges* (Zürich: Manesse, 1988).

church'.[40] Voltaire embodies the European Enlightenment—for some, he embodies Europe itself—when he praises Peter the Great for having 'favorisé tous les cultes dans son vaste empire'.[41]

Under the European Convention on Human Rights, freedoms of religion (Article 9) and speech (Article 10), have certainly generated controversial case law.[42] But so has the US First Amendment. One would be hard pressed to find, in the respective European and US case law as the whole, evidence of fundamentally different freedoms on either side of the Atlantic. Europe and the US have long shared the background aim of securing a public sphere for the robust exchange of ideas. Everyday experience equally supports my preference for trans-Atlantic cultural comparisons that are more grey than black-or-white. One need merely look at the public sphere throughout most European states as it actually exists, and not merely as it might be speculatively theorized. While hate speech bans are indeed of genuine concern for the legitimacy of law in a democratic society, let us not forget that virtually all open discussion and debate that can be waged in the US can be, and is, waged throughout the established European democracies. I have yet to find myself scurrying over to Amazon.com (ie, the US branch) because it can provide massive quantities of books banned on Amazon.co.uk, Amazon.de, or Amazon.fr.

If we consider issues that have dominated political discussion in recent decades, from national elections, to social welfare, to armed conflict, to third-world development, to environmental pollution, to education, drugs, smoking, abortion, gay rights, or countless other issues of public concern, it would be ludicrous to suggest that fundamental freedoms of public participation are identifiably stronger—or the outcomes of such open debates identifiably better—on one or the other side of the Atlantic. That is not to deny the genuine problem that arises if, for example, someone wishes to read or hear, say, racist material, or an argument denying the Holocaust. Speakers able to disseminate such views freely in the US may be barred from doing so in Europe. Post rightly suggests that such exclusion poses problems of democratic principle, or democratic ideals of equal citizenship. It does not, however, indicate significantly lower levels of overall freedom of speech in Europe. Post continues:

The [US Supreme] Court has . . . interpreted the freedom of expression clause of the First Amendment in a manner analogous to the Amendment's Establishment Clause, which requires government to be neutral as between the many different religious sects that in America have sought to control the state. Since the 1940s, the Supreme Court has been

---

[40] J. Locke, *A Letter Concerning Toleration* Ed. J. H. Tully, Trans. W. Popple (Indianpolis: Hackett, 1983 [1689]), 1.

[41] Voltaire, '*Traité sur la Tolérance*', in Voltaire, *L'affaire Calas* Ed. J. van den Heuvel (Paris: Gallimard, 1975), 107, Peter the Great 'supported all beliefs in his vast empire.'—my translation.

[42] See eg, *Otto-Preminger-Institut* v. *Austria* (Appl. No. 13470/87), ECHR, Ser. A, No. 295-A [1994]; *Jersild* v. *Denmark* (Appl. No. 15890/88), ECHR, Ser. A, No. 298 [1995]; *Wingrove* v. *United Kingdom* (Appl. No. 17419/90), ECHR 60 [1996].

reluctant to allow the state to enforce community norms in public discourse. In effect, the First Amendment pressures the state to be neutral with respect to the many competing communities that seek to control the law by enforcing their own particular ways of distinguishing decency from indecency, critique from hatred[.][43]

Of course, that observation, too, is subject to qualifications. The Supreme Court's rationales for upholding general prohibitions even on obscene materials not depicting children or non-consenting adults[44] cannot easily be reconciled with the concept of a mature citizenry responsible for autonomous choices in matters of mental-emotional experience and expression. It suspends any notion of content neutrality, allowing the state to enforce community norms in public discourse. In maintaining that obscenity plays 'no essential part of any exposition of ideas', the Court altogether imposes upon public discourse some assumption about what counts as an 'idea'.[45] Nevertheless, in areas of political and social concern, as more traditionally understood, Post does state a dominant principle of US free-speech jurisprudence that has prevailed since its civil-libertarian turn.

Insofar as Post is elucidating a constitutional principle, he describes (A) 'the public sphere in America' as 'an arena for the competition of many distinct communities'. On first glance, that statement may seem broad. Insofar as it is true, however, it can only mean something rather narrower, namely, (B) 'the public sphere in America is an arena for the *formally even-handed* competition of many distinct communities'. In other words, that 'competition' need not be substantively even-handed—each community allowed only to participate with equal resources, which would require a totalitarian level of state control, and even then would hardly be practicable. Rather, it is even-handed 'competition' in the sense that each 'community' has a chance to use the public sphere to put its case.

The difference between (A) and (B), then, is two-fold. On the one hand, if there is value to the First Amendment's hostility towards the state-sponsored enforcement in public discourse of the norms of any particular community, it lies in the value of fair play—in a formally equal chance for each of those communities to speak. Hence a legally imposed requirement of equal treatment of all such communities, insofar as speech is concerned. On the other hand, the First Amendment does not require, for example, that poorer or otherwise disempowered communities

---

[43] See n. 23 above, p. 133.

[44] See eg, *Miller* v. *California* 413 US 15 (1973).

[45] Ibid., 20. Not entirely helpfully, the Court in *Miller* adopts the following criteria to decide which non-'ideas' might be excluded by government from the public sphere, as 'obscenity', without violating the Constitution: 'The basic guidelines for the trier of fact must be: (a) whether "the average person, applying contemporary community standards" would find that the work, taken as a whole, appeals to the prurient interest; (b) whether the work depicts or describes, in a patently offensive way, sexual conduct specifically defined by the applicable state law; and (c) whether the work, taken as a whole, lacks serious literary, artistic, political, or scientific value.' Ibid., 24, internal citations deleted. On problems that arise in applying that standard, see ibid., 37, Douglas, J. dissenting, discussing problem of vagueness. See also *Paris Adult Theatre I* v. *Slaton* 413 US 49, 73 (1973), Brennan, J. dissenting discussing problems of vagueness and overbreadth.

or individuals be funded to provide material equality with wealthier ones; or that less powerful entities be given greater air time in order to offset their lack of influence vis-à-vis more dominant ones.

That distinction between formal norms and their social contexts is crucial. Of particular concern to the American civil liberties tradition, as Post notes, is the risk that viewpoints of a dominant community might be enforced to the detriment of less influential communities. It has never been the case, however, that norms of strictly formal neutrality, even of constitutional stature, can fully avert that risk. They do so only imperfectly, since informal, social inequalities can operate as coercively as formally discriminatory norms. Nowhere has that discrepancy emerged more forcefully than in the Southern United States, whose governments long acquiesced in the values and practices of white supremacy—ie, in preferring the norms favoured by one community—regardless of any First Amendment requirement of purely formal government neutrality with respect to various communities' conflicting values. The landmark cases of *Heart of Atlanta Motel, Inc.* v. *United States*[46] and *Katzenbach* v. *McClung*[47] showed how, well into the 1960s, racial segregation still dominated Southern American life with at least a passive imprimatur of state and local law. Those cases involved businesses typical in the South from the nineteenth century through to the 1960s, which openly refused to provide equal services for blacks and whites. They mirrored, in the commercial sphere, the doctrine of 'separate but equal' which had been enshrined as constitutional precedent in the 1896 case of *Plessy* v. *Ferguson*.[48] Those cases show that, even if certain manifestations of political, economic, and social power imbalances may not be enforced within formally enacted law (or within other government conduct, insofar as judicially reviewable), social and economic power imbalances may nevertheless prevail in countless ways that are supported within the overall apparatus of the legal system.

That insight has long stood as a cornerstone of 'outsider jurisprudence', including Critical Legal Theory, Critical Race Theory, LatCrit, radical feminism, or queer theory.[49] Those movements bar us from claiming, 'Well, yes, *purely social factors* may "enforce" such imbalances, but the *law* does not follow suit', since, in such instances, no clean and simple line can be drawn between 'law' and 'society'. Insofar as broader social practices are effectively supported (even if not expressly endorsed) within the full framework of law, they cannot be said to exist in a universe utterly distinct from law. The problem is not merely that 'the law cannot be perfect, and will falter in practice even when its norms are sound in principle'. The problem is that those norms can only ever encompass part of the problems they are supposed to solve—certainly in the United States, where the

---

[46] *Heart of Atlanta Motel, Inc.* v. *United States* 379 US 241 (1964).
[47] *Katzenbach* v. *McClung* 379 US 294 (1964).
[48] *Plessy* v. *Ferguson* 163 US 537 (1896).
[49] On the concept of outsider groups and outsider jurisprudence, see eg, M. Matsuda (n. 5 above), 18–20.

Constitution, both in its black letter and in its subsequent interpretation, avoids tampering even with overwhelming social power imbalances.[50]

Post's analysis does, then, present US constitutional ideals of strictly formal neutrality, and their underlying attitudes of government non-preference for the norms of certain communities over others. However, those ideals reveal little about the social and economic realities of a society whose legal regime has, throughout history, sustained colossal social and economic power imbalances. Those social and economic power imbalances assure that the values and norms of dominant communities are overwhelmingly enforced through the legal regime that sustains their power and privilege. It would be a simplistic essentialism to assume (and Post rightly avoids making any such assumption) that a First Amendment norm of formal neutrality expresses overall patterns of political, economic or cultural even-handedness within the broader American society; that poor blacks, for example, enjoy the same effective freedom of expression enjoyed by wealthy whites, even if they all enjoy the same formal freedom of expression.

I shall re-formulate Post's observations, then, not to contradict them, but to display more explicitly the limits of formal norms from a legal-realist perspective (the italics representing my interpolations to Post's words quoted above):

Formally, the First Amendment requires that the state be neutral with respect to the many competing communities that seek to control the law by enforcing their own particular ways of distinguishing decency from indecency, critique from hatred, *even if in practice within the broader society and culture that are held in place by that same legal system, such enforcement of particular communities' norms may be present and even pervasive. Accordingly,* in the United States public discourse is an arena for the *formally even-handed* competition of many distinct communities, *even if such differentials as status, class, wealth, ethnicity, gender, or sexuality, also held in place within the totality of the legal system, systemically preclude even-handedness in practice.*

My aim is not to deny all reality to Post's view of the American public sphere, although he describes a First Amendment ideal that departs dramatically from the reality actually lived by socially and economically disempowered communities and individuals within that legal regime. I overwhelmingly endorse the American civil libertarian approach to free speech, but we must avoid any conclusion that current First Amendment jurisprudence creates 'an arena for the competition of many distinct communities' of a kind that does not fundamentally exist in the legal regimes of other Western democracies. Hate speech bans are indeed incompatible with the ideal of such an arena, but, as implemented in most European states, are far from wholly destroying it. For the most part, US approaches to free speech promote 'an arena for the competition of many distinct communities' precisely in the ways that European approaches promote such an

---

[50] On the proposition that the US Constitution does not include or imply social or economic rights, ie, individual rights to compel government provision of social services, see eg, *De Shaney* v. *Winnebago Social Services Dept.* 489 US 189 (1989).

arena. US civil libertarian norms promote that open, participatory 'arena' through formal norms, largely indifferent to gross material inequities; European social welfare states promote their own open, participatory 'arenas' through attention to actual material circumstances, sometimes sacrificing the formal even-handedness of the First Amendment. Whilst I would maintain that European states can achieve the same result without making that sacrifice, I would not maintain that the European public sphere is, in view of the totality of formal *and* real conditions, less free or open than the American. Nor would I dismiss Post's view as 'idealistic' in a derogatory sense. Values and ideals matter in law. They maintain an ongoing and fluid relationship with everyday attitudes and practices.[51] In the US Supreme Court, sheer ideals hold enormous power to influence social practices and attitudes. Nevertheless, as Tolstoy warned, we must be wary of a 'science of jurisprudence' that risks treating 'the State and power as the ancients regarded fire—namely, as something existing absolutely'.[52] The US Supreme Court is a mighty force, but is still only one force in a complex society, whose social patterns do not always mirror the Court's dominant values, and may actively thwart them.

For reasons that Post has rightly stated in various writings, European hate speech bans raise real concerns about government regulation of public discourse in societies that depend upon an open and transparent system of participatory democracy for the very legitimacy of their laws;[53] however, the ways in which European social democracies may have enhanced substantive even-handedness in political empowerment and participation by rectifying gross social or economic balances must be considered if trans-Atlantic legal ideals are to be compared not in a vacuum, but as real social forces operating in real societies. There is no straightforward sense in which one or the other continent achieves greater overall even-handedness in the power and influence of their constituent communities. The American First Amendment does provide more rigorous, formal even-handedness to all speakers, albeit against a backdrop of strong deference to substantive, material imbalances that allow gaping disparities in the real power and influence of privileged communities. The established European democracies admittedly allow very limited compromises of formal even-handedness, but, unlike the US, have actively sought to promote greater substantive even-handedness by overcoming excessive social and economic disparities—certainly, though misguidedly, through restrictions on speech thought to exacerbate those disparities, but also, more importantly, through greater minimum social and economic protections (themselves, to be sure, stronger in some European states than others). Indeed, as I have argued elsewhere, longstanding, stable, and prosperous European social welfare states can and should eliminate hate speech

---

[51] See generally eg, Dworkin, n. 33 above.

[52] L. Tolstoy, 'Second Epilogue', in *War and Peace* Trans. L. Maude and A. Maude (Ware, UK: Wordsworth Classics, 1993), 936. '[T]he State and power', Tolstoy continues, 'are merely phenomena, just as for modern physics, fire is not an element but a phenomenon.'

[53] See n. 23 above.

bans, *not* because, as Post may appear to suggest, they somehow lack any fundamental overall even-handedness that the United States possesses, but because hate speech bans simply fail to serve their aims of achieving greater social or economic balance.[54] General economic and social protections suffice to further those aims, without the necessity of restricting speech.

Marxists and many post-Marxist critical theorists would take the analysis a giant step further, arguing that US Supreme Court jurisprudence is nothing but 'superstructure' (*Überbau*), nothing but a fiddle played by forces that actively engineer the very inequalities that the Court may nominally purport to combat, but, in practice, only ever serves to perpetuate. We need not venture quite so far in our search for the real America lurking behind the elite, 'hegemonic' values of its legal culture. Today's critical theorists generally recognize the real and distinct power of formal legal norms and processes.[55] However, their writings warn against any culturally essentialist view that norms applied by courts straightforwardly recapitulate those that govern social or economic life.

Essentialism looms when one feature of a society is allowed to eclipse other, contrary elements. The First Amendment's requirement of formal even-handedness does indeed promote the crucial democratic value of open and robust public discourse. However, it would be an exaggeration to infer that Europe's hate speech bans alone, or even the broader moral choices they represent, suffice to destroy that value altogether, or even to weaken the equally robust sphere of controversy and debate in Europe. If we wish to understand the relationship between government and public discourse, in order to assess the health of public discourse on either side of the Atlantic, we must look at informal, social elements as well as the formal-legal elements that are relevant to that relationship. That is no easy task—which is why we must avoid any suggestion that differences in specific legal norms yield easy or obvious conclusions about broader cultural differences.

6. Formal and Substantive Freedoms: An Age-Old Dilemma

A classic political idea, notable from Plato through to Rousseau and Hegel, is that we achieve 'real' freedom through certain restrictions on freedom. A child loses free choice when compelled to attend school, to do homework, or to learn good manners; yet we commonly believe that the child's overall empowerment, the child's later horizons and opportunities—professional, personal, social—are enhanced through those sacrifices imposed early on. A child lacking such constraints is likely to find doors shutting later in life; and fewer choices mean less overall freedom throughout the individual's lifetime. Famously arguing that society must sometimes 'force one to be free',[56] Rousseau provided a counterpart

---

[54] See n. 22 above, 578–81.   [55] See n. 6 above, pt. II.
[56] 'Hence for the social compact not to be an empty formula, it tacitly includes the following engagement which alone can give force to the rest, that whoever refuses to obey the general will shall

to classical, liberal 'hands-off' notions that would equate state coercion with diminished freedom.

That 'less is more' ideal of freedom operates not only individually, but also collectively, when limits on the freedoms of some are seen as legitimate means of enhancing the freedoms of others. Advocates of hate speech bans often see such limits as utterly minimal diminution of liberty, on the view that no serious social value can be served by crude expressions of racism, antisemitism, Islamophobia, homophobia or other hate speech. The cost of what is seen as a wholly minimal restriction on the expressive activities of some speakers is deemed to be out-weighed by the benefit of an enhancement of the real freedom of out-groups to participate more fully in democracy, without being hunted into the fringes of society through hostile public discourse. Many Europeans might well argue, just as American Critical Race Theorists have argued, that a reduction of the freedoms of hate mongers promotes the freedoms of out-groups by creating a more wel-coming social environment. On that view, public discourse that casually accepts intolerant speech marginalizes out-groups, sending them subtle yet constant messages that they are not equal, full-fledged members of the political commu-nity, however much their purely formal rights and freedoms may suggest that they are.[57] Hate speech bans aim at moving from purely formal rights of citizenship—fully enjoyed as real rights only for the privileged on top of the heap—to more inclusive rights that can genuinely be enjoyed by those at the bottom. By regu-lating such speech, the state sends a message to blacks or gays that their partici-pation is welcome.

There are certainly some practical problems with that view. It makes a causal assumption that hate speech deters participation in public discourse, yet its proponents have never undertaken or cited serious empirical research to show that, in longstanding, stable, and prosperous democracies any such causal rela-tionship exists (as opposed to societies such as Rwanda or the former Yugoslavia, where undeveloped public discourse could indeed lead to mass atrocities), no more than it has been shown that violence in the media breeds systemic social violence. And it is questionable whether speech should be penalized on grounds of a wholly speculative causal link. In other words, there is no evidence that these aims of social inclusion are in fact promoted through hate speech bans.

---

be constrained to do so by the whole body: which means nothing other than that he will be forced to be free; for this is the condition which, by giving each Citizen to the Fatherland, *guarantees him against all personal dependence*; the condition which is the device and makes for the operation of the political machine, and alone renders legitimate civil engagements which would otherwise be absurd, tyrannical, and liable to the most frightful abuses.' J.-J. Rousseau, 'The Social Contract, I.7(8)', in J.-J. Rousseau, *The Social Contract and Other Later Political Writings* Trans. and Ed. V. Gourevitch (Cambridge: CUP, 1997), 53, emphasis added.

[57] See generally, M. J. Matsuda, C. Lawrence III, R. Delgado, and K. W. Crenshaw (eds.), *Words that Wound: Critical Race Theory, Assaultive Speech and the First Amendment* (Boulder, CO: Westview Press, 1993).

That does not, however, make those aims unworthy. Through much of the twentieth century, the Dutch system of *verzuiling* ('pillarization') structured a state that, albeit geographically small, has long contained among the world's highest population densities (at 16 millions today, its head count lags only slightly behind the combined population of Denmark, Sweden, and Norway, making the Netherlands demographically more of a medium-sized than a small-sized European state). Centuries of rivalry among varieties of religious, secular, and political groups—itself a microcosm of the broad social conflicts from which modern Europe had emerged—were acknowledged by the system of *verzuiling*. Control of important public functions, such as education and media air time, were delegated to various constituent communities, with considerable shares going to religious organizations. That attempt to avoid domination by any one group aimed at enhancing public participation overall.[58]

Such an arrangement would have been unthinkable in the US, under the Supreme Court's Establishment Clause jurisprudence. Nor is that a surprise. The Dutch and American systems differed because their respective histories and demographics differed. Each grew out of attempts within political and legal institutions, over centuries, to learn from past ills and to avoid future ones. Each reflects strong values, even if not precisely the same institutional balances, of democracy, republicanism, liberalism, and pluralism. Certainly, by the 1960s and 1970s, those arrangements had to yield to a system more attuned to changing politics, economics, and demographics.[59] Nevertheless, however irreducibly Dutch the specific concept of *verzuiling* may be, it vividly shows a European state pursuing an 'arena for the competition of many distinct communities', albeit in a way very different from the American.

Under the French concept of *laïcité,* the purely formal, 'hands-off' approach of the US Supreme Court shows the US to be rather lukewarm in promoting the public sphere as an arena for the competition of distinct communities, insofar as US law fails to address the problem of the substantive, informal, or social power of the more dominant communities. French law and practice require that the state-sponsored educational system be used for the systematic promotion of critical analysis of all belief systems, religious and secular.[60] Again, as with US First Amendment principles, the precepts of *laïcité* are only ideals, which may not always reflect the concrete, socio-economic realities France's marginalized, 'outgroup' communities.[61] Nevertheless, it is that injunction of critically-minded education which imposes upon the French state the task of providing primary

---

[58] See eg, Parlementair Documentatie Centrum (Universiteit Leiden), 'Verzuiling', in *Parliament en Politiek,* <http://www.parlement.com/9291000/modulesf/g72bd2vo>, Dutch (last accessed 13 June 2008).

[59] Ibid.

[60] See generally H. Pena-Ruiz, *Qu'est-ce que la laïcité?* (Paris: Gallimard, 2003).

[61] See L. Mucchielli et al., *Quand les banlieues brûlent... Retour sur les émeutes de novembre 2005* (Paris: La Découverte, 2007).

schooling.[62] By contrast, when dominant religious faiths or credos *do* slip into the American public sphere with the imprimatur of the Supreme Court, with no equitable representation of minority beliefs, the practice is approved on grounds of 'tradition',[63] suggesting a comparative lack of vigilance over the neutrality of that 'arena' in comparison to French *laïcité*. While I do not propose to examine either the philosophical merits, or the execution in practice, of *laïcité*, it strikingly contrasts with the US in the way in which it envisages a rigorously neutral 'arena for the competition of many distinct communities'. Much of the history of Europe, then, is nothing but an attempt to build such arenas, albeit not always in the ways Americans were doing it.

Cultural essentialism poses dangers on all sides of the hate speech debate: on the European side as well as the American; on the side of hate speech prohibitionists as well as the side of free-speech 'absolutists'. For example, David Fraser, in this collection, endorses prohibitions on Holocaust denial in several European states, rejecting the US position. From (a) the evil of the Holocaust, Fraser infers (b) the evil of a legal norm that would permit certain forms of oral or written publication of (c) the evil of Holocaust denial. We can assume without discussion (a) the evil of the Holocaust, and (c) the evil of Holocaust denial. And we can assume that (c) follows from (a). It is questionable, however, whether (b) follows from (a), certainly as a matter of sheer logic, but, more importantly, as a matter of either utility or moral right. Michael Whine's chapter in this volume, and Fraser's as well, show that bans on Holocaust denial have by no means proved either effective or desirable as means of combating Holocaust denial. Prosecutions for Holocaust denial are precisely what nourish it: high profile trials engender sensational media attention, lending quasi-credibility to Holocaust deniers, which, in turn, contrary to the aims of the bans, actively encourages ongoing doubts about the existence or gravity of the Nazi extermination programmes. No American Holocaust deniers have attained anything like the stature of Robert Faurisson in France, or indeed David Irving throughout much of Europe. To the contrary, the absence of bans and the consequent absence of prosecutions in the US leave such figures consigned to the obscurity they deserve.

Whilst this is not the place to examine that issue in depth, the only danger I would note is that advocates of bans on Holocaust denial may, too, slip into essentialist modes of argument. Once we have recognized that such bans would be doomed under the American First Amendment principles, arguments about essential differences between American and European culture, extrapolating wholly from black-letter norms, may provide an all-too-facile means of arguing that the American civil liberties approach, arising from an essentially alien legal and cultural mentality, is simply irrelevant to Europe: 'It may be fine for

---

[62] See n. 60 above, 96–116.
[63] See eg, *Marsh v. Chambers* 463 US 783 (1983), upholding legislative prayer on grounds of 'history and tradition'.

Americans, but it's not the way we in Europe do things'. As I've tried to suggest, such culturally essentialist reasoning does not invite engagement with the specific reasoning of American civil liberties principles, testing their applicability to European law, culture, or democracy. It merely invites the jurist to dismiss them out of hand. And, of course, the problem of Holocaust denial is linked to questionable assumptions about a specifically 'European' history, a matter to which I shall return after a brief excursion into American history.

7. Ahistoricism

Post explains his view of a distinctly American public arena with the aid of the following quotation from *Cantwell* v. *Connecticut*,[64] a landmark Supreme Court case decided in1940:

To persuade others to his own point of view, the pleader, as we know, at times, resorts to exaggeration, to vilification of men who have been, or are, prominent in church or state, and even to false statement. But the people of this nation have ordained in the light of history, that, in spite of the probability of excesses and abuses, these liberties are, in the long view, essential to enlightened opinion and right conduct on the part of the citizens of a democracy. The essential characteristic of these liberties is, that under their shield many types of life, character, opinion and belief can develop unmolested and unobstructed. Nowhere is this shield more necessary than in our own country for a people composed of many races and of many creeds.[65]

The Supreme Court in *Cantwell* provides a classic statement of the American civil liberties ethos. Even a harsh critic of US politics could not seriously challenge the force of such ideals in the history of American liberalism. Once again, however, there arises a question about the degree to which we can extrapolate from that ideal to an accurate depiction of the ways in which Americans have actually been able to enjoy such rights. When *Cantwell* was decided, racial segregation remained iron-clad law throughout the southern United States, under a 'separate but equal doctrine' that had been enshrined by the Supreme Court. An African-American could be lynched, with the complicity of the entire legal system, simply for failing to say 'Yes Sir' to a white man, let alone indulge in 'vilification', or standing on a street corner in Atlanta or Birmingham to plead for equal rights—which even a white person could not safely do. Nor in northern or other non-segregationist states did African Americans (and some other minorities) enjoy full civil rights in any real sense.[66] For African Americans the formal existence of such constitutional 'liberties' failed to provide any meaningful kind of 'shield' under which 'many

---

[64] *Cantwell* v. *Connecticut* 310 US 296 (1940).

[65] See n. 23 above, p. 133, quoting *Cantwell*, 310.

[66] The literature is vast. For a variety of perspectives, see eg, R. Delgado and J. Stefancic (eds), *Critical Race Theory: The Cutting Edge*, 2nd edn. (Philadelphia, PA: Temple UP, 2000).

types of life, character, opinion, and belief [could] develop unmolested and unobstructed'. Nor did American law overall show much evidence that 'this shield' was indeed 'necessary' in an America 'composed of many races and of many creeds'. In no way was 'the public sphere' in America providing anything like 'an arena for the competition of many distinct communities'. It is altogether unclear what 'history' the *Cantwell* Court is referring to, aside from a largely mythologized one—not in the sense of being wholly false, but in the sense of idealizing one very partial reality while overlooking many realities that contradict it.

What status are we to assign, then, to *Cantwell's* lofty vision of the 'shield' of civil liberties for America's diverse communities? Again, we must avoid both the idealist-essentialist Scylla of allowing sheer aspirations to speak for reality, and the materialist-reductionist Charybdis of refusing to see any reality at all in the ideals. *Cantwell's* dictum was real if only because it was prophetic, foreseeing the gradual emergence of the 'public sphere', genuinely open to all Americans, that Post describes. But did that 'public sphere' ever fully emerge? On 17 May 1954, more than a decade after *Cantwell*, the Court took a decisive step in its steady break from *Plessy* with *Brown* v. *Board of Education*.[67] Yet not even the most naïve formalist could maintain, and indeed no one has seriously argued, that a full-fledged arena of open public discourse emerged that same day. No one makes that argument because no one can stretch quite so far in reading sheer legal norms, however momentous, into lived reality.

More than 20 years after *Cantwell*, the Supreme Court was still confronted with pervasive racial inequality,[68] betokening fundamental social incapacities within the *real* 'public arena', whatever legal guarantees may have been functioning to protect a wholly formal, wholly idealized one. So when shall we say that a pervasively free and open American 'public arena' actually emerged? Any socially and culturally contextual reading teaches that such a question is not so much a matter of fact but of interpretation, indeed of highly controversial interpretation. As we have seen, many theorists within the various critical movements, while not denying some genuine gains, would argue that it still has not fully emerged; that an abstract legal discourse of equality or inclusion means little when social forces, held in place through law, systematically undermine those values.[69]

I do not wish to insist too strongly on an unbreachable chasm between the traditional civil liberties position and the insights of critical theory. Indeed, I have recently questioned that divide, and chastized some critical theorists for adopting, in their eagerness to dismiss altogether some core values of the American civil liberties tradition, a selective legal realism that can become as pernicious as wholly

---

[67] *Brown* v. *Board of Education* 347 US 483 (1954), holding unconstitutional state enforced racial segregation in public schools.

[68] See eg, *Heart of Atlanta Motel, Inc.* v. *United States* 379 US 241 (1964).

[69] See generally, Delgado and Stefancic in n. 66 above.

idealized formalisms.[70] That is why, as I have mentioned, the force of First Amendment ideals should not be underestimated. Critical theorists have nevertheless persuasively suggested that inclusiveness and even-handedness within the public sphere are elusive, unstable, historically contingent ideals. Questions as to whether they exist at all are not amenable to a simple yes-or-no. The American public sphere that Post describes is a recent historical creation. Throughout most of US history, the public sphere was a debilitated place; nor can such a history be easily swept away by a relatively recent line of Supreme Court cases. The problem of ahistoricism arises, then, when a snapshot of one historical moment is used to provide a general depiction of the society, eclipsing other, contrasting histories. The emergence of the civil-libertarian ideal expressed in *Cantwell*, though clearly important, must not overshadow contrary social realities dating, in one form or another, from the founding of the United States to the present day. Any straightforward characterization of 'America' shorn from that historical bedrock runs the risk of an ahistoricism entailing the same errors as the aforementioned cultural essentialism.

Like essentialism, ahistoricism poses dangers on all sides of the hate speech debate. Scepticism towards free speech in Europe, for example, is often explained in simplistically historical terms. It is often argued that the unbridled freedom to utter racist and antisemitic hate speech under the Weimar Republic led to the most brutal, genocidal regime in history, showing that a rights-based democracy in itself provides no guarantee that free speech will generate any kind of robust 'marketplace of ideas'; it may lead to the utter abrogation of such a society. However, that recourse to history is more ahistorical than historical in any critically minded way. The Weimar democracy cannot seriously compare with today's democracies in any relevant respect. Arguably, such a view assumes them to be similar for no reason other than that they all are nominally called 'democratic'. Today's Council of Europe world, in which Europeans are inculcated from the youngest age, in school and through the media, with values of rights and open debate, fundamentally differs from the nineteenth- and early twentieth-century Concert of Europe world of authoritarian, bellicose states (and, in the case of Weimar, a notoriously weak one), more inclined to promote values of obedience and conformity than values of vigorous, broad-based discourse. Nor, by extension, is such historical reasoning valid to justify bans on Holocaust denial. It is for that reason as well that I do not advocate abolition of hate speech bans always and everywhere, but limit my focus to stable, prosperous, and longstanding democracies—terms admittedly uncertain, but which have been given more precise meaning through general principles governing the derogations jurisprudence of such bodies as the European Court of Human Rights, pursuant to ECHR Article 15 or the UN Human Rights Committee, pursuant to ICCPR Article 4.

---

[70] See n. 6 above.

Attempts to draw such straightforward moral lessons from complex histories are generally hazardous. As an abstract proposition, one might indeed argue that the history of European fascism teaches the necessity of regulating speech; yet one might just as plausibly argue that European fascism teaches the necessity of avoiding any trace of that government-imposed content regulation which stands as a hallmark of the period. A sufficiently offhand or simplified historical account will support either view; which is why such accounts must not be used to short-circuit more serious examination of the character of the world's various democratic societies, and how they may resemble, or differ from, other democracies in history.

8. Conclusion

Legal realism and critical theory have long taught that surface, black-letter norms may reveal little about lived reality, including the lived reality of the law. That insight must be carried over into cross-cultural comparisons of legal regimes and legal cultures. The 'public sphere' of open, democratic discourse is a real, yet also ineffable thing. We cannot draw a neat line around it, showing where it stops and starts. The realities that shape it do not reduce to the formal norms governing it. And if that observation applies to the public sphere within any one society, then it applies when we compare societies. No comparison of two or more societies' respective public spheres can proceed solely on an analysis of black-letter norms. Euro-American differences that may at first appear black-or-white can turn out to be more complicated—on both sides of the Atlantic, and on both sides of the debate about adopting or abolishing bans on extreme speech. Robert Post and James Weinstein join a host of American scholars who have provided trenchant arguments for preserving free speech as a matter of democratic legitimacy, many of which, in my view, transfer readily to the democratic cultures Europe and other societies. The reflections on democratic citizenship explored in much of their work can readily be assimilated into a European political, cultural, and legal idiom, as long as we guard against reading vast cultural differences into the wholly limited differences of trans-Atlantic norms regulating hate speech.

11

Incitement and the Regulation of Hate Speech in Canada: A Philosophical Analysis

L. W. Sumner

Every liberal democracy approaches the regulation of hate speech in its own particular way. In this paper I draw on the experience, and the particularities, of the hate speech laws that have been in place in Canada since 1970. But I also bring to the issue a principled framework for locating the boundaries of free speech, one which derives from John Stuart Mill and has subsequently been operationalized by the Canadian Supreme Court. The conclusion I reach is that, while the best-known piece of Canadian hate speech legislation cannot be justified under this framework, a lesser-known offence has a better chance of success. In the distinction between these offences there are, I suggest, important lessons for the boundaries of free speech.

1. Mill's Tests

I begin with two unargued assumptions: (1) in liberal democracies there is a strong presumption in favour of protecting at least certain core kinds of highly valued speech, a presumption which is codified (in one way or another) in the form of a legal right; (2) this presumption is rebuttable, thus there are justifiable limits to free speech rights. In Canada the presumption is codified in section 2(b) of the Charter of Rights and Freedoms, which guarantees, inter alia, the right to free expression, while the terms of the rebuttal are set out in section 1, which stipulates that all of the specific rights enumerated in the Charter are subject to 'reasonable limits'.[1] Where hate speech is concerned, therefore, the Canadian

---

[1] Canadian Charter of Rights and Freedoms, Schedule B of the Constitution Act, 1982; enacted as Schedule B to the Canada Act 1982 (U.K.) 1982, ch. 11:

s. 2: Everyone has the following fundamental freedoms:

... (b) freedom of thought, belief, opinion and expression, including freedom of the press and other media of communication; ...

s 1: The Canadian Charter of Rights and Freedoms guarantees the rights and freedoms set out in it subject only to such reasonable limits prescribed by law as can be demonstrably justified in a free and democratic society.

Charter is a convenient vehicle for raising a familiar question: Is the regulation of such speech, by means of criminal sanctions, a reasonable limit on freedom of expression? Is this a form of speech for which the presumption in favour of freedom can be rebutted?

These were the questions faced by the Canadian Supreme Court in its 1990 *Keegstra* case.[2] James Keegstra was a secondary school teacher in Eckville, Alberta who used his classroom to advocate his antisemitic opinions. He taught his students that a worldwide Jewish conspiracy has been responsible for depressions, wars, anarchy, and revolution and that the Jews created the myth of the Holocaust in order to gain sympathy for themselves. He was charged under section 319(2) of the Canadian Criminal Code, first enacted in 1970, which prohibits the wilful promotion of hatred against groups identified by such characteristics as race and religion.[3] In *Keegstra* a constitutional challenge was raised against this section, primarily on the ground that it was an unjustifiable infringement of section 2(b) of the Charter. In its judgment the Court upheld the constitutionality of the hate promotion law by a narrow majority of 4–3. The majority and the minority on the Court agreed that hateful expression was covered by section 2(b), thus that the law did indeed infringe the *Charter* right. The issue therefore was whether this infringement was justifiable under the terms of section 1. In deciding this question the Court utilized the tests which it had set out in its 1986 *Oakes* decision.[4] In order for a limit on a *Charter* right to be 'reasonable' it must pass two tests, one concerning its end and the other concerning the means it employs to achieve that end:

1. *Legislative objective.* The purpose of the legislation must be sufficiently 'pressing and substantial' to justify limiting the right.
2. *Proportionality.* The means employed by the legislation must be proportional to the objective to be achieved. The proportionality test subdivides in turn into three parts:
   (a) *Rational connection.* There must be reasonable grounds for expecting the legislation to be effective in achieving its objective.
   (b) *Minimal impairment.* The legislation must limit the right no more than is necessary in order to achieve its objective.
   (c) *Proportional effects.* The costs of the limitation must not exceed the benefits to be gained from achieving the objective.

---

[2] *R.* v. *Keegstra* (1990) 3 S.C.R. 697.
[3] Criminal Code, R.S., 1985, ch. C-46:

S. 319(2): Every one who, by communicating statements, other than in private conversation, wilfully promotes hatred against any identifiable group is guilty of
(a) an indictable offence and is liable to imprisonment for a term not exceeding two years; or
(b) an offence punishable on summary conviction.

. . .

(7) In this section, "identifiable group" means any section of the public distinguished by colour, race, religion, ethnic origin, or sexual orientation.

[4] *R.* v. *Oakes* (1986) 1 S.C.R. 103.

In applying these tests to the hate promotion law the majority and the minority also agreed that the objective of the law—which they saw as the protection of vulnerable minorities against harms likely to result from the spread of contempt or enmity directed toward them—was sufficiently pressing and substantial to justify the limitation. The issue on which the Court divided, therefore, was the application of the proportionality test, which requires that the expected benefits of the hate speech law be balanced against its expected costs. The rational connection requirement is intended to ensure that the benefits promised by the legislation will actually be delivered. It must therefore be shown at this stage that criminalizing hate speech will succeed in reducing its circulation, with corresponding gains in self-esteem and other important social goods for the members of target minorities. With the minimal impairment step we move to the cost side. Both sides have agreed that, even if hate speech has little to contribute to such core values as democracy or the pursuit of truth, restricting it nonetheless compromises at least one of the interests served by expressive freedom: the autonomy or self-fulfilment of the speakers themselves. The question now is whether this cost is greater than it need be in order to yield the legislation's expected benefits. If comparable benefits for minorities could be achieved at less cost to expressive freedom, then the legislation will fail this part of the proportionality test. Finally, the proportional effects requirement brings the cost and benefit sides together, in order to determine whether the benefits of the legislation are worth securing in the face of its predictable costs.

So understood, the *Oakes* tests bear a striking resemblance to the factors highlighted by John Stuart Mill's harm-based approach to justifying restrictions on liberty. Mill's statement of his general principle of liberty is well known: 'the only purpose for which power can be rightfully exercised over any member of a civilized community, against his will, is to prevent harm to others'.[5] This principle entails that any legislative measure restricting liberty of expression must first pass a *harm test*: the government must be able to show that the particular kind of expression in question (hate speech, for instance) threatens to impose serious harm on third parties. The kind of harm threatened must be serious, as opposed to merely slight or trivial, in order to compete with the very substantial value of free expression. This threshold requirement corresponds to the first *Oakes* test, which stipulates that the restriction must be in service of a pressing and substantial objective. Absent such an objective (which is to say, absent evidence of serious harm to be prevented), the restriction cannot be justified.

If the restrictive legislation manages to pass the harm test it does not follow, however, that it is justified by Mill's liberty principle. That principle makes harm to others a necessary condition for limiting liberty, but not a sufficient one.[6] The

---

[5] J. S. Mill, 'On Liberty' in J. S. Mill, *Essays on Politics and Society* Ed. J. M. Robson (Toronto: Univ of Toronto Press, 1977), 223.

[6] Ibid., 292: '... it must by no means be supposed, because damage, or probability of damage, to the interests of others, can alone justify the interference of society, that therefore it always does justify such interference.'

legislation must also pass a *cost-benefit test*: restricting the expression in question must yield a better balance of benefits over costs than leaving it unregulated.[7] This requirement of a positive cost-benefit balance does not provide a simple algorithm for deciding whether, and when, the state is entitled to enforce restrictions on forms of expression in those cases in which the harm test has been satisfied. However, it does suggest the kinds of factors which will be relevant. First, the restriction must have some reasonable expectation of success. While it may be thought desirable to inhibit or suppress some form of expression by legal means, it is a further question whether doing so is possible. To the extent that the restrictions can be readily circumvented, by an underground market or by technological innovations such as the Internet, the case for them is weakened. Second, there must be no less costly policy available for securing the same results. Even when it promises to be effective in preventing some significant social harm, censorship abridges personal liberty and deprives consumers of whatever benefits they may derive from the prohibited forms of expression. It should therefore be the last, not the first, resort of government for preventing the harm in question. Where less coercive measures (education, counterspeech, etc.) promise similar results they should be preferred. Where a narrower infringement of freedom of expression will be equally effective it too should be preferred. Third, the expected benefits of the restriction must, on balance, justify its costs. Censorship can compromise other important social values, such as vigorous engagement in public debate. It can have a 'chilling effect' on legitimate forms of expression (literary, artistic, etc.). However well intended the restriction might be, in practice it will be administered by police, prosecutors, judges, or bureaucrats who may use it to justify targeting unpopular, marginal forms of literature with no significant capacity for social harm. On balance, the benefits to be gained by legal restraints on expression must be great enough to justify the collateral costs.

Mill's cost-benefit condition has its counterpart in the second *Oakes* test of proportionality, with its components of rational connection, minimal impairment, and overall positive cost-benefit balance. In this way both Mill and the Canadian Supreme Court take us to the same harm-centred issues: the (actual or potential) harms of hate speech and the cost-benefit balance of measures designed to regulate such speech. To these issues, therefore, we now turn.

2. The Harms of Hate Speech

For the purposes of this discussion I will consider hate speech to be any form of expression whose dominant purpose is to insult or denigrate members of a social

---

[7] Ibid., 276: 'As soon as any part of a person's conduct affects prejudicially the interests of others, society has jurisdiction over it, and the question whether the general welfare will or will not be promoted by interfering with it, becomes open to discussion.'

group identified by such characteristics as race, ethnicity, religion, or sexual orientation, or to arouse enmity or hostility against them. Since I have dealt with the harms that can be done by such speech at greater length elsewhere,[8] my treatment of the question here will be brief. In contrast with the putative links between pornography and harms to women, social scientists have given relatively little attention to the harms of hate speech. In order to sort through what is available, it will be convenient to distinguish two different (though not mutually exclusive) causal pathways by means of which hate messages targeting a particular minority might harm the members of that minority. We will say that the harm is *direct* if it results from exposure to the messages by members of the target group themselves. This may occur when individuals are subjected to verbal abuse in the form of racist epithets or insults, but also when hate messages intrude upon the lives of their targets in the form of anonymous telephone calls or notes, graffiti spraypainted in public spaces, crosses burned in front yards, pamphlets delivered through the mail, the desecration of sacred places, or other means. Mari Matsuda has enumerated these direct harms as follows:

Victims of vicious hate propaganda experience physiological symptoms and emotional distress ranging from fear in the gut to rapid pulse rate and difficulty in breathing, nightmares, post-traumatic stress disorder, hypertension, psychosis, and suicide...

Victims are restricted in their personal freedom. To avoid receiving hate messages, victims have to quit jobs, forgo education, leave their homes, avoid certain public places, curtail their own exercise of speech rights, and otherwise modify their behavior and demeanor. The recipient of hate messages struggles with inner turmoil...

As much as one may try to resist a piece of hate propaganda, the effect on one's self-esteem and sense of personal security is devastating. To be hated, despised, and alone is the ultimate fear of all human beings. However irrational racist speech may be, it hits right at the emotional place where we feel the most pain.[9]

Even if there were no empirical evidence to support Matsuda's claims, they have a pretty secure footing in common sense. After all, hate messages directed at members of their target group are not meant to engage the audience in a rational debate or persuade them of some important truths. Rather, they are meant to hurt—by insulting, humiliating, or intimidating—and it would scarcely be surprising if they were often to succeed in this aim. Many of the immediate responses Matsuda describes are the ones all of us evince when subjected to abuse or insult, whether motivated by prejudice or not. Fortunately, however, we do not need to rely solely on common experience here: there is also scientific support for the attribution to victims of hate speech of these kinds of emotional,

---

[8] L. W. Sumner, *The Hateful and the Obscene: Studies in the Limits of Free Expression* (Toronto: Univ of Toronto Press, 2004), s. 5.5.

[9] M. J. Matsuda, 'Public Response to Racist Speech: Considering the Victim's Story', M. J. Matsuda, C. Lawrence III, R. Delgado, and K. W. Crenshaw (eds.), *Words that Wound: Critical Race Theory, Assaultive Speech and the First Amendment* (Boulder, CO: Westview Press, 1993), 24–5.

attitudinal, and behavioural effects.[10] It is also worth noting that they bear more than a passing resemblance to some of the short-term effects on children of sexual abuse, and on women of sexual violence. There is no clean line here between abusive speech and abusive conduct—or, rather, the former is just one type of the latter.

The harms of hate speech, however, do not end with its direct impact on its victims. We will say that the harms are *indirect* if they work through the mediation of attitudes and conduct on the part of an audience other than the target groups themselves. The two broader social conditions to which hate messages are most frequently said to contribute are the social inequality of target minorities and violence against members of these minorities. These outcomes are not, of course, really distinct, since the experience of living in fear of racist or homophobic violence is itself one form of social inequality. However, for analytic purposes I will deal with them separately, first with inequality and then, finally, with violence.

Whatever their precise content, hate messages preach the inferiority of the groups they choose to single out and implicitly or explicitly advocate discrimination against the members of those groups. Actual discriminatory practices against minorities would therefore count as success for the producers and distributors of these messages. But members of hate groups typically have little power to impose such practices beyond the confines of their own narrow circles. Success therefore will necessarily require enlisting a much wider public in the cause. That, in turn, will require an impact on the attitudes of non-members of the target minorities—members, that is, of the dominant social groups. It is this mechanism of subtle and pervasive attitudinal change that Matsuda also attributes to hate speech:

Research in the psychology of racism suggests a related effect of racist hate propaganda: At some level, no matter how much both victims and well-meaning dominant-group members resist it, racial inferiority is planted in our minds as an idea that may hold some truth. The idea is improbable and abhorrent, but because it is presented repeatedly, it is there before us. 'Those people' are lazy, dirty, sexualized, money grubbing, dishonest, inscrutable, we are told. We reject the idea, but the next time we sit next to one of 'those people', the dirt message, the sex message, is triggered. We stifle it, reject it as wrong, but it is there, interfering with our perception and interaction with the person next to us.[11]

Clay Calvert has pointed to the same effect: 'It is a long-term, cumulative harm that accrues with repeated use of racist epithets directed at targeted minorities. The harm is the subordination of racial minorities, including the perpetuation

---

[10] See, for instance, C. Calvert, 'Hate Speech and its Harms: A Communication Theory Perspective' (1997) 47(1) *J. Communication* 4; L. Leets, 'Experiencing Hate Speech: Perceptions and Responses to Anti-Semitism and Antigay Speech' (2002) 58(2) *J. Social Issues* 341; L. B. Nielsen, 'Subtle, Pervasive, Harmful: Racist and Sexist Remarks in Public as Hate Speech' (2002) 58(2) *J. Social Issues* 265.

[11] See n. 9 above, 25–6 (citation omitted).

and reinforcement of discriminatory attitudes and behaviors. In brief, use of racist expressions creates and maintains a social reality of racism that promotes disparate treatment of minorities.'[12]

We are obviously dealing here with an alleged causal relationship between the incidence of hate speech within a society and the discriminatory treatment of that society's target minorities. This connection has a strong basis in common sense since hate speech often openly advocates an unequal social status for minorities. However, advocacy is one thing and successful advocacy quite another. It is plausible to suppose that hate speech makes some contribution toward the unequal social status of minorities such as blacks, Asians, Jews, aboriginals, and gays and lesbians. But no serious scientific attempt has been made to factor out and measure the extent of this contribution, nor is it easy to see how this could be done. It seems that in the territory of equality few advances are possible beyond what common sense and experience can teach us.

Things are rather different when we turn to the issue of violence. Hate violence takes the form of assault on a person or damage to property motivated by hostility toward the group with which the person or property is associated. Most legal jurisdictions now classify certain cases of murder, assault, public mischief, and the like as hate crimes on the basis of evidence of such motivation. Whereas the literature on the effects of hate speech may be limited, there is ample evidence of the damage that hate crimes can do both to their immediate victims and to other members of the target communities.[13] None of this, of course, is surprising: we know that being the victim of racist or homophobic violence is a harm, just as we know the same for sexual violence. The question in this case, as in the earlier, is whether there is a causal connection back to a particular form of expression. In brief: does hate speech cause hate crimes?

Many hate messages either imply or openly advocate the legitimacy of violence against minorities. By so doing, it is arguable—indeed highly plausible—that they contribute to a climate which fosters hate crimes and which members of vulnerable minorities experience as threatening or intimidating. The extent of this contribution is, of course, difficult to measure with any degree of certainty but we can point to one quite tangible link in the causal chain from speech to crime.

---

[12] See Calvert (n. 10 above), 6.
[13] See, for instance, K. T. Berrill and G. M. Herek, 'Primary and Secondary Victimization in Anti-Gay Hate Crimes: Official Response and Public Policy' (1990) 5(3) *J. Interpersonal Violence* 401; L. Garnets, G. M. Herek, and B. Levey, 'Violence and Victimization of Lesbians and Gay Men: Mental Health Consequences' (1990) 5(3) *J. Interpersonal Violence* 366; J. Levin and J. McDevitt, *Hate Crimes: The Rising Tide of Bigotry and Bloodshed* (New York: Plenum Press, 1993); A. Barnes and P. H. Ephross, 'The Impact of Hate Violence on Victims: Emotional and Behavioral Responses to Attacks' (1994) 39(3) *Social Work* 247; K. M. Craig, 'Retaliation, Fear, or Rage: An Investigation of African American and White Reactions to Racist Hate Crimes' (1999) 14(2) *J. Interpersonal Violence* 138; G. M. Herek, J. R. Gillis, and J. C. Cogan, 'Psychological Sequelae of Hate-Crime Victimization among Lesbian, Gay, and Bisexual Adults'(1999) 67(6) *J. Consulting and Clinical Psychology* 945; G. M. Herek, J. C. Cogan, and J. R. Gillis, 'Victim Experiences in Hate Crimes Based on Sexual Orientation' (2002) 58(2) *J. Social Issues* 319.

While some hate messages are disseminated by isolated individuals, most of them are generated by organized hate groups. For these groups the primary purpose of the materials they circulate, largely now through websites, is not to contribute to a broad public debate concerning Jews or blacks or gays. Rather, the materials are used to reinforce the shared ideology that binds the group together and to recruit new group members.[14] For a hate group, hate speech is its creed or ideology, and its call to action. That action frequently involves acts of violence against members of target groups or their property. It is impossible to determine with any accuracy what proportion of the overall incidence of hate crimes can be attributed to individuals affiliated with hate groups.[15] Some studies have suggested that most such crimes are committed for thrills or in defence of 'turf' against 'outsiders', and only a small proportion by individuals for whom racism or homophobia is a long-term mission.[16] On the other hand, we have good evidence that many hate groups have a history of involvement in racist violence.[17] Furthermore, there have been a number of prominent instances of hate violence in recent years where the perpetrator has had a personal history of involvement with a hate group.[18] When the group has advocated violence against members of a particular minority and one of its adherents comes to practise just such violence, it is difficult to resist a cause-and-effect conclusion. If that conclusion is at least sometimes justified then hate messages can do more than merely legitimize or endorse violence against target minorities—they can also encourage or even instigate it.

[14] A. Tsesis, *Destructive Messages: How Hate Speech Paves the Way for Harmful Social Movements* (New York and London: NYU Press, 2002), 117: '... during opportune times, [hate speech] inflames and recruits persons who can be catalyzed to wreak havoc on outgroups. Discriminatory oratory functions to unify ingroups through a mutually captivating ideology. It distinguishes ingroups from minorities, expresses the superiority of the dominant group, and organizes for collective action against outgroups.'

[15] This is especially so with some of the most frequently reported types of hate crime, such as vandalism and harassment, which, because usually anonymous, result in a lower arrest rate.

[16] B. Perry, *In the Name of Hate: Understanding Hate Crimes* (New York and London: Routledge, 2001), 142: '... [I]t is clear that hate groups are not the primary perpetrators of bias-motivated crime. The vast majority is committed—singly or in groups—by people who are not directly connected to any organized form of hate.') See also Levin and McDevitt, n. 13 above; J. McDevitt, J. Levin, and S. Bennett, 'Hate Crime Offenders: An Expanded Typology' (2002) 58(2) *J. Social Issues* 303.

[17] For Canada, see League for Human Rights of B'Nai Brith Canada, *Skinheads in Canada and Their Link to the Far Right* (Downsview, ON: B'nai Brith Canada, 1990); W. Kinsella, *Web of Hate: Inside Canada's Far Right Network* (Toronto: HarperCollins, 1994). Comprehensive accounts of hate groups in the United States can be found in J. Ridgeway, *Blood in the Face* 2nd edn. (New York: Thunder's Mouth Press, 1995) and K. Stern, *A Force Upon the Plain: The American Militia Movement and the Politics of Hate* (New York: Simon and Schuster, 1996); for a briefer overview see Perry, ibid., ch. 6.

[18] In 1999, Benjamin Smith, an adherent of the World Church of the Creator, killed two people and wounded twelve during a shooting rampage in Indiana and Illinois in which he was targeting blacks, Jews, and Asians. Later that same year Buford Furrow, who had been affiliated with Aryan Nation-Church of Jesus Christ, shot five people in a Jewish community centre in Los Angeles and then killed a Filipino postal worker an hour later.

3. Promoting and Inciting

The foregoing is the merest sketch of the harms commonly associated with hate speech. It will, however, suffice to help us determine how the regulation of hate speech fares with respect to the two tests proposed by Mill and operationalized by the Canadian Supreme Court. Recall that the harm test essentially sets a threshold for the very idea of regulation. Where conduct falls below that threshold—by causing no significant harm to others—the issue of subjecting it to coercive interference does not even arise. For such conduct the default presumption of liberty stands unrebutted. It is worth noting that this threshold for regulation is particularly high in the case of the criminal law, due to the seriousness of the sanctions attached to transgression, the stress and expense of the trial process, and the social stigma that is carried by the acquisition of a criminal record. Liberal societies should be particularly reluctant to employ criminal measures to prevent or control antisocial conduct: 'Since many acts may be "harmful", and since society has many other means for controlling or responding to conduct, criminal law should be used only when the harm caused or threatened is serious, and when the other, less coercive or less intrusive means do not work or are inappropriate.'[19] The stringency of this test is also reflected in the Supreme Court's requirement that the objective of the restrictive legislation be 'pressing and substantial'. Stringent though it might be, however, some conduct—and surely some expressive conduct—will surmount the threshold, which will bring the second, cost-benefit, test into play: the restriction must be worth purchasing at its cost to expressive freedom.

The harms of hate speech are most visible and verifiable when they are direct, in the form of abusive or insulting language used against its target group. While the criminal law does not ordinarily protect citizens against verbal abuse, it may do so when the abuse reaches the level of harassment, threat, or intimidation. There seems little doubt that racist or homophobic abuse can reach that level. However, when it does then the means chosen for delivering the message will itself constitute an offence: criminal harassment, uttering a threat, public mischief, and so on. Where there is evidence that the offence is hate-motivated, which will generally be provided by the content of the message, then it can be prosecuted as a hate crime for the purpose of seeking an enhanced penalty.[20] In other cases, such as neo-Nazi rallies in Jewish neighbourhoods, time, manner, or circumstance restrictions should suffice to ensure that the offending messages are

---

[19] Government of Canada, *The Criminal Law in Canadian Society* (Ottawa, 1982).

[20] I take no stand here on the justifiability of penalty enhancement for hate crimes, nor on the issue of whether this is itself a free speech restriction; for arguments on both sides of these issues see J. B. Jacobs and K. Potter, *Hate Crimes: Criminal Law and Identity Politics* (New York: OUP, 1998) and F. M. Lawrence, *Punishing Hate: Bias Crimes Under American Law* (Cambridge, MA: Harvard UP, 1999).

not imposed on an unwilling target audience. In none of these instances does there seem to be a need to address the problem by imposing a general content restriction on hate speech.

In any case, it is evident that legislation like the hate promotion statute in the *Criminal Code* is not meant to protect minorities against the direct harms of hate speech. In criminalizing speech that wilfully promotes hatred, Parliament was concerned with the impact of such speech on audiences other than the target minorities themselves. Put otherwise, the aim was not to prevent members of minorities from hating themselves but to prevent them from being hated by others. The concern was with the kind of attitude change that hate speech might effect in members of the dominant majority—those in a position to treat minorities prejudicially through the mechanisms of discrimination and/or violence. As noted in the previous section, those who are subjected to racist or homophobic discrimination or violence doubtless suffer harms serious enough to warrant legal protection. But that is not the issue—or at least not all of the issue —where the regulation of hate speech is concerned. The law already has resources —both human rights law and criminal law—adequate, at least in principle, for protecting citizens against these harms. The free speech issue requires us to answer a different question: to what extent can the undoubted harms of discrimination and violence be imputed to speech that wilfully promotes hatred?

I am not going to attempt a general answer to this question, if only because the right answer for a particular society will surely reflect the particular situations of vulnerable minorities in that society. So I will confine myself in what follows to the Canadian context and the Canadian law. The time has now come to take a closer look at that law, more specifically at the gravamen of the offence it defines: the wilful promotion of hatred. All three of the key terms in that phrase are in need of explication, which the Court attempted to provide in its *Keegstra* decision. We begin with hatred, which Dickson CJ, writing for the Court, glossed in the following way: 'Noting the purpose of s. 319(2), in my opinion the term "hatred" connotes emotion of an intense and extreme nature that is clearly associated with vilification and detestation . . . Hatred in this sense is a most extreme emotion that belies reason; an emotion that, if exercised against members of an identifiable group, implies that those individuals are to be despised, scorned, denied respect and made subject to ill-treatment on the basis of group affiliation.'[21] In confining hatred in this way to the most extreme forms of contempt or enmity, Dickson was attempting to fend off the charge, brought by the dissenting minority, that the hate promotion law failed the minimal impairment test due to overbreadth. But he was also trying to preserve the rational connection between the terms of the law and its 'pressing and substantial' objective, which had been agreed to be the protection of minorities against the harms likely to result from the spread of contempt or enmity directed toward them—the harms, that is, of discrimination

---

[21] See n. 2 above, 777.

and violence. Because of its high pitch of intensity, hatred, as Dickson understood it, is the feeling or attitude most likely to motivate these practices.

The burden of requiring that the promotion of hatred, in this sense, must be wilful is to make the offence one of specific intent: the speaker must 'intend or foresee as substantially certain a direct and active stimulation of hatred against an identifiable group'.[22] The Court was very clear that the offence consists in the intent of the speech rather than its (probable or certain) effect: no evidence need be adduced of any hatred actually promoted by the speech in question. In defence of this provision of the law Dickson wrote that 'it is clearly difficult to prove a causative link between a specific statement and hatred of an identifiable group. In fact, to require direct proof of hatred in listeners would severely debilitate the effectiveness of section 319(2) in achieving Parliament's aim.'[23] The law does require that the speech be public—or, rather, 'other than in private conversation'—but it is not clear that it requires that there be any listeners at all. Putting hateful messages on my telephone answer machine or my personal website would doubtless be an offence even if no one ever dialled my number or accessed my site. Furthermore, in those cases where the speech does have listeners, the reaction of the audience is immaterial. I might be a spellbinding orator able to stir up extreme enmity against the people I happen to hate on the basis of their skin colour or the god they choose to worship or the partners they choose to sleep with, but as long as this is my intent I commit the offence no less if I am inept enough to put my audience to sleep or reduce them to helpless laughter.

Dickson's further defence of the intent provision leads him to fall back onto the notion of risk: 'It is well accepted that Parliament can use the criminal law to prevent the risk of serious harms, a leading example being the drinking and driving provisions in the *Criminal Code*.'[24] But this is clearly to shift ground. The offence of driving while impaired requires no specific intent: it is both necessary and sufficient that one's blood alcohol level exceed some stipulated minimum. It is true, of course, that the offence does not rest on doing any harm on the particular occasion: I commit it even if I manage to drive home safely from the party without causing any injury to persons or property. But it does rest on an objective assessment of risk: driving in that condition on any occasion increases the probability of such injury by some degree which it is in principle possible to calculate. Applying this analogy to the case of hate speech would first require demonstrating that hate speech, as a general phenomenon, increases the probability of discrimination or violence against minorities. That is, it would be necessary to show that the incidence of these prejudicial practices in a country like Canada is, or would be, higher in the presence of hate speech than in its absence. But this is just the kind of social-scientific evidence about the effects of hate speech which we lack. Furthermore, even if this general evidentiary burden could

---

[22] Ibid.   [23] See n. 2 above, 776.   [24] Ibid.

be discharged, it would also be necessary to show that this heightened level of risk is present on every particular occasion on which some speaker aims to promote hatred, regardless of whether there is any realistic chance of achieving that aim.

The third notion in need of explication is promotion. What is it to promote hatred? Once again, Dickson takes on the interpretive task: 'Given the purpose of the provision to criminalize the spreading of hatred in society, I find that the word "promotes" indicates active support or instigation. Indeed the French version of the offence uses the verb *"fomenter"*, which in English means to foment or stir up. In "promotes" we thus have a word that indicates more than simple encouragement or advancement.'[25] Dickson has doubtless given the term the reading it needs in order for the hate promotion law to have any chance of passing the minimal impairment test, but he also leaves us wondering why, if this is what is meant, Parliament chose the language of promotion in the first place. In ordinary English to promote something—a cause, let us say, or an event—is to do something to bring it about or help it to succeed. In short, promotion need be no more than 'simple encouragement or advancement'; it need not rise to the level of instigating, fomenting, or stirring up. On the other hand, there is a perfectly good ordinary English term which has its uses in the law and which does have this further connotation, namely incitement. 'Incite' derives from the Latin root *citare*, which means to set in rapid motion, rouse, or stimulate ('excite' has the same root). The *Oxford English Dictionary* offers the following as approximate synonyms for 'incite': spur on, stir up (see 'foment', above), animate, stimulate, provoke, instigate. What these various notions seem to have in common is the idea of (1) galvanizing someone into action by (2) appealing to the passions rather than to reason. Inciting to action thus contrasts with counselling, or advising, or persuading: it works through getting the subject worked up or agitated rather than by offering a convincing argument.

So what Dickson has told us, in effect, is that when Parliament spoke of promoting hatred what it really meant was inciting hatred. But if that is what Parliament meant, why did it not say so? Why did it use the seemingly more innocuous language of promotion, rather than incitement? Its terminological choice seems all the stranger when we note that incitement is the common notion in comparable hate speech regulations in most European jurisdictions. In England, for instance, incitement to racial hatred has been an offence since the passage of the Race Relations Act 1965 and is currently defined as such under Part 3 of the Public Order Act 1986. In 2006 incitement to religious hatred was added to the Act as a comparable offence.[26] So why is Canada out of step here? Now

---

[25] See n. 2 above, 776–7.

[26] There are significant differences between the two offences. See I. Hare, 'Crosses, Crescents and Sacred Cows: Criminalising Incitement to Religious Hatred' (2006) *Pub. L.*, 521, and K. Goodall, 'Incitement to Religious Hatred: All Talk and No Substance?' (2007) 70(1) *Modern L. Rev.* 89. Both racial and religious hatred have been included from the beginning under Canada's hate promotion law.

Parliament did, as it happens, have a good reason not to speak of inciting rather than promoting hatred in section 319(2) of the *Criminal Code*, and I will return to this reason shortly. But meanwhile, it is worth noting that in at least one crucial respect the crime of inciting racial (or religious) hatred is somewhat anomalous. The notion of incitement has its uses in the law outside of this particular context.[27] *Black's Law Dictionary* defines 'incite' as 'to provoke or stir up (someone to commit a criminal act, or the criminal act itself)' and includes incitement, along with attempt, conspiracy, and solicitation, in the roster of inchoate offences. Now it is in the nature of an inchoate offence that its unlawful status is, as it were, parasitic on a principal or substantive offence. Attempted murder, therefore, is an offence in its own right because murder is, and conspiracy to defraud is an offence because fraud is. Likewise, in the criminal law in general incitement is a criminal act only where the act incited is itself criminal. However, incitement of hatred is a conspicuous exception to this rule. Hatred is not itself a criminal offence, not even when it is directed at a group defined by such markers as race, religion, or sexual orientation. So it is somewhat odd, to say the least, that it should be unlawful to incite someone to a state or condition that is not itself unlawful. It is difficult to think of other examples in the criminal law, though assisting (counselling, aiding or abetting) a suicide does come to mind. Here the principal act is not criminal, though assisting it is. But at least in this case it is an act, on the part of a second party, on which the collateral offence is defined. The further oddity of the crime of inciting hatred is that the thing incited is a feeling, or emotion, or attitude, rather than a concrete act. The problem here is not that hatred is incapable of being incited: one can incite feelings in another just as much as, or in addition to, acts. Indeed, as indicated earlier, it seems part of the very meaning of incitement that the other is moved to act by the arousal of passion. No, the difficulty lies in figuring out why inciting a feeling, where there is no requirement of any subsequent criminal act, itself deserves the status of a criminal act.

The hate promotion law, therefore, seems doubly unlikely to pass Mill's tests, since the offence it defines is doubly removed from the harms of discrimination and violence which it aims to prevent.[28] First, because the offence consists entirely in the intent to incite hatred, there is no requirement that any hatred has actually been incited, and, second, even if the incitement has been successful there is no requirement that it has resulted in, or even increased the likelihood of, any criminal, or otherwise antisocial, act. For these reasons, the principal argument in favour of the hate promotion law—that it can play an important part in preventing discrimination or violence against vulnerable groups by reducing the general level of hostility toward them—appears to be insufficient.

---

[27] Though, curiously, not in the Canadian *Criminal Code*, which speaks only of counselling the commission of a criminal offence, not inciting one.

[28] I leave it open here whether the law would fail to surmount the threshold of 'significant harm' or, alternatively, would yield insufficient benefits to justify its costs to expressive freedom.

We should not conclude from this, however, either that hate speech should be subject to no regulation nor that the notion of incitement has no role to play in such regulation. It is time now to return to the question I posed earlier: if Dickson is right that Parliament in 1970 meant to prohibit the incitement of hatred why did it speak instead of the promotion of hatred? The straight answer, I think, is that it had already utilized the notion of incitement to define a distinct offence. In Canada virtually all discussion of hate speech regulation has focused on section 319(2) of the *Criminal Code*—the hate promotion law that was at stake in the *Keegstra* case. Much less attention has been devoted to section 319(1), which prohibits the incitement of hatred against an identifiable group 'where such incitement is likely to lead to a breach of the peace'.[29] In framing its hate speech restrictions Parliament elected to define two distinct offences, one of inciting hatred and the other of promoting hatred.[30] While both speak of stirring up or provoking a feeling or passion, only the former requires the crucial further link to an unlawful act. Unlike the hate promotion law, the hate incitement law therefore retains an important element of the notion of incitement as an inchoate offence. We can, of course, still side with Dickson in thinking that by 'promoting hatred' in section 319(2) Parliament meant the same as 'inciting hatred' in section 319(1). But it seems to me more plausible to conclude that it had a narrower notion of incitement in mind—one which tied it to the commission of a substantive offence and which was therefore inapt for the further offence of hate promotion. However this might be, the important point is that the incitement offence requires what the promotion offence does not, namely some contribution to the (actual or potential) commission of an unlawful act (such as a hate crime against members of a protected minority). In this respect it seems designed to deal with the final category of indirect harm identified in the previous section: instances in which speakers use inflammatory rhetoric to inspire listeners to commit acts of racist or homophobic violence.

It is worth noting here that Mill himself acknowledged that restrictions on incitement to violence could pass his tests for justifiable limits to free speech. Having concluded his absolutist defence of 'the fullest liberty of professing and discussing, as a matter of ethical conviction, any doctrine, however immoral it

---

[29] S. 319(1): Every one who, by communicating statements in any public place, incites hatred against any identifiable group where such incitement is likely to lead to a breach of the peace is guilty of

    (a) an indictable offence and is liable to imprisonment for a term not exceeding two years; or

    (b) an offence punishable on summary conviction.

[30] 385. It defined a third as well:

S. 318(1) Every one who advocates or promotes genocide is guilty of an indictable offence and liable to imprisonment for a term not exceeding five years.

(2) In this section, "genocide" means any of the following acts committed with intent to destroy in whole or in part any identifiable group, namely,

    (a) killing members of the group; or

    (b) deliberately inflicting on the group conditions of life calculated to bring about its physical destruction.

may be considered',[31] he then turned to the question 'whether the same reasons do not require that men should be free to act upon their opinions'. Unsurprisingly, in answering this question he invoked the harm test—the action must be 'at their own risk or peril'—and then applied this test to the special case of the expression of opinions: '...even opinions lose their immunity, when the circumstances in which they are expressed are such as to constitute their expression a positive instigation to some mischievous act. An opinion that corn-dealers are starvers of the poor, or that private property is robbery, ought to be unmolested when simply circulated through the press, but may justly incur punishment when delivered orally to an excited mob assembled before the house of a corn-dealer, or when handed about among the same mob in the form of a placard.'[32] Here we have the familiar ingredients of unlawful incitement: the use of fiery speech to ignite strong passions which will in turn drive listeners to commit unlawful acts. Mill touched on the same themes in his treatment of the doctrine of tyrannicide, where he defended the right to circulate it as a general thesis but then continued: '...I hold that the instigation to it, in a specific case, may be a proper subject of punishment, but only if an overt act has followed, and at least a probable connexion can be established between the act and the instigation.'[33]

By 'instigation' Mill evidently means something very similar to what we normally understand as incitement. Similar, but not quite identical. As Mill makes clear, he would treat instigation as an offence 'only if an overt act has followed'. But this requirement is at odds with the common conception of inchoate offences, whose commission does not require that the principal offence actually be carried out. This is necessarily true in the case of attempts, which by their very nature preclude the successful commission of the act, but it can be contingently true of all other inchoate offences: my conspiracy to defraud may be overheard in wiretapped conversations, my solicitation to murder may be made to an undercover police officer, and my exhortation to go out and beat up on Jews or gays may be greeted by my audience with shrugs and yawns. Mill may still be right in requiring 'a probable connexion...between the act and the instigation', but this requirement would be satisfied if it could be shown that the incitement at least created a significant risk that the offence would be committed. This condition is what Parliament seems to have had in mind in stipulating that the incitement must be 'likely to lead to a breach of the peace', whether or not any such breach actually occurs.

In the previous section I noted that messages disseminated by hate groups can have the function both of recruiting new members and of motivating adherents to commit hate crimes against members of target groups. This latter function makes for a much more direct causal relationship between the message and the violence,

---

[31] See n. 5 above, 228n.
[32] See n. 5 above, 260.
[33] See n. 5 above, 228n.

one which is not mediated by shifts in the overall climate of public opinion about minorities. However, it also opens up the possibility of treating the communication of hate messages, under certain circumstances, as incitement to this violence. Where hate crimes have been committed by members, or former members, of known hate groups and have clearly been inspired by hate messages disseminated by those groups, there seems no reason not to regard the latter as having incited the violence and as being liable to prosecution on that basis. The Canadian offence of inciting hatred seems to target just such cases.

There remains a question, however, not about the legitimacy of such an offence, but about its necessity. Recall the earlier discussion of the direct harms of hate speech: the injuries inflicted on members of vulnerable minorities when they are the unwilling audience of such speech. While no one doubts the reality or the seriousness of such injuries, there is a legitimate question whether any special protection against them is necessary, alongside the general prohibition of such antisocial acts as threats, harassment, intimidation, and vandalism. The same question arises where the indirect harm of incitement to violence is concerned. If it is in general unlawful to counsel or solicit an act of violence, then why is it necessary to define a special offence for the particular case of incitement of a hate crime? Unlike the case of the hate promotion law, there is no ground for principled objection to both of these other speech-related offences on free speech grounds. Neither constitutes a broad content restriction on speech; instead, each prohibits hate speech only in a concrete context in which it can be reliably linked to harm, or the risk of harm, against assignable victims. The issue, rather, is one of redundancy, the special cases being included under broader offences in which hate need not be an issue.[34] It may, of course, be possible to defend the redundancy, whether for the symbolic importance to minorities of acknowledging their particular vulnerability, or for publicly communicating the message that racism and homophobia have no place in a liberal social order, or for singling out certain uses of speech as hate crimes for the purpose of penalty enhancement. These are matters which a liberal society may be left to decide on pragmatic grounds without concern that it is thereby unjustifiably infringing free speech rights.

4. Conclusion

At the outset I posed the question whether the presumption in favour of free speech is rebutted in the case of hate speech. Using the Canadian hate speech laws as my working example, and utilizing the harm-centred tests for the justifiable

---

[34] Recall that neither of Mill's instigation cases, discussed above, involve hate speech. Neither corn-dealers nor tyrants constitute an 'identifiable social group' for the purposes of Canada's hate speech laws.

restriction of speech derived from Mill and operationalized by the Canadian Supreme Court, I have reached the following conclusions. First, it is entirely legitimate to protect minorities against the injuries they suffer when insulting or abusive language is directed at them as an unwilling audience; however, there are (or should be) adequate means in the law to provide such protection without legislation specifically targeting hate speech. Second, legislation, such as the hate promotion law, which merely targets the intent to stir up hatred without any closer connection to an unlawful (discriminatory or violent) act is too remotely and speculatively linked to harms to minorities to satisfy Mill's tests. The notion of incitement utilized in this legislation has been disengaged from its stricter and narrower meaning elsewhere in the law. Third, there is no similar objection to legislation, such as the hate incitement law, which is more narrowly aimed at speech that constitutes an instigation to an unlawful act, especially to a hate crime. Even here it could be argued that no law specifically regulating hate speech is necessary, if in general it is unlawful to incite the commission of a criminal offence. However this might be, singling out hate speech in this way need not fail Mill's tests and may be appropriate for the support it provides for vulnerable social groups.

12

Hate Speech, Extreme Speech, and Collective Defamation in French Law

Pascal Mbongo

Strictly speaking, the concepts of 'hate speech', 'extreme speech', and 'collective defamation' are not juridical categories in France. Here we will treat these concepts more as analytical categories, which, when employed by administrative authorities and judges, interfere with freedom of expression. While the concept of 'extreme speech' may be applied to speech directed towards, among others, institutions, authorities, and state symbols,[1] here we will only be interested in speech directed towards individuals or groups of individuals on the basis of a characteristic, whether it be race, ethnicity, religious belief, gender, physical capability (for example, disabilities) or sexual orientation (for example, homosexuality).[2] From this perspective, the concept of speech will refer to all statements, and to all representations in written and printed form, in drawings, engravings, paintings, emblems, and images.

The general question relating to these interferences is whether they constitute a shift, or even a rupture, in the French notion of freedom of expression or whether, on the contrary, they maintain something of the nature of this core right. Apart from the genealogical argument, which rests on the particularly recent creation of the legal mechanisms involved, we find very little in support

---

[1] French criminal law contains numerous qualifications that aim to restrict expressions of this type of speech. As such, French criminal law punishes any abuse, defamation, and affront directed towards the courts, tribunals, the army, public services, civil servants, the police force etc. In addition to this, French criminal law restricts apologies for crimes or offences (in particular, apologies for war crimes or terrorist acts) as well as incitement to commit a crime or offence. Finally, the penal code since 2003 (Art. 433-5-1) enforces the penalty of a fine in the case of 'public affront to the national anthem or to the French tricolour' in the course of a protest organized or regulated by public authorities.

[2] Malicious acts have a specific sense in the French penal code. Technically, French law does not define malicious crimes as such. However, when an act punishable in itself (eg, discrimination, murder, etc.) has been committed with malicious intent on the basis of the victim's race, gender, sexual orientation, disability, etc., the enforceable penalty is necessarily greater than it would otherwise be.

for the first hypothesis.[3] What is more probable is that these interferences appear like mirrors, not only of the French notion of freedom of expression, but also of the relationship that the French state maintains with society. The French notion of freedom of expression has in fact always been relativistic if only because, by constantly establishing a balance between freedom of expression and 'law and order',[4] French constitutional texts have never brought about a debate comparable to the American debate relating to the First Amendment's provision that Congress shall make no law abridging freedom of speech.[5] This is true even if we exclude the periods of authoritarian regimes such as the Restoration (1814–1830) or the Second Empire (1852–1870). As a matter of fact, the constancy of this balance between freedom of expression and 'law and order' tells us something about a certain form of 'paternalism' that is particularly characteristic of the French state in its relations with society. This paternalism is said to be justified, rightly or wrongly, by the political presupposition that society is incapable of governing itself. From this perspective, it is only logical that freedom of expression should not be defined *exclusively* in terms of the search for truth or as the concrete guarantee of democracy. It is for precisely this reason that the right to 'dignity and worth of the human person' tends to become (in France as well as more generally in Europe) the basis of the legal mechanisms used in the struggle against hate speech and extreme speech, in place of the classic 'law and order' argument (in French law) or of the necessary 'protection of the rights and liberties of others' (under the European Convention on Human Rights (ECHR)).

In the pages which follow, we will bring to the fore (1) the systematic attempts by which French law aims to control extreme speech and (2) assess the rigour that is characteristic of the suppression of collective defamations.

1. Systematic Control of Hate Speech and Extreme Speech

This control is the result of a combination of administrative and penal regulations.

---

[3] Contemporary French legislation on racist speech or on the denigration of religious beliefs dates back to the 1970s (law of 1 July 1972), whereas the suppression of other types of speech only began to develop in the 1990s.

[4] Freedom of expression is codified by Arts.10 and 11 of the 1789 Declaration of the Rights of Man and of the Citizen: 'No one shall be disquieted on account of his opinions, including his religious views, provided their manifestation does not disturb the public order established by law' (Art. 10) and 'The free communication of ideas and opinions is one of the most precious of the rights of man. Every citizen may, accordingly, speak, write, and print with freedom, but shall be responsible for such abuses of this freedom as shall be defined by law' (Art. 11).

[5] We are all familiar with the famous assertion of Judge Hugo Black ('No law means no law') that aimed to deny the very principle of regulation in matters concerning freedom of expression.

(i) Administrative Law

French administrative law offers the government or regulatory agencies a certain number of prerogatives that can be employed to control the content of speech. These prerogatives are defined by texts specific to each type of medium through which the speech is communicated, with nevertheless an important difference: in the case of written publications, of videograms and computer programs, of radio and television, these prerogatives make possible *administrative suppression*, whereas in the case of cinema they allow for a more *preventative administrative control.*

Administrative control of the content of written publications that is exercised *a posteriori* is codified by a law of 16 July 1949 relating to 'publications intended for young people'.[6] Article 14 of this law gives the Minister of the Interior the triple authority to ban publications (books, reviews, whether or not they are sold in sealed packaging)[7] that 'represent a danger for young people': the power to ban the sale of such a publication to those younger than eighteen years; the power to ban the public display of such a publication; and the power to ban all publicity in the press or audiovisual media that is in favour of such a publication. Incidentally, the law permits the Minister to combine many of these bans. In the exercise of these powers, the Minister may be advised by a 'Committee for publications dangerous for young people' established by law. There is, however, no obligation for the Minister to consult the Committee and, if he or she does choose to, he or she is not obliged to follow its advice.[8] One will observe that the Council of State (the highest level of French administrative jurisdiction) deemed that Article 14 of the 1949 law was not a violation of the ECHR.[9] It is important to recognize that the title of this law is deceptive, since the text is in fact also applicable to publications intended for adults. It is equally deceptive in the sense that the concept of a 'danger for young people', which forms the basis of the ministerial powers, has a very broad meaning: It is applied not only to publications of a licentious or pornographic nature, but equally to publications that give prominence to crime or violence, that are xenophobic, that condone violence or hatred (whether it be racial, sexist, homophobic, or on the basis of religious belief), that condone the use, possession, or trafficking of drugs, that defend suicide, and so on.

In the case of documents recorded on magnetic media, on digital media with optical readers, and on semiconductors,[10] the law of 17 June 1998 'relating to the

---

[6] For a political history of this text, see in particular B. Joubert, *Dictionnaire des livres et des journaux interdits par arrêtes ministériels de 1949 à nos jours* (Paris: Editions du Cercle de la Librairie, 2007).

[7] CE, 20 December 1985, SARL, Editions du Pharaon, Rec. 391.

[8] CE, 19 January 1990, Sté française des revues SFR et Sté des éditions de la fortune, Rec. 908; CE 19 July 1994, Sidos, Rec. 751, 1086, 1093.

[9] CE, 28 July 1995, Association 'Alexandre', Rec. 794 and 951.

[10] This refers to videograms (eg, video cassettes recorded on magnetic tape or videodisks recorded on electronic media) and computer programs such as those used by computer games.

prevention and suppression of sexual offences as well as the protection of minors' gives the Minister the triple authority to ban such documents on the basis of the 'danger for young people' that the content represents. As such, the Minister has the authority: to ban the rent or sale of such a document to those younger than eighteen years; to ban the public display of such a document; and to ban the publicity of such a document in the press or in audiovisual media. Though the concept of 'danger for young people' that justifies this authority may be defined in terms equally broad as those used for written publications, the administrative control over videograms and computer programs does differ from the former on two points: the Minister may only combine two bans where videograms are concerned (bans on recommending, giving, renting, or selling to under eighteens, and bans on favourable publicity in all media forms); moreover he or she cannot prescribe one or more of the aforementioned measures without having consulted an administrative commission responsible for advising on whether videograms or computer programs present a 'danger for young people'.

Where radio broadcasts and television are concerned, the law of 1986 relating to audiovisual communication[11] defines the authority over content control in radio and television broadcasts, which has been devolved to the regulatory authority of these media, the *Conseil supérieur de l'audiovisuel* (the French equivalent of the British Ofcom). This authority may prescribe a variety of sanctions (suspending programmes, withdrawing permission to broadcast, imposing fines) on a radio or television operator who broadcasts a programme containing illicit material, such as pornographic content, prominence of crime or violence, incitement to violence or hatred (on the basis of race, gender, sexual orientation, religious belief, as well as towards the police force, and so on), xenophobic speech, and incitement to the use, possession, or trafficking of drugs.

In relation to administrative control over the content of cinematic works, this is codified by the *Code de l'industrie cinématographique* (Cinematic Industry Code). In accordance with the Code, a film may not be shown in French cinemas unless it has received authorization from the Minister of Culture following a consultation with a committee:[12] the *Commission de classification des films* (Committee for Film Classification).[13] Pursuant to this law, both the opinion of the Committee for Film Classification and the Minister's decision must take into consideration the need to 'protect children and adolescents from undesirable effects that certain cinematic works may have on their personality and development'. Since the Minister generally follows the Committee's advice, this advice will be the focus of our attention. As such, every film that is intended for public projection in French cinemas must first be subjected to a collective viewing of the whole film, including the trailer, by the Committee. After this, the Committee

---

[11] This text has often been amended, but not on the subject in which we are interested here.
[12] Art. 19 of the Cinematic Industry Code.
[13] Decree of 23 February 1990 taken to implement Art. 19 of the Cinematic Industry Code.

may advise the Minister to: grant authorization for screenings for all ages (equivalent to a U certificate); impose an age limit on the film and/or its trailer (in France, the age limits are set at 12, 16, and 18 years); impose an X certificate (films that are pornographic or contain incitement to violence);[14] or impose a total ban, in the case of works that are 'incompatible with the respect for fundamental values, for example in films that are damaging to human dignity, or that comprise incitement to hatred or violence for reasons of religious belief or race'.

It must be understood that many resources are available to the Committee and the Minister, depending on whether the film contains explicit or ambiguous speech. A total ban on a film tends to be applied when the content is *explicitly* racist, antisemitic, sexist, homophobic, or xenophobic (whether as an apology for, or as an incitement to, racial, sexist, homophobic, or xenophobic hatred), when it is seen as an apology for crime, et cetera,[15] and the X certificate tends to be applied when the content of the film is explicitly pornographic or obscene. In other cases (for example, the age limits of 12, 16, and 18 years), the Committee is equally vigilant with regard to the *risk* of hate speech and extreme speech. Indeed, when making decisions on these bans, the Committee, the Minister, and, at a later stage, judges having the authority to rule on a ministerial decision, all use the concept of 'protecting young people' in a generic, broad, and, at the very least, subjective sense.[16] This concept applies not only to works containing images or speech that have sexual connotations, and those that *give particular prominence* to crime or violence (violence or hatred on the basis of race, gender, sexual orientation; the use, possession, or trafficking of drugs; torture and inhumane or degrading behaviour, and so on), but it is also applied to any work 'whose complexity or narrative mode may lead to confusion in the way it is received by young audiences', in other words, a work that lacks 'clear markers of behaviour' which results in the risk of children and adolescents identifying with the material.[17] Moreover, the Committee (and the Minister) may go as far as recommending that the screening of the film be accompanied by a warning to the viewer regarding the content of the work or some of its characteristics. This is the

---

[14] An X certificate does not mean a film is banned, however: it is banned for under eighteens, it may only be screened in specialist cinemas that come under a specific distribution network, the operators of such cinemas will not receive public subsidies that are available to operators of normal cinemas, and taxes will be higher for these specialist X certificate cinemas.

[15] The Committee has not, however, recommended a total ban since 1981. It prefers to leave it to tribunals to pronounce such a ban in accordance with the criminal law.

[16] The Committee itself agrees with this criticism in one of its reports: 'In comparison with certain practices abroad, the general framework in which classification should take place, as regards the very practice of control, relates neither to a methodology, nor to an evaluation grid that would help to determine directly the age group for which the film is suitable, nor to precise criteria... upon which the Committee may base its decisions. Classification is to a considerable degree a subjective exercise and a difficult one to theorize. Nevertheless, the practice of these controls does bring to light certain "praxis" of classification' (*Commission de classification des œuvres cinématographiques*, Rapport 2004, 28).

[17] On the interpretive work in which the Committee is engaged each time, see ibid., 28–9.

case particularly for films that, 'in terms of content, cross the boundaries that warrant informing the public, but do not justify imposing an age limit of 18 years'.[18]

To complete this picture of administrative control we must consider a well-known text that organizes administrative control over certain activist and radical groups. The law of 10 January 1936 'relating to fighter groups and private militia'[19] institutes a procedure for the administrative dissolution of certain groups. This dissolution may be decreed by the President of the Republic during Cabinet meetings and may target groups for one of many reasons set out by the law, including: inciting armed demonstrations in the street; organizing a 'fighter group' or private militia; aiming to undermine by force 'the republican form of government' or 'territorial integrity'; promoting racist or xenophobic ideas (since an amendment of the law introduced in 1972); and engaging in acts of terrorism (since an amendment of the law introduced in 1986).[20] The 1936 law calls for three further specifications. What we must first consider is that it is not only applicable to the material acts of certain radical or extremist groups, but equally to certain opinions expressed by these associations (for example, racist, antisemitic, xenophobic opinions, and so on). Moreover, it is useful to note that each decision to dissolve an association that the President of the Republic makes on the basis of this law may be contested before the *Conseil d'Etat* (Council of State). Thirdly, given that the French Council of State has always felt that the measures of this law do not contradict the ECHR, its control over presidential decisions consists more

[18] *Commission de classification des œuvres cinématographiques*, Rapport 2007, 12. The compromise of lowering the age limit to 16 years but accompanying the screening with a warning to the viewer has been applied, eg, to *Shortbus* by John Cameron Mitchell. The Committee's opinions and the Minister's decisions do not escape (far from it) criticism that strives to make it seem like 'censorship'. These criticisms are nevertheless somewhat paradoxical: the arguments triggered by the Committee's opinions are often very animated, whereas arguments relating to age restrictions of 18 and 16 years are very rare and proportionately less numerous that in the 1950s, 1960s, or 1970s. One of the most discussed cases of recent years is *Saw III* by Darren Bousman, taking into account the fact that the film was given an 18 certificate, a classification which supposes the presence of 'scenes of non-simulated sex or of very strong violence, but which, due to the manner in which they are filmed or the nature of the subject represented', do not justify a more severe classification, ie, an X certificate. The application of these criteria to *Saw III* on the basis of 'very strong violence' triggered a dispute between the *Société des réalisateurs de films* (Society of Filmmakers) on the one hand, and the Committee for Film Classification and the Minister of Culture on the other, the former reproaching the latter group for not taking into consideration the fact that they were dealing with an 'exploitation film'.

[19] See P. Mbongo, 'Actualité et renouveau de la loi du 10 janvier 1936 sur les groupes de combat et les milices privées' (1998) 3 *Revue du droit public* 715.

[20] The application of this law has hardly been hindered by the jurisprudence of the ECtHR, pursuant to which political parties 'play an essential role in the smooth running of democracy', and so restrictions of freedom of association set out in Art. 11(2) of the Convention must therefore be interpreted in a strict way. As such, dissolving a political party can only be justified by 'pressing and convincing reasons' (*United Communist Party of Turkey* v. *Turkey* (1998) 26 ECtHR 121; *Socialist Party* v. *Turkey* (1998) 27 EHRR 51; and *Freedom and Democracy Party* v. *Turkey* ECtHR, 8 December 1999).

in saying whether the President of the Republic is justified in applying the law to contentious groups.

The law of 10 January 1936 has been implemented on numerous occasions, and this has often been justified by the ideologies of certain political groups. The most recent case involved the dissolution of the group 'Tribu Ka' by the President on 28 July 2006. This group of black activists was charged with having engaged, through press releases, publications on its website, and statements made by its officials, in: the propagation of ideas and theories striving to justify and encourage discrimination; the propagation of racial hatred and violence, notably towards people who are not black; the propagation of antisemitism; and the encouragement of threatening behaviour towards people of Jewish confession. The decision to dissolve the group was contested before the court by members of the group but the President's decision was deemed to be legal.[21] The judges felt that 'if the dissolution constituted an abridgement of freedom of expression, this abridgement [was] justified by the seriousness of the dangers posed to law and order and to public security by the activities of the group concerned'.

(ii) Criminal Law

This administrative regulation is complemented by penal legislation, the implementation of which lies with penal jurisdictions. As such, radical speech, extreme speech, or hate speech may be prosecuted by way of one of the following penal categories set out by the Law on the Freedom of the Press of 29 July 1881: (a) provocation or incitement to commit certain crimes or offences; (b) apology for certain crimes or offences (for example, murder, theft, war crimes, crimes or offences of collaboration with the enemy, terrorism, and so on); (c) the provocation of hatred, violence, or discrimination on the basis of adherence or non-adherence to a certain ethnic group, race, religious belief, or gender, on the basis of sexual orientation or disability (henceforward referred to as adherence or non-adherence to a certain ethnic group); (d) abuse directed towards a person or group on the basis of adherence or non-adherence to a certain ethnic group; (e) defamation of a person or group on the basis of adherence or non-adherence to a certain ethnic group (Article 29 al. 2 L. 1881): and (f) impugning the existence of one or more crimes against humanity as they are defined by Article 6 of the charter of the Nuremberg Tribunal of 1945. The scope of these charges is so broad that they are applicable whatever kind of media is used. In other words, they are applicable to speech expressed through one of many types of written media (for example, books, reviews, pamphlets, drawings, engravings, posters, paintings, and emblems), through existing means of audio-visual communication (for example, radio broadcast, television, cassette, DVD, and so on), and through means of electronic communication. Moreover, the rigour of French criminal law

---

[21] CE, 17 November 2006, Tribu Ka.

with regard to certain types of speech is such that the law punishes hate speech even if it has not been pronounced publicly.[22] Such is the case of abuse or defamation directed towards a person or a group on the grounds of his/her/its race, religious belief, ethnicity, gender, sexual orientation, or physical disability.

(iii) General Observations

Given that all these laws have been accepted in principle by French judges, an understanding of French law in terms of extreme speech or hate speech consists rather in seeing how administrative authorities and judges implement these measures on a day to day basis, and how they decide whether a given speech, image, or representation constitutes either: a violation of a legal proscription (hypothesis 1), or on the other hand, a speech that contributes to public debates, to intellectual understanding (for example, philosophical, theological, historical, and so on), to literary, artistic, or humorous creation (hypothesis 2). These are all examples of legal reasons that the author of a contentious speech may use in his or her defence.

The manner in which French administrative authorities and judges proceed is interesting in itself if we compare it to the ECtHR's statement, according to which 'freedom of expression constitutes one of the essential foundations of a democratic society and is applicable to ideas that offend, shock, or disturb'.[23] It is apparent that when French administrative authorities and judges are called upon to consider a case, they do not begin by asking themselves whether or not they are in the presence of the type of speech that 'offend[s]', 'shock[s]', or 'disturb[s]', from which they should be protected according to Article 10 of the ECHR. The first, and sometimes the only, question they ask is more often that of whether or not the legal criteria have been fulfilled: either with a view to taking administrative measures to ban a publication or to dissolve a group, or with a view to pronouncing a criminal conviction. One might say that French administrative and judicial authorities only use the ECtHR's statement in the case of *Handyside* v. *United Kingdom* as a subsidiary argument in order to reinforce their decision not to abridge freedom of expression in contentious cases. And yet this constitutes neither a paradox, nor a mark of distrust on behalf of French jurisdiction vis-à-vis the ECtHR. Rather, it is a logical 'mechanism' if we accept that: first, the ECtHR's proposition (according to which freedom of expression protects, amongst others, opinions that shock, offend, or disturb) does not itself lead to any specific resolutions in cases of freedom of expression;[24] and, secondly, this mechanism is consistent with the casuistic method of qualifying contentious speech or remarks that French administrative authorities and judges must carry

---

[22] Art. R. 624-4 of the Penal Code.

[23] *Handyside* v. *United Kingdom* (1976) 1 ECtHR 737.

[24] See P. Mbongo, 'Le traitement juridictionnel des offenses aux convictions religieuses', in J.-F. Lachaume, *Mélanges en l'honneur de M. Jean-François Lachaume* (Paris: Dalloz, 2007), 691–708.

out, since the legal qualifications concerned are those of national law and since, as we have seen, these qualifications were deemed to be compatible, in principle, with the ECHR.

Finally, aside from making a purely speculative reflection on the legitimacy of laws whose principles are for the most part accepted in France[25] as well as by the ECtHR, the question is rather whether, and how, the French administrative or legal authorities claim to avert the risk of an ideological and moral conformity masked by these laws.

2. A Particular Rigour for Certain Types of Speech

(i) Overview of Collective Defamations

There are six 'identities'[26] that French law protects from negative or depreciatory speech: racial identities, religious identities, ethnic identities, gender identities (for example, women), physical identities (for example, people with disabilities), and homosexuality. As we have seen, these 'identities' are protected by administrative law either under the generic category of speech that presents a 'danger for young people', or under the more specific category of speech that is racist, sexist, homophobic, that denigrates religious beliefs, and so on.

As regards criminal law (the French Constitution obliges the law to define offences 'in clear and precise terms'), these 'identities' are protected against certain types of speech according to three categories of offences: abuse on the grounds of race, ethnicity, gender, sexual orientation, religious belief, or disability;[27] defamation on the grounds of race, ethnicity, gender, sexual orientation, religious belief, or disability;[28] and provocation of discrimination or hatred on the grounds of race, ethnicity, gender, sexual orientation, religious belief, or disability.[29]

---

[25] This French consensus pertains notably to the fact that none of the successive political majorities has even considered abrogating any of these legal mechanisms. On the contrary, they have reinforced them over the years. For example, it was a conservative majority that made the following additions to French law, by means of a law of 30 December 2004 relating to the struggle against discrimination: offences of abuse or defamation on the grounds of gender, sexual orientation, and disability. They also reinforced penal suppression of abuse and defamation on the grounds of race and religious belief.

[26] Here the concept of 'identity' is used simply as a linguistic convention, considering the theoretical and practical problems that this term generally raises. Does 'race' constitute an identity? Does being a woman constitute an identity? Does 'homosexuality' express a simple sexual preference or an identity (especially considering the different understandings of identity across generations)? The term 'minorities' could also have been retained if the laws in question had not been equally easy to invoke by majority groups (eg, 'whites', for legislation relating to racist speech, and 'Catholics', for legislation relating to speech that denigrates religious beliefs).

[27] The sentence is six months imprisonment and a fine of €22,500 (Art. 33 of the Press Law of 29 July 1881).

[28] The sentence is one year imprisonment and/or a fine of €45,000 (Art. 24 of the Press Law of 29 July 1881).

[29] The sentence is one year imprisonment and/or a fine of €45,000 (Art. 24 of the Press Law of 29 July 1881).

The first observation suggested by these penal categories relates to the question of whether one should see them as suppressing collective affronts and defamations. Although French law may deny this (neither texts, nor judges, nor analysts seem to be aware of the notion of a 'collective affront' or 'collective defamation'), one must nevertheless reply in the affirmative for at least two reasons: first, because this is authorized by the wording of these offences;[30] and, secondly, because, in accordance with French law, registered associations that strive to put a stop to certain forms of discrimination may file a lawsuit against the author of a speech that challenges the 'identity' of the groups represented by these associations.

The second observation suggested by the penal regulation of collective defamation is linked to the independence of the notions of abuse, defamation, and provocation. In the context of French criminal law, abuse is understood to be 'any offensive expression, term of contempt, or invective that does not impute any fact'. Consequently, in order for speech to be defined as 'abuse' on the grounds of race, gender, sexual orientation, religious belief, et cetera, a contentious speech must constitute an 'offensive expression, term of contempt, or invective' directed towards a person or group of people on the grounds of their race, gender, religious belief, and so on. Where defamation is concerned, it is understood to be 'any allegation or imputation of a fact that damages the honour of or consideration for the person or group to whom the fact is imputed'. This being the case, racial, sexist, or religious defamation supposes the presence of an allegation 'that damages the honour of or consideration' for a person or group of people on the grounds of their race, gender, religious belief, et cetera.

Taking into consideration the terms of these legal definitions of collective defamation, it is not easy for judges to demonstrate that the constitutive criteria of these offences have been fulfilled,[31] to the point where their conclusions are often far from clear, to the point where differences of opinion are common between the judge presiding over the original case, the appeal judge, and finally the Court of Cassation (the highest judicial authority). This is particularly evident when one examines certain cases arising from the two principal sources of contention in courts, that is, cases of religious abuse and defamation, and cases of racial abuse and defamation.[32]

---

[30] The law applies as much to speech directed at 'a person' (eg, a speaker referring to his interlocutor as a 'Negro' or a 'Yid') as to 'a group of people' (eg, 'Blacks', 'Catholics', 'women', and so on).

[31] This is all the more difficult in the case of abuse and defamation on the grounds of race, gender, religious belief, and sexual orientation, to the point where a judge almost has to distance himself from his own feelings as well as from those of the plaintiff in order to decide 'objectively' whether or not he is in the presence of a contemptuous expression or an allegation damaging to the honour of an individual or group of individuals on the grounds of their race, gender, religious beliefs, or sexual orientation.

[32] Since sexist and homophobic speech was not integrated into the law until 2004, courts have not yet had to deal with many cases. The most well-known case of conviction for 'abuse directed towards homosexuals' concerns a Deputy of the political right, Mr. Christian Vanneste, who, during interviews with two newspapers, maintained that homosexuality was 'inferior' to heterosexuality and that homosexuality would be 'dangerous for humanity if it became universal'. Paradoxically, the public

(ii) Religious Abuse and Defamation

As an example from recent years dealing with religious abuse and defamation,[33] we may cite the criminal proceedings taken against the writer Michel Houellebecq for the following remarks taken from an interview granted by the latter to a literary magazine: '[A]fter all, the stupidest religion is Islam. When you read the Koran you're appalled (. . .) appalled'. The writer was nevertheless acquitted.

The *Giniewski* case is no less remarkable in terms of the difficulty of the task faced by the judiciary. This case concerned an article published in a journal in 1994 that was very critical towards Pope John-Paul II's encyclical *The Splendour of the Truth* (Veritatis Splendor, 1993). The author of the article, Paul Giniewski, a writer, historian, and theologian, was prosecuted for religious defamation damaging to Catholics because of certain passages in his article, and in particular, the following:

> The Catholic Church institutes itself as the sole guardian of divine truth . . . It loudly proclaims the fulfilment of the Old Covenant in the New, the superiority of the latter . . . Many Christians have recognized that scriptural anti-Judaism and the doctrine of "fulfilment" of the Old Covenant in the New led to anti-Semitism and prepared the ground in which the idea and implementation of Auschwitz took seed.

Giniewski was initially convicted for the article. His conviction was later annulled before a court of appeal, the ruling of which was then annulled by the Court of Cassation. A new court of appeal was charged with judging the case and convicted the author for religious defamation. The case was brought before the ECtHR, who concluded that France's conviction of Giniewski constituted a violation of freedom of expression.[34]

The initial judgement in favour of convicting Giniewski was justified by the court in the following terms:

> . . . Thus, according to the author of the text, not only the idea, but the execution of the massacres and horrors committed at Auschwitz, symbol of the Nazi death camps, are necessary continuations of the foundations of the Catholic doctrine, namely the doctrine of fulfilment of the Old Covenant in the New, thereby making Catholics, and to a more general extent, Christians, directly responsible [for these crimes]. Such an assertion is evidently damaging to the honour of and consideration for Christians and particularly for the Catholic community, and comes under the provisions of Article 32, paragraph 2 of the law of 29 July 1881 . . . The link of causality between belonging to a religious faith and the fact imputed by the contentious remark is obvious: It is because they belong to a religion presumed to have an anti-Semitic past, and because they recognise the value of the Pope's encyclical, and the doctrine of the fulfilment of the Old Covenant in the New

---

prosecutor felt that the remarks were all the more reprehensible coming from a Deputy, whereas Mr. Vanneste's lawyer maintained (in vain) that his remarks were all the more protected precisely because they came from a Deputy.

[33] See n. 24 above.   [34] *Giniewski* v. *France* (2007) 45 ECtHR 23.

asserted in it, that it is suggested that Christians and Catholics are to a certain degree responsible for the massacres of Auschwitz... The defendant was indeed within his rights to denounce Christian anti-Semitism in history and to warn readers against any new manifestation or resurgence of this sentiment, by reminding them that, in the past, Christian churches have sometimes accepted and even encouraged the idea of 'teaching contempt' for the Jewish people, who have been presented as being guilty of deicide. However, nothing gave him the authority to use extreme terms upon the release of the Pope's new encyclical reasserting the doctrine of 'fulfilment' and, by means of confusion, to attribute responsibility for the Nazi massacres committed at Auschwitz to the Catholic community.

Conversely, the first court of appeal that acquitted Giniewski felt that:

... the meaning of Paul Giniewski's remark can be summarised thus: Certain principles of the Catholic religion tinged with anti-Semitism favoured the Holocaust... the court is well aware of the reactions that can be provoked by such an article within the Catholic community, even if the author claims to be voicing the opinions of 'many Christians'... however... by criticising the encyclical 'The Splendour of the Truth' so vigorously, Paul Giniewski has raised a theological and historical debate on the repercussions of certain religious principles and on the roots of the Holocaust;... since the theory maintained by the author is based exclusively on the doctrinal debate, it does not legally constitute a specific fact likely to characterise a defamation...

In its French incarnation, the Mohammed Cartoons[35] controversy came about when a French satirical periodical (*Charlie Hebdo*) reprinted the famous drawings initially published in Denmark. In this context, French Muslim organizations called for a ban against the publication of the contentious issue of *Charlie Hebdo,* but this request was unsuccessful due to a technical irregularity. At the same time, these organizations took legal action against these publications for religious abuse. After much debate, these complaints were rejected by the criminal court in Paris in a ruling on 22 March 2007. The court began by setting out the premises of its argument:

Given that *Charlie Hebdo* is a satirical paper containing numerous caricatures that no one is obliged to buy or read, as opposed to other media such as posters displayed on public highways; given that a caricature is defined as a portrait that goes beyond good taste in order to fulfil a parodic function... Given that the literary genre of caricatures, although deliberately provocative, contributes in this respect to freedom of expression and to the communication of thoughts and opinions...'

The judges then carried out a semeiological and iconographic analysis of the contentious drawings and concluded that only one of them (the drawing in which the prophet Mohammed is represented wearing a turban shaped like a bomb with a lit fuse)

---

[35] See P. Mbongo, 'Les caricatures de Mahomet et la liberté d'expression' (2007 May) *Esprit*, 145.

suggests that terrorist violence is inherent to the Muslim religion, a fact which would justify a conviction for religious abuse. However, the court observed that 'though the scope of the drawing is such that, in its own right and when taken in isolation, it may be likely to offend adherents of this faith and to damage consideration for them on the grounds of their observance...it cannot be evaluated in relation to criminal law, separated from the context of its publication...

The court also noted that 'the drawing in question is included in a special issue, in which the front cover "editorialises" the content and serves as a general presentation of *Charlie Hebdo*'s position'. The court concluded that:

although the character of this caricature may be shocking, even insulting, to Muslim sensitivities, the context and the circumstances of its publication in the paper *Charlie Hebdo* arose independently of any deliberate intention to directly and gratuitously offend people of Muslim faith; that the acceptable limits of freedom of expression have not, therefore, been exceeded.

These cases involving religious abuse and defamation call for a final observation. French criminal law theoretically accords all religions with the same protection against abuse or defamation. This equality is not, however, confirmed in reality, in that the majority of trials (and therefore the majority of convictions) concern speech directed towards Christianity (and almost exclusively towards Catholicism) and Islam. Many explanations exist for this situation: the continued existence of a certain French anti-Catholicism maintained by the suspicion over the Catholic Church's claim to govern minds and public morals;[36] the will of certain social actors to fight against the development (real or imagined) of 'Islamophobia' in France;[37] the fact that judges apprehend speech directed towards Jews under the category of racial, rather than religious, abuse and defamation (denigrating public speeches directed towards Judaism as a doctrinal corpus are virtually non-existent in France[38]); the tendency of French law to exclude a certain number of beliefs deemed to be more or less dangerous from the provisions guaranteeing religious freedom, and, in doing so, limiting the likelihood that

[36] R. Rémond, and M. Leboucher, *Le nouvel antichristianisme* (Paris: Desclée de Brouwer, 2005). The history of the separation of the church and the state in France ('the eldest daughter of the Church') has been chaotic, even murderous, ever since the declaration of religious freedom by the French Revolution (1789). This separation was only imposed definitively in 1905, following a break in diplomatic relations between France and the Holy See (Pius X) and the nationalization of Catholic and Protestant churches and synagogues. On the contemporary issues concerning the law of separation of 1905, see P. Mbongo, 'La loi de séparation des Églises et de l'État: une survivance?', in *La Semaine Juridique: Édition générale*, 7 December 2005, 2239.
[37] V. Geisser, *La nouvelle islamophobie* (Paris: Editions la Découverte, 2003); T. Deltombe, *L'Islam imaginaire: La construction médiatique de l'islamophobie en France, 1975–2005* (Paris: Editions la Découverte, 2005).
[38] This rarity is notably the result of a combined ebb in Catholic anti-Judaism (notably since the Second Vatican Council abandoned the theology of substitution) and in the practice of Catholicism in France.

the people concerned by these beliefs will invoke these provisions as their right to legal measures relating to speech directed against religious beliefs.[39]

(iii) Racial Abuse and Defamation

The Edgar Morin case relates to the publication of an article entitled 'Israel-Palestine: the Cancer', co-signed by three well-known intellectuals, Edgar Morin, Sami Naïr, and Danièle Sallenave, in the newspaper *Le Monde* on 4 June 2002. This article maintained:

One is hard pressed to imagine that a nation of fugitives, descended of the people subjected to the most long-standing persecution in the history of humanity, having been subjected to the worst humiliations and the deepest contempt, should be able to transform itself in two generations into a dominating and self-assured people and, with the exception of an admirable minority, a contemptuous people taking satisfaction in humiliating others; the Jews of Israel, descended of an apartheid named the ghetto, are ghettoizing the Palestinians. The Jews, who were humiliated, despised, and persecuted, are humiliating, despising and persecuting the Palestinians. The Jews, who were the victims of a merciless order, are imposing their merciless order on the Palestinians. The Jewish victims of inhumanity are displaying a terrible inhumanity. The Jews, scapegoats for every evil, are 'scapegoating' Arafat and the Palestinian Authority, who are made responsible for attacks that they are prevented from preventing.

These assertions led to complaints against the authors from the Union of Jewish Students of France and from an association of lawyers, on the grounds that the authors of the article had committed an offence of racial defamation.

Though the initial court hearing the case found that the contentious article did not constitute racial defamation, the court of appeal concluded differently and convicted the three intellectuals. By means of a textual analysis appropriate to this type of trial, the court of appeal proposed that the first contentious paragraph of the article did indeed constitute racial defamation in that it imputed to the entirety of the Jewish population in Israel 'the specific fact of humiliating Palestinians and of taking satisfaction in this, by stigmatizing their behaviour in light of their common history'. The second paragraph appeared equally defamatory to the court of appeal, in that:

[I]t imputes to Jewish people, as a whole and beyond simply the Jews of Israel (which the pejorative repetition in an incantatory tone of the term 'the Jews' clearly suggests), the

---

[39] A law of 12 June 2001 has reinforced the suppression of 'religious sects' in France. Among other measures, the law of 12 June 2001 instituted two new charges: The offence of 'mental manipulation' and the offence of promotion of sectarian movements. Moreover, the law has increased the penalties applicable to the offence of 'fraudulent abuse of ignorance or weakness committed by sectarian groups'. The Mormon Church, the Church of Scientology, and Jehovah's Witness, to cite only the world-famous groups, all feel threatened by this law just as even more obscure movements do. As such, their legal strategy for gaining legal recognition as a 'religion' consists precisely in trying to win the court cases they file against their opponents for religious abuse or defamation.

fact of persecuting Palestinian people in exactly the same manner in which they themselves had been persecuted; it uses the terms 'imposing a merciless order, inhumanity' to qualify the behaviour imputed to Jewish people with respect to the Palestinians, in a manner that is damaging to the dignity of all Jewish people; and it imputes to them a particularly undignified and cruel form of duplicity in their dealings with Arafat and the Palestinian Authority, supposedly employed to make the latter appear responsible for the attacks that Jewish people are presumed to favour or, ultimately, promote.

Finally, the court of appeal made it clear that these two passages should be distinguished from the rest of the article: on the one hand, those two paragraphs contained an 'outrageous accusation of specific facts', by which the law defines defamation; on the other hand, the rest of the article consisted of the 'expression of the authors' personal convictions in the context of a political debate, and whose largely polemical nature is justified by the very nature of the conflict and by the heightened passions that such a conflict elicits in the protagonists'.

The Court of Cassation eventually sided with the ruling of the initial hearing, and therefore with the accused intellectuals, by settling the question of whether the disputed passages comprised only (as maintained by the defendants, but rejected by the court of appeal) 'a virulent criticism of Israeli policy', a criticism testified to paradoxically by the comparison made by the authors between 'the behaviour to which the Jewish people were subjected, and the behaviour imputed to them'. After noting that the contentious remarks were 'isolated within an article criticizing Israeli government policy with regard to the Palestinians', the Court of Cassation added that these remarks 'do not impute any specific fact likely to be damaging to the honour of or consideration for the Jewish community as a whole on the grounds of it belonging to a nation or religion, rather they are the expression of an opinion having its roots in the intellectual debate'.[40]

The *Dieudonné* case also deserves mention as an illustration of the random nature of trials for racial abuse or defamation. 'Black' (or rather mixed-race) professional comedian and political activist Dieudonné M'Bala had given an interview with a Lyons newspaper during the 2002 presidential elections in which he wished to be a candidate. To the question '[W]hat do you think of the rising anti-Semitism amongst young 'beurs' (North-Africans born in France)?', he replied:

Racism was invented by Abraham. 'The Chosen People', that's the beginning of racism. Muslims today are retaliating tit for tat. For me, Jews and Muslims, it doesn't exist. So anti-Semitism doesn't exist, because Jews don't exist. These two notions are just as stupid as each other. No one is Jewish or else everyone is. I don't understand any of it. In my opinion, Jewish, it's a sect, a scam. It's one of the most serious ones because it was the first. Some Muslims take the same route by reviving concepts like 'the Holy war'...

---

[40] Court of Cassation, First Civil Law Chamber, Bulletin d'information n° 395, 12 July 2006, 340.

The court of appeal acquitted Dieudonné by stating that 'returned to their original context, the terms "Jewish, it's a sect, a scam" is rooted in a theoretical debate on the influence of religions and does not constitute an attack on the Jewish community as human community'. For its part, the Court of Cassation (bearing in mind that it does not cite the activist in the same way) argued that 'the affirmation "Jewish, it's a sect, a scam". It's one of the most serious ones because it was the first" is not grounded in the free criticism of a religious fact contributing to a debate of general interest, but constitutes abuse that targets a group of people on the grounds of its origin. The suppression of this abuse is therefore a necessary abridgement of freedom of expression in a democratic society'.

13

Towards Improved Law and Policy on 'Hate Speech'—The 'Clear and Present Danger' Test in Hungary

Peter Molnar[1]

1. Introduction

There is a widely acknowledged view that the United States prohibition of content-based 'hate speech' laws is exceptional. Kevin Boyle writes about 'the distinctive position of the United States' in this matter,[2] and Sandra Coliver phrases it as 'the United States' dramatically different approach from that of Europe and the rest of the world',[3] while she argues that a 'number of lessons may be drawn from the US experience which may be applicable to other legal systems'.[4] James Weinstein writes that the 'American free speech doctrine is

[1] I would like to thank John Harbord, Ivan Hare, Leslie Newman, Robert C. Post, Nadine Strossen, and James Weinstein for their especially helpful, detailed written comments on the drafts of this essay. I am also grateful to many other friends and colleagues who shared with me their insights on the regulation of 'hate speech', and to the Faculty of the Cardozo School of Law for the great opportunity to give a talk for them on the main points of this article and for their thoughtful questions and remarks following my lecture.
    This article will analyse only the prohibition of 'hate speech' in the criminal law in Hungary without exploring the civil law or media law responses. For examples supporting the argument that a media-specific regulation is needed in the case of broadcasting insofar as it works differently from other forms of communication, see R. Gillette, 'Kosovo: Media and the Riots of March 2004', in S. Nikoltchev (ed.), *Political Debate and the Role of the Media: The Fragility of Free Speech* (Strasbourg: European Audiovisual Observatory, 2004), 101–3; I. Al-Marashi, 'The Dynamics of Iraq's Media: Ethno-Sectarian Violence, Political Islam, Public Advocacy, and Globalization' (2007) 25 *Cardozo Arts & Ent. L. J.* 95, 113–8.
    When used in legal parlance, the colloquial expression 'hate speech' seems to presuppose that the state can define with legal precision the particular forms of content that should be regulated as 'hate speech'. Because I regard this implicit assumption as questionable, I shall use 'hate speech' only in quotation marks. I do not mean to imply that many clear instances of obvious 'hate speech' cannot be identified; I mean only to stress that a reliable definition of this term, if possible at all, cannot be taken for granted.
[2] 'Overview of a Dilemma: Censorship Versus Racism', in S. Coliver (ed.), *Striking a Balance: Hate Speech, Freedom of Expression and Non-Discrimination* (London: Art. 19, 1992), 4.
[3] 'Hate Speech Laws: Do They Work?' in *Striking a Balance* (ibid.), 372.
[4] Ibid., 372.

unique among democracies in forbidding even a narrow ban on racist speech'.[5] Michel Rosenfeld notes the distinction, writing that, 'In the United States, hate speech is given wide constitutional protection while under international human rights covenants and in other Western democracies,[6] such as Canada, Germany, and the United Kingdom, it is largely prohibited and subjected to criminal sanctions.'[7] Frederick Schauer writes that 'American free speech exceptionalism is as manifest with respect to incitement to racial hatred and other forms of "hate speech" as it is with respect to libel and slander.'[8]

The aim of this article is to highlight the relevant jurisprudence of Hungary, a post-Holocaust, post-communist, Central European democracy, and to show that the search for effective law and policy on 'hate speech' benefits from a fresh, open look at the best practices wherever they have developed.

Part 2 of this essay provides a short description of the social context in Hungary, the most important elements of which are: the Hungarian freedom struggles in the nineteenth and twentieth centuries which always passionately advocated freedom of speech and freedom of the press; decades of totalitarian censorship; the largest Jewish community remaining in Central Europe after the Holocaust, mostly concentrated in Budapest; antisemitism; and the hatred against Roma Hungarians. The prevailing argument was that adopting the American approach to 'hate speech' was the best possible choice; risky, but still the most prudent.

Part 3 analyses how the Hungarian Constitutional Court ('the Constitutional Court') and the other courts in Hungary have adopted the 'clear and present danger test' of the Supreme Court of the United States ('the Supreme Court').[9] I show how the Constitutional Court laid down the constitutional interpretation of freedom of speech for the Republic of Hungary—referencing the 'clear and present danger test', but still permitting restrictions the Supreme Court would not tolerate —and how the Hungarian Supreme Court and the lower courts construe that interpretation in their decisions, narrowing it in ways that affirm the American approach. I examine cases where the 'clear and present danger' test has not been

---

[5] 'Hate Speech, Viewpoint Neutrality, and the American Concept of Democracy', in T. R. Hensley (ed.), *The Boundaries of Freedom of Expression & Order in American Democracy* (Kent, OH: Kent State UP, 2001), 166.

[6] In addition to Canada, Germany, the United Kingdom, and the United States, Ronald Krotoszynski includes Japan in his comparative book on freedom of speech, but he also compares only established democracies. See *The First Amendment in Cross-Cultural Perspective: A Comparative Legal Analysis of the Freedom of Speech* (New York: New York UP, 2006).

[7] 'Hate Speech in Constitutional Jurisprudence: A Comparative Analysis' (2003) 24 *Cardozo L. Rev.* 1523.

[8] 'Media Law, Media Content, and American Exceptionalism' in *Political Debate and the Role of the Media* (n. 1 above), 63.

[9] For a detailed history of the test see G. R. Stone, *Perilous Times: Free Speech in Wartime from the Sedition Act of 1798 to the War on Terrorism* (New York: W. W. Norton & Co., 2004), 135–233.

applied properly and I also provide an example to show the effect of the exceptional criminal law ban on the public display of certain totalitarian symbols.

Finally, in light of related Hungarian jurisprudence, I explore what might be the most helpful policy on this issue, the most difficult of all questions of free speech theory.

2. The Social Context of 'Hate Speech' in Hungary

It is almost taken for granted that the tragic European history of the twentieth century triggers a more restrictive legal treatment of 'hate speech' than the history in the United States,[10] although as Ronald Dworkin writes: 'There is nothing like the Holocaust in American history, but slavery is bad enough.'[11] Instead of accepting arguable presumptions on the different cultural environments of alleged 'hate speech', a careful analysis of the social context is necessary in each country in order to find the best law and policy.

For the new, post-communist democracies of Central and Eastern Europe, still in transition, history provided a unique sense of freedom (including freedom of speech) derived from generations that experienced both dictatorship and demo-cracy. But this perspective had to overcome the hardships of learning freedom, learning to organize one's life, living in a free political community, and identifying with a nationwide community without exclusive nationalism. As András Sajó observes:

After all, racism and incitement to hatred against ethnic (national) groups (primarily but not exclusively minorities) present a major social and regulatory problem in the post-communist period. Extremist nationalist propaganda was often part of the self-assertion of nationalist political movements and often became part of the official government ideology. Extremist nationalist speech played a major role in the escalation of the Yugoslav conflict, contributing ultimately to genocide. Given the strong endorsement of nationalism by many political actors, including some governments, in many countries extremist speech, irrespective of the legal provisions, became socially normalized to an extent.[12]

How can law and policy influence a socio-cultural environment where 'extremist speech, irrespective of the legal provisions, became socially normalized to an extent'? Is there any chance that a 'hate speech' law can accomplish its desired impact under such circumstances? Can the criminal prohibition of 'hate speech' work in the absence of social consensus against such communication? Can criminal prohibition educate a society; can it help create and strengthen basic

---

[10] For different approaches to 'hate speech', see *Striking a Balance* in n. 2 above; *Words & Deeds: Incitement, Hate Speech & the Right to Free Expression* (London: Index on Censorship, 2005).

[11] *Freedom's Law: The Moral Reading of the American Constitution* (Cambridge, MA: Harvard UP, 1996), 225.

[12] *Freedom of Expression* (Warsaw: Institute of Public Affairs, 2004), 128.

moral values including a clear rejection of racism? Is it not ersatz displacement instead of focusing on what the educational-cultural institutions and organizations could do to change the deeply rooted prejudices of many families? On the other hand, how can such countries avoid abusing laws on hate/extremist speech to suppress political dissent? An example of misusing such laws is the Russian statute 'On countering extremist activity', enacted in 2002, and amended in 2006. Andrei Richter writes:

According to analysts, the main idea behind the changes was to shield the authorities from discontent. Extremism now included spreading material that explained or justified it, disseminating public calls to engage in it and also promoting or facilitating it through the media. Publicly defaming state officials by maliciously accusing them of committing acts of an extremist nature also became an act of extremism.[13]

Most former communist states in Central and Eastern Europe regulate 'hate speech' on the basis of its content. Some of the post-communist countries, post-Soviet states such as Russia, Estonia and Lithuania, the post-Yugoslav republics, and Romania, incorporated the prohibition of incitement to hatred in their constitution.[14] Emerging nationalist, ethnic, and religious conflicts after the fall of the communist regime that suppressed different groups certainly played a part in establishing bans on 'hate speech' at the constitutional level.

Hungary, after several suppressive regimes,[15] took the opposite road, reflecting a deep distrust of government regulation of public discourse and the dangers of content-based restrictions of speech. The explanation for this choice by a Central European, post-Holocaust, post-communist country, in the words of Kevin Boyle, 'must include its history as a society born in rebellion against, among other things, censorship'.[16] Boyle wrote this as part of his 'explanations for the distinctive position of the United States' on the 'hate speech' issue. Yet, the same sentence describes the historical background of free speech jurisprudence in Hungary. Demanding the right to freedom of speech and freedom of the press was at the forefront not only during the non-violent, negotiated transition from communism to democracy[17] (in the phrase of Vaclav Havel, the 'velvet revolution' of 1989), but also in a chain of earlier revolutions in Hungary.

---

[13] *Post-Soviet Perspective on Censorship and Freedom of the Media* (Moscow: UNESCO, 2007), 227.

[14] See n. 12 above, 128–32.

[15] The political leaders of Hungary allied with Nazi Germany and in March 1944, German troops occupied the country. The Soviet army liberated Hungary, but the liberation turned to another suppression. As Peter Hanak writes, 'Oppression was followed by oppression, dictatorship by dictatorship, devastation by devastation. It is not easy for democracy and freedom to take firm root in this battered region of Europe.' 'Hungary on a Fixed Course: An Outline of Hungarian History', in J. Held (ed.), *The Columbia History of Eastern Europe in the Twentieth Century* (New York: Columbia UP, 1992), 204.

[16] See n. 2 above, 4.

[17] See A. Arato, *Civil Society, Constitution and Legitimacy* (Lanham, MD: Rowman & Littlefield Publishers, 2000), 81–127.

The 1848 revolution and freedom fight against Habsburg absolutism[18] was introduced by a liberal period that Istvan Bibo describes as follows: '... Hungary between 1825 and 1848... reacted to the movement of European democracy and patriotism with such energy that' it filled the 'Western European contemporaries with the greatest hopes'.[19] Lajos Kossuth, the leader of the revolution, who was celebrated both in England and in the US after the defeat of the revolution, became nationally known through his *Parliamentary Reports,* distributed in 1833 in about 70, later 100 subscribed, handwritten copies around the country by mail. The then existing system of censorship did not cover private letters, but as Istvan Deak points out, 'Kossuth's mailing campaign clearly contradicted the laws on the press.'[20] Still, the laxity of the censorship allowed this particular press to function, although as Deak writes, 'the personal authorization of the monarch was needed to set up even a single printing press, and censorship was both extensive and irrational'.[21] But when in 1833, Kossuth secretly bought a lithographic press in Vienna to print his *Parliamentary Reports,* his press was confiscated.[22] He had to continue his reports without being able to print them, until 1836: the end of the four years long session of the Parliament. Then he started the *Municipal Reports,* but as he was not allowed to use the mail any longer to distribute his particular press, he had to rely on travellers to carry the copies of the biweekly reports. Finally, as Deak writes, 'the twenty-fourth issue of the *Reports* was confiscated and in the spring of 1837 he was arrested... and charged with disloyalty and sedition'.[23] He was convicted, but released after three years, and at the beginning of 1841, he became the editor of the then started, printed newspaper, *Pesti Hírlap* (*Pest News*). Until 1844, when he was removed, he could run 'an almost free press', with a circulation higher than five thousands copies.[24] In Deak's explanation, perhaps it was made possible, besides the tactical moves of the government, by 'the sympathy of the censors, who, as teachers and ecclesiastics, were not immune to the liberal and nationalist[25] sentiments sweeping the educated public'.[26]

---

[18] The 1848 revolution was also a fight for Hungary's independence from the Habsburg Empire. It was the longest lasting among the 1848 revolutions in Europe, and was suppressed with the help of the troops of the Russian tzar in 1849. As Paul Ignotus writes: 'The Hungarian War for Freedom against Habsburg absolutism in 1848–49 was a unique feat of valour which mesmerized liberal world opinion and resounded for decades to come in the poems of Swinburne and W. S. Landor and Matthew Arnold, of Francois Coppée and Heinrich Heine.' *Hungary* (London: Benn, 1972), 57.

[19] I. Bibo, 'The Distress of East European Small States', in I. Bibo and K. Nagy (eds.), *Democracy, Revolution, Self-Determination: Selected Writings* (Highland Lakes: Atlantic Research and Publications, 1991), 32.

[20] I. Deak, *The Lawful Revolution: Louis Kossuth and the Hungarians 1848–1849* (New York: Columbia UP, 1979), 29.

[21] Ibid.

[22] As Istvan Deak describes, 'the government was so timid, or so generous, that it amply paid Kossuth for his financial loss'. See ibid., 30.

[23] Ibid., 31–3.   [24] Ibid., 41.

[25] It was nineteenth-century nationalism, in which, as Ignotus writes, 'the currents towards national and human liberty united, at least for a while'. See n. 18 above, 49–50.

[26] See n. 20 above, 41.

At the beginning of the 1848 revolution, the revolutionaries, led by poet Sandor Petofi, issued 'the first uncensored Hungarian leaflets'.[27] Petofi and his fellow rebels, as Deak writes, 'seized the largest printing shop' in Budapest and 'leaflets containing the Twelve Demands and the National Song[28] were printed on the spot and thrown to the multitude. Thus freedom of the press was established by one peaceful stroke.'[29] Among the twelve demands of the revolution, the first one was the abolishment of censorship and the freedom of the press.

Few days before the 1918 revolution[30] actually took place on 30th October, the National Council of the upcoming revolution, as one of its members, Oscar Jaszi recalls, 'contented itself with issuing its proclamation of October 26, 1918, in all the papers, in defiance of the censorship'.[31] Following the tradition of the 1848 revolution, the National Council published its programme in twelve points. As Mihaly Karolyi, the prime minister of the revolution writes, 'the censorship of the press was abolished by the arbitrary action of the journalists, who simply refused to submit their manuscripts to the censor'.[32] The revolution turned Budapest, in the words of Jaszi, 'into a gigantic debating society'.[33]

The memory of the first uncensored leaflet in Hungarian also inspired the students and other revolutionaries of the 1956 revolution. On the evening of 23 October, the first day of the revolution, the students (like Petofi and his fellows in 1848) wanted freedom of the press, in the words of Justice Brandeis, 'both as an end and as a means'.[33a] They were determined to let the public know about their claims (listed in points as the Twelve Demands in 1848)[34] through the most effective mass communication tool of their time which in 1956 in Hungary was the national radio. But this time a peaceful stroke was not enough to succeed. The staff of the radio refused to broadcast the students' Points in full. Instead it aired a speech by one of the infamous leaders of the dictatorship who brutally accused the 'provocateurs' and 'enemies' of the communist party. It led to the seige of the radio building. When the crowd that pulled down the monumental Stalin statue at the edge of the City Park heard that the political police had started to fire on and kill demonstrators at the radio, people rushed there.

As Francoise Fejto writes:

It was like the Danube during the spring floods.... The radio was the voice of the nation, but it was an enslaved voice, distorted, void of meaning. It was by means of the Budapest

---

[27] See n. 18 above, 54.

[28] The National Song, written by Sandor Petofi, was the emblematic poem of the revolution and the fight for Hungary's independence.

[29] See n. 20 above, 71.

[30] After a few months, the 1918 revolution was followed by a communist dictatorship which, after another few months, was followed by counter-revolution.

[31] O. Jaszi, *Revolution and Counter-Revolution in Hungary* (New York: Howard Fertig 1969), 31.

[32] M. Karolyi, *Faith Without Illusion* (London: Jonathan Cape, 1956), 107.

[33] See n. 31 above, 42.   [33a] *Whitney* v. *California*, 274 US 357 (1927), 375.

[34] See n. 18 above, 236–7.

radio that the regime had always flooded the country with lies. The Hungarians rose in arms because they wanted the truth to take over the radio.[35]

By the next morning, after tragic bloodshed, the revolutionaries took over the radio building while already late at night they occupied the premises of the *Szabad Nep*,[36] the daily newspaper of the communist party, and published an extra edition that condemned the political police that guarded the radio.[37] In the words of Paul Ignotus, there was a 'pouring-out of Points'.[38] As Fejto, Istvan Bibo —the last member of the government who stayed in the Parliament building until the Soviet troops occupied it on 4 November—also writes that the 1956 revolution, among its other fundamental goals, expressed 'opposition to the authority that arbitrarily distorts reality, news, ideas, and teachings in the service of its own interests, leading to a demand for truth and honesty in public and cultural life' and 'freedom of criticism, communication of facts as they are'.[39]

During the years when Hungary was a communist country (between 1948 and 1989) the primary use of the incitement provision of the criminal code was to protect the ruling totalitarian ideology from dissent. The ideological character of the Criminal Code of the communist system is well captured in its provision on 'insult against a community' that included 'socialist conviction' among the listed targets, instead of including political conviction in general.[40] The communist, soviet-type constitution declared rights, but as empty slogans. Freedom of the press could be practised only in line with the presumed interest of the socialist society, an interest as defined by the totalitarian party.

A free press existed only underground, from the end of the 1970s. At the beginnings of the *samizdat*[41] in Hungary, publications like Kossuth's *Reports* multiplied, producing a few copies by using typewriters with indigo. But soon, a whole underground system was developed with secretly located stencil machines and collective personal distribution, the latter similar to the spread of the *Municipal Reports*. The samizdat-producing, so-called democratic opposition took freedom of the press and other rights seriously, as if they were free citizens.[42]

---

[35] F. Fejto, *Behind the Rape of Hungary* (David McKay Company, Inc. 1957) 185, 187.

[36] The hypocritical title of the infamous propaganda paper means 'free people' in Hungarian.

[37] See n. 18 above, 238–9.

[38] Ibid., 244.

[39] 'The Hungarian Revolution of 1956: Scandal and Hope', in n. 19 above, 343–4.

[40] '... insult against a community included using, in front of others, an offensive or denigrating expression against the Hungarian nation and groups or persons, based on their nationality, religion, race, or socialist conviction, or committing other similar acts [original s. 269 para. (2)]', Decision 30/ 1992 (V. 26.) AB, 3,<http://www.mkab.hu/content/en/en3/13589104.htm>(last accessed 24 July 2008).

[41] *Samizdat* is the Russian word for the underground literature in the communist regimes. The largest collection of *samizdat* publications can be found in the Open Society Archives, in Budapest, <http://www.osa.ceu.hu> (last accessed 24 July 2008).

[42] See T. Judt, 'The Dilemmas of Dissidence: The Politics of Opposition in East-Central Europe', in F. Feher and A. Arato (eds.), *Crisis and Reform in Eastern Europe* (New Brunswick, NJ: Transaction Publishers, 1991), 258–64. As Andrew Arato writes: 'The major independent activities, at

One of the leading dissidents, Miklos Haraszti, wittily captures the absurd way in which public discourse was exercised under communist rule, the Orwellian circumstances in which the memory[43] of the already deeply traumatized society also suffered great damage:

Real communication takes place only between the lines. And it is public life itself that is the space between the lines... Actually, we have no idea what our message would be if it could be freely articulated... If state artists fight for anything between the lines, it is solely for the survival of this space.[44]

As a result of overall censorship, there was no opportunity freely to discuss public matters including the Holocaust and Hungary's part in it.[45] Most of the Jewish Hungarians of the countryside were killed in 1944; Budapest is a city of many Holocaust survivors.[46] Antisemitic speech in Budapest can be compared to neo-Nazi speech in Skokie, Illinois where antisemites were allowed by the courts to march in a neighbourhood largely populated by Holocaust survivors.[47] But Budapest, with the largest remaining Jewish community of Central Europe,[48] is a city where the persecution actually took place in the most horrific ways. There could scarcely be more painfully sensitive racist speech than has existed in this

least until 1986–87, were publishing, lecturing, discussing, and teaching, and the key hope seemed to have been the building of the moral bases of democratic structures and practices'. 'Social Theory, Civil Society, and the Transformation of Authoritarian Socialism' in *Crisis and Reform in Eastern Europe* (this note), 22.

[43] Reclaiming memory against the 'contract of forgetting' (in the phrase of one of the leading dissidents, Janos Kis, quoted by Tony Judt) was a central theme of the democratic change at the end of the communist system. See Judt in n. 42 above, 280. See also T. G. Ash, *We The People—The Revolution of '89 Witnessed in Warsaw, Budapest, Berlin & Prague* (Cambridge: Granta Books, 1990), 47–60.

[44] M. Haraszti, *The Velvet Prison: Artists Under State Socialism* Trans. K. and S. Landesmann and S. Wassserman (New York: Basic Books, 1987), 144, 145, 147. In Hungary, Haraszti's book was published in *samizdat*, with the following title: *The Aesthetics of Censorship*. Since 2004, Haraszti has been the OSCE (Organization for Security and Cooperation in Europe) Representative on Freedom of the Media.

[45] For an in-depth analysis of Hungarian society's responsibility for the Holocaust, see I. Bibo, 'The Jewish Question in Hungary after 1944 (1948)' in n. 19 above, 153–322.

[46] See K. Frojimovics, et al, Jewish Budapest: Monuments, Rites, History Ed. G. Komoroczy (Budapest: Central European UP, 1999).

[47] *Collin v. Smith* 447 F. Supp. 676 (N.D. Ill.), *aff'd*, 578 F.2d 1197 (7th Cir.), *cert. denied* 439 US 916 (1978). For a description and analyses of the case, see eg, S. Walker, *Hate Speech: The History of an American Controversy* (Lincoln, NE: Univ of Nebraska Press, 1994), ch. 6.

[48] Milan Kundera writes about Central Europe: 'Indeed, no other part of the world has been so deeply marked by the influence of Jewish genius. Aliens everywhere and everywhere at home, lifted above national quarrels, the Jews in the twentieth century were the principal cosmopolitan, integrating element in Central Europe. They were its intellectual cement, a condensed version of its spirit, creators of its spiritual unity.' 'The tragedy of central Europe', *The New York Review of Books*, 26 April 1984. About changes in Jewish identity in Hungary, see A. Kovacs, 'Changes in Jewish identity in modern Hungary', in J. Webber (ed.), *Jewish Identities in the New Europe* (Oxford: Centre for Postgraduate Hebrew Studies, 1994), 150–60, and A. Kovacs, 'Jewish groups and Identity Strategies in Post-Communist Hungary', in Z. Gitelman, B. Kosmin and A. Kovács (eds.), *New Jewish Identities: Contemporary Europe and Beyond* (Budapest: Central European UP, 2003), 211–42.

Central-European country. Undoubtedly, therefore, Hungary is one of the political communities with a strong reason to impose criminal prohibitions on antisemitic and other racist speech. According to a 1999 survey among the interviewed Jewish Hungarians '85 per cent consider it acceptable to place legal restrictions on the public expression of antisemitic views, while 59 per cent support such sanctions against Holocaust deniers'.[49]

Besides antisemitism, an equally important argument for using criminal law to ban racist speech is the hatred against Roma Hungarians, the largest, Holocaust-surviving minority in Hungary. Roma Hungarians (who are disadvantaged by unemployment rates much higher than average, income much lower than average, and life expectancy much shorter than average) face not only prejudice and denigration, but segregation in schools[50] and discrimination in employment,[51] in hospitals,[52] and in law enforcement.[53]

According to the website of *Radio C*,[54] a not for profit Roma, community radio station in Budapest since 2001, about 200,000 Roma Hungarians live in and around Budapest, more than 100,000 of them in Budapest. But data on the number of Hungarian Roma is contested, because 'according to census data gathered once every 10 years (and based on self-identification), the number of Roma in Hungary was half the number calculable on the basis of the school data. Such distortion was apparent even in the 2001 census.'[55] Under the law on the protection of personal data,[56] sensitive personal data (such as data concerning ethnic identity) can be accessed and processed only if the data subject provides her written, informed consent, without coercion. This regulation is in sharp

---

[49] A. Kovács (ed.), *Jews and Jewry in Contemporary Hungary: Results of a Sociological Survey, Report No. 1—2004* (Budapest: Institute for Jewish Policy Research, 2004), 44.

[50] See the Thematic Reports of the European Roma Rights Centre (ERRC, <http://errc.org>, last accessed 24 July 2008); 'The Impact of Legislation and Policies on School Segregation of Romani Children' (2007), <http://www.errc.org/cikk.php?cikk=2743> (last accessed 24 July 2008); 'Stigmata: Segregated Schooling of Roma in Central and Eastern Europe, a Survey of Patterns of Segregated Education of Roma in Bulgaria, the Czech Republic, Hungary, Romania, and Slovakia' (2005), 80–5, <http://www.errc.org/cikk.php?cikk=1892> (last accessed 24 July 2008).

[51] See the Thematic Report of the ERRC, 'The Glass Box: Exclusion of Roma From Employment' (2007), <http://www.errc.org/db/02/14/m00000214.pdf> (last accessed 24 July 2008).

[52] See R. Izsák: ' "Gypsy Rooms" and Other Discriminatory Treatment Against Romani Women in Hungarian Hospitals' (2004), <http://www.errc.org/cikk.php?cikk=2063&archiv=1> (last accessed 24 July 2008). See also the recent decision of the European Court of Human Rights that ruled against the Czech Republic in a school segregation case: *D.H. and Others* v. *the Czech Republic* (Application No. 57325/00), 13 November 2007. This landmark decision will have an impact on segregation in Hungarian schools as well.

[53] See 'Roma Rights: Police Violence against Roma' (Winter 1998), <http://www.errc.org/cikk. php?cikk=475> (last accessed 24 July 2008); see also *Rights Denied: The Roma of Hungary* (Helsinki: Human Rights Watch, 1996).

[54] <http://www.radioc.hu/>, in Hungarian (last accessed 24 July 2008).

[55] F. Babusik, 'Legitimacy, Statistics and Research Methodology—Who Is Romani in Hungary Today and What Are We (Not) Allowed to Know About Roma', *Roma Rights: Ethnic Statistics* (2004), <http://www.errc.org/cikk.php?cikk=1937> (last accessed 24 July 2008).

[56] Act LXIII of 1992 on the Protection of Personal Data and Disclosure of Information of Public Interest.

contrast with recent anti-Roma discriminatory practices in data processing. As Gyorgy Kerenyi, founding editor of *Radio C*, writes, '... until the 1960s, the Roma had identity cards of distinct color. Until 1989 Roma criminals (and their families) were registered separately with the police'.[57]

We have tremendous data about widespread anti-Roma prejudice. As Kerenyi writes, 'According to a 1995 survey, 67 per cent of Hungarians are convinced that the inclination to commit crime is inherent in "Gypsies" blood.'[58] Particularly negative portrayal in the media against the Roma reinforces bad stereotypes. Jeno Zsigo, president of the Roma Parliament, a civil organization of the Hungarian Roma described the sole exception where the Roma are positively portrayed as follows: 'The only image of us they tolerate is that of the dancing slave.'[59]

As Helen Darbishire writes, 'some speech which is undoubtedly offensive, does not constitute hate speech, even though it may contribute to a climate of prejudice and discrimination against minorities'.[60] The results of a 1996–1997 content analysis of the national and regional daily newspapers describe the design of anti-Roma press reports, obviously effective, whether or not they constitute 'hate speech':

Almost two-thirds (60 per cent) of the articles presented individual Roma without indicating any particular qualities other than their ethnicity; these persons were presented simply as 'gypsies', embodiments of the whole group. In addition, only 25 per cent of the Roma in the sample could speak directly; in the remaining three quarters of the cases, the reader could only learn about Romani opinions through the mediation of a third person. This ratio is striking when compared to non-Roma: 64 per cent of them had the opportunity to express their opinions directly in articles on Romani issues.[61]

Under such circumstances, it would be imperative for democratic parties and all other forces to unite against all forms of racism and discrimination. But this response is not embedded in the political culture, so is almost completely absent. Recently, a journalist, Zsolt Bayer wrote in a daily newspaper, *Magyar Hirlap*, about Jewish journalists 'they are our reason-Jews, meaning their bare existence is a reason for anti-Semitism'. The article was condemned by the leader of the centre-right Hungarian Democratic Forum, Ibolya Dávid, Budapest's liberal Alliance of Free Democrats mayor Gábor Demszky, the Hungarian Journalists' Association (MÚOSz), and several other politicians and professional organizations. Some institutions, among them 'Budapest City Hall, announced they had

---

[57] G. Kerenyi, 'Roma in the Hungarian Media' (Fall 1999) *After the Fall: Media Studies J.* 141.
[58] Ibid.
[59] Quoted in n. 57 above, 147.
[60] 'Hate speech: New European Perspective', *Roma Rights: Romani Media/Mainstream Media* (1999), <http://www.errc.org/cikk.php?cikk=1129> (last accessed 24 July 2008).
[61] G. Bernáth and V. Messing, 'Seen from Afar: Roma in the Hungarian Media', *Roma Rights: Romani Media/Mainstream Media* (1999), <http://www.errc.org/cikk.php?cikk=1168> (last accessed 24 July 2008).

cancelled their *Magyar Hírlap* subscriptions.'[62] But the publisher of *Magyar Hírlap*, 'entrepreneur, media owner and one of the Hungary's wealthiest people, Gábor Széles has publicly defended'[63] Bayer, and leaders of the allegedly centre-right Federation of Young Democrats—Civic Alliance, a party much larger than the Hungarian Democratic Forum, publicly kept Bayer company at the birthday celebration of their party. Jean-Yves Camus includes a similar example in his study on the use of racist, antisemitic, and xenophobic elements in political discourse: 'In January 2004 an Israeli flag was burned during a demonstration by the Civic Circles, a political association set up by the former Conservative Prime Minister Viktor Orbán just after his defeat in the 2002 general election'.[64]

Although the racist Hungarian Life and Justice Party,[65] elected to the parliament in 1998, lost its seats in 2002, there is no clear common platform to reject the prevalent appearances of undeniable racism. In the autumn of 2004, the Parliament passed a declaration, supported by all the four parliamentary parties at the time, which condemned the activity of a group advocating a programme similar to that of Hungary's extreme National Socialist Arrow Cross party that was in power for some months beginning in October 1944. However, condemning a small group of extremists is ersatz displacement when coded and sometimes overt racism can be heard from allegedly moderate, democratic circles.

3. The Application of the 'Clear and Present Danger Test' in Hungary

(i) The 'Hate Speech' Decisions of the Hungarian Constitutional Court

The Constitutional Court, in the years since its establishment in 1989, has embodied the liberal spirit of the post-communist transition by establishing freedom of speech as a core value of the new democracy. The first profoundly important Constitutional Court decision on 'hate speech' came in 1992.[66] It did not review a case because the Constitutional Court provides abstract constitutional adjudication of the laws.[67] The Supreme Court and the lower courts

---

[62] 'Anti-semitic' journalist defended', *The Budapest Sun*, 2 April 2008, <http://www.budapestsun.com/cikk.php?id=28067> (last accessed 24 July 2008).

[63] Ibid.

[64] J.-Y. Camus, 'Study on the use of Racist, anti-Semitic and Xenophobic Elements in Political Discourse', *The Use of Racist, anti-Semitic and Xenophobic Elements in Political Discourse* (Council of Europe: European Commission against Racism and Intolerance, 2005), 38.

[65] As András Kovács argued, 'Extreme right wing parties today (...) are dangerous primarily not because they *create* xenophobia but because they attempt to *organize* it into a conceptual system and link it to existing serious socio-economic problems', 'Xenophobia, Anti-Semitism and the Extreme Right in Europe', *Racism in Central and Eastern Europe and Beyond: Origins, Responses, Strategies. Report* (Budapest: Open Society Institute, 2000), 55.

[66] See n. 40 above.

[67] See L. Sólyom and G. Brunner (eds.), *Constitutional Judiciary in a New Democracy: The Hungarian Constitutional Court* (Ann Arbor, MI: Univ of Michigan Press, 2000).

decide the cases and they can request the Constitutional Court to review the regulation they have to apply. In this complex system, the Supreme Court and the lower courts, when they construe the law, have to follow the law's abstract interpretations presented in the Constitutional Court decisions.[68]

Decision 30/1992 reviewed the 'hate speech' provision of the Criminal Code. Despite the tragic history of the country, or because of it, the reasoning of Decision 30/1992 calls upon the famous 'clear and present danger' test of the Supreme Court, as it was first formulated by Justice Holmes in the opinion he wrote in the *Schenk* case[69] and in his landmark dissent in the *Abrams* case.[70] The rich and beautiful language of the best parts of the Constitutional Court's free speech decisions written in the early nineties reveal the writers' familiarity with the great texts of free speech opinions of the Supreme Court.[71]

Decision 30/1992 played a decisive role in the Hungarian constitutional argument about freedom of speech and public debate.[72] The reasoning of the decision mirrors the political climate of a freshly post-dictatorial country, where liberty was rare and where people appreciated the value of free expression that had not existed for long decades:

Historical experience shows that on every occasion when the freedom of expression was restricted, social justice and human creativity suffered and humankind's innate ability to develop was stymied. The harmful consequences afflicted not only the lives of individuals, but also that of society at large, inflicting much suffering while leading to a dead end for human development. Free expression of ideas and beliefs, free manifestation of even unpopular or unusual ideas is the fundamental requirement for the existence of a truly vibrant society capable of development.[73]

The Court's reasoning reflects the sensibility of a people who have first-hand experience of freedom denied. It highlights not the risk of allegedly or really dangerous speech, but rather the risk of restricting freedom of speech on the basis of its content, the danger of censorship. Secondly, the decades of enforced silence under communist rule did not allow open discussion of the Holocaust or of the communist system itself, including its darkest, Stalinist years. Further restrictions on the free expression of ideas on the basis of their content, even under

---

[68] About different models of constitutional adjudication see A. Sajo, *Limiting Government: An Introduction to Constitutionalism* (Budapest: Central European UP, 1999), 225–44.

[69] *Schenk* v. *United States* 249 US 47 (1919).

[70] *Abrams* v. *United States* 250 US 616 (1919). For analysis of Holmes' theory of the First Amendment as described in his dissent in the *Abrams* case, see V. Blasi, 'Holmes and the Marketplace of Ideas' (2004) *Sup. Ct. Rev.* 1.

[71] The political elite in Hungary maintains a long tradition of familiarizing itself with American democracy. For example, liberal leaders in nineteenth-century Hungary (most of them enlightened aristocrats and noblemen) were well-versed in Alexis de Tocqueville's famous work about the American democratic system.

[72] For a critical assessment of the decision see A. Sajo, 'Hate Speech for Hostile Hungarians' (1994) 3 *E. Eur. Const. Rev.* 84.

[73] See n. 40 above, 6–7.

democratic circumstances, could have a chilling effect on the free debate of tragic events and periods in the country's history. Thirdly, both the lack of freedom of speech and the country's terrible record on discrimination and persecution left the drafters of the new constitutional system (among them Jewish Hungarians) keen to avoid providing any opportunity for the state to discriminate against people and their opinions. These considerations led to an especially strong commitment to the constitutional value of freedom of speech. As the Court stated,

> ...A change of political system is inevitably accompanied by social tensions.... [but just because of these]...unique historical circumstances...a distinction must be made between incitement to hatred and the use of offensive or denigrating expressions.[74]

The Court did not use Hungary's burdensome history and the unavoidable difficulties of the democratic transition as reasons to justify the content-based prohibition of 'hate speech'. Instead, the Court's constitutional argument separated incitement to hate from speech that is offensive but does not incite to hate. The Court drew a distinction between constitutionally protected and unprotected speech, the latter of which can be banned by criminal law, by holding that the content-based criminal prohibition of derogatory speech (as opposed to incitement that is not banned on the basis of its content, but only if it leads to a clear and present danger) was unconstitutional. The Court struck down the second provision of Article 269 of the Criminal Code, which stated that:

Anyone who in front of a large public gathering uses an offensive or denigrating expression against the Hungarian nation, any other nationality, people, religion or race, or commits other similar acts, is to be punished for the offence by imprisonment for up to one year, corrective training or a fine.[75]

The Court ruled that only the first provision of Article 269 of the Criminal Code contained a constitutional, necessary, and proportionate restriction on freedom of speech, a right the court considered to be 'the "mother right" of...the so-called fundamental rights of communication',[76] which include the right to free speech, freedom of the press, freedom of information, and in a broader sense, artistic and scientific freedoms. The first provision of Article 269 states that:

A person who, in front of a large public gathering, incites hatred against
a) the Hungarian nation,
b) any national, ethnic, racial or religious group, further against certain groups among the
   population, commits a felony and is to be punished by imprisonment for a period of
   up to three years.[77]

The decision deduced the criminal legal limitation of freedom of expression partially from the disturbance of public peace, but the Court in the key part of its argument reasoned about the incitement of hatred as follows:

---

[74] Ibid., 16.   [75] Ibid., 2.   [76] Ibid., 5.   [77] Ibid., 2.

The disturbance of the social order and peace . . . also contains the danger of the large-scale violation of individual rights: whipped-up emotions against the group threaten the honour, dignity (and in the more extreme cases, also the lives) of the individuals comprising the group, and by intimidation restrict them in the exercise of their other rights as well (including the right of freedom of expression). The behaviour criminally sanctioned . . . poses a danger to individuals' rights, too, which gives such weight to public peace that . . . the restriction on the freedom of expression can be regarded as necessary and proportionate. . . . [T]his reasoning considers not only the intensity of the disruption of public peace which—above and beyond a certain threshold ("clear and present danger")—justifies the restriction of the right to freedom of expression. What is of crucial importance here is the value that has become threatened: the incitement endangers subjective rights also having prominent places in the constitutional value system.[78]

A closer analysis of the Court's reasoning illuminates the applied interpretation of the 'clear and present danger' test, and this phrase is quoted in English. Once public peace is disrupted, we can hardly worry that it might be disturbed. The decision, although using the clear and present danger standard in a sentence about disturbance of the public peace, emphasizes that what is pivotal to meet the test is that individual rights are endangered. Therefore, the constitutionally punishable crime of incitement is completed only when the rights that are threatened when the public peace is disturbed are in a state of clear and present danger.

In this way, the case by case analysis, required under Decision 30/1992, may determine whether the particular expression disturbed the public peace to an extent where individual rights were clearly and presently endangered, thus justifying the restriction of freedom of expression. The Court held that it is not sufficient merely to analyse whether public peace has been disturbed to determine the relevant criminal legal boundaries of speech. If we did not make the clear and present endangerment of individual rights a condition for curtailing freedom of expression, the majority could unduly restrict public discourse by claiming that the respective speech disturbed the public peace. As a result, the Roma's response to anti-Roma speech, which could offend the non-Roma majority, may be jeopardized and might fall outside the constitutional protection of the right to freedom of expression. At the same time, the customary use of denigrating language about Roma would likely be protected expression, because as part of the traditional local discourse it could be considered by the biased majority to be speech that does not disturb the public peace.

The Court argued in its *Decision 30/1992* that 'the decision does not exclude the possibility for the legislature to extend the scope of criminal sanctions beyond incitement to hatred'.[79] But when Parliament, responding to public pressure aroused by the acquittal of leaders of racist organizations actually extended the related regulation in 1996, 2003, and 2008, the Court repeatedly struck down the

---

[78] Ibid., 14–15.   [79] Ibid., 17.

new, broader criminal restrictions on speech.[80] In Decision 12/1999 the Court argued:

In addition to incitement to hatred, ordering the punishment of other acts suitable for the arousal of hatred as new forms of conduct constituting the offence reflect the legislature's intention to punish specific conducts beyond the scope of incitement to hatred... the constitutional threshold of culpability.... [I]t is only incitement that incorporates a level of danger "above a certain limit" that may allow the restriction of the freedom of expression. Punishing other acts suitable for the arousal of hatred would diminish the threshold of culpability. If the level of danger reaches the scale of incitement, there is no need to specify "other acts" as the statutory definition of incitement covers such conduct.[81]

Andras Sajo wrote in 1994, that in fact 'the Hungarian Court failed to recognize the overbroadness of the incitement provision'.[82] Since then, while the Constitutional Court has been persistent in upholding its 1992 decision, the Supreme Court and lower courts (building on the Constitutional Court's interpretation of incitement to hatred) have provided a rather narrowly tailored understanding of the Hungarian 'clear and present danger' test, construing it as a 'clear and present danger of violence' test, close to the rule set up in the *Brandenburg* case.[83]

In its third related decision, in 2004, the Constitutional Court stressed that equality also triggers state restraint from content-based regulation of speech, because:

... the state may not prohibit the expression and the dissemination of any views merely on the basis of their contents, nor may certain opinions be declared more valuable than others, as this would violate the requirement of treating individuals as persons of equal dignity (such a prohibition would result in preventing certain groups of people from expressing their personal convictions), and—by excluding certain views—prevent the development of a free, lively and open debate involving all relevant opinions, even before a political discourse could emerge.[84]

But should even racist speech be part of public discourse? Is racism a 'relevant opinion'? What would require a democracy to tolerate racist expressions in its political debates? The answer lies in what Robert Post calls the 'paradox of public discourse',[85] 'the First Amendment, in the name of democracy, suspends legal enforcement of the very civility rules that make rational deliberation possible'.[86]

---

[80] Decision 12/1999 (V. 21.) AB, <http://www.mkab.hu/content/en/en3/12069604.htm> (last accessed 24 July 2008); Decision 18/2004 (V. 25.) AB, <http://www.mkab.hu/content/en/en3/09360304.htm> (last accessed 24 July 2008).

[81] Decision 12/1999 (V. 21.) AB ibid. 6–7.

[82] See n. 72 above, 86.

[83] *Brandenburg* v. *Ohio* 395 US 444 (1969).

[84] Decision 18/2004 (V. 25.) AB in n. 80 above, 7.

[85] See 'The Constitutional Concept of Public Discourse: Outrageous Opinion, Democratic Deliberation, and *Hustler Magazine v. Falwell*' (1990) 103 *Harv. L. Rev.* 601, 643.

[86] 'Racist Speech, Democracy, and the First Amendment' (1991) 32 *Wm. & Mary L. Rev.* 267, 287.

Of course, making public discourse possible is only one of the many reasons for prohibiting racist speech. But the 'paradox of public discourse' includes the equality argument of the Constitutional Court. As Post writes:

> The norm of equality violated by racist speech... is substantive;... It is the kind of norm that ought to emerge from processes of public deliberation. Although the censorship of racist speech is consistent with this substantive norm of equality, it is inconsistent with the formal principle of equality, because such censorship would exclude from the medium of public discourse those who disagree with a particular substantive norm of equality. Such persons would thus be cut off from participation in the processes of collective self-determination.
>
> First Amendment doctrine has tended to resolve the paradox of public discourse in favour of the principle of formal equality, largely because violations of that principle limit *pro tanto* the domain of self-government, whereas protecting uncivil speech does not automatically destroy the possibility of rational deliberation.[87]

The Constitutional Court seems to follow the same logic in its 2004 decision, emphasizing that only the consequentionalist approach (as opposed to one that is content-based) can meet the strict constitutional requirement to protect freedom of speech: 'Even in the case of extreme opinions, it is not the contents of the opinion but the direct and foreseeable consequences of its communication that justify a restriction of free expression and the application of legal consequences...'[88]

In its Decision 30/1992 the Court states that 'abusive' language (or other equivalent forms of expression) should be answered by a public that should develop its critical ability to respond to such speech through cleansing debate:

> Only through self-cleansing may a political culture and a soundly reacting public opinion emerge. Thus one who uses abusive language stamps himself as such and in the eyes of the public he will become known as a 'mudslinger'. Such abusive language must be answered by criticism.[89]

The Court's argument for the need to answer 'abusive' speech with criticism reflects the American free speech literature. The wording may remind the reader familiar with the landmark First Amendment cases of the famous concurring opinion of Justice Brandeis in *Whitney*:

> Those who won our independence by revolution were not cowards... If there be time to expose through discussion the falsehood and fallacies, to avert the evil by the processes of education, the remedy to be applied is more speech, not enforced silence.[90]

The distinction made by the Constitutional Court between incitement to hate and the use of denigrating expressions can be understood as the distinction between speech that allows the opportunity 'to expose through discussion the falsehood and fallacies, to avert the evil by the processes of education', and speech

---

[87] Ibid., 304.　　　　[88] Decision 18/2004 (V. 25.) AB in n. 79 above, 7.
[89] Decision 30/1992 (V. 26.) AB in n. 40 above, 17.
[90] See Justices Brandeis and Holmes concurring in *Whitney* v. *California* 274 US 357 (1927).

that causes danger without allowing time for answer by criticism. In the latter case, in the words of Justice Holmes, 'an immediate check is required to save the country'.[91] Of course, averting the evil by criticism requires engagement, which is presumably less comfortable than relying on the state to prohibit, for example, racist speech. But, even the criminal prohibition of racist expressions cannot work without the engagement of the overwhelming majority of the political community in a rejection of racism. If such a rejection exists, prohibition becomes an additional, rather symbolic act. If such a rejection does not exist, the prohibition of racist speech is likely to be abused against the very minorities the regulation allegedly aims to protect.

Rejection by engaged criticism should be understood in the broadest possible sense. Most importantly, it should involve the widespread, creative use of all educational opportunities to build not only tolerance, but mutual understanding between the different communities, the mutual respect of the coexisting cultures based on knowledge and a consciously crafted, rich network of personal connections and cooperation.

Such an engagement is particularly important in newer democracies like Hungary, where the experiences of authoritarian regimes discouraged participation in public matters. Thus, active rejection of racism can contribute to build a participatory citizenry. It can also help the development of good character in the members of society, in the sense as Vincent Blasi writes,

...a regime of free speech can help to develop character by requiring those who would beat back bad ideas and contain evil demagogues to pursue those worthy objectives in the most arduous way: engagement rather than prohibition...In this view, the most dangerous ideas can be defeated only by strong persons, not by repressive laws.[92]

Another aspect of civic engagement could be the use of civil law against denigrating speech.[93] This is suggested by the Constitutional Court, and the Court

---

[91] *United States* v. *Abrams* 250 US 616, 630 (1919).

[92] V. Blasi, 'Free Speech and Good Character' (1999) 46 *UCLA L. Rev.* 1567, 1573–4.

[93] The Constitutional Court also mentioned that besides criminal sanctions 'there are other means available, such as expanding the possible use of moral damages, to provide effective protection for the dignity of communities'. But in the *Hegedus Jr.* case (the facts and criminal court aspects of which I will describe later in this article) except in one lower court decision which was reversed by the appellate court, civil courts have refused to grant standing to persons who were not personally identified in an antisemitic article written by Hegedus Jr., but had tried to sue for damages.

An amendment of the Civil Code, accepted in Parliament in October, 2007, would have provided standing for members of minority groups if their group is targeted by 'hate speech', but in July 2008, the Constitutional Court held the amendment unconstitutional (Decision 96/2008 (VII.3) AB). In September 2008, the Minister of Justice introduced a new bill to Parliament in the hope that it will not only be accepted but will also pass the constitutional muster.

The only plaintiff successful in suing for damages in such a case was a Roma-Hungarian bus driver who sued because of an anti-gypsy article that alleged that Romas are threatening and even killing the Hungarians. The bus driver could successfully claim standing because the anti-gypsy article (published in *Magyar Forum*, an extreme-right weekly, edited by the president of MIEP) he challenged had accused only Roma Hungarians of a village in Pest county where he lives, and the article had also described a 'K-clan' as the worst Roma group in the village, where the first letter of the

stresses that criminal law should be applied as a last resort, and it should not be considered a means to improve the style of public discourse:

The prospect of a large amount of compensation is also part of this process. However, criminal sanctions must be applied in order to protect other rights and only when unavoidably necessary, and they should not be used to shape public opinion or the manner of political discourse, the latter approach being a paternalistic one.[94]

The desire to avoid paternalistic control by the state derives from the experience under the dictatorships from which democracy in Hungary emerged. The distrust of state regulation in setting the boundaries of public discourse is similar in Hungary and in the United States: two countries with very different histories. Yet, it is a sensibility shared by Americans and Hungarians. Pursuant to this deeply rooted belief in freedom of speech, exercising caution means braving free public debate. It is an idea that reflects the most important paradox of 'hate speech' laws because such laws are at least partially based on the conviction that insofar as 'hate speech' is dangerous (as it is in many instances) a cautious society should prohibit it by criminal law. The American-Hungarian approach realizes rather the danger of arbitrary restrictions on freedom of speech, starting with the difficulties of defining 'hate speech', considers the lack of content-based prohibition of alleged 'hate speech' by the criminal law as the cautious approach, and relies on robust public rejection of expressions of hatred.

The question is whether the strong statements in the relevant decisions of the Constitutional Court will become a shared cultural frame of reference in Hungarian society? In the United States, although the Holmes and Brandeis dissenting and concurring opinions reflected the minority view on the Supreme Court at the time, they inaugurated the modern understanding of the First Amendment.[95] Stretching the boundaries of freedom of speech as far as possible through the decisions of the Constitutional Court, the challenge for the political community in Hungary is to develop a broad consensus against overt and coded forms of racist speech, a consensus that should be strongly reinforced whenever such expressions occur.

But those who follow the political environment of Hungary might wonder to what extent this post-Holocaust, post-communist society is ready to reject racist expressions. Andras Sajo, one of the strongest advocates of freedom of speech in Hungarian constitutional discourse, two years after the 1992 landmark decision of the Constitutional Court, ventured the opinion that the Court might be

---

plaintiff's last name was 'K' and his wife actually belongs to the family called 'K-clan' by the article. The civil court granted him standing and awarded him moral damages that are awarded in cases of non-propriety loss, for causing significantly harder living and working conditions for the plaintiff.

[94] See n. 40 above, 17.

[95] See A. Lewis, *Make No Law: The Sullivan Case and the First Amendment* (New York: Random House, 1991), chs. 8–9.

compelled to change its position.[96] The discouraging examples might outweigh the encouraging ones, but a recent development provides some hope. At the end of August 2007, the flag of the Hungarian Guard, an extreme-right paramilitary organization, was blessed by a representative of each of the three major Christian denominations (Catholic, Evangelical, and Reformed Church), without the knowledge or authorization of their churches.[97] Yet, in January 2008, a regional head of the Catholic Church in Veszprem (in Western Hungary) did not allow the blessing of the flag of the Guard.

'Only through self-cleansing may a political culture and a soundly reflexive public opinion emerge,' wrote the Constitutional Court in 1992. How far has the process of 'self-cleansing' gone since the Court laid down its argument? Has 'self-cleansing' worked in the 16 years following Decision 30/1992? Is 16 years enough time for a society to go through the psychological process necessary to change cultural behaviour and attitudes? Do the European Union, the Council of Europe, the Organization for Security and Cooperation in Europe, and other international organizations (Hungary is a member in all of them) provide sufficient defence against the danger of hateful ideas while allowing for a longer period of 'self-cleansing'? Finally, how can tolerating 'hate speech' contribute to 'self-cleansing'?

As Frank Michelman writes, 'we need not credit Nazis marching through Skokie with expanding the menu of visions from which individuals choose their truths.'[98] John Stuart Mill however, at the end of the second chapter of his essay on liberty recapitulates the four grounds that in his view justify the liberty of thought and discussion, including the value of letting even obviously wrong opinions be freely expressed. Although we can immediately cast off his first two reasons because racist speech cannot be true, or cannot even 'contain a portion of truth,'[99] Mill's next arguments appear pertinent to the 'hate speech' debate. He writes:

> Thirdly, even if the received opinion be not only true, but the whole truth; unless it is suffered to be, and actually is, vigorously and earnestly contested, it will, by most of those who receive it, be held in the manner of a prejudice, with little comprehension or feeling of its rational grounds. And not only this, but, fourthly, the meaning of the doctrine itself will be in danger of being lost or enfeebled, and deprived of its vital effect on the character and conduct: the dogma becoming a mere formal profession, inefficacious for good, but cumbering the ground and preventing the growth of any real and heartfelt conviction from reason or personal experience.[100]

---

[96] 'It remains to be seen whether tragic historical experience and burning social conflicts do not, in effect, compel constitutional courts to "constitutionalize" specific content-based restrictions on speech in order to protect racial groups and other minorities.' See n. 72 above, 87.

[97] Z. Balla, 'Hungarian guard formed', *The Budapest Sun*, 29 August 2007, <http://www.budapestsun.com/cikk.php?id=27108> (last accessed 24 July 2008).

[98] 'Universities, Racist Speech and Democracy in America: An Essay for the ACLU' (1992) 27 *Harv. C. R.-C. L. L. Rev.*, 339, 354, n. 52.

[99] J. S. Mill, *On Liberty*, E. Rapaport (ed.), (Indianapolis, IN: Hackett Publishing Co. Inc. 1978), 50.   [100] Ibid.

The Hungarian Civil Liberties Union (HCLU) offers a similar reflection, but goes even further than Mill. In the view of the HCLU, banning opinions that would challenge the truth not only results in accepting the truth 'in the manner of a prejudice' or as a 'dogma' as Mill writes, but might make the general public reluctant to believe the factual statements of historians. The HCLU explicitly mentions Holocaust denial as an example, and argues that:

prohibiting the expression of any views, even those which are obviously false, may harm the community. As long as it is not forbidden to deny an established truth (eg, that the Holocaust took place), the general public has good reason to believe that what the experts say about the facts of history is true. If it becomes forbidden publicly to deny a thesis,[101] the general public will be deprived of any basis for its belief in what the expert says.[102]

Free speech theories[103] provide many more explanations for the American-Hungarian approach to 'hate speech'. In addition to the argument for truth, another instrumental justification for freedom of speech is that, without it, democratic self-government simply cannot work. Alexander Meiklejohn argued that: 'When men govern themselves, it is they—and no one else—who must pass judgment upon unwisdom and unfairness and danger . . . To be afraid of ideas, any idea, is to be unfit for self-government.'[104] The self-government rationale for freedom of speech is connected to the idea of limiting government in order to create and maintain open, robust public discourse which serves as a fundamentally important check on governmental power. Vincent Blasi called it the 'the checking value' in the First Amendment of the US Constitution. As Blasi writes:

. . . free expression is valuable in part because of the function it performs in checking the abuse of political power,[105] . . . While a proponent of the checking value may regard free expression as important partly because of its contributions to progress, wisdom, community, and the realization of individual potential, he is likely to value free expression primarily for its modest capacity to mitigate the human sufferings that other humans cause. Much of that suffering is caused by persons who hold public office.[106]

As opposed to instrumental justifications of freedom of speech, the argument based on individual autonomy supports the free communication of information and ideas as an independent value, not as a value that serves another goal. Dworkin emphasizes that the constitutive justification of freedom of speech— that does not rely on the instrumental value of it—provides the necessary broad

---

[101] Here, the HCLU should have written about restriction on the denial of 'facts' instead of 'a thesis', because there is a fundamental difference between questioning historical facts and challenging opinions.
[102] 'HCLU Policy Paper on Freedom of Expression', 3, <http://pdc.ceu.hu/archive/00001392/01/4.pdf> (last accessed 24 July 2008).
[103] See eg, E. Barendt *Freedom of Speech*, 2nd edn. (Oxford: OUP, 2005), 1–38.
[104] *Political Freedom: The Constitutional Powers of People* (New York: Harper, 1960), 27.
[105] 'The Checking Value in First Amendment Theory' (1977) *Am. Bar Found. Research J.* 521, 528.
[106] Ibid., 538.

protection for all forms of expression.[107] Beside the speaker's point of view, Dworkin also lays down a clear argument from the perspective of the listeners: 'We retain our dignity, as individuals, only by insisting that no one—no official and no majority—has the right to withhold an opinion from us on the ground that we are not fit to hear and consider it.'[108]

Edwin Baker argues that freedom of speech has to be respected because it is 'central to individual liberty':

... freedom of speech is fundamental less because of its instrumental value or the value of reasoned arguments and more because freedom to engage in self- expressive acts is central to individual liberty ... Part of the reason to protect speech ... is a commitment to the view that people should be able to participate in constructing their world.[109]

The individual autonomy-based arguments stress the point that all of us have the right to express what we wish to say, and to hear what others wish to express. Robert Post, in his participatory theory, analyses how the open public debate provides individuals' authorship in democracy even if their opinions do not attain majority support.[110] Without the opportunity of such authorship, the very legitimacy of the democracy is undermined.

Even if it is arguable that the search for truth in the marketplace of ideas supports a constitutional ban on content-based 'hate speech' laws, other theories (some examples of which were mentioned above) provide stronger justifications for the American-Hungarian approach. It is no accident that the Constitutional Court combines the argument for individual freedom with an analysis of the social process of open public discourse:

The Constitution guarantees free communication—as an individual behaviour or a public process—and the fundamental right to the freedom of expression does not refer to the content of the opinion. Every opinion, good and damaging, pleasant and offensive, has a place in this social process, especially because the classification of opinions is also the product of this process. . . . With the freedom of the press having become a reality no-one speaking out publicly may invoke external compulsion, and with every line penned he gives himself out and risks his entire moral credibility.[111]

(ii) The *Hegedus Jr.* Case and Its Aftermath: The Failure Properly to Apply the Test

One telling example of how the 'clear and present danger' test has been applied in Hungary is the *Hegedus Jr.* case, although the lower court, the Municipal Court of Budapest, did not apply the 'clear and present danger' test. Hegedus Jr., a

---

[107] For Dworkin's distinction between the instrumental and constitutive justification for freedom of speech see n. 11 above, 199–202.
[108] Ibid., 200.
[109] 'Of Course, More Than Words' (1994) 61 *U. Chi. L. Rev.* 1181, 1197, 1204.
[110] See 'Reconciling Theory and Doctrine in First Amendment Jurisprudence' (2000) 88 *Cal. L. Rev.* 2353.
[111] See n. 40 above, 15–7.

Protestant (Reformed Church) minister, was prosecuted for an article, titled *Christian Hungarian State*, in which he, in unmistakable code words, called for the exclusion of Jewish people from Hungarian society:

... as a result of the self-renunciation of the Compromise of 1867,[112] the hordes of the vagabonds of Galicia had ... invaded it; who, as if they were the old self of man without salvation, in an ancient onslaught fretted and are still scrunching this homeland, which, despite all this, is capable of resurrection from its ruins, on the heaps of the bones of our heroes. With their Sion of the Old Testament lost because of their sins and rebellions against God, let the most promising eminence of the moral order of the New Testament, the Hungarian Sion be irretrievably perished.

... And because it is not possible to burn out every single Palestinian from the banks of river Jordan with Fascist methods very often surpassing even those of the Nazis, they come to the banks of the Danube, sometimes as internationalists, sometimes as nationalists, and sometimes as cosmopolitans, to kick into the Hungarians once again, because they feel like it.

They become hysterical even from the salutation: CHRISTIAN HUNGARIAN STATE. They say: it is exclusion ...

Now let you Hungarians listen to the one single message of survival over the thousandth year of the Christian Hungarian state, which has been based on the ancestral inheritance and continuity of right: EXCLUDE THEM! FOR IF YOU DO NOT EXCLUDE THEM, THEY WILL EXCLUDE YOU!

Of this message we are warned by the misery of thousand years, by the inheritance nevertheless existing 'high above' of our country that has been robbed and looted a thousand times, and last but not least by the stone-throwing sons of Ramallah.[113]

The article was published in 2001, in 12,000 copies in a Budapest district newspaper of the then parliamentary Hungarian Life and Justice Party of which Hegedus Jr. was vice president, as well as member of Parliament. The Municipal Court of Budapest sentenced Hegedus Jr. to imprisonment for a period of one year and six months (suspended to probation for three years).[114] But the Municipal High Court of Appeal of Budapest acquitted Hegedus Jr.,[115] and the reasoning of the two courts illustrates very different applications of Decision 30/1992.[116] The Municipal Court of Budapest recalled that the exclusion of Jewish people from

[112] This historic agreement, called *Compromise,* created the Austro-Hungarian Monarchy in 1867. The 'liberalism of the dualistic era', as Peter Hanak characterizes it, the 'good old years', as people in Hungary remembered this period that lasted for half of a century, ended with the dissolution of the monarchy in 1918. See n. 15 above, 165. See also O. Jaszi, *The Dissolution of the Habsburg Monarchy* (Chicago: Univ Chicago Press, 1929) (n. 19 above), 13–86.

[113] Quoted by Municipal Court of Budapest Case No. 13.B.423/2002/7 in *Anti-Semitic Discourse in Hungary in 2002-2003* (Budapest: B'nai B'rith Budapest Lodge, 2004), 324–5, <http://www.hagalil.com/antisemitismus/ungarn/antisemitism-2003.pdf> (last accessed 24 July 2008).

[114] Municipal Court of Budapest Case No. 13.B.423/2002/7 in ibid.

[115] Municipal High Court of Appeal of Budapest Case Reg. No. 3.Bf.111/2003/10 in ibid.

[116] See G. Schweitzer, 'License for verbal exclusion? Or the Sentencing and Acquittal of Lorant Hegedus Jr.' in ibid., 247–53.

Hungarian society in fact took place by formally legitimate anti-Jewish laws in Hungary between 1938 and 1945.[117] The Municipal Court stated:

The final aim of this article was, and the accused was aware of it, that the aroused hatred might as well erupt from the enclosed world of emotions and manifest itself for others. This conduct constitutes and qualifies as incitement against the community as stated in the statutory provision in Article 269. b) of the Hungarian Criminal Code.[118]

The Municipal Court of Budapest did not find that the article had to create a clear and present danger in order to constitute the crime of the incitement to hatred. But the Municipal High Court of Appeal of Budapest, relying on the decisions of the Constitutional Court, took a sharply different approach, requiring the clear and present danger of violence as a precondition to finding that incitement to hatred existed. The Municipal High Court of Appeal of Budapest stated that the lower Municipal Court of Budapest 'failed to address the extent of the danger'.[119] and held that incitement of hatred should be construed, following the reasoning of the Constitutional Court and the related case decisions of the Supreme Court[120] as:

...the person who
  -calls to violent acts,
  -calls to the performance of such an action or conduct, where
  -the danger is not only assumed but there are actual rights endangered and there is a
   direct threat of a violent act,
is deemed not as someone who exercises the right to the freedom of expression of opinion, but one who commits incitement to hatred.[121]

The acquittal of Hegedus Jr. prompted Parliament to amend the relevant provision of the Criminal Code to extend the criminal restriction on 'hate speech'. This led to the third related decision of the Constitutional Court in 2004. In this way, indirectly, the Constitutional Court became involved in the case. Sajó, besides criticizing the acquittal of Hegedus Jr., calls attention to the fact that:

...ordinary courts became very reluctant to apply the incitement to hatred provisions. The prosecution does not find it applicable to anti-Semitic chants at football games (such as 'the trains are ready for Auschwitz')...The terms 'exclude them' were identical to those used in the preparation of race laws of the Hungarian fascist regime. This was found to fall outside Article 269 because of the lack of a clear and present danger. It was argued that in

---

[117] The Municipal Court of Budapest mentions Act No. IV of 1939 on the limitation of the social and economic expansion of the Jews and Act No. VIII of 1942 on the regulation of the legal status of the Israelite denomination in ibid., 331.

[118] Municipal Court of Budapest Case No. 13.B.423/2002/7 in ibid., 331–2.

[119] Municipal High Court of Appeal of Budapest Case Reg. No. 3.Bf.111/2003/10 in ibid., 342.

[120] Case decisions No. BH.1997/165. and BH. 1998/521. of the Supreme Court of the Republic of Hungary in ibid., 340.

[121] Municipal High Court of Appeal of Budapest Case Reg. No. 3.Bf.111/2003/10 in ibid., 340–1.

the current political situation one can rule out that such statements will result in the use of legislation covering racial discrimination.[122]

The reluctance of the prosecution to apply the incitement to hatred provisions to antisemitic chants at football games precludes such racist speech from even becoming a court case. It shows that instead of repeatedly enacting stricter laws that would be found unconstitutional by the Constitutional Court,[123] proper application of the crime of incitement to hatred should become part of the fight against 'hate speech'. The article of the racist cleric might or might not fall under Article 269 of the Criminal Code, and this question is still unresolved in Hungary.[124] But antisemitic chants at football stadium gatherings should be prosecuted and sentenced under the Criminal Code. These are clear-cut crimes even if we follow the most narrowly tailored approach of the Hungarian Civil Liberties Union, the first organization on earth that copied its English name from the name of the American Civil Liberties Union:

... when an agitated crowd is incited to violent action, and the potential victim is on the scene, then the danger that the speech is followed by violent action is clear and present. When, however, a speaker addresses indifferent passers-by, who are hurrying about to do their business, and the potential scapegoat is not present, the danger is negligible.[125]

The lack of proper application of the narrowly tailored criminal prohibition is connected to the lack of overall political condemnation of racist speech. Jean-Yves Camus paints a rather dark picture on the political atmosphere in Hungary. As he describes:

... [a] distinctive feature of the situation in Hungary is that anti-Semitism is also considered perfectly respectable on newsstands, where the MIEP's[126] monthly '*Magyar Forum*'[127] is on sale. The list of books available by mail order from the newspaper in 2003–2004 is undoubtedly unique in Europe, since it offers books applauding the

---

[122] 'Background Paper IV: The Legislative Framework and Judicial Review Concerning Racist and Discriminatory Expression in a Selected Number of European Countries', *Combating Racism While Respecting Freedom of Expression* (Council of Europe: European Commission against Racism and Intolerance, 2007), 141.

[123] In February 2008, the Parliament accepted a new amendment of the Criminal Code, trying again to define 'hate speech' and to prohibit it on the basis of its content. László Sólyom, the President of the Republic of Hungary, the first Chief Justice of the Constitutional Court, one of the authors of *Decision 30/1992*, found that the new law would be unconstitutional and, before signing the bill, he sent it to the Constitutional Court and initiated its previous constitutional review. In July 2008, the Constitutional Court held the bill unconstitutional. Decision 95/2008 (VII. 3.) AB.

[124] An important part of the debate is to what extent it has to be taken into consideration that Hegedus Jr., and other Parlimentarians represented in Parliament the extreme right wing Hungarian Life and Justice Party when the article was published.

[125] See n. 101 above.

[126] MIEP is the acronym of the Hungarian Life and Justice Party in Hungarian.

[127] See Z. Mihancsik, 'Revealing Quotes: Magyar Fórum, Magyar Demokrata, Vasárnapi újság (Abridged)' in *Anti-Semitic Discourse in Hungary in 2000* (Budapest: B'nai B'rith Budapest Lodge, 2001), 155–162, <http://www.hagalil.com/antisemitismus/ungarn/antisemitism-2000.pdf> (last accessed 24 July 2008).

Hungarian Waffen SS ... a negationist book on Auschwitz and a translation of a 1930s French classic on the judeo-masonic plot theory—many of them illustrated by drawings and caricatures like those produced by the Nazi Stürmer.[128]

(iii) The Prohibition of the Public Display of Certain Totalitarian Symbols

Riots on the streets of Budapest on the 50th anniversary of the anti-Stalinist revolution in 1956 provided a convincing example for the argument that even unfettered racist speech can contribute to democratic public opinion. On 24 October, the *New York Times* in the centre of its front page displayed a photograph of the street riots on 23 October, the starting day of the revolution. The photograph focused on a demonstrator whose face was distorted by hate and who was holding a huge red and white striped flag. The article that followed did not mention the flag. No doubt, the overwhelming majority of the readers did not know what kind of flag was in the picture. Perhaps, many of them thought that it was the Hungarian national flag. The readers of the *New York Times* were able to learn about the flag two days later from a short, scarcely noticeable letter to the editor that many readers probably missed, written by István Deák, a Hungarian emeritus professor of history at Columbia University:

Your caption did not mention that the demonstrator pictured in the foreground is not waving the Hungarian flag but the striped, so-called Arpad flag of the Arrow Cross, Hungary's extreme National Socialist party.

The Arrow Cross was in power for a few months beginning in October 1944, during which time Hungary was devastated by the war and thousands of Jews were rounded up and killed.

During the recent demonstrations in Budapest, the flag of the Hungarian Nazis has been conspicuous.[129]

This example is not about a mistake even the best newspapers can make when they fail to provide an accurate description of the relevant historical-cultural background of an event. The story of this photo is an instance of coded racism. It had to be coded, because in Hungary, the criminal law prohibits the public display of certain listed totalitarian symbols, among them the swastika and the arrow cross. The Constitutional Court took this provision of the Criminal Code as an exception, holding it constitutional with the thoroughly unconvincing argument that symbols are such special forms of expression that they can trigger specific criminal prohibition.[130] Section 269/B of the Criminal Code says that:

---

[128] See n. 64 above, 38.

[129] 'To the Editor: Re "Clashes Disrupt Hungarians' Celebration of Anti-Soviet Revolt in '56" (front-page photograph, Oct. 24)', *The New York Times*, 26 October 2006.

[130] Decision 14/2000 (V. 12.) AB, <http://www.mkab.hu/content/en/en3/06079304.htm>.

(1) Anyone who
    a) distributes;
    b) uses in front of a large public gathering;
    c) exhibits in public a swastika, the SS sign, an arrow-cross, the hammer and sickle, a
       five-pointed red star or a symbol depicting the above commits a misdemeanour—
       unless a graver crime is realised—and shall be punishable by fine.
(2) The person who commits an act defined in paragraph (1) for the purposes of dis-
    seminating knowledge, education, science, or art, or for the purpose of information
    about the events of history or the present time shall not be punishable.[131]

Consequently, extreme right demonstrators could not have displayed the arrow cross or the swastika, or the red and white striped flag with an arrow cross on it: the flag of the Arrow Cross, the Hungarian Nazi Party. They can only use a red and white striped flag without the arrow cross on it. The Federation of Young Democrats—Civic Alliance, the leading right-wing party, after a short hesitation endorsed the use of the striped flag stating that it is just a historical Hungarian flag. But while some versions of the red and white striped flag are historic Hungarian flags indeed, the flag became strongly associated with the Arrow Cross Party. Since 1944–45, the flag has been a symbol of the most horrible terror and cannot be separated from this meaning.[132]

The criminal prohibition of the public display of certain totalitarian symbols could not stop the use of a similar totalitarian symbol. The exceptional content-based criminal law ban on symbolic speech led to coded racist speech in Hungary. It deprived the global community of the opportunity to understand a profound aspect of the reported political turmoil in a post-Holocaust, post-communist, Central-European democracy. The result of the regulation is that most non-Hungarian foreigners could not decode the message of the flag that they saw on the front page of one of the world's most respected newspapers.

Endorsing the use of the striped flag at anti-government demonstrations[133] by the Federation of Young Democrats—Civic Alliance provides a clear example of coded speech that is hard to understand abroad. This makes it much easier for the leading right-wing party of Hungary to engage in doublespeak, using democratic language when talking to foreigners, while mixing with extreme right groups and ideas when talking to a domestic audience. As this illustration shows, limiting

---

[131] Act XLV of 1993 on the amendment of Act IV of 1978 on the Criminal Code introduced this provision into the Criminal Code under the title 'Use of Symbols of Despotism'.

[132] The failure to accept that the red and white striped flag cannot be separated from the terror it symbolizes is somewhat similar to the continued public display of the confederate flag (the flag of the Confederacy organized by the Southern states in 1861) that cannot be separated from slavery in the US.

[133] László Sólyom, the President of the Republic of Hungary, in a speech he gave at the opening meeting of the autumn sessions of Parliament on 10 September, 2007, at least asked demonstrators 'to respect the victims and the pain of the survivors by not using this flag as a symbol, to be humane, to think about what they cause with this'.

public discourse by prohibiting totalitarian symbols significantly contributed to the spread of racist speech instead of reducing it.

4. Conclusion

I have always been convinced that freedom of speech in new democracies needs the maximum protection in order to overcome the long history of suppression and the fear of speaking freely.[134] As the HCLU argues:

> when democratic institutions work well, and the people who fill the main institutional roles are united in rejecting antidemocratic radicalism, extremism has no appeal beyond a very limited section of the public. It is indeed imperative to take resolute action against racism, but that should not be done with instruments of the penal law in the first place.[135]

Through my personal experiences as a lawmaker in the first two terms of the freely elected post-communist parliament of the Republic of Hungary in the 1990s, I became persuaded that legislation has a limited capacity to change the mindset of a political community that had lived under dictatorship for long decades. I also learned that only carefully planned law and policy can enable the political community to develop the culture of liberal constitutional democracy in the fastest way possible.

Instead of repeatedly questioning the Hungarian 'clear and present danger' test, efforts against 'hate speech' should focus on the single most important remedy: education that can fight ignorance and prejudice, the roots of hatred. In addition, clear-cut political condemnation of racist speech and other expressions of hatred, combined with a proper application of the criminal law prohibition of incitement to hatred could at least to some extent enable the political community to build a healthier society.

Hungary, as a case study, also shows that each country has to choose the best anti-'hate speech' policy for itself. Instead of taking for granted that in the constitutional treatment of 'hate speech' there is a deep divide between the US and all other countries, it would be more helpful to look openly at possible policy directions. The constitutional prohibition of content-based regulation of 'hate speech' can be useful outside the US as well. In each case, the law has to be carefully designed to include all available substantive safeguards that facilitate the constitutional application of the statute. All possible procedural safeguards should be also employed, such as the one in Canada where in instances of alleged hate speech '... no prosecution may be initiated without the *consent* of the Attorney

---

[134] See P. Molnar, ' "... without uncertainty, compromise and fear," or Should the New York Times Rule be Introduced in Hungary?' (Shorenstein Paper, 2000), <http://www.ksg.harvard.edu/presspol/research_publications/papers/working_papers/2000_15.PDF> (last accessed 24 July 2008).
[135] See n. 102 above, 3.

General'.[136] Lack of content-based regulation should not mean that even incitement to hatred that creates the imminent danger of violence is not prosecuted. Content-based regulation should be as narrowly tailored and applied as possible and should build on all the best practices that have been developed to at least reduce the likelihood of the misuse of the 'hate speech' law to suppress political dissent.[137] International organizations should review their policies to take into consideration that the weaker a democracy, the more likely the abuse of a content-based 'hate speech' law. The United Kingdom is certainly an established democracy, but as Nadine Strossen writes about the controversial application of the British Race Relations Act of 1965: 'In perhaps the ultimate irony, this statute, which was intended to restrain the neo-Nazi National Front, instead has barred expression by the Anti-Nazi League.'[138] The same content-based ban, even if it is not abused in established democracies, might be easily abused in rather fragile ones.

[136] I. Cotler, 'Hate Speech, Equality, and Harm Under the Charter: Towards a Jurisprudence of Respect for a "Free and Democratic Society"', in G.-A. Beaudoin and E. Mendes (eds.) *Canadian Charter of Rights and Freedoms,* 4th edn. (Toronto: Butterworths, 2005), 1488.

[137] See eg, the Amicus Curiae brief in *Ferdinand Nahimana, Jean-Bosco Barayagwiza and Hassan Ngeze* v. *The Prosecutor* (ICTR Case No. ICTR-99-52-A) from the Open Society Justice Initiative to the International Criminal Tribunal for Rwanda, in collaboration with African and international human rights and freedom of speech/expression groups, <http://www.justiceinitiative.org/db/resource2/fs/?file_id=17874> (last accessed 24 July 2008).

[138] N. Strossen, 'Balancing the Rights to Freedom of Expression and Equality: A Civil Liberties Approach to Hate Speech on Campus' in *Striking a Balance* (n. 2 above), 307.

14

Cumulative Jurisprudence and Hate Speech: Sexual Orientation and Analogies to Disability, Age, and Obesity

*Eric Heinze**

1. Introduction

On the evening of 13 September 2002, three boys, aged 16–20 entered a city park in Reims, France. Their plan was to 'smash an Arab' (*'casser de l'Arabe'*). Instead they found François Chenu. Chenu was 29 years old, an openly gay man. So they decided to 'smash a faggot' (*'cassé du pédé'*). They taunted him, beat him, then threw him in a pond, where he was later discovered drowned.[1]

Queer bashing is never just about physical assaults. A society casual about words like 'queer' or 'poof' is one in which sexual minorities[2] are maimed and murdered. Queer bashing without words is like a dirge without music. Queer bashing is that torrent of blows and words, every kick and punch chanted with 'queer', 'poof', 'faggot', 'cocksucker' or 'lesbo'; like a racist, antisemitic or Islamaphobic attack, the same kinds of words spewed with the same kinds of blows.

* This piece appears with the kind permission of *International Journal of Human Rights*, Special Double Issue: *Protection of Sexual Minorities since Stonewall: Progress and Stalemate in Developed and Developing Countries* (published also as an anthology by Routledge), edited by P. C. W. Chan, where it is published under the title, 'Cumulative Jurisprudence and Human Rights: The Example of Sexual Minorities and Hate Speech'. The ideas presented in this piece benefited from a staff seminar held at Durham University, Spring Term 2007, chaired by Erika Rackley and facilitated by Helen Fenwick and Gavin Phillipson, and from a subsequent one-day conference at Durham entitled 'Sexuality, Hatred and Law,' 6 May 2008, organized by Neil Cobb and Gavin Phillipson. Thanks are due also to James Weinstein and two anonymous reviewers for their detailed comments.

[1] See *Au-delà de la Haine*, a documentary film directed by Olivier Meyrou (2005); C. Constant, 'Leçon d'humanité', *L'Humanité*, 14 March 2007, http://www.humanite.presse.fr/journal/2007-03-14/2007-03-14-847695 (last accessed 15 June 2008).
[2] Like concepts of 'race', 'ethnicity', or 'religion', concepts of 'sexual orientation' and 'sexual minorities' may be fluid and are not amenable to conclusive definitions. For the limited purposes of human rights law, the term 'sexual minorities' may be used generally 'to denote people whose preferences, intimate associations, lifestyles, or other forms of personal identity or expression actually or imputedly derogate from a dominant normative-heterosexual paradigm'. See E. Heinze, *Sexual Orientation: A Human Right* (Dordrecht, NL: Martinus Nijhoff, 1995), 61.

In recent years, that violence of words has provided powerful justifications for hate speech bans.[3] It is understandable that sexual minorities would seek protection under them as part of a broader effort to combat prejudice. In so doing, they would be pursuing an otherwise legitimate and often successful strategy, which I shall call 'cumulative jurisprudence'. Gains for sexual minorities have frequently resulted from activists, lawyers, and scholars citing protections, such as privacy, free expression, free association, or non-discrimination, which may not originally have been adopted with sexual minorities in mind, but then showing how those protections can and should be interpreted to include sexual minorities. In the following discussion, I shall argue that cumulative jurisprudence is appropriate for sexual minorities as a general matter, but should not be assumed to apply mechanically to all norms that may emerge within the human rights corpus, without any deeper enquiry into the legitimacy of the underlying norms themselves. Norms against hate speech provide an example.

I shall begin by examining the concept of cumulative jurisprudence as a systematic application of general human rights norms to categories of persons not expressly named or intended in leading human rights instruments. A cumulative jurisprudence has allowed sexual minorities to gain increasing recognition within human rights systems, and might seem prima facie to justify the extension of hate speech bans to include sexual minorities. I shall then argue, however, that hate speech bans pose a dilemma intolerable for human rights law: either they promote discrimination by unfairly limiting the protected categories and individuals; or, if they were to include all similarly situated categories and individuals, they would represent more than just minimal limits on free speech. I conclude that sexual minorities should generally enjoy all guarantees available within human rights law, but should not seek refuge in bans that may serve more to betray fundamental principles of human rights law than to promote them.

2. Sexual Minorities and Cumulative Jurisprudence

Michel Foucault's publication of *Histoire de la sexualité*[4] in 1976 sparked a revolution in our understandings of dominant and subordinated social groups. Foucault described the post-Enlightenment appropriation of sexuality within the sphere of scientific enquiry. Purportedly neutral, objectivist—professionalized and therefore exclusive—scientific discourses of sexuality, presupposing unacknowledged standards of normativity and deviance,[5] came to pervade

---

[3] For a landmark text, see eg, M. J. Matsuda, C. Lawrence III, R. Delgado, and K. W. Crenshaw (eds.), *Words that Wound: Critical Race Theory, Assaultive Speech and the First Amendment* (Boulder, CO: Westview Press, 1993). For other works, see eg, authors cited in R. Delgado, 'About Your Masthead: A Preliminary Inquiry into the Compatibility of Civil Rights and Civil Liberties' (2004) 39 *Harv. C.R.-C.L. L. Rev.* 1.

[4] *Histoire de la sexualité I: La volonté de savoir* (Paris: Gallimard, 1976).

[5] See also M. Foucault, *Histoire de la folie à l'âge classique* (Paris: Gallimard, 1972).

language and consciousness to the extent that what we now know as 'hetero-sexuality', 'homosexuality', 'transsexualism', and a long train of similar terms came to construct, and thereby to control, our everyday sense of sexual experience and sexual identity. The objectivist, scientific discourses have persisted, of course, providing ample fodder for debates between 'essentialist' and 'social construc-tionist' approaches. Foucault nevertheless shed real light on how dominant social discourses regiment everyday experiences and attitudes.

Social constructionism reminds us that when gay bashers cry 'queer', 'poof', 'faggot' and 'cocksucker', they are not merely describing some 'outside world' which 'contains' such individuals. Rather, they are 'constructing' that world, to control those individuals. Compare a story told by Randall Kennedy:

Although they typically travelled on public buses, my mother had failed to notice that her mother, Big Mama, always took her to the back of the bus where Negroes were segregated. One day, Big Mama asked my mother to run an errand that required her to catch a bus on which they had often ridden together. This errand marked the first time that my mother rode the bus on her own. She stood at the correct stop, got on the right bus, and deposited the appropriate fare. Being a bit scared, however, she sat down immediately behind the bus driver. After about a block, the driver pulled the bus over to the curb, cut the engine, and suddenly wheeled around and began to scream at my mother who was all of about eight or nine years old—'Nigger, you know better than to sit there! Get to the back where you belong'![6]

Randall Kennedy's mother was not born a 'nigger'. She was made one, as Chenu was made a *pédé*, within a world whose fundamental relationship to such indi-viduals was one of social dominance and subordination.

The phrase 'hate speech' is recent, having arisen in the 1980s in the United States. More recently, the phrase has been adopted in Europe and elsewhere.[7] But the problem itself is ancient. Blasphemy laws, for example, may not in every sense be identical to current hate speech laws, as they have often protected beliefs themselves, regardless of whether any groups or individuals might be personally offended by speech against those beliefs, which, moreover, have generally been the ideas of the dominant group, and not of a minority.[8] Functionally, however, they have served to protect sensibilities and to avoid offence. In recent jurisprudence, blasphemy laws have often been maintained precisely insofar as they serve the same aims as hate speech laws—prohibiting speech likely to be found offensive or unduly disruptive.[9]

---

[6] *Nigger: The Strange Career of a Troublesome Word* (New York: Vintage, 2003), xii.

[7] See eg, K. Boyle, 'Hate Speech: The United States Versus the Rest of the World?' (2001) 53 *Me. L. Rev.* 487, 489.

[8] See eg, *Otto-Preminger-Institut* v. *Austria* (Appl. No. 13470/87), ECHR, Ser. A, No. 295-A [1994], upholding a blasphemy law protective of the Roman Catholic majority). See also *Wingrove* v. *United Kingdom* (Appl. No. 17419/90), ECHR 60 [1996].

[9] See E. Heinze, 'Viewpoint Absolutism and Hate Speech' (2006) 69 *Modern L. Rev.* 543, 558–59; E. Heinze, 'Towards the Abolition of Hate Speech Bans: A "Viewpoint Absolutist" Per-spective', in T. Loenen and J. Goldschmidt (eds.), *Religious Pluralism and Human Rights* (Antwerp: Intersentia, 2007), 295.

Article 20(2) of the International Covenant on Civil and Political Rights (ICCPR),[10] currently binding on 160 states,[11] provides that 'any advocacy of national, racial, or religious hatred that constitutes incitement to discrimination, hostility, or violence shall be prohibited by law'. Drafted in the 1960s, the ICCPR does not use the phrase 'hate speech'. However, it captures the overall aims that have emerged in post-WWII regulations of speech deemed to be highly offensive.

From the perspective of sexual minorities, it might well be argued that the enumeration of three specific kinds of target groups in Article 20(2)—national, racial, or religious—should be deemed only 'illustrative', and not final or exhaustive.[12] On that approach, it could be argued that Article 20(2) represents only an early attempt to deal with intolerance through human rights instruments, which can grow to encompass additional target groups as each groups' history and circumstances comes to light. In support of that approach, it could be noted that, like similar provisions in other international, regional, or national instruments, Article 19(3), which limits freedom of expression on grounds of 'public order', 'morals', or even 'rights or reputation of others', remains amenable to hate speech bans protective of sexual minorities.[13] Some national legal systems have already extended hate speech bans to protect gays, either by specific legislative amendment or through subsequent judicial interpretation.[14]

The International Convention on the Elimination of All Forms of Racial Discrimination[15] (CERD), also drafted in the 1960s, includes a detailed prohibition of hate speech, which, albeit expressly limited to race, exemplifies the broad reach of hate speech bans that have been promoted within international law and institutions.[16] Article 4 requires that states parties,

(a) Shall declare an offence punishable by law all dissemination of ideas based on racial superiority or hatred, incitement to racial discrimination, as well as all acts of violence or incitement to such acts against any race or group of persons of another colour or ethnic origin ...

---

[10] 993 U.N.T.S. 3, entered into force 3 January 1976.

[11] For periodically updated data on ratifications, accessions, successions, reservations and declarations for international human rights treaties, see eg, Office of the United Nations High Commissioner for Human Rights (UNHCR), 'Ratifications and Reservations', <http://www2. ohchr.org/english/bodies/ratification/> (last accessed 15 June 2008).

[12] See eg, n. 2 above, s. 12.3; E. Heinze, 'Equality: Between Hegemony and Subsidiarity' (1994) 52 *Review of the International Commission of Jurists* 56; M. Bossuyt, *L'interdiction de la discrimination dans le droit international des droits de l'homme* (Brussels: Bruylant, 1976).

[13] See 'Viewpoint Absolutism and Hate Speech' in n. 9 above, 556–9.

[14] See eg, ibid., 544, discussing the French case of Dominique Vanneste. See also eg, J.-P. Loof, 'Freedom of Expression and Religiously-Based Ideas on Homosexuality: European and Dutch Standards', in T. Loenen and J. Goldschmidt (eds.), *Religious Pluralism and Human Rights* (Antwerp: Intersentia, 2007), 267–78.

[15] 660 U.N.T.S. 195, entered into force 4 January 1969.

[16] See n. 11 above.

(b) Shall declare illegal and prohibit organizations, and also organized and all other propaganda activities, which promote and incite racial discrimination, and shall recognize participation in such organizations or activities as an offence punishable by law.

CERD is of particular interest, insofar as post-WWII movements for the rights of sexual minorities have often followed in the footsteps of anti-racism movements, as illustrated, for example, in the United States, where the African-American civil rights movements of the 1950s and 1960s, joined by the feminist movements of the 1960s and 1970s, became decisive in inspiring America's gay rights movements.[17] In the post-WWII period, gay rights movements have frequently pursued a strategy of cumulative (or 'analogical') jurisprudence, whereby rights first recognized for racial, ethnic, religious, or national minorities, or women, would be seen to set the stage for rights of sexual minorities.[18]

The question I am asking is whether the considerable success of a cumulative jurisprudence in achieving rights for sexual minorities should be applied so as to extend hate speech bans to embrace sexual minorities. In the mid-1990s, when sexual minorities were first beginning[19] to gain attention within the United Nations, I had argued that their rights must not primarily be seen as 'innovations'. They must be seen as necessary applications of existing international norms, without which the interpretation of those norms would be inherently contradictory. I recommended some jurisprudential principles for the recognition of rights of sexual minorities within existing international human rights law.[20] One of them, which I called the 'Principle of Extant Rights', was formulated as follows: 'Rights of sexual orientation are required by extant human rights law to the degree, and only to the degree, that they derive from extant rights'.[21]

By including the restriction 'only to the degree', I conceded the minor, arguably tautological, point that fundamental rights for sexual minorities could not be said to exist *already* within the existing international human rights corpus except insofar as those rights existed within the corpus for human beings generally. That slight limitation having been acknowledged, the more important point was that protections already existing for human beings generally had to be extended *ipso facto* to sexual minorities. Cumulative jurisprudence has provided an important vehicle for realizing the Principle of Extant Rights.

The aim of the Principle of Extant Rights was to play both descriptive and prescriptive roles. As a prescriptive matter, it suggests that fundamental

---

[17] For some standard accounts, see, eg, J. D'Emilio, *Sexual Politics, Sexual Communities: The Making of a Homosexual Minority in the United States, 1940–1970* (Chicago: Univ of Chicago Press, 1983); T. Marotta, *The Politics of Homosexuality* (Boston: Houghton Mifflin, 1981). Similarly, Marxist and left-wing approaches in Europe tended to aggregate the interests of outsider groups. See eg, M. Mieli, *Elementi di critica omosessuale* (Turin: Giuliu Einaudi, 1977).

[18] See text accompanying notes 32–44 below.

[19] See n. 2 above, 12 n. 54, noting limited attention to sexual orientation within the UN through the 1980s.

[20] Ibid., ch. 8.   [21] Ibid., 136.

international human rights must be construed to apply to sexual minorities if they are to avoid falling into internal contradiction. As a descriptive matter, it provides a sense of how, in general, advocacy for rights of sexual minorities has in fact tended to proceed: once the post-World War II frameworks for human rights were already firmly in place—originally drafted with little regard to rights for sexual minorities—sexual orientation and identity have subsequently been incorporated at international, regional, and national levels, be it through national legislation and adjudication, or through the judgments or opinions of international or regional human rights bodies.[22]

In its prescriptive role, the Principle of Extant Rights takes as axiomatic—that is, it merely assumes, insofar as international human rights count as norms within positive international, regional, or national law—that existing rights within the international corpus are normatively legitimate, in particular such fundamental norms as privacy, expression, association, or non-discrimination. In proposing it, I conceded from the outset that human rights may not be historically or cross-culturally universal. They may be artefacts of specific historical, political, and economic circumstances. Or, even if we take as given a general corpus of human rights, certain rights within that corpus might be challenged in their formulation or interpretation.[23] Many a human rights norm—such as privacy, expression, association, non-discrimination—could be independently contested on its own terms, before any more specific inquiry into its applicability to sexual minorities would even arise. Is the norm genuinely universal? Does it, in all cases, stand as a legitimate 'trump' over worthy, competing interests?

The prescriptive approach, then, simply assumes the validity of the general corpus of fundamental human rights, without undertaking any inquiry into the overall validity either of any specific right, or of the human rights corpus, as such. Its role is merely to state that, insofar as the existing corpus *is* accepted and applied, it must be applied equally to sexual minorities. For nuts-and-bolts human rights practice, that assumption poses few problems. Everyday advocacy can assume, as a general matter, that sexual minorities as such merit, say, privacy,[24] freedoms of expression or association,[25] or non-discrimination[26] insofar as all human beings merit it.

The cumulative jurisprudence of non-discrimination for sexual minorities has not been mechanical or straightforward. Consider the US example. Having adopted the most demanding standard of judicial review, 'strict scrutiny', for racial classifications,[27] the road to gender equality was rockier, starting from a

---

[22] See text accompanying notes 32–44 below.
[23] See n. 2 above, ch. 3.
[24] Ibid., ch. 10.
[25] Ibid., ss. 14.3–14.5.
[26] Ibid., chs. 12 and 13.
[27] See *Korematsu* v. *United States* 323 US 214 (1944); *Brown* v. *Board of Education* 347 US 483 (1954); *Loving* v. *Virginia* 388 US 1 (1967).

highly deferential 'rational basis' standard,[28] then swinging towards a strict
scrutiny standard,[29] until finally settling upon a standard of intermediary review
('heightened', but not always 'strict'), which—often in the interest of respecting
gender differences that would accrue to women's advantage—had to take into
account complexities of difference that tend to be specific to gender.[30]

The road for sexual minorities was at least as rocky. After a major defeat in the
1986 case of *Bowers* v. *Hardwick*,[31] the US Supreme Court began to recognize
rights for gays only in the 1996 case of *Romer* v. *Evans*,[32] then the 2003 case of
Lawrence v. *Texas*.[33] Even in those cases, the Court has created the oddity of
applying a remarkably rigorous standard of review in practice, while remaining
ambivalent about declaring the adoption of a stricter level of scrutiny as a formal
or final matter.[34] Despite that erratic approach, it seems that, overall, a jurisprudence originating in anti-racist movements has expanded to encompass other
targets of discrimination,[35] with sexual minorities gradually included through a
cumulative jurisprudence.[36]

In Europe, the evolution of Article 14 of the European Convention on Human
Rights[37] also provides an example of cumulative jurisprudence. Article 14 sets
forth a standard non-discrimination provision,

The enjoyment of the rights and freedoms set forth in this Convention shall be secured
without discrimination on any ground *such as* sex, race, colour, language, religion, political
or other opinion, national or social origin, association with a national minority, property,
birth *or other status*. (emphasis added)

---

[28] See *Reed* v. *Reed* 404 US 71 (1971). Since the Supreme Court in *Reed* did strike down the
gender discrepancy in dispute, however, it could be argued that the Court was already anticipating a
more stringent approach.
[29] See *Frontiero* v. *Richardson* 411 US 677 (1973). The application of strict scrutiny by a plurality
of only four Justices, however, suggested a continuing unease about the appropriate judicial standard.
[30] See *Craig* v. *Boren* 429 US 190 (1976); *United States* v. *Virginia* 518 US 515 (1996).
[31] *Bowers* v. *Hardwick* 478 US 186 (1986).
[32] *Romer* v. *Evans* 517 US 620 (1996).
[33] *Lawrence* v. *Texas* 539 US 558 (2003).
[34] See the various views taken on the Supreme Court's standards of review in eg, R. E. Barnett,
'Justice Kennedy's Libertarian Revolution: Lawrence v. Texas' (2003) 21 *2002–2003 Cato Sup. Ct.
Rev.* 21; L. H. Tribe, 'Lawrence v. Texas: The "Fundamental Right" that Dare Not Speak Its Name'
(2004) 117 *Harv. L. Rev.* 1893.
[35] Although *Lawrence* was not decided primarily on grounds of equal protection (non-discrimination), the Court noted the consistency of its holding with equal protection principles. *Lawrence*
539 US 558 (2003) at 574–5, describing as 'tenable' a disposition of the case on equal protection
grounds. See also 579, O'Connor, J., concurring, arguing that the sodomy statute should be struck
down on equal protection grounds.
[36] See eg, J. E. Nowak and R. D. Rotunda, *Constitutional Law*, 6th edn. (St. Paul, MN: West
Publishing, 2000), 786–926.
[37] Convention for the Protection of Human Rights and Fundamental Freedoms, 213 U.N.T.S.
222, entered into force 3 September 1953, as amended by Protocols Nos. 3, 5, 8, and 11, entered
into force 21 September 1970, 20 December 1971, 1 January 1990 and 1 November 1998,
respectively.

Whilst specifically referring to sex (originally construed as applying to men and women), race, colour, and other categories, the 'such as' and 'other status' clauses have long been interpreted to mean that the expressly enumerated categories are not exhaustive. In *Marckx* v. *Belgium*, the European Court of Human Rights held discriminatory treatment of unwed mothers to be in violation of Article 14.[38] In *Inze* v. *Austria*, the Court interpreted 'other status' to encompass children born out of wedlock.[39] In *Darby* v. *Sweden*, the Court extended the clause further to include persons not registered as resident.[40] Recognition of homosexuality came as early as 1981, with *Dudgeon* v. *United Kingdom*[41] (although subsequent developments, notably for transsexuals, have not been uniformly positive[42]). The UN Human Rights Committee, too, has increasingly recognized sexual orientation[43] along with other classifications under the 'other status' clauses of ICCPR.[44]

3. Cumulative or Contradictory?

Is there a limit to the Principle of Extant Rights, in particular, to the axiomatic assumption of the overall validity either of the corpus in general or of any given background norm? How shall we proceed when it is by no means obvious that a particular norm *should* carry the kind of authority that can be accorded to norms such as privacy, expression, association, or professional or educational non-discrimination? Should sexual minorities accept the overall, background norm of prohibitions on hate speech wholesale, insisting on equal protection under them, without any independent analysis into the merit of those norms themselves?

CERD Art. 4 may refer only to race, and ICCPR Art. 20(2) may include only the two other categories of nationality and religion. Sexual minorities might nevertheless reason as follows: once we have shown that homophobic speech is similarly harmful, easily associated with precisely the kinds of danger or violence

---

[38] See *Marckx* v. *Belgium* (Appl. No. 6833/74), judgment of 13 June 1979, ECHR, Ser. A, No. 31.

[39] See *Inze* v. *Austria* judgment of 28 October 1987, ECHR, Ser. A, No. 126.

[40] See *Darby* v. *Sweden* judgment of 23 October 1990, ECHR, Ser. A, No. 187.

[41] *Dudgeon* v. *United Kingdom* (Appl. No. 7525/76), judgment of 22 October 1981, ECHR., Ser. A, No. 45.

[42] See generally eg, E. Heinze, 'Sexual Orientation and International Law: A Study in the Manufacture of Cross-Cultural "Sensitivity"' (2001) 22 *Mich. J. Int'l L.* 283.

[43] See eg, *Toonen* v. *Australia*, Communication No. 488/1992, UN GAOR, Human Rights Committee, UN Doc. CCPR/C/50/D/488/1992 (1994); 'Concluding Observations of the Human Rights Committee: Colombia', para. 16, UN Doc CCPR/C/79/Add.76 (1997); 'Concluding Observations of the Human Rights Committee: Sudan', para. 8, UN Doc. CCPR/C/79/Add.85 (1997); *Young* v. *Australia*, Communication No. 941/2000, UN Doc CCPR/C/78/D/941/2000 (2003). But see eg, *Joslin* v. *New Zealand*, Communication No. 902/1999, UN Doc A/57/40 at 214 (2002); n. 42 above, 292.

[44] See S. Davidson, 'Equality and Non-Discrimination', in A. Conte, S. Davidson, and R. Burchill (eds.), *Defining Civil and Political Rights: The Jurisprudence of the United Nations Human Rights Committee*, (Aldershot, UK: Ashgate, 2004), 161, 172–4.

that those provisions sought to avert, extending hate speech bans to encompass sexuality should proceed as a matter of course. Some states have already begun to protect sexual minorities under hate speech bans.[45] In 1997, a resolution of the Committee of Ministers of the Council of Europe (COM-COE) urged a more extensive regime of hate speech bans. Unlike CERD Art. 4 or ICCPR Art. 20(2), it is worded more like a standard non-discrimination norm, employing an open-ended 'other forms' clause, suggesting a potentially unlimited range of individuals or groups for protection under hate speech bans. Sexual minorities would count as obvious candidates. The resolution calls upon member states to combat,

... statements ... which may reasonably be understood as hate speech, or as speech likely to produce the effect of legitimising, spreading or promoting racial hatred, xenophobia, anti-Semitism *or other forms* of discrimination or hatred based on intolerance.[46]

Although that resolution is non-binding, such a statement represents an authoritative synthesis of views, either on the current status, or on a plausible further evolution of their respective states' approaches. To date, the European Court of Human Rights has accepted a principle of wide latitude towards states' decisions to censor speech found to be offensive,[47] and UN Human Rights bodies have advised European states to strengthen further their censorship activity.[48] The more specialized European Commission against Racism and Intolerance (ECRI) has also continued to push for stronger censorship.[49]

Standard non-discrimination norms aim to secure benefits and burdens spread throughout society, without any individuals or groups unfairly treated[50] on grounds

---

[45] See text accompanying n. 14 above.

[46] Recommendation No. R (97) 20 (1997), Principle 1 (my emphasis). See eg, n. 7 above, advocating incorporation of sexual orientation within hate speech bans.

[47] See eg, *Otto-Preminger-Institut* v. *Austria* (Appl. No. 13470/87), ECHR, Ser. A, No. 295-A [1994]; *Wingrove* v. *United Kingdom* (Appl. No. 17419/90), ECHR 60 [1996]. In *Jersild* v. *Denmark* (Appl. No. 15890/88), ECHR, Ser. A, No. 298 [1995], the Court struck down a penalty imposed for the broadcast of racist views solely because they were broadcast within the context of expository journalism, not presented as the views of the journalist or broadcaster. There was no suggestion that the original speakers merited any freedom of speech.

[48] See eg, Conclusions and Recommendations of the Committee on the Elimination of Racial Discrimination, Denmark, UN Doc CERD/C/304/Add.2 (1996), para. A.3, suggesting that, notwithstanding the European Court's judgment, Denmark retained an obligation under CERD to punish the offensive speech in *Jersild*. See generally eg, Committee on the Elimination of Racial Discrimination, General Recommendation 7, Measures to Eradicate Incitement to or Acts of Discrimination (Thirty-second, 1985), UN Doc A/40/18 at 120 (1985), reprinted in Compilation of General Comments and General Recommendations Adopted by Human Rights Treaty Bodies, UN Doc HRI\GEN\1\Rev.6 at 199 (2003).

[49] See eg, ECRI General Policy Recommendation No. 1: Combating racism, xenophobia, anti-Semitism and intolerance, adopted on 4 October 1996; ECRI General Policy Recommendation No. 7: On national legislation to combat racism and racial discrimination, adopted on 13 December 2002; ECRI General Policy Recommendation No. 8: On combating racism while fighting terrorism, adopted on 17 March 2004; ECRI General Policy Recommendation No. 9: On the fight against antisemitism, adopted on 25 June 2004.

[50] On the concept of 'treatment' under non-discrimination norms, see E. Heinze, *The Logic of Equality: Part I* (Aldershot, UK: Ashgate, 2003).

of irrelevant characteristics. The modern non-discrimination norm is amenable to a cumulative jurisprudence because it is cumulative in its conception.[51] To exclude one group holding a claim that is equal in merit to that of an included group, is, itself, to discriminate. Any such disparity impeaches the non-discrimination norm altogether. To expand the norm's scope—as long as that expansion retains the aim of eliminating such recourse to irrelevant characteristics in the distribution of burdens and benefits—is to perfect it, and thus to perfect the whole of the human rights corpus. The same is true of any legitimate extensions of norms of privacy, expression, association, and the like.

That observation cannot be made about hate speech bans. Consider an analogy to persons who are mentally or physically disabled.[52] That analogy reveals flaws in hate speech bans, and distinguishes such bans from rights of privacy, employment, speech, association, and other human rights. Bringing the disabled within the scope of a standard non-discrimination norm may occasionally pose practical problems (for example, questions about expenditure for 'reasonable accommodation'[53]); however, under today's non-discrimination norms, it can no longer be denied that a given handicapped individual who, for all relevant purposes, is equally situated to others in terms of qualifications for such matters as housing, education, or employment, must be accorded equal access.

Similarly, unless their specific health or welfare dictate otherwise, arguments can scarcely be made against their equal rights of expression, association, belief, right to life, and other fundamental rights. Nor can it be claimed that their enjoyment of such rights in any serious way diminishes the rights of others. In a word, taking into account any such pragmatic considerations, the application of 'other status' clauses to encompass the physically or mentally disabled within non-discrimination norms would widely be seen today not merely as feasible, but as a moral imperative.

What would it mean, however, to include the disabled within hate speech bans? Consonant with concepts of social constructionism, advocates of hate speech bans argue that, insofar as derogatory terms remain standard within ordinary speech, their underlying prejudices—Blacks are inferior, Jews are greedy, sexual minorities are dangerous deviants or predatory perverts—are expressly or tacitly disseminated and reinforced as social norms.[54] Similarly, words like 'idiot', 'moron', 'spas', 'spack', 'lame', 'pscyho', 'loony', or 'schizo' construct physical, mental, or psychological disability as inferior, inept, bumbling, misbegotten, or ridiculous.[55] They are so engrained within our language and usage as to seem

---

[51] See Bossuyt in n. 12 above.
[52] See generally eg, 'What is Disability', at *Disability Knowledge and Research*, <htt//www.disabilitykar.net/learningpublication/whatisdisability.html> (last accessed 15 June 2008), noting controversy about the concept of 'disability'.
[53] See n. 50 above, ch. 16.
[54] See eg, Matsuda et al., in n. 3 above.
[55] See eg, J. Shapiro, 'Label falls short for those with mental retardation', *National Public Radio*, 22 January 2007, <http://www.npr.org/templates/story/story.php?storyId=6943699> (last accessed 15 June 2008).

innocuous, not unlike the casual racism or homophobia of earlier times, when words like 'nigger' or 'queer' passed easily in polite society. According to guidelines adopted by the American Psychological Association, 'The use of certain words or phrases can express gender, ethnic, or racial bias, either intentionally or unintentionally. *The same is true of language referring to persons with disabilities*, which in many instances can express negative and disparaging attitudes.'[56]

Nor has disability been the only category generally excluded from protection under hate speech bans. Age is another. Epithets like 'old bag' or 'senile' stigmatize both real and mythical infirmities of age.[57] Consider also physical fitness or appearance: 'fatso' or 'fat slob' degrade those who are overweight (leaving aside questions of when overweight would count as a disability), even through medical conditions beyond their control, such as congenital diabetes.[58] Eddie Murphy's 2006 film *Norbit* was rebuked for courting laughter at the expense of obesity.[59] Had his portrayals featured similarly conceived caricatures of groups, such as racial, ethnic, or religious groups, protected under hate speech bans in European states, serious questions of censorship could have been raised about the film's European distribution.[60] In the words of the COM-COE resolution, such a film can 'reasonably be understood' to be 'spreading or promoting' discriminatory attitudes.

In 1999, the England Football Association manager Glenn Hoddle publicly stated that individual disabilities were justly deserved, through 'bad karma' accumulated in former lives. Hoddle lost his job thereafter,[61] but only as a matter of public relations, due to his high profile, and not through the application of any hate speech ban. Even in the rare cases where physical, mental, or psychological disability has been contemplated for inclusion under hate speech bans,[62] no serious attempt has been made to explain how that inclusion could occur without either massive, or wholly random, censorship of speech. Either whole categories such as physical, mental or psychological disability, age, or overweight, must be excluded; or, if they are included, essentially random, and therefore individually

---

[56] American Psychological Association (APA), 'Guidelines for Non-Handicapping Language in APA Journals', <http://apastyle.apa.org/disabilities.html> (last accessed 15 June 2008), emphasis added.

[57] On age discrimination generally, see eg, American Association of Retired People (AARP), 'Age Discrimination at Work', <http://www.aarp.org/money/careers/jobloss/a2004-04-28-agediscrimination.html> (last accessed 15 June 2008).

[58] See eg, The Obesity Society, http://www.obesity.org/ (last accessed 15 June 2008).

[59] See eg, R. W. Butler, 'Norbit movie review', *Guidelive.com* 9 February 2007, <http://www.guidelive.com/portal/page?_pageid=33,97283&_dad=portal&_schema=PORTAL&item_id=52579>, reprinted from *The Dallas Morning News* (last accessed 15 June 2008).

[60] See text accompanying nn. 46–7 above.

[61] See eg, 'Sport: football: Hoddle sacked', *BBC Online Network*, 3 February 1999, <http://news.bbc.co.uk/1/hi/sport/football/270194.stm> (last accessed 15 June 2008).

[62] See eg, T. Branigan and A. Travis, 'Straw moves to ban incitement against gays', *The Guardian*, 9 October 2007, <http://www.guardian.co.uk/gayrights/story/0,,2186690,00.html> (last accessed 15 June 2008).

discriminatory, choices must be made about which members of those groups will
and will not be protected from terms so ubiquitously used.

A cardinal aim of hate speech bans is to protect groups or individuals with scant
political influence. While ethnic or religious minorities in several Western
countries have organized visible political movements, the disabled are often
isolated; limited in their ability even to associate effectively, let alone to mobilize
strategic lobbying efforts. They are often restricted in their ability to earn, let
alone to pool resources, and can generally direct few of their resources towards
activities like anti-hate speech campaigns, given the ongoing and more pressing
expenses of primary care.[63] It would come as no surprise nowadays for leading
celebrities or commentators to shun terms like 'nigger', 'dirty Jew', or 'queer',
while directing terms like 'idiot' or 'moron' at leading political figures, indeed in
the belief that they are speaking in the same socially critical vein. Obvious
examples have included US President George W. Bush or Vice President Dan
Quayle, not to mention countless uses of such terms, sometimes passionately,
sometimes nonchalantly, in everyday speech.[64] The problem arises not from the
prospect of offence caused to a Bush or a Quayle. Rather, the problem is that such
terms offend all persons whose psychological conditions are thereby degraded.[65]

That shift in focus—from the disparagement of a classification targeted against
someone belonging to that classification, to its use against someone not belonging
to it—requires some explanation, as it may appear to change considerably the
nature of the hate speech concerned. As James Weinstein, for example, has
commented on a previous statement of my views,

It is very rare nowadays that anyone, at least in the US or UK, would use a term to
knowingly disparage the mentally retarded or physically handicapped. Nor is there a
massive amount of hate speech readily available on the Internet against the mentally
retarded or the physically disabled, as there is with respect to blacks, Jews and gays. There
is not nearly the same reason to try to use the force of law to eradicate 'hate speech' against
these groups. People nowadays simply do not hate the mentally retarded or physically
disabled in the way that too many people hate blacks, Jews, or gays. I think the same is
true of the elderly. There may be more hostility towards this group, but nothing like that
directed towards people on the basis of race, ethnicity or religion. Moreover and more
significantly, though there may be cases of people using 'fighting words' against the
elderly, the disabled, or the obese in the street when the get annoyed, there is to my

---

[63] At a global level, most people with disabilities lack the basic services they require. See eg,
Committee on Economic, Social and Cultural Rights, General Comment No. 5: Persons with
disabilities (Eleventh session, 1994), UN Doc E/1995/22 at 19 (1995), reprinted in Compilation of
General Comments and General Recommendations Adopted by Human Rights Treaty Bodies, UN
Doc HRI/GEN/1/Rev.6 at 24 (2003).

[64] Recall the popular jibe long directed against Bush, 'Somewhere in Texas a Village is missing an
idiot!' See eg, M. Honigsbaum, 'Divided we stand', *The Observer*, 17 October 2004, <http://
observer.guardian.co.uk/review/story/0,6903,1329057,00.html> (last accessed 15 June 2008).

[65] To draw an analogy, it is not merely Falstaff, but Jews who are smeared when Mistress Page
disparages Falstaff's deceit by calling him 'A Herod of Jewry'. W. Shakespeare, *The Merry Wives of
Windsor* II. i. 20.

knowledge no hate literature against these groups at all, and even if there is some, it is nothing like the virulent tracts directed against Jews, Blacks and sexual minorities.[66]

Weinstein's objection is empirical. There is no evidence of widespread hostility towards the mentally or physically disabled, elderly, or obese, comparable to that against certain racial, ethnic, religious, or sexual categories. Therefore, by definition, there can be no substantial causal link between derogatory language against those groups and any such hostility.

If that objection were correct governments, courts and human rights bodies would endorse hate speech bans only if some threshold level of hostility against protected group could be demonstrated. In *Otto-Preminger-Institut* v. *Austria*,[67] however, the European Court of Human Rights rejected any such condition placed on a state's prerogative to combat intolerance through censorship. The Court did not require any showing of systemic hostility or discrimination towards Roman Catholics in Austria, who have long constituted the overwhelming numerical and socio-cultural majority of the country's population.[68] The prosecution was originally brought under traditional blasphemy principles, and not a hate speech ban in the modern sense. The European Court upheld the conviction on general grounds of overall tolerance,[69] and not on grounds of any *sui generis* exceptions to free speech principles, specifically created for blasphemy laws.

In essence, the Court treated anti-Catholic expression as an evil in itself, evil simply on grounds of its expression of intolerance, and not merely as evil on the condition that some independent history, or future possibility, of material detriment be adduced. Nor, despite some criticism of *Otto-Preminger-Institut,* is that decision an aberration. The Court reiterated its view in *Wingrove* v. *United Kingdom,* in which it, once again, upheld censorship on grounds that the material in question offended Christians or Christian beliefs. No international human rights body has recommended any principles that would contradict or limit such an approach. (The censorship in *Otto-Preminger-Institut* and *Wingrove* were not 'hate' materials in any straightforward sense. They were merely art-house films, which, respectively, lampooned and sexualized Christian symbols.)

Nor could these human rights bodies easily do otherwise, once they had started down the road of endorsing hate speech bans. To require threshold showings of

---

[66] Private communication of 24 December 2007.

[67] *Otto-Preminger-Institut* v. *Austria* (Appl. No. 13470/87), ECHR, Ser. A, No. 295-A [1994].

[68] According to the *Encyclopaedia Britannica,* 'More than four-fifths of Austrians are Christian. The overwhelming majority of Christians are adherents to Roman Catholicism; Protestants (mainly Lutherans) and Orthodox Christians form smaller groups. Islam has a small but important following, mainly among the Bosniac and Turk populations. Vienna's Jewish population, which was all but destroyed between 1938 and 1945, has increased steadily since that time but remains tiny. More than one-tenth of the population is nonreligious.' *Britannica Online,* <http://www.britannica.com/eb/article-274941/Austria> (last accessed 15 June 2008).

[69] See ECHR, Ser. A, No. 295-A [1994], para. 47, interpreting ECHR Art. 9 as protecting 'the religious feelings of believers' from 'provocative portrayals of objects of religious veneration'.

some sufficient number of acts of hostility would entail a 'more-victim-than-thou' jurisprudence, which, far from combating discrimination, would only entrench it. Intolerant attitudes may disadvantage the designated groups or individuals in ways subtler than concerted campaigns of hate. For example, if someone who is mentally or physically disabled is denied housing or employment despite possessing the competence to fulfil all requirements—precisely as if a person belonging to a racial, ethnic, religious, or sexual minority is denied—it may be impossible in any given case to determine whether or to what degree overall social attitudes were a contributing factor.

Unsurprisingly, advocates of hate speech bans have not insisted upon rigorously empirical evidence to demonstrate links between broader attitudes and discrete detriments suffered in particular instances. The crucial premise of hate speech bans has never been that hate speech *demonstrably* causes detriment to the disparaged groups, as no such evidence has been adduced for longstanding, stable, and prosperous democracies,[70] no more than it has been shown that violent films promote social violence, or that pornography augments incidents of rape. Rather, advocates of hate speech bans proceed on the broader assumption that hate speech *might plausibly* cause such detriment, indeed in ways which are often subtle and pernicious, and therefore not amenable to precise empirical observation.

Nor can it be argued that Blacks, Jews, or sexual minorities have more burdened histories. Nazism showed how the physically or mentally disabled, along with all the propaganda—hate speech—concerning their threats to Aryan purity and perfectability, led them to extermination on grounds of their putative sub-humanity.[71] Might Chenu's attackers not just as eagerly have assaulted someone mentally or physically disabled, or someone elderly or obese? Can anyone argue that such an attack would not have been motivated by a cultural arsenal stockpiled with age-old barbs of 'idiot', 'spas', 'old bag', and 'fat slob'? It would require a leap of sociological imagination to argue that such an assault would be ignited by a consciousness promoted by hate speech when racially motivated, but not when motivated by stereotypes of mental or physical condition.

At first blush, one might wonder whether such disparities between classifications included within, and excluded from, hate speech bans are insurmountable. One might argue, in the spirit of the COM-COE resolution, that *any* actual or potential victims of discrimination should be protected by hate speech bans. But what would it mean to extend the bans so widely? We can safely assume that the films, newspaper or magazine articles, radio, and television shows or websites in

---

[70] Despite their advocacy of hate speech bans, Richard Delgado and Jean Stefancic have inadvertently noted that racist and other discriminatory incidents had *increased* in Europe after hate speech bans were introduced. 'A Shifting Balance: Freedom of Expression and Hate-Speech Restriction' (1993) 78 *Iowa L. Rev.* 737, 745. See critically, See 'Viewpoint Absolutism and Hate Speech' in n. 9 above. 577–8.

[71] See eg, Disability Rights Commission, 'The Holocaust—perfection is the issue, says Disability Rights Commission', 26 January 2001, <http://83.137.212.42/sitearchive/DRC/newsroom/news_releases/2001/the_holocaust_-_perfection_is.html> (last accessed 15 June 2008).

which terms like 'idiot' and 'moron' appear—the same media that would no longer use 'nigger' or 'queer' in non-ironic or non-critical contexts—are innumerable. Remarkably broad censorship of both the media and everyday speech, backed up by legal penalties, would be required. Hate speech bans can only succeed either through enormous measures of censorship or through discriminatory selection of target categories or individuals.

To date, of course, the latter course has been chosen. Few have seriously proposed massive censorship. Rather, leading proponents of hate speech bans, often justifying bans as necessary means of listening to society's unheard, excluded voices, have generally excluded physical, mental, or psychological disability, age, or overweight from the categories for which they seek protection.[72] Indeed, so common is the use of terms degrading to members of these groups that proponents of bans on racial and ethnic hate speech unwittingly use these terms. For instance, Richard Delgado, a leading Critical Race Theorist and passionate advocate of penalties for racist speech, has used the word 'schizophrenic' derisively to mean 'inept',[73] As Delgado states elsewhere, 'we *are* our current stock of narratives, and they us'.[74]

It might be argued that, in view of increasing numbers of vocal elderly and overweight, they are now able to defend themselves in the public arena. However, the relative political stature of an otherwise numerical minority has not generally been deemed by advocates of hate speech bans to constitute grounds for excluding the affected members from protection. Again, in *Otto-Preminger-Institut,* the fact that Roman Catholicism has long been Austria's overwhelmingly dominant faith, far from preventing censorship, was cited by Austrian authorities, unchallenged by the European Court, to suggest that there was *ipso facto* 'a pressing social need for the preservation of religious peace'.[75]

Hate speech bans collide, then, with either of the following two principles of human rights law. (1) If they are narrowly drawn so as to limit their application, they violate the principle of non-discrimination by censoring or punishing some offences, while permitting similar offences against equally vulnerable persons. (2) If they are broadly drawn to include all target groups or individuals, they potentially capture large quantities of expression. In applying the Principle of Extant Rights, then, my concerns about the inclusion of sexual minorities within hate speech bans stems not from any specific characteristics of sexual minorities, but from the inadequacies of hate speech bans themselves. The fact that some or

---

[72] See eg, Matsuda et al., in n. 3 above; Delgado in n. 3 above.

[73] See n. 3 above, 15.

[74] R. Delgado and J. Stefancic, 'Images of the Outsider in American Law and Culture,' in R. Delgado and J. Stefancic (eds.), *Critical Race Theory: The Cutting Edge*, 2nd edn. (Philadelphia, PA: Temple UP, 2000), 131, 225, 229, reprinted as 'Images of the Outsider in American Law and Culture: Can Free Expression Remedy Systemic Social Ills?'(1992) 77 *Cornell L. Rev.* 1258, original emphasis.

[75] ECHR, Ser. A, No. 295-A [1994], para. 52. See R. A. Lawson and H. G. Schermers, *Leading Cases of the European Court of Human Rights*, 2nd edn. (Leiden: Ars Aequi Libri, 1999), 573.

all sexual minorities *might* be amenable to inclusion under hate speech bans provides no moral compensation for the exclusion of other equally vulnerable groups or individuals. Sexual minorities, or any groups—racial, ethnic, religious—cannot legitimately accept the protections of such norms within a framework of *fundamental, universal rights,* when equally vulnerable groups or individuals are excluded.

4. Some Objections and Replies

Hate speech bans may be required as temporary measures within weak or newly emerging democracies, or under legitimately declared states of emergency. Such circumstances cannot, however, overcome either the bans' discriminatory character. Within longstanding, stable and prosperous democracies, it becomes questionable whether sexual minorities, or any other groups, should be seeking protection from norms that are fundamentally exclusive of some of society's most vulnerable.

I cannot examine all possible objections to my criticism of hate speech bans, as any such discussion would require a full-blown analysis of the overall problem of hate speech bans, which has been the subject of countless scholarly studies. It is worthwhile, however, to note some concerns arising specifically from an understanding of cumulative jurisprudence as a central instrument of rights for sexual minorities.

An anonymous reviewer of this piece objected that I have noted 'no ground peculiar to sexual minorities' use of hate speech, which ... makes them particularly vulnerable to its misapplication'.[76] That objection effectively makes the following assumption: if some groups or individuals, such as sexual minorities, are satisfied with the protections they can receive from hate speech bans, the bans are therefore legitimate *for those groups.* Yet that is precisely the assumption I am rejecting. The view of human rights I am assuming is the opposite: even if a hate speech ban could be both drafted and applied so as to protect some groups, or some individuals, in ways generally seen as beneficial, we would still be contradicting the founding assumptions of the leading human rights norms—certainly, of all those that have been central to rights of sexual minorities—if we were to maintain that a norm is legitimate even if it cannot be enjoyed equally by all similarly situated persons.[77]

The premise of international human rights since the Universal Declaration of Human Rights (UDHR)[78] has been that norms of the human rights corpus can

---

[76] Report of anonymous reviewer for publication in the *International Journal of Human Rights,* delivered to me via electronic communication on 2 August 2007.

[77] See E. Heinze, 'Even-handedness and Human Rights: A Legitimacy Test for States, NGOs, IGOs and Public Debate' (2008) 21 *Harv. Hum. Rts. J.* 7.

[78] G.A. res. 217A (III), UN Doc A/810 at 71 (1948).

claim universal legitimacy only insofar as they can, in principle, be framed and applied so as to encompass all human beings.[79] For sexual minorities, or any other actual or potential beneficiary group, to claim protection of norms that cannot be extended to other equally vulnerable groups should prompt the gravest ethical concerns about whether such norms properly belong within the international human rights corpus (except, again, as temporary measures in unstable states), despite the fact that hate speech bans have been endorsed within international human rights law.[80]

The same reviewer objected that '[n]one of the international laws ... or indeed national hate speech laws that exist internationally, defines every insult or offence as hate speech. To do so would be ridiculous. Yet [Heinze] argues ... that every insult against an overweight or disabled or elderly should be considered hate speech as the only alternative is to discriminate selectively, which is anathema to human rights principles.'[81] I have not had to argue, however, that *every* such insult would have to count as hate speech. No such broad claim is required to demonstrate the discriminatory nature of hate speech bans. It suffices to ask whether there is *any* body of insults that can be covered under leading international and regional norms without either discriminatory application, whereby *equally dangerous or hurtful* terms go unregulated, or highly rigorous censorship.

Even avid proponents of, for example, race-based hate speech bans, do not generally insist that 'every' racist insult be banned, for the simple reason that insults are context-bound, and not amenable to exhaustive enumeration. 'Queer bastard' might be benign if used, for example, in an ironic, comical or in-group situation. Meanwhile, 'funny gay man' might be offensive in an overtly anti-gay context. In view of the grey areas that render many contexts ambiguous, neither I nor anyone else could provide any conceptually exhaustive account of what counts as 'every' insult against any given category of persons. The view that '[t]o do so would be ridiculous' is, then, precisely the problem. Any serious step towards non-discriminatory application of hate speech bans, even in cases of overall parity in the level of offence to the targeted group or individual ('easy cases'), would indeed be a step towards a 'ridiculously' censorious regime, whereby much freedom of speech would be exercised not as a right, but as a contingent government concession. Yet any step away from that order of censorship becomes a step towards discriminating between protected and unprotected victims of speech acts that are otherwise equally offensive.

One might also raise a more pragmatic objection. Consider the following argument: 'Perhaps terms like 'idiot' or 'old bag' are indeed difficult to eradicate. However, the fact that we cannot protect all individuals does not mean we should protect none. We do not live in an ideal world. We must achieve what we can,

---

[79] UDHR Arts. 1, 2, 7, 28.
[80] See nn. 46–9 above.
[81] Report of anonymous reviewer. See n. 76 above.

even if we cannot achieve everything.' That objection might carry some weight in many other areas of law (it may be legitimate to renovate Hyde Park even if there is not enough money to clean up St James Park, or to catch more speeding motorists on the M1 than on the M4), but raises grave concerns for human rights. By analogy, there is no doctrine of human rights law which states that torture of some is justified as long as torture of most can be prevented; or that privacy, or freedom of conscience, are justified for some, even if they cannot be extended to all (such results may often occur in practice, for reasons of material constraint or political will, but are never justified by any principle of human rights law). Everyday legislation on ordinary issues must certainly deal in horse-trading and compromises, which presumably underlies much routine legislative activity: 'We'll agree to reduce taxes on the wealthy if you agree to reduce them on the poor'; 'We'll agree to raise the speed limit if you agree to build safety ramps'. That reasoning cannot transpose *simpliciter* to human rights law.[82] Even under a validly declared state of emergency, we could hardly adopt approaches such as, 'We don't have enough money to protect the Catholics, so we'll just protect the Protestants' or 'If you agree not to torture the children, we'll allow you to torture the adults'. One reason for the credibility of such fundamental rights to life, privacy, expression, and non-discrimination is that, despite breaches in practice, there is absolutely no conceptual difficulty in postulating their universal application in principle. Insofar as hate speech bans are not, and cannot be, extended to protect all vulnerable individuals or groups, they violate that principle of universality.

Where does this all leave François Chenu? In calling for coherence in human rights, does one risk overlooking some of the concrete problems that hate speech bans might help to solve? Not at all. Another error among advocates of hate speech bans is their frequent failure to distinguish between, on the one hand, a broader arena of public discourse—the arena of radio, television, film, the press, or the speaker in the public common—and, on the other hand, invective specifically and immediately directed by certain individuals against other, more-or-less specifically targeted individuals in face-to-face situations.[83] Opponents of hate speech bans rarely deny that offensive speech of the second type may legitimately be proscribed. In the United States, the doctrine of 'fighting words' allows the punishment of personally targeted insults in live, hostile encounters.[84] In principle, the protections afforded by that traditional doctrine are far broader than those afforded by modern hate speech ban; they allow punishment of *any* kind of strongly offensive remark, which may include, yet need not be limited to, insults on grounds of race, ethnicity, religion, or other such identity. Certainly,

---

[82] See generally eg, R. Dworkin, *Taking Rights Seriously* (London: Duckworth, 1977), distinguishing between concepts of 'policy' and 'principle').

[83] See eg, Matsuda et al., in n. 3 above.

[84] See *Chaplinsky* v. *New Hampshire* 315 US 568, 571–3 (1942). See eg, 'Viewpoint Absolutism and Hate Speech' in n. 9 above, 575–7.

traditional bans on 'fighting words' require periodic review as to their content or application, in view of changing social conditions. However, in itself, an approach like the US Supreme Court's upholding of bans on fighting words contains all that is required to protect *all* individuals from direct and unduly hostile verbal assaults. Moreover, as to actual crimes, involving non-speech acts such as killing, battery, theft, rape, or vandalism, the US Supreme Court has found that no violation of free speech arises when hate speech is used as evidence of a hate-based criminal motive, or that crimes motivated by racial or other group-based animus may be punished more harshly than others.[85]

Again, my focus in this article has been on stable, longstanding, and prosperous democracies. What makes a democracy sufficiently stable, longstanding and prosperous to be able to abolish hate speech bans? There will always be room for debate in borderline cases. But, as a general matter, Western European states certainly fill the bill. At the very least, some sufficiently stable, longstanding, and prosperous democracy is presupposed by any binding civil rights instrument, as suggested (1) by the inclusion, in modern instruments, of derogations clauses, authorizing suspension of certain rights during legitimately declared states of emergency,[86] as well as (2) the judicial application of derogation principles to older instruments.[87] Derogation principles effectively require that a state guarantee rights unless it is rendered materially unable to do so.[88] Certainly, many states, in Europe and internationally, albeit not fully stable, longstanding and prosperous democracies, are parties to the ICCPR or the European Convention on Human Rights (ECHR), without regularly invoking the derogations clauses. However, as to weaker or emerging democracies, the totality of their political, social, and economic standards would warrant them to invoke those clauses against political or social unrest with far greater latitude (both under the ICCPR 'proportionality' principle and under the ECHR 'margin of appreciation' doctrine) than would be expected for the wealthier and more stable Western European members.[89]

It is stable, longstanding, and prosperous democracies that I have had in mind in noting that no correlation has been shown between levels of hate speech and incidence of hate crime. However, it is by no means certain that such correlation is absent today in weaker or newly emerging democracies. In some emerging

---

[85] See *Wisconsin* v. *Mitchell* 508 US 476 (1993).

[86] European Convention on Human Rights (ECHR) Art. 15; International Covenant on Civil and Political Rights (ICCPR) Art. 4.

[87] See eg, *Korematsu* v. *United States* 323 US 214 (1944), finding that national security may constitute a compelling government interest in abridging a constitutionally protected right.

[88] See ECHR Art. 1; ICCPR Art. 2(2).

[89] Thus, for example, the UN Human Rights Committee's reference to 'exigency' inevitably presupposes levels of available resources to prevent violence or harm. Human Rights Committee, General Comment 29: States of Emergency (Art. 4), UN Doc CCPR/C/21/Rev.1/Add.11 (2001), reprinted in Compilation of General Comments and General Recommendations Adopted by Human Rights Treaty Bodies, UN Doc HRI/GEN/1/Rev.6 at 186 (2003).

democracies, for example, is has been suggested that a newly liberalized press can harshly impact vulnerable groups without the democratic institutions or trad-itions, or the sheer resources, required to redress the effects.[90] Meanwhile, in such societies, attitudes towards sexual minorities have often remained harsh and have even worsened.[91] Accordingly, I have refrained from taking a position on hate speech in such societies. Bans may indeed be required where some likely causation from hate speech to hate crime can be shown. Overall, however, the growing strength of democratic institutions and practices, along with the resources to protect vulnerable groups, should be displayed in a society's gradual ability to reduce its reliance on hate speech bans.

Today, as opposed to just a few decades ago, the increasing disdain for persons who casually drop epithets like 'nigger', 'dirty Jew', or 'queer' gives testimony not so much to the efficacy of prosecutions, which have scarcely had any systematic character in Europe, but to the fact that, in essentially open, liberal democracies, maintaining faith in the free and robust exchange of ideas,[92] informal, social pressures have always had the potential to effectuate needed change without the need for coercive laws which, at best, accomplish nothing, and, at worst operate in unjustifiably discriminatory ways. In general, sexual minorities have been right to follow a cumulative jurisprudence—to insist that norms of even-handedness intrinsic to the very idea of human rights be rigorously implemented and respected in practice. However, cumulative jurisprudence is only as worthy as the norms to which it is applied. Hate speech bans, despite their wide acceptance within international law and in most national jurisdictions, raise grave concerns about both their conceptual and practical compatibility with the norms and principles of human rights law.

5. Conclusion

A cumulative jurisprudence of human rights has been and remains an important means of advancing the interests of sexual minorities within the dominant con-temporary framework of international, regional, and national human rights regimes. Even non-discrimination norms not originally conceived to apply to sexual minorities have been interpreted to extend to them with little conceptual or practical difficulty. That does not mean, however, that it should be applied willy-nilly to any norm that may emerge within human rights regimes. Hate speech

---

[90] See eg, Conclusions and recommendations of the Committee on the Elimination of Racial Discrimination: Bulgaria, para. 8–9, UN Doc CERD/C/304/Add.29 (1997), expressing concern about hate speech and hate crimes in Bulgaria.

[91] See European Parliament resolution of 26 April 2007 on Homophobia in Europe, P6_TA (2007)0167, with special emphasis on Poland, <http://www.europarl.europa.eu/sides/getDoc. do?Type=TA&Reference=P6-TA-2007-0167&language=EN> (last accessed 15 June 2008).

[92] For a classic judicial statement, see eg, *Whitney* v. *California* 274 US 357 (1927), Brandeis J. concurring.

bans are by definition conceived as limitations on fundamental rights of speech and expression. They cannot be applied in a non-discriminatory way without raising serious questions about the fundamental status of free speech. Again, any step away from discriminatory application becomes a step towards massive censorship; and any step away from massive censorship becomes a step towards discriminatory application. Either hate speech bans must arbitrarily exclude persons who are just as vulnerable as those who enjoy protection, or the bans must extend so far as to undermine the right of free speech and expression. Hate speech bans have no place within longstanding, stable, and prosperous democracies, which have ample means at their disposal to protect sexual minorities and other vulnerable groups from hate crime and discrimination, without having to impose inevitably arbitrary limits on speech.

PART III

INCITEMENT TO RELIGIOUS HATRED AND RELATED TOPICS

15

Blasphemy and Incitement to Religious Hatred: Free Speech Dogma and Doctrine

Ivan Hare

Religion has been central to discussions of freedom of expression since the first sustained writings in English about the extent of free speech, whether in Milton's *Areopagitica*, Locke's *A Letter Concerning Toleration*, or Mill's *On Liberty*.[1] Indeed, it is arguable that by removing the sole source of religious authority, the Reformation of the Christian church in the sixteenth century was responsible for provoking many of the founding documents of political philosophy. However, two recent legal developments make it fruitful to reflect again on the relationship between religion and freedom of expression in English law. They are: the entry into force of primary legislation criminalizing incitement to religious hatred;[2] and Parliament's decision to abolish the offence of blasphemy.[3] The structure of this chapter is as follows. In Part 1, I set out the historical basis for the common law protection of (certain) religious doctrines from criticism. In Part 2, I explain how the two developments described above came about. In Part 3, I assess the consistency of these developments with free speech principle.

1. The Historical Relationship between Speech and the Protection of Religion: Blasphemy

The relationship between public law and religion in the United Kingdom is large and complex with many aspects which I do not propose to address here. For

---

[1] J. Milton, *Areopagitica and Education* Ed. G. H. Sabine (Arlington Heights, IL: Harlan Davidson, 1951); J. Locke, *The Second Treatise of Civil Government and a Letter Concerning Toleration* (Oxford: Basil Blackwell, 1946); and J. S. Mill, *On Liberty* (Harmondsworth: Penguin, 1974).

[2] The relevant parts of the Racial and Religious Hatred Act 2006 (amending parts of the Public Order Act 1986) came into force on 1 October 2007.

[3] The Criminal Justice and Immigration Act 2008, s. 79 (which entered into force on 8 July 2008). The repeal followed the decision in *R (on the application of Stephen Green)* v. *The City of Westminster Magistrates' Court & Ors* [2007] EWHC 2785 (Admin) (the *'Jerry Springer'* case) which is described in further detail below. Blasphemy is used to cover both oral and written (known as blasphemous libel) forms.

example, the Church of England remains the established Church with the sovereign at its head as Defender of the Faith. Non-communicant members of the Church of England continue to be subject to certain disabilities in relation to succession to the throne.[4] Also, despite recent reforms, certain senior members of the Church of England retain seats as of right in the upper house of the legislature, the House of Lords.[5] These matters are beyond the scope of this paper as their impact on freedom of expression is generally oblique.[6] On the other hand, laws on incitement to religious hatred and blasphemy have a direct impact on the exercise of free speech rights. The two topics are also related in another way since one of the ostensible reasons for passing the incitement law was to remove the discrimination between different faiths which meant that only the established Church was protected by the law of blasphemy and other faiths could be subject to scurrilous abuse without criminal liability.

Offences against religion were originally exclusively within the jurisdiction of the ecclesiastical courts and papal canon law. They only attracted the attention of the legislature and the common law courts at the time of the Reformation when ultimate secular and religious authority was unified in the King.[7] For some time after the Reformation, the list of religious offences was long. Along with blasphemy, Blackstone included apostasy, heresy, 'profane and common swearing and cursing' and, finally, 'witchcraft, conjuration, inchantment or sorcery'.[8] Blasphemy was one of four types of libel which were subject to criminal punishment. The others were seditious libel, obscene libel, and criminal defamatory libel and are discussed further below.[9]

The first recorded case of an indictment for blasphemy before the ordinary courts is *R* v. *Taylor*.[10] Taylor has been described as a 'blasphemer of unusual thoroughness' and the particulars of his offence included statements that 'Christ is a whoremaster, and religion is a Cheat ... I am Christ's younger brother and that

---

[4] Act of Settlement 1700, ss. 2 and 3.

[5] C. Smith, 'Bishops in the House of Lords: a Critical Analysis' [2008] *Pub. L.* 490.

[6] The modern relationship between church and state in the United Kingdom is discussed in detail in F. Cranmer, J. Lucas, and R. Morris, *Church and State: A Mapping Exercise* (London: Constitution Unit, 2006). For the position in Scotland, see C. Munro, 'Does Scotland Have an Established Church?' (1997) 4 *Eccl. L. J.* 639. The existence of an established church does not of itself violate Art. 9 of the European Convention on Human Rights (ECHR) (*Darby* v. *Sweden* (1990) 13 EHRR 774, para. 45).

[7] W. S. Holdsworth, *History of English Law, Vol. VIII* (London: Methuen, 1903–26), 402. For the history of blasphemy before 1660, see G. D. Nokes, *A History of the Crime of Blasphemy* (London: Sweet & Maxwell, 1928), 1–42.

[8] W. Blackstone, *Commentaries on the Laws of England*, 8th edn. (Oxford: Clarendon Press, 1778), Book IV, ch 4. Blackstone defined blasphemy, ibid., 59, as: 'denying [the Almighty's] being or providence; or by contumelious reproaches to our saviour Christ. Whither also may be referred all profane scoffing at the Holy Scripture, or exposing it to contempt or ridicule. These are offences at common law punishable by fine and imprisonment, or other infamous corporal punishment: for Christianity is part of the laws of England'.

[9] See notes 66–9 below and associated text.

[10] (1676) 3 Keb 607; 84 ER 906.

Christ is a bastard'.[11] Chief Justice Hale explained the jurisdiction of the Court of King's Bench over such matters in the following terms:

These words, though of ecclesiastical cognisance, yet that religion is a cheat, tends to the dissolution of all government, and therefore punishable here, and so of contumelious reproaches to God, or the religion established. An indictment lay for saying the Protestant religion was a fiction for taking away religion, all obligations to government by oaths etc ceaseth, and Christian religion is a part of the law itself, therefore injuries to God are punishable as to the King, or any common person.[12]

Several different rationales are discernible for the closeness of the relationship between established religion and the state. One element of the justification for treating blasphemy so harshly was the instrumental value of the Protestant religion to the functioning of the legal system. As Hale CJ makes clear, if an individual is prepared to say that the Protestant religion is a fiction, he would be under no obligation to give truthful testimony in court simply because he has sworn on the Bible. The use of oaths was crucial to the validity of a number of forms of legal document outside court too.[13]

However, the second rationale is the more significant. If the state is so closely identified with the religion it has established and the head of state is also the head of that church, then to subvert the doctrine of the established church is to undermine the authority of the state itself. This is the origin of the relationship between blasphemous libel and sedition. One further particular characteristic of the relationship merits explanation and that is the notion that the citizen's secular and religious loyalty ought not to be divided. In *A Letter Concerning Religious Toleration*, Locke was keen to promote a distinction between secular and religious authority, at least as far as the differences between sects within the Protestant religion were concerned.[14] As between Protestant sects, secular

---

[11] A. Cromartie, *Sir Matthew Hale 1609–1676: Law, Religion and Natural Philosophy* (Cambridge: CUP, 1995), 74–5.

[12] The other report of *Taylor's case* (1 Vent 293; 86 ER 189) states: 'Christianity is parcel of the laws of England; and therefore to reproach the Christian religion is to speak in subversion of the law.' It has been pointed out that Hale relied on an inaccurate translation of one of his authorities (C. S. Kenney, 'The Evolution of the Law of Blasphemy' (1922) 1 *Camb. L. J.* 127, 130–1). Cromartie also quotes Hale from the Fairhurst Papers in Lambeth Palace Library on the power to suppress religious dissent: 'the reasonableness and indeed necessity of this coercion in matter of religion is apparent for the concerns of religion and the civil state are so twisted one with another that confusion and disorder an[d] anarchy in the former must of necessity introduce confusion and dissolution of the latter', Cromartie (ibid.), 177. See further, W. Hawkins, *A Treatise of the Pleas of the Crown*, 8th edn. (London: S. Sweet, 1824) Bk. 1, 358.

[13] 'Promises, covenants, and oaths, which are the bonds of human society, can have no hold upon an atheist' J. Locke, *Concerning Toleration* (n. 1 above), 156. See further, Blackstone (n. 8 above), 43. It has been argued that maintaining the authority of the oaths used in commercial activity among an itinerant and unruly population was a more important function of blasphemy than ensuring religious conformity in medieval Germany (D. Nash, 'Analyzing the History of Religious Crime: Models of "Passive" and "Active" Blasphemy Since the Medieval Period' (2007) 41 *J. Soc. Hist.* 5).

[14] J. Locke, *Concerning Toleration*, n. 1 above.

authority (represented by the magistrate) ought not to interfere in 'articles of faith, or forms of worship' since secular authority was enforced through penalties and such coercive measures are not likely to persuade the individual to alter his fundamental beliefs.[15] However, in Locke's view, the state retained a legitimate interest in suppressing those who enter another religion which involves believers in 'deliver[ing] themselves up to the protection and service of another prince'.[16] Locke illustrated his point by reference to the 'Mahometan' who 'acknowledges himself bound to yield blind obedience to the Mufti of Constantinople, who himself is entirely obedient to the Ottoman Emperor'.[17] However, this rationale is plainly equally applicable to Catholics who were said to bind themselves to the ultimate authority of Rome in preference to the secular and religious sovereign in England.

As the values of the Enlightenment spread and relative religious stability returned to England, the breadth of the definition of blasphemy was narrowed to some extent.[18] As such, sober and temperate discussions of the basic tenets of Christianity and even the denial of the truth of the Christian religion or the scriptures (if carried out with restraint) were permissible.[19] The limit of tolerance was reached where it was perceived that criticism of Christianity or the Church of England tended to 'endanger the peace then and there, to deprave public morality generally, to shake the fabric of society, and to be a cause of civil strife'.[20]

Any thought that the offence of blasphemy had lapsed through desuetude in the later part of the last century was scotched when the conservative campaigner Mary Whitehouse brought a successful private prosecution for blasphemy against the editor and publishers of *Gay News* in 1977.[21] Mrs Whitehouse objected to the

---

[15] Ibid., 128.   [16] Ibid., 155.   [17] Ibid., 156.

[18] Lord Cozens-Hardy MR in *In re Bowman* [1915] 2 ch. 447, 462, commented on the decision in *Ramsay* (n. 19 below) and stated that mitigation of the rigours of the offence was required to ensure that figures such as Charles Darwin and Thomas Huxley were not prosecuted. In parallel with this development, the penalties for religious offences were reduced (eg, the writ of *De Haeretico Comburendo* (by which heretics were burned) was abolished by 29 Car. 2, c. 9 and the Ecclesiastical Courts Act 1813 abolished excommunication (with certain exceptions)). At the same time, a long series of Acts removed various disabilities which had formerly affected non-communicants of the Church of England (such as the Toleration Act 1689 (for dissenting Protestants), the Roman Catholic Emancipation Act 1829 and the Religious Disabilities Act 1846 (for Jews)).

[19] *R* v. *Hetherington* (1841) 4 St Tr NS 563, 590 (Lord Denman CJ) and *R* v. *Ramsay and Foote* (1883) 15 Cox CC 231, 236 (Lord Coleridge CJ).

[20] *Bowman* v. *Secular Society Ltd* [1917] AC 406, 466–7, per Lord Sumner. Lord Coleridge CJ in *Ramsay* drew the line more restrictively (ibid.), 236: 'A wilful intention to pervert, insult, and mislead others, by means of licentious and contumelious abuse applied to sacred subjects, or by wilful misrepresentations or wilful sophistry, calculated to mislead the ignorant and the unwary, is the criterion and test of guilt.' As its title suggests, *Bowman* did not concern a prosecution for blasphemy, but whether a bequest to the Secular Society (whose aim was to promote the philosophy that human conduct should be based upon natural knowledge, and not upon super-natural belief) was valid. The House of Lords held that it was (Lord Finlay LC, 423; Lord Dunedin, 433; Lord Parker of Waddington, 445–6; and Lord Buckmaster, 470). Gifts for non-Christian purposes had not always been upheld in the past. For example, a gift for the advancement of the Jewish religion was held to be unlawful in *De Costa* v. *De Paz* (1754) 2 Swanst 487.

[21] The history of the offence was traced in detail by Roskill LJ in the Court of Appeal (*R* v. *Lemon* [1979] QB 10, 18G–24C). In the House of Lords, Lord Diplock referred to blasphemy's 'long and at

publication of the poem, 'The Love that Dares to Speak its Name' by Professor James Kirkup, which was accompanied by a drawing of Christ. The publication was described as portraying in explicit detail acts of sodomy and fellatio with the body of Christ immediately after the moment of his death and ascribing to Christ promiscuous homosexual practices with the Apostles and other men during his lifetime. In *Whitehouse* v. *Lemon*, the House of Lords confirmed the continued existence and breadth of the offence at common law, although there was some difference of opinion about its definition.[22] The majority of the House affirmed the convictions on the ground that there was no requirement that the prosecution should prove any intention beyond that of publishing material which was in fact blasphemous.[23] The minority would have allowed the appeal on the ground that the mental element of blasphemy should be rendered more in tune with modern criminal law by requiring an intention to shock or arouse resentment.[24]

The law remained in essentially this state for almost 30 years, until the decision in *Jerry Springer* which is discussed in greater detail below. The one area where there was judicial activity in the interim related to attempts to extend the law of blasphemy to other religions. For example, Mr Choudhury sought unsuccessfully to prosecute Salman Rushdie and the publisher of *The Satanic Verses* for blasphemous libel.[25] In *Choudhury*, the Divisional Court concluded that it was not now open to it to extend the law of blasphemous libel to other religions even if it had considered it desirable to do so which (given the difficulties of definition) it did not.[26]

2. Legislating Against Hate and the Repeal of the Law of Blasphemy

In this section, the background to the legislation on incitement to religious hatred and that repealing the offence of blasphemy are addressed in turn.

---

times inglorious history in the common law' (*Whitehouse* v. *Lemon* [1979] AC 617, 633B). The last prosecution in Scotland was in *Henry* v. *Robinson* 1843 1 Brown 643, making it arguable that the offence there has lapsed.

[22] Ibid.

[23] Ibid., Viscount Dilhorne, 645F–656C; Lord Russell of Killowen, 657G–658A; and Lord Scarman, 665F–G. The editor of *Gay News*, Denis Lemon, was originally sentenced to nine months' imprisonment (suspended for 18 months) and fined £500; the publishers were fined £1000. The Court of Appeal quashed the custodial elements of Lemon's sentence and left the fines in place.

[24] Ibid., Lord Diplock, 635H–636B; and Lord Edmund-Davies, 656B–E.

[25] *R* v. *Chief Metropolitan Stipendiary Magistrate, ex p Choudhury* [1991] 1 QB 429. In *R* v. *Gathercole* (1838) 2 Lew 237, 254; 168 ER 1140, 1145, Alderson B stated: 'A person may, without being liable to prosecution for it, attack Judaism or Mahomedanism, or even any sect of the Christian religion, save the established religion of the country; and the only reason why the latter is in a different situation from the other is, because it is the form established by law, and is therefore part of the constitution of the country.' See J. Waldron, 'Rushdie and Religion', in J. Waldron (ed.), *Liberal Rights-Collected Papers 1981–1991* (Cambridge: CUP, 1993) and C. Munro, 'Prophets, Presbyters and Profanity' [1989] *Pub. L.* 369.

[26] *Choudhury* (ibid.), 447B–448E (Watkins LJ).

(i) Incitement to Religious Hatred

The discriminatory coverage of the common law of blasphemy was one of the principal arguments relied upon by those who advocated the introduction of a new offence of incitement to religious hatred. To this unfairness was added the partial coverage of the statutory offence of incitement to racial hatred which prohibits threatening, abusive or insulting words or behaviour or displays of written material where the defendant intends thereby to stir up racial hatred or whereby racial hatred is likely to be stirred up.[27] As a result of the manner in which the concept of race has been interpreted under the race relations legislation, certain religious denominations (which were also found to be 'ethnic groups') were entitled to the protection of the law on incitement to racial hatred.[28] This protection extended to Jews and Sikhs, but not to Christians, Muslims, or Hindus. Something must now be said about the nature of the offence of incitement to hatred in English law.

The statutory offence of incitement to racial hatred was not introduced until the Race Relations Act 1965 ('the 1965 Act'), but had common law antecedents in the laws of sedition and public mischief.[29] Stephen's definition of sedition included:

an intention . . . to raise discontent or disaffection amongst Her Majesty's subjects, or to promote feelings of ill-will and hostility between different classes of such subjects.[30]

Prosecutions have been brought under this offence for conduct which would be regarded today as examples of incitement to racial or religious hatred.[31] The common law alternative to sedition was public mischief which (if possible) was even more broadly defined to include 'all offences of a public nature, that is, all such acts or attempts as tend to the prejudice of the community'.[32] However, such offences were not an effective deterrent since their inherent vagueness discouraged prosecutions and, by the late 1960s, sedition would only be relied upon where there was a direct incitement to violence or public disorder.[33]

The first legislative attempt to prohibit incitement to religious hatred was made at the time of the passage of the Public Order Bill 1936 and was urged again

---

[27] S.18 of the Public Order Act 1986.

[28] I. Hare, 'Race Discrimination', in S. Gregory and E. Temperton (eds.), *Tolley's Discrimination in Employment Handbook* (London: LexisNexis Butterworths, 2008), para. 6.5.

[29] The background to the offence of incitement to racial hatred is described in greater detail in P. Leopold, 'Incitement to Hatred: The History of a Controversial Criminal Offence' [1977] *Pub. L.* 389; D. Williams, *Keeping the Peace: the Police and Public Order* (Hutchinson, London, 1967), 169–78; and A. Lester and G. Bindman, *Race and Law* (Penguin, Harmondsworth, 1972), 344–60.

[30] *Stephen's Digest of the Criminal Law*, 9th edn. (London: Sweet and Maxwell, 1950), art 114 (an earlier version of which was approved in *R* v. *Burns* (1886) 16 Cox CC 355, 360, per Cave J).

[31] Eg, *R* v. *Osborne* (1732) 2 Swanst 503n. Such prosecutions were not always successful: *R* v. *Caunt* (1947), unreported, described by E. C. S. Wade, 'Seditious Libel and the Press' (1948) 64 *L. Q. R.* 203.

[32] *R* v. *Manley* [1933] 1 K.B. 529, 534, per Lord Hewart C.J.

[33] D. Williams, *Keeping the Peace* (n. 29 above), 198.

during consideration of the 1965 Act.[34] However, the rise in ethnic tensions and violence which had followed the increase in immigration since the 1950s was regarded as placing incitement to racial hatred in a class of its own. Further attempts to add religion to the offence of incitement to racial hatred occurred during the passage of the Criminal Justice and Public Order Bill 1994. These proposals also included provisions abolishing the offence of blasphemy.[35]

More recent initiatives include the Anti-Terrorism, Crime and Security Bill 2001–02 and the Religious Offences Bill 2001–02. As originally drafted, the Anti-Terrorism Bill followed the familiar pattern of adding religion to the existing offence of incitement to racial hatred. However, the clause was dropped from the Bill after the House of Lords had voted to remove it on two occasions.[36] The Lords' objection was based principally on the inappropriateness of including such a reform in a Bill directed at terrorism. In response to this withdrawal, Lord Avebury introduced the Religious Offences Bill (as a private members' bill) which would have had substantially the same effect as the aborted government measure.[37] The Government then established the Select Committee on Religious Offences in England and Wales which delivered its Report in 2003.[38] The Committee was unable to reach a firm conclusion on whether incitement to religious hatred should be criminalized.[39]

This indecisiveness did not deter the Government which came forward with further legislative proposals of its own in the Serious Organised Crime and Police Bill which would again have added religious hatred to the existing provisions on racial hatred in the 1986 Act, but the incitement provision fell in the run-up to the general election in 2003. The Religious Hatred Act finally became law in 2006.[40] After a lengthy process of negotiation between the Upper and Lower House, the Lords successfully persuaded the Commons to accept four significant

---

[34] K. D. Ewing and C. A. Gearty, *The Struggle for Civil Liberties: Political Freedom and the Rule of Law in Britain, 1914–1945* (Oxford: OUP, 2000), 307–26, discussing the background to the 1936 Act which was passed briskly through Parliament in November to December 1936, a month after the Battle of Cable Street.

[35] C. Unsworth, 'Blasphemy, Cultural Divergence and Legal Relativism' [1995] 58 *Modern L. Rev.* 658.

[36] Rt. Hon. David Blunkett, M.P., HC Deb., 13 December 2001, Cols. 1112–3.

[37] HL Bill 39, 2001/02.

[38] HL Paper 95-I (10 April 2003).

[39] Report (ibid.), paras. 131–8.

[40] The Religious Hatred Bill as originally drafted simply amended the offences in ss. 18–23 of the 1986 Act by substituting 'racial or religious hatred' for the current references to 'racial hatred'. The definition of religious hatred is contained in a new s. 17A of the 1986 Act which provides that it 'means hatred against a group of persons defined by reference to religious belief or lack of religious belief'. Incitement to religious hatred has been prohibited in Northern Ireland since the Public Order (Northern Ireland) Order 1987 (see B. Hadfield, 'The Prevention of Incitement to Religious Hatred— An Article of Faith?' (1984) 35 *N.I.L.Q.* 231 and T. Murphy, 'Incitement to Hatred: Lessons from Northern Ireland' in S. Coliver (ed.), *Striking a Balance: Hate Speech, Freedom of Expression and Non-discrimination* (London: Art. 19, 1992).

modifications of the Government's original proposals.[41] First, the new offence of incitement to religious hatred would not simply be tacked on to the existing offence of racial hatred, but merited its own legislative provision. Secondly, unlike racial hatred, the *actus reus* of the offence would be confined to 'threatening' words or behaviour and would not include those which were merely abusive or insulting. Thirdly, and again unlike racial hatred, it would not be sufficient that religious hatred was likely to be stirred up: the speaker must have intended his speech to produce that effect. The new provision in the 1986 Act now reads:

29B(1) A person who uses threatening words or behaviour, or displays any written material which is threatening, is guilty of an offence if he intends thereby to stir up religious hatred.

Fourthly, the Lords inserted a new clause intended to remind the prosecuting authorities and the courts of the limits of the new prohibition:

29J Nothing in this Part shall be read or given effect in a way which prohibits or restricts discussion, criticism or expressions of antipathy, dislike, ridicule, insult or abuse of particular religions or the beliefs or practices of their adherents, or of any other belief system or the beliefs of its adherents, or proselytising or urging adherents of a different religion or belief system to cease practising their religion or belief system.

Whether these amendments have quieted the free speech concerns raised by the original proposal is addressed below.[42]

(ii) Repeal of the Law of Blasphemy

There have been numerous attempts to amend, repeal, or replace the law of blasphemy. Professor Kenny introduced a Bill in 1885 which would have repealed the law of blasphemy and replaced it with a provision based on the Indian Penal Code. The Indian Penal Code makes it an offence to speak or display a symbol or act with the intention of wounding a person's religious feelings within such a person's sight or hearing.[43] The first attempt at outright abolition appears to have been that introduced by Charles Bradlaugh in 1889 and was repeated in 1923 and 1925.[44] Tony Benn MP introduced a Bill to abolish blasphemy to the House of Commons in 1989 and Lord Avebury introduced a similar Bill to the Upper House in 1995. In 1994, Lord Lester of Herne Hill QC

---

[41] A. Lester, 'Free Speech and Religion—The Eternal Conflict in the Age of Selective Modernization' in A. Sajo (ed.), *Censorial Sensitivities: Free Speech and Religion in a Fundamentalist World* (Utrecht: Eleven International, 2007).

[42] The 2006 Act is further discussed in I. Hare, 'Crosses, Crescents and Sacred Cows: Criminalising Incitement to Religious Hatred' [2006] *Pub. L.* 520.

[43] Indian Penal Code, s. 298.

[44] The history is described in *Choudhury* (n. 25 above), 447H–448A. Charles Bradlaugh had himself been prosecuted unsuccessfully for blasphemy arising out of the same matters as the defendants in *Ramsay and Foote*, n. 19 above, *R* v. *Bradlaugh* (1883) 15 Cox CC 217.

proposed amendments which would have abolished the law of blasphemy and introduced an offence of incitement to religious hatred.[45] Further attempts were made in 2001, 2002, and 2005. All of these initiatives failed and it appeared that no Parliament would be willing to risk offending the limited constituency which continues to support the existence of the offence.[46] However, the aims of those seeking abolition have now been substantially achieved without any real debate or consultation by a side-wind in *Jerry Springer* and the parliamentary reaction to it.[47]

Jerry Springer was another example of the law of blasphemy being invoked to seek to punish artistic expression.[48] In January 2007, Stephen Green sought to bring a private prosecution for blasphemous libel in the City of Westminster Magistrates' Court. Mr Green was the national director of an organization called the Christian Voice which describes itself as a prophetic ministry. The named defendants to the proposed prosecution were Jonathan Thoday, the producer of the stage play *Jerry Springer: The Opera* which ran between April 2003 and July 2006 at various locations, and Mark Thompson, the Director General of the BBC, who broadcast a version of the production on national television in January 2005. *Jerry Springer* is a parody of the television chat show of the same name and Mr Green objected particularly to Act Two in which the character of Mr Springer descends into hell and there meets various characters from the earlier parts of the play who now represent religious figures. For example, in the course of Act Two, there is an argument between Satan and Christ (who is dressed in a large baby's nappy and accepts that he has coprophiliac tendencies) in which the latter admits to being 'a little bit gay' and, holding up his hand, tells Satan to 'Talk to the stigmata'; the figure of God is portrayed as inadequate and in need of therapy; and the chorus chants *Jerry Eleison* (a parody of the *Kyrie Eleison* which features in many Christian services). The District Judge refused to issue the summonses on two principal grounds: first, the prosecution was prevented by the Theatres Act 1968 and the Broadcasting Act 1990; and, secondly, there was no prima facie case of blasphemous libel. Mr Green then brought the present challenge to the District Judge's decision in the Divisional Court.

The Divisional Court rejected the challenge and upheld both bases for the lower court's decision. Taking the second ground first, the Court upheld the

---

[45] These proposals are discussed in D. Feldman, *Civil Liberties and Human Rights in England and Wales*, 2nd edn. (Oxford: OUP, 2002), 917, n. 63. See further, I. Bryan, 'Suffering Offence: The Place, Function and Future of the Blasphemy Laws Revisited' (1999) 4 *J. Civil Liberties* 332.

[46] The House of Lords Select Committee Report (n. 38 above), paras. 32–6.

[47] N. 3 above.

[48] The use of Christian imagery is a frequent and controversial part of the history of twentieth century art from George Grosz's work 'Shut Up and Soldier On' which depicted Christ on the cross wearing a gas mask and army boots in the 1920s to Andre Serrano's 'Piss Christ' and Chris Offili's 'The Holy Virgin Mary' in the 1990s. The Archbishop of Melbourne sought an injunction to restrain the National Gallery of Victoria from showing a photograph of Serrano's work: *Pell* v. *The Council of Trustees of the National Gallery of Victoria* [1998] 2 VR 391. See the literary examples quoted at n. 77 and associated text below.

finding that the play could not be regarded as an attack on Christianity, but was really aimed at the exploitative television chat show. Further, the fact that the play had been performed regularly for two years without any evidence that it under-mined society or occasioned civil strife or unrest meant that there was no prima facie case of blasphemous libel.[49] More significant is the first finding. It was based on s. 2(4) of the Theatres Act which provides (as relevant):

No person shall be proceeded against in respect of a performance of a play or anything said or done in the course of such a performance—

(a) for an offence at common law where it is of the essence of the offence that the performance or, as the case may be, what was said or done was obscene, indecent, offensive, disgusting or injurious to morality...

Mr Thompson was entitled to the protection of an identical provision in paragraph 6 of Schedule 15 to the Broadcasting Act 1990. There can be no dispute that blasphemy is a common law offence or that the essence of the crime is offensiveness.[50] However, it is remarkable that *Jerry Springer* was decided on the basis of provisions which make no reference to blasphemy and were enacted without any parliamentary debate about their impact on the law of blasphemy.

The outcome is even more surprising when the provisions of the Theatres Act and the Broadcasting Act are examined in context. Section 2 of the The-atres Act begins by prohibiting the performance of *obscene* plays and incorp-orates the test of a tendency to 'deprave and corrupt' from the Obscene Publications Act 1959 referred to below.[51] Similarly, Schedule 15 to the Broad-casting Act is entitled the 'application of the Obscene Publications Act 1959 to television and sound programmes' and paragraph 6 is expressly stated to be without prejudice to section 2(4) of the 1959 Act.[52] Further support is provided by the legislative histories of the Theatres and Broadcasting Acts. The Theatres Act is the more significant since the Broadcasting Act merely applied the same form of words to a different medium. There are no references to blasphemy in the parliamentary debates which preceded the Theatres Act (in contrast the lengthy debates about the abolition of blasphemy referred to above).[53] Indeed, it is clear that section 2(4) was regarded as confined to obscenity by all those who participated. For example, Lord Stow Hill stated:

[49] N. 3 above, paras. 32–3 (Hughes LJ). This argument reveals the importance of a strong presumption against prior restraints: unless such expression can take place and demonstrate its overall harmlessness to the stability of society, this argument would be unavailable to defenders of free speech.

[50] Ibid., paras. 19–20 (Hughes LJ).

[51] N. 67 below. Indeed, the side-heading for s. 2 of the Theatres Act is 'Prohibition of presen-tation of *obscene* performances of plays' (emphasis added).

[52] S. 2(4) of the 1959 Act replaces the common law of obscene libel with the new statutory test.

[53] See HL Deb., 28 May 1968, Vol. 292, Cols. 1044–104; HL Deb., 20 June 1968, Vol. 293, Cols. 908–82; HL Deb., 19 July 1968, Vol. 295, Cols. 592–640; HC Deb., 23 February 1968, Vol. 759, Col. 825–74; and HC Deb., 10 May 1968, Vol. 764, Col. 760–84.

[S]ubsection (4) prevented the institution of certain criminal proceedings in respect of what I think can be broadly called offences analogous to those covered by Clause 2(1) [that is, the prohibition on obscene plays][54]

As such, it is clear that the provisions relied on by the Divisional Court relate to the common law of obscenity and were not intended to have any impact on the law of blasphemy. It is disappointing that the Divisional Court chose this route to reach an obviously desirable result, rather than addressing directly the compatibility of the offence of blasphemy with the protection of free speech. *Jerry Springer* is therefore a further example of the reluctance of English courts to engage in principled decision-making on matters of freedom of expression.[55]

The decision in *Jerry Springer* is even more striking when one considers that the result of the decision cannot sensibly be confined to theatre and television. It is widely accepted by courts in the United Kingdom and in Strasbourg that the state is entitled to subject broadcasting to more rigorous restrictions than printed matter in the interests of pluralism and because of the immediacy of the impact of broadcast images.[56] If the state has found that restrictions on blasphemy are not necessary for television, it becomes difficult to argue that prosecutions against the printed word are proportionate. As such, *Jerry Springer* was likely to have swept away the law of blasphemy in all areas except for face-to-face utterances between individuals. The Divisional Court had thus almost fully achieved what the House of Lords said in *Lemon* was not possible by judicial decision.

The legislative response to the decision in *Jerry Springer* was rapid. On 9 January 2008, the Government gave a commitment that it would propose abolition of the common law offences of blasphemy and blasphemous libel after a short period of consultation.[57] The Archbishops of Canterbury and York stated in a letter to the Secretary of State for Communities and Local Government that they did not oppose abolition on the rather obscure condition that 'provisions are in place to provide the necessary protection to individuals *and to society*' (emphasis added).[58] On 5 March 2008, Baroness Andrews introduced the relevant clauses to the House of Lords by way of amendment to the Criminal Justice and Immigration Bill. Baroness Andrews gave three reasons for the abolition: first, that the current law had fallen into disuse and therefore carried the risk of bringing the law in general into disrepute; secondly, that legislation on incitement to religious

---

[54] HL Deb., 19 July 1968, Vol. 295, Col. 592. To similar effect, see Lord Lloyd of Hampstead in ibid., Vol. 293, Col. 914, introducing an amendment to add the common law offence of conspiracy to corrupt public morals.

[55] See J. Weinstein and I. Hare chs. 2 and 3 respectively in this volume.

[56] E. Barendt, *Freedom of Speech*, 2nd edn. (Oxford: OUP, 2005), 444–9.

[57] HC Deb., 9 January 2008, Col. 454. The Government was said to have 'every sympathy for the case for formal abolition'. This was in response to the proposal by the Liberal Democrat MP, Dr. Evan Harris, that blasphemy should be abolished as 'ancient discriminatory, unnecessary, . . . and non-human right compliant' (ibid.), Col. 442.

[58] HL Deb., 5 March 2008, Col. 1118.

hatred and religious discrimination was now in place and that this would provide adequate protection to individuals; and, thirdly, the existence of the offences hindered the UK's efforts to challenge oppressive blasphemy laws in other jurisdictions.[59]

The first reason, although ostensibly principled, is hardly a justification for introducing the amendment so late in the day and only in response to a proposal from a member of another political party. There is some irony in the second reason since the discriminatory coverage of the law of blasphemy was used as a justification for the introduction of the law on incitement to religious hatred. The fact that the proposal was tacked onto existing legislation in response to the combined effect of a court decision and a non-governmental parliamentary initiative also undermines the third justification: the weight the abolition is likely to carry as a tool of international free speech diplomacy. In any event, the amendment was passed by a substantial majority, although several members of the House criticized the lateness of its introduction and the effect this had of limiting debate.[60]

3. Free Speech Principle and the Protection of Religious Sensibilities

Underlying the whole of the normative debate on the above questions is the issue of whether it is appropriate for the law to protect religious doctrine and sensibilities from criticism and offence. In this section, I consider whether such restrictions are consistent with a strong commitment to the importance of free speech. There is not adequate space here to set out a principled justification for the protection of free speech as it applies to religion. In any event, the general principle is better set out in other contributions to this collection.[61] However, a couple of points can be briefly made. First, speech on matters of religious controversy will very often be at the core of protected speech since religious perspectives are a frequent part of political debates on matters ranging from when life begins to when it ends (and many matters in between). Secondly, principle recognizes that offensiveness is not a valid basis for restrictions on free speech and that debate is substantively as well as procedurally hampered by legal attempts to impose civility norms.[62] I now turn to consider whether the law of blasphemy and incitement to religious hatred infringe a robust conception of free speech.

---

[59] Ibid., Cols. 1118–21. The Joint Committee on Human Rights also supported the proposed abolition and suggested that the Strasbourg jurisprudence had moved on since *Wingrove* (Fifth Report, *Legislative Scrutiny: Criminal Justice and Immigration Bill* (HL 37/HC 269), 25 January 2008, paras. 1.56–1.60).

[60] Eg, Baroness O'Caithan, the Bishop of Chester and Lord Neill of Bladon (ibid., Cols. 1131, 1140 and 1142).

[61] See Weinstein, ch. 2 in this volume.   [62] Ibid.

(i) Blasphemy

The law of blasphemy was plainly objectionable on a number of grounds. First, it was an anachronistic survivor of the various forms of criminal libel which the common law developed to deal with even mildly expressed criticisms of the social and political status quo. The closeness of the link between seditious and blasphemous libel is clear from Stephen's definition referred to above and from the fact that the two offences were treated as essentially interchangeable in some of the ancient authorities.[63] For example, Keach was prosecuted before Aylesbury Assizes for sedition (and not blasphemous libel) for publishing a book contrary to the doctrine of the Church of England and its ceremonies.[64] Despite the proximity of the relationship between the two offences, seditious libel is substantially narrower than the modern form of blasphemous libel since the former requires the prohibited expression to have a tendency to incite public disorder and violence against constituted authority and the defendant must have intended to incite such violence or disorder.[65] Further, judicial indications are that it is impossible to envisage circumstances in which a prosecution for seditious libel would be appropriate today.[66]

The common law of obscene libel has been much confined by legislation. Obscene material must be more than merely offensive to justify prosecution: it must have a tendency to deprave and corrupt.[67] Further, there is a defence of public good where publication can be shown to be in the interests of science, literature, art or learning, or other objects of general concern.[68] Finally, the law of criminal defamatory libel now requires either that the person defamed should be likely to be provoked into committing a breach of the peace or that it should be in the public interest that criminal proceedings should be brought.[69] In any event, it is now almost never relied upon. As such, the law of blasphemous libel was an anomaly which had survived the amendment or narrowing of its sister offences without any express parliamentary endorsement.

---

[63] Perhaps the most striking illustrations of the relationship between blasphemy and sedition is that it was a combination of both that led to the death sentences imposed on both Socrates and Jesus Christ (A. W. Jeremy, 'Religious Offences' (2003) 7 *Eccl. L. J.* 127, 128).

[64] *R* v. *Keach* (1665) 6 St Tr 701. See further J. R. Spencer, 'Criminal Libel—A Skeleton in the Cupboard' [1977] *Crim. L. Rev.* 383.

[65] *R* v. *Burns* (1886) 16 Cox CC 355 and *Choudhury* (n. 25 above), 453C–E.

[66] *Green* (n. 3 above), para. 22 (Hughes LJ). As the court noted, there has been no prosecution for seditious libel since the nineteenth century except for the unusual case of *R* v. *Caunt*, n. 31.

[67] Obscene Publications Act 1959, s. 1(1).

[68] S. 2(4) of the 1959 Act prevents prosecutions at common law where the essence of the offence is that the matter is obscene. S. 4 provides the defence of public good. On the availability of defences of public good, see P. Kearns, 'Obscene and Blasphemous Libel: Misunderstanding Art' [2000] *Crim. L. Rev.* 652 and J. Jaconelli, 'Defences to Speech Crimes' [2007] *Eur. Hum. Rts. L. Rev.* 27.

[69] 'It is ranked amongst criminal offences for its supposed tendency to arouse angry passion, provoke revenge, and thus endanger the public peace' (*R* v. *Holbrook* (1878) 4 QBD 42, 46 (Lush J)) and *Gleaves* v. *Deakin* [1980] AC 477. All forms of common law libel were abolished by s. 73 of the Coroners and Justice Act 2009 with effect from 12 January 2010.

Secondly, the offence was potentially very broad in its application. As is clear from *Lemon*, there was no need to prove an intention to cause shock or resentment. As such, the offence was effectively one of strict liability which is unorthodox and undesirable for a crime which carries an unlimited penalty. The *actus reus* was also wide and, according the House of Lords, may cover publications which 'shock and arouse resentment among believing Christians' or 'which contains any contemptuous, reviling, scurrilous, or ludicrous matter relating to God, Jesus Christ, or the Bible, or the formularies of the Church of England as by law established'.[70] These formulations are wide and not entirely consistent. More recently, the Divisional Court has proposed a somewhat narrower definition of the 'gist' of the offence as involving 'material relating to the Christian religion, or its figures or formularies, so scurrilous and offensive in manner that it undermines society generally, by endangering the peace, depraving public morality, shaking the fabric of society, or tending to be a cause of civil strife'.[71] As a result of the confused state of the authorities, the Law Commission wrote that it was 'hardly an exaggeration' to assert that whether or not a publication constitutes a blasphemous libel can only be judged with confidence after the jury has delivered its verdict.[72] This has led to inconsistent results with different juries acquitting or convicting defendants in relation to the same material.[73] Some courts have regarded this breadth and uncertainty as fatal to the continued recognition of the offence at common law. For example, the Irish Supreme Court found it impossible in 1999 to authorize a prosecution for blasphemy in light of the lack of clarity surrounding its definition.[74]

Thirdly, as a result of this uncertainty and breadth, the law plainly posed a serious threat to free speech. I have already referred to the fact that the penalty was unlimited and many of the early cases involved the infliction of severe punishment.[75] I have also mentioned above that, as late as 1977, the editor of *Gay News*

---

[70] *Lemon* (n. 21 above), Lord Diplock, 635D; and Lord Scarman, 665G respectively. It should be remembered that the House was not concerned with the *actus reus* of blasphemy in *Lemon*.

[71] *Green* (n. 3 above), para. 16 (Hughes LJ). For many, 'shaking the fabric of society' is one of the most important functions of free speech.

[72] Law Commission Working Paper, No. 79, 1981, para. 6.1.

[73] The Law Commission refers to the example of William Hone who was tried and acquitted of blasphemy on three occasions in 1817 while Joseph Russell was convicted in 1819 (and sentenced to six months' imprisonment) for selling the same works (ibid., fn. 19).

[74] *Corway* v. *Independent Newspapers (Ireland) Ltd* [1999] 4 IR 484. The consent of the High Court is required for all criminal prosecutions for libel against a newspaper by the Defamation Act 1961, s. 8. The attempted prosecution concerned a cartoon which depicted a number of politicians waving goodbye to a priest holding the Eucharist while saying 'Hello progress—bye bye Father'. This was a pun on some of the campaign literature issued by those opposing the recent divorce referendum which read 'Hello divorce—bye bye daddy'. Mr. Corway maintained that he had suffered offence and outrage as a result of the contempt shown for the Eucharist. See P. O'Higgins, 'Blasphemy in Irish Law' (1960) 23 *Modern L. Rev.* 151, 155–66, reviewing the Irish cases.

[75] Eg, Taylor was pilloried three times. In 1821, Mary Carlisle was found guilty of blasphemous libel for selling a pamphlet alleging that the Old Testament was full of contradictions and wickedness. She was fined the substantial sum at the time of £500, imprisoned in Dorchester gaol for 12 months with her release conditional on finding sureties of £1,000 for her good behaviour for the next five years

was originally sentenced to imprisonment (albeit suspended). The very closeness of the relationship between sedition and blasphemy made it inevitable that blasphemy has been used as a tool to suppress speech on matters of intense public controversy. For example, the publisher of Thomas Paine's *The Age of Reason* was sentenced to a year's hard labour after which he was required to enter recognisances of £1,000 to secure his release.[76] There is also a lengthy history of prosecutions being brought in relation to substantial works of literature, including Ben Jonson's *Volpone*, Shelley's *Queen Mab* and Siegfried Sassoon's *Stand To*.[77]

Fourthly, it is difficult to identify an adequate justification for the offence of blasphemy in its present (or any foreseeable) form. Four potential justifications were put forward by the Law Commission in its Report in 1985:[78] the protection of religion and religious beliefs; the protection of society; the protection of individual feelings; and protection of public order. Dealing with these justifications in turn, the protection of religion cannot provide an adequate basis for criminalization. The link between blasphemy and the protection of the state is no longer regarded as valid and is fundamentally undermined by the increasingly secular and religiously diverse nature of British society.[79] Similarly, it is now widely regarded as objectionable that the protection of the law of blasphemy should only extend to the Christian faith. The protection of society is a nebulous concept and each generation appears to fear that certain forms of conduct will lead to its disintegration. This justification ultimately collapses into the others and is therefore equally vulnerable. Any supposed justification based on the protection of individual feelings is subject to the objection that religious feelings in a broadly secular society are entitled to no greater protection from the criminal law than those which may be as strongly held on other matters of controversy such as politics or loyalty to other social groups based on familial or sporting ties.[80] In any event, an analysis of the history of prosecutions fails to reveal a single example

---

(*R* v. *Carlile (Mary)* (1821) 1 St Tr NS 1033, 1045). Where a prisoner was not able to find such sureties, they remained in gaol (*R* v. *Woolston* (1728) Fitzg 64; 94 ER 655). As late as 1922, Gott was sentenced to nine months' imprisonment with hard labour (Lord Trevethin CJ commenting, apparently without irony, that this sentence would make it more likely that the prison authorities would pay attention to the prisoner's poor health than otherwise (*R* v. *Gott* (1922) 16 Cr App R 87, 90)).

[76] *R* v. *Williams* (1797) 26 St Tr 653, 705. At trial, it was said that the second instalment of the work had 'excited a general avidity to read the book, particularly among the middling and lower classes of life' (ibid., 653).

[77] *R* v. *Moxon* (1841) 4 St Tr NS 693 (successful prosecution of a bookseller for selling *Queen Mab*). See further H. B. Bonner, *Penalties Upon Opinion*, 3rd edn. (London: Watts & Co., 1934) and J. R. Spencer, 'Blasphemy: The Law Commission's Working Paper' [1981] *Crim. L. Rev.* 810, 817–8.

[78] The Law Commission, *Criminal Law: Offences Against Religion and Public Worship* (Law Com. No. 145, 18 June 1985). The Commission recommended abolition. Interestingly, the Commission rejected the idea of replacing blasphemy with a new offence of outraging religious feelings.

[79] D. Feldman, *Civil Liberties and Human Rights* (n. 45 above), 907–11.

[80] The ECtHR has acknowledged that views on matters other than religion may be of equal importance under Art. 9 of the Convention to 'atheists, agnostics, sceptics and the unconcerned' (*Kokkinakis* v. *Greece* (1994) 17 EHRR 397, para. 31).

of proceedings being brought to protect the interests of persecuted believers: instead, blasphemy was habitually employed against those expressing minority and unorthodox positions.[81] Public order cannot be an adequate justification since the courts have repeatedly held that there is no requirement that there should be an imminent, or even potential, breach of the peace before the offence of blasphemy can be made out.[82] In any event, there is no evidence that existing public order offences are inadequate to deal with any threat to public peace.

The absence of a positive justification for the offence and the definitional uncertainty surrounding it might have suggested that blasphemy was likely to be condemned in Strasbourg. The law clearly interfered with freedom of expression and so the relevant questions were whether the interference was 'prescribed by law' and was necessary in a democratic society in the interests of public safety, the prevention of disorder, the protection of morals or the protection of the rights of others.[83] Surprisingly, the ECtHR held in *Wingrove* that the English law of blasphemy was sufficiently clear to satisfy the requirement that it should be prescribed by law.[84] The case concerned a challenge to the British Board of Film Classification's refusal to certify for sale or distribution the film *Visions of Ecstasy* on the ground that it was blasphemous.[85] However, the limits of this ruling should be noted. First, the Court's finding was based on an express concession by the parties.[86] Secondly, the Court referred to the 'degree of flexibility' to be accorded to national authorities in defining inherently vague concepts such as blasphemy.[87] There is no reason why this would apply to review by a domestic court.

More disappointing was the decision of the ECtHR that the law of blasphemy fulfilled the legitimate aim of protecting the rights of Christians (and its sympathizers) not to suffer outrage to their feelings and that the refusal to certify the film was a proportionate means of achieving that end.[88] It is possible to overstate the significance of these decisions for a number of reasons. First, the Court relied heavily on the doctrine of the margin of

---

[81] Spencer (n. 77 above), 816.

[82] *Gott* (n. 75 above), 88–9, 90 (Avory J and Trevethin LCJ), *Bowman* (n. 20 above), 459–60 (Lord Sumner) and *Lemon* (n. 21 above), 662 (Lord Scarman).

[83] See I. Hare, 'Extreme Speech Under International and Regional Human Rights Standards', ch. 3 in this volume.

[84] *Wingrove* v. *United Kingdom* (1997) 24 EHRR 1. The Commission's earlier decision to the same effect in *Gay News Ltd and Lemon* v. *United Kingdom* (1982) 5 EHRR 123, para. 10 is of limited usefulness given its age and status. See S. Ghandi and J. James, 'The English Law of Blasphemy and the European Convention on Human Rights' [1998] *Eur. Hum. Rts. L. Rev.* 430.

[85] The film portrayed St Theresa of Avila in a state of ecstasy at the contemplation of Christ which could not be entirely explained by his power as a religious symbol.

[86] *Wingrove* (n. 84 above), para. 43.

[87] Ibid., para. 42.

[88] Ibid., para. 48. The decision was in line with the Court's earlier finding in *Otto-Preminger Institut* v. *Austria* (1994) 19 EHRR 34 that the seizure and forfeiture of the film *Das Liebeskonzil* (Council in Heaven) was compatible with Art. 10 in order to protect religious peace and the feelings of Roman Catholics.

appreciation.[89] Secondly, there were powerful dissents in both cases and the conclusions of the Court were contrary to the firmly expressed views of the Commission that there was a violation of Article 10.[90] Thirdly, the Court appears to be moving towards a more protective approach to free speech in this context as evidenced by the recent decision in *I. A. v. Turkey*.[91] Although the Court upheld an author's criminal conviction for blasphemy in this case, it did so by a narrow 4–3 margin. Significantly, the dissenting Judges Costa, Cabral Barreto, and Jungwiert made the following points: that a democratic society is not a theocratic one and that the time had come to revisit the *Otto-Preminger* and *Wingrove* judgments which, in their view, placed too much emphasis on conformism or uniformity of thought and reflected an overcautious and timid conception of freedom of the press.[92] Further, the Court has shown itself less willing to protect religious sensibilities in recent cases concerning criticism of secularism and calls for the introduction of Sharia in Turkey and suggestions that aspects of Catholic doctrine may have contributed towards the causes of the Holocaust.[93]

For the above reasons, the abolition of the offence is to be welcomed. However, two reservations must be entered. First, it was pusillanimous for Parliament to create the new offence of incitement to religious hatred in 2006 at least in part to remove the anomalies created by the discriminatory application of the Public Order Act, but not to have addressed the continued and more offensively partial coverage of blasphemy until two years later. Secondly, Parliament did not engage in the kind of principled argument in its recent blasphemy debate that might have been expected. The Government was spurred into action by a judicial decision (itself based on questionable reasoning) and an amendment proposed by a member of another political party. The quality of the debate was not high. A flavour of this is given by the fact that Baroness Andrews on behalf of the Government stated (incorrectly) that her researches revealed only two blasphemy prosecutions in the history of the offence. If one of the reasons for supporting abolition was that this would provide support to the UK's opposition to the draconian application of blasphemy laws overseas, this was an unedifying background to the reform. Having mentioned the relationship between blasphemy and incitement to religious hatred, I now turn to this development.

(ii) Incitement to Religious Hatred

There are three main arguments advanced by those who sought to have incitement to religious hatred criminalized which I propose to discuss in turn before

---

[89] *Wingrove* (n. 84 above), para. 58 and *Otto-Preminger* (ibid), para. 50.

[90] *Wingrove* (ibid), paras. 65-9 and *Otto-Preminger* (ibid), paras. 75–81.

[91] (2007) 45 EHRR 30. It may be that the Court is moving towards a more protective role in relation to extreme speech, see Hare, n. 83 above.

[92] Ibid., paras. 0I-5-8.

[93] See *Gunduz* v. *Turkey* (2005) 41 EHRR 5, paras. 43–8 and *Giniewski* v. *France* (2007) 45 EHRR 23, paras. 50–2.

considering some of the difficulties of principle and practice to which it gives rise. The arguments in favour are: first, that a new offence is necessary to address the serious social problem of incitement to religious hatred in Great Britain; secondly, that such an offence is required to remove the discriminatory protection presently afforded to Jews and Sikhs by the Public Order Act's provisions on incitement to racial hatred; and thirdly, that the offence is required to comply with the UK's international legal obligations.

The rise in anti-Islamic statements which is said to have followed the 11 September 2001 attacks on the World Trade Centre in New York and the London bombings of July 2005 is well documented.[94] However, even if true, this is not a plausible reason for the new offence for a number of reasons. First, when the Racial and Religious Hatred Bill was first introduced, the Government expressly denied that it thought that incitement to religious hatred was commonplace.[95] Secondly, if the new offence was required to address a serious social problem, it is very surprising that the Government delayed bringing the Racial and Religious Hatred Act into force for well over a year in the immediate aftermath of serious Islamist terror attacks in the United Kingdom.

More importantly, any increase in incitement to religious hatred would only require new legislation if it was clear that existing provisions were incapable of dealing with it. However, there is no suggestion that this is the case.[96] The existing offence under section 5 of the Public Order Act is committed by the use of threatening, abusive, or insulting words or behaviour within the sight or hearing of a person likely to be caused harassment, alarm, or distress. The similar offence under section 4A (which requires an intent to cause harassment, alarm, or distress) may be punished with imprisonment. These offences cover harassment, alarm, or distress and are wider than the new offence of incitement to religious hatred in several respects. Moreover, as a result of amendments introduced in 2001, the offences under sections 4A and 5 of the Public Order Act are both subject to penalty enhancement up to a maximum of two years imprisonment where they are committed with religious aggravation.[97] Religious aggravation means that at the

---

[94] Eg, C. Milmo, 'Muslims feel like "Jews of Europe"', *The Independent*, 4 July 2008 (previewing a Channel 4 documentary called 'It Shouldn't Happen to a Muslim' broadcast on the second anniversary of the London bombings).

[95] Paragraph 69 of the letter from Caroline Flint, MP, Parliamentary Under Secretary of State for the Home Office (3 February 2005) in response to the Joint Committee on Human Rights' *Fourth Report of 2004–05: First Progress Report*, HL Paper 26, HC 224 and annexed in Appendix 2a of the Committee's Eighth Report, HL 60/HC 388.

[96] The only example which the minister was able to provide when the matter returned to the Commons was of 'a poster that depicts women, some of whom are white British and some of whom are not, wearing the burqa and that includes quotations from the Koran. The poster states that such women cannot be trusted because they are recruited in various parts of the world as suicide bombers and asks what they are hiding under their ugly clothes', Paul Goggins MP, HC Deb., 31 January 2006, Col. 194. This example would plainly not fulfil the definition of incitement under the Act.

[97] Crime and Disorder Act 1998, s. 31 (as amended by the Anti-terrorism, Crime and Security Act 2001).

time of committing the offence (or immediately before or after doing so), the offender is motivated by, or demonstrates hostility towards, the victim based on the victim's actual or presumed membership of a religious group.[98] As *Norwood* demonstrates, the Public Order Act has been used in a number of cases which would also fall within the ambit of the new offence of incitement to religious hatred even though there was no evidence in that case that any Muslim had seen Norwood's sign.[99] The only reason why an individual would be likely to be charged with incitement to religious hatred would therefore appear to be because of the longer maximum penalty. It is unsurprising that the police and prosecutors will continue to rely on other methods of social control where they do not have to get over the hurdles included in the Racial and Religious Hatred Act.[100]

Turning to the second supposed argument in favour of the new offence, it is true (as explained above) that the earlier version of the Public Order Act did provide some protection for Sikhs and Jews, but not for Muslims, Hindus, or Christians. However, this protection was not provided to them as religious groups, but because of their status as ethnic groups within the Race Relations Act. As such, it is not accurate to say that Sikhs and Jews are treated more favourably as *religions*. In any event, the effect of this distinction may be exaggerated. First, there are so few prosecutions for incitement to racial hatred that it may be said not to provide substantial protection for those it covers. Secondly, there are many cases of anti-Muslim incitement which may be analysed as incitement to racial hatred since they are really directed at members of, for example, the Bangladeshi or Pakistani communities. There is no requirement that the words or behaviour which give rise to a prosecution for incitement to racial hatred should themselves be racist. For example, the first prosecution in Scotland for incitement to racial hatred was against David Wilson, a member of the BNP, who had distributed leaflets in the Pollokshields area of Glasgow which alleged that 'Muslim racists' were 'running amok' and attacking white residents. Evidence was given at trial that the majority of Muslims in Pollokshields were of South Asian origin and the Sheriff concluded that the terms Muslim and Pakistani were used interchangeably in that community.[101] Wilson was convicted.

[98] Ibid., s. 28. In *R* v. *Barrie* [2005] EWCA Crim 1318; [2006] 1 Cr App R (S) 40, the defendant had stated to two Muslims: 'You should go and blow some buildings up. That's your job. You're good at that.' The Court of Appeal upheld a custodial sentence of six months, referring to the 'obvious fact' that since 11 September 2001, 'whole communities have lived in fear because of the inflammatory comments made by some ill-informed people about the Islamic religion and about Muslim communities in the United Kingdom' (ibid., para. 6). The free speech issues raised by penalty enhancement provisions are addressed in I. Hare, 'Legislating Against Hate: The Legal Response to Bias Crimes' (1997) 17 *O. J. L. S.* 415.

[99] *Norwood* v. *DPP* [2003] EWHC 1564 (Admin).

[100] Since 2002, the police and local authorities also have the Anti-Social Behaviour Order at their disposal which may be applied to cases involving incitement to racial or religious hatred.

[101] *PF* v. *Wilson*, 24 October 2002 (unpublished), cited in K. Goodall, 'Incitement to Religious Hatred: All Talk and No Substance?' (2007) 70 *Modern L. Rev.* 89, 95–6. The conviction was affirmed on appeal (*Wilson* v. *PF* [2005] HCJAC97, 2005 SCCR 686).

Thirdly, and in any event, it is logically as valid a method of removing any perceived anomalies in the coverage of the law on incitement to racial hatred to repeal that offence rather than further to extend it. This is not the appropriate forum to discuss the offence of incitement to racial hatred, but it is strongly arguable that it is both objectionable as a matter of free speech principle and, at best, ineffective in practice.[102] The analogy between incitement to racial and religious hatred is also not manifestly sound. Whatever advances have been made in defining race as a social (as opposed to a purely biological) construct,[103] it remains the case that for the vast majority who live in liberal democracies, religious adherence is a matter of choice rather than birth and the law does not usually provide the protection of the criminal law for vilification based upon the life choices of its citizens.[104] Indeed, it is arguable that greater latitude should be given to free discussion on religious matters than on those concerning race for a number of additional reasons. The first is that a substantial part of the aim of most religions is to persuade and convert new adherents. Thus religions are in a competitive position with regard to one another.[105] Secondly, religions inevitably make competing and often incompatible claims about the nature of the true god, the origins of the universe, the path to enlightenment, and how to live a good life and so on. These sorts of claims are not mirrored in racial discourse. In addition, unlike most minority groups who are the victims of racial incitement, many religious entities are highly organized and well-funded and therefore have the resources to counter extreme speech against them.[106] Finally, religious groups make influential, voluntary contributions to debates on matters of profound public controversy, including abortion, homosexuality, and the place of women in society.[107]

[102] Hare, 'Crosses, Crescents and Sacred Cows' (n. 42 above), 533–4.

[103] R. Miles, *Racism After 'Race Relations'* (London: Routledge, 1993) and J. Richardson and J. Lambert, *The Sociology of Race* (Ormskirk: Causeway Press, 1985).

[104] 'Expression that advocates hatred and stereotyping of people on the basis of immutable characteristics is particularly harmful to the achievement of these values as it reinforces and perpetuates patterns of discrimination and inequality' (*Islamic Unity Convention* v. *Independent Broadcasting Authority* 2002 (4) SA 294, para. 45, per Langda DCJ).

[105] J. Waldron, *Liberal Rights* (n. 25 above), ch. 6. The US Supreme Court invalidated the conviction of Jesse Cantwell, a Jehovah's Witness, for inciting a breach of the peace when he played a record in public which described all organized religions (and the Roman Catholic Church in particular) as the work of Satan (*Cantwell* v. *Connecticut* 310 US 296 (1940)). See R.C. Post, 'Cultural Heterogeneity and Law: Pornography, Blasphemy, and the First Amendment' (1988) 76 *Cal. L. Rev.* 297.

[106] Supplementary submission to the Religious Offences Committee by the British Humanist Association (4 December 2002), Report (n. 38 above), Vol. II, 74.

[107] P. Cumper, 'Freedom of Thought, Conscience and Religion', in D. Harris and S. Joseph (eds.), *The International Covenant on Civil and Political Rights and United Kingdom Law* (Oxford: Clarendon Press, 1995), ch. 11. In *An Application for Judicial Review by the Christian Institute and Others* [2007] NIQB 66, a number of Christian groups challenged the Northern Ireland Regulations prohibiting harassment on the ground of sexual orientation on the basis that the ban infringed their right to convey their religious views on homosexuality.

The third argument for reform is not powerful. The Strasbourg jurisprudence establishes that there is no requirement under the ECHR to legislate in order to protect individuals from incitement to religious hatred. Indeed, even the old and discriminatory coverage offence of blasphemy was found not to breach the Convention.[108] Nor is it arguable that the UK is bound by its other international obligations to enact such legislation. The UK entered a reservation to Article 20 of the International Covenant on Civil and Political Rights and has not proposed to review that position.[109]

So much for the arguments in favour. What difficulties of principle and practice are caused by the new offence? The new offence would not be objectionable as a matter of free speech principle if it were confined to face-to-face threatening speech which has a limited claim to be protected expression.[110] However, the definition of the threatening words or behaviour is likely to be treated (like the other cognate terms in the Public Order Act) as a question of fact and as such there is a powerful risk that broad interpretations will remain uncorrected on appeal.[111] There is a further risk to free speech that the new offence will come to be used as a precedent for prohibiting incitement on other grounds and that the current limitations on its use will be whittled away. It was possible to argue that the offence of incitement to racial hatred was justified on historical grounds given its longevity or that it is legitimate for the law to treat race differently. However, once it is conceded that other forms of incitement may be prohibited, it becomes more difficult to resist the argument that incitement to hatred should cover the same grounds as prohibited discrimination and therefore extend to gender, disability, age, and so on.[112] This prediction has already come true since the Criminal Justice and Immigration Act 2008 has added incitement to hatred on the grounds of sexual orientation to religious hatred in a provision closely modelled on the religious offence.[113] The second fear arises from the history of the offence of incitement to racial which has been incrementally extended since its original formulation.[114]

---

[108] *Choudhury* v. *United Kingdom* (1991) 12 *Hum. Rts. L. J.* 172.

[109] See Hare, n. 83 above.

[110] See Weinstein ch. 2 in this volume.

[111] *Brutus* v. *Cozens* [1973] AC 854. Some of the difficulties caused by the appellate reluctance to interfere are clear from the disappointing decisions in *Director of Public Prosecutions* v. *Collins* [2006] UKHL 40; [2006] 1 WLR 2223 and *Connolly* v. *Director of Public Prosecutions* [2007] EWHC 237 (Admin); [2008] 1 WLR 276.

[112] See Heinze, ch. 14 in this volume. The Fabian Society has recently suggested that the word 'chav' should be prohibited as likely to incite class hatred. See 'Stop using chav: It's deeply offensive', *Fabian Society*, <http://fabians.org.uk/publications/extracts/chav-offensive> (last accessed 2 August 2008).

[113] Schedule 16 to the 2008 Act. Canada provided a further example when, in 2004, homophobic hate speech was added to the prohibition on racial hate speech in s. 319 of the Canadian Criminal Code. For further examples, see L. McNamara, *Human Rights Controversies: The Impact of Legal Form* (Abingdon: Routledge-Cavendish, 2007), 161–2.

[114] See Hare, 'Crosses, Crescents and Sacred Cows' (n. 42 above), 534.

As a matter of practice, the narrow definition of the offence and the existence of the free speech defence make it unlikely that the police and prosecutors will rely on it rather than the numerous more broadly defined legal tools referred to above.[115] Indeed, it is arguable that the new offence may turn out to be almost impossible to prosecute as it appears to have confused two distinct audiences for inciting speech. Speech which incites hatred against a particular group is not generally threatening towards members of that group because it is intended to incite hatred within those the speaker regards as at least potentially like-minded. As such, it is much more likely to be abusive or insulting towards members of the impugned group. On the other hand, speech which is simply threatening is itself unlikely to incite hatred against a particular group. The decision to confine incitement to religious hatred to threatening speech has therefore probably narrowed the new offence to the point of non-existence.

4. Conclusion

It is difficult to draw optimistic conclusions from the story of English law's recent treatment of religion and free speech. The United Kingdom is in fact a post-Christian, secular society, but government appears to be unable or unwilling to accept the ramifications of this. The welcome repeal of blasphemy did not proceed out of a principled concern for equality or free speech, but a hastily assembled political compromise. The new law on incitement was not a balanced response to a pressing social problem, but a cynical sop to a vocal, minority population who felt themselves to have been disproportionately the victims of recent Government initiatives on terrorism. Both reforms took place without the meaningful debate about the ramifications for free speech which one might expect. Current policy towards religion therefore resembles less that of a modern democracy and more that of the Roman Empire:

The various modes of worship which prevailed in the Roman world were all considered by the people as equally true; by the philosopher as equally false; and by the magistrate as equally useful.[116]

---

[115] See Sir Leslie Scarman's criticisms of the (now repealed) requirement of intent in the offence of incitement to racial hatred and its impact on police decision-making in *Red Lion Square Disorders of 15 June 1974: Report of Inquiry by the Rt Hon Lord Justice Scarman*, OBE, Cmnd 5919, (London: HMSO, 1975).

[116] E. Gibbon, *The Decline and Fall of the Roman Empire, Vol. I* (New York: Modern Library, 1932), 25.

16

The Danish Cartoons, Offensive Expression, and Democratic Legitimacy

*Ian Cram**

1. Introduction

The publication in the Danish newspaper *Jyllands-Posten* of cartoons depicting the Prophet Muhammed in 2005 (and their subsequent re-publication in media outlets across Europe) provoked a series of protests from outraged Muslims. One of the cartoons depicted the Prophet wearing a turban in the shape of a bomb. Another image had the Prophet informing a suicide bomber that Paradise has run out of virgins. Danish food exporters were among the first to experience the wrath of the protestors as boycotts of Danish food products occurred in a number of the Middle East states. At the formal level of diplomatic relations, protests were made to the Danish Prime Minister by the ambassadors of several Muslim countries. Syria and Saudi Arabia went further, recalling their ambassadors, whilst Libya closed its entire embassy in Copenhagen. Sadly however, responses elsewhere to the cartoons went beyond restrained expressions of official regret. In February 2006, the Danish Foreign Ministry felt obliged to advise its nationals in Indonesia to leave the country, warning of a 'significant and imminent danger' from extremists who were looking to 'actively seek out Danes...'[1] In Pakistan, hundreds of students protested in Lahore and Multan. Effigies of the Danish Prime Minister were burnt after he refused to bow to pressure to punish the newspaper. Protestors also set fire to a church, a number of cinemas, and American-owned

* I wish to acknowledge the helpful contributions of those who commented on an earlier version of this chapter presented at a conference Extreme Speech and Democracy hosted by the Centre for Public Law, at Cambridge University in April 2007. An especially heavy debt of gratitude is owed to Professor Robert Post, of the Yale Law School whose work is discussed in the latter sections of this chapter and who was tireless in his support and helpful advice during its drafting. The chapter has also benefitted from the careful editing and thoughtful comments of Professor Jim Weinstein of Arizona State University on an earlier draft. Responsibility for the views expressed below remains with the author.

[1] J. Aglionby and G. Fouché, 'Danes told to leave Indonesia after terrorist threat reported', *The Guardian*, 13 February 2006.

food outlets. Two persons died in clashes with the police.[2] In Africa, clashes in Libya claimed the lives of eleven persons whilst in the Nigerian provinces of Borno and Katsina, sixteen lives were lost as churches were burned amidst riotous scenes.[3]

There were varying outcomes for media organizations caught up in the dispute. A court in Aarhus, Denmark rejected a libel action brought by seven Danish Muslim groups against *Jyllands-Posten* after state prosecutors declined to bring a criminal prosecution.[4] The editor of *France Soir*, Jacques Lefranc, was removed from his post after his newspaper reprinted the cartoons under the headline 'Yes, we have the right to caricature God'. This dismissal provided the news context for the BBC to show the carton images as they appeared in *France Soir*. In so doing, the corporation became the first news organization in the United Kingdom to broadcast the images (or some of them at least) at the centre of the controversy. Hours earlier the European Trade Commissioner, Peter Mandelson, had urged media organizations to refrain from broadcasting material that in his view 'was bound to offend'.[5] Students involved in the editing of college magazines found themselves subject to internal disciplinary proceedings. In the United States, a student editor at the University of Illinois was fired after republishing the cartoons,[6] whilst a student at Clare College, Cambridge University was reprimanded by the College Dean and required to make a public apology for the 'deep offence and hurt to very many people' caused by his decision to reprint the cartoons.[7] The 19-year-old student had earlier been interviewed by the police under caution before being taken to an unknown location for his own safety as copies of the magazine were impounded by the college.

Denied the possibility of a prosecution under domestic blasphemy laws,[8] protestors in the United Kingdom gathered outside the Danish Embassy in

---

[2] '70,000 gather for violent Pakistan cartoons protest', *The Times Online*, 15 February 2006.

[3] A. Hill and A. Asthana, 'Nigeria cartoon riots kill 16', *The Observer*, 19 February 2006.

[4] G. Fouché, 'Danish court dismisses Muhammed cartoons case', *The Guardian Unlimited*, 27 October 2006.

[5] The British Council of Muslims nonetheless supported the decision to show the images as part of the developing news story involving *France Soir* and considered that the BBC's motives were entirely different from certain newspapers which had intended to attack Islam. See I Marland and S. Bell, ' "Blasphemous" cartoons shown on British TV as Muslims vent outrage', *The Scotsman*, 3 February 2006.

[6] 'National Briefing: Midwest: Illinois: Editor Fired Over Muslim Cartoons', *The New York Times*, 15 March 2006.

[7] 'Islam cartoon student apologises for offence', *Cambridge Evening News*, 16 April 2007.

[8] The common law offences of blasphemy and blasphemous libel have now been abolished by s. 79 of the Criminal Justice and Immigration Act 2008. Previously, the common law protected the Anglican variant of Christianity only and so afforded no protection to Muslims, see *Whitehouse* v. *Lemon* (1978) 68 Cr App R 38 and *R* v. *Bow Street Magistrates' court ex parte Choudhury* [1991] 1 All ER 306. *Whitehouse* made clear that the attack on Christianity had to be expressed in a sufficiently scurrilous or outrageously indecent manner. Additionally, as *Bowman* v. *Secular Society* [1917] AC 406, 466–7 reminded us, the attack must have had a 'tendency to endanger then and there, to deprave public morality generally, to shake the fabric of society and to be cause of civil strife'. Given these onerous conditions, it was hardly surprising that the offence had fallen into disuse. There were

London. Some carried placards that called for the beheading of those who insult Islam. Demonstrators also chanted 'Bin Laden on his way', 'Europe you will pay with your blood', and 'Bomb, bomb the UK'. One speaker called for UK soldiers serving in Iraq to come back to Britain in body bags. Subsequently, several participants were convicted at the Old Bailey of the offences of soliciting murder and incitement to racial hatred.[9]

Although the publication and re-publication of the cartoons raise profound ethical questions for journalists and editors, the central concern in this paper is a legal and constitutional examination of the legitimacy of 'offence' as a ground for limiting expression by the coercive force of law. A government seeking to assuage hurt feelings and court quick popularity among Muslim groups (and, even more broadly, religious communities who might have similar anxieties about satirical expression about religion) might be tempted to devise new restrictions on expression about religious matters. This chapter sets out to tackle a number of questions. First, I discuss the likely outcome of a challenge before the European Court of Human Rights to national authorities' restrictions on expressive activities, where those restrictions rest on the claim that the expression in question does or is likely to cause offence to genuinely held religious beliefs.[10] From a media freedom perspective, the record of the Court in cases such as *Otto Preminger Institut*, *Wingrove*, *Murphy* and *I. A. v. Turkey* (each of which will be discussed below) is far from encouraging. However, a re-evaluation of the Court's hitherto relaxed approach to national authorities' blasphemy-based restrictions may be afoot. In 2005, the minority joint dissent of the European Court of Human Rights (Second Section) in *I. A. v. Turkey* argued that the time had come to 'revisit' the *Otto Preminger Institut* and *Wingrove* line of case law which it was claimed had tended to place

---

no prosecutions in the period after the enactment of the Human Rights Act 1998. In December 2007, the High Court declined to interfere with a refusal to issue a summons for blasphemous libel against the producer of the play *Jerry Springer–The Opera* and the BBC who had subsequently broadcast it, see *The Queen (on the application of Stephen Green)* v. *The City of Westminster Magistrates' Court* [2007] EWHC 2785. In the play, an actor representing the chat show host imagines his descent into hell and encounters Satan, God, Christ, Mary, and Adam and Eve. Among other passages in the play, the characters swear at each other, Eve fondles Jesus' genitals, and Mary makes reference to a failed condom. Critically, there was no evidence that the play (then having been performed regularly in major theatres for two years) had caused civil strife. Had the common law offences remained extant, it is entirely possible that they would have been challenged under the non-discrimination provisions of Art. 14 of the ECHR.

[9] F. Yeoman, 'Four jailed for hate crimes at cartoon protest', *The Times Online*, 18 July 2007.

[10] For the purposes of the present discussion, I assume that it is possible to distinguish between expression that 'merely' offends listeners and viewers on the one hand and, on the other hand, expression that produces hatred of others in listeners. Under Strasbourg jurisprudence, hateful expression is treated as falling outside the protective ambit of Art. 10 either because of the derogating provisions of Art. 10.2 or, more fundamentally, because of Art. 17 which allows the Court a basis for declaring as manifestly ill-founded Convention claims which are 'aimed at the destruction of any of the rights or freedoms set forth herein'. See *Glimmerveen & Hagenbeek* v. *Netherlands* Application Nos. 8348/78 and 8406/78, 18 DR 187.

too much emphasis on conformism or uniformity of thought and to reflect an overcautious and timid conception of freedom of the press.[11]

A substantial focus of the first section is on methodological aspects of the supranational's court supervisory approach to intervention in cases of offensive expression. I argue here that the application of the margin of appreciation doctrine has been confused with the result that an excessive degree of discretion has accrued to national authorities in their regulation of offensive expression. Then, there is the question of whether under Convention jurisprudence there is an individual 'right' to be protected from offensive expression (effectively a right to have one's religious views respected in public discourse) or, alternatively, whether this protection is best characterized as a countervailing societal interest. Again, the argument in this essay is that the relevant Convention jurisprudence is marked by an ambivalence that has not served the interests of unorthodox speakers. The foregoing criticisms tend however to presume the importance to liberal, democratic societies of expression that injures genuinely held religious belief. I examine that presumption by discussing some reasons in favour of tolerating offensive expression, including what for many is the least deserving form of offensive expression, namely, 'gratuitously offensive' speech. Finally, some issues around the outer limits of offensive expression are explored. Is there, to put it starkly, a 'tipping point' for offensive material beyond which democratic states should prohibit offensive expression? Here I am concerned at a more abstract level with how liberal democratic states might accommodate and reconcile ideas of individual autonomy, collective decision-making as well as formal and substantive notions of equality. I will draw heavily here on the concept of 'democratic legitimacy' that has been cogently developed in the work of Robert Post, a leading American First Amendment scholar.

2. Offensive Expression in European Convention Jurisprudence—*Handyside* Rhetoric and Reality

The European Court of Human Rights has emphasized on numerous occasions that the freedom conferred in Article 10 is not to be seen as confined to information or ideas that are favourably received or deemed inoffensive. In *Handyside* v. *UK*, freedom of expression was said to be a 'fundamental feature of democratic society'. It is not limited 'to information or ideas that are favourably received or regarded as inoffensive' but extends to ideas that 'offend, shock, or disturb the State or any sector of the population'.[12] Allowing such expression was said in *Oberschlick* v. *Austria* to follow from the demands of pluralism, tolerance and

---

[11] Judgment of 13 September 2005, Application No. 42571/98, Joint Dissent of Judges Costa, Cabral-Barreto and Jungwiert, para.8.
[12] *Handyside* v. *UK* (1979–80) 1 EHRR 737.

broadmindedness 'without which there is no democratic society'.[13] However, in respect of expression that touches upon religious subjects, freedom of expression has proved something of a chimera as the Strasbourg Court (though sometimes opposed by the Commission) has readily backed away from interfering with national authorities' interference with expression. In *Otto Preminger Institut* v. *Austria*[14] for example, the Court upheld the seizure and forfeiture of a film which it considered was 'gratuitously offensive' to the religious feelings of others (including Roman Catholics) as a lawful restraint on the applicant film institute even though it was intended that the film would only be shown to a paying audience with an interest in 'art cinema' type films who had, in any event, been given prior warning of its nature. The usual reason that is offered for this unwillingness to second-guess national authorities' decisions is that national authorities are better placed than the supervisory, supranational authorities to understand where to draw the line between permitted and improper expression about religious matters.

Consider thus *Wingrove* v. *UK* where the British Board of Film Classification (BBFC) refused to issue a certificate to the video *Visions of Ecstasy* which concerned the erotic visions of a character that was supposed to be St. Teresa of Avila—a sixteenth-century Carmelite nun.[15] The refusal of a certificate meant that the video could not be lawfully distributed. In effect, this was a prior restraint on publication. By a majority of 7–2, the Court held that there had been no violation of Article 10. In his separate concurring judgment, Judge Bernhardt, the President of the Court stated that, after having viewed the film, he had not been convinced that the film should have been effectively banned by the refusal to classify it. However, where basis of the restriction was the religious feelings of others and moral standards more generally, the role of the international judge was limited to those cases where the national decision could not be 'reasonably justified'. In his view, the domestic authority's margin of appreciation had not been exceeded here and, accordingly, there had been no violation of Wingrove's Article 10 rights. Any other conclusion, Judge Bernhardt concluded, would have the unfortunate effect of turning the Strasbourg Court into an appellate body on taste and decency standards. In an academic article approving of what he labelled the 'subsidiarity' of the approach in *Wingrove*, the then-Deputy Registrar of the Court Paul Mahoney cited the fact that

culturally diverse European democratic society has not yet developed a common value to the effect that blasphemy laws are themselves and as a matter of principle repugnant to the dictates of free speech.[16]

The majority in *Wingrove* adopted without qualification the national authorities' description of the film as offering the viewer 'a voyeuristic erotic experience' and

---

[13] (1995) 19 EHRR 389.
[14] (1995) 19 EHRR 34.
[15] (1997) 24 EHRR 1.
[16] P. Mahoney, 'Universality Versus Subsidiarity in the Strasbourg Case Law on Free Speech: Explaining Some Recent Judgments' (1997) 4 *E.H.R.L.R.* 364, 375.

this may have disinclined the Court to apply at face value *Handyside*'s protection of shocking and offensive ideas. But be this as it may, rather than upholding what was in effect a complete ban on the film's distribution, the Court could nonetheless have insisted that the BBFC devise some less intrusive means of protecting the sensibilities of Christians such as the use of an '18' certificate with explicit warnings on the front cover. Judge Bernhardt's reliance upon the margin of appreciation within which national authorities' might regulate a vital Convention right such as expression in order to safeguard a competing public interest points up a problematic aspect of this jurisprudence that is developed in the next section. It is worth noting in passing here, however, that the conceptual murkiness surrounding the margin of appreciation was exacerbated by the reference in *Wingrove* to the need to strike a 'balance' between the Article 10.1 right and Article 10.2 countervailing interests. In his concurring judgment Judge Pettiti commented upon the

difficult balancing exercise that has to be carried out . . . where religious . . . sensibilities are confronted by freedom of expression . . . [17]

'Balancing' sits oddly alongside established features of Article 10 jurisprudence that require any interference with expression to be both (i) 'convincingly established' and (ii) based on 'relevant and sufficient' grounds.[18] This is commonly thought to give a presumptive priority to the principle of freedom of expression and a correspondingly narrowed scope for national interference with expressive activity. 'Balance' seems to undercut much of this presumptive priority as virtually all criticism of a religion or the religious practices of its adherents is likely to cause offence and, as such, become eligible to be put onto the scales by national authorities who are best placed to judge the need for restriction. As *Murphy* v. *Ireland* illustrates, the notion of 'balance' is especially corrosive of freedom of expression where the message is unpopular and causes offence to listeners across a number of sections of the community.[19] In *Murphy* the Strasbourg Court declined to interfere with a ban imposed on an advertisement intended for broadcast on commercial radio submitted by the *Irish Faith Centre*—a small, Dublin-based evangelical grouping. The ban on all religious advertising in the audio-visual sector was challenged in the Irish courts as an unconstitutional limitation of the qualified right to communicate in Article 40(3)(1) of the Irish Constitution. In the High Court of Ireland, Geoghegan J upheld the constitutionality of the ban as a reasonable limitation on the right.

It is sufficient, in my view, if there were good reasons in the public interest for the ban. Irish people with religious beliefs tend to belong to particular churches and that being so religious advertising coming from a different church can be offensive to *many people . . .* (emphasis added).[20]

---

[17] (1997) 24 EHRR 1, 36.
[18] See thus *Goodwin* v. *UK* (1996) 22 EHRR 123, para. 40.
[19] (2004) 38 EHRR 13.   [20] Ibid., para.12.

In its judgment, the European Court of Human Rights noted how religion had been a 'divisive factor' in Ireland and adopted Geoghegan J's observations about religious advertising on television or radio causing offence to those belonging to a different religious affiliation (although curiously the same 'offensive' impact would not apparently be felt by readers of newspapers or magazines).[21]

3. The Margin of Appreciation and the Absence of Consensus

The aspiration towards universal standards of human rights protections is compromised by the doctrine of the margin of appreciation. Under the doctrine, core freedoms that are said to lie at the heart of any democratic society take on fundamentally different complexions across signatory states. The expanded application of the doctrine from beyond its original context of national security,[22] to other rights and freedoms permits local and temporary political majorities to curtail a range of individual entitlements for self-interested reasons.[23] In the context of offensive expression, the doctrine permits the censoring of unpopular or controversial expression, thereby preventing orthodoxies being held up to critical examination.[24]

As was noted earlier, the justification for a more relaxed form of supra-national scrutiny in religious offence cases centres upon the absence across Council of Europe states of a consensus on moral matters in general or religious beliefs more specifically. In each of these circumstances, the argument is advanced that national authorities with their local knowledge are best placed to make line-drawing decisions, demarcating the boundary between permitted and excessive expression. National authorities are, after all, explicitly charged under Article 1 of the Convention with securing for everyone within their jurisdiction the rights conferred under the Convention.[25]

---

[21] Ibid, para. 73. On the more immediate impact of broadcast (as opposed to print) media, see *Jersild* v. *Denmark* (1994) 19 EHRR 1, and, under the US First Amendment, *FCC* v. *Pacifica Foundation* 438 US 726 (1978).

[22] *Lawless* v. *Ireland* (No. 3) (1961) 1 EHRR 15. For commentary, see F. Ni Aolain, 'The Emergence of Diversity: Differences in Human Rights Jurisprudence' (1995) 19 *Fordham Int'l L. J.* 101; E. Benvenisti, 'Margin of Appreciation, Consensus and Universal Standards' (1999) 31 *N.Y.U. J. Int'l L. & Pol.* 843, 845–846 and R. St. J. Macdonald, 'The Margin of Appreciation', in R. St. J. Macdonald, F. Matscher, and H. Petzold (eds.), *The European System for the Protection of Human Rights* (Dordrecht: Martinus Nijhoff, 1993).

[23] The actual range of the margin of appreciation will be heavily context dependent. See further R. St. J. Macdonald, ibid., 85.

[24] Benvenisti is particularly concerned by the tendency for minority interests to be compromised by the application of a relaxed standard of review at the supra-national level. See Benvenisti (n. 22 above), 849 *et seq.*

[25] See *Handyside* v. *UK* (1979–80) 1 EHRR 737, para. 48 for an early example of the emphasis upon the role of national authorities in securing Convention rights in the context of expression that conflicts with public morals 'especially in our era which is characterised by a rapid and far-reaching evolution of opinions on the subject'.

Whilst accepting that the absence of a consensus on moral matters such as abortion could be plausibly established, there is clearly a need for some methodological clarity from the courts about how this empirical claim is supported. Thus, issues arise about the sources to which the Court should turn for information on a matter that is as fluid and dynamic as moral standards. In the case of religious beliefs, should the Court refer to the published statements of church officials, rabbis and imams, or to opinion poll surveys of practising adherents of the faith? In *Handyside* (which dealt with obscene materials) by contrast, the absence of a consensus on the requirements of morals is simply asserted. We are asked to take it as beyond dispute that no pan-European consensus exists.[26] There is, in short, neither empirical evidence cited in support of this claim nor an explicit methodology to sustain it. Sometimes, the Court has been confronted with the claim by national authorities that moral standards vary *within* the state from region to region. In *Muller* v. *Switzerland* the Court seems to have taken on trust the Swiss authorities' claims that, unlike the rest of Switzerland, the people of Fribourg were particularly sensitive to the sexually explicit art of Muller, although it appears from the record that the Fribourg prosecutor only acted to seize the paintings after just one man complained that his daughter had reacted violently to the exhibited materials.[27]

Leaving to one side for a moment these methodological objections and accepting, for the sake of argument, that the absence of a European-wide consensus on a matter of morals generally or the causing of religious offence more specifically could be satisfactorily established, does the Court's record in such circumstances point consistently away from intervention with rights-infringing decisions of national authorities? *Dudgeon* v. *UK* would seem to suggest not. Although the Court spoke of greater tolerance towards adult homosexual conduct across Council of Europe States by 1981, not even the majority in *Dudgeon* was able to claim that a *new European norm* of equal respect and tolerance towards practising homosexuals had evolved. In Northern Ireland itself, opinion was divided on whether Northern Ireland should decriminalize homosexual conduct between males over the age of 21 years.[28] Nonetheless, the majority held that the possibility of criminal proceedings against consenting adult homosexuals had not been shown to correspond to a pressing social need and as such violated

---

[26] Ibid.

[27] (1991) 13 EHRR 212. There is a suggestion that the Court might have taken a less indulgent view of the seizure had access to the exhibition been limited rather than open and free of charge to all members of the public. Moreover, had the art consisted of political satire rather than sexually explicit images, this feature too would have strengthened arguments for supervisory review.

[28] Most religious groups (in both the Roman Catholic and Protestant communities) were generally opposed to reform, as were some political parties such as the Democratic Unionists. Support for reform came from groups representing homosexuals and social work agencies. The General Synod of the Church of Ireland also favoured decriminalization, whilst disputing that homosexuality was as acceptable in the eyes of God as heterosexuality. See further *Dudgeon* v. *UK* (1981) 3 EHRR 40, 43–4.

Dudgeon's Article 8 right to respect for his private life. From *Dudgeon* then, we can see that the absence of consensus need not point inexorably to relaxed supranational scrutiny. In the context of a vital Convention right—the right to respect for one's private life—the Court was prepared to take a searching supervisory look at national restrictions and strike down a disproportionate interference with the right.[29]

4. A 'Right' to be Protected from Offensive Expression?

The protection from offence that religious beliefs undoubtedly enjoy in European human rights law inevitably raises questions about the juridical basis of this protection. Does the Convention for example recognize a 'right' to be protected from having one's religious views insulted or offended? If so, where does this right come from? Two possible candidates for such a right can be identified in the Court's reasoning. The first is the 'rights of others' derogation on freedom of expression in Article 10(2). Alternatively, it has been argued that the right to freedom of thought, conscience and religion in Article 9 provides the true locus of this entitlement. At the outset, it should be noted that neither the Article 10(2) derogation nor the Article 9 right guarantees in express terms the right to protection of religious feelings, a fact pointed out by the joint dissenting judgments in *Otto Preminger Institut* v. *Austria*.[30] Such textual considerations aside, the case law points in divergent directions.[31] *Otto Preminger Institut* seems to suggest that 'the rights of others' in Article 10(2) can only be understood by reference to the Article 9 right to religious freedom. In contrast, Judge Pettiti, one of the majority in *Wingrove*, declares without further elaboration that Article 9 cannot be 'in issue'[32] in cases of offence to religious feelings and that the 'rights of others' restriction in Article 10(2) is capable of serving as a self-standing ground of restraint. Judge Pettiti's denial that Article 9 is relevant here seems correct. It is difficult to see how, outside of wholly exceptional circumstances, public insults and criticisms of religious belief and practices by others[33] might engage Article 9

---

[29] Under the US Constitution, the state's legitimate interest in preserving and enforcing general moral standards does not permit the restriction of a fundamental constitutional right. See *Lawrence* v. *Texas* 539 US 558 (2003), 571–4, 578 and the discussion in J. Weinstein, 'Democracy, Sex and the First Amendment' (2008) 31 *N.Y.U. Rev. L. & Soc. Change* 865, 884, 895–7 and accompanying footnotes.

[30] (1995) 19 EHRR 34, Joint Dissenting Opinion, para. 6. See the majority in *I. A.* v. *Turkey* who argued that certain forms of conduct (including writing books) could be repressed if judged 'incompatible with respect for the freedom of thought, conscience, and religion of others'. (2007) 45 EHRR 30, para. 41.

[31] See on this point C. Evans, *Freedom of Religion under the European Convention on Human Rights* (Oxford: OUP, 2001).

[32] (1997) 24 EHRR 1, 34.

[33] I intend the reference to 'others' here to refer solely to private individuals. If, to the contrary, the insulting expression emanates from the state (or even powerful corporations), it is perhaps less difficult to conceive of situations in which Art. 9 might be engaged.

by effectively restraining believers' freedom of religion, or the public/private manifestation of religious beliefs.[34] At bottom, the claim that an individual's freedom of religion is somehow dependant upon (and may be improperly curtailed by) what others say about that individual's religious beliefs effectively allows religious beliefs to dictate what may be said in the public sphere. This position is extremely difficult to reconcile with modern understandings of liberalism.

If the 'rights of others' in Article 10(2) is felt to offer a free-standing basis for restraining offensive expression, there needs to be some clarity about the reach of this particular derogation. It would appear beyond argument that each enumerated Convention right and freedom is a 'right or freedom' for the purposes of Article 10(2). However, as we have just seen, ordinarily offensive expression will not interfere with the exercise of Article 9 freedoms. Instead, it could be claimed that the 'rights of others' is something of a 'catch-all' derogation[35] capable of extending more widely to rights and freedoms not enumerated in the Convention and that this is where we find the juridical basis of the right not to be offended. Consistent with this view, the Court employed this derogating provision loosely in *Kokkinakis* v. *Greece* to hold that there was a 'right' to be protected from the religious proselytism of others.[36] Such a potentially limitless pool of 'countervailing rights' is deeply unattractive and troubling, threatening as it does to swallow up the right to freedom of expression.

An alternative and more plausible means of giving protection to religious feelings under the Convention is to contend that there is at best a countervailing societal or public interest in not offending the feelings of religious persons. This countervailing interest in preventing offence could be said to reflect overarching Convention values such as tolerance, mutual respect, and dignity.[37] If the dispute in the Danish cartoons case is properly characterized as the exercise of an Article 10(1) *right* versus a *public interest* in the preservation of tolerance towards the religious beliefs of others, then, if it is to be meaningful constraint befitting a

---

[34] It is accepted in Convention jurisprudence concerning Arts. 8 (right to respect for private life) and 11 (freedom of association) that the state may come under a positive obligation to secure the Convention rights of an individual where the interference occurs by virtue of the actions of a third party. See *X & Y* v. *Netherlands* (1986) 8 EHRR 235 (Art. 8) and *Plattform Artze fur das Leben* v. *Austria* (1998) 13 EHRR 204 (Art. 11). No equivalent ruling has been made in respect of Art. 9 although where it could be shown that another individual prevented the exercise of Art. 9 rights, a failure on the part of the state to protect religious freedom could be said to put the state in breach of its duty under Art. 1 of the Convention to 'secure' Convention rights. For general discussion, see A. Clapham, *Human Rights in the Private Sphere* (Oxford: OUP, 1993) and D. J. Harris, M. O'Boyle, and C. Warbrick, *Law of the European Convention on Human Rights* (London: Butterworths, 1995), 19–22.

[35] M. D. Evans, *Religious Liberty and International Law in Europe* (Cambridge: CUP, 1997), 328.

[36] (1994) 17 EHRR 397. The Greek authorities had failed however to specify sufficiently clearly the reason why the applicant had been found to have 'improperly proselytised' under Greek law and so his conviction in the domestic courts was deemed to violate the right to freedom of religion under Art. 9.

[37] Note however the comment of Professor David Feldman in 'Human Dignity as a Legal Value' (1999) *Pub. L.* 682 that dignity can easily serve 'as a screen behind which paternalism or moralism are elevated above freedom in legal decision-making'. 697.

fundamental individual right, the Convention right to freedom of expression must be given strict priority over the policy goal of a tolerant society. On this view, expression ought only to be interfered with when there is a demonstrable and serious threat to that policy goal and then only to the extent strictly needed to safeguard it. The evidential burden on Contracting States in such circumstances ought to reflect the strong priority afforded to freedom of expression.

5. Offence as a Contents-Based Ground for Restricting Expression

American First Amendment jurisprudence is instructive as to why we should be sceptical about the regulation of public discourse by reference to its viewpoint or content.[38] One of its core precepts is that allowing the state to restrict public debate on the basis of its content is highly dangerous to democratic self-governance and to the intellectual growth and fulfilment of individuals both in their capacities as speakers and listeners.[39] Thus, in *Boos* v. *Barry* the Supreme Court observed

[I]n public debate our citizens must tolerate insulting and even outrageous speech in order to provide 'adequate breathing space to the freedoms protected by the First Amendment'.[40]

Selective treatment of particular topics raises the prospect that the state might even be able to excise certain disfavoured ideas or images from public discourse altogether.[41] The decision of the House of Lords in *R (Pro-Life Alliance)* v. *British Broadcasting Corporation* provides an instructive domestic example of the failure to grasp the dangers of content regulation.[42] In that decision, the House of Lords upheld as a lawful exercise of broadcaster's discretion the BBC's refusal to

---

[38] For an interesting collection of essays on methodological issues surrounding the use and abuse of comparative constitutional materials, see S. Choudhry (ed.), *The Migration of Constitutional Ideas* (Cambridge: CUP, 2006). My justification for drawing upon First Amendment jurisprudence in the above section of materials is that these materials help to uncover the normative underpinnings of our supra-national system of rights protection. Asking why the US Supreme Court has taken a particular stance can inform a European discussion as to why our human rights court reason in the way that it does. The outcome of the process may be to conclude either that existing European rules are not justified and ought to be modified or discarded, or alternatively, that any emergent differences with the comparator system are in fact justified because of specific historical or cultural reasons or differences in prevailing commitments in political philosophy. In my view, the reasons why content-based restrictions have been found constitutionally problematic in the US also make such restrictions problematic under the European Convention on Human Rights.

[39] See thus *New York Times* v. *Sullivan* 376 US 254, 270 (1964) per Brennan J. and *Police Department of the City of Chicago* v. *Mosley* 408 US 92, 95 (1972) per Marshall J.

[40] 485 US 312, 322 (1988) quoting from *Hustler Magazine* v. *Falwell* 485 US 46, 56 (1988).

[41] *Simon & Schuster Inc.* v. *Members of New York State Crime Victims Board* 502 US 105, 116 (1991).

[42] [2003] 2 WLR 1403.

broadcast actual footage of a suction abortion showing the dismembered limbs and head of an aborted foetus on grounds of 'offence to public feeling'. That the censorship in question occurred during a General Election campaign and, further, that the images were to be shown in a Party Election Broadcast to be broadcast in Wales by the anti-abortion *Pro-Life Alliance*—a registered political party with candidates standing in Welsh constituencies—underscores that their Lordships neglected to incorporate into their reasoning a principled understanding of the vital importance of political expression to democratic self-governance.[43]

Politicians may well seek to suppress 'offensive speech' for reasons which have more to do electoral advantage than a genuine commitment to the values of tolerance and respect. Indeed, the values of tolerance and pluralism can even be placed in jeopardy where a powerful majority acting through their political representatives invoke 'offence' to stifle minority or unpopular viewpoints. The temptation to acquiesce in the official suppression of views with which we disagree or even loathe, because their public expression offends our sensibilities should additionally be resisted because, on a subsequent occasion, it may be our speech or that belonging to persons with whom we agree that is targeted. According to the American philosopher Joel Feinberg, the causing of offence rarely constitutes a sound basis for restraining speech or conduct.[44] He observes that people take offence at many socially useful or even necessary activities. Furthermore, offence will readily result where the audience possesses bigoted attitudes. He offers the example of the undoubted offence that would have been caused as recently as several decades ago in parts of the United States by mixed race couples strolling arm in arm down the main street. We might build upon Feinberg's argument and observe that if suppression of speech were allowed merely to prevent offence to religious belief expression is liable to be curtailed by reference to the standards of some of the least tolerant, most easily outraged members of society. Such a basis for prohibiting expression would produces the ironic result for liberal democracies that, in trying to accommodate differences out of a commitment to pluralism and the equal worth of alternative conceptions of the good life, the lack of tolerance on the part of certain of the accommodated groups provides the basis for curtailing the freedoms of the rest.

In addition to the costs associated with suppressing offensive speech, as John Stuart Mill demonstrates there are benefits to both society and the individual that may accrue from expression that causes 'moral distress' in others with religious beliefs.[45] As Jeremy Waldron has cogently argued, Mill's Harm Principle—far from sanctioning restrictions upon expression and conduct that outrages others

---

[43] For critical commentary, see I. Hare, 'Debating Abortion—The Right to Offend Gratuitously' (2003) 62 *Cambridge L. J.* 525 and I. Cram, *Contested Words—Legal Restrictions on Freedom of Speech in Liberal Democracies* (Aldershot: Ashgate, 2006), 50–7.

[44] *The Moral Limits of the Criminal Law—Volume 2 Offense to Others* (New York: OUP, 1985), 25.

[45] J. S. Mill, *On Liberty* in *Three Essays: On Liberty, Representative Government, the Subjection of Women* (London: OUP, 1975).

and causes genuine moral distress—actually encourages offensive expression.[46] Upon initial consideration, this conclusion may seem odd if we count the very real feelings of hurt that can result when the beliefs of faithful adherents to a religion are attacked as a 'harm' in the Millian sense. However, it is important to recall that the presence of 'harm' for Mill is merely a threshold requirement before individual liberty can be limited by the state. Those who favour restriction must then additionally show that the costs of preventing moral distress resulting from the damaging impact of censorship are outweighed by the benefits of preventing this moral distress. Waldron argues that Mill saw the causing of moral distress not as a cost but rather as a positive consequence of exposure to rival accounts of the good life. The outrage that a Christian or Muslim or Jew might feel on reading a blasphemous book or seeing a blasphemous image is 'something to be welcomed, nurtured, and encouraged in the free society that Mill is arguing for'.[47] Waldron labels the clash between rival accounts as an 'ethical confrontation' and contends that Mill's commitment to societal progress in matters of morals would allow a range of expressive activity in matters of religion from verbal debates to the flaunting of alternative lifestyles in public. That he contemplated a vigorous, disrespectful, and even abusive exchange of opinion in public is evident from the fact that at one point in *On Liberty,* Mill speaks of the necessity for truth to emerge from the 'rough process of a struggle between combatants fighting under hostile banners'.[48] Apart from the enhanced moral development of society, Mill also believed that the individual benefited morally and intellectually from participation in such a confrontation and suggested that where no spontaneous dissent exists, it might even have to be manufactured for the benefits described above to accrue. For these reasons, a Millian approach to offensive expression would strongly uphold an uncensored liberty to publish the images of the Prophet as a satirical commentary on the links between Islam and terrorist violence.

Mill's defence of offensive expression rests upon instrumental arguments about the benefits to the audience or society that flow from such speech. It is possible of course to frame a non-instrumental account of offensive expression that stresses its intrinsic worth to speakers. At the end of this chapter, I discuss Robert Post's work on democratic legitimacy to explore how one such non-instrumental approach might play out in the context of offensive expression.

6. Expression about Islam as 'Political Speech'

A specific reason for according a significant degree of protection on speech about Islam arises from the overt desire of certain Islamic groups to attain political power so that they might advance their goal of creating a theocratic state. Thus,

---

[46] 'Mill and the Value of Moral Distress' (1987) 35 *Pol. Studies* 410.
[47] Ibid., 413. [48] See n. 45 above, 59.

the fourteenth-century scholar and jurist Ibn Taymiyya, considered by Islamists and jihadis to offer a valid interpretation of sharia law, is credited with first making the argument that Islam requires state power to bring about the Caliphate. Tamiyya urged the forcible overthrow of those rulers of Islamic lands who were unbelievers and used laws other than sharia and would not repent. Today, Tamiyya's work provides a justification for jihadis in their violent struggle against both 'unbelievers' and 'sinning' Muslim leaders who fail to implement sharia.[49] Certain fundamentalist forms of Islam can be seen as having an overtly political character in that they advocate disobedience to secular, democratically constituted authorities and contest elections on platforms that seek either to replace secular laws and secular authority by sharia law and sharia courts, or to have the latter co-exist alongside the former. As the Court recognized in *Refah Partisi (the Welfare Party)* v. *Turkey*,[50] the policies of the Turkish Islamist *Welfare Party* would, if implemented, oblige individuals to obey rules laid down by an entity other than the state, and, further, treat persons differently on the basis of their religious beliefs. Sharia law, it was observed, also diverged from Convention values in respect of the criminal law, criminal procedure, and the legal status of women. In all these regards, the *Welfare Party* advocates had placed arguments about the desirability of a Caliphate in mainstream political debate.[51]

In their protests about the Iraq war, justifications for suicide bombings and their broader critiques of western imperialism and decadence, imams and others claiming to be within the Islamic tradition have entered the public sphere of societal discourse and politics. As such, comments about Islam whether by its defenders or its critics (including the cartoonists) would appear to fall within Professor Eric Barendt's definition of political speech as expression 'relevant to the development of public opinion on the whole range of public issues which an intelligent citizen should think about'.[52] Accordingly, the appropriate intensity of review by the supranational authorities in Strasbourg of national authorities' restrictions on expression about Islamic links to terrorist activity ought to be that accorded to restrictions on political expression. Without such close supervision over national authorities' restrictions, there will likely be self-censorship on the part of commentators with the result that the violent protests on behalf of those who have been 'insulted' will have succeeded in creating a 'chill' on freedom of expression that robs the public domain of a range of opinion concerning the links between religious fundamentalism and terrorism.

---

[49] M. R. Habeck, *Knowing the Enemy: Jihadist Ideology and the War on Terror* (New Haven: Yale UP, 2006), ch. 2.

[50] (2003) 37 EHRR 1.

[51] Not all Islamist parties are hostile to democracy, however. In Turkey, the AK (Justice and Development Party), which gained power in the 2007 elections, is apparently 'committed to the democratic process'. See n. 49 above, 4.

[52] *Freedom of Speech* (Oxford:, Clarendon Press, 1985), 152. Barendt's definition was adopted by the High Court of Australia in *Theophanous* v. *The Herald and Weekly Times Limited* (1994) 182 CLR 104.

7. The Problem of Gratuitously Insulting or Gratuitously Offensive Speech

It is one thing to mount a defence of expression *intended* as a serious contribution to public affairs that others may find disagreeable or offensive on religious grounds. Within offensive expression, however, there lies a sub-class of speech labelled 'gratuitously offensive' speech that is considered the least deserving of protection. Thus the majority in *I. A.* v. *Turkey* talked of the 'duty on speakers to avoid expressions that are gratuitously offensive'.[53] The *Oxford English Dictionary* defines 'gratuitous' as 'without any good ground or reason; not required or warranted by the circumstances of the case'.[54] In the context of offensive expression, two distinct meanings can be discerned. The first concerns offensive expression that is groundless, lacking an objective basis in fact or reason whilst the second involves some form of unnecessary or needless expression that offends members of the audience.

If we first consider 'groundless' offensive expression, the criticism of the speaker is that the facts do not lend any support whatsoever to his assertions (even though the speaker nonetheless intends to make a serious contribution to public debate and is mistaken about the existence of certain facts). This appears to be the sense in which the term is used by the Court in *I. A.* v. *Turkey* to describe a passage in a philosophical novel *The Forbidden Phrases* whose publisher had been convicted of blasphemy and fined in the Turkish courts. One passage in the novel stated that the Prophet Muhammad broke his fast 'through sexual intercourse, after dinner and before prayer. Muhammad did not forbid sexual intercourse with a dead person or a live animal.'[55] The allegation here is factual although 'unwarranted'[56] in the Court's view since established and orthodox accounts unequivocally reject this version of events in the life of the Prophet. In a tersely worded majority opinion that could find no violation of Article 10, the Court referred to the gratuitous nature of the offensive words and declined to intervene with the Turkish authorities' assessment on the blasphemy charge, noting that the latter could not be said to have overstepped their margin appreciation.

In principle, the lack of protection for gratuitously offensive speech appears eminently sensible. Little or no contribution to public debate or understanding is made or is intended to be made by groundless utterances and where gratuitously offensive speech is regulated, it could be argued that legal controls play a role in fostering a civilized and respectful discourse among individuals who wish to participate in public debate. This could be one way of furthering the value of individual respect and dignity that underscores the Convention.

---

[53] (2007) 45 EHRR 30.
[54] 2nd edn. (Oxford; OUP, 1989).
[55] See n. 53 above, para. 44.   [56] Ibid.

One of the problematic aspects of the *I. A.* v. *Turkey* ruling however is the way in which a characterization of 'groundless' or 'unwarranted' offence plays out in the context of a novel. Here there is by definition no *necessary* historical grounding for the novel, and yet such works may be read as offering a particular critique of a religious tradition as in the case of Salman Rushdie's *Midnight's Children* or *The Forbidden Phrases*. Neither is it clear from the report whether the publisher was given an opportunity under Turkish law to mount a defence of literary or other merit and adduce expert evidence to support this claim and challenge the prosecution's case.[57] Second, whilst the motivation for the prosecution seems to have been the atheistic attack on religious belief in general, the selection of particular passages in the novel as constituting the gratuitously offensive or abusive attack on Islam is open to the criticism that the prosecution was allowed to cherry-pick the most offensive parts of the novel without having to concede the context in which they were written. Finally, the medium of communication needs to be considered. As a novel, *The Forbidden Phrases* lacked the immediate impact and reach of a video (such as *Wingrove*), film (*Otto Preminger Institut*) or television broadcast (*Murphy*). According to its own jurisprudence, the Strasbourg Court should have been wary of endorsing the national courts' ruling.[58] Instead, the censorious views of the majority of Turkish society were indulged and an alternative, minority, and non-Islamic conception of the moral life stifled for fear of upsetting the prevailing religious sentiments of the community.

It may have been more credible to treat the passages complained of in *The Forbidden Phrases* under the second sense of 'gratuitous' identified above, namely 'needlessly' causing offence. Here, 'gratuitous' looks to describe the manner of expression and links to notions of abusive or excessive speech. A good example of this form of gratuitously offensive speech would be the 'Fuck the Draft' message on Paul Cohen's jacket which he wore in a Los Angeles courthouse.[59] Cohen's expression was held by a narrow majority of the US Supreme Court to be protected under the First Amendment.[60] For the dissenting justices however, opposition to the Vietnam War could have been expressed in other, less offensive terms. The dissent accords perhaps more closely with the dominant European approach as revealed by the ruling in *Otto Preminger Institut*.[61] It would have been possible for the film makers in the latter instance to have made their criticisms of the Roman Catholic Church without resorting to the 'provocative' portrayals of God, Jesus, and Mary.[62] By analogy, it might be argued that persons wishing to comment upon the links between Islam and terrorism could have done so equally

---

[57] In a report to the Istanbul Court of First Instance, a panel of three academics confirmed the view of the Dean of Theology at Marmara University that the novel was blasphemous. Ibid., paras. 22–5.

[58] Ibid. para. 44.

[59] *Cohen* v. *California* 403 US 15 (1971).

[60] The state was not entitled under the First Amendment to 'cleanse' public to the point where this sort of emotive speech was censored.

[61] (1995) 19 EHRR 34.

[62] Ibid., paras. 16, 22, and 56.

effectively without publishing a cartoon of the Prophet with a bomb-shaped turban. In the case of the written word, the author of a controversial work like *The Forbidden Phrases* might have been able to deploy a metaphor or some other allegorical device to hint at the substance of his provocative claims.

The chief difficulty that confronts this version of gratuitous offence is that it confers upon the state wide and vaguely defined powers to prescribe the *manner* in which ideas and opinions are expressed. It constrains the speaker by ruling out emotively charged language which, as the majority of the US Supreme Court recognized in *Cohen*, might often constitute the most powerful communicative style available to him. The 'cleansing' of public debate that results may please the squeamish but only at a cost to public discourse as the norms of a particular section of society are privileged.[63]

8. Putting the Breaks on Offensive Expression: Tipping Points and the Concept of Democratic Legitimacy

The foregoing arguments in favour of robust protection for offensive expression leave unexplored the important issue of the outer limits of the freedom to engage in offensive expression. If *Otto Preminger Institut, Wingrove, Murphy* and *I. A.* v. *Turkey* all erred in upholding national restrictions that bolstered majoritarian, religious sentiments, then it is right to ask how much more protective ought the Strasbourg Court have been. It is worth noting at the outset that some commentators are troubled by what they would classify to be an excessive degree of expressive freedom. Michael Ignatieff recently put it thus:

No one defending freedom of expression can be happy defending a cultural climate in which freedom exposes religious minorities to a daily drizzle of cheap jokes on television, ignorant remarks in the supermarket and the public house, and the occasional taunt or epithet on the way to the mosque or temple.[64]

One useful way of thinking about the circumstances in which liberal democracies might conceivably restrict offensive expression is provided by the idea of 'democratic legitimacy' that has been developed in the work of Robert Post and the tension he explores between individual autonomy and substantive equality.[65]

---

[63] This point is well made by Robert Post in 'The Constitutional Concept of Public Discourse: Outrageous Opinion, Democratic Deliberation, and *Hustler Magazine v Falwell*' (1990) 103 *Harv. L. Rev.* 605, 632.

[64] 'Respect and the Rules of the Road', in L. Appignanesi (ed.), *Free Expression is No Offence* (London: Penguin, 2005), 128. Ignatieff here classes together a range of different types of speech, some of it public and others that are less obviously so.

[65] See n. 63 above; 'Racist Speech, Democracy, and the First Amendment' (1991) 32 *Wm. & Mary L. Rev.* 267; 'Community and the First Amendment' (1997) 29 *Ariz. St. L. J.* 473; 'Democracy and Equality' (2006) 603(1) *ANNALS of the Am. Acad. Pol. & Soc. Sci.* 24; 'Religion and Freedom of Speech: Portraits of Muhammad' (2007) 14(1) *Constellations* 72.

Post's account starts from a definition of democracy as active and mediated self-rule by the citizens. In his view, for citizens to experience government as their own government, each person must 'have the warranted conviction that they are engaged in the process of governing themselves'.[66] A vital component of this conviction is the perception that the state is responsive to the values of each citizen and that each one of us has the potential to influence the outcome of public discourse through our ideas and arguments. The opportunity to participate in public discourse promotes individual identification with the state and its decision-making processes even if the actual outcomes of public discourse are at odds (as they must be from time to time) with our own preferences. To enable this identification with the state, each person must within the realm of public discourse be treated equally with other citizens and as an autonomous, self-determining individual. If, to the contrary, the state were to exclude an individual from participating in the speech by which public opinion is formed, those so excluded will experience a loss of 'democratic legitimacy' and feel alienated from the process of self-government. This alienation of the censored, however, could be justified where the consequence of allowing the censored expression 'alienates *all other citizens* from participating in public discourse'.[67] The silencing of the speaker in this scenario serves to preserve the very existence of *public* discourse. More problematic in Post's view is suppression of the speech of Citizen A on the grounds that it will have the effect of 'alienating' citizens from group B.[68] Here, the restriction on A is rationalized on the ground that it will promote the fuller participation of citizens from group B in public discourse. Where A is prohibited from speaking because citizens in group B find A's contributions to be offensive, a questionable trade-off occurs whereby the loss to democratic legitimacy that happens when A's autonomy is curtailed (and he is thereby alienated from public discourse) is sacrificed in the pursuit of a more inclusive polity. Post is critical of

---

[66] See 'Democracy and Equality' in ibid., 26.

[67] Ibid., 31, emphasis added. A type of speech that Post suggests might fit this scenario is 'fighting words' (ie face-to-face personal insults) as classically occurred in *Chaplinsky* v. *New Hampshire* 315 US 568 (1942) where on the streets of Rochester, New Hampshire the defendant accused the city marshal of being a 'damned fascist' and a 'racketeer'. This was treated by the Court as an instance of personal abuse in a private fracas rather than public discourse, although it would seem that the subject matter of the defendant's remarks did relate sufficiently to matters of public concern for the speech to be treated as a contribution to public discourse. Had Chaplinsky directed his remarks at a crowd, rather than the marshal directly, the case for extending First Amendment protection to the speech might have been stronger. I understand Post's position to be that expression which might otherwise qualify as a contribution to public discourse may nonetheless be suppressed because of the very language used by the speaker. This of course raises questions about what it means to participate in public discourse and involves normative judgments about whether the expression goes beyond personal abuse. It is plainly possible for speech that is personally abusive to also make a contribution to political debate. We have in the end to accept with Post that the peripheries of public discourse will remain vague.

[68] The literature on the 'silencing' effect of racist and other speech includes M. J. Matsuda, 'Public Response to Racist Speech: Considering the Victim's Story' (1989) 87 *Mich. L. Rev.* 2320 and R. Delgado and J. Stefancic, *Understanding Words That Wound* (Oxford: Westview Press, 2004).

such a strategy. The individualistic basis of public discourse through which each of us participates in collective self-determination dictates that the freedom of speakers' such as A must trump the claims from groups 'injured' by speech. The latter are required to demonstrate a degree of fortitude and self-confidence to enter the arena of public discourse unaided by the state. Otherwise, as Post himself observes, in large heterogeneous countries 'populated by assertive and conflicting groups, the logic of circumscribing political discourse to reduce political estrangement is virtually unstoppable'.[69]

This stance may be contrasted with a communitarian approach to speech regulation where the curtailment of A's speech and the consequent loss of autonomy is considered less problematic. In a communitarian society, the state is not neutral between conceptions of the good life, but seeks to promote a substantive version of the 'common good' and actively strives to create the public and private virtues needed for society to attain that end.[70] Liberal ideas of personal autonomy underpinned by notions of individual rights are rejected as missing the collective dimension of existence and fostering instead an atomized hedonism. Communitarians perceive individuals as having social characters grounded in the communities in which they live.[71] The good of the individual is not conceivable unless understood within some broader view of the good of the community. For communitarians, rules of civility found in the common law (for example in the laws of defamation and privacy) or in statutes regulating public morals, express dominant community norms and thus community identity. Restraints on offensive and racist expression (and thus on autonomy) can thus be cast and defended as the product of majoritarian rule-making that reflects prevailing norms such as tolerance and the equal worth of individuals and are enforced for the good of the whole community. Here, the protection of religious (or other group) feeling may be prioritized over the value of democratic legitimacy, or these legitimacy concerns may simply be seen as a non-issue and ignored altogether.

As Post himself has concluded, the relationship between speech and community is 'highly dependent upon contingent matters of history and culture'.[72] The detailed discussion of European freedom of expression jurisprudence earlier in this chapter revealed that the Strasbourg Court has shown considerable deference to local communities' perceptions of the boundary between permitted and prohibited expression and thus to local determinations of what the demands of civility require. This raises the question of whether these majoritarian restrictions are compatible with the demands of modern liberal democratic practice. The

---

[69] 'Racist Speech, Democracy and the First Amendment', see n. 65 above, 316.

[70] On communitarian thinking in general see, M. J. Sandel, *Liberalism and the Limits of Justice* (Cambridge: CUP, 1982), C. Taylor, *Philosophy and the Human Sciences: Philosophical Papers Volume II* (Cambridge: CUP, 1985), and M. Walzer, *Spheres of Justice: A Defence of Pluralism and Equality* (Oxford: Blackwell, 1983).

[71] A. C. McIntyre, *After Virtue: A Study in Moral Theory* (London: Duckworth, 1981).

[72] 'Community and the First Amendment', in n. 65 above, 483.

Court's failure to address the problem of offensive speech within a framework of arguments about the democratic legitimacy of regulation constitutes a serious omission. The idea of democratic legitimacy brings to the surface the often difficult balancing exercises that are at issue in free speech cases. Had the Court in cases like *Wingrove, Otto Preminger Institut, Murphy,* and *I. A.* looked to the alienating impact of the respective acts of national censorship upon the speakers and then balanced this alienation against any 'silencing' of Christians in the UK, Roman Catholics in the Austrian Tyrol, non-evangelicals in Ireland, or Muslims in Turkey, it is difficult to see how any of these restrictions could have been sustained. In the case of the Danish cartoons, allowing the offensive expression appeared to embolden a number of those who claimed to be offended. Public discourse in Europe was inundated by a range of Muslim perspectives and responses to the cartoons. Indeed, far from alienating Muslims from the state, or silencing them in public discourse, it could be argued that these participants in public debate demonstrated a healthy commitment to the idea that they could shape the contours of public policy. In so doing, those protesting against the right to engage in speech offensive to particular religious communities ironically revealed the fortitude that can be demanded of all of us in a pluralistic liberal democracy.

17

Criminalizing Religiously Offensive Satire: Free Speech, Human Dignity, and Comparative Law

*Amnon Reichman**

1. Introduction

Should satire that ridicules a religious figure or the core tenets of a religious belief receive different constitutional protection than that afforded to political satire? As the on-going Danish Cartoons affair reveals, this is a difficult question involving a potential clash between the values underlying freedom of expression and those underlying freedom of religion. This chapter will examine two possible models that seek to resolve the tension in principle: the US model, under which freedom of speech enjoys pre-eminence, and the Israeli model, that protects human dignity as the principal value. In outlining the Israeli approach, the chapter will analyse an Israeli case that led to the first criminal conviction for the violation of an act prohibiting the publication of material calculated to outrage religious sentiments. The chapter will then address some normative and institutional features that separate the US and the Israeli approaches. Moving beyond comparative legal analysis, the chapter will put forward the hypothesis that the source of the difference in jurisprudence arises at least in part out of a different cultural perception regarding the core meaning of 'speech' or 'expression' in these two jurisdictions. Drawing upon this cultural understanding, the chapter will suggest that perhaps it is passion, not merely reason, that organizes the realm of public discourse. The chapter will conclude with a brief comment on the possible limits of relying on foreign sources in some (passion-based) cases.

* A previous and expanded version of this chapter appeared in *Fordham International Law Journal.* Special thanks to James Weinstein for his careful reading of previous drafts and most conducive comments.

2. The *Suszkin* Case

On June 27, 1997, Tatyana Suszkin entered an area under the control of the Palestinian Authority in Hebron, carrying posters, designed and produced by her, depicting a hand-drawn pig wearing a Muslim headdress (Kafia) with the name Muhammad in Arabic and English sketched on its torso. The swine—considered particularly vile and defiling by Islam—held a pencil in one of its hooves and appeared to be writing the Koran while stepping on it. Suszkin carried glue and spray-paint, and was wearing a Kahane Chai[1] T-shirt. Israeli soldiers detained her and handed her over to the Israeli police. The following day, while on bail, she hurled a stone at a Palestinian vehicle driving in the Hebron area. She was convicted in the district court, inter alia, of attempting to outrage[2] religious feelings (§173 of the Israeli Penal Code) and received a sentence of three years in jail.[3] The Israeli Supreme Court denied her appeal.[4]

Justice Or, writing for the Supreme Court, noted that while the offence has been on the books since the British Mandate,[5] this case represented the first time the Court had addressed and applied the criminal prohibition against outraging

---

[1] Rabbi Meir Kahane formed a political party that advocated the strict application of biblical law towards non-Jews, primarily Arabs, which would have resulted in the confiscation of all Arab property, the disenfranchisement of Arab voters in elections for the Israeli parliament (the Knesset), the invalidation and prohibition of any interfaith marriage between Jews and non-Jews, and, ultimately, the deportation of Arabs from Israel into neighbouring Arab countries. In 1990 Kahana was murdered in the United States and his followers established a movement called Kahane-Chai (Kahane is alive.) After his followers turned to actions against Arabs, the movement was declared a terror organization under Israeli law. For a review of these events, see EA 11280/02 *Central Elections Committee for Sixteenth Knesset* v. *MK Tibby* [2003] IsrSC 57(4) 1, 52–3.

[2] The section as enacted by the British stated that it is a crime (carrying up to one year of imprisonment) for a person to publish any print, writing, effigy or image calculated or tending to outrage the religious feelings or beliefs of others, or to utter in a public place an in the hearings of another person any word or sound calculated or tending to outrage such feelings and beliefs. This provision was part of a chapter on offences relating to religious and public monuments. The Hebrew translation of this section of the Code, which became the official version upon the establishment of the State of Israel, carries a slightly different meaning, as the words 'calculated or tending to outrage' connote in Hebrew 'having the capacity of inflicting gross harm'. This essay will use the original British language, but it should be kept in mind that under Israeli law the notion of harm is explicit in the words of the statute.

[3] CrimC (Jer) 436/97 *Israel* v. *Suszkin*, [1997] IsrDC 97(5) 730. Suszkin was convicted of an attempt only, since there was no sufficient evidence that she actually distributed or posted the poster. She was also convicted for violating the prohibition against committing a racist act (§ 144D1(a) of the Penal Code (1977)), for attempting to deface property, for endangering life on a highway and for supporting a terror organization (§ 4(g) of the Prevention of Terror Ordinance (1948), as amended in 1980).

[4] CrimA 697/98 *Suszkin* v. *Israel* [1998] IsrSC 52(3) 289.

[5] The statute was originally enacted in 1936 by the British as s. of the Criminal Code Ordinance (Palestine). The statute was enacted by the High Commissioner—since the original design to have a local representative body as a legislature failed—and embodied provisions similar to those enacted in other parts of the empire. See N. Bentwich, 'The New Criminal Code for Palestine' (1938) 20 *J. Comp. Legis. and Int'l. L.* 71.

religious sentiments. The Court did not review the constitutionality of the section of the penal code on its face because the relevant Basic Law (Human Dignity and Liberty, enacted in 1992)[6] applies only with respect to prospective legislation. The Court nonetheless was called upon to interpret the section in order to ensure its application was consistent with the principles underlying the Basic Law. The Court upheld the conviction without committing itself to a narrow reading of the statute. It did not set a particularly high bar for 'outrage' (or in its Hebrew version, 'gross infliction of harm to sentiments') nor did it read the statute as requiring the showing of high likelihood of disturbance of the peace or violence which may result from such infliction. Placing this case in a comparative perspective reveals the significant gap that exists between the US and Israeli approaches to free speech. Had such a conviction been obtained in the United States, it would, in all likelihood, have been invalidated on the grounds that a statute criminalizing speech that outrages religious sentiments is invalid on its face under the First Amendment.[7] While it is unlikely that the Israeli legislature would have enacted this British Mandate-era statute today (if only because of the wide discretion it confers upon the prosecutors), the Knesset nonetheless did not see fit to revoke the Act or otherwise amend it after the conviction.[8]

3. Offensive Speech: Diverging Normative Justifications

As a normative matter, the status of freedom of expression relative to other rights provides a key theoretical distinction between the Israeli and American systems. The Israeli system follows, as a general matter, Mill's teachings, according to which basic liberties are legally protected, subject to the principle of harm: I am at liberty to move my hands until I hit my neighbour's nose, at which point I cause her harm and therefore am not at liberty to proceed.[9] The principle of harm is not restricted, conceptually, to physical harm. Although Mill suggested that speech

---

[6] As amended by Basic Law: Human Dignity and Liberty, 1994, S.H. 90.

[7] Above all else, the First Amendment means that government has no power to restrict expression because of its message, its ideas, its subject matter, or its content. *Police Department of City of Chicago* v. *Mosley* 408 US 92, 95–6 (1972), but see *Beauharnais* v. *Illinois* 343 US 250 (1952), in which the court relied on the then recent events of WWII and on the history of interracial violence in Illinois to uphold the criminalization of group libel. The validity and scope of *Beauharnais* are unclear. In *New York Times Co.* v. *Sullivan* 376 US 254 (1964) the court ruled that contrary to *Beauharnais* libel is protected under the First Amendment, yet the case did not address the issue of group libel (as distinct from libel of a public figure) nor the issue of the likelihood for violence, both central to *Beauharnais*. The court was reluctant to review the matter in *Smith* v. *Collin* 439 US 916 (1978) (*cert denied*), and let the decision of the lower courts, according to which *Beauharnais* is no longer good law, stand.

[8] The text of the statute was in fact amended by the Knesset in 1988 but not with respect to the 'tendency to outrage' section; the Knesset replaced the enumerated modes of publication (print, writing, etc.) with the generic term 'publication'.

[9] J. S. Mill, *On Liberty with the Subjection of Women and Chapters on Socialism* (Cambridge: CUP, 1989), 20, 56.

should be protected against the religious forces seeking to suppress it, it is clear that speech may cause harm to the individual, not only indirectly, such as through libel, but also directly, by harming one's mental state through verbal abuse. And while a moral agent has the liberty to express her autonomy through deeds and speech, others have the right to be free from the harm caused by such actions and expressions. This basic understanding results in a structure of rights that does not automatically place a premium on the protection of expression over other rights. Nor does it necessarily distinguish between rights applicable to state action and rights applicable in the private realm. From the perspective of the victim, it matters less whether her right was infringed by the state or by a private actor acting under the laws of the state.[10] Under the 'general rights' model, speech is indeed instrumental to the pursuit of truth and for self-fulfilment, but other rights play an equally instrumental role in furthering equally important values, such as the protection of the self and other aspects of autonomy. It is therefore not surprising that in most of the common law world freedom of expression is not deemed as necessarily 'weightier'—whatever that may mean—than other fundamental rights.[11] Consequently, to the extent that constitutional bills of rights were enacted to protect fundamental rights—as is the case in Canada—and to the extent that the function of the state is to protect human rights or at least to govern while guarding against violation of human rights—as is the case in several post-WWII civil law and common law jurisdictions—freedom of expression is protected, but does not enjoy pre-eminence over other rights.

It is against that background that the US constitutional structure is innovative. The US Constitution protects speech specifically, and does not protect, for example, the freedom from emotional harm (to the extent that such harm may be caused by state action). Neither is the right to be free from libel specifically protected, so if the legislature revokes the statutory or the common law protections against libel, the US Constitution need not be directly engaged. It would seem, then, that the basic assumption under the US model is that the ordinary common law and legislative processes could provide adequate protection against emotional harm (or any other 'civil' or 'private') harm, and it is not the business of the Federal constitution to guard against harms the regulation of which could be entrusted to the ordinary structures of (accountable) governance, such as legislatures. The right to the free expression of ideas, however, receives specific protection from the legislative process itself, even if such protection entails limiting the protection the legislature (or the courts) could provide against emotional harm.

---

[10] C. R. Sunstein, 'Neutrality in Constitutional Law (With Special Reference to Pornography, Abortion, and Surrogacy)' (1992) 92 *Colum. L. Rev.* 1; C. R. Sunstein, *The Partial Constitution* (Cambridge, MA: Harvard UP, 1993), 71–5; L. M. Seidman and M. V. Tushnet, *Remnants of Belief: Contemporary Constitutional Issues* (New York: OUP, 1996), 89.

[11] See D. Feldman, *Civil Liberties and Human Rights in England and Wales*, 2nd edn. (Oxford: OUP, 2002), 765–74.

The fact that the US Constitution does not view freedom of expression as one liberty coequal with others and instead views it as a constitutive element of democratic sovereignty, demands normative justification. Traditional justifications, exemplified by Alexander Meiklejohn, highlight the importance of speech to the democratic voting process: speech is essential to informing people how to cast their ballot.[12] Yet these justifications are subject to the objection that voting is a rather crude and incomplete method of participation, and therefore a risk of alienation of social segments which values have not played a meaningful part *de facto* in the formation of policy on point is not insignificant. More recent and interesting justifications focus on the relationship between speech, values, and community more generally. According to these arguments, expressive participation—not only through voting but also, if not mainly, through the voicing of one's opinion—is central to the processes of establishing (and maintaining) the bonds between the various segments of heterogeneous societies, bonds which transform the various communities into a 'people' or a sovereign. Put bluntly: 'I am allowed to speak—therefore I belong.' Furthermore, scholars have noted that in heterogeneous societies a clash of values is almost inevitable, and thus it is almost inevitable that voicing some opinions would offend members of some communities. In order to avoid the risk of imposing values of one community on another by proscribing speech that offends one community but expresses the values of another, a sound policy would be to establish a public sphere where members of all communities may express their values and opinions in a nearly unfettered way. Such a sphere stands to mitigate the loss of loyalty by members of the community whose values would have been declared 'inferior' had the sphere allowed for content-based regulation. If the values of all communities are equally subjected to criticism, including ridicule, then the risk of fraying the social fabric —a risk which exists given the limited ability of the participatory voting processes to provide meaningful opportunity to influence the outcome of public debate—is lower. Moreover, such sphere allows—if not invites—participation by members holding diverse values, and in that respect, the claim is, the 'legitimacy' of the system is maintained (or enhanced). Such sphere enables members of the various communities to examine their values and determine whether (or not) to transform and adopt other values (or practices). In that respect, a public sphere where freedom of expression reigns is consonant with the underlying premise of democracy—the demand for the availability of mechanisms to curtail the exercise of state power and the promise of the potential for social transformation.[12a]

---

[12] *Free Speech and Its Relation to Self-Government* (New York: Harper, 1948).

[12a] Robert Post, 'Meiklejohn's Mistake: Individual Autonomy and the Reform of Public Discourse', 64 *U. Colo. L. Rev.* 1109, 1124–35 (1993); Robert Post, 'Community and the First Amendment' 29 *Arizona State L. J.* 473 (1997); Robert Post, 'Between Democracy and Community: The Legal Constitution of the Social Form', in Democratic Community: *Nomos* XXXV 163–90 (John W. Chapman and Ian Shapir eds., 1993); Robert Post, 'The Constitutional Concept of Public Discourse: Outrageous Opinion, Democratic Deliberation and Hustler Magazine v. Falwel', 103 *Harv. L. Rev.* 601 (1990).

The upshot of these inter-related justifications is the constitutional protection of a sphere of debate and exchange of ideas structured around the concept of public reason: we seek to convince each other by putting forward arguments that we believe resonate better with the principles of reason and best reflect our sense of justice as an expression of our experience. To the extent that public discourse is about 'legitimacy', then legitimacy, morally speaking, is an expression of reason.

Clearly, this normative argument also has sociological dimensions. The United States was formed as a nation of immigrants, not as an organic ethno-political unit with shared history, customs, and mores. It is no surprise, then, that the protection of speech was necessary in order to generate 'peoplehood'. As Robert Post demonstrates, contrary to the common law model where speech is seen as a threat to solidarity, to the community mores and to loyalty to King and Country, speech in the United States, given its highly heterogeneous social fabric, plays an essential role in the formation of a political community. Therefore the constitutional protection of speech can be seen as protecting that which binds the American meta-community (or community of communities) together. Post also suggests that given the heterogeneous nature of the US society, the constitutional protection of speech allows members of various communities, with differing values, to maintain their faith in (or loyalty to) the American nation. As is apparent, under this sociological approach emotions play a role as central as reason, and therefore a tension arises between the normative justification for public discourse (which is centred around reason) and the sociological (or cultural) approach to the importance of public discourse which presumes a loss of legitimacy if passion-based claims are unprotected. The US jurisprudence is less than consistent on this point by protecting emotive speech[13] while highlighting the importance of public discourse as a reason-based instrument.[14]

While not all US scholars are convinced that the US model is necessarily superior,[15] it is difficult to ignore its influence. In contrast, for the time being at least, the constitutional right that organizes the Israeli system is human dignity. In enacting Basic-Law: Human Dignity and Liberty, the Knesset deliberately omitted the express protection of speech.[16] We can assume that this was so, at least in part, because the Knesset felt that granting freedom of speech constitutional status would excessively limit governmental powers to balance (or appease) the different interests at stake: those of the humanistic 'liberals,' who

---

[13] *Cohen* v. *California* 403 US 15 (1971); *Hustler Magazine, Inc.* v. *Falwell* 485 US 46 (1988).

[14] *Dun & Bradstreet* v. *Greenmoss Builders* 472 US 749 (1985) 787, Justice Brennan (dissenting): 'The breadth of this protection evinces recognition that freedom of expression is not only essential to check tyranny and foster self-government but also intrinsic to individual liberty and dignity and instrumental in society's search for truth' (citing *Bose Corp.* v. *Consumer's Union of the United States, Inc.* 466 US 485, 503–504 (1984); *Whitney* v. *California* 274 US 357, 375 (1927), Brandeis, J, concurring.

[15] See eg, F. Schauer, 'Must Speech Be Special?' (1983) 78 *Nw. U. L. Rev.* 1284.

[16] For the political background that led to the adoption of the basic laws, see J. Karp, 'Basic Law: Human Dignity and Liberty—A Biography of Power Struggles' (1993) 1 *Mishpat Umimshal* 323.

would like to be able to criticize all edifices of power by empowering individual critique (as an expression of human dignity), and those of the 'religious conservatives', who would like to ensure the respect toward 'basic values', including the dignity of religion (and of man, created in God's image).[17]

It could be argued that behind the choice to place human dignity, rather than expression, at the core of the Basic Law lies the realization that Israel is even *more* heterogeneous than the United States; the bonds that tie the various communities into a 'polity' are threatened by *truly* deep divides. Whereas the people of the United States share the American dream—the pursuit of liberty (and wealth)— the various communities that comprise the Israeli society have radically different notions regarding the identity of the state. Consequently, it is unclear that enshrining speech, rather than human dignity, will serve well as the uniting value over which the various communities form their loyalty to the polity. As courts interpret the Basic Law, they will have to decide whether the right of human dignity (situated at the constitutional level) also encompasses the protection of freedom of expression (already recognized as a fundamental right in Israeli administrative law), and if so, what the contours of protected speech are within the right of human dignity.

In any event, it is easy to see that the statute underlying *Suszkin* would fare better in Israel than it would in the United States: while freedom of expression could be derived from human dignity, so could the freedom from dignitary harm.[18] In fact, it seems that freedom from dignitary harm is at least as closely connected to human dignity as freedom of expression. After all, one's dignity is offended if one cannot freely expresses one's attitude, but one's dignity is equally (if not more directly) offended if one is shamed or humiliated (at least if dignity is taken to mean also 'honourable standing' or 'equal membership'). Speech or an expressive act that humiliates Muslim worshipers, therefore, has a weaker claim to heightened constitutional protection in Israel because that very speech violates other aspects of the right of human dignity, such as a Muslim's right to be free from dignitary harm on account of their religious beliefs. A different ordering of democratic values, expressed in a different structure of rights, thus appears to be separate the Israeli system from its US counterpart.

4. Offensive Speech: Is Religion Normatively Special?

The Israeli statute goes a step further in separating itself from the US approach: it singles out a certain class of speech—that which offends religious sensibilities— over other classes of offensive speech, and is thus content-oriented and

---

[17] Ibid. See also Justice Dorner in PPA (Prisoner Petition Appeal) 4463/94 *Golan* v. *Prison Services* [1996] IsrSC 50(4) 136.

[18] In the *Miller* v. *Minister of Defense* (1995) IsrSC 49(4) 94 at 131, Justice Dorner says that there is no doubt that the purpose of the Basic Law is to prevent humiliation.

discriminates on the basis of the speaker's viewpoint. Under Israeli law there is no offence that criminalizes infliction of emotional harm as such (other than torture, which includes emotional torture[19]). Do religion and religious feelings have an independent value? According to the standard liberal model, all rights deserve equal respect and thus the law should equally protect against harm to all types of sentiments, not just religious ones. Some Israeli scholars have indeed suggested that singling out harm to religious sentiments is problematic—a legal artefact left from pre-liberal times[20]—and that perhaps the court should interpret the statutory scheme to mitigate differences between types of emotional harm.

Others, in contrast, have suggested that religious beliefs are unique because religion is an institutionalized normative regime that competes with the legal regime of the modern state on a fundamental level.[21] On this view, it is prudent to accord religious sentiments a greater margin of tolerance, so as not to push believers into having to choose between the authority of the state and the authority of their religion (namely, the authority of God). Just as state and religion may clash over issues such as service in the (secular) military, so could state and religion clash when religion contains duties to suppress certain types of speech (protected by the secular constitution). It is therefore no wonder that the British legislature saw fit to prohibit speech derisive to other religions: not only would such speech likely result in actual violence, but of equal importance such speech would bring the foundation upon which the modern state (and the rule of law) rests into direct conflict with the foundation upon which religion (and religious law) rest, to the detriment of both. This tension may be especially acute in Israel, a Jewish democracy that does not separate state and religion.

While the US Constitution, which does separate state from religion, can be seen as playing the role of an all-encompassing civil religion,[22] such a role in Israel would amount to a direct clash between state and deity-based religion.[23] While in the US public discourse is, as an essential part of this civil religion, taken to be the sacred domain of thought and critique, this may not be so in societies where a deity-based religion is not separated from the state and where public discourse is not sacred for the sake of discourse (thought, deliberation, etc.) but rather may be either sacred or sacrilegious, depending on whether the speech (and its regulation) force citizens to chose between their loyalty to God (and God's community) and

---

[19] The one exception is the s. 368c of the Penal Code (1977) that criminalizes emotional abuse among the offences against minors and helpless.

[20] D. Statman, 'Hurting Religious Feelings', in M. Mautner et al (eds.), *Multiculturalism in a Jewish and Democratic State* (Tel Aviv: Ramot Univ Tel Aviv, 1998).

[21] I. Englard, *Religious Law in the Israel Legal System* (Jersualem: Harry Sacher Institute For Legislative Research and Comparative Law, Hebrew Univ, 1975), 33–46.

[22] R. N. Bellah, 'Civil Religion in America' (1967) 96 *Daedalus: J. Am. Acad. Arts and Sci.* 1; R. N. Bellah and P. H. Hammond, *Varieties of Civil Religions* (San Francisco: Harper & Row, 1980). See also M. Cristi, *From Civil to Political Religion: The Intersection of Culture, Religion and Politics* (Waterloo, Ont.: Wilfrid Laurier UP, 2001), 47–89.

[23] G. Sapir, 'The Boundaries of Establishment of Religion' (2005) 8 *Mishpat Umimshal* 155.

their loyalty to the state (and fellow citizens). While the civil religion of the US encourages people to fight to protect the rights of all citizens to express their views, the various religions that comprise the religious fabric in Israel face certain explicit religious duties if certain statements are expressed, including the religious duty to suppress future expression of these sacrilegious views. The recent clashes with the Muslim world over the cartoons of Muhammad demonstrate this attitude. In light of human history, some would say that securing against such religious offences is also pragmatically wise.

Moreover, those who call for treating religion distinctively could remind us that in religion, speech plays a unique role by connecting a person to God positively (prayer) or negatively (blasphemy). It is not 'just an opinion'. Moreover, religious speech, such as prayer, is often a communal act and thus the community has a direct stake in the content of the speech. Such speech may bring good (blessing) or harm (curse) to others, and thus the others, namely the community, are directly involved in the act of religiously-relevant speech, if only because it is the religious duty of the community to care for its members.

Those who view the challenge posed by religion as unique suggest that the state, including the judiciary, should demonstrate extra-sensitivity to religious sentiments of all. According to this approach, the potential chill emanating from the prohibition against religiously offensive speech could be mitigated by sound prosecutorial policy to restrict prosecution to the most extreme cases (for prosecution would not only directly violate the liberty of the speakers but also risk further deepening social rifts by making martyrs out of the jailed speakers).

Notwithstanding the arguments raised above, it is far from clear that religion should indeed receive special treatment. Beliefs as strongly held as religion—such as ideological commitments—may also clash and pose an equal threat to the social fabric, and some ideologies may include a moral duty to suppress speech detrimental to its core values. Moreover, it is not clear that heightened civility is the only logical solution to religious clashes. It could still be the case that a sphere where it is accepted that all are free to express their sentiments, including (religious) sentiments that offend the (religious) sentiments of others would allow for co-existence without fracturing society. Stifling the expression of offensive sentiments—for example: the Jews are the chosen people and are therefore 'superior'; the Jews have sinned for not accepting Jesus; or that Muhammad is the bearer of truth and the last prophet that ought not be ridiculed—may equally lead to alienation of some (if not all) groups. Attempting to chart a 'correct' balance between religious sentiments, sentiments in general, and free speech appears ever more elusive. As the debate regarding the appropriate protection speech (and religious beliefs) should be accorded continues, the law on the Israeli books remains, and amending it or declaring its application unconstitutional would require marshalling good enough reasons. Thus far, the practical solution in Israel has been to leave the law on the books but to enforce it only in the rarest circumstances (*Suszkin* being the only documented one in recent memory).

5. Citizens, State, and Speech

The regulation of speech—and in particular hate speech—also calls to our attention the different attitudes regarding the relationship between state and citizen. The US approach to the protection of speech (and constitutional rights in general) assumes some degree of adversity between citizen and state: while the three branches of government are there to govern on behalf of the people, the state nonetheless remains a threat individual liberty. The Leviathan is dangerous and it is natural and desirable that the people should distrust the exercise of power by state agents (as these agents may have an interest in broadening and consolidating their power).

This adversary position is not necessarily shared in other common law democracies. The notion of responsible government—that we should trust the government to carry out the public mandate granted to it—is prevalent in countries such as Canada.[24] The idea that the representatives can be trusted to protect the rights and interests of their constituencies was often raised as an argument against the necessity of enacting a constitutional bill of rights in Canada,[25] and when one was adopted it was not a result of a crisis in the protection of human rights, but rather as a vehicle to establish common identity upon which all Canadians would unite.[26] The Canadian Charter of rights— which enshrines all basic civic and political rights, except, interestingly, property rights—was not taken by the courts as necessarily establishing adversity between the government and the citizenry but rather as reinforcing the basic fiduciary duty officials owe the public.

In this respect, the situation in Israel is even more complex. The Jewish people struggled for sovereignty for years. The establishment of the state of Israel, as a national home for the Jewish people, creates a special relationship between the community and the state: it represents the affirmation of dreams and aspirations rather than a dangerous Leviathan.[27] Approached from this angle, Israel is more Canadian than Canada. Nevertheless, centuries of living in the Diaspora have taught Jews to view the official branches of the state as something that ultimately

---

[24] P. W. Hogg, *Constitutional Law of Canada* (Scarborough, Ont.: Carswell, 1997), 251; J. L. Hiebert, 'New Constitutional Ideas: Can New Parliamentary Models Resist Judicial Dominance When Interpreting Rights?' (2004) 82 *Tex. L. Rev.* 1963, 1963–4.

[25] See M. Mandel, *The Charter of Rights and the Legalization of Politics in Canada* (Toronto: Thompson Educational Publishing, 1994), 39–46.

[26] See Hogg (n. 24 above), 694; A. Cairns, *Charter versus Federalism: The Dilemmas of Constitutional Reform* (Montreal; Buffalo: McGill-Queen's UP, 1992); R. Gwyn, 'Trudeau: The Idea of Canadianism', in A. Cohen and J. L. Granatstein (eds.), *Trudeau's Shadow: The Life and Legacy of Pierre Elliott Trudeau* (Toronto: Random House of Canada, 1998).

[27] Israel's declaration of independence emphasizes the historical bond between the Jewish people and the state, and calls the Jewish Diaspora to join the historical act of building a Jewish nation. Official Paper (1) 14.5.1948, 1 (14 August 1948).

may be captured by forces that would harm the Jewish people.[28] Jews have therefore insisted on maintaining social structures that are separate from the state, and are often at odds with the state. The Israeli Court must therefore steer a course between the attitude that the state is the manifestation of peoplehood (and thus cannot be viewed as 'the enemy'), and on the other hand the remnants of Diasporaic attitudes reflecting the culture of collective autonomy from state law and hints of illegalism (or disrespect towards civil authority).[29] The ambivalent attitude in Israel toward law as 'our' norms and law as 'their' decrees thus adds a layer of complexity to the justifications the Court provides for its doctrine and intervention. Put differently: if in the United States the court acts on behalf of the Constitution as embodying the values and symbols of 'We, the People' by protecting the individual members of the people from the power of the executive and the legislature—on behalf of whom, and against whom, does the Israeli Court act?

Until 1995, the Israeli Court positioned itself as protecting the people against the executive by acting as the agent of the legislature in reviewing the acts of the bureaucracy. The Court refrained from exercising constitutional judicial review of statutes and restricted itself to administrative review (which included the development of a judicially created bill of rights). Although the Basic Laws enacted in 1992 did not expressly provide for judicial review of legislation, in 1995 the Court construed these laws as conferring such authority upon it, and consequently the tension between the Court as the agent of the state and the Court as an agent of the people intensified. More specifically, in exercising judicial review for the protection of speech the Israeli Court faces the following dilemma: on the one hand, it could portray free speech as a fundamental civic value (and thus portray itself as acting in the name of the people against the state). This position is problematic, however, because the values of the Jewish people may be noble and just, but free speech is not prominent among them. Therefore the Court might be perceived as imposing civic values which are not home-grown, thereby placing itself in an even greater adversarial position vis-à-vis the State of the Jewish people. If, on the other hand, the Court portrays itself as a formalist agent of the state and its laws, it would require some creative rhetoric to justify striking down laws of the state on behalf of the state, especially given the legislative silence on the matter of judicial review and its decision not to enumerate speech as a protected right.

---

[28] The objection toward civil authority is a central motive of the Jewish Diaspora folklore and was central in the clandestine efforts to bring Jews to Israel and settle the land under British rule. See the story 'Hadrasha', in H. Haim, *Hadrasha and Other Stories* (Tel Aviv: Dvir, 1991), 127. See E. Shprinzak, *Every Man Whatsoever Is Right In His Own Eyes: Illegalism In Israeli Society* (Tel Aviv: Sifriat Poalim, 1986).

[29] Eg, see the contrasting opinions expressed by Justices Zamir and Cheshin in HCJ 164/97 *Conterm Ltd.* v. *Ministry of Finance, Department of Customs and VAT* [1998] IsrSC 52(1) 289, regarding the desirable relationship between the state and the individual, and especially the fiduciary duty owed by the individual toward the state.

The relationship between citizen, state and speech is complicated for yet another reason: the decisions of the Court are themselves also speech. The court's speech (about speech) is an essential component in the formation of the national ethos. While this ethos addresses the aforementioned tension between responsible government and limited government, its main thrust is the formation of membership in the community, including the formation of what this membership entails. Put differently, in deciding matters of hate speech, such as the *Suszkin* case, the court is engaged not only in manoeuvring between 'our law' and 'their decrees' but also between 'us' and 'them.' In legal disputes over what constitutes hate speech and whether such speech is nonetheless protected, it is often the case that the court informs us that hate should not be expressed at 'them,' because they are in fact (the court argues) part of 'us'.[30] By making pronouncements on what it means to be a member of the Israeli community—and what rights and obligations come along with that membership—the court thus impacts Israel's delicate politics of identity. The court's legally binding speech is therefore a factor in establishing the shared beliefs that bind the different factions of the Israeli society into a polity. However, since Israelis have yet to reach a shared understanding of the nature of the state (Jewish and/or democratic), the court's pronouncements regarding who We the People are (what we stand for and what duties we owe our fellow citizens) are bound to offend some and appear to others as illegitimate ventures into the sphere best left to political parties and the general populace. The vagueness of the term 'human dignity' allows the court to navigate between a universalist notion of a community of moral agents to which all belong—and which the court protects against the state—and a particularistic notion of the Israeli community, where group membership matters, where accommodation of the various groups is central, and where the court plays the role of a state agent in ensuring such accommodation.

6. The Cultural Significance of Speech

A fuller explanation for the different approaches to the protection of free speech adopted in the United States and Israel requires us to delve even deeper by exploring the meaning of speech itself. Each society may have a different collective conception of what it means to 'speak'. As alluded to earlier, the cultural understanding of 'speech' raises the possible singularity of religious speech. But there are other cultural elements that suggest that 'speaking' in the United States may not necessarily be the same as 'speaking' in Israel. Although scant reliable empirical data on point exists, it is nonetheless submitted that in Israel, the

---

[30] M. J. Matsuda, in 'Public Response to Racist Speech: Considering the Victim's Story' (1989) 87 *Mich. L. Rev.* 2320, 2345–8, says that the prohibition should guarantee that minorities can be an equal and safe part of society.

meaning of words—spoken and written—is different; this is so because the power of the word is different. According to this hypothesis, in the United States, the word is the opinion of the speaker to which he or she is entitled. In Israel, words have an independent force; nearly mystical. Somewhat paradoxically, words are taken more seriously in Israel than in the United States, and therefore receive lower legal protection. In Israel words are more dangerous—not necessarily because of the reaction they may elicit from others but because of their very nature—and therefore the speaker should beware (and the state may perceive a stronger justification for regulation). Words are seen as having the power to constitute reality.[31] In the United States, one person's word does not necessarily have substantial weight when it clashes with another person's word. Not so in Israel. Each speaker is taken as having a formative power, and once a word is spoken it cannot be taken back. Public discourse, therefore, is not only about a political exchange of ideas based upon persuasion; rather public discourse in infused with transformative speech acts. As if the speaking of the word has a role both in reflecting and constructing the world around us, where images and symbols, rationality and emotions, passion and reason, truths and believes, past and future, human autonomy and divine intervention are all interlaced.

From the perspective of an informed observer it seems that words spoken by a person regarding another person in the Israeli society tie both the speaker and the subject of the speech to the collective, in a different manner than in the United States. In the United States—to the extent that we may talk about the United States in singular terms—a prevailing narrative is that people define themselves through their own speech, and, to an extent, take pride in having a 'thick skin' that allows them to tolerate disagreeable and even offensive expressions of others. In Israel, on the other hand, the prevailing narrative—again, grossly generalizing—is that the status of a person and her belonging in the collective is determined in no small degree by what people say about her. Thus, in Israel, 'thick skin' means detachment, alienation, and perhaps uncaring, a position seen as reflecting negatively on the moral fibre of the person.

While in a rather heterogeneous society like the United States speech forms the common ground which citizens as speakers share, speech in Israel, a hyper-heterogeneous society, is often perceived as a threat to the complex mechanism of keeping the various social units together. At least as far as political speech is concerned, the American system acts as if there exists an 'all-American' sphere

---

[31] The Biblical saying: 'Death and life are at the behest the tongue' (Proverbs 18, 21), is used frequently. The importance of words in the Israeli public sphere is reflected in the high interest and public reaction to the mystical-religious 'pulsa de-nura' rituals held by national religious extremists in order to bring a curse upon Prime Ministers Rabin and Sharon. See A. Balint et al., 'A "pulsa de-nura" ritual was held for Prime Minister Sharon: "If he dies there will be no disengagement"', *Ha'aretz* 28 July 2005. See also S. Ilan, 'Curse and tell', *Ha'aretz* 28 July 2005, noting that the ritual had become a media event without much religious content.

where speech is not only the emblem of individual liberty, but its protection serves to unite the different individuals (and the different communities) into members in that all-American collective. In Israel, this all-national sphere is infused with identity symbols that do not necessarily sanctify each individual as a speaker in the democratic discourse, but rather value the collective and the struggles it is facing: 'We are all Israelis since we all face the same challenges and missions; inflicting harm on the mosaic of beliefs that form the Israeli fabric would thus endanger maintaining the ensemble'. Moreover, this all-Israeli sphere—to the extent that it exists—would not necessarily be governed by reason; it could well be in the domain of passion, where the common currency is one of deep commitment to ideologies and desire to promote causes. If this is the case, the Court would be hard pressed to fully adopt the US approach towards community-building through free speech. While it might be the case that the Court would urge all members of the society to view the commitment to free speech as the bedrock principle upon which to establish membership, the different meaning of speech itself might limit the success of such efforts.

If these hypotheses indeed capture a glimpse of the social reality, they provide further insights into some of the differences between Israel and the US discussed above. As mentioned, the Israeli Court, as an organ of the state, has to chart its course not only between opposing attitudes towards the state as 'ours' or 'theirs' but also with respect to its own role, given the tension between the civil religion (liberalism) and the deity-based religions of Judaism and Islam. On the one hand, the Court is expected to appear as a neutral body, devoid of any value-laden tilt toward one conception of the state or another, let alone one ideology over another. Public confidence rests on the assumption that judges separate themselves from the passionate battle of ideals, energetically fought in the Israeli public sphere. On the other hand, the notion that the court is fully separated from the other organs of state governance or from a certain ideology—a virtue, under the US model of separation of powers—is seen not only as unrealistic by some, but as undesirable in Israel.[32] In the final analysis, all the organs of the state are burdened with the collective mission of creating and sustaining a Jewish democracy; the courts should get no leave of absence. The idea that the court is disengaged and detached would strike at least some as heresy: is a court in Jewish democracy just like a court in any other liberal democracy? From its inception, Israel sought to be more than yet another nation-state; it sought to express Jewish values. It is therefore no wonder that the Court, while striving to ensure the robust sphere of the exchange of ideas, ideologies, and beliefs as the tenets of liberal democracy everywhere demand, is nonetheless careful to note that it is a genuinely Israeli constitutional law that the Court is

---

[32] According to Daphne Barak-Erez, the identification of the Israeli Supreme Court with the national ideology is the source of the public confidence in it. See her *Milestone Judgments of the Israeli Supreme Court* (Tel Aviv: Ministry of Defense and the Broadcast UP, 2003), 128.

developing.[33] Comparative law, while informative and inspirational, is therefore only a limited source of law according to the Israeli Court, not only because it lacks formal authority, but because its origins are rooted in systems with different social conditions and legal conceptions.

7. Legal Cultures—Balancing Words

Paying attention to the rhetorical tools available to judges in addressing offensive speech reveals another significant difference between US and Israeli doctrine: the use of 'balancing'. Whereas in the US the notion of balancing freedom of expression with other rights has met with notable opposition,[34] judges and scholars in Israel have wholeheartedly embraced the balancing methodology.[35] Moreover, what resembles in the US the language of 'balancing' is often applied in a manner that is not. Many of the doctrines that imply a balance of sorts (between the 'price' of suppressing speech and the weight of the governmental interest) predetermine the resulting outcome. This is most evident with respect to the 'strict scrutiny' that the Court applies to content-based restriction on public discourse which requires the state to show that the regulation serves a 'compelling' state interest and is narrowly tailored to achieve this interest.[36] While it could be argued that implicit in this doctrine is the relative 'weights' of the value underlying the state interest and the value of free speech, in fact the doctrine is set and applied so only in very limited circumstances will the Court find that the state interest is compelling enough and that the means used by the state are narrowly

---

[33] See Chief Justice Barak in HCJ 1715/97 *Lishkat Menahaley Hashka'ot* v. *Minister of Finance* [1997] IsrSC 51(4) 367 at 403: 'Indeed, comparative law reassures the judge that the interpretation given to the legal text is accepted and works well in other jurisdictions. However, comparative inspiration ought not lead to imitation and disparagement. The ultimate decision must always be "local." Moreover, we should also be aware of the limitations of comparative law. The law reflects the society, and our society is different from other societies.'

[34] See T. A. Aleinikoff, 'Constitutional Law in the Age of Balancing' (1987) 96 *Yale L.J.* 943. The most prominent opponent of balancing on the US Supreme Court was Justice Hugo Black. See eg, *New York Times Co.* v. *United States* 403 US 713, 714–20 (1971), Black, J., concurring; H. L. Black, 'The Bill of Rights' (1960) 35 *N.Y.U. L. Rev.* 865.

[35] In HCJ 153/83 *Levi* v. *Southern Dis. Commissioner* [1988] IsrSC 38(2) 393, 400, Justice Barak says that balancing is recognized in the Israeli law as an expression of the non-absolute status of rights. See also G. Pessah, 'Freedom of Speech and the Legal Foundation of the Press' (2000) 31 *Mishpatim* 895; E. Benvenisti, 'Regulating Speech in a Divided Society' (1999) 30 *Mishpatim* 29.

[36] *Boos* v. *Barry* 485 US 312 (1988); *Carey* v. *Brown* 447 US 455, 461 (1980). But see *Burson* v. *Freeman* 504 US 191(1992); *Austin* v. *Michigan Chamber of Commerce* 494 US 652 (1990). This type of balancing was referred by scholars as 'definitional' or 'principled' balancing, contrasted with 'ad-hoc' balancing. See M. B. Nimmer, *Nimmer on Freedom of Speech: A Treatise on the Theory of the First Amendment* 2-15–2-24 (1984); S. H. Shiffrin, *The First Amendment, Democracy and Romance* (Cambridge, MA: Harvard UP, 1990), 32. The 'definitional' v. 'ad-hoc' are similar to the Israeli 'vertical' v. 'horizontal' but are not identical. Eg, 'ad-hoc' balancing implies an 'all things considered' decision, whereas 'horizontal' balancing may entail a principled analysis of the relative 'weight' of the rights at stake (as well as a principled analysis of the alternative ways available at minimizing the overall infringement of the clashing rights).

enough tailored to pass muster. In Israel, this is referred to as 'vertical' balancing:[37] the public interest is placed 'above' the right—or is 'weightier' than the right—but it will trump the right only if the state demonstrates that there is near certainty that the interest will sustain a serious injury if the speech will not be suppressed. The term 'balancing' notwithstanding, the Court in these cases is engaged in a formalistic methodology that provides rule-like protection to certain types of speech.

A different kind of balancing is what the Israeli Court calls 'horizontal' balancing:[38] the balancing between two rights, when the court actually has to 'weigh' the importance of each right (ie, the value it protects) and how much of each right is being infringed by the state action.[39] This is indeed true balancing, since the court is seeking a 'margin of accommodation' for both rights, a 'compromise' between the two rights[40] that reflects their exact weight under the circumstances. Despite the scientific precision the test implies, horizontal balancing is subject to the obvious criticism of the absence of a shared metric[41] and that this amorphous process allows the court to reach ad hoc, result oriented decisions. As obvious as the methodological difficulties of horizontal balancing may be, the Israeli legal culture expressed, until recently, little or no reservations regarding its application.

In *Suzkin*, the need to balance arose as the Court tried to determine whether the lower courts had struck the right balance between freedom of expression and the value of tolerance of religious beliefs. Recall that Ms. Suszkin was not charged with violating an ordinary 'breach of the peace' offence, and thus the Court was not required to examine whether her expressive conduct would bring about riots and whether such riots, under the circumstances, would be a form of a heckler's

---

[37] The Israeli Court applies the vertical test when faced with a clash between a compelling governmental interest and a fundamental human right. In HCJ 448/85 *Daher* v. *Minister of Interior* [1986] IsrSC 40(2) 701, the clash was between the interest of public safety and the freedom of movement. In CrimA 126/62 *Disenchik* v. *Attorney General* [1963] IsrSC 17(1) 179, the clash was between the interest of maintaining an independent judiciary (that ensures due process to all) and the freedom of expression. This could be compared to the language the US courts use in applying the strict scrutiny standard when the government uses race as a criterion for its action: such action will be allowed to stand only if it is absolutely necessary for achieving a compelling state interest and the use of race is narrowly tailored to such an achievement. See *Korematsu* v. *US* 323 US 214 (1944), where the court ruled that exclusion of citizens of Japanese ancestry from certain West Coast areas was justified because of the compelling need to prevent sabotage.

[38] See HCJ 2481/93 *Dayan* v. *Wilk, Jerusalem District Commander* [1994] IsrSC 48(2) 456, 480.

[39] Justice Dorner says in HCJ 1514/01 *Gur-Aryeh* v. *Second Television and Radio Authority* [2001] IsrSC 55(4) at 285 that 'the purpose of the horizontal balance is to minimize the infringement of both rights' by allowing a minimal infringement of each right by the other. 'If the co-existence isn't possible, the right that will outweigh the other is the one that the consequence of its infringement inflicts greater harm for the individual.'

[40] Compare, in the US context, the clash between the right to vote and the right to speak in *Burson* v. *Freeman* 504 US 191(1992).

[41] See Aleinikoff in n. 34 above.

veto.[42] Rather, the harm the specific offence set to prevent is the harm to religious feelings.[43] The Court wondered whether the prosecution should show that it is nearly certain that the speech will cause such harm, or whether the prosecution need show only that it is probable, or highly probable, but not nearly certain that the publication would outrage religious sentiment.[44] The answer to that question depends on the relative weight (or importance) of the governmental interest. The more compelling the interest is, the greater the harm its frustration would impose, and therefore the longer the leash the Court would accord the state in demonstrating the likelihood that the harm would in fact materialize. What is the weight of outraging religious sentiments? In Israel—perhaps in all democracies, but certainly in Israel—that would be a hard question to answer. After somewhat serpentine reasoning, the Court left the matter undecided. It found that in any event, the 'near certainty' test was met: it was nearly certain that had the posters been posted or handed to Palestinians in Hebron, serious harm to religious sentiments would have been inflicted.[45] Yet the Court expressed no reservations in principle to go down the path of horizontal balancing, had the evidence been different.

Part of the Court's relative comfort with horizontal balancing rests on an unusual institutional feature which was not present in *Suszkin,* a criminal appeal, but which is present in almost all administrative and constitutional cases. In Israel, the Supreme Court sitting as a high court of justice has original jurisdiction in petitions against the state, and therefore its balancing doctrine is rarely applied in lower courts. It is therefore not surprising that the Israeli Court approves of horizontal balancing, knowing that such balancing grants it greater latitude to reach the desired balance in each case without delegating such discretion to lower courts. In the US, in which the Supreme Court exercises exclusively appellate jurisdiction in free speech cases over myriad lower courts, horizontal balancing might prove unmanageable and undermine the law's duty to treat like cases alike.

---

[42] HCJ 2481/93 *Dayan v. Wilk, Jerusalem District Commander* [1994] IsrSC 48(2) 456; HCJ 153/83 *Levi v. Southern District Commander* [1984] IsrSC 38(2) 393, and HCJ 148/79 *Sa'ar v. Interior Minister* [1980] IsrSC 34(2) 169, all addressing directly or indirectly, whether opposition from the possible audience is a legitimate concern for not providing a permit for a demonstration. Compare, in the US *Forsyth County Georgia. v. Nationalist Movement* 505 US 123 (1992). Perhaps the most famous US case on point is the Skokie affair, dealing with the rights of Neo-Nazis to march in the streets of the village of Skokie, a town with a large Jewish population including survivors of and those who had relatives who perished in the Holocaust). See *Collin v. Smith* 447 F.Supp. 676 (N.D. Ill, 1978), affirmed 578 F.2d 1197 (7th Cir, 1978).

[43] In determining what outrage to religious feelings is, the Court relied on an article by Statman in n. 20 above, and stated that 'one outrages another person religious feelings when his behaviour causes anger, frustration, insult, etc and these feelings were not stirred hadn't the other person been religious.'

[44] CrimA 697/98 *Suszkin v. Israel* [1998] IsrSC 52(3) 289, 306–7.

[45] The Court rejected Suszkin's claim that only an expert can determine the intensity of the suffering or the harm caused to the religious feelings of Muslim believers (*Suszkin* IsrSC 52(3) at 311). Some criticize the reliance on probabilities in this context: either a certain statement *does* offend sentiments, or it *does not*, and the court, like any member of society, is equipped with the necessary social understandings to make this determination. See HCJ 806/88 *Universal City Studios Inc. v. Film & Play Review BD* [1989] IsrSC 43(2) 22, 42.

This unusual institutional feature of the Israeli system is, however, in the process of changing, as the jurisdiction over public law matters is being transferred, slowly but surely, to the district court level (the intermediate level in Israel, above the courts of the peace). One can expect that unless matters of constitutional law are restricted solely to the Supreme Court sitting as a constitutional court—an idea that is being discussed but which raises a host of problems—the application of the balancing doctrine in lower courts in Israel is likely to raise serious issues of uniformity.[46]

8. Beyond Differences: The Doctrine of Fighting Words

It has been assumed, without discussion, that the statute at hand would have been struck down by the courts had it been adopted in the US. The statute criminalizes protected speech, and does so in a vague and overbroad manner. But more fundamentally, it seeks to proscribe speech simply because it is offensive to some, and thus clashes with the cornerstone of First Amendment principle against content discrimination. But what would have been the result if Suszkin had been charged not under this statute but for breach of the peace or breach of public order? US courts have long concluded that in some cases—rare but identifiable— offensive speech is proscribable as a breach of the peace if it constitutes 'fighting words'—'abusive remarks directed to the person of the hearer'.[47] Conceptually, face-to-face cursing at another human being is not a mode of communication of ideas, thoughts, facts, or opinions deserving of much constitutional protection. In *Suszkin* the judges in the lower courts found that Suszkin intended nothing but to 'retaliate' against the Arabs, insult for insult.[48] She had no intention of engaging anyone in dialogue or debate, nor was she trying to make a point through satire by provoking thought or reflection. This subjective intent matches the objective meaning of her action. Under the circumstances,[49] posting this pamphlet in Hebron, and thereby making the residents of houses on which the posters would be glued a captive audience, constitutes an act of aggression (albeit committed through words). Had Suszkin been indicted on a general breach of the peace offence, and had the Court resorted to the doctrine of 'fighting words', it could

---

[46] Such issues might burden the appellate docket of the Supreme Court, and may require the Supreme Court to 'discipline' lower courts of differing views. Given the diverging opinions among Israeli jurists regarding the proper balance between values, the Supreme Court might in fact lose some of its institutional capital as a result of such strife.

[47] *Cantwell* v. *Connecticut* 310 US 296 (1940); *Chaplinsky* v. *New Hampshire* 315 US 568 (1942).

[48] CrimC (Jer) 436/97 *Israel* v. *Suszkin* [1997] (unpublished), 9.

[49] 100,000 Palestinians and 500 Jews live in Hebron, which is probably the most sensitive point of friction between Jewish and Palestinian civilians in the occupied territories. The peak of the tension was the massacre of Muslim worshipers in Tomb of the Patriarchs on February 1994 by a Jewish settler. The situation in Hebron is described in *The Report of the Official Investigation Committee for the Massacre in Cave of Machpela* (1994).

have sidestepped the quagmire of selectively protecting religious sensibilities. Furthermore, the judges would not have had to go down the slippery slope of probabilities—whether it was likely, probable, highly probable, or nearly certain that feelings would be hurt. Nor would they have needed to determine the 'degree of injury' or the extent of emotional harm suffered (or likely to be suffered) by the audience. Had Suszkin been indicted for attempting to breach the peace it is not far-fetched to assume that her indictment would have been allowed to stand even in the United States. If calling a police officer 'a damned Fascist'[50] constitutes fighting words unprotected by the First Amendment, than it stands to reason that so would gluing these highly offensive posters on Muslims' houses in Hebron.[51]

The unique facts of *Suszkin* differentiate the case from other cases—and, for that matter, from the Danish cartoons incident—where arguably equally offensive speech was posted on internet sites, in newspaper caricatures, as part of art shows, dance shows and exhibitions, or as part of a motion picture. In such cases the Israeli Supreme Court has systematically ruled in favour of freedom of expression, despite the fact the feelings were hurt, sensibilities offended and emotions injured.[52] In all these cases, the Israeli Court was sensitive to the centrality of expression in a democratic regime, even when such speech may have infringed upon other rights. Between maintaining solidarity—not hurting any groups' feelings—and managing conflicts through allowing expression (including harsh or insensitive expressions), the Court developed the Israeli administrative law doctrine in favour of the latter (as long as no specific legislation on point ordered differently).[53] As these examples reveal, the Israeli Court realized that the media through which satire was communicated—precisely because it was mediated—was an integral part of public discourse, whereas in *Suszkin* the speech was directed at individuals in their domicile and in a manner that did not seek to provide them with any meaningful information or engage them in any conversation. It would

---

[50] *Chaplinsky* v. *New Hampshire* 315 US 568 (1942).

[51] In *R.A.V.* v. *City of St. Paul, Minnesota* 505 US 377 (1992) the United States Supreme Court was willing to assume that the burning of a cross in the yard of a black family with the intention to intimidate would constitute fighting words. The situation in *Suszkin* is not that dissimilar.

[52] In HCJ 14/86 *Laor* v. *Film & Play Review BD* [1987] IsrSC 41(1) 421, the court ruled in favour of showing of a play even though it offended the feelings of the Jewish public since it compared the Israeli army to the Nazis. In CA 316/03 *Bachri* v. *Movies' Review Council* [2003] IsrSC 58(1) 249, the Court struck down the decision of the council to refuse a license to show the movie 'Jenin Jenin' by Bachri, even though the film described the events in the refugee camp in April 2002 'in a distorted way that hurt the feelings of soldiers and families of slain soldiers'. In HCJ 606/93 *Kidum Enterprise and Publishing (1981) Ltd* v. *Broadcasting Authority* [1994] IsrSC 48(2) 1, the Court again allowed the broadcasting of an advertisement that had a sexual *double-entendre*. In *Gur-Aryeh* in n. 39 above, the Court ruled in favour of broadcasting a TV show on Saturday (the Jewish Sabbath) despite the injury to the religious feelings of participants in the show. All these decisions were based on the assertion that the injuries caused by those expressions should be tolerated in a democracy.

[53] Justice Barak in EA 11280/02 *Central Elections Committee for Sixteenth Knesset* v. *MK Tibby* [2003] IsrSC 57(4) 1, 21 emphasized that it is better for democracy that undemocratic pressures would be relieved through democratic channels of expression, than through non-democratic channels that might include violence.

seem, then, that the different social context—the medium—makes a difference. In other words, it could very well be the case that had the *Suszkin* poster been published in the satire section of a newspaper, the Court might have found the indictment unconstitutional as applied, in part because such publication would not amount to 'fighting words' given the lack of proximity.

In any event, faced with an indictment based on a rather peculiar and very rarely used statute, the Israeli Court did not attend to comparative law in this case—notwithstanding the clear comparative tendencies of the court in freedom of expression cases—and thus the fighting words doctrine is not yet an official part of Israeli law.

9. Some Heretical Reflections on Speech Theory and the Role of Passion

The general normative baseline in relation to which current (and most of the historic) debate concerning freedom of speech rests is the baseline of public *reason*. When Habermas writes on the importance of speech and discourse in modern democracy he assumes at least a minimal level of knowledge of the facts, competence to analyse them and the use of a reason-based methodology with which to achieve a decision and convince others.[54] According to Habermas, and to Rawls, reason is the basis for moral legitimacy. As mentioned earlier, the primary justifications for the supremacy of freedom of speech over other rights and freedoms are reason based. These justifications are based on the correlation between democracy and deliberation. It is not surprising, therefore, that the speech protected by the First Amendment is, at its core, speech that conveys a discursive message, speech that begins (or is a part of) a conversation which is based on—and which fosters—reasoned arguments. 'Fighting words' reside outside the scope of the First Amendment protection precisely because they cannot be justified as part of the reason-based sphere of public discourse. This baseline is challenged once the assumption is no longer that people assess the facts, debate rationally over matters, or engage in reason-based self-reflection over values. If a competing baseline is identified, where reason and reason-based critique resides alongside passion and passion-based argument, then the traditional justifications of constitutional protection for freedom of speech need reexamination.

As mentioned above, some scholars recognize the centrality of emotive speech, and thus base First Amendment jurisprudence on a quest for social legitimacy achieved by providing a space for members of the various sub-communities to participate by expressing their passionately held values. Under this conception, public discourse is a sphere where communication sustains the quilt of communities from disintegration and participation maintains a sense of loyalty to the overall

---

[54] J. Habermas, *Knowledge and Human Interests* Trans. J. Shapiro (London: Heinemann, 1972).

constitutional order.[55] This analysis, however is almost by definition society-specific, not only because various societies may be more or less heterogeneous (and therefore more or less threatened by emotionally challenging dissenting speech) but also because perceived as such, legitimacy is a social fact (nothing more, nothing less). As such, the people of Canada, Israel, or Germany, may either view their system as legitimate, or may not, and their attitude may be formed regardless of whether the US speech doctrines were adopted in these jurisdictions or not, or whether they found its underlying rationale convincing or not. We may only speculate on the possible explanation for the degree of legitimacy any given system enjoys, with little to say about possible alternative explanations (lacking the alternative universes in which to test out our hypothesis) or, worst, lacking a foundation from which to engage in a normative critique. An attempt to bridge the sociological and the normative approaches—the facts and the norms—is conceptually taxing, and perhaps unattainable. Yet it seems that a deeper examination into sociological legitimacy and normative legitimacy is nevertheless required. One possible way to do that would be to look closer at moral legitimacy as based also on passion.

Modern research in various fields acknowledges that reason and rationality might in fact not be the sole, or dominate, feature of public (and private) decision-making or reflection.[56] Additionally, it may very well be that moral judgment cannot be fully separated from moral sentiment, such as passion (or outrage). It could very well be the case that we are convinced, at the end of the day, by what we *feel*. If indeed reason-based deliberation is not the sole mode governing interpersonal ethical engagement with public (and private) matters, and if indeed it is also through the expression of passion that we form our identity, we must further inquire into the scope of the constitutional protection of speech.[57] If speech is an expression of passion, should we grant it less protection, because it does not further the quest for truth or the Habermasian notion of legitimacy-generating discourse? Or, conversely, if at the end of the day moral judgment is a matter of sentiment, should we not be more tolerant of passion-based expression, and allow passion a longer leash? Suszkin's expression was certainly passionate; should we strive to rein in such expression, as I suggested earlier, through the fighting words doctrine? Or should we develop a sphere where passion is recognized as an important element in moral judgment, and thus view Suszkin's

---

[55] R. C. Post, 'The Constitutional Concept of Public Discourse: Outrageous Opinion, Democratic Deliberation and *Hustler Magazine v. Falwell*' (1990) 103 *Harv. L. Rev.* 601, 642.

[56] D. Kahneman, P. Slovic, and A. Tversky (eds.), *Judgment under Uncertainty: Heuristics and Biases* (Cambridge: CUP, 1982); A. R. Damasio, *Descartes' Error: Emotion, Reason, and the Human Brain* (New York: Putnam, 1995); S. Blackburn, *Ruling Passions: A Theory of Practical Reasoning* (Oxford and New York: OUP and Clarendon Press, 1998), 252.

[57] See M. Nussbaum, *Love's Knowledge: Essays on Philosophy and Literature* (Oxford and New York: OUP, 1990), 81–2, arguing that 'theorizing needs to be completed with intuitive and emotional responses'. See also R. C. Solomon, *A Passion for Justice: Emotions and the Origin of the Social Contract* (Reading, MA: Addison-Wesley, 1990), 44.

expression as deserving protection? Assume for the sake of argument that Suszkin handed out leaflets, instead of seeking to glue a poster on private property; would it not follow that her speech should be protected as the kind of speech that provokes the polity into moral debate (which itself cannot be divorced from passion)? This, of course, is *not* to say that the moral outrage the poster incident raises should prevent or forestall an unequivocal moral denunciation of Suszkin's act. The content of the poster (as well as the attempt to glue it uninvited on private property) should be condemned. But on first impression, accepting passion as an organizing matrix of public discourse should accord it greater breathing room.

On the other hand, if passion is taken seriously, can we maintain the faith—the passionate faith—in a constitutional order that bars any criminal prosecution of Suszkin's provocation? It could very well be the case that in a society where passion is central, the Court would have been perceived as acting illegitimately had it *not* convicted Suszkin. After all, the Court itself must perform its role in passionately rejecting a passionate challenge to the very fabric of co-existence between Muslims and Jews in Israel (especially given the fact that the offense occurred in Hebron). Perhaps *Suszkin* provides a rare example of a passionate articulation of values by the Court itself, intended to sustain the passionate belief in the constitutional order in Israel. This of course should not be read as implying that because we protect passionate speech of individuals we should necessarily invite (or accept) passionate speech by judicial state institutions. Yet if passion matters, we should explore its contours.

As can be seen, re-organizing the sphere of public discourse to accommodate for passion along with reason-based critique might lead to a significantly different understanding of the normative principles underlying the regulation of speech. Much is still to be explored in this field, and the above discussion only marks a possible starting point in the comparative domain.[58]

10. Conclusion

Outraging religious sensibilities is an offence most courts would be wary of implementing. It places the court in the thicket of defining what religious sentiments are, what outrages them, why these feelings deserve greater protection than do other sentiments, and above all, it places the court in the position of taking sides in what may often be a heated debate about the values underlying freedom of speech versus the values underlying a given religion (and the values underlying freedom of religion in general), a position from which most courts

---

[58] For an extensive debate in the US see J. Weinstein, 'Democracy, Sex and the First Amendment', a response by A. Koppelman, 'Free Speech and Pornography' and a reply by J. Weinstein, 'Free Speech Values, Hardcore Pornography, and the First Amendment' (2007) 31 *N.Y.U. Rev. L. & Soc. Change* 865, 885–8, 921.

would stay away at nearly all costs. *Suszkin* is thus a unique case. This chapter suggests that the best way to understand Suszkin is under the US fighting words doctrine, though the Israeli Court made no mention of this doctrine.

This chapter suggested that even if the Knesset adds freedom of expression to the list of enumerated rights in the Israeli Basic Laws, the Knesset, and subsequently the courts, will have to decide whether to grant freedom of expression the special status it enjoys in the US over other liberties, or whether to adopt the competing, 'general rights' model, prevalent, for example, in Canada. This chapter also suggests that the language of human dignity, which stands at the foundation of the general rights model, is more favourable for restricting group-based offensive speech than is the US model.

Furthermore, the chapter pointed to the tension between normative justifications for freedom of expression, resting primarily on the concept of public reason, and cultural justifications of freedom of expression, resting on the notion of social legitimacy in heterogeneous societies 'blessed' with diverse values. In that context, the fact that human dignity is placed as the core constitutional legal right in Israel invites the Court and its students to examine to what extent passion-based speech, which may be an expression of dignity but which almost by definition offends the dignity of others, deserves as strong a constitutional protection as reason-based speech. Human dignity, as a feature of the moral universe, is inalienable on account, or as an expression of, humans possessing the capacity to reason right from wrong. Seen as closely related to the capacity to reason, human dignity could be interpreted as protecting reasoned-based arguments, and granting less protection to passion-based speech. This conclusion may be reinforced given that people may perceive their dignity infringed by passion-based speech. On the other hand, failing to protect speech, including passion-based offensive speech, is also an infringement of the expression of human dignity. The Court thus could reach a conclusion that recognizing the importance of passionate speech might lead to protection of religiously outrageous speech even on a human dignity model. As we have seen, the Court in *Suszkin* chose to sidestep this issue by treating human dignity as the foundational value upon which Israel's hyper-heterogeneous society rests. In so doing the Court found that the state may prosecute speech which seeks to deeply fracture the co-existence between members of the various faiths, all deserving the protection of fundamental human rights.

In this context we should note the Court's own judgments have a hand in shaping the sphere of public discourse including its nature as reason-based or passion-based. Thus far, the Israeli Court has been treading on both mills. The court's jurisprudence contains rhetoric rich with values and identity-shaping pathos, and thus participates in constituting national ideology, akin to the US civil religion.[59] This line of reasoning resonates with the early American cases,

---

[59] In HCJ 6126/94 *Senesh* v. *Broadcasting Authority Management.Board* [1999] IsrSC 53(3) 817, Justice Barak writes about the Jewish heritage of freedom of expression, beginning in the days of the

where judges like Brandeis told the American people what its forefathers fought for, thereby resting the decision primarily on passion and identity arguments.[60] Another line of argument that the Israeli Court follows on occasion adopts a 'colder' approach that places speech as part of a rather formal system of constitutional protections, emphasizing institutional roles, structures and conceptual fit in a somewhat dispassionate tone of reason and critique.[61]

In the final analysis, *Suszkin* is far more than a case about a Jewish settler distributing offensive posters in Hebron. If we read the decision carefully, it is a about the role the forum state's unique history, culture, and religious sensitivities play in the decision of a domestic court, and consequently, about the inference we can draw from such a decision regarding the dynamics of the emerging global discourse on human rights. Significantly in this regard, the Israeli Court was not willing to rely on external sources, even though it often turns to such sources, and even though such sources could have proven helpful. Perhaps the Court thought that an explicit dialogue with foreign law would have undermined its strong emphasis on core elements of Israeli identity. Specifically, the Court may have feared that relying on First Amendment jurisprudence would have invoked, at least in part, a transnational, if not universal, basis for its decision. If it had relied on such external sources, the Court would have been tripped by the wire weaved into Suszkin's claim, namely that the jurisprudence the Court was developing was not sensitive enough to the Jewish character of Israel. The subtext of Suszkin's argument was that Israel's Jewish character is under threat, and that Jews should fight back; relying on US jurisprudence would have only highlighted the threat. The Court thus answered Suszkin in her own terms, basing the decision on domestic (ie, Jewish) values and symbols. It stressed the importance Judaism places on respecting human dignity of all those created in God's image and referred to the harassments Jews experienced in other countries on account of their belief.

Bible. As to 'other values', see Justice Barak in HCJ 6698/95 *Qa'adan* v. *Israel Land Administration*, [2000] IsrSC 54(1) 258, 280.

[60] *Whitney* v. *California* 274 US 357, 375 (1927), Brandeis, J, concurring.

[61] In HCJ 651/03 *The Association for Civil Rights in Israel* v. *Chairman of Central Elections Committee for Sixteenth Knesset* [2003] IsrSC 57(2) 62, 72, Justice Procaccia sidestepped the charged issue in that case by relying on the formulaic necessity of free speech for the democratic election process. In CA 316/03 *Bachri* v. *Movies' Review Council* [2003] IsrSC 58(1) 249, Justice Dorner similarly stated that censoring the movie on the ground of falsehood will hurt the democratic process by giving the authorities the power to choose right from wrong instead of such truth emerging from the 'market place of ideas', suggesting that this market place is the domain of analytical and rational reasoning.

PART IV

RELIGIOUS SPEECH AND EXPRESSIVE CONDUCT THAT OFFEND SECULAR VALUES

18

Religious Speech that Undermines Gender Equality

Carolyn Evans[*]

1. Introduction

The struggle for gender equality has often been in direct conflict with religious teachings and other forms of religious speech enunciated by religious leadership: the speech of the priest, the mufti, the lama, or the rabbi.[1] This chapter addresses the issue of religious speech that offends the value of gender equality and the question of how a liberal state should respond to such speech. In it, I develop an argument that attempts to take seriously the legitimate claims of both religious speakers and women who are committed to gender equality, while also acknowledging that these two groups are not mutually exclusive.

In pluralistic, democratic societies we do not merely disagree over whether particular examples of speech should be permitted or regulated. We also disagree on more fundamental issues about what speech is valuable, when regulation is justified, and the types of harm that speech can do. Our legal and political system (while ostensibly liberal and secular) in fact also takes into account other, older models of speech. In particular it makes space for religious conceptions of speech.[2] Recently, it has made space to a lesser degree for some secular feminist views of

[*] I am grateful to Adrienne Stone, Simon Evans, and Stephen Donaghue for their comments on an earlier draft and to Kirsty Souter and Duncan Kauffman for their research assistance. This paper is part of a broader project on Religious Freedom and Non-discrimination Laws undertaken as a Discovery Project for the Australian Research Council.

[1] This is not to suggest that there are not important differences between the construction of gender between different religious groups and in different parts of societies. See D. Sullivan, 'Gender Equality and Religious Freedom: Toward a Framework for Conflict Resolution' (1992) 24 *N.Y.U. J. Int'l L. & Pol.* 795, 811: '[r]ace, ethnicity, class, the relationship between state institutions and religious authority, and gender itself all mediate the effects of religion on other human rights'.

[2] For a discussion of this in the American context and a critical reflection on the way in which this accommodation of religious speech is changing, see C. Olsen, 'In the Twenty-First Century's Marketplace of Ideas, Will Religious Speech Continue to be Welcome?: Religious Speech as Grounds for Defamation' (2005) 37 *Tex. Tech L. Rev.* 497.

speech.[3] Various groups compete within societies to have their conception of speech given recognition and legitimacy by the legal and political system, either through the mandating of particular types of speech (for example, gender neutral language) or the prohibition of particular types of speech (for example, blasphemy). In a pluralistic society, it is important to ensure that a wide variety of groups are given a chance to articulate and defend their conceptions of how and when speech should be regulated. In this chapter, I argue that one group of people whose conceptions of speech is given inadequate space in our legal and political system is religious women. This is not to suggest that religious women should be given any particular privilege, but rather that their voices should not be assumed to be adequately represented by either conservative male religious leadership or secular feminist voices.

To illustrate these points, I will first give some examples of religious speech that is harmful to notions of gender equality. I will then outline two models of speech (one liberal and one religious) and explain why neither gives adequate support to religious women who live in communities where religious speech that undermines gender equality is commonplace. Finally, I will argue that the liberal state should respond to religious speech that promotes gender inequality by the adoption of certain policies that empower women inside religious communities, enabling transgressive speech and refusing to give legitimacy to women-hating speech (even if not directly banning it).

2. Religious Speech that Offends against Gender Equality

The extent to which religious practices, traditions, and beliefs play a role in perpetuating religious inequality is a complex issue which has been analysed in some detail by others. Here I will draw out two examples of religious speech that are offensive to the notion of gender equality.[4] The first is the construction of essentialized gender roles and the creation of a hierarchy of men and women. The second is speech that expressly encourages or implicitly condones violence against women. While I discuss these as two distinct categories, they are linked. Speech that conveys a message of gender inequality places women in a subordinate position relative to the men who are (statistically) most likely to harm them: husbands and fathers in particular. As much domestic violence takes at least the ostensible form of

---

[3] In Australia, one example of this is that the drafting guidelines for legislation in all jurisdictions require gender neutral language to be used. See eg, Australian Government, Office of Parliamentary Counsel, *Drafting Direction No. 2.1: English Usage, Gender-Specific and Gender-Neutral Language, Grammar, Punctuation and Spelling* (2006), [13]–[24], <http://www.opc.gov.au/about/draft_directions.htm> (last accessed 10 April 2008).

[4] I have deliberately chosen the majority (although not all) of my detailed examples from Christianity. This is to play a small part in redressing the over-emphasis on Islam as the exclusive or predominant 'problem' religion from the point of view of women's rights and on Christianity as more compatible with modernity and equality.

punishment for transgressions, speech that legitimates men's roles in controlling women and gives men responsibility over women's compliance with sexual and personal codes of conduct creates fertile ground in which violence can grow.

In making this argument, I do not want to paint a picture of religion being in an inevitable and eternal conflict with women's rights. Religions differ on gender issues and even within the one religion there are different voices. I will return to the importance of transgressive women's voices within religious traditions later. But the views about gender difference and hierarchy that I outline here are the ones that are common to many religions, are still prevalent in many mainstream religions, and have played an important role in influencing the law and culture of many societies and the place of women in those societies for centuries.

(i) Construction of Gendered Hierarchies

The construction of a gender hierarchy whereby women are subject to the authority of men (what Courtney Howland calls the 'obedience rule'[5]) is common to the conservative branches of many religions. Positions of authority within the family, the religious organization, and (preferably) the state, are said to be the legitimate place of men only. Within the Christian tradition, this was defended in part on biblical authority (the sin of Eve having condemned her to subordination), but also by reference to the law of nature itself. Both St Augustine,[6] and Thomas Aquinas,[7] for example, argued for women's subordination to men on the basis of theology and natural law. Continuing resistance in many Christian denominations to women as priests or bishops traces its roots to a similar mixture of biblical authority and the naturalness of gender differentiation.[8]

The hierarchy of men over women within the Church is also reflected in the authority of husband over wife in the domestic sphere. This relationship of authority of husband over wife meant that within conservative Christian quarters there have been concerns over social changes that take women out of the primary role of wife and mother.[9] For example, the conservative Anglican organization, *Equal but Different*, has the following to say about gender relations and the biblical imperative to preach differential gender roles:

Equal but Different is committed to the historic and Biblical understanding of men and women as individuals created in the image of our loving Creator God, equally fallen in our

---

[5] C. Howland, 'The Challenge of Religious Fundamentalism to the Liberty and Equality Rights of Women: An Analysis Under the United Nations Charter' (1997) 35 *Colum. J. Transna'l L.* 271, 282.

[6] St. Augustine, *Questions on the Heptateuch*, Book I, para. 153.

[7] T. Aquinas, *Summa Theologica I*, qu. 92, Art. 1, ad 2.

[8] For an interesting discussion of the ostensible arguments against women's ordination and some musings on other possible explanations for the strong emotions that this debate evokes, see M. Porter, *The New Puritans* (Melbourne: Melbourne UP, 2006), ch. 4.

[9] S. E. Merry, 'Rights, Religion, and Community: Approaches to Violence Against Women in the Context of Globalization' (2001) 35 *Law & Soc'y Rev.* 39, 63–4.

human nature and equally able to be saved by our Saviour the Lord Jesus Christ, so that we might honour him and serve each other in relationships of *loving male leadership and intelligent, willing female submission in the family and the church*. This applies to single and married women alike in the life of our Christian community, although it has a special relevance to marriage and the raising of children. The church can *model for all society* the beauty of right relationships, as men and women cooperate within *their distinctive roles* as God intended. We realise this is counter-cultural in our feminist society but believe the *teaching of the Bible is clear and relevant* to our day, despite the passage of time and cultural change.[10]

Of course, Christianity is far from alone in pursuing such views of the inherent difference and subordination of women: from the use by Hindu conservatives of the story of Suti who sacrificed her life to prove her chastity and to preserve her husband's honour; to the violent enforcement of modest dress codes for women in some Muslim communities; to the saying that a Jewish woman is first under obedience to her father, then her husband, then her son and never fit for independence, there is a long history of patriarchy in most religious traditions.[11] Further, these traditions are being revived and reinvented by conservative and fundamentalist politico-religious groups all over the world.[12] In one recent example, the female Pakistani minister Zilla Huma Usman was shot by a gunman claiming to be acting on the will of God, because she did not dress sufficiently modestly and because women should not participate in public life.[13]

(ii) Incitement or Condoning of Violence against Women

As the example of Zilla Huma Usman demonstrates, this political revival of the concept of a divinely-mandated authority held by men over women can have physically dangerous consequences for women.[14] This is because a second way in which some religious speech can offend the value of gender equality is by explicitly encouraging or implicitly condoning violence against, or abuse of,

---

[10] Taken from the About Us page of the website <http://www.equalbutdifferent.org> (emphasis added). It is interesting to note the injection of the liberal idea of equality into the title of the organization and some of its rhetoric. However, the conjunction with the concept of 'submission' makes it clear that difference, rather than equality, is the key principle of the organization. It is also clear from numerous parts of its website that this women's organization bases its positions on what it claims to be clear biblical authority and the importance of advocating positions in compliance with these biblical mandates.

[11] For an overview of religious fundamentalism in five world religions, see Howland (n. 5 above), 285–324. See also F. Raday, 'Culture, Religion and Gender' (2003) 1 *International Jo. of Constitutional Law* 663, 672–6.

[12] Sullivan (n. 1 above), 812.

[13] B. Loudon, 'Preacher Kills MP Over Veil', *The Australian* (Sydney), 22 February 2007, 9. The killer (who had been linked to the deaths of several prostitutes in the past) allegedly said that he would 'kill all those women who do not follow the right path' if freed again.

[14] For a discussion of the connection between the obedience rule and violence against women, see Howland (n. 5 above), 283.

women and girls. This particularly applies to those women who defy the religious conception of good womanhood.[15]

Recently, in Australia, a furor broke out over comments by Sheik Taj el-Din al-Hilali who compared women who did not veil to uncovered meat. He argued that adultery (under which heading he appeared to include rape) was the responsibility of women 90 per cent of the time.

> Because the woman possesses the weapon of seduction. She is the one who takes her clothes off, cuts them short, acts flirtatious, puts on make-up and powder, and goes on the street dallying. She is the one wearing a short dress, lifting it up, lowering it down, then a look, then a smile, then a word, then a greeting, then a chat, then a date, then a meeting, then a crime, then Long Bay Jail, then comes a merciless judge who gives you 65 years. But the whole disaster, who started it? The Al-Rafihi scholar says in one of his literary works, he says: 'If I come across a crime of rape—kidnap and violation of honour—I would discipline the man and teach him a lesson in morals, and I would order the woman to be arrested and jailed for life.'[16]

While his sermon was marked by particularly provocative and offensive language and caused a huge public outcry, the idea that women are the cause of sexual assaults (particularly if they fail in some way to comply with the religious notion of a good woman) is hardly one exclusively referable to him.[17] Indeed a number of Australian Christian leaders were muted in their response to the controversy, not wanting to be associated with the way in which the idea was put, but giving some credence to the notion that the way a woman dresses makes her responsible to some degree for any sexual harm that comes to her.[18]

Another example of speech, this time one that seems on its face to condemn violence against women, but which has the effect of implicitly enabling it, can be found in East Timor, which is an overwhelmingly Catholic country. Domestic violence (including serious assaults) against women is commonplace there. The East Timorese Catholic Church leadership has officially condemned domestic violence and participated in some programmes to help eliminate it. However, it has consistently spoken out against attempts to allow for divorce in East Timor. It has also condemned women's groups that provide shelter to those who have escaped abusive marriages and has been hostile to women working outside the

---

[15] G. Stopler, 'The Free Exercise of Discrimination: Religious Liberty, Civic Community and Women's Equality' (2004) 10 *Wm. & Mary J. Women & L.* 459; Raday (n. 11 above), 671–2.

[16] This quotation is taken from a translation of the Ramadan sermon of Sheik al-Hilali undertaken by an Australian newspaper: 'Revealed: The Mufti Uncut', *The Australian* (Sydney), 28 October 2006, 29.

[17] It is also, of course, not one shared by all Muslims. Many Australian Muslims condemned his statements. See R. Kerbaj, 'Muslim Leader Blames Women for Sex Attacks', *The Australian* (Sydney), 26 October 2006, 1.

[18] Many conservative Christian churches also deny that domestic violence is a problem and focus blame on the women who 'provoke' such violence: Merry (n. 9 above), 62.

home.[19] While husbands are chided for beating their wives, wives who break out of the traditional model of wife and mother to escape this abuse are vilified and condemned as home-breakers.[20] This reflects the position of the Catholic Church's doctrines more generally. In the Catechism, the clearest and most detailed injunctions concerning the family are in relation to the protection of the institution of marriage and the sinfulness of divorce. While sexual abuse of children in a family is condemned, there is no mention of the sinfulness of sexual or physical abuse of spouses.[21] In a traditional, Catholic society, these teachings create serious hurdles for women attempting to leave abusive relationships and for those who attempt to assist them through such initiatives as providing shelters for abused women and children. It may also undermine the speech of the church leaders who officially condemn domestic violence, by shifting the blame for a broken marriage onto the woman who leaves rather than the man whose abuse has caused her to leave. Some men may also interpret such condemnations of women who attempt to leave marriages as an excuse for further violence against them.

These are but a few number of examples from a wide range of ways in which religious speech can be hostile to women's rights, using tactics from the construction of stereotyped roles for 'good' women to encouragement of violence against women who do not conform to this stereotype.

3. Two Models of Speech

Having considered some ways in which religious speech may undermine gender equality, I now turn to flesh out briefly two possible and contrasting perceptions of speech: the first liberal and the second, a particular and conservative model of religious speech—a model primarily associated with influential conservative, institutionalized religions but one that also has some resonances for other religious modes. I begin by acknowledging that both are relatively simple models. As a result of the diversity of liberal thought and the diversity of religious thought, there are some people who would describe themselves as liberal who do not accept the first model, and there are many people who would describe themselves as religious who do not accept the second model. They are, nonetheless, helpful models of two types of ways of conceiving of speech and its roles in society, and each has something different to say about whether, and when, the state should intervene in religious speech that undermines gender equality.

---

[19] S. H. Rimmer, 'The Roman Catholic Church and the Rights of East Timorese Women' in A. Whiting and C. Evans (eds.), *Mixed Blessings: Laws, Religions and Women's Rights in the Asia-Pacific Region* (Leiden: Martinus Nijhoff, 2006), 161.

[20] For other Christian churches that take the same approach, see Merry (n. 9 above), 64–6.

[21] Catholic Church, *Catechism of the Catholic Church* (2000), [2384], <http://www.vatican.va/archive/ENG0015/_P87.HTM> (last accessed 10 April 2008).

(i) The Liberal Model

I will outline the liberal model of speech only briefly because it is well known and explored in many papers in this book. The liberal model of speech is grounded in several different, inter-related justifications. Jim Weinstein, in his chapter in this collection, suggested two: democracy and political equality (with political equality being closely linked to autonomy). Another might be that truth, or ever-closer versions of it, emerges best from an open, vigorous, uncensored discussion and debate. The liberal model is reluctant to see the regulation of speech in the private realm and requires good justifications for regulation of speech in the public realm. (Exactly what is a good justification and when it applies will differ between different types of liberalism and different liberal, legal orders.) The model generally rejects the notion of content-based regulation: if one person is allowed to make a speech about the need for greater equality in family relationships, then another speaker has to be allowed to speak about the benefits of traditional family models.[22] While rejecting content-based regulation, the model does allow for distinguishing between various types of speech such as political, commercial, and so forth. Greater justification is required before intervening in core liberal speech, such as political speech, than is required for less valuable forms of speech such as commercial speech, although justification is still required for both.

These justifications for free speech and consequent differential valuing of different types of speech in order to determine how compelling the government's reasons must be before intervening are well known and I do not intend to dwell on them.

What response might the liberal model have to religious speech that undermines gender equality? For the liberal model (or, at least, many liberal models), one of the challenges presented by religious speech that threatens women is that such speech often occurs in realms where the liberal is reluctant to see state intervention:[23] in the church, temple, synagogue, or mosque (a protected private religious domain) and in the home (the protected private domestic domain). The private/public divide underlies liberal justifications for regulating some speech more than others and it assumes that people have both significant public and private elements to their lives.

Yet the so-called private domestic and religious domains are for some women the places where they live a great deal of their lives. At the extreme, women in some small, close-knit, conservative religious communities may have almost no life in what the liberal world-view conceives of as the public realm. In such communities, education for women ceases at as early an age as the legal system will allow and paid employment is forbidden. They spend most of their time

---

[22] For a useful discussion of content neutrality in relation to even highly inflammatory speech, see I. Hare, 'Inflammatory Speech: Cross Burning and the First Amendment' (2003) *PL* 408.

[23] L. G. Jacobs, 'Adding Complexity to Confusion and Seeing the Light: Feminist Legal Insights and the Jurisprudence of the Religion Clauses' (1995) 7 *Yale J. L. & Feminism* 137, 153.

within their home or the homes of co-religionists and participation in religious celebrations is the closest that they come to public participation. When liberalism keeps the state out of these realms, the speech environment in which women live is saturated with messages, uncontestable because of their divine origin, of inferiority, difference, and obedience.[24]

The liberal model is also problematic from a women's point of view because of its general insistence on demonstrable and direct harm arising from speech before intervention is permissible.[25] Most liberal societies are ambivalent about whether speech that encourages differential gender roles is harmful and are reluctant to intervene in structures of hierarchy in domestic relations. I argued earlier that the creation of a relationship in which the husband is given authority over, and responsibility for, his wife creates fertile ground for violence against women. With its aversion to content-based regulation, liberalism sometimes has little to offer abused women other than the theoretical right to speak out against the abuse or to leave the abusive relationship. Both rights can be rather illusory in circumstances of violence or when women are regularly subjected to speech reminding them of their inferiority and their husband's rightful authority over them.

(ii) A Religious Model

Let me now contrast this well-known liberal understanding of the role and place of speech in society with one religious model of speech.[26] As noted earlier, this model of speech is particularly associated with conservative, institutional forms of religion, but may also throw light on attitudes towards speech that have relevance to a wider group of religions. This model is not grounded in democracy or equality, but rather sees speech as an element of a relationship with the divine.[27] All speech under this model has a hearer beyond the temporal realm and all speech

---

[24] This constructs around them what Young describes as 'social structures that inhibit the capacities of some people. An account of someone's life circumstances contains many strands of difficulty or difference from others that, taken one by one, can appear to be the result of decisions, preferences, or accidents. When considered together, however, and when compared with the life story of others, they reveal a net of restricting and reinforcing relationships' (I. M. Young, *Inclusion and Democracy* (Oxford: OUP, 2000), 93.

[25] This is one of the issues that has made the debate over pornography and its potential to harm women so complex for liberals and feminists. For a good overview, see R. Graycar and J. Morgan, *The Hidden Gender of Law*, 2nd edn. (Sydney: Federation Press , 2002), 410–20.

[26] For a somewhat different discussion of similar issues, see S. H. Williams, 'Religion, Politics, and Feminist Epistemology: A Comment on the Uses and Abuses of Morality in Public Discourse' (2002) 77 *Ind. L. J.* 267, 270; Olsen, n. 2 above; and R. Ahdar and I. Leigh, *Religious Freedom in the Liberal State* (Oxford: OUP, 2005), ch. 12.

[27] The point is made more generally by Raday (n. 12 above), 668: 'The fundamental tenets of monotheistic religions are at odds with the basis of human rights doctrine. Human rights doctrine is humancentric; it is based on the autonomy and responsibility of the individual ... and systematic-rational principles ... Monotheistic religion, in contrast, is based on the subjection of the individual and the community to the will of God and on a transcendental morality.'

has the potential to strengthen or weaken the relationship between the speaker and the divine listener.

There are at least three categories of speech in such a model: sacred speech; speech as a religious duty; and forbidden speech.

(a) Sacred Speech

The first category is sacred speech. This might take the form of prayer, ritual, the reading of sacred texts, chants, songs, or spoken elements of meditation. The act of speaking these words is often heavily circumscribed. The person who speaks them, the office of the speaker, the place in which the words are spoken, the language that is used, the precise wording that is used, and the time at which they are spoken may all be prescribed in a form that the believer understands to be unchangeable and divinely mandated. These are not matters for negotiation, critical evaluation, or development over time (even if the reality is that they have in fact been negotiated and developed over time). The speech loses its sacred quality if the rules for speaking are not adhered to. From one Catholic viewpoint, for example, to allow someone who calls herself a woman priest to speak the words of the Catholic Mass is not to simply substitute in a different (possibly less appropriate or qualified) speaker while still maintaining the underlying integrity of the speech. It is to fundamentally change the sacred *nature* of the words themselves—to rob them of their power of transubstantiation and to transform them instead into a kind of blasphemy.

For the state to regulate this area of the sacred, to *require* religions to give women the opportunity to serve as religious leaders or to mandate gender neutral language in religious ritual, is thus completely unacceptable, since it amounts to a state imposition of conduct diametrically opposed to religious belief. Under this religious model, the secular state has no role in regulating the sacred and no authority recognizable by people who adhere to this model to do so.[28] The important role played by this sacred speech means that, at least for some religious people, in a hierarchy of forms of speech that are in need of protection sacred speech would rank very highly. It is the core or paradigmatic case of religious speech. (This may be contrasted with the liberal view that perceives the central case of speech to be 'public discourse'[29] or discourse which aids participation in self-government.[30] By contrast, religious rituals that have no political content, no

---

[28] Of course, the reality is usually that there has been significant change in religions over time, including their concept of the sacred, but it is portrayed as unchanged in fundamentals and unchangeable.

[29] See R. C. Post, 'The Constitutional Concept of Public Discourse,' (1990)103 *Harv. L. Rev.* 601, where he argues that free speech in the First Amendment does not cover all speech but rather the speech by which Americans engage in self-government.

[30] See J. Weinstein, 'Democracy, Sex and the First Amendment' (2007) 31 *N.Y.U. Rev. L. & Soc. Change* 865, 879, who argues: 'the right to participate in democratic self-governance, both as a speaker and auditor is properly referred to as the core free speech norm.'

relevance for self-government and may sometimes take place in private tend to be at the periphery of liberal free speech protections or to even fall outside them.[31])

(b) Speech as a religious duty

The second type of speech is speech as a religious duty or obligation. Rather than conceiving of speech as a liberal right that the right holder may choose to freely exercise or refrain from exercising for whatever reason, this type of speech is a duty placed on the speaker either by the requirements of the external deity or by a commitment to a transcendent moral or spiritual order. An example of such speech is the requirement of proselytism in some religions. To attempt to convert others to one's own religion is not merely about trying to bring someone else to see the truth and is thus not simply analogous to trying to convince others of the superiority of a particular political, social, or other position.[32] It is also a personal religious obligation placed on the speaker to speak the truth—even to an unwilling listener. It is an obligation in Christian terms to preach the gospel 'in season and out'.

Also included in this type of speech is the prophetic tradition—the denunciation of sinfulness and immorality of the world and the call for a return to righteousness.[33] Again, the fact that listeners may reject the prophetic words and continue to live in immorality, perhaps even violently retaliating against the speaker, is perfectly consistent with this prophetic tradition. As the speech is an obligation rather than a right, utilitarian compromises about whether, how, or to whom to convey the message are unacceptable. While those in the world may close their ears, the prophet also speaks to and for the divine, and strengthens that transcendent relationship even while suffering the fate of prophets and being reviled in the temporal world.

---

[31] The United States Supreme Court, however, rejected an argument that a university could treat groups wishing to use a space for religious worship differently from other groups. The university claimed that it had not breached the First Amendment on the basis that its protection did not extend to religious worship (even though it extended to other forms of religious speech). The Court rejected this 'novel' argument on the basis that its content was not intelligible, that it would require the courts to become unduly entangled in judging religious issues and that the distinction was not relevant to the purposes of the First Amendment. See *Widmar* v. *Vincent* 454 US 263 (1981) at 274. However, Justice White, in dissent, described the notion that religious worship was indistinguishable from First Amendment protected speech as 'plainly wrong' at 284.

[32] For a useful discussion of how to balance this obligation and the rights of listeners in the context of the workplace, see T. C. Berg, 'Religious Speech in the Workplace: Harassment or Protected Speech?' (1999) 22 *Harv. J. L. & Pub. Pol'y*, 959.

[33] For one of many examples, see the Lord's injunction to Jeremiah: 'And I will utter my judgments against them touching all their wickedness, who have forsaken me, and have burned incense unto other gods, and worshipped the works of their own hands. Thou therefore gird up thy loins, and arise, and speak unto them all that I command thee: be not dismayed at their faces, lest I confound thee before them.' Jeremiah 1: 16–17 (Authorized King James Version). Much of the rest of this book deals with the prophecies made by Jeremiah, the price that he paid for making them (see particularly Jeremiah 20) and the punishment of the people of Israel for refusing to heed them.

For some religious leaders and groups, teaching differential gender roles is conceived of as part of this religiously-obliged speech. For them, the heightened participation of women in the workforce, the increased control that women have over their sexual lives and reproduction, the rejection by many women of traditional roles as wives and mothers, are forms of sinfulness that they are duty-bound to warn the world of. The extract from *Equal but Different* set out above is an example of such religious motivation. The group does not merely argue that feminism is a bad idea or has particular social costs, but that it is forbidden by biblical authority. Again, in those circumstances, for the state to attempt to intervene and prevent a religious person from speaking out and warning the world of the errors that it is falling into by attempting to treat men and women as equal, is to create a conflict between the obligation to God and state law. Under the religious model, the obligation to God must take precedence.

(c) Forbidden speech

The third type of speech is forbidden speech. This is speech which is positively dangerous either because it encourages listeners to turn to untrue beliefs or immoral ways or because it is speech which damages the speaker in the saying. Blasphemy, apostasy, heresy, and other religious speech offences fall into this category. This speech is spiritually dangerous to speakers, even if no one else ever hears them say it and it has no effect on other people. It damages, in serious cases even severs, the relationship between the speaker and the divine.

Such speech is also forbidden because of the effect that it has on others and on the moral and social order. Speech that denies creationism, argues for the equality of people regardless of sexuality, or promotes moral relativism are all types of speech that certain religious speakers have argued need to be forbidden because of their corrupting effect on society.

In certain contexts, the speech of some religious women will also fall into the forbidden category, for example, the speech of women who attempt to adopt the religious speech that is perceived by others as reserved for men: Jewish women praying at the Western Wall,[34] Muslim women leading community prayers in North America,[35] and women fighting for recognition as Buddhist monks in Thailand.[36] At the more extreme edge, even speech that defends women's equality, from religious or non-religious women, may be interpreted as forbidden speech because it might convince women to behave in a way that some religious leaders consider incompatible with a woman's divinely mandated role. Any

---

[34] Raday (n. 11 above), 688–9.

[35] For views on a range of religious issues, including women led prayer, from progressive American Muslims see <http://www.progressiveislam.org/eid_al_fitr_prayer_2006> (last accessed 9 September 2008).

[36] L. Peach, 'Sex or Sangha? Non-normative Gender Roles for Women in Thai Law and Religion' in A. Whiting and C. Evans (eds.) *Mixed Blessings* (n. 19 above), 54–7.

attempt to engage the state in suppressing such speech because of its forbidden religious nature would, of course, bring the religious model into sharp conflict with the liberal model.

The religious model differs from the liberal in part because under this religious model of speech, who speaks, what they say and the context in which they say it are all far more important than they are under the liberal model. Yet when it comes to intervening in sacred or obliged speech, the liberal model tends to leave space for religious speech even when it is damaging to women's equality. The religious speakers are effectively claiming a negative liberty to prevent state intervention, which liberalism is generally prepared to grant. It is only when the religious model desires state involvement in prohibiting forbidden speech that the two have a profound conflict; and as we see from blasphemy laws in the United Kingdom, the liberal model has not invariably won out in such a conflict.[37]

4. Empowering Religious Women's Speech

(i) The Importance of Religious Women's Speech

Given the inadequacy of both models of speech for women, some religious women who are also committed to gender equality are creating their own forms of speech that neither wholly reject nor wholly accept either the religious or liberal.[38] Such speech draws deeply from the particular religious tradition of which women are a part—embracing the concept of the sacred but seeking out new ways of understanding and experiencing it; working within the prophetic tradition, but using that tradition to call for justice for women.[39] It may also draw from liberalism's challenging of received wisdom and commitment to multiple speakers and its various conceptions of equality. Learning from both liberalism and

---

[37] See S. Stokes, 'Blasphemy and Freedom of Expression under the European Convention on Human Rights: The Decision of the European Court in *Wingrove* v. *United Kingdom*' (1997) 2 *Entertainment L. Rev.* 71, 72, for a discussion of blasphemy laws in England. For a criticism of the European Court of Human Rights' preparedness to uphold blasphemy laws that protect only one religion, see S. Palmer, 'Contempt, Free Press and Fair Trial: A "Permanent Shift"?' (1997) 56 *Cambridge L. J.* 467. For useful discussion of the way in which the preservation of English blasphemy laws that protect the Church of England are tied to the question of establishment and the role of the Church within the state, see C. Unsworth, 'Blasphemy, Cultural Divergence and Legal Relativism' (1995) 58 *Modern L. Rev.* 658, 664. For an analysis of recent developments, see Ivan Hare's essay in ch. 15 of this collection.

[38] As Jacobs notes in a discussion about ways in which feminist perspectives can cast light on the First Amendment of the United States Constitution, the 'feminist experience of striving towards gender freedom informs efforts to define other types of freedoms as well.' (n. 23 above), 137.

[39] Examples include the Jewish women who have petitioned for the same right as men to pray at the Western Wall in Jerusalem (discussed in A. Gutmann, *Identity in Democracy* (Princeton: Princeton UP, 2003, 6); the nineteenth-century 'women's movement' in the United States (discussed in E. B. Clark, 'Religion, Rights, and Difference in the Early Woman's Rights Movement' (1987) 3 *Wis. Women's L. J.* 29).

feminism, it is wary of relying too heavily on the regulatory power of the patri-archal states, but is keenly aware of the potential harm to religious women done by unregulated speech:[40] harm by religious speakers who denigrate religious women's political and moral equality but also (although I do not deal with this here) done by secular liberal speakers who denigrate their religiosity.[41]

In a response to secular, feminist criticisms of Islam's treatment of women, Dr. Mona Siddiqi exemplifies such an approach of drawing from a variety of speech traditions. She argues that:

An immense amount of work is being done by academics, activists and ordinary women around the Islamic world to raise consciousness of many of the issues to which [a particular feminist] rightly refers. Importantly, however, most of these women are not rejecting the Muslim faith in their struggles for better societies. Most . . . are revisiting the scriptural traditions in the claim that the Koranic worldview is essentially egalitarian in spirit and that society has failed to translate this world into any meaningful reality.[42]

These types of transgressive, transforming speech and women's movements within religions are an important part of changing religious speech that is harmful to women, and they have already had great success over time.[43] It is often for-gotten that in countries such as the United States, United Kingdom, and Aus-tralia, the early women's movement had a strong religious influence and religious standards were often used by women to criticize the structures of government, law, and even church.[44] They used a powerful mixture of liberal legal concepts

[40] Young (n. 24 above), 8, argues that '[c]ontrary to many today who find in civil society the primary basis for social change to promote justice, however, I argue that those who wish to undermine injustice cannot turn their backs on state institutions as tools for that end.'

[41] Ibid., 9: 'Many people rightly distrust projects of cosmopolitan governance, however, because they fear cultural homogenization or a failure to respect and recognize the specificity of peoples.' For similar reasons, religious women may be wary of some of the claims of liberation made by secular liberalism, fearing that such liberation comes only at the price of abandoning a religious or spiritual dimension that is central to their experiences and a fundamental element of the communities that are important to them. See, for an example of the everyday importance of religion in the lives of a particularly vulnerable group of women and the way that it acts as a source of strength for them, McMichael's discussion of the way in which Islam creates a stable 'home' for Somali refugee women living in Australia (C. McMichael, '"Everywhere is Allah's Place": Islam and the Everyday Life of Somali Women in Melbourne, Australia' (2002) 15 *J. Refugee Studies* 171, 172). Volpp also has a useful discussion of the way in which much liberal feminist speech is denigrating to the culture or religion of minority women while not acknowledging all the problems of patriarchy, violence and oppression in Western society (L. Volpp, 'Feminism Versus Multiculturalism' (2001) 101 *Colum. L. Rev.* 1181).

[42] M. Siddiqui, 'Islam and Feminism: Are they Poles Apart?' *Sunday Herald*, 7 May 2006, 15. For a similar argument see M. Badran, 'Understanding Islam, Islamism, and Islamic Feminisms' (2001) 13 *J. of Women's History*, 47.

[43] Volpp (n. 41 above), 1211, for example, discusses the importance of 'agency within patriarchy' and the nature of many women's experiences as not fitting neatly into either the category of 'victim' or 'agent.'

[44] For a discussion of the integral role religious ideas played in the women's movement in the United States, see Clark (n. 39 above), 40. She summarizes the views of many women involved in the movement: 'As they did with the church, women reformers castigated law as a human corruption of a divine institution.' This mixture of religious, prophetic language, and liberal political reform made for a very powerful combination.

(referring to the Bill of Rights, for example, in the US context) in conjunction with the religious, prophetic language of judgment, and the need for repentance and reform. In disrupting the power of men over their lives, they could call on a higher power, a view summarized by feminist historian Elizabeth Clark in the phrase: 'Resistance to tyranny is obedience to God.'[45] It was a style of speech that has been used in other fights for justice as well by speakers such as Martin Luther King, Ghandi, and Desmond Tutu.[46] It has potentially great potency, but is often overlooked or marginalized by feminists who perceive of religion as simply being conservative and inegalitarian rather than a potential source of liberation.

In considering the regulation of religious speech in liberal societies, the importance of this transgressive religious women's speech should not be forgotten. It is easy enough for male legislators and judges to negotiate with male religious leaders and to come to forms of accommodation of religion within liberal frameworks that take the interests of both groups into account, but that fail to consider the position of women. Yet the viewpoints of religious women should not be assumed to be the same as those of the male leaders of their communities— leaders whose selection, after all, is often made without the input of women. Space needs to be made in considerations about regulations that affect religions (including the regulation of religious speech) to acknowledge the distinctive roles and interests of women. This becomes particularly important when religious speech is used to emphasize the inequality of women, because transformative movements within religions are one of the most powerful tools against this type of speech. This transformative speech may well be far more effective than heavy-handed state intervention to ban directly anti-equality speech, which may be both provocative to particular religious communities and ineffective because it clashes with the religious model of speech to which many religious people (including religious women) will give precedence.

(ii) Practical Strategies for Empowering Religious Women's Speech

What are some of the concrete ways in which a liberal society might be able to empower religious women within religious communities to find distinctive voices and to ensure that these voices are heard? Let me pause and note that I say voices rather than voice. I have discussed the transgressive possibilities of religious women's speech, but we must acknowledge that some religious women will prefer

[45] Ibid., 41.

[46] As Seyla Benhabib has argued, '[r]ights, and other principles of the liberal democratic state, need to be periodically challenged and rearticulated in the public sphere in order to enrich their original meaning. It is only when new groups claim that they belong within the circles of addressees of a right from which they have been excluded in its initial articulation that we come to understand the fundamental limitedness of every rights claim within a constitutional tradition as well as its context-transcending validity' (*The Rights of Others: Aliens, Residents and Citizens* (Cambridge: CUP, 2004), 196–7).

to work within conservative paradigms and will feel most comfortable with the conservative religious speech model and with being represented in the public realm by a male leadership. Insofar as the state creates processes and supports that ensure that this is a real choice and that it is not simply assumed by both male religious leaders and the state to be the natural state of affairs, I have no objection to it.[47] But these are significant caveats and ones that are often not given serious attention by those who defend religious women's subordination as a 'voluntary choice'.

Let me outline some ways in which a liberal state that is reluctant to ban speech on the basis of content and reluctant to regulate directly the religious sphere might none the less help to ensure that religious women have a chance to develop independent voices and for those voices to be heard. Some of these policies are not directly related to speech, but to creating the conditions in which women are given the tools and opportunities to make a real choice about religious issues and to articulate those choices. They include providing high quality education for children and ensuring that there is no exemption for religious groups to school leaving ages (that is, no *Wisconsin* v. *Yoder*)[48] that deprives children of their right to an education long enough to allow them to develop their critical faculties. It also gives girls within the community a greater chance to develop skills that may make them more employable outside a religious community if they choose to leave it, a decision that currently can have very stark economic costs for women in some close-knit religious communities.[49]

Similarly, there needs to be strong protection against domestic violence and a refusal to accept religious or cultural justifications for the perpetuation of such violence. This is also an area in which speech bans might well be considered; those who advocate or justify violence against women might well be penalized even if they do so on the authority of the Bible or the Koran or the Torah. The concept of incitement to racial and religious hate, prohibited in a number of jurisdictions, is capable of also being extended to inciting gender hatred. Domestic violence against women is at least as serious, costly, and widespread a social harm as violence based on religion or belief. There is no reason that similar measures to those that have been taken to protect racial and religious groups from hate that aims to stir violence against them should not equally be deployed against

---

[47] Note, however, the warning of Raday (n. 11 above), 699–700, arguing that the consent of oppressed sub-groups within a community cannot be assumed: '[t]heir sharing of the community understanding—where that understanding is based on a patriarchal tradition—cannot be taken for granted, even if they do not express dissent.' For an alternative viewpoint, arguing that women can and do voluntarily embrace traditional and subordinate roles, see D. M. Smolin, 'Will International Human Rights be Used as a Tool of Cultural Genocide? The Interaction of Human Rights Norms, Religion, Culture and Gender' (1995–6) 12 *J. L. & Relig.*, 143, 162–9.

[48] *Wisconsin* v. *Yoder* 406 US 203 (1972). In that case, the United States Supreme Court accepted the right of Amish families to take their children from school at an earlier age than was required by law in order to protect the integrity of the Amish way of life.

[49] J. Norton, 'Insular Religious Communities and the Rights of Internal Minorities: A Dilemma for Liberalism' (2000–3) 9 *Auckland Univ Law Rev.* 404, 417–8.

those who aim to stir hate or legitimize violence against women. Such a law would, of course, not only apply to religious leaders, but neither would there be any good reason for exempting them from it as religions are not usually exempted from general criminal and public order laws. Extending a law such as s. 29B of the Racial and Religious Hatred Act 2006 (United Kingdom)[50] to prohibiting acts that stir up hatred against women—or even requiring a more stringent test of inciting violence against women—demonstrates a commitment to taking hatred on the basis of gender as seriously as hatred on the basis of race or religion. The free expression guarantees in Article 10(1) of the European Convention on Human Rights and other similar treaty and statutory protections of human rights are not absolute but can be limited inter alia to protect the 'rights and freedoms of others' (Article 10(2)). The European Court of Human Rights has upheld proportionate race and religious hate laws on the basis of respect for 'the equal dignity of all human beings'[51] and, although the Court has not yet dealt specifically with the issue, there is every reason to claim the same entitlement to equal dignity to women who face violence and denigration on the basis of their sex, as there is to protect those who face it on the basis of their race.

While domestic violence might not seem directly linked to speech, some women pay a direct, physical cost for speech that challenges established gender hierarchies within their religious communities or homes. It is often claimed by religious leaders that women embrace a differentiated social role to men and voluntarily accept patriarchal religious teachings. Women's silence, however, cannot be interpreted as acquiescence to the status quo if it is obtained through fear—including fear of violence or fear of the economic consequences of leaving the community. As Frances Raday puts it, 'subjection to patriarchal authority inherently reduces the capacity for public dissent'.[52] By vigorously enforcing current laws prohibiting domestic violence and by introducing laws that prohibited inciting hatred or violence on the basis of gender, the state can open up spaces for women to be able to speak without fear of violent retribution. The relatively minor cost in free speech for those who seek to encourage violence

---

[50] This section sets out that someone who uses 'threatening words or behaviour, or displays any written material which is threatening, is guilty of an offence if he intends thereby to stir up religious hatred.'

[51] For a useful summary of the relevant principles see *Gündüz* v. *Turkey* (Application No. 35071/97) 4 December 2003: 'the Court would emphasise, in particular, that tolerance and respect for the equal dignity of all human beings constitute the foundations of a democratic, pluralistic society. That being so, as a matter of principle it may be considered necessary in certain democratic societies to sanction or even prevent all forms of expression which spread, incite, promote or justify hatred based on intolerance (including religious intolerance), provided that any "formalities", "conditions", "restrictions" or "penalties" imposed are proportionate to the legitimate aim pursued (with regard to hate speech and the glorification of violence, see mutatis mutandis, *Sürek* v. *Turkey* (No. 1) [GC], No. 26682/95, § 62. ECHR 1999-IV). Furthermore, as the Court noted in *Jersild v. Denmark* (judgment of 23 September 1994, Series A No. 298, p. 25, § 35), there can be no doubt that concrete expressions constituting hate speech, which may be insulting to particular individuals or groups, are not protected by Art. 10 of the Convention.'

[52] Raday (n. 11 above), 702.

against or hatred of women is a proportionate price to pay for the protection of women's rights to physical integrity and free speech.

Finally, there are a range of other measures that governments can take to encourage (but not coerce) religions into taking the voice of women more seriously. Governments make all sorts of calculations in engaging with religious issues and there is no reason that gender equality should not be one. Perhaps tax exemptions should only be available to religious groups that voluntarily accept compliance with discrimination laws. Perhaps only religious institutions that can demonstrate that they have engaged in a consultative process that includes women should have their views accepted by government as representative of the views of their community. Perhaps they should, at least, be *asked* to justify any claims that they are speaking for all of their people when they attempt to influence policy or legal outcomes. Perhaps all government representatives or advisory bodies (including religious ones) should have minimum representation of women. Such schemes to encourage religions to treat seriously internal constituencies that they have historically marginalized may, of course, extend beyond issues of gender. Tax exemptions, for example, might well only be made available to religious institutions that adhere to all the non-discrimination laws that apply to similarly placed non-religious institutions. Yet there is a strong claim for women's equality to be a particular focus in liberal democracies, because it is around gender (and the related area of sexuality) equality that the resistance of most religions to non-discrimination remains strongest. Very few religions claim the right in liberal democracies to discriminate on the basis of race, ethnicity, physical disability, and so forth and where these claims are made they tend to be given short shrift by legislators (in every state in Australia, for example, exemptions to non-discrimination laws for religious schools do not permit discrimination on the basis of race, but do permit discrimination on the basis of gender and sexuality).

The policies suggested above do not coerce religious communities into changing deeply held positions on the role of women, but all create incentives to do so, signal that the state has a commitment to gender equality and give support to those within all religious groups who argue for greater gender equality within their tradition.

5. Conclusion

Religious speech continues to be powerful and influential in many communities across the world. Sometimes that speech has been used to challenge the status quo and move societies towards greater freedom, equality and dignity for all. But there is also a long tradition of religious speech being used in ways that perpetuate and legitimize gender inequality. The liberal state, which should have a commitment to both religious freedom and equality, is thus faced with a conflict between two important sets of rights.

In this chapter, I have outlined some suggested reforms that are generally non-coercive and respectful of religious freedom, while still seeking to influence religious groups to take gender equality seriously. All of these proposals would have implications for religious freedom and religious autonomy.[53] But religious freedom and autonomy, important though they are, are not the only values of a liberal society.[54] Gender equality is also claimed to be an important value. The speech of religious women has played an important and distinctive role in Western societies: sometimes that speech complemented the messages of the religious institutions to which they belonged, but not uncommonly such speech brought them into conflict with both the religious and political leadership of the day. If the regulation of religious speech is left only to men who are assumed to speak on behalf of women, then the powerful and potentially transforming nature of that unique women's speech is lost and a religious rhetoric of gender inequality will be allowed to flourish.

---

[53] For criticisms of a similar 'liberating' approach to culture, see C. Kukathas, 'Are There Any Cultural Rights?' (1992) 20 *Pol Theory* 105, 122–3, and D. E. Bernstein, 'Sex Discrimination Laws vs Civil Liberties' (Working Paper No. 20, School of Law, George Mason University, 2000).

[54] See M. C. Nussbaum, *Women and Human Development: The Capabilities Approach* (Cambridge: CUP, 2000), 202, arguing that the 'state and its agents may impose a substantial burden on religion only when it can show a compelling interest. But ... protection of the central capacities of citizens should always be understood to ground a compelling state interest'.

19

Homophobic Speech, Equality Denial, and Religious Expression

*Ian Leigh**

1. Introduction

This chapter discusses legal responses to an increasingly contested question: whether or in what way religious traditionalists have the right to express their belief that homosexual conduct is immoral.[1] Is this homophobia or equality denial and therefore appropriately punished as a form of hate speech? Or is it protected religious speech?

It is arguable that we are witnessing in Britain a fascinating reversal of a famous intellectual contest—the celebrated mid-twentieth century 'Hart-Devlin' debate.[2] Now, as then, a central issue is public attitudes towards homosexuality. Then H. L. A. Hart, widely seen as the champion of liberal forces, argued against the Devlin thesis that society was entitled to enforce its shared morality over sexual conduct. Five decades later matters have changed and moved far beyond the Wolfenden Committee's proposals for de-criminalization of homosexual conduct that gave rise to Hart-Devlin controversy. By a series of bold legislative and judicial measures discrimination against homosexuals and lesbians has been made unlawful, by repealing or amending discriminatory laws (for example, with regard to the age of consent and in the introduction of civil partnerships), and by

* Earlier versions were presented at the Extreme Speech and Democracy Conference, Centre for Public Law, University of Cambridge, 21–22 April 2007 and at the Expert meeting on Religious Pluralism in Europe, 9–11 May 2006, University of Utrecht. The chapter draws partially on material published in I. Leigh, 'Religiously-Motivated Discriminatory Speech: "Homophobia" and Equality Denial', in M. L. P. Loenen and J. E. Goldschmidt, (eds.), *Religious Pluralism and Human Rights in Europe: Where to Draw the Line* (Antwerp: Intersentia, 2007). I am grateful to Jim Weinstein for extensive comments on an earlier draft.

[1] For an earlier analysis of clashes over the same issues in education and employment law, see I. Leigh, 'Clashing Rights, Exemptions and Opt-Outs: Religious Liberty and "Homophobia"', in R. O'Dair and A. Lewis (eds.), *Law and Religion*, (Oxford: OUP, 2001).

[2] H. L. A. Hart, *Law, Liberty and Morality* (London: OUP, 1963); P. Devlin, *The Enforcement of Morals* (London: OUP, 1965).

prohibiting private discrimination, as regards employment and the provision of goods and services.

Most proponents of gay and lesbian rights would be surprised to be described as moral enforcers in the mould of Lord Devlin. And yet the parallels are unmistakable, as first regulators[3] and then the police and the courts have begun to treat dissent from the new orthodoxy of sexual orientation equality as offensive to public opinion. In the twenty-first century equivalent of the Hart-Devlin debate 'homophobia' is the new homosexuality and sexual orientation equality is the new shared morality. By a strange irony it is religious conservatives who are now out of step with the new morality and find themselves in need of the protection of liberal principles.

This new orthodoxy about homosexuality has troubling implications for free speech: people who now voice in print or in broadcasting their private beliefs that homosexual conduct is immoral may find themselves under police investigation following a complaint for provoking a 'hate incident', as happened to both the Anglican Bishop of Chester and the Secretary-General of the Muslim Council of Great Britain following public remarks disapproving of homosexual conduct.[4] Even in advance of the enactment in English law of incitement of an offence of hatred on grounds of sexual orientation,[5] there was a growing list of examples of people with traditional religious objections to the morality of same-sex intercourse who had been penalized by legal or informal sanctions for expressing those views.

In 2004 an elderly street preacher, Harry Hammond, was convicted for a public order offence for displaying a sign in the centre of Bournemouth on a Saturday afternoon stating 'Stop Immorality. Stop Homosexuality, Stop Lesbianism'.[6] In 2005 a retired Christian couple was interviewed by Lancashire police for 80 minutes following their phone call to Wyre Borough Council complaining of its sexual orientation policies.[7] In 2006 the Edinburgh University Christian Union— a student religious society—faced penalties from the University and the National Union of Students for using a bible-study course advocating heterosexual marriage as the only appropriate channel for sexual expression.[8] Even in advance of the enactment in English law of an offence of incitement to hatred on grounds of sexual orientation in February 2007 the Joint Committee on Human Rights argued that children should be protected from offensive teaching in schools in religious education classes that same-sex behaviour is immoral[9], although the

---

[3] See pp. 382–3 below.

[4] See p. 382 below.

[5] The new offence created by s. 74 of the Criminal Justice and Immigration Act 2008 is discussed at pp. 384–7 below.

[6] See pp. 388–90 below.

[7] In December 2006, the police and the council admitted acting wrongfully and paid an out-of-court settlement of compensation and legal costs: S. Doughty, '£10,000 apology by police to Christians hounded in gay row', *Daily Mail*, 23 December 2006.

[8] Christian Institute, *Defending Your Christian Union*, (Newcastle, 2007), 3.

[9] Sixth Report for 2006/7, *Legislative Scrutiny: Sexual Orientation Regulations*, HL Paper 58/HC 350, para. 67.

Committee would allow factual presentations of what religions believe about homosexuality. This comes close to instituting the mirror image of the much-criticized section 28[10]—a mere seven years after its repeal. Putting these developments together the Devlinization of gay rights is, it seems, all but complete.

Now that the elimination of prejudice and discrimination against homosexuals and lesbians has become a goal of public policy requiring the coercive and symbolic use of law, how should those who continue to express dissent on religious grounds from the new orthodoxy be treated? Should the public teaching of these newly heretical positions be allowed outside religious communities, although it may slow down the inevitable march towards the new Jerusalem of a society free of sexual prejudice? Should dissidents be confined to religious ghettos where they may be permitted to continue to believe and teach each other traditional ideas about heterosexual marriage, provided they do not spread the contagion outside? Or should the 'equality police' be sent into churches and mosques to root out these dangerous teachings and practices and to confiscate the offending texts? This is an exaggeration, of course, but these parodies are recognizable distortions of real arguments now taking place in a number of Western liberal states.

The arguments for prohibiting religious expression criticizing homosexuality involve the deployment of two contentious labels: 'homophobia' and 'hate speech'. The first treats disapproval (including, on some versions, failure to positively approve) of homosexuality as a form of fear or hatred of homosexuals, lesbians, and bisexuals as a group. It follows that to publicly express these views is to engage in 'hate speech', in that it may create a threatening or intimidating environment disapproving of homosexuality, encourage prejudice, or, directly or indirectly, incite 'homophobic' violence'.[11] The position of religious institutions is pivotal because, according to Professor Robert Wintemute, they are 'one of the prime sources of insults against, or incitement of hatred towards LGBT individuals'.[12]

Advocates of hate speech laws urge that the state is entitled to regulate expression where social conditions stifle debate and marginalize certain groups.[13]

---

[10] The colloquial name for s. 2A Local Government Act 1986, which prohibited local education authorities from intentionally promoting homosexuality or promoting the teaching in any maintained school of 'the acceptability of homosexuality as a pretended family relationship'. The provision was repealed by the Local Government Act 2000. See n. 1 above, 253–61.

[11] See the recitation by the Supreme Court of Sweden in the *Green* case (discussed below), 4:

'The *travaux préparatoires* specified that homosexuals are a vulnerable group in society, and are often victims of crimes as a result of their sexual orientation and that Nazis and other groups with racist ideologies agitate against homosexuals and homosexuality, as a part of their propaganda and inter-linked with their general racist and anti-Semitic campaigns (Govt. Bill 2001/02:59, page 32 *et seq.*).'

[12] 'Religion vs. Sexual Orientation: A Clash of Human Rights?' (2002) 1 *J.L. & Equal.*, 126, 150. It is clear that Wintemute would, however, support granting a private space to religious institutions to continue to practice in way that is otherwise discriminatory. For a measured treatment of the conflict see also W. N. Eskridge, *Gaylaw: Challenging the Apartheid of the Closet* (Cambridge, MA: Harvard UP, 1999), ch. 9.

[13] O. Fiss, *The Irony of Free Speech* (Cambridge, MA: Harvard UP, 1996).

Such laws are, they contend, justified because of the adverse effects of hate speech, particularly the propagation of racism and homophobia.[14] An analogy is drawn with racist speech and racial discrimination. By prohibiting the public expression of 'homophobic hate speech' advocates hope to cut off the roots from 'homophobia'. Critics of hate speech laws argue, in contrast, that such laws single out certain forms of free speech simply because they express an unpopular or unorthodox idea.

The argument that members of religious groups have a right to express dissent from the new orthodoxy about homosexuality, however, focuses on scriptural teachings: the Old Testament, the New Testament and the Qur'an all contain teaching against homosexual behaviour, although not all contemporary adherents of these religions take these texts literally.[15] On this basis these religions at least require the ability to exclude from membership or leadership (for example, through ordination) practising homosexuals and to refuse to recognize or perform ceremonies of 'marriage' for same-sex couples. Those interests have been recognized by exceptions for religious organization in sexual orientation discrimination provisions[16] or their exclusion from requirements to perform such ceremonies.[17]

Beyond this, however, adherents of these religious groups may seek freedom to publicly express these views as part of religious expression (for example, by calling on homosexuals to repent) or to oppose or reverse changes recognizing gay rights as harmful to society. In this way not just the right of freedom of religion, but also of a broader right of freedom of association and of freedom of expression may be at stake. Iain Benson of the Centre for Cultural Renewal argues: 'just as the State cannot properly coerce religion, it should not coerce sexual practice acceptance'.[18] Robert Gagnon levels a more general criticism of the overreach of equality arguments. He points out that the label 'homophobic' is a part of the 'politics of personal destruction', conveying 'the impression of a psychiatric disorder', as a 'strategy of intimidation to forestall genuine debate and belittle dissenters'.[19] As a

---

[14] For criticism, W. Sadurski, 'On "Seeing Speech Through an Equality Lens": A Critique of Egalitarian Arguments for Suppression of Hate Speech and Pornography' (1996) 16 *O.J.L.S.* 713.

[15] For a sustained theological analysis of the biblical texts, see R. Gagnon, *The Bible and Homosexual Practice: Texts and Hermeneutics* (Nashville, TN: Abingdon Press, 2001).

[16] Eg Employment Directive 2000/78, Art. 4(1) and (2). For analysis of this and many other comparative examples, see R. Ahdar and I. Leigh, *Religious Freedom in the Liberal State* (Oxford: OUP, 2005), ch. 10.

[17] The need for an exemption under Canadian constitutional law in a law to extend civil marriage to same-sex couples was recognized by the Supreme Court of Canada in holding that state compulsion of religious officials to perform same-sex marriages contrary to their religious beliefs would violate s. 2(a) of the Charter: *Reference re Same-Sex Marriage* [2004] 3 S.C.R. 698, 721–3. In the UK, see Civil Partnerships Act 2004, s. 6.

[18] 'A Civil Argument About Dignity, Beliefs and Marriage' Being a Brief for an Appearance Before the Special Legislative Committee of the House of Commons on Bill C-38, *The Civil Marriage Act,* <http://www.culturalrenewal.ca/downloads/sb_culturalrenewal/BriefBillC38.pdf> (last accessed 8 June 2008).

[19] See n. 15 above, 26–7; see also G. Colwell, 'Turning the Tables with "Homophobia"' (1999) 16 *J. Applied Phil.* 207.

result, in a growing number of countries religious dissenters from sexual orientation equality now run the risk of prosecution for inciting hatred.

2. Laws Prohibiting Homophobic Expression

A number of countries have extended laws that prohibit the incitement of hatred against ethnic, racial, or religious groups to include groups identified by sexual orientation.[20] Thus the Netherlands Criminal Code penalizes insults expressed publicly for the purpose of discriminating on a variety of grounds (Article 137c): incitement to hatred, discrimination, and violence on grounds of, inter alia, race (Article 137d); and publicizing or disseminating these expressions, other than for objective publication (Article 137e). Homosexuality is not expressly mentioned but Article 90 of the Code defines discrimination as any distinction, any exclusion restriction or preference, which has the purpose or effect of nullifying or impairing the recognition, enjoyment, or exercise, on an equal footing, of human rights and fundamental freedoms in the political, economic, social cultural, or any other field of public life.[21]

Similarly under Section 135a of the Criminal Code of Norway it is an offence punishable by up to two years imprisonment to publicly threaten, insult, or subject to hatred, persecution, or contempt any person or group of persons because (inter alia) of their 'homosexual bent, life-style, or inclination'. In Iceland the Criminal Code makes it an offence for any person, by mockery, slander, insult, threat, or other means, to publicly attack a person or a group of persons on the grounds of their sexual orientation.[22] A comparable offence exists in Lithuania.[23]

In Canada the Criminal Code contains offences of inciting hatred in a public place against an 'identifiable group' (where such hatred is likely to lead to a breach of the peace) and (regardless of place or breach of the peace) of 'willfully' promoting hatred against an identifiable group (Article 319(1) and (2)). An 'identifiable group' means 'any section of the public distinguished by colour, race, religion, ethnic origin, or sexual orientation'.[24] It is noteworthy, however, that Canadian law gives a religious defence: under Article 319(3)(b), it is a defence

---

[20] See OSCE Office for Democratic Institutions and Human rights, *Combating Hate Crimes in the OSCE Region: An Overview of Statistics, Legislation and National Legislation* (Warsaw: OSCE, 2005). In addition to the examples discussed here, see the Swedish legislation discussed below.

[21] See further below.

[22] S. 223a.

[23] Section 170 of the Criminal Code of Lithuania provides: 'Any person who by public statements orally, in writing or through mass media mocks, expresses contempt, incites hatred or discrimination against a group of people or an individual belonging to such group on account of their ... sexual orientation ... shall be punished by fine or restriction of freedom, or arrest, or imprisonment up to 2 years.'

[24] Criminal Code, ss. 319(7) and 318(4).

(inter alia) if the defendant 'in good faith ... expressed or attempted to establish by argument an opinion on a religious subject'.[25]

3. International Responses

There has been a mixed response from domestic courts in different countries to hate speech offences.[26] At the international level[27] the UN Human Rights Committee has upheld a French law concerning Holocaust denial.[28] The position under the European Convention on Human Rights is also mixed. The European Court of Human Rights has recognized that limited and proportionate hate speech offences can be compatible with Article 10 (which protects freedom of expression),[29] stating that:

tolerance and respect for the equal dignity of all human beings constitute the foundations of a democratic, pluralistic society. That being so ... it may be considered necessary in certain democratic societies to sanction or even prevent all forms of expression which spread, incite, promote or justify hatred based on intolerance (including religious intolerance), provided that any 'formalities', 'conditions', 'restrictions' or 'penalties' imposed are proportionate to the legitimate aim pursued.[30]

---

[25] See *Ross* v. *New Brunswick School District No. 15* [1996] 1 S.C.R. 825, in which the Supreme Court of Canada upheld a provincial human rights board of inquiry order to transfer a teacher who had publicly disseminated (though not in class) his religiously-based view that Christian civilization was being destroyed by a Jewish conspiracy. The Supreme Court found, however, that the order that he be dismissed from the non-teaching post if he continued publicizing his views infringed on his freedom of conscience and religion under s. 2(a) of the Charter.

[26] See *RAV* v. *City of St Paul, Minnesota* 505 US 377 (1992). The US Supreme Court holds unconstitutional as unjustified content-based regulation of speech ordinance that prohibited placing on public or private property any symbol including 'a burning cross or Nazi swastika' which 'arouses anger, alarm, or resentment in others on the basis of race, color, creed, religion or gender ... '); *Virginia* v. *Black et al* 155 L.Ed.2d 535 (2003), upholding the constitutionality of a statute forbidding cross-burning on another person's property or on public property with intent to intimidate a person or group. In Canada see *R* v. *Keegstra* [1990] 3 S.C.R. 697, conviction for racist propaganda, Holocaust revisionism survived Charter challenge); *R.* v. *Zundel* [1992] 2 S.C.R. 731, reversing conviction for Holocaust denial under law prohibiting spreading false information.

[27] See J. Cooper and A. M. Williams, 'Hate Speech, Holocaust Denial and International Human Rights Law' (1999) *E.H.R.L.R.* 593; D. McGoldrick and T. O'Donnell, 'Hate Speech Laws: Consistency with National and International Human Rights Law' (1998) 18 *L.S.* 453.

[28] *Faurisson* v. *France*, 2 BHRC 1, Communication No. 550/1993, UN Doc CCPR/C/58/550/1993 (1996).

[29] '1. Everyone has the right to freedom of expression. This right shall include freedom to hold opinions and to receive and impart information and ideas without interference by public authority ... 2.The exercise of these freedoms, since it carries with it duties and responsibilities, may be subject to such formalities, conditions, restrictions or penalties as are prescribed by law and are necessary in a democratic society in the interests of national security, territorial integrity or public safety, for the prevention of disorder or crime, for the protection of health or morals, for the protection of the reputation or the rights of others ... '

[30] *Gündüz* v. *Turkey* (2005) 41 EHRR 59, para. 40, holding that the applicant's conviction for inciting religious hatred violated Art. 10.

Consequently applications from people convicted of racial hate speech or holo-caust denial, complaining of violation of the right of freedom of expression, have been declared inadmissible in a number of instances.[31]

However, in its most fully reasoned hate speech decision—a case from Denmark involving a journalist convicted of aiding the spread of racist speech for interviewing extremists who expressed racist views on a television documentary—the Court noted that although the remarks of the interviewees were not protected the pro-gramme itself was a serious attempt to inform the public rather than to propagate racist views and therefore held that Article 10 had been violated by the conviction.[32]

In *Gündüz v Turkey*, the European Court of Human Rights specifically addressed religiously intolerant speech, recognizing that although

expressions that seek to spread, incite or justify hatred based on intolerance, including religious intolerance, do not enjoy the protection afforded by Article 10 of the Convention [,] the mere fact of defending sharia, without calling for violence to establish it, cannot be regarded as 'hate speech.'[33]

This decision seemingly gives some protection under Article 10 to points of view antithetical to Convention values, provided they do not incite violence or hatred. Although the Convention jurisprudence is not without ambiguities, it would appear that this will include the right of a religiously motivated speaker to attack contemporary secular and pluralist values.[34] The Strasbourg Court has, however, not yet considered restrictions on homophobic expression, irrespective of religious motivation,[35] although, as we shall see, in one instance the Supreme Court of Sweden has found such a prosecution to be incompatible with the Convention.[36]

4. The UK Position

Until very recently the UK did not have an offence of 'homophobic hate speech' as such. In October 2007, however, the government announced proposals

---

[31] These range from *Glimmerveen and Hagenbeek* v. *the Netherlands*, 8348/78, 18 D&R 187 to *Garaudy* v. *France* 65831/01, ECtHR 2003-IX and *Witzsch* v. *Germany,* 7485/03, 13 December 2005.

[32] *Jersild* v. *Denmark* (1995) 19 EHRR 1; and see *Lehideux and Isorni* v. *France* (2000) 30 EHRR 665. Contrast the admissibility decision in *Garaudy* v. *France,* Appl. 65831/01, 24 June 2003.

[33] *Gündüz* v. *Turkey* (2005) 41 EHRR 59, para. 51. Note also that the European Court has ruled in two recent instances that convictions of national courts under religious defamation laws violated Art. 10 by excessively curtailing public criticism of religious figures or groups: *Giniewski* v. *France,* Appl. 64016/00, judgment of 31 January 2006; *Klein* v. *Slovakia,* Appl. No. 72208/01, judgment of 31 October 2006.

[34] Limits on a similar party political programme may, however, be permissible. See A. Nieu-wenhuis, 'The Concept of Pluralism in the Case Law of the European Court of Human Rights' (2007) 3 *Eur. Const. L. Rev.* 367, 380–2.

[35] The *Hammond* case (below) was declared inadmissible because of the death of the applicant. *Fairfield* v. *UK,* Appl. No. 24790/04, 8 March 2005.

[36] See pp. 391–3 below.

(considered below) to enact such an offence, punishable by up to seven years' imprisonment. Prior to this hate speech against homosexuals was likely to be punished indirectly by the requirement that in sentencing a criminal offender courts must consider as grounds for increasing the sentence that 1) at or near the time of committing the offence the offender demonstrated towards the victim hostility based on the sexual orientation (or presumed sexual orientation) of the victim or 2) the offence was motivated wholly or partly by hostility towards persons who are of a particular sexual orientation.[37] In practice this aggravation is likely to be demonstrated by comments made at the time of the offence. Another way that present law punishes homophobic hate speech is that, applying a widely drawn Code of Practice, the police are now regularly responding to alleged homophobic 'hate incidents' where the harm involves no more than the public expression of disapproval of homosexual conduct, regardless of whether or not an offence might have been committed.[38] For these purposes the threshold is very low. A 'hate incident' is regarded as 'any incident, *which may or may not constitute a criminal offence,* which is *perceived by the victim or any other person,* as being motivated by prejudice or hate'.[39]

On this basis police investigations were launched following complaints from members of the public against both the Anglican Bishop of Chester and the Secretary-General of the Muslim Council of Great Britain for broadcast remarks disapproving of homosexual conduct. Although neither resulted in prosecution, the effect on chilling religious speech is obvious; with respect to the later investigation, a group of Muslim leaders wrote to *The Times* in January 2006 to complain of intimidation and bullying and of an attempt to silence dissenting views.[40]

Regulatory control of the media also has been used to punish speech, including religious speech, deemed homophobic. In an adjudication in June 2004, OFCOM[41] upheld a complaint from a viewer against a UK-based Christian TV Channel, Revelation TV, for comments made by the presenter of its *World In Focus* programme.[42] During the controversy surrounding the appointment of

---

[37] S. 146, Criminal Justice Act 2003. On the question of aggravated offences (discussed in relation to race) see I. Hare, 'Legislating Against Hate—the Legal Response to Bias Crimes' (1997) 17 *O.J.L. S.* 415.

[38] F. Bennion, 'New Police Law Abolishes the Reasonable Man (and Woman)' (2006) 170 *Justice of the Peace* 27; J. Freedland, 'How police gay rights zealotry is threatening our freedom of speech', *The Guardian*, 18 January 2006.

[39] Association of Chief Police Officers and Home Office Standards Unit, *Hate Crime: Delivering a Quality Service* (London: Home Office, 2005), para. 2.2.1(emphasis added). Similarly, the Crown Prosecution Service's policy is to treat an incident as 'homophobic' where it is perceived to be so by the victim or any other person, <http://www.cps.gov.uk/news/pressreleases/archive/2006/134_06. html> (last accessed 9 June 2008).

[40] Letter to the Editor, *The Times*, 14 January 2006.

[41] The Office of Communications, established under the Communications Act 2003.

[42] OFCOM, Programme Complaints Bulletin, 28 June 2004, 3, <http://www.ofcom.org.uk/tv/ obb/prog_cb/pcb_12/pcb_pdf12.pdf> (last accessed 9 June 2008).

openly gay bishops, the programme presenter gave what OFCOM described as 'a four minute polemic about his views on homosexuality in general as well as homosexuality within the Church'. This it found was in breach of parts of the Programme Code dealing with respect for human dignity and avoidance of denigration of others' beliefs.[43] Five years previously, OFCOM's predecessor, the Independent Television Commission, had handed out considerably harsher treatment to the God Channel, a Christian cable and satellite television channel. The channel was fined £20,000 for four breaches of the Commission's Advertising Code. One of the infringements involved a passage (of fifteen seconds duration in a presentation of 28 minutes promoting a forthcoming conference) in which homosexuality was referred to as 'an abomination' (quoting from the book of Leviticus in the King James Version). The channel argued that however unpopular such a view might be it was a protected manifestation of religious belief under Article 9 of the ECHR and, moreover, that its freedom of expression under Article 10 was at stake. The ITC rejected this claim, finding that the passage was 'grossly offensive' to public feeling.[44]

Some forms of homophobic speech are also covered by anti-discrimination law. The definition of harassment applicable to sexual orientation discrimination in employment includes 'creating an intimidating, hostile, degrading, or offensive environment'.[45] Critics of this legislation feared that it might be used to penalize employees who during casual conversation explain their religious beliefs concerning homosexuality which the other person found contentious or upsetting.[46] A partially successful attempt was made to challenge a comparable provision in Northern Ireland legislation dealing with discrimination in goods and services.[47] In the context of considering a challenge to the Equality Act (Sexual Orientation) Regulations (Northern Ireland) 2006, Weatherup J. appeared to accept the possibility of a potential conflict between the right to express one's religious beliefs

---

[43] OFCOM Programme Code, ss. 1.8 and 7.6. For discussion of the Programme Code and religious liberty see Ahdar and Leigh (n. 16 above), 389–95.

[44] ITC Determination, 20 December 1999.

[45] Employment Equality (Sexual Orientation) Regulations 2003, SI 2003/1661, reg. 5(1). Before the introduction of these regulations it had been held that abuse of a teacher on grounds of her orientation did not amount to *sex* discrimination: *Pearce* v. *Mayfield Secondary School Governing Body* [2002] ICR 198.

[46] See *Peterson* v. *Hewlett-Packard Co.* 358 F.3d 599 (9th Cir, 2004) in which the court affirmed summary judgment for an employer that had dismissed a devout evangelical employee for responding to the employer's diversity poster featuring a gay employee by prominently displaying a poster with biblical texts that condemn homosexuals to death. In *Bodett* v. *Coxcom, Inc.* 366 F.3d 736 (9th Cir, 2004) an employee's Title VII religious discrimination claim was dismissed. The plaintiff's employment had been terminated for repeatedly telling a lesbian subordinate of her religious objections to homosexuality in violation of the employer's anti-discrimination and harassment. See further J. Moldover, 'An Employer's Dilemma: When Religious Expression and Gay Rights Cross', *New York Law Journal*, 31 October 2007. I am grateful to Simon Calvert for pointing out these references.

[47] The equivalent British regulations covering discrimination in goods and services, made under the Equality Act 2006, do not cover harassment. And (in the UK) see *Apelogun Gabriels* v. *London Borough of Lambeth* (2006) ET 2301976/05.

and the statutory definition of harassment on grounds of sexual orientation.[48] The applicants had argued that the definition violated their rights under Article 9 of the European Convention on Human Rights. The situation envisaged was where a religious service provider gave an explanation of its reasons of orthodox belief for not offering the service (for example, adoption or relationship counselling) on equal terms to same-sex couples as those of different sexes. Such an explanation ran the risk, it was argued, of falling within the ambit of 'creating an intimidating, hostile, degrading, or offensive environment'. The judge, however, treated this point as moot in view of his decision to strike down the regulations for procedural impropriety in the consultation process, holding that this issue was more appropriately addressed in the redrafting process.[49]

The government, however, introduced provisions to create an offence of incitement to homophobic hatred into the Criminal Justice and Immigration Bill 2007–8 and—in modified form—these have become law.[50] Groups such as Stonewall have lobbied for an offence of this kind as an equalizing measure that would bring the treatment of sexual-orientation equality into line with race and religious equality.[51] They claim also that such speech restrictions are justified because of a link between inciting hatred and homophobic violence.[52] The new offence takes the form of an extension of the existing racial hatred legislation, modelled on the recent offence of incitement to religious hatred law.[53]

Under section 74 and schedule 16 of the Criminal Justice and Immigration Act 2008 it has become an offence to use threatening words or behaviour or to

---

[48] *An Application for Judicial Review Brought by the Christian Institute et al* [2007] NIQB 66 (11 September 2007).

[49] Ibid., para. 84.

[50] The intention to do so was announced by the Minister of Justice (Rt. Hon. Jack Straw, MP) during the Second Reading of the Criminal Justice and Immigration Bill. Hansard HC Debs. Vol. 464 Col. 67–8 (8 October 2007).

[51] Note, however, that there is no equivalent offence in UK law as regards sexual equality (ie, no offence of inciting sexual hatred) and that the International Covenant on Civil and Political Rights, Art. 20 applies only to 'advocacy of national, racial or religious hatred that constitutes incitement to discrimination, hostility, or violence'.

[52] The link between speech and violence is controversial, especially where religious expression is concerned. In 2006 an adjudication of the Advertising Standards Authority (a non-statutory industry body) concerned a newspaper advertisement placed by the Gay Police Association in *The Independent* newspaper under the heading 'in the name of the father', which described a 74 per cent rise in reported homophobic incidents where the religious belief of the perpetrator was the sole or primary motivating factor. It depicted a Bible next to a pool of blood. The advertisement prompted more than 500 complaints to the ASA on grounds that it was offensive and derogatory towards Christians, that it vilified, stereotyped, and could incite violence towards Christians, and that it suggested that Christian beliefs were responsible for or condoned homophobic violence. The ASA rejected the claims that it had these specific effects but nevertheless found it to be misleading and untruthful, and the alleged link between religious views and homophobic violence to be unsubstantiated. The GPA was instructed by the ASA to ensure that future campaigns were not presented in a way that could cause undue offence or use imagery that gave misleading messages. See Advertising Standards Authority Adjudication, 18 October 2006, <http://www.asa.org.uk/asa/adjudications/Public/TF_ADJ_41843.htm> (last accessed 9 June 2008).

[53] Racial and Religious Hatred Act 2006; see n. 60 below.

display any written material which is threatening if it is intended to stir up hatred on grounds of sexual orientation. Hatred 'on the grounds of sexual orientation' is defined to mean:

hatred against a group of persons defined by reference to sexual orientation (whether towards persons of the same sex, the opposite sex or both).

Just as in the debate over religious hatred, critics argued that this further extension of the law was unnecessary in view of the application of other criminal offences, that it relied on a false comparison between race and homosexuality (which some religious critics see as a practice, rather than a status), and that there was a risk to free speech and religious debate. Gay activist Peter Tatchell argued that the offence could be a threat to free speech and that existing laws—were they to be enforced— were already capable of dealing with the harm caused by rap artists or Islamic preachers who advocate violence against homosexuals.[54] Ron Liddle, writing in *The Spectator,* objected to the contradictory outcome of an enforced culture of civility in debates concerning religion, sexual orientation, and toleration:

[A] Muslim who espouses one of its fundamental tenets—that homosexuality is wicked and a sin—might find himself banged up by the old bill for inciting homophobic hatred. And if I were then to say what I believe—that, partly because of its attitude towards gay people, Islam is a vindictive, bigoted and repressive ideology—then I might be banged up, too. This is surely ludicrous.[55]

As with incitement to religious hatred, the difficulty in defining 'hatred' was central to the issue. Critics argued that it would be difficult if not impossible to distinguish 'hatred' from vigorous and open debate on religious and other grounds about the morality of same-sex conduct and equality.[56] Even leaving aside difficulties of what 'homophobia' means, to draw a line between derogatory homophobic abuse, on the one hand, and reasoned, if contentious, religious opinion, on the other, is problematic. The difficulty led in one of two directions. Supporters of the reform argued that the good sense of the prosecuting authorities and of juries and magistrates as fact-finders should be trusted so as not to penalize expression in the latter category. In the light of the *Hammond* decision and the

---

[54] P. Tatchell, 'Hate speech v free speech', *Guardian Unlimited,* 10 October 2007, <http://commentisfree.guardian.co.uk/peter_tatchell/2007/10/hate_speech_v_free_speech.html> (last accessed 9 June 2008). See also M. Paris, 'We gays are not so weedy we can't take insults', *The Times,* 11 October 2007 and 'Free speech demands a bit of give and take, m'luds', *The Times,* 24 April 2008.

[55] 'Laws that constrain free speech bring out the childish bigot in me', *The Spectator,* 10 October 2007.

[56] Memorandum to the Public Bill Committee on the Criminal Justice and Immigration Bill from the Department for Christian Responsibility and Citizenship, Catholic Bishops' Conference of England and Wales, and the Mission & Public Affairs Council of the Church of England, 22 November 2007, <http://www.cofe.anglican.org/news/pr11307.html> (last accessed 9 June 2008); Christian Institute, *The 'Homophobic Hatred' Offence, Free Speech and Religious Liberty,* (Newcastle, 2008), <http://www.christian.org.uk/issues/2007/gay_rights/hatecrime/briefing_jan08.pdf> (last accessed 9 June 2008).

police investigations already mentioned into broadcasters and clergymen, the scepticism of opponents and distrust of prosecutorial discretion was at least understandable. Moreover, even if good sense prevails speech anywhere near to the boundary would nonetheless be chilled. From this opponents of the proposed offence conclude that it would be better not to legislate against expression of hatred against homosexuals beyond the provision providing increased sentences for bias motivated crimes.

Rather than arguing for a defence for good faith arguments on a religious subject[57], or based on Article 9 of the European Convention on Human Rights (for example teaching within religious organizations or religious services[58]), religious critics of the legislation instead put their weight behind a more general free speech defence. Their first attempt at revising the Bill was an unsuccessful cross-party backbench amendment which failed to pass at the House of Commons Report stage in January 2008.[59] The proposed amendment would have protected from prosecution 'discussion of, criticism of, or expressions of antipathy towards, conduct relating to a particular sexual orientation, or urging persons of a particular sexual orientation to refrain from or modify conduct related to that orientation'.

The proponents argued that the focus upon *conduct* rather than criticism of homosexuals as a group was in keeping with the spirit of the new offence and that the main purpose was to provide reassurance to those whose speech—whether religiously motivated or not—might otherwise be chilled.[60] The government claimed, however, that these interests had already been protected by confining the scope of the offence to 'threatening' words and behaviour (rather than insulting or abusive words or behaviour) and that the police and prosecutors would receive guidance on distinguishing unlawful words or behaviour from unpopular criticism of homosexuality.

In many ways the debate was a reprise of arguments raised by the Lester amendment to the Racial and Religious Hatred Bill 2006. That amendment to the offence of incitement to religious hatred introduced a strong free speech protection[61] supported by, among others, those fearful for the effect on religious

---

[57] See Canadian Criminal Code, Art. 319(3)(b).

[58] See the Supreme Court of Sweden's discussion in the *Green* case (pp. 391–3 below) to 'sermon-like' situations.

[59] Hansard HC Debs. Vol. 470 Col. 448 ff. (9 January 2008).

[60] Albeit in markedly weaker terms than the comparable defence under the incitement to religious hatred offence. There was no reference to 'dislike, ridicule, insult, or abuse'—all of which are protected with reference to religions, beliefs, and religious practices under s. 29J of Public Order Act 1986 (as amended by the Racial and Religious Hatred Act 2006). See n. 53 above.

[61] S. 29J of the Public Order Act 1986 provides that:

'Nothing in this Part shall be read or given effect in a way which prohibits or restricts discussion, criticism or expressions of antipathy, dislike, ridicule, insult, or abuse of particular religions or the beliefs or practices of their adherents, or of any other belief system or the beliefs or practices of its adherents, or proselytizing or urging adherents of a different religion or belief system to cease practising their religion or belief system.'

freedom. On this occasion, however, the amendment to the Criminal Justice and Immigration Bill was defeated by a government majority of 159.

Undeterred, critics of the proposals re-phrased their objections in milder language which referred solely to criticism of sexual conduct and on 21 April 2008 the former Conservative Home Secretary Lord Parker of Waddington successfully moved an amendment at the Lords' Committee stage. This amendment, which passed by a majority of 81 to 57, states that:

for the avoidance of doubt, the discussion or criticism of sexual conduct or practices or the urging of persons to refrain from or modify such conduct or practices shall not be taken of itself to be threatening or intended to stir up hatred.[62]

The government continued to maintain that the amendment was unnecessary because the proposed offence could only be committed by use of words that were 'threatening' and that mere criticism would not fall within the ambit of the offence. Supporters of the amendment stressed, however, that it was designed to provide reassurance to those whose speech might otherwise be 'chilled' and to prevent over-zealous policing. Ministers preferred that the latter question be addressed through guidance but critics pointed out that the existing guidance on hate incidents was misleading and appeared to have encouraged the police to intervene in an over-bearing fashion. Although the government succeeded in removing the amendment in the House of Commons[63] when the House of Lords inserted the amendment for a second time ministers, anxious to secure speedy passage of the other powers in the Bill, conceded defeat.[64]

Despite this outcome, unfortunately it remains all too likely (based on experience in other jurisdictions) that the new offence will result in further legal skirmishes between religious traditionalists and gay rights advocates. The police, however, now have a clearer legislative basis to turn away requests to investigate religious speech that may be counter-cultural in its stance on sexual orientation but which is not threatening. It is noteworthy, however, that the Act does nothing to change the previous interpretations given to lesser public order offences. Even where the words of street preachers, clergymen, and other religious critics clearly fall short of the 'threatening' threshold under the new offence there remains therefore the possibility of liability under lesser public order offences which cover 'abusive' or 'insulting' words likely to cause harassment, alarm or distress.[65] Consideration of the European Convention jurisprudence is therefore necessary.

---

[62] Inserted as s. 29JA Public Order Act 1986 by sched. 16, para. 14 of the Criminal Justice and Immigration Act 2008.

[63] Hansard HC Debs. Vol. 475 Col. 598 ff. (6 May 2008).

[64] Hansard HL Debs. Vol. 701 Col. 594 ff. (7 May 2008).

[65] As occurred in the *Hammond* case, below.

5. The Status of Religiously-Motivated Speech

Despite the protections for freedom of belief and religion and freedom of expression that feature in the International Covenant on Civil and Political Rights and the European Convention on Human Rights,[66] there is no right of religious expression as such, nor is religiously-motivated speech given special privileges or protections.[67] The UN Declaration on the Elimination of All Forms of Intolerance and Discrimination Based on Religion or Belief 1981 is more explicit in treating free speech as an aspect of religious liberty.[68] Article 6 of the Declaration states that freedom of religion includes the freedoms: '(d) To write, issue and disseminate relevant publications in these areas', and '(e) To teach a religion or belief in places suitable for these purposes'. The Declaration is, however, a non-binding text. Nevertheless, the European Court of Human Rights adopts a somewhat similar approach by giving some recognition to freedom to manifest one's religion through teaching, preaching, and bearing witness under Article 9 of the European Convention. In *Kokkinakis* v. *Greece*,[69] the Court held that Article 9 had been violated when two Jehovah's Witnesses were convicted by the Greek courts of the offence of proselytism. Less happily from the point of view of free speech, the majority of the judges promulgated a distinction between proper bearing witness and 'improper proselytism'. Apart from this interpretation of Article 9, however, there is no distinctive protection for religious speech as such in the Convention; it falls under the general protection for free speech under Article 10.

Speaking of Article 10, the European Court famously said in the case of *Handyside* v. *United Kingdom* that it

encompasses the right to express not only ideas 'that are favourably received or regarded as inoffensive, but also . . . those that offend, shock or disturb the State or any sector of the population. Such are the demands of that pluralism, tolerance and broadmindedness without which there is no "democratic society" '.[70]

(i) The *Hammond* Case

Handyside's admonition that freedom of speech encompasses ideas that 'offend, shock, and disturb', which religious speech certainly has the capacity to do, did

---

[66] See ICCPR Arts. 18 and 19 and ECHR, Arts. 9 and 10.

[67] For an argument that religious speech is routinely accorded less protection than political speech see A. Geddis, 'You Can't Say "God" on the Radio: Freedom of Expression, Religious Advertising and the Broadcast Media after *Murphy v Ireland*' (2004) 9 *E.H.R.L.R.* 181. In *Murphy* v. *Ireland* (2004) 38 EHRR 212, the European Court of Human Rights held that a ban prohibiting any form of religious advertising on the radio did not violate Art. 10.

[68] The Declaration was adopted by General Assembly Res. 36/55, 36 UN GAOR, Supp. (No. 51), 171. See M. Evans, *Religious Liberty and International Law in Europe* (Cambridge: CUP, 1997), ch. 9; D. J. Sullivan, 'Advancing the Freedom of Religion or Belief through the UN Declaration on the Elimination of Religious Intolerance and Discrimination' (1988) 82 *Am. J. Int'l L.* 487.

[69] (1993) 17 EHRR 397.   [70] (1979) 1 EHRR 737, para. 49.

little to avail the defendant in *Hammond* v. *DPP*,[71] the UK decision mentioned earlier. Harry Hammond was an elderly street preacher who preached in the centre of Bournemouth on a Saturday afternoon while holding a large sign with the words: 'Stop Immorality', 'Stop Homosexuality', 'Stop Lesbianism', and 'Jesus is Lord'. A hostile crowd of some 30 to 40 people had formed, some of whom reacted violently by assaulting Hammond. After his refusal to desist from preaching, and following substantial debate among themselves (and after representations by members of the crowd), the police decided to arrest Hammond rather than his opponents. The Magistrates Court convicted him of displaying an 'insulting' sign causing 'alarm or distress' contrary to section 5 of the Public Order Act 1986,[72] fined him £300, and confiscated the sign.

Hammond's appeal on a point of law against the magistrates' conviction was dismissed. The Divisional Court rejected his argument that his right to religious freedom under Article 9 of the Convention and his right to free expression under Article 10 had been violated. The decision turned on the reluctance of the court to interfere with the first instance tribunal's findings that Hammond's behaviour amounted to displaying an 'insulting' sign causing 'alarm or distress'. Noting that freedom of expression was 'an axiomatic freedom'[73] and there was a danger of a 'heckler's veto'[74] stifling public speech, May LJ., giving judgment for the court, admitted he did not find the case 'easy' and it was 'not without hesitation'[75] that he deferred to the magistrates' findings. Nevertheless, he found that it was open to the magistrates to find that the sign was 'insulting' and also open to them to find that Hammond's conduct had not been 'reasonable' (a defence under section 5(3)(c) of the Act).[76]

This is a profoundly unsatisfactory decision that is inconsistent with the Convention jurisprudence recognizing the protection for expression of shocking ideas given by decisions on Article 10 at Strasbourg.[77] It is doubtful that it would have withstood substantive analysis in the European Court of Human Rights—an avenue closed, however, by Hammond's death before the petition was determined.[78] The Divisional Court's deference—despite misgivings—to the magistrates' findings is arguably inconsistent with the responsibility of *all* courts under section 6 of the Human Rights Act 1998 not to violate a person's Convention rights. That Act also required the Public Order Act 1986 be given a Convention-

---

[71] [2004] EWHC 69 (Admin).

[72] The Public Order Act 1986, s. 5(1), creates a wide-ranging offence of using 'threatening abusive or insulting' words, signs, or behaviour 'within the hearing or sight of a person likely to be caused harassment, alarm, or distress thereby'.

[73] [2004] EWCH 69 (Admin), para. 6.

[74] Ibid., para. 29.

[75] Ibid., para. 32.

[76] Ibid., paras. 32–4.

[77] *Handyside* v. *UK* (1979) 1 EHRR 737, para.49.

[78] An application to the European Court of Human Rights was declared inadmissible because Hammond had by that time died. *Fairfield* v. *UK*, Appl. No. 24790/04, 8 March 2005.

compatible reading so far as possible.[79] Andrew Ashworth has pointed out that the Divisional Court should therefore have narrowed the interpretation of 'distress' in section 5 of the Public Order Act 1986 to protect free speech.[80]

In a powerful critique Andrew Geddis argues that the Divisional Court's interpretation in *Hammond* is a 'pro-civility'[81] judgment. The implicit demand that the speaker re-phrase his public dissent from social orthodoxy into more acceptable (that is, less distressing to his hearers) terms would in this instance, he argues, change not only the manner but also the *content* of the message, since it was the equation of homosexuality with immorality on the defendant's sign that had been found by the court to be offensive. In effect *Hammond* criminalizes public expression of this view altogether.[82] In that sense it is a deeply illiberal ruling since, on the shakiest of factual foundations about disturbance of public order, it allows public expression of an entire religious viewpoint to be prohibited. In contrast, a 'transformative' view, by which the state teaches its citizens that they should learn to tolerate the existence and expression of 'a full panoply of beliefs', would be a stronger recognition of the core democratic values of diversity and pluralism and, moreover, be more consistent with the Convention approach.[83]

Arguably, just such an approach can be found in *Redmond-Bate* v. *DPP*, an earlier Divisional Court ruling quashing the conviction of one of three young, female 'Christian fundamentalist' preachers for obstructing a police constable by refusing the officer's request to stop street preaching in the face of some hostile elements in a crowd of more than a hundred. Sedley LJ. observed:

Free speech includes not only the inoffensive but the irritating, the contentious, the heretical, the unwelcome and the provocative provided it does not tend to provoke violence. Freedom only to speak inoffensively is not worth having... From the condemnation of Socrates to the persecution of modern writers and journalists, our world has seen too many examples of State control of unofficial ideas.[84]

Hammond can be contrasted also with decisions in the Netherlands and in Sweden. In the Netherlands in 2002 a court acquitted Imam el-Moumni of inciting hatred or discrimination against a group of people because of their homosexual orientation.[85] In May 2001, on the television programme *Nova*, he

---

[79] Human Rights Act 1998, s. 3.
[80] 'Case Comment', (2004) *Crim. L.R.* 851, 853.
[81] Geddis explains that on this view:

'the state legitimately can require that anyone wishing to espouse or discuss matters of general public or political interest respect the sensibilities of others, and act in a fashion which preserves a measure of decorum in society as a whole. Shaping or conditioning of the realm of public discourse in this fashion reflects a communitarian ethos; the rights of individual speakers should not be allowed to trump the wider collective social interest in establishing standards that govern what is an acceptable contribution to the public debate over matters of common, current importance.' In 'Free Speech Martyrs or Unreasonable Threats to Social Peace?—"Insulting" Expression and Section 5 of the Public Order Act 1986' (2004) *P. L.* 853, 869.
[82] Ibid., 866–7.   [83] Ibid., 871.   [84] (1999) 7 BHRC 375, (1999) *Crim. L.R.* 998.
[85] The prosecution was brought under article 137 of the Criminal Code. See p. 379 above.

had denounced homosexuality as 'harmful to Dutch society' and a 'contagious disease'. He was acquitted and, on appeal by the prosecutor to the Court of Appeal, the acquittal was upheld.[86] The court found that his statements were permitted as a manifestation of his religious freedom of expression as an Imam. Similarly, in 2005 the Supreme Court of Sweden quashed the conviction of pastor Åke Green, who had been sentenced to a month's imprisonment in 2004 for inciting hatred on grounds of sexual orientation, following his trenchant criticism of homosexuality in a church sermon. This decision contains the fullest judicial analysis to date of the issue of whether such religious speech is protected.

(ii) The *Åke Green* Case

In the *Green* case[87] the Supreme Court of Sweden had to consider the conviction of a Pentecostal pastor for the offence of agitation against a group on the basis of their sexual orientation[88] arising from a sermon preached on 20 July 2003, in Borgholm, before about 50 persons. The title of the sermon was 'Is homosexuality congenital or the powers of evil meddling with people?'. According to the Court's summary:

Åke Green linked homosexuality with the origin and spread of AIDS . . . [H]e speaks of sexual abnormalities (apparently including homosexuality in this group) as a deep cancerous growth, and about sexual use of animals in connection with a Biblical verse from Leviticus 18:22–30, which begins 'you shall not lie with a man, as a man lies with a woman,' but also refers to bestiality. In the third section, he refers to the First Epistle to the Corinthians, using the expressions 'corrupter of boys,' 'perverted people' and 'paedophiles' when speaking of homosexuals. Finally, before addressing the First Epistle to the Corinthians 6:18, he characterizes homosexuality as something sick, and a corrupted thought that displaces a pure one.[89]

---

[86] G. Coughlan, 'Dutch court clears anti-gay Imam', *BBC News*, 9 April 2002, <http://news.bbc.co.uk/1/hi/world/europe/1917905.stm> (last accessed 9 June 2008). Ministerie van Binnenlandsezaken en Koninkrijksrelaties, *Policy Document on Fundamental Rights in a Pluralistic Society* (Netherlands: 2004), 17. See also the acquittal on appeal (upheld by the Supreme Court on 9 January 2001) of a member of the Lower House, Mr. Van Djke, for likening homosexual behaviour to theft in a magazine interview, ibid., 18. See further Jan-Peter Loof, 'Freedom of Expression and Religiously-Based Ideas on Homosexuality: European and Dutch Standards' in Loenen and Goldschmidt (n. 1 above).

[87] *Prosecutor General* v. *Åke Ingemar Teodor Green*, the Supreme Court of Sweden, Case No. B 1050–05, issued in Stockholm on 29 November 2005. An English version is available on the Supreme Court's website, <http://www.domstol.se/Domstolar/hogstadomstolen/Avgoranden/2005/Dom_pa_engelska_B_1050-05.pdf> (last accessed 9 June 2008).

[88] Under ch. 16, s. 8 of the Swedish Criminal Code a person is guilty of agitation against a group by making a statement or otherwise spreading a message that threatens or expresses contempt for the group with reference (inter alia) to their sexual orientation. This category was added to protections for groups with reference to their race, skin colour, nationality, ethnic origin, or religious belief by an amendment of the law on 1 January 2003.

[89] *Prosecutor General* v. *Green*, 7. Green also stated, however, that not all AIDS sufferers were homosexual and that not all homosexuals were paedophiles. See n. 87 above, 2–3.

The issue for the Supreme Court was whether applying the offence under the Criminal Code in Green's case would violate the Swedish Constitution or the European Convention on Human Rights, both of which guaranteed freedom of religion and freedom of expression. The Supreme Court found that there would no violation of the Constitution but that, having regard to the jurisprudence of the European Court of Human Rights, the conviction was a disproportionate restriction under Articles 9 and 10 of the Convention. Accordingly, a restricted interpretation of the offence of agitation against a group was required.[90]

It is noteworthy that when the offence of agitation against a group had been extended to cover sexual orientation in 2003, the Swedish Council of Free Churches had lobbied unsuccessfully to exclude words spoken in a church sermon from the offence. The government provided reassurance by making clear that the intention was not to prevent or 'restrict free and objective debate' about homo-sexuality whether in churches or elsewhere, that not every statement 'that includes judgments regarding a group' was to be criminalized, and that only discussion that overstepped 'the limits of objective and responsible discourse regarding the group in question' would be an offence. The context and motivation for the words would be relevant.

Merely citing and discussing religious scriptures, for example, does not fall within the purview of criminalized behaviour pursuant to this proposal. However, it should not be permissible to use this kind of material to threaten, or to express contempt for, homosexuals as a group, any more than it would be permissible to use religious texts to threaten, or express contempt for, Muslims or Christians. It is important here to distinguish between statements and communications that refer to sexual orientation, *per se,* and express threats or contempt against the collective on these grounds, from other statements and communications that relate to behaviour or the expression of a sexual preference, but in no way intend to insult or threaten the entire group of people who have that sexual orientation.[91]

The Constitution Committee of the Riksdag had also rejected the idea of special rules for statements made in sermons. It argued that: 'in sermon situations, citing

---

[90] See *Hugh Owens* v. *Saskatchewan Human Rights Commission* [2006] SKCA 41 in which the Saskatchewan Court of Appeal held that s. 14(1)(b) of the Saskatchewan Human Rights Code, S.S. 1979, c. S-24.1 which made it unlawful to publish an article or statement that tends or exposes a class of persons to hatred, ridicule, belittling, or affront to their dignity had to be interpreted narrowly to protect freedom of expression and of religion. The appellant, who had published a newspaper advertisement, depicting two stickman holding hands, with a prohibited sign superimposed and reference to various Biblical passages, was found not to have violated s. 14 (1)(b). The provision had to be interpreted as applying only to statements conveying intense feelings and a strong sense of detestation, calumny, and vilification of homosexuals. The Court found that a reasonable person who understood the context of the public debate about sexual identity in Canadian society and the nature of fundamental religious texts would not interpret the advertisement as reaching this standard. I am grateful to Gavin Phillipson for drawing my attention to this decision.

[91] Govt. Bill. P. 41 et seq., cited in n. 87 above, 6.

scripture, and only urging an audience to adhere to the precepts contained therein, should normally not lie within the criminalized area'.[92]

The Supreme Court found that Green had acted out of his 'Christian conviction to improve the situation of his fellow man' and 'what he considered to be his duty as a pastor'. The Court also found, however, that his sermon contained insulting judgments of homosexuals as a group and went beyond the direct expression of biblical verses. The Court rejected Green's argument that it was homosexual *behaviour* and not the group per se that he condemned as sinful according to biblical standards, and found that his remarks were essentially directed at the sexual preference per se rather than the practice of homosexuality. Because he had overstepped the limits of objective and responsible discourse, his behaviour constituted expressing contempt for homosexuals as a group, contrary to the Criminal Code.

However, the Supreme Court found that under Article 9, free speech in a 'sermon-like situation' protected thoughts and ideas based on a religion. Therefore it needed to be considered whether it was necessary in a democratic society to restrict Green's freedom to preach. The Article 9(2) jurisprudence of the European Court of Human Rights on proportionality is notoriously underdeveloped in view of the regrettable tendency of the Court to hold under Article 9(1) that contested practices are not a manifestation of religious belief, rather than to consider whether the restriction is necessary.[93] Nevertheless, the Supreme Court approached the question by analogy with Article 10 (where proportionality analysis is commonplace). A comprehensive assessment of circumstances, including the context was required in 'hate speech' cases to determine if the restriction was proportionate in relation to the purpose and whether the reasons were relevant and sufficient. Particular stress was laid upon the fact that political speech where no incitement to violence was involved had been found to be protected under Article 10.[94] The Court applied this approach to find that Green's statements could not be said to encourage or justify hatred of homosexuals and that to convict him in these circumstances would therefore violate the Convention. Consequently, the offence of agitation against a group had to be interpreted restrictively, even though this meant the offence was narrower than the *travaux préparatoires* indicated.

6. Adjudicating Rights Conflicts

The Supreme Court of Sweden's judgment in *Green* is one model of how clashes of equality, non-discrimination, freedom of expression, and of religion can be

---

[92] Report 2001/02:KU23, p. 36 et seq., cited in n. 87 above, 7.
[93] Ahdar and Leigh (n. 16 above), 122–5.
[94] *Yasar et al* v. *Turkey*, application 42713/98, 23 September 2004, unpublished.

approached—through proportionality analysis. This requires the state to justify restrictions on religious expression according to strict criteria even when acting to protect other individuals from discrimination. Proportionality entails demonstrating a rational basis for protecting a legally permissible interest in a way that impairs the enjoyment of right no more than necessary. We can better appreciate its advantages by comparing an alternative strategy—so-called definitional balancing of rights.[95] This method deals with apparent inconsistencies between the protection of religious liberty and protection from discrimination on grounds of sexual orientation by in effect defining away one of the rights involved.

An example of the dangers to free speech of a definitional balancing approach is provided by a New Zealand High Court decision which involved an attempt to censor video recordings (produced by a US religious organization) on the grounds that their teaching on homosexuality incited hatred. *Living Word Distributors Ltd* v. *Human Rights Action Group Inc (Wellington)*[96] concerned a challenge to a decision of the Film and Literature Board of Review classifying two videos distributed in New Zealand and produced as 'objectionable' under section 3 of the Films, Videos and Publications Classification Act 1993. The videos were a religious and political polemic against the 'homosexual lifestyle', dealing with AIDS and with sexual orientation equality. The Board had concluded that the videos tended to represent that a class of persons were inherently inferior by reason of sexual orientation, a ground which was a prohibited ground of discrimination under section 21(1) of the Human Rights Act 1993. The High Court endorsed that approach and the Board's preference for non-discrimination over freedom of expression.[97]

---

[95] Care is needed in use of terminology. The distinction between 'definitional balancing' and 'ad hoc' balancing of rights originates in discussion of US First Amendment jurisprudence. See M. B. Nimmer, 'The Right to Speak From *Times* to *Time*: First Amendment Theory Applied to Libel and Misapplied to Privacy', (1968) 56 *Cal. L. Rev.* 935, arguing in favour of definitional balancing especially on grounds of certainty. However, 'ad hoc' balancing of rights criticized by some First Amendment scholars is qualitatively different from proportionality discussed in this chapter. This is due to the significantly different way in which the rights concerned are expressed under the European Convention on Human Rights, Arts. 9 and 10 (notably the more detailed specification of the right and of the stipulations for limitation) which invites a structured analysis by the court. See in the UK *de Freitas* v. *Permanent Secretary of Ministry of Agriculture, Fisheries, Lands and Housing* [1999] 1 AC 69 and *R(Daly)* v. *Secretary of State for the Home Department* [2001] UKHL26 [2001] 2 AC 532. Arguably, the same point applies to the New Zealand Bill of Rights Act 1990 and the Canadian Charter of Rights, although in each case the limitation provisions are general (s. 5 of the NZBORA and s. 1 of the Charter) rather than tied to specific rights. See, respectively, *Moonen* v. *Film and Literature Board of Review* [2000] 2 NZLR 9; *R* v. *Oakes* [1986] 1 S.C.R. 103 (and applying the method to hate speech, *R* v. *Keegstra* [1990] 3 S.C.R. 697). For systematic discussion of proportionality with respect to free speech, H. Fenwick and G. Phillipson, *Media Freedom Under the Human Rights Act*, (Oxford, OUP, 2006); and with regard to religious freedom, Ahdar and Leigh (n. 16 above), ch. 6.

[96] See (1997) 4 HRNZ 422. See R. Ahdar, *Worlds Colliding: Conservative Christians and the Law* (Aldershot: Ashgate, 2001), 251–5; A. Butler, 'Limiting Rights' (2002) 33 *V.U.W. L. Rev.* 537, 548–9.

[97] Protected under ss. 19 and 14 respectively of the New Zealand Bill of Rights Act 1990.

The Court of Appeal, however, found that the High Court had erred in law, quashed the decision and remitted the matter back to the Board.[98] The Court of Appeal found that the Board had interpreted its power over 'objectionable' material unduly widely. The Board had wrongly conflated factors to be weighed in relation to objectionable subject matter (which under the legislation concerned depictions of various sexual activities) with the grounds for censorship, so that it blurred the line between censorship and anti-discrimination legislation.[99] Moreover, the Board and High Court below had wrongly given primacy to the non-discrimination provision over freedom of expression by assuming that on the facts that the two clashed and that the latter should be restricted:

But in terms of the statutory scheme there is no direct clash of rights . . . The Bill of Rights is a limitation on governmental, not private conduct. The ultimate inquiry under s 3 involves balancing the rights of a speaker and of the members of the public to receive information under s14 of the Bill of Rights as against the State interest . . . in protecting individuals from harm caused by the speech. And the fundamental error on the part of the High Court was in treating s19 as prevailing over s14.[100]

Whereas freedom of expression was *directly* in issue, non-discrimination was not.[101] To give full effect to freedom of expression under the Bill of Rights Act therefore required a restricted reading of the Board's powers over objectionable material.[102] If the High Court's use of a definitional balancing approach can be faulted for giving too little weight to free speech, the Court of Appeal's ruling might appear artificially to exclude consideration of arguments concerning discrimination. Its virtue, however, is enforce the discipline of justification upon the regulatory body to justify restrictions on freedom of expression, rather than permitting a generalized 'trade off' between competing rights.[103]

In religious liberty cases one common definitional balancing technique is to invoke the belief-action distinction—to limit religious freedom to freedom of *belief*. Thus, believers are free to believe that same-sex conduct is immoral but not to *act* on that belief to another person's detriment. The Supreme Court of Canada partially followed this approach to resolving the conflict in *Trinity Western University* v. *British Columbia College of Teachers*,[104] holding that the

---

[98] [2000] 3 NZLR 570. Per Richardson P, Gault, Keith, and Tipping JJ.; Thomas J. found that the Board lacked jurisdiction to classify the publication under s. 3 and accordingly there was no reason to remit the decision to the Board.

[99] [2000] 3 NZLR 570, 582.

[100] Ibid., 584.

[101] Ibid., 583–4.

[102] The New Zealand Bill of Rights Act 1990 requires courts to give preference to possible readings of legislation that conform with the ICCPR (s. 6), subject to reasonable limitations demonstrably justified in a free and democratic society (s. 5).

[103] See Butler (n. 96 above), 549.

[104] [2001] 1 S.C.R. 772. See further I. Benson and B. Miller, 'Pluralism and the Respect for Religion' (2001) *Lex View*, <http://www.culturalrenewal.ca/qry/page.taf?id=58> (last accessed 9 June 2008).

body responsible for regulating teacher training in British Columbia, the British Columbia College of Teachers ('BCCT'), had acted unlawfully in denying accreditation to a programme to be run at a private Christian university. Students at Trinity Western signed a comprehensive statement of 'Community Values' affirming their belief in, and intention to abide by, a number of aspects of Biblical behaviour, including abstention from same-sex sexual relationships. The BCCT considered that this appeared to follow discriminatory practices and refused to accredit the course. The majority of the Supreme Court (L'Heureux-Dubé J. dissenting) held that the apparent conflict between the equality right under section 15 of the Charter and the right of religious freedom under section 2(a) could be resolved by the belief-action distinction. In the Court's view, freedom of religion includes the right to believe that same-sex conduct is immoral, but not to act on those beliefs, by discriminating against a practising homosexual or lesbian.[105]

The danger of this approach is that confining religious liberty to matters of belief in this way relieves the state of the burden of justifying restrictions on the right. In *Trinity Western* this danger was less apparent because, as the majority ruled, failure by BCCT to correctly understand the scope of freedom of religion had led to the unlawful conflating of it with the equality right under section 15. The BCCT had erroneously concluded that even the signing by the students of the statement of Community Values, which concerned *their own* beliefs and personal conduct, was evidence of 'homophobia'. The Supreme Court, however, found that here was no evidence that Trinity Western produced teachers who had or would discriminate in the classroom.[106] Moreover, the majority held that even if some homosexual students would be deterred from applying to Trinity Western this would not close alternative avenues to them qualifying as teachers in British Columbia. BCCT had thus failed to correctly weigh the various rights and had acted without sufficient evidential basis to justify the restriction on freedom of religion involved in denying accreditation.[107]

The majority judgment appears, therefore, to waiver between the definitional balancing and proportionality approaches. Despite these shortcomings the *Trinity Western* decision makes some valuable distinctions between statements of personal beliefs and discriminatory acts that could profitably be learned in discussions about religiously-motivated 'homophobic hate-speech'.

When definitional balancing is applied to silence in the name of non-discrimination any views other than those positively approving of homosexual lifestyles, equality is in effect dominant over freedom of religion and freedom of expression. This is a contentious outcome and one that is at odds with a vision of liberal society based on John Rawls' 'overlapping consensus' among people of

---

[105] [2001] 1 S.C.R. 772, 814-5. L'Heureux-Dubé J, dissenting, rejected this distinction and analysed the conflict under s. 1 rather than s. 2(a).
[106] Ibid., 816.
[107] Ibid., 814.

different 'comprehensive views'.[108] As two Justices of the Supreme Court of Canada have argued, equality should not be allowed to 'obliterate' freedom of belief, nor vice versa:[109]

Thus, persons who believe that homosexual behaviour, manifest in the conduct of persons involved in same-sex relationships, is immoral or not morally equivalent to heterosexual behaviour, for religious or non-religious reasons, are entitled to hold and express that view. On the other hand, persons who believe that homosexual behaviour is morally equivalent to heterosexual behaviour are also entitled to hold and express that view. Both groups, however, are not entitled to act in a discriminatory manner.[110]

As Justice Albie Sachs of the South African Constitutional Court, has said in ruling that despite religious objections to such unions, the denial of same-sex marriage was unconstitutional:

The objective of the Constitution is to allow different concepts about the nature of human existence to inhabit the same public realm, and to do so in a manner that is not mutually destructive and that at the same time enables government to function in a way that shows equal concern and respect for all.[111]

Definitional balancing of equality, freedom of religion and freedom of expression risks favouring one such comprehensive view at the expense of another. It can also leave unpopular viewpoints vulnerable—as demonstrated by the strand in European Convention jurisprudence that denies expression that it disapproves of the protection of free speech at all, on the grounds that it serves no social purpose.[112]

The better approach, it is submitted, is to reconcile clashes between equality and freedom of expression and religion by proportionality analysis that considers whether there was a reasonable limitation on freedom of religion and of expression. This allows for a more structured and analytical approach than definitional balancing between rights. As in the *Green* judgment, it allows for the context of speech disapproving of homosexuality to be fully considered, including such factors as whether a religious text was being expounded, the nature of the occasion (for example, whether it was in a church sermon or in a radio broadcast), the

---

[108] John Rawls, *Political Liberalism*, (New York: Columbia UP, 1993), 1.

[109] *Chamberlain* v. *Surrey School District No. 36* [2002] 4 S.C.R. 710, 788 (Gonthier J dissenting, joined by Bastarache J.). The majority in *Chamberlain* ruled that a School Board had acted unlawfully in considering, even indirectly, the religious objections by parents to the use in a kindergarten of books depicting same-sex couples, since to do so violated a statutory requirement in provincial law to conduct schools 'on strictly secular and non-sectarian principles' (School Act R.S.B.C. 1996, c. 412, s.76).

[110] Ibid., 784.

[111] Constitutional Court of South African, *Minister of Home Affairs and Another* v. *Fourie*, Case CCT 60/04, 1 December 2005, para. 94.

[112] In *Otto-Preminger Institut* v. *Austria* (1995) 19 EHRR 34, para. 49, the Court refers to 'expressions that are gratuitously offensive to others and thus an infringement of their rights, and which therefore do not contribute to any form of public debate capable of furthering progress in human affairs'.

composition of the audience, and so on. Proportionality also lends itself better to consideration of the respective costs to non-discrimination and antipathy to homosexuals, on the one hand, and to freedom of expression and manifestation of religious belief, on the other, of criminalizing or permitting homophobic speech. Whereas a definitional balancing approach requires a hard edge between these clashing rights, proportionality adopts a more tapered or over-lapping approach which does not deny the relevance of one right merely because it is displaced in a particular situation by the other. Rather, proportionality acknowledges that the balance between the rights may be tipped in one direction or the other depending on sensitive differences in the context or the words used.

7. Conclusion

The clash between religious expression and 'homophobic hate speech' laws poses a genuine challenge for the system of human rights based on tolerance and pluralism. As Lord Walker has remarked: 'in matters of human rights the court should not show liberal tolerance only to tolerant liberals'.[113]

There are two clear alternative ways for the courts to deal with the challenge of the clash of religious expression and sexual orientation equality within a liberal human rights framework. One approach is to limit one of these rights to accommodate the other through 'definitional balancing'. The alternative approach, advocated here, and demonstrated by the Supreme Court of Sweden in the *Green* case, is to face up to the inherent clash of values through use of the proportionality test.

Undoubtedly, however, much of the vague argument surrounding 'homophobia' could be avoided in the legal arena through careful use of definitions. For example, complaining to a council about its expenditure on promoting gay rights, expressing the view on radio that homosexual couples should not be permitted to adopt children, or publicly advocating that homosexuals seek counselling—all of which have been investigated by the police in Britain as 'hate incidents'[114]—are nothing of the kind. At most they are expressions of dissent from the orthodoxy of sexual orientation equality and well within the bounds of civil public debate in a liberal democracy.

Legislation prohibiting incitement of hatred on grounds of sexual orientation can and should be framed tightly to distinguish more clearly between 'sexual orientation equality denial', and 'homophobia'. Two key differences are whether there is an individual 'target' or 'victim' and whether there is any intention or likelihood of violence to an individual. Hostility aimed towards homosexuals as a

---

[113] Lord Walker of Gestingthorpe in *R* v. *Secretary of State for Education and Employment Ex p Williamson* [2005] UKHL 15, para. 60.
[114] See Bennion (n. 38 above), 28–30.

group would therefore need to be clearly linked with harm to identifiable victims; otherwise it shades into criminalizing criticism of homosexual practice as such (as in the *Hammond* decision). Countries with more tightly drawn hate offences usually mark out this category of offences by reference to an individual *victim's* identifiable characteristics. Whereas in other wider instances it is the alleged intolerance motivating the offender that is determinative. It is here that clashes with freedom of religion are most likely to occur.

Although the new offence under UK law sets the threshold relatively high in referring to 'threatening' words or behaviour intended to incite 'hatred', much will depend on how these terms are applied in specific contexts. A broad interpretation could still risk interference with legitimate religious expression, although the general defence in section 29JA will certainly protect some religious expression commenting on or aimed at homosexual and lesbian practice. A specific clause protecting public discourse or a defence for religious expression (as in Canadian legislation) might have been preferable in dealing explicitly with clashes between equality, freedom of speech, and freedom of religion. Even in the absence of an explicit defence, however, under the Human Rights Act 1998 the UK courts would be obliged to read the incitement to homophobic hatred offence in the light of the Convention right in Article 9 to manifest one's religious beliefs. This may produce an approach similar to that of the Supreme Court of Sweden in the *Green* case.[115]

It remains to be seen whether the new orthodoxy on sexual orientation is sufficiently liberal to accommodate its religious dissenters.

---

[115] The same approach may lead to reconsideration of the outcome in *Hammond* (pp. 388–90 above) as regards the lesser offence under s. 5 of the Public Order Act 1986.

20

Extreme Religious Dress: Perspectives on Veiling Controversies

Dominic McGoldrick

1. Introduction

This essay examines 'extreme religious dress', in particular, the wearing of the Islamic headscarf-*hijab*.[1] The headscarf-*hijab* is a complex communicative symbol.[2] It has become the subject of legal challenges in jurisdictions across the world. The regulation of it and other aspects of religious dress can involve the intersection of a number of national and international human rights.[3] The issues can be analysed from a variety of perspectives, but the focus here is predominantly a legal one that seeks to apply human rights standards and categorizations. Section 2 considers the relationships between speech and religious dress. Section 3 examines how headscarf-*hijab* cases have been, and can be, constructed in terms of international human rights law. It considers, in particular, individual applications to national courts and international human rights bodies, individual and group identities and the human right to freedom of religion. Section 4 considers the narrower educational context that has been the locus of so many of the controversial cases. Section 5 considers the issue from religious, race, and gender discrimination perspectives. Section 6 widens the perspective to embrace fundamental values of autonomy and consent. Section 7 notes the role of the margin of appreciation in explaining human rights outcomes. Finally, Section 8 locates the importance of religious dress issues, and in particular that of the Islamic headscarf-*hijab*, within broader contemporary political and philosophical debates.

---

[1] Using 'dress' in a wide sense to cover veiling, clothing, and religious symbols.

[2] See L. Abu-Odeh, 'Post-Colonial Feminism and the Veil: Considering the Differences' (1992) 26 *New Eng. L. Rev.* 1527. J. Heath (ed.), *The Veil: Women Writers on its History, Lore, and Politics* (Berkeley, CA: California UP, 2008).

[3] See D. McGoldrick, *Human Rights and Religion: The Islamic Headscarf Debate in Europe* (Oxford: Hart, 2006).

2. Speech and Religious Dress

Extreme speech, and particularly extreme political speech, may be afforded a very high degree of protection because speech is seen as central to the democratic process. While philosophical justifications for freedom of religion in terms of self-development, self-determination, and individual autonomy may parallel those for expression, religious expression arguably has a weaker philosophical basis in terms of any contribution to the democratic process.[4] 'Extreme speech' is usually associated with communication via speech. Such communications can be criminalized, repressed, or regulated in various ways because of the relationship between the particular 'speech' and certain values which are considered to be 'extreme': for example, racial or religious hatred, propaganda for war, terrorism, and so on. In some contexts, speech and religious expression may overlap. Freedom of speech/expression can be framed as the right to identify publicly with any group, community or philosophy by choice of speech, dress, or symbols.[5] Words and symbols can appear on dress. Forms of dress can expressly carry speech (for example, words on a T-shirt) or symbolize ideas or causes. The act of wearing or not wearing an Islamic headscarf-*hijab* can be a political and symbolic one.[6] Where religious dress is associated with conveying an element of political speech or as part of a political process it might be expected to benefit from the high protection afforded to political speech and so restrictions on it would be difficult to justify.[7] However, as we shall see, such religious expression via dress has not been as highly protected and restrictions have been more readily accepted as justified in a variety of contexts.

The context for religious dress controversies is normally rather different from those concerning extreme speech, but the rationale can be similar. Religious dress can be repressed or regulated because of the relationship between the particular 'religious dress' and certain values which are considered to be 'extreme': viz, religious fundamentalism. However, the relationship can be a very diffuse one in which there is no suggestion that the particular individual was advocating fundamentalism. Similarly in the French[8] and Turkish[9] contexts the dress is

---

[4] '[T]here are significant problems with identifying a coherent and subjectively appropriate philosophical rationale for the right to religious freedom', T. Lewis, 'What Not To Wear: Religious Rights, the European Court, and the Margin of Appreciation' (2007) 56 *Int'l & Comp. L. Q.* 395, 405.

[5] See E. Barendt, *Freedom of Speech,* 2nd edn. (Oxford, OUP, 2005), 1–23.

[6] The veil was a symbol of colonial resistance in Algeria and Egypt and of communist resistance in Afghanistan.

[7] See eg., *The Moscow Branch of the Salvation Army* v. *Russia,* Application No. 72881/01, ECHR 5 October 2006 (on the importance to democracy of associations, including religious associations).

[8] See J. Robert, 'Religious Liberty and French Secularism' (2003) 2 *BYU L. Rev.* 637; J. Baubérot, 'Secularism and French Religious Liberty: A Sociological and Historical View' (2003) 2 *BYU L. Rev.* 451; and M. Troper, 'French Secularism, or Laïcité' (2000) 21 *Cardozo L. Rev.* 1267.

[9] See O. Denli, 'Between *Laicist* State Ideology and the Modern Public Religion: The Head-Cover Controversy in Contemporary Turkey', in T. Lindholm, W. Cole Durham and B. G. Tahzib-Lie (eds.), *Facilitating Freedom of Religion or Belief: A Deskbook* (Leiden: Nijhoff, 2005) 497; R. Mandel, 'Turkish Headscarves and the "Foreigner Problem": Constructing Difference through Emblems of Identity' 46 *New German Critique* (Winter, 1989) 27, who deals extensively with the situation in Turkey.

'extreme' only in the sense of being the 'other' to the state values of secularism or neutrality. The French headscarf affair (*L'Affaire du Foulard*) that has run since 1989 has been premised on the place of secularism in French history and society.[10] The most recent expression of this was the Law of 2004 prohibiting the wearing of signs or dress by which school pupils overtly manifest a religious affiliation.[11] In Turkey in 2007, a million people marched in defence of a secularist, democratic philosophy they perceived as being challenged by a proposed Islamist President whose wife wears the headscarf-*hijab*.[12] In a context where the state's values are much weaker or non-existent, then the same dress does not carry the same degree or connotation of 'extremity' but may still be repressed or regulated in particular contexts and spaces because of its perceived symbolism.[13]

3. Human Rights Perspectives

(i) Individual Applications to National Courts

Domestic remedies must be exhausted before international remedies can be invoked. National courts in Germany, Switzerland, and Turkey have upheld headscarf-*hijab* bans as consistent with their respective constitutions. In the *Ludin*[14] case in Germany, the focus was on the principle of neutrality and the distribution of powers in a federal state.[15] In Switzerland, the main emphasis was on the principles of neutrality, secularism, and gender equality. In Turkey, the emphasis was on the principle of secularism and the equality of women. The UK has no written constitution and has not specifically sought to ban headscarves-*hijab* in any particular context. The UK courts have accepted that schools and employers may, consistently with the ECHR and European Union directives on

---

[10] See J. R. Bowen, *Why the French Don't Like Headscarves: Islam, the State, and Public Service* (Princeton: Princeton UP, 2007). On the French controversy over the veil see J. W. Scott, *The Politics of the Veil* (Princeton: Princeton UP, 2007).

[11] *Loi encadrant, en application du principe de laïcité, le port de signes ou de tenues manifestant une appartenance religieuse dans les écoles, collèges et lycées publics*, Loi No 2004–228 du 15 mars 2004, (17 March 2004) 17 *Journal Officiel* 5190.

[12] See M. Fletcher and S. Erdem, 'Is this just a headscarf—or really a threat to democracy?', *The Times*, 1 June 2007.

[13] See A. D. Renteln, 'Visual Religious Symbols and the Law' (2004) 47(12) *Am. Behav. Scientist* 1573.

[14] BVerfG, 2 BvR 1436/02 (24 September 2003), <http://www.bundesverfassungsgericht.de/entscheidungen/rs20030924_2bvr143602.html>[German] (last accessed 23 July 2008).

[15] See A. F. von Campenhausen, 'The German Headscarf Debate' (2004) 2 *BYU L. Rev.* 665; D. Schiek, 'Just a Piece of Clothing? German Courts and Employees with Headscarves' (2004) 33 *Industrial L. J.* 68; O. Gerstenberg, 'Germany: Freedom of Conscience in Public Schools' (2005) 3 *Int'l J. Const. L.* 94; M. Mahlmann, 'Religious Tolerance, Pluralist Society and the Neutrality of the State: The Federal Constitutional Court's Decision in the Headscarf Case' (2003) 4(11) *German Law Jo.*, <http:www.germanlawjournal.com/article.php?id=331> (last accessed 23 July 2008).

religious discrimination, be able to justify drawing a line on certain aspects of Islamic dress.[16]

(ii) Individual Applications to International Human Rights Bodies

Individual applications under the European Convention on Human Rights (ECHR),[17] the First Optional Protocol (OP1) to the International Covenant on Civil and Political Rights (ICCPR)[18] or the Optional Protocol to the UN Convention on the Elimination of All Forms of Discrimination Against Women (CEDAW)[19] against headscarf-*hijab* restrictions are possible if the relevant state is a party. As of the end of 2008, the French headscarf-*hijab* issue had not arisen before any of the international human rights decision-making bodies. There may be future cases once French domestic remedies have been exhausted. Claims can be formulated differently because there are some differences between the ECHR and the ICCPR.[20] Both treaties protect freedom of religion (Article 9 ECHR, Article 18 ICCPR), but only the ICCPR has an express guarantee of minority rights (Article 27 ICCPR). A French Declaration with respect to Article 27 precludes such a claim with respect to France. By contrast, minority rights can only form part of the context of ECHR jurisprudence.[21] However, there are an increasing number of judgments of the European Court of Human Rights in which the issue concerning minority rights appears to be the central one.[22] The ICCPR also has a freestanding equality and non-discrimination guarantee (Article 26 ICCPR).[23] Until recently the ECHR contained only a parasitic non-discrimination guarantee in Article 14 ECHR (which includes discrimination on grounds of religion). Protocol 12 (2002) to the ECHR has remedied this to some degree and it is now in force. However, a significant number of

---

[16] See S. Knights, *Freedom of Religion, Minorities, and the Law* (Oxford: OUP, 2007), 117–20 (on education) and 149–51 (on employment); Parts 4 and 5 below.

[17] 47 states parties as of 1 January 2008.

[18] There were 160 states parties to ICCPR and 110 states parties to OP1 as of 1 January 2008.

[19] There were 185 states parties to CEDAW and 90 states parties to the OP to CEDAW as of 1 January 2008.

[20] See G. Pentassuglia, *Minorities in International Law: An Introductory Study* (Strasbourg: Council of Europe, 2002).

[21] See G. Gilbert, 'The Burgeoning Minority Rights Jurisprudence of the European Court of Human Rights' (2002) 24 *Hum. Rights Q.* 736.

[22] See eg, *Connors* v. *UK* (2005) 40 EHRR 9 (on the vulnerable position of gypsies) and *Nachova* v. *Bulgaria*, Application Nos. 43577/98 and 43579/98, 6 July 2005 (on the Roma).

[23] Article 26 ICCPR provides: 'All persons are equal before the law and are entitled without discrimination to the equal protection of the law. In this respect, the law shall prohibit any discrimination and guarantee to all persons equal and effective protection against discrimination on any grounds such as race, colour, sex, language, religion, political or other opinion, national or social origin, property birth or other status'. See M. Nowak, *CCPR—Commentary*, 2nd edn. (Kehl: Engel, 2005) 397–434; S. Joseph, J. Schultz, and M. Castan, *The ICCPR—Cases, Materials and Commentary*, 2nd edn. (Oxford: OUP, 2004).

members of the Council of Europe have not ratified it, including France, Turkey, and the UK.[24]

The issue of the Islamic headscarf-*hijab* had been dealt with in a number of international human rights bodies. In applications against Turkey concerning the wearing of Islamic headscarves-*hijab* by university students, the European Commission on Human Rights found no violations of the ECHR. In *Karaduman* v. *Turkey*[25] the Commission acknowledged that the manifestation of the obser-vances and symbols of the religion of the great majority, without restriction as to place and manner, might constitute 'improper pressure on students who do not practice that religion or those who adhere to another religion'. In Turkey, the restrictions on the headscarf-*hijab* affect the majority. By contrast, in France and most other countries, the restrictions on the headscarf-*hijab* affect the minority. International human rights law tends to focus on the need for minority protection.[26] By contrast, international human rights law tends to assume that the majority can look after itself.

In *Dahlab* v. *Switzerland*,[27] the European Court of Human Rights considered the issue of a schoolteacher in a primary school who was prohibited from wearing an Islamic headscarf-*hijab* when teaching. It found no violation. It stressed, inter alia, the impact that the 'powerful external symbol' conveyed by her wearing a headscarf-*hijab* could have. It also questioned whether it might have some kind of proselytizing effect, seeing that it appeared to be imposed on women by a precept laid down in the Koran that was hard to reconcile with the principle of gender equality. Thus the Court found that Switzerland was entitled to place restrictions on the wearing of the Islamic headscarf-*hijab,* as it was compatible with the pursued aim of protecting pupils by preserving religious harmony. The Court addressed the issue of a university student, as distinct from a school teacher, being prohibited from wearing a headscarf for the first time in 2004 (Chamber) and 2005 (Grand Chamber) in *Leyla Şahin* v. *Turkey*.[28] Neither the Chamber nor the Grand Chamber found a violation of any of the provisions of the ECHR. The Grand Chamber considered that the paramount consideration underlying the ban on the wearing of religious symbols in universities was the principle of secularism. It accepted Turkey's two central contentions, namely that secularism (i) was consistent with the values of the ECHR and (ii) was necessary to protect the democratic system in Turkey that was required to support the ECHR.[29] The

[24] It entered into force in April 2005. As of 23 October 2008, there were 17 states parties. See S. Lagoutte (ed.), *Prohibition of Discrimination in the Nordic Countries: The Complicated Fate of Protocol 12 to the European Convention on Human Rights* (Oslo: Danish Institute for Human Rights, 2005).

[25] (1993) 74 DR 93, para. 108.

[26] GC 23, Art. 27, UN Doc CCPR/C/21/Rev.1/Add.5 (1994).

[27] Application No. 42393/98, ECHR 2001-V.   [28] (2007) 44 EHRR 5.

[29] See C. D. Belelieu, 'The Headscarf as a Symbolic Enemy of the European Court of Human Rights' Democratic Jurisprudence: Viewing Islam Through a European Legal Prism in Light of the *Sahin* Judgment' (2006) 12(2) *Columb. J. Eur. L.* 573. N. Nathwani, 'Islamic headscarves and human rights: a critical analysis of the relevant case law of the European Court of Human Rights' (2007) 25 *Netherlands Quarterly of Human Rights* 221–54.

decisions under the European Convention concerning the headscarf-*hijab* in Turkish universities and in Swiss primary schools have essentially focused on freedom of religion. In *Şahin,* the Grand Chamber also considered it in terms of the right to education, but found no violation. None of the international human rights decisions to date has focused on freedom of expression or on the right of parents to have children educated in accordance with their religious and philosophical convictions. There has also been one inadmissibility decision by the Committee on the Elimination of Discrimination Against Women regarding a complaint against Turkey holding that the applicant had not exhausted her domestic remedies.[30]

The only finding to date of international human rights law being violated by a headscarf-*hijab* ban is that of the Human Rights Committee (HRC) in *Hudoyberganova* v. *Uzbekistan,* which considered the compatibility of a headscarf-*hijab* ban in state universities in Uzbekistan with Article 18 (freedom of religion) of the ICCPR.[31] However, that decision was very much a default decision in the absence of proper justification by the state. It constitutes a very limited precedent.

(iii) Individual and Group Identities and Rights

The wearing of the Islamic headscarf-*hijab* can be seen as part of an individual's expression of cultural or religious identity.[32] Identity is protected by a combination of human rights including religion, expression, and privacy. In its General Comment No. 22 on 'The Right to Freedom of Thought, Conscience and Religion' (on Article 18 of the ICCPR), the HRC stated: 'The observance and practice of religion or belief may include not only ceremonial acts but also such customs as . . . the wearing of distinctive clothing . . . '[33] Some Muslim girls and women clearly regard wearing the headscarf-*hijab* as part of their individual and group identity.[34] In *Şahin,* the Grand Chamber of the European Court of Human Rights noted: 'Those in favour of the headscarf-*hijab* see wearing it as a duty and/or form of expression linked to religious identity . . . '[35]

As noted, freedom of expression can also be framed as the right to identify publicly with any group, community, or philosophy by choice of speech, dress, or symbols.[36] Choice of dress would also clearly come within the ambit of private life.[37] In terms of the philosophical justifications for religion, expression, or privacy it

---

[30] *Rahime Kayhan* v. *Turkey* in 2006, Communication No. 8/2005.

[31] UN Doc CCPR/C/82/D/931/2000 (18 January 2004. The Views of the HRC are not legally binding.

[32] See S. Mullally, *Gender, Culture and Human Rights: Reclaiming Universalism* (Oxford: Hart, 2006); R. Coomaraswamy, 'Identity Within: Cultural Relativism, Minority Rights and The Empowerment of Women' (2002–03) 34 *Geo. Wash. Int'l L. Rev.* 483.

[33] GC 22, para 4, UN Doc CCPR/C/21/Rev.1/Add.4, adopted on 29 July 1993.

[34] See F. Mernissi, *The Veil and the Male Elite: A Feminist Interpretation of Women's Rights in Islam* (Reading, PA: Addison-Wesley, 1991); J. Henley, 'Europe faces up to Islam and the veil', *The Guardian,* 4 February 2004.

[35] See *Şahin* (n. 28 above), para. 35.   [36] See Barendt, n. 5 above.

[37] See generally W. J. F. Keenan (ed.), *Dressed to Impress: Looking the Part* (Oxford: Berg, 2001).

would be part of self-development, self-determination, or individual autonomy. For example, some French Muslim women are passionately opposed to the ban even if they themselves do not wear a headscarf-*hijab*. They believe that women should be able to choose.[38] Identity is an aspect of individual human dignity, autonomy, and self-determination. It is thus an aspect of privacy that allows individuals to function freely and to enjoy the possibility of self-definition and self-determination.[39] In the context of the right to privacy, the European Court of Human Rights has referred to these underlying values of self-determination and autonomy.[40]

A good example of an applicant arguing that restrictions on headscarf-*hijab* violate a range of human right is *Şahin*.[41] The applicant alleged that a ban on wearing the Islamic headscarf-*hijab* in higher education institutions violated her rights and freedoms under Articles 8 (private life), 9 (religion), 10 (expression), and 14 (non-discrimination) of, and Article 2 of Protocol 1 (right to education) to, the European Convention. The Grand Chamber found no violations.[42]

Whilst both Article 9 ECHR and Article 18 ICCPR protect some communitarian aspects of freedom of religion, they do so via individual rights, not group rights.[43] Group identities have become increasingly politicized in many states and 'collective identity' has been perceived as a human right. This has encouraged, enforced, and legitimized forms of solidarity.[44] The degree of recognition of a particular group reflects its power relationship with the state.[45] The headscarf-*hijab* issue is thus often conceived of in terms of identity recognition.[46] Liberals may conceive differences as reducible to individual claims but for French Muslims, for example, the facial equality of French law is not enough. It ignores its quest for group recognition of its identity. They are not seeking merely equality of treatment, but rather equality of respect.

(iv) Minority Rights and Cultural Rights

Under Article 27 ICCPR, religious minorities shall not be denied the right to profess and practise their religion and ethnic minorities shall not be denied the

---

[38] See S. Bell, 'France finds its cover girl for veil battle', *The Sunday Times*, 25 January 2004.

[39] L. G. Loucaides, 'Personality and Privacy under the European Convention on Human Rights' (1990) 61 *British Year Book Int'l. L.* 175.

[40] *Pretty* v. *United Kingdom* (2002) 35 EHRR 1, para. 61; *Goodwin* v. *United Kingdom* (2002) 35 EHRR 18, para. 90. J. Marshall, 'Conditions for Freedom? European Human Rights Law and the Islamic Headscarf Debate' (2008) 30 *Human Rights Quarterly* 631.

[41] See n. 28 above.

[42] Ibid., paras. 164–5. See J. Marshall, 'Freedom of Religious Expression and Gender Equality: *Sahin* v *Turkey*' (2006) 69 *Modern L. Rev.* 452.

[43] See eg, *Cha'are Shalom Ve Tsedek* v. *France* (2000) 9 BHRC 27.

[44] C. El Hamel, 'Muslim Diaspora in Western Europe: The Islamic Headscarf (*Hijab*), the Media and Muslims' Integration in France' (2002) 6(3) *Citizenship Studies* 293, 306.

[45] See R. Kastoryano, *Negotiating Identities: States and Immigrants in France and Germany* (Princeton, NJ: Princeton UP, 2002), 138.

[46] See A. E. Galeotti, 'Citizenship and Equality: The Place for Toleration' (1993) 21(4) *Pol. Theory* 585, 599–600; L. Köker, 'Political Toleration or Politics of Recognition: The Headscarves Affair Revisited' (1996) 24(2) *Pol. Theory* 315.

right to enjoy their own culture.[47] Article 30 of the Convention on the Rights of the Child (CRC) parallels this for minority children.[48] A claim that headscarf-*hijab* restrictions violate Article 27 could not be brought against states parties to the ICCPR where Muslims are the majority population, for example, in Turkey and Uzbekistan.[49] A claim could not be brought against France because of its Declaration to Article 27 ICCPR, which the HRC regarded as a reservation. A claim could not be brought against the UK because the UK has not accepted the right of individual petition under the OP1 to the ICCPR and there are no direct minority rights under the ECHR. Article 27 does not expressly provide that the rights of the protected minorities can be subject to limitation. However, the jurisprudence of the HRC has held that restrictions may be placed upon the rights of an individual member of a minority if they are shown to have a reasonable and objective justification and to be consistent with the other provisions of the ICCPR read as a whole, including the provisions against discrimination.[50] In addition, any limitations cannot destroy the essence of the right.

(v) The Right to Freedom of Religion

The core of religious freedom is obviously that of internal religious belief.[51] Under the ECHR and the ICCPR, that element is absolute. However, external manifestations of religious belief are subject to the possibility of greater limitation under Articles 9(2) ECHR and 18(3) ICCPR. It is helpful to recall the terms of these provisions:

Article 9(2) ECHR:
Freedom to manifest one's religion or beliefs shall be subject only to such limitations as are prescribed by law and are necessary in a democratic society in the interests of public safety, for the protection of public order, health or morals, or for the protection of the rights and freedoms of others.

Article 18(3) ICCPR:
Freedom to manifest one's religion or beliefs may be subject only to such limitations as are prescribed by law and are necessary to protect public safety, order, health, or morals or the fundamental rights and freedoms of others.

Given the widespread practice of wearing the Islamic headscarf-*hijab*, it will be treated an as aspect of religious belief that is at, or close to, the core or essence of the right, but not part of the 'inviolable core of freedom of religion'. This does not

---

[47] On Art. 27, see Nowak (n. 23 above), 406–36; Joseph et al, (n. 23 above), 635–67; S. Wheatley, *Democracy, Minorities and International Law* (Cambridge: CUP, 2005) 11–43; S. Poulter, 'The Rights of Ethnic, Religious and Linguistic Minorities' (1997) 2 *Eur. Hum. Rights L. Rev.* 254.

[48] There is no individual petition system under the CRC.

[49] See *Ballantyne, Davidson and McIntyre* v. *Canada*, Human Rights Committee, UN Doc CCPR/C/47/359/1989 (5 May 1993) (the English speaking population in Quebec was not a minority for Art. 27 purposes because it was a majority in Canada as a whole).

[50] See Nowak (n. 23 above), 666–7.

[51] See L. M. Hammer, *The International Human Right to Freedom of Conscience: Some Suggestions for Its Development and Application* (Aldershot: Ashgate, 2001).

preclude the possibility of this manifestation of religious belief being limited, but it puts a heavier burden on the state to justify the limitation as being, in the language of Article 9(2) ECHR, 'necessary in a democratic society'. Of the permissible grounds of limitation, the ones that are most commonly invoked are the 'protection of public order' and the 'protection of the rights and freedoms of others'. In this context 'public order' includes the prevention of public disorder but also extends to the wider concept of the ordering of public affairs in the state, which the French refer to as *l'ordre public*.[52] However, this wide interpretation may be open to question under the ICCPR as it uses the expression the English expression *public order* but not the French expression *l'ordre public*.

(vi) Negative and Positive Aspects of a Human Right

With many (but not all) human rights, a positively formulated right (for example, freedom of religion, expression, or association) also carries its negative (for example, the right not to believe in a religion, to silence or not to associate), although the negative aspect may not always be afforded the same level of protection as the positive aspect.[53] So the express right to do something may carry the implied right not to do it. It has been argued that, 'if a society objects to anyone being forced to wear a headscarf, then it should equally object to everyone being forced not to wear one'.[54] In some states, for example Iran and Saudi Arabia, it is compulsory by law for women to wear headscarves, even if they are merely visiting the country. One might intuitively think that this violates international human rights law but none of the international human rights bodies has yet suggested that it does.[55] Individual applications against those states under OP1 to the ICCPR are not possible because they are not party either to the ICCPR (Saudi Arabia) or to the OP1 (Iran). However, during the periodic reporting processes some critical comments have been made by individual experts. If compulsory veiling does not violate international human rights law, it might suggest that a state could also prohibit the wearing of a headscarf-*hijab* in particular circumstances or contexts. From the perspective of an individual woman, there may be no difference as in each case they are being told what to do. Their individual beliefs are irrelevant, and 'attempts to "liberate" women my removing

---

[52] The expression *l'ordre public* was used 14 times in the *Report of the Commission de reflexion sur l'application du principe de la laïcité dans la République* (hereinafter *Stasi Report*): see <http://les-rapports.ladocumentationfrancaise.fr/BRP/034000725/0000.pdf> (last accessed 23 July 2008). The Report recommended what became the Law of 2004.

[53] See *Sorenson* v. *Denmark* (2008) 46 EHRR 29 (Art. 11 ECHR included the right not to join a trade union), finding a violation by 12 votes to 5.

[54] Leader, 'A threat to no one', *The Guardian*, 11 February 2004; P. Weil, 'A nation in diversity: France, Muslims and the headscarf', *Open Democracy*, 25 March 2004, <http://www.open-democracy.net/faith-europe_islam/article_1811.jsp> (last accessed 23 July 2008).

[55] See eg, the exchange with Iran in the UN Committee on Economic, Social and Cultural Rights, UN Doc E/C.12/1993/SR.8 (4 December 1993).

the veil ... replaced one form of social control with another'.[56] While the compulsion to wear veils in Iran and Saudi Arabia is more wide-ranging—it affects everyone, even non-believers, and applies in all public places—the prohibition on wearing the headscarf-*hijab* is more limited in scope in, for example, France, Germany, Turkey, and Belgium. It covers only particular individuals and/or particular places. Such factors would clearly be relevant to the aim and proportionality of such a measure. The proposal in Belgium to ban the *burqa* in all public places and not just in state offices or institutions, is the most extreme proposal that has yet been publicly aired in a European context. It is notable that the arguments made in support of it related to public safety and security rather than to the specific rights and freedoms of others. In September 2008 the Dutch government announced its intention to ban the wearing of garments that cover the face at all primary and secondary schools, secondary vocational colleges, and adult education centres. It aimed to introduce a bill to this end in the House of Representatives by mid-2009. The rationale was that good education depends on teachers and students being able to see each other. If one of them wore a face-covering garment, good communications became impossible. The ban will apply to all school premises, including outdoor areas, and to anyone on those premises, including visitors, parents, school personnel, and delivery personnel.[56a]

(vii) The Human Rights Context of Church–State Relations under the ECHR

The European Court of Human Rights views the state's role as the neutral and impartial organizer of the practicing of various religions, denominations, and beliefs and considers that this is conducive to religious harmony and tolerance in a democratic society.[57] States are required to ensure mutual tolerance between opposing groups in a pluralist context. However, individuals and groups have to make concessions that are justified in order to maintain and promote the ideals and values of a democratic society.[58] A balance between the fundamental rights of each individual thus has to be found. Deciding on human rights questions in the context of church-state relations, on which opinion in a democratic society may reasonably differ widely, was necessarily difficult for international human rights institutions and so particular weight *is* given to the role of national decision-making bodies.[59] By stressing the special importance of the national decision-making body, the absence of any uniform European conception of the

---

[56] See N. J. Hirschmann, 'Western Feminism, Eastern Veiling, and the Question of Free Agency' (1998) 5(3) *Constellations* 345, 350.

[56a] See 'Face-covering garments to be banned at school'. <http://www.government.nl/News/ Press_releases_and_news_items/2008/September/Face_covering_garments_to_be_banned_at_school>.

[57] *Şahin* (n. 28 above), para. 107.

[58] Ibid., paras. 106–8.

[59] Ibid., para. 109.

significance of religion in society, the varying national traditions and requirements, and the dependence of regulations on the domestic context, the Court is
affording states a wide margin of appreciation.[60]

(viii) Limitations on Religious Freedoms on the Basis of the 'protection of public order' and the 'protection of the rights and freedoms of others'

Of the permissible grounds of limitation on religious freedom, those that are most
commonly invoked in the context of the headscarf-*hijab* are the 'protection of
public order' and the 'protection of the rights and freedoms of others.' The issue is
whether, in the particular context, the limitations on the individual's right can be
justified. For example, the individual's right to express their religious identity is
challenged by communal/communitarian rules, such as the French Law of 2004
prohibiting the wearing of signs or dress by which school pupils overtly manifest a
religious affiliation, the Turkish educational rules in the *Leyla Şahin* case or the
German civil service rules in the *Ludin* case. There is no real suggestion that a
Muslim headscarf-*hijab* is inherently offensive to a particular individual as such
(although some people are offended by its symbolism)[61] or that it hurts or
threatens anyone in any physical manner. In that sense, it is different from
restrictions on religious or cultural rights based on the prevention of physical or
psychological injury,[62] or expression that can be restricted because of its obscene
or offensive nature.[63] With respect to France and Turkey the basis for the prohibitions on the headscarf-*hijab* are in maintaining fundamental organizational
principles of the state—*laïcité*/secularism.[64] In Germany, the central governing
principle is neutrality. However, in each case the real substance of the human
rights argument is that the restriction is necessary to protect the human rights
system in general and thereby to protect the human rights of others. This is the
French thinking behind *laïcité*. In the *Sahin* case, the European Court of Human
Rights accepted this systemic human rights protection argument with respect to
the headscarf-*hijab* ban in Turkish universities. Turkey had starkly warned the

---

[60] Ibid., para 110. See s. 7 below.
[61] M. Parris, 'Never mind what this woman thinks, wearing a veil is offensive to me', *The Times*, 27 August 2005.
[62] Eg, female genital mutilation.
[63] See *Otto-Preminger-Institut* v. *Austria* [1994] ECHR 26 (a film considered offensive to religious sensitivities); *Wingrove* v. *United Kingdom* [1996] ECHR 60 (a video might outrage and insult the feelings of Christians). More generally though, the European Court's consistent jurisprudence has been that freedom of expression covers ideas and information that offend, shock, or disturb. The one dissentient in the *Sahin* case (n. 28 above), Judge Tulkens, stressed that the majority's decision was inconsistent with its approach to freedom of expression.
[64] See T. Asad, 'Reflections on *Laïcité* and the Public Sphere' (2005) 5(3) *Social Science Research Council*, <http://www.ssrc.org/publications/items/v5n3/index.html> (last accessed 23 July 2008); B. Gökariksel and K. Mitchell, 'Veiling, Secularism, and the Neoliberal Subject: National Narratives and Supranational Desires in Turkey and France' (2005) 5(2) *Global Networks* 147.

Court that secularism was the basis of its human rights system and, indeed, was the only way it considered that it could ensure compliance with the ECHR. Turkey did not base its restriction of the rights of Leyla Şahin on her as an individual harming anyone, pressuring anyone, or engaging in proselytism.[65]

In other contexts, the European Court has similarly accepted that restrictions on rights were consistent with the ECHR even if no harm could be proved.[66] Thus it found no violations in the dissolution of a political party in Turkey[67] or in banning of a commercial religious broadcast in Ireland even though it was accepted that it was not offensive.[68] Ireland stressed that religious division had characterized Irish history. Thus the Court may accept that restrictions are consistent with the ECHR even though there is no evidence that the specific individual applicant is considered to be a threat, has harmed anyone, has engaged in any harmful activity, or has sought directly to interfere with the rights and freedoms of others.

4. Educational Contexts

(i) Children's Rights

The locus for many of the controversial cases has been the educational context.[69] The headscarf-*hijab* issue can be viewed from a child rights perspective.[70] The starting point would then be the individual pupil's right to freedom of religion and their right to education. The threshold question is whether there is an 'interference' with the right concerned.[70a] There may not be if there is alternative provision which the child can be expected to access even at the cost of some

---

[65] See C. Evans. 'The "Islamic Scarf" in the European Court of Human Rights' (2006) 7 *Melbourne J. Int'l L.* 52.

[66] See S. Langlaude, 'Indoctrination, Secularism, Religious Liberty, and the ECHR' (2006) 55 *Int'l. & Comp. L. Q.* 929. On secularism in a non-European context, see L. Thio, 'Religious Dress in Schools: The Serban [Muslim turban] Controversy in Malaysia' (2005) 55 *Int'l. & Comp. L. Q.* 671.

[67] See *Refah Partisi (the Welfare Party) and Others* v. *Turkey* (2003) 37 EHRR 1 (dissolution of a political party). See K. Boyle, 'Human Rights, Religion and Democracy: The *Refah Party* Case' (2004) 1 *Essex HR Rev.* 1; P. Cumper, 'Europe, Islam and Democracy—Balancing Religious and Secular Values under the Eurpoean Convention on Human Rights' (2003/04) 3 *European Yearbook of Minority Issues* 163.

[68] *Murphy* v. *Ireland* (2004) 38 EHRR 13. See A. Geddis, 'You Can't Say "God" on the Radio: Freedom of Expression, Religious Advertising and the Broadcast Media after *Murphy* v. *Ireland*' (2004) 9 *EHR L. Rev.* 181. Compare the European Court's stricter approach to restrictions on political advertising in *VgT Verein Gegen Tierfabriken* v. *Switzerland*, (2002) 34 EHRR 159.

[69] See S. Knights, 'Religious Symbols in the School: Freedom of Religion, Minorities and Education' (2005) 10 *EHR L. Rev.* 499, and J. Finnis, ch.21 in this volume.

[70] See generally G. Van Bueren, *The International Law on the Rights of the Child* (Dordrecht: Nijhoff, 1995). Still another perspective is that of the parent's rights as concerns the education of their children. On the limits of this, see *Konrad* v. *Germany*. Application No. 35504/03, ECHR 18 September 2006, [2007] ELR 435.

[70a] See S. Leader, 'Freedom of Futures: Personal Institutional Demands and Freedom of Religion' (2007) *Modern L. Rev.*

inconvenience. This was the view of the majority of the House of Lords in the *Begum* case.[71] Begum sought to wear a *jilbab* (a loose fitting cloak) but the school refused as this was inconsistent with its uniform policy. The majority found no interference because she could have attended a school which would have permitted her to wear the *jilbab*.[72] If there is judged to be an interference (for example, where the child is expelled or refused access to school and there is no alternative provision), then the state will have to justify the limitation on the rights.[73] This was successfully done on the *Begum* case where all five members of the House found that, in the circumstances, B's expulsion was not a violation of her rights to religion and education.[74] Although *Begum* lost her case, it attracted worldwide publicity and attendant public discussion of Muslim integration, respect for religious beliefs, and multiculturalism. However, it was arguably a poor test case. The challenge was made in the context of a strongly multicultural school, clear sensitivity to Muslim issues and cross-cultural and cross-gender support for an agreed school uniform. Indeed, some of the responses to the case questioned whether there had been too much accommodation of non-Christian religious beliefs in a historically Christian state.

Adverse comparisons with the allegedly favourable treatment received by Muslims were drawn with what was perceived to be the scant regard paid to Christian values in the *Playfoot* case.[75] Miss Playfoot applied for judicial review of a decision of the defendant governing school body not to permit her to wear a purity ring while a pupil at the school. The school was a maintained, non-denominational girls' secondary school. Under the school uniform policy, there was a general ban on the wearing of jewellery, although the school had previously granted an exemption to some pupils to wear certain items on the grounds that they were considered to be requirements of their faith. This included the headscarf-*hijab*. Playfoot asserted that she had worn the ring to school because she was a committed Christian with a genuine belief that she should remain sexually abstinent before marriage and that the ring was a sign of that belief. Relying on the policy, the school had asked Playfoot to cease wearing the ring on school premises. The governing body endorsed this view and decided not to grant Playfoot an exemption from the policy. It found no evidence or explanation linking the belief in sexual abstinence to wearing the ring so that it could conclude

---

[71] *R. (Begum)* v. *Denbigh High School Governors* [2006] UKHL 15; [2007] 1 A.C. 100. See N. Gibson, 'Faith in the Courts: Religious Dress and Human Rights' (2007) 66(3) *Cambridge Law Jo.* 657; G. Davies, 'The House of Lords and Religious Clothing in *Begum* v. *Head Teacher and Governors of Denbigh High School*' (2007) 13 *Eur. Pub. L.* 423.

[72] The *Begum* non-interference approach was followed in *R (on the application of X)* v. *Headteacher of Y School*, (2007) EWHC 298 (Admin); [2008] 1 All ER 249.

[73] For the argument that this is the better jurisprudential approach, see M. Hill and R. Sandberg, 'Is Nothing Sacred? Clashing Symbols in a Secular World' (2007) *Pub. L.* 488.

[74] See L. Gies, 'What Not To Wear: Islamic Dress and School Uniforms' (2006) 14(3) *Fem LS* 377.

[75] *R. (Playfoot (A Child))* v. *Millais School Governing Body* [2007] EWHC 1698 (Admin), [2007] H.R.L.R. 34. See H. Stout, 'Case Reports' (2007) 8(4) *Education Law Jo.* 273; R. Syal, 'Christian pupil challenges school ban on chastity ring', *The Times*, 23 June 2007.

that wearing it was a manifestation of Playfoot's belief. Playfoot submitted that the governing body's decision not to permit her to wear the ring breached Article 9 of the European Convention and that she had been discriminated against in breach of Article 14 as girls of other religions at the school were permitted to wear items that fell outside of the policy.

The application was refused. Playfoot was under no obligation, by reason of her belief, to wear the ring. Accordingly, she was not manifesting her belief by wearing the ring and Article 9 was not engaged. Her Article 9 rights were not interfered with as she voluntarily accepted the uniform policy of the school which did not accommodate the wearing of the ring and there were other means open to her to practice her belief without undue hardship or inconvenience. The uniform policy was prescribed by law and served a number of important functions, including fostering the school identity and an atmosphere of allegiance, discipline, equality, and cohesion and allowing children to learn in an environment which minimized the pressures that resulted from marking difference on grounds of wealth and status. Those functions were in similar terms to those previously upheld as legitimate and proportionate. The school was fully justified in acting as it did. It recognized exceptions to its general ban on jewellery where the imposition of the strict rule would impose a disproportionately harsh result on a pupil. However, none of those exceptions applied in the instant case, including the exception where enforcing the policy would be likely to result in an unlawful breach of a pupil's human rights. Finally, there was no evidence that the school unlawfully discriminated against Playfoot in breach of Article 14. Instead, the evidence suggested that it reached carefully considered decisions on each occasion it was called upon to permit exceptions to the uniform policy. The result may be explicable in Convention terms, but the public perception of it was that Muslims and other religious groups were once again being accorded rights that were being denied to the Christian community.[76]

It was argued that the French Law of 2004 was wrong in principle because it was directed at school children and had the effect of obstructing dialogue.[77] A child's perspective might start from the premise that schools should teach children the value of diversity and difference. There is value in children experiencing diversity in schools and the meaning of neutrality in schools can be questioned.[78] Tolerance develops through experience and interaction.[79] As one French

---

[76] See J. Aston and C. Gordon, 'Teenager loses "purity ring" legal battle', *The Independent*, 16 July 2007.

[77] See F. Magnion, 'Muslim Headscarves and French Secularism' (2003), <http://www.francismangion.btinternet.co.uk/headscarf.htm> (last accessed 23 July 2008). See also <http://www.headscarf.net/index2.htm> (last accessed 23 July 2008).

[78] Pew Forum, n. 146 below. On the presentation of partisan political views in UK schools see *Dimmock* v. *Secretary of State for Education and Skills (now Secretary of State for Children, Families and Schools)* [2007] EWHC 2288 (Admin), [2008] ELR 98.

[79] M. Levinson, 'Liberalism Versus Democracy? Schooling Private Citizens in the Public Square' (1997) 27(3) *British J. Pol. Sci.* 333, 341 and 358. See also J. Bell, 'Religious Observance in Secular Schools: A French Solution' (1990) 2(3) *Education and the Law* 121, who argued that, in an educational context, the 'State has to err on the side of diversity' 127.

schoolgirl commented, 'It is for the teachers to be neutral, not the children.'[80] Excluding religion from classrooms may create a neutral atmosphere, but it could potentially also be a rather sterile environment. Much would depend on the teachers and the curriculum.[81] Critics of French schools in particular have argued that the absence of religious symbols in school means that an important opportunity is being missed that could provide a focus for discussing various religions and cultures.[82] In a German headscarf-*hijab* context, it has similarly been argued that the environment in schools can be a crucial one for learning tolerance.[83]

In June 2004, the United Nations Committee on the Rights of the Child specifically discussed the French Law of 2004. Its Concluding Observations expressed concern that the legislation might be counterproductive by neglecting the principle of the best interests of the child and the right of the child to access to education. It recommended that France continue closely to monitor the situation of girls being expelled from schools as a result of the new legislation and ensure that they enjoyed the right of access to education.[84]

(ii) Teachers' Rights and Children's Rights

As well as the child and the parents, there is also the position of the teacher to consider. In France, it is an important principle that representatives of the state (which includes teachers) must appear neutral.[85] Therefore, they must not display any religious affiliation. An important element in the decision of European Court of Human Rights in the *Dahlab* case was that a teacher is a 'representative of the State'.[86] The Court was concerned at the 'powerful external symbol' that could be conveyed by a primary school teacher—a representative of the state—wearing a headscarf-*hijab* and questioned whether it might have some kind of proselytizing effect.[87] As for the representative element there are two related themes. The first is the representative function. The teacher is the state and must reflect the neutrality of the state. They have an obligation of restraint (*devoir de réserve*).

The second is that the teacher (or other civil servant) is the employee of the state. The European Court of Human Rights has accepted that voluntary employment can carry with it limitations on rights.[88] For example, in *Kalac*

---

[80] Comment of J. Farouk, cited in A. D. Smith, 'France divided as headscarf ban is set to become law', *The Observer*, 1 February 2004.

[81] On the difficulties of getting the right balance of knowledge about religion into a curriculum see *Folgero* v. *Norway, Grand Chamber*, (2007) 23 B.H.R.C. 227; [2007] ELR 557; *Leirvag* v. *Norway* (Communication No. 1155/2003) UN Human Rights Committee, 23 November 2004, 19 B.H.R. C. 635.

[82] See C Killian, 'The Other Side of the Veil—North African Women in France Respond to the Headscarf Affair' (2003) 17(4) *Gender & Society* 567, 578–9.

[83] See Gerstenberg, n. 15 above.

[84] UN Doc CRC/C/15/Add 240, paras. 25–6 (30 June 2004). See also CRC/C/SR 967 and 968, para. 33 (2 June 2004).

[85] See McGoldrick (n. 3 above), ch. 2, para. 2.14.

[86] Ibid., ch. 4, para. 4.6.   [87] Ibid., ch. 4, para. 4.5.

[88] See also *Ahmed and Others* v. *United Kingdom* (2000) 29 EHRR 1 (restriction of political rights of public servants at municipal authorities); *Stedman* v. *United Kingdom* (1997) 23 EHRR CD 168 (complaint inadmissible because of acceptance of contractual obligations in the private sector). See Leader, n. 70a above.

v. *Turkey*[89] the state could restrict the freedom to manifest religious beliefs of a military judge who was alleged to have adopted unlawful fundamentalist opinions the manifestation of which breached military discipline and infringed the principle of secularism. Similarly, restrictions on a teacher's right to manifest their religion may be justifiable if there is evidence that it has a qualitative effect on their work.[90] This was the situation in *Azmi* v. *Kirklees MBC*.[91] Mrs Azmi had been suspended from her school teaching assistant role after persistently refusing to follow an instruction not to wear a full-face veil when in class with pupils, assisting a male teacher. Observations of her work by the local authority had led to the conclusion that her performance of her duties when veiled was less effective because the children were deprived of non-verbal signals, which were an important part of communication. Azmi's proceedings alleging direct and indirect discrimination on the grounds of her Muslim religion against the council failed. Rather than receiving support, the applicant was criticized by members of the Muslim community, Muslim politicians and even the head of the Commission for Racial Equality. The case arguably engendered an anti-Muslim backlash directed at their perceived refusal to integrate and complaints of lack of protection for Christian beliefs.

European Convention jurisprudence clearly supports some restrictions on employees' manifestations of their religion. However, employees and pupils can be distinguished in two ways. First, there is no right to employment and an employment relationship is contractual. The school–pupil relationship is not based on contract. A pupil has a human right to education and the pupil's parents have a duty to send them to school or otherwise educate them. Secondly, a pupil at school or a student at university is not a 'representative of the state' at all, or certainly not in the same way as a teacher. In this sense they cannot be argued to convey a 'powerful external symbol' as the Swiss Federal Court and the European Court of Human Rights found that a primary school teacher did in the *Dahlab* case.[92] In the French school context, an analogous argument is made that there can be demands for religious restraint by pupils.[93] The second element in the *Dahlab* case was that the European Court raised the question of whether the

---

[89] (1999) 27 EHRR 552, para. 28.

[90] The position can be the same for someone exercising a profession. In 2006 a Muslim solicitor, Shabnam Mughal, was asked by an immigration judge to remove her veil because he could not hear her. She refused, left the court and was later taken off the case. A subsequent practice ruling accepted that veils could be worn as long as it was consistent with the administration of justice. Presumably it is not so consistent if the judge cannot properly hear the advocate. See N. Britten, 'Lawyer in a veil is taken off case', *The Daily Telegraph*, 15 November 2006, and 'Guidance on the wearing of the full veil, or niqab, in Court' in Judicial Studies Board, Equal Treatment Bench Book, (March, 2008) <http://www.jsboard.co.uk/downloads/ettb_veil.pfe>.

[91] [2007] ICR 1154; [2007] ELR 339, EAT.

[92] See McGoldrick (n. 3 above), ch. 4, para. 4.5. See also von Campenhausen, n. 15 above, on a civil servant's voluntary relinquishment of some degree of religious freedom when entering the job.

[93] C. Laborde, 'Secular Philosophy and Muslim Headscarves in Schools' (2005) 13(3) *J. Pol. Phil.* 305, 322, 325–6.

teacher's wearing a headscarf-*hijab* might have 'some kind of proselytizing effect'. The Court cited no evidence for this. By contrast, the majority opinion in the German Constitutional Court decision on headscarves-*hijab* (the *Ludin* case) did look at this issue. Interestingly, it noted that little was known about the effect of religious symbols worn by teachers on the development of children.[94]

(iii) Universities

The prohibition of headscarves-*hijab* in universities is more difficult for states to justify in human rights terms. Generally speaking, university students will be mature adults who are in a context where tolerance is essential and diversity is often valued. Adults might be expected to be capable of dealing with or resisting any negative pressures emanating from another person's religious clothing or its external symbolism. In France, the prohibition on headscarves-*hijab* in the Law of 2004 did not extend to universities. The Stasi Commission distinguished universities from schools on the basis that students were adults and that universities had to be open to the world.[95] In *Şahin*, the European Court of Human Rights considered the issue of a student, as distinct from a teacher, being prohibited from wearing a headscarf-*hijab*. It appeared that no other state in the Council of Europe prohibited headscarves-*hijab* in universities.[96] Nonetheless, the European Court still held that the restrictions were within Turkey's margin of appreciation and found no violations of the ECHR. Any limitation must not impair the essence of an individual's rights. In *Şahin v. Turkey,* the Grand Chamber found that the restriction in question did not impair the very essence of the applicant's right to university education.[97] Finally, restrictions on university students wearing headscarves-*hijab* in Uzbekistan were found to constitute a violation of Article 18(2) ICCPR by the Human Rights Committee.[98] However, as we noted, that was very much a default decision.

5. Discrimination

(i) Religious Discrimination and Islamophobia

Restrictions on the wearing of the Islamic headscarf-*hijab* are also challenged on the basis that the restrictions are directly or indirectly discriminatory against Muslims or against religions which attach a particular importance to aspects of dress.[99] In

---

[94] See Mahlmann (n. 15 above), paras. 23–4.
[95] *Stasi Report* (n. 52 above), para. 4.2.2.2. Universities are to be exempt from the measures announced by the Dutch Government in 2008, see text to n. 56a above.
[96] See the dissenting opinion of Judge Tulkens, in *Şahin*, (n. 28 above), who stressed this point.
[97] *Şahin*, n. 28 above, para. 161.   [98] See n. 31 above.
[99] See C. D. Baines, '*L'Affaire des Foulards*—Discrimination, or the Price of a Secular Public Education System?' (1996) 29 *Vand. J. Transnat'l L.* 303; A Riley, 'Headscarves, skull caps and crosses', <http://www.muslim-lawyers.net/news/index.php3?aktion=show&number=248> (last

Şahin, one of the complaints was put forward in terms of Article 14 (non-discrimination), taken individually or together with Article 9 of the Convention (freedom of religion) or the first sentence of Article 2 of Protocol 1 (right to education). The Court noted that the applicant had not provided detailed particulars in her pleadings before the Grand Chamber. Furthermore, the regulations on the Islamic headscarf-*hijab* were not directed against the applicant's religious affiliation, but pursued, among other things, the legitimate aim of protecting order and the rights and freedoms of others and were manifestly intended to preserve the secular nature of educational institutions. Consequently, the reasons which led the Court to conclude that there had been no violation of Article 9 or Article 2 of Protocol 1 'incontestably also apply to the complaint under Article 14, taken individually or together with the aforementioned provisions'.[100]

In France, several polls in 2003 suggested that a large majority of French Muslims (78 per cent) favoured the principle of *laïcité*, on the basis that it was supportive of religious freedom.[101] However, some French Muslims perceived the headscarf-*hijab* ban as one of many examples of religious discrimination.[102] They considered that it was racist,[103] motivated by anti-Islamic sentiment, and constituted part of the general 'post 9/11' Islamophobia. It was argued that the Law of 2004 was an attempt to curb Islam.[104] Some members of the French Muslim community also considered that the headscarf-*hijab* issue was being used for political manipulation when the, 'real issues for us are high unemployment in the Muslim community, violence and harassment, discrimination in jobs, and housing'.[105] Such views are supported by the fact that the only recommendation in the Stasi Report that has been acted upon is the recommendation on religious clothes and signs in public schools.[106] It appears to be generally accepted, including by the Stasi Commission itself, that French Muslims face extensive discrimination, poverty, alienation, and economic and social exclusion.[107] The French Government vehemently denied that the Law of 2004 discriminated on

accessed 23 July 2008); n. 46 above. More generally, see E. Holmes, 'Anti-Discrimination Rights Without Equality' (2005) 68(2) *Modern L. Rev.* 175.

[100] *Şahin* (n. 28 above), para. 165.

[101] Cited in J. Vaïsse, 'Veiled Meaning: The French Law Banning Religious Symbols in Public Schools' *US-France Analysis Series* (March 2004), n. 9, <http://www.brookings.edu/fp/cusf/analysis/vaisse20040229.pdf> (last accessed 23 July 2008). See also J. R. Bowen, 'Why Did the French Rally to a Law Against Scarves in School' (2008) 68 *Droit et Société* 33–52.

[102] As did the Sikhs when they were affected by it.

[103] Using the term 'racist' in a more general political sense, rather than in a necessarily legal one.

[104] C. Caldwell, 'Veiled threat: Can French secularism survive Islam?', *The Weekly Standard*, 19 January 2004, <http://www.weeklystandard.com/Content/Public/Articles/000/000/003/583lxmcr.asp> (last accessed 23 July 2008).

[105] Karim Bouzid, a Muslim leader, cited in J. Henley, 'French MPs reappraise plan to outlaw veils', *The Guardian*, 20 January 2004. See T. D. Keaton, *Muslim Girls and the Other France: Race, Identity Politics and Social Exclusion* (Bloomington: Indiana UP, 2006).

[106] See Weil, n. 54 above.

[107] See J. Willms, 'France unveiled: Making Muslims into citizens?', *Open Democracy*, <http://www.opendemocracy.net/faith-europe_islam/article_1753.jsp> (last accessed 23 July 2008).

religious grounds. It recalled that the 1905 Law on Separation prohibited discrimination on the basis of faith.[108] Some commentators expressed a more general fear that the French prohibition on headscarves-*hijab* might ultimately cause more harm than good.[109] Even those that might have been persuaded of the case for the ban were concerned at the possibility that it would stigmatize and polarize the Muslim community, be perceived as persecution, and would in turn promote Islamic extremism and fundamentalism.

(ii) Religious Discrimination and the European Union

Some aspects of French restrictions on the headscarf-*hijab* could arguably be contested in the French courts as religious discrimination under the European Union's 2000 Directive on Equal Treatment in Employment and Occupation.[110] The Directive provides protection for school teachers, university staff, or civil servants as employees,[111] but does not extend to pupils or students.[112] The facial neutrality of the French Law of 2004 may exclude direct discrimination, but a teacher could complain of indirect religious discrimination, the test for which has been relaxed under Article 2 of the Directive. In a UK context, it has been agued that under this more modern test, a prohibition on a teacher wearing the *jilbab* (the issue at stake in the *Begum* case, but there involving a pupil) would probably always raise a prima facie case of religious discrimination.[113] If so, the school or local education authority would then have to show that the measure was justified, that is, a 'proportionate means of achieving a legitimate aim'.[114] The standard of justification required in cases of alleged religious discrimination could be a high one. However, the justifications that have been accepted by the European Commission and Court of Human Rights for restrictions to the ECHR rights would be likely to be given very significant weight. It has been argued that France may well be found to be in breach of the Directive because its courts interpret discrimination in general (and indirect discrimination and positive action in particular) much more narrowly than other EU states and, perhaps more importantly, than the ECJ.[115]

---

[108] See Law of 9 December 1905, *Journal Officiel*, 11 December 1905, 7205; J. McManners, *Church and State in France 1870–1914* (London: Church Historical Society, 1972).

[109] See J. Freedman, 'Secularism as a Barrier to Integration? The French Dilemma' (2004) 42(3) *International Migration* 5; N. Walter, 'When the veil means freedom', *The Guardian*, 20 January 2004; M. Bunting, 'Secularism gone mad', *The Guardian*, 18 December 2003.

[110] Council Directive 2000/78/EC of 27 November 2000, OJ L303/16, 2 December 2000. See N. Addison, *Religious Discrimination and Hatred Law* (London: Routledge, 2006).

[111] It would also cover a member of university staff as an employee.

[112] See A. Blair and W. Aps, 'What Not to Wear and Other Stories: Addressing Religious Diversity in Schools' (2005) 17(1–2) *Education and the Law* 1, 16.

[113] Ibid., 14. For the UK's implementation, see the Employment Equality (Religion or Belief) Regulations 2003, 2 December 2003 (2003 Regulations).

[114] Regulation 3(b)(iii) of the 2003 Regulations.

[115] K. Berthou, 'The Issue of the Voile in the Workplace in France: Unveiling Discrimination' (2005) 21(2) *Int'l J. Comp. L. & Ind'l. Rel.* 281.

In the UK in 2006 an incident related to religious dress in a Christian context drew wide publicity and again adverse comparisons were drawn with the allegedly favourable treatment received by non-Christian religions.[116] In the *Eweida* case, the claimant challenged a British Airways policy which had the effect of banning workers from wearing visible symbols of Christianity.[117] Eweida wished to wear a small Christian cross on a chain around her neck. She lost her case before an employment tribunal, but the company attracted severe public criticism from politicians, including the then Prime Minister Tony Blair, church leaders,[118] and even from the United Nations High Commissioner for Human Rights. It was again presented as a situation in which the Christian community was being disadvantaged. The wearing of headscarf-*hijabs*, turbans, and Sikh bracelets was permitted by the company.[119] Eventually, the airline announced that it was climbing down from its policy, which banned workers from wearing visible symbols of Christianity, after conducting what it said was a comprehensive review. The review concluded that the uniform policy should be amended to allow a lapel-pin symbol of faith, such as a Christian cross or a Star of David, with some flexibility for individuals to wear a symbol of faith on a chain.[120] In January 2008, after rejecting an out of court settlement, Eweida lost her case. It was rejected on the grounds that she had breached the firm's regulations without good cause. The tribunal's report highlighted several other issues regarding her conduct at BA. It rejected all her claims of religious discrimination and harassment, and criticized her for her intransigence, saying that she, '... generally lacked empathy for the perspective of others ... her own overwhelming commitment to her faith led her at times to be both naive and uncompromising in her dealings with those who did not share her faith'.[121]

(iii) Racial Discrimination

A large number of states, including France, are parties to the UN Convention on the Elimination of Racial Discrimination.[122] The Committee on the Elimination of Racial Discrimination (CERD) raised the issue of the French headscarf-*hijab* ban in February 2005.[123] France has also implemented the 2000 EU Directive on

---

[116] 'Cross row stokes Christian anger', *BBC News* 15 October 2006, <http://news.bbc.co.uk/1/hi/uk/6051486.stm> (last accessed 23 July 2008).

[117] There is no published report of the decision of the employment tribunal. She lost her appeal; see *Eweida v. British Airways*, [2008] EAT 123_08_2011.

[118] The Archbishop of Canterbury, Dr Rowan Williams, threatened to sell the Church of England's £9 million worth of shares in the company if it did not change its policy.

[119] See J. McCaffrey, 'If a Muslim can wear her veil to work why is my cross forbidden?', *Daily Mirror*, 16 October 2006.

[120] See P. Foster, 'BA backs down and ends ban on crosses', *The Times*, 20 January 2007.

[121] T. Sanderson, 'A cross to bear', *The Guardian*, 17 January 2008, <http://commentisfree.guardian.co.uk/terry_sanderson/2008/01/a_cross_to_bear.html> (last accessed 23 July 2008).

[122] 173 states parties as of 18 July 2007. The general prohibition on racial discrimination is widely accepted as part of customary international law.

[123] CERD/C/SR.1675, paras. 36, 49–50, 57 (28 February 2005).

the principle of equal treatment between persons irrespective of racial or ethnic origin.[124] It is arguable that the headscarf-*hijab* ban can be contested under this Directive.[125] Many French Muslims perceive the headscarf-*hijab* ban as racial discrimination in general and discrimination against *immigrés* (literally meaning immigrants, but widely used to include those of a different ethnic origin even if of French nationality) in particular.[126] However, in legal terms it is more difficult to analyse the Islamic headscarf-*hijab* ban in terms of racial discrimination unless the terms 'racial or ethnic origin' are interpreted very widely. Muslims are followers of the religion Islam, but they are not a race as such.[127]

(iv) Gender Discrimination and Feminist Perspectives

Prohibitions and restrictions on the headscarf-*hijab* can raise issues of gender discrimination.[128] CEDAW has been widely ratified. However, it has also been the subject of a higher number of reservations than the other major UN human rights treaties. Some of the reservations by Islamic states take the form of a general reservation to any obligations inconsistent with *sharia* law.[129] An Optional Protocol adopted in 1999 permits individual petitions. The first decisions under CEDAW on individual petitions were taken in 2003. The headscarf-*hijab* restrictions in Turkey were challenged under CEDAW in *Rahime Kayhan* v. *Turkey* in 2006.[130] Ms Kayhan was a teacher. She wore the headscarf-*hijab* from 1991 to 2000 until she was dismissed for wearing it. She submitted that there had been a violation of Article 11 of the Convention concerning discrimination in relation to work. Turkey submitted that the regulations on the attire of civil servants applied to both male and female civil servants and that there was no

---

[124] Council Directive 2000/43/EC, 29 June 2000, OJ L180/22.

[125] See Mahlmann, n. 15 above; Blair and Aps, n. 112 above.

[126] Some British Muslims also perceive their treatment as racist: see M. Franks, 'Crossing the Borders of Whiteness? White Muslim Women Who Wear the *Hijab* in Britain Today' (2000) 23(5) *Ethnic and Racial Studies* 917.

[127] See *Mandla* v. *Dowell Lee* [1983] 2 AC 548. As a result (before the 2003 Regulations), Muslims in the UK had to argue that discrimination against them was indirectly against them as Asian and thus racial; see *Walker* v. *Hussain* [1996] IRLR 11. In *R (Watkins Singh)* v. *Governing Body of Aberdale Girls' High School and Rhondda Cynon Taf Unitary Authority* [2008] EWHC 1865 (Admin), [2008] ELR 00, WS, a Sikh schoolgirl, successfully claimed indirect racial discrimination on the basis of the school's refusal to allow her to wear a Kara, a plain steel bangle, which she regarded as a manifestation of her religion of exceptional importance.

[128] See D. Lyon and D. Spini, 'Unveiling the Headscarf Debate' (2004) 12(3) *Fem. L. S.* 333; Malik (n. 159 below). For an argument based on gender equality in the French Constitution, see G. Coq, 'Foulard islamique: pour un retour à la loi république', *Liberation*, 6 November 1996.

[129] For the text of reservations see <http://www.un.org/womenwatch/daw/cedaw/reservations-country.htm> (last accessed 23 July 2008). On limitations on gender equality, see V.M. Moghadem, *Towards Gender Equality in the Arab/Middle East Region: Islam, Culture and Feminist Activism*, United Nations Development Programme, Occasional Paper 2004/6, <http://hdr.undp.org/docs/publications/background_papers/2004/HDR2004_Valentine_Moghadam.pdf> (last accessed 23 July 2008).

[130] See n. 30 above, Communication No 8/2005, <http://www.un.org/womenwatch/daw/cedaw/protocol/decisions-views/8_2005.pdf> (last accessed 23 July 2008).

element of its content or application that constituted discrimination against women.[131] It also stressed the individuals wishing to join the civil service knew that there were rules on attire. The Committee on the Elimination of Discrimination Against Women declared the application inadmissible for failure to raise the issue of discrimination based on sex during the exhaustion of domestic remedies.[132]

The rights in the ICCPR and ICESCR are to be respected on a non-discriminatory basis (Article 2 of each Covenant specifically refers to sex discrimination) and the equal right of men and women to enjoy all of the rights in the Covenants must be ensured (Article 3 of each Covenant). Article 26 ICCPR on equality and non-discrimination (which expressly includes sex discrimination) has been interpreted as a free-standing provision. Article 14 ECHR (non-discrimination) is more limited. Sex discrimination is one of the illustrative grounds. For the parties to it Protocol 12 ECHR now provides a free-standing non-discrimination guarantee similar to that in Article 26 ICCPR.

There are an estimated two million Muslim women in France. The Law of 2004 prohibiting the wearing of conspicuous religious signs is on its face neutral but it clearly affects a much higher proportion of females than males and so can be viewed as indirectly discriminatory on the basis of gender. It would thus require justification by reference to a legitimate aim and objective grounds. Human Rights Watch, a non-governmental organization, argued that by disproportionately affecting Muslim girls the law was discriminatory.[133] Obviously only women wear the headscarf-*hijab*. It is also predominantly women who wear Christian crosses. However, only Jewish males wear skullcaps.

In *Dahlab*[134] the applicant argued, inter alia, that the prohibition imposed by the Swiss authorities on her wearing an Islamic headscarf-*hijab* while teaching amounted to discrimination on the ground of sex within the meaning of Article 14 of the European Convention in that a man belonging to the Muslim faith could teach at a state school without being subject to any form of prohibition.[135] The European Court reiterated that 'the advancement of the equality of the sexes' was a major goal in the Member States of the Council of Europe and that therefore 'very weighty reasons' would have to be advanced before a difference in treatment on the ground of sex could be regarded as compatible with the Convention. However, it considered that the prohibition was not directed at her as a member of the female sex but pursued the legitimate aim of ensuring the neutrality of the state primary education system. Such a measure could also be applied to a man who, in similar circumstances, wore clothing that clearly identified him as a member of a different faith. Accordingly, there was no

---

[131] Ibid., para. 4.4.   [132] Ibid., paras. 7.6–.7.

[133] See 'France: Headscarf Ban Violates Religious Freedom', Human Rights Watch, Statement of 27 February 2004, <http://hrw.org/english/docs/2004/02/26/france7666.htm> (last accessed 23 July 2008).

[134] See *Dahlab*, n. 27 above.   [135] Ibid., 8.

discrimination on the ground of sex.[136] This response illustrates the limitations of a formal non-discrimination discourse. Factually, the Court is quite correct. However, it can be argued that it 'ignores the social reality that the dispute surrounded headscarf wearing by *women* and [that] there was little evidence of equivalent difficulties for men'.[137] In *Dahlab,* the Court also noted that the headscarf 'appeared to be imposed on women by a precept laid down in the Koran' that was 'hard to square with the principle of gender equality'.[138] This was again stressed in the Şahin case.[139] As noted, the advancement of the equality of the sexes is a major goal of the Member States of the Council of Europe.[140]

There is a perspective that views the headscarf-*hijab* as offensive because of its repressive symbolism in terms of relations between the sexes.[141] Symbolism is historically significant in French political and social thinking, but is also relevant in many other European states. The headscarf-*hijab* is troublesome for Western thinkers because it suggests a belief system in which women are inferior to men.[142] French feminist communities were divided on the headscarf-*hijab* issue.[143] More generally Western feminists tend to be hostile towards the veil although some view it more positively as preserving culture and symbolizing resistance to Westernization.[144] Most French feminists appear to regard the headscarf-*hijab* as a symbol of the oppression of women.[145] Thus, in general, most women's groups were on the side of the secularists and in favour of the new law.[146] In December 2003, sixty prominent French women issued a petition urging a ban on 'this visible symbol of the submission of women'.[147] The

---

[136] Ibid., 14.

[137] Lyon and Spini (n. 128 above), 338 (commenting on the French context, emphasis in original).

[138] See *Dahlab* (n. 27 above), 13.

[139] *Şahin* (n. 28 above), para 111.

[140] See *Dahlab*, n. 27 above, and *Abdulaziz, Cabales and Balkandali* v. *United Kingdom* [1985] 7 EHRR 471.

[141] See S. Poulter, 'Muslim Headscarves in School: Contrasting Legal Approaches in England and France' (1997) 17 *O.J.L.S.* 43, 69–72.

[142] M. Marrin, 'Comment: Cry freedom and accept the Muslim headscarf', *The Times,* 1 February 2004.

[143] See J.W. Scott, 'Symptomatic Politics: The Banning of Islamic headscarves in French Public Schools' 23(3) *French Politics, Culture & Society* (Winter 2005), 106.

[144] See Hirschmann (n. 56 above), 349.

[145] See Femmes Publiques, 'Être féministe, ce n'est pas exclure!', 23 October 2003, <http://sisyphe.org/article.php3?id_article=677> [French] (last accessed 23 July 2008). For a more general argument, see S. M. Okin (ed.), *Is Multiculturalism Bad for Women?* (Princeton: Princeton UP, 1999).

[146] This included the group called '*Ni putes, ni soumises.*' See *The Veil Controversy: International Perspectives on Religion in Public Life* (2004) Pew Forum, <http://pewforum.org/events/? EventID=55> (last accessed 23 July 2008), hereinafter Pew Forum. See the evidence to the Stasi Commission (n. 52 above), <http://www.ladocumentationfrancaise.fr/brp/notices/034000725. shtml> [French] (last accessed 23 July 2008).

[147] The magazine *Elle* sponsored a petition, signed by several intellectuals and politicians, against the veil, describing it as 'intolerable discrimination' and the 'visible symbol of the submission of women in public'. See S. Louet, 'Chirac stokes Muslim veil debate', *Human Rights Without Frontiers,* 8 December 2008.

headscarf-*hijab* was sometimes compared to the yellow star worn by Jews during the Nazi era.[148] Many women in the west find the headscarf-*hijab* deeply problematic.[149]

The support of women's and feminist groups for the Law of 2004 was generally based on a conceptualization of the headscarf-*hijab* as a disempowering instrument for the oppression of women.[150] In response, it has been argued that that this opinion confuses the issue between women who are forced to wear the *burqua* (an almost complete covering of the female form) and denied even a minimum of civil and political rights, and women who prefer to wear a headscarf at work. The approach evidences the 'Western hegemonic thinking with a touch of assimilationism.'[151] Christine Delphy, a leading French feminist, criticized the French Government for using feminism for its own purposes and for its exceptional treatment for Islamic insignia. She argued that girls should not be excluded.[152] Feminists have also observed that the Government's response falls into the classic public/private divide.[153] It is willing to take action in respect of a public element of the treatment of women. Thus, polygamy and female genital mutilation are illegal in France.[154] However, women experience discrimination in a range of areas.[155] Domestic violence and sexual harassment continue to be major problems.[156] The situation of Muslim women is often described in terms of their being caught between two worlds.[157] It has been observed that it is often difficult for women to step out of their cultural frame and argue for secularism and human rights.[158]

Public schools in France are seen as vital arenas to inculcate values of sexual equality and independent, critical thought. Some Muslim parents took the view that they would ask their daughters to de-veil before sacrificing their education.

---

[148] See P. Silverstein, 'Headscarves and the French Tricolor', *Middle East Report Online*, 30 January 2004, <http://www.merip.org/mero/mero013004.html> (last accessed 23 July 2008).

[149] Walter, n. 109 above, (emphasis added).

[150] E. Badinter, quoted in n. 80 above.

[151] Berthou (n. 115 above), 309. See also the dissenting opinion of Judge Tulkens in the *Şahin* case, holding that it was not the Court's role to make a unilateral and negative appraisal of a religion or religious practice, just as it was not its role to determine in a general and abstract way the significance of wearing the headscarf or to impose its viewpoint on the applicant.

[152] See C. Delphy, 'L'affaire du foulard: non à l'exclusion', 1 November 2003, <http://sisyphe.org/article.php3?id_article=728&var_recherche=foulard> [French] (last accessed 21 April 2008).

[153] See Carolyn Evans' chapter in this volume.

[154] Inasmuch as these practices represent an affirmation of cultural identity, that identity is not accepted in Western European states.

[155] See the 'Concluding Observations of the Committee on the Elimination of Discrimination Against Women: France' (27 January 1993) UN Doc. A/48/38, paras. 327–58.

[156] Though the state has taken a number of measures, ibid., para. 335. See also <http://www.avft.org> [French] (last accessed 21 April 2008).

[157] See M. Simons, 'Muslim women in Europe claim rights and faith', *The New York Times*, 29 December 2005. On the separate lives of Muslim men in western states see M. Sifaoui, *Inside Al Qaeda: How I Infiltrated the World's Deadliest Terrorist Organization* (London: Granta Books, 2003).

[158] M. A. Helie-Lucas, 'The Preferential Symbol for Islamic Identity: Women in Muslim Personal Laws', in V. Moghadem (ed.), *Identity Politics and Women: Cultural Reassertions and Feminisms in International Perspective* (Boulder, CO: Westview, 1994) 391, 402.

However, there were concerns that some parents might take their female children out of school early (the leaving age is 15) or altogether. There were also fears that the ban would force girls out of school. If Muslim girls had stayed out of public schools, this would have run contrary to France's general policy of integration. The early evidence on the effect of the Law of 2004 suggested that the worst fears of critics had not been realized. A French Education Ministry Report published a year after the law's adoption argued that it had been successful and had been implemented with relatively little difficulty. Indeed, some Muslim families had found it a liberating experience.

(v) Intersecting Discrimination

Finally, the headscarf-*hijab* ban could be an example of multiple or intersecting discrimination or complex inequality based on sex, religion, and ethnic origin.[159] In *Khanum* v. *IBC Vehicles Ltd.*,[160] a Muslim woman who suffered adverse treatment at work when she began to wear a headscarf-*hijab* was held to have been discriminated against on the basis of both race and sex.

6. Autonomy and Consent

The interpretation and application of human rights texts in particular contexts can be assisted by locating their underlying values or principles.[161] In the wider feminist community, there is a strong commitment to the overriding priority of individual autonomy because, without it, 'women remain vulnerable to the claims of nation, religion, or community'.[162] However, that community found the headscarf-*hijab* issue a difficult one because it juxtaposed fundamental principles of toleration, self-determination, and choice.[163] Individual voluntarism or consent would not necessarily be accepted by major religions as the primary

---

[159] See M. Malik, 'Complex Equality: Muslim Women and the "Headscarf"' (2008) 68 *Droit et Société* 127–52 For a United States perspective, S. Hannett, 'Equality at the Intersections: the Legislative and Judicial Failure to Tackle Multiple Discrimination' (2003) 23 *O.J.L.S.* 65. See also, A. Vakulenko, '"Islamic headscarves" and the European Convention on Human Rights: an inter-sectional perspective' (2007) 16 *Social and Legal Studies* 183–99.

[160] IT 1200058/97, 2 March 1998, 15 Sept 1999, EAT, unreported, available on Westlaw 1999 WL1556547. See also [2002] EmpLR 713 re: *Hussain* v *Midland Cosmetic Sales Limited* on the regulation of the *hijab* on health and safety grounds. A point related to Art. 9 ECHR (freedom of religion) was raised, but not pursued.

[161] '[T]he notion of personal autonomy is an important principle underlying the interpretation of the guarantees in Art. 8 ECHR, *Pretty* v. *United Kingdom* (n. 40 above). See also Leader, n. 70a above.

[162] S. Mullally, 'Feminism and Multicultural Dilemmas in India: Revisiting the *Shah Bano* Case' (2004) 24 *O.J.L.S.* 671, 687.

[163] See Killian, n. 82 above, who provides evidence that age and education were significant determining factors in women's responses and whether they used a discourse of rights and equality or an essentially religious one. See also the discussion in 'Voile ou foulard', <http://sisyphe.org/rubrique.php3?id_rubrique=49 [French] (last accessed 23 July 2008).

factor.[164] At best, they might put it on the same level as norms relating to cultural, community, and family membership. However, the consent issue is a particularly difficult one for human rights lawyers. Consent is usually a very powerful human rights principle based on autonomy. The empirical evidence is that different members and generations within the same family can take different views on the headscarf-*hijab*. A grandmother might wear it, a mother not. One daughter then follows the grandmother, the other the mother. A wife might wear it even though her husband would prefer that she did not. In an immigration context, the first generation may seek to be invisible so as to gain acceptance, while the second and subsequent generations seek to be visible so as to gain recognition. If each individual seems to make their own free and informed decision then a very strong interest would be needed to override their views.

So should the analysis be different if some women want to wear the headscarf-*hijab* when others, including other women, consider it to be an instrument of oppression? Does this make their 'consent' a false or limited one? Is the headscarf-*hijab* really an instrument of oppression?[165] Has male pressure become so prevalent that it has become unconscious and made women instruments of their own oppression?[166] Who decides? Consent is not an absolute principle. For example, in many states women cannot consent to prostitution, slavery, polygamy, or female genital mutilation. As Nancy Herschmann has argued:

The *act of choosing* is necessary but not sufficient. What is also needed is the ability to *formulate choices*, and this requires the ability to have meaningful power in the construction of contexts.[167]

In terms of principle, one would be looking for evidence of pervasive oppression before considering that consent can be rendered problematic.[168] Even if one accepted the argument that the headscarf-*hijab* is an instrument of oppression by parents and the male Islamic community, is this ethically worse than governmental compulsion not to wear it?

Some French Muslim women's groups were in favour of the headscarf-*hijab* ban specifically because of the phenomenon of increased violence against, and social domination of, Muslim women.[169] It was also notable that some of the

---

[164] See Hirschmann, n. 56 above.

[165] On western images of Muslim women see G. Martín-Muñoz, 'Islam's women Under western eyes', *Open Democracy*, 10 September 2002, <http://www.opendemocracy.net/faith-europe_islam/article_498.jsp> (last accessed 23 July 2008); M. Tavokili-Targhi, 'Women of the West Imagined: The Farangi Other and the Emergence of the Women Question in Iran' in Moghadem, *Identity Politics* (n. 158 above), 98. On Muslim images of 'western women' see E. Tarlo, 'Reconsidering Stereotypes: Anthropological Reflections on the *Jilbab* Controversy' (2005) 21(6) *Anthropology Today* 13.

[166] See Hirschmann (n. 56 above), 357–9.

[167] Ibid., 361 (emphasis added).

[168] See Lyon and Spini (n. 128 above), 341.

[169] Some such groups have been engaged in re-interpreting Islam. For a feminist critique of the origins and interpretation of the headscarf-*hijab*, see F. Mernissi, *Women and Islam: A Historical Theological Enquiry* (Oxford: Blackwell, 1991). See also M. Sunder, 'Piercing the Veil' (2003) 112 *Yale L. J.* 1399.

younger French Muslim women also supported the French Law of 2004, 'in order to continue their own fight against what they see as male oppression, especially in the tough French "*banlieues*" where girls are regularly harassed, gang-raped, and even burnt to death for going bareheaded and wearing western-style clothes.'[170] Some Muslim women in France considered that the issue was not one of freedom of religion, but was 'about saving schoolgirls from a kind of apartheid that is increasingly imposed by the men in their community'.[171] They saw the veil as putting women into a position of submission. Its prohibition in schools served to protect girls from bullying by fundamentalist Muslims. Women would now have the defence of having to comply with the law. From the perspective of Islamic teaching, the woman would in effect be acting under coercion or necessity (*darura*) emanating from a non-Muslim state.[172] Some French women who had come from more fundamentalist Islamic states (such as Algeria) favoured the headscarf-*hijab* prohibition in schools because they had observed at first hand the rise of the Islamists. A poll in *Le Monde* in November 1989 found that among Muslims, older people (67 per cent) were more opposed to the veil than younger people (44 per cent); and women (49 per cent) were more opposed to it than men (43 per cent). Only 30 per cent of Muslims supported veiling in school, and 22 per cent were indifferent.[173] The French philosopher Bernard-Henry Levy argued that the law would actually support the mainstream Islamic faith by challenging the fundamentalist approach to women.[174]

Many observers would think it natural and logical to approach the headscarf-*hijab* issue from the gender perspective. However, it is important to bear in mind that, although there are a plurality of Muslim opinions on gender equality,[175] a Muslim perspective would not proceed from an equality of women perspective in the first place.[176] Such a perspective on gender is at radical odds with those of the Council of Europe and the European Union. While prohibitions on the headscarf-*hijab* can always be seen as insignificant and trivial, they do represent a line in the sand against, and a rejection of, an Islamic perspective that does not regard or treat women as equals. The argument is that if the line is not drawn at the headscarf-*hijab*, more extensive veiling will follow, and then a more general claim for the application of *sharia* law.[177]

---

[170] 'Fighting the veil', Letter to *The Sunday Times*, 1 February 2004.
[171] Cited in C. Bremner, 'Chirac bans use of Muslim headscarf in all state schools', *The Times*, 18 December 2003.
[172] See B. Lewis, 'Legal and Historical Reflections on the Position of Muslim Populations Under Non-Muslim Rule', in B. Lewis and D. Schnapper (eds.), *Muslims in Europe* (London and New York: Pinter, 1994).
[173] See Killian (n. 82 above), 573.
[174] B.-H. Levy, 'Off with their headscarves', *The Sunday Times*, 1 February 2004.
[175] See H. Beilefeldt, 'Muslim Voices in the Human Rights Debate' (1995) 17 *Hum. Rights Q.* 587.
[176] M. H. A. Reisman, 'Islamic Fundamentalism and its Impact on International Law and Politics', in M. W. Janis and C. Evans (eds.), *Religion and International Law* (The Hague: Nijhoff, 1999), 357.
[177] The European Court of Human Rights has held that individual advocacy of the introduction of *Sharia* law is protected by Art. 10 of the ECHR: the mere fact of defending *sharia*, without calling for violence to establish it, could not be regarded as hate speech (*Gündüz* v. *Turkey* (2005) 41 EHRR 5.

7. Explaining Differential Human Rights Outcomes: The Margin of Appreciation

This essay has sought to apply human rights standards, values, and categorizations to restrictions on wearing the headscarf-*hijab*. It is submitted that the categories used here are helpful in exploring and exploding the human rights implications of the headscarf-*hijab*. It is evident that a human rights approach embodies a certain set of concepts, boundaries, and discourse. Within each human rights categorization, there can be found a complex balancing of claims and interests. The balance is very context-dependent and may reveal tensions that pull in different directions. The human rights outcome for a headscarf-*hijab* dispute may thus vary from one state to another. Within the ECHR system, the European Court will explain this by reference to the 'margin of appreciation'.[178] By contrast, under the ICCPR, the Human Rights Committee never refers to a margin of appreciation doctrine. Although this could be taken to suggest that it might apply a more intensive standard of scrutiny than the European Court of Human Rights, this is not necessarily the case. On identical facts, the Committee might reach the same conclusion as the European Court but simply do so without reference to the margin of appreciation. Domestic courts may apply analogous doctrines by reference to which they accord a significant degree of deference to democratic legislative decisions on how to resolve conflicting human rights claims.[179]

8. Locating the Debates on Religious Dress

Historically, differences and plurality, especially of a religious kind, have been more destructive than constructive.[180] The importance of religious dress issues, and in particular that of the Islamic headscarf-*hijab*, thus has to be located within broader contemporary political and philosophical debates. Religiosity has not withered on the vine in the face of secularism and modernity. In Europe, the issue of religious dress and, in particular, that of the Islamic headscarf-*hijab* debate has become a microcosm of wider debates on integration,[181] tolerance,[182] cultural

---

[178] See J. A. Sweeney, 'Margins of Appreciation: Cultural Relativity and the European Court of Human Rights in the Post-Cold War Era' (2005) 54(2) *Int'l. & Comp. L. Q.* 459; Lewis, n. 4 above.

[179] The domestic legislative decision may be to afford the individual schools a significant degree of discretion, as in the *Begum* case, (n. 71 above). See, in particular, Lord Hoffman in *Begum*, paras. 62–4.

[180] J. Nielsen, *Muslims in Western Europe* (Edinburgh: Edinburgh UP, 1992), 165.

[181] See M. Mirza, A. Senthilkumaran, and Z. Ja'far, *Living Apart Together: British Muslims and the Paradox of Multiculturalism* (Policy Exchange, 2007), <http://www.policyexchange.org.uk/images/libimages/246.pdf> (last accessed 23 July 2008).

[182] On the effects of seeing differences as opposites, see W. Brown, *Regulating Aversion: Tolerance in an Age of Identity and Empire* (Princeton: Princeton UP, 2006) 176 on 'Tolerance as in Civilizational Discourse'.

pluralism, and diversity[183] and multiculturalism generally,[184] but specifically with respect to Muslims.[185]

The headscarf-*hijab* debate is thus part of broader questions that are not new, but which are becoming more acute: how do people who disagree over profoundly different matters live together and will this necessarily involve some limited, but positive, accommodation in the public sphere?[186] Three recent incidents exemplify some of the sensitivities and tensions involved. First, in 2006 in the United Kingdom a wide and controversial public debate was occasioned by comments by the then Leader of the House of Commons, Jack Straw, that he found speaking to a veiled woman uncomfortable. He described the veil as a 'visible statement of separation and difference'.[187] The then Prime Minister, Tony Blair, expressed general support for the views of Mr Straw. An interesting aspect of the responses was that even the value of a public debate was put at issue. Some questioned Mr Straw's motives and expressed concern that the comments would fuel extremists and fundamentalists. Others considered that the debate was a proper part of wider discussion of multiculturalism and British identity.

Secondly, in 2007, a million people marched on the streets of Turkey in defence of secularism. The context of the marches was the nomination by the ruling Justice and Development Party (AKP), which has Islamic roots, of Abdullah Gül for the post of President. His wife wears the headscarf-*hijab*. The Turkish Army, which sees itself as having a central role in the defence of the secular republic and has overthrown four previous governments, issued an ominous public statement that could be read as threatening intervention if necessary.[188] After a rebuff in the Parliament (by 411 votes to 103), the ruling party called an early general election and was returned to power. Gül was re-nominated and elected President. In 2008, the Turkish Parliament approved an amendment to the Turkish Constitution that would see a relaxation of the headscarf-*hijab* ban in Universities. The government-sponsored measure would

---

[183] See S. Benhabib, *The Claims of Culture: Equality and Diversity in the Global Era* (Princeton: Princeton UP, 2002); N. Harris, *Education Law and Diversity* (Oxford: Hart, 2007), especially chs. 1 and 7; W. Kymlicka, *Multicultural Odysseys: Navigating the New International Politics of Diversity* (Oxford: Oxford UP, 2007); A. Phillips, *Multiculturalism Without Culture* (Princeton, Princeton UP, 2007).

[184] T. Modood, A. Triandafyllidou, and R. Zapata-Barrero (eds.), *Multiculturalism, Muslims and Citizenship: A European Approach* (London: Routledge, 2006); D. McGoldrick, 'Multiculturalism and its Discontents' (2005) 5(1) *Hum. Rights L. Rev.* 27; T. Modood, *Multiculturalism: A Civic Idea (Themes for the 21st Century)* (Cambridge: Polity, 2007).

[185] See J. S. Fetzer and J. C. Soper, *Muslims and the State in Britain, France, and Germany* (Cambridge: CUP, 2005).

[186] See W. Kymlicka, *Multicultural Citizenship: A Liberal Theory of Minority Rights* (Oxford: Clarendon, 1995).

[187] See M. Taylor and V. Dodd, 'Take off the veil, says Straw—to immediate anger from Muslims', *The Guardian*, 6 October 2006.

[188] The text, attributed to General Yasar Buyukanit, the head of the army, and posted on the military's web site, stated: 'Our nation has been watching the behavior of those separatists who can't embrace Turkey's unitary nature and centers of evil that systematically try to corrode the secular nature of the Turkish Republic.'

amend two articles of the Constitution relating to access to education to ensure that no student was prevented from going to state-backed universities because of his or her style of dress, President Abdullah Gül approved the changes.[189] Opinion polls reportedly showed a majority of Turks backed an easing of the ban.[190] However, the opposition CHP (Republican People's Party) and the DSP (Democratic Left Party) applied to the Constitutional Court for the annulment of the changes on the grounds that they violated the principle of secularism in Article 2 of the Constitution. On 5 June 2008 the Constitutional Court, by nine votes to two, rules the amendments unconstitutional because they conflicted with the principle of secularism in Article 2 of the Constitution.[191]

Even if the reforms had survived constitutional scrutiny, women professors as well as civil servants would still have been prohibited from wearing the headscarf. The fear of opponents was that this was the first step in an Islamization of Turkey. Once again, tens of thousands of people staged protest rallies against the changes. Such developments at the national political level highlight a point that is often forgotten, namely that a judgment of the European Court finding no violation returns the matter to the domestic political and constitutional forum.

Thirdly, and finally, the acute sensitivities of affording greater legal accommodation and recognition to Islamic customs and practices (*sharia* law) within the law of the land was exemplified by the extremely hostile reaction to a such a suggestion by the Archbishop of Canterbury, Dr Rowan Williams, in a lecture in 2008.[192] At least part of the hostility was founded on the view that such a step would inevitably lead to some members of religious communities, and women in particular, having their national and international human rights restricted to a much greater extent than at present.[193] Further controversy followed after support for this approach from Lord Phillips, the then Lord Chief Justice (and future President of the Supreme Court).[194]

---

[189] See 'Secularists' lament' *The Economist*, Vol. 384 Issue 8548, 53–4 (29 September 2007); P. De Bendern, 'Secular Turks rally against Muslim headscarf reform', *International Herald Tribune*, 2 February 2008.

[190] See V. Boland 'Turkey moves to ease headscarf ban', *Financial Times*, 7 February 2008; J. Turner, 'Islam and the great Cover-Up,' *The Times* (2), 18 July 2008.

[191] Human Rights Watch 'Turkey: Constitutional Court Ruling Upholds Headscarf Ban' (7 June 2008) <http://www.hrw.org/english/docs/2008/06/06/turkey19050.htm>.

[192] Archbishop of Canterbury, 'Civil and Religious Law in England: a Religious Perspective', 7 February 2008, <http://www.archbishopofcanterbury.org/1575> (last accessed 23 July 2008).

[193] See D. Gadher, A. Taher and C. Morgan, 'Rowan Williams faces backlash over sharia', *The Sunday Times*, 10 February 2008; Editorial, 'Wounded and Wiser', *The Guardian*, 12 February 2008.

[194] See his speech on 'Equality before the Law', East London Muslim Centre, 3 July 2008. See also A. Taher, 'Revealed: UK's First Official Sharia Courts' *The Sunday Times*, 14 September 2008.

21

Endorsing Discrimination Between Faiths: A Case of Extreme Speech?

John Finnis

Propositions about a religious faith which differs decisively from others were foundational to the House of Lords' decision in *Shabina Begum*.[1] But they were articulated tersely, and commentaries have neglected them. Whether this neglect stems from oversight, or from the prudent timidity now customary in these matters,[2] is unclear. The propositions are drawn out below, by reference to their fuller articulation by the European Court of Human Rights (ECtHR), and a question is then raised: when articulated by editorials, letters to the editor, placards and public speeches, academic articles, or political programmes, do these propositions become instances of 'extreme' (or 'hate') speech?

1. Legitimate, if not Necessary, School Ban on a Garment

Begum displays the unsatisfactory conceptual and argumentative state[3] of contemporary human rights law. This is worth noticing, on the way to unearthing the decision's real but understated premises.

The case's main holding, for present purposes, is that Denbigh High School's prohibition of Shabina Begum's attending school dressed in a jilbab (long shapeless gown) was a limitation of her freedom to manifest her beliefs which was 'necessary in a democratic society in the interests of . . . the protection of the rights

---

[1] *R (on the application of Begum)* v. *Denbigh High School Governors* [2006] UKHL 15, [2007] 1 AC 100.

[2] On the significance of intimidation in this context, see J. Finnis, 'Religion and State: Some Main Issues and Sources' (2006) 51 *Am. J. Juris.* 107, 126.

[3] For some instances, see J. Finnis, 'Nationality, Alienage and Constitutional Principle' (2007) 123 *L. Q. Rev.* 417.

and freedoms of others'.[4] There was a secondary holding:[5] her religious freedom was not limited (infringed, interfered with, or violated) at all, since she was free to go to other schools in or near Luton which would permit her to wear the garment. Though significant, this holding is of more limited practical relevance. For, until Islamization, multiculturalism or sheer informality proceed a good deal further, there will be many areas of the country in which persons like Miss Begum would not have the luxury of this option.

The Lords, even the reluctantly concurring Baroness Hale, make light work of explaining why what was evidently not 'necessary for the protection of the rights and freedoms of others' in at least two nearby schools *was* necessary in Denbigh High School. Indeed, that way of framing the issue is conspicuously absent, save in a fleeting and oblique mention by Lord Bingham. Summarizing an argument by counsel for Miss Begum to the effect that the school was 'refusing permission when some other schools permitted it,' Lord Bingham responds simply that 'different schools have different uniform policies, no doubt influenced by the composition of their pupil bodies and a range of other matters. Each school has to decide what uniform, if any, will best serve its wider educational purposes.' Here, as in much of the Lords' discussion of justification under Article 9(2), the issue of *necessity*—whether for protection of rights or for anything else—seems sidelined in favour of the question whether the school made *a reasonable judgment* about what would '*best* serve' the interests of its pupils.

The same goes for Lord Hoffmann's parallel statement: the school 'had decided that a uniform policy was in the general interests of the school and then tried to devise a uniform which satisfied as many people as possible and took into account their different religions'.[6] Here again there is no attention to the question whether

---

[4] European Convention on Human Rights (1950) Art. 9:

(1) Everyone has the right to freedom of thought, conscience, and religion; this right includes freedom to change his religion or belief and freedom, either alone or in community with others and in public or private, to manifest his religion or belief, in worship, teaching, practice, and observance.

(2) Freedom to manifest one's religion or beliefs shall be subject only to such limitations as are prescribed by law and are necessary in a democratic society in the interests of public safety, for the protection of public order, health, or morals, or for the protection of the rights and freedoms of others.

The main holding in *Begum* includes a decision that the limitation on her freedom was 'prescribed by law' in so far as it was prescribed by the school rules made by and for this particular state-maintained school.

[5] Lords Bingham, Hoffmann and Scott; Lord Nicholls and Baroness Hale doubting. There are two further holdings: (i) that her right to education was not engaged, for analogous reasons, and (ii) that she had not been 'excluded' for the purposes of the ill-drafted School Standards and Framework Act 1998. These both come over from the companion case of *Ali* v. *Lord Grey School Governors* [2006] UKHL 14, [2006] 2 AC 363.

[6] *Begum,* para. 67. Lord Hoffmann is here dealing with the Court of Appeal's ruling that the school violated Article 9 by failing to adopt the right procedures (including a review of the obligations of public authorities under the Human Rights Act 1998 and the ECHR) when determining its policy on school uniforms. That ruling would have had wide significance had it not been utterly rejected by the Lords in *Begum,* and need not be considered further here.

it was not merely 'in the general interests' of the school but, rather, *necessary* to restrict anyone's freedom to manifest religious belief. And that question seems out of focus even when Lord Hoffmann says, or implies, that the trial judge had held that 'the school was entitled to consider that the rules about uniform were necessary for the protection of the rights and freedoms of others'; for the passage he quotes from Bennett J's judgment says nothing about necessity; it instead finds that the policy on uniforms 'promotes a positive ethos and a sense of communal identity' and '*aims* to protect [the] rights and freedoms' of those Muslim female pupils who otherwise would 'feel pressure on them either from inside or outside the school' to wear a garment they do not wish to wear.[7] That the school was *aiming* to protect rights is clearly relevant. It was perhaps indispensable to a demonstration that the policy was necessary, or was judged necessary, for that purpose. But, in the absence of any comparison with alternative assessments of the need and alternative policies for meeting it, it demonstrates neither necessity nor even a judgment of necessity by the school.

Instead, the articulated argumentation of the Lords' judgments looks to (1) *proportionality* (see especially Lord Bingham at para. 26) and (2) *margin of appreciation* or, rather, *deference* to the *area of judgment* (Lord Hoffmann at para. 64) to be accorded to the national constitutional order's non-judicial parts: notably Parliament and the head teachers and governors of maintained secondary community schools.

So one must ask, first, why proportionality, in the context of justification under Article 9(2), did not require of the school's policy formation more than the abundant care and good judgment admired by the Lords. Does not Article 9(2), taken with the Strasbourg jurisprudence, require that any policy restricting manifestations of religious or philosophical belief (a) be doing so in response to a 'pressing social need', and (b) be, among otherwise appropriate measures, 'the measure that is *the least restrictive*' of the right to manifest such belief? This is the question which Judge Tulkens presses in dissent against the other sixteen judges of the Grand Chamber (and the seven judges of the Fourth Section) of the ECtHR in *Sahin v Turkey*.[8] The question is met with resounding silence both in the Grand Chamber and the Lords. The conceptually relaxed and undemanding criteria employed in those tribunals—legitimacy of aim and proportionality of means—seem more appropriate to justifying some allegedly discriminatory differentiation between persons than to showing that a well-intentioned measure is '*necessary* in a democratic society'.

The same goes, I think, for the Lords' deference to the area of judgment they treat as accorded to the school. To be sure, the Court of Appeal was misguided in demanding that the school explicitly attend to the European Convention on

---

[7] *Begum,* para. 58 (emphasis added). Since Lord Scott agreed fully with the judgments of Lords Bingham and Hoffmann, and Lord Bingham agreed fully with Lord Hoffmann's, the latter's, if not also Lord Bingham's, is a judgment commanding majority support.

[8] *Sahin* v. *Turkey* (2007) 44 EHRR 5, see paras. 2, 5, 8, and 13 of her dissenting judgment.

Human Rights (ECHR) when adopting school rules. But did the trial judge investigate precisely whether—and if so, why—the school judged *necessary* what nearby schools judged unnecessary? As we have seen, he seems instead to have been content to find that the school was *aiming* to protect the rights and freedoms of girls who did or would otherwise 'feel pressure on them either from inside or outside the school' to wear a garment they do not wish to.

In sum, the Lords' judgments on the justifiability of banning the jilbab from Denbigh School seem thin, conclusory, and result-oriented. Even Baroness Hale, who was more impressed by Judge Tulkens than by the views of the other twenty-two Strasbourg judges in *Sahin*, does not really face up to the question whether the school's policy on uniforms was necessary in the face of alternative policies which would have permitted the jilbab. She does hold, importantly, that 'the justification which Judge Tulkens found lacking' is supplied by the evidence of other girls' fear of being pressured. But what she concludes from that, directly and immediately, is no more than that the school's policy was 'a thoughtful and proportionate response to reconciling the complexities of the situation' given 'the social conditions in that school, in that town, and at that time'.[9] The conceptual slackness of human rights law-in-action is impressive.

2. Necessary State Ban on a Party and Government

Yet the result in *Begum* seems right. The school's determination to hold onto its policy[10] in the face of threatened and actual litigation is some evidence of its own judgment that its policy was indeed necessary, and alternative policies quite inappropriate. In deferring to this opinion, the Lords found *Sahin* 'valuable guidance,' and strong support.[11] To a far greater extent than the judgments disclose, counsel for the school had rested his argument about justification squarely and almost exclusively on *Sahin*,[12] where both chambers of the Strasbourg Court had deferred, with little sign of strain, to the rulings of the Turkish courts and other authorities. It is in *Sahin* that the real premise and thrust of *Begum* can be found.

The issue in *Sahin* arose out of a ruling of the Turkish Constitutional Court in 1989, striking down a 1988 enactment about dress in universities. This enactment, while requiring 'modern dress' in all educational institutions, allowed that 'a veil or headscarf covering the neck and hair may be worn out of religious

---

[9] *Begum*, para. 98.

[10] The school being about 80 per cent (sometimes over 90 per cent) Muslim, and its (female) headteacher being of Muslim origin, its policy approved (besides English-style uniforms) several kinds of Islamic-type attire less constricting than the jilbab (and less redolent of Islamic political movements such as the Muslim Brotherhood and its offshoots).

[11] *Begum*, paras. 32 (Lord Bingham), 59 (Lord Hoffmann). Baroness Hale, as we have seen, was doubtful.

[12] See *Begum* [2007] 1 AC 100, 104, 107 (Richard McManus QC).

conviction'. The Constitutional Court held it subversive of the constitutional guarantee of secularism, and thus a violation of the underlying values and rights of conscience, of religious freedom, and of equality. That ruling is foundational for the decisions of both chambers at Strasbourg in *Sahin*. They defer to the judgment of the Turkish authorities, judicial and non-judicial, about the threat that even a *permission* to use Islamic dress will pose, where Islam is the religion of the majority, to freedom of conscience and religion.

The precise contours and grounds of this judgment, one that would have been found surprising by many British readers (at least in 1989, if not so much so in November 2005), are explored in section 3 below. For the present, they can be summarized by reference to a statement which, on its surface, seems not to discriminate (differentiate) between religions: 'when a particular dress code [is] imposed on individuals by reference to a religion, the religion concerned [is] perceived and presented as a set of values that [are] incompatible with those of contemporary society'.[13] That incompatibility, however, is elaborated in terms of two further but related considerations: the equality rights of women; and the rights and freedoms of all those, whether Muslim, ex-Muslim, or non-Muslim, who choose not to conform to what some Muslims perceive and present as a religious duty—a right, in other words, to be free from intimidation or pressure. Moreover, thirdly, 'there are extremist political movements in Turkey which seek to impose on society as a whole their religious symbols and conception of a society founded on religious precepts... [E]ach Contracting State may... take a stance against such political movements, based on its historical experience'. Measures such as those in issue in *Sahin*, forbidding the Islamic headscarf, 'have to be viewed in that context and constitute a measure intended to achieve the legitimate aims' of protection of rights and freedoms and public order.[14]

Microcosmically, *Begum* tracks this line of thought. It upholds the school's judgment that wearing the jilbab is impermissible because permitting it would result[15] in a threat to the rights of other children, if not of apparent volunteers such as Miss Begum herself. Obviously, the use of a religious symbol to manifest

---

[13] *Sahin* (n. 8 above), para. 39, paraphrasing the reasoning of the Constitutional Court of Turkey.

[14] *Sahin*, ibid., Grand Chamber para. 115 quoting Fourth Section paras. 107–9. See also n. 22 below, quoting what the Grand Chamber said about the matters in issue in *Sahin* in advance of its judgment in that case. The elaborate discussion of *Sahin* by Stephen Breyer, Justice of the Supreme Court of the United States, in his *Active Liberty: Interpreting a Democratic Constitution* (Oxford: OUP, 2008), 132–41, fails entirely to recognize that the pressure on women to wear the scarf was envisaged by the Turkish and European courts, and *mutatis mutandis* in the English courts in *Begum*, as pressure not so much from fellow students (or pupils) as from persons outside the educational institution (whether parents and other relatives, or religious leaders, or political parties or miscellaneous activists). Justice Breyer's apparent unawareness of the passage quoted in n. 22 below, and of the entire historic case in which that passage was pronounced, only accentuates his inattention to the *modus operandi* of the politico-religious forces under consideration by these courts.

[15] The causality here is what Aquinas would call *removens prohibens*: removing the ban would allow those (inside and outside the school) who wish to demand that all (Muslim) girls wear this garment to make that demand much more efficaciously than before. The ban blocks the pressure.

one's personal belief can threaten the rights of others only if it is associated with a definite and particular kind of religious culture. To be the matrix for a threat of this kind, a religious culture must have one or more of a cluster of features: a disrespect for equality (here the equality of females, especially girls and young women); a denial of immunity from coercion in religious matters (including matters of apostasy from that religion or rejection of all religion), the immunity now central to Christian political teaching;[16] a mandating, encouragement, or permission of intimidation of apostates, backsliders and others; and a treatment of all arenas, educational or political, as in principle subject to threatening pressure, indeed compulsion, in the name of religious truths and precepts and of promoting adherence to them.

All this lies just below the surface of the Lords' terse allusions to the school's predictions(?) of 'adverse repercussions' if they allowed the jilbab;[17] to measures 'to protect girls against external pressures', with mention also of 'an extremist version of the Muslim religion';[18] to 'patriarchal dominance of... families;'[19] and to the 'quite unnecessarily confrontational' behaviour, verging on the 'threatening,' of the two men who accompanied Shabina Begum at her first wearing of the jilbab to school.[20] All these can be treated as incorporating by tacit reference the allusion to 'pressing social need' made by both chambers of the Strasbourg Court in *Sahin*.[21]

Turkey's 'historical experience' of political and social life in the context of adherence by 94 per cent of its population to the same religion as that of 80–90 per cent of the children at Denbigh School, supplied the Lords in *Begum* with interpretative premises more realistic than are generally available in British public discourse or had been elaborated by counsel or the lower courts. Lessons of that experience are crystallized both in *Sahin* and in the much more important case which made the outcome in *Sahin* easy to predict, *Refah Partisi (The Welfare Party) and Others* v. *Turkey*.[22] The Refah [Welfare] Party was the largest in

---

[16] See Finnis, 'Religion and State' (n. 2 above), 117–22.

[17] *Begum*, para. 34 (Lord Bingham).   [18] Ibid., para. 65 (Lord Hoffmann).

[19] Ibid., para. 98 (Baroness Hale).

[20] Ibid., paras 79, 80 (Lord Scott); at para. 10 Lord Bingham records that the deputy headteacher who was thus confronted 'felt that their approach was unreasonable and he felt threatened'.

[21] Para. 115 of *Sahin* quoting the judgment of the Fourth Section: 'As has already been noted (see... *Refah Partisi*...), the issues at stake include the protection of the "rights and freedoms of others" and the "maintenance of public order" in a country in which the majority of the population, while professing a strong attachment to the rights of women and a secular way of life, adhere to the Islamic faith. Imposing limitations on freedom in this sphere may, therefore, be regarded as meeting a pressing social need by seeking to achieve those two legitimate aims, especially since, as the Turkish courts stated..., this religious symbol has taken on political significance in Turkey in recent years.'

[22] *Refah Partisi (No. 2)* v. *Turkey* (2003) 37 EHRR 1. In para. 95 of its judgment, the Grand Chamber addressed matters before it, not in the case in hand, but in *Sahin* (on which proceedings the European Court of Human Rights had not yet pronounced):

> 95. In a country like Turkey, where the great majority of the population belong to a particular religion, measures taken in universities to prevent certain fundamentalist religious movements from exerting pressure on students who do not practise that religion or on those who belong to another religion may be justified under Article 9 §2 of the Convention. In that context, secular

Turkey's Parliament, and in the governing coalition, when in January 1998 it was dissolved, and its assets confiscated, by the Constitutional Court on the ground that the Party was a 'centre of activities contrary to the principle of secularism'. The decision was upheld 4:3 in the Third Section at Strasbourg in July 2001,[23] and reaffirmed unanimously by the Grand Chamber (seventeen judges) in February 2003.

The Strasbourg Court's grounds for upholding such drastic action were that the Refah Party had been sufficiently shown to advocate and intend the introduction of Islamic law, *sharia*, either for everyone or as part of a plural system of laws for citizens of different faiths, and that its leaders' statements about *jihad* did not clearly rule out resort to force to achieve its aims. Even in the absence of threats of force, both *sharia* and plural religiously based legal systems are in themselves, even if democratically adopted, inherently incompatible (so the Court finds) with the ECHR and the conceptions of democracy and the rule of law which it enshrines. The Grand Chamber also unanimously rejected the view of the dissenting judges (including the English judge) in the Third Section that dissolution was disproportionate to the danger and could safely await concrete steps to put the Refah Party's programme into effect by enacting it.

In the course of this, the Grand Chamber in *Refah* briefly restated the well-known thesis of Strasbourg jurisprudence: 'the State's duty of neutrality and impartiality is incompatible with any power on the State's part to assess the legitimacy of religious beliefs'.[24] But only if that thesis is read in an extremely refined and limited sense can it be regarded as compatible with what the Court (in Turkey and in Strasbourg) actually held and did in *Refah*. For *sharia*, not to mention quasi-*millet* legal pluralism and forcible *jihad*, can hardly be thought of as extraneous to the religion under consideration; and the finding that they are each and all simply incompatible with the ECHR is equivalent to an assertion of their illegitimacy. Moreover, these are findings about a particular religion, not all religions; for there is no reason to think that other significant religions today share any of these illegitimate tenets or projects, or any similar tenets or projects.

The Strasbourg Court's willingness—as shown by its actions—thus to discriminate between one faith and others made it easy for the Lords in *Begum* to reject an equality or non-discrimination argument which Miss Begum's counsel made a main part of her submissions on the (un)justifiability of the jilbab ban:

A school that favours some religious symbols but not others is also guilty of discrimination which is a wrong in itself. By refusing to allow the claimant to wear the jilbab the school

universities may regulate manifestation of the rites and symbols of the said religion by imposing restrictions as to the place and manner of such manifestation with the aim of ensuring peaceful co-existence between students of various faiths and thus protecting public order and the beliefs of others (see *Karaduman* v. *Turkey*, No. 16278/90, Commission decision of 3 May 1993, DR 74, p. 93).

[23] *Refah Partisi (No. 1)* v. *Turkey* (2002) 35 EHRR 3.
[24] *Refah Partisi (No. 2)* (n. 22 above), para. 91.

prevented her alone from expressing her particular religious belief while permitting others to express theirs. The exclusion treated the claimant and her religious beliefs less favourably than other pupils and that was contrary to Article 14 of the Convention.[25]

The Lords rejected this; they simply treated it as unarguable once a pressing social need had been shown, in relation to Article 9(2), for restricting the relevant manifestations of the particular religious belief in question.[26]

3. A Certain Religion's Unacceptable Political Purposes

In resolving the little local difficulty about jilbabs in Denbigh High School, the Lords accepted counsel's invitation to place much weight on the Strasbourg Court's *Sahin* decision on the wider but still limited question of headscarves in Turkish universities. But that decision in turn refers us, at its key points,[27] to *Refah*'s use of a similar principle of 'militant democracy'[28] to resolve great national

---

[25] *Begum*, 107 (Cherie Booth QC). As Richard McManus QC said in reply, the argument from Art. 14 had not been advanced in earlier phases of the proceedings (though, as Lord Bingham observes at para. 13, Miss Begum's solicitors had appealed to Art. 14, inter alia, in their initial statement of reasons why the school should take her back, a month after the initial sending-home), and none of the Lords' judgments consider it worthy of mention: a finding that restriction of religious rights is justified under Art. 9(2) is tantamount to a finding that the relevant discrimination in relation to religion (or that religion) is justified (or, to speak more closely in line with the way Art. 14 uses the word 'discrimination', is differential treatment without discrimination). Art. 14:

> 14. *Prohibition of discrimination.* The enjoyment of the rights and freedoms set forth in this Convention shall be secured without discrimination on any ground such as sex, race, colour, language, religion, political, or other opinion, national, or social origin, association with a national minority, property, birth, or other status.

[26] On the imperative need (for the sake of justice and respect for religious rights) to distinguish (discriminate) between particular religions, and on a recent plain albeit limited acknowledgement of this by the British Parliament, see Finnis, 'Religion and State' (n. 2 above), 124–7, quoting (125) the Equality Act 2006, s. 52(4)(g), which authorizes certain public decisions 'taken on the grounds ... (ii) that a religion or belief is not to be treated in the same way as certain other religions or beliefs'.

[27] *Refah* is cited by the Grand Chamber in *Sahin* (*No. 2*) in paras. 35, 107, 108 and most decisively in paras. 114–5.

[28] 'Militant democracy' is explained in the Third Section's summary of the Turkish Government's case:

> 62. The Government asserted that, when confronted with the risk which political Islam represented for a democratic regime based on human rights, that regime was entitled to take measures to protect itself from the danger. 'Militant democracy', in other words a democratic system which defended itself against all political movements which sought to destroy it, had been born as a result of the experience of Germany and Italy between the wars with fascism and national-socialism, two movements which had come to power after more or less free elections. In the Government's submission, militant democracy required political parties, its indispensable protagonists, to show loyalty to democratic principles, and accordingly to the principle of secularism. The concept of militant democracy and the possibility of repressing political groups which abused freedom of association and freedom of expression were set forth in the Constitutions of European States (for example, in Art. 18 and Provisional Art. XII of the Italian Constitution and Arts. 9 § 2, 18 and 21 § 2 of the German Basic Law).

issues. So it is easy to picture sensible British politicians or citizens finding much food for thought in *Refah*, when deliberating about great issues touching their own country.

For the findings and certain uncontested arguments in *Refah* have wide relevance. Recall the three grounds for dissolving Refah, the Prime Minister's political party:

> . . . Refah advocated [i] setting up a plurality of legal systems, introducing discrimination between individuals on the ground of their religious beliefs and functioning according to different religious rules for each religious community, in which [ii] sharia would be the applicable law for the Muslim majority of the country and/or the ordinary law. In addition, . . . [iii] Refah did not exclude the possibility of recourse to force in certain circumstances in order to oppose certain political programmes, or to gain power and retain it.[29]

The Government of Turkey, the Turkish Constitutional Court, the Third Section (including the dissenting judges), and the entire Grand Chamber all stressed that each of these policies is incompatible with democracy, the rule of law, and the ECHR;[30] that they are policies rooted in Islam itself; and that they represent a standing danger to any democratic state in which Muslims are sufficiently numerous to hope to impose their will on the political community. The Turkish Constitutional Court had considered them 'specific features of Islam'.[31] The Government of Turkey, observing that Turkey was 'the only Muslim country where there was a liberal democracy after the Western model,'[32] argued before the Third Section of the Strasbourg Court that:

> political Islam did not confine itself to the private sphere of relations between the individual and God but also asserted the right to organise the State and the community. In so doing, it showed the characteristics of a totalitarian regime. In order to attain its ultimate goal of replacing the existing legal order with sharia, political Islam used the method known as '*takiyye*', which consisted in hiding its beliefs until it had attained that goal.[33]

The phrase 'political Islam' may suggest that there is a non-political Islam, or that the politics in political Islam come from outside Islam. But such suggestions—often

---

[29] *Refah Partisi (No. 1)* (n. 23 above), para. 76 (internal numbering added).

[30] For the ways in which each of these policies of Refah is incompatible with democracy and the rule of law, see eg, *Refah Partisi (No. 1)*, ibid., para. 70.

[31] Ibid., para. 24.

[32] Ibid., para. 61. Even the dissenting judges in the Third Section held that Turkey 'remains the only State with a substantially Islamic population which adheres to the principles of a liberal democracy. The example provided by States governed by fundamentalist Islamic regimes underlines the risk to democracy posed by a departure from the secular ideal'. There are 57 states in the intergovernmental Organization of the Islamic Conference: over 40 of these have a Muslim majority and in a further seven, half the population is Muslim.

[33] Neither the Third Section nor the Grand Chamber made any finding about Islamic *takiyye* (a practice which had not been denied by the applicants), but each observed more broadly that political parties and movements may conceal their aims and profess their adherence to democracy and the rule of law until it is too late to prevent them overthrowing both: *Refah (No. 1)*, ibid., at paras. 48 and 80; *Refah (No.2)* (n. 22 above), para. 101.

conveyed by speaking of 'Islamism'[34]—find no support in the judgments of either chamber. The Third Section found that 'the establishment of a theocratic regime' was a possibility in Turkey, not only because of its past (which had included an 'Islamic theocratic regime')[35] but because of 'the fact that the great majority of its population are Muslims'.[36] In a passage adopted by the Grand Chamber:

... the Court considers that sharia, *which faithfully reflects the dogmas and divine rules laid down by religion, is stable and invariable*. Principles such as pluralism in the political sphere or the constant evolution of public freedoms have no place in it... a regime based on sharia... clearly diverges from Convention values, particularly with regard to its criminal law and criminal procedure, its rules on the legal status of women and the way it intervenes in all spheres of private and public life in accordance with religious precepts. [A] political party whose actions seem to be aimed at introducing sharia... can hardly be regarded as an association complying with the democratic ideal that underlies the whole of the Convention.[37]

As to the third ground for banning Refah, namely its leaders' threats to resort to violence and the use of force, the Turkish Government had characterized jihad as 'the most generalized and absolute violence', characteristic of all '"holy war"'.[38] The Grand Chamber gives a well-informed but straightforward interpretation of 'jihad':

... The Court considers that, whatever meaning is ascribed to the term 'jihad'... (*whose primary meaning is holy war and the struggle to be waged until the total domination of Islam in society is achieved*), there was ambiguity in the terminology used [in the speeches of Refah leaders] to refer to the method to be employed to gain political power. In all of these speeches the possibility was mentioned of resorting 'legitimately' to force in order to overcome various obstacles Refah expected to meet in the political route by which it intended to gain and retain power.[39]

Those intimidatory pressures for conformity which are a main ground for the headscarf ban in Turkey and the jilbab ban in Denbigh High School are often—and thus in any actual or anticipated instance may reasonably if not correctly be treated by public authorities as—early precursors of jihad.

4. Applying the Findings: Extreme Speech or Belated Warning?

Confronted by the grave warnings thus issuing from courts of great pan-European authority, citizens of countries whose Muslim population is increasing very

---

[34] Notice that, according to the dissenting judges in *Refah* (*No. 1*) n. 23 above, 'the Government in the present case indeed argue that it is a feature of Islamic politics to conceal one's true intentions and to achieve one's aims by surreptitious means'. In many circles it is *de rigueur* to replace 'Islamic' with 'Islamist' in making such a claim, but in *Refah* both Government and judiciary decline to muffle their point.

[35] *Refah Partisi* (*No. 1*), ibid., para. 76.　　[36] Ibid., para. 65.

[37] Ibid., para. 72 (emphasis added); *Refah Partisi* (*No. 2*), para. 123. The French version of the passage I have emphasized is at least as clear: 'la cour reconnaît que la *Charia*, reflétant fidèlement les dogmes et les règles divines édictées par la religion, présente un caractère stable et invariable.'

[38] *Refah Partisi* (*No. 1*), para. 63.　　[39] *Refah Partisi* (*No. 2*), para. 130 (emphasis added).

rapidly by immigration and a relatively high birth rate may ask themselves whether it is prudent, or just to the children and grandchildren of everyone in their country, to permit any further migratory increase in that population, or even to accept the presence of immigrant, non-citizen Muslims without deliberating seriously about a possible reversal—humane and financially compensated for and incentivized—of the inflow. Such thoughts, and the corresponding proposals that might be put forward for reflective deliberation, could not rightly be described as extreme, unless the judgments of both chambers of the Strasbourg Court in *Refah* are extreme. And such proposals themselves would, *mutatis mutandis*, be in line with the Turkish solution upheld so strongly in *Refah*: excluding from public political life the country's largest party and many of its leaders.

Yet when a small and peaceful demonstration was attempted in Brussels, on 11 September 2007, to urge 'Against the Islamization of Europe', the Secretary-General of the Council of Europe—the body responsible, together with the Strasbourg Court, for implementing the ECHR—issued a statement[40] condemning the demonstrators as bigots who endanger Europe:

The fact is that Europe and its values are indeed under threat, but the danger is not coming from Islam. Our common European values are undermined by bigots and radicals, both islamists[41] and islamophobes, who exploit fears and prejudice for their own political objectives.

The rights of freedom of speech and assembly, guaranteed by the Convention, 'should not be regarded as a licence to offend', he said, ignoring the many cases in which the Court has held, as it reiterated in *Refah*, that:

freedom of expression as enshrined in Article 10 is applicable, subject to paragraph 2, not only to 'information' or 'ideas' that are favourably received or regarded as inoffensive or as a matter of indifference, but *also to those that offend*, shock, or disturb (see, among many other authorities, the *Handyside* v. *United Kingdom* judgment of 7 December 1976, Series A no. 24, p. 23, § 49, and the *Jersild* v. *Denmark judgment* of 23 September 1994, Series A no. 298, p. 26, § 37).[42]

More disturbing than the demonstrators' urging that the Islamization of Europe be lawfully and peacefully halted is the Secretary-General's concluding declaration that such urging is vicious and immoral:

It is very important to remember that the freedom of assembly and expression can be restricted to protect the rights and freedoms of others, including the freedom of thought, conscience and religion. This applies to everyone in Europe including the millions of

---

[40] Council of Europe, Press Release 590 (2007) dated 11 September 2007, and headed '*Europe is threatened by bigots—not by Islam*. Statement by Terry Davis, Secretary General of the Council of Europe, on the march "Against the Islamisation of Europe" today in Brussels'.

[41] In no way, however, did the courts in *Refah Partisi* give comfort to the idea that 'islamism' is a product of 'fears and prejudice' rather than of religious dogmas: see *Refah* (*No. 2*) quoted at n. 37 above.

[42] Ibid., para. 89 (emphasis added).

Europeans of Islamic faith, who were the main target of today's shameful display of bigotry and intolerance.

These claims about targeting and bigotry cannot be sustained coherently without finding *Refah* a 'shameful display of bigotry and intolerance' and (mis)reading it as a ruling that Turkish law could rightly 'target' the millions of Turks of Islamic faith who supported the party and government dissolved for seeking to implement that faith's 'stable and invariable' and eminently political 'dogmas'.[43] The odious violence with which the Belgian police enforced the Mayor of Brussels' ban on the demonstration is matched by the extremism of the Secretary-General's statement.

To read *Refah* reflectively, aware of Europe's demographic trends and immigration policies, is to wonder whether the future of democracy and the rule of law, and of much else besides, is not imperilled here and now by the relentless defaming of all who try to initiate public deliberation about political and legislative action to counter, effectively, the bad and ever-increasingly unavoidable effects of those trends and policies. Such defamation is a kind of extreme speech as potent for ill as many other kinds, and certainly more dominant (and seemingly more reckless about its own long-term effects) than most.

[43] See the judgments of the Third Section and Grand Chamber quoted at n. 37 above.

PART V

INCITEMENT TO, AND GLORIFICATION OF, TERRORISM

22

Incitement to, and Glorification of, Terrorism

Eric Barendt

1. Introduction

The Terrorism Act 2006 introduced into UK law a new offence of encouragement of terrorism. Statements which are likely to be understood as a direct or indirect encouragement or other inducement to the commission of terrorist acts may be caught by the offence. One clause in the Act was particularly controversial: it provides that among the statements likely to be understood as indirectly encouraging an act of terrorism are those glorifying such acts, at least where members of the public would reasonably infer that they should emulate them. It was vigorously argued by critics of the Bill, including the Joint Committee of the House of Lords and House of Commons on Human Rights, that this clause was unacceptably vague;[1] it might on one view criminalize a speech, say, expressing understanding for suicide bombers from Gaza, when that speech could be understood as encouraging others to emulate that conduct. The government argued that a prosecution would rarely, if ever, be brought in those circumstances, but the Bill's opponents pointed out that the mere existence of the provision on the statute book would deter or 'chill' freedom of speech.

I want to examine here the free speech arguments relevant to the new offence of encouragement of terrorism, in particular whether the offence is compatible with the freedom of political speech required by a commitment to liberal democracy. I am less concerned with the particular 'glorification' offence; if the general encouragement offence is suspect on free speech grounds, as I think it is, it follows that the inclusion of glorification of terrorism among the statements caught by that general offence is wrong. Doubts about the compatibility of the encouragement offence with free speech principles are just that much stronger with regard to glorification. I am largely concerned with arguments of general principle, but will also examine how the new offence might fare in the United States, where the

---

[1] 'Counter-Terrorism Policy and Human Rights: Terrorism Bill and related matters', 3rd Report of Joint Committee on Human Rights 2005–6 (HL Paper 75-I, HC 561-I), paras. 27–8.

Supreme Court in *Brandenburg* v. *Ohio*[2] formulated a strong free speech protective rule to immunize extremist political speech from prosecution. In contrast, I am not concerned in this paper with the argument that the offence would not survive scrutiny before the European Court of Human Rights, or with the question whether the introduction of the offence was necessary, given other provisions in UK criminal law proscribing incitement to violence and criminal conduct.[3] These are important issues, which were fully considered by the Joint Committee on Human Rights in its examination of the Bill,[4] and again more recently when the Committee concluded that the offence did not satisfy the safeguards for freedom of expression implicit in the European Terrorism Convention.[5]

2. The Terrorism Act 2006

It is important to understand the scope of the offence of encouragement of terrorism introduced by section 1 of the 2006 Act.[6] The section applies to:

a statement that is likely to be understood by some or all members of the public to whom it is published as a direct or indirect encouragement or other inducement to them to the commission, preparation or instigation of acts of terrorism...

An offence is committed only if the person publishing the statement *intends* members of the public to be directly or indirectly encouraged by it to commit, prepare, or instigate terrorist acts, or is *reckless* whether members of the public will be so encouraged: section 1(2). As already mentioned, among the statements likely to be understood as indirectly encouraging terrorist acts are included statements which glorify the commission or preparation, whether in the past, in the future, or generally, of such acts, provided they are statements from which 'members of the public could reasonably be expected to infer that what is being glorified is being glorified as conduct that should be emulated by them in existing circumstances': section 1(3).[7] Other features of the offence are as follows:

1. How a statement is likely to be understood, and what members of the public could reasonably be expected to infer from it, are to be determined by regard to its contents and the circumstances in which it is published: section 1(4).

---

[2] 395 US 444 (1969).

[3] In *R* v. *El-Faisal* [2004] EWCA Crim 456, the Court of Appeal upheld the conviction for the offence of soliciting murder contrary to the Offences against the Person Act 1861 of a Muslim minister who had made taped speeches encouraging his listeners to kill the enemies of Islam, in particular Americans, Jews, and Hindus. No *particular* acts or victims were identified. The new offence of encouragement of terrorism presumably covers speech falling short of this sort of incitement or solicitation; otherwise it would be an unnecessary addition to the statute book.

[4] See n. 1 above, paras. 21–41.   [5] 1st Report of Session 2006–7, HL Paper 26, HC 247.

[6] The Act also creates a new offence of disseminating terrorist publications (s. 2) and contains provisions applying the offences under ss. 1 and 2 to Internet publications: s. 3.

[7] Glorification is defined as 'any form of praise or celebration': s. 20(2).

2. It is irrelevant (a) whether the statement is likely to be understood as encouraging *particular* acts of terrorism, rather than terrorist acts generally; and (b) whether any person is in fact encouraged to commit a terrorist offence: section 1(5).
3. There are defences where it is not proved that the publisher intended to encourage terrorist acts, viz., where the publisher was reckless. It is then a defence to show (a) that the statement did not represent his views, and (b) that it was clear that it did not express them: section 1(6).

In short, the offence is committed if a statement, assessed in relation to its content and the circumstances of its publication, is likely to be understood as encouraging terrorism, and if its maker or publisher intended to encourage members of the public to commit such offences or was reckless with regard to that effect. The significance of these tests or criteria will be discussed later;[8] they raise the difficult question whether it is compatible with free speech principles to proscribe expression which is understood, perhaps very reasonably, by the audience as encouraging terrorism (or some other offence), but which the speaker did not intend to bear that meaning. Further, not only need the prosecution not show that anyone was in fact encouraged by the statement to commit any terrorist offence, it need not show that the commission of such an offence was a *likely* consequence of its publication. It will be argued that this is a serious omission.[9]

3. The Encouragement of Terrorism and Freedom of Speech

How far should the general encouragement of terrorism be regarded in a liberal democracy as an exercise of freedom of speech? And insofar as it is, are there substantial reasons for proscribing it? We should first distinguish from the expression of general encouragement, or of a defence, of terrorism, the expression of a strong imperative to someone about to detonate a bomb or pull a trigger ('Kill him' or 'Slaughter these infidels'). The latter is so closely linked to the violent act that it should be characterized as conduct or action, rather than speech, and so falls altogether outside a freedom of speech principle. The expression is communicated immediately before the act, perhaps as an instruction to start it, so it seems right to treat it as part of the conduct itself. Alternatively, we could take the view that, although it is speech, it loses its immunity from regulation. As Mill said in a much quoted passage:[10]

An opinion that corn-dealers are starvers of the poor, or that private property is robbery ... may justly incur punishment when delivered orally to an excited mob assembled before the house of a corn dealer, or when handed about among the same mob in the form of a placard.

---

[8] See pp. 455–9 below.   [9] See pp. 458–9 below.
[10] J. S. Mill, *On Liberty and Other Essays* (Oxford: OUP, 1991), 62.

The important point here is that the speech in Mill's passage was made before 'an excited mob'; if the opinion had been circulated in other circumstances, it would have been covered by his free speech principle and could not have properly been prosecuted.

Mill also wrote, it should be remembered, that the instigation of tyrannicide should only be punished if the deed followed from the speech and a 'probable connection [was] established between the act and the instigation.'[11] Otherwise its advocacy should be treated as speech; it expressed the view that the murder of a tyrant is an act of civil war, not simply an assassination. Mill's point might be put this way: a general encouragement of terrorism should be regarded as a statement of political aspirations, or a challenge to conventional understandings of liberal democracy, rather than necessarily as a real incitement to terrorist atrocities or other criminal conduct. On this perspective, the encouragement of terrorism would certainly amount to an exercise of freedom of speech; or, in the language of freedom of speech analysis, should be treated as covered by a free speech or free expression principle.[12] We then need strong arguments to justify its proscription, for example, persuasive evidence to show that it does induce specific acts of terrorism.

Mill's point is reflected perhaps in the well-known distinction drawn by US courts between the abstract advocacy of insurrection or violence and the incitement to, or instigation of, a particular act of violence. The former may be treated as a legitimate exercise of political speech, while the latter can properly be proscribed as closely connected to violent or other criminal conduct. On this line of argument we might also distinguish, as Greenawalt does, between the public ideological encouragement of crime and private non-ideological solicitation.[13] The former is intended, or should be regarded, as a contribution to debate on important questions: 'Are our institutions really democratic?' and 'Is disorder, even violence, the only way to compel government to listen to grievances about its foreign policy?' In contrast, private solicitation intended only for a few ears, generally those of criminal conspirators, has no strong claim to protection as an exercise of free speech rights. This is particularly clear when the solicitation has no political or ideological content—the incitement is to commit a murder, say, for purely financial gain or for personal vengeance. I also think that the incitement in private by, say, a spiritual leader to a few of his followers to slaughter infidels does not engage freedom of speech: it can hardly be regarded as a contribution to public discourse, for it allows for no response or debate.[14] The democratic

---

[11] Ibid., footnote to pp. 20–1.

[12] For the distinction between the *coverage* and *protection* of a free speech clause, see F. Schauer, *Free Speech: A Philosophical Enquiry* (Cambridge: CUP, 1982), 89–92.

[13] *Speech, Crime, and the Uses of Language* (New York: OUP, 1989), 261–6.

[14] The extent to which private communications engage freedom of speech is a relatively neglected question: for a brief treatment, see E. Barendt, *Freedom of Speech* 2nd edn. (Oxford: OUP, 2005) 29–30.

justification for freedom of speech only applies to expression which can plausibly be seen as contributing to political debate or discourse. That may include some types of racist and other extremist speech, but hardly incitements to action delivered in private.

The general encouragement of terrorism or other criminal conduct should also be distinguished from remarks made in the course of an agreement to commit such acts. The latter do not engage freedom of speech. Speech involved in the planning and preparation of criminal offences should not be immune from general conspiracy laws, as they do not form part of any public discourse or debate. Nor generally should threats of violence be regarded as an exercise of freedom of speech; they are intended to intimidate, or are understood as intimidating, their audience, so they chill, rather than contribute, to public debate. However, as will be seen later, courts may find it difficult to draw clear lines between those threats and verbal conspiracies which fall outside the scope of freedom of speech, on the one hand, and the threats and other extreme speech which are regarded as part of legitimate public protest, on the other.[15]

4. Scanlon's Argument

One argument for treating the encouragement of terrorism as fully protected speech is that made by Thomas Scanlon in a classic article.[16] He argued there that government should not interfere with freedom of speech, if it does so in order to stop people forming false beliefs, or from acting on those beliefs, for example, the belief that it is legitimate to rob banks because they are conspiracies against the poor. He described this, rather oddly, as the Millian principle:[17]

There are certain harms which, although they would not occur but for certain acts of expression, nonetheless cannot be taken as part of a justification for legal restrictions on these acts. These harms are: (a) harms to certain individuals which consist in their coming to have false beliefs as a result of those acts of expression; (b) harmful consequences of acts performed as a result of those acts of expression, where the connection between the acts of expression and the subsequent harmful acts consists merely in the fact that the act of expression led the agent to believe (or increased their tendency to believe) those acts to be worth performing.

Scanlon's Millian principle would certainly cover the general encouragement of terrorism, at least in circumstances falling short of an immediate incitement to detonate a bomb or pull a trigger. It would preclude government from intro-ducing legislation to ban encouragement either because it thought it wrong for

---

[15] For relevant US cases on threats and criminal conspiracy, see pp. 453–61 below.

[16] 'A Theory of Freedom of Expression' (1972) 11 *Phil. & Pub. Aff.* 204, reprinted in R. M. Dworkin (ed.), *The Philosophy of Law* (Oxford: OUP, 1977), 153.

[17] Ibid., 213. Scanlon's description of his principle as 'Millian' is odd, because it does not argue that freedom of expression is important because it contributes to the discovery of truth.

the audience to form a belief that, all things considered, terrorism is (at least sometimes) justified, or even because it thought that the dissemination of these messages would make more likely the commission of terrorist atrocities. The law may punish those who commit such atrocities, but it would be wrong for the law to punish those who advocate, urge, or encourage them. Scanlon's argument, it should be noted, goes further than Mill's; on its basis it would always be wrong to proscribe the advocacy of tyrannicide, however clear the link between that advocacy and an actual instance of the act.

The arguments which might be made for this principle have rightly been found unconvincing.[18] First, the fact that, say, a bank-robber or terrorist may be punished for acting on his belief that his conduct is right does not mean that it is wrong also to punish those who have encouraged the conduct. It is counter-intuitive to conclude that a terrorist's decision to act entirely breaks any causal connection between the encouragement and the atrocity. Moreover, those encouraging terrorism surely share some moral responsibility for the atrocities they persuade others to commit. It would certainly be right to ascribe responsibility when the encouragement comes from preachers or other leaders in positions of authority vis-à-vis the people they are addressing, but those advocating a course of conduct still have some moral responsibility whatever their position. It is generally right, of course, to impose greater penalties on those actually committing the terrorist (or other criminal) acts, but that does not mean that others who encourage such conduct should be immune from liability.

The discussion in this last paragraph assumes that some act *has occurred* as a result of the encouragement; there is no knockdown argument for exculpating the persuaders in those circumstances. Is there a good argument, however, against banning expression which may persuade others to act, irrespective whether they in fact do so? Scanlon's argument is that such a ban would interfere with the autonomy of members of the audience to form their own judgement about the truth or falsity of the beliefs they are invited to consider, and in particular whether to comply with any laws which outlaw the conduct urged on them. The import of Scanlon's theory is that it would be wrong to criminalize the encouragement of terrorism, because the state would then have the ability to deprive its citizens of hearing arguments whether it is right for them to comply with the laws criminalizing terrorism. It would in his view be incompatible with individual autonomy to surrender a right to hear those arguments.

There are a number of difficulties with this part of Scanlon's argument. First, he was surely wrong to argue that the Millian principle is necessary to allow individuals to hear the case for breaking the law against terrorism. A ban on the encouragement of terrorism would certainly not deprive citizens of the opportunity to hear arguments that there is too much ill-considered legislation dealing with terrorism and that much of it should be repealed or challenged in the

---

[18] See in particular R. Amdur, 'Scanlon on Freedom of Expression' (1980) 9 *Phil. & Pub. Aff.* 287.

courts.[19] I doubt also whether it would deprive them of access to arguments that, all things considered, it is sometimes right to disobey the law, even the laws proscribing terrorism. It deprives them only of speech encouraging terrorism. Would an autonomous citizen necessarily object to that? Amdur has argued, I think rightly, that sometimes we might choose to surrender our autonomy or freedom to consider particular arguments, because we appreciate that we are not only speakers and listeners, but also the potential *victims* of dangerous speech.[20] Or we might consider that in some circumstances audiences are not to be trusted to consider properly extremist claims made to them and that speech in those circumstances should, therefore, be regulated or even proscribed. That argument might be applicable to many cases of hate speech, and certainly can be invoked to justify the regulation of speech encouraging terrorism; autonomous citizens might well choose, for example, to impose limits on what political (or religious) speakers can say to the public for fear that otherwise as potential members of an audience (or congregation) they, or least the more gullible among them, would be persuaded to engage in terrorist atrocities.

There are other shortcomings of the Millian principle, and Scanlon himself no longer endorses it. In a later article he has doubted whether unrestricted speech is always conducive to the ability of autonomous listeners to determine what beliefs to adopt or what courses of action are appropriate for them.[21] Arguably, they are unable, for example, to determine what to believe when advertisers make rival claims about the merits of different products, or perhaps even when politicians engage in saturation advertising on television. In the context of extremist speech urging the necessity of acts of terrorism, it could be said that some members of its likely audience are unable to assess its merits, either because they are not sufficiently exposed to relevant counter-arguments or because they have been brought up automatically to accept arguments made to them by their political or religious leaders. However, this point cannot be pressed too far. It could be employed to undermine any argument for freedom of political speech, because it can always be said that the people cannot be trusted properly to assess the claims made to them. Nevertheless, Scanlon's argument does not provide a strong basis for the protection of speech encouraging terrorism; it is very doubtful if we surrender our autonomy by outlawing the dissemination of such extremist expression.

5. A Speaker's Right to Encourage Terrorism?

Ronald Dworkin criticized Scanlon's argument for freedom of expression on the ground that it gave more weight to the interests of the listeners or audience than

---

[19] See H. H. Wellington, 'On Freedom of Expression' (1978) 88 *Yale L.J.* 1105, 1124–5.
[20] See n. 18 above, 299.
[21] 'Freedom of Expression and Categories of Expression' (1979) 40 *U. Pitt. L. Rev.* 519.

those of the speaker.[22] On another perspective, freedom of expression is primarily concerned to protect the rights of speakers to participate in a functioning democracy, as well as perhaps to enable them to express themselves artistically and in other ways to promote their own self-development. So it may be argued in this context that the proscription of encouragement of terrorism improperly infringes the rights of extremist speakers to contribute to public discourse. They are not allowed to make their argument that democracy is so rotten that it should be attacked, or that state institutions may legitimately be destroyed as a step towards its radical reconstitution. If they are denied that right, then they have no duty to comply with the general law enacted and enforced by those institutions. Now this argument can be made plausibly by other extremist speakers, for example, the peddlers of hate speech who argue against racial integration or express hostility to religious groups. It is much more difficult, however, for the advocates of terrorism to claim these same foundational free speech rights as a condition of their acceptance of the obligation to obey democratically enacted laws. Advocates of terrorism do not consider that they have any obligation to obey these laws, even if they are allowed to speak freely. They are not even claiming a right to participate in democratic debate or to contribute to public discourse; indeed, they deny the point of this type of discourse, which seeks to bring about change through the democratic process, not by force. The argument that a terrorist has a free speech right to assert the value of his style of life can also be summarily rejected.[23] We must look elsewhere for plausible arguments for holding that encouragement of terrorism is covered by freedom of political speech.

6. Other Arguments

The failure of these important arguments does not mean, however, that we should not have some reservations about the proscription of speech encouraging terrorism in circumstances which fall well short of incitement to commit an imminent offence. At the very least, it must be conceded that general encouragement or advocacy is hard to distinguish from political speech. For example, when demonstrators in London marching against the Danish cartoons carried placards displaying death threats to infidels, they were surely expressing their strong political views, albeit violently. The threats were not targeted at any particular individuals and did not urge any specific assassination. On one view, therefore, they were less of an incitement to violence than are the chants, commonly heard at football matches, directed at specific footballers, or referees. Nevertheless, one demonstrator on the cartoons protest march was successfully

---

[22] See his Introduction to *The Philosophy of Law* (n. 16 above), 14–6.

[23] Joseph Raz's arguments for free expression as validating different forms of life does not apply to 'ways of life . . . without redeeming features'. See 'Free Expression and Personal Identification' (1991) 11 *OJLS* 303, 319.

prosecuted for incitement to murder.[24] The possibility that this case was singled out for prosecution as a result of the widespread public disquiet at the reaction of some Muslims to the publication of the Danish cartoons provides another reason for reluctance to countenance criminalizing this speech: our distrust of government in the free speech context.[25] To extend the scope of the criminal law by proscribing speech encouraging terrorism is dangerous, because it enables the government to prosecute extreme political speech it dislikes, perhaps for very good reason, while not intervening in other circumstances where it is more sympathetic to the speech. A further reason for disquiet is that the Terrorist Act offence may well exercise some 'chilling effect' on freedom of political speech which the government accepts is not caught by the new law.

There is also, I think, a real public interest in hearing extremist views of this kind, not because we might consider them right, or might wish at some stage to act on them, as Scanlon argued, but because it is vital for us to know that they are held and held sufficiently strongly that some people wish to communicate them to others. We also need to know who holds these views and why they are held. We can only respond intelligently to undesirable extremist attitudes, and remove or reduce the reasons why they are held, if we allow them, to some extent, to be disseminated. Moreover, the argument that the appropriate response to bad speech is not proscription, but the communication of better speech, is not an empty slogan.[26] Although there are some circumstances, for example, a public emergency, when this does not apply, normally it is the most prudent course; the danger of proscription is that public speech will be driven underground and will then resurface when it is too late to counter it.

The question then is how the line should be drawn between general encouragement of criminal conduct on the one hand, and incitement on the other. The former is covered by a freedom of speech or expression principle, while the latter either falls outside it altogether or, even if covered by this principle, we can easily accept that it nonetheless may be proscribed. United States courts used to draw a distinction between abstract advocacy and incitement, but as Holmes J. said in his dissent in *Gitlow* v. *New York*,[27] all ideas are incitements: '[t]he only difference between the expression of an opinion and an incitement in the narrower sense is the speaker's enthusiasm for the result'. It is unhelpful, or perhaps even futile, to attempt to distinguish in abstract or general terms between the *advocacy* of violence or terrorism and its *incitement*. The law should provide criteria which enable distinctions to be drawn, and these should respect, so far as possible, both

---

[24] Umran Javed was convicted of soliciting murder when he shouted 'Bomb, bomb USA' and 'Bomb, bomb Denmark' during his speech outside the Danish Embassy, see <http://www.timesonline.co.uk/tol/news/uk/article1289958.ece> (last accessed 26 May 2008).

[25] For a short discussion of this argument, see Barendt (n. 14 above), 21–3.

[26] See the judgment of Brandeis J. in *Whitney* v. *California* 274 US 357, 375–8 (1927) for the classic exposition of this argument.

[27] 268 US 652, 673 (1925).

the values of free political speech and the imperative requirement to protect the public from acts of violence and terrorism with which extreme speech may be intimately associated.

7. *Brandenburg* v. *Ohio*

Some criteria are suggested by the decision of the Supreme Court in *Brandenburg* v. *Ohio*,[28] the leading case on subversive political speech in the United States. Brandenburg, an organizer of the Ku Klux Klan in Ohio, had been convicted under the state Criminal Syndicalism law of advocating 'the necessity, or propriety of crime, violence, or *unlawful methods of terrorism* as a means of accomplishing political reform . . .' (my emphasis). At a poorly attended rally held on a farm, Brandenburg declared that although the Klan was not a 'revengent organization', it was possible that 'there might have to be some revengence taken' if the federal government 'continues to suppress the white, Caucasian race . . .'. He then stated that the Klan would be 'marching on Congress' on 4 July. The Ohio appellate courts affirmed his conviction for the statutory offence. The Supreme Court in a per curiam opinion held the law unconstitutional on its face, deriving from recent decisions.

the principle that the constitutional guarantees of free speech and free press do not permit a State to forbid or proscribe advocacy of the use of force or of law violation except where such advocacy is directed to inciting or producing imminent lawless action and is likely to incite or produce such action.[29]

The derivation of this principle from decisions of the Court in the 1950s and 1960s is controversial. Arguably, it is based on a generous interpretation of the Supreme Court's decision in *Dennis* v. *US*,[30] where it had upheld the conviction of leaders of the Communist Party for the offence of advocating the overthrow of the government, even though there was no evidence that they were in any position to bring about such a revolution. Moreover, its relationship to the 'clear and present danger' test first formulated by Holmes J. in his judgment for the Court in *Schenk* v. *US*[31] is unclear. In separate concurring judgements in *Brandenburg*, Black and Douglas JJ repudiated the 'clear and present danger' test as having no proper place in First Amendment jurisprudence; it was too easy, in their view, for it to be manipulated to justify the proscription of speech on the ground that its dissemination created a clear risk of an imminent threat to state security or public

[28] 395 US 444 (1969).   [29] Ibid., 447.
[30] 341 US 494 (1951). But in later cases the Court had struck down convictions for comparable offences, finding only 'abstract advocacy' of abstract political doctrine creating no danger of violence: *Yates* v. *US* 354 US 298 (1957) and *Noto* v. *US* 367 US 290 (1961).
[31] 249 US 47, 52 (1919).

order. Whatever these difficulties, the test has been applied by the Supreme Court in subsequent cases and remains authoritative.[32]

The Court's decision assumes that all speech inciting force or lawless action is covered by the First Amendment guarantee of free speech, and formulates a test to delimit the circumstances in which it may be proscribed without violating that guarantee. In all other circumstances the expression of such advocacy or incitement is protected. The *Brandenburg* formula represents, it has been said, a compromise between two positions:[33] that which would concede to the state power to ban any speech which it regards as dangerous to its security or good order, and that urged by Scanlon's Millian principle, under which the state is denied any power to ban speech because the public may be persuaded to act on it. Compromise may be a pejorative term.[34] But it is possible to take a more benevolent view of tests which attempt to balance freedom of speech against other important public goals. Indeed, the adoption of some such tests seems inevitable except to a free speech absolutist. The question then is whether the elements in the formula are justifiable in principle and can be applied relatively easily in practice. I propose to examine four aspects of the *Brandenburg* formula, applying them to the offence created by the UK Terrorism Act 2006; I then add a few remarks about its application to acts of terrorism, as distinct from other violence or public disorder.

(i) The Words Used by the Speaker or Writer

The opinion in *Brandenburg* refers to the *advocacy* of the use of force or of law infringement. But it is doubtful whether the Court meant that only the use of specific words explicitly advocating or urging the use of force or law violation could be held criminal, compatibly with the First Amendment guarantee of freedom of speech. Any speech which is understood by its audience as inciting the use of force or law violation might be held a criminal offence, provided the *Brandenburg* criteria are satisfied. As Larry Alexander argues, there is no justification for exempting from the criminal law speech which incites violence or terrorism through the use of irony or by providing information simply because it uses these means to urge on the audience to commit these crimes, rather than the conventional language of explicit incitement or solicitation.[35] Marc Antony's ironic funeral oration, to take a familiar example, clearly solicited reprisals against

---

[32] *Hess* v. *Indiana* 414 US 105 (1973); *NAACP* v *Claiborne Hardware Co.* 458 US 886 (1982), discussed below at p. 460. The Court also applied a similar approach in a case decided the same year as *Brandenburg*, when it held the conviction of the defendant for making a joking remark about shooting the President incompatible with the First Amendment: *Watts v US* 394 US 705 (1969).

[33] L. Alexander, 'Incitement and Freedom of Speech' in D. Kretzmer and F. K. Hazan (eds.), *Freedom of Speech and Incitement against Democracy* (Hague: Kluwer, 2000) 101, 116.

[34] Ibid., 116 describes the *Brandenburg* Court opinion as a 'non-principled compromise'.

[35] Ibid., 106.

the assassins of Julius Caesar.[36] It is for this reason that I have no particular quarrel with the inclusion of 'glorification' of terrorism as among the statements which may be understood as indirectly encouraging terrorist acts. If the celebration of acts of terrorist violence is understood by listeners as encouraging them to emulate them, in circumstances where it is also likely that they will soon commit further terrorist acts, then there is no reason of principle why a speaker glorifying the acts should not be held as guilty as a speaker using more direct language. Similarly, it is right to penalize a defendant for making threats which put the targeted victims in fear for their life, whether or not he articulated the threats explicitly or expressed them indirectly through posting notices indicating that they would be treated in the same way as others who had been shot.[37]

(ii) Advocacy Directed to Inciting or Producing Unlawful Action

One interpretation of the Supreme Court's *Brandenburg* opinion is that it introduced a constitutional requirement that the advocacy must be *intended* to incite or bring about violence or other unlawful action for the incitement offence to be compatible with the First Amendment. But it has been pointed out that this would run counter to principles developed in other areas of free speech juris-prudence where the intention of the speaker is not decisive;[38] the assessment, for example, whether hard core pornography is 'obscene' and so outside the coverage of the First Amendment does not depend on the writer's or artist's intention, but on whether the publication appeals to a prurient interest in sexual matters, portrays such conduct in a patently offensive way and lacks serious merit. These are objective tests. The intention of the writer might at most be a factor in applying them to the publication; he would, and should, not succeed in a free speech argument merely by establishing that he published shocking sexually explicit images with the intention of provoking vigorous public debate on the scope of state pornography laws. Nor would, or should, someone charged with incitement to terrorism or other violence be able to escape liability by arguing, however persuasively, that he intended the incitement as a joke, or that he did not think anyone would take his advocacy seriously, though they in fact did so.

The offence in the UK Terrorism Act attracted criticism because it was not limited to the intentional encouragement of terrorist acts, but also criminalized statements likely to be understood as encouraging such acts, where the author was 'reckless as to whether members of the public will be directly or indirectly

---

[36] *Julius Caesar,* Act III, Scene ii, 79ff. The example apparently troubled commentators on early free speech jurisprudence: see G. Gunther, 'Learned Hand and the Origins of First Amendment Doctrine: Some Fragments of History' (1975) 27 *Stan. L. Rev.* 719, 773.

[37] See *Planned Parenthood of the Columbia/Williamette Inc* v. *American Coalition of Life Activists* 290 F.3d 1058 (9th Cir, 2002), discussed below.

[38] F. Schauer, 'Intentions, Conventions, and the First Amendment: the Case of Cross-Burning' (2003) *Sup. Ct. Rev.* 197, 216–24. Also see n. 33 above, 107–9.

encouraged...' to commit them: section 1(2)(b)(ii). As the Joint Committee on Human Rights pointed out, this does not even require subjective recklessness:[39] someone might be convicted, it seems, even if it never occurred to him that the readers of his pamphlet might be encouraged to perpetrate terrorist acts. That may be very undesirable as a matter of criminal law, but I am not sure that we should raise freedom of speech objections to the provision.

(iii) The Requirement of Imminent Unlawful Action

The requirement that the advocacy be directed to inciting or producing *imminent* lawless action has been followed by the Supreme Court in a later case.[40] There are perhaps similar requirements in comparable areas of English law. For example, under the UK Public Order Act 1986, to prove an offence of the use of threatening, abusive, or insulting words, with intent to provoke violence, or in such a way that the other is likely to fear it, the prosecution must show that *immediate* violence is feared or provoked.[41] The strict liability rule in contempt of court law only applies when the publication—for example, a press report discussing the criminal record of someone facing trial—creates a *substantial risk* of serious prejudice to the legal proceedings.[42] Courts have frequently held that there is no substantial risk when proceedings are not due to take place for a number of months.[43] That is similar to a requirement of relative imminence. Recently, the House of Lords has held that the police have no common law power to detain demonstrators and stop them proceeding to the place of protest, because they fear a breach of the peace or disorder as a real possibility.[44] It must be imminent: 'it was wholly disproportionate to restrict [the applicant's] exercise of her rights [to freedom of expression and assembly] because she was in the company of others some of whom might, at some time in the future, breach the peace'.[45] In all these cases the English courts emphasized that the danger must be relatively imminent in time; it is however difficult to disentangle the part played by this factor from the theoretically separate consideration whether the conduct at issue was likely to bring about the danger.

An imminence requirement can be justified for two reasons. First, the advocacy of disorder, even terrorism, at some unspecified, perhaps indefinite, time in the

---

[39] See n. 1 above, paras. 30–3.
[40] *Hess* v. *Indiana* 414 US 105 (1973), where the Court reversed a state court conviction for disorderly conduct of a demonstrator who had said: 'We'll take the fucking street later...' One reason for the reversal was that the words did not clearly indicate an intention to produce imminent disorder, rather than to act at some unspecified future time.
[41] *R* v. *Horseferry Road Metropolitan Stipendiary Magistrate, ex p Siadatin* [1991] 1 QB 260, DC.
[42] Contempt of Court Act 1981, s. 2(2).
[43] *Attorney-General* v. *News Group Newspapers Ltd* [1987] 1 QB 1, 16; *Attorney-General* v. *ITN* [1995] 2 All ER 370, 382–3.
[44] *R (on the application of Laporte)* v. *Chief Constable of Gloucestershire* [2007] 2 All ER 529.
[45] Ibid., para. 55 per Lord Bingham.

future is not sufficiently closely connected with any likely or intended act; abstract advocacy of this sort—the preaching of revolution by academic Marxists is an obvious example—has more in common with archetypical political speech, than it does with the incitement to commit a specific act of terrorism or insurrection immediately or even in the near future. The requirement is therefore closely linked with that of the likelihood that the encouragement will bring about such an act—to be considered shortly. Of course, there may be nice and difficult questions how imminent the action advocated need be to satisfy the requirement, but that surely does not mean that it should be abandoned.

The second reason for the imminence requirement is that the advocacy or encouragement of terrorism can be countered in the long term by other speech: the advocacy of other courses of action, the dissuasion of prospective terrorists from their course. Alexander rightly points out that counter-speech may be ineffective, or that in some circumstances it will be unclear to whom it should be addressed.[46] He is unsure that it is appropriate to treat the requirement as one of free speech law, rather than the criminal law. Yet, in conjunction with the first reason considered in the previous paragraph, this argument does make a powerful free speech point. We know that inflammatory, seditious, or racist speech may all be dangerous—by, for instance, undermining our support for democracy and its institutions or by promoting distrust and suspicion, and eventually violence, between different racial groups. But we tolerate such speech, because we believe that it can be countered by other speech. Implicit in the free speech argument from democracy is the conviction that the democratic process ensures that in the long term better, more liberal, ideas will prevail over those advocating its destruction. We are confident that over a period of years public discourse will not destroy our democratic institutions. So it should be for speech encouraging terrorism, in the absence of evidence that it is likely to cause a terrorist atrocity.

(iv) Likely to Incite or Produce Unlawful Action

This fourth aspect of the *Brandenburg* formula is crucial. It ensures that the publisher of ineffective, idle threats, or incitements cannot be convicted, if, irrespective of the words he used, his statements are unlikely to encourage anyone to commit terrorist or other unlawful acts.[47] In United States constitutional language, unless the advocacy is likely to incite unlawful action, it creates no clear and present danger and it would infringe freedom of speech to penalize its communication. The insistence on the objective likelihood of disorder is a feature of other areas of US free speech jurisprudence and is reflected in decisions in other

---

[46] See n. 33 above, 109–10.

[47] It is incompatible with the First Amendment to penalize [empty threats] to kill the President: *Watts* v. *US* 394 US 705 (1969).

jurisdictions on public order offences.[48] But it is not an element of the Terrorism Act offence of encouraging terrorism. As discussed above, the writer of a pamphlet likely to be read as encouraging terrorism could be convicted of the offence, provided he had the necessary intention or was reckless with regard to how it would be understood, even if it was circulated only to a small handful of people and was quite unlikely to persuade them to commit terrorist offences.[49] As the Joint Committee on Human Rights pointed out in its recent report on the Council of Europe Convention, the lack of a requirement of danger omits an important safeguard which reduces the inhibiting effect of the new offence on freedom of expression.[50]

There is no obvious explanation for the omission of this requirement. Perhaps the government takes the view that any encouragement of terrorism necessarily creates a risk that the offence will be committed. On this view, the speech itself constitutes a clear and present danger, and it is foolish to ask for more. Even if this view is tenable now in the climate of fear engendered by 9/11 and the London bombs in July 2005, it could not be held if and when the terrorist threats recede. As Hans Linde argued in his classic article on the *Brandenburg* case,[51] laws criminalizing incitement to subversion may become more or less constitutional vis-à-vis the First Amendment as the dangers which they are designed to prevent appear or recede.

8. The *Brandenburg* Principle Inapplicable to Threats and Conspiracy

It was argued earlier that speech encouraging terrorism should be distinguished from speech disseminated in the course of a criminal conspiracy and from threats to commit violence, as well as from a clear incitement to commit immediate violence ('Kill Him' or 'Slaughter the Infidels').[52] While there are good reasons for holding the former covered by a free speech clause, serious threats of violence and conspiracies to commit it are not entitled to immunity from regulation, even though they take the form of speech. These distinctions are reflected in leading US case law. In the *Planned Parenthood* case,[53] a 6–5 majority of the Ninth

---

[48] See the Australian High Court decision in *Coleman* v. *Power* (2004) 220 CLR 1, and the discussion in n. 14 above, 296–8.

[49] See the discussion at pp. 446–7 above, and n. 1 above, para. 34.

[50] See n. 5 above, paras. 35–7.

[51] '"Clear and Present Danger" Reexamined: Dissonance in the *Brandenburg* Concerto' (1970) 22 *Stan. L. Rev.* 1163.

[52] See p. 447 above.

[53] *Planned Parenthood of the Columbia/Williamette Inc* v. *American Coalition of Life Activists* 290 F.3d 1058 (9th Cir, 2002). Also see the less controversial decision of the 2nd Circuit Court of Appeals in *US* v. *Kelner* 534 F.2d 1020 (1976), in which the defendant was convicted for uttering threats of violence at a press conference (such as 'We have people . . . who intend to make sure that Arafat and his lieutenants do not leave this country alive') just before Yasser Arafat landed in New York.

Circuit Court of Appeals, sitting en banc, held that actions of a militant anti-abortion activists organization in publicly disclosing on posters and websites the names and addresses of abortion providers amounted to true 'threats of force', and were unprotected by the First Amendment. The Court distinguished *Brandenburg* on the ground that the activists had named individual abortion providers; here there was an implicit threat to their life, as the defendants must have appreciated that other named doctors on similar posters and sites had been killed. The majority of the Court rightly characterized the notices as threats of violence, rather than as a form of strong public protest. It also distinguished the decision of the Supreme Court in *NAACP* v. *Claiborne Hardware Co.*,[54] where black leaders had called for an economic boycott of white traders in protest against racial discrimination. Although the speech of one of the leaders suggested that strong measures would be taken against blacks who did not participate in the boycott, the Court did not regard it as falling outside the *Brandenburg* principle; the language amounted to a strong plea for black unity, and violence occurring weeks or months later could not be regarded as imminent.

The First Amendment does not give defendants any immunity from criminal conspiracy laws, even though their conspiracy takes the form of a verbal or written agreement and is therefore literally speech. The First Circuit Court of Appeals applied this principle in the controversial *Spock* case, where the defendants had been charged with solicitation of, and conspiracy to counsel and abet, refusal to serve in the armed forces during the war in Vietnam.[55] The Court distinguished between the general expression of moral support for those refusing to register for the draft on the one hand, and on the other an agreement to encourage illegal draft evasion, which the court held not to be an exercise of free speech rights. This decision was followed in the *Rahman* case[56] where the defendants had been convicted of conspiracy and other offences for plotting to bomb office buildings and to assassinate the President of Egypt and Rabbi Meir Kahane, a prominent extreme Zionist. It was immaterial that the role of the leading defendant, Abdel Rahman, a Muslim preacher, had taken the form of verbal instructions to his followers. He was not immune from prosecution, because he participated in the conspiracy 'through the medium of political speech or religious preaching'.[57] The Court considered it was immaterial in this context whether the words had been uttered in public or in private.

The courts are right to hold serious threats and verbal conspiracies unprotected by freedom of speech, because the expression in these contexts cannot plausibly be

---

[54] 458 US 886 (1982). Stevens J. for the Court generously characterized a speech promising that black people who did not respect the boycott would 'have their necks broken' as emotionally charged rhetoric which did not exceed the limits of the *Brandenburg* test.

[55] *US* v. *Spock* 416 F.2d 165 (1st Cir, 1969). The Court reversed the defendants' convictions, holding their speech amounted to moral advocacy and was not part of a criminal conspiracy.

[56] *US* v. *Rahman* 189 F.3d 88 (2nd Cir, 1999).

[57] Ibid., 117.

treated as a contribution to the public discourse which lies at the foundation of a participatory democracy. Of course, it may be difficult to distinguish sometimes between hyperbole amounting to no more than an empty threat in the course of vigorous political protest from a true threat which puts its victims in real fear for their lives, safety, or property. But generally the context in which the speech is communicated or disseminated will indicate clearly enough on which side of the line it falls: factors such as the language used, the primary audience addressed, and the position of the speaker with regard to that audience are all relevant. It was relevant in *Rahman*, for example, that the preacher urging the assassinations had the power to dispense fatwas, so it was hard to characterize these urgings as mere persuasion. In contrast, a general encouragement of terrorism, including assassination of political leaders, where no *immediate* acts are incited, should be regarded as a contribution to political or public discourse, and so falls under a freedom of speech or expression principle. That at least is what *Brandenburg* and later US jurisprudence suggests.

9. The Relevance of *Terrorism*

The Terrorism Act 2006 singles out statements encouraging *terrorism* for proscription. Comparable statements encouraging, but not inciting, ordinary violence, or burglary, or other criminal conduct, are not caught by the criminal law. If they were, it was unnecessary to introduce any provisions designed to make special provision for speech inducing terrorist offences. In the context of our general commitment to freedom of speech, is it justifiable to impose more stringent restrictions on expression which encourages terrorism than those imposed on expression encouraging other criminal conduct? Leaving aside the political reasons for the introduction of this legislation—to reassure an anxious public and to persuade it that the government is in charge of affairs—one argument can be made in support of especially tight free speech restrictions in this context. In the leading US case on subversive speech before *Brandenburg*, a plurality of the Supreme Court approved the version of 'clear and present danger' adopted by Learned Hand J. in the lower court:

In each case [courts] must ask whether the gravity of the 'evil', discounted by its improbability, justifies such invasion of free speech as is necessary to avoid the danger.[58]

This is clearly a gloss on the 'clear and present danger' test as formulated by Holmes J, and a gloss which dilutes it considerably.[59] Government can always argue that some dangers are so serious that, even making allowance for their

[58] *US* v. *Dennis* 183 F.2d 201, 212 (2nd Cir, 1950), affirmed by the Supreme Court, 341 US 494, 510 (1951) per Vinson CJ.
[59] For commentary, see B. Schwartz, 'Holmes versus Hand: Clear and Present Danger or Advocacy of Unlawful Action?' (1994) *Sup. Ct. Rev.* 209, 231–6.

improbability, it is right to suppress all speech which might contribute to bringing them about. The argument is not, however, a silly one, and at times of a real pressing emergency it should be accepted.

The difficulty in accepting this argument as a justification for the offence of encouraging terrorism is the broad definition of 'terrorism' in UK legislation;[60] it encompasses, among other things, the use or threat of serious damage to property, as well as serious violence against a person, which is designed to influence the government of any country, and which is made for the purpose of advancing any political, religious, or ideological cause. It is immaterial whether the targeted government is democratic or authoritarian. Thus the advocacy of tyrannicide, allowed by Mill unless it was clearly linked to the actual act,[61] would clearly be caught by the new offence introduced by the 2006 enactment; that would even be the case if the assassination was thought necessary to the introduction of a new, democratic, regime.[62] It is hard to believe that such advocacy, plainly regarded as an exercise of liberty of speech by Mill, is outlawed in the United Kingdom 150 years after the publication of his famous essay. But it is, and that should at the least make all democrats or libertarians uneasy.

---

[60] Terrorism Act 2000, s. 1, applied to the offences under the Terrorism Act 2006 by s. 20 of the later legislation: see C. Walker, 'The Legal Definition of "Terrorism" in United Kingdom Law and Beyond' (2007) *P.L.* 331, 337–41.

[61] See p. 448 above. It should be noted that Mill considered that only the targeted government (not presumably that in London) was entitled to take proceedings against the speaker who advocated the assassination.

[62] *R* v. *F (Terrorism)* [2007] 2 All ER 193, CA: no defence to a prosecution for an offence under the Terrorism Act 2000 that act of terrorism at issue would be directed at Libya, an authoritarian regime. The same principle would apply to a prosecution for the encouragement offence under the 2006 Act.

23

The Terrorism Act 2006: Discouraging Terrorism

Tufyal Choudhury

1. Introduction

The United Kingdom faces a serious threat of terrorist attack from 'home-grown' and international sources, but the scale of the threat and its likely duration are unknowable to the general public. The security services can identify 2000 individuals who pose a direct threat to national security and public safety and warn of the 'radicalisation, grooming and indoctrination' by terrorists of children as young as 15 to carry out attacks.[1] In proposing new laws directed at proscribing speech that encourages acts of terrorism the Home Secretary, Charles Clarke MP, cited fears of growing violent radicalization:

[The 7 July 2005 terrorist attacks in London] indicate that there are people in this country who are susceptible to the preaching—and I do not use that in the religious sense—of an argument or a message that terrorism is a worthy thing, a thing to be admired, a thing to be celebrated and then act on the basis of that . . . What this Bill is about is trying to make that more difficult, that transition from people encouraging, glorifying to then an act being undertaken.[2]

During parliamentary debate of the legislation the government emphasized the ideological nature of the threat the UK faced:

It is not driven by poverty, social exclusion or racial justice. Those who attacked London in July and those who have been engaged in or committed the long list of previous terrorist atrocities were not the poor and the dispossessed. They were, for the most part, well educated and prosperous . . . [I]deas drive those people forward.[3]

---

[1] R. Norton-Taylor, 'Al-Qaida recruiting teenagers to attack targets in Britain, warns MI5 chief', *The Guardian*, 6 November 2007, <http://www.guardian.co.uk/uk/2007/nov/06/alqaida.politics> (last accessed 31 May 2008).

[2] Draft Terrorism Bill 2005: Oral evidence, Tuesday 11 October 2005 HC (2005-6) 515-I Q3.

[3] Hansard HC Vol. 438 Col. 325 (26 October 2005).

They drew particular attention to the role of free speech in giving oxygen to ideas that lead to violent radicalization:

We should not ignore the contributory role that radical texts and extremist pamphlets have in radicalisation. They serve to propagate and reinforce the extremist and damaging philosophies which attempt to justify and explain the motivations of terrorists. We should not underestimate the role that such literature can have in radicalising vulnerable and susceptible young people, particularly changing Muslims from law-abiding members of the community to potential terrorists.[4]

The government argued that new offences relating to the encouragement of terrorism were needed to, 'deal with those who . . . contribute to the creation of a climate in which impressionable people might believe that terrorism was acceptable'.[5] Its principle legal response to this, in section 1 of the Terrorism Act 2006, is to make it an offence for a person to publish statements that directly or indirectly encourage or induce a person to the commission, preparation, or instigation of acts of terrorism. These new 'encouragement offences' constitute a significant restriction on the exercise of the fundamental right of free expression. Its threat to free speech arises not only from specific prohibitions and prosecutions but also the wider chilling effect on expression. Of course, freedom of speech is not an absolute right. However, any interference with such rights should be drawn narrowly and to the extent strictly required to meet its purpose. The centrality of free speech to liberal democratic society requires that less restrictive responses are exhausted before restrictions on free speech are introduced.

This chapter examines the potential contribution the new offence might make to the government's desired aim of preventing violent radicalization. It looks at the efficacy of the legislation in two respects: firstly, the role that the impugned statements play in the radicalization process; and, secondly, the potential for the criminalization of such statements to be counter-productive and undermine the government's broader counterterrorism strategy. It is argued that radicalization is largely a private process. Public statements that encourage acts of terrorism may contribute to this process but are not central to it. Furthermore, the provisions in the legislation that aim to proscribe such statements are drafted with a degree of breadth and vagueness that increases the risks of the legislation becoming counterproductive. The uncertainty surrounding the scope of the new offences and the discretion needed to enforce the legislation in a climate of distrust and fear between parts of the Muslim community and public institutions will reinforce perceptions of discrimination and unjust enforcement of counter-terrorism laws, which in turn will undermine the broader counterterrorism strategy.

---

[4] Hansard HL Vol. 677 Col. 551 (17 January 2006).
[5] Hansard HC Vol. 438 Col. 334 (26 October 2005).

2. The CONTEST Strategy

CONTEST, the name given to the government's overarching counterterrorism strategy, provides a wider policy context for understanding the specific provisions of the Terrorism Act 2006. This is a multi-dimensional strategy corresponding to the multi-faceted nature of terrorism. The strategy has four strands—Prevention, Pursuit, Protection and Preparedness.[6] *Prevention* takes in long-term goals, such as working to reduce tendencies leading to 'radicalisation', for instance through helping resolve international disputes which terrorists can exploit; addressing issues of inequality, discrimination, and social exclusion, which 'strengthens society and its resistance to terrorism';[7] fighting the 'battle of ideas';[8] deterring those who facilitate terrorism and those who encourage others to become terrorists, thus 'changing the environment in which extremist and those radicalising others can operate'.[9] *Pursuit* goes wider than actually seeking to prevent terrorist attacks and includes the disruption of terrorist activities, through better understanding of their capabilities and intentions; prosecutions, deportations, control orders, and proscriptions of organizations; working with communities; making it harder for terrorists to operate domestically and abroad; and targeting their funds. *Protection* entails working to safeguard critical national infrastructure and other sites at risk and maintaining border security. *Preparedness* means ensuring effective contingency arrangements are in place.

The Government places the 'encouragement offences' in the Terrorism Act 2006 within the 'prevent' strand of CONTEST.[10] The 'encouragement offences' are not the only legal tools in the 'prevent' strand. They do, however, appear to permit intervention by the criminal law at a much earlier point in time than the others. The framing of UK anti-terrorism laws in terms of the 'prevention of terrorism' is suggestive of the extent to which the legal policy focuses on a 'control' over a 'criminalisation' approach. Control Orders, detention without trial, proscription, port controls, and data mining fall within the 'control' category. While other measures such as arrest, interrogation, and stop and search, 'could legitimately be included in either strategy'.[11] Given the perceived nature of the threat, 'control' is at the core of the CONTEST strategy: '[e]ven "pursuit" which includes prosecution, is invoked in the context of "disrupting terrorist activity"'.[12]

Legal offences and powers form only a small part of the overall 'prevent' strand of CONTEST. Conditions of socio-economic disadvantage, as well as experiences

---

[6] Prime Minister and Secretary of State for the Home Department, 'Countering International Terrorism: The United Kingdom's Strategy' (Cm 6888, 2006).

[7] Ibid., 9.   [8] Ibid., 13.

[9] Ibid., 1.   [10] Ibid., 12.

[11] C. Walker, 'Keeping Control of Terrorists without Losing Control of Constitutionalism' (2007) 59 *Stan. L. Rev.* 1395, 1400.

[12] Ibid., 1401.

of discrimination are recognized as relevant background factors that increase the risks of radicalization. Policies aimed at addressing these issues, which contribute towards work within the 'prevent' strand, range from the enactment of legislation to prohibit discrimination on the grounds of religion or belief in the provision of goods, services, facilities, education, and exercise of public functions by public bodies through to action on reducing the ethnic minority employment and educational attainment gap.[13] The location of the government's 'Preventing Extremism Unit' within the Department for Communities and Local Government (CLG) underlines the emphasis on non-legal tools in preventing extremism. The Department's primary task is to 'enable "local communities...to challenge robustly the ideas of...extremists"'.[14] Its strategy, entitled 'Preventing Violent Extremism: Winning Hearts and Minds', is focused around four themes: promoting shared values, supporting local solutions, building civic capacity and leadership, and strengthening the role of faith institutions and leaders.[15]

3. The Terrorism Act 2006

In addition to forming part of the government response to the attacks in July 2005, the encouragement offences in the Terrorism Act 2006 are also a response to the need for the United Kingdom to give effect to its obligations under the Council of Europe's Convention on the Prevention of Terrorism (CECPT), signed in May 2005.[16] The Convention requires state parties to, 'adopt such measures as may be necessary to establish public provocation to commit a terrorist offence...when committed unlawfully and intentionally, as a criminal offence under its domestic law'.[17] The Convention defines, the 'public provocation to commit a terrorist offence' as, 'the distribution, or otherwise making available, of a message to the public, with the intent to incite the commission of a terrorist offence, where such conduct, whether or not directly advocating terrorist offences, causes a danger that one or more such offences may be committed'.[18] Terrorist offences are identified as those contained in the international treaties listed in the appendix to the treaty.[19] A working group of the Council's Committee of Experts on Terrorism, which drafted the Convention, reviewed the nature of the existing laws on 'incitement to terrorism'. They concluded that while direct provocation to terrorism was covered in most legal systems, a *lacuna* remained in respect of indirect provocation.[20]

---

[13] Equality Act 2006.
[14] Department for Communities and Local Government, 'Preventing Violent Extremism: Winning Hearts and Minds' (London: Department for Communities and Local Government, 2007), 4.
[15] Ibid., 5–10.   [16] CETS No. 196.   [17] CECPT, Art. 5(2).
[18] Ibid., Art. 5(1).   [19] Ibid., Art. 1.
[20] 'Explanatory Report of the Council of Europe's Convention on the Prevention of Terrorism', para. 97.

The Terrorism Act 2006 contains three measures targeted at restricting activities used to encourage acts of terrorism. First, the Act makes it an offence to 'publish' or cause to be published:

[A] statement that is likely to be understood by some or all members of the public to whom it is published as a direct or indirect encouragement or other inducement to them to the commission, preparation, or instigation of acts of terrorism or Convention offences.[21]

A 'statement' includes, 'a communication of any description, including a communication without words consisting of sounds or images or both'.[22]

'Publishing' includes, 'providing electronically any service by means of which the public have access to the statement'.[23] The scope of 'publication' appears to extend to internet service providers (ISP), as well as those who run websites where people can post statements.[24] Thus, section 1 'will catch persons who run websites which allow people to post messages on forums or bulletin boards...where an impugned statement is posted on such a forum, the poster of the statement, the person running the website, and the ISP, will all be "publishers" of the statement' for the purposes of section 1.[25]

Section 2 makes it an offence to disseminate a 'terrorist publication'.[26] Dissemination covers a wide range of conduct including distribution, circulation, giving, lending, offering, or electronic transmission of the content of a publication and even extends to the possession of a terrorist publication with a view to its distribution.[27] A 'terrorist publication' includes a publication with matter contained in it that is likely 'to be understood, by some or all persons to whom it is or may become available as a consequence of that conduct, as a direct or indirect encouragement or other inducement to them to the commission, preparation, or instigation or acts of terrorism'.[28]

Section 3 of the Terrorism Act 2000 already allowed for the proscription of an organization that promotes or encourages terrorism. The 2006 Act amends this to make it clear that promotion or encouragement of terrorism includes 'any case in which activities of the organisation include the unlawful glorification of the commission or preparation (whether in the past, in the future, or generally) of acts of terrorism' or where the organization's activities 'are carried out in a manner that ensures that the organisation is associated with statements containing any such glorification'.[29]

---

[21] Terrorism Act 2006, s. 1.   [22] Ibid., s. 20(6).
[23] Ibid., s. 20(4)(b).
[24] A. Hunt, 'Criminal Prohibitions on Direct and Indirect Encouragement of Terrorism' (2007) *Crim. L. Rev.* 441, 444.
[25] Ibid.
[26] Terrorism Act 2006, s. 2.
[27] Ibid., s. 2(2).
[28] Ibid., s. 2(3)(a).
[29] Ibid., s. 21(5A)(b).

Both the section 1 and 2 offences cover direct and indirect 'encouragement' or 'other inducement'. It is not clear whether 'encouragement' places the threshold for the offence below 'incitement'. In attempting to unpack the provisions of the statute, Adrian Hunt suggests a significant distinction can be drawn between 'saying something that may have encouraging effects, and prohibiting the saying of something that is likely itself to be understood as an encouragement'.[30] However, the difficultly in drawing this distinction arises from the introduction of an undefined 'indirect' 'mode' of encouragement.[31] The model of anti-discrimination laws, which differentiate between direct and indirect discrimination, may suggest one possible way of approaching this issue. Under such an approach, the distinction between direct and indirect encouragement would lie precisely in the fact that, in the case of direct encouragement, a suggestion of encouragement can be found on the face of the statement; indirect encouragement, in contrast, includes statements which have the effect of encouragement even though this cannot be gleaned from the face of the statement. This would then potentially bring within the scope of the law statements that have an encouraging effect. Given the breadth of statements that could potentially come within the scope of the law, if under this approach a statement is found to be indirectly encouraging, to safeguard freedom of expression it would be important to consider whether the encouraging statements could be justified on grounds unrelated to encouraging terrorism.

The statute itself remains largely silent on the crucial issue of what constitute direct or indirect encouragement or other inducement. In respect of indirect encouragement there is some limited elucidation. The statute provides that indirect encouragement includes 'every statement which glorifies the commission or preparation (whether in the past, in the future, or generally) of' acts of terrorism or Convention offences.[32] Glorification is initially drawn in very broad terms: it 'includes' but is not limited to 'any form of praise or celebration'.[33] However, the scope for liability for glorification is narrowed by the need for the statement to be one from which a reasonable inference can be drawn by those to whom the statement is made, that the conduct being glorified 'is being glorified as conduct that should be emulated by them in existing circumstances'.[34]

The glorification of terrorism was originally proposed as a stand alone offence, separate from indirect encouragement. Opposition to this approach led to its amended inclusion as an instance of indirect encouragement. Given this amended position, the necessity of its continued inclusion was questioned. The government put forward three arguments for its continued and explicit inclusion. Firstly, they pointed to the commitment in the 2005 Labour Party election manifesto to introduce laws against those who 'glorify or condone acts of terror'.[35] While the manifesto commitment provides a strong argument that the legislation covers

---

[30] See n. 24 above, 453.   [31] Ibid.
[32] Terrorism Act 2006, ss. 1(3)(a) and 2(4)(a).
[33] Ibid., s. 20(2).   [34] Ibid., ss. 1(3)(b) and 2(4)(b).
[35] 'Britain: Forward Not Back', (The Labour Party Manifesto, 2005), 53.

actions that glorify acts of terrorism the reference to 'condoning' terrorism in the manifesto would not appear to necessitate an explicit subsection dedicated to condoning as a further example of indirect encouragement. Secondly, it was argued that the inclusion was necessary because the term was specifically used in UN Security Council Resolution 1624.[36] The Security Council Resolution, while '*repudiating* attempts at the justification or glorification of terrorist acts (*apologie*) that may incite further terrorist acts', is a non-binding resolution that does not place any obligation on states to introduce laws to prohibit glorification.[37] Thirdly, the Home Secretary argued that the explicit reference to glorification was needed as this was the main form of indirect encouragement used for radicalization:

[I]t is perfectly clear that people who seek to recruit terrorists do so not just by directly encouraging terrorism or by provoking people to commit violent acts but by glorifying terrorism and terrorists. They may emphasise that terrorists are heroes whose actions should be copied; that terrorists go straight to paradise when they die; that terrorists undertake glorious acts that deserve to be emulated; or that terrorists are simply better humans than those of us who are not terrorists. The single word that best captures that is 'glorification'. It is the word that, we all recognise, covers such forms of indirect encouragement. It does not, as I have explained, cover all forms of indirect encouragement, but it does cover those forms. It is that clarity of meaning that makes the word 'glorification' so important... those who seek to recruit terrorists know what it means.[38]

The Home Secretary placed particular emphasis on the signal that the legislation would send, and argued that failure to explicitly include glorification as a form of indirect encouragement would send the signal that glorification is acceptable.[39]

While the statute identifies 'glorification' as an illustration of indirect encouragement it provides no further guidance on what else comes within the scope of indirect encouragement. In fact, the legislation extends beyond indirect encouragement to 'other inducements' which may also be direct or indirect.

Much parliamentary time was taken in trying to penetrate the meaning of these terms. During debate opponents cited examples of the types of statements they feared would fall foul of the new law, including statements by the Prime Minsters' wife Cherie Blair[40] and the Liberal Democrat MP Jenny Tonge[41] expressing

---

[36] Hansard HC Vol. 442 Col. 1429 (15 February 2006).

[37] UNSC Res 1624 (14 September 2005) UN Doc S/RES/1624.

[38] Hansard HC Vol. 442 Col. 1437 (15 February 2006).

[39] Hansard HC Vol. 442 Col. 1437–8 (15 February 2006).

[40] See eg, G. Jones and A. La Guardia, 'Anger at Cherie "sympathy" for suicide bombers', *The Daily Telegraph*, 19 June 2002, <http://www.telegraph.co.uk/news/worldnews/middleeast/jordan/1397696/Anger-at-Cherie-%27sympathy%27-for-suicide-bombers.html> (last accessed 31 May 2008).

[41] See eg, N. Watt, 'Lib Dem MP: Why I would consider being a suicide bomber', *The Guardian*, 23 January 2004, <http://www.guardian.co.uk/politics/2004/jan/23/israel.liberaldemocrats> (last accessed 31 May 2008).

understanding of the motives of those who carry suicide bombings.[42] The Joint Committee on Human Rights accepted that the government was trying to draw a distinction between encouraging and glorifying terrorism on the one hand and explaining or understanding it on the other. The difficulty with such a distinction is that it 'is not self-executing: the content of comments and remarks will have to be carefully analysed in each case, including the context in which they were spoken, and there will be enormous scope for disagreement between reasonable people as to whether a particular comment is merely an explanation or an expression of understanding or goes further and amounts to encouragement, praise, or glorification'.[43]

A further difficulty relates to the test for determining the impact of impugned statements. In the section 1 offence, the impact of a statement that encourages acts of terrorism is measured by reference to its likely understanding by members of the *public* to whom it is published. The public/private distinction is therefore critical to the scope of the section 1 offence.[44] During the passage of the Bill, the government repeatedly emphasized that the section 1 offence did not encompass private conversations.[45] Furthermore, 'public' includes the public or a section of the public, in any country or territory.[46] Where a statement is made to the world in general, it is not clear which members of the public will be used as the barometer for the likelihood test.

The encouragement must relate to either 'acts of terrorism' or 'Convention offences'. The latter is aimed at giving effect to the provisions of the Council of Europe's Convention on the Prevention of Terrorism. The distinction drawn in the statute between 'acts of terrorism' and 'Convention offences' reflects one of several points at which the 2006 Act go beyond the requirements of the UK's obligations under CECPT. In addition to the very specific and carefully defined set of 'Convention Offences', the 2006 Act adopts the very board definition of 'acts of terrorism' found in the Terrorism Act 2000. This includes the use or threat of action that involve serious violence against a person, serious damage to property, endangering another person's life, creating a serious risk to the health and safety of the public or a section of the public, and action designed seriously to interfere with or seriously disrupt an electronic system.[47] These actions become 'acts of terrorism' where two conditions are met. Firstly, the use or threat of action is designed to influence the government or to intimidate the public or a section of

---

[42] Hansard HC Vol. 438 Col. 350, 368 (26 October 2005); Hansard HC Vol. 438 Col. 845, 857 and 874 (2 November 2005); Hansard HC Vol. 439 Col. 399 (9 November 2005); Hansard HL Vol. 675 Col. 1468 (21 November 2005); Hansard HC Vol. 442 Col. 1443 (15 February 2006).

[43] Joint Committee on Human Rights, 'Counter-Terrorism Policy and Human Rights: Terrorism Bill and Related Matters', HC (2005/06) 561-I, 18–9.

[44] In the s. 2 offence, encouragement via the dissemination of a terrorist publications, the impact of such material is measured by reference to its likely understanding by 'all or some of the *persons* to whom it is or may become available' (emphasis added).

[45] Hansard HL Vol. 676 Col. 435 (5 December 2005) and Vol. 677 Col. 583 (17 January 2006).

[46] Terrorism Act 2006, s. 20(3).   [47] Terrorism Act 2000, s. 1(2).

the public. Secondly, the use or threat of action is designed to further a political, religious, or ideological cause.[48] The broad nature of the definition of 'acts of terrorism' in the 2000 Act was justified in the basis that its primary role was to provide a platform for allowing the use of investigative police powers, and was not a term on which a criminal offence is based.[49] Its adoption as the basis for the substantive encouragement offences in the 2006 Act risks over breadth in criminal law. The broad definition, when combined with the provisions of sections 1(5)(a) and s2(7) of the Act 'facilitates the criminalisation of a form of direct encouragement to engage in terrorism in a general and undifferentiated way that would not previously have been caught by common law incitement'.[50]

The encouragement offences, in respect of 'acts of terrorism' do not entail extra-territorial jurisdiction. The definition of 'acts of terrorism' in the 2000 Act, however, provides that the 'use' or 'threat' of 'action' includes, 'action' outside the United Kingdom.[51] The encouragement offences therefore cover the direct or indirect encouragement, in the United Kingdom, of actions outside the United Kingdom. This brings within the scope of the legislation statements by individuals that provide direct or indirect encouragement of acts of terrorism to those involved in political resistance to any government, irrespective of the nature of the regime or the opportunities for non-violent resistance. By utilizing the definition of 'acts of terrorism' in the 2000 Act, the legislation fails to allow for distinctions to be made between impugned statements that encourage serious violence towards innocent civilians and violence directed at seriously damaging the property or apparatus of an oppressive state. The Home Office Minister Hazel Blears also resisted arguments in the House of Commons for the legislation to allow distinctions to be made between 'freedom fighters' and 'terrorists':

The Bill will not affect the ability to say that people who are fighting oppression should be supported. It will prevent people saying such things, when they know, believe or have reasonable grounds for believing that the people to whom they are speaking are likely to see such remarks as an inducement or encouragement to emulate that behaviour. The legislation is precise, and it is targeted at people who know that when they say such things, they might not incite people to a specific terrorist act, but they are creating a climate in which resorting to terrorism is seen as a valid response . . . [I]f people attack the apparatus of the state, they could well injure innocent civilians. If someone attacked a railway station an innocent person could be involved.[52]

It seems likely, for example, that the offence would have covered impugned statements made by anyone in the UK that encouraged Iraqi civilians to seriously damage or destroy statues of Saddam Hussein in Bagdad.

---

[48] Ibid., s. 1(1).
[49] Hansard HC Vol. 346 Col. 410 (15 March 2000). See also C. Walker, *Blackstone's Guide to the Anti-Terrorism Legislation* (Oxford: OUP, 2002).
[50] See n. 24 above, 448.   [51] Terrorism Act 2000, s. 1(4)(a).
[52] Hansard HC Vol. 438 Col. 871–4 (2 November 2005).

In contrast to 'acts of terrorism', the encouragement of 'Convention offences' does entail extra-territorial jurisdiction.[53] While, this is a requirement of CECPT, the Terrorism Act, by omitting crucial limitations found in the equivalent provisions in the CECPT, goes beyond what is needed by the Council of Europe. In particular, CECPT requires an 'intention' to incite the commission of a terrorist offence; furthermore, the statement must cause a danger that one or more such offences will be committed.[54] By contrast, the encouragement offences in the Terrorism Act can be committed recklessly and it is irrelevant for the purpose of the offence whether a person is in fact encouraged or induced by the statement.[55] The role of the Attorney-General in authorizing prosecutions was identified as a safeguard built into the 2006 Act in extra-territorial cases.[56] Where the offence has been committed 'for a purpose wholly or partly connected with the affairs of a country other than the United Kingdom' the Act also requires the consent of the Attorney General, or in the case of Northern Ireland, the Advocate General. The Terrorism Act creates new opportunities for oppressive regimes to seek to have their dissidents prosecuted by UK courts. The role of the Attorney General in this process makes it harder for a British government to resist pressure with the argument that the decisions for such prosecutions are purely a matter for the prosecuting authorities.

The potential breadth of the encouragement offences and their chilling impact on free speech is further reinforced by the fact that the offences can be committed recklessly.[57] The government justified the broad drafting of the offences on the basis that the widely drawn provisions would be read narrowly and compatibly with human rights norms in light of the duty of the courts under the Human Rights Act 1998.[58]

Hunt argues that in light of the constraints of the HRA and the need to narrowly construe the provisions of the offences to avoid disproportionate interference with human rights, the legislation, while extending the law beyond existing provisions on incitement to cover incitement to terrorism in general rather than specific acts of terrorism, has not been successful in ensuring that it covers oblique or indirect encouragement.[59] The chilling effect on free speech from these offences, however, does not rest primarily on the specific parameters of the offence, vital though this is, nor the number of prosecutions. Rather, the new offences aim to send out a signal to those who indirectly encourage terrorism and to challenge the climate in which statements that indirectly encourage terrorism are viewed as acceptable. Thus, 'the real impact will be found in the thousands of hidden acts of self-censorship and informal censorship that are likely to result,

---

[53] Terrorism Act 2006, s. 17.   [54] CECPT, Art. 5.
[55] Terrorism Act, 2006 s. 1(5).
[56] Ibid., s. 19; Hansard HC Vol. 438 Col. 873 (2 November 2005).
[57] Terrorism Act 2006, ss.1(2)(b) and 2(1)(c).
[58] '[W]e bring forward these provisions with a proper understanding that the constraints imposed by the Human Rights Act and other legislation should bite on this.' Hansard HL Vol. 677 Col. 582 (17 January 2006).
[59] See n. 24 above, 44.

preventing the very discussions that need to be allowed if the causes of terrorism are to be honestly examined'.[60]

4. The Radicalization Process

The extent to which the encouragement offences can play a part in preventing violent radicalization is difficult to determine. Understanding the process of violent radicalization, and the role of the impugned statements in that process, however, provides some indication of their potential to do so. Three elements of the radicalization process are of particular note in our evaluation of the encouragement offences in the Terrorism Act 2006: firstly, the importance of experiences and perceptions of discrimination and unfair treatment by those subject to this process; secondly, the extent to which radicalization is a group process that takes place in private spaces hidden away from the wider community; and thirdly, the 'religious literacy' or state of knowledge about their religion prior to radicalization among those radicalized.

Any discussion of the radicalization process is confronted by that fact that our understanding of the process remains in its early stages and, of course, the process itself is constantly changing. In evidence to the UK Security and Intelligence Committee, the police acknowledged that the London terrorist attacks of 7 July 2005 showed that 'there was no clear profile of a British Islamist terrorist'; the police were 'working off a script' which was completely discounted by the events of 7/7.[61]

An analysis by the Dutch government suggests that three aspects play a role in the process of radicalization: the individual process, the interpersonal dynamic, and the effect of circumstances. In the first of these, the individual process, violent radicalization is seen as one possible outcome from the search for identity. For young people in particular the search for identity is part of the process of defining one's relationship with the world that usually takes place without violent radicalization. Such radicalization therefore also requires the second aspect, an interpersonal interaction with other actors who stimulate and influence the radicalization process.[62] It is to this interpersonal interaction that statements covered by the Terrorism Act 2006 are most likely relevant. At the same time, the third aspect, the effect of circumstances, which includes the wider social, economic and political context including state anti-terrorism laws and policies, also contributes to radicalization.

---

[60] A. Kundnani, *The End of Tolerance: Racism in 21st Century Britain* (London: Pluto Press, 2007), 179.

[61] Intelligence and Security Committee, 'Report into the London Terrorist Attacks on 7 July 2005' (Cm 6785, 2006), 29–30.

[62] Directorate of General Judicial Strategy, 'Policy Memorandum on Radicalism and Radicalisation' (Ministry of Justice, 2005), 8–10. See also M. Slootman and J. Tille, *Processes of Radicalisation: Why Some Amsterdam Muslims Become Radicals* (Amsterdam: Institute of Migration and Ethnic Studies, 2006).

Another model examines the 'attitudes' of individuals at 'high risk' of radical-ization, using ten indictors weighted according to their importance to the process.[63] The four most important 'essential' factors are 'acceptance',[64] 'equal opportunities',[65] 'integration',[66] and 'acceptance of social values'.[67] Four factors identified as having 'average importance' are 'toleration/welcome',[68] 'entitle-ment',[69] 'loyalty', and 'language competence'.

While research can identify some 'risk factors', 'pinpointing exactly why or when someone becomes radicalised is extremely difficult as it is a complex process that does not follow a linear path'.[70] Anecdotal reporting, analysis and profiling of personality, and behavioural characteristics of extremists have enhanced our understanding.[71] But these take place after individuals have been captured.

Quintan Wiktorowicz's study of *Al-Muhajiroun* is of particular relevance, since *Al-Gurabba* and *The Saved Sect* the only two organizations to be proscribed for glorifying acts of terror, were offshoots that developed from *Al-Muhajiroun* after it was disbanded in 2004.[72] Wiktorowicz explored the factors that explain initial

---

[63] D. E. Pressman, *Countering Radicalisation: Communication and Behavioural Perspectives*, (The Hague: Clingendal Centre for Strategic Studies, 2006).

[64] Ibid., 11, the 'Acceptance' scale rating is based on the perceived level that an individual feels he or she has been accepted into society. In this model a very low score is considered a precipitating factor for discontent and anger.

[65] Ibid., 12, the 'equal opportunities' scale rates the person's perception of fairness and discrim-ination in the workplace.

[66] Ibid., 11, 'Integration' is measure by the extent to which individuals feel integrated in the general community and the participation in activities outside their own ethnic and religious group.

[67] Ibid., 12, the model does not define social values but asks respondents to identify what they perceive to be the main values of society and the extent to which they accept and agree with these values.

[68] Ibid., 11, the 'welcome' scale aims to determine whether an individual actually feels welcomed by society or merely feels tolerated.

[69] Ibid., 'Entitlement' refers to the extent to which an individual has expectations of society which if they are not met lead to greater disappointment. Pressman suggests that the second and third generation children of immigrants have a much higher sense of entitlement/expectation and there-fore, a greater and more intense sense of frustration when those expectations are not realised.

[70] A. Pargeter, 'North African Immigrants in Europe and Political Violence' (2006) 29 *Studies on Conflict and Terrorism* 731, 737.

[71] See generally M. Sageman, *Understanding Terror Networks* (Philadelphia: Univ of Pennsylvania Press, 2004); F. Khosrokhavar, *Suicide Bombers: Allah's New Martyrs* Trans. D. Macey (London: Pluto Press, 2005).

[72] Q. Wiktorowicz, *Radical Islam Rising: Muslim Extremism in the West* (Lanham, MD: Rowman and Littlefield, 2005). *Al-Muhajiroun* was first founded in Saudi Arabia in 1983 by exiled Syrian Omar Bakri Mohammed. He later moved to the United Kingdom and became leader of the British section of *Hizb-ut-Tahrir* (see n. 86 below). In 1996, following disagreements with its leadership, Bakri Mohammed resigned his position in *Hizb ut-Tahrir* and re-launched *Al-Muhajiroun* in Britain. Both organizations are committed to the creation of a unified Islamic state, the Caliphate. However, *Hizb ut-Tahrir* see this as occurring in the Muslim world while *Al-Muhajiroun* argue that attempts at creating the Caliphate should be made wherever its members are found, including in western European states. *Al-Muhajiroun* came to public prominence after 2001 when its provocative, public, and vocal support for Osama bin Laden and praise for the 9/11 attackers as the 'Magnificent 19' drew significant media attention. The organization was formally disbanded in October 2004. However, in November 2005 some of its followers created two successor organizations, the Saved Sect and *Al-Gurabba*. See K. Conner, 'Islamism in the West: The Life-span of the Al-Muhajiroun in the United Kingdom' (2005) 25 *Journal of Muslim Minority Affairs* 117.

interest and eventual membership of such organizations. He suggests that those wanting to join *Al-Muhajiroun* must have a willingness to expose themselves to the movement's message. This 'cognitive opening', which creates 'the willingness to listen to their views' can be the product of a crisis that shakes certainty in previously accepted beliefs and renders an individual more receptive to the possibilities of alternative views and perspectives. Where the existing belief system does not provide an adequate explanation then the individual will be open to other views. Types of crisis that create cognitive openings are economic, (losing a job, blocked mobility) social and cultural (sense of cultural weakness, experiences of racism, and humiliation), political (repression, torture, and political discrimination), and personal (bereavement, victimization of a crime).[73] Wiktorowicz identifies some of the factors that opened members of *Al-Muhajiroun* up to new perspectives about religion:

Encounters with racism as well as Islamophobia prompted these individuals to think about how they fit into British society and the role of Islam for Muslim minorities in the United Kingdom. Others experienced cognitive openings...through discussions with familiars and strangers alike...Eventual joiners who responded to the opening through religious seeking found mainstream religious institutions and figures wanting. For these individuals, local imams and mosques failed to provide guidance on specific concerns of British Muslims. As a result they were more amenable to experimentation outside the mainstream.[74]

Akil Awan refers to these moments as 'Transitional Religiosity Experiences', (TRE).[75] Among those that become radicalized, the TRE provides a point of bifurcation and rupture in their life narrative. They, 'construct a harsh dichotomy between the two life phases'; a process Awan calls 'contextual bifurcation'.[76] Thus, 'the past life and all that it entailed is now diametrically opposed to the present life'.[77] This is often accompanied by cutting off ties with previous family and social networks. He places emphasis on the attempts to reconcile minority and majority cultural identities as an antecedent of TRE. Among those whose TRE leads to radicalization there is a, 'staunch repudiation of one's minority culture'.[78] The reasons for this are varied but include oppressive experience of parental culture. Awan notes that both Omar Khan Sharif, a British citizen whose suicide bomb-belt failed to detonate during a terrorist attack on a Tel Aviv pizzeria and Mohammed Siddique, the leader of the 7 July 2005 bombers had gone against parents in their choice of marriage partners. This experience of their parent's culture as oppressive can also be reinforced by clan-based power structures which have the effect of 'divesting youth of any real tangible control over their lives' and

---

[73] Ibid., 19–20.   [74] Ibid., 24.

[75] 'Transitional Religiosity Experiences: Contextual Disjuncture and Islamic Political Radicalism', in T. Abbas (ed.), *Islamic Political Radicalism: A European Perspective* (Edinburgh: Edinburgh UP, 2007).

[76] Ibid., 210.   [77] Ibid.   [78] Ibid., 215.

undermining confidence in political institutions.[79] In this context, 'the repudiation of one's ethnic culture and its appurtenances can in itself symbolise a form
of self empowerment'.[80] Biographies of violent radicals reveal an individual who
is, 'ensconced within the majority culture prior to their radicalisation...
comfortably immersed in popular, mainstream youth culture, lax in religious
praxis but also, critically, one who clearly retains some vestiges of his *minority*
cultural and religious identity'.[81] Events or incidents then bring this religious
identity to the foreground. Alienation from, or 'gradual lack of identification'
with, both the *minority* and *majority* cultures together with socio-
economic deprivation and political disaffection creates a state of anomie. The
TRE does not resolve the resulting feelings of alienation and purposelessness. By
contrast radical political Islam becomes attractive, precisely because it is claiming
to be part of a global movement that is not anchored to any particular nationality,
and precisely because it has a revolutionary political agenda. It offers the
opportunity to be part of a global elite.[82]

Central to the 'identity crisis' and trying to understand what it means to be
Muslim in a non-Muslim country is the widespread perception that Muslims are
not accepted by British society. Individuals drawn to *Al-Muhajiroun*, find that
experiences of Islamophobia belie society's claims of tolerance:

The experience of both racial and religious discrimination has prompted some young
Muslims to think about their identity and how they fit into British society. This is
particularly true of young university students who suffer from a sense of blocked social
mobility.[83]

The leaders of *Al-Muhajiroun* identify this group as their most important
recruitment pool, because it is the upwardly mobile group that, 'believes that they
face a discriminatory system that prevents them from realising their potential.
They grew up in Britain but are not considered British by many in society'.[84]
Omar Bakri Mohammed, the leader of *Al-Muhajiroun*, emphasizes the importance of this identity crisis triggered by discrimination in attracting potential
joiners: '[I]f there is no racism in the west, there is no conflict of identity... If
there is no discrimination or racism, I think it would be very difficult for us'.[85]
Thus, the leaders of *Al-Muhajiroun* are clear that their role is to provide an
identity of empowerment in the midst of the identity crisis. Studies of *Hizb-ut-
Tahrir*,[86] another radical organization in which Omar Bakri Mohammed was the

---

[79] Ibid.   [80] Ibid., 215–6.   [81] Ibid., 217–8.   [82] Ibid., 219–20.
[83] See Wiktorowicz (n. 72 above), 90.
[84] Ibid., 91.   [85] Ibid.
[86] Founded in the Middle East, in the 1950s, and with branches now in the UK, *Hizb-ut-Tahrir*
does not engage in terrorism or any direct action but in 'ideological struggle'. It has been accused of
being a 'conveyor belt for terrorists'; an organization that 'indoctrinates individuals with radical
ideology, priming them for recruitment by more extreme organizations where they can take part in actual
operations'. It occupies as 'grey zone of militancy, with its activities involving more than mere expression
of opinion but less then terrorism'. Z. Baran, 'Fighting the War of Ideas' (2005) 84(6) *Foreign Affairs* 68.

UK leader, also suggest that individuals come into contact with them as part of a search for 'shelter from racism and Islamophobia'.[87]

The government, in arguing for the need for the encouragement offences, placed emphasis on the ideological drive of those that carry out terrorist bombings and played down the relevance of socio-economic deprivation. The Home Secretary argued that violent radicalism 'it is not driven by poverty, social exclusion, or racial justice... they were not the poor and the dispossessed. They were, for the most part, well educated and prosperous... ideas drive those people forward'.[88] The examples of Ahmed Omar Saeed Shiekh,[89] Sajid Badat,[90] and Omar Khan Sharif[91]—who all attended private schools—or Mohammed Siddique Khan, the leader of the 7 July 2005 bombers—who was a university graduate—challenges a simple deprivation/violence nexus. However, the history of political violence has rarely suggested a straightforward relationship between deprivation and the mobilization of individuals towards violence:

[M]obilisation is not about rich or poor leaders and/or perpetrators. It stands to reason that those most able to mobilise should be the educated strategists. These types of individuals are not above instrumentalising the belief or suffering of others; nor are they immune to a genuine sense of responsibility in the name of a community, on whose behalf they decide to act.[92]

Focusing on the circumstances of individuals underestimates the impoverished nature of the communities from which they hailed, and 'which held a profound resonance for them'.[93] Thus, the individual socio-economic circumstances of the 7 July 2005 bombers may not be as significant as that fact that three of them grew up in an area of Leeds where 10,000 of the 16,300 residents had living standards that are amongst the worst three per cent nationally.[94] The government recognizes the need to address social and economic deprivation within its CONTEST strategy. Action taken on discrimination and deprivation does not, of course, preclude the need to also prohibit statements that encourage terrorism.

An important question that goes to the heart of the necessity of the section 1 offence is the role that the prohibited statements play in violent radicalization. The Internet is regarded as the key platform for the dissemination and mediation

---

[87] S. Hamid, 'Islamic Political Radicalism in Britain: The Case of *Hizb-ut-Tahrir*', in T. Abbas (ed.), *Islamic Political Radicalism: A European Perspective* (Edinburgh: Edinburgh UP, 2007), 150.

[88] Hansard HC Vol. 438 Col. 325 (26 October 2005).

[89] Convicted in Pakistan for involvement in the murder of Daniel Pearl in 2002.

[90] Pleaded guilty in 2005 to planning to blow up aircraft with a shoe bomb.

[91] Involved in suicide bombings in Tel Aviv in 2003.

[92] R. Briggs, C. Fieschi, and H. Lownsbrough, *Bringing it Home: Community Based Approaches to Counter Terrorism* (London: Demos, 2006), 45–6.

[93] See n. 75 above, 213.

[94] 'Report of the Official Account of the Bombings in London on 7th July 2007', HC 1087 (2005-6), 13.

of the culture of violent extremism.[95] Its appeal lies in several factors, including its cost, accessibility, anonymity, lack of censorship, speed, immediacy, scope, reach, and interactivity. While violent extremists groups see the Internet as an important site for virtual radicalization and recruitment, its efficacy in actual radicalization is extremely difficult to ascertain. Awan argues that 'viewing and surfing habits are no indication of extremist proclivities or terrorists inclinations. Rather, Jihadist fora can in many cases ... be completely innocuous and actually serve a cathartic role'.[96] Similar assumptions about the Internet's ability to negatively influence the audience are not automatically made about other forms of graphic violence such as pornography.

In the US, government analysts have not found any direct evidence specifically linking the Internet to recruitment of individuals to mainstream established terrorist organization or movements.[97] The evidence of 'self-radicalization' by individuals from material seen on the Internet remains limited.[98] Research in the Netherlands has found two cases in which individuals have becomes radicalized 'under the influence of the Internet'. Thus it was concluded that 'propaganda via the internet makes a contribution towards radicalisation'.[99] On the other hand, the study finds that, while recruitment on the Internet by international terrorist groups is theoretically possible, it is not very likely. Rather, the Internet provides an opportunity for those who have stepped over the threshold to contact such groups.[100] The move towards violent radicalization requires personal contacts and for individuals to be linked into existing terrorist networks and structures. Friendship ties and pre-existing relationships were important factors in the recruitment of individuals to al-Qaida in 68 per cent of cases.[101]

The section 1 offences prohibit statements made to the 'public'. It does not extend to private communications. Pushed to justify this distinction during debate in the House of Lords, the government stated only that it was not 'appropriate' for the offence to target private communication. The only further hint of explanation for the protection of private communication was the government's assertion that it was 'trying to be liberal'.[102] Crucially, however, public statements appear to have a limited role in the radicalization process. For groups like *Hizb-ut-Tahrir* and *Al-Muhajiroun*, initial contact and recruitment of new

---

[95] See G. Weimann, *Terror on the Internet: The New Arena, The New Challenges* (Washington: United States Institute for Peace, 2006); S. Atran, 'The "Virtual Hand" of Jihad', (2005) 3 *Global Terrorism Analysis* 8; G. R. Bunt, *Islam in the Digital Age: E-Jihad, Online Fatwas and Cyber Islamic Environments* (London: Pluto Press, 2003).

[96] 'Virtual jihadist media: Function, legitimacy and radicalizing efficacy' (2007) 10 *European Journal of Cultural Studies* 389, 404.

[97] B. Hoffmann, *The Use of the Internet by Islamic Extremists* (Santa Monica, CA: RAND, 2006), 16.

[98] P. R. Neumann, 'Europe's Jihadist Dilemma' (2006) 48(2) *Survival* 71, 77.

[99] National Coordinator for Counterterrorism, 'Jihadis and the Internet' (The Hague: The National Coordinator for Counterterrorism, 2007), 74.

[100] Ibid., 81.

[101] See Sageman in n. 71 above, 154.

[102] Hansard HL Vol. 676 Col. 435 (5 December 2005).

members may come from outreach work, such as public leafleting and stalls at public events. However, the actual indoctrination takes place through private communication with individuals after they have been screened, and involves 'a period of intense immersion in to the party ideas and literature for periods of between six months to three years'.[103] The official report into the 7/7 bombings noted that radicals increasingly use private homes as meeting places in order to avoid detection. Individual mentors play a critical role in the grooming process. Initially, mentors place an emphasis on being a devout Muslim, without introducing an extremist agenda. Potential recruits are then subjected to propaganda illustrating the abuse and persecution of Muslims around the world. Religious justifications from the Quran and *hadith* are then given for violent jihad and, in the case of suicide attacks, the importance and rewards of martyrdom are emphasized.

Detailed theological and legal arguments underpinning a theory of violent jihad and justifying suicide bombings are also a key feature of extremist websites.[104] Such statements may lie at the centre of the kinds of statements that the offence of indirect encouragement of terrorism is seeking to reach. State intervention that has the effect of regulating religious disputes over matters of theology and law by proscribing unacceptable doctrines threatens to infringe core free speech rights.[105] Such intervention is therefore not justified at least until less restrictive responses have been exhausted.

Wiktorowicz finds that a common characteristic among those who are members of *Al-Muhajiroun* is that they were not particularly religious and did not have any significant religious education prior to their 'cognitive opening', religious seeking and exposure to radical movements.[106] The activists he interviewed 'were irreligious prior to their seeking and involvement in the movement. They describe their prior selves as secular and typically British'.[107] Religious seekers that are drawn to *Al-Muhajiroun* 'are not in a position to objectively evaluate whether *Al-Muhajiroun* represents an accurate understanding of Islam. Most are religious novices exploring the faith in depth for the first time'.[108] Rachel Briggs also notes that 'most Al-Qaida recruits are not highly religious before they make the decision to join the *jihad*; only 17 per cent received Islamic primary or secondary

---

[103] See n. 87 above, 149. See also Wiktorowicz (n. 72 above), 47–55. For a detailed personal account of this process from a former member of *Hizh-ut-Tahrir*, see E. Hussain, *The Islamist* (London: Penguin, 2007).

[104] See n. 75 above, 222.

[105] H. C. Keehn, 'Terroristic Religious Speech: Giving the Devil the Benefit of the First Amendment Free Exercise and Free Speech Clauses' (1998) 28 *Seton Hall L. Rev.* 1230.

[106] See n. 72 above, 85–133.

[107] Ibid., 102.

[108] Ibid., 127; See also A. S. Moussaoui and F. Bouquillat, *Zakarias Moussaoui: The Making of a Terrorist* (London: Serpent's Tail, 2003). Written by the brother of Zacarias Moussaoui, this book too emphasises the lack of religious education and understanding among recruits to extremist organizations.

education and very few came from highly religious backgrounds'.[109] Bruce Hoffman argues that much of the material on the Internet produced by radical groups is successful because it goes unchallenged. The absence of speech and ideas to counter the radical views of *Hizb ut-Tahrir* is also suggested to be a key factor in their continued appeal.[110] Thus, the success of such groups in the UK is, in part, down to the 'failure of mainstream Sunni traditions to connect with Muslims educated and socialised in Britain'.[111]

The difficulties of connecting, socially, intellectually, and linguistically to young Muslims has been identified as one of main challenges facing the South Asian *ulema* in trying to transmit Islam to the next generation. Furthermore, this has to be achieved at a time when their monopoly as custodians of Islam is challenged within South Asia by what Philip Lewis calls 'modernists' and 'Islamists'. The South Asian *ulema* also have to compete with well funded Saudi Wahhabi/Salafi tradition, and on university campuses with groups like *Hizb-al-Tahrir*.[112] Jonathan Birt places emphasis on the role of Saudi funding for the success of *Salafi* groups. This ensures that in the Islamic book market, *Salafi* literature is cheap, well-produced and has a print run that is five to ten times that of any other British based sectarian publication, aggressively targeted at a global English speaking audience.[113] He also estimates that the number of British graduates from the Islamic University of Medina number in the hundreds.[114]

All this suggests that the appropriate policy response from government to statements that encourage acts of terrorism should be focused on facilitating, supporting, and encouraging more speech that challenges the ideas underpinning violent radicalization. Such an approach would be consistent with a view of free speech as a fundamental value of a liberal democracy, protected because of its essential role in discovering truths. As Justice Brandeis argued in his concurrence (joined by Justice Holmes): 'If there be time to expose through discussion the falsehood and fallacies, to avert the evil by the processes of education, *the remedy to be applied is more speech, not enforced silence...*' and 'the fitting remedy for evil counsel is good ones'.[115] On this basis interference with free speech is justified when ideas do not have the opportunity to enter the market place to face scrutiny and rebuttal from competing ideas.

---

[110] See n. 97 above, 158.

[111] P. Lewis, 'Only Connect: Can the *Ulema* Address the Crisis in the Transmission of Islam to a New Generation of South Asians in Britian?' (2006) 15 *Contemporary South Asia* 165, 169.

[112] Ibid., 166. Salafism (also referred to as Wahhabism) is a particular tradition within Sunni Islam that is dominant in Saudi Arabia but is found in Muslim communities across the world.

[113] J. Birt, 'Wahhabism in the United Kingdom: Manifestations and Reactions', in M. al-Rasheed (ed), *Transnational Connections and the Arab Gulf* (London: Routledge, 2005), 169.

[114] Ibid., 170.

[115] *Whitney* v. *CA* 274 US 357 (1927) (emphasis added).

5. The Counterproductive Potential of Counterterrorism Laws

The extent to which the statements covered by the Terrorism Act section 1 contribute to violent radicalization remains unclear. Even if the encouragement offences may contribute towards the prevention of violent radicalization, this benefit has to be weighed against the potential counterproductive impact of these offences on overall counterterrorism strategy. If the government overreacts, counterterrorism measures themselves may feed and sustain terrorism, creating a well of sympathy and silence among sections of society, especially if these measures increase repression, stigmatize, and alienate these groups.[116] Thus, the State's counterterrorism measures 'can profoundly affect the nature and lethality' of terrorist violence. Any analysis of the causes of terrorism which does not consider the possible counterproductive effect of counterterrorism measures runs the risk of being dangerously 'limited and flawed'.[117]

The British government's response to terrorism in Northern Ireland provides a cautionary tale. The oppressive nature of the action by the security services was central to increasing recruitment and support for the Provisional Irish Republican Army (PIRA). It was the 'crude and oppressive security policies' of the British army in the 1970s that gave 'many previously uninvolved Catholics ample reason to hate the RUC and British Army' and led to recruitment en masse. A good example of this were the 1183 raids on Catholic homes that took place during two months in 1970 involving 'carpets and floorboards being pulled up, doors kicked in, walls and ceiling being knocked open with drills and sledgehammers. Yet in only 47 cases were weapons actually found.'[118] In fact, Andrew Silke suggests that 'the IRA worked to provoke harsh measures from the unfortunate security services, knowing full well the benefits it would reap in terms of support and recruits'.[119] Internment of 2,357 people of whom 1,600 were released without charge led to further recruitment by the PIRA. Kieran McEvoy concludes that:

Apart from the political fallout, in purely military terms internment was an unmitigated disaster. The degree and intensity of the violence in the aftermath of internment has not been matched either before or since. The principal justification for internment had been to take the principal players out of action and then make further inroads on their operations by gaining intelligence through interrogations. In the seven months prior to internment, eleven soldiers, and seventeen civilians died; in the five months following internment, thirty-two British soldiers, five members of the Ulster Defence Regiment,

---

[116] A. Silke 'Fire of Iolaus: The Role of State Countermeasures in Causing Terrorism and What Needs to be Done', in I. Bjorgo (ed.), *Root Causes of Terrorism: Myths, Realities and the Ways Forward* (London: Routledge, 2005), 241.
[117] Ibid.   [118] Ibid., 244.   [119] Ibid.

and ninety-seven civilians were either shot dead or blown up. The intended objectives of internment had clearly not been achieved.[120]

According to Paddy Hillyard:

[T]he lessons from Northern Ireland are clear. Widespread violation of human rights in the so called 'war against terrorism' is counterproductive. It erodes democracy by undermining the very principles on which social order is based and alienates the communities from whom the authorities need support in dealing with political violence.[121]

In particular, 'people are not going to report incidents or crucial information to the police when either their last contact was at best unpleasant and at worst humiliating and abusive or that they have heard how a neighbour or relative has been treated. Good intelligence is essential to prevent acts of terror, yet the authorities still appear to lack an understanding of the crucial role of good police community relations in this endeavour.'[122]

Anti-terrorism legislation and policy needs to take account of the impact on the communities whose cooperation is needed. Community engagement is the cornerstone of effective counterterrorism policy. As Briggs notes, those who argue that 'Muslims should tolerate inconveniences for the greater good, effectively put up and shut up... lack understanding about how security is really delivered in practice—always through consent, never through force'.[123] The need to build trust and support with communities is recognized in the National Policing Plan 2005–08. It provides that the counterterrorism strategy of Government is underpinned by 'strong community ties to build and increase trust and confidence within minority faith communities'.[124]

Building cooperation and trust with Muslim communities is critical not only in gathering intelligence but also in countering the strategic aims of terrorists to exploit the sensitivity of democratic societies to the insecurities of the majority of citizens and so provoke an overreaction from the State. This overreaction in turn will further alienate the minorities that are the focus of suspicion and thus make it easier for terrorists to exploit the situation and exacerbate community tensions.

In the House of Lords debates on the on pre-trail detention of up to 90 days, Lord Condon, the former Metropolitan Police Commissioner, warned that 'the battle against terrorism is a battle that will last for decades. It is a battle for hearts and minds...' He feared that, on balance, 'and it is a very fine balance', the extension of detention without charge might be counterproductive 'in the sense of

---

[120] *Paramilitary Imprisonment in Northern Ireland* (Oxford: OUP, 2001), 214–5.

[121] 'The "War on Terror": Lessons from Ireland' in *Essays for Civil Liberties and Democracy in Europe* (European Civil Liberties Newtwork, 2005), 4, <http://www.ecln.org/essays/essay-1.pdf> (last accessed 1 June 2008). See also C. Campbell and I. Connelly, 'Making War on Terror? Global Lessons from Northern Ireland' (2006) 69 *MLR* 935.

[122] Ibid., 2–3.   [123] See n. 92 above, 15.

[124] Home Office, 'National Policing Plan 2005–8: Safer, Stronger Communities' (London: HMSO, 2008), 22.

encouraging martyrdom rather than preventing it'. The struggle in his view was one that was 'a philosophical struggle that would endure for several decades'. In this context measures, such as 90 days detention 'would have enormous tactical advantage in the short term ... but that longer term and strategically it could be counterproductive'. Thus, the question for Parliament to decide was:

[H]aving heard what the police and intelligence agencies are advocating, what does this House and the other place feel is in the long-term benefit of the country in the fight against terrorism? Even though in one, two or three individual cases an extension to 90 days may help, my fear is what that might generate in terms of helping in the propaganda of terrorism. Often there is a misunderstanding about what *al-Qaeda* is. It is not a finite list of several hundred people and, once we have ticked them off and got them before a court and convicted, we will have stopped terrorism ... The huge publicity that has surrounded this debate has already generated enormous fear in law-abiding communities in parts of this country. If we now go back and make it look as though we are going to challenge yet again the point of 28 days that we have reached, I fear that it will play into the hands of the propagandists, who will encourage young men and women—to all other intents and purposes, they are good people—to be misguided.... [125]

There is concern that the use of powers under anti-terrorism laws is already having counterproductive impact on community cooperation. One particular area of concern is the increased use of stop and search powers under section 44 of the Terrorism Act 2000. The Muslim Council of Britain claimed that 'the police are misusing their new powers ... We think that the institutional racism highlighted by the McPherson report is morphing into institutional prejudice against Muslims. We are worried a generation of young Muslim men is being criminalized...' [126] Britain's most senior Muslim police officer, Assistant Commissioner Tarique Ghaffur, has commented that the impact of stop and search and passenger profiling has been to create 'a strong feeling of mass stereotyping within Muslim communities'. He believes that incidence such as the raid by anti-terrorism police on a house in Forrest Gate in East London during June 2006 that turned out to be based on unreliable intelligence and led to the shooting of an innocent young Muslim 'drip feeds into vulnerable communities and gradually erodes confidence and trust'. He also warns of 'a very real danger that the counterterrorism label is also being used by other law-enforcement agencies to the effect that there is a real risk of criminalising minority communities. The impact of this will be that just at the time we need the confidence and trust of these communities, they may retreat inside themselves. We therefore need proper accountability and transparency round all policy and direction that affects communities.' [127]

---

[125] Hansard HL Vol. 676 Col. 1174-5 (13 December 2005).

[126] R. Cowan, 'Young Muslims "Made Scapegoats" in Stop and Search', *The Guardian*, 3 July 2004. See also Liberty, *The Impact of Anti Terrorism Powers on the British Muslim Population* (London: 2004), <http://www.liberty-human-rights.org.uk/publications/6-reports/anti-terror-impact-brit-muslim.PDF> (last accessed 1 June 2008).

[127] Assistant Commissioner Tarique Ghaffur, speech to the Association of Black Police Officers (6 August 2006).

The government emphasized the importance of the signal that was being sent to terrorists by the explicit inclusion of glorification in the Terrorism Act 2006. The government needs to be equally cognisant about the signals sent out to the wider Muslim community by the introduction of legislation with such potentially broad and opaque terms. The former Home Office Minister John Denham M. P. placed the creation of the encouragement offences in the broader context of the overall counterterrorism strategy:

[This] ... is not a battle over what people are allowed to say; it is a question of how we win arguments. The battle is for hearts and minds. We must persuade young British people from the Muslim community who feel angry about what is happening in the world ... and who feel that in the west their Muslim lives are less valuable than others and their rights less valued than others, that engagement in politics, democracy, public life, and argument is the way to achieve change, not terrorism ... [A]gainst us are extremists who are arguing the opposite—that there is no way forward for them in western democracy; that it is a sham, an illusion and a dead end; and that terrorist violence is not only justified but the only way. We must be careful not to feed that argument. As the Bill stands, however, it is more helpful to the propaganda of extremists than it is to winning hearts and minds.[128]

The all encompassing definition of acts of terrorism found in the Terrorism Act 2000 and the failure to allow for distinctions between the indiscriminate killing of innocent civilians and attacks on the property and apparatus of a repressive state criminalizes all support for any political violence irrespective of the circumstance. The Act in Denham's view impedes the potential for nuanced response to the different context in which violence takes place:

It allows the extremists, in arguments that will take place in communities ... to argue that ... it is not even possible to support people who they regard as their brothers, and who are fighting occupation and winning elections, without being silenced. They will say that it is not possible to advocate a Muslim state without being silenced ... They will say that the terrorist route is the only way. That is the argument that will be advanced in streets and communities up and down the country, and what we must ask ourselves is whether the phrasing of clause 1 will help us to win the argument for democracy and engagement.[129]

The Report of the Working Groups set up by the Home Office in the aftermath of the July 2005 London bombings also expressed concerns about the impact of encouragement offences on political debate:

Inciting, justifying, or glorifying terrorism as currently formulated could lead to a significant chill factor in the Muslim community in expressing legitimate support for self-determination struggles around the world and in using legitimate concepts and terminology because of fear of being misunderstood and implicated for terrorism by the authorities.[130]

---

[128] Hansard HC Vol. 438 Col. 369–70 (26 October 2005).
[129] Hansard HC Vol. 438 Col. 370–1 (26 October 2005).
[130] Home Office, 'Preventing Extremism Together Working Groups August–October 2005' (London: HMSO, 2005), 77.

The view that this legislation was aimed to circumscribe the boundaries of acceptable political debate for Muslims was reinforced by perception that the provision in the 2006 Act to allow the proscription of organizations that glorify terrorism were targeted at *Hizb-ut-Tahrir*, an organization whose main achievement has been in shifting the debate within Islamist groups on the issue of the need for a new Caliphate and the centrality of religious identity over other national or ethnic ties.[131] This view was further reinforced by the Home Secretary Charles Clarke in his speech to the US Heritage Foundation in October 2005 where he declared that 'there can be no negotiation about the re-creation of the Caliphate; there can be no negotiation about the imposition of *Sharia* law'. Along with free speech and gender equality, these matters, he said, were 'simply not up for negotiation'.[132] For some Muslims this was a clear signal that such issues are outside the bounds of political debate. For them 'the main problem here is not that our governments disagree with the concept of the *Khilafah* (the re-creation of the Caliphate) and *Shariah* law. What is disturbing is the way in which they are determined to close debate and to tighten the boundaries of inclusiveness in mainstream society.'[133]

Attitudes and treatment based on stereotypes and prejudice are one of the ways in which Muslims encounter discrimination. Young Muslim men have emerged as the new 'folk devils' of popular and media imagination, being represented as the embodiment of fundamentalism. To be a British Muslim is defined 'solely in terms of negativity, deprivation, disadvantage, and alienation'.[134] In public discourse Muslim men are not only conceptualized as 'dangerous individuals' with a capacity for violence and terrorism, but also as 'culturally dangerous', as threatening 'the British way of life/civilisation'.[135]

There is a risk that the encouragement offences will exacerbate and reinforce the prejudice and discrimination directed towards Muslims, which in turn plays a significant role in increasing vulnerabilities for radicalization. As the encouragement offence can be committed without any intent to encourage terrorism but recklessly, individuals who do not want to risk violating the law will have to carefully consider whether a statement is 'likely to be understood by some or all

---

[131] See n. 86 above.

[132] 'Contesting the Threat of Terrorism' (Speech to the Heritage Foundation, Washington DC, October 2005), <http://www.heritage.org/Research/HomelandSecurity/upload/84232_1.pdf> (last accessed 1 June 2008).

[133] 'In Blunkett's Footsteps' 7 *Reflections* 1, reproduced at <http://reimagginingtheummah.blogspot.com/search?q=footsteps> (last accessed 1 June 2008); see also O. Saeed, 'The Return of Caliphate', *The Guardian*, 1 November 2005, <http://www.guardian.co.uk/politics/2005/nov/01/religion.world> (last accessed 1 June 2006).

[134] C. E. Alexander, *The Asian Gang: Ethnicity, Identity, Masculinity* (Oxford: Berg, 2000), 6.

[135] L. Archer, *Race, Masculinity and Schooling: Muslim Boys and Education*, (Maidenhead: Open UP, 2003), 157. See also L. Fekete, 'Anti-Muslim Racism and the European Security State' (2004) 46 *Race and Class* 3.

members of the public to whom it is published as a direct or indirect encouragement or other inducement'. As discussed earlier, there is great uncertainty how this provision of the Act will be applied, especially where a statement is made to a wide audience. This lack of clarity creates space for stereotypes and prejudice to slip in unconsciously in the application of this provision. In trying to explain the provision, the Home Office Minster argued that 'for an offence to be committed, the audience has to understand that what is being said is an inducement for them and no one else to commit terrorist acts. For example, no offence will be committed if a member of an audience at an academic lecture thinks, "Well, I am not encouraged to commit terrorist acts, but I can quite imagine that, *if this sentiment was expressed at a gathering of young Muslim men*, it could have an encouraging effect on them"' (emphasis added).[136] Implicit in the thought that the Minister attributes to the person listening to the lecture is the shared assumption that 'young Muslim men' as a group need to be treated with caution because of the potential risk of their radicalization. To stay within the law, ordinary law abiding citizens may, just like the person in the lecture theatre, consider what impact their statement may have on 'young Muslim men' when such men form the public, or a section of the public, to whom their statement is made. In this way, the legislation perpetuates the construction of young Muslim men as a dangerous threat to society.

6. Conclusion

There is no doubt that the United Kingdom faces a serious threat from both 'home grown' and international terrorism. Overall, the government is pursuing a sensible medium term counterterrorism strategy that recognizes the need to take steps to address the background social, economic, and political factors that increase the risks of violent radicalization. The need of community engagement is broadly accepted, if not always perfectly achieved.[137] The law has a role to play in helping to tackle terrorism. However, new offences, particularly those that are preventative and place restriction on fundamental rights must be necessary to be justified. The encouragement offences in the Terrorism Act 2006 aim to prevent violent radicalization by prohibiting public statements which contribute to the creation of a climate 'in which impressionable people might believe that terrorism was acceptable'.[138] It is not clear, however, that public statements covered by the legislation play a significant role in a process of radicalization that takes place largely through private communication. Radical websites may contain extensive

[136] Hansard HC Vol. 439 Col. 391 (9 November 2005).

[137] B. Spalek and A. Imtoual, '"Hard" Approaches to Community Engagement in the UK and Australia: Muslim Communities and Counter-Terror Responses' (2007) 27(2) *Journal of Muslim Minority Affairs* 185.

[138] Hansard HL Vol. 675 Col. 1385 (21 November 2005).

legal and theological arguments that justify and thereby encourage, directly or indirectly, acts of terrorism. But the persuasiveness of these statements often rests on the absence of alternative speech rebutting and challenging the arguments made. Even if the encouragement offences may contribute towards the prevention of violent radicalization, in judging their efficacy this benefit must be weighed against the potential counterproductive impact of these offences on the overall counterterrorism strategy. Here, the potential breadth of the encouragement offences, together with the lack of certainty produced by several of their central aspects, have created a serious risk that any short term benefits to be gained from this law is outweighed by the long term damage it may inflict on the overall counterterrorism strategy. The Terrorism Act of 2006 thus blurs rather than clarifies the lines between radicals and terrorist. It fails to draw a distinction between those who resist oppressive regimes without endangering the lives of innocent civilians and those that indiscriminately kill innocent people. It requires people to construct an image of the potential terrorist and thereby risks reinforcing perceptions of young Muslim men as a dangerous threat to society. All this leaves one wondering, who exactly is encouraging terrorism?

24

Radical Religious Speech: The Ingredients of a Binary World View

Sara Savage and Jose Liht

1. Introduction: The Shaping Power of Language

What power does extreme speech have to incite violence? Do people simply imbibe it and march according to its orders? In this chapter we argue that a confluence of social and psychological factors affecting young Muslims living in the West can augment the persuasiveness of radical Islamist discourse in such a way that the discourse is taken to describe 'how things really are'. We argue that actions (such as religiously motivated violence or civic non-participation) are not automatically sparked by extreme religious speech, but rather these actions 'make sense' and become more likely if its hearers possess a social construction of reality to which the 'story' of radical Islamism readily connects.

Foucault argues that ways people use language form the building blocks of social reality. Discourses, that is, any socially shared body of speech or text, are understood as 'practices that systematically form the objects of which they speak'.[1] By virtue of the way language selects some features of reality, and rejects others, a particular version of reality is constructed. A category, word, or sentence inevitably points to 'this', and not 'that'. Language therefore cannot provide a neutral one-to-one correspondence with infinitely complex reality. Rather, it plays an active role in selectively constructing that reality. Accordingly, Foucault asserts that the one who defines the world, controls it. For example, by studying the history of madness, Foucault identified the power of psychiatric labels to define and control those to whom they were applied. A diagnosis of 'schizophrenia' is likely to shape the entire life of the person so labelled, whether that label is warranted or not.[2] Language is therefore a terrain for power struggles.

Whereas clearly discourses are not neutral, we argue that Foucault's 'hard' archaeological approach to discourse tends to reify language, as if language itself is

---

[1] M. Foucault, *The Archaeology of Knowledge* (New York: Pantheon Books, 1972), 54.
[2] M. Foucault, *History of Madness*, J. Khalfa (ed.), (London: Routledge, 2006).

the agent acting in society. In reality, humans are the agents. Our approach in this chapter is to explore the cognitive and social processes that operate *upon* and *through* extreme religious discourse, thus activating its latent potential. Discourses only have power when they speak to a given construction of reality that people already possess. A discourse which fails to connect with listeners' own experience and construction of reality will appear bizarre and irrelevant, but speech that conveys a worldview that makes sense of listener's experience will be absorbed into the already existing framework of beliefs, altering, over time, that framework.

Three main concerns are addressed in this chapter. In Section 2, we examine the key structural features of Islamist radical religious speech and their likely cognitive consequences. Key structural features considered here are: the three-part narrative echoing primitive and dualist world views resulting in low levels of complexity, rhetorical strategies, the 'rationalistic' word-based emphasis that avoids the nuancing influence of symbolic aspects of the sacred text, the closed way in which the belief system is organized, and the mutual misrepresentation afflicting both Islamists and the West through the 'myth of pure evil'. In Section 3, we explore the need for a positive social identity to which extreme religious discourse appeals, particularly among second and third generation young Muslims living in Europe and Britain. The authors' current work is to design and test de-radicalizing educational resources for young Muslims in Britain and Europe, and our expertise lies with this population. The Muslim diaspora in Britain and Europe share certain historical and cultural factors that are distinct from Muslim populations in other parts of the world. Thus, section 3, pertaining to identity issues, describes in particular the experience of young Muslims in Britain and Europe. Extreme speech is most powerfully 'activated' under totalist group conditions. A totalist group seeks to become a members' main social and cognitive universe, thus amplifying the group's influence. Totalist groups intensify group-based identity at the expense of individual identity. In Section 4, we explore the implications for policy-makers of the now widespread Islamist discourse. Do-it-yourself assembly kits of this binary vision are now widely available at thousands of radicalizing websites. By flooding the marketplace of ideas, this particular version of social reality is gaining the *'of course'* status of the everyday among many young Muslims. Thus, while sacrificing its revolutionary patina as 'extreme' speech, it extends its reach.

2. Structural Features of Islamist Radical Religious Discourse

(i) Narrative

A basic narrative, or story, has become widespread, encouraging and legitimating the new pattern of religiously motivated violence. Terrorism in previous decades has aimed at achieving concrete, political goals. The recent pattern of terrorism, as in the attack on the Twin Towers, differs in its absence of prior bargaining, the suicide of the terrorists, and the goal of maximum loss of life and damage to social structures (as symbolized by the destruction of the World Trade Centre). These features suggest that the main goal of current terrorism perpetrated against western targets is to achieve a sweeping revision concerning which groups have most status and influence on the world stage, well beyond immediate, practical gains.

What kind of story can make sense of such actions? Stories are a major cognitive tool that people use to make sense of the world. Stories account for the links between events (causation) and provide a sense concerning the way life should unfold (teleology). Children (of all ages) are gripped by a good story and are frustrated if the ending is missed out, or is somehow incongruent. Stories work by building up a dramatic tension, and providing a resolution. The power of story is subtle, but all the more influential for being less than explicit. According to Griemas, all basic stories, such as folk tales or fairly tales, comprise three parts: (1) an initial sequence; (2) the obstacle and the help; and (3) the resolution.[3] Versions of reality that take this three-part structure make sense to people; such accounts already have 'a foot in the door' in common-sense understanding. A thumbnail sketch of the 3-part storyline, following the contours of radical Islamist thought (deriving from the writings of Maududi and Murad,[4] Qutb,[5] and Nabhani[6] in combination with Saudi Salafi literalism), is as follows:

(1) The initial sequence:

There once was a golden age of Islam.

(2) The obstacle and the help:

The West intervened through colonization, the imposition of secular states, support of Israel, and a host of illegitimate wars. The purity of Islam was compromised within the Muslim world and Muslims are now oppressed around the world by the secular and godless West. There is one solution, enshrined (purportedly) as the centrepiece of the Qur'an: it is the duty of all Muslims to struggle for the institution of Sharia law and to reinstate the Caliphate in order to usher in the perfect Islamic society.

(3) The resolution:

The prestige, power, and purity of Islam vis-à-vis the West is a zero-sum game that Islam will win. The perfect Islamic society is the will of Allah; martyrs will be rewarded. Both internal (compromised Muslims) and external (Western) enemies are fair game.

Thus, the traditional, socially conservative, and peaceful role of religion in Muslim societies has been turned into a mobilizing narrative and this has been

---

[3] N. T. Wright, *Christian Origins and the Question of God* (Minneapolis, MN: Fortress Press, 1992). Wright uses a version of A. J. Griemas' narrative analysis for his own literary analysis.

[4] S. A. A. Maududi and K. Murad, *The Islamic Movement: Dynamics of Values, Power, and Change* (Leicester: Islamic Foundation, 1984).

[5] A. Bergesen (ed.), *The Sayyid Qutb Reader: Selected Writings on Politics, Religion, and Society* (New York: Routledge, 2007).

[6] T. Nabhani, *The Islamic State* (New Delhi: Milli Publications, 2001).

exported worldwide thanks to the Internet and an avalanche of Saudi-backed resources. This mobilizing narrative serves several important goals. First, it deflects attention from the internal troubles within Islamic countries by concentrating on both real and perceived harm caused by past and present Western policies. Secondly, by finding a scapegoat outside itself, the cohesion of Muslim society and its religious worldview is saved. Thirdly, diaspora Muslims are given a rallying call to identify with, and defend, the transnational *umma* (the wordwide community of Muslim believers).

A number of scholars argue that this narrative structure fosters a psychological state of 'splitting' where the in-group is seen as all good and the out-group as all bad.[7,8] The term 'splitting' is rooted in the post-Freudian work of Klein, who theorized that infants typically deal with their experience of frustration (and terror) in response to mothering that fails to meet their needs by 'splitting'. In this defensive position, the infant's concept of the 'good', caring mother (or breast) is split off from the 'bad', uncaring mother. This is a split that preserves the fantasy of the all-good, all-caring mother upon whom the infant so literally depends (although a separate, all-bad mother now also 'exists').[9] A similarly binary vision is evidenced in various ancient narrative structures such as 'the myth of redemptive violence' identified by Ricœur. In this narrative structure, based in primitive myths preceding the monotheisms, violence is seen as necessary and redemptive. It is necessary to exterminate the bad in order to preserve the good.[10] The myth of redemptive violence first appeared in the ancient Babylonian myth of creation: the Enuma Elish. In this myth, chaos and evil are seen as primordial and absolute and must be continually conquered by force, lest they overwhelm the given order. This myth voices the struggle of the ancient empires to impose their control. All crimes against the polity are thus crimes against heaven and are violently crushed for threatening the cosmic order. As chaos and evil are understood as the basic substratum of reality, pre-emptive force is continually required to keep it at bay. Violence is redemptive: it is the only way that good can be maintained.

Our argument is that, when activated in contemporary discourse, the basic story-line of 'redemptive violence' screens out the more peaceful, integratively complex and universalizing aspects of Islam. A number of religious scholars concur that the theological world views of all three monotheisms (Christianity, Judaism, and Islam), each with their own particular, yet internally heterogeneous and often nuanced approaches to the problem of evil, can be collapsed into primitive states of splitting.[11] This is particularly the case when people feel they

---

[7] C. T. Davis, 'Seeds of Violence in Biblical Hermenuetics' in J. H. Ellens (ed.) *The Destructive Power of Religion* (Westport, CT: Greenwood Press, 2004), 35.

[8] J. Piven, 'On the Psychosis (Religion) of Terrorists', *The Psychology of Terrorism*, Vol. 3 (Westport, CT: Greenwood Press, 2004), 119.

[9] M. Klein, *Developments in Psycho Analysis (Psychoanalysis Examined and Re-Examined)*, J. Riviere (ed.), (New York: Da Capo Press, 1983).

[10] P. Ricœur, *Fallible Man* (New York: Fordham UP, 1986).

[11] W. Wink, *Naming The Powers* (Philadelphia: Fortress Press, 1984).

are under threat. Violence against the 'evil' that threatens is then seen to be 'good'.

Another ancient narrative structure is described by Girard, who argues that the myth of 'the violent sacred' has surfaced at times of crisis throughout the process of hominization, the long journey of early humans towards a shared, humaning culture. In the myth of the violent sacred, the substitutionary death of a scapegoat is required in order to save the social group. Girard argues that this scapegoating narrative underlies the three monotheisms and can be activated in times of threat. This narrative, along with its urge towards a violent resolution, comes into play in times of extreme rivalrous crisis between social groups.[12] It is arguable that globalization and immigration patterns are having the effect of 'shrinking' geographic space and increasing competition between groups for the available social resources (such as status and prestige) and physical resources (shrinking also due to global warming). When groups become locked in a rivalry so advanced that the existence of all is threatened, if a scapegoat can be found (usually randomly selected but having some odd or distinctive features) and violence enacted upon it, the ensuing catharsis saves the wider society from self-destruction. 'Evil' is externalized as outside the group and then expunged. Both the powerful drive to kill the enemy and preserve the group are fulfilled through scapegoating.

Scholars agree that the initial goal of Islamism was to subvert and overthrow compromised Muslim regimes, such as in Egypt or Saudi Arabia. These attempts failed, and only secondly has attention has been turned to an external (Western) enemy.[13] In Islamist extreme speech, suicide bombers are exhorted to expunge evil through the killing of random civilian targets, thus winning for themselves a 'heroic' martyrdom. The terrible logic of these otherwise incomprehensible acts is clarified to some degree when seen through the lens of the redemptive violence and scapegoating narratives, with their fantasy, cathartic resolutions to highly threatened states.

Our argument here is that although awareness of primitive narratives underlying an ideology is usually less than conscious, such narrative forms present deeply familiar ways of making sense of powerful emotions and conflicts in daily life. They secretly add their weight to contemporary Islamist discourse. Mythical narratives functioned similarly in the case of Nazi ideology. Such narratives, we argue, invite 'regression' to more constricted psychological states.

(ii) Rhetorical Strategies

Whenever people use language, they do so to *accomplish* certain aims: to persuade, to accuse, to justify, to encourage, to control. Islamist discourse is no exception in

---

[12] R. Girard, *The Scapegoat* (Baltimore: Johns Hopkins UP, 1986).
[13] G. Kepel, *The War for Muslim Minds: Islam and the West* (Cambridge, MA: Belknap Press/ Harvard UP, 2004).

this respect. It is fair game that most speakers employ rhetorical strategies to achieve their goals and that they seek to present their version of reality as self-evidently correct.[14] Religious and political discourses are typically heavily ladened with rhetorical strategies. There are five distinct stages of classical rhetoric: *inventio* (invention); *dispositio* (arrangement); *elocutio* (style); *memoria* (memorization); and *pronuntiatio* (delivery). Seven strategies, described below, largely fall into the third stage of style (*elocutio*).[15]

(a) 'Us' and 'Them'

Cognitively, people tend to think in simple contrasts, in binaries.[16] Indeed, all mental activity, including visual perception, proceeds on the basis of contrast; neurons have only one 'word'. They either fire ('on') or they do not fire ('off'). These 'words' have the job of conveying a rich, subjectively experienced reality. Reality is so complex, and yet short-term memory and attentional capacities are so restricted, that it is necessary for humans to impose simplifying categories upon the incessant flow of stimuli. Categories are the building block of our cognitive system. The most basic categorical distinctions people make involve the categorization of something into two parts: the good and the bad, us and them, in-groups and out-groups. The primitive archaic narratives and infant states of splitting (into good/bad) described above illustrate this tendency.

An analysis of the communications of Osama Bin Laden, illustrates the way Bin Laden employs splitting in his depictions of Muslims versus Westerners. Presented as polar opposites, Muslims are categorized as all good; Westerners as all bad. The West is presented as the antithesis of the perfection Bin Laden preaches: pious, moral, chaste, ascetic, disciplined. The achievements of the West are ignored or downplayed, whereas its flaws and problems are highlighted. Labels such as 'infidels,' routinely used of Westerners, insinuate a sense of threat to the Islamic religious worldview, thus increasing the likelihood of splitting into a binary vision. In a state of threat, cognitive constriction occurs, critical reasoning is restricted, and blind, uncritical acceptance of a discourse can readily ensue.[17]

(b) Caricatures

Caricatures operate like 'straw men'. Instead of responding to a real person or a fair portrayal of a differing viewpoint, this rhetorical strategy exaggerates features

---

[14] J. M. Atkinson and J. Heritage (eds.), *Structures of Social Action: Studies in Conversation Analysis* (Cambridge: CUP, 1984).

[15] E. P. J. Corbett and R. J. Connors, *Classical Rhetoric for the Modern Student*, 4th edn. (New York: OUP, 1999).

[16] B. D. Reed, *The Dynamics of Religion: Process and Movement in Christian Churches* (London: Darton, Longman and Todd, 1978).

[17] J. Unrath, Integrative Complexity Analysis in the Discourse of Osama bin Laden from 1994 to 2007 (Unpublished MPhil project, University of Cambridge, 2007).

that can be exploited, and downplays other aspects that would counteract the exaggeration. A caricature, for example, of George Bush as a Zionist, Crusader, and murderer, is a way of maintaining clear in-group/out-group category boundaries, as the leader is held to be a prototype of the group. In Bin Laden's communications, he routinely attributes the responsibility for every negative aspect of Muslim experience to the 'Jewish-Crusader alliance'. Shorthand terms such as 'Great Satan' encapsulate the caricature and its underlying arguments. As discourses are shared and reinforced by a social group, to disagree with, or even to modify, a prevailing caricature is to set oneself outside the boundaries of the moral community.

(c) Foot in the Door

The author or speaker draws you in just enough to get your attention and sympathy, and gets his foot in the door through a shared interest. By selectively quoting from the Qur'an, radical Islamist discourse presents itself as a valid, pious interpretation of Islam. This strategy is most successful among secularized young Muslims who lack the in-depth knowledge of Islam that could enable them to critique the radical discourse. This strategy is particularly effective among 'bad' Muslims, those in prison or otherwise excluded from the Muslim community. Prison populations offer rich recruiting grounds, as the radical discourse gets a 'foot in the door' by offering an opportunity for shamed young men to atone for their otherwise unforgivable sins. By taking up the call to join a training camp or terrorist cell, the new adherent can atone for his sin and return to the *umma* as a hero.

(d) Thin Edge of the Wedge

If we allow x, then y will happen. This rhetorical strategy is not really arguing against x, but against y. If, for example, European Muslims were to vote in Western democracies (x), then the will of Allah (the ideal Islamic society) will be prevented (y). Those who use this rhetorical strategy are linking something that *they* oppose (non-violent methods of civic protest, voting and civic participation in democratic societies) to something that most *'right thinking people'* oppose (the will of Allah), claiming that support of one entails support of the other.

(e) Domino Reasoning

As an extension of the 'thin edge of the wedge', not only y will happen, but x, z, q, w will happen, and then everything will collapse. The end-point is catastrophic. For example, if women are allowed to be unveiled, their honour is tainted, then the honour of their families will be degraded, the men will be shamed, resulting in the breakdown in the family, eventually leading to a *total loss of moral and spiritual values*. This rhetorical strategy links the initial focus of opposition with a loss so huge that any other viewpoint is overwhelmed. The predicted outcome is so disastrous that it must be avoided at all costs.[18]

(f) Emotional Tone, Flow, Rhythm and Metaphor

Unrath describes the style of language used by Bin Laden when addressing a Muslim audience as emotive, duty-oriented, and poetic in a style very reminiscent of the sacred texts of Islam. Bin Laden's phraseology, word choice, and the short rhythmic sentences echo the sacred texts in such a way as to suggest to followers that his words are the *only* true and correct tradition dating back to Mohammad himself. His style of language is reinforced by the visual symbolism of Bin Laden's dress, manner, and ascetic (cave) habitation, all of which emulate the Prophet's manner of living. As all Muslims are enjoined to emulate the Prophet's way of life, Bin Laden provides a potent visual and verbal reminder of this injunction.[19]

(g) Appearance of Rationality

In sharp contrast, when addressing the West, Bin Laden uses clear reason and logic. He speaks very plainly and matter-of-factly.

... [his words] are carefully chosen, plainly spoken, and precise. He has set out the Muslim world's problems as he sees them; determined that they are caused by the United States; explained why they must be remedied; and outlined how he will try to do so.[20]

However, Unrath argues that even though he uses a more logical rhetoric when addressing a Western audience, Bin Laden relies mainly on "if... then" statements and absolutist demands which are conceptually simple.[21]

An appearance of rationality marks even the most basic tracts and pamphlets produced by radical Islamists. Rightly acknowledging the pivotal role Islamic scholars played in philosophy, mathematics, and science during Islam's Golden Age (while Europe lagged behind during the Dark and Middle Ages), the appearance of rationality evokes a (historically-based) positive, distinctive sense of Islamic identity, while at the same time giving a legitimating 'nod' in the direction of the current prestige of contemporary scientific rationality. While radical Islamist discourse is, in fact, heavily ladened with emotional tone and rhetorical strategies (as are most political discourses), this is cloaked with an appearance of rationality.

(iii) Propositional, Word-Based Processing

We have just argued that radical Islamist discourse seeks to present purportedly correct religious knowing in terms of word-based, rationalistic assertions. The

[18] S. Savage and E. Boyd-Macmillan, *The Human Face of Church* (London: SCM/Canterbury Press, 2007).
[19] See n. 17 above.   [20] See n. 17 above, 5.   [21] See n. 17 above.

claim that the highest purpose of a Muslim is to struggle for the Caliphate is well-served by demoting non-political, symbolic, devotional, or mystical aspects of Islam. The symbolic aspects of traditional Islam that could nuance and broaden this message are thereby obscured.

Watts argues that religious knowing entails two distinct kinds of processing: a word-based (propositional) knowing (as in doctrine) and a dense, implicational, symbolic, metaphorical knowing too deep for words. Implicational knowing layers and integrates input from ritual, emotions, and bodily states. These two distinct ways of processing ideally function as a holistic system: propositional statements are best served when understood in a rich implicational context and ritual practices are enriched by the rational understanding provided by the tradition. Religious devotees normally possess a reservoir of word-based and implicational knowledge with which to understand the multiple meanings of religious content.[22] Under these ideal conditions, polarized conclusions from religious discourse are usually avoided. However, Islamist radical discourse appears to isolate implicational from propositional (word-based) content, thus destroying the polyvalent nature of religious knowing. Clear-cut, extreme conclusions are thereby promoted.

A degree of doublespeak is afoot. While extreme speech gives the appearance of rationality concerning its belief tenets and the obligations it lays on it hearers, it simultaneously seeks to evoke intense emotion, not least through the rapid fire, arousing, intense delivery of a number of high-profile radical preachers. Basic emotions like shame, rage, and fear are evoked as listeners are invited to identify with the injustices and sufferings of Muslims worldwide. Shame is a highly aversive emotional state and is likely to be even more so in an honour culture, where to fail to take up the invitation to right the wrongs of injustice is to remain in an intolerably shamed state.

(iv) Intratextuality

Another feature of extreme speech concerns its logical structure, a feature that would fall under classical rhetoric's *dispositio* (arrangement). Hood, Hill, and Williamson argue that fundamentalist belief systems (whether Christian, Islamic, Jewish, or other) are typically organized as a closed system: in their parlance, as an intra-textual system.[23] Whether a belief system is organized in a closed or open way has systematic cognitive consequences.[24] A closed belief system is one that is organized around a central authority belief. The validity of all other beliefs logically descends from the inviolate, sacred authority belief. Beliefs are true

---

[22] F. N. Watts, 'Implicational and propositional religious meanings' *Int'l J. Psychology of Relig* (submitted 2007).

[23] *The Psychology of Religious Fundamentalism* (New York: Guilford Press, 2005).

[24] M. Rokeach, *The Open and Closed Mind: Investigations into the Nature of Belief Systems and Personality Systems* (New York: Basic Books, 1960).

because, for example, 'the Bible tells me so' or 'the Qur'an says'. Disconfirming evidence is not allowed to modify the authority belief, and is systematically screened out. As conflicting perspectives are routinely excluded, arguments within a closed belief system show lower integrative complexity. Islamist speech is organized in this way, intra-textually, around a central authority belief (the Qu'ranic message, but highly selectively interpreted by radical discourse).[25] All other beliefs must be validated in a one-way direction from the authority belief to peripheral beliefs (such as dress, diet, family structure, political allegiances). What the Qu'ran says (as interpreted by radicalizers) is what ordinary people must believe and do. Never do the peripheral beliefs or practices of ordinary believers modify the authority belief. It is a one-way direction of validation, and this protects the authority belief from reality-testing. It is convenient that authority beliefs (concerning God) are usually of an abstract, unfalsifiable nature, whereas peripheral beliefs ('voting is unIslamic'), are somewhat more vulnerable to reality-testing. It is a malign coincidence that a closed system is precisely what a recruiter could wish for in a successful, obedient terrorist who does not ask questions or entertain alternate perspectives.

On the positive side, intra-textual systems have the capacity to provide adherents, in the face of secular culture, with a robust sense of meaning and purpose. They provide a coherent religious discipline through which people can seek to transform their lives. Whereas the creators and disseminators of radical Islamist discourse appear to be transparently motivated towards political ends, we argue that *followers* of the discourse become genuinely religiously motivated. Their intensified religiosity, often sincerely motivated, takes on a life of its own, innocent, to some degree, of the ultimate aims of the discourse creators. It is not incidental that Islamist extreme speech purports to connect young Muslims to God. If you are seeking to mobilize people to kill themselves and others, people are reluctant to venture into that territory unless they believe they have God on their side, and that they are fighting 'evil'. The complex reality is that sincere, devotional motives become enmeshed with the pleasure that a sense of certainty, group superiority and the promise of vindication (or revenge) supply. The rhetorical strategies described thus far are well designed to achieve that powerful mixture.

(v) Integrative Complexity

The 'us' and 'them' rhetorical strategy described above is typical of low integrative complexity. What characterizes extreme religious speech is its lack of complexity: an all-good, in-group is pitted against a dominant, all-bad, illegitimate out-group. The complexity of information processing is a powerful predictor of inter-group confrontation. Integratively complex thinking recognizes the legitimacy of

[25] See n. 23 above.

different evaluative viewpoints and is capable of higher-order synthesis of these viewpoints. Low integrative complexity thinks in terms of, for example, binary, black, and white contrasts with little or no integration of the perspectives.[26] In previous research, IC analysis—the coding of complexity in verbal material on a 1 to 7 scale—has predicted the course of major international crises leading to either the outbreak of war or to peaceful compromise.[27,28] Dozens of studies on the IC of communications delivered by decision-making elites show that when international crises ensue and IC maintains peacetime baseline levels, conflict is resolved without recourse to violence. However, when IC plummets, war typically follows.

Unrath's examination of the integrative complexity of Bin Laden's speeches and sermons, using IC analysis, provides evidence that Bin Laden's speeches and sermons significantly dropped to very levels of integrative complexity directly before 9/11, and again just before the foiled attempt to blow up aeroplanes in June 2006. These findings are in line with predictions that drops in IC predict violent confrontation and lends further support the evidence that Bin Laden was planning both those attacks.[29] The research, prevention, and conflict resolution potential of examining the IC of extreme Islamist speech are discussed in Section 4.

(vi) Thinking as Arguing

Any discourse is part of an ongoing 'conversation' within a particular zeitgeist. In line with Gadamer's hermeneutic principle, a statement (or argument) only makes sense when the underlying question that it addresses is understood. Thus any discourse is part of a 'conversation' involving the discourse speakers and the discourse audience (or adversaries).[30] Billig argues that the form of argument (for example, the statement of a proposition and its antithesis) characterizes much social dialogue. It is characteristic of most dyadic arguments that one person will take a somewhat extreme position on an issue (thesis), 'in order to make a point', expecting that the counter argument (antithesis) will be provided by the other person. It is understood that the caveats and qualifications omitted from the thesis will be duly mopped up by the antithesis. Typically, both parties involved in an argument will take extreme positions (with their consequently lower IC) implicitly knowing that both contributions are needed to provide the bigger

---

[26] P. Suedfeld, K. Guttieri, and P. E. Tetlock, 'Assessing Integrative Complexity at a Distance: Archival Analysis of Thinking and Decision Making' in J. M. Post (ed.), *The Psychological Assessment of Political Leaders: With Profiles of Saddam Hussein and Bill Clinton* (Ann Arbor, MI: Univ Michigan Press, 2003), 246.

[27] J. M. Satterfield and M. E. P. Seligman, 'Military Aggression and Risk Predicted by Explanatory Style' (1994) 5 *Psychological Sci.* 77.

[28] P. E. Tetlock and A. Tyler, 'Churchill's Cognitive and Rhetorical Style: The Debates over Nazi Intentions and Self-Government for India' (1996) 17 *Pol. Psychology* 149.

[29] See n. 17 above.

[30] H. G. Gadamer, *Truth and Method* (London: Continuum, 2004).

picture (with the potential for higher integrative complexity if opposing perspectives are integrated). Billig has further pointed out that much of our thinking follows this rhetorical 'arguing' form.[31] Following this, much of our intra-individual 'inner speech' may lack the qualifying arguments that would be presented by the implied conversational partner, or 'adversary', which then tends to be marked by low IC.

Radical Islamist discourse is no exception. The discourse is an argument that locates the causes of problems within Islamic societies (and diaspora) squarely on the shoulders of the secular West. In diagnosing the problem in this way, this solution logically follows: a return to an intensified, literalist, politicized Islam. How the Western media represents this discourse is not irrelevant to the unfolding of the drama being played out.

(vii) The Myth of Pure Evil

When Western media covers the activities inspired by radical Islamic discourse, the accounts are often clothed within the 'myth of pure evil'.[32] This story line, so prevalent in the popular media accounts of violence (for example, tabloid press, horror films, and TV news coverage of crime, terrorism, and violence) replays, in simplified form, features of the myth of redemptive violence:

- a thoroughly evil actor perpetrates violence
- against a completely innocent victim
- for no reason other than the selfish gain of the perpetrator/s, and/or his/their sadistic pleasure in harming others.

When a crime of violence is portrayed in this binary, good versus evil manner, the required response is clear: fight back furiously. The myth of pure evil serves a number of purposes: it inspires sympathy for the victims by portraying the violence as sheer evil; it galvanizes action against the outrage; and it counters the subtle bias to 'blame the victim' (a function of the widely held 'Just World theory' in which victims are believed to get what they deserve). Many people, victims and audience alike, report that they 'feel better' when the world is portrayed in the simplified terms of the myth of pure evil. It is comforting when evil is viewed as entirely 'other'.

The myth of pure evil also resonates with the memory bias of victims. This binary account will appear intuitively correct, as well, to those who side with the victims of an outrage. Baumeister describes the bias that regularly attends the thinking and perception of victims and contrasts this with the bias of perpetrators. Not surprisingly, both biases show some self-serving elements. Victims of violent crime regularly (and understandably) see the harm caused by the offence as

---

[31] M. Billig, *Arguing and Thinking: A Rhetorical Approach to Social Psychology* (Cambridge: CUP and Paris: Maison des Sciences de l'Homme, 1996).

[32] R. F. Baumeister, *Evil: Inside Human Cruelty and Violence* (New York: W. H. Freeman, 1997), 17.

extreme, long-lasting (if not permanent), completely unwarranted, unprovoked, and undeserved. Perpetrators of violent crime regularly minimize the damage they cause, argue that they 'didn't mean it', or that the harm inflicted could not have been 'that bad', or that they were acting in self-defence, or that there were other mitigating factors. In fact, violent people often view themselves in the role of the victim: they simply were *finally* reacting to the party who they feel has victimized them for so long.[33]

Baumeister's research into the thinking and selective memories of both victims and perpetrators presents us with some uncomfortable truths. While not minimizing the incalculable harm resulting from violent crime, most often, in reality, both perspectives have some validity. Most acts of violence are embedded within a spiral of increasing mutual harm that leads up to the final violent drama that publicly cements the roles of victim and perpetrator. The mutual aggression *mounts* throughout the spiral of mutual harm (verbal, physical, economic, or military); it rarely appears out of nowhere. Based on criminal records and trial proceedings, statistically, this is almost always so in the case of domestic violence, and collective or state violence usually follows the same pattern. Rarely is the victim victimized entirely out of the blue.[34]

In the 'War on Terror', the myth of pure evil, as advanced both by the victims of religious violence (the West and other victims of recent terrorism) and its perpetrators (Islamists who consider themselves in the role of victims reacting to long term damage), obfuscates the complexity of this social reality. The act of terrorism is a violent punctuation mark to a spiral of mutual harm. This in turn perpetuates the cycle of violence as the new victim now has a reason to retaliate with an even higher level of violence. Offences that publicly shame or damage an inflated ego are especially likely to provoke extreme retaliation as the perpetrator seeks to restore a desired superior social status. Thus, efforts at de-radicalizing young Muslims need to take this wider picture into account and the systematic mutual misrepresentation in the worldwide media.

3. The Appeal of Islamist Extreme Speech

We now discuss the social psychological needs to which Islamist extreme speech appeals, particularly among young British and European Muslims. Why would British and European Muslims turn against the society that has offered them education, social welfare, and employment prospects? Our argument is that the erosion of the traditional religious world in these western countries leads to self-definitional uncertainty among young Muslims. This is particularly the case with second or third generation Muslims who imbibe two cultures (communally-based Muslim and individualistic Western culture), in contrast to their parents who are

---

[33] Ibid.   [34] Ibid.

often firmly embedded within their own ethnic community of origin. This is internalized as self-definitional uncertainty: the 'Who am I?' question so vital for young people. Uncertain identities (and related underachievement) create an opening which can be filled by a new Islamist group identity robust enough to withstand identity threat.

This aversive state of identity uncertainty, along with threats to their religious/cultural world view, motivates young people to gain a new group identity to withstand identity uncertainty and dissonance experienced within the host society. Totalist, radical groups re-evoke the collective, communal nature of Muslim traditional culture, and provide an opportunity to belong to, and merge with, a valued group. Uncertainty Reduction Theory demonstrates that group identity is better able to defend against uncertainty than are individual identities.[35] Tightly boundaried groups requiring high levels of conformity and obedience are particularly effective at warding off feelings of uncertainty. In the case of Islamist radical groups, the extremist, totalist group leader (usually male) becomes the prototype around which vulnerable identities can model themselves.

It so happens that into this context of identity uncertainty, an abundance of Saudi Salafist Islamist discourse has arrived, employing a mobilizing narrative in which the prestige of Islam vis-à-vis the West is the central concern. Groups are formed through adhering to the discourse. Once Islamist group identity becomes a salient way to deal with self-definitional uncertainty, thinking and problem-solving shift from individual-based strategies to group-based strategies. Given that upward mobility for individual young Muslims is often not very likely (for example, due to widespread educational underachievement of British Muslims), a group strategy, rather than an individual attempt at raising one's status, is often adopted. If individual upward mobility were more readily available, individuals perhaps would be more likely to take that path instead.

The argument here is that salience of group identity is the 'pull' factor. Those who are eager to define themselves through a group identity are primed for Islamist discourse; there is a ready match between their construction of social reality and that of Islamist discourse.

A robust body of literature shows that humans have a cognitive mechanism to impose order on chaotic aggregates of people and transform them into orderly groups. These groups share commonalities, and are distinct from others. People categorize the disorderly perceptual field into meaningful perceivable groups with incredible ease. Controlled experiments show that, even in randomly allocated groups of people, once people categorize others into groups, they will automatically show biased preference towards the group of inclusion. The extent and ease with which this evidence can be replicated across cultures has made scientists

---

[35] M. A. Hogg, 'Uncertainty and Extremism: Identification with High Entitativity Groups under Conditions of Uncertainty' in V. Yzerbyt, C. M. Judd, and O. Corneille (eds.), *The Psychology of Group Perception: Perceived Variability, Entitativity, and Essentialism* (New York: Psychology Press, 2003), 401.

think that this mechanism might have given early hominids a survival advantage in that it made it possible to identify individuals that would be good reciprocators versus groups that would not, thus maximizing the investment/return ratio for societal exchange.[36]

The process of categorizing people into meaningful groups to which one belongs, and to prefer those groups over others, is a powerful cognitive mechanism. Once categorization takes place and meaningful groups are perceived, individuals will selectively perceive the information that confirms that members of the in-group share prototypical characteristics that distinguish them from out-group members who are equally perceived as homogeneous (but less good) entities. This reinforces the tendency for people to accept group-based attitudes and behaviours. By selecting the information that confirms a particular perception of the group, individuals unconsciously suppress the attitudes and thinking that differs from the group prototype.[37]

Besides perceiving groups as homogeneous, experiments show that once categorization takes place, people treat the groups to which they belong in such a way as to ensure their supremacy over other groups. Even if there are no 'realistic' goods which are available, individuals will invest in having their group fair better than other perceived groups. It seems that individuals build their self-concept partly from the information attached to their membership groups. The need for positive self-evaluation exerts an important motive to compare positively to other membership groups. Therefore, understanding the group with which an individual identifies and the perception of that group's status versus other groups in the theatre of social-hierarchies, is important for understanding how individuals will respond to speech directed at advancing their group-based positive self-evaluation.[38]

Although individuals identify with many groups and there is flexibility to their self-concept and allegiances, perceptual parsimony, culture, historical fact, experience, and active elite communications restrict the fluidity of identities and determine the pool of possible identities. Highly visible characteristics will be hard to resist as bases of identity and differentiation. Furthermore, the more a socially-constructed group category maps onto perceived reality and is useful for people to parsimoniously explain experience, the more that particular category will be used by people and will form the basis of group-based solidarity and conflict.

Political leaders as well as extremists intuitively tap into the propensity of categorization into an in-group and an out-group. They consciously exploit identity cleavages based on shared narratives and symbols. The confluence of identity, status, and the legitimacy of prevailing group hierarchies are key in fostering support for collective causes. In fact, it could be argued that without

---

[36] D. M. Abrams, M. A. Hogg, and J. M. Marques (eds.), *The Social Psychology of Inclusion and Exclusion* (New York: Psychology Press, 2005).

[37] See n. 35 above.

[38] M. A. Hogg and D. M. Abrams, *Social Identifications: A Social Psychology of Intergroup Relations and Group Processes* (London: Routledge, 1988).

catalysing a group identity and pitting it against an out-group, mobilization is unlikely to occur.

Even though members of groups (such as European Muslims) that compare negatively to other more dominant groups (such as Western nations) find that this impacts on their self-concept negatively, it is only when other alternatives are subjectively entertained and deemed possible that group members will venture to try to achieve a revision of the hierarchy. When groups see the status relationship situation as non-permanent and unstable, together with the perception that the current situation is illegitimate and unfair, these perceptions combine to catalyse collective mobilization to bring about change.[39] In this vein, we posit that for many of the disaffected, 9/11 introduced new possibilities for a revision of group status hierarchies.

Thus, when a group stops seeing itself as inevitably subordinate to another and when altering its inferior status becomes a realistic possibility, a radical shift in ideology typically ensues in order to challenge the hierarchy of the dominant group. Ideologies arising for this task will include a justification for using various means of challenging the status quo, whether peaceful resistance (as in Gandhi's *satyagraha*) or terrorism (distorting and over-extending concepts of jihad).[40]

Radical Islamist discourse in Europe is a current exemplar of framing a social problem, diagnosing it, and offering a solution in a way that intensifies categorization. For example, radical Islamic discourse tries to displace local and national identities by a transnational *ummah* and pit it against an undifferentiated, morally decadent, and oppressing West.[41] By having the West stand for exploitative capitalism, decadent morality, and a host of Islamophobic conspiracy theories, the problems afflicting Muslims are framed in a language of 'clash of civilisations' that reifies the *ummah* and the West as tangible groups to identify/disidentify with. Individuals' dissatisfaction with race relations, diminishing development opportunities, and identity crises play into a narrative of the West's global war on Islam and Muslims.[42] The solution to problems then prescribed is the religious duty to struggle for the re-institution of the perfect Islamic society.[43]

Taking a social movement, theoretical approach (sociology) to Islamic radicalization in the UK, fieldwork on al-Muhajiroun shows how dissatisfaction with unfulfilled economic expectations and race relations provide openings for radicalizers to pitch their take on things.[44] Once the basic philosophy that radicalizers offer becomes credible, recruitment into a group is easily facilitated. Once recruited into the group, a gradual process that allows normal individuals to

---

[39] F. M. Moghaddam, *From the Terrorists' Point of View: What They Experience and Why They Come to Destroy* (Westport, CT: Praeger Security International, 2006).

[40] See n. 38 above.

[41] O. Roy, *Globalized Islam: the Search for a New Ummah* (New York: Columbia UP, 2004).

[42] Q. Wiktorowicz, *Radical Islam Rising: Muslim Extremism in the West* (Lanham, MD: Rowman & Littlefield, 2005).

[43] M. Juergensmeyer, 'Terror in the Name of God' (2001) 100 *Current History* 357.

[44] See n. 42 above.

become indiscriminate killers can take place over time. Uncertainty reduction research might partly hold the key for understanding how this unfolds. Through controlled experiments and survey research, studies show how individuals afflicted by ambivalence towards self-defining issues can be particularly vulnerable to recruitment by totalist groups. Through a process in which individuals resolve internal ambivalence by fully identifying with a leader, group members become depersonalized.[45] Depersonalization seems to erode socially acquired inhibitions to attack others. Psychological assessment of incarcerated Islamic terrorists confirms that, although psychologically normal in every sense, their individual sense of self has been completely overtaken by the aims and ideology of the group.[46] In other words, their individual identity has been replaced by a prototypical shared identity, which both incites them to commit violent acts and absolves them from the normal guilt that would accompany such acts.

To recap, we suggest that a pathway towards receptivity to the ideology of radicalizers follows this kind of process: the erosion of traditional religious and communal world views in Europe leads to self-definitional uncertainty among young Muslims. Uncertain identities are subsumed into a radical Islamist group identity that is well-defended from identity threat. Once group thinking is in place, religious speech intensifies perceptions of in-group and out-groups, in which the in-group is viewed as illegitimately subordinate to the oppressive out-group, yet in a status hierarchy that is deemed unstable and liable to change (post-9/11). Extreme speech is most powerfully 'activated' under totalist group conditions, although do-it-yourself assembly kits for this binary vision are now widely available at thousands of radicalizing web-sites.

4. Implications

We have argued that discourses only have power when they 'speak' to a given construction of reality that people already have. Section 3 argues that there is a degree of match between radical Islamist speech and some young, Western Muslim's construction of social reality. This final section deals with implications for policy-makers concerned with racial and religious hatred or incitement to terrorism legislation and prevention.

Speech that explicitly incites racial or religious hatred or glorifies or incites to terrorism rightly comes under the authority of government, policing, and legislative bodies. Extreme speech that does not explicitly cross this line, yet presents a social construction of reality that could pave the way for religious/racial hatred or terrorism, presents a grey area. We suggest that, while this grey area of speech

---

[45] See n. 35 above.

[46] J. M. Post, 'When Hatred is Bred in the Bone: Psycho-Cultural Foundations of Contemporary Terrorism' (2005) 26 *Pol. Psychology* 615.

should not be ignored, nor should it be suppressed. It offers researchers working in tandem with terrorism-prevention strategies a key opportunity to detect and identify budding 'hot spots'.

The first level of analysis is the discourse itself. Speech can be analysed for the markers of the archaic narrative structures and rhetorical strategies, discussed in Section 2. The more these features are present, the more likely that the discourse will have the effect of constricting cognitive processes (shutting down critical reasoning) for those who the discourse connects. 'Splitting' into the all-good in-group and the all-bad out-group, along with an unquestioned acceptance of the discourse, are the two likely consequences.

A second level of analysis following identification of the discourse features is the level of integrative complexity (IC) of the discourse (communicated by elites) and of those using the discourse (followers). The implications of IC research for extreme religious speech are worth considering. IC can provide a reliable scientific measurement of the simplification of religiosity akin to fundamentalism and post-modern religious fanaticism. Moreover, IC coding can provide insight into the possibilities of negotiation and compromise between parties and the type of resolution (peaceful or otherwise) that religious conflicts engender.

More than being simply epiphenomenal to the direction of conflict, manipulation of IC levels might help induce higher complexity in a negotiation or conflict atmosphere and help resolve crises through compromise. Evidence from Tetlock and Liht et al. points out that a rise in IC by one of the parties in a conflict might produce greater IC reciprocity in the counterpart, thus helping to foster conflict resolution through mutual concession. Through the use of time series, Teltlock analysed UN ambassadors' communications by the US and the Soviet Union in a period of three decades. He found that the IC level of communications of both governments depended to an important degree on the IC level of the last thing their opponent had said.[47] Moreover, in a study examining the IC of face-to-face peace negotiations between the Mexican Government and the Zapatista peasant insurgency, Liht et al. found a similar effect, but running in a single direction. When the IC of government representatives elevated, both the mediator's and the insurgents' levels rose. Nevertheless, neither the mediator nor the insurgents had the capacity to influence the government or each other. Although the level of IC per day was significantly associated to the degree of advance made in the negotiations as reported in the press (high IC being coterminous with advance and concession in the negotiations for peace, land, and regional autonomy from the federal government), Liht et al. concluded that the asymmetric status and prestige of a party to a conflict might determine who has the power to influence who.[48]

---

[47] P. E. Tetlock, 'Integrative Complexity of American and Soviet Foreign Policy Rhetoric: A Time-Series Analysis' (1985) 49 *J. Personality and Social Psychology* 1565.

[48] J. P. Liht, P. Suedfeld, and A. Krawczyk, 'Integrative Complexity in Face-to-Face Negotiations Between the Chiapas Guerrillas and the Mexican Government' (2005) 26 *Pol. Psychology* 543.

Although IC research seems central to public speech, including extreme religious speech, it is not clear if IC can be manipulated wilfully to induce a beneficent disposition towards the other party. While some studies point out that people can be guided to think in more complex terms than they would usually do through prompts,[49] it is not clear if this could be done in a purely strategic way (apart from the authentic views and attitudes of the party to the conflict) in a conflict or negotiation. It might be hard consciously to manipulate the complexity of one's communications without having achieved a change of attitudes through the negotiation process itself or from some external change in circumstances. Extremely low IC in deceptive UN-delivered communications during the planning phases of surprise attacks show that IC is resistant to deception and conveys the real intentions of communicators. The IC of speeches of Arab and Israeli representatives to the UN across several wars show that whilst the content of communications was trying to hide and misinform about true intensions to attack, IC levels reflected true intentions by plummeting to negligible levels.[50]

Pending further research on the pragmatic application of IC, the strategic manipulation of IC in key communications might help induce more propitious conditions for negotiation and compromise between parties. Although high IC might entail an openness to compromise with immoral positions, the tactical delivery of well-planned communications that evoke a softening of the opposition might be used in conjunction with deterrents as part of an integrated approach to diplomacy and containment of religiously fuelled sectarianism.

A third line of research concerns those who are the hearers and users of extreme speech. The question to ask is how people are constructing the social world around them. In section 3, we have argued that people who are primed to mobilize show a particular way of perceiving the social world. It is as if the complex social world is now seen through a 'lens' that organizes perception of human groupings in the following way:

(1) The social world is chopped up into a sharply demarcated, impermeable in-group ('my group') and out-group (the 'other', 'enemy' group). For example, radical Islamism depicts the world in terms of two camps: Muslims versus the West.
(2) The in-group is viewed as subordinate to the out-group.
(3) The higher status of the out-group is considered illegitimate (morally or politically).
(4) Further, if there is a perception that the given social hierarchy has become unstable, the opportunity for radical change now appears.

An analysis of these social/cognitive templates can provide insight into which social niches in a population will most readily connect with the Islamist narrative. These two influence each other in an increasing spiral; distinguishing 'chicken'

---

[49] B. Hunsberger, J. Lea, S. M. Prancer, M. Pratt, and B. McKenzie, 'Making Life Complicated: Prompting the Use of Integratively Complex Thinking' (1992) 60 *J. Personality* 95.

[50] P. Suedfeld and S. Bluck, 'Changes in Integrative Complexity Prior to Surprise Attacks' (1988) 32 *J. Conflict Resolution* 626.

from 'egg' may not be possible. The authors are currently researching this double line of enquiry with the aim of: (a) systematically identifying the meaningful social niches (through clustering analysis) that comprise the Muslim community of UK young people (ages 18–35); (b) assessing niches' socio-cognitive processes that predict mobilizations aimed at contesting the social hierarchy of groups (making them vulnerable to being groomed for religiously motivated violence); and (c) through in-depth group interviewing, exploring niches' immersion in radical discourse and examining the role of extreme religious discourse in legitimating or weakening the polity and of violent versus civic activism to produce social change. This project provides just one example of research on the trail of extreme speech, with the aim of identifying points of access where specifically tailored community and educational programmes can be effective for long-term terrorism prevention.

5. Conclusion

In this chapter we have outlined key ingredients of Islamist radical religious speech, and the social psychological needs to which they appeal, particularly among second and third generation young Muslims living in Europe. Key structural features of Islamist radical religious speech include: a three-part narrative, echoing primitive and dualist world views resulting in low levels of complexity, rhetorical strategies, the closed way in which the belief system is organized, and the 'rationalistic' word-based emphasis that avoids the nuancing influence of symbolic aspects of religious knowing. In Section 3, we discussed the social psychological needs to which the extreme speech appeals. A pathway through these elements is as follows: the erosion of traditional religious worldviews in Europe leads to self-definitional uncertainty among young Muslims. Uncertain identities are subsumed into a radical Islamic group identity that is well-defended from identity threat. Once group thinking is in place, religious speech intensifies perceptions of in-group and out-groups, in which the in-group is viewed as illegitimately subordinate to the oppressive out-group, yet in a status hierarchy that is deemed unstable and liable to change (post-9/11). Extreme speech is most powerfully 'activated' under totalist group conditions, although do-it-yourself assembly kits for this binary vision are now widely available at thousands of radicalizing websites. Research on the trail of extreme speech can help identify those social niches most likely to mobilize (based on IC and SIT indicators) and are well-placed to inform societally based long-term terrorism prevention programmes.

PART VI

HOLOCAUST DENIAL

'On the Internet, Nobody Knows You're a Nazi': Some Comparative Legal Aspects of Holocaust Denial on the *WWW*

David Fraser

1. Introduction

The principal legal questions which arise around efforts to act against the phenomenon known as Holocaust denial on the World Wide Web (*WWW*) predate the arrival of the Internet and the Information Technology age. An underlying theme in debates about the pernicious nature of Holocaust denial on the *WWW* is that of the impact of technological developments in relation to the mischief in question. Is the incidence (or impact) of such activity on the Web merely a quantitatively superior incidence of the same phenomenon from the era of print or even of cable television, or is it qualitatively different by the simple fact of technology? I argue that the jurisprudential dilemma of the quantitative versus qualitative debate is, in fact, no dilemma at all. It matters not whether we assert and prove that the *WWW* permits more people easier and quicker access to Holocaust denial literature/propaganda or that we go beyond this to prove some kind of geometrically increased harm as a result of the new technologies. In fact, we can elide complex and ultimately futile debates, both about causality in relation to hate speech more broadly construed and about Holocaust denial more specifically, by adopting another approach.[1]

What is not in dispute is that Holocaust denial continues to flourish and to spread regardless of the technology in question. While such speech is protected in the United States under the First Amendment, in Europe and elsewhere, legislative intervention and judicial actions have been undertaken to attempt, at least, to slow down the flow of this particular form of hatred and to make life more

---

[1] See eg, *Mugesera* v. *Canada (Minister of Citizenship and Immigration)* 2005 SCC 40. For a discussion of the case, see generally J. Rikhof, 'Hate Speech and International Criminal Law: The *Mugesera* Decision by the Supreme Court of Canada' (2005) 3 *J. of Int'l Crim. Justice* 1121.

difficult for its perpetrators.[2] Whatever answers one gives to the epistemological dilemma of cyber-hate, the difficulties and strategic issues which are raised will remain the same.

We must revisit the basic legal and social norms which are at play. At a political and then at a positive legal level, we must convincingly establish either that Holocaust denial causes harm or that it is a kind of *malum in se*. Only if there is a solid jurisprudential, social, and political foundation to this basic deontological issue can we begin to talk about, analyse, and deploy various legal tactics against deniers. Second, we must examine the most effective ways in which the state and other actors might wish to combat this social evil, as a social, political, and legal matter. The technological issue thus becomes one of legal regulatory technique, rather than one which we address as a new epistemological paradigm. James E. Young argues that all memory laws:

> ... are negotiated in human time and space and that their codification by no means ends this negotiation but, in fact, invites their constant reinterpretation in new times and circumstances. Process might thus be regarded as the lifeblood of memorial mandates, with the end of process regarded as the foreclosure of memory over time.[3]

The broader epistemological problem arises not just in relation to laws prohibiting or criminalizing Holocaust denial but in relation to so-called 'memory laws' more generally. Legislative interventions in the field of collective or national memory can take several forms, from laws of simple recognition such as the UK's establishment of a Holocaust Remembrance Day, to laws criminalizing denial of a legislatively recognized historical fact, for example, the Holocaust, such as the French *Loi Gayssot*.[4] This French statutory intervention into the fields of law and history came about in a set of particular historical, political, and legal circumstances. It coincided temporally and politically with the prosecution of wartime collaborationist killer, Paul Touvier, and the surrounding controversies about state and the Roman Catholic Church's collaboration in keeping Touvier out of the hands of the French police and away from the courts for forty years. It also came into being at the time of one of the frequent resurgences of high profile public examples of Holocaust denial in France.

---

[2] See eg, L. Greenspan and C. Levitt (eds.), *Under the Shadow of Weimar: Democracy, Law and Racial Incitement in Six Countries* (Westport, CT: Praeger, 1993); I. Nemes, 'Regulating Hate Speech in Cyberspace; Issues of Desirability and Efficacy' (2002) 11 *Information & Communications Technology Law* 193; H. W. K. Kaspersen, *Cyber Racism and the Council of Europe's Reply* (Sydney: Human Rights and Equal Opportunities Commission, 2003), ch. 7. For specific law reform proposals uniting public and private regimes, see, J. Bailey, 'Private Regulation and Public Policy: Toward Effective Restriction of Internet Hate Propaganda' (2004) 49 *McGill L. J.* 59; R. A. Kahn, *Holocaust Denial and the Law: A Comparative Perspective* (New York: Palgrave Macmillan, 2004).

[3] 'Mandating the National Memory of Catastrophe', in A. Sarat, L. Douglas, and M. Merrill Umphrey (eds.), *Law and Catastrophe* (Stanford: Stanford UP, 2007), 131.

[4] Loi n°90–615 du 13 juillet 1990, Loi tendant à réprimer tout acte raciste, antisémite ou xénophobe, JORF, 14 July 1990.

Several prominent French historians have publicly called for the abolition of all memory laws (*lois mémorielles*), arguing that they constitute an unwarranted and dangerous political intrusion into the domain of objective historical inquiry.[5] The ire of the historical experts was raised as a result of a series of legislative measures which were seen as politicizing history, from laws recognizing the slave trade as a crime against humanity to a legislative edict qualifying events in Armenia in 1915 as 'genocide'. Space does not permit a detailed examination of all of the issues raised more broadly in these French debates. One can argue however, *pace* Young, that the *Loi Gayssot* which criminalizes Holocaust denial arose out of particular historical circumstances in a political and social context which included a growing awareness of the direct and voluntary involvement of the Vichy regime in the killing of the Jews of France in the Second World War and the rise of the Far Right as a renewed political force at the time the law was passed and which continues to trouble the French body politic today. Opponents of memory laws in France have always insisted on and continue to adopt the position that such pieces of legislation are *per se* objectionable, whether they take the form of simple acts of remembrance and recognition or that of penal statutes. Proponents argue that such measures are required in order to ensure not just a place in collective memory for certain historical events but, in those instances such as the *Loi Gayssot* which criminalize denial, to protect that collective memory in the Republic from anti-democratic forces. In other words, the criminalization of Holocaust denial in France was and is the result of a widespread and engaged political debate in a vibrant democracy.

Much of the analysis which follows is grounded in the position that the *WWW* is simply part of the means through which a particular evil takes place. It is not, as is often asserted in debates surrounding regulation of the Internet more generally, *sui generis* in any special jurisprudential sense. International or global crime is not a new phenomenon; the failures of national legal systems to regulate or interdict trans-border criminality are not part of some jurisprudential revolution; the idea that the state can and should play a role in criminalizing a social evil does not shock the paradigms of legal theory. In other words, if Holocaust denial is an evil, if it causes harm or is a *malum in se*, then the means through which the evil occurs, or the place in which it is situated, simply establish the practical limits and requirements of both the form and substance of legal regulation; they do not fundamentally alter them.

It is undoubtedly true that from the moment the *WWW* permitted trans-border information migration, Holocaust deniers have sought to internationalize their politics through easily accessible technology. At the same time, they have attempted to nationalize their practices. They have sought a geographical, legal, and physical space for their activities from which they can then benefit from a new borderless cyber-world. They have sought to shelter themselves from legal

---

[5] René Rémond, *Quand L'État Se Mêle à L'Histoire* (Paris: Stock, 2006).

sanctions by situating their operations in jurisdictions, most particularly the United States, where they perceive themselves to be beyond the reach of other legal systems.[6]

This chapter does do not deal with the details and complexities of the free speech paradigm. It does not present, on this issue in particular, a free speech absolutist position.[7] This does not mean that the free speech paradigm is without its importance, nor that the debate is not an interesting one. Instead, the chapter focuses on a discussion of several comparative instances in which legal regulation of Holocaust denial has been dealt with in contexts which do not adopt the uniquely American view that Nazis should be allowed to say whatever they want. Sovereign legislatures in many jurisdictions, unhampered by the text and ideology of the free speech paradigm or the marketplace of ideas, have decided (by implication or explicitly) that it is socially and politically desirable to regulate and to prohibit Holocaust denial and other forms of hate speech wherever these speech acts manifest themselves. The analysis proceeds on the dual bases that legal positivism permits the acceptance of these legislative interventions as jurisprudentially sound and interesting and from the moral, political view that Nazis are evil. The decision as to whether it is best to simply recognize and remember the Shoah as is the case in the United Kingdom or whether more active regulation or criminalization is required is always a matter of politics, history, and context.

Nonetheless, this conflict between legal worldviews and paradigms of free speech versus regulation of the content of speech remains a central issue.[8] But it is not and will not be the main focus here. That is a task for others who believe that an American-centric jurisprudential and political context is the most valuable, if not the only, area for our attention and interest.

2. The Context of Holocaust Denial

This chapter focuses in particular on the phenomenon of Holocaust denial. Other models of regulation and criminalization of speech which denies genocide or crimes against humanity do exist. Article 261 *bis* of the Swiss Penal Code

---

[6] See eg, A. Brown, 'Internet activists foil ban on Nazis', *The Independent*, 3 February 1996; 'Des Croix Gammés Sur L'Internet, *Le Nouvel Observateur*, 3–9 April 1997; E. G. Olson, 'As Hate Spills Onto the Web, a Struggle Over Whether, and How, to Control It', *The New York Times*, 24 November 1997; L. Despins, 'Le racisme surfe sur le web, *L'Express*, 30 July 1998; P. Finn, 'Neo-Nazis find safety net in the land of free speech', *Sydney Morning Herald*, 24 December 2000; I. DeFreitas, 'Worldwide web of laws threatens the Internet', *The Times*, 9 January 2001; Y. Laurent, 'Le webmaster d'un site néo-Nazi, SOS-Racaille, a été interpellé par les polices française et russe', *Le Monde*, 8 August 2003; M. Imbleau, *La Négation du Génocide Nazi: Liberté d'expression ou Crime Raciste?* (Paris: L'Harmattan, 2003).

[7] See D. Fraser, 'Memory, Murder and Justice: Holocaust Denial and the "Scholarship" of Hate', in C. Cunneen, D. Fraser, and S. Tomsen, (eds.), *Faces of Hate: Hate Crime in Australia* (Sydney: Hawkins Press, 1997).

[8] See the discussion of the *YAHOO!* cases below.

establishes an offence for any act which denies or minimizes genocide or crimes against humanity. The Council of Europe in its Framework Decision on Racism and Xenophobia in April 2007 called on member states to criminalize all acts which deny or grossly trivialize crimes against humanity, war crimes and genocide as defined in the Statute of the International Criminal Court. This 'genocide model' as opposed to the 'Holocaust denial' model presents its own problematic questions not the least of which is one of temporality in relation both to certain historical events and the applicability of penal statutes. The central epistemological difficulty with this approach as applied to certain circumstances rapidly becomes apparent. This difficulty is highlighted in current debates surrounding the atrocities committed by Turkish forces against the Armenian civilian population in 1915 and 1916. The concept of 'genocide' did not exist until Raphael Lemkin's study popularized the term in 1944.[9] As a matter of historical and lexical accuracy therefore, one must ask if it is possible to apply this term retrospectively to events which pre-dated the concept of 'genocide' itself. As a matter of criminal law, can one apply the concept and the prohibition to the denial of such events today. Pragmatically, can a trial court engage in the necessary historical inquiry to determine which specific historical event falls under which particular heading of a generalized criminalization of denial? In other words, in order to apply such general prohibitions to a denial of the Armenian genocide, a real issue in today's world, a court would first have to determine that events in Turkey in 1915 did in fact constitute genocide, a concept which by necessity would have to be applied retrospectively to the historical facts in order to impose criminal liability today. This is not to suggest that such an inquiry and determination are practically beyond the realm of judicial competence, but it does point out that general criminalization provisions have their own inherent problems. Indeed, it might be argued that in such cases, a specific legislative 'recognition' of the Armenian genocide would make such prosecutions easier and would greatly facilitate the courts' task.

The chapter focuses on Holocaust denial for two other important reasons. First, the Holocaust, the Shoah, the destruction of European Jewry by the Nazis and their allies was, for reasons which cannot be fully explored here, a unique historical phenomenon. In those countries in which the Holocaust and its precursor events occurred, it is quite simply a defining moment of national identity and collective memory. Those who seek to deny its facticity today engage in acts which directly assault the democratic body politic, a body politic constructed through a long process of coming to terms with the tragedy which was the Shoah. Second, the targeting of Jews, as opposed to other identifiable groups, was central to Nazi ideology and the worldview of the Thousand Year Reich, a condition

---

[9] *Axis Rule in Occupied Europe: Laws of Occupation, Analysis of Government, Proposals for Redress* (Washington, D.C.: Carnegie Endowment for International Peace, 1944).

precedent for which was a Europe which was *Judenrein*, free of Jews. It was specific to European Jewry. The members of no other group were targeted for complete and instant annihilation simply because they were racially identified as belonging to the enemy race. In the well-known formulation, 'Not all victims of the Nazis were Jews, but all Jews were victims of the Nazis'. This does not mean that other groups did not suffer; nor does it mean that they were not victims of crimes against humanity or in some cases perhaps genocide. Homosexual men were targeted but under the guise of a criminal code provision which predated the Nazi rise to power. They could, in the Nazi worldview, 'convert' and escape further persecution. Gypsies, (Roma and Sinti) were racially 'Aryan' and were in principle persecuted as asocial or criminal elements. Only in Hungary and some parts of Eastern Europe were they targeted for elimination. The majority of French Gypsies for example were interned but released when they could demonstrate that they had a fixed abode to which they could return. In other words, their nomadic lifestyle was targeted, not their racial or religious identity. Jews were Jews and were targeted for elimination as such. The fate of other victims of the Nazis was horrible and to deny it should perhaps be a criminal offence but the fate of the Jews was worse and it is the rightful focus of the legislation examined here.[10]

A brief summary of the issues at play in legal debates concerning the regulation or prohibition of Holocaust denial is perhaps useful. All right-thinking people accept that millions of Jews (and others) were killed by the Nazis and their allies and collaborators in World War Two.[11] We also accept that the extermination of European Jewry was part of the Nazi worldview and political agenda and that much, but not all, of the killing took place through the use of poison gas in death camps. This generally accepted view of the events we call the Holocaust is subject to subtle analyses, historiographical refinement, and ideological positioning on various issues, none of which is important or central to the issues of concern here. Historians continue to uncover archival records which allow for a more complete, nuanced understanding of specific events, places, and times relating to the Shoah. None of these discoveries or advances in knowledge, however, permits any questioning of the Holocaust as a historical fact. What remains important is this fact and the historical, moral, and ethical lessons which might follow on this truth.

Holocaust deniers (who prefer to call themselves 'revisionists' in order to cloak their activities in a scholarly garb)[12] reject almost all of these facts of the

---

[10] M. Berenbaum, *A Mosaic of Victims: Non-Jews Persecuted and Murdered by the Nazis* (New York: NYU Press and London: I.B. Tauris, 1990).

[11] For an intriguing presentation of the moral and legal issues at stake and an argument about the proper taxonomy for these issues, see S. Fish, 'Holocaust Denial and Academic Freedom' (2001) 35 *Valparaiso U. L. Rev.* 499.

[12] Ibid.

Holocaust. For them, the Holocaust is the 'so-called Holocaust'. They argue and assert inter alia that:

1. The Holocaust did not occur because there is no so-called Hitler document: a written order from Hitler requiring the killing of Jews.
2. There were no gas chambers used for killing Jews and others in the camps. Gas was used to decontaminate prisoners' clothing. The deaths in the various prison or concentration camps were due to a combination of disease, deprivation caused by war, and Allied bombing attacks.
3. Eyewitness testimony of 'survivors' is untrustworthy either because of the psychological illnesses of the witnesses or their personal stake in obtaining compensation.
4. The compensation industry is a plot by international Jews/Zionists to extract payments from an innocent and victimized Germany.[13]

The defamation trial of American historian Deborah Lipstadt, who was pursued by the notorious denier David Irving, put many of these claims before the public once again,[14] as did Irving's later conviction by an Austrian court and imprisonment for denial-related crimes.[15] Yet an important legal question remains. Absent free speech absolutism, regulation and prohibition by the state of Holocaust denial can easily fit within our traditional understandings and paradigms of criminal, quasi-criminal, and regulatory intervention. But such interventions must be based on a supportable finding of harm or a demonstration that Holocaust denial constitutes a *malum in se*.

The first level of epistemological and jurisprudential difficulty which is left largely unarticulated in many of the debates around decided cases arises in this context. There can be no doubt that Holocaust denial is morally repugnant, politically dangerous, and demonstrably false. Nor, given a full understanding of

---

[13] See generally, B'nai Brith Anti-Defamation League, *Hitler's Apologists: The Anti-Semitic Propaganda of Holocaust 'Revisionism'* (New York: ADL, 1993); Simon Wiesenthal Center, *Holocaust Denial: Bigotry in the Guise of Scholarship* (Los Angeles: Simon Wiesenthal Center, 1994).

[14] For the start of the story, see D. Lipstadt, *Denying the Holocaust: The Growing Assault on Truth and Memory* (New York: Free Press/Macmillan, 1993). See *Irving* v. *Penguin Books Ltd & Deborah Lipstadt* [2001] EWCA Civ 1197. For analyses of the trial and the issues surrounding it, see D. D. Guttenplan, *The Holocaust on Trial* (New York: W. W. Norton & Company, 2001); R. J. Evans, *Lying About Hitler: History, Holocaust and the David Irving Trial* (New York: Basic Books, 2001). See also D. Lipstadt, *History on Trial: My Day in Court with David Irving* (New York: Ecco/HarperCollins, 2005). More recently, a parallel case was brought in France by Robert Faurisson against former *Garde des Sceaux* Robert Badinter for remarks made by Badinter in which he is alleged to have called Faurisson a 'falsifier of history' (*un faussaire de l'histoire*). See C. Boltanski, 'Faurisson, négationniste impétitent face à Badinter', *Libération*, 13 March 2007; J. Coignard, 'Le négationniste Faurisson à nouveau traité de "faussaire"', *Libération*, 3 April 2007. Faurisson, like Irving, lost, 'Faurisson perd son procès contre Badinter', *Libération*, 21 May 2007.

[15] See I. Traynor, 'Behind bars, but liberals defend Irving', *The Guardian*, 28 November 2005; T. Garton Ash, 'This is the moment for Europe to dismantle taboos, not erect them', *The Guardian*, 19 October 2006. See also J. Howard, 'Muslim leader sent funds to Irving', *The Observer*, 19 November 2006. He was released from Austrian prison just before Christmas 2006. ' "Holocaust denier" Irving freed from jail', *The Independent*, 20 December 2006. He took up the Holocaust denial almost immediately thereafter. T. Crichton, 'Holocaust denier reneges on regret', *The Sunday Herald*, 24 December 2006.

the history, politics, and ideologies of Holocaust denial, can there be any real doubt that the phenomenon is informed by a virulent antisemitism which underlies specific and intentional political programmes. For many, none of these reactions can, in and of themselves, justify legal prohibition of the criminal type in modern liberal democratic societies; unless and until clearly articulated legal norms are enunciated and enforced. Not only free speech principles themselves, but broader liberty concerns (of both a democratic and a republican nature) must and do come to the fore. Within the democratic rule of law paradigm, these can be countered by demonstrating harm or *malum in se* which would justify and support state intervention. What then, is the harm of Holocaust denial and how does that harm fit into our current legal taxonomical structures?

Lipstadt argues that Holocaust denial is an 'assault on truth and memory'.[16] Yet, only in exceptional circumstances such as criminal libel, blasphemy, and fraud, assaults on truth are not normally subject to criminalization, assaults on memory even less so. With the exception of assertion number 4 above (that there is a Jewish/Zionist compensation industry behind claims that the Holocaust occurred), more subtle and legally aware Holocaust deniers do not generally even identify the targets of their ideological politics in a direct fashion. Instead, they cloak themselves in the garb of academic inquiry and the search for historical accuracy and truth. Their underlying, but central, antisemitism is generally articulated in vague, coded terms understandable and understood by their closed circle of adherents. Traditional criminal law categories, like incitement or con-spiracy, are difficult if not impossible to apply in such cases. A legally know-ledgeable Holocaust denier has little difficulty in writing of 'Zionists' and 'Marxists,' or of 'survivors' in scare quotes or in asserting that 'our traditional enemies' are behind the claims that the Holocaust occurred. While direct semiotic attacks on 'Jews' for example will easily and uncontroversially fall afoul of most non-American legal regimes aimed at prohibiting racial, religious, and ethnic hate speech, more subtle encodings may prove more difficult to regulate. The most recent case in Canada involving David Ahenakew, a former leader in Canada's aboriginal communities, indicates the difficulties of dealing with instances of promotion of racial hatred within the traditional paradigms of criminal law.[17]

The taxonomical issues at play in regulating and prohibiting Holocaust denial on the *WWW* can appear to be even more fundamental to our jurisprudential traditions and understandings. Who, in particular (to pick but one example from the credo of denial) is harmed by an assertion that there were no gas chambers for killing at Auschwitz? Clearly, history is challenged, mocked, and ignored, but

---

[16] It is important to underline here that true to her position as an American academic, Lipstadt rejects on free speech grounds legal regulation of Holocaust denial.

[17] See *R. v. Ahenakew* [2005] SJ No. 459; [2006] SKQB 272; 2006 Sk. C. LEXIS 345; K. Harding, 'Ahenakew unapologetic after conviction', *The Globe and Mail*, 8 July 2005; K. Harding, 'Ahenakew stripped of Order of Canada', *The Globe and Mail*, 11 July 2005.

history has no standing as a plaintiff. Holocaust survivors and specifically those who escaped Auschwitz might find themselves traumatized by such a statement. The reality of their lived experience in the Nazi killing apparatus is denied. The infliction of mental distress is only criminalized in very limited circumstances in the English criminal justice system, as an extension of the law of assault and more recent stalking offences. Consistent with criminal law principles, such cases typically require the presence of a specific or, at least, a foreseeable victim and more importantly, the presence of the *mens rea* of intention as an element of the crime which must be proved beyond a reasonable doubt by the prosecuting authorities. These problems might well be avoided or at least minimized, by legislative recourse (as is the case in both Canada and Australia) to a civil standard and the use of an objective test of the likelihood of harm. The basic issues of causation remain however even under the likelihood standard, as do concerns about the appropriate mental element, and its provability.

There is no real, practical doubt, in the world of Holocaust denial as a political and ideological position and strategy, that Jews are the target. But the idea that such statements as 'There is no Hitler order' or 'No one was gassed at Auschwitz' fit into established criminal law categories such as assault or that they create the likelihood of a specific harm to foreseeable victims such as Holocaust survivors, or that they are likely to incite others to acts of antisemitic violence, is each extremely problematic, without even entering into issues of free speech or good faith. Assertions that eyewitness survivors are greedy or motivated by a desire to see Germany punished or that they are mentally ill fall afoul of similar taxonomical difficulties, as well as falling awkwardly within our traditional understandings of the *mens rea* elements of criminal liability. The idea of harm and the concomitant role of law in reducing or eliminating harm are, in this context, more difficult to deploy than many might believe. Again, there is no doubt in the real world about the ideology and political beliefs which inform Holocaust deniers. There can be no political doubt about their antisemitism. There can be no practical or deontological doubt about their pernicious political agenda. But none of these statements leads us to the inevitable result as a matter of law that Holocaust denial targets specific victims or that the perpetrators of Holocaust denial have identifiable targets in mind. There must be serious doubt within the traditional confines and limitations of criminal law discourse that Holocaust denial causes or is likely to cause specific and identifiable harm.

Instead, many proponents of criminalization simply assert, perhaps to avoid such discussion, that society and therefore the state through its criminal (or human rights) justice system owes a duty to the traumatized survivors and to the memory of the victims of Nazi killings. The basis of legislation then becomes perhaps somewhat clearer. There are victims, both dead and living, of Nazi atrocities and we owe them a duty: a duty to minimize further harm and to memorialize their suffering. This argument for criminalization appears close to the basis of blasphemy laws (there is a truth and it must be defended) or else it approaches the *malum in se* position. Law's role in protecting and enshrining history, truth, and memory is at the very least problematic and probably impossible.[18] Yet the *malum in se* position appears to be the only one which remains available to justify and support state intervention in such activities. This idea, of a moral and ethical judgment about the nature and existence of evil, sits uncomfortably with some understandings of modernity and the role of the state within a rational, modern, technologically sophisticated world.[19] Yet, an ethics in relation to the Holocaust is all that is available to us.[20] Again this is the core of arguments and debates about memorialization and law more generally. The necessary social and political discussion and dialogue identified by James E. Young is at the heart of these statutory interventions. They occur only as the result, as in France, Germany, and Austria, for example, after considered public debate about core values of present-day democratic national identity and the place of the Shoah historically in each country. Prohibition is the result not just of such democratic deliberation about memory and history but flows from a decision that denial is a pernicious manifestation of the same ideological and political phenomena which gave rise to the historical tragedy of extermination. Indeed, such a clearly articulated position as the one informing legislative action would also have the potential to remove complex and fraught issues of victimhood from political and especially legal discourse about hate crime more generally. It could go some way to remove barriers in those jurisdictions where standing to bring cases against Holocaust deniers is problematic.[21]

Legal regulation of Holocaust denial then is best justified by a collective social, ethical, and political decision that Holocaust denial is an evil which we cannot permit or tolerate because the ethics of the Holocaust as perpetuated by deniers is the denial of all ethical possibilities within human existence.[22] This largely unarticulated legal and jurisprudential position is at the heart of the often heated debates which surround both the basic question of whether to criminalize Holocaust denial and the next level of inquiry concerning the particular difficulties of the interdiction of denial on the *WWW*. Indeed, it is perhaps the case that the apparently amoral nature of the technological developments in question exacerbates the primary ethical and deontological problem. The *WWW* is just bits and bytes, zeroes, and ones. It is (as a whole) as it is in its various components, without morality and ethical concern. Yet, as opponents of criminalization are

[18] See D. Fraser, *Law after Auschwitz: Towards a Jurisprudence of the Holocaust* (Durham, NC: Carolina Academic Press, 2005).

[19] See T. Murphy and N. Whitty, 'The Question of Evil and Feminist Legal Scholarship' (2006) 14 *Feminist Legal Studies* 1.

[20] For an introduction to some of the complex issues arising here see, inter alia, Z. Bauman, *Modernity and the Holocaust* (Ithaca, NY: Cornell UP, 1991) and *Postmodern Ethics* (Oxford: Blackwell, 1993).

[21] See the discussion of Australia below.

[22] The difficult and complex issues which support this assertion are beyond the scope of this chapter.

prone to assert, 'Information longs to be free'. And freedom is an ethical state. At its core, the debate over *WWW* regulation and hate speech/Holocaust denial must be recast in its true form, as a debate about truth and ethical existence. Whether law can even approximate either of these deontological states is perhaps a question for another day.

3. YAHOO!, the *WWW*, and French Legal Regulation of Holocaust Denial

Perhaps the most well-known case of attempts to regulate Nazis on the Internet is the litigation in France concerning the *WWW* entity YAHOO!.[23] Indeed, the *YAHOO!* case gained international notoriety not just because it raised the issues of Nazis on the Internet, but because it brought into stark contrast the two dominant legal paradigms: French intervention in substantive regulation of speech and the American First Amendment approach. While *YAHOO!* is not a case which deals with Holocaust denial per se, it plays a central part in on-going debates on hate speech and Nazis on the Internet issues.

Some context is perhaps required. France was occupied by the Germans during the Second World War. Jews in France were sent to the death camps by the Germans and by their French collaborators, including agents of the French state. Issues of memory, justice, history, and law as they relate to the Holocaust have long been at the forefront of French political debate.[24] France is also the home and birthplace of Holocaust denial. Beginning in the late 1940s, a thread of French political thought denying the historical fact of the Holocaust has been present.[25] French Holocaust denial is important not just because it was first, but also because it has a complex political and ideological history, combining the not so surprising elements of Nazi sympathizers and neo-fascist racists, with a strong presence of radical left-wing theorists and practitioners.[26] Holocaust denial has also made successful inroads into the French academy, seeking thereby to establish its self-professed role as an intellectually worthy and informed part of debate over questions of history. The role of intellectuals and the place of the French university as a site for Holocaust denial are key points in any

[23] La Ligue Contre Le Racisme et L'Antisémitisme-LICRA et L'Union des Étudiants Juifs de France-UEJF c. La Société YAHOO! INC et La Société YAHOO! France, Tribunal de Grande Instance de Paris, RG :00/05308.

[24] See n. 18 above, ch. 5.

[25] See F. Brayard, *Comment L'Idée Vint à M. Rassinier: Naissance du Révisionnisme* (Paris: Fayard, 1996).

[26] See N. Fresco, 'Les Redresseurs de Morts', *Les Temps Modernes*, 1980, 21; P. Vidal-Naquet and L. Yagil, *Holocaust Denial in France: Analysis of a Unique Phenomenon* (Tel Aviv: Tel Aviv University Project for the Study of Anti-Semitism, 1994); A. Bihr, G. Caldiron and D. Daeninckx, et al. (eds.), *Négationnistes: les chiffonniers de l'histoire* (Paris: Golias/Syllepse, 1997).

understanding of the nature of the phenomenon in that country.[27] Deniers position themselves as pursuing an intellectually rigorous form of Holocaust revisionism, an accepted and acceptable version of revisionism in history more generally. A primary mover has been Robert Faurisson, a literature professor and apparent antisemite.[28] The movement has spread to some French university departments which have controversially awarded advanced research degrees for Holocaust denial theses. In one notorious instance, Jean Plantin was allowed to regain his university awards from the Université de Lyon, which had been stripped from him. The decision removing his degrees was unlawful because it had been taken outside the four-month period after which all degree awards become final under French law.[29] At around the same time as he achieved his administrative law victory, Plantin became the first person in French legal history to be sentenced to prison for publishing material denying the Holocaust.[30]

With the rise of antisemitism and racist attacks related to Middle Eastern political events and an anti-Zionist, 'pro-Palestine' taxonomy as a new code for antisemitism in France, these historical developments are of current and on-going importance for a fuller understanding of attempts to regulate Holocaust denial and other incidents of hate speech on the *WWW* and for a specific comprehension of the *YAHOO!* case.

Again, it is important to note that the *YAHOO!* case is not a case which deals with Holocaust denial. The plaintiffs, LICRA, and UEJF, instituted proceedings against YAHOO! because the company allowed the sale of Nazi memorabilia in France, through its online auction site. They alleged that such sales aided and abetted neo-Nazism.

One can find there a number of emblems (Swastikas and the SS insignia of concentration camp guards being the most numerous) in many forms (knives, photographs, flags), including the most unexpected ones (cushions, plates, Swastika computer mouse pads...)

---

[27] See H. Rousso, *Le Dossier Lyon III: Le rapport sur le racisme et le négationnisme à l'Université Jean Moulin* (Paris: Fayard, 2004) ; O. Bertrand and E. Davidenkoff, 'Négationnisme: Lyon-III pas facho mais complaisant', *Libération*, 6 October 2004; 'Bruno Gollnisch (FN) émet des doutes sur l'existence des chambres à gaz et relativise l'ampleur de la Shoah', *Libération*, 12 October 2004; O. Bertrand, 'Négationnisme: le prof Gollnisch forcé de sécher à Lyon-III', *Libération*, 23 October 2004; 'Bruno Gollnisch poursuivi pour "contestation de crimes contre l'humanité"', *Le Monde*, 29 November 2004; 'Gollnisch cède et "reconnaît" l'extermination', *Libération*, 8 November 2006; 'Procès Gollnisch à Lyon: mea-culpa bien stratégique', *Libération*, 9 November 2006; 'Bruno Gollnisch (FN) condamné pour ses "insinuations" sur l'Holocauste', *Le Monde*, 20 January 2007; 'Prison avec sursis pour Gollnisch', *Libération*, 18 January 2007.

[28] See P. Vidal-Naquet, *Assassins of Memory: Essays on the Denial of the Holocaust* (New York: Columbia UP, 1992); 'Le négationniste Robert Faurisson a été condamné à trios mois de prison avec sursis', *Le Monde*, 3 October 2006.

[29] See O. Bertrand, 'Plantin récupère ses titres universitaire', *Libération*, 23 June 2003; S. Landrin, 'L'universitaire négationniste Jean Plantin retrouve ses diplômes lyonnais', *Le Monde*, 25 June 2003.

[30] O. Bertrand, 'Prison ferme pour le négationniste Jean Plantin', *Libération*, 26 June 2003; 'Prison ferme pour Jean Plantin', *Le Monde*, 27 June 2003.

By their very nature and their price, the 'articles' displayed every day for several months by YAHOO clearly target a neo-Nazi clientele.

The 'Auction' service thereby serves as a vulgar mail order catalogue which includes pages dedicated to Nazism...which YAHOO! INC makes available to sellers.

Technically, its server (Yahoo.com) connected to the Internet is the place where computer files inherent for these operations (text and images) are stored, housed and disseminated.[31]

LICRA and the UEJF invoked the provisions of a regulation adopted by the Conseil d'Etat which makes it criminal, with certain historical and artistic exceptions:

...to wear or to exhibit in public a uniform, insignia, or emblem resembling the uniforms, insignia, or emblems worn or exhibited (...) by members of an organization declared a criminal organization under Article 9 of the statute of the International Military Tribunal annexed to the London Agreement of 8 August 1945.[32]

The basis for this French law, as for the law more specifically prohibiting Holocaust denial,[33] is a specific historical incorporation of the Trials of Major War Criminals before the International Military Tribunal at Nuremberg into French legislation as a form of *de jure* incontestable truth. While there are several aspects of this particular method which raise problematic legal and historical issues (which are beyond the scope of this chapter), the French legislative framework does offer clear guidance as to how to create a *malum in se* prohibition. The plaintiffs argued that YAHOO! breached these provisions of the *Code Pénal* by offering French *WWW* users access to goods which were illegal in that country. YAHOO! offered several defences to the action. It asserted that its current technology prevented it from adequately screening for country of origin either those who used its facilities to offer goods for sale or those who sought to purchase such goods. It also argued that because it was an American company whose primary server and customers who placed goods for sale were situated in the United States (where the display of such items was clearly legal), the French legal system was over-reaching in its attempts to criminalize its online activities.

This is the new technology/free speech nexus which so troubles many dealing with the issue of regulating hate on the *WWW*. First, the new technologies of web-site posting and Internet commerce make it impossible to monitor and filter goods or individuals. The world of virtual commerce makes the idea of a situated vendor or purchaser both epistemologically problematic and practically impossible. Secondly, in an argument which appears to contradict the assumptions of the first, recourse is had to a more traditional view of the world in which the web-site, or the server, or the client in fact takes on a corporeal, physical reality. They are situated in a real sense outside of France and therefore they cannot be

---

[31] *UEJF v. YAHOO! INC and YAHOO! France* Assignation en Référé, May 2000, Tribunal de Grande Instance de Paris (author's translation).
[32] Code Pénal- Partie Réglementaire- Décrets en Conseil d'Etat, R645-1 (author's translation).
[33] See discussion below.

regulated by French law. This becomes a traditional application of arguments about the sovereign territory of the nation state, extra-territoriality and the application of penal law. Nor are proponents of regulation necessarily on more solid epistemological ground. They are compelled, within the constraints of traditional legal discourse, to assert a different physical reality: that the corporate personality is situated in France, that access is gained in France by French citizens sitting at French computers and over French telephone lines. The wine of new technologies fits into old legal bottles with little difficulty no matter on which side of the regulation debate one might fall.

After ordering a series of expert opinions on the possibility of effective regulation by YAHOO!, the Court issued its interim decisions ordering the *WWW* provider to filter its French site and to prevent French users from gaining access to such materials as were clearly prohibited by the operative provisions of French law.[34] The story did not end there. YAHOO! immediately filed an action in the United States District Court in San Jose, California, seeking a judicial declaration that the French judgment was not enforceable in the United States.[35] Once again the disembodied Internet, the *WWW* beyond our narrow, outdated notions of the nation state by its very technological essence, immediately reappears as required in an embodied corporate and corporeal form in the judicial forum as practical and legal necessity demand. Instead of new technology, we find simple old-fashioned notions of private and public international law.

While this Court must and does accord great respect and deference to France's sovereign interest in enforcing the orders and judgments of its courts, this interest must be weighed against the United States' own sovereign interest in protecting the constitutional and statutory rights of its residents.[36]

There can be no doubt, once the balancing act of legal reasoning rears its ugly head in a United States Federal Court, who and what will triumph. Indeed, the very global nature of the Internet requires and demands a return to embodied national normativity.

Many nations, including France, limit freedom of expression on the Internet based upon their respective legal, cultural, or political standards. Yet because of the global nature of the Internet, virtually any public web-site can be accessed by end-users anywhere in the world, and in theory any provider of Internet content could be subject to legal action in countries which find certain content offensive.[37]

Thus while the trial judge is careful to underline that the majority of Americans as well as he, find the display of Nazi memorabilia 'profoundly offensive,'[38] the

---

[34] See inter alia, *Ordonnance de Référé*, 22 May 2000; *Ordonnance de Référé*, 11 August 2000; *Ordonnance de Référé*, 20 November 2000 ; Tribunal de Grande Instance de Paris.

[35] *YAHOO! INC* v. *La Ligue Contre Le Racisme et L'Antisémitisme* 145 F. Supp. 2d 1168 (N.D. Cal. 2001).

[36] Ibid., 1178.   [37] Ibid., 1179.   [38] Ibid., fn. 7.

public interest of democracy, free speech, and American First Amendment jurisprudence require that the Court refuse to give effect and recognition to the French decision.

Such is the public face of the *YAHOO!* case.[39] It is a battle between social and legal policy in certain parts of Europe which forbids Holocaust denial and related phenomena and the American First Amendment tradition which protects just such activities in the service of the jurisprudence of freedom and democracy.

A key point which follows from the French political and legislative decisions to criminalize such speech is that there is a publicly stated, principled stance that such discourse has no place in the French Republic. The Holocaust as found and laid out by the International Military Tribunal is an historical reality officially recognized by, and incorporated within, the basic normative renderings of French republican legality. Yet the public nature of the French prohibitions hides an intriguing and important legal phenomenon. The prime proponents and actors against hatred on the *WWW* were and continue to be, not the French state and its representatives, but socially engaged bodies corporate whose primary political, social, and legal aim is the struggle against hate. French rules of civil and criminal procedure permit and perhaps even encourage such actions before the courts of justice by such *'parties civiles'*. LICRA and UEJF act as parts of civil society and represent an engaged citizenry in its struggles against Nazi apologists and other hate-mongers within the republic.

This underlines an important aspect of the political and ideological legal struggle against Holocaust denial and related phenomena in the French context. At one level, the struggle is privatized. It can be seen to disengage the state from direct involvement in such cases. One might argue that the pedagogical function of such actions, the vision of the *République Française* underlying and informing the pursuit of YAHOO! and others, is somewhat diminished by the absence or low-key presence of explicit state intervention. At the same time, this privatization of criminal proceedings permits the involvement of a politically aware and informed citizenry in engaging Nazis and racists directly in the legal forum.

The involvement of these bodies and similar groups allows us access to another aspect of the French context. While lawyers and commentators are particularly interested in the issues of the utility or appropriateness of legal mechanisms in dealing with these disputes, the groups themselves (LICRA and UEJF) see and deploy legal mechanisms as only one part of their political armoury in the struggle against hate-mongers. Litigation and law are tools, instrumentalized as part of a

---

[39] It is important to note however that on appeal, the Circuit Court decided that given the interim nature of the French court's orders and YAHOO!'s apparent *de facto* compliance therewith, the case was not in fact ripe for adjudication. The appellate court also left open the substantive question as to whether First Amendment protections were relevant and available to YAHOO! in the instant case. See *YAHOO! INC v. La Ligue contre le Racisme et l'Antisémitisme*, 433 F. 3d 1199, *cert. denied*, 2006 US LEXIS 4180 (US, May 30, 2006). See also, A. Ben-Ezer and A. L. Bendor, 'Conceptualizing *YAHOO! v. L.C.R.A.*: Private Law, Constitutional Review, and International Conflict of Laws', (2003–4) 25 *Cardozo L. Rev.* 2089.

broader political strategy in these battles. This does not mean that law and its ideological and pedagogical force are underestimated by these actors.[40] It does mean that law is not the be all and end all of the political struggle against Holocaust denial and other forms of racial, ethnic, and religious hatred on the *WWW*.[41] This is perhaps the best and most valuable lesson we can learn from the *YAHOO!* case and similar proceedings in France.

There are other, perhaps more strictly legal, lessons which arise from the French experience. These legal issues here and elsewhere appear in particular legal and ideological (not to mention social and historical) contexts, which cannot be ignored. A succinct examination of other French cases dealing with the criminalization of Holocaust denial and hate speech serves briefly to highlight some related issues and questions.

The French *Loi sur la liberté de la presse*, of 29 July 1881 (as amended) is the primary legal mechanism by which France deals with issues of hate speech and Holocaust denial. Article 23 of the Law, introduced in December 1985, deals with 'crimes and offences committed by the press or by any other means of',[42] including 'audiovisual communication'. Article 24, introduced in January 2002, criminalizes the

(Incitement) to discrimination, hatred or violence towards a person or a group of persons based on their origin or their membership or non-membership in an identified ethnic group, nation, race or religion.[43]

Finally, Section 24 *bis*, in force since March 1994, makes Holocaust denial a criminal offence. It is a violation of French law to use the press or any other form of public written communication, including the Internet or *WWW*, to deny the existence of crimes against humanity as defined by the London Agreement and committed by members of a criminal organization as defined by the Nuremberg International Military Tribunal.

There are, of course, several important factual, historical, and legal issues which arise under the French legislation, not the least of which is the permanent memorialization and juridification of some of the historically problematic findings of the Nuremberg Tribunal. It seems clear however that no form of legislation criminalizing denial is perfect. The issues which would arise in relation to the Armenian genocide serve as one example of this. Likewise the Council of Europe's reference to war crimes, crimes against humanity and genocide as defined in the statute of the International Criminal Court does little to elide

---

[40] See A. David, 'Militants, Encore un Effort!' in A. David (ed.), *Racisme et Antisémitism: Essai de Philosophie sur l'Envers des Concepts* (Paris: Ellipses, 2001), 295 *et seq.*

[41] See eg, J. Coignard, 'L'hébergeur d'un site néonazi devant la justice', *Libération*, 20 April 2000; S. Zappi, 'Le MRAP dénonce la naissance sur l'Internet d' "une nouvelle extrême droite arabophobe" ', *Le Monde*, 17 July 2003.

[42] Author's translation.   [43] Author's translation.

practical dilemmas for adjudication. What is important for the purposes of this chapter is that the French legal system clearly outlaws the incitement of racial hatred and discrimination and, in addition, specifically criminalizes Holocaust denial. A series of litigious matters has shed some light on the law and politics of Holocaust denial and related phenomena in France.

In 1998 for example, criminal proceedings were instituted against 'F,' in fact, Robert Faurisson, one of the leading Holocaust deniers in the world.[44] In this case, Faurisson was accused of allowing the posting on the Internet site Anciens Amateurs de Récits de Guerres et d'Holocaustes (AARGH) of material denying the Holocaust in violation of Articles 23, 24, and 24 *bis*. The writing in question began with the assertion that the Holocaust is a fiction. The defendant raised a number of matters which have since become the standard fare in such cases. He first asserted that the facts alleged against him did not occur on the '*territoire national*' of France and therefore that the Court had no jurisdiction. The Court had no trouble in asserting the applicability of Article 113–2 of the *Code pénal* which gives jurisdiction to French courts where any constitutive act of the offence has been committed on French soil. Since publication takes place wherever the material is disseminated, the jurisdictional issue is easily dealt with by applying traditional legal norms and rules.[45]

More importantly for future attempts to regulate Holocaust denial and hate speech on the *WWW*, however, Faurisson asserted a factual defence, that there was no evidence that he was the publisher or writer of the material in question or that he had any control over the website where the offending material appeared. The court agreed with the defendant, finding that there was no evidence that he was responsible for the website or had any control over it. The simple fact that his writings appeared or that the site contained many references to his writings or various legal actions against him could not, as a matter of proof in a criminal case, be used to create an evidentiary presumption of his guilt. Similarly, his refusal to take any steps to remove the writings or to request or demand their removal could not constitute an implicit confession (*aveu implicite*) of his culpability or involvement. The court found that given the complete absence of any investigation or evidence concerning the website management, control or access thereto, the charge could not stand.

Three important elements in relation to the legal regulation of Holocaust denial on the *WWW* under French law arise. First, the French courts have experienced little, if any, difficulty in exercising national jurisdiction over the content of the *WWW*. Of course, the efficacy of such regulation raises many other issues which cannot be specifically addressed here.[46] Secondly, the French courts

---

[44] *F*, Tribunal de Grande Instance de Paris, No. 9727603115, 13 November 1998.

[45] See also *CJL*, Cour de Cassation, Chambre Criminelle, No. Y 01-80, 134 FS-P+F Z 01-80. 135, 27 November 2001.

[46] It is important to note here that French courts are aware of these difficulties. They are clearly concerned about the creation of 'Internet havens' to which ISPs will resort in order to avoid the

have had no difficulty in applying the standard normative taxonomy of criminal law. As the case of *F* demonstrates quite clearly, even Holocaust deniers as notorious and as obnoxious as Faurisson have rights and benefit from the rule of law in a western liberal democracy. Finally, it is clear that the protagonists, particularly among the *parties civiles*, learned the lessons of the case of *F*. Careful investigation of web-site ownership and control questions as well as a more specific and strategic targeting of ISPs have come to characterize subsequent French cases. The legal battle against Holocaust denial on the *WWW* in France is, and has always been, construed and conceived as part of a broader struggle against fascist forces. Cutting them off from the power of the *WWW* is the main goal of such cases. If indirect targeting of ISPs is the most effective means of doing so, then so be it.

Another case from France highlights these points. In 2002, UEJF took an action against LYCOS France in order to prevent the service provider from giving Web access to a site labelled 'nsdap': the German appellation for the Nazi Party.[47] UEJF sought the details of the owners of the site from the ISP and damages in negligence for LYCOS' failure to filter the site in the first place. They used the doctrine of French law to piggyback civil liability on breaches of criminal statutory duties. This case once again turned on the application of traditional norms, this time in terms of delictual responsibility under French law. The Internet, *WWW*, web hosting, et cetera created no more difficulty for French law than any other factual scenario.

Here the defendant successfully invoked a defence which asserted that it had not been negligent. The Court accepted LYCOS' assertion that while terms such as 'Jew', 'heil', 'Nazi', or 'Hilter' might well raise red flags for a wary and socially concerned ISP, the term 'nsdap' was far too specialized to cause the ordinarily prudent Internet provider to suspect nefarious content.[48] Indeed, LYCOS demonstrated its bona fides by adding the phrase to its search engine filter as soon as it was made aware of its significance by the complainants.[49] The substantive issue of the content and the applicable French legal norms were not discussed by the courts since the normal operation of the rules of civil law meant that the defendant had not acted in a negligent fashion.

Of course, this means that in those cases where breaches of the law can be demonstrated and sufficient proof of liability established, the normal operation of the law will permit *parties civiles* to intervene successfully to shut down access to

---

consequences of French justice. See eg, *J'Accuse c. Société General Communication et al*, Tribunal de Grande Instance de Paris, No. RG :01/57676, 30 October 2001. M.-J. Gros, 'Le portail néonazi échappe au filtrage', *Libération*, 31 October 2001.

[47] *UEJF c. S. A. Multimania Production devenue LYCOS France*, Cour d'Appel de Versailles, R.G. No. 00/05502, 16 May 2002.

[48] Ibid., 3 (author's translation).

[49] Ibid., 5.

websites, to have severe monetary penalties imposed, and to gain the subsidiary but crucial publicity benefits of such actions.[50]

The French example demonstrates some of the strengths and weaknesses of attempts to regulate and interdict Holocaust denial on the Internet. Even in the absence of First Amendment hegemony, the battle against the evil of Holocaust denial and the powerful dissemination capacities of the *WWW* is a difficult one which calls, first and foremost, for the actions of an engaged body politic.[51] The struggle continues. Meanwhile, other jurisdictions have faced similar issues.

4. Canada: Zundel, the Web, and the Success (?) of Law

The story of Holocaust denial in Canada is, without too much exaggeration, the story of one man. Ernst Zundel was born in Germany and came to Canada in the 1950s. He started a successful photo refinishing business and quickly associated himself with fascist circles in Canada and elsewhere. The story of his struggles with the Canadian legal system is well known.[52] Some of the issues arising out of his most recent brushes with the law and hate on the *WWW* are pertinent to the present discussion.

Somewhat ironically perhaps, Zundel became one of the biggest publishers and distributors of Holocaust denial literature in the world using the old-fashioned technology of printing. It was this technology which was in question in the first series of actions against him. More recently, Zundel and those around him have discovered the power of the *WWW* and the *Zundelsite* has become a favourite of hate-mongers and neo-Nazis everywhere. From 1996 until 2002, the Canadian Human Rights Commission (CHRC) undertook investigations into and proceedings against Zundel and his Internet-based activities. Sabina Citron, a Holocaust survivor living in Canada, was the prime instigator in the CHRC actions against Zundel. After Citron overcame technical standing questions and institutional reluctance to proceed against Zundel a second time, the CHRC finally moved against Zundel under Section 13(1) of the Canadian Human Rights Act which prohibits telephonic communications of:

... any matter that is likely to expose a person or persons to hatred or contempt by reason of the fact that the person or those persons are identifiable on the basis of a prohibited ground of discrimination.[53]

---

[50] See eg, *Association J'Accuse, Acton Internationale pour la Justice (AIPJ) & UEJF c. Nos Racines*, Tribunal de Grande Instance de Paris, No. RG :02/57758, 8 August 2002; *T*, Tribunal de Grande Instance de Paris, No. 0028602422, 26 March 2002.

[51] See also, R. Planchar, 'Un négationniste de Bruxelles arrêté', *La Libre Belgique*, 20 November 2006.

[52] See, eg, G. Weimann and C. Winn, *Hate on Trial: The Zundel Affair, the Media, and Public Opinion in Canada* (Oakville, Ontario: Mosaic Press, 1986) and R. A. Kahn, 'Rebuttal versus Unmasking: Legal Strategy in *R. v. Zundel*' (2000) 34 *Patterns of Prejudice* 3.

[53] Canadian Human Rights Act, Section 13(2), Hate Messages.

Section 2 prohibits discrimination on the basis of 'race, national, or ethnic origin . . . [and] religion,' among other grounds.[54]

The Commission was met again with a series of technical and legal arguments.[55] Zundel's lawyer raised the ground that the *Zundelsite* was based in California and therefore was beyond the jurisdictional remit of the Commission. The Commission and Tribunal were also faced with Zundel's on-going assertions of technological ignorance and passivity. He argued throughout that he did not know anything about the *WWW* and had no connection with those who chose to use his name without his active intervention. Several other objections, some based in constitutional free speech positions, and others grounded in technical arguments about the meaning of 'telecommunications' under the relevant statute were also in issue.

In relation to Holocaust denial on the *WWW*, the CHRC and the Tribunal specifically addressed the question as to the nature of the mischief in question. The Tribunal heard evidence from two expert witnesses, Professor Gary Prideaux on discourse analysis and Professor Frederick Schweitzer on 'Historical Motifs in Anti-Semitism'. This quasi-judicial body engaged in a specific inquiry as to the nature of Holocaust denial as a legal phenomenon in order to determine whether the information or speech on the *Zundelsite* was in violation of the legislative provisions in question.

Prideaux identified techniques deployed by the speaker in order that the listener understand exactly the meaning intended to be conveyed. Among the identified techniques were:

1. generalization and the use of scare quotes;
2. specifically chosen vocabulary;
3. use of repetition;
4. targeting a particular group; and
5. coding and metaphor.[56]

Prideaux's conclusion that the *Zundelsite* met these criteria and was fundamentally antisemitic can serve as an important point for future debate about Holocaust denial and other forms of hate speech on the *WWW*. There can be no doubt that statements like 'Kill the Jews' are meant to, and do, convey certain messages. Indeed, such statements probably fall under our traditional understandings of incitement. But Zundel, his acolytes, and fellow Jew-haters are not always so blatant and obvious in their discourse. Some of the examples on which Prideaux

---

[54] Ibid., Section 2, Purpose.
[55] *Sabina Citron and Canadian Human Rights Commission and Ernst Zündel and League for Human Rights of B'nai Brith Canada*, Reasons for Decision, Canadian Human Rights Tribunal, T.D. 1/02 2002/01/18.
[56] Ibid., 123.

gave expert testimony and which were accepted by the Tribunal are more complex and more controversial than simple and crude Jew-baiting.

Prideaux asserted for example that the use of the terms 'Marxist' or 'Zionist' 'would expose Jews to hatred and contempt'.[57] This is ridiculous unless one is willing to create complex arguments about context and history, about who is speaking and who is listening and so on. To a greater or lesser extent, the Tribunal in this case ignored these subtleties, or at least paid no attention to the potential implications of its own discursive practices. The question which arises here is not just one of historical complexities of what is 'Zionism' and whether all Jews are Zionists, but is also about assumptions which seem to be built into the very legal semiotics of prosecutions of Holocaust deniers. There can be no doubt that Zundel and his acolytes are antisemites and neo-Nazis or even unreconstructed Nazis. When they use the term 'Marxist,' for example, there can be little practical question that this is deployed in the context of the historical equivalence between 'Jew' and 'Marxist' in Western antisemitic ideology. However, what we know as political truth may not always be the same thing as what we know as a legal matter or what we are permitted to know under operative legislative language. The traditional coding of 'Marxist' (or 'capitalist' or 'banker') equals 'Jew' leaves unanswered two basic factual questions from which important legal consequences are drawn. Who is listening to or reading these codes and what causal consequences do these codes have on the listener?

It is plausible to argue that Zundel and his readers in fact have access to the same code, that their semiotic universe is identical. Indeed communication of the ideology and its underpinnings would seem almost by definition to be grounded in the recipient's ready access to, or knowledge of, the linguistic code at play. Antisemites know that 'Zionist' and 'Marxist' are code for 'Jew' and more importantly they know that 'Jew' signifies 'bad.' In other words, the signifying sequence is not likely to subject Jews to hatred and contempt since Jews are already subjected to hatred and contempt by those who deploy and invoke it. The hermeneutic circle of Holocaust deniers is a closed one. As a matter of law, this must be intimately connected to the question of causation and/or causality. If a third party, one living behind a Rawlsian veil of ignorance, heard or was exposed to the *Zundelsite*, what would s/he understand? Could they break the code? Would they hate Jews as a result? Would they, as the law requires, be likely to act so as to 'expose a person or persons to hatred or contempt'? This is a much more complex question than the one which is found in the Tribunal's summary of Prideaux's evidence. Yet without such a careful analysis, the legal basis of the Tribunal's decision against Zundel is, to put it mildly, problematic.

The evidence of Professor Schweitzer was meant to fill in this possible lacuna. Schweitzer's evidence pointed out various instances where he found clear

[57] Ibid., 127.

expressions of various antisemitic stereotypes on the *Zundelsite*. Simply by removing references to 'Jews', a clever denier could avoid liability unless the court or tribunal can accept as a matter of law, a combined reading of texts based on Prideaux's and Schweitzer's analyses. For example, substitute one of David Irving's favourite phrases, 'our traditional enemies,' for any reference to 'Jews'. 'Our traditional enemies are liars.' 'Our traditional enemies are out to dominate the world.' Unless we bring to the legal hermeneutics of regulating Holocaust denial under the Canadian human rights model, a pre-understanding of the history of antisemitism and of the codes of antisemites, we cannot read these statements as subjecting Jews to ridicule, contempt, or hatred.[58]

Similarly, if there is a causal requirement even of the 'likely to' variety, it seems, as a matter of law, extremely difficult to prohibit legally antisemitism of more subtle and advanced kind. First of all, the difficulty of the code means tha only those already likely to understand it and share its goals and assumptions will understand. Consequently, those who do not understand are not 'likely to' hate anyone as a result. What appears to be happening in *Zundel* and in other similar proceedings is that a basic prejudgment has been made by the Tribunal, that Holocaust denial is antisemitic and therefore prohibited. It appears highly problematic, given this example, to argue that general legal human rights and anti-discrimination mechanisms, with only broad concepts of hatred, contempt, race, ethnicity, and religion, can and do, in and of themselves, adequately prohibit Holocaust denial. What *Zundel* demonstrates is that such regimes must at some level institutionally pre-judge statements and then operate a kind of legalized backing and filling to appear to comply with internal rule of law standards. The French and European positions which specifically embody the unassailable truth of the Holocaust avoid such unsatisfactory legal gymnastics.

A preliminary finding by the Human Rights Tribunal in *Zundel* illustrates this point. As he had in his earlier criminal trial, Zundel attempted to raise a defence of truth.[59] He wanted to be able to prove that the Holocaust did not take place. If he succeeded then the prosecution against him would collapse. 'Hatred' and 'contempt' would be irrational and therefore arguably unforeseeable or unintended (as a matter of law) responses to truth. A speaker, according to Zundel's legal position, could not be held responsible for the irrationality of his listeners in such cases. Moreover, if Holocaust denial is true, then any contempt which might fall upon Jews would not be the result of anything to do with their race or religion but would instead be attributable to their acts as liars or mentally ill people who created the fantasy of the Holocaust. Such is the juridical world created by the legal discourse of Holocaust denial.

[58] On this point at a higher level of generality, see Fish, n. 11 above.
[59] Canadian Human Rights Tribunal, Interim Decision, 25 May 1998.

The Tribunal found that truth was not a defence under Section 13. The statute deals with 'effects' and not with 'intention' or 'truth'. Its goal was to prevent the consequences of contempt, ridicule, or hatred. Its aim is to protect the victim, not to punish the perpetrator.

> ...it is the effect of the message on the recipient, and ultimately on the person or group vilified, that is the focus of the analysis. The truth in some absolute sense really plays no role. Rather, it is the social context in which the message is delivered and heard which will determine the effect that the communication will have on the listener. It is not the truth or falsity per se that will evoke the emotion but rather how it is understood by the recipient.[60]

This is, to say the least, when read in the context of the Tribunal's decision on the merits, a solipsistic mess. Truth in an absolute sense is not relevant but a contextualized understanding of the content of the statements is. The truth of statements is not important, but the message of those statements is crucial. Again, in those who already hate Jews, the message will in fact and in law, have no real effect at all. Moreover, the actual impact on the victims of Holocaust denial is not legally relevant here since the statute itself focuses, as the Tribunal makes clear, on the listener and her/his reaction to the message.[61] Whether the Holocaust happened at all is irrelevant as far as Canadian human rights legislation is concerned. Surely, if we accept the assertion as a matter of ethical necessity and of the duty to memory, that denial is a *malum in se*, this is an unacceptable, if perfectly legal, solution to the mischief of denial and other forms of hate speech.[62]

At some level then, it would appear that general legal anti-discrimination codes and statutes like the Canadian one are more difficult to deploy as tools against Holocaust denial than specific provisions like the French statute which identify Holocaust denial as a *malum in se*. Only if one ignores the meaning of the legal rules, as the Canadian Human Rights Tribunal appeared to do in *Zundel*, can the law be effective against subtle and informed Holocaust denial. Recent experience in Australia confirms this.

---

[60] Ibid., 3.   [61] See also, *Warman* v. *Kyburz*, 2003 CHRT 18.

[62] The fate of Zundel the person provides an interesting footnote. Zundel found true love and moved to the United States where he married Ingrid A. Rimland, a US citizen and webmaster of the *Zundelsite*. He vowed never to return to Canada where he was persecuted for speaking the truth. Unfortunately for Zundel, he failed properly to notify the US immigration authorities of his marriage and to apply for a change of his status. He was deported to Canada, where, despite his many years of residence, he had never taken out citizenship. Recent changes to Canadian law meant that permanent residents like Zundel who had, again like Zundel, spent more than six months outside the country, could be stripped of their status. Canadian Intelligence Services officers testified that Zundel was, because of his links to neo-Nazis, a national security threat. The government sent Zundel back to his native Germany despite his claims that because he faces imprisonment there as a result of a conviction for Holocaust denial activities, he is a political refugee. He was sentenced to five years in prison by a court in Mannheim in February 2007: 'Zundel sentenced to five years in German prison' *The Globe and Mail*, 15 February 2007; P. Cheney, 'Zundel verdict satisfies camp survivor', *The Globe and Mail*, 16 February 2007.

5. Australia, the Law, and Holocaust Denial

Holocaust denial in Australia also features an expatriate German resident, in this instance Fredrick Töben. Töben is in charge of the Adelaide Institute, which despite its grand title, is a focal point for Holocaust denial in Australia. Töben had been charged with hate speech offences in his native Germany and in 2002, he found himself before the Federal Court of Australia following a Human Rights and Equal Opportunity Commission (HREOC) determination that he had violated provisions of Section 18C of the Racial Discrimination Act. The Australian Constitution, as interpreted by the High Court, requires that HREOC decision be enforced and sanctions applied by the Federal Court.[63] The relevant provision of the Act prohibits public conduct which:

> ... is reasonably likely, in all the circumstances, to offend, insult, humiliate, or intimidate another person or group of people;[64]

Race, colour, and national or ethnic origin are protected categories.

The complaint alleged that the Adelaide Institute website contained Holocaust denial material as well as more general antisemitic items attacking the 'Jewish lobby'.[65] The case involved many familiar themes and issues. The Australian court simply accepted the findings of the Canadian Tribunal in relation to the nature and function of the Internet and the *WWW* as sites for information dissemination. Töben admitted to being the director of the Adelaide Institute and controlling the website. The Australian court then piggybacked on developments and issues already well-aired in France and Canada.

As in *Zundel*, the court here had to decide whether the denial of the Holocaust was material 'likely to offend' under the statute.

> There is no direct evidence before the Court tending to establish that any person was offended, insulted, humiliated, or intimidated by the material from the Adelaide Institute website... The court must make an objective assessment itself as to what is reasonably necessary.[66]

This difference in statutory language between the Australian provision and the Canadian is important. The latter requires the likelihood of 'contempt' or 'hatred,' while the former focuses on the impact on the 'victim' of the language. It protects feelings of offence, insult, humiliation, or intimidation. While it was trumped or sloughed off by the Federal Court by invoking an objective test of likelihood, the problem of causation still remains a central dilemma to the

---

[63] Another aspect of the Australian legislative scheme is that the original complaint was filed against Töben by Jeremy Jones, of the Executive Council of Australian Jewry. The legislation allows aggrieved individuals standing to complain to the Commission.

[64] Racial Discrimination Act of 1975, s. 18C (1)(a).

[65] *Jones* v. *Töben* [2002] FCA 1150.   [66] Ibid., 84.

satisfactory jurisprudential resolution of such cases. Indeed, the whole of the court's judgment seems characterized by a jurisprudential sloppiness which greatly diminishes the ideological impact of its substantive finding that Töben did violate Australian law.

As was the case in *Zundel*, the Australian Court was faced with the issue of whether the Holocaust did happen. The basic factual and ethical basis for the struggle against Holocaust denial was however once more elided. While recognizing that it is generally accepted that the Holocaust occurred, the court specifically pointed out that:

> ... it is not for the court in a case of this kind to seek to determine whether or not the Holocaust occurred... The role of the court is to determine whether the applicant has substantiated his complaint that the respondent engaged in conduct rendered unlawful.
> ... [67]

This judicial reluctance or refusal to deal with the central issue of the historical fact of the Holocaust leads to a bizarre and unsatisfactory conclusion on the substantive merits of the claim. In reaching its conclusions on the issues of likelihood and harm as defined in the statute, the court writes:

> The applicant gave evidence that the Australian Jewish community has the highest percentage of survivors of the Holocaust of any Jewish community in the world outside of Israel. Each of the first two of the imputations identified... above thus challenges and denigrates a central aspect of the shared perception of Australian Jewry of its own modern history and the circumstances in which many of its members came to make their lives in Australia rather than in Europe. To the extent that the material conveys these imputations it is, in my view, more probable than not that it would engender feelings of hurt and pain in the living by reason of its challenge to deep seated belief as to the circumstances surrounding the deaths, or the displacement, of their parents or grandparents. For the same reason, I am satisfied that it is more probable than not that the material would engender in Jewish Australians a sense of being treated contemptuously, disrespectfully and offensively.[68]

The question remains, in Australian law, did the Holocaust happen? While the complainants led some evidence, the court concluded only that there is a 'shared perception' among Australian Jews, one which is a 'deep seated belief' about the deaths of their families. In other words, while finding that Töben engaged in antisemitic acts and speech, the court was only willing to recognize harm as required under the law as damage to the victims' 'belief' and 'shared perception'. In other words, the Federal Court treated the Holocaust not as historical fact, not as a reality of life within western modernity which defines and delimits our notions of civilization, but as a matter of group psychology and theology.

Survivors in Sydney, Melbourne, and Perth are not legally survivors of the Holocaust, but people who share a collective historical belief and theological

---

[67] Ibid., 89.   [68] Ibid., 93.

perspective about the disappearance of their families in Europe. The *Einsatz-gruppen*, the killing vans, the crematoria, are all for Australian law, simply matters of 'belief'. This deep-seated psychological state cannot be attacked on the basis of singling out a specific ethnic, religious, or racial group.

The Adelaide Institute website continues to flourish, largely by providing links to denial and antsemitic sites in other jurisdictions. It also carries the following:

Dr. Frederick Töben's disclaimer

I am operating under a Federal Court of Australia Gag Order that prohibits me from questioning/denying the three pillars on which the 'Holocaust' story/legend/myth rests: 1. During World War II, Germany had an extermination policy against European Jewry; 2. of which they killed six million; 3. using as a murder weapon homicidal gas chambers. It is impossible to discuss the 'Holocaust' with such an imposed constraint. I therefore am merely reporting on matters that I am not permitted to state. For example, if I state the 'Holocaust' is 1. a lie; 2. six million Jews never died, or 3. the gas chambers did not exist, then I would claim that I am merely reporting on what expert Revisionists such as Professors Butz/Faurisson, et al, are stating in public.[69]

The law is obeyed. But the law as set out in the Australian human rights context, like its Canadian counterpart, is inherently inadequate. The reliance upon technical legal reasoning which must conform to general anti-discrimination statutory provisions ignores the historical reality of the Holocaust and denies in its own way the reality of the Shoah. The European solution of specifically worded legislation embodying the empirical reality of the Holocaust within the textual practices of national legality, whatever the difficulties inherent in that situation, clearly offers a preferable and more ethically acceptable position in the face of the pernicious practice of Holocaust denial. The Canadian and Australian cases simply demonstrate the inherent difficulty of manipulating law to avoid truth.

6. Conclusion

This brief survey highlights some of the issues and dilemmas, legal, historical, political, and now theological, which arise out of attempts to regulate Holocaust denial on the *WWW*. Each jurisdiction deals with the same issue in its own particular way, by invoking differing substantive legal norms, different procedural and judicial mechanisms, and apparently dissimilar jurisprudential perspectives on the issues at hand. The real question in each case is not whether we must combat Holocaust denial on the *WWW*, but how the struggle should be waged.

Only an unequivocal public and legal semiotics of incorporating the Holocaust into our social and political practice as societies can permit us to engage in a direct and ethically informed battle against Holocaust denial, whatever its form. The

---

[69] <http://www.adelaideinstitute.org>, accessed 23 July 2008.

Canadian emphasis on the impact such statements are likely to have on those to whom the ideas are communicated and the Australian court's insistence on the traumatization of members of the Jewish community, both suffer from the same epistemological, ideological, and political defects. The focus in each, directly and indirectly, is on the idea of the signifying chain survivor/victim/Jew. Jews did suffer as the principle victims of Nazi ideology and practice. The trauma which does surround denial for many members of various Jewish communities must not be dismissed or diminished. But soon the biological reality of historical experience will take its final toll. There will be no more survivors. This is one reason why the Canadian/Australian invocation of general human rights or discrimination paradigms focusing on an identified group or individual is unsatisfactory. In the near future, these systems will be forced to recognize a kind of communitarian, idealized second, and third generation traumatization in order to justify further legal intervention. That too must suffer serious, if not fatal, epistemological (not to mention slippery slope) difficulties.

Instead, the European approach which translates and imposes the Holocaust as a signifying event with universal meaning and importance within modernity comes much closer to the historical and political reality and truth of the Shoah. Only if and when we recognize in explicit and public terms the *malum in se* of denial's attacks on our Western, twenty-first century memory and truth can we serve not just memory and truth but justice, in the past, present, and future.

26

Expanding Holocaust Denial and Legislation Against It

Michael Whine

Holocaust deniers, and the media they use, are changing as a consequence of international political developments. It is necessary to update earlier analyses by this author of Holocaust denial in the United Kingdom.[1] Those works noted, to begin with, that the media for promoting denial had been revamped in light of technological advances, just as the nature of the propaganda itself was changing. New forms of this propaganda encompassed pseudoscientific books and papers; crude denial material, usually published in leaflet form by small neo-Nazi groups; and what can be called political denial, which includes the most recent and increasingly potent source, namely, Islamists as well as Internet and television transmissions within some Muslim states.

Many of the pseudoscientific publications available internationally were published under cover of fictitious academic publishing houses. These works included, for example, *The Hoax of the Twentieth Century* by Arthur Butz, *Did Six Million Really Die?* by Richard Harwood, and *The Leuchter Report*. Historians challenged these and rebutted their false theses. The very public destruction of David Irving's already tarnished reputation, as a result of his libel case against Deborah Lipstadt, effectively undermined the position of the pseudoscientific deniers, as did the more recent conviction of Germar Rudolf.[2] Some years ago

---

[1] M. Whine, 'Holocaust Denial in the United Kingdom', in J. Herman Brinks, S. Rock, and E. Timms, (eds.), *Nationalist Myths and Modern Media: Contested Identities in the Age of Globalisation* (London: Tauris Academic Studies, 2005), <http://www.thecst.org.uk/docs/Holocaust%20Denial %20in%20the%20UK.pdf> (last accessed 23 July 2008); M. Whine, 'Progress in the Struggle against Anti-Semitism in Europe: The Berlin Declaration and the European Union Monitoring Centre on Racism and Xenophobia's Working Definition of Anti-Semitism' (2006 February 1) 41 *Post-Holocaust and Anti-Semitism*, <http://www.jcpa.org/phas/phas-041-whine.htm> (last accessed 23 July 2008); M. Whine, 'Cyberhate, Antisemitism, and Counterlegislation' (2006 August 1) 47 *Post-Holocaust and Anti-Semitism*, <http://www.jcpa.org/phas/phas-047-whine.htm> (last accessed 23 July 2008).

[2] 'German Holocaust denier Rudolf jailed for 30 months,' *Deutsche Presse-Agentur*, 15 March 2007.

Fred Leuchter attempted to prove technically that Zyklon B was not used in the gas chambers. His lack of any engineering qualification was the subject of a successful criminal action in the American courts and his capacity to comment was curtailed.[3]

In Britain, distribution of the crude leaflets published by Lady Jane Birdwood's English Solidarity Organisation, Combat 18, and the National Front was halted after the criminal convictions of some of the main actors. These only took place after the Criminal Justice and Public Order Act (1994) and the Crime and Disorder Act (1998) came into force.[4] These measures gave the police powers of arrest for the distribution of material that incites racial hatred, and of immediate arrest without a warrant for suspected racially motivated public-order offences. They effectively put a stop for some years to the widespread dissemination of Holocaust-denial material in Britain by the far Right.

Thus, whereas in the 1980s and 1990s Britain became a world centre for publishing Holocaust-denial material, in many languages and for many markets, the British courts have successfully prosecuted such works despite the lack of specific Holocaust-denial legislation, where it contained material that incited hatred against Jews.[5]

This author's previous work also reviewed the genesis and progress of international agreements against antisemitism and Holocaust denial, including that promoted online. In this regard, too, there are new developments.

1. Holocaust Denial and the Internet

An increasing amount of Holocaust denial and trivialization propaganda comes from the Middle East. It is being transmitted primarily through the Internet, and also through print media and television. This, in turn, appears to be encouraging the far Right in several countries to resume promoting denial after a lull of several years, and even after the criminal convictions of some of its earlier proponents. Holocaust trivialization and inversion have also become more

---

[3] *Commonwealth of Massachusetts* v. *Fred A. Leuchter, Jr.*, Cambridge District Court, Cambridge, MA, 11 June 1991. By reaching a consent agreement with the court, Leuchter avoided a custodial sentence and a fine for practicing engineering without a license.

[4] Criminal Justice and Public Order Act 1994, <http://www.opsi.gov.uk/acts/acts1994/Ukpga_19940033_en_1.htm>; Crime and Disorder Act 1998, <http://www.opsi.gov.uk/acts/acts1998/19980037.htm> (both last accessed 23 July 2008).

[5] For example, Lady Jane Birdwood was convicted in April, 1994 for possessing and distributing threatening, abusive, and insulting literature that contained Holocaust-denial statements; Charlie Sargent, Will Browning, and Martin Cross were convicted for stirring up racial hatred in 1994 for publishing *Combat 18*, a magazine that denied the Holocaust; Nick Griffin and Paul Ballard were convicted in April, 1998 for publishing *The Rune* magazine, which contained denial material; Simon Sheppard was convicted in June 2000 for publishing leaflets that contained statements ridiculing the Holocaust.

common, possibly because outright denial itself has been criminalized in some jurisdictions.[6]

The trivialization argument is usually that far fewer Jews were murdered from 1939 to 1945 than the generally agreed figure of around six million, that the majority died of illness contracted in the death camps, or that the plight of the Palestinians in 1948 was worse than what befell the Jews. The inversion argument portrays Israel and the Jews' behaviour toward the Palestinians as being at least as bad as that of the Nazis toward the Jews.

In all cases the logic follows a similar route: to shift the moral responsibility for genocide, and to portray the victims as the new perpetrators. The promoters of these arguments come from a wider range than the outright deniers and may include the Arab and Muslim states, non-state propagandists within those countries, as well as some ideologues and activists on the political far Left.[7]

The promotion via the Internet of Holocaust denial, trivialization, and inversion poses new challenges. The founders of the Internet intended it to be a domain for free speech, unhindered by any restrictive legislation. Over the past ten years this ethos has been challenged by anti-racist and Jewish NGOs, and recently by some governments concerned that political extremists have seized on the freedoms of cyberspace to spread incitement and hatred. Of increasing concern is that those most influenced are the young, who may be less able to differentiate authoritative and factual material from propaganda.[8] The governments of those countries most affected by the Nazi takeover of Europe, and the Holocaust, have most strongly called for legislation to criminalize denial propaganda, including that online.

A second challenge posed by online Holocaust denial is one of jurisdiction, even if states have laws that criminalize it. Canada, Australia, France, and Germany, adopting different approaches, have recently brought successful criminal prosecutions against deniers, and the sites that published their material, within their own jurisdictions. But jurisdictions stop at states' borders.

Hence, denial and racist sites have relocated to jurisdictions where no supervisory regime exists or where there are no legal sanctions. One of the Internet's founding fathers recently asserted that the Internet should not allow itself to be used for hate promotion.[9] Nevertheless, the influence of the First Amendment to the US Constitution plays an important part in determining international attitudes toward online hate. Internet service providers in the United States and

[6] See M. Gerstenfeld, 'Holocaust Inversion: The Portraying of Israel and Jews as Nazis' (2007 April 1) 55 *Post-Holocaust and Anti-Semitism*, <http://www.jcpa.org/JCPA/Templates/ShowPage.asp?DRIT=0&DBID=1&LNGID=1&TMID=111&FID=381&PID=0&IID=1526&TTL=Holocaust_Inversion:_The_Portraying_of_Israel_and_Jews_as_Nazis> (last accessed 23 July 2008).

[7] For discussion of the issues, see Ibid.; M. Gerstenfeld, 'Ahmadinejad, Iran, and Holocaust Manipulation: Methods, Aims, and Reactions' (2007 February 1) 551 *Jerusalem Viewpoints*, <http://jcpa.org/JCPA/Templates/ShowPage.asp?DBID=1&LNGID=1&TMID=111&FID=442&PID=0&IID=1495> (last accessed 23 July 2008).

[8] The issues and potential remedies were debated at the OSCE Meeting on the Relationship between Racist, Xenophobic and Anti-Semitic Propaganda on the Internet and Hate Crimes, Paris, June 2004, <http://www.osce.org/documents/cio/2004/09/3642_en.pdf> (last accessed 23 July 2008).

[9] S. Nebehay, 'Web co-inventor backs licensing', *Reuters*, 27 November 1999.

elsewhere, however, have generally proved responsive to criticism that they host denial and other hate sites, and have enforced contractual non-hate terms-of-service obligations on users.[10]

2. International Agreements

Diplomatic pressure from some states, and particularly from NGOs, has prompted European intergovernmental organizations to pass resolutions and conclude agreements commemorating the Holocaust and condemning its denial or trivialization. These include:

the Declaration of the Stockholm International Forum on the Holocaust, by which the signatory states agreed to institute educational programmes and national commemorative initiatives; the European Parliament Resolution on remembrance of the Holocaust, antisemitism and racism; and the various declarations of the Organization for Security and Cooperation in Europe (OSCE), including the Permanent Council Resolution (2004), the Berlin Declaration (2004), the Cordoba Declaration (2005), the Brussels Declaration of the OSCE Parliamentary Assembly (2006), and a Resolution passed by the Parliamentary Assembly of the Council of Europe in 2007.[11]

In 2005, the European Monitoring Centre on Racism and Xenophobia (EUMC) (reconstituted in March 2007 as the European Union Agency for Fundamental Rights) published the Working Definition of Antisemitism, intended as a guide for criminal justice agencies. The RAXEN network of focal points monitoring racist violence identifies Holocaust denial as a specific form of antisemitism. The Working Definition notes, among other things, that:

Contemporary examples of antisemitism in public life, the media, schools, the workplace, and in the religious sphere could, taking into account the overall context, include, but are not limited to:

Denying the fact, scope, mechanisms (for example, gas chambers) or intentionality of the genocide of the Jewish people at the hands of National Socialist Germany and its supporters and accomplices during World War II (the Holocaust).[12]

---

[10] Whine, 'Cyberhate,' n. 1 above.

[11] Declaration of the Stockholm International Forum on the Holocaust, Stockholm, 26–28 January 2000; Resolution on the Holocaust, anti-Semitism and Racism, European Parliament, Brussels, 27 January 2005; Combating Anti-Semitism, Decision No. 607, Permanent Council, Organization for Security and Cooperation in Europe, PC.DEC/607, 22 April 2004, <http://www.osce.si/docs/mc-dec_12-04.pdf> (last accessed 23 July 2008); Berlin Declaration, Bulgarian Chairmanship, the Chairman-in-Office, Berlin, 2004, <http://www.osce.org/documents/cio/2004/04/2828_en.pdf> (last accessed 23 July 2008); Cordoba Declaration, Slovenian Chairmanship, Chairman-in-Office, Cordoba, 9 June 2005, <http://www.osce.org/documents/cio/2005/06/15109_en.pdf> (last accessed 23 July 2008); Resolution on Combating Anti-Semitism and Other Forms of Intolerance, Declaration of the OSCE Parliamentary Assembly, Brussels, 3–7 July 2006; Resolution 1563, Combating anti-Semitism in Europe, Parliamentary Assembly, Council of Europe, Strasbourg, 27 June 2007.

[12] Working Definition of Antisemitism, European Monitoring Centre on Racism and Xenophobia, Vienna, 16 March 2005, <http://eumc.europa.eu/eumc/material/pub/AS/AS-WorkingDefinition-draft.pdf> (last accessed 23 July 2008).

At the international level, the United Nations was finally persuaded to address the issue of the Holocaust. In 2005, it established 27 January as the International Day of Commemoration in Memory of Victims of the Holocaust. It now marks this day annually at Security Council headquarters in New York.[13] In January 2007, the UN General Assembly unanimously passed a resolution condemning Holocaust denial, with only Iran dissenting. This states:

Noting that 27 January has been designated by the United Nations as the annual International Day of Commemoration in memory of the victims of the Holocaust,
1. *Condemns without any reservation* any denial of the Holocaust;
2. *Urges* all Member States unreservedly to reject any denial of the Holocaust as a historical event, either in full or in part, or any activities to this end.[14]

A recent poll of the OSCE's 56 member states reported that 39 (71 per cent) have now established a Holocaust Memorial Day (HMD) or commemorate Holocaust victims. Of these, 19 (33 per cent) have HMD on 27 January and 15 (27 per cent) on a different day; 6 (11 per cent) incorporate commemoration of Holocaust victims into their national memorial days.[15]

Thus, Holocaust denial is now universally recognized as a specific form of hate. Many states deem it to constitute criminal behaviour that is subject to sanction. Until recently, however, the Additional Protocol to the Council of Europe Convention on Cybercrime had been the only international agreement requiring states to criminalize denial. Article 6 of the Additional Protocol states:

1. Each Party shall adopt such legislative measures as may be necessary to establish the following conduct as criminal offences under its domestic law, when committed intentionally and without right: distributing or otherwise making available, to the public through a computer system, material which denies, grossly minimises, approves or justifies acts constituting genocide or crimes against humanity, as defined by international law and recognised as such by final and binding decisions of the International Military Tribunal, established by the London Agreement of 8 August 1945, or any other international court established by relevant international instruments, and whose jurisdiction is recognised by that Party.
2. A Party may either
   a) require that the denial or the gross minimization referred to in paragraph 1 of this article is committed with the intent to incite hatred, discrimination or violence against any individual or group of individuals, based on race, colour, descent, or national or ethnic origin, as well as religion if used as a pretext for any of these factors, or otherwise.

---

[13] Resolution adopted by the General Assembly on the Holocaust Remembrance, A/RES/60/7, New York, 1 November 2005, <http://www.un.org/holocaustremembrance/docs/res607.shtml> (last accessed 23 July 2008).
[14] Holocaust denial, Resolution adopted by the General Assembly, 61/255, A/RES/61/255, New York, 22 March 2007.
[15] List of OSCE Participating States that Have Established Holocaust Memorial Days, OSCE ODIHR, Tolerance and Non-Discrimination Programme, Warsaw, 12 October 2006.

b) reserve the right not to apply, in whole or in part, paragraph 1 of this article.[16]

To date, 30 states have signed this protocol and eleven have ratified it.[17]

3. National Legislation

Fourteen separate European states have now criminalized Holocaust denial. All have adopted the basic premise that deniers are extremists who use denial as a means to rehabilitate Nazism. Thus, denial activity strikes at the heart of democratic governance in a continent that was torn apart from 1939 to 1945. An additional consideration is that deniers use Holocaust denial to incite hatred against Jews. They usually claim that Jewish demands for reparations and restitution for property stolen during the Nazi era are specious and based on a falsification of history. There was no Holocaust, or the consequences were much less serious than Jews say they were, hence Europeans and European governments are being conned by the Jews. Almost invariably this constitutes incitement against Jews and Jewish communities, and frequently has led to violence against Jews and Jewish institutions. Again this undermines fundamental concepts of civil liberty and fundamental rights.

The assumption that Jewish organizations urge legislation against Holocaust denial because it constitutes offensive speech is not completely correct. They also do so because they know from experience that the Jews are always the first in line; a society's treatment of its Jews is a paradigm for how it will treat all minorities. Jews' experience in the post-World War II era suggests that their rights are best protected in open and tolerant democracies that actively prosecute all forms of racial and religious hatred. Holocaust survivors themselves have been an important source of support for legislation. In France, for example, they have pressed for prosecutions under the Gayssot Act of 1990 (see note 21 below).

The European states that now criminalize Holocaust denial posit that such denial constitutes an attempt to justify crime, incites hate crime, or seeks to undermine the findings of the International Military Tribunal of August 1945 (the Nuremberg Tribunal). Criminal prosecutions have also taken place in Canada and Australia, but using other legislation. In both cases, though in different ways, this legislation addresses the issue of 'offending speech' to a defined section of the community.

---

[16] Additional Protocol to the Convention on Cybercrime, concerning the criminalization of acts of a racist and xenophobic nature committed through computer systems, Council of Europe, Strasbourg, 28 January 2003, <http://conventions.coe.int/treaty/en/treaties/html/189.htm> (last accessed 23 July 2008).

[17] Treaty open for signature by the states which have signed the Treaty ETS 185, <http://conventions.coe.int/Treaty/Commun/ChercheSig.asp?NT=189&CM=8&DF=3/28/2007&CL=ENG> (last accessed 23 July 2008).

In Austria, Article 3h of the Prohibition Act (Verbotzgesetz) states that:

[A] person shall also be liable to a penalty under Art. 3g if, in print or a broadcast or in some other medium, or otherwise publicly in any manner accessible to a large number of people, if he denies the National Social genocide, or other National Socialist crimes against humanity, or seeks to minimise them in a coarse manner or consents thereto or to justify them.

Punishment is by imprisonment for one to ten years, and if the offender or his activities are considered particularly dangerous, for up to twenty years.[18]

In Belgium, Article 1 of the law of 23 March 1995 states that:

Whoever, in one of the circumstances indicated by Article 444 of the Penal Code, denies, grossly minimises, tries to justify or approves of the genocide committed by the German National-Socialist regime during the Second World War will be punished by imprisonment of eight days to one year and a fine of twenty six to five thousand francs.[19]

In the Czech Republic, Article 261a of the amended constitution of 16 December 1992 states that:

[T]he person who publicly denies, puts in doubt, approves or tries to justify Nazi or communist genocide, or other crimes against humanity of Nazis or communists will be punished by prison of six months to three years.[20]

In France, Article 24 *bis* of the amended Press Act of 29 July 1881 states that:

those who have disputed, by one of the means stated in Article 23A, the existence of one or more crimes against humanity as they are defined by the article of the statute of the International Military Tribunal, annexed to the London Agreement of 8 August 1945, and which were committed by members of an organization declared criminal by the application of Article 9 of the above-mentioned statute or by a person found guilty of such crimes by a French or an international tribunal, will be punished with the penalties foreseen by the sixth paragraph of the Article 24.[21]

In Germany, Article 130 of the amended Penal Code of the Federal Republic of Germany states that:

(3) Whoever publicly, or at a meeting, denies, diminishes, or approves an act committed under the regime of National Socialism, of the kind described in Article 220A, paragraph 2, in a way likely to disturb public peace ... shall be punished by imprisonment up to five years, or a monetary fine.[22]

---

[18] Osterreich, StGBI 13/1945, amended version BGBI 148/1992, cited in N. Osin and D. Porat (eds.), *Legislating against Discrimination: An International Survey of Anti-Discrimination Norms* (Leiden and Boston: Tel Aviv University and Martinus Nijhof, 2005), 87.

[19] Ibid., 117.

[20] *Hate Crime Legislation in European Union Member States* (Paris: European Jewish Congress, 2007).

[21] Law of 29 July 1881, as amended by Act No. 90–615 of 13 July 1990, cited in n. 18 above, 306.

[22] *Federal L. J.*, 1994, cited in n. 18 above, 330.

In Liechtenstein, Article 283 of the Penal Code states that:

Public denial or trivialization or attempts to justify genocide or other crimes against humanity constitute a criminal act.[23]

In Lithuania, Holocaust denial is illegal with prison sentences of two to ten years and a fine.[24]

In Luxembourg, Article 457-3 of the revised Criminal Code states that:

It is forbidden to contest, trivialise, justify, or deny publicly the existence of crimes against humanity or war crimes linked to the Holocaust.[25]

4. Successful Prosecution

In the Netherlands, there is no primary legislation against Holocaust denial but Article 137 of the Criminal Code, which criminalizes defamation and religious and racial incitement, has been the basis for two successful prosecutions. The first was against Siegfried Verbeke, a Belgian national whose appeal against the May 1996 verdict by a Hague court was turned down on 25 November 1997.[26] The second occurred on 21 December 2004 when the District Court of Hertogenbosch convicted Ivo Janssen for having deliberately insulted Jews on his website by posting links to denial sites, including one that published the book *Did Six Million Really Die?*[27]

In Poland, denial of the Nazi crimes committed during between 1939 and 1945, and of Communist-era crimes, is illegal under Article 55 of the 1998 Law on the Institute of National Remembrance—Commission for the Prosecution of Crimes against the Polish Nation. This states that:

He who publicly and contrary to facts contradicts the crimes mentioned in Article 1, clause 1 shall be subject to a fine or a penalty of deprivation of liberty of up to three years. The judgment shall be made publicly known.[28]

---

[23] *Combating Hate Crimes in the OSCE Region: An Overview of Statistics, Legislation, and National Initiatives* (Warsaw: OSCE/ODIHR, 2005), 135–6, <http://www.osce.org/publications/odihr/2005/09/16251_452_en.pdf> (last accessed 17 April 2008).

[24] See n. 20 above.   [25] See n. 23 above, 138.

[26] 'Netherlands,' Country Reports, Stephen Roth Institute for the Study of Contemporary Antisemitism and Racism, Tel Aviv University, 1998, <http://www.tau.ac.il/Anti-Semitism/asw97-8/holland.html> (last accessed 23 July 2008); also <http://www.meldpunt.nl/index.php?link=revisionismee> [Dutch] (last accessed 23 July 2008).

[27] D. Verhuist, 'Conviction for Holocaust Denial on Website,' Institute for Information Law, University of Amsterdam,<http://merlin.obs.coe.int/iris/2005/2/article35.en.html> (last accessed on 23 July 2008).

[28] Act of 18 December 1988 on the Institute of National Remembrance—Commission for the Prosecution of Crimes against the Polish Nation, <http://www.ipn.gov.pl/portal/en/32/46/> (last accessed 23 July 2008).

In Portugal, Article 240(2) of the Criminal Code punishes anyone who

in a public meeting, in writing intended for dissemination, or by any other means of social communication, defames or insults an individual or group of individuals on grounds of their race, colour, or ethnic, national or religious origin, particularly by denying war crimes and crimes against peace or humanity, with the intention of inciting to or encouraging racial or religious discrimination.[29]

In Romania, Emergency Ordinance 31/2002 of the Penal Code prohibits publicly denying the Holocaust and its consequences. Penalties range from fines to fifteen years' imprisonment.[30] In the Slovak Republic, an amendment to Section 261 of the Criminal Code, which punishes public sympathy for fascism or any similar movement, allows the criminal prosecution of

public negation, doubts, acceptance or justification of fascist crimes or other similar movements.[31]

In Switzerland, article 261 *bis* of the Penal Code states that:

He who publicly incites hatred or discrimination toward a person or group of persons because of their racial, ethnic, or religious adherence;

He who, publicly, propagates an ideology with the intention to belittle or denigrate in a systematic manner members of a race, ethnic group, or a religion;

He who, for the same reason, organises, or encourages actions of propaganda or participates in them;

He who, publicly, by word of mouth, in writing, by image, by gesture, by assault, or in any other way, belittles or discriminates in a way which affects the human dignity of a person or a group of persons because of their race, their ethnic belonging to their religion or who, for the same reason, denies, grossly minimises or tries to justify a genocide or other crime against humanity;

He who refuses to give to a person or group of persons, because of their racial, ethnic, or religious belongings, a prestation destined for public use, shall be punished with imprisonment or with a fine (prison: three years maximum; fine: up to Sfr. 40,000).[32]

In a recent setback in Spain, the Constitutional Court overturned the legislation that criminalized Holocaust denial in an appeal case initiated by far Right activist Pedro Varela. According to government leaders, however, the legislation seems likely to be reinstated. Foreign Minister Miguel Ángel Moratinos asserted: 'Even if this means changing the penal code, we must overturn this decision' and added that the current or any other government 'will never permit Spain to become a center for neo-Nazi activity'.[33]

---

[29] See n. 23 above, 144–5.

[30] Monitorul oficial al României, 28 March 2002, cited in 'Final Report of the International Commission on the Holocaust in Romania', presented to President Ion Iliescu, Bucharest, 11 November 2004, 36.

[31] See n. 23 above, 149.   [32] See n. 18 above, 869.

[33] 'Spanish FM: Constitutional Court Decision "Must Be Overturned"', *European Jewish Press*, 15 November 2007, <http://www.ejpress.org/article/21780> (last accessed 23 July 2008).

Adversaries of legislation against Holocaust denial have argued that such laws restrict the basic human right of freedom of expression. An authoritative answer was given by the European Court of Human Rights (ECHR) in its judgment of 24 June 2003 against French denier Roger Garaudy. He had appealed against the dismissal of his earlier appeal by the French Court of Cassation following his conviction for several offenses involving denial. The ECHR noted that:

[T]here are limits to freedom of expression: the justification of a pro-Nazi policy cannot enjoy the protection of Article 10 and the denial of clearly established historical facts— such as the Holocaust—are removed by Article 17 from the protection of Article 10. As regards the applicant's convictions for denying crimes against humanity, the Court refers to Article 17: in his book the applicant calls in question the reality, degree and gravity of historical facts relating to the Second World War which are clearly established, such as the persecution of Jews by the Nazi regime, the Holocaust and the Nuremberg trials. Denying crimes against humanity is one of the most acute forms of racial defamation towards the Jews and of incitement to hatred of them.[34]

5. The European Common Framework

The European Parliament is now moving to rationalize and make consistent European states' laws against racial and religious hatred. Early in 2007, the German Presidency announced its plan to ensure the passage of the Common Framework Decision, which had been the subject of negotiation since 2001 and requires European states to legislate against racism in general, encompassing Holocaust denial.[35] This was agreed in Luxembourg on 19 April 2007. Article 1 of the Common Framework states that:

1. Each Member State shall take the measures necessary to ensure that the following intentional conduct is punishable:
   (a) publicly inciting to violence or hatred directed against a group of persons or a member of such a group defined by reference to race, colour, religion, descent, or national or ethnic origin;
   (b) the commission of an act referred to in point a) by public dissemination or distribution of tracts, pictures, or other material;

---

[34] Information Note No. 54 on the case law of the Court, European Court of Human Rights, Strasbourg, June 2003, <http://www.echr.coe.int/Eng/InformationNotes/INFONOTEN o54. htm> (last accessed 23 July 2008). Art. 17 of the Convention for the Protection of Human Rights and Fundamental Freedoms (ECHR) is designed to prevent abusers of rights from claiming protection that might be conferred by other articles. It states that: 'Nothing in this Convention may be interpreted as implying for any state, group or person any right to engage in any activity or perform any act aimed at the destruction of any of the rights and freedoms set forth herein or at their limitation to a greater extent than is provided for in the Convention.'

[35] J. Paulick, 'Germany moves to silence Holocaust deniers across Europe', *Deutsche Welle*, <http://www.dw-world.de/dw/article/0,2144,2317216,00.html> (last accessed 23 July 2008); Framework decision on Racism and Xenophobia, Press Release 8665/07 (Presse 84), Council of the European Union, Luxembourg, 19 April 2007.

(d) publicly condoning, denying, or grossly trivializing the crimes defined in Article 6 of the Charter of the International Military Tribunal appended to the London Agreement of 8 August 1945, directed against a group of persons or a member of such a group defined by reference to race, colour, religion, descent, or national or ethnic origin where the conduct is carried out in a manner likely to incite violence or hatred against such a group or a member of such a group.[36]

Article 1(c) refers to denial of genocide, as defined in Articles 6, 7, and 8 of the Statute of the International Criminal Court.

The Framework Decision had hitherto been held up by objections from Italy, Ireland, the UK, and some Scandinavian countries, which see blanket legislation against Holocaust denial as an infringement of the free-speech prerogative their states guarantee. To meet these objections, additions were made to the draft document that allow prosecutions only where Holocaust denial is carried out in a manner likely to incite violence or hatred (Article 1c). This was further reinforced by a codicil stating that:

1a) **For the purpose of paragraph 1** Member States may choose to punish only conduct which is either carried out in a manner likely to disturb public order or which is threatening, abusive, or insulting.

1b) For the purpose of paragraph 1, the reference to religion is intended to cover, at least, a conduct which is a pretext for directing acts against a group of persons or a member of such a group defined by reference to race, colour, descent, or national or ethnic origin.

2. Any Member State may, at the time of the adoption of this Framework Decision by the Council, make a statement that it will make denying or grossly trivializing the crimes referred to in paragraph 1(c) and/or (d) punishable only if the crimes referred to in these paragraphs have been established by a final decision of a national court of this Member State, and/or an international court or by a final decision of an international court only.[37]

The additional clauses meet the objections raised by the UK in particular, and allow for prosecution only where Holocaust denial is intended to incite hatred. An academic publication where specific aspects of the Holocaust might be debated, however inaccurate historically, would therefore be permissible. European states now have two years to enact legislation which ratifies the Framework Decision, if they do not have laws which meet the common criteria.

6. Recent Convictions

The momentum to institute criminal proceedings, however, has not diminished in recent years, and some states continue to demonstrate their commitment to

---

[36] Proposal for a Council Framework Decision on combating racism and Xenophobia, 8544/07, DROIPEN 34, Justice and Home Affairs Council of the European Union, Brussels, 17 April 2007.
[37] Ibid.

prosecute offenders. According to the Austrian authorities, for example, more than two hundred criminal convictions were secured under their prohibition statute from 1999 to 2006.[38]

Ernst Zündel, a German citizen formerly domiciled in Canada, was sentenced in February 2007 to five years on fourteen counts of incitement at his trial in Mannheim, Germany. For more than twenty years Zündel had been a prominent publisher of neo-Nazi and denial material in Canada, which he illegally exported to Germany and Austria. His first trial some months earlier had been terminated because of the behaviour of his defence attorney Sylvia Stolz.[39]

In the 2007 trial, Stolz was finally banned from the court on the ground that she was trying to sabotage her client's trial, and she had to be replaced. She has also now been charged with incitement, attempting to thwart a prosecution, and using symbols of a banned organization. During Zündel's first trial she repeatedly disputed the mass murder of Jews by the Nazis, called for hatred against Jews, and ended a legal document with the words 'Heil Hitler'.[40]

In March 2006, Germar Rudolf, whom the United States had extradited to Germany, was also convicted by a court in Mannheim for denying the Holocaust in his pseudoscientific *Rudolf Report*. He was sentenced to two and a half years in prison.[41]

In March 2007, Bruno Gollnisch, a French Member of the European Parliament and deputy head of the National Front, was fined $6,450 and given a three-month suspended sentence for publicly disputing the facts of the Holocaust. He also was ordered to pay $71,200 in compensation to those who had brought the action against him, and was suspended for five years from his teaching post at Jean Moulin University in Lyon.[42]

John Gudenus, a former representative of the far Right Freedom Party in the Austrian Bundesrat, was sentenced to a year's probation in April 2006 after publicly claiming that there were no gas chambers. He had been forced to resign from the Austrian National Council in 1995 for a similar public statement.[43]

In September 2006, however, in Torun, Poland, prosecutors dropped a criminal case against Radio Maryja commentator Stanislaw Michalkiewicz. They accepted that a broadcast he had made on 27 March 2006 did not constitute an intentional action ridiculing or denigrating the Holocaust, and that he had not denied the Nazi crimes in Poland. Michalkiewicz had labelled restitution efforts

---

[38] See n. 20 above.
[39] 'Zündel sentenced to five years in German prison', *Associated Press*, 15 February 2007.
[40] 'German lawyer for Zündel charged with incitement', *The Globe and Mail*, 20 March 2007.
[41] See n. 2 above.
[42] 'Fine for Gollnisch', *Jewish News*, 25 January 2007.
[43] 'Austria', Country Reports on Human Rights Practices 2006, US Department of State, Washington, D.C., 6 March 2007, <http://www.state.gov/g/drl/rls/hrrpt/2006/78800.htm> (last accessed 23 July 2008).

by Polish Jews as extortion and had belittled the facts of the Holocaust but was not guilty of a criminal offence.[44]

Back in December 1999, a court in Opole (Silesia) had found history professor Dariusz Rarajczak guilty of denial. He received no punishment because the book he had written, *Tematy niebezpieczne* (Dangerous Themes), had only a limited distribution. He was, however, barred from teaching for three years.[45]

In July 2007, the leader of the Hessen branch of the German National Democratic Party, Marcel Woll, was imprisoned by the Friedberg county court for publicly proclaiming that state-sponsored school trips to former concentration camps amounted to 'brainwashing'.[46]

In August 2007, the Austrian denier Gerd Honsik was arrested in Spain in connection with an outstanding conviction for publishing books and leaflets disputing the number of Jews killed. He had fled to Malaga to escape imprisonment.[47]

In Greece, the public prosecutor brought a case under Law 927/1979 of the Criminal Code against Kostas Plevris, author of the book *Jews: The Whole Truth* and publisher of the extreme-Right weekly *Eleftheros Kosmos*, both of which allegedly deny the Holocaust. An amendment to this law, which criminalizes 'acts or initiatives aiming at racial discrimination,' allows the public prosecutor to bring charges ex officio.[48] On 13 December 2007, Plevris was convicted and sentenced to 14 months imprisonment.[49]

In Belgium, the Forum of Jewish Organisations in Flanders filed a complaint against former senator Roeland Raes of the Vlaams Blok party (now reconstituted as the Vlaams Belang) for denying the existence of Nazi death camps during an interview on Dutch television. Raes was indicted in March 2007 and his trial was due to reconvene in December.[50]

In France, Vincent Reynouard was sentenced to a year's imprisonment and fined 10,000 euros in November 2007 for denying the Holocaust in a pamphlet he had published in 2005. *Holocaust? The Hidden Facts* was sent to museums and town halls across the country and described the Holocaust as an 'old propaganda theme'. His sentence is stated to be the heaviest handed down to date in France.[51]

---

[44] 'Poland', Country Reports on Human Rights Practices 2006, US Department of State, Washington, D.C., 6 March 2007, <http://www.state.gov/g/drl/rls/hrrpt/2006/78832.htm> (last accessed 23 July 2007).

[45] M. Weber, 'Polish Professor Fired for Dissident History Book' (2000) 19 *J. Historical Rev.* 25, <http://www.ihr.org/jhr/v19/v19n3p25_Weber.html> (last accessed 23 July 2008).

[46] 'Neo-Nazi to serve time for Holocaust denial', *Jewish Telegraphic Agency*, 7 August 2007, <http://www.jta.org/cgi-bin/iowa/breaking/103484.html> (last accessed 23 July 2008).

[47] 'Arrested', *Jewish News*, 30 August 2007.

[48] See n. 20 above.

[49] Correspondence between author and Central Board of Jewish Communities in Greece, 13 November 2007.

[50] 'Belgian ex-senator on trial for "Holocaust Denial" ', *United Press International*, 4 April 2007; email to author from Forum of Jewish Organizations, 17 July 2007.

[51] 'Frenchman convicted for Holocaust denial', *Expatica News*, 9 November 2007.

7. The Iranian Government's Initiative

As stated, the latest and most determined impetus to promote denial comes from the Middle East. Unlike previous initiatives, this has the clear backing of governments.

In February 2006, in what was clearly an Iranian-government-initiated response to the Danish cartoon controversy, the Tehran daily *Hamshahri* launched an international competition to find the best twelve cartoons about the Holocaust. Masoud Shojai, organizer of the exhibit for the cartoons, said, 'You see they allow the Prophet to be insulted. But when we talk about the Holocaust, they consider it so holy that they punish people for questioning it.'[52] The winner of the competition, Abdollah Derkaoui of Morocco, received $12,000 for his work depicting an Israeli crane piling cement blocks on Israel's security fence, on which was a picture of Auschwitz, thereby obscuring the Al-Aqsa Mosque in Jerusalem.[53]

The Tehran Holocaust Conference, held in December 2006 by the Iranian government, should be seen in the light of the government's other long-term strategies. These include, among others, the Shiite challenge to the Sunni and particularly Saudi leadership of the Muslim world, extending Iranian power in the Gulf region, and the campaign to delegitimize Israel and gain control of Jerusalem. Israel having in part been established as a haven for Holocaust survivors, one aim of the Tehran conference was to cast doubt on the Holocaust and therefore on the necessity for Israel.[54]

The conference was organized by the hitherto respected Institute for Political and International Studies, linked to the Foreign Ministry. Sixty-seven participants came from thirty countries, and particularly noteworthy was the wide range of the participants' backgrounds and beliefs. They included David Duke, the American white supremacist and former Ku Klux Klan leader; European neo-Nazi propagandists; members of the Jewish anti-Israeli Neturei Karta sect; Shiraz Dossa, political science professor at St. Francis Xavier University in Nova Scotia; and an anti-Hindu campaigner for Dalit ('untouchable') rights.[55]

The conference came in the wake of an aborted March 2006 conference, also organized by Iranian government-linked entities, which was abandoned when the German authorities withdrew the passports of the would-be participants from that

---

[52] 'Iran displays Holocaust cartoons', *BBC News*, 15 August 2006, <http://news.bbc.co.uk/1/hi/world/middle_east/4795709.stm> (last accessed 23 July 2008).

[53] 'Moroccan wins Iran Holocaust cartoon contest', *Associated Press*, 2 November 2006, <http://www.msnbc.msn.com/id/15525133> (last accessed 23 July 2008).

[54] See Gerstenfeld, 'Ahmadinejad', n. 7 above.

[55] 'Tehran International Conference, "Review of the Holocaust: Global Vision" 10–12 December 2006', <http://www.adelaideinstitute.org/2006December/contents_program1.htm> (last accessed 23 July 2008).

country. As a consequence only two of the foreign invitees, the Australians Frederick Toben and Richard Krege, attended alone and instead embarked on a lecture tour of Iranian universities.[56]

Toward the end of the two-day December conference, the Iranian government announced the establishment of the Foundation of Holocaust Studies to promote 'the study of the Holocaust'—that is, denial. The director, Mohammad Ali-Ramin, plans follow-up conferences and announced the appointment of a group of advisers who include the UK-domiciled Michelle Renouf, supporter of David Irving and other deniers.[57] Other members are Christian Lindtner of Denmark, the abovementioned Frederick Toben of Australia, Serge Thion of France, and Bernhard Schaub of Switzerland.

On her return from the Tehran conference to London in early 2007, Renouf began to write and lecture on denial. Although her only audiences in Britain so far have been tiny neo-Nazi groups such as the New Right Group on 14 January and the British People's Party on 20 January, she also has spoken in the United States and has given interviews on Iranian television.[58]

8. David Irving

The Iranian initiative coincided with renewed far Right activity, particularly in Central and Eastern Europe where right-wing parties sometimes constitute the main parliamentary and extraparliamentary opposition. Although Holocaust denial is not part of these parties' platforms, their presence has made it easier for David Irving, for example, to visit several countries since his early release on probation and lecture there to invited audiences. He had served eighteen months of a three-year sentence received in Austria in 2005 for Holocaust-denial offenses committed in 1989.

In January 2007, Irving visited several former death camps in Poland and carried out research for a new book.[59] In March he was in Hungary, to which he had been invited by his new publishers Sandor and Tibor Gede, to launch the Hungarian version of his book *Nuremberg: The Last Battle*. He also spoke on 15 March at an open-air rally of the far Right Justice and Life Party, which ended in a

---

[56] 'The Mashhad 'Holocaust' Conference—6 March 2006', Adelaide Institute, <http://www.adelaideinstitute.org/Iran/conference_program2.htm> (last accessed 23 July 2008).

[57] 'Constituting the International 'Holocaust' Research Foundation—IHRF: Interim Committee, Tehran 13 December 2006', <http://www.adelaideinstitute.org/2006December/Holocaust_Stiftung.htm> (last accessed 23 July 2008).

[58] 'Leeds BPP Meeting a Huge Success', British People's Party, 20 January 2007, <http://www.bpp.org.uk/leeds20thmeet.html> (last accessed 23 July 2008).

[59] 'Real History, and a Radical's Diary', <http://www.fpp.co.uk/docs/Irving/RadDi/2007/020307.html> (last accessed 23 July 2008).

riot with police arresting scores of neo-Nazi demonstrators though this was after Irving had left.[60]

In April, Irving exhibited his books at a book fair in Barcelona and spoke at a meeting organized by the abovementioned Pedro Varela.[61] However, he was denied a place at the 52nd Warsaw Book Fair after complaints to the organizers, and was asked to remove his stand and books after he had set them up.[62]

On 23 March, Irving was interviewed on the Italian SKY TG24 documentary programme *Controcorrente* (Countercurrent). He claimed that engineering techniques supported his contention that mass gassings could not have occurred at Auschwitz.[63] An Italian bill to outlaw denial was recently withdrawn by the government because of free-speech concerns, though Irving had been refused entry into the country during the 1990s.

9. Future Outcomes

Irving's renewed activity will provide a boost to Holocaust denial. As Medoff and Grobman note:

The prosecution and imprisonment of prominent Holocaust-deniers in Europe dealt a serious blow to the Holocaust-denial movement in 2006. Some civil libertarians decried the use of laws prohibiting Holocaust-denial, but there was a noticeable decline in denial activity, following the jailing of the movement's best-known figure, David Irving, in Austria, and the prosecution of prominent activists Ernst Zundel, and Germar Rudolf in Germany. The release of Irving from prison in December 2006, after serving about one third of his three year sentence, is likely to reinvigorate the denial movement in the year ahead.[64]

Likewise, the Iranian government's encouragement and assistance will provide a further boost, and possibly financial rewards.

Recent initiatives include the International Holocaust Revisionist Conference organized by Eric Gliebe of the white-supremacist National Alliance, which took

---

[60] 'David Irving: Controversial historian in Hungary for book signing, speeches', *Budapest Sun*, 14 March 2007, <http://www.budapestsun.com/cikk.php?id=25958> (last accessed 23 July 2008); 'Hungarian protests turn violent', *BBC News*, 15 March 2007, <http://news.bbc.co.uk/go/pr/fr/-/1/hi/world/europe/6453183.stm> (last accessed 23 July 2008); R. Hodgson, 'Holocaust denier guest of honour', *The Budapest Times*, 14 March 2007, <http://budapesttimes.vitalcomp.hu/index.php?do=article&id=2261> (last accessed 23 July 2008).

[61] 'Real History and a Radical's Diary', <http://www.fpp.co.uk/docs/Irving/RadDi/2007/300407.html> (last accessed 23 July 2008).

[62] L. Owen, 'Irving booted out of Warsaw fair', *The Bookseller*, 24 May 2007. Video footage of Irving's expulsion is also available on YouTube at <http://wideo.gazeta.pl/wideo/0,0,4143632.html> (last accessed 18 April 2008).

[63] 'British historian denies WWII gassings', *Associated Press*, 23 March 2007.

[64] 'Holocaust Denial: A Global Survey—2006', David S. Wyman Institute for Holocaust Studies, Washington, D.C., 2, <http://www.wymaninstitute.org/articles/HolocaustDenial2006.pdf> (last accessed 23 July 2008).

place in Hillsboro, West Virginia, on 26–27 May 2007. Among the speakers were Canadian Paul Fromm, Michelle Renouf, and veteran deniers Arthur Butz and Willis Carto.[65] The far Right Argentinian Second Republic Movement plans to hold a '[m]ulti-disciplinary International Conference' in Buenos Aires in 2008 to establish 'the true nature of power and leverage exerted by International and Local Zionists [*sic*] organizations and interests in our country'.[66]

It does not appear that the international criticism, and the criminalization of public denial activity in almost half the states of the European Union, will stop the denial promoters. Instead they may shift the focus of their activity to those states where no criminal sanctions exist. The legal and political environment in the states that have legislation may be too hostile to risk further prosecution, particularly for the older activists such as Faurisson or Irving who have previous convictions and may now face severe penalties if convicted again.

The United States will continue to allow Holocaust-denial activity because of the First Amendment guarantees, although mainstream Internet service providers have been prepared, when requested, to remove posters of hate speech from their sites. Deniers may therefore have to rely increasingly on sympathetic hosts. The United States also will continue to present an attractive destination for deniers, particularly the older, better-known activists whose entry is not barred as their criminal convictions are not for crimes recognized by American courts. Moreover, paid personal appearances and book-sale opportunities provide a source of income otherwise denied them in Europe.

Former Soviet Union and EU accession states may be particularly reluctant to legislate against speech, however offensive and even if it incites hatred. They are still affected by their experiences in the twentieth century when freedom of speech was severely curtailed by the Nazis and then by the communists. Hatred promotion will continue in some former Soviet-bloc states such as Ukraine, where the privately funded MAUP university in Kiev offers courses on anti-Zionism and publishes antisemitic texts, and where David Duke has lectured. In these states there currently is no legislation and no political will to confront denial activity, though the Ukrainian government has recently been responsive to criticism over MAUP.

Holocaust denial will continue throughout the Arab and Muslim world, promoted by the state-controlled and private media, for the reasons noted above. This is despite the recognition by some local political leaders and spokesmen of the harm that denial activity causes to these countries' international reputation, as

[65] R. Forbes, 'Nationalist free speech meeting a success despite sabotage gambits', *National Alliance News*, <http://www.natallnews.com/story.php?id=5253> (last accessed 23 July 2008). See also 2007 Holocaust Revisionist Conference DVD, Catalog Item 891, National Vanguard Books, available at <http://www.natvanbooks.com/cgi-bin/webc.cgi/st_prod.html?p_prodid=104>1 (last accessed 23 July 2008).

[66] 'New Holocaust Debate to be Held in Argentina, Statement from the Argentine Second Republic Movement', British People's Party, <http://www.bpp.org.uk/argentinedebate.html> (last accessed 23 July 2008).

in a recent statement by Egyptian Ahmed Aboul Gheit. On 21 April 2007, he pointed out that Egypt had voted for the abovementioned UN General Assembly Resolution and supported the EU Common Framework Decision.[67]

On 8 June 2007, in a fence-mending exercise at an OSCE intergovernmental conference, the Egyptian representative denied that there was antisemitism in the Arab world.[68] It is, though, a fact that antisemitism and Holocaust denial are now endemic in the Arab world and that state institutions play the key role in impelling them.

10. The Necessity of Holocaust Education

The existence of legislation that criminalizes Holocaust denial, and a history of prosecuting it in a particular country, may seem to be a sufficient deterrent in itself. But the fact that there are repeat offenders such as Faurisson suggests that this is not the case. Prominent activists in those EU countries that maintain a hostile legal environment have not stopped publishing denial material nor making public statements, sometimes via their national media, denying all or important elements of the Holocaust. As noted, they may merely shift the locus of their activity.

The abovementioned Stockholm Declaration has led to a proposal for a more comprehensive education regime for the young entailing mandatory courses for all students. Such a programme is now being put in place by the International Taskforce and the OSCE Office for Democratic Institutions and Human Rights (ODIHR). This more realistic and effective solution would create an environment where denial activity would find little or no support. At the time of writing, seven OSCE participating states have begun to use teaching materials developed by the Anne Frank House in Amsterdam in their education systems, and a further three are working with ODIHR to do the same.[69]

At the Holocaust Memorial Museum in Washington, D.C., information officers from UN Information Centres in eleven Latin and Central American states recently launched a programme titled 'The History of the Holocaust: Confronting Hatred, Preventing Genocide and Cultivating Moral

---

[67] 'Egyptian minister reacts to EU decision on criminalizing anti-Holocaust remarks,' *MENA News Agency* [Arabic], *BBC Monitoring*, 21 April 2007.

[68] Rauf Saad, assistant to the minister of foreign affairs of the Arab Republic of Egypt, Plenary Session 1, OSCE Conference on Combating Discrimination and Promoting Mutual Respect and Understanding, PC.DEL/543/07, Bucharest, 8 June 2007, <http://www.osce.org/documents/cio/2007/06/24998_en.pdf> (last accessed 23 July 2008).

[69] C. Strohal, Address by Ambassador Christian Strohal, Director of the OSCE Office for Democratic Institutions and Human Rights (ODIHR), 672nd Session of the Permanent Council, Vienna, 28 June 2007, <http://www.osce.org/documents/odihr/2007/06/25361_en.pdf> (last accessed 23 July 2008). See also 'ODIHR tackles anti-Semitism with innovative education materials', *OSCE Highlights*, 31 May 2007.

Responsibility'. In an address to participants, Kiyo Akasaka, UN under-secretary general for communications and public information, stated that: 'History has shown that the Holocaust was intimately linked to the founding of the United Nations. I urge you to be curious, ask questions and reflect on ways in which you can enhance outreach activities in your respective countries in the areas of Holocaust remembrance, human rights and genocide prevention.'[70]

To defeat denial, more effective than laws alone is education—coupled with the widespread understanding that denial is a means to undermine or falsify the established facts of history, promote neo-Nazi ideology, attack democracy, and delegitimize the State of Israel. However, from a moral and historical perspective it is equally important that European states legislate to outlaw this form of hatred, which has the capacity to unravel the cohesion that these states have worked to achieve since 1945.

---

[70] 'UN joins with Holocaust Museum to foster genocide prevention, remembrance', *UN News Service*, 15 May 2007, <http://www.un.org/apps/news/story.asp?NewsID=22556&Cr=holocaust& Cr1=> (last accessed 23 July 2008).

27

The Holocaust Denial Decision of the Federal Constitutional Court of Germany

Dieter Grimm

In Germany, Holocaust denial was made a crime in 1994 by an amendment to section 130 Penal Code (instigation to hatred). A previous attempt to criminalize it had failed ten years earlier.[1] But before Holocaust denial was specifically outlawed in 1994, it had already been punished under more general provisions of the Penal Code: section 185 (libel and slander), section 189 (revilement of the memory of defunct persons) and section 130 in its original form, which did not explicitly refer to the atrocities committed under national socialist rule, but to incitement of hatred against segments of the population, call for violent or arbitrary measures against them etc.[2]

Such broad interpretation of these provisions had drawn some criticism as excessively stretching the text. But the interpretation had found the approval of the *Bundesgerichtshof* (Germany's highest court for civil and criminal law), which upheld a conviction for Holocaust denial under the unamended section 130. In doing so the Court stated:

The historical fact itself that human beings were singled out according to the criteria of the so-called 'Nuremberg Laws' and were robbed of their individuality for the purpose of extermination puts Jews living in the Federal Republic into a special personal relationship

---

[1] See E.Stein, 'History against Free Speech: The New German Law against the "Auschwitz"—and other—"Lies" (1986) 85 *Mich. L. Rev.* 277.

[2] Section 130 Penal Code as amended in 1994 did not explicitly mention the Holocaust denial either, but referred to 'acts committed under national socialist rule of the sort mentioned in s. 220a (1) Penal Code'. This section, in turn, criminalized several acts that were regarded as, or as contributing to, genocide. S. 130(3) Penal Code in its present form reads: 'Whoever publicly or in a meeting approves of, denies or renders harmless an act committed under the rule of National Socialism of the type indicated in s. 6 subsection (1) of the Code of Crimes against International Criminal Law, in a manner capable of disturbing the public peace shall be punished with imprisonment for not more than five years or a fine.' S. 6(1) Code of Crimes against International Criminal law is more or less identical with s. 220a Penal Code, which was abolished when the Code of Crimes against International Criminal Law was enacted in 2002.

vis-à-vis their fellow citizens; what happened is also present in this relationship today. It is part of their personal self-perception to be comprehended as belonging to a group of people who stand out by virtue of their fate and in relation to whom there is a special moral responsibility on the part of all others and that this is a part of their dignity. Respect for this self-perception is virtually, for each individual, one of the guarantees against repetition of this kind of discrimination and forms a basic condition of their life in the Federal Republic. Whoever seeks to deny these events denies, vis-à-vis each individual, the personal worth due to each [Jewish person]. For the person concerned this means continuing discrimination against the group to which he belongs and, as part of that group, against himself.[3]

The Holocaust denial case that I shall focus on in this chapter and of which I was the judge rapporteur is a 1994 decision by the German Constitutional Court. Decided before the amendment of section 130, the case did not concern a criminal conviction, but rather arose out of an administrative proceeding. The complainant was the Munich/Upper-Bavarian section of the National Democratic Party of Germany (NPD), a small right-wing party not represented in the *Bundestag*, the federal parliament. The NPD had planned a public meeting in the city of Munich where David Irving was supposed to speak. According to the announcement by the NPD, the speech would deal with the alleged Jewish blackmailing of German politics by exploiting the Holocaust.

The municipal authorities of Munich, who had been notified of the planned assembly by the NPD, issued an order prohibiting Irving, other speakers, and the participants of the assembly from denying the persecution of Jews during the Third Reich. In case of non-compliance, the assembly would be dissolved. The order was based on section 5(4) of the Statute on Assemblies (*Versammlungsgesetz*), which allows for a prohibition of an assembly if there is evidence that the organizer or his followers will express opinions or allow utterances that constitute a crime. The municipal authorities were of the view that Holocaust denial constituted a crime punishable under the provisions of the Penal Code mentioned above.

After having opposed the order without success in the administrative courts, the NPD filed a constitutional complaint based on Article 5 (freedom of speech) and Article 8 (freedom of assembly) of the German Basic Law. The Federal Constitutional Court rendered its decision on 13 April 1994.[4] The Court started from the assumption that the order would pass constitutional muster if the prohibition on denying the Holocaust was compatible with freedom of expression under Article 5. The Court reasoned that prohibited speech does not become

---

[3] BGHZ 75, 160, 162–3 (1980). English translation from N. Dorsen, M. Rosenfeld, A. Sajo, and S. Baer, *Comparative Constitutionalism: Cases and Materials*, (St. Paul: Thomson/West, 2003), 913.
[4] BVerfGE 90, 241 (1994). An English translation may be found in *Decisions of the Bundesverfassungsgericht*, Vol. 2 (Baden-Baden: Nomos, 1998), 620; D. P. Kommers, *The Constitutional Jurisprudence of the Federal Republic of Germany*, 2nd edn. (Durham: Duke UP, 1997), 382; Dorsen, et al. (ibid.), 913.

lawful just because uttered in the context of an assembly.[5] Conversely, a violation of freedom of expression by the order would have entailed a violation of freedom of assembly. This is why the emphasis was laid on Article 5.

According to Article 5 everybody has the right to freely express and disseminate his opinion in speech, writing, and pictures. The formulation 'freedom of opinion' is narrower than 'freedom of expression'. It covers only a segment of speech. This gives rise to the question whether statements of fact come within the protection of 'freedom of opinion'. According to the Constitutional Court's established jurisprudence, statements of fact fall within the protection of Article 5 only if they are related to opinions, either because the facts are the object of an opinion or because they are used as evidence supporting or refuting an opinion.

Opinions and statements of fact differ in that opinions are characterized by the subjective relationship between the expression and its object. They are personal assessments of a matter or value judgements, whereas statements of facts are characterized by an objective relationship between the expression and its object. The speaker alleges that what he says is in fact the case, independently of his personal views. Hence, opinions as subjective expressions cannot be qualified as right or false, while statements of facts can. According to the jurisprudence of the Court, the question of truth or falsehood of a statement of fact is relevant to the degree of protection. False statements of fact are less protected than true ones or opinions. A deliberate lie or a statement of fact whose falsehood was already clearly established before the statement was made is not protected at all. This distinction, which had been made long before this Holocaust denial case,[6] became relevant here. The Holocaust denial was found to be a false statement of fact whose falsehood was undoubtedly established by numerous reports of witnesses, historical research, and not least by the Auschwitz trial of 1964/65 in Frankfurt.

In order to clarify what is and what is not a statement of fact when historical occurrences are at stake, I want to mention another case that was decided three months before the Holocaust denial case. The case concerned a book entitled (in English translation) *Truth for Germany: The Question of Guilt for the Second World War*.[7] The author tried to show that it was the allies not Hitler who was responsible for the outbreak of World War II. The book was banned under a statute protecting juveniles (*Jugendschutzgesetz*) because it was found false and could mislead young persons about national socialism. The Constitutional Court reversed the ban, finding that the author's thesis on the war guilt question was not a statement of fact but an opinion based on a complex set of facts. The fact that

---

[5] I leave aside that the decision concerned a prior restraint because it is not of relevance in the present context.

[6] See BVerfGE 54, 208, 219 (1980); BVerfGE 61, 1, 8 (1982); BVerfGE 85, 1, 15 (1991). For an English translation, see *Decisions of the Bundesverfassungsgericht* (n. 4 above), 189, 244, 542.

[7] BVerfGE 90, 1 (1994). For an English translation, see *Decisions of the Bundesverfassungsgericht* in n. 4 above, 570.

the author's conclusion contradicted the findings of historical research alone was no sufficient ground for a ban as long as any denial, justification, or glorification of NS deeds was avoided. The Court remarked that the right way to deal with publications like this is discussion rather than suppression. As we shall see, this decision has a direct bearing on the Holocaust denial case, to which I now return.

Finding that the denial of the Holocaust was a false statement of fact whose falsehood was undoubtedly established at the time when the NPD wanted to hold its assembly should have ended the case. If the Holocaust denial was not protected by Article 5 of the Basic Law, this right could not have been violated by the order. The same was true for Article 8. Nevertheless the Court continued its examination, perhaps to avoid the impression that it had chosen an easy way to circumvent the crucial question, or maybe because it was aware of the difficulty of clearly distinguishing between opinions and statements of fact. So it went on to inquire whether the result would be different if Holocaust denial, seen in the context of the meeting to discuss alleged Jewish blackmailing of German politics by exploiting the Holocaust, were regarded as an opinion.

Under this approach, it became necessary to balance the fundamental right limited by the order (freedom of speech) and the interest protected by the statute (depending on the relevant provision of the Penal Code, the honour of the Jews living in Germany, the memory of the Jews who had lost their lives in concentration camps, or public peace). The balancing requires an answer to two hypothetical questions and a conclusion: (1) what would be the loss for freedom of speech if the interests protected by the statute prevail? (2) what would be the loss for these interests if freedom of speech prevails? (3) which loss weighs more heavily? Here again, the doubtless falsehood of the statement on which the opinion was based comes in, this time, however, not to exclude the expression from fundamental rights protection but as relevant to the weight of free speech in the balancing process. The answer was: the weight of an opinion that is based on an evidently false statement of fact is slight.

This modest weight alone, however, would not be sufficient to justify the suppression if the harm that speech causes to the interests protected by the statute were even smaller. So what was the harm? Here the Constitutional Court referred to the personality rights of the Jews currently living in Germany. These rights were protected by section 185 Penal Code, which, in turn, concretized Article 2 Section 1 (free development of one's personality) in connection with Article 1 Section 1 (human dignity) of the Basic Law. The Jews were regarded as a group capable of being insulted.[8] The Court quoted the reasoning of the *Bundesgerichtshof* discussed above, thereby affirming that the persecution of Jewish people during the Nazi era had become part of the identity of the present generation of Jews in Germany. Denial of the Holocaust therefore denies their identity. If the

---

[8] In German law the requirements for group libel are less severe than in common law, see eg, BVerfGE 93, 266, 299–303 (1995)—'Soldiers are murderers'.

German state allows such denial of Jewish identity, it contributes to creating an atmosphere of insecurity for German Jews or at least nourishes the impression that Germany no longer distances itself from what it had done to the Jews, whereas an official recognition that these events happened and that their denial will be prosecuted provides a safeguard against their repetition. These considerations weighed more heavily than the interest in uttering an opinion which contained an evidently false statement of fact.[9]

Decisive for the outcome was not the assumption that the Holocaust had been 'the evil as such',[10] but a concrete evaluation of what the Holocaust denial still meant seventy years after the events. In the final analysis, it is the German responsibility for the Holocaust that explains the decision. It has become part of the identity of post-war Germany that atrocities like these should never happen again under the responsibility of the German state. The criminalization of the Holocaust denial symbolizes this deep conviction and thus is a uniquely German justification. As such, this justification would not be applicable to a prohibition of Holocaust denial in countries that do not have to bear the same historical responsibility.

This is of interest, since the criminalization of the Holocaust denial is not limited to Germany or countries where government agencies or parts of the population collaborated with the Nazi regime. It is therefore remarkable that the European Court of Human Rights had no objection against punishment of the Holocaust denial in countries other than Germany. Although this Court routinely emphasizes the importance of freedom of speech for a democratic society, it found that any justification of a pro-national socialist policy is not covered by Article 10 of the European Convention on Human Rights. In the Court's eyes there is a category of clearly established historical facts—among them the Holocaust—where denial is stripped from Article 10 protection because of Article 17, which prohibits any misuse of the Convention rights.[11] This decision goes even farther than the German Constitutional Court's jurisprudence.[12]

---

[9] Since the Holocaust denial would have violated s. 185 of the Penal Code the Court saw no need to discuss whether ss. 189 and 130 would have been violated as well.

[10] See D. Fraser in this volume.

[11] See most recently *Garaudy* v. *France*, Case No. 65831/01 of 24 June 2003.

[12] Upon an initiative of the German presidency the European Union recently resumed earlier attempts to enact a Framework Decision on combating racism and xenophobia. If enacted it would oblige the Member States to take the measures necessary to ensure that 'publicly condoning, denying or grossly trivializing crimes of genocide, crimes against humanity and war crimes as defined in Arts. 6, 7 and 8 of the Statute of the International Criminal Court, directed against a group of persons or a member of such a group defined by reference to race, colour, religion, descent, or national or ethnic origin when the conduct is carried out in a manner likely to incite to violence or hatred against such a group or a member of such a group' is punishable (see Doc. 8544/07 of the Council of the European Union of 17 April 2007). A political agreement on the Framework Decision was reached in the Council in April, 2007 and in the European Parliament in November, 2007. The formal enactment is still pending.

28

The Politics of Memory: Bans and Commemorations

Patrick Weil*

1. Introduction

Since the beginning of 2005, a heated debate has developed in France over the manner in which to commemorate discrimination or collective persecutions which the French State witnessed or in which it participated, and whether or not to ban the act of denying that these acts ever took place. This debate has its origins in two events. The first was the passage of Article 4 of the law of 23 February 2005, related to the 'Nation's recognition of the contributions made by repatriated French citizens', which stated:

School curricula shall recognize in particular the positive role played by French citizens living overseas, notably in North Africa, and will accord to the soldiers of the French army who served in these territories the prominent historical role they deserve.[1]

Very quickly, this provision of the law provoked strong reactions. Petitions circulated first on March 25 (by Claude Liauzu, Gilber Meynier, Gerard Noiriel, Frederic Regent, Trinh Van Thao, and Lucette Valensi), then on 13 April (by the Human Rights League) brought together thousands of signatures demanding its revocation.[2] On 27 March, another historian, Guy Pervillié, responded by suggesting that Article 4 of this law was in fact based on Article 2 of the law of 21 May 2001 (the Taubira Law), which recognized slavery as a crime against humanity. This line of argument was echoed by Alain-Gérard Slama in an article in *Le Figaro* on 18 April 2005.

* This text had its origins in a lecture entitled 'Law, Memory, and History' that was presented on 5 October 2006 at Port-Louis, Mauritius, at the invitation of Fred Constant, who I thank here. I also thank Bruce Ackerman, Claire Andrieu, Olivier Beaud, Stéphane Dufoix, Michel Giraud, Laurent Joly, Emmanuel Macron, Frédéric Regent, Anne Simonin, and Pierre Vesperini for their contributions to the development of this article. This chapter is a development of an article originally published in French in *Esprit* 2/2007. Trans. Josh Gibson.

[1] For more on the controversies tied to the passage of this law, see R. Bertrand, *Mémoires d'empire, La controverse autour du 'fait' colonial* (Broisseux (73), Editions de Croquant et Savoir/Agir, 2006).
[2] See G. Manceron and C. Liauzu, *La Colonisation, la loi et l'histoire*, preface by Henri Leclerc (Paris: Syllepse, 2006).

A few months later, the historian Olivier Pétré-Grenouilleau, author of an important book on the slave trade,[3] came under intense questioning after having declared in a interview with the *Journal du dimanche*, published 12 June 2005:

It is also a problem with the Taubira Law that considers the European slave trade as a 'crime against humanity', including in this conclusion a comparison with the Holocaust. The slave trade was not a genocide. [...] The Jewish genocide and the slave trade were different processes. There is no Richter Scale of suffering.

Olivier Pétré-Grenouilleau was immediately thereafter sued by a group of residents of the Antilles, Guyana, and Reunion who opposed his statement, which they considered to be 'revisionist'. A few months later, on 13 December 2005, several famous historians co-authored a joint appeal in the daily newspaper *Libération* entitled 'Freedom for History'. After expressing their strong emotional reaction in light of 'increasingly frequent political statements recognizing events of the past and judicial trials involving historians and intellectuals', they stated:

Historians do not accept any dogma, nothing is prohibited to them, they know no taboos. [...] It is not the role of historians to praise or to condemn, but to explain. History is not a slave to current events. Historians do not impose contemporary ideological schemes onto past events and they do not introduce today's sensibilities into past events.

History is not memory. The historian, using a scientific approach, gathers the memories of different individuals, compares them, holds them up against documents, objects, historical remnants, then establishes the facts. History takes memory into account, but cannot be reduced to mere memory alone.

History is not a judicial object. In a free country, it is not up to the Parliament or the judicial authorities to define historical truth. The politics of the Nation State, even motivated by the best intentions, is not the politics of history.

It is in violation of these principles that a succession of laws, notably those of 13 July 1990, 29 January 2001, 21 May 2001, and 23 February 2005 have restricted the liberty of historians, having said to them, under threat of punishment, what they could research, what they should find, having prescribed them methods and imposed them real limits.

The historians (Jean-Pierre Azéma, Élisabeth Badinter, Jean-Jacques Becker, Françoise Chandernagor, Alain Decaux, Marc Ferro, Jacques Julliard, Jean Leclant, Pierre Milza, Pierre Nora, Mona Ozouf, Jean-Claude Perrot, Antoine Prost, René Rémond, Maurice Vaïsse, Jean-Pierre Vernant, Paul Veyne, Pierre Vidal-Naquet, and Michel Winock) concluded their appeal by demanding the revocation of these laws because they were 'unworthy of a democratic state'. Which laws were they referring to in parallel with the law of 23 February that was previously mentioned?

---

[3] *Les traites négrières, Essai d'histoire globale* (Paris: Gallimard, 2004).

First, the law of 13 July 1990, known as the 'Gayssot Law', made it punishable by law to deny: 'One or several crimes against humanity as defined by Article 6 of the Code of the Military Tribunal of Nuremburg, as amended to the London Agreement of 8 May 1945...'.[4] Particularly targeted here were denials of the existence of extermination camps, gas chambers, crematoria, and the extermination of the Jews. Secondly, they were referring to the law of 29 January 1990, which had just one article: 'France publicly recognizes the Armenian genocide of 1915.'[5] Last to be included in their list was the law of 21 May 2001,[6] in which the French republic recognized:

the transatlantic slave trade and the slave trade in the Indian Ocean, as well as slavery itself, perpetrated starting in the Fifteenth Century in the Americas, the Caribbean, the Indian Ocean, and in Europe against African, Amerindian, Malagasy, and Indian constitutes a crime against humanity.

Article 2 of the law adds that 'school curricula as well as history and social science research programs will allocate to the slave trade and slavery the important place they deserve'. Article 4 of the law mandates the creation in mainland France of an annual day of commemoration of the abolition of slavery. Four years later, in 2006, after consulting the Committee for the Commemoration of Slavery, the Government chose 10 May, the date of the unanimous adoption of the law by the French Senate.[7]

In addition to wanting to maintain their academic liberty, these historians justified their demands for the cancellation of the laws in other ways. First, they argued that the notion of a crime against humanity is not properly used to describe slavery in the 2001 Taubira Law (Pierre Nora):

The idea of applying the concept of crimes against humanity to past events, no matter how revolting they are, is dangerous and disturbing in the eyes of historians. This is because the concept is precisely defined. It includes two elements which are, by definition, foreign to historians: a moral condemnation, which assumes that humanity is constant and based in the past on the same criteria of judgment used today; and a principle of 'imprescriptibility', which assumes a time identical to itself, while history is first and foremost a lesson in the differences between times. The application of the term 'crimes against humanity' to contemporary mass killings, since they are visible, tangible is understandable. But with the slave trade and slavery targeted by the 2001 law, we are two

---

[4] Art. 24 *bis* of the law of 29 July 29 1881 on the freedom of the press created by the law of 13 July 1990 adds '[...] and those which were committed either by members of an organization having been declared in violation of the law under the application of Article 9 of this statute, or by a person found guilty of such crimes by a French or international jurisdiction'. Law Number 90–615 of 13 July 1990 to stop all racist, antisemitic or xenophobic acts, Journal officiel de la République française (JORF), 14 July 1990, 8333.

[5] Law Number 2001–70 of 29 January 2001, JORF, n°25, 30 January 2001, 1590.

[6] Law Number 2001–434 of 21 May 2001, JORF, n°119, 23 May 2001, 8175.

[7] The choice of the date was announced by President Jacques Chirac on 30 January 2006.

to five centuries behind. And which perpetrators of these crimes will be prosecuted, if not the historians who discuss these events in terms unauthorized by law?[8]

The context[9] in which this declaration was made was for Pierre Nora distinctive of a new wave of demands for recognition and of misuse of special groups' memories. 'From now on, each minority will demand in the name of collective memory to be re-inserted into our common history';[10] for René Rémond it was a context of confusion between memory and history: 'Memories are naturally particular, while history tends to be general. Memories are emotional; history is based on rational order. By campaigning for a law to officially recognize them, memories seek to become history.'[11]

Yet, the demands for the repeal of these laws met with strong opposition from both historians and lawyers. As early as 20 December 2005, an appeal entitled 'Let's Not Confuse Everything', signed by 32 well-known individuals, stated that by passing the laws of 1990 and 2001, 'The legislator is not getting mixed up in the territory of the historian, he is supporting it.'[12] From another perspective, Henry Rousso, initially not a supporter of the Gayssot Law ('without a doubt, to fight denial we should have used the existing legal arsenal, rather than passing a contested law') declared on 24 December that 'abolishing the law today would be an even less appropriate political act'.[13] Gérard Noiriel, for his part, disputed the privileged position historians created for themselves in the debate over the memorial laws.[14] For him, Article 4 of the Law of 23 February 2005 infringed the autonomy of historians, imposing value judgments in education and in historical research, while their role is only 'to understand and explain the past. None of the laws cited in the "Appeal of the Nineteen" cross this limit.'

In the end, only Article 4 of the Law of 23 February was revoked, having been ruled unlawful by the Constitutional Council on 31 January 2006[15] as falling into the domain of rulemaking, or of the application of the law, which is reserved to the executive branch, rather than the legislature. On 3 February, the complaint against O. Pétré-Grenouilleau was withdrawn. But the debate was far from being resolved.

Does this selective reaction by public authorities have any particular meaning? Is it not really just the result of an abdication of responsibility in favour of certain

---

[8] 'J. Buob and A. Frachon, Pierre Nora et le métier d'historien', *Le Monde 2*, No. 105, February 2006.

[9] On this context, see S. Dufoix, 'Historiens et mnémographes' (June 2006) 2 *Controverses* 15.

[10] Ibid.

[11] 'Pourquoi abroger les lois mémorielles?' (November 2006) 325 *Regards sur l'actualité* 23.

[12] Appeal signed notably by Yves Chevalier, Bernard Jouanneau, Serge Klarsfeld, Claude Lanzmann, and Frédéric Encel.

[13] 'Mémoires abusives', *Le Monde*, 24 December 2005.

[14] On the 'liberty of the historian,' see <http://cvuh.free.fr/debat/noiriel.liberte.historien.html> [French] (last accessed 25 July 2008).

[15] The Constitutional Council was asked to review this law less than one week earlier, on 25 January 2006.

minority groups? Let us put aside the Law of 29 January 2001 on the Armenian Genocide, which only has a declarative, rather than a legal, impact.[16] The two other still-contested laws reflect three kinds of legislative action: a radical ban that breaks with certain rights such as free speech; the recognition of slavery as a crime against humanity; and the choice to place certain events into the collective memory through national commemorations.

I want to demonstrate here that none of these types of public action are new: the French Republic has previously recognized slavery as crime against humanity and has adopted such radical bans and celebrations: in 1848, at the time of the permanent abolishment of slave trade and slavery; and in the 1880s, when the Republic was definitively put into place as France's form of government. Examining the circumstances in which these institutionalizations took place will permit us to understand the more recent laws in a historical context.

2. Permanent Elimination of Slavery in 1848

Slavery in France was permanently eliminated by the decree of 27 April 1848 (it had been banned previously in 1794 but was reintroduced in 1802).[17] Article 8, Section 1 of this decree bans any French citizen from owning, acquiring, or selling slaves or even participating indirectly in the slave trade, *under penalty of loss of French citizenship.*

This sentence was the most severe penalty on citizens available in the French justice system, bar none. What other situation could lead to deprivation of citizenship and a possible situation of statelessness without a trial, as a result of a simple administrative procedure? Even if a French citizen were to kill the President, he would retain his citizenship, but not if he took part in the slave trade.

Clearly, the practical reach of this penalty was limited: Section 2 of Article 8 provided for a three-year period during which a French citizen who owned slaves could dispose of them. The law of 11 February 1851 increased this delay to ten years, and the law of 28 May 1858 provided an exemption for French citizens having owned slaves before 1848.[18] Thereafter, the law only applied to the practice of the slave trade or the purchase of slaves after 27 April 1848. The law was actually put into application, however: for example, the automatic deprivation of citizenship stopped the descendants of one 'Du Repaire de Truffin', based in Cuba, from successfully claiming French citizenship decades later.[19]

---

[16] S. Garibian, 'Pour une lecture juridique des quatre lois "mémorielles" ' (February 2006) *Esprit* 158.

[17] On this first ban, see L. Dubois, *A Colony of Citizens: Revolution and Slave Emancipation in the French Caribbean, 1787-1804* (Chapel Hill: UNC Press, 2004) and F. Régent, *La France et ses esclaves, De la colonisation aux abolitions (1620–1848)* (Paris: Grasset, 2007).

[18] Grenoble Court of Justice, 10 June 1891, Leandri (Clunet, 91.1232).

[19] See French Diplomatic Archives, Contentieux, Affaires diverses, 377.

This radical outcome was disputed by France's best-known jurists of the time.[20] For Andre Weiss, this was:

An anomaly, an exception... of a more severe penalty than judicial interdiction, civic degradation, that could be legally incurred by one of our fellow citizens, without any judgment, without there even being a court competent to judge him.[21]

People were aware at that time that they were punishing what we would now call 'crimes against humanity'. A committee formed to prepare for the pending abolition of slavery (formed 4 March 1848, chaired by Victor Schoelcher) wrote in its report to the Minister of the Navy and the Colonies, that slavery was a crime of 'lèse humanité'.[22] Later, in 1883, at the beginning of the debate that would result a few years later in the important nationality law of 1889, the Council of State was consulted. Council reviewer Camille Sée proposed eliminating all the exemptions and exceptions to the ban on owning slaves and its consequences, and only allowing a one year grace period for French citizens who had previously acquired a slave through inheritance, marriage, or as a gift to dispose of them. Otherwise, they would face the penalty of deprivation of French citizenship.[23] In the Senate, rapporteur Anselme Batbie, a professor at Paris' law school, was, like most legal scholars, of the opposite view. They preferred the 1848 provision to be repealed, for its implementation could provoke statelessness:

People object that this Frenchman [the possessor of a slave] has put himself outside human rights... but there are many other criminals who put themselves outside of the laws of humanity for much graver offenses.[24]

Even if the exact same terminology is not used at that time, the concept of a crime against humanity certainly is *de facto* present. The House of Deputies did not, however, follow the Senate, and left in place, for the slave trade and for slavery itself, this extraordinary penalty of loss of French nationality, regardless of whether the individual concerned had another nationality. Those who would start practicing slavery would therefore become unworthy of being French. They would be banished from France and placed at the fringes of humanity. This provision was not retroactive: it did not punish past acts, it just prevents future ones. The provision remained in place for almost a century, until the Nationality Act of 19 October 1945,[25] at which time the former French colonies took on the egalitarian common law legal status of overseas departments. The earlier penalty

---

[20] *Traité élémentaire de droit international privé* 2nd edn. (Paris: Larose & Tenin, Vol.1, 1907), 563 *et seq.*

[21] Ibid., 566.

[22] *Esclavage et colonisation* (Paris: PUF, 2007), 141.

[23] Conseil d'Etat, Report Number 44.113 of Camille Sée, first appendix to Number 428, distributed 25 April 1883, 126.

[24] Senate session of 8 February 1887.

[25] See H. Batiffol, *Traité élémentaire de droit international privé* (Paris: LGDJ, 1949), 149.

was extraordinary, one could even say legal customs, a basic political law in its purest form, of the kind used either to preserve or to re-establish the political foundations of a society.

3. Consecration of the Republic

Some twenty years after the abolition of slavery, in 1870, the Second Empire fell. In 1875, the Republic was restored, first fragilely, in 1875 with a one-vote majority, and then with increasing majorities in each subsequent year. The 1880s were the period when the new republican form of government settled in for the long term. It was through the law of 6 July 1880 that July 14 was selected as the annual national work holiday.[26] 'A new political order cannot be put into place until devices are created that publicly bind together members of the same community', according to the analysis of Olivier Ihl,[27] who has studied the creation and implementation of this republican celebration.

The organization of a series of national holidays, reminding people of the memories that tie them to their existing political institutions, is a necessity that all governments recognize and put into practice.

This was stated by M. Achard, the sponsor of the legislation in the Chamber of Deputies, adding:

Only our republic... has been deprived of any solemnity that could consecrate it in a striking manner. We, elected through full universal suffrage, have the duty to rectify this situation, which has made of the Republic a mere governmental abstraction.[28]

Even though today 14 July is the only national holiday commemorating the Republic itself, it was not necessarily the obvious or only available option. It was chosen after 4 September, the anniversary of the fall of the Empire which was commemorated for some time, and after the failure of the commemoration of the centenary of Voltaire's death on 30 May 1878, as well as the special patriotic holiday, unrelated to any particular historical event, that took place on 30 June 1879.[29]

The selection of 14 July, an anniversary already commemorated by popular celebrations, provoked much opposition from the political right, but was not lacking a certain deliberate ambiguity: 'it called to mind, said the bill's sponsor in the Chamber, the storming of the Bastille on 14 July 1789 and the great Fédération feast that was celebrated on 14 July 1790'.[30] The Bill's sponsor in the Senate, Henri Martin, also emphasized this double dimension to the celebration

---

[26] This was the sole article of the law of 6 July 1880.
[27] *La fête républicaine* (Paris: Gallimard, 1996), 25.
[28] Annales de la Chambre des Députés, séance du 8 juin 1880, 237–8.
[29] See n. 27 above, 101–10.   [30] See ibid., 237–8.

of 14 July 1789, reminding his colleagues of the chronology of the events that leaded to 14 July 1789:

On 17 June 1789, the Third Estate was declared the National Assembly. On 20 June, the meeting room of the National Assembly was closed by order of the courts. On 23 June, a declaration of the king cancelled all acts of the National Assembly and summoned its members to disperse themselves. The Assembly did not break up. The Court seemed to give way. But, on 11 July, the popular Minister who was the intermediary between the Court and the country, M. Necker, was dismissed and replaced by a ministry of coup d'etat; in the meantime, an entire army consisting mainly of foreigners was called to surround Paris. [...] That same day, in Paris, you remember what happened at the Palais Royal, the famous episode which led to the massive social movement that followed over the next three days. This small act of war ... by demonstrating the force of the people, annihilated all the plans set against the National Assembly; this small act of war saved France's future. But do not forget that after the day of 14 July 1789, there was also the day of 14 July 1790. No one can criticize that day for leading to a single drop of blood shed, or for causing any division in the country. That day was the consecration of French unity. Yes, it consecrated what the former royalty had prepared.

After having tried to convince the monarchists that they could rally to the cause of 14 July without disowning their own principles, the Bill's sponsor added: 'If some among you have concerns about the first 14 July, you certainly cannot have any about the second one'.[31]

The celebration of 14 July 1789 and/or 1790 was the first non-religious national holiday. It was a citizen celebration founded on 'the quasi-contractual adherence to republican memory'.[32] It was also the first non-religious work holiday,[33] although the time off work only came into practice gradually.[34] A few years later, in 1892, it was proposed that new national holidays be created on 10 August and 21 or 22 September to celebrate the fall of the monarchy, or the institution of the Republic,[35] yet nothing came of this effort. 14 July remained the only national holiday for the Republic.

In the meantime, four years after the creation of the 14 July national holiday, Parliament gathered as the full National Assembly[36] to revise the constitutional laws of 1875. Advocates of the Republic definitively triumphed, since the elections of 1881 provided the Republican majority with a clear mandate: a mandate for wholesale revision of constitutional law. This mandate consisted of

---

[31] JORF, Sénat, 30 June 1880, 7236–237. See also F. A. Aulard, *Histoire politique de la révolution française, Origines et développement de la démocratie et de la république, 1789–1804* (Paris: Armand Colin, 1901), 35–66, 83.

[32] See n. 27 above, 119.   [33] Ibid., 23.

[34] Originally only applied to civil servants and municipal employees, it was extended on 2 November 1892 to various segments of commerce and industry, yet even then it was not fully respected in practice by employers. Ibid., 142–3.

[35] Ibid., 130–1.

[36] It was under the Third republic, the name of the reunion of the house of deputies and of the senate, who had the power to establish and revise Constitutional laws.

eliminating the President's ability to dissolve the Chamber of Deputies and the weakening, if not total elimination, of the Senate. Jules Ferry, President of the Council, manoeuvred to approve a limited revision, eliminating public prayers and senators-for-life, a reform in how Senators were elected,[37] and finally a revision that stated:

The republican form of government cannot be the subject of a Constitutional revision. Members of families having reigned over France are ineligible to be President of the Republic.[38]

The second sentence, which was subsequently eliminated, helps to clarify the context in which this proposal was approved: it was intended as a ban on the return of the monarchy. This is made clear by Jules Ferry's comments during the debate over the law:

From the day you approve this protective law, it will no longer be permitted, at least in the Parliament, to propose a return to the monarchy.[39]

Concretely, this means that it is forbidden to introduce or to debate in Parliament a bill that would call into question the republican form of government in France. M. Boucher, speaking for the opposition, was not fooled:

When you have eliminated all of the limitations that previous laws imposed on the freedom of the press, the freedom of assembly[40] ... can you, without renouncing your own principles, limit the propaganda of ideas, the discussion of principles? Should only the form or the name of a political institution be held inviolable?

Nonetheless, this is what the National Assembly decided. The Constitution of the Fifth Republic has preserved these terms, which compose, in a slightly modified form, paragraph 5 of Article 89 of the Constitution of 1958: 'The Republican form of government cannot be subject to constitutional revision.' Still today, members of Parliament, who have the right to amend the Constitution, face an explicit limit to this right in one area: 'The Republican form of government in France'.[41]

Thus, at the end of two major periods of division among the French people, one between slaves and citizens, the other among citizens regarding their form of government, the republic created two extraordinary, radical bans. They were contested by legal scholars as offending legal traditions (free speech, due process, et cetera), but were nonetheless included permanently in French law. In addition, as early as 1848, slavery was already recognized as a crime against humanity. And

---

[37] Law of 14 August 1884 providing partial reform of constitutional law.

[38] These terms came at the end of para. 3 of Art. 8 of the law of 25 February 1875.

[39] JORF, Parliamentary Debates, Assemblee Nationale, 12 August 1884, 96.

[40] The law guaranteeing freedom of press was passed on 29 July 1881 and that on freedom of assembly, 30 June 1881.

[41] On the reality and the nature of this limit, see O. Beaud, *La puissance de l'Etat* (Paris, PUF, 1994), 329–57.

finally, after its definitive victory over other forms of government, the republic organized a celebration of its creation by its fellow citizens. A sort of 'commemoration/ban' configuration appears to be a mode of political intervention in these particular historical moments: the conditions for unification of the people are put into place by the celebration of a new unit, while a ban of ideas and practices that would bring back unacceptable division among the people and would threaten social or political peace is decided.

4. Commemorations and Bans with Respect to the Genocide of the Jews in Europe

It is this coupling of commemoration and ban that exists regarding the genocide of the Jews of Europe perpetrated during World War II. At the beginning of the 1970s, the vision of resistant France during World War II inspired by the Gaullists and the Communists started to break down.[42] The Vichy Regime and the attitude of the French people during the period of the occupation began to appear more clearly in their full complexity. The release of the movie 'Sorrow and Pity', the pardon provided to militia-man Paul Touvier, and the book *Vichy France* by Robert Paxton[43] each contributed to this change. The testimony of those who had been deported, most often Jews, was increasingly listened to. The Eichmann trial brought to a larger public understanding the scale of the genocide suffered by European Jews. Among the key elements that contributed to the rebirth of a Jewish identity that was marked by the persecutions suffered under Vichy were: the forced migration of the repatriated populations of Algeria, Morocco, or Tunisia; the Six Day War and the genocidal anguish it caused; and finally, the intense emotion provoked by the words of De Gaulle who spoke, during his press conference of November 27, 1967: 'the Jews, an elite people, sure of themselves and dominating'.[44]

It was in this context that, on 28 October 1978, the weekly magazine *L'Express* published an interview with the Vichy regime's former General Commissioner for Jewish Affairs, Louis Darquier de Pellepoix, sentenced to death in absentia in 1947. In this interview, entitled 'At Auschwitz, we only gassed lice', Darquier justified the deportation: 'No matter what, we needed to get rid of these foreigners, these immigrants, these thousands of stateless individuals who were the cause of all of our problems'. He denied the reality of the genocide: 'I will tell you, myself, exactly what happened at Auschwitz. We did use gas. Yes, that is true. But we gassed lice.'

---

[42] See H. Rousso, *The Vichy Syndrome: History and Memory in France Since 1944* Trans. A. Goldhammer (Cambridge: Harvard UP, 2006).

[43] *Vichy France: Old Guard and New Order, 1940–1944* (New York: Columbia UP, 2001).

[44] A. Wieviorka, *l'Ere du témoin* (Paris: Hachette Littératures, 2002), 135–40.

The Darquier de Pellepoix scandal immediately made headlines; it crystallized the feeling of malaise tied to a fear of the trivialization of Nazism. A few days later, in the magazine *Historia*, the widow of Reinhard Heydrich, described as 'indomitable', 'valiant', and 'very National-Socialist', not denying 'any of its commitments', was particularly shocking. Mrs. Heydrich demonstrated a shameless antisemitism, justifying the Holocaust ('It is undeniable that something had to be done to prevent the Jews from doing harm') before calling its reality into question: the extermination of six million Jews seemed technically impossible to her. The commentary of the journalist was as follows: 'For Mrs Heydrich, passions have calmed, and it is time to allow History to decide, and History should be objective.'[45] On 1 November 1978, Robert Faurisson wrote to numerous newspapers:

I hope that some of the statements that the journalist Philippe Ganier Raymond has recently attributed to Louis Darquier de Pellepoix finally lead the public to discover that the supposed massacres in 'gas chambers', and the supposed 'genocide' are parts of the same lie.[46]

A week later, a journalist from *Le Matin* interviewed Faurisson, and in its 16 November 1978 edition, the paper ran the prominent headline 'The Gas Chambers Didn't Exist'.[47] On 29 December, *Le Monde* published an opinion piece by him: 'The Problem of the Gas Chambers or the Problems of Auschwitz'.[48] Reactions were numerous, and very intense. In Parliament, as early as 17 November 1978, Pierre Sudreau, Deputy from the Loir-et-Cher, demanded an investigation.[49]

In court, Faurisson and Darquier de Pellepoix faced lawsuits. Among historians, reactions were numerous and unanimous.[50] It was in this context that on 27 July 1979, the Senate debated and unanimously approved (over the Prime Minister's opposition) a bill making the celebration of 8 May a public holiday.

The history of the celebration of the victory of the Allies over Germany on 8 May 1945 is chaotic.[51] In 1946, the date of the commemoration of the victory was fixed as 8 May if it falls on a Sunday, or otherwise on the following Sunday. The law of 23 March 1953 made 8 May a holiday. In 1959, the celebration of 8 May was moved to the second Sunday in May before being replaced in 1968 by a celebration on the actual day of the anniversary, but only at the end of the day.

---

[45] A. Zarca, 'Que sont devenus les enfants des chefs Nazis?', *Historia*, October 1978. See also L. Joly, *Darquier de Pellepoix et l'antisémitisme français* (Paris: Berg International, 2002), Introduction.

[46] V. Igounet, *Histoire du négationnisme en France* (Paris: Le Seuil, 2000), 222.

[47] Ibid.   [48] Ibid., 235–6.   [49] Ibid., 232.

[50] On the various responses described above, see the collection of comments by P. Vidal-Naquet, *Assassins of Memory: Essays on the Denial of the Holocaust* (New York: Columbia UP, 1992).

[51] On the various responses described above, see C. Andrieu, 'Vu du parlement: les clivages politiques relatifs à l'image des dernières guerres françaises, 1945–2003 (Seconde guerre mondiale, guerre d'Indochine, guerre d'Algérie)', presented at 'The New Cleavages in France' conference held at Princeton University, 9–12 October 2003, conference proceedings to be released in 2008.

On 8 May 1975, Valery Giscard d'Estaing sent the nine members of the European Council a letter in which he informed them of his decision no longer to celebrate the anniversary of the 1945 victory. The 11 November holiday would continue, however, as 'an opportunity to commemorate the sacrifice of all who gave their lives to safeguard national independence'.[52] This decision led to a unanimous reaction from veterans' groups. Thereafter, eighteen bills were proposed in Parliament by people of all political stripes. Ceremonies held on the local level received ever-increasing attendance.

In the minds of the Senators who decided in June of 1979 to make 8 May a national holiday, it wasn't just a question of celebrating the victory against Germany, but against Nazism as well: 'As such, it represents the attachment of the French people to public liberties and respect for human dignity'. And the rapporteur of the bill in the senate added:

The recent statements by the former 'Commissioner for Jewish Affairs' in France have shown that evil has not disappeared and that today, agents of Nazism feel they are allowed to make the most unworthy declarations. Signs of the resurgence of fascism are numerous, and we must fight against them in the most energetic way possible.[53]

The Senate was unanimous in its support, but President Giscard d'Estaing opposed the reinstitution of the holiday, and blocked its discussion in the National Assembly. The election of Francois Mitterrand changed the situation. On 23 September 1981, before the National Assembly, bill sponsor M. Hautecoeur once again made reference to the recent denial of the genocide of the Jews to justify the return of the 8 May celebration:

The former commissioner for Jewish affairs from the Vichy government, Darquier de Pellepoix, has not hesitated in taking pride in his former responsibilities [...] The celebration of 8 May is in response to this.[54]

The law of 2 October 1981[55] fully established the day of the victory of 8 May 1945 as a public and a work holiday, and was the first response—(via a celebration) to the cover-up or the negation of the Nazi crimes.

Less than ten years later, it would be through a radical ban that Parliament would intervene. In the meantime, the ideas of Faurisson continued to have easy access to the media (at least, newspapers and radio) through the incessant exercise of the right to respond which requires that equal media airtime be provided to those with opposing viewpoints on an issue. On 15 June 1985 at the University of Nantes, Henri Roques defended his PhD thesis, which was later invalidated for administrative irregularities, on 2 July 1986. In the thesis, views such as these are

---

[52] JORF, Parliamentary Debates, Senate, 16 May 1979, report by M. Touzet, 1284.
[53] Ibid.
[54] JORF, Parliamentary Debates, National Assembly, 23 September 1981, 1265. The National Assembly voted in support of the bill by a vote of 481 to 1.
[55] Ibid., 3 October 1981, 2698.

found: 'It is impossible to go verify on site the veracity of these appalling stories that we are saturated with'. He asserts that there is 'a new religion that seeks to be imposed on us ... the religion of the Holocaust'.[56] First publicized in the writings and media of the extreme right, on 15 May 1986 the thesis was the lead headline in the press in Nantes. On 23 May 1986, Henri Roques was invited to be a guest on radio station Europe 1's show 'Recoveries'. By the end of 1986, more than 1,500 copies of the thesis were circulating in France and more than 4,000 in Germany in a German-language version.[57] A few weeks after the Barbie trial resulted in a life prison term, Jean-Marie Le Pen, appearing on the political radio talk show 'RTL-Le Monde' mentioned the gas chambers as 'a detail of the Second World War'.[58] Le Pen at that point held a seat in Parliament, along with 34 other National Front Deputies. A few months later, the Government of Michel Rocard agreed to a discussion about a bill which originated in the Parliament. What would later become known as the 'Gayssot Law' was the synthesis of two bills: one Communist, and one Socialist (introduced in 1987 by Guy Ducoloné and in 1988 by Georges Sarre). It was the Socialist bill that originally proposed to penalize any denial of a crime against humanity that occurred during World War II, going beyond the Law of 31 December 1987 which had made being an apologist for a crime against humanity a criminal offence.[59]

During the debate in full plenary session, on 2 May 1990, Gaullist MP Jacques Toubon criticized the measure since it could put in danger the freedom of university research. But the right did not ultimately oppose the adoption of the Bill by a vote of 307 (deputies from the left) to one (Deputy Stirbois of the National Front).[60]

As soon thereafter as 4 May 1990, in the newspaper *Libération*, Madeleine Rebérioux stated her opposition to the text, and reaffirmed it in 1996 on the following grounds.[61] First, it attributes to the law what belongs to a normative order, and to the judges in charge with its implementation, the responsibility to state the historical truth even though historical truth refuses all official authorities. 'The USSR paid too dearly for its behaviour in this domain to allow the French Republic to follow in its footsteps.' Secondly, it will almost unavoidably lead to an extension into other areas besides the genocide of the Jews: other genocides and other assaults against what will be declared 'historical truth'. Thirdly, it allows the Holocaust deniers to present themselves as martyrs, or at least like persecuted individuals.

It was Michel Troper, looking into the constitutionality of the Gayssot Law,[62] who provided the most relevant response. He first reminds us that Article 10 of

---

[56] See n. 46 above, 408.   [57] Ibid., 421.   [58] Ibid., 657, 13 September 1987.
[59] See E. Bleich, *Race Politics in Britain and in France: Ideas and Policymaking Since the 1960s* (Cambridge: CUP, 2003), 153–5.
[60] JORF, National Assembly, Parliamentary Debates, Second Session of 2 May 1990, 954–7.
[61] 'Contre la loi Gayssot', *Le Monde*, 21 May 1996.
[62] 'La loi Gayssot et la Constitution' (1999) 54(6) November/December *Annales Histoire Sciences Sociales* 1239.

the French Declaration of the Rights of Man and Citizens, which belongs to the current Constitution, sets up a distinction between opinions and their expression: 'No one shall be disquieted on account of his opinions ... provided their manifestation does not disturb the public order as established by law'.[63] He also emphasizes the following fact:

A large part of social life, in the most liberal systems, takes place under the empire of truths that it is forbidden to discuss ... A university would not even accept the application of a supposed historian who held that Napoleon won the battle of Waterloo ... There is thus, in any social group, theories that are presumed false. The Gayssot Law makes documents denying the Holocaust a crime that a court can punish without having to first prove that these writings are false. The incrimination results, therefore, of a presumption created by the legislator.

Liberal adversaries of the Gayssot Law correctly make the point that it is not up to the courts to determine historical truth, but this argument in reality only provides an additional justification for the law, because it avoids making judges play a role that they are not qualified for.[64]

And when Serge Klarsfeld stated that 'the negation of the facts has the character of propaganda to it, and it causes emotional damage to those who lost their relatives in the camps. Those who are against this law do not live amongst the survivors and do not hear their cries,'[65] one cannot stop oneself from thinking that this new provision in French law is within the parameters of what has been done in past periods, following great division, or great trauma. Here again, national representatives have decided to take extraordinary, albeit legal measures to insure civil and social peace. Other democracies—(Germany or Austria) that have experienced the same trauma, as Rene Rémond has recognized, turned to the same kind of measures.[66]

5. And Slavery...?

So, where does slavery stand in this context? The radical ban instituted in 1848, implicitly recognizing slavery as a crime against humanity, but how can we explain the lack of a celebration of this event?

First, by the initial reaction of former slaves and their immediate descendants, who would not have so much wanted to forget their status as slaves, but 'in a

[63] The concept of 'public order' covers in the French Constitutional Council Jurisprudence 'good order, security, public hygiene and the public peace'. See *Libertés et ordre public. Les principaux critères de limitation des droits de l'homme dans la pratique de la justice constitutionnelle* at <http://www.conseil-constitutionnel.fr/divers/documents/libpub.htm>, Services du Conseil constitutionnel (2003).

[64] See n. 62 above.

[65] Interview with Serge Klarsfeld, 19 February 1996 (n. 46 above), 446.

[66] *Quand l'Etat se mêle de l'histoire* (Paris: Stock, 2006), 19.

demand for equality, for integration as citizens',[67] but gave priority to a fight for a complete political equality; they would only acquire it after a century, in 1946, with the departmental status attributed to Guadeloupe, Martinique, Guyana, and Reunion. During the revolts that led to the first abolition, it was the values of the French Revolution, liberty and equality, which were invoked, as Laurent Dubois demonstrates.[68]

From the point of view of the republican authorities at the time abolition was definitively decreed in 1848, there was no official, institutionalized national holiday at all, since the celebration of 14 July would not be put into place until 1880. Under the Third Republic, the celebration of transatlantic citizenship had erupted in a context where the majority of the Empire's subjects did not have citizenship.

Abolition will never become a key moment in the historical, cultural, or political narrative. It is pointed out, but as a moment emptied of its meaning. It is not part of history. It does not belong to French narrative identity. Descriptions of 1848 mention the decree abolishing slavery, but do not linger on it. The new access to liberty by tens of thousands of people enslaved by France does not warrant any commentary.[69]

The demand for the recognition of this event began to develop in the 1960s. Identity movements developed in the Overseas Departments to reinstitute the image of the slave and his experiences.[70] Already in 1983, a regulation requires that on 27 April, primary schools, middle schools, and high schools should dedicate one hour of teaching about the abolition of slavery. Additionally, in each Overseas Department, a holiday is created to celebrate liberation.[71] But, at the time of the coincident increased presence of former residents of the Overseas Territories in mainland France and the celebration of the 150th anniversary of the abolition of slavery, a demand for the recognition of slavery as a crime against humanity emerged. In mainland France, former residents of the Overseas Territories suffered discrimination and discovered that French citizenship is no protection against racism. They began a search for their specific identity and the historical causes of the discrimination or the inferior representation they faced. On the occasion of the celebration of the 150th anniversary of slavery's abolition, 23 May 1998, 40,000 people from Martinique, Guadeloupe, Guyana, Reunion, French people of African origin, and Africans marched from *Place de la République* to *Place de la Nation* in Paris, under the organization of the Committee for a Single Commemoration of the Abolition of the Slavery of Blacks in the French Colonies.[72]

---

[67] M. Giraud, 'Les enjeux présents de la mémoire de l'esclavage', in P. Weil and S. Dufoix (eds.), *L'esclavage, la colonisation, et après… France, Etats-Unis, Grande-Bretagne* (Paris: PUF, 2005), 534.
[68] 'Histoires d'esclavage en France et aux Etats-Unis', (2007 February) *Esprit*, 71.
[69] F. Vergès, *La mémoire enchaînée, Questions sur l'esclavage* (Paris: Albin Michel, 2006), 71.
[70] Ibid., 89.   [71] JORF, Decree 83–1003, 23 November 1983, 3407.
[72] See n. 69 above, 90.

France discovers today a cultural difference that had already existed for a long time within the country, but which it has chosen to ignore, forgetting, even concealing, its history.[73]

Missing was an event of the standing of 14 July marking the end of slavery, in the sense that as Olivier Ihl reminds us, in order to 'celebrate similarity', a moment of simultaneous interdependence. This moment is what the Taubira Law created. The remembrance of the abolition of slavery would be celebrated, but all of the demands which had at one point been made and discussed and which could have divided the national community (for example reparations or a formal apology) were not part of the law that was passed. The recognition of slavery and the slave trade as crimes against humanity was made explicit, whereas it was only implicit in the 1848 law. And just like in the 1848 law, this was done in the name of the French nation for the responsibility which was directly that of the French.

Thus, these two controversial laws can be seen in the context of a series of actions that, at certain key moments, the Republic initiates. These actions are always triggered by the end of times of great division, with a goal of creating a new feeling of common citizenry, a new unity surrounding fundamental values, through two paired means: celebration and a radical ban. Today, the Taubira Law completes a process begun in 1848 (by a radical ban), by reminding us that slavery is a crime against humanity, and celebrating its abolition, the value of equality of all citizens, new and old, independent of their colour or origin. Similarly, the Gayssot Law complements the law of 2 October 1981, reinstituting the celebration of the victory over Nazism, by excluding from public space the denial of the crime of genocide against the Jews of Europe, in the name of the unacceptable pain that the survivors of this crime and a number of people who lived during this period of History would continue to suffer if Holocaust denial could be freely undertaken. That was the perception of the majority of the French Parliament, of Serge Klarsfeld who played a major role in the passing of the law and of other public intellectuals. For Pierre Vidal-Naquet, 'the denier is viewed as a kind of 'paper Eichmann'.[74] And for Frederic Worms, '[t]he denial is a re-doubling of the first violation; it is itself an atrocity . . . the denier does to the witness what the executioner has done to the victim'.[75] Tied to these terms, a national day of commemoration of racist and antisemitic persecution is held 16 July, the date of the anniversary of the round-up of the Velodrome d'hiver,[76] to which is added homage to the Righteous of France.[77]

---

[73] See n. 69 above, 39.   [74] See n. 50, above.

[75] 'La négation comme violation du témoignage', in C. Coquio (ed.), *L'Histoire trouée, Négation et témoignage* (Nantes: L'Atalante, 2004), 96.

[76] Or on the following Sunday if the 16th falls during the week. See the decree of 3 February 1993 creating a national day of commemoration for racist and antisemitic persecutions committed under the authority of the so-called 'government of the French state (1940–1944)', JORF, 4 February 1993.

[77] Law of 10 July 2000 creating a national day of commemoration for the victims of racist and antisemitic crimes by the French state, and in homage to the 'Justes' of France, JORF, 11 July 2000, 10483.

Nothing in these mechanisms limits the liberty of historians already under the restrictions, admittedly quite rare, dictated by the courts: good faith, accuracy, impartiality, and 'conscience of the responsibilities of objectivity' are requested by common law.[78] Slavery was already considered under the law of 1848 as a crime against humanity, and if 'the Gayssot Law can be perceived as a restriction on the freedom of the historian, it can also be considered as 'a direct product of the rigor required by the historical discipline; it is nothing more than a reminder of the obligation of truth'.[79]

Nothing in the two laws can symbolize the victory of 'minorities' against the 'majority', quite the contrary. The celebration of the French citizens recognized as 'Righteous Among the Nations' alongside the Jewish victims as a part of the yearly 16 July ceremony provides (from the perspective of the historical memory of the Occupation) 'the framework for the reconciliation of the nation with itself'.[80] Following the advice of Tzvetan Todorov,[81] it takes from traumatic memories the exemplary value that the reversal of memory into a plan for the future can only make relevant. Following this same advice, the incorporation into the national memory of historic facts related to slavery and its abolition can allow citizens born from this history to feel like more of a stakeholder in the nation. To other citizens, it allows them better to understand that it was in the French territories in the Caribbean and in Reunion that the founding principles of the Republic (Liberty, Equality, and Fraternity) were first put into practice following the Revolution.

Certainly, the Taubira Law intervenes in the domain of school curricula by requiring that history and social science classes dedicate substantial time to the history of the slave trade and of slavery. This is a benign intrusion in administrative power—in France, it is the responsibility of the Prime Minister and his Cabinet, and not that of Parliament, to define curricular and educational research priorities. But it is not a question of normative limitation, as Article 4 of the Law of 23 February 2005 would have been, by requiring that history teachings discuss colonialization from a 'positive' angle.

It is also clear that, in regard to the repertoire of actions that we have elucidated, the involvement of the French legislature regarding the Armenian genocide seems disconnected from national history. But, for the moment, the law that is in effect, that of 29 January 2001, has only a declarative value.

One can question the date chosen for the celebration of the abolition of slavery. 10 May, the date of the final vote on the Taubira Law by the Senate lacks any link

---

[78] See n. 16 above, 172.

[79] C. Lanzmann, 'Universalité des victimes,' (2006) *Justice et histoire, histoire et mémoire,* <http://www.droitshumains.org/hist-mem/debat12.htm> [French] (last accessed 25 July 2008).

[80] S. Gensburger, 'Les figures du "Juste" et du résistant et l'évolution de la mémoire historique française de l'occupation' (2002) 52 (2–3) *Revue française de science politique* 314.

[81] *Les abus de la mémoire* (Paris: Arléa, 1995), cited by P. Ricœur, *La mémoire, l'histoire, l'oubli* (Paris: Le Seuil, 2000), 105.

to the past. As if the primary work had been done by modern legislators who owed nothing to their forebears (slaves and descendants of slaves, politicians, and militant abolitionists) despite our having shown here that the Law of 1848 already implicitly recognized slavery as a crime against humanity. The date of 4 February, commemorating the first abolition of slavery (1794), would perhaps have been more relevant, calling to mind an abolition won by slaves and philanthropists, and obtained without any payment of compensations to slave owners.

To place the Gayssot and Taubira Laws into a genealogy of historical interventions demonstrates an evolution in national priorities. In the past, the unity of the French around the republican regime merited an extraordinary political intervention. Protection of fundamental human rights and a concrete respect for equality among citizens have now become the priorities of the French Republic.

PART VII

GOVERNMENTAL AND SELF-REGULATION OF THE MEDIA

29

Shouting Fire

From the Nanny State to the Heckler's Veto: The New Censorship and How to Counter It

David Edgar*

Who would have thought it? Nearly fifty years after the Lady Chatterley trial, nearly forty years after the abolition of the Lord Chamberlain, censors and self-censors are stalking the land. A group of Sikhs attack a theatre and force its management to stop performances of a play. Another theatre removes the burning of the Koran from its production of Marlowe's *Tamberlaine*, and a third insists that three references to Mohammad are removed from a production of a play about a prison riot. An art gallery removes an exhibit in which copies of the Bible, the Torah, and the Koran are enclosed in glass. And, of course, a Danish magazine publishes cartoons of the Prophet Mohammad and provokes violent demonstrations around the world.

Despite the presumptions of pundits and prime ministers alike, Muslims and Sikhs are not alone. In the same period as the above, CBS was fined half a million dollars when a singer's nipple was accidently exposed for 1.7 seconds during a live broadcast of the half-time concert at the Super Bowl. The BBC withdrew its comic animation *Popetown* (at a cost of £2m) after protests by Catholics, as did Madame Tussauds' a waxwork of Posh and Becks playing Mary and Joseph in a nativity scene. *Christian Voice* published the home phone numbers of BBC executives as part of its campaign against *Jerry Springer—The Opera*, and were joined by the BNP in picketing performances of a national tour; while Sainsbury and Woolworth's withdraw DVDs of the show from sale. Meanwhile, British Hindus demanded that Asia House withdraw an exhibition of works by an Indian artist (with a Muslim name) depicting Hindu goddesses in the nude.

* This article is a revised and updated version of a paper given at Gagging, a conference held at the University of Hull on 25 March 2006, published in earlier versions as 'Shouting Fire: Art, Religion and the Right to Be Offended' (2006) 48 *Race and Class* 61 and in 'Gagging—Forum on Censorship' (2007) 17 *Contemporary Theatre Rev.* 524. It also contains material first used in 'In defence of evil', *The Observer*, 30 April 2000 and in 'Rules of engagement', *The Guardian*, 22 October 2005.

Simultaneously, the painter Damien Hirst was pressured to shelve plans to make a photorealist recreation of a photograph of two forensic experts at a murder scene, and reporter Jane Kelly was fired from the *Daily Mail* for painting a picture of Myra Hindley. Labour went to the country on a manifesto which promised to outlaw insulting religion and glorifying or condoning political violence. Subsequently, the Metropolitan Police demanded the right to proscribe protest chants and placard slogans on demonstrations. Playwright Gary Mitchell's house and family were attacked by paramilitaries in protest against his plays about the Belfast Protestant community. And the New York Theatre Workshop cancelled its run of *My Name is Rachel Corrie*, a drama based on the emails and diaries of a peace campaigner killed by Israeli bulldozers in Gaza.

These are not new phenomena. Paintings of and plays about Myra Hindley are regularly attacked for insensitivity, as are plays or television dramas about or referring to the killing of James Bulger (in 2001, the *Daily Express* attacked an episode of a police series which showed a fictional small boy being abducted from a shopping mall). In 1998, Michael Howard said that Gitta Sereny's book about Mary Bell would have been better not written, while Tessa Jowell asserted more recently, that paedophilia was too powerful a topic to be the subject of satire. Meanwhile, artists face legal threats from the copyright owners of their subjects, films, books, and even pop songs are cited as inspiring hideous crimes and criminals sell the dramatization rights in their stories to support their defence. In 1989, a film about 'the ecstatic and erotic visions of St Teresa of Avila' (Visions of Ecstasy) was banned by the British Board of Film Classification in case it contravened the blasphemy laws. Twenty-five years ago, Mary Whitehouse had the director of Howard Brenton's *The Romans in Britain* indicted for pimping. Thirty years ago, she secured the conviction of *Gay News* for blasphemous libel after the magazine published a poem by James Kirkup about a Roman centurion's gay fantasy about the crucified Christ. And it is worth remembering that up until the abolition of stage censorship in 1968, British playwrights could not show two men in bed together, mention venereal disease, criticize the Royal Family, insult friendly foreign powers, or represent God.

Following the acquittal of Penguin Books in the 1960 Lady Chatterley trial and (even more) the abolition of theatre censorship in 1968, it was possible to think that the battle for free speech had been won, that any further prosecutions (say, of the Schoolkids OZ or Gay News) were merely the death rattle of a discredited dogma, and that—finally—acceptable infringements of free speech had been narrowed down to Oliver Wendell Holmes' proverbial 1919 proscription against 'shouting fire in a crowded theatre and causing a panic'. Today, fears about the influence of sexual and violent images, the commodification of all forms of culture, a growing concern for the victims of crime, and the emergent movement against criticism of religion are among many factors which have widened the net. Now, Holmes' proscription is no longer just a matter of preventing a stampede: today, shouting fire can be censured for distressing the relatives of people killed in other fires, infringing the rights of the firemen, offending religions for whom fire is a sacred object, and glorifying, condoning, or encouraging arson. All of which possibilities arise out of the idea that, fundamentally, deep down, to shout 'fire' is to start one.

Many current arguments for censorship draw on or extend the idea that to represent is to enact. The most important aspect of the prosecution of *The Romans in Britain*—in which an actor playing a Roman soldier mimed buggering another actor playing a Druid—was that the director Michael Bogdanov was arraigned for 'procuring an act of gross indecency' between the two actors. The Romans case itself fell apart in unsatisfactory circumstances, after the judge had been informed in chambers that what appeared to be actor Peter Sproule's penis was actually his thumb. Its most dangerous legacy was not the well-worn notion that the representation of something encourages people to do it, but the new if related idea that to portray *is* to do. In the trial, Mary Whitehouse's solicitor claimed that there was no material difference between people being portrayed making love on stage or in film and a couple having sex in the street.[1] This idea is at the root of the American anti-pornography campaigner Catherine MacKinnon's argument that 'in terms of what men are doing sexually, an audience watching a gang rape in a movie is no different from an audience watching a gang rape that is re-enacting a gang rape from a movie, or an audience watching any gang rape'.[2]

Many of those who accept that there is a difference between portrayal and enactment nonetheless happily espouse the literalist idea that to portray is to promote. Much of the criticism of the horror films collectively dubbed videonasties—a moral panic which erupted shortly after Brenton's play—was based on the idea that watching a represented act was on a continuum with the commission; that while the blinding of Gloucester was *not the same as* putting out someone's real eyes, it was somehow en route to it. This notion has been exploited in criminal trials: over the last quarter of a century, the game of hunt the guilty movie (or teleplay, or video) became *de rigueur* for newspapers, judges, and indeed defendants seeking to explain violent behaviour. In 1985, a rapist nicknamed the Fox was persuaded to blame a video called Sex Wish for his crime.[3] The 10-year old killers of James Bulger were said to have been influenced by a video, *Child's Play 3*, which there is no evidence either of them watched.[4] In 1997, John Grisham attempted to hold Oliver Stone and Warner Brothers legally responsible for the killing of his friend Bill Savage by two youngsters who claim to have watched *Natural Born Killers* over 20 times (two years later the Supreme Court 'let

---

[1] J. Sutherland, *Offensive Literature: Decensorship in Britain 1960–1982* (London: Junction Books, 1982), 189.

[2] Quoted in *The Independent*, 29 May 1994.

[3] *The Guardian*, 3 March 1985; *London Evening Standard*, 27 February 1985.

[4] D. Sharrock, M. O'Kane, and E. Pilkington, 'Two youngsters who found a new rule to break', *The Guardian*, 25 November 1993.

stand' the judgement that the film had 'inspired' robbery and shooting).[5] In 1999 two Kent students who murdered, dismembered, and buried a colleague were found to have a copy of the video of *Shallow Grave* in their room.[6] For that matter, the two killers at Columbine High School in Colorado were inspired by a Leonardo de Caprio film *The Basketball Diaries*, John Lennon's assassin was one of a number of lone killers who were obsessed with *Catcher in the Rye*, and Charles Manson's murderous rampage was inspired by the Beatles' track 'Helter Skelter'. And, as it happens, the two Kent students appear to have been actually provoked into murder when their victim likened them to Wallace and Gromit.

Nonetheless, there were a number of high-profile recantations by actors and writers involved in violent films: in 1993 Anthony Hopkins, Kim Basinger, Michael Caine, and Clint Eastwood came out against film violence (though Hopkins subsequently changed his view).[7] A year earlier, Anthony Burgess wrote a piece in *The Observer* declaring that 'Physical violence is the monopoly, at least in our own age, of the inferior artist'. Not restricting himself to our age, he removed two of the usual counter-examples by lambasting *Titus Andronicus* as cheap opportunism, and describing the blinding of Gloucester in *King Lear* as 'a gratuitous sop to the corruption of the viewer'. Declaring his conversion to the thesis that art can be dangerous, Burgess quoted Lady Snow's remark after the Moors Murders that 'if the burning of all the books in the world were necessary to save one child's death, we should not hesitate to incendiarise'.[8]

Parallel to the idea that to portray is to promote is the equally literalist notion that to dramatize is to condone. The most extreme and obvious example of this is the popular (and on occasions, professional) response to any attempt by artists to explain or understand violent and sexual crimes against children. In October 1999, the American novelist A. M. Holmes' novel *The End of Alice*, of which the narrator is an imprisoned paedophile murderer, was attacked by the NSPCC, not on the grounds of its veracity ('she seems to have gone right inside the mind of the offender', a spokesman said)[9] but on the grounds that it portrays the belief by the paedophile that the children he abuses are willing participants. In his piece on the NSPCC's demands for the book to be withdrawn, *The Guardian's* Social Services correspondent wrote: 'It becomes hard to distinguish fantasy from fact and the reader is lured into sharing the paedophile's view of children as complicit in sex acts'.[10] In another piece on the scandal, Dea Birkett reported how, in recent years, 'the term "illegal fantasy" has become widely accepted' among anti-abuse professionals. So, by simply articulating paedophiliac desires, Holmes' book 'is deemed to be complicit with them. And, by implication, the author herself is

---

[5] 'Natural born copycats', *The Guardian*, 20 December 2002.
[6] A. Gentleman, 'Horror videos inspired student killers', *The Guardian*, 8 May 1999.
[7] *Sunday Telegraph*, 14 March 1993.
[8] 'Stop the clock on violence', *The Observer*, 14 March 1993.
[9] *The Guardian*, 28 October 1997.   [10] *The Guardian*, 27 October 1997.

complicit in this first step towards abuse'.[11] Similarly, Paula Vogel's *How I Learnt to Drive*, a play about child sexual abuse presented at the Donmar Warehouse the following June, was attacked by Cornelia Oddie, deputy director of Family and Youth Concern, who told the *Independent on Sunday* that every time paedophilia is portrayed in drama she believes the crime is perceived as less shocking and more acceptable.[12] Significantly (though coincidentally), *The End of Alice* was published the same month as the opening of the *Sensation* exhibition, which included Marcus Garvey's notorious portrait of Myra Hindley, made up of children's handprints.

The peculiarly hysteria which erupts whenever anyone seeks to represent or mention Myra Hindley is the most obvious example of the idea that to represent is to exalt. This presumption is at the core of attacks on plays about the Bulger killings, Mary Bell and the Wests. In 2000, I was subject to similar accusations, when I adapted Gitta Sereny's biography of Hitler's architect and armaments minister Albert Speer for production at the National Theatre in London.[13] In addition to genuinely mixed reviews, the play was discussed in the comment sections of several newspapers. In the *Daily Mail*, Tom Bower attacked 'the contrived humanization of monsters like Hitler and Speer' in Sereny's book and my play.[14] In a similar attack, the Conservative historian Andrew Roberts claimed that at no point in the play was Hitler presented as 'anything other than fascism with a human face'.[15] In a letter to *The Times*, Charles Spencer (not the *Daily Telegraph* drama critic) argued that insofar as my play presented Speer's anguish and Hitler's charm, my play revealed 'the danger, and to some the offensiveness, of fictionalizing historical characters responsible for ghastly crimes. The process inevitably humanizes such monsters and invokes understanding, if not forgiveness. This is evident even in the plays of Shakespeare'.[16]

Well, there it is. As the French have it, *tout comprendre c'est tout pardonner*; or, as Lord Acton put it, 'Too much explaining leads to too much forgiving', of Macbeth as much as Myra Hindley. In the same year as Albert Speer, the *Mail on Sunday's* front page story concerned a projected 'political uproar' over plans by the BBC 'to spend millions of pounds of licence-payers' money on a dramatized account of two of the IRA's most notorious terrorists', Seamus and Dermot Finucane, who had masterminded the mass breakout from the Maze. As the BBC wanly explained, this project was at that stage merely a proposal, there was no script. To his credit, David Trimble commented that 'if it told the truth it would be an interesting exercise'. But, for the *Mail's* leader writer, 'the very process of dramatization almost inevitably makes the audience see things from the central character's point of view'.[17]

[11] *The Guardian*, 28 October 1997.
[13] *Albert Speer*, London, 2000.
[15] *Sunday Telegraph*, 28 May 2000.
[17] *Mail on Sunday*, 30 July 2000.

[12] *Independent on Sunday*, 21 June 1998.
[14] *Daily Mail*, 27 May 2000.
[16] *The Times*, 14 June 2000.

How has this happened? How has the notion that to represent is to enact morphed into the idea that to dramatize is to condone? The answer is that the latter concept has been dramatically strengthened by two mutually-supporting phenomena, which have allowed a shift in the ideology and indeed location of the free speech debate. In the *Chatterley* trial, the state sought to protect weak consumers from corrupting influence (exemplified in the prosecution counsel's famous question to the jury: 'Is it a book that you would even wish your wife or your servants to read?')[18] Now, individuals or groups seek to suppress material which causes them distress or offence, turning the free speech debate from a question of state power into an issue of consumer rights. The phenomena which have enabled if not brought about this change are, first, the commodification of art (which has tended to diminish the moral status of artists) and, second, the rise of victim power in and beyond the criminal justice system.

In 1992–3, the three major US television networks all produced dramatizations of a single true life story: that of Amy Fisher, the so-called Long Island Lolita, who attempted to murder the wife of a garage owner with whom she claimed she was having an affair. The truth or otherwise of this claim was tested by CBS from the point of view of the husband (Joey Buttafuoco), by NBC from the point of view of Amy herself, and by ABC from the trial transcripts, albeit dramatized as the investigation by a concerned feminist journalist into a case which seemed morally clear-cut at the outset but became less so as her sympathetic and insightful investigation proceeded.

In addition to providing the clearest possible example of how the same set of facts can be dramatized to give three quite different meanings (the model of the Kurasawa film *Rashamon* and John Hopkins' quartet of television plays *Talking to a Stranger*) the Amy Fisher case was significant for another reason: Fisher's selling of her story to NBC financed her defence. The increasing commodification of the information on which fact-based dramas are based is one of the factors which have tended to devalue them. Following his release from jail, the newspapers speculated that Nick Leeson would make up to £3 million from the dramatization of his biography *Rogue Trader*.[19] Having been castigated for putting her side of the story of her arrest, trial, and imprisonment for the alleged murder of a fellow nurse in Saudi Arabia, Deborah Parry announced plans to use television drama to try and clear her name.[20] One of the many complications in Lucy Gannon's 1996 Carlton teleplay *Beyond Reason*—a dramatization of another case of spurned young lover attacking lover's wife—was the fact that the victim's husband had a financial relationship with a tabloid.[21]

But the commodification of cultural artefacts goes way beyond real life dramatizations of criminal cases. The playwright John Guare heard the story of a New York conman who pretended to be the son of Sidney Poitier, and used it as

---

[18] See n. 1 above, 23.
[20] *Sunday Telegraph*, 8 November 1998.

[19] *The Guardian*, 18 June 1997.
[21] *The Guardian*, 13 April 1995.

the jumping off point for his play *Six Degrees of Separation*; the conman took him to court.[22] Four of the Beirut hostages protested against Granada's drama-documentary on their captivity, on the grounds that the film infringed their own rights to their own stories. The official British artist of the Gulf War, John Keene, faced protests and legal threats from the Disney Corporation for having painted a picture of the devastation of a Kuwait beach which included a Mickey Mouse doll. Another British artist, David Haslam, faced legal action from the owners of the copyright of Noddy; the American artist Rick Rush was taken to court for painting a picture of Tiger Woods. While both the Canadian Mounted Police and the Los Angeles Police Department have sought to copyright their own logos for the purpose of commercial exploitation, and a mock photograph in an art exhibition of Di and Dodi lookalikes cuddling a mixed-race baby is berated on the grounds of the infringement of copyright in Princess Diana's image. Talking of image, the British Broadcasting regulator upheld former athlete David Bedford's complaint against 118 for using an image of two David Bedford lookalike runners to advertise their directory inquiry service.[23] And significantly, these mechanisms slip across into journalism: when Paddy Ashdown took the *Sunday Telegraph* to court over the printing of a minute of a secret meeting with Tony Blair, one of his grounds was that the words of the minute had a commercial value.[24]

The commodification of culture—the idea that writers and artists are only in it for the money—makes it much easier for critics to judge artistic work literalistically, and so set it in the scales against the distress it does or might cause. The rights of victims and their families, principally to avoid distressing memories of crimes, were cited in the case of Lucy Gannon's *Beyond Reason* as well as Jimmy McGovern's drama-documentary about the Hillsborough football stadium tragedy and (most recently) Michael Caton-Jones' film about the 1994 Rwandan massacres, *Shooting Dogs*. (One of the reasons why there are currently so few drama-documentaries on the BBC is because stringent regulations require them to consult not only the living, but the relatives of dead people represented in them.) It is the basis of all the attacks on representations of Myra Hindley, of which the most emblematic was Diane Dubois' 1998 Edinburgh Festival Fringe play about Hindley's continued iconic influence, which had to move from the Gilded Balloon, one of the big three fringe venues, ostensibly 'for technical reasons', when backer Calder's Cream Ale threatened to withdraw sponsorship. A spokesman explained that 'Calder's is committed to the light-hearted side of the fringe', but it was also suspected that that it had been subject to pressure from the *Sun*, which described the play as 'twisted and sick' and Justice for Victims (Scotland), which insisted: 'Please put Hindley's innocent victims and their

---

[22] Programme note (Royal Exchange Theatre, Manchester), April 2004.
[23] 'Phone inquiries ad broke code', *The Guardian*, 28 January 2004.
[24] S. Lockyear, 'When Paddy met Tony', *The Guardian*, 30 July 2001.

families before greed'.[25] The play it should be said was not a biography, but concerned five media studies students one of who whom was trying to create a treatment for a TV documentary about Hindley. (It is doubtful, on the greed front, that it made anyone very rich.) On response to the scandal, Conservative culture spokesman Peter Ainsworth stated: 'It is difficult to say that there should be some no-go areas for any artistic endeavour—but it's an extraordinarily tricky area: there are questions of taste and decency and there is a need to protect the families involved'.

The assertion of the rights of victims' families to be protected from distress leads easily to the demands of larger groups to be protected from offence. For the *Daily Express*, an episode of *Mersey Beat* in which a child's abduction was witnessed by CCTV was not only offensive to James Bulger's parents, 'but to anyone who was touched by the toddler's tragic plight'.[26] In December 2006, James Bulger's mother was reported as 'boiling with rage' at the idea that her son's death might be referred to in a historical exhibition in the Museum of Liverpool, asking 'what kind of callous people would think of doing this in the name of art and culture?' When the *Guardian* serialized Gordon Burn's book about Frederick West, *Happy Like Murderers*, readers protested not only to protect West's victims, but to protect a general readership from the 'suffering, despair, and pain involved in the subject matter'.[27]

It will be noticed that the terrain has shifted: *Mersey Beat* was a fiction, the proposed exhibit in the Museum of Liverpool (and Gordon Burns' book) were works of fact. The problem with the language of victim power is that it draws no necessary distinction between factual, fictionalized, and fictional treatment of events. Exactly the same arguments against the use of Frederick West's taped confessions as a source for drama were reproduced, some time later, when Channel 4 used the tapes in a documentary. In April 2007, the need to protect victims' relatives and others from distress was cited both by the BBC, to justify postponing the broadcast of Hanif Kureishi's short story about the murder of a hostage in Iraq (while captured BBC reporter Alan Johnson's fate remained uncertain), and against NBC's broadcast of Virginia Tech assassin Cho Sung-Hue's videos. In the same week, Channel 4 postponed broadcast of Tony Merchant's fictional film about British soldiers in Iraq, *A Mark of Cain*, for fear that it would encourage the Iranian government to delay the release of the British sailors it was then holding.

The desire to protect two groups from offence underpins the two pieces of legislation that provoked the most alarm among free speech advocates. The perceived offensiveness of statements supporting terror attacks was the impetus behind Labour's 2005 manifesto commitment to outlaw not just glorification,

---

[25] *The Guardian*, 11 August 1998, and 'Myra play causes a stir', *BBC News Online*, 13 August 1998, <http://news.bbc.co.uk/2/hi/entertainment/149756.stm> (last accessed 24 July 2008).
[26] *Daily Express*, 16 July 2001.   [27] *The Guardian*, 12 September 1998.

but also the condoning of terrorism. In the first draft of the actual Bill, the offence of glorifying, exalting, or celebrating acts of terrorism (condoning had been dropped) was proposed in addition to (and on top of) the offence of encouraging terrorism, and was thus intended to be applied against statements which could not be proved to have encouraged anyone to do anything. Conscious that the applicable definition of terrorism (according to the Terrorism Act 2000, any action 'the use or threat' of which 'is designed to influence the government or to intimidate the public . . . for the purpose of advancing a political, religious or ideological cause') would certainly embrace the ANC and the Easter Rising (if not the Boston Tea Party), the government promised a list of officially disapproved terrorist events more than 20 years old to which the bill would apply.

Subject to a barrage of criticism, the government revised the bill. In its new form, 'glorification' (but no longer exaltation nor celebration) was made part of the offence of indirectly encouraging terrorism. However, the terrorist acts so glorified could be 'in the past, the future, or generally'. So a laudatory speech, play, or pamphlet about the ANC, Irgun, or the Vietcong could still fall within the net, but only if the speaker intended members to be encouraged to emulate it in existing circumstances.

It is this clause which the House of Lords sought and failed to remove in January 2006, substituting a clause which defined 'indirect encouragement' in pretty much the same terms as glorification. What it did not have was the word 'glorify'. The difference between the Commons and the Lords was not about encouragement of terrorism, which is clearly criminalized. It is about the expression of an opinion.

Where the representational arts specifically get into trouble is in relation to the only allowable defence, which in both versions is for the accused to show that the glorification or encouragement neither expressed his/her views nor had her/his endorsement. As with the Conservative Government's Section 28 prohibition of the 'promotion' of homosexuality by local authorities, the problem is, 'How do you tell?' By having lesbians as their protagonists, do Lillian Hellman's *The Children's Hour* or Frank Marcus' *The Killing of Sister George* thereby 'promote' their sexuality? Even when protagonists are clearly unheroic, does their centrality invite us to see things from their point of view? (Is Edward II's sexuality his fatal flaw or his saving grace?) Similarly, now, does a laudatory biography, documentary drama, or (in due time) eulogy 'endorse' the terrorist actions of Nelson Mandela or Gerry Adams in a way that might encourage disenfranchized minorities to take up arms, like they did? These questions will confront juries at a time when, as we have seen, the distinction between portrayal and promotion, expression and endorsement, representation, and its object is subject to considerable confusion, in newspaper columns, on picket lines, and among government agencies. *Christian Voice* picketed the tour of *Jerry Springer—The Opera* on the grounds that a metaphorical dramatization of a TV presenter's nightmare was a literal representation of Jesus Christ. In February 2006, actors playing

Guantanamo inmates were interrogated under terror laws at Luton Airport (one was asked 'Did you become an actor mainly to do films like this . . . ?').[28] A week before that, the Welsh Assembly issued guidelines which appeared to ban kissing in school plays.[29]

The Lords gave in on glorification on 22 March 2006, and that clause is now law. The statute that is often paired with it—that relating to religious hatred— was considerably amended. Not only did the Commons insist that incitement to racial hatred be intended and threatening (rather than 'threatening, insulting and abusive'), it also passed a Lords' amendment specifically protecting criticism, abuse, insult, or ridicule of any religion from prosecution.

The problem, of course, is that some Muslims saw the glorification clause as an attack on their freedom of speech (on the grounds of preventing offence), while many saw the religious hatred clause as a defence of their right not to be offended. For civil libertarians, the presumption at the heart of the *Behzti* protests at the Birmingham Repertory Theatre and the Danish cartoon affair is the most manifestly wrongheaded presumption of all: that to represent is to insult. And even if it is not the most wrongheaded, the militancy with which this notion has been defended makes it clearly the most immediately dangerous. To correct a popular misconception, *Behzti* was not closed after protests by the Sikh com- munity in anything other than a strictly chronological sense: it was closed after a small group of young Sikh men physically attacked a theatre whose frontage consists almost entirely of glass just before the evening performance of a children's show. Other institutions have not waited to be attacked before pulling risky material. In September 2005, Tate Britain withdrew John Latham's *God is Great*, a piece in which the Koran, the Bible, and the Torah are apparently embedded in a sheet of plate glass, on the grounds that—after the 7 July London attacks—it might be seen as insensitive.[30] In November, the Bristol Old Vic altered the scene in Marlowe's *Tamberlaine* in which the central character burns the Koran and berates the prophet; the director stating that the decision was artistic, his co-artistic director stating that the original text would have been 'unnecessarily inflammatory'.[31] Before rehearsals of Richard Bean's *Up on Roof*—a play about the 1976 Hull prison riot for Hull Truck—Bean was asked to remove three mentions of Mohammad's name, on the grounds that the Board of Trustees felt these lines might represent a 'non-quantifiable risk to our staff' (the same excuse given by the Deutsche Opera in Berlin for cancelling performances of a pro- duction of Mozart's *Idomeneo* featuring the severed heads of Buddha, Christ, and Mohammad). Richard Bean decided to go along with these changes, and the rift

[28] D. Rose, 'Using terror to fight terror', *The Guardian*, 26 February 2006.
[29] 'School play love scene "ban" fear', *BBC News Online*, 17 February 2006, <http://news.bbc.co. uk/2/hi/uk_news/wales/4721998.stm>, (last accessed 24 July 2008).
[30] D. Smith, 'Artist hits at Tate "cowards" over ban', *The Observer*, 25 September 2005.
[31] *The Observer*, 27 November 2005.

has healed, but (along with Tate Britain and Bristol) it can be seen as another example of a growing and predictable trend to self censorship.

I am clear in my own mind that 'to represent is to insult' is as dangerous—if not more dangerous—than any of the other concepts that are threatening hard-won rights to free expression. So why, on the religious issue, do I find myself unexpectedly, uncomfortably, and unusually tempted by the fence? It is partly because of the way in which the eyes of the free speech lobby concentrate on Muslim (and Sikh) protesters, and pay little attention to years and years of attempts by Christians to suppress images of which they disapprove. It is also because—thus far and by and large—Sikhs and Muslims have only been concerned to protest against images of things they regard as sacred, while Christians have been happy to try and impose their non-religious opinions as well. (Usually non-violently, of course: Christian campaigners burnt no British flags in protest against the Rolling Stones' supposedly offensive lyrics at the half-time concert in a recent Super Bowl. But then, they did not need to. CBS had just been fined $550,000 for Janet Jackson's 2004 'wardrobe malfunction' and so ABC decided to play it safe and mute them.)

My unease is also exacerbated by the ahistorically Whiggish reading of Enlightenment and post-Enlightenment history of those who pit the progressive west against backward Islam: in fact, the enlightenment project survived centuries of religious, political, and sexual censorship without the golden thread snapping. But the thing that worries me most is the tone of the enlightenment's proponents today.

I am an atheist. I do not believe in God, the afterlife, miracles, or the resurrection. I do not see why belief in the supernatural should give your opinions particular weight, or require that particular sensitivity to be shown to you, or restrict my freedom of speech in any way. I think that the influence of people who believe in the supernatural is increasing, and that that poses probably the greatest immediate threat to peace and wellbeing throughout the world. I wish it was not so. I wish that people agreed with me that religion is irrational and can be dangerous. Most of all, I wish that young Britons of Pakistani and Bangladeshi heritage would pursue the redress of their economic and political grievances—which remain justified and considerable—through secular political and industrial activity, as they did in the 1970s. But I understand why they do not. I understand why, in particular, the language of Marxism failed them, because it failed all of us. I understand why the vocabulary of protest is drawn from the sacred, why angry young Sikhs and Muslims campaign for the suppression of books and plays rather than fascist propaganda, why religious rights have superseded industrial rights, and schoolchildren protesting about school uniform campaign to wear the jilbab rather than jeans. And I also understand why, against the constant drumbeat of execration and demonization in the popular newspapers, the endless jibes against 'political correctness', the lordly governmental strictures handed down about dress and language, the presumptive association of Islam with terrorism, Muslims see the publication of the Danish cartoons not as the exercise of a right but as the prelude to a pogrom. And, hence, that there are perfectly intelligent and sensible people in this country who do not think that the value of unrestricted free expression is a given, people for whom the slogan 'Enlightenment, Enlightenment, Enlightenment' is not enough.

And is there not—in the pronouncements of German newspaper editors and British newspaper columnists on the principles at stake in the Danish cartoons affair—something uncomfortably smug, self-satisfied, and patronizing? I have no objection to men kissing in the street or pictures of topless women on beaches, but is not there something actually rather childish about the Dutch insisting that all applicants for Dutch citizenship watch, study, and be quizzed on a DVD containing these images? (This is the country in which architectural designs for mosques are rejected as 'too Islamic'.) And, when we read progressive and liberal thinkers condemning young Muslims and Sikhs for attacking free speech, do we not hear echoes of previous generations of progressives who felt betrayed by the people they were standing up for, and used that feeling of betrayal as an excuse for abandoning them? In particular, are we not reminded of the first generation of American neo-conservatives, who used what they saw as the excesses of the late 60s—particularly the criminalization of the Black Panthers—as an excuse for abandoning the civil rights struggle? Thank goodness, we heard them saying, Black political leaders are thugs, we can now abandon our concern with racial disadvantage. And similarly, now, in the columns of *Prospect* and *The Guardian* as much as those of *Jyllands-Posten* or *Die Welt*, do we not hear something between relief and glee: oh, how wonderful, the poorest and most wretched and most exploited in our society are on the wrong side, they are homophobic and sexist, they believe in fatwas and forced marriages, and putting women in black bags, we do not have to bother about them anymore?

So, lest we forget, while *liberté* is a necessary condition of social wellbeing and justice, it is not a sufficient condition. Indeed, in the absence of *égalité* and *fraternité*, there are circumstances in which *liberté* can be a tool of rejection and exploitation. While individual free speech is an absolute (though, in its current form, a very recent) gain, it does not stand alone. People who were made invisible by a criminalization of which censorship was an important constituent—I am thinking particularly of gays—won their liberation from those constraints by collective political action.

Applying those principles to a particular case, it was right that the first response to the forced closure of *Behzti* was an unconditional defence by authors and theatre-makers (though few arts administrators and politicians) of the Birmingham Rep's right to present Gurjeet Kaur Bhatti's play in the form in which she wrote it. That defence gives those who made it permission to address related and perhaps knottier questions about how theatres who want to represent the communities around them should respond when parts of those communities do not like what they hear.

There were three basic lines on the *Behzti* affair: the straight-up, post-Enlightenment, freedom of artistic expression argument trumpeted by Nick Hytner's ringing declaration of the theatre's right to be offensive. Then there is the argument that this right is not absolute, that theatres financed by taxpayers need and should pay attention to the sensitivities of the communities they serve—an argument which pays attention, in this case, to the distress caused to a generally invisible community who, when at last they find themselves represented theatrically, discover it is in a play which appears to argue that their temples are hotbeds of corruption and rape. But, third, there is the proposition that the communities to which theatres should perhaps be sensitive are by no means monolithic, that the protests against *Behzti* were overwhelmingly male, and that the sexual abuse of a young Sikh woman by an older Sikh man struck a chord among young Asian women from all faiths. In this reading, *Behzti* and other Asian plays *are* being sensitive to the feelings of a marginalized and silenced community—it is just, it is a dissident community. And the credibility of this argument is sustained by what happened at the Birmingham Rep in the months after *Behzti*, during which a previously announced programme of Black and Asian plays dealt with issues as bland and uncontroversial as Afro-Caribbean gun crime, Muslim brothels, terrorism, communalism, and teenage sex. During this season, the Rep kept a rough head-count of its non-white audiences for all its shows. In the studio theatre, Asma Dar's *Chaos* (set in a Muslim home, concerned with careerism, communalism, and terrorism) gained a 40 per cent, largely Asian non-white audience; about the same as Yasmin Whittaker Khan's *Bells*, a play about Muslim brothels in London. A revival of Kwame Kwei-Armah's *Elmina's Kitchen* (co-produced with the National Theatre) achieved the largest Black audience of its pre-London tour (nearly a third) in the Rep's 900 seat main house. While over 60 per cent of the audience for a short run of Roy Williams' *Little Sweet Thing* (co-produced with Ipswich and Nottingham) was non-white.

Although all of these plays had tough and challenging content, *Little Sweet Thing* was probably the most controversial of all. Roy Williams' story of a Black ex-con who tries but fails to break free from a criminal sub-culture contained two white characters, both of which are threatened and bullied by Black characters, whom they seek first to emulate and then to out-do. The idea that emulating Black urban culture can turn weak nice people into strong nasty ones is a pretty brave notion for a Black writer to express. I think if it had been expressed in an interview or an article it would have been rejected angrily. On stage, it was recognized and accepted. This is because its audiences understood the most basic thing about theatre, that it provides a site in which you can say things that are riskier and more extreme than the things you can say elsewhere, because what you say is not real but represented. Of all people, the marginalized and the demonized have an interest in preserving the rights of free expression, particularly in a space where the rules of engagement allow our most extreme and violent emotions and desires to be confronted under secure conditions: as Sir Philip Sidney reminds us, no-one believes they really *are* the Gates of Thebes, and that is the whole point of the exercise. The Greeks paired theatre with democracy as the twin pillars of their polity precisely because it is all pretend.

The lesson of the best Black and Asian theatre in Britain is that drama, like the other arts, gives voice to the silenced and the excluded. Like the Greeks, we should defend the arts, not because they are not important, but because they are. The empowering character of free expression might seem less immediately obvious if you do not have access to the microphone. But the answer to that is to open up the airwaves rather than close them down.

I have tried to show that the new censoriousness has been enabled by a largely ignored but sustained campaign over many years, to devalue and trivialize the business and purpose of art. Lady Snow's desire to burn all the books in the world to protect a single child is echoed (albeit in a minor key) in the Welsh assembly guidelines on physical contact in school plays, which insist that school play directors 'should not rely on arguments about the artistic integrity of the text', as if artistic integrity did not matter very much. Similarly, when home office minister Fiona Mactaggart says that the rights of artistic expression have to be set against the rights of communities to be secure and safe (in a BBC Radio 4 *Today* programme interview immediately after the closure of *Behzti*), she diminishes activities that are essential to bringing those ends about.

Behind all of this is the idea that there are subjects too important, too profound, too dangerous for writing (and painting, and performing, and even reporting) to touch. Behind that is an assumption that fiction writing in particular has no a positive value, that it is a trivial pursuit, a luxury pastime which if it proves to be dangerous to its consumers should be suppressed for the greater good, like high-risk sports, keeping attack dogs, or eating meat off the bone. We have been intimidated by such accusations—aided and abetted as they have been by post-modern critics in the universities—into ignoring or devaluing the positive role of art in our lives. We need to assert that the telling and hearing of stories (in whatever medium) is not an optional extra. It is central to our being as humans. Indeed, certain crucial aspects of humanness could not exist without it. The most obvious is our ability to imagine other worlds and other times through stories told either from or about them. The second is our capacity to plan, which relies on the ability to imagine a series of actions and their consequences, and on the basis of that speculation, to choose between them.

But, thirdly, fiction teaches us to empathize. Behind the criticism of Gitta Sereny's studies of Albert Speer and Mary Bell, lies a refusal to accept the humanity of those who behave inhumanely. When James Bulger's mother describes her son's killers as evil monsters it is understandable, but it is not true. When, again understandably, the parents of Mary Bell's victims write that 'Mary Bell is not worthy of consideration as a feeling, human being',[32] they are letting

---

[32] In *The Sun*, quoted in the *Sunday Telegraph*, 3 May 1998.

the rest of us off the hook. I portrayed Hitler as a human being, because that is what he was. Indeed, to refuse to accept that is to echo that very lack of empathy which characterizes violent criminals. In her study of the 1961–2 Eichmann trial, Hannah Arendt noted that the decisive flaw in Adolf Eichmann's character was 'his almost total inability ever to look at anything from the other fellow's point of view'.[33] The children who murdered James Bulger appear not to have understood that the child was a human being like they were, capable of experiencing terror and suffering. They were in this sense not so much evil, as lacking an essential human skill without which it is impossible to be good.

The point of writing about evil is not to discourage it by pointing out the inevitability of its come-uppance; 'Don't do this at home' is as misleading a description of what writing counsels us as 'go thou and do likewise'. The awful truth is that the response most great writing about wickedness provokes in us is neither 'yes please' nor 'no thanks' but 'you too?' Shakespeare's Richard III advocates, celebrates, nay glorifies brother-drowning, nephew-smothering, and tyranny-imposing. True, he gets his just desserts. But what the first half of the play does is confront us with the fact that this appalling man is the most vivid, thrilling and inspiring person on stage. Similarly, as the great critic Eric Bentley argues, we watch *King Lear* in fascination, not because any of us have thrown our father out into the storm, but because all of us have, at some time or another, wanted to.

By enabling us to imagine what it is like to see the world through other eyes (including through the eyes of the violent and the murderous), artistic representation develops capacities without which we cannot live together in societies at all. Thus, defence of free speech is not primarily a matter of the rights of the speaker, but the rights of the listener. In that sense, we all have the right not only to offend but to be offended. Without it, we are all impoverished and disarmed.

To promote that complex but vital idea requires, first, levelling the playing field by repealing the blasphemy laws. If we are to resist retightening of the (correctly) emasculated Religious Hatred Act, then we need also to repeal the equally illiberal glorification clauses of the Terrorism Act. We need to understand why Muslims and Sikhs get angry, and an acknowledgement that they are not the only religions involved in these controversies. But it also requires us to assert the importance of free expression for the marginalized and the excluded, and to defend and protect fiction's right to portray, to explain, to represent, to shock, to inspire, and to imagine. After all, what happens at the beginning of *Henry V*? A man shouts 'fire' in a crowded theatre.

[33] *Eichmann in Jerusalem: A Report on the Banality of Evil* (New York: Penguin, 1994), 47–8.

30

Extreme Speech and American Press Freedoms

David J. Bodney

1. Introduction

Extreme speech has played a dramatic role throughout American legal history. From the very beginning, radical rhetoric has figured prominently in the storyline of America. Yet no sooner had this fledgling country committed itself to freedom of speech and of the press, did the young republic take steps to punish the publishers of politically volatile expression. To say we Americans have had conflicting views about the role of extreme speech in our experiment with ordered liberty is understatement indeed.

In the beginning, even before the 'miracle' birth of our written constitution in 1787,[1] Americans engaged in speech of the most extreme kind. In the eighteenth century, what Thomas Paine called 'common sense' the British governors viewed as radical instigation.[2] Nevertheless, Paine's pamphleteering quickly came to be seen by Americans as a classic form of speech, reflective of one's patriotic duty. Ultimately, if not imminently, Paine's speech sparked a revolution and established a tradition of vigorous political expression deserving of judicial protection.

The author of America's Declaration of Independence, Thomas Jefferson, expressed the view—extreme at the time—that truth should be a defence to defamation claims.[3] The law of the day held quite the opposite: *truthful* defamation was even more damaging than falsehood. 'The greater the truth the greater the libel' was the law in early eighteenth-century America, especially when

---

[1] C. D. Bowen, *The Miracle of Philadelphia: The Story of the Constitutional Convention May to September 1787* (Boston: Little, Brown and Co., 1966).

[2] '[Thomas] Paine considered aristocratic government, established by a parasitic caste of the pedigreed and privileged, as the chief author of human misery.' S. Wilentz, *The Rise of American Democracy: Jefferson to Lincoln* (New York: W.W. Horton & Co., Inc., 2005), 24. Indeed, '[a] Philadelphia patriot worried that Paine's proposals would stir "the multitude in a perpetual ferment like the ocean in a storm."' Ibid.

[3] A. Dershowitz, *Finding Jefferson: A Lost Letter, A Remarkable Discovery, and the First Amendment in an Age of Terrorism* (Hoboken, NJ: John Wiley & Sons, Inc., 2008), 65.

truthful libels were aimed at public officials. Indeed, when a New York jury accepted truth as a *defence* to the charge of seditious libel in the 1734 trial of John Peter Zenger, it created a maxim of defamation law that has stood the test of time.[4] Truth is now an absolute defence to libel lawsuits in the United States, and the Zenger trial paved the way for American courts to protect robust speech— with some rather notable exceptions—ever since.

Over the years, American jurisprudence has endeavoured to draw a workable line between vigorous and even caustic political and social critique, which must be protected in a free and democratic society, and incitement to imminent violence, which is undeserving of such protection. At the same time, the law has encouraged the market—if not the marketplace of ideas—to set the boundaries of offensive speech. While the law punishes libellous, obscene, and truly threatening communications, social mores, and watchdog groups play an increasingly powerful role in curbing extreme speech in a marketplace where earnings per share are dominant constants.[5] However defined, extreme speech has played an exalted part in the unfolding American drama, pushing and probing the political conversation in often uncomfortable ways, and turning the wheels of profit at paces and in directions we Americans variously abhor and applaud, but ultimately embrace as part of our way of life.

As the foregoing suggests, extreme speech is a highly elastic term, broad enough to encompass the writings of Jefferson, the pages of *Hustler* magazine and the torch-lit passages of *Mein Kampf.* In the context of 'extreme speech,' one challenge of assessing governmental and self-regulation of the press, then, is definitional. By extreme speech, do we mean only hate speech? Or do we also mean to include defamatory speech, invasion of privacy and intentional infliction of emotional distress? Does the topic include obscenity, pornography, and laws intended to protect the tender sensibilities of minors? To what extent does the conversation involve a discussion of criminal laws, regulatory processes, and that rarity in American law, 'prior restraints' against the press? By the 'press,' do we consider only mainstream media—newspapers, magazines, books, television, and radio—or do we mean to include the Internet, bloggers, and 'citizen journalists'?

American law, especially in this field, has not developed in a neat or systematic way. But it has taken root over time and in patterns that allow one to generalize about the law's treatment of speech. What follows, then, are the general contours of the American constitutional framework for addressing the challenge of extreme speech, with particular emphasis on the rights of the press.

---

[4] Ibid.

[5] For an interesting perspective on the origins of American market ambitions, see W. McDougall, *Freedom Just Around the Corner: A New American History 1585–1828* (New York: HarperCollins, 2004), 4–5 ('Who is this new man, this American? As [Herman] Melville would certainly have it, he or she is a hustler... To suggest Americans are, among other things, prone to be hustlers... is simply to acknowledge Americans have had more opportunity to pursue their ambitions, by foul means or fair, than any other people in history... No wonder American English is uniquely endowed with words connoting a swindle.').

2. The Sedition Act

The principal protection of the press lies in the First Amendment to the Constitution of the United States. Ratified in 1791, the First Amendment provides that 'Congress shall make no law . . . abridging the freedom of speech, or of the press . . .'. Within a mere seven years of the First Amendment's ratification, Congress passed the Sedition Act of 1798, which gave the federal government broad powers to punish speech critical of it or its officials. Indeed, the publication of any 'false, scandalous, and malicious writing . . . with intent to defame' could result in an exorbitant monetary fine or imprisonment.[6] As Professor Geoffrey Stone has written, when a Federalist Congress passed the Sedition Act—an Act aimed to stifle criticism of the Adams administration by a Republican press—'the Federalists (and the U.S. government) declared war on dissent' in America.[7]

For over two centuries, volumes have been written on the meaning of the First Amendment and its compatibility with laws such as the Sedition Act, and debate over the correct interpretation continues to this day. Jefferson, a Republican, described life under the Sedition Act as a 'reign of witches,' when Federalist prosecutors issued 17 indictments for seditious libel.[8] Though Federalists justified the Act by invoking images of spies and conspirators in their midst, their true target was the presidential election of 1800, and their strategy was 'to silence every leading Republican newspaper as the contest between Adams and Jefferson grew nigh'.[9] Federalists designed the Act to expire on the last days of John Adams' term of office, lest it be used against the Federalists in the event Jefferson defeated Adams in the election, which he did.[10]

With his inaugural address in 1801, Jefferson's presidency began on a conciliatory note: 'We are all Republicans—we are all Federalists.' One of his first official acts in office was to pardon all those convicted under the Sedition Act and free those still in jail. To Jefferson's mind, the Act functioned as a 'nullity as absolute and as palpable as if Congress had ordered us to fall down and worship a golden image'.[11]

3. *Near, Sullivan,* and *Brandenburg*

More than a century and a half later, the US Supreme Court expressly recognized the unconstitutionality of the Sedition Act, and it did so in a case of profound

---

[6] G. R. Stone, *Perilous Times: Free Speech in Wartime from the Sedition Act of 1798 to the War on Terrorism* (New York: W.W. Norton & Co., Inc., 2004), 36.
[7] Ibid. The Republican party of the eighteenth century was an entirely different political party than today's Republican party. It was sometimes referred to as the Democratic-Republican party, and today's Democratic party traces its origins to the party of Thomas Jefferson.
[8] Ibid., 46–8.   [9] Ibid., 48.   [10] Ibid., 67.   [11] Ibid., 73.

significance to press freedoms in America. In 1964, a unanimous Supreme Court decided *New York Times* v. *Sullivan*, a libel case that declared our 'profound national commitment to the principle that debate on public issues should be uninhibited, robust, and wide-open'.[12] The Court recognized that the press must therefore be allowed to publish 'vehement, caustic, and sometimes unpleasantly sharp attacks on government and public officials'.[13] So when an Alabama official sued the *New York Times* for libel over an advertisement soliciting support for the civil rights movement, the Court held that a public official must prove constitutional 'actual malice'—knowledge of falsity or reckless disregard of truth, by clear and convincing evidence—before the official can collect damages against the press under the First Amendment. Recognizing that 'erroneous statement is inevitable in free debate,' Justice William Brennan's opinion for the Court in *Sullivan* noted that even false statements must be protected 'if the freedoms of expression are to have the 'breathing space' that they 'need ... to survive'.[14] To support the Court's decision, Justice Brennan analogized the civil law of libel as applied by the Alabama court in this case to the Sedition Act of 1798 and observed, that 'although the Sedition Act was never tested in this Court, the attack upon its validity has carried the day in the court of history'.[15]

More than three decades before *Sullivan*, the Supreme Court had previously used the First Amendment to protect press freedoms profoundly. In *Near* v. *Minnesota*, the Court invalidated a Minnesota statute that permitted a judge to block the publication of a newspaper if the court found its content 'obscene, lewd, and lascivious,' or 'malicious, scandalous, and defamatory'.[16] Writing for a majority of the Court, Chief Justice Charles Evan Hughes found that prior restraints on the press are presumptively unconstitutional, striking at the very core of the First Amendment, and can be tolerated only in the most exceptional cases —for example, to halt the publication of troop movements in time of war.[17]

If *Sullivan* gave the media 'breathing room' to publish defamatory falsehoods about public officials (and later public figures),[18] *Near* 'stiffened the backbone of countless editors and publishers and helped stave off periodic attempts by politicians, judges, and prosecutors to muzzle the journalistic watchdog'.[19] *Near* and *Sullivan* have come to assure the American media that their stories cannot be enjoined—except in the rarest of circumstances—and that subsequent punishment for libel and related claims cannot be meted out except upon clear and convincing proof of actual malice.[20] With *Near* and *Sullivan* standing as twin

---

[12] *New York Times Co.* v. *Sullivan* 376 US 254, 270 (1964).   [13] Ibid.
[14] Ibid., 271–2.   [15] Ibid., 276.
[16] *Near* v. *Minnesota* 283 US 697 (1931).
[17] K. Hall, J. W. Ely, and J. B. Grossman, (eds.), *The Oxford Companion to the Supreme Court of the United States*, 2nd edn. (New York: OUP, 2005), 675.
[18] *Curtis Publishing Co.* v. *Butts* 388 US 130 (1967).   [19] See n. 17 above, 675.
[20] By 1971, *Near*'s rejection of prior restraints had become bedrock First Amendment law in the United States. Hence, when the Nixon administration sought to enjoin the *New York Times* from publishing a classified document on the history of America's involvement in the Vietnam War, the

pillars of press freedoms, the Supreme Court decided a third case that serves to protect the publication of speech that comes close to incitement, but not all the way.

In *Brandenburg* v. *Ohio*, the Court reviewed a conviction under an Ohio criminal syndicalism statute. The case involved heated advocacy at a televised Ku Klux Klan rally. After reviewing the Court's 50-year history of trying to develop a workable test to separate protected from unprotected advocacy of illegal conduct, the Court adopted a test allowing the punishment of speech advocating illegal action, but only when 'such advocacy is directed to inciting or producing *imminent* lawless action and is *likely* to incite or produce such action'.[21] By requiring that the speech in question constitute incitement and not just mere advocacy of illegal conduct, *Brandenburg*, provided an important supplement to the old 'clear and present' danger test, which, despite its name, frequently allowed the criminalization of speech if it had even a 'tendency' to encourage or cause lawlessness.

With *Near, Sullivan,* and *Brandenburg,* the Supreme Court established a strong and lasting framework for the protection of extreme speech in America. All three cases involved speech that was in some sense extreme, or at least offensive to a community with power to suppress it. *Near* invalidated a judge's attempt to enjoin rabid, antisemitic remarks in the *Saturday Press,* a weekly newspaper. Though Near was 'an unsavoury character—anti-Catholic, antisemitic, anti-black, and anti-labour'—the Court overturned an arguably well-intentioned law (and reversed the judge who sought to apply it) on First Amendment grounds.[22] The *Sullivan* case focused on a few false and arguably defamatory statements contained in a paid advertisement titled 'Heed Their Rising Voices', a fundraising solicitation for the defence of Dr. Martin Luther King, Jr. and the Struggle for Freedom in the South.[23] *Brandenburg* arose from the conviction of a man over racist statements uttered at a televised KKK rally. In these cases, 'uninhibited, robust, and wide-open' speech was given wide berth—wide enough to withstand the state's attempts to enjoin publication, collect money damages, and imprison someone for deeply offensive speech.

Supreme Court, in a per curiam decision, found that the government had failed to meet its heavy burden of proving a need for prior restraint. Three justices dissented, objecting to the rush of the proceedings. In a separate concurring opinion, Justice Byron White emphasized that publishers could be prosecuted for criminal violations of national security laws regulating the dissemination of classified information, but only *after* publication. *New York Times* v. *United States* 403 US 713, 733 (1971). In dissent, Chief Justice Warren Burger expressed his 'general agreement' with Justice White's views on the availability of 'penal sanctions' for possession or dissemination of documents or information relating to the national defence. Ibid., 752.

[21] *Brandenburg* v. *Ohio* 395 US 444, 447 (1969), emphasis added.

[22] See n. 17 above, 675.

[23] *New York Times Co.* v. *Sullivan* 376 US 254, 256–9 (1964). See also T. Branch, *Parting the Waters: America in the King Years 1954–63* (New York: Simon and Schuster, 1988), 288–9.

4. Rhetorical Hyperbole, Vigorous Epithets, and Parody

Once the Supreme Court interpreted the First Amendment to require proof of actual malice before public officials could prevail in defamation cases, the First Amendment became a ready source of protection for a wider variety of speech. In short order, the actual malice doctrine was expanded to protect the media in libel cases brought by public figures [24] And, contrary to the common law rule imposing strict liability on publishers of certain types of defamatory material, the First Amendment was soon held to require even a private figure to show the defendant at fault in making the false statements.[25] In some states, drawing on the logic of *Sullivan*, even private figures would be obliged to prove actual malice when the reporting at issue involved matters of public concern.[26] And shortly after *Sullivan*, two Supreme Court cases paved the way for full-blown judicial protection of biting, offensive speech.

In *Greenbelt Cooperative Publishing Association, Inc.* v. *Bressler*, the Court protected a newspaper's use of the word 'blackmail' to describe a developer's negotiations with a city council. Characterizing the use of that term in that context as 'no more than rhetorical hyperbole, a vigorous epithet,'[27] the Court, moreover, went beyond the qualified privilege of *Sullivan* to protect a particular type of speech absolutely. The protection of 'rhetorical hyperbole' and the 'vigorous epithet' found further support from the Court a few years later in a case involving use of the word 'traitor' to define a labour union 'scab'. In *Letter Carriers* v. *Austin*, the Supreme Court broadened its definition of 'rhetorical hyperbole' to protect speech used in a 'loose, figurative sense'.[28] Although the case did not involve a media defendant (and indeed arose in the context of a labour dispute), it lent First Amendment cover to 'merely...a *lusty and imaginative expression* of the *contempt* felt by union members'.[29]

If the modern constitutional era of press freedom blossomed in the 1960s under the liberal Supreme Court of Chief Justice Earl Warren, then it took full root decades later under the Court's conservative counterpart, Chief Justice William Rehnquist. Writing for a unanimous Court in *Hustler Magazine* v. *Falwell*,[30] Rehnquist extended the actual malice privilege to protect the media in cases involving parody and satire, even when such expression is 'outrageous' or vicious and cruel. The case involved a mock Campari ad in *Hustler* magazine that depicted the evangelist Reverend Jerry Falwell as an inebriated participant in an incestuous sexual escapade in an outhouse with his mother. A federal jury declined to find the parody libellous, because no reasonable reader would have

---

[24] *Curtis Publishing Co.* v. *Butts*, 388 US 130 (1967).
[25] *Gertz* v. *Robert Welch, Inc.* 418 US 323 (1974).
[26] See *Walker* v. *Colorado Springs Sun, Inc.* 538 P.2d 450, 457 (Colo, 1975).
[27] 398 US 6, 14 (1970).   [28] *Letter Carriers* v. *Austin* 418 US 264 (1974).
[29] Ibid., 286, emphasis added.   [30] 485 US 46 (1988).

believed it to contain any statement of fact about Falwell. Still, the jury awarded $200,000 in damages to Falwell on a separate claim of intentional infliction of emotional distress, which required no proof of a false statement of fact.

In effect, the Supreme Court ruled that plaintiffs could not circumvent the First Amendment protections of *Sullivan* by taking a libel claim and denominating it otherwise—here, 'intentional infliction of emotional distress'. The Court held that before a public figure can recover for intentional infliction, the plaintiff must establish constitutional actual malice, which requires that the defendant recklessly or knowingly publish some *false statement of fact* about the plaintiff, a showing that could not be made in that case or most cases involving parody or satire. The defendant's *intention* to inflict emotional suffering, and the *outrageous* character of the expressions themselves, are insufficient to vitiate the First Amendment privilege. Thus *Hustler* resulted in a rule of law that protects the most outlandish, inherently unbelievable speech, while leaving more factual statements at greater risk of liability. Drawing on America's rich tradition of caustic lampoonery, especially in the form of cartoons aimed at our public figures, the Court recognized the importance of safeguarding the press from liability based on a public figure's hurt feelings.

5. Incitement, True Threats, and Fighting Words

One state supreme court recently had occasion to determine whether extreme speech aimed at Muslims could give rise to liability for intentional infliction of emotional distress. The case involved a daily newspaper's publication of a letter to the editor about the war in Iraq. In pertinent part, the letter stated:

We can stop the murders of American soldiers in Iraq by those who seek revenge or to regain their power. *Whenever there is an assassination or another atrocity we should proceed to the closest mosque and execute five of the first Muslims we encounter.*

After all this is a 'Holy War' and although such a procedure is not fair or just, it might end the horror. Machiavelli was correct. In war it is better to be feared than loved . . . [31]

The case was brought by two Islamic-Americans, ostensibly on behalf of 'all Islamic-Americans who live in the area covered by the circulation of the *Tucson Citizen*, including the reach of the Internet website published by the *Tucson Citizen*'.[32]

The Arizona Supreme Court unanimously ruled that the First Amendment absolutely protects newspapers from tort suits involving speech on matters of public concern unless the plaintiff can prove that the speech fits squarely into one of the few exceptional categories recognized by the US Supreme Court. The

---

[31] *Citizen Publishing Co.* v. *Miller* 205 513, 115 P.3d 107 (Ariz. 2005), emphasis added. The author served as counsel to Citizen Publishing Co. and argued the case on 24 March 2005 to the Arizona Supreme Court.
[32] Ibid.

Arizona high court identified three possible exceptions to the general rule of First Amendment protection of political speech—and rejected each of them in turn.

First, the court analysed a possible 'incitement' exception under the *Brandenburg* rule, but discarded it because the letter did not advocate '*imminent lawless action*'.[33] Second, the court made short shrift of plaintiffs' asserted application of the 'fighting words' doctrine.[34] Under that doctrine, the First Amendment does not protect words 'which, by their very utterance inflict injury or tend to incite an imminent breach of the peace'.[35] Underscoring the importance of context, the supreme court noted that 'fighting words' must be addressed to the target of the remarks, and that the doctrine has generally been limited to 'face-to-face' interactions. Finally, the court considered whether the letter could constitute a 'true threat' under a line of precedent arising from a case in which an anti-war protestor was convicted for threatening the president's life for exclaiming at an anti-war rally that '[i]f they ever make me carry a rifle the first man I want to get in my sights is L. B. J'.[36] In *Watts* v. *United States*, the Supreme Court distinguished certain actionable threats from constitutionally protected speech, found the defendant's remark to be a form of crude political hyperbole and reversed the conviction. Following *Watts* and cases decided thereafter, the Arizona Supreme Court emphasized that context is essential. Harkening back to Justice Oliver Wendell Holmes' famous line, the court observed, 'there is a vast constitutional difference between falsely shouting fire in a crowded theatre and making precisely the same statement in a letter to the editor'.[37] It also found that 'plainly political messages' are far less likely to be true threats than statements directed 'purely at other individuals'.[38]

At bottom, the *Citizen Publishing* case is emblematic of the judiciary's approach toward the media's use of extreme speech. Rhetorically, the court described the language in the letter to the editor as 'no doubt reprehensible' and 'offensive'.[39] Still, the Supreme Court recognized the fundamental importance of protecting 'the free flow of ideas and opinions on matters of public interest and concern,'[40] and ordered dismissal of the lawsuit.

6. The Marketplace and Evolving Norms of Civility

As a practical matter, the American media's usage of extreme speech is regulated less by laws than by market factors and evolving norms of civility.[41] Today more

---

[33] Ibid., 112–3 (emphasis added).
[34] *Chaplinsky* v. *New Hampshire* 315 US 568, 572 (1942).   [35] Ibid.
[36] *Watts v. United States* 394 US 705, 706 (1969).   [37] See n. 31 above at 115.
[38] Ibid.   [39] Ibid., 113.
[40] Ibid. at 111, quoting *Hustler Magazine* v. *Falwell* 485 US 46, 50 (1988).
[41] I borrow the term 'evolving norms of civility' from Professor Robert Post, who used it at the conference on which this volume is based ('Extreme Speech and Democracy', 22 April 2007) to

than ever, the media endeavours to produce what sells. Advertisers are matched with audiences to maximize profits in a rapidly changing media marketplace. Adaptation to the World Wide Web presents a serious challenge to traditional media outlets. To cynical eyes, Justice Holmes' notion of an exalted 'marketplace of ideas' has become little more than the marketplace.[42]

In recent years, mainstream media have largely overcome their fears about written ethics guidelines. Those fears may have been rooted in their lawyers' worries about plaintiffs' counsel using internal standards of care as evidence against media defendants in libel and breach of privacy lawsuits. In any event, newsroom ethics policies now abound and are having a salutary effect. When major media companies can pledge themselves to treat people with 'respect and compassion' and observe 'common standards of dignity,' they are doing as much to elevate the level of discourse—and reduce the repetition of hate speech—as the dicta in any lengthy judicial opinion.

In April 2007, just as the conference on which this volume is based was taking place, CBS Radio was scrambling to address the fallout from certain offensive speech used on-air by one of its most popular talk show hosts, Don Imus. The controversy presents an interesting case study of constraints imposed by the marketplace and evolving civility norms rather than by the force of law. Imus had described certain black female student athletes at Rutgers University as 'nappy-headed ho's'. It was not the first time he had spewed insults on air about blacks or, for that matter, other groups, using such terms as 'thieving Jews,' 'faggots' and 'lesbos'.[43] Pressure mounted on CBS to fire Imus. Network employees called on management to take action against him as did civil rights leaders and advertisers. In short order, the popular 'Imus in the Morning' was no more—at least not on CBS. To the extent litigation ensued, it involved only breach of contract claims. By definition, the Federal Communications Commission could not punish Imus' remarks as 'indecent'.[44] Months later, a repentant Imus found a new home on another network.

---

describe one key aspect of the informal regulatory framework that constrains the American media in the publication of extremist messages.

[42] *Abrams* v. *United States* 250 US 616, 630 (1919), dissenting opinion. '[W]hen men have realized that time has upset many fighting faiths, they may come to believe even more than they believe the very foundations of their own conduct that the ultimate good desired is better reached by free trade in ideas—that the best test of truth is the power of the thought to get itself accepted in the competition of the market, and that truth is the only ground upon which their wishes safely can be carried out. That, at any rate, is the theory of our Constitution. It is an experiment, as all life is an experiment.'

[43] D. Carr, 'Networks condemn remarks by Imus', *The New York Times*, 7 April 2007; A. Peyser, 'Ugly "diss" jockey can take the unfunny and run', *The New York Post*, 15 August 2007.

[44] The FCC consistently has defined an indecent broadcast as one that includes 'language or material that, in context, depicts or describes, in terms patently offensive as measured by contemporary community standards for the broadcast medium, sexual, or excretory organs or activities', <http://www.fcc.gov/cgb/consumerfacts/obscene.html> (last accessed 24 July 2008). See also *FCC* v. *Pacifica Foundation* 438 US 726 (1978).

Happily, there is little place for jail terms in America for messengers who stir the pot. As the Supreme Court said nearly 60 years ago, reversing a conviction for breach of peace, 'a function of free speech under our system of government is to invite dispute. It may indeed best serve its high purpose when it induces a condition of unrest, creates dissatisfaction with conditions as they are, or even stirs people to anger.'[45]

With its *Sullivan* decision in 1964, the Supreme Court ended the debate over the constitutionality of the Sedition Law. For the past half century, the Court has built strong judicial ramparts to protect the press from legal claims over various kinds of 'extreme' speech. At the same time, the press has become more dependent than ever on its acceptance by the public in the marketplace which, in turn, has found itself driven by a host of factors, including public pressure to improve civility and journalistic ethics. Indeed, the American marketplace, where civility competes with crudity for profit, functions as a loose regulatory framework for curbing extreme speech. The marketplace may be an imperfect enforcement mechanism, but it compliments and informs the judicial protections that the American media enjoy.

In America, we rely on speech and the press—and an informed public—to extinguish the fires of hate. But it requires constant vigilance. As Judge Learned Hand wrote in 1944: 'Liberty lies in the hearts of men and women; when it dies there, no constitution, no law, no court can save it.'[46]

---

[45] *Terminiello* v. *City of Chicago* 337 US 1, 4 (1949).
[46] *The Spirit of Liberty*, 3rd edn. (New York: Alfred A. Knopf, 1974), 189–90.

31

Extreme Speech and the Democratic Functions of the Mass Media

Jacob Rowbottom

A number of recent events have highlighted the difficult questions faced by the media when handling extreme speech. Such issues include whether the media should be free to publish the cartoons of the Prophet Mohammad that were at the centre of the Danish controversy, whether the broadcasters of *Celebrity Big Brother* in 2007 gave a platform to racist behaviour, and whether the media incited racial hatred by broadcasting a documentary featuring an Islamic preacher. These issues can be viewed from a range of different angles, such as the impact of the mass media on public order or its power to shape people's attitudes. However, this chapter will focus largely on the arguments to carry and restrict extreme speech that relate to the democratic functions assigned to the mass media, and examine some of the UK laws and regulations.

The term extreme speech is vague and can be used to describe a wide variety of expression, such as holocaust denial, extreme pornography, and speech inciting hatred or likely to provoke public disorder. The way the mass media should handle extreme speech will depend on the type of speech and its context, making any precise rules difficult to formulate. This chapter will merely attempt to sketch a general approach across a range of different types of expression and consider how the position of the mass media differs from that of the individual citizen. While recognizing the broad range of expression that can be labelled extreme, this chapter will primarily use the term to refer to expression that is seen to be discriminatory or perpetuate discriminatory attitudes. Given the theme of this volume in looking at the relationship between extreme speech and democracy, the focus will be on the democratic justification for media freedom. In particular, it will focus on the approach to news and current affairs in the media, rather than broader issues concerning, say, drama or entertainment, although these too may perform important functions in a democracy.

1. Media Freedom and Democracy

Many of the chapters in this volume focus on the impact of extreme speech on expression rights held by individual citizens. For example, Professor James Weinstein gives an account of freedom of expression as a channel of participation required by the commitment to political equality and popular sovereignty.[1] While freedom of expression and media freedom are closely related and are often treated as equivalents in UK law,[2] the premise of this chapter will be that the two are not to be treated identically. Greater emphasis tends to be given to the instrumental role of the media in serving the democratic needs of society and the audience.[3] Unlike the citizens' rights of freedom of expression, the protection of the media is not justified as a vehicle for the journalist, editor, or owner to pursue his or her own political views, but in the way it serves the audience and public as a whole. Consequently, under this approach the mass media may be subject to some burdens or have privileges that would be more problematic in the case of an individual citizen. Both the privileges and burdens applicable to the media may impact on its treatment of extreme speech and will be considered in the following sections.

On a number of occasions the European Court of Human Rights (ECtHR) has stressed the important democratic functions to be performed by the mass media. In *Observer and Guardian* v. *United Kingdom*, the ECtHR emphasized the importance of media freedom in the following terms:

Whilst it must not overstep the bounds set, inter alia, in the 'interests of national security' or for 'maintaining the authority of the judiciary', it is nevertheless incumbent on it to impart information and ideas on matters of public interest. Not only does the press have the task of imparting such information and ideas: the public also has a right to receive them. Were it otherwise, the press would be unable to play its vital role of 'public watchdog'.[4]

Under most accounts of democracy, the media will be expected to perform these functions. While the role of imparting information and ideas, and the 'public watchdog' function are generally taken together, the two could have different implications for the treatment of extreme speech. The public watchdog role will generally emphasize the need for protection against state interference and may require some special safeguards. The function of imparting information and ideas

---

[1] See ch. 2.

[2] For example, see *Attorney General* v. *Guardian Newspapers (No 2)* [1990] 1 AC 109, 183.

[3] For a discussion of the relationship between media freedom and freedom of expression, see J. Lichtenberg, 'Foundations and Limits of Freedom of the Press' in J. Lichtenberg (ed.), *Democracy and the Mass Media* (Cambridge: CUP, 1990); E. Barendt, *Freedom of Speech*, 2nd edn. (Oxford: OUP, 2005), 419–24; and H. Fenwick and G. Phillipson, *Media Freedom under the Human Rights Act* (Oxford: OUP, 2006), 20–32.

[4] (1992) 14 EHRR 153, para. 59.

is more complex and can be pursued in a number of different ways. The relationship between these functions and extreme speech will be considered in greater detail below.

(i) Public Watchdog

The term public watchdog suggests that the media performs its democratic function by holding the government and other public institutions to account, and exposing abuses of power.[5] Restrictions on the use of extreme speech could potentially hamper the media in performing this role. A blanket rule prohibiting the dissemination of racist statements could prevent a journalist from reporting primary evidence of, for example, racist attitudes within the police force.[6] There is also a concern that restrictions on extreme speech could be abused to censor certain viewpoints, such as some contributions to the debate on asylum and immigration. These concerns do not mean that there should be no restrictions on extreme speech, but rather that such restrictions should be framed in a way that preserve the scope for the media to investigate the government and other powerful institutions.

The ordinary laws that restrict extreme speech will normally apply to the media. Consequently, media entities may be prosecuted for expression that, for example, stirs up racial hatred, encourages terrorism, or is obscene. The issue is whether the application of such laws hampers the media's performance of the watchdog function. The jurisprudence of the ECtHR resolves this question by distinguishing between those directly expressing hate speech and those that are merely reporting on the views held by others. In the well-known case of *Jersild* v. *Denmark*, the ECtHR held that the conviction of a journalist for broadcasting the statements of a far right-wing group in a documentary violated freedom of expression under Article 10 of the European Convention on Human Rights (ECHR).[7] By contrast, a prosecution of the members of the group for making the neo-Nazi statements would be permitted, as such statements fall outside the scope of Article 10.[8] The distinction has been justified as the journalist merely informed the public of views that are held within the society, whereas the members of the group itself were advocating the extreme viewpoint. Such a distinction may seek to protect professional reporting that conveys events with a level of detachment.

---

[5] Under Art.10 jurisprudence this goes beyond investigating state institutions and can, for example, extend to major companies. See *Fressoz and Roire* v. *France* (1999) 5 BHRC 654, para. 50.

[6] For example, the BBC documentary *The Secret Policeman* broadcast on 21 October 2003 contained footage of officers using racist terms.

[7] (1995) 19 EHRR 1. The protection is not granted to the media as an institution, but rather to the activities normally undertaken by the media.

[8] See *Lehideux and Isornia* v. *France* (1998) 5 BHRC 540, para. 53.

The distinction made in *Jersild* is not always an easy one to apply. It is not clear what level of detachment is necessary to claim the role of reporter rather than advocate: whether it is sufficient to make clear that the views are not those of the journalist, or to challenge those views, or to condemn them.[9] The difficulties are also highlighted where a documentary maker edits the expression of others to give it the most sensational appearance.[10] Furthermore, if the effect of the content is to cause gross offence or stir up racial or religious hatred, then it may be questioned why the purpose of the journalist is so important.[11] This will be the case particularly where the reproduction of an image or use of a word is seen to cause harm regardless of the context. For example, the publication of the Danish cartoons or a pornographic image may cause the same offence regardless of whether it is part of a report.

While the Article 10 jurisprudence gives some leeway to journalists on the techniques to be used in reporting,[12] including 'recourse to a degree of exaggeration, or even provocation',[13] this is not without limits. Media institutions are to act responsibly when disseminating extreme speech, with reference to the particular context. For example, the ECtHR stated in *Surek and Ozdemir* v. *Turkey*, that the duties and responsibilities required of media professionals have 'special significance in situations of conflict and tension' and that they should take care not to incite violence against the state, and warned that the media should be cautious to ensure that it does not 'become a vehicle for the dissemination of hate speech and the promotion of violence'.[14] More recently, in *Stoll* v. *Switzerland*, the ECtHR stated that in light of the influence of the mass media, the protection given to journalists when reporting is 'subject to the proviso that they are acting in good faith and on an accurate factual basis and provide "reliable

---

[9] See the dissenting opinions of Judges Ryssdal, Bernhardt, Spielmann and Loizou in *Jersild* (n. 7 above), para. 3. The difficulties in applying this standard were recently highlighted in *Lindon* v. *France* [2007] ECHR 21279/02, in which the author of a novel that contained statements about the French *Front National* and its leader Jean-Marie Le Pen was convicted under French defamation laws. As a reaction against the conviction, the newspaper *Libération* published extracts from the novel and disputed that the content was defamatory. The newspaper was subsequently convicted under defamation laws. The ECtHR held that the liability of the newspaper did not violate Art.10 on the grounds that the newspaper did not show a sufficient level of detachment. Contrast with the partly dissenting opinion of Judges Rozakis, Bratza, Tulkens, and Šikuta.

[10] In *Jersild*, ibid., the dissenters highlighted that the journalist had 'cut the entire interview down to a few minutes, probably with the consequence or even the intention of retaining the most crude remarks'. The concern about the Channel Four documentary, *Undercover Mosque*, was that its editing may have distorted the views of the Islamic clerics featured. See *The Daily Telegraph*, 9 August 2007.

[11] E. Heinze, 'Viewpoint Absolutism and Hate Speech' (2006) 69 *Modern L. Rev.* 543, 561.

[12] *Jersild* (n. 7 above), para. 31.

[13] *Prager and Oberschlic* v. *Austria* (1996) 21 EHRR 1, para. 38.

[14] (1999) 7 BHRC 339, para. 63. On the facts, a conviction for publishing an interview with the leader of a proscribed organization violated Art. 10. Even though the interview was one-sided, the Court found it had 'a newsworthy content' in allowing the public 'to have an insight into the psychology of those who are the driving force behind the opposition to official policy in south-east Turkey', para. 61. See also *Erdogdu and Ince* v. *Turkey* [1999] ECHR 25067/94, para. 54.

and precise" information in accordance with the ethics of journalism.'[15] Consequently, heightened protection does not give the media carte blanche to publish
whatever it wants and the possible consequences of disseminating extreme speech
can be considered. Article 10 merely strikes a different balance to give the media
greater leeway when contributing to public debate. While the distinction between
advocating and reporting a particular viewpoint may not be watertight, it at least
provides some scope for media institutions to discharge their public function
responsibly, while preserving the goal of the hate speech laws.

The extent to which UK law follows the distinction made in *Jersild* is unclear.
Section 79 of the Criminal Justice and Immigration Act 2008 abolishes the
common law offence of blasphemy. Prior to its abolition, the media could have
been prosecuted for blasphemy, in theory at least, even if merely disseminating
the views of others, as that offence required intent to publish the material, rather
than specific intent to blaspheme.[16] Given the rarity of prosecutions under this
law, it was always unlikely that it would be used to curb media reporting. One
recent attempt to bring a private prosecution against the BBC for broadcasting
Jerry Springer the Opera failed on the grounds that the broadcasting laws shield
broadcasters from this offence, and in any event the public order elements of the
offence had not been made out.[17] While the chances of a prosecution were always
remote, the abolition of the offence will remove any remaining concerns.

A number of offences under the Public Order Act 1986 concern expression
that incites racial hatred.[18] For example, it is an offence to broadcast or include in
a programme or a cable service content that involves threatening, abusive, or
insulting visual images or sounds, if it is intended (by the broadcaster, producer,
director, or speaker) to stir up racial hatred or is likely in all the circumstances to
stir up racial hatred.[19] A similar offence applies to the publication or dissemination of written material that stirs up racial hatred.[20] As such offences can be
committed without the intent to stir up racial hated, it is possible that a media
entity could be prosecuted when reporting the racist speech of others. While there
are a number of defences available to those not intending to stir up racial hatred,
there is no broad defence that such expression was in the context of a news
report.[21] However, the chances of such a prosecution being brought are narrowed

---

[15] *Stoll* v. *Switzerland* [2007] ECHR 69698/01 at para. 103.

[16] *R* v. *Lemon* [1979] AC 617. There was speculation that the broadcaster Joan Bakewell would
face prosecution for reading excerpts of the poem in question in *Lemon* in a BBC TV series in 2001,
The Observer, 3 March 2002.

[17] *R (on the application of Green)* v. *City of Westminster Magistrates' Court* [2007] EWHC 2785
(Admin). The claimant, a member of the group *Christian Voice*, challenged a District Judge's refusal
to issue a summons for a private prosecution of the Director General of the BBC. The statutory
protection for broadcasters is provided under Broadcasting Act 1990, Sched. 15.

[18] The Public Order Act 1986, s. 17 defines racial hatred as 'hatred against a group of
persons ... defined by reference to colour, race, nationality (including citizenship) or ethnic or
national origins'.

[19] The Public Order Act 1986, s. 22.   [20] The Public Order Act 1986, s. 19.

[21] Fenwick and Phillipson (n. 3 above), 514.

by the requirement for the Attorney General's consent.[22] Furthermore, the reference to the likelihood of racial hatred being stirred up in 'all the circumstances' where there is no intent makes it less likely that statements made in the context of a media report will constitute an offence.[23] However, the potential for such a provision to be invoked against the media when reporting is real and the prosecution of programme makers has been considered on some occasions.[24]

By contrast, the position with the offence of inciting religious hatred is clearer as the offence is drawn more narrowly than racial hatred laws. The expression has to be 'threatening' and intent to stir up religious hatred is necessary.[25] The religious hatred offence also contains a broad defence to protect freedom of expression that is likely to protect the media when reporting.[26] The offence of 'encouragement of terrorism' enacted in 2006 should also preserve the scope for the media to report the views of others given that the publisher must intend or be reckless as to whether the statement will encourage others to commit terrorism offences.[27] Even if a media entity can be shown to be reckless to such an effect, it is still a defence for those without intent to encourage acts of terrorism, to show 'that the statement neither expressed his views nor had his endorsement' and that this was clear in all the circumstances.[28] While the law on racial hatred appears least clear in relation to the position of the media, the more recently enacted restrictions on extreme speech appear to give some protection to the *Jersild* principle.

(ii) Diverse Information and Ideas

While most accounts of the media in a democracy stress the importance of the watchdog function, this suggests a relatively narrow role for the media in serving democratic needs. The other function emphasized by the ECtHR is imparting ideas and information. The *Jersild* principle will be just as important in this function, where the media report on the views of others. This role for the media can be taken to mean something much more for a democracy than the simple

---

[22] The Public Order Act 1986, s. 27.

[23] Fenwick and Phillipson (n. 3 above), 514.

[24] For example, the Crown Prosecution Service considered prosecuting Channel 4 for the documentary *Undercover Mosque* broadcast in January 2007, but concluded there was insufficient evidence. See Crown Prosecution Service press release, 8 August 2007.

[25] The Public Order Act 1986, ss. 29B–F. The offence of inciting religious hatred applies only to statements that are threatening, whereas racial hatred laws apply to those which are threatening, abusive, and insulting.

[26] The Public Order Act 1986, s. 29J provides 'Nothing in this Part shall be read or given effect in a way which prohibits or restricts discussion, criticism, or expressions of antipathy, dislike, ridicule, insult, or abuse of particular religions or the beliefs or practices of their adherents, or of any other belief system or the beliefs or practices of its adherents, or proselytizing or urging adherents of a different religion or belief system to cease practising their religion or belief system'.

[27] Terrorism Act 2006, s.1.

[28] The Terrorism Act 2006, s. 1(6). See also s. 2(9) for a defence to the dissemination offence and s. 3 for the notice and take down provisions applicable to Internet Service Providers.

delivery of information and can be subdivided into a range of more specific functions, such as providing diverse viewpoints, acting as a space for political actors to participate, and a forum for deliberation.[29] Such functions extend the role of the media beyond the provision of information and education of the audience and suggest a further purpose of serving citizens as participants in the democratic process. Given that most citizens cannot speak on, or participate in, the mass media, this broader function will still be performed through the provision of content to a wide audience. For example, allowing citizens to see their views and interests represented in the media can foster a sense of inclusion in the democratic process. Broadly speaking, this function for the media in providing a range of information and views can be consistent with differing accounts of democracy that prescribe varying levels of direct participation for the citizen. This chapter does not seek to examine all the ways the media can serve different democratic theories, but will consider two contrasting approaches to the media: the public service media and that of a partisan media, to illustrate how the concerns about extreme speech can vary.

(a) A Public Service Model

Under the public service model, one goal for the media is to provide a range of different viewpoints to a wide audience comprising different sections of society. It enables citizens to hear views and information of which they were not previously aware and with which they may disagree. The media acts as a space in which citizens can be persuaded by new views and can see ideas and arguments being contested. In this way, the public service model designates the media as a type of forum for deliberation among different views and interests. Its goal need not be consensus or agreement, but at least allows the points of disagreement to be understood and gives a place for mediation between the different views. James Curran describes the public service media as a place:

> where people come together to engage in a reciprocal debate about the management of society . . . It reports the news with due impartiality, and gives space to different views.[30]

In the United States, such a model for the mass media is sometimes described as a 'republican model', which Edwin Baker describes as having the following features:

> First, the press should be thoughtfully discursive, not merely factually informative. It should support reflection and value or policy choice. Second, this discursive press must be

---

[29] For a discussion of the relation between models of democracy and journalism, see J. Strömbäck, 'In Search of a Standard: Four Models of Democracy and Their Normative Implications for Journalism' (2005) 6 *Journalism Studies* 331; C. E. Baker, *Media, Markets, and Democracy* (Cambridge: CUP, 2002), chs. 6–8. The account of the different functions given in this chapter draws on the work of James Curran and Edwin Baker.

[30] J. Curran, *Media and Power* (London: Routledge, 2002), 245, looking to the German broadcasting model as an example.

inclusive. The democratic pursuit of, and hopefully agreement on, a real common good requires an inclusive public discourse... The press ideally should be civil, objective, balanced, and comprehensive—although some slippage in the first three might be allowed if necessary in order to not overly restrict participation.[31]

Such a model requires that the media be impartial in its coverage of politics, in which no particular viewpoint is to be privileged, and emphasizes professional standards in reporting. It also permits some level of internal pluralism, in which the media provides a range of partial views, but an overall variety ensures that no single perspective dominates the coverage of news and current affairs.

How these elements should be combined and whether the public service is best served by focusing on impartial reporting or a diverse range of partial sources is a continuing debate in media policy. While there are different approaches to public service media, the important point at present is that it seeks to serve the public as a whole. The public service media is not reduced to a passive conduit for others and plays an active role in interpreting political stories and critically analysing the approaches taken by political actors. In these roles, the public service media acts as a trusted source of information and analysis. However, the public service media is distinct from other political actors operating within the forum and itself constitutes a place for participants in the political process to engage with one another.[32] The requirement that the media be inclusive may lead to demands that those extreme speakers whose activities are lawful receive some impartial coverage in the public service media. This question will be considered more fully in relation to the UK broadcast media below.

The position in relation to extreme speech is additionally complicated as some limits on expression in the public service media may be imposed to further its functions in exchanging ideas and mediating between different views. As Professor Baker notes, there may be some demand under this model for civility in the media as, if 'discourse is to be inclusive, then speech that denigrates other potential participants in the debate is not helpful'.[33] Professor Curran similarly states that if the public service media is to be a place for conciliation and compromise, then it should be governed by norms including:

civility, a way of expressing disagreement that does not seek to delegitimate or marginalize opponents through personal invective; *empathy*, a desire to comprehend other groups through sympathetic understanding; *mutuality*, a feeling of being connected to society, and being concerned about the well-being of others...[34]

Such norms may justify the restriction of certain forms of extreme speech, and the manner in which it is expressed. Civility requires that expression in the public service media respect the dignity and moral status of other citizens. Such limits

---

[31] Baker (n. 29 above), 148–9. [32] J. Lichtenberg (n. 3 above), 123.
[33] Baker (n. 29 above), 173.
[34] J. Curran, 'Reinterpreting the Democratic Roles of the Media' (2007) 3 *Brazilian Journalism Research* 31, 40.

may be thought to be central to the goals of the media as a universal forum, in creating a climate for views to be received with an open mind. The dissemination of extreme speech through the mass media could emphasize and heighten divisions in society, which in turn undermines the capacity for any mediation between these diverse views. Civility norms can also help ensure that the public service media retains its universal appeal, without driving away certain sections of society that feel their status has been attacked. This may result in additional restrictions being imposed on expression that would otherwise be lawful if said by a citizen off the media. This is not to give a licence for censorship on the public service media. However, the factors determining the necessity of such a restriction on the public service media are different from those considered in relation to an individual citizen.

Consequently, there is a difficult balancing act involved in the public service media. On the one hand, there is the need to include a wide range of views held within society, including the unpopular and controversial. On the other, some limits based on civility may be required to pursue those public service goals.

(b) A Partisan Media

The second model, labelled here the partisan media, does not aim to bring together all different parts of society, but attempts to permit the media to represent different views without being constrained by balance or impartiality. This still aims to permit diverse views and information to be accessed by the citizens, but does so through external pluralism in which a range of different media outlets pursue a partisan line. This differs from the public service model in that the media does not attempt to mediate between competing viewpoints, but will advocate a particular view. The media still performs a social function and is still justified instrumentally, but its role is closer to that of a citizen.[35] When viewed in this way, the partisan media is connected to freedom of association in which groups of like-minded citizens come together to pursue a view or interest. However, its role as an advocate means that it may lack the detachment necessary to benefit from the *Jersild* principle where there are general limitations on extreme speech.

Such a role is sometimes associated with a liberal pluralist model for the media, in which politics is characterized as a competition between different factions and bringing conflict into the open.[36] Along these lines, the media may play a role in the overall bargaining process between different parts of society.[37] Under this approach, the media entity may communicate views it claims to represent, mobilize that audience to a particular cause or issue, and reinforce some of the audiences' views. However, this model need not be tied to the pluralist account of politics. For example, an account that sees politics as pursuing the common good

---

[35] J. Lichtenberg, n. 3 above.   [36] Baker, n. 29 above.
[37] See D. Hallin and P. Mancini, *Comparing Media Systems: Three Models of Media and Politics* (Cambridge: CUP, 2004), 132–3.

may still assign a partisan role to some media entities and allow other institutions to perform the function of mediation.

Under the partisan model, the media will be under no duty to carry or engage with extreme speech. However, it may choose to do so, whether to advocate or criticize such a point of view. Such an approach is more likely to be sceptical of extreme speech restrictions that can inhibit the capacity of the media to advocate particular views. For example, if an extreme political party or interest group produces its own newsletter, this may include extreme speech as part of its own message. Given that it is not performing a universal or mediating role, the demands for civility advanced above will be weaker.

However, there will still be concerns about extreme speech. If it is decided that there is no place for a particular view in political life, for example in instances where a political party is banned or certain speech is made illegal, then similar curbs may be imposed on the partisan press. Even in less extreme circumstances, there may be calls for limits. Whatever harms are to be attributed to extreme speech (for example through a silencing effect or inciting hatred and violence), these are potentially brought about on a much greater scale if widely disseminated through the media. Similarly, some extreme speech restrictions may arguably be justified on the grounds that the particular media is intrusive. There may also be restraints demanding accuracy in the content of such media, which may indirectly restrain some extreme speech. While some restrictions may be justified along these lines, it is distinct from the broader demands of the public service model, and care will need to be taken to ensure that it does not undermine the capacity of the media to act as an advocate or representative in this sector.

The partisan media should not simply be equated with a free market. State support could be used to ensure that a diverse range of media is available. For example, the state can provide a subsidy to establish media titles that represent minority viewpoints or give funding to a political party to establish its own communications. If external pluralism is pursued in the broadcast media through a range of partisan channels,[38] then licences may be distributed in a way that ensures that each channel reflects a distinct view or outlook. This model could also be pursued through other policies such as internal pluralism, although unlike the public service model, it will seek to serve a more limited audience rather than bring diverse views to the public as a whole. The partisan model for the media need not be a space completely free of regulation, but it will be more resistant to restrictions imposing civility norms.

There are many variations of the different democratic functions of the media, and the two models presented above are given as examples on different ends of the spectrum. There are many other models and variations that sit between the two extremes. Furthermore neither model needs to describe the entirety of the media in any system. Some scholars have called for a mix of these different models with

---

[38] Ofcom discussion document, *New News Future News*, July 2007, 71.

different sectors of the media following the partisan and public service media approach.[39] The models above need not spell any specific legal restrictions and it may be argued that self-regulation/restraint on the part of the media entity is sufficient to fulfil these goals. While neither of these goals need be explicitly stated as the purpose of UK media regulations, the remainder of this chapter will examine the regulations and consider how these different democratic functions are reflected.

2. Extreme Speech and Media Regulation

As stated above, some regulations to further these democratic functions may be permissible on the mass media, which would not be appropriate for an individual citizen. Before looking at the content of the regulations, a few points should be noted about the nature of media regulation. While hate speech laws are often criticized as too blunt, media regulations tend to permit greater flexibility in guiding media institutions to perform their functions responsibly and meet certain standards, rather than seeking rigid enforcement. Unlike criminal law sanctions, media regulations do not completely banish the extreme speech from political debate, but rather prevent its communication in certain forums. The consequences of a breach may be less severe, such as a formal reprimand or fine. Such flexibility raises other concerns, including the clarity of the standards and consistency of enforcement. The regulations also place much discretion in the hands of the regulator, as the courts have generally been reluctant to interfere with their decisions. While regulations may be permitted to promote these democratic functions, care should be taken to ensure that such regulations are not used to mask an ulterior motive and that the power to formulate and apply the standards is not abused.

In the UK, the broadcast media, other than the BBC, is regulated by a statutory body, Ofcom, which is charged with the task of drafting and enforcing a Code of Practice for broadcasting standards.[40] The BBC is established by Royal Charter and standards are enforced by the BBC Trust.[41] By contrast, newspapers are subject to a Code of Practice drawn up and enforced by a self-regulatory body, the Press Complaints Commission (PCC).[42] Despite the differences between the

---

[39] Curran (n. 30 above), ch. 8. For a similar argument concerning the different regulatory regimes for the print and broadcast media in the US, see L. Bollinger, 'Freedom of the Press and Public Access: Toward a Theory of Partial Regulation of the Mass Media' (1976) 75 *Mich. L. Rev.* 1.

[40] Ofcom Broadcasting Code, July 2005, <http://www.ofcom.org.uk/tv/ifi/codes/bcode/> (last accessed 24 July 2008). If a breach of the Code is found, Ofcom can impose the following sanctions on broadcasters: a direction not to repeat a programme; a direction to broadcast a correction or a statement of Ofcom's finding; a financial penalty; or shortening/revoking a broadcast licence (not applicable to the BBC, S4C, and Channel 4).

[41] Although some standards, including those on offensiveness, can be referred to Ofcom.

[42] The PCC will first attempt to resolve complaints informally. However, if such a resolution is not reached and a breach of the Code is found, then the publication has to publish the adjudication in full in its own pages.

print and broadcast media, it is worth noting that in so far as both codes target discriminatory treatment, both go beyond racial and religious hatred that are normally the target of hate speech laws. The PCC Code of Practice states that the press must avoid prejudicial or pejorative references not only to an individual's race, colour, or religion, but also to their gender, sexual orientation, or any physical or mental illness, or disability. For example, newspapers should not use terms such as 'nutter' to describe someone with a mental illness.[43] While no law forbids such a statement from being made by an individual citizen, it would fall foul of the media regulations.

(i) The Broadcast Media

In the UK, different broadcasters are subject to varying levels of public service obligations.[44] While these obligations serve a range of purposes, one set of rules about news and current affairs seems related to the public service model described above. All news on the broadcast media must be reported and presented with 'due impartiality'.[45] Similarly, television and national radio services must preserve due impartiality 'on matters of political or industrial controversy and matters relating to current public policy', although this standard can be met in a single programme or 'generally in relation to a series of programmes taken as a whole'.[46] This permits broadcasters to include programmes that advance a particular viewpoint in greater depth, but alternative viewpoints must be included in other programmes on that service. The rules also prohibit editorializing by a broadcaster. Special impartiality rules apply at the time of an election to ensure that political parties and candidates are treated fairly, although major political parties will be given greater attention.[47] Given that the courts in the UK have generally been reluctant to intervene in the decisions of the regulators concerning these impartiality rules,[48] broadcasters and regulators have considerable discretion in deciding how to pursue these public service goals.

---

[43] See PCC Guidance Note, *On reporting mental health issues* (2006). Before the PCC guidance was published, *The Sun* on 23 September 2003 published the headline 'Bonkers Bruno Locked Up', referring to the former boxer Frank Bruno's treatment for depression. The public response forced *The Sun* to change its headline for later editions to 'Sad Bruno in Mental Home'.

[44] See Communications Act 2003, pt. 3 ch. 4.

[45] See Communications Act 2003, s. 319(2)(c); Department of Culture Media and Sport, *Broadcasting: An Agreement Between Her Majesty's Secretary of State for Culture, Media and Sport and the British Broadcasting Corporation*, Cm 6872 (2006) (BBC Agreement), cl. 44; For further guidance see BBC Editorial Guidelines (2005), s. 4 'Impartiality and Diversity of Opinion', and Ofcom Broadcasting Code, s. 5.

[46] Communications Act 2003, s. 320. Local radio services are subject to a requirement not to give 'undue prominence' to any particular view or body.

[47] Ofcom Broadcasting Code, s. 6.

[48] T. Gibbons, *Regulating the Media*, 2nd edn. (London: Sweet & Maxwell, 1998), 118. See *Lynch* v. *BBC* [1983] NI 193; *R* v. *BBC, ex p Referendum Party* [1997] EMLR 605; *R* v. *BCC, ex p Owen* [1985] QB 1153; *R (on the application of Boyd Hunt)* v. *ITC* [2002] EWHC 2296 (Admin). For examples where the courts in Scotland have been willing to intervene, see *Wilson* v. *Independent Broadcasting Authority* [1979] SC 351 and *Houston* v. *BBC* [1995] SC 433.

These obligations lead to the question of whether the broadcast media needs to include extreme speech as part of its impartial coverage. A broadcaster need not cover, or be impartial towards, viewpoints that are contrary to fundamental democratic principles and will generally oppose racism and intolerance, for example.[49] This is unsurprising given that that the public service media is deemed to be a place that brings different sections of society together in the name of democracy. While speech challenging fundamental values may be included in coverage, it will tend to be subject to criticism. However, one difficulty with this approach is that it will not always be clear which types of viewpoint are truly opposed to fundamental values, as very few speakers will admit such a position openly. Some speakers may express extreme views but claim to work within the parameters of the constitutional system. How such speakers should be treated raises more difficult issues for the broadcaster dealing with provisions on impartiality.

The rules do not require strict neutrality on all political matters or equality among all viewpoints or political actors.[50] Instead, the requirements of 'due impartiality' depend on factors such as the subject matter and expectations of the audience. Given the difficulties in selecting the different sides to an argument and determining the leading representatives, there is no requirement that views held by a minority or on the fringes of political debate are given equal coverage or prominence as is given to other more mainstream views. The selection of issues and views in the BBC's coverage of politics was at one time 'anchored to views already expressed in Parliament'.[51] However, such an approach has its limits and would exclude those views that have not organized themselves within the formal political process.[52] Such exclusion could undermine the public service function if it encourages some sections of the audience to turn to other media sources that do reflect their views.[53] A broader view of diversity allows those outside formal politics to be represented in the media. This would include giving greater prominence to interest groups and may also require journalists to search further for views that have not been organized and have no high-profile advocates.

---

[49] See Lord Annan (Chairman), *Report of the Committee on the Future of Broadcasting,* Cmnd 6753, Annan Committee, (London: HMSO, 1977), para. 17.21. However, compare the view of the Annan Committee (para. 18.14) on access programmes, in which broadcasters may have to let strongly opinionated groups express views that 'stir up hatred over issues such as immigration'. See also Gibbons, ibid., 108–109.

[50] Ofcom Broadcasting Code, s. 5: '"due impartiality" does not mean an equal division of time has to be given to every view, or that every argument and every facet of every argument has to be represented.' For the BBC, see the BBC Editorial Guidelines (2005), s. 4.

[51] BBC Trust, *From Seesaw to Wagon Wheel: Safeguarding Impartiality in the 21st Century* (June 2007), 33.

[52] *New News Future News,* (n. 38 above), para. 5.42 refers to concerns that under current impartiality rules views 'that do not fit easily within a conventional "both sides of the argument" approach can struggle to be heard'. See also A. Boyle, 'Political Broadcasting, Fairness and Administrative Law' [1986] *Pub. L.* 562, 574.

[53] BBC Trust (n. 51 above), 64. See also *New News Future News,* ibid., paras. 5.22–5.28.

However, if such a broader approach is taken, it becomes harder to determine which views should be covered and how much weight and attention given to each view. If the level of coverage is not roughly proportionate to popular support for that position, then it may increase the demand to include more extreme viewpoints.[54]

While broadcasters do look beyond parliamentary politics, there are arguments that they should do so to a greater extent. The traditional approach of public service broadcasting is thought to be under increasing strain as a result of various changes in the political landscape (such as the changes in traditional party divisions, polarization on some issues, and the role of single-issue groups), so that politics can no longer be seen to be about balancing two main sides of an argument.[55] A report from the BBC in 2007 stated that the 'parameters of "normality" and "extremism" have shifted' and the broadcaster should be more willing to bring in diverse views that may be thought of as extreme.[56] Similarly, in late 2006 Peter Horrocks, Head of Television News at the BBC, called for a model of 'radical impartiality' in which audiences should 'be prepared to hear from those whose views many of our viewers may find abhorrent'. Horrocks elaborates:

Instead I believe we need to consider adopting what I like to think of as a much wider 'radical impartiality'—the need to hear the widest range of views—all sides of the story. So we need more Taleban interviews, more BNP interviews—of course put on air with due consideration—and the full range of moderate opinions. All those views need to be treated with the same level of sceptical inquiry and respect . . . This wider range of opinion is a worthwhile price to pay to maintain a national forum where all can feel they are represented and respected.[57]

Some demand for such an approach can also be found in the quantative research commissioned by the BBC, which showed that 83 per cent of those surveyed thought that 'broadcasters should report on all views and opinions, however unpopular or extreme some of them may be'.[58]

Peter Horrocks also stated that allowing such diverse of views to be heard creates 'a common approach to understanding'.[59] Consequently, under this view, the BBC should not simply become a conduit for competing views and Horrocks would maintain the role of the broadcaster as a forum for mediation, fitting with the account of a public service media given above. It is unclear whether such a broader approach to impartiality is simply to cover such views through mediated politics and subject them to rigorous criticism, or whether it should also entail more authored programmes in which the extreme speaker can advance his or her

---

[54] See Gibbons (n. 48 above), 110.   [55] BBC Trust (n. 51 above), 36.

[56] BBC Trust (n. 51 above), 37.

[57] P. Horrocks, 'Finding TV news' lost audience', a lecture to the *Reuters* Institute of Journalism and St Anne's College, Oxford, 28 November 2006.

[58] BBC Trust (n. 51 above), 20–1.   [59] Horrocks, n. 57 above.

views. The latter approach is likely to be the more controversial. However, under either approach, if the obligations on a public service broadcaster lead to the inclusion of some extreme views, then it may create a tension with the civility norms outlined above that are thought to be an element of a public service media.

Protection of such civility norms can be found in the broadcasting regulations. For example, clause 2.3 of the Ofcom Broadcasting Code provides that 'broadcasters must ensure that material which may cause offence is justified by the context' and then specifies:[60]

Such material may include, but is not limited to, offensive language, violence, sex, sexual violence, humiliation, distress, violation of human dignity, discriminatory treatment or language (for example on the grounds of age, disability, gender, race, religion, beliefs and sexual orientation).

While not specifically concerned with extreme speech, the rule could limit the potential for such material to be broadcast. While such restrictions are often justified in terms of the pervasiveness of the broadcast media,[61] this can partly be related to the universality of the public service function. The argument that those potentially offended can simply turn over to another channel may defeat the purpose in bringing everyone together to see new and challenging views. This does not mean that every programme must never offend, that television should avoid controversy, or that niche programmes are not permitted. However, such programming must be considered in relation to the public service function. Similarly, the Ofcom Code provides special rules on the coverage of religion and states: 'religious views and beliefs of those belonging to a particular religion or religious denomination must not be subject to abusive treatment'.[62] The Ofcom Code further provides that material that encourages or incites the commission of a crime is not to be included in broadcast material,[63] which limits expression that is likely to incite religious or racial hatred. Regulations of accuracy may also impose some indirect limits on extreme speech and the way such messages are conveyed.[64]

The broadcasting regulations also aim to prevent stereotypes being used to perpetuate discriminatory attitudes.[65] This partly addresses the concern that hate

---

[60] For similar provisions, see the BBC Editorial Guidelines (2005), s. 8, 'Harm and offence'. The Television Without Frontiers Directive, Art. 22, also requires that material that incites racial hatred is not broadcast.

[61] See Barendt (n. 3 above), 446, and *R (on the application of ProLife Alliance) v. BBC* [2003] UKHL 23, [2004] AC 185, paras. 20–1.

[62] Ofcom Broadcasting Code, s. 4; BBC Editorial Guidelines (2005), in s. 12, provides 'we recognize our duty to protect the vulnerable and avoid unjustified offence or likely harm. We aim to achieve this by ensuring our output is not used to denigrate the beliefs of others.'

[63] Ofcom Broadcasting Code, s. 3; BBC Editorial Guidelines (2005), s. 7 on inciting crime, and s. 11 on covering terror and emergencies.

[64] Ofcom Broadcasting Code, s. 5; BBC Editorial Guidelines (2005), s. 3.

[65] Ofcom Broadcasting Code Guidance Notes on s. 2 (August 2007) provides 'Broadcasters should take particular care in their portrayal of culturally diverse matters and should avoid

speech laws are ineffective and merely force the discriminatory speech into more subtle and persuasive forms, such as stereotyping. Such a rule also reflects the concerns that the broadcast media does shape social attitudes and shows how broadcasters must take care when dealing with extreme speech on account of their trusted status. While it is hard to enforce a provision in relation to stereotyping, it does operate as a guideline for broadcasters and in cases where such a stereotype has been used, Ofcom can provide a warning. This does, of course, raise the very difficult question of when a particular characterization can be deemed to be a stereotype, but the more flexible provisions of the regulatory code are better suited to this task than criminal law sanctions.

The tension between the civility norms and the requirement to carry diverse views can be seen in the case of party election broadcasts. Major political parties and registered parties contesting one sixth of the seats up for election qualify for at least one free broadcast on certain channels.[66] Such a system represents a limited form of internal pluralism in which the political parties have direct, unmediated access to the broadcast media. On a number of occasions, parties such as the British National Party (BNP) have qualified for an election broadcast. For example, in the 2004 European elections, the BNP sought to air an election broadcast on Channel Five concerning allegations of anti-white crimes being committed by Asian men in West Yorkshire.[67] Channel Five refused to show this broadcast on the grounds that it was likely to stir up racial hatred, as prohibited by the broadcasting regulations, and required a number of parts to be cut. The BNP decided not to pursue its original message in the broadcast, but used the broadcast to complain of censorship.[68] Despite the number of cuts, complaints were made to Ofcom about this and other BNP broadcasts. Ofcom rejected the complaints and found that, after the cuts, the broadcasts were not inflammatory or offensive as the content was not targeted at Muslims in general.[69]

While Channel Five's main concern was that the broadcast would incite racial hatred (raising the concerns about public order and potential criminal liability), the broadcaster's discretion is not restricted to such extreme cases. For example, if a political party seeks to broadcast content that does not incite hatred, but does rely on a stereotype of an ethnic minority to communicate its message, there is an

---

stereotyping unless editorially justified. When considering such matters, broadcasters should take into account the possible effects programmes may have on particular sections of the community'. See also the BBC Editorial Guidelines (2005), s. 8.

[66] See Ofcom Rules on Party Political and Referendum Broadcasts (2004). For the BBC see cl. 48 of the BBC Agreement, n. 45 above.

[67] Ofcom Programme Complaints Bulletin, Issue 18, 20 September 2004.

[68] 'BNP forced to edit election film', *BBC News*, 29 May 2004, <http://news.bbc.co.uk/1/hi/uk_politics/3757641.stm> (last accessed 24 July 2008).

[69] Ofcom Programme Complaints Bulletin, Issue 18, 20 September 2004. A similar complaint about a BNP party election broadcast was also rejected by Ofcom's predecessor, the Independent Television Commission (ITC), on the grounds that it did not refer race and immigration, but solely to EU membership (ITC adjudication, 1 June 1999).

arguable case that the broadcaster could refuse to air it on the grounds that it would violate the broadcast regulations discussed above. It is unlikely that a court would hold that such a restriction violates freedom of expression under Article 10 following the decision in *Prolife Alliance*, in which the House of Lords upheld an application of the taste and decency standards to a party election broadcast.[70] This example highlights the tension faced by broadcasters in providing access to diverse views while maintaining civility rules, but also shows how the two can co-exist.

Such tensions could increase if the broader approach to impartiality discussed above is taken. The regulations do not amount to an outright prohibition on offensive words or content, but require that the inclusion of material that may cause offence be 'justified by the context'.[71] This permits the broadcast of controversial and challenging material, but there should be some warning to shape audience expectations and it should not be broadcast at a time when children are watching. The approach permits the reporting of extreme and offensive views under the *Jersild* principle outlined above. For example, Ofcom's predecessor, the Independent Television Commission (ITC), rejected complaints about giving the individuals accused of murdering Stephen Lawrence airtime on an interview with Martin Bashir, on the grounds that they had not been given a platform but had been subject to difficult questioning by the interviewer.[72] However, the broadcaster cannot merely act as a conduit for the extreme speaker and must challenge the views being presented. Outside the context of politics, in the high profile ruling on *Celebrity Big Brother* in 2007, Channel Four argued that in broadcasting some incidents that could be interpreted as racist, it was merely conveying what the contestants had said and done and in so doing stimulated a debate about race that was of public value. Despite accepting similar arguments in previous rulings,[73] Ofcom found that Channel Four did not sufficiently moderate the incidents and did not do enough to challenge the allegedly racist behaviour.[74] Exactly what level of moderating is required is difficult to state with any precision, which again highlights the difficulties faced by a broadcaster in showing the necessary level of detachment.

The broadcast regulations have been interpreted in a way that permits provocative authored programmes that advance a particular viewpoint on sensitive topics, such as immigration, and are critical of religion or particular faiths.[75]

---

[70] *ProLife Alliance*, n. 61 above.   [71] Ofcom Broadcasting Code, s. 2.
[72] ITC adjudication, 1 June 1999.
[73] Ofcom Broadcast Bulletin, Issue 50, 19 December 2005.
[74] Ofcom Content Sanctions Committee, 24 May 2007.
[75] Ofcom Broadcast Bulletin, Issue 61, finding that Richard Dawkins' *The Root of All Evil* did not breach the Code as the broadcaster had made clear it was an opinion piece and had also broadcast other views; Ofcom Broadcast Bulletin, Issue 59, finding that a Channel Four programme that was critical of evangelical christianity was not in breach of the Code; Ofcom Broadcast Bulletin, Issue 48 finding that a Channel Four documentary, *Immigration Is a Time Bomb*, was not in breach even though it included interviews with the BNP: 'The programme dealt with a series of uncomfortable

However, care must be taken to ensure that the controversial stance does not cross the line breaching the rules on offensiveness outlined above. The competing pressures faced by broadcasters can be seen from the Channel Four documentary *The Edge of the City*, which followed the activities of social workers in Bradford. The programme featured allegations that a paedophile ring organized by Asian men targeted white girls and highlighted the difficulties in bringing charges against them. The documentary was criticized for publicizing the allegations in a way that emphasized the racial dimension.[76] However, further concerns arose from the impact on public order. The documentary was not shown in the run-up to the May 2004 local elections (as originally planned) following a request from the West Yorkshire police fearing that it could stir up racial tensions in the area and after the documentary had been seized upon by the BNP during their campaign. That the documentary was eventually shown in August 2004, after the elections had taken place, shows how the content that can be broadcast varies according to the surrounding circumstances. Even though the programme investigated the views of others, the principle stated by the ECtHR in *Surek* outlined above emphasizes the need to take into account the context. While such concerns about the provocation of violence and racial tensions apply across all the mass media, the public service sector may have special responsibilities. By reaching a wide audience and through its status as a trusted source of information, the public service media has a powerful impact and should avoid exacerbating social divisions. Even if its own programme is not hate speech, some consideration must be taken of the danger that it could be seized upon by extreme speakers. This is not to criticize the broadcast of such programmes, but is rather to highlight the care that must be taken by the public service media and competing pressures faced in making such programmes.

One element of public service broadcasting has been considered which reflects the need for a common forum. This does not prevent the production of niche and specialist programmes and the common forum function may be achieved in a range of ways, such as programmes targeting specific cross sections of the public. From the cases considered above, the imposition of standards requiring impartiality and some civility norms do not appear to deter broadcasters from making controversial programmes on political issues. If broadcasters wish to go further down this path (with the broader approach to impartiality discussed above), there is scope within the regulations to do so. The approach does, however, mean the broadcaster will face a number of competing pressures. Furthermore, the standards to be met are hard to state with precision and will often depend on the context. This also increases the danger of seemingly inconsistent decisions by

---

issues and did so in a way which was provocative, but not racist or anti-Islamic. A distinction was made between those Muslims with more "radical" views and those with moderate interpretations of Islam.'

[76] See T. Branigan, 'Blame on the Edge', *The Guardian*, 17 August 2004.

the regulators. However, such difficulties are arguably less problematic in the case of media regulations, as opposed to criminal sanctions that apply to all speakers, and should not deter the broadcast regulators from attempting to manage such competing pressures.

(ii) The Press

The press covers a wide range of media performing different democratic functions and it is difficult to make generalizations. Some print media titles will clearly represent the partisan press described above, such as publications produced by a political party or magazines catering to a niche audience. Political magazines such as the *Spectator* and the *New Statesman* also tend to represent and advocate a particular political outlook. It is more difficult to categorize the national press. At first sight, it may appear to fit into the category of the partisan press as such titles can editorialize and pursue its own political stance. However, the days of the overt link between political parties and national newspapers through direct ownership are long gone. Instead the claim to represent its audience tends to be derived from its response to readers' preferences in the marketplace. However, the capacity of the market to provide media that truly represents its audience has been doubted,[77] and it is distinct from the party-controlled press. Furthermore, advocacy is not the sole function of the national press. In the case of the so-called quality newspapers at least, the press aims to provide professional journalism, which is evidenced in the division between reporting and commentary. How the balance is struck between the two varies among titles and concern has been expressed recently that the boundary between the two is becoming blurred.[78] The national press therefore seems to occupy a position that is somewhere between the partisan and public service models. Even if not truly representative, the partisan element is seen to provide a form of external pluralism, which is combined with a model of professional reporting that aims to be fair and accurate. The mixed roles suggest that restrictions on extreme speech may be seen as a greater interference with its democratic functions, but does not completely rule out such limits.

Under the PCC Code of Practice, extreme speech is most directly engaged by Clause 12, which deals with discriminatory speech:

i) The press must avoid prejudicial or pejorative reference to an individual's race, colour, religion, gender, sexual orientation, or to any physical or mental illness or disability.
ii) Details of an individual's race, colour, religion, sexual orientation, physical or mental illness, or disability must be avoided unless genuinely relevant to the story.

As the Press Complaints Commission has emphasized on many occasions, the Code relates to individuals rather than to groups of people and complaints from

---

[77] See Curran (n. 30 above), 227–31.
[78] For example, in his speech to *Reuters* on 12 June 2007, Tony Blair referred to 'the confusion of news and commentary' in the print media.

third parties are not normally accepted. If a British newspaper published the Danish cartoons, it would not fall within the jurisdiction of the PCC Code. Consequently, newspapers can make statements that are generally racist and can engage in stereotyping without the PCC having jurisdiction to hear the complaint. This has its roots in the fact that print media regulations are trying to ensure that individuals are not subject to unfair treatment by the press, rather than to secure more general standards of content.

The complaint commonly made against the PCC is that when complaints do fall within its jurisdiction, it places greater weight on the industry's interests and, even when a breach is found, its sanctions are not sufficient to force papers to conform to the standards.[79] As an example of the protective approach to press freedom, a complaint that a cartoon depicting Ariel Sharon eating a baby, in a reference to a Goya painting, was discriminatory in invoking the blood libel was rejected by the PCC on the grounds that the cartoon was not intended to have this effect and that politicians are likely targets for satire. The PCC concluded:

it would be unreasonable to expect editors to take into account all possible interpretations of material that they intend to publish, no matter what their own motive for publishing it. That would be to interpret the Code in a manner that would impose burdens on newspapers that would arguably interfere with their rights to freedom of expression.[80]

Without commenting on the conclusion of that adjudication, the reasoning employed by the PCC shows the weight that it places on editorial freedom in choosing how to report stories and advance viewpoints.

One area of particular concern has been newspaper reporting of asylum and immigration and when dealing when some ethnic minorities. In this context, the issue is not the extreme speech of a lone dissenter, but speech that appeals to popular prejudices and reinforces existing discriminatory attitudes. It is a type of hate speech that may still be acceptable to a large proportion of the population and such sensationalized stories can help to boost sales. When *The Sun* and the *Daily Mail* ran stories about organized gangs of asylum seeking gypsies from Romania going begging in the UK, complaints were made to the PCC that the references to specific women as gypsies were discriminatory and would incite racial hatred.[81] The PCC rejected the complaints and found that the article was on a matter of public interest and the references to gypsies were justified given the

---

[79] For discussion see House of Commons, Culture, Media and Sport Committee, *Privacy and media intrusion* HC 458-I, Fifth Report of 2002–3; House of Commons, Culture, Media and Sport Committee, *Self-regulation of the press* HC 375, Seventh Report of 2006–7.

[80] Complaint made on behalf of the Embassy of Israel and Ariel Sharon against *The Independent*, Press Complaints Commission Report 62.

[81] Complaint made by Asylum Aid and others against *The Sun* and complaint made by Asylum Rights Campaign against the *Daily Mail*, Press Complaints Commission Report 50.

subject of the story. While the PCC will point to those instances where it has upheld such complaints,[82] critics argue that cases such as those above show that when the PCC does find a complaint to be within its jurisdiction, it tends to give much greater weight to the newspaper's freedom.[83] Critics also point to reports that journalists have been pressured into writing sensationalized stories in order to boost circulation.[84] Aside from the specific provisions of the Code, the PCC has provided more specific guidance on using the correct terminology while covering asylum and immigration issues and avoiding misleading terms such as 'illegal asylum seeker'.[85]

While such guidelines still permit newspapers to pursue highly emotive political campaigns, it at least acknowledges the concern that such reports can perpetuate discriminatory attitudes. Despite these changes, the Joint Committee on Human Rights found in 2007 that the PCC Code 'is not sufficiently robust to protect asylum seekers and other vulnerable minorities from the adverse effects of unfair and inflammatory media stories'.[86] The question is then whether further steps are required to curb such reporting (such as stronger self-regulation), or whether this would unduly hamper the role that has been allocated to the newspapers. The way this question is addressed will partly depend on which democratic function is assigned to the media. The advocates of stronger controls have tended to emphasize the obligations of professional reporting, rather than to see the print media as a purely political vehicle. This can be seen in the Joint Committee's recommendation that the PCC provide further guidance on reporting asylum and immigration.[87] Such guidance would emphasize the obligations of responsible journalism, with the Committee drawing a comparison with the professional code in the United States that draws a clear line between reporting and commentary and provides protection for vulnerable groups.[88] A further strategy to demand stronger controls on extreme speech may be to go beyond professional requirements and suggest that some public service obligations could be imposed on the print media. This may arise in recognition of the argument that the print media does not merely represent the preferences of its audience, but shapes its views. Arguments for some public service obligations on the press may also point to the lack of an equivalent partisan media for some minorities to respond to the negative reports featured in the national press and are

---

[82] See Memorandum submitted by the PCC to the Joint Committee on Human Rights, *The Treatment of Asylum Seekers*, Vol. 2, HL Paper 81-II, HC 60-II, Tenth Report of Session 2006–2007, Ev 445–6.

[83] See C. Frost, 'The Press Complaints Commission: a study of ten years of adjudications on press complaints' (2004) 5 *Journalism Studies* 101, 108–13.

[84] See discussion in the Joint Committee on Human Rights, Vol. 2 (n. 82 above), Ev 61.

[85] PCC Guidance Note, *Refugees and Asylum Seekers* (October 2003).

[86] Joint Committee on Human Rights, *The Treatment of Asylum Seekers*, Vol. 1, HL Paper 81-I, HC 60-I, Tenth Report of Session 2006–7, para. 364.

[87] Ibid., para. 366.   [88] Ibid., para. 363.

therefore largely excluded from the debate.[89] The call for some public service responsibilities may therefore be to correct the imbalances generated by the market.

In rejecting such calls, the PCC and some newspapers have relied on the argument that it would restrict the freedom of the press to pursue its editorial line. Such a claim is reflected in the written evidence of the *Daily Express* to the Joint Committee on Human Rights, stating that it approaches the issue of asylum and immigration:

with an agenda we believe to be in the public interest and make no apology for doing so. As a newspaper we are sceptical about the impact of the asylum system on national life and indeed about the alleged benefits of continued large scale immigration in general. In this we reflect the overwhelming views of our readers. We are one component of a free and diverse press and are not—and should not be—constrained by the sort of rules and regulations on coverage which bind, for example, broadcasters during general election campaigns.[90]

The argument advanced appeals to the partisan nature of the national press and distinguishes it from the public service sector. The newspaper sees itself as one participant in the broader media system rather than a common forum and consequently places greater emphasis on its expression rights. These competing arguments highlight the contested nature of the democratic functions that the national press performs and how the different functions will be emphasized by those supporting and opposing some limits on extreme speech.

3. Conclusion

In this chapter, the approach taken towards the media in relation to extreme speech has been distinguished from that taken towards the individual. The media may require some protection to pursue its watchdog function when reporting speech that is illegal when advocated by an individual. However, some restraints may be imposed on the media in relation to extreme speech that is legal when spoken by a citizen. This chapter has approached the issue from one particular angle: the justification of media freedom by reference to its democratic functions and how this may permit some regulations that enhance those goals. There are many other perspectives that may be considered in relation to extreme speech and the media, such as whether restrictions on extreme speech would be

---

[89] See eg, Evidence of Oxfam to the Joint Committee on Human Rights, Vol. 2 (n. 82 above), at Ev 381–2: 'Asylum seekers and refugees themselves, despite many research efforts which have shown how their voices are ignored in favour of elite sources, continue to have little influence on how these issues are portrayed and yet are the most directly affected by them'.

[90] Evidence of the *Daily Express* to the Joint Committee on Human Rights, Vol. 2 (n. 82 above), Ev 454. See also, the Committee's report (n. 86 above), at paras. 359–62.

counter-productive, the effects on the audience, and how the media may be responsible for public order. This chapter has also omitted any discussion of the Internet. Despite concerns that the new media will eventually render the public service model obsolete, the considerations outlined in this chapter could also be used to shape new media policies.[91] The approach taken in this chapter does not provide a green light to all regulations concerning extreme speech and does not provide a clear-cut answer to the permissibility of a particular regulation and its compatibility with freedom of expression. However, rather than dismissing demands for limits on extreme speech as an unwarranted interference, the claims of media freedom should be assessed in the light of the functions that the media is to perform in a democracy.

---

[91] See J. Rowbottom, 'Media Freedom and Political Debate in the Digital Era' (2006) 69 *Modern L. Rev.* 489.

Index

advertising
  religious, ban on 316–17
African Charter on Human and People's
    Rights
  economic, social and cultural rights,
      treatment of 68–9
  freedom of expression under 74
  parties to 68
agreements
  compromise 115
American Convention on Human Rights
  entry into force 68
  freedom of expression under 74
  response to rise of fascism, as 75
anarchism
  expression of 3
anti-discrimination
  norms, growth of 76
Arab Charter of Human Rights
  freedom of belief, thought and opinion
      under 74
  provisions of 69
Australia
  bill of rights, absence of 11
  Holocaust denial, regulation of 534–7
autonomy
  citizen, conception of democracy
      demanding 145
  democratic legitimacy 143
  formal 142–4
  legal legitimacy 143
  political, exercise of 175
  speaker 142–6
  state, respect by 142

blasphemous libel
  abolition of offence 299
  anomaly, as 301
  broad application, potential 302
  definition 127
  free speech, threat to 302–3
blasphemy
  abolition of offence
    background 296–7
    proposal for 295
    repeal of law 296–300

anti-Catholic expression 277
common law offence 103
  scope of 293
Danish law 132
discriminatory coverage of law 293
Euro-US comparisons 187–8
film, refusal to certify on grounds
    of 304–5
first indictment for 290–1
function of laws 266
Gay News, case against 292–3, 584
harsh treatment, reasons for 291
Jerry Springer case 297–9
jurisdiction over 290
justification of offence, difficulty
    of 303–4
narrowing of definition 292
objectionable law, as 301
prosecutions 305
sedition, link with 303
speech and protection of religion,
    relationship of 289–93
style and content 127
UK law, attempt to abolish 131
US Constitution, prohibition under 132–3
breach of the peace
  Hammond case 30–40
  violence, provoking 31
  words or behaviour likely to lead to 103
broadcasting
  civility norms, protection of 622–3
  common forum, need for 625
  discriminatory treatment, targeting
      622–3
  diverse views, allowing 621
  extreme speech, inclusion of 620
  fairness issue 16
  freedom of 15–17
  impartiality 624
  neutrality 620
  obscene, prohibition 298
  party political broadcasts by BNP 623
  provocative programmes 624–6
  public service regulation 619, 621
  racial hatred, incitement of 612–13
  regulation 618–26

broadcasting *(cont.)*
    self-censorship 583–4

Canada
    Charter of Rights and Freedoms
        free expression, right to 204
        limit on rights, reasonable 205–6
    extreme speech, protection of 79
    hate speech
        Keegstra case 205
        laws against 204
        presumption in favour of free speech,
            rebutting 219–20
        regulation 212
            reasonable limit on freedom of
                expression, as 205–6
    Holocaust denial, regulation of 529–33,
        537, 549
censorship
    arguments for 585
    Bulger, representations of 585, 590, 596
    distress or offence, material causing 588
    encouragement of terrorism, offence
        of 590–1
    evil, writing about 597
    Hindley, pictures and dramas concerning
        584, 587, 589–90
    important subjects of 596
    portrayal and enactment, difference
        between 585
    religious grounds, on 593
    self-censorship 583–4
    theatre, abolition 584
Central and Eastern Europe
    freedom, unique sense of 239
    hate speech, regulation of 240
children's rights
    religious dress, wearing of 411–14
citizenship
    rights of as natural right 162
communism
    expression of 3
community
    democratic, Meiklejohn's view of 174
    dominant, viewpoints of 193
    meaning 129
    social formulation inculcating norms,
        as 172
    speech, relationship with 329
**Convention on the Prevention and
    Punishment of the Crime
    of Genocide**

    entry into force 65
copyright
    commercial value 589
    image, commercial exploitation 589
Council of Europe
    European Convention on Human Rights
        65–8 *see also* **European Convention
        on Human Rights**
    foundation of 65
    institutional structure 66
crime
    encouragement of 461
crimes against humanity
    denial of 4, 514–15
        French law 564
    past events, application of concept to 564
    slavery 562–8
cultural rights
    religious dress, wearing of 405–6
culture
    commodification 588–90
    social differences and struggles 130
    totality of norms 129

Danish cartoons
    Britain, protesters in 312–13
    clash of values, representing 331
    demonstrations against 452
    ethical questions 313
    globalized conditions, freedom of speech
        under 17
    Iranian government, initiative of 551–2
    libel actions against 312
    media organizations, impact for 312
    persons claiming to be offended,
        emboldening 330
    principles at stake 594
    publication of 311
    reaction to 311–12
defamation
    group 58–9, 87–8
        France, not juridical category in 221
        see also **France**
    individuals, against 59
    truth as defence 598
democracy
    absolute sovereignty, people possessing 1
    anti-democratic speech, exclusion from
        public discourse 47–50
    civility rules, depending on observance of
        173
    constitutionalism, and 12

deliberative 111–13, 115
  extremists, internal and external critique
    117–18
free speech, marriage with 1–5
liberal *see* **liberalism**
media freedom 609–18
militant 14
normative principle of equal respect,
  embodying 146
people, faith in 155–7
personality rights linked with 13
political rule, as 14
popular sovereignty 26
public reason, based on 112–13
democratic participation
core free speech right 25–30
equal, commitment to 28
individual right of 27–9
right to 25–30
weight of individual interest in 38
disabled people
bad karma, disability resulting from 275
disparaging terms used against 276–7
isolation of 276
Nazi threats to 278
non-discrimination against 274–5

elderly people
ability to defend themselves 279
degrading speech against 275
insults against, nature of 281
elections
free 14
equality denial
hate speech, whether 375
equality rights
conflict, adjudicating 393–8
natural rights, as 162
Europe
Islamization 440
European Agency for Fundamental Rights
role of 68
European Convention on Human Rights
Church-State relations, human rights
  context 409
coming into force 66
Council of Europe, role of 65
destruction of rights set out in, no right of
  78–9
enforcement mechanisms 66
extreme speech, protection of 73
freedom of expression under 72–4

freedom of religion, right to 407–8
French law in relation to 228–9
limitations on exercise of rights 67
margin of appreciation, doctrine of 67–8,
  77, 427
offensive expression, application
  to 314–17
religion, freedom of 191
religious dress, provision relating to 403–5
reservations 67
rights protected by 66
sexual minorities, rights of 270–1
speech, freedom of 191
speech offending religious sensibilities,
  protection of 73–4
unmarried mothers, rights of 271
European Court of Human Rights
decisions, nature of 21
supervisory approach to intervention 314
European Union
social policy 76–7
women's rights 77
xenophobia, measures against 77
extreme speech
appropriate response to 120
concept of 221
criminalizing 99–105
  attempts at 96
current attempts to suppress 4
discredited restrictions on 6
elastic term, as 599
extremist views, public interest in hearing
  453
France, in *see* **France**
hearers and users of 506–7
integrative complexity 505–6
international human rights movement,
  alien to 76
intratextuality 496–7
Islamist
  appeal of 500–4
  caricatures 493–4
  domino reasoning 494–5
  emotional tone, flow, rhythm and
    metaphor 495
  foot in the door 494
  group identity, salience of 501–3
  identity uncertainty, context of 501
  implications 504–7
  integrative complexity 497–8
  intratextuality 496–7
  narrative 489–90

extreme speech *(cont.)*
  propositional, word based processing 495–6
  pure evil, myth of 499–500
  rationality, appearance of 495
  rhetorical strategies 492–5
  structural features of 489–500
  thin end of the wedge 494
  thinking as arguing 498–9
  us and them 493, 497
  laws restricting 610
  legal regulation of 99–105
  media, questions faced by 608
  political 96
  political ideas, advocacy of 3
  power to incite violence 488
  religion, centrality to regulation 4
  religious dress, and 401–2
  scope of 599, 608
  threats, nature of 5
  use of term 608
extremists
  claims of 114
  classification of 116
  discourse ethics 111–13, 115
  discussion of 97
  engaging with 114–16
  groups, liberal critique of 116–17
  identification of 97–9
  ideologies 114
  individual acts, dealing with 98
  internal and external critique 117–18
  irrational, unreasonable and mad doctrines, containing 107–9
  liberal democracies, discussion in 97
  markers of 99
  political space for, creating 109–11
  rational liberal consensus 107–9
  religious, approach to 107
  rules of the game, application of 115–17
  vulnerable individuals, protection of 116

fascism
  expression of 3
film
  gratuitously offensive 315–16
formal norms
  social contexts of 193
France
  activist and radical groups, administrative law controls 226–7
  annual national holiday 568–9

antisemitism 522
celebration of victory of the Allies over Germany 572–3
cinematic works
  administrative law controls 224–5
  authorizations for screenings 225
collective defamation
  juridical category, not 221
  negative or depreciatory speech, identities protected from 229
  offences, definition of 229–30
  overview 229–30
  penal regulation, notions relating to 230
  racial abuse 234–6
  religious abuse 231–4
constitutional law, revision of 569–70
digital or magnetic media, control of
  administrative law 223–4
  young people, danger for 224
education system, laicization 198–9
European Convention on Human Rights, law in relation to 228–9
extreme speech
  administrative law controls 223–7
  criminal law controls 227
  juridical category, not 221
  systematic control of 222–9
  understanding of law on 228
freedom of expression
  constitutional texts 222
  interferences with 221–2
  notion of 221
French citizens overseas, positive role of 562–4
genocide of Jews, commemorations and bans 571–5
hate speech
  administrative law controls 223–7
  criminal law controls 227
  juridical category, not 221
  law on 526
  systematic control of 222–9
  understanding of law on 228
Holocaust denial, regulation of 521–9, 571–5
July 14, significance of 568–9
memory bans, debate on 562–5
new political order 568
Nuremberg trials, incorporation into law 523
occupation 521
periods of division in 570

racial abuse, proceedings against 234–6
radio and television broadcasts
  administrative law controls 224
  criminal law controls 227
  illicit material in 224
religious abuse, proceedings against 231–4
religious dress, law on *see* **religious dress**
Republic, restoration of 568
sexual equality and independence, values of 423–4
slavery
  abolition, lack of celebration 575–9
  crime against humanity, as 562–7
  former slaves, reaction of 575–6
  permanent elimination of 566–8
written publications
  administrative law controls 223
  criminal law controls 227

freedom
formal and substantive 196–200
less is more ideal 197
restrictions, effect of 196

freedom of expression
concepts threatening 593
contents-based ground for restricting, offence as, 321–3
essential foundation of democratic society, as 33
European Convention on Human Rights 72–4
France, in *see* **France**
fundamental feature of democratic society, as 314
human rights instruments, under
  International Convention on the Elimination of All Forms of Racial Discrimination 71–2
  International Covenant on Civil and Political Rights 69–72
  regional 72–4
ideas or beliefs, challenging 180–1
insulting, expression being
  Hammond case 30–40
  Norwood case 44–52
law violation, advocacy of 42
legitimate protest, going beyond 32
nature of 11–14
objectionable material, powers over 395
other rights, relative to 333
presumptive priority 316
reasonable protest 45
religion, centrality of 289

rights conflict, adjudicating 393–8
social welfare, contribution to 37–8

freedom of speech
Act of Parliament infringing, judicial interpretation of 43–4
American exceptionalism 140
Australia, in 11
boundaries of
  framework for 204
  Mill's tests 204–7
Britain, in 2
broader framework of rights, within 163
Canada, in *see* **Canada**
civility norms, offending 55–8
constitutions, in 11–14
core area essential for democratic government 42–3
core principle 23–4
cross-cultural normative critique 23
democracy
  functionalization in interests of 13
  marriage with 1–5
democratic participation, right to 25–30
English cases 24
fighting words 52–3
foundational approach 144
globalized conditions, under
  Danish cartoons 17
  religion, protection of 17–19
  uniformity of law 19–22
group defamation 58–9, 87–8
Hammond case 30–40
individual right, valued as 61
instrumental justification 256–7
judicial protection of 42
justifications 30
law violation, advocacy of 53–5
mainstream opinion, speech offending 29
meaning 11–17
minority protection, relationship with 106
national culture, law as part of 22
new democracies, in 263
Norwood case 44–52
other protected values, balance with 13
overprotection, strategy of 52–9
presumption in favour of protecting 204
  rebutting 219
protection of
  clear and [present danger test 24–5
public reason, baseline of 350
raison d'etre, derivation 12

freedom of speech *(cont.)*
  religious sensibilities, protection of
    blasphemy 301–5
    English law, conclusions as to treatment
      in 310
    generally 300
    religious hatred, incitement to 305–10
  social policy, as to 28
  socialist constitutions, in 11
  sound choice, assisting electorate in 61
  speaker autonomy 142–6
  speech at periphery of core 52–9
  unpopular ideas, expression of 60
  US doctrine *see* **United States**
  valuation, grounds for 139

gender equality
  gendered hierarchies, construction of 358–60
  religious speech offending against
    extent of 358
    gendered hierarchies, construction of
      358–60
    reforms 374
    violence against women, incitement or
      condoning 360–2
  religious teachings, in conflict with 357
  struggle for 357
genocide
  concept of 515
  denial of 514–15
    European Common Framework 547–8
  hate, pervasion of 139
  moral responsibility, shifting 540
  small and powerless group, against 170
  speech, conviction based on 155
Germany
  broadcasting, freedom of 15–17
  freedom of speech in 559
  hate speech, prohibitions 146
  Holocaust denial
    crime, as 557
    evaluation of 561
    litigation 557–61
  political parties, banned 14

hate speech
  bans
    abolition, ability of 284
    detriment, link to 278
    disabled people, relating to 274–5
    elderly, inclusion of 275
    extensive regime, call for 273

  human rights groups, endorsement by
    277–8
  human rights principles, collision with
    279
  justification 279
  obese people, inclusion of 275
  objections and replies 280–84
  protection, aim of 276
  temporary 280
  Canada, in *see* **Canada**
  Central and Eastern Europe, regulation in
    240
  crimes, motivating committing of 218–19
  criminalizing, attempts at 96
  critique, and 126
  cultural essentialism, dangers of 199
  cultural policy 105–7
  differing regulation of 23
  discriminatory nature of 209–10
  Euro-US comparisons
    absolute divide 187
    ahistoricism 200–3
    centre of gravity 186
    comparative method 183
    formal and substantive freedoms 196–200
    formal law 189–90
    informal power 187–8
    issues, divisive 182
    locus of 184–7
    political and social realities, in 183
    realism and essentialism 190–96
  European bans, issues raised 195
  European conferences on 182
  European, control of content 188
  evil consequences of 134
  extreme emotions 123–4
  extreme speech regulation 84
  France, in *see* **France**
  Germany, prohibition in 146
  harms of
    direct 208, 219
    discrimination and violence, imputing
      213
    indirect 209, 219
    minorities, protection of 213
    nature of 207–11
    visible and verifiable 212
  hate crime, and incidence of 283–4
  homosexuals, against 377
    censorship 273
    harmful, being 272
    see also **homophobia**

Hungary, in *see* **Hungary**
intent provision 214
low ranking 144
meaning 92, 123, 127, 207
media regulation 105–7
minorities, protection of 101–3
non-legal responses to 105–7
Norwood case 44–52, 84
participation on public discourse,
    deterring 197
political, imposing norms of community 173
Post's approach to 171–2
private, restriction of 164
promoting and inciting 212–19
promotion of hatred 215–17
public
    appropriate regulation of 178, 180
    context of 178–9
    equal rights of others, denying 167
    First Amendment, protection by 165–81
    lawful political speech, as 176
    other forms of discourse, not distinguished
        from 181
    other rights, impact on 165–9
    personal security, effect on 165
    personality rights, effect on 166
    political character, protection due to 169–
        77
    presumptively wrong 169
    right of recognition, effect on 166–9
    rights-based analysis, refining 177–81
    social order, rights within 178
racist *see* **racist hate speech**
real harms caused by 156–7
regulation
    business leaders favouring 153–4
    discrimination, prevention of 135
    evils caused by 150–5
    exacerbation hypothesis 149–50
    fabrication of pretexts for 134
    formal autonomy, restricting 143
    harmful effects, suppressing 133–4
    justifications, effect of 154–5
    logic of 128
    objections to 146–50
    operation of 134–5
    political energy, diversion of 153
    principle created by 154
    state and citizen, relationship of 340–2
    US and European contrasted 137–8
sexual minorities, extension of bans to *see*
    sexual minorities

social consensus against 239
style of presentation, punishments 127
United Kingdom, historical overview in
    92–5
United States, doctrine in *see* **United States**
US position as anomaly 186
use of denigrating expressions, and 252
use of expression 267
verbal abuse 212
violence
    causing 135–6
    issue of 210–11
wilful 214
hatred
disagreement, and 126–7
law, indispensability to 124
legal attempts to suppress 125
legal condemnation 125
oldest legal prohibition 124
proper place, in 124
Holocaust
continuing impact, evaluation of 561
denial *see* **Holocaust denial**
European Jewry, extermination
    of 516
groups targeted 515–16
historical reality, as 525
international Holocaust Revisionist
    Conference 553–4
Memorial Museum 555
unique historical event, as 515
Holocaust denial
Arab and Muslim world, in 554–5
Australia, in 534–6
bans, advocacy of 199
battle against 536
Britain, publications in 539
context of 514–21
criminalization of 513
    argument for 519–20
deniers
    arguments of 517
    changes in 538
    facts, rejection of 516–17
    Irving 552–3, 558–61
    media used by 538
    revisionists, as 516
education, necessity of 555–6
European Common Framework 547–8
European history, link with 200
France, regulation in 571–5
future outcomes 553–5

Holocaust denial *(cont.)*
  Germany
    crime, as 557
    litigation in 557–61
  harm of 518
  international agreements 541–43
  internationalization of 513
  Iranian government, initiative
      of 551–2
  legal and social norms 512
  legal questions 511
  legal regulation
    basis of 519
    collective social, ethical and political
        decision, as 520
    contexts of 514
    France, in 521–9
    international agreements 541–3
    issues 516, 536
    justification 517
    national legislation 543–5
    taxonomical issues 518
  national legislation 543–5
  prosecutions, successful 545–7
  pseudoscientific publications 538
  punishment of 127
  recent convictions 548–50
  repugnancy 517–18
  restrictions prohibiting 89–90
  scope of 519
  specific form of hate, as 542
  spread of 511
  survivors, traumatizing 519
  trivialization argument 540
  truth and memory, assault on 518
  United States, in 554
  World Wide Web, on
    Australian legislation 534–7
    Canadian legislation 529–33, 537
    efforts to act against 511
    French litigation 521–9
    interdiction of 520
    jurisdiction, challenge of 540
    Middle East, material from 539
    trivialization argument 540
homophobia
  anti-discrimination laws, speech covered
      by 383–4
  conduct, focus on 386–7
  group, hostility to 398–9
  hate incidents 382
  hate speech

    anti-discrimination laws, speech covered
        by 383–4
    media regulatory control of 382–3
    offences, international responses
        to 380–1
    UK position 381–7
    whether being 375
  immorality, belief in 395–7
  incitement, offence of 384
  laws forbidding expression of 379
  personal destruction, politics of 378
  religious 382
  religious groups, of 378
  religiously-motivated speech
    balancing approach to 396–7
    Hammond case 388–91
    human rights system, challenge for 398
    Netherlands, decision in 390–1
    status of 388–93
    street preaching 390
    Sweden, Green case 391–3
  rights conflict, adjudicating 393–8
  scope of 377
  videos, challenge to 394–5
homosexuality *see also* **sexual minorities**
  Hart-Devlin debate 375–6
  homophobic speech *see* **homophobia**
  immorality, linked with 30–40
  insulting ideas, exclusion from public
      discourse 33–5
  new orthodoxy as to 376
    dissent, expression of 378
  Northern Ireland, law in 318
  physical assaults 265
  prejudice and discrimination against 377
  promotion of sexuality 591
  queer bashing 265
  religious disapproval of 4
  same-sex marriage, denial of 397
  United States, recognition of rights
      in 271
  violence of words against 265
human rights
  conflict, adjudicating 393–8
  differential outcomes, explaining 427
  general corpus, validity of 270
  margin of appreciation 427
  negative and positive aspects 408–9
  Principle of Extant Rights 269–70, 272
  protection
    consensus, absence of 317–19
    margin of appreciation 317–19

underlying values 424
human rights instruments
anti-discrimination Conventions and
    Declarations 76
growth of concept 63
international
    content and impact of 62
    Convention on the Prevention and
      Punishment of the Crime of
      Genocide 65
    extreme speech, protection of 74–9
    history and structure of 62–9
    International Convention on the
      Elimination of All Forms of Racial
      Discrimination 64–5
    International Covenant on Civil and
      Political Rights 64–5
    Universal Declaration 62
regional
    African Charter on Human and People's
      Rights 68–9
    American Convention on Human
      Rights 68
    Arab Charter of Human Rights 69
    content and impact of 62
    European Convention on
      Human Rights 65–8
      see also **European Convention
      on Human Rights**
    extreme speech, protection of 74–9
    history and structure of 62–9
Hungary
Budapest, Jewish community in 244
censorship in 241–4
Civil Liberties Union 256
denigratory speech, use of civil law
    against 253
freedom of expression
    criminal legal limitation 248–9
    denial, experience of 248
    effect of restricting 248–9
    instrumental justification 256–7
    strict constitutional requirement to
      protect 252
freedom of the press 241–3
hate speech
    antisemitism 244, 246, 257–60
    clear and present danger test, application
      of 247–63
    Constitutional Court, decisions
      of 247–61
    content-based prohibition 249, 251

Criminal Code, review of provisions of
    248–9
free speech theories, and 256
Hegedus Jr. case 257–60
Jews, call for exclusion from society
    257–60
jurisdiction 240
offensive speech, and 249
overbroadness of provision 251
participatory citizenry, rejection
    leading to 253
policies, deciding 263
public discourse, racist speech as part of
    251
racist, reasons for imposing criminal
    prohibitions on 244
rejection, whether country ready for 254
Roma Hungarians, hatred against 245–7
social context 239–47
special order and peace, disturbance of
    250–1
strong statements against 254
incitement provisions 243
liberal period in 240–1
paternalistic control, avoidance of 254
public discourse, exercise of 244
racism 247
restriction on freedom of speech, approach
    to 240
Roma 245–6
totalitarian symbols, prohibition of public
    display 261–3

image
commercial exploitation 589
immigration
Muslim population, increase in 439–40
incitement
criminal conspiracies 459–60
disaffection, to 93
hatred, to
    harm, risk of 105
    history of 104
    powerless minorities, not protecting 105
    racial *see* **racial hatred, incitement to**
    religious *see* **religious hatred, incitement to**
    themes of 104
Hungary, criminal code 243
instigation, and 218
law violation, speech advocating 454–5
mutiny, to 93

incitement *(cont.)*
offences of 4, 93
racial hatred, to *see* racial hatred,
  incitement to
unlawful action
  advocacy directed at 456
  imminent, advocacy of 457–8
  likelihood of inciting or producing 458–9
use of force, speech advocating 454–6
violence against women, of 360–62, 372
violence, of 217–18
  immediate 459
insulting speech
gratuitous 325–7
intellectual and spiritual freedom
rights of as natural rights 162
International Convention on the Elimination
    of All Forms of Racial Discrimination
entry into force 64
freedom of expression under 71–2
hate speech, prohibition of 268–9
Islamic headscarf-hajib, prohibition on
    wearing as issue 419–20
racial superiority or hatred, prohibiting
    dissemination of ideas based on 185–6
rights of sexual minorities, analogous to 269
speech condemned by 125
States' performance, monitoring 186
US ratification 186
International Covenant on Civil and Political
    Rights
adoption of 63
advocacy of national, racial or religious
    hatred, prohibition 177, 184–5, 268
freedom of expression under 69–72
Human Rights Committee 64
  political speech, protection of 70–1
political speech, protection of 70–1
reservations 64, 185
rights in 63
Internet
free speech, as domain for 540
hate promotion on 540
hate, regulation of 523
Holocaust denial, regulation of
  see Holocaust denial
regulation, debates 513
violent radicalization, role in 477–8, 480
World Wide Web, transborder information
    migration through 513
Ireland
religious advertising, ban on 316–17

Israel
freedom of expression, status of 353
public discourse, sphere of 353–4
religious satire law 332–3, 336–7
speech, cultural significance 342–5
state and citizen, relationship of 340–2
words, balancing 345–6

jurisprudence
outsider 193

language
power struggles, terrain for 488
shaping power of 488–9
libel
blasphemous *see* blasphemous libel
obscene, law of 301
liberalism
common values, search for 98
core values 111
egalitarian reciprocity 98
extremism
  discourse ethics 111–13, 115
  discussion of 97
  engaging with 114–16
  groups, critique of 116–17
  individual acts, dealing with 98
  irrational, unreasonable and mad
      doctrines, containing 107–9
  markers of 99
  political space for, creating 109–11
  rational liberal consensus 107–9
  religious, approach to 107
freedom of exit and association 99
ideological foundations 119
illiberal doctrines, motivation to engage
    in 98
misuse of concept of democracy 119
political 107–8
radically different groups, place
    of 110
rational consensus 109
voluntary self-ascription 99
liberty
external rights 161
general principle of 206
justification of restrictions on 206–7

marketplace of ideas
Holmes's theory of 169–70
media
broadcast

civility norms, protection of 622–3
common forum, need for 625
discriminatory treatment,
    targeting 622–3
diverse views, allowing 621
extreme speech, inclusion of 620
impartiality 624
neutrality 620
party political broadcasts by BNP 623
provocative programmes 624–5
public service regulation 619, 621
regulation 618–26
dictatorships, control in 14
diverse information and ideas, dissemination
    of 613–18
extreme speech
    approach to 629–30
    limits on expression 615
    political parties or speech, ban on 617
    questions arising 608
    regulation 618–29
forum produced by 15
freedom and democracy 609–18
freedom of 14–17
government, separation from 15
hate speech regulation 105–7
homophobic 382–3
journalistic techniques 611–12
partisan model 616–18
press
    discriminatory speech 626
    emotive political campaigns 628
    ethnic minorities, reporting 627
    extreme speech 626
    industry, interests of 627
    meaning 599
    regulation 618, 626–9
    scope of 626
public discourse 29–30
public service model 614–16
public watchdog, as 610–13
regulation
    broadcast media 618–26
    discriminatory treatment, targeting 619
    newspapers 618, 626–9
    press, of 618, 626–9
views of others, reporting 613
written ethics guidance 606
memory laws
    French historians' call for abolition of 513
    legal interventions 512

negotiation of 512
minority rights
    religious dress, wearing of 406–7

natural rights
    citizenship, of 162
    equality, to 162
    external 161
    freedom of speech, background to 159–60
    intellectual and spiritual freedom, of 162
    personality, of 162
Netherlands
    verzuiling (pillarization), system of 197–8

obese people
    ability to defend themselves 279
    degrading speech against 275
    insults against, nature of 281
obscenity
    obscene libel, law of 301
    plays and broadcasts, of 298–9
offensive expression
    balancing, use of 345–8
    communitarian approach to 329
    consensus, absence of 317–19
    costs of suppressing 322–3
    democratic legitimacy, concept of 327–30
    European Convention jurisprudence, in
        314–17
    film, in 315–16
    freedom to engage in 327
    gratuitous 325–7
    groundless 325–6
    Islam, about 322–3
    legitimacy as ground for limiting free speech
        313
    normative justifications, diverging 333–7
    outrage provoking 321–3
    politicians seeking to suppress 322
    religion, whether normatively special 337–9
    right to be protected from, whether 319–21
    tipping points 327–30

paedophilia
    drama, portrayed in 584, 586–7
personality
    rights of
        natural right, as 162
        public hate speech, effect of 166
plays
    Black and Asian theatre 596
    black urban culture, relating to 595

plays *(cont.)*
  forced closure, response to 594–5
  obscene, prohibition 297–8
  self-censorship 583–4
  theatre censorship, abolition 584
political discussion
  issues dominating 191
political speech
  definition 324
  expression about Islam as 323–4
pornography
  anti-censorship feminists, view of 153
  harms to women, link with 208
  portrayal and enactment, difference
      between 585
  regulation of 153
press, freedom of *see also* **media**
  private capacity, publication of pictures of
      celebrities in 20
privacy, right to
  demarcation 21
  private capacity, publication of pictures of
      celebrities in 20
  rape victim, publication of name of 160–1
public discourse
  ambiguous political rhetoric, interpretation
      of 50–2
  anti-democratic speech, exclusion of 47–50
  civility norms
    imposed on 33
    offending 55–8
  content-based regulation 81
  controversial speech, punishment for 40–4
  democratic, limits of 118–20
  dignity and respect, norms of 174
  ethics 111–13, 115
  expression forming part of 29–30
  fighting words 52–3
  government authority in US, legitimation of
      137
  group defamation 58–9, 87–8
  Hungary, in 244
  importance of right to participate in 61
  insulting, expression being
    Hammond case 30–40
    Norwood case 44–52
  insulting ideas, exclusion of 33–5
  insults, protection from 85
  Israel, in 353–4
  law violation, advocacy of 53–5
  legal restriction, freedom from 172–3
  mutual recognition 174–7

  participation in, suppression of 136
  personal abuse distinguished 35–7
  Post's theory of 169–74, 190–5
  preconditions 172
  protection, meriting 145
  public sphere 203
  respect for others, mandating 172
  right of, weight of 37
  Roman Catholic Church, attacking 35–6
  settings of 29–30
  social welfare, contribution to 37–8
  tone of 56
  violation of right to participate in 32
public order
  ethnic groups, protection of 307
  Hammond case 30–40
  incitement to racial hatred *see* **racial hatred,
      incitement to**
  Norwood case 44–52
  religious aggravation of offences 306–7
  religious dress, perspectives on wearing on
      410–11
  speech threatening 5–6
  threatening or insulting words or behaviour,
      use of 31

racial hatred, incitement of
  public order offences 612–13
  anomalies on scope 308
  current provisions 100
  introduction of offence 294
  offence of 93–5, 99
  protected groups 100
  public order concerns 100
  religious hatred, overlap with 101
racist hate speech
  causal claim 147
  prohibition
    democratic self-understanding, reducing
        152–3
    effectiveness 149
    enforcement 148–9
    evils caused by 150–5
    exacerbation hypothesis 149–50
    genocidal results, producing 156
    justifications, effect of 154–5
    negative effects 149
    oppression, increasing sense of 152
    political energy, diversion of 153
    pragmatic justification 147–8
    principle created by 154
  refusal to tolerate 151

social toleration 151
recognition
  Hegel, philosophy of 168
  Hobbes, writings of 167
  Locke, writings of 167–8
  mutual
    conflict, resolving 168
    foundation of right, as 175
    public discourse, and 174–7
    speech, relationship with 175
    structures of 175
  natural rights theory, roe in 169
  right of, effect of public hate speech 166–7,
    172
  roots of concept 167
religion
  adherence, nature of 308
  advertising, ban on 316–17
  blasphemy *see* **blasphemy**
  Church of England, position of 290
  debate, contributions to 308
  dress *see* **religious dress**
  extreme speech regulation, central to 4
  freedom of
    religious dress, wearing of 407–8
    right of 18
  freedom of expression, central to 289
  institutionalized normative regime, as 338
  liberty, restriction to matters of
    belief 396
  mutually exclusive beliefs, separation of 18
  offence, protection from 319–21
  offences against 290
  public law, relationship with 289–90
  religious feelings, hurting 19
  religious people, public interest in not
    offending 320
  Roman Catholic Church, attacking 35–6
  secular state, place in 18–19
  sensibilities, outraging 352
  speech
    protection from 17–19
    role of 339
  state and citizen, relationship of 340–2
  state, separation from 338
  women's rights, in conflict with 358–9
religious aggravation
  meaning 306–7
  penalty enhancement for 306
religious dress
  autonomy and consent, issues of 424–6

children's rights 411–14
Christian context, in 419
controversies, context for 401
cultural rights 406–7
discrimination
  European Union, in 418–19
  feminist perspectives 420–2
  gender 420–2
  intersecting 424
  Islamophobia 416–18
  racial 419–20
educational context, in
  children's rights 411–14
  French law 413–14
  jewellery, rule forbidding 412–13
  modern dress, requirement of 433
  school ban on garment, legitimate 430–33
  teachers' rights 414–16
  uniform policy, conflict with 412,
    431–3
  universities, prohibition in 416, 433
freedom of religion, right to 407–8
human rights perspectives
  Church-State relations, human rights
    context 409
  cultural rights 406–7
  freedom of religion, right to 407–8
  individual and group identities and rights
    405–6
  international human rights bodies,
    individual applications to 402–5
  minority rights 406–7
  national courts, individual applications to
    402
  negative and positive aspects 408–9
  public order, and 410–11
incompatible values 434
individual and group identities and rights
  405–6
international human rights bodies, individual
  applications to 402–5
Islamic headscarf-hajib
  autonomy and consent, issues of 424–6
  children's rights 411
  Church-State relations, human rights
    context 409
  communicative symbol, as 400
  cultural rights 406–7
  feminist perspectives 420–4
  freedom of religion, right to 407–8
  French context, in 401–2
  gender discrimination 420–4

religious dress *(cont.)*
    individual and group identities and rights
        405–6
    international human rights bodies,
        individual applications to 403–5
    intersecting discrimination 424
    Islamophobia, challenges based on
        416–18
    issues 400
    legal challenges to 400
    minority rights 406–7
    national courts, individual applications
        to 402
    negative and positive aspects 408–9
    political and symbolic wearing or not
        wearing 401
    public order perspectives 410–11
    racial discrimination 419–20
    repressive symbolism of 422
    teachers' rights 414–16
    Turkish context, in 401–2, 428–9,
        433–41
    universities, prohibition in 416
    Islamophobia 416–18
    location of debate 427–9
    minority rights 406–7
    national courts, individual applications to
        402
    rights of other people, threat to 430–5
    school ban on garment, legitimate 430–3
    speech, and 401–2
    unacceptable political purposes, expressing
        437–9
religious hatred, incitement of
    nature of 613
    anti-Islamic attacks, combating 306
    anti-terrorism provisions 295
    arguments for criminalization 305–8
    background 294–6
    ECHR, no requirement to protect
        individuals under 309
    ethnic groups, protection of 307
    existing provisions, adequacy of 306
    extension of racial provisions to 101–2
    first legislative attempt to prohibit 294–5
    free speech defence 386–7
    groups covered by 97
    jokes, outlawing 103
    legislative provision 296
    limits of prohibition 296
    Muslim minorities, protection of 101–2
    narrow definition 310
    offence of 102

    opponents of criminalization 102–3
    pressure for offence of 94
    principle and practice, difficulties of 309–10
    racial hatred, overlap with 101
    social problem of 306
religious speech
    forbidden 367–8
    gender equality, undermining 357–74
        see also **gender equality**
    homophobic
        balancing approach to 396–7
        Hammond case 388–91
        human rights system, challenge for 398
        Netherlands, decision in 390–91
        status of 388–93
        street preaching 390
        Sweden, Green case 391–93
    ideas that offend, shock and disturb 388–9
    Islamist radical discourse
        caricatures 493–4
        domino reasoning 494–5
        emotional tone, flow, rhythm and
            metaphor 495
        foot in the door 494
        integrative complexity 497–8
        intratextuality 496–7
        key ingredients of 507
        narrative 489–92
        propositional, word based processing
            495–6
        pure evil, myth of 499–500
        rationality, appearance of 495
        rhetorical strategies 492–5
        social problem, diagnosis and solution
            to 503
        structural features of 489–500
        thin end of the wedge 494
        thinking as arguing 498–9
        us and them 493, 497
    model of 364–8
    power and influence of 373
    religious duty, as 366–7
    reluctance to ban 372
    sacred 365
    satire
        constitutional protection, whether
            receiving 331
        Danish cartoons *see* **Danish cartoons**
        extra sensitivity to 339
        Israeli law 332–3, 336–7
        models for resolving tension 331
        posting, place of 349

religion, whether normatively special 337–9
Suszkin case 332–3, 354
violence against women, inciting 360–2, 372
women, by
  empowering 368–73
  encouragement to take seriously 373
  forbidden 367–8
  importance of 368–70
  practical strategies for empowering 370–3
  regulation of 370

Russia
extremist activity, countering 240

sedition
blasphemy, link with 303
definition 294
model of 103–4
United Kingdom courts, in 92
United States legislation 1–2, 600
  unconstitutionality 600–2, 607
seditious libel
common law offence 103
suppression of 124–5
sexual minorities
cumulative jurisprudence
  contradictory, or 273–81
  European Convention on Human Rights 272
  interests, advancing 284–5
  non-discrimination, of 271–2
  scope of 266–72
fundamental rights 269
hate speech bans
  extension to 269
  protection under 273
ICCPR, application to 268
insults against, nature of 281
International Convention on the Elimination of All Forms of Racial Discrimination, analogy of 268–9
non-discrimination norms 273–4
Principle of Extant Rights 269–70, 272
violence of words against 265
sexual orientation
agitation against group on grounds of 391–3
criticism or antipathy, free speech defence 386
equality denial 398
hatred on grounds of 376
hatred, stirring up on grounds of 385–6, 398–9

laws forbidding homophobic expression 379
Northern Ireland, regulation in 383–4
slavery
crime against humanity, as 562–7
France, in
  abolition, lack of celebration 575–9
  crime against humanity, as 562–7
  former slaves, reaction of 575–6
  permanent elimination of 566–8
social norms
aspects of 129
identity, importance to 128
intersubjective 129
law enforcing 130
meaning 128
reinforcement 129
totality of 129
sovereignty
popular 26
speech
balancing, use of 345–8
cultural significance 342–5
fighting words, doctrine of 52–3, 82, 86, 282, 348–50, 605
forbidden 367–8
freedom of *see* **freedom of speech**
hate *see* **hate speech**
homophobic *see* **homophobia**
models of
  contrasting 362
  liberal 363–4
  religious 364–8 *see also* **religious speech**
offensive *see* **offensive expression**
passion, role of 350–2
pluralist society, regulation in 357–8
religious *see* **religious speech**
state and citizen, relationship of 340–2
theory, heretical reflections 350–2
state
legitimacy 142–6

terrorism
activists, religious background 479–80
acts of, definition 484
CONTEST strategy 465–6
encouragement, offence of
  acceptable political debate, circumscribing boundaries of 485
  acts of terrorism, relating to 470–1
  agreement to commit acts, remarks in course of 449
  argument for 477

terrorism *(cont.)*
  causal connection with act 450
  censorship, as 590–2
  conspiracy, and 459
  Convention offences, relating to 470, 472
  direct and indirect 468
  European obligations, implementing 466
  extra-territorial jurisdiction, not involving 471
  free expression, restriction on 464
  free speech arguments 445, 447–9
  free speech, impact on 472
  fully protected speech, argument for treatment as 449–51
  impugned statements, impact of 470–1
  indirect 591
  inducement 468
  interpretation of terms 469–70
  introduction of 445
  justification 462
  media, reporting by 613
  need for 464
  organizations, proscription of 467
  private communications 478
  public, statements to 478
  publications, dissemination of 467
  radicalization process, impact on 473–80
  reservations as to proscription 452–4
  Scanlon, argument of 449–51
  scope of 446–7, 460
  statements, publication of 467
  statutory provisions 446–7, 466–73
  United States, in 445–6
  unlawful action, inciting 456–9
  violent radicalization, contribution to prevention of 464, 487
  extremist views, public interest in hearing 453
  freedom fighting, and 471
  glorification of 120, 468–9, 484
    acts of 445
    freedom of speech, attack on 592
    illiberal clauses on 597
    law against 592
  imminent unlawful action, advocacy of 457–8
  incitement to 88–90
  laws countering
    communities, impact on 482–3
    counterproductive potential of 481–6
    mass stereotyping 483, 485
    legislation against, argument as to 450–1

  new offences, justification of 486
  Northern Ireland, response to 481–82
  pre-trial detention, length of 482–3
  radicalization *see* **violent radicalization**
  speaker's right to encourage 451–2
  UK, threat to 463–4, 486
thought and belief
  freedom of 168

United States
  ahistoricism 200–3
  blasphemous speech, prohibition 132–3
  blasphemy laws 188
  civil liberties ethos 200–1
  criminal conspiracy laws 459
  distinct communities, competition of 192
  extreme speech
    curbing 599
    incitement 604–5
    market factors and evolving norms of civility, regulation by 605–7
    parody 603–4
    pre-Constitution 598
    protection of 602
    rhetorical hyperbole 603–4
    role in history 598
    true threats 604–5
    vigorous epithets 603–4
  free speech doctrine
    child pornography, exclusion of 82
    clear and present danger, speech presenting 461
    community-building, approach to 344
    constitutional element of democratic sovereignty, as 335
    content discrimination, rule against 81–90
    extreme speech protection 91
    fighting words 82, 86, 281, 348–50, 604–5
    hate speech 84–8
    Holocaust denial 89–90
    imminent unlawful action, advocacy of 457–8
    incitement to law violations 82
    law violation, speech advocating 454–6
    likelihood of inciting or producing unlawful action 458–9
    merits of 80
    model of 334–6
    obscenity, exclusion of 82
    other democracies, differing from 90–1

prohibition of hate speech laws,
exceptional 237–8
public concern, matters of 83
racist expression, suppression of 85–7
scrutiny of 13
subversive political speech 454–5
terrorism, encouragement of 445–6
terrorism, incitement to 88–90
true threats 82, 87
unlawful action, advocacy directed at 456
use of force, speech advocating 454–6
viewpoint discriminatory speech
regulation 85–7
freedom of speech
broader framework of rights, within 163
constitutional protections 133
constitutional text 159
democratic self-governance, relevant to 171
democratic deliberation, essential to 174
exceptionalism 140
First Amendment, foundations and limits
of 159–64
formal evenhandedness, effect of
requirement 196
general account of rights, within 161
illegal conduct, advocacy of 602
interpretation of 191–2
natural rights background 159–60
public hate speech, whether protecting
165–81
public speech promoting hatred, extending
to 158
rape victim, publication of name of 160–1
reform of jurisprudence 163
relational right, as 177
rights-based conception 160
social interests, conflicts between 160
gay rights, recognition of 270–1
hate speech bans
extreme speech regulation 84
group defamation 87–8
insulting statements 84–5
Norwood case, likely treatment of 84
public order rationale for proscription 87
hate speech, regulation of 137–8
Holocaust denial, permitted 554
individualism, norms of 137
militant anti-abortion activists, threats by
459–60
nation of immigrants, as 336
pervasive racial inequalities 201
political and social critique 599

political dissent, obstacles to 141
press freedoms, protection of 601
racist ideas, ban on public expression of 23
Sedition Act 1–2, 600
unconstitutionality 600–2, 607
speech, cultural significance 342–5
state and citizen, relationship of 340
terrorism, incitement to 88–90

videos
violence, inspiring 585–6
violence
against women, inciting 360–2, 372
encouragement of 461
films and videos, on 585–6
hate 210
incitement, restrictions on 217–18
instigation 218
minorities, against 210–11
mobilization of individuals to 477
violent radicalization
activists, religious background 479–80
aspects of 473
contribution of legislation to prevention of
464, 487
dissatisfaction as opening for 503–4
high risk individuals 474
identifying 474
Internet, role of 477–8, 480
Islamophobia, and 476
organizations, joining 474–5
process of 473–80
prohibited statements, role of 477–8
public statements, role of 478–9, 486
radicalizers, receptivity to ideology of 504
recruitment 476, 478–9
socio-economic factors 477
speech challenging acts underpinning 480
statements contributing to 481
Transitional Religiosity Experiences 475–6
understanding of 473

war
ambiguous political rhetoric, interpretation
of 50–2
protest, convictions for 40–4
vehement protest against 3
war crimes
denial of 515

xenophobia
measures against 77